March 7–11, 2017
Oslo, Norway

Association for
Computing Machinery

Advancing Computing as a Science & Profession

CHIIR'17

Proceedings of the 2017
Conference Human Information Interaction and Retrieval

Sponsored by:

ACM SIGIR

In cooperation with:

ACM SIGCHI

Supported by:

Oslo and Akershus University College & City of Oslo

Association for
Computing Machinery

Advancing Computing as a Science & Profession

The Association for Computing Machinery
2 Penn Plaza, Suite 701
New York, New York 10121-0701

ISBN: 978-1-4503-4677-1 (Digital)

ISBN: 978-1-4503-5446-2 (Print)

Additional copies may be ordered prepaid from:

ACM Order Department
PO Box 30777
New York, NY 10087-0777, USA

Phone: 1-800-342-6626 (USA and Canada)
+1-212-626-0500 (Global)
Fax: +1-212-944-1318
E-mail: acmhelp@acm.org
Hours of Operation: 8:30 am – 4:30 pm ET

Printed in the USA

CHIIR 2017 Chairs' Welcome

It is our great pleasure to welcome you to Oslo and to the *Second ACM SIGIR Conference on Information Interaction and Retrieval (CHIIR'17).* The number of contributed papers and short papers, and the number of conference attendees, clearly demonstrate the value of this unique forum for researchers and students interested in the user-centered aspects of information interaction and information retrieval. We have participants from all five continents, there is a good combination of senior and aspiring researchers among the presenters, and we have attracted interesting workshops and tutorials – in sum, we feel that the program for CHIIR'17 validates the decision of ACM SIGIR to continue to fully sponsor the conference.

We would like to recognize the people and institutions who have contributed to making CHIIR'17 a success. We first thank the authors for providing the content of the conference program. The three Program chairs, Luanne Freund, Birger Larsen and Dan Russel have invested a lot of time and effort in organizing the paper selection process both for the full and short papers, and in putting together a very interesting program, with the help of more than 80 members of the Senior program committee and the Program committee. We are grateful for the efforts of the Tutorials and Workshops chair, Preben Hansen, the organizer of the Doctoral consortium, Katriina Byström, and the Publications chair, Sampath Jayarathna. Our colleagues at OAUC, Erik Eileng and Kjetil Iseli have offered invaluable support with respectively the financial organization and the website management. The three keynote speakers, Ann Blandford, Norbert Fuhr and Håkon Wium Lie, were all immediately willing to share their insights as veterans in the field.

Finally, we thank the hosting organization, Oslo and Akershus University College, for generous sponsorship and all the practical support we could wish for, our colleagues at the Department of Archivistics, Library and Information Science for help with all the logistics of the conference, and the City of Oslo for inviting us into the City Hall for the welcome reception.

We hope that you will find the program interesting and thought-provoking and the interaction with old and new friends and colleagues engaging and stimulating, - and that you will enjoy the amenities of the OAUC and the city of Oslo!

Ragnar Nordlie
General Co-chair
Oslo and Akershus University College

Nils Pharo
General Co-chair
Oslo and Akershus University College

CHIIR 2017 Program Chairs' Welcome

It is an honour to present the program for the second ACM SIGIR Conference on Human Information Interaction and Retrieval (CHIIR 2017), held in Oslo, Norway from March 7 to March 11, 2017. CHIIR offers the opportunity to present and discuss research on user-centered approaches to information retrieval, information access and information interaction, including studies of interactive systems, searcher behaviour, novel interaction paradigms, interface design, new evaluation methods, and a range of related areas. CHIIR is an interdisciplinary event in which researchers, students and practitioners working across several areas, including information retrieval, information science and human computer interaction, come together to think creatively about the challenges and opportunities afforded by digital information systems. Welcome to all the CHIIR-ists joining us this year!

The CHIIR 2017 program consists of Full Papers (10 pages), Perspectives Papers (10 pages) and Short Papers (4 pages). We received a total of 112 submissions: 48 Full Papers, 9 Perspectives Papers and 55 Short Papers. Of these, we accepted 19 Full Papers (40%), 5 Perspectives Papers (56%) and 36 Short Papers (65%). We also accepted one Full Paper as a Short Paper. We were pleased to receive so many strong Perspectives Papers, which are meant to present novel ideas or insights, and we hope these will inspire some great discussions. Each Full and Perspectives paper is allocated a 30-minute presentation slot in the program. Short papers are presented as posters during a special evening session, beginning with a short boaster presentation.

In addition to contributed papers, the CHIIR program features three keynote talks by prominent academic and industry researchers, representing the breadth of interests in the CHIIR community: Norbert Fuhr (University of Duisburg-Essen, Germany) , Ann Blandford (University College London, UK) and Håkon Wium Lie (Opera Software, Norway). In addition to these speakers and the main conference program, CHIIR features a Doctoral Consortium, two Tutorials, and three Workshops.

We would like to acknowledge the excellent work of the Organizing Committee, including the Doctoral Consortium Chair, Katriina Byström (Oslo and Akershus University College of Applied Sciences, Norway); the Workshops and Tutorials Chair, Preben Hansen (Stockholm University, Sweden), and the Proceedings Chair, Sampath Jayarathna (California State Polytechnic University Pomona, USA). The paper reviewing and selection process was enabled by an outstanding 12 member Senior Program Committee and a diverse and international general Program Committee consisting of 77 members. Our thanks and the credits for creating a high quality technical program go to them.

We would also like to thank the general chairs, Ragnar Nordlie and Nils Pharo, both of Oslo and Akershus University College of Applied Sciences, Norway, who placed their trust in us, provided guidance when needed, and contributed substantially to the excellent program in place for the conference. A final thanks and enthusiastic cheer (!) for the authors and attendees who are contributing their work and ideas here in Oslo at this second CHIIR conference. We hope that you find the CHIIR 2017 program interesting and thought-provoking and that you return home with exciting research plans.

Luanne Freund
CHIIR 2017 Program Co-Chair
University of British Columbia, Canada

Birger Larsen
CHIIR 2017 Program Co-Chair
Aalborg University, Denmark

Daniel M. Russell
CHIIR 2017 Program Co-Chair
Google, Inc., USA

Table of Contents

Paper Session: Search Dynamics

Paper Session: Social Signals

Paper Session: Searching and Learning

Paper Session: Personal Information Management and Collaborative Search

Short Papers

Doctoral Consortiums

Tutorials

Workshops

CHIIR 2017 Conference Organization

Conference Chairs:	Ragnar Nordlie (*Oslo & Akershus University College of Applied Sciences, Norway*) Nils Pharo *(Oslo and Akershus University College of Applied Sciences, Norway)*
Program Chairs:	Luanne Freund *(University of British Columbia, Canada)* Birger Larsen *(Aalborg University, Denmark)* Dan Russel *(Google, USA)*
Workshop & Tutorial Chair:	Preben Hansen *(Stockholm University, Sweden)*
Proceedings Chair:	Sampath Jayarathna *(California State Polytechnic University Pomona, USA)*
Doctoral Consortium Chair:	Katriina Byström *(Oslo and Akershus University College of Applied Sciences, Norway)*
Senior Program Committee:	Leif Azzopardi *(University of Glasgow, UK)* Jaap Kamps *(University of Amsterdam, Netherlands)* Diane Kelly *(University of Tennessee, USA)* Gary Marchionini *(University of North Carolina at Chapel Hill, USA)* Andreas Nuernberger *(Otto-von-Guericke University of Magdeburg, Germany)* Heather O'Brien *(University of British Columbia, Canada)* Ian Ruthven *(University of Strathclyde, UK)* Chirag Shah *(Rutgers University, USA)* Catherine Smith *(Kent State University, USA)* Paul Thomas *(Microsoft, Australia)* Peiling Wang *(University of Tennessee, USA)* Ryen W. White *(Microsoft Research, USA)*
Program Committee:	Dirk Ahlers *(Norwegian University of Science and Technology, Norway)* Omar Alonso *(Microsoft, USA)* Robin Aly *(University of Twente, Netherlands)* Judit Bar-Ilan *(Bar-Ilan University, Israel)* Klaus Berberich *(Max Planck Institute for Informatics, Germany)* Nicholas Belkin *(Rutgers University, USA)* Ralf Bierig *(National College of Ireland, Ireland)* Kathy Brennan *(University of North Carolina at Chapel Hill, USA)* Peter Bruza *(Queensland University of Technology, Australia)* George Buchanan *(City University, London, UK)* Robert Capra *(University of North Carolina at Chapel Hill, USA)* Ed H. Chi *(Google, Inc., USA)* Charles Cole *(McGill University, Canada)* Michael Cole *(LexisNexis, USA)* Anita Crescenzi *(University of North Carolina at Chapel Hill, USA)* Tina Du *(University of South Australia, Australia)* David Ellis *(Aberystwyth University, UK)* Nicola Ferro *(University of Padua, Italy)*

Program Committee (continued):

Ingo Frommholz *(University of Bedfordshire, UK)*
Wai-Tat Fu *(University of Illinois, USA)*
Norbert Fuhr *(University of Duisburg-Essen, Germany)*
Elke Grefeneder *(Humboldt University, Germany)*
Matthias Hagen *(Bauhaus-Universität Weimar, Germany)*
Preben Hansen *(Stockholm University, Sweden)*
Morgan Harvey *(Northumbria University, UK)*
Claudia Hauff *(Delft University of Technology, Netherlands)*
Jiyin He *(Centrum Wiskunde & Informatica, Netherlands)*
Daqing He *(University of Pittsburgh, USA)*
Brent Hecht *(University of Minnesota, USA)*
Jeff Huang *(Brown University, USA)*
Isto Huvila *(Uppsala University, Sweden)*
Peter Ingwersen *(University of Copenhagen, Denmark)*
Hideo Joho *(University of Tsukuba, Japan)*
Gareth Jones *(Dublin City University, Ireland)*
Yvonne Kammerer *(Knowledge Media Research Center, Germany)*
Noriko Kando *(National Institute of Informatics, Japan)*
Saraschandra Karanam *(Utrecht University, Netherlands)*
Jussi Karlgren *(Gavagai & KTH Royal Institute of Technology, Sweden)*
Jaana Kekäläinen *(University of Tampere)*
Claus-Peter Klas *(GESIS - Leibniz Institute for Social Sciences, Germany)*
Rick Kopak *(University of British Columbia, Canada)*
Udo Kruschwitz *(University of Essex, UK)*
Sanna Kumpulainen *(Tampere University of Technology, Finland)*
Dirk Lewandowski *(Hamburg University of Applied Sciences, Germany)*
Christina Lioma *(University of Copenhagen, Denmark)*
Suzanne Little *(Dublin City University, Ireland)*
Chang Liu *(Peking University, China)*
Jingjing Liu *(University of South Carolina, USA)*
Qiaoling Liu *(CareerBuilder LLC, USA)*
Ying-Hsang Liu *(Charles Sturt University, Australia)*
Andreas Lommatzsch *(Technische Universität Berlin, Germany)*
Irene Lopatovska *(Pratt Institute, USA)*
Marianne Lykke *(Aalborg University, Denmark)*
Andrew Macfarlane *(City University London, UK)*
Athanasios Mazarakis *(ZBW / Kiel University, Germany)*
Dana Mckay *(Swinburne University of Technology Library, Australia)*
Peter Mutschke *(GESIS – Leibniz Institute for the Social Sciences, Germany)*
Gabriella Pasi *(Università degli Studi di Milano Bicocca, Italy)*
Edie Rasmussen *(University of British Columbia, Canada)*
Rebecca Reynolds *(Rutgers University, USA)*
Soo Young Rieh *(University of Michigan, USA)*
Stefan Rueger *(Knowledge Media Institute, Open University, UK)*
Tony Russell-Rose *(UXLabs, UK)*
Alan Said *(University of Skövde, Sweden)*
Ladislao Salmeron *(University of Valencia, Spain)*
Eero Sormunen *(University of Tampere, Finland)*

Program Committee (continued):

Jaime Teevan *(Microsoft Research, USA)*
Anastasios Tombros *(Queen Mary University of London, UK)*
Andrew Trotman *(University of Otago, New Zealand)*
Pertti Vakkari *(University of Tampere, Finland)*
Suzan Verberne *(Radboud University Nijmegen, Netherlands)*
Barbara Wildemuth *(University of North Carolina at Chapel Hill, USA)*
Iris Xie *(Universty of Wisconsin-Milwaukee, USA)*
Xiaojun Yuan *(University at Albany, State University of New York, USA)*
Pengyi Zhang *(Peking University, China)*
Yan Zhang *(University of Texas at Austin, USA)*
Yong Zheng *(Illinois Institute of Technology, USA)*

CHIIR 2017 Sponsors & Supporters

Sponsors: SIGIR Special Interest Group on Information Retrieval — SIGCHI

Supporters: Oslo and Akershus University College of Applied Sciences — Oslo and Akershus University College

City of Oslo — City of Oslo

Modeling Interactive Information Retrieval as a Stochastic Process

Norbert Fuhr
University of Duisburg-Essen
Germany
norbert.fuhr@uni-due.de

ABSTRACT

Stochastic models have a long history in IR, starting from probabilistic models for (non-interactive) IR, and later for evaluation measures like e.g. average precision or discounted cumulated gain. The probabilistic ranking principle defines the order in which a user should inspect the documents retrieved by the system, for maximizing the retrieval quality experienced by the user. In a similar way, for interactive IR, the interactive probabilistic ranking principle (IPRP) defines a framework for the optimum ordering of suggestions / possible actions to be considered by the user.

For modeling sequences of interactions, different variants of Markov models have been proposed by a number of researchers. Here a user moves stochastically between different model states, which are not directly observable; instead, some signal is emitted along with each transition. In the simple Markov model, there is a unique mapping from signal sequences to state sequences, while hidden Markov models drop this assumption. In partially observable Markov models, some transitions may not be observable at all. Orthogonal to this distinction, in Markov decision processes, it is additionally assumed that the user achieves a certain gain with each transition.

Although the theoretic foundations of these models are well-known, their application to interactive retrieval raises a number of research questions. In the ideal case, we would like to model search progress at a level that is comparable to cognitive models. Thus, as a basic requirement, the states should have some semantic meaning and correspond to different cognitive tasks / states of the user. Moreover, search progress should be somehow reflected by the sequence of states the user passes through. As basic 'signals' we have the user's actions which are typically recorded in the system log, and thus easily available for experimentation. Furthermore, other observation data can be collected, such as key logging, mouse movements, eye tracking or EEG data (the latter two types only in lab experiments)

There are three major applications of these models. First, and most important, as a realization of the IPRP, they can be used for user guidance. Second, the analysis of these models serves for a detailed, user-oriented analysis of a interactive IR system, pointing out e.g. where users spend most of their time, or where the transition probabilities of specific actions is below the expectation. Third, the models can be used for more realistic stochastic simulations of interactive IR.

In this talk, after illustrating the basic concepts, we present some recent research results illustrating the general feasibility of research along these lines.

CHIIR '17, March 7–11, 2017, Oslo, Norway.

ACM ISBN 978-1-4503-4677-1/17/03.

DOI: http://dx.doi.org/10.1145/3020165.3020190

1. REFERENCES

[1] N. Fuhr. A probability ranking principle for interactive information retrieval. *Information Retrieval*, 11(3):251–265, 2008. http://dx.doi.org/10.1007/s10791-008-9045-0.

[2] Vu T. Tran and Norbert Fuhr. Using eye-tracking with dynamic areas of interest for analyzing interactive information retrieval. In William R. Hersh, Jamie Callan, Yoelle Maarek, and Mark Sanderson, editors, *Proceedings of the 35th international ACM SIGIR conference on Research and development in Information Retrieval*, pages 1165–1166. ACM, 2012.

[3] Vu T. Tran and Norbert Fuhr. Markov modeling for user interaction in retrieval. In *SIGIR 2013 Workshop on Modeling User Behavior for Information Retrieval Evaluation (MUBE 2013)*, August 2013.

[4] Yinan Zhang and Chengxiang Zhai. Information retrieval as card playing: A formal model for optimizing interactive retrieval interface. In *Proceedings of the 38th International ACM SIGIR Conference on Research and Development in Information Retrieval*, SIGIR '15, pages 685–694, New York, NY, USA, 2015. ACM.

[5] Yinan Zhang and Chengxiang Zhai. A sequential decision formulation of the interface card model for interactive ir. In *Proceedings of the 39th International ACM SIGIR Conference on Research and Development in Information Retrieval*, SIGIR '16, pages 85–94, New York, NY, USA, 2016. ACM.

Engaging In Information Interaction

Ann Blandford
University College London (UCL)
London, UK
a.blandford@ucl.ac.uk

ABSTRACT

People interact with information in a myriad of ways [1]. As well as actively seeking information, people also encounter it, and there have been various efforts to design systems that support encountering and keeping track of encountered information [2,3]. But what people engage with depends: on how it fits with their ongoing activities as well as whether they recognize its potential value [4]. Sometimes, people are open to engaging with information, and may experience information encountering as serendipitous; at other times, a similar encounter might feel like overload or distraction [5]. The design of systems that support effective engagement will ideally take account of people's practices and contexts as well as their interests.

Perhaps paradoxically, serendipitous encounters rarely happen by chance: people invest in various ways in increasing the likelihood of valuable information encounters that enable them to keep up-to-date and make creative leaps [6,7]; again, good design can facilitate productive interactions with information [8]. In this talk, I will discuss various qualitative studies of how people fit information encountering into their lives, how they experience serendipity, and some of the ways they invest up-front effort in future information interactions; I will also highlight opportunities to design to support people in making best use of information they find.

Author Keywords

Serendipity; information interaction; situated use

BIOGRAPHY

Ann Blandford is Professor of Human–Computer Interaction at UCL and former Director of UCL Interaction Centre. She started her career in industry, but soon moved into academia, where she developed a focus on the use and usability of computer systems. She leads research on how people interact with and make sense of information, and how technology can better support people's information needs, with a focus on situated interactions. Within this, she has led studies on information encountering and how we can design to support serendipitous encounters with information. She has over 200 international, peer-reviewed publications, including a Synthesis Lecture on "Interacting with Information" [1].

CHIIR'17, March 7–11, 2017, Oslo, Norway.
ACM ISBN 978-1-4503-4677-1/17/03.
http://dx.doi.org/10.1145/3020165.3038293

REFERENCES

1. Blandford, A., & Attfield, S. (2010). Interacting with information. *Synthesis Lectures on Human-Centered Informatics*, *3*(1), 1-99.
2. Jones, W., Bruce, H., & Dumais, S. (2001, October). Keeping found things found on the web. In *Proceedings of the tenth international conference on Information and knowledge management* (pp. 119-126). ACM.
3. Adams, A., Blandford, A., Budd, D., & Bailey, N. (2005). Organizational communication and awareness: a novel solution for health informatics. *Health Informatics Journal*, *11*(3), 163-178.
4. Makri, S., & Blandford, A. (2012). Coming across information serendipitously-Part 1: A process model. *Journal of Documentation*, *68*(5), 684-705.
5. Pontis, S., Kefalidou, G., Blandford, A., Forth, J., Makri, S., Sharples, S., ... & Woods, M. (2015). Academics' responses to encountered information: Context matters. *Journal of the Association for Information Science and Technology.*
6. Dantonio, L., Makri, S., & Blandford, A. (2012). Coming across academic social media content serendipitously. *Proceedings of the American Society for Information Science and Technology*, *49*(1), 1-10.
7. Pontis, S., Blandford, A., Greifeneder, E., Attalla, H., & Neal, D. (2015). Keeping up to date: An academic researcher's information journey. *Journal of the Association for Information Science and Technology.*
8. Makri, S., Blandford, A., Woods, M., Sharples, S., & Maxwell, D. (2014). "Making my own luck": Serendipity strategies and how to support them in digital information environments. *Journal of the Association for Information Science and Technology*, *65*(11), 2179-2194.

CSS and User-Adapted Web Presentations

Håkon Wium Lie
Opera Software
Oslo, Norway
howcome@opera.com

ABSTRACT

Håkon Wium Lie proposed Cascading Style Sheets (CSS) while working with Tim Berners-Lee at CERN in 1994. CSS has become a cornerstone web technology which enables beautiful web pages across a range of devices. The CSS specification was developed while Håkon worked for W3C, and as CTO of Opera Software he shepherded CSS implementations.

He is now the chairman of YesLogic, which makes the Prince CSS-to-PDF formatter. He holds a MS from MIT's Media Lab, and a PhD from the University of Oslo.

In his keynote, Håkon will discuss how CSS was designed to allow web content to be presented in different contexts, serving different user needs.

BIOGRAPHY

Håkon Wium Lie proposed CSS in 1994 and is still hard at work on CSS specifications. He is the CTO of Opera Software and a champion for CSS compliance in all browsers. Lie is also a director of YesLogic, the company behind the CSS-based Prince formatter, which was used to produce a book he co-authored: Cascading Style Sheets: Designing for the Web. He has a Masters degree from the MIT Media Lab and a PhD from the University of Oslo. He is an advocate of Acid2, the video element, web fonts, and growing apples. Real apples.

CHIIR '17, March 07-11, 2017, Oslo, Norway
ACM 978-1-4503-4677-1/17/03.
http://dx.doi.org/10.1145/3020165.3038294

User Interests in German Social Science Literature Search – A Large Scale Log Analysis

Daniel Hienert
GESIS – Leibniz Institute for the Social Sciences
Cologne, Germany
daniel.hienert@gesis.org

ABSTRACT

The social sciences are a broad research field with a lot of sub- and related disciplines. Accordingly, user interests in a digital library for the social sciences are manifold. In this study we analyzed nine years log data of a social science digital library to get an overview of the fields, categories, topics and detailed information needs users are interested in. Based on the log data we have built interactive visualizations which give an overview and concurrently let us look at the detailed interests of users. The underlying log data and the created visualizations are then used to analyze user interests at different hierarchical levels and on a temporal view. The results show that there are topical interests of the users in specific fields and topics of the social sciences but at the same time there exists a diversity of different information needs. Based on these findings we analyze in detail the gap between the indexing language of the system used to annotate documents and the language users apply to articulate their information needs.

Keywords

Log Analysis; User Interests; Social Sciences; Digital Library

1. INTRODUCTION

The nature of the *Social Sciences* to describe the social relationships between humans and their interactions within the society makes them an interdisciplinary field with relations to a lot of other disciplines. The Social Sciences incorporate disciplines such as Sociology, Demography, Ethnology, Political Science, Education, Psychology, Communication Studies, Economics, Social Policy, Interdisciplinary and Applied Social Sciences and related areas such as the Humanities, Legal and Administrative Science, Natural Sciences, Technology and Medicine[1]. Maurice B. Line summarized the characteristics of the social sciences as a challenging discipline for bibliographic control pointing out that there is, among other points, an inherent instability of the subject matter and a lack of terminology that was common over time and across countries [18].

This complexity is also mirrored in digital libraries which collect and offer bibliographic (and other) information for the social sciences. On the level of documents and databases, document collections from different sub fields of the social sciences need to be collected from different origin databases or as a part of larger multidisciplinary databases to get a complete view of the whole field. On the level of semantic integration, knowledge organization systems try to solve the challenges of the complex taxonomy and the multiple database problem with their different thesauri and classification systems. On the human side, there is the challenge that users with a diversity of information needs in the different fields of the social sciences are looking for information. Understanding these information needs and classifying them in a more abstract classification system is a first step to understand the topical interests of users and to build better supporting services.

To observe and capture the complexity of the social sciences on the base of user-system interaction we concentrate in this work on the following two research questions: (1) "*What are the user interests in the (German) Social Sciences on different topical levels and over a long period of time?*" and (2) "*Are knowledge organization systems such as thesauri good enough to capture these user interests?*"

To this purpose we analyze nine years log data from Sowiport, a digital library for the Social Sciences. The goal is to capture the user interests at different levels of main and sub- categories, topics and user information needs. Based on the log data we created different interactive visualizations which allow analyzing the topical interests from overview to detail and on a temporal basis. We will especially investigate the differences between the controlled language used for the indexation of documents and the language used by the users to address their information needs.

2. RELATED WORK

In this section we first report on the characteristics of log analysis in general. Then we will show which insights have been captured with log analysis in different domains. The last sub section in particular refers to the information seeking behavior of social scientists.

2.1 Log Analysis in General

Log analysis is a method to analyze the interaction between the user and the search system. Kelly [15] arranges log analysis in the middle of a research continuum, one step towards the system`s focus. It can be a compromise between the system and the human focus as user interactions are captured in logs, but the method is scalable and can identify usage patterns for a mass of end users. Peters [25] contributes a literature review about the history and development of Transaction Log Analysis (TLA) until the mid-

[1] see for example the definition of the UNESCO at http://portal.unesco.org/en/ev.php-URL_ID=13135&URL_DO=DO_TOPIC&URL_SECTION=201.html in section "Group I - Social sciences, including" or the browsable Universal Decimal Classification (UDC) for the field of the Social Sciences at http://udcdata.info/18549

CHIIR '17, March 07 - 11, 2017, Oslo, Norway

ACM 978-1-4503-4677-1/17/03…$15.00
DOI: http://dx.doi.org/10.1145/3020165.3020168

90s. The article shows the diversity of applications for which TLA can be used: from computing basic statistical data such as the average session length or average keywords entered per user to the field of analyzing more complex user behavior, e.g. to find out what makes a session successful. Jansen [11] gives a good overview of the possibilities and limitations of log analysis and describes that it can identify trends and typical interactions, but cannot record the user's perception of the task, the underlying information need or the underlying situation and context of the search. Agosti et al. [1] explicitly distinguish between web search engine log analysis (WSE) and digital library log analysis (DLS). In WSE users query a search engine with diverse information needs and the retrieved documents are webpages (or other types such as images, videos etc.). In DLS users are searching in a specialized domain or around a specific topic. Here, retrieved documents are (mostly) bibliographic records. These documents are structured and organized in a knowledge organization system (KOS) such as thesauri and classification systems. A second aspect is that domain or topic knowledge can influence search behavior. Wildemuth [29], for example, showed that search tactics of medical students changed over time when the domain knowledge changed. Kelly and Cool [16] show the influence of topic familiarity on searching efficacy and reading time. White et al. [28] conducted a large-scale analysis of web search logs and showed that domain experts had different search behavior than non-experts.

2.2 Log Analysis in Different Domains

Log analysis has been conducted in different domains to derive knowledge about the specific information seeking behavior of users in different scientific communities.

Islamaj Dogan et al. [10] for example analyzed the search behavior of *biomedical* users in PubMed by the investigation of one month log data. Among other things they annotated a subset of 10,000 randomly chosen search queries with semantic categories and found that searches by author name, gene/protein and by disease were most frequent. Natarajan et al. [23] conducted a small scale log analysis of an electronic health record system. Here, queries were manually classified to different semantic categories such as "Laboratory or Test Result" or "Disease or Syndrome". Nicholas et al. [24] addressed the issue of integrating log files from five different sources of health information. They present a method to categorize web page titles to health categories on a large scale. For the domain of *chemistry* Davis et al. [2,3] examined transaction logs of electronic journal downloads of 29 journals from the American Chemical Society (ACS) servers. Their studies are based on the prior observation that chemists rely heavily on journal literature. First, they found that the majority of users downloaded only few articles and consulted only few journals [3]. To answer the question how scientists locate published articles in ACS they found that most people came from the electronic library catalog and from bibliographic databases [2]. Ke et al. [14] report results and findings from a transaction log analysis in the domain of *Science, Technology and Medicine.* This work investigates large logs from Elsevier's ScienceDirect website in Taiwan offering bibliographic information and full-text articles from 1,300 journals and about 625,000 users. The authors describe different usage patterns, for example, that full-text article viewing is the most active category; about different user actions (34% browse vs. 13% search) or about the average length of search queries with about 2.27 terms. They also report on common query terms ("acid", "review", "cell" etc.), but did not further process them. Jones et al. [13] contribute a study with a transaction log analysis of user activity in the *Computer Science* Technical Reports Collection of the New Zealand Digital Library. This collection includes about 46,000 technical reports and the authors analyzed a log of 61 weeks with about 30,000 queries. In summary, they found very short sessions, few queries per user, simple queries and small changes for reformulating and, that only the first results were viewed. The authors also present a list with commonly appearing query terms ("compression", "object", "software" etc.) and state that this data could serve as a basis to identify user groups whose information needs have been met or not. Another work in the field of *Computer Science* [20] analyzed six months of usage of the Research Index digital library and found that users preferred relatively brief queries and had short session times. Yi et al. [30] conducted a log analysis of two fields under the umbrella of the social sciences: *Psychology* and *History*. Besides basic query statistics they conducted a more sophisticated analysis of query terms and their ability to categorize queries to subjects. They tested with (1) single query terms, (2) co-occurring word pairs and (3) multiword terms and found that the last method worked best for that purpose. Within the analysis of a multi-disciplinary OPAC (including the field "social sciences and law") Villen-Rueda et al. [27] studied and compared the distribution of queries with author, title or subject search. In their analysis they found low values for subject searches of about 14% in contrast to related literature which report values between 26% and 83%.

Apart from [30] we could not find any transaction log analysis which use specifically logs from a social science digital library. Most work in TLA concentrates very much on statistical measures of session lengths, average query terms etc. In this work we rather want to focus on the topical interests of users on different levels of abstraction.

2.3 Information Seeking Behavior of Social Scientists

A study in 1993 by Ellis et al. [5] identified six basic information seeking strategies of social scientists: (1) *starting* (initial search for information), (2) *chaining* (following referential connections such as references), (3) *browsing* (e.g. by scanning of journals or tables of contents), (4) *differentiating* (between sources to filter materials), (5) *monitoring* (the field of interest by following sources such as journals, conferences) and (6) *extracting* (relevant material from sources). In 2006, after the long-time establishment of digital libraries and web-based information retrieval systems, Meho & Tibbo [22] mainly confirmed Ellis' model, but added some new behavior features such as (7) *accessing* (the material found with methods above), (8) *networking* (with colleagues to exchange information), (9) *verifying* (the accuracy of the information), and (10) *information managing* (by archiving and organizing the information).

All lot of these activities are nowadays (at least in a basic manner) supported by modern digital libraries. Users can search for information, follow references and citations, browse in journals or proceedings, see citation counts, access the full text, store information found and make alerts for new search results. This gives some evidence that user`s interests in this field can be concluded from user interaction within digital libraries with large populations.

3. A DIGITAL LIBRARY FOR SOCIAL SCIENCE LITERATURE INFORMATION

Sowiport[1] is a digital library for social science information [9] and contains more than nine million bibliographic records, full texts and research projects from twenty-two different databases with German-language and English-language content. The portal reaches about 25,000 unique visitors per week, mainly from German speaking countries.

The bibliographic records contained in Sowiport are mostly annotated with keywords and sometimes with category information depending on the source database. For example, for records of the most requested German database SOLIS (Social Science Literature Information System) both information are available. Here, 475,000 documents are manually annotated with keywords from the thesaurus for the social sciences (TheSoz[2]) with about 12,000 entries and categorized with the classification for the social sciences[3] with 14 main classes and 145 sub classes. However, other databases included in Sowiport use different thesauri and classification systems what makes it difficult to deploy an overall indexing and classification system. To solve this issue we have created the heterogeneity service (HTS) which expands the user's search query with equivalents from other thesauri. The HTS contains cross-concordances [21] for 25 different thesauri with about 513,000 controlled terms. When a search query is submitted by a user of Sowiport it will be internally expanded with equivalent terms from the HTS. For example, the query term "workforce" is expanded with terms like "labor force", "manpower", "employees" and "workers".

A second service is the Search Term Recommender (STR) [19] which can map arbitrary user terms to controlled terms from a subject-specific vocabulary. The system is based on a co-occurrence analysis with free terms from titles and abstracts and controlled terms from descriptors. A logarithmically modified Jaccard similarity measure is used to rank term suggestions for a given input term. The STR service is included in the term recommender of Sowiport to propose controlled terms for free user inputs. If, for example, the user enters the term "hunger" into the search bar, the system proposes terms like "nutrition", "food", "poverty", "Third World" and "developing country".

4. LOG DATA PROCESSING

In this section we describe the different preprocessing steps from raw log data files to explicit user actions with keyword and category information.

4.1 Building User Actions

The transaction logs for the analysis of user interest in the social sciences were generated by two different technical systems underlying Sowiport. From 2007 until April 2014 Sowiport based on an own-developed JAVA framework and a SOLR search engine (sowiport-old). Since 2014 the digital library framework VuFind (sowiport-new) with a SOLR search engine is used.

For both frameworks all search actions were logged in a database table. This table was expanded for each search query with the first ten search results as a list of document IDs. These IDs have been either recorded in separate Tomcat log files and were matched in a preprocessing step by the session-id and the search query (for sowiport-old) or were directly logged in the database table (sowiport-new). Additionally, all search engine robots in the table were marked with the help of a heuristic. All rows with the same IP and with more than 100 rows in the table were compared to a number of patterns which indicate a link call from URLs that had been propagated in search engines. If only these patterns were matched and no other actions were found the IP was marked as a bot and excluded from further processing. For sowiport-new bots have been additionally excluded from logging if the request header has been given any evidence for a bot.

We only used *initial searches* from users which (1) entered new or add additional terms in the simple or advanced search form and submitted the search or (2) initiate a new search by clicking on authors, keywords, classifications, journals or proceedings. We did not take search modifications such as paging, sorting, filtering, faceting, exporting or any other adaption into account. This way, search topics are not count multiple times per user.

In a next step we extracted two user actions from these tables: (1) a user viewing the detailed information for a document record ("*view_record*") and (2) a search query conducted by a user ("*search*"). Both actions were identified with different patterns for sowiport-old and sowiport-new and the actions with session-id, date, action type, user search terms, viewed document-ids or search results list ids were copied to a new table. The final table contains 8,799,694 user actions from November 2007 to July 2016 with 2,148,414 searches and 6,651,280 record views.

4.2 An Overall Keyword & Classification System

In the next processing step we want to apply keyword and category information to each user action. The information therefore derives from the record which has been viewed (for the *view_record* action) or from the results of the search query (for the *search* action). In the previous section we already addressed the issue of different thesauri and classification systems of the twenty-two different source databases included in Sowiport. Consequently, documents appearing in our user actions are annotated with different thesauri and classification information. To achieve a canonical categorization we decided to use the thesaurus for the social sciences TheSoz and the classification for the social sciences (explained in Section 3) as an overall classification system. This has some benefits: (1) a large part of the viewed documents and search results contain SOLIS documents (the log data shows that more than half of user actions contain SOLIS records), (2) TheSoz descriptors and classifications are manually added to SOLIS documents and the system is of a high quality and has been improved over the years by information professionals, (3) we have already developed a set of services such as HTS and STR (see Section 3) with which we can transform keywords from other thesauri and from uncontrolled terms to descriptors of the thesaurus for the social sciences.

For user actions which already included one or more SOLIS documents (about 4.8 million actions) we directly used the keyword and category information. In particular, for a *view_record* action we used the top three keywords and the main classification of the viewed document. For a *search* action we computed the most assigned keywords and classification from the resulting documents and used the top three keywords and the most common classification.

[1] http://sowiport.gesis.org

[2] http://www.gesis.org/en/services/research/tools-zur-recherche/social-science-thesaurus/

[3] http://www.gesis.org.org/unser-angebot/recherchieren/tools-zur-recherche/klassifikation-sozialwissenschaften/

For user actions without SOLIS documents (about 3.8 million actions) we applied a number of processing steps. If the record(s) contained keyword information we transformed those to equivalent SOLIS keywords with the help of the HTS service. If not, we used the title of the record and user search terms, cleaned them from stop words and other specialized characters and transformed them to SOLIS keywords with the help of the STR service. If the action then has SOLIS keyword information we applied the top category learned from the existing actions for the top three keywords.

We are aware that the application of these methods gives only an abstraction of the users' true information needs. The quality of capturing them thereby depends on the quality of the document collection, on the ranking functionality and the quality of the HTS and STR services. However, the application of these methods allowed large scale clustering of search interests and we were able to add keywords and categories to 8,605,189 user actions.

5. VISUALIZATIONS

The main question for the visualization part is how we can achieve a clear and meaningful presentation of more than eight million user actions including categorization, keywords and user search terms. The main focus here is to get an instant overview of user interests at each level of detail. We have therefore created an interactive visualization which allows an easy analysis of specific sub fields without getting lost in the data. To this aim we exploited the hierarchy of the classification system and decided to arrange the user actions on four zoomable levels: (1) main categories, (2) subcategories, (3) keywords, and (4) user search terms. A path in this hierarchy can be for example: Sociology → Sociology of Economics → Income → Social Inequality. The prototype can be found at http://vizgr.org/social-science-topics.

The first level gives an overview of the 14 main categories from the classification for the social sciences. For the visualization we used the circle pack layout[4] of the D3.js framework. In this visualization type the circle radius of the main categories (level one) and the subcategories (level two) is built recursively by keywords with more than 500 user actions on the third level (this amount is still doable by the framework). This way, the visualization is an abstraction of all user actions and shows only the most interesting categories and topics users are interested in. Exact proportions given in the tables of this paper are computed from the database table. In Figure 1, we can get an instant overview on which top categories were most frequently accessed by users. For example, the third largest main category is "Interdisciplinary and Applied Field of the Social Sciences".

With a mouse click on a category we can zoom in. Now, all categories within the top category are shown. 145 sub classes are ordered in the top categories. Here, the circle radius encodes the number of actions within this category. This way we can get an instant overview on which categories were most frequently accessed by users. For example, in Figure 2, we can see the subcategories of "Interdisciplinary and Applied Field of the Social Sciences".

With a second mouse click on a category bubble we can zoom into that certain category. Now, all keywords with more than 500 user actions are shown (Figure 3 shows the topics for the category "Social Problems"). Again, the circle radius encodes the number of user actions with this keyword. We can see which topics appear most frequently in this specific category.

With a third mouse click on a keyword bubble we can zoom into that keyword. Now we see most frequent user search terms combinations for this keyword (here for the topic "Discrimination" shown in Figure 4). For this we used a tree layout[5]. The tree layout is separated by several levels from left to right. On the first level (tree node) we see the document keyword. On the second level it is shown which user search terms were frequently used for this document keyword. The strength of relationship is visualized by the ordering (from top to bottom) and additionally by different edge width and the node radius. On the second level we can then see which second user term has been combined with the prior term (and so on). This way, we can see instantly which user search term combinations appear most frequently for a given document keyword.

6. ANALYSIS

Having applied the same classification system to all user actions, we now have a good overview on which main categories, subcategories and topics users are interested in. The visualization gives us the chance to dive into the data and to have an instant overview on what is interesting.

6.1 Main Categories

The clustering by main categories gives us an overview on an abstract level which broad fields of the social sciences our users are interested in. Table 1 shows the main categories ordered by the percentage of user actions. The top 5 main categories are (M1) Sociology, (M2) Interdisciplinary and Applied Fields of the Social Sciences, (M3) Political Science, (M4) Education and Pedagogics and (M5) Science of Communication. The percentage of user actions shows that a good portion of about 73% of the users is interested in these five fields. Of these, Sociology is by far the largest category with about 28%, followed by Interdisciplinary and Applied Fields of the Social Sciences with 15% and Political Science with 13%.

We find it hard to identify subject distributions from prior studies on the social science domain that we could compare our findings to. In fact, even the term "social sciences" is not defined consistently in the literature. In 1983, Haart [7] gives an overview of the different definitions of social sciences in different countries and classification systems (Dewey, UDC, UNESCO). For Germany, the selection of the main fields of the social sciences in his and our table is nearly identical. Some evidence about the distribution is given from the field of citation analysis. Early work from Earle & Vickery [4] in 1965 found Politics, Economics, Education and Sociology to be the largest subjects by citation count in social science literature of the UK. Line [17] in 1981 found Psychology, Sociology and economics to be predominant from citation counts of 300 monographs and 140 serials. Haart in 1983 [7] reports from the DISISS project with 2,760 serials that the subjects Economics, Education, Political Science and Psychology were prominent. We were unable to find more recent material showing the distribution of social science subjects by citation analysis with an adequate distinction of subject fields.

[4] https://github.com/mbostock/d3/wiki/Pack-Layout

[5] https://github.com/mbostock/d3/wiki/Tree-Layout

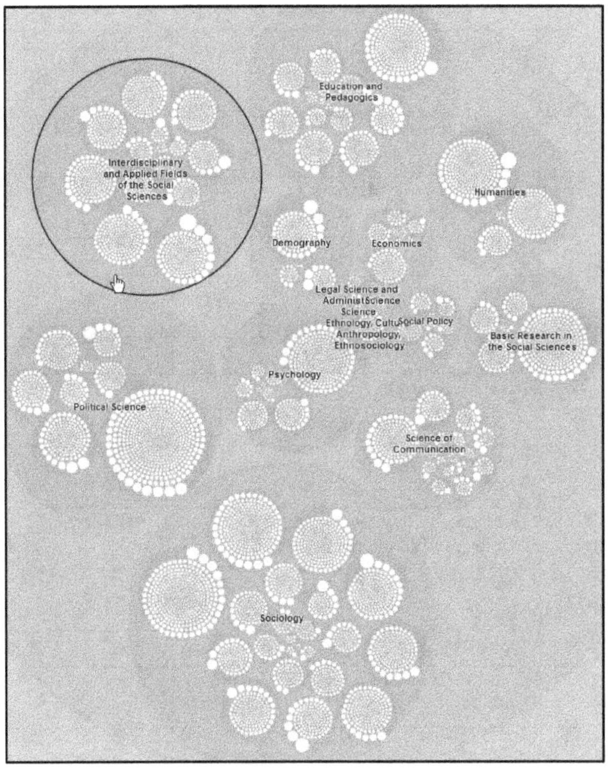

Fig. 1. First level: Overview of the main categories

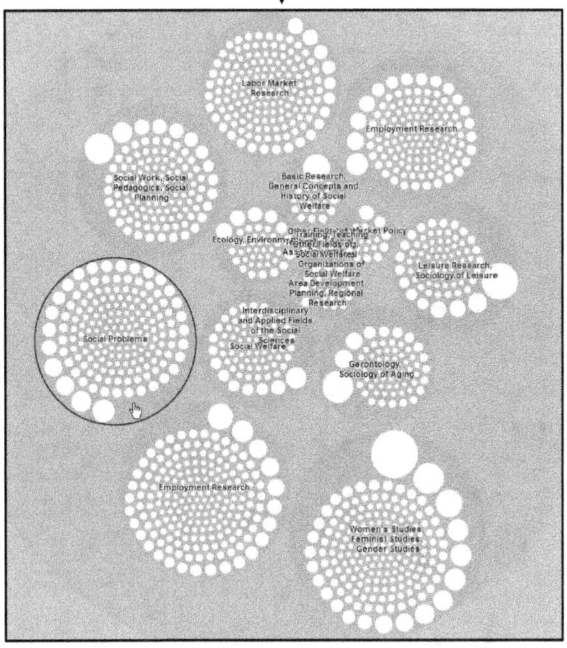

Fig. 2. Second level: Overview of the subcategories in "Interdisciplinary and Applied Field of the Social Sciences"

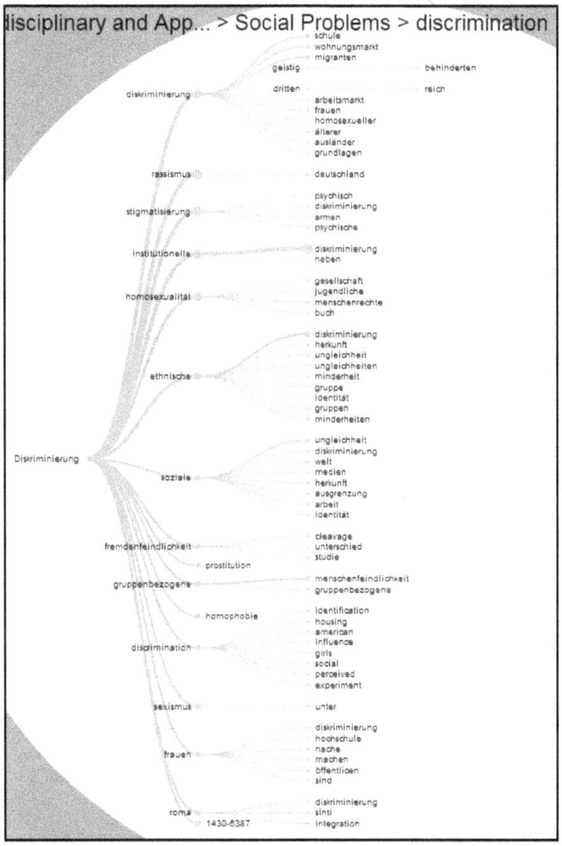

Fig. 4. Fourth level: User search terms for the topic "Discrimination". Not translated as these are user terms.

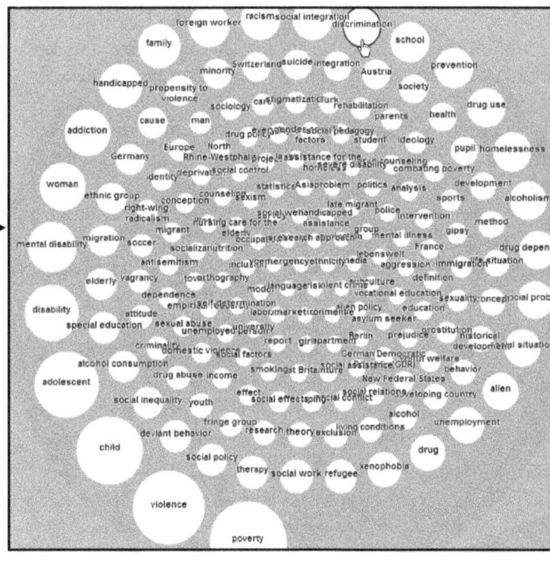

Fig. 3. Third level: Topics in the category "Social Problems"

6.2 Subcategories

On the second level we want to have a look at the subcategories users are interested in. Table 2 gives an overview of the top twenty subcategories. The top five subcategories are (S1) Political Process, Elections, Political Sociology, (S2) General Sociology, (S3) Social History, (S4) Methods and Techniques of Data Collection and Data Analysis and (S5) Sociology of Education. These five subcategories make up about 20% of all user actions.

Table 1. Main categories ordered by user interest.

#	Main category	Percent of User Actions
M1	Sociology	28.00%
M2	Interdisciplinary and Applied Fields of the Social Sciences	14.99%
M3	Political Science	13.27%
M4	Education and Pedagogics	10.53%
M5	Science of Communication	5.99%
M6	Humanities	5.98%
M7	Psychology	5.88%
M8	Basic Research in the Social Sciences	5.61%
M9	Demography	2.99%
M10	Economics	2.78%
M11	Social Policy	2.28%
M12	Ethnology, Cultural Anthropology, Ethnosociology	0.70%
M13	Legal Science and Administrative Science	0.68%
M14	Science, Engineering, Medicine	0.29%

The visualization in Figure 1 allows us some interesting observations: (I) It instantly clarifies that top subcategories are distributed over the top nine main categories (we can see that there is at least one big bubble in the first nine main categories). This lets us conclude that any user's interest is usually well distributed over the main classes. (II) The main category Sociology contains a lot of specialized sociologies. Here, the structures and processes of thematic sub-areas or social groups are examined. Eight subcategories are included in the top 20 (see Table 2) with all different aspects of Sociology such as Education, Culture, Art, Family, Industry and Work, Youth, Criminality, Medicine, Communication, Religion and so on. However, also all other specialized sociologies are frequently questioned by users (compare Figure 1 to see the number and size of bubbles included in Sociology) which in sum makes Sociology the most prominent main category. (III) The main category Political Science contains two important subcategories: (a) Political Process, Elections, Political Sociology and (b) Peace and Conflict Research, International Conflicts. (IV) The main category "Interdisciplinary and Applied Fields of the Social Sciences" is represented by three important subcategories from Table 2: (a) Woman's and Gender Studies, (b) Employment Research and (c) Social Problems. (V) Beyond the classification by main categories, the topic Education plays an important role with the two subcategories "Sociology of Education" (S5) from M1 and "Education and Pedagogics" (S7) from M4 forming together 6.07 % of all user actions.

To follow the distribution of subcategories over time, we built another visualization. Fig. 5 shows the distribution of categories from 2007 to 2016 for the top ten categories in percent of user actions per month in this category. It can be seen that the overall trend for most categories seems to be relatively constant with variations of a few percentage points. We examined this for the top 30 categories and found that there is a solid and constant level of interest in the categories. Exceptions are the subcategories that deal with the topic Education. Here, we can see a growing interest over time, especially in the beginning of 2014 when the Sowiport portal was relaunched.

Table 2. Top 20 subcategories users are interest in.

#	Subcategory	Main category	Percent of user actions
S1	Political Process, Elections, Political Sociology	M3	5.98%
S2	General Sociology, Basic Research, General Concepts and History	M1	4.02%
S3	Social History	M5	3.30%
S4	Methods and Techniques of Data Collection and Data Analysis	M7	3.23%
S5	Sociology of Education	M1	3.20%
S6	Social Psychology	M8	2.93%
S7	Education and Pedagogics	M4	2.87%
S8	Women's Studies, Feminist Studies, Gender Studies	M2	2.36%
S9	Cultural Sociology, Sociology of Art, Sociology of Literature	M1	2.28%
S10	Family Sociology, Sociology of Sexual Behavior	M1	2.07%
S11	Employment Research	M2	2.04%
S12	Peace and Conflict Research, International Conflicts	M3	2.02%
S13	Sociology of Work, Industrial Sociology, Industrial Relations	M1	1.90%
S14	Migration, Sociology of Migration	M9	1.88%
S15	Science of Communication	M6	1.81%
S16	Social Problems	M2	1.78%
S17	Criminal Sociology, Sociology of Law	M1	1.73%
S18	Medical Sociology	M1	1.72%
S19	Philosophy, Religion	M5	1.68%
S20	Sociology of Youth, Sociology of Childhood	M1	1.57%

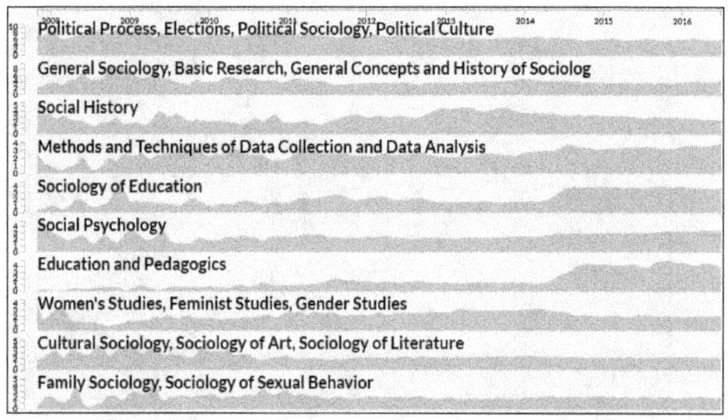

Fig. 5. Top ten categories from 2007 to 2016

6.3 Topics in Categories

On the third level we can explore which topics appear in a category with at least 500 matching user actions. Subcategories with many diverse topics may encounter a lot of aspects of the topic (e.g. for S2 General Sociology: Social theory, Society, Social Change etc.). Additionally many geographic aspects can appear (e.g. for S1 Political Process, Elections: Great Britain, France, Developing Country etc.). Also, temporal aspects can be

Table 3. Main topics for subcategories.

#	Subcategory	Top five topics
S1	Political Process	democracy, party, politics, Great Britain, right-wing radicalism
S2	General Sociology	sociology, sociological theory, theory, society, social inequality
S3	Social History	teaching materials, mathematics instruction, vocational education, school, sports
S4	Data Collection and Analysis	qualitative method, interview, measurement, empirical social research, research
S5	Sociology of Education	school, education, teaching, university, Germany

found (e.g. in S2 Social History: 20th century, 19th century etc.). This level spans thus a network with all different aspects that touch the subject. This view on categories is new as it is not explicitly discarded in the category system but implicitly built by keywords of viewed and searched documents in this category and chosen by user interaction. Table 3 shows the main topics for the five most viewed subcategories.

A more detailed example is shown in Figure 3 with the topics for the subcategory S16 "Social Problems". Here, about 111 different aspects of social problems are visualized. From generic problems such as poverty, violence, disability, addiction, alcoholism, racism to social units such as child, youth, woman, parents to different social groups such as foreign employee, foreigners, elder people, disabled peoples, refugees, Turks and countries such as Suisse, Austria, France to provisions such as rehabilitation, prevention, social integration, therapy and so on.

6.4 User terms for a topic

On the most specific level we leave the predefined classification system of categories and keywords curated by information professionals and enter the world of user search terms. This level explicitly indicates in which aspects users are interested by presenting their query terms in combination. We computed the count of user terms for all search actions and found that on average users enter 2.21 terms per query. This is similar to the average count of terms found in web search by Jansen et al. [12] with 2.21 terms. For domain-specific search different values reported: for Health Records: 1.2 terms [23], for E-journals in medicine: 2.27 terms [14] and for Pubmed: 3.54 terms [10]. For Psychology: 3.16 terms and History 3.42 terms [30] and for the field of Computer Science: 2.43 terms [13] and "three or fewer" [20].

As an example for this level of user terms we use Figure 4. It shows the word tree for the topic "discrimination". On the first level important user terms are discrimination, racism, stigmatization, institutional, xenophobia, prostitution, ethnic, social, sexism, homophobia, homosexuality, women, group-focused, sexual, antiziganism, prejudice and Roma. On the second level these terms combine for example to "discrimination school", "discrimination migrants", "institutional discrimination" or "group-focused enmity".

7. INDEXING LANGUAGE VS. USER LANGUAGE

Another aspect we want to address here is what differences exist between keywords applied to documents by information professionals (level 3 in our visualization) and the terms users apply for searching (on level 4). This issue has been addressed in research as the "vocabulary problem" [6]. Users use a different vocabulary to articulate their information needs than the vocabulary used to index the documents in a collection.

To investigate this issue in detail it is helpful to understand the way how information professionals assign index keywords to documents. As already described the thesaurus for the social sciences contains about 12,000 entries with 8,000 descriptors and 4,000 synonyms (non-descriptors) which refer to these descriptors. All entries are linked with semantic relationships such as "related", "broader", "narrower", "use instead", "used for" and are enriched with notes for disambiguation and a classification assignment. Similar to the constant development of a scientific discipline, also a thesaurus is in constant further development. So, new descriptors and non-descriptors are included in the thesaurus after carefully weighing up their importance. The vocabulary of a thesaurus should be as small as possible to make the indexing process consistent and retrieval results precise, but also as large as necessary to capture all phenomena of a scientific discipline. One method is to set each descriptor in nominative singular to avoid all declinations of a term. A second methodology to keep the vocabulary relatively small is the principle of semantic decomposition. Compound terms such as "bittersweet" are decomposed into individual terms like "bitter" and "sweet" as long as no significant loss of meaning is accompanied. These copulative compounds are very frequently used in the German language. As a result the content of documents is described with several equally weighted descriptors (post-coordinate indexing [26]).

There are several approaches to mitigate the problem of different languages of users and the system, for example with term recommenders. In Sowiport we have included such a recommender which helps the user in the process of formulating the search query. This is done with two methods: first, by autocompleting user entries with thesaurus terms and second, by showing descriptors that are semantically near [9]. In a long term evaluation we could show that the term recommender in Sowiport is used in 10% of the cases and has a largely positive effect for the following search processes [8].

However, users still use their own language for several reasons. First and foremost, users might not be aware that using a controlled vocabulary leads to search results with higher precision and recall. Here, the difference between web search engines and domain specific digital libraries becomes visible. Web search engines nearly always return results due to the immense corpus of web pages. In domain specific digital libraries the usage of knowledge organization systems is still doable and leads to better results if the vocabulary is used. A second reason might be that the users have information needs that cannot be expressed with the existing vocabulary. Be it new phenomena in a discipline that still cannot be represented with thesaurus terms or are circulated under several different terms, or phenomena in detail that are under the level of existing (combinations of) descriptors.

7.1 Comparing user search queries to thesaurus terms

In the following we will measure the overlap and especially the difference between vocabulary used on the system and on the user side. This can in particular show if information needs of real users can be expressed with the existing thesaurus and on the other side which needs cannot be expressed and are possible candidates for the inclusion in the thesaurus.

Table 4. Example user search terms not found in the thesaurus.

#	Original Term	English Translation	Example Search Query	Thesaurus	Category
1	tokyo	tokyo	city development tokyo	Could be included, used in more than 5,930 docs	Basic
2	freiwilligenmanagement	voluntary management	voluntary managment elderly	Can be described by separate descriptors	Remain current
3	jugendgewalt	youth violence	youth violence xenophobia	Can be described by separate descriptors	Basic
4	seniorenarbeit	work with elderly	community oriented work with elderly	Can be described by separate descriptors	Basic
5	pegida	pegida (far-right movement founded in Dresden in October 2014 which promotes anti-islamic positions)	refugee pegida	Could be included, used in more than 30 docs	Lately
6	pflegende	nourishing	nourishing relatives	Exists in nominative singular	Basic
7	kita	abbreviation for "Kindertagesstätte" - day nursery	day nursery studies	Could be included as non-descriptor	Remain current
8	dating	dating	online dating	The German (broader) term "Partnersuche" could be included and "dating" as a synonym	Remain current
9	kontakthypothese	contact hypothesis	contact hypothesis xenophobia	Could be included, used in more than 49 docs	Specialized
10	ttip	ttip	ttip public opinion	Could be a narrower term for "Freihandel"	Lately
11	geschlechterrollen	gender roles	children gender roles	Could be included as non-descriptor	Basic
12	blame	blame	culture of blame	Could be included as translation	Basic
13	eurokrise	euro crisis	solidarity euro crisis	Could be included, used in more than 280 docs	Remain current
14	praise	praise	praise and blame	Could be included, used in more than 2,728 docs	Basic
15	sharing	sharing	sharing economy	Could be included, used in more than 24,409 docs	Remain current
16	migrantinnen	migrant woman	older migrant woman	Can be described by separate descriptors	Basic
17	internetnutzung	internet use	internet use youth	Can be described by separate descriptors	Basic
18	herkunftseffekte	social origin factors	primary and secondary effects of social origin factors	Could be included, used in more than 86 docs	Specialized
19	zukunftsplanung	future planning	personal future planning	Could be included, used in more than 280 docs	Specialized
20	ageing	ageing	ageing population	"Ageing society" could be included	Basic
21	willkommenskultur	welcome culture	refugees welcome culture	Could be included, used in more than 64 docs	Lately
22	bildungsvererbung	education inheritance	Education inheritance and health	Could be included, used in more than 30 docs	Specialized
23	lebensweltorientierung	lifeworld orientation	social work and lifeworld orientation	Could be included, used in more than 200 docs	Specialized
24	biografiearbeit	biography work	biography work dementia	Could be included, used in more than 200 docs	Basic
25	heimatgefühl	sense of home	sense of home and identity	Could be included, used in more than 70 docs	Lately

For the analysis we used the same dataset as in the previous chapter. In particular we used all search queries from users that had been entered into a search form (simple or advanced) with the field type set to "all" (default) or "keyword" with about 1.7 million search queries. We found that users often copy ISSNs of journals or enter person names into the search bar. We filtered these queries as first approach with regular expressions. We then tokenized each query into individual tokens, applied a German and English stop word list, filtered special characters and finally used a German Porter stemmer to reduce declinations to their word stem. We found that there were still a large number of person names that are hard to capture by regular patterns. Therefore, we compared tokens to all author names from Sowiport (about 35,000 distinct first and last names) and, if found, erased them from the test set. Finally, each token was compared to all German and English translations in the thesaurus to find if it was included or not. For all terms not found in the thesaurus we also counted the frequency.

As a final result we found that about 88.26% of the user terms could be found in the thesaurus. That is really a large part, which means that most information needs could be expressed with the existing vocabulary of the thesaurus.

However, much more insight can be given by the part which could not be found. After all filtering steps 11.74% of the terms in user search queries could not be found in the thesaurus (143,934 of 1,226,503 terms; 40,965 distinct terms). Figure 6 shows that the frequency distribution of the missing terms follows a really long tail. That means that only a few new terms have been entered by users regularly, but there is a really long tail of terms which has been entered only once or twice. Even in this filtered list, we still have a lot of terms which have no specific topical meaning ("approach", "based", "way", "related", "versus", "survey", "handbook") and which make only sense when used with a second or third term.

Table 4 shows some examples of frequent terms which have not been found in the thesaurus. Among them are very recent social

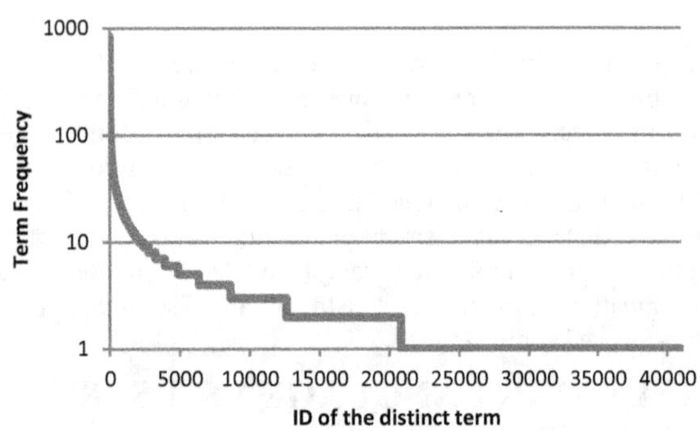

Fig. 6: Frequency of user search terms which have not been found in the thesaurus

phenomena or movements such as "Pegida" (since 2014), "TTIP" (since 2014), "welcome culture" (2015) or "sense of home" (2015). "Pegida" is a far-right movement founded in Dresden in October 2014 which promotes regularly anti-islamic demonstrations. "TTIP" is a trade agreement between the US and the European Union under ongoing negotiations since 2013 and which is discussed controversially. "Welcome culture" in this context means the opening of the German society towards refuges within the European migrant crisis in 2015. "Sense for home" is a reoccurring phenomenon in Germany where sense for home is enforced by the globalized and highly industrialized world. Characteristic is that all of these terms show only small numbers of documents in the collection.

Furthermore, there are several topics and phenomena which already run over some years, but also started lately in our logs. For example the "euro crisis" has started in 2010. The topic of "sharing" has started with "file sharing" in 2009 and then developed over "car sharing", "job sharing", "music sharing", "bike sharing" and "house sharing" until 2016. The topic "day nursery" started in 2010. Day nursery is a recent topic in Germany, especially for children from one to three years old. In 2013 a law went into effect that states a legal claim for a nursery place for this group of children. For the next topic "voluntary management" there is much more experience and literature in the Anglo-American World and it has come up in Germany lately and in our logs since 2012.

Then we can compare between basic concepts on the one side and specialized concepts on the other. "Tokyo" seems to be requested very often and can be found regularly in the literature. It seems that the thesaurus has not focused on that yet. "Biography work" is an essential method in the social sciences and could also be included. The topics "pflegende (nourishing)" and "Migrantinnen (migrant woman)" show the limits of the principle of semantic decomposition for indexing in the German language: "Migrant UND Frau" is not the same as "Migrantinnen", as the first describes "migrant AND woman" and the second "female migrants". The same applies for the second example: "pflegende Eltern" is not the same as "Pflege UND Eltern" as the first describes "parents who are nourishing" and the second describes "care and parents". Specialized terms such as "kontakthypothese" ("contact hypothesis"), "herkunftseffekt" ("social origin factors"), "zukunftsplanung" ("future planning"), "bildungsvererbung" ("education inheritance") or "lebensweltorientierung" ("lifeworld orientation") have a similar challenge in the German language (as opposed to the English language) as the semantic decomposition of these terms do not describe the same concept as the compound term.

However, as we can see the comparison between the system- and the user language can show important new and recent topics and aspects of user interest.

8. CONCLUSION

To answer *research question (1)* "What are the user interests in the (German) Social Sciences on different topical levels and over a long period of time?" we have analyzed nine years transaction logs from a digital library for the social sciences to study the topical interests of German users in this field. On the level of main categories there is a strong interest for (1) Sociology, (2) Interdisciplinary and Applied Fields of the Social Sciences, (3) Political Science, (4) Education and Pedagogics and (5) Science of Communication. Sociology is by far the most important category with about 28% of interest. The analysis on the level of subcategories show a strong interest in (a) Political Process, Elections, Political Sociology, (b) General Sociology, (c) Social History, (d) Methods and Techniques of Data Collection and Data Analysis and (e) Sociology of Education. The top subcategories are evenly distributed over the main categories with a strong focus on Sociology. This means on the one hand that the user's interest is well distributed over all main categories and on the other that there is a strong focus on Sociology and its sub disciplines. We could see that on the level of subcategories the user interests are stable over time. On the next more specific level, the level of topics, we can see the diversity of interest within a subcategory chosen by user interaction. On the fourth level we then finally show user search terms and here we can see which user search terms were used in combination. All in all, the categorization of user actions into the classification system is a good method to handle the topical complexity of the field of social sciences.

Research question (2) asked "Are knowledge organization systems such as thesauri good enough to capture these user interests?". We therefore compared in detail the indexing language on level 3 and the user language on level 4. We found that a large part of over 88% of user search terms can be found in the thesaurus, which shows the power and topical coverage of the thesaurus system. Thus, the thesaurus seems to be an important instrument to cover a majority of user interests but at the same time to allow precise retrieval. On the other hand, the 12% of the topics which could not be found in the thesaurus show interesting trends of longer lasting and very recent new research questions. These user topics are good candidates for the inclusion into the thesaurus. Comparing indexing and user language seems to be a good method to identify actual strengths and weaknesses of a thesaurus. This allows among others to find topics and themes which are no longer interesting (or have never been) and can therefore be deleted.

ACKNOWLEDGMENTS

This work was partly funded by the DFG, grant no. MA 3964/5-1; the AMUR project at GESIS. The author thanks the focus group IIR at GESIS for fruitful discussions and suggestions.

9. REFERENCES

1. Maristella Agosti, Franco Crivellari, and Giorgio Maria Di Nunzio. 2011. Web log analysis: a review of a decade of studies about information acquisition, inspection and interpretation of user interaction. *Data Mining and Knowledge Discovery* 24, 3: 663–696. https://doi.org/10.1007/s10618-011-0228-8
2. Philip M. Davis. 2004. Information-seeking behavior of chemists: A transaction log analysis of referral URLs. *JASIST* 55, 4: 326–332. https://doi.org/10.1002/asi.10384
3. Philip M. Davis and Leah R. Solla. 2003. An IP-level analysis of usage statistics for electronic journals in chemistry: Making inferences about user behavior. *Journal of the American Society for Information Science and Technology* 54, 11: 1062–1068. https://doi.org/10.1002/asi.10302
4. Penelope Earle and Brian Vickery. 1969. Social science literature use in the UK as indicated by citations. *Journal of Documentation* 25, 2: 123–141. https://doi.org/10.1108/eb026468
5. D. Ellis, D. Cox, and K. Hall. 1993. A comparison of the information seeking patterns of researchers in the physical and social sciences. *Journal of Documentation* 49: 356–356.

6. G. W. Furnas, T. K. Landauer, L. M. Gomez, and S. T. Dumais. 1987. The Vocabulary Problem in Human-system Communication. *Commun. ACM* 30, 11: 964–971. https://doi.org/10.1145/32206.32212
7. H. P. Hogeweg-De Haart. 1983. Characteristics of social science information: A selective review of the literature. Part I. *Social Science Information Studies* 3, 3: 147–164. https://doi.org/http://dx.doi.org/10.1016/0143-6236(83)90021-2
8. Daniel Hienert and Peter Mutschke. 2016. A Usefulness-based Approach for Measuring the Local and Global Effect of IIR Services. In *Proceedings of the 2016 ACM on Conference on Human Information Interaction and Retrieval* (CHIIR '16), 153–162. https://doi.org/10.1145/2854946.2854962
9. Daniel Hienert, Frank Sawitzki, and Philipp Mayr. 2015. Digital Library Research in Action: Supporting Information Retrieval in Sowiport. *D-Lib Magazine* 21, 3/4. https://doi.org/10.1045/march2015-hienert
10. Rezarta Islamaj Dogan, G. Craig Murray, Aurelie Neveol, and Zhiyong Lu. 2009. Understanding PubMed user search behavior through log analysis. *Database : the journal of biological databases and curation* 2009: bap018. https://doi.org/10.1093/database/bap018
11. Bernard J. Jansen. 2006. Search log analysis: What it is, what's been done, how to do it. *Library & Information Science Research* 28, 3: 407–432. https://doi.org/http://dx.doi.org/10.1016/j.lisr.2006.06.005
12. Bernard J. Jansen, Amanda Spink, and Tefko Saracevic. 2000. Real Life, Real Users, and Real Needs: A Study and Analysis of User Queries on the Web. *Inf. Process. Manage.* 36, 2: 207–227. https://doi.org/10.1016/S0306-4573(99)00056-4
13. Steve Jones, Jo Sally Cunningham, Rodger McNab, and Stefan Boddie. A transaction log analysis of a digital library. *International Journal on Digital Libraries* 3, 2: 152–169. https://doi.org/10.1007/s007999900022
14. Hao-Ren Ke, Rolf Kwakkelaar, Yu-Min Tai, and Li-Chun Chen. 2002. Exploring behavior of E-journal users in science and technology: Transaction log analysis of Elsevier's ScienceDirect OnSite in Taiwan. *Library & Information Science Research* 24, 3: 265–291. https://doi.org/http://dx.doi.org/10.1016/S0740-8188(02)00126-3
15. Diane Kelly. 2009. Methods for Evaluating Interactive Information Retrieval Systems with Users. *Found. Trends Inf. Retr.* 3, 1—2: 1–224. https://doi.org/10.1561/1500000012
16. Diane Kelly and Colleen Cool. 2002. The Effects of Topic Familiarity on Information Search Behavior. In *Proceedings of the 2Nd ACM/IEEE-CS Joint Conference on Digital Libraries* (JCDL '02), 74–75. https://doi.org/10.1145/544220.544232
17. Maurice B. Line. 1981. The structure of social science literature as shown by a large-scale citation analysis. *Social Science Information Studies* 1, 2: 67–87. https://doi.org/http://dx.doi.org/10.1016/0143-6236(81)90001-6
18. Maurice B Line. 2000. Social Science Information-The Poor Relation. *IFLA Journal-International Federation of Library Associations* 26, 3: 177–179.
19. Thomas Lüke, Philipp Schaer, and Philipp Mayr. 2012. Improving Retrieval Results with Discipline-Specific Query Expansion. In *TPDL* (Lecture Notes in Computer Science), 408–413. Retrieved from http://arxiv.org/abs/1206.2126
20. Malika Mahoui and Sally Jo Cunningham. 2001. Search Behavior in a Research-Oriented Digital Library. In *Research and Advanced Technology for Digital Libraries: 5th European Conference, ECDL 2001 Darmstadt, Germany, September 4-9, 2001 Proceedings*, Panos Constantopoulos and Ingeborg T. Sølvberg (eds.). Springer Berlin Heidelberg, Berlin, Heidelberg, 13–24. Retrieved from http://dx.doi.org/10.1007/3-540-44796-2_2
21. Philipp Mayr and Vivien Petras. 2008. Cross-concordances - terminology mapping and its effectiveness for Information retrieval: Crosskonkordanzen - Terminologie Mapping und deren Effektivität für das Information Retrieval. In *World Library and Information Congress*. Retrieved from http://archive.ifla.org/IV/ifla74/papers/129-Mayr_Petras-en.pdf
22. Lokman I. Meho and Helen R. Tibbo. 2003. Modeling the Information-seeking Behavior of Social Scientists: Ellis's Study Revisited. *J. Am. Soc. Inf. Sci. Technol.* 54, 6: 570–587. https://doi.org/10.1002/asi.10244
23. Karthik Natarajan, Daniel Stein, Samat Jain, and Noémie Elhadad. 2010. An Analysis of Clinical Queries in an Electronic Health Record Search Utility. *International journal of medical informatics* 79, 7: 515–522. https://doi.org/10.1016/j.ijmedinf.2010.03.004
24. David Nicholas, Paul Huntington, and Janet Homewood. 2003. Assessing used content across five digital health information services using transaction log files. *Journal of Information Science* 29, 6: 499–515. https://doi.org/10.1177/0165551503296007
25. Thomas A. Peters. 1993. The history and development of transaction log analysis. *Library Hi Tech* 11, 2: 41–66. https://doi.org/10.1108/eb047884
26. M. Taube and Documentation Incorporated. 1953. *Studies in Coordinate Indexing*. Documentation Incorporated.
27. Luis Villen-Rueda, Jose A. Senso, and Felix Moya-Anegon. 2007. The Use of OPAC in a Large Academic Library: a transactional log analysis of subject searching. *The Journal of the Academic Librarianship* 33: 327–337. https://doi.org/10.1016/j.acalib.2007.01.018
28. Ryen W. White, Susan T. Dumais, and Jaime Teevan. 2009. Characterizing the Influence of Domain Expertise on Web Search Behavior. In *Proceedings of the Second ACM International Conference on Web Search and Data Mining* (WSDM '09), 132–141. https://doi.org/10.1145/1498759.1498819
29. Barbara M. Wildemuth. 2004. The Effects of Domain Knowledge on Search Tactic Formulation. *J. Am. Soc. Inf. Sci. Technol.* 55, 3: 246–258. https://doi.org/10.1002/asi.10367
30. Kwan Yi, Jamshid Beheshti, Charles Cole, John E. Leide, and Andrew Large. 2006. User search behavior of domain-specific information retrieval systems: An analysis of the query logs from PsycINFO and ABC-Clio's Historical Abstracts/America: History and Life. *Journal of the American Society for Information Science and Technology* 57, 9: 1208–1220. https://doi.org/10.1002/asi.20401

SearchGazer: Webcam Eye Tracking for Remote Studies of Web Search

Alexandra Papoutsaki
Brown University
alexpap@cs.brown.edu

James Laskey
Brown University
jlaskey@cs.brown.edu

Jeff Huang
Brown University
chiir@jeffhuang.com

ABSTRACT

We introduce SearchGazer, a web-based eye tracker for remote web search studies using common webcams already present in laptops and some desktop computers. SearchGazer is a pure JavaScript library that infers the gaze behavior of searchers in real time. The eye tracking model self-calibrates by watching searchers interact with the search pages and trains a mapping of eye features to gaze locations and search page elements on the screen. Contrary to typical eye tracking studies in information retrieval, this approach does not require the purchase of any additional specialized equipment, and can be done remotely in a user's natural environment, leading to cheaper and easier visual attention studies.

While SearchGazer is not intended to be as accurate as specialized eye trackers, it is able to replicate many of the research findings of three seminal information retrieval papers: two that used eye tracking devices, and one that used the mouse cursor as a restricted focus viewer. Charts and heatmaps from those original papers are plotted side-by-side with SearchGazer results. While the main results are similar, there are some notable differences, which we hypothesize derive from improvements in the latest ranking technologies used by current versions of search engines and diligence by remote users. As part of this paper, we also release SearchGazer as a library that can be integrated into any search page.

Keywords

web search behavior; remote user studies; online eye tracking; user interactions; gaze prediction

1. INTRODUCTION

Search is a visual activity. Users examine search results to determine what is relevant to them and their task. Knowing what a searcher has examined, or is looking at, has been the focus of numerous studies in information retrieval. Typically, the goal is to understand searcher behavior and apply that information to improve the search systems. Traditionally, these studies are done in lab with specialized eye trackers, or inferred using remotely collected interaction data like clicks or cursor activity.

We explore a new approach to understanding visual attention in search that leverages the advantages of both types of studies: scalability across millions of users, naturalistic environments, and real webcam-based gaze tracking. SearchGazer is a pure JavaScript eye tracking library that infers the gaze behavior of users in real time. The eye tracking model self-calibrates by watching searchers interact with search pages and trains a mapping between features of the eye and positions on the screen. Huang et al. [15] have shown that when a user clicks on a web page, they will first look at the target where they intend to click. Webcam images during these user interactions can be collected and used as cues for what the user's eyes look like. Future observations of the eye can be matched to similar past instances to infer the eye-gaze, even when the user is not interacting.

SearchGazer can be added to any search page for standard eye tracking and for identifying which search elements the user is looking at. In this paper, we investigate the utility of SearchGazer in the context of web search, assessing its ability to substitute or at least approximate specialized eye trackers. Currently, while there have been software artifacts that use webcams for eye tracking (typically by processing the video stream offline), there is no published research describing the implementation or application of browser-based webcam eye trackers (e.g. [32]). Further, we ask the question, "can SearchGazer *really* be useful for search behavior studies?"

We investigate this by directly replicating some of the main results of three past studies: Cutrell et al. [8] and Buscher et al. [5] presented highly-cited eye tracking studies which investigated searcher behavior on the presentation of search results and search advertisements respectively. Lagun et al. [21] used the cursor as a restricted focus viewer, also a remote behavior capture technique, but which obscures most of the search page, hindering the user experience. Therefore, we directly substitute the specialized eye tracker or cursor-as-a-viewer interface with SearchGazer. While we briefly report on the accuracy of SearchGazer in Section 3, the focus is on the ultimate evaluation: whether researchers conducting a prior study performed with an eye tracker would reach similar conclusions with SearchGazer, performed remotely, online, and in real time without any special equipment.

These studies were conducted simultaneously with crowdworkers, with more participants at a lower cost (in terms of time and money). Indeed, many of the main results are quite similar, and we show the original charts and heatmaps side-by-side with corresponding charts and heatmaps generated

CHIIR '17, March 07 - 11, 2017, Oslo, Norway

ISBN 978-1-4503-4677-1/17/03...$15.00

DOI: http://dx.doi.org/10.1145/3020165.3020170

by SearchGazer. For the results that are different, we discuss plausible explanations, primarily due to the change in search technology since the original study and differences in the diligence of in-lab participants and remote crowd-workers.

The main contributions of this work are: 1) the description and evaluation of our real-time online webcam eye tracker, SearchGazer (with source code publicly available at `http://webgazer.cs.brown.edu/search`), and 2) the investigation of results from replication of three seminal web search behavior papers, when SearchGazer is substituted for specialized eye trackers or interfaces.

2. RELATED WORK

2.1 Webcam Eye Tracking

There are relatively few academic publications about using webcams for eye tracking, with most webcam eye trackers typically being video streams processed offline (not real-time) and involving an explicit calibration phase. There has been work on eye tracking self-calibration using image saliency to estimate user gaze for calibration purposes [30], but this is a very rough estimate of where a user is looking. Alnajar et al. [1] introduced a webcam eye tracker that self-calibrates with pre-recorded gaze patterns instead of predicted saliency. Although more accurate, it still requires users to view stimuli for which "ground truth" gaze patterns have been recorded. Xu et al. introduced TurkerGaze [32], a webcam eye tracker deployed on Amazon Mechanical Turk for image saliency prediction. It requires calibration which is performed during a game phase where users lock their gaze on a specific target. Moreover, it requires an offline training component. Huang et al. [17] developed PACE, a standalone desktop application that performs eye tracking using user interactions. SearchGazer is distinguished by self-calibrating in real time via gaze-mouse interaction relationships which are readily available, as well as being able to be used on any web page without any software installation or configuration. In addition, it can predict both the absolute gaze location and the corresponding search element on the screen. These attributes make SearchGazer ideal for remote online studies and experiments, especially in the context of web search.

Several software artifacts for eye detection have been made available online, though without much formal evaluation. OpenGazer [34] is an open source desktop application that performs eye detection using computer vision algorithms from OpenCV; it has been abandoned since 2010. Camgaze.js [31] is a JavaScript library that predicts the pupil location and gaze direction in real-time, but does not map it to the screen. Clmtrackr [25] is a JavaScript library that performs facial feature tracking through constrained local models. SearchGazer adopts clmtrackr for eye detection and uses our own algorithms for mapping the gaze on the screen.

There have also been commercial forays into online webcam eye tracking for usability studies. Tobii Technologies has spun off a company called Sticky that helps websites optimize advertisements based on visual behaviors. One of the earlier services to offer webcam eye tracking was GazeHawk, which was acquired by Facebook in 2012 and is now shut down. Like our work, their system tracked the user in their natural environment from the browser, without the need to install software. However, their approach is significantly different as they transmitted the webcam video to their own servers for offline processing. They did so because at that time, laptops were not capable of processing the video data in real time [personal communication with GazeHawk founders]. Additionally, they required a phase of user calibration and did not include user interactions. Finally, a recent startup called Xlabs focuses on head tracking to determine the gaze position and has built a Chrome browser compatible software extension that can be installed by its users.

2.2 Examination Behavior in Web Search

Lab studies involving eye tracking during web search have been commonly used to trace visual attention. Past research has found a correlation between gaze and cursor positions in search behavior [11, 28]. Guo and Agichtein [11] reported that the distance between cursor and gaze positions was larger along the x-axis, and was generally shorter when the cursor was placed over the search results. Their model could predict with 77% accuracy when gaze and cursor were strongly aligned using cursor features. Huang et al. [15] note that the notion of gaze and cursor correlation is overly naive; instead their relationship greatly depends on what the user is doing at that time. They show that the two are highly correlated when users aim at or hit a target, but the correlation is poor when the cursor is idle. Navalpakkam et al. [26] investigate the gaze-cursor relationship on non-linear page layouts which, in search, may represent cases when information or advertisements are shown in a second column. Furthermore, they perform gaze prediction using a non-linear model and identify particular regions of interest. Xu et al. [33] created a computational model that predicts spatio-temporal visual attention on graphical interfaces based on cursor movements, keyboard activity, and the UI components. Boi et al. [2] created a method for segmenting content groups in pages that based on mouse movements identifies the user-perceived group of contents with a 20% mean pixel-based error. Lagun et al. [22] devised an approach that combines user interactions and salience of the web page to infer visual attention in search. Liu et al. [23] extended this work by using visual saliency maps derived from image content to predict users examination behavior on an experimental browser.

Numerous studies of web search use eye tracking or some proxy (like cursor activity) as a tool for understanding searchers and design better search systems. Buscher et al. [4] used eye tracking features to infer user interest and show that this can yield great improvements when personalizing search. Huang et al. [16] have investigated the meaning behind cursor interactions, and how they can improve our understanding of searcher behavior along with the relevance of search results for future users. Buscher et al. [6] and Dumais et al. [9] notice that users have different gaze behavior patterns, but can be clustered into different personalities: exhaustive examiners, economic examiners focused on the organic results or also on the ads. Liu et al. [24] tap into the different phases of gaze behavior in web search by developing a two-stage model that examines the "skimming" and "reading" phases. Finally, beyond traditional web search, Kules et al. [20] understand gaze behavior in a faceted search interface and find that as part of examining results, users spend half the time looking at facets, prompting "task building that incorporates consideration of the dimensions of the task."

3. SEARCHGAZER

We have developed SearchGazer, a self-calibrated client-side eye tracking library that extends WebGazer [27] and trains a regression model which maps eye features to gaze locations and search page elements during user interactions. In addition to predicting the gaze of a user within any device display which has a browser that supports access to the webcam, SearchGazer also identifies gaze periods over regions of interest on the search results page for analysis. A few lines of JavaScript code are enough to integrate SearchGazer in any search page and perform eye tracking once the user starts interacting with the page naturally. The software is open source and available at `http://webgazer.cs.brown.edu/search`.

SearchGazer is relatively simpler than trackers with explicit 3D reasoning [12]. This simplicity allows it to run in real time through browser JavaScript. The primary novelty of SearchGazer is to constantly self-calibrate based on cursor-gaze relationships. Not only does this eliminate the need for explicit calibration sessions, it means users are free to move and SearchGazer will learn new mappings between eye features and screen coordinates.

Any facial feature detection library can be plugged in SearchGazer; it only needs the location of the eyes within the video. Here, SearchGazer uses clmtrackr [25] and accepts as input the smallest rectangle that fits the eye contour.

3.1 Eye Features

SearchGazer relies on a regression model that maps video pixels to gaze locations. To detect the eye features we follow the same procedure with TurkerGaze [32] and represent each eye region as a resized 6×10 image patch. The two eye regions are processed with gray-scaling and histogram equalization, resulting to a 120D feature that will be input to the regression algorithm described below. Unlike TurkerGaze, SearchGazer does not post-process offline and retrains in real time.

3.2 Mapping to Screen and Self-Calibration

Matching the computed eye features to screen coordinates requires a mapping between the 120D vectors and the coordinates of the user's gaze on the device screen. This complex relationship depends on the 3D position and rotation of the head with respect to the camera and screen. These 3D properties can be estimated, but generally require careful calibration and expensive computation. SearchGazer avoids this by using a simpler mapping between eye features and display coordinates. In addition, it relies on continual self-calibration through user interactions that naturally take place in web search and do not disrupt the user experience.

We base our model on the assumption that when a user interaction occurs, the gaze locations on the screen match the screen coordinates of that interaction. In a web search study, Huang et al. showed that the gaze-cursor distance averages 74 pixels [15] during a click. Research on attention control and its allocation mechanisms led to similar findings [10]. For simplicity, we assume that the gaze and cursor align perfectly during clicks.

The click history and the corresponding gaze predictions are stored locally in the browser, thus avoiding privacy concerns of storing eye features in a remote location. No data are transmitted from the user's computer to the website hosting the SearchGazer code, other than the continuous predictions and their corresponding cursor positions in the case of clicks. SearchGazer's predictions are not affected by scrolling and are projected within the window viewport. Whenever the user is not directly interacting with the page, the camera still captures eye features, and applies the regression model.

3.2.1 Mapping Eye Features

To map the eye pixels to gaze locations we implement a ridge regression model which maps the 120D eye feature vector to the display coordinates (D_x, D_y) for each click. The simplicity of this regularized linear regression allows it to provide relatively accurate predictions in real time and with only a few clicks needed for training.

Without loss of generality, we consider the ridge regression model function for the x-coordinate prediction: $f(\mathbf{v}) \rightarrow D_x$. This function is $f(\mathbf{v}) = \phi(\mathbf{x})^T \mathbf{w}$, where $\phi(\mathbf{x})$ is a basis function and $\mathbf{w}$ is a vector of weights which satisfy:

$$\min_{\mathbf{w}} \sum_{x_i \in \mathbf{x}} ||D_{x_i} - f(x_i)||_2^2 + \lambda ||\mathbf{w}||_2^2 \tag{1}$$

Here the last term λ acts as a regularization to penalize overfitting. In our study we set $\lambda = 0.00001$.

3.2.2 Sampling Cursor Movements

Past studies have shown that when users move their cursor to perform an action there is a strong correlation between cursor and gaze location [13]. This distance grows when the cursor remains idle. We extend the ridge regression model, taking into consideration that the location of the cursor is a good signal for the gaze location when the cursor is active. Our assumption for clicks remains the same. When cursor moves, we assume it matches the true gaze location. Unlike click coordinates though, cursor locations contribute to the regression model for at most 200ms, a duration comparable to that of a gaze fixation. Therefore, when the cursor is idle and no new cursor location has been introduced, our model falls back to the original simple ridge regression where only clicks contribute to the training of SearchGazer.

3.2.3 Mapping to Search Elements

The predicted gaze coordinates are combined with the DOM structure of the underlying search page and mapped to examined page elements such as links, snippets, and ads.

4. EVALUATION

In [27], we conducted two user studies—one online and one in-lab—with a total population of 87 participants. Gaze predictions from SearchGazer were compared to those made by the commercial eye tracker Tobii EyeX. The mean error was 128.9 pixels with an average visual angle of 4.17° or 1.6 inches. Figure 1 shows the average distance (in pixels) between the predictions made by SearchGazer's regression model and the true gaze locations across 50 clicks. These results are promising as they show that SearchGazer can predict relatively accurately eye-gaze locations.

To further investigate the applicability and utility of SearchGazer in web search, we replicate the studies found in three seminal papers in the area of information retrieval that used eye tracking to better understand web search behavior. We conducted all three replication studies remotely, recruiting participants through the Amazon Mechanical Turk crowdsourcing platform. All crowd-workers passed a qualification test which ensured they had a webcam and their browser supported the getUserMedia() API that provides access to the webcam stream. To ensure lack of bias each study was conducted with a unique population of crowd-workers.

The gaze predictions made by SearchGazer are not fine-grained enough to identify fixations. Instead, we rely on

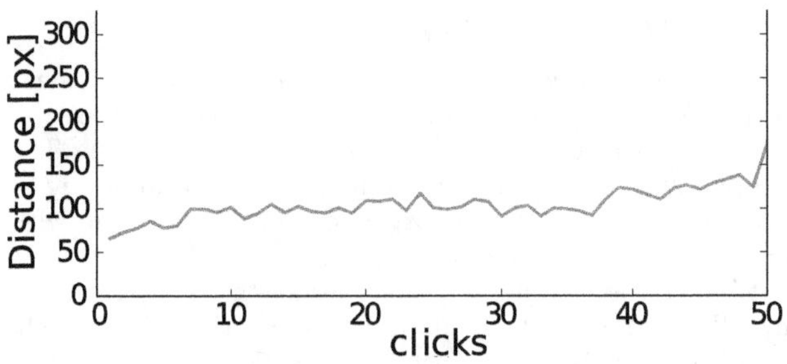

Figure 1: Average distance in pixels between SearchGazer and the true gaze locations across 50 clicks.

raw gaze data when comparing our findings to previous studies. In addition, each of the heatmaps included in the following sections was created according to the color palette of the corresponding original study. In the following sections we report the results when replicating the three seminal studies. Due to lack of the original reference data we cannot perform any rigorous statistical analysis to assess our findings. Instead, we report average differences and high-level metrics that give a general quantified measure of the similarities between SearchGazer and the original studies.

5. RESULT EXAMINATION BEHAVIOR STUDY

The first study we reproduce is [8], a prominent early study that used eye tracking in web search. Cutrell et al. conducted an in-lab user study with 22 participants, exploring the effects of changes in the presentation of search results, i.e. the snippet length, on 6 informational and 6 navigational queries that were submitted to MSN Search. A Tobii x50 eye tracker was used to identify gaze coordinates.

5.1 Experimental Design and Procedure

To replicate this study we performed a few modifications as some of its specifications are outdated. Given that MSN Search does no longer exist as an independent search engine, we used its successor, Bing. One of the navigational queries ("Pinewood") was also changed to a current software company ("Symantec"). In contrast to [8], our participants were only allowed to look for the answer within the first page of returned results and could not manipulate the given query. For each of the 12 queries, the first search engine result page (SERP) was downloaded from Bing, without snippet length manipulation. All ads were removed so that the SERPs resembled as much as possible the MSN Search, leading to 8 instead of 10 organic results. SearchGazer was added on each of the 12 SERPs to predict and log in real time the gaze locations.

Our version of the study started with instructions and a consent form. As tasks designed for crowd-workers tend to be shorter than in-lab studies, we included an explicit calibration step, during which crowd-workers had to click on a circular target that appeared in a 5×3 grid. The calibration step was conducted again at the middle of the study. Crowd-workers proceeded with the 12 search tasks presented in a randomized order. For each task, a description of the search goal and a corresponding query was given. After a search, crowd-workers provided their answer or declared they were unable to successfully acquire the target information. After the study, they filled an online demographic questionnaire.

5.2 Participants

49 crowd-workers performed this study. 13 participants were excluded due to abandoning the task, not following the instructions, or due to technical issues with data logging in our server. The final population consisted of 36 participants (14 female, 22 male). They were 20 to 49 years old (M=30.1, SD=7.24). 22 had normal vision, 8 wore glasses and 6 contact lenses. All participants received 2USD at the end of the experiment. To ensure they completed the whole study, they provided an ID they were handed with the questionnaire. The study lasted on average 10.11 minutes (SD=4.13). In total, there were 610 clicks and 76,389 gaze predictions.

5.3 Results

Cutrell et al. provided preliminary results on the general characteristics of search results, along with changes in the web search behavior when varying the snippet length. We focus on the former, as those findings are more generalizable and applicable to modern search engines.

Viewing order and fixation duration: Research in information retrieval has repeatedly shown that users tend to examine results from top to bottom when presented with SERPs that have a single-column linear layout [18]. Figure 2 shows in circles the mean time for the gaze to arrive at each organic result. Cutrell et al. confirmed previous findings, showing in Figure 2a that the mean time for the gaze to arrive at each result is roughly linear, with lower ranked results attracting attention last. Figure 2b shows the corresponding mean arrival times for the data obtained through SearchGazer. Note that in our replication studies a SERP contained at most 8 organic results. We observe that the arrival times also follow a linear fashion but the slopes are significantly different. For lower ranked results, arrival times are higher in our study, with result 8 being reached on average after 14.2 seconds. We hypothesize that as search engines have become more powerful web searchers tend to trust the first ranks even more, exploring the bottom of the page only after careful consideration of the first results. After normalization, the average difference between the original study and our findings is 14.75%.

The second component of Figure 2 is the average fixation duration for each result, depicted in bars. As shown in Figure 2a from [8], most gaze activity was directed at the first results, which attracted far more attention. In Figure 2b, SearchGazer's predictions demonstrate similar total visual attention towards lower-ranked results. Following [19], we assume that the power law fits the data better than any other common distribution. Fitting two power law curves on the original and SearchGazer's results, we find that the exponents are 0.7235 and 0.7906, respectively. After normalization, the average difference between the fixations in the original study and our findings is 5.09%. We observe that the curves have similar slopes, although the crowd-workers of our experiment spent less time examining each result. This can be perhaps explained by the difference in nature of a remote and an in-lab study. As crowd-workers are unattended and use Amazon Mechanical Turk as their source of income, they tend to go through the tasks faster and possibly not as diligently. In addition, crowd-workers often come from different countries, with English being a secondary language and therefore they might approach the tasks differently than in-lab participants who are often native speakers.

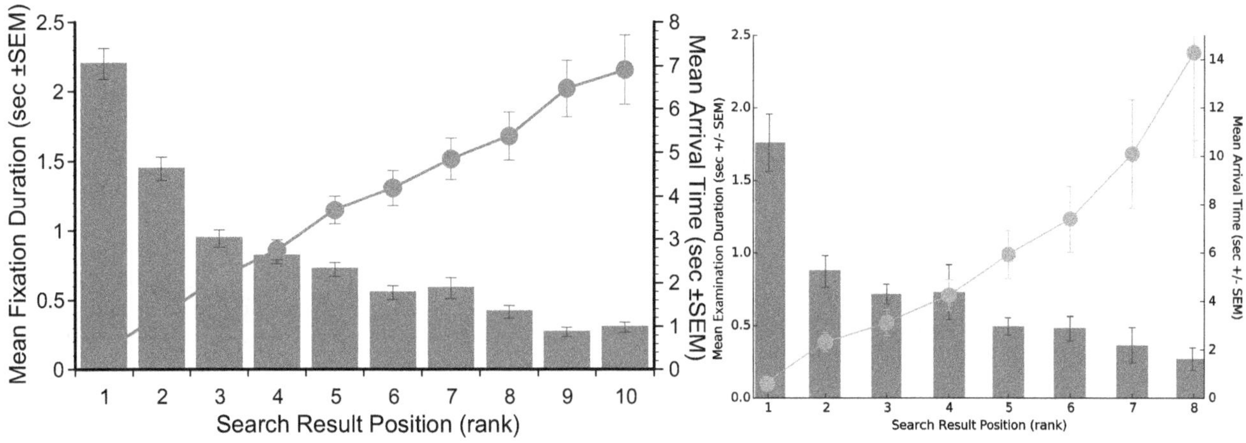

(a) Result Examination Behavior Study (b) SearchGazer

Figure 2: Mean fixation/examination duration (bars) and mean time for gaze to arrive at each result (circles).

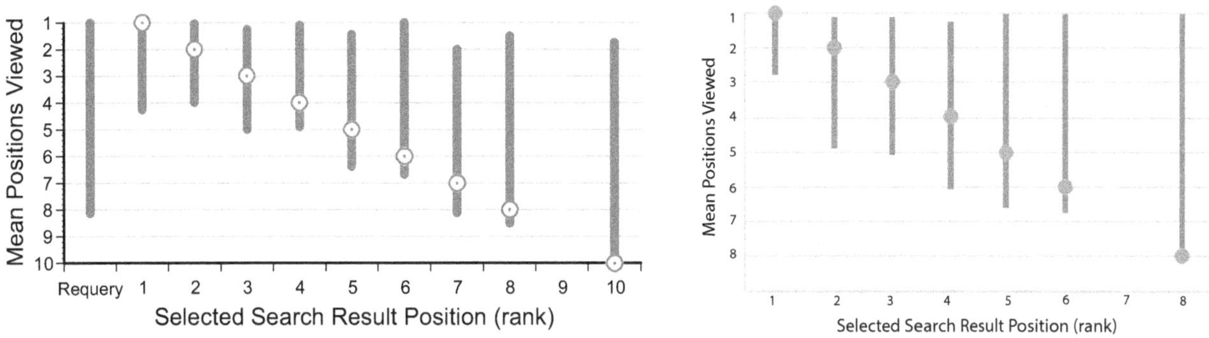

(a) Result Examination Behavior Study (b) SearchGazer

Figure 3: Mean number of search results looked at before users clicked on a result (above and below that result).

Results Viewed before a click: An interesting measure of saturation is how many results were viewed on average before a click occurred on a result. Figure 3 shows the average number of results ranked higher and lower than the one that the user clicked on. For example, in Figure 3a, users from [8] who clicked on result 5, on average looked at almost all items above it and about 1.5 results below it. Figure 3b shows our findings when we analyzed SearchGazer's predictions. Crowd-workers that clicked on result 5, on average look at 4 items above and 1.6 below it. The average difference between the two studies is 0.28 results for those ranked higher and 0.61 results for those ranked lower than the one clicked. Missing the reference data prevents us from running any rigorous statistical test, but on average it seems that SearchGazer can replicate similar studies relatively accurately.

6. AD EXAMINATION BEHAVIOR STUDY

Buscher et al. [5] investigated contemporary search engines that contain ads and related searches in addition to organic results. They conducted a lab user study, varying the type of task (informational or navigational) and the quality of ads (relevant or irrelevant). The experiment was conducted with 38 participants that were provided with custom generated SERPs for each of the above combinations, for a total of 32 search tasks. A Tobii x50 eye tracker was used to measure visual attention across different areas of interest (AOIs).

6.1 Experimental Design and Procedure

The authors of [5] provided the list of 32 queries along with the corresponding SERPs that were used in the original study. Each query could return one of two SERPs that varied in the quality of ads (relevant or irrelevant to the query). SearchGazer was added on all SERPs to predict gaze locations in real-time. To keep the study short and remotely practical, we only worked with 12 of the original queries (6 informational, 6 navigational). The experimental design was identical to the procedures followed in the "result examination behavior study" described in Section 5. The ordering of tasks was also randomized across all participants but for the ad quality we followed the same protocol as [5]. Each participant was assigned to one of three ad quality blocks. Each block contains 12 trials, with ads being mostly good (relevant), bad (irrelevant) or randomly selected.

6.2 Participants

Forty-four crowd-workers performed this study. Nine were filtered out due to incomplete or abandoned tasks. The resulting 35 participants consisted of 17 female and 18 male, with ages ranging from 21 to 59 years (M=30.4, SD=9.1).

Of these participants, 19 had normal vision, 13 wore glasses and 3 contacts. The study lasted on average 9.75 minutes (*SD*=7.05) and in total there were 88,438 gaze predictions.

6.3 Measures

The following two measures were used as defined in [5]:

AOIs: Each SERP was broken into separate AOIs that correspond to 10 organic results, 3 top ads, and 5 rail ads.

Fixation Impact: Buscher et al. used the measure of fixation impact [3] which spreads the duration of a fixation to all AOIs that fall close to the fixation center using a Gaussian distribution. They used Tobii Studio to detect fixations, for which the exact technique is unknown. We instead used raw gaze predictions and a smaller radius Gaussian.

6.4 Results

General Gaze Distribution on SERPs: The gaze heatmap in Figure 4a demonstrates the distribution of visual attention across all participants in [5]. The data have been aggregated across all queries and the background SERP serves as an example. Figure 4b shows the corresponding heatmap created by the predictions of SearchGazer across all 12 queries and 35 participants. We observe that both heatmaps follow the golden triangle, with the majority of visual attention focused in the first three organic results. For SearchGazer there is a wider spread of predictions across the whole SERP, as it is not as stable as a commercial eye tracker. Nevertheless, it is worth noting that the aggregated data can lead to similar conclusions between the two studies.

Figure 5 shows the mean fixation impact for each AOI across all participants and tasks. The results from [5] in Figure 5a show that most visual attention falls on the top results. Figure 5b shows the corresponding SearchGazer results. Our findings have the same linear decay across organic results, with the exception of the 7th and 8th which are examined for longer. This is perhaps due to the page-fold falling near them or because crowd-workers are more deliberate in the examination of lower results. In addition, our study shows smaller overall examination durations. Surprisingly, the five right ads attract much higher visual attention. SearchGazer predictions could lack precision, as we noticed that the inferred gaze positions were more scattered along the x-axis. After normalization, the average difference between the mean fixation impact as seen across the two studies is 28.78%.

Effects of Task Type: Figure 6 shows the mean fixation impact for AOIs, split between informational and navigational tasks. Both [5] and our results show in Figures 6a and 6b respectively that participants spent more time on SERPs for informational tasks. This additional time was mostly spent on the organic results. After normalization, the average difference between the mean fixation impact is 21.85% for informational and 29.52% for navigational tasks.

Effects of Ad Quality: Figure 7 shows the mean fixation impact for AOIs, separated based on ad quality (good or bad). Buscher et al. did not find any statistical difference between the time spent in SERPs with good and bad ads, but showed that participants devoted about twice as much visual attention to top ads when the ads were of good quality. In contrast, participants paid less attention to the organic results when good quality ads were displayed, as shown in Figure 7a. Our findings in Figure 7b indicate in many cases a totally different picture, revealing that webcam eye tracking can miss such subtle differences. The fact that our study included 12 instead of 32 tasks might have also reduced the effect that ads normally have. After normalization, the average difference between the mean fixation impact is 23.63% for pages with good ads and 25.48% for bad ads.

7. RESTRICTED FOCAL VIEW RESULT EXAMINATION STUDY

Lagun and Agichtein [21] created ViewSer, a tool that automatically modifies the appearance of a SERP to show one result at a time, while blurring the rest of the interface using a restricted focal view. The participant can uncover only one result using their cursor, thus the search engine knows which result a user is examining. Although ViewSer is an interface and not an eye tracker, it allows researchers to infer web search behavior remotely without the need of additional equipment. Our work with SearchGazer builds on ViewSer's idea of capturing examined regions of the search page at scale, and their assessing the feasibility of the work through crowd-workers. The authors validated the utility of ViewSer by running a remote user study with 106 crowd-workers. Each worker went through a list of 25 benchmark search tasks from the Web Track of the TREC 2009 competition. The results were compared to an in-lab study that was performed with 10 participants using a Tobii x60 eye tracker. Clickthrough and viewing rates were comparable between participants using ViewSer and those tracked using the physical eye tracker.

7.1 Experimental Design and Procedure

We did not have access to the original SERPs, so instead replicated this study using Google and focusing on 12 queries. We downloaded the 12 Google SERPs and added SearchGazer on each. As with all 3 replication studies crowd-workers were allowed to only click within the first page of returned results and could not manipulate the query. The rest of the protocol was the same as the Result Examination Behavior Study.

7.2 Participants

Forty-seven crowd-workers performed this study. Eleven were excluded due to incomplete and abandoned tasks, resulting to 36 participants (12 female, 24 male). Their ages ranged from 21 to 63 years (*M*=31.97, *SD*=10.42). Twenty-five had normal vision, 10 wore glasses and 1 wore contacts. The study lasted on average 10.36 minutes (*SD*=6.83). Across all participants there were 630 clicks and 76,602 gaze predictions.

7.3 Results

Gaze Distribution: Figure 8 shows an example heatmap of the relative viewing time spent on the SERP that corresponds to the query "toilet". For [21] this heatmap can be created only with data collected from the in-lab eye tracking study, as shown in Figure 8a. Data gathered from ViewSer can be visualized with vertical colorbars as shown in Figure 8a, as colorbar (b). The (a) colorbar corresponds to data gathered from the in-lab eye tracking study. SearchGazer which predicts in real-time the gaze locations as screen coordinates can lead to both types of visualizations, allowing for richer information. Figure 8b shows the corresponding heatmap created with our data. As the organic results in the two SERPs are not identical, it is hard to compare them directly. It is worth noting though, that as the task is informational ("Find information on buying, installing, and repairing toilets"), participants tend to spend more time on the SERP, examining even lower-ranked results.

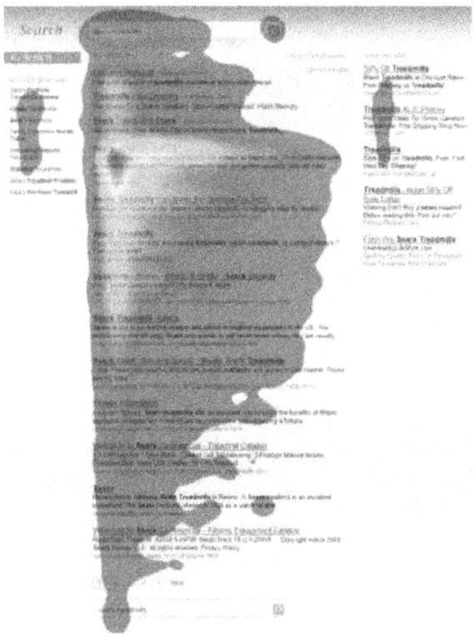

(a) Ad Examination Behavior Study

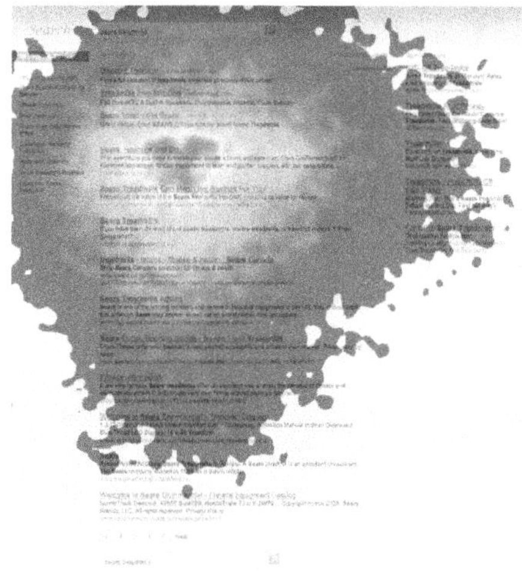

(b) SearchGazer

Figure 4: Gaze heatmap aggregated across all participants and queries and projected on a sample SERP.

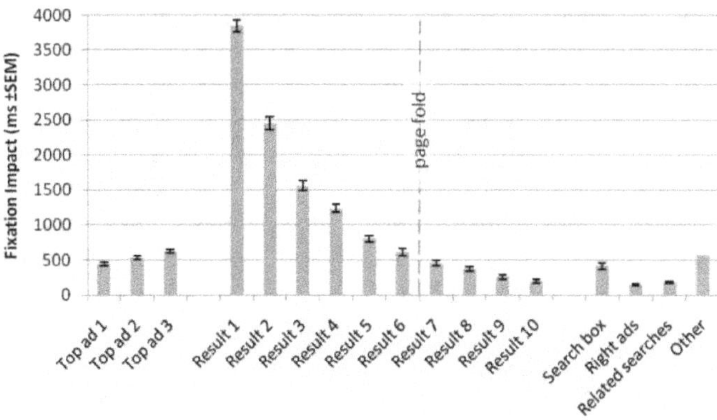

(a) Ad Examination Behavior Study

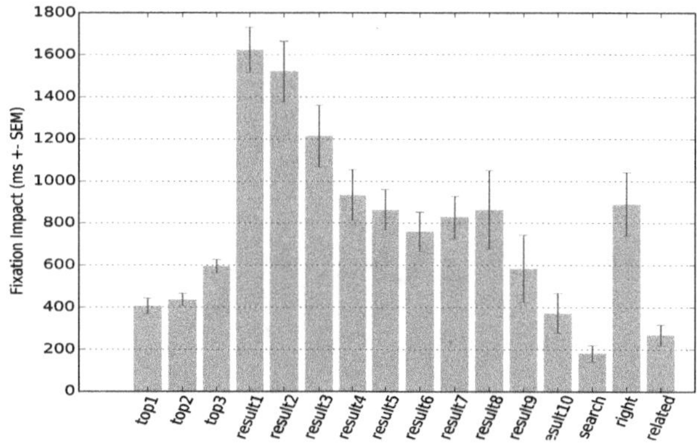

(b) SearchGazer

Figure 5: Mean fixation impact on SERP elements in milliseconds.

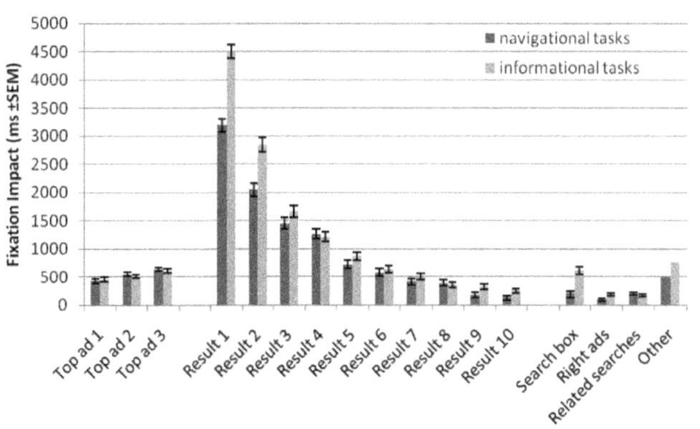

(a) Ad Examination Behavior Study

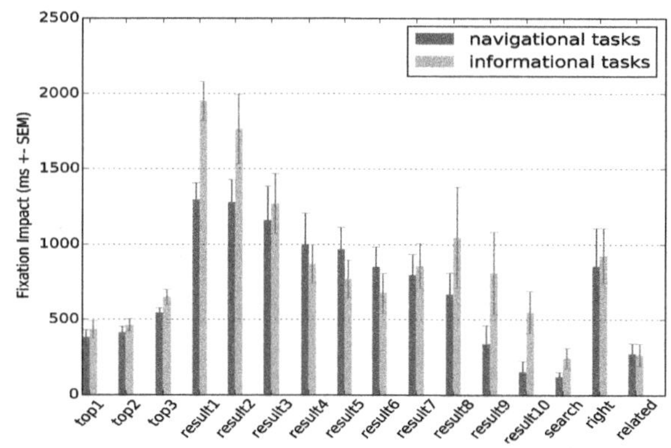

(b) SearchGazer

Figure 6: Comparison of mean fixation impact on SERP elements for navigational and informational tasks.

SERP Examination and Clickthrough: Figure 9 depicts the viewing and clickthrough rates across all queries and participants. As shown in Figure 9a, the data gathered from the ViewSer group demonstrate that both viewing and clickthrough rates decay in a linear fashion, with lower ranked results attracting less attention. Figure 9b shows the corresponding data gathered from the predictions made by SearchGazer. It is worth noting that even though the same linear trend is observed the rates are lower. After normalization, the average difference between the viewing rate is

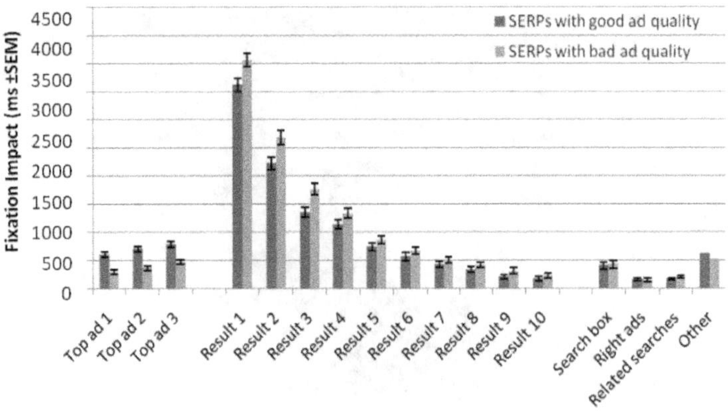

(a) Ad Examination Behavior Study

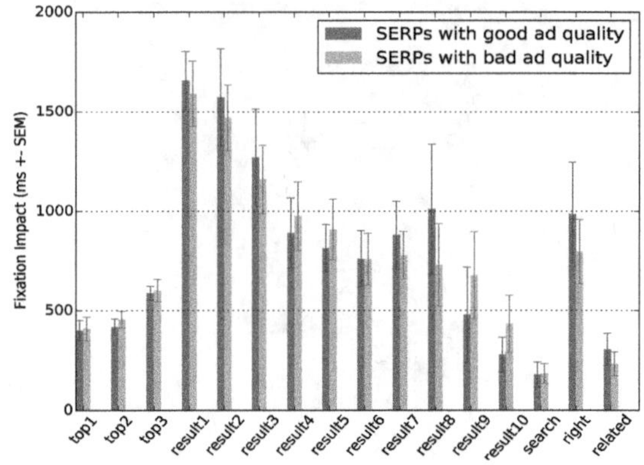

(b) SearchGazer

Figure 7: Comparison of mean fixation impact on AOIs for SERPs displaying good or bad ads.

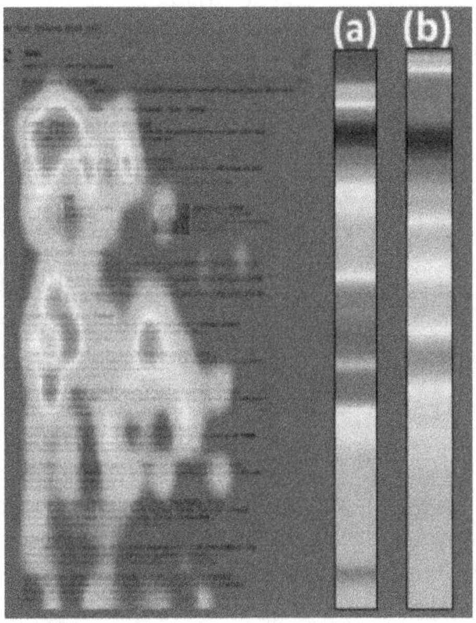

(a) Result Examination Behavior Study via Restricted Focal View. Colorbar (a): eye tracking group. Colorbar (b): ViewSer group.

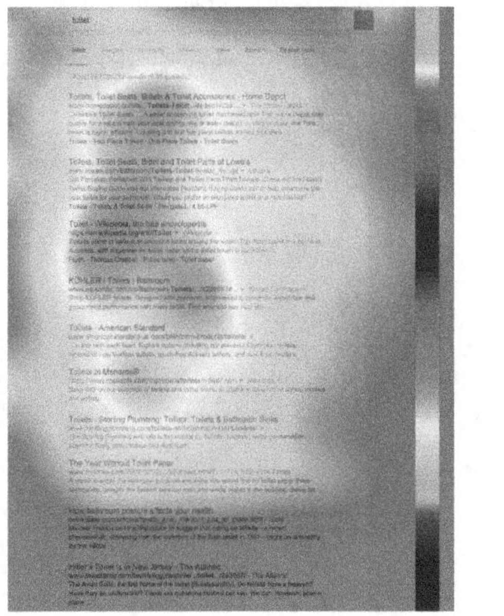

(b) SearchGazer. SearchGazer allows the creation of gaze heatmaps, unlike ViewSer which is restricted to density colorbars.

Figure 8: Attention heatmap over a SERP for the query "toilet" and its corresponding colorbar showing the heatmap density.

14.11% and 28.54% for the clickthrough rates. This could be a result of the differences in the user experience across the two studies. Restricted focus viewing can lead users to carefully examine more results instead of just scanning them, as they now have to move their cursor to reveal one result at a time. At the same time, ViewSer can lead to a closer examination of results that would otherwise be overlooked, leading to higher clickthrough rates in lower ranked results. In our study, the bottom results attracted less attention and even fewer clicks. As many of the informational tasks were vague and acceptable target information existed in many results, it is not unlikely that our crowd-workers ended up clicking on the first few results, trusting the search engine.

8. DISCUSSION

Replicating these three studies revealed both the potential and limitations of performing webcam eye tracking in place of specialized equipment and interfaces. Many of our findings, such as Figure 3, achieved similar conclusions compared with the original studies, showcasing that SearchGazer can be successfully used in experiments where the goal is to measure the distribution of gaze locations. SearchGazer was able to recreate general trends and even highlight differences in viewing times across individual organic results. In comparison to a restricted focus viewer [21], SearchGazer does not disturb the user experience by blurring the SERP. Once users consent to giving access to their webcam, they can continue navigating the web page as they would normally do, while SearchGazer collects interactions and predicts gaze activity in the background. Overall, using SearchGazer we were able to reproduce three studies with numerous charts and heatmaps at a fraction of cost, effort, and time it would normally take if those studies were conducted in lab. Multiple crowd-workers performed the study simultaneously and without the need of

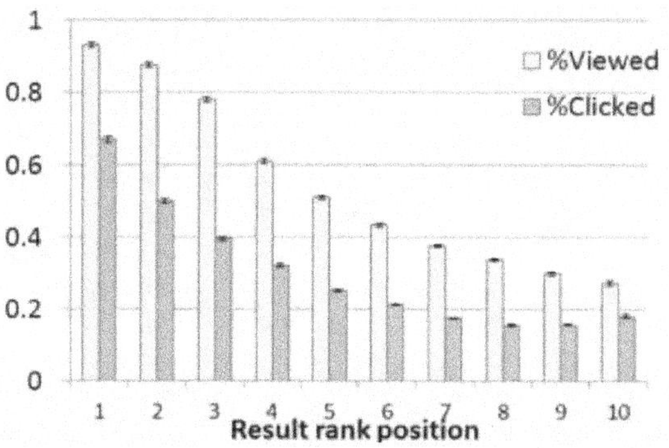

(a) Result Examination Behavior Study via Restricted Focal View

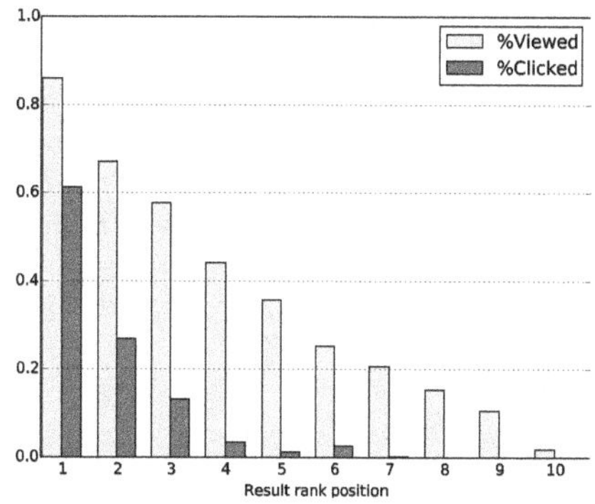

(b) SearchGazer

Figure 9: Viewing and clickthrough rates for each rank, aggregated across all queries and participants.

monitoring, allowing us to test SearchGazer with far richer and more diverse computational and ambient environments.

On the other hand, there are certain limitations that we cannot ignore. Although [5] is the closest to what we could replicate most precisely, there were specific differences that were surprising and demonstrate the need to expand our understanding of SearchGazer's constraints. A possible explanation for those differences is our lack of an algorithm to identify fixations, relying instead on raw gaze data. Although the overall aggregated data were almost always very close to the original studies, we can hypothesize that removing saccades would lead to a clearer picture that would allow replication of more fine-detailed studies. Coming up with an algorithm custom-built for SearchGazer to identify fixations as is available in existing eye trackers is one future direction. Further, SearchGazer assumes that the location of clicks and cursor movements is equal to that of the gaze. Temporal and spatial differences in this relationship might bias our model. Since our studies were conducted remotely, we lack information about the nature of SearchGazer's errors. In the future, we are interested in pursuing in-lab studies and extensively compare SearchGazer with physical eye trackers to better understand its behavior, strengths, and limitations.

Our current implementation of SearchGazer is simply a prototype demonstrating webcam eye tracking. It is not intended to be the most optimal or accurate version of online webcam eye tracking. Part of why we are releasing the software online as open source is so other researchers and developers can refine its computer vision components. The software is completely modular and different eye detectors, regression models, or interaction-based learning algorithms can be completely swapped out. In fact, we have successfully tried 3 publicly available eye detectors, 2 regression models, and multiple ways of using user interactions to train the model. The version selected for the study replications was chosen as it performs well across many peoples' facial appearances and environmental conditions. For a more extensive evaluation of SearchGazer in generic sites see [27].

8.1 Privacy

Ultimately, the use of webcams in online applications poses privacy risks, but there can be significant benefits if used appropriately, allowing websites to improve their usability or conduct experiments to better understand human behavior. Hong et al. [14] state that users will accept the privacy risks only if there are clear benefits that outweigh them.

SearchGazer is opt-in, as browsers request access to the webcams and the gaze predictions are computed in real time on the user's computer so the video stream is not sent over the web (unlike webcam eye trackers like Sticky or GazeHawk). Therefore, users decide between the trade-off of transmitting their eye-gaze behavior, in exchange for some benefit from the search engine. We imagine scenarios where users are compensated or offered other incentives, like an advertising-free search interface or additional gaze-based search features.

9. CONCLUSION

We proposed SearchGazer, a real-time online eye tracker using only the common webcam as a way to determine users' examination behavior on search pages. Using SearchGazer, we revisit in today's search environments the key findings from: a search results page examination study from CHI 2007, a search advertisement examination study from SIGIR 2010, and study of a restricted focus viewer based on the cursor from SIGIR 2011. The findings from reproducing past web search studies showed that the approach of conducting remote eye tracking studies through webcams is not unreasonable.

This new approach can be transformative, as examination behavior can be understood at scale for diverse search scenarios: when users perform infrequent queries, when search interface designers seek to test new features or layouts. In fact, numerous information retrieval models seek to infer which search results a user has examined (e.g., [7, 29]); clearly, this signal is important to the web search community, even when not measured perfectly. Compared to lab studies, remote crowd-workers can perform tasks whenever and wherever they choose, without the need for any special equipment or software installation. Remote webcam eye tracking is therefore considerably cheaper than an in-person lab study required for typical eye trackers, saving time for both the participants and experimenters. Additionally, experimenters are able to release the tasks which can be performed by remote crowd-workers immediately and simultaneously, allowing for faster feedback to inform search engine design.

10. ACKNOWLEDGMENTS

This research is supported by NSF grants IIS-1464061, IIS-1552663, and the Brown University Salomon Award.

11. REFERENCES

[1] F. Alnajar, T. Gevers, R. Valenti, and S. Ghebreab. Calibration-free gaze estimation using human gaze patterns. In *Proc. ICCV*, pages 137–144, 2013.

[2] P. Boi, G. Fenu, L. D. Spano, and V. Vargiu. Reconstructing user's attention on the web through mouse movements and perception-based content identification. *ACM TAP*, 13(3):15:1–15:21, 2016.

[3] G. Buscher, E. Cutrell, and M. R. Morris. What do you see when you're surfing?: using eye tracking to predict salient regions of web pages. In *Proc. CHI*, pages 21–30, 2009.

[4] G. Buscher, A. Dengel, and L. van Elst. Eye movements as implicit relevance feedback. In *Proc. CHI Extended Abstracts*, pages 2991–2996, 2008.

[5] G. Buscher, S. Dumais, and E. Cutrell. The good, the bad, and the random: an eye-tracking study of ad quality in web search. In *Proc. SIGIR*, pages 42–49, 2010.

[6] G. Buscher, R. White, S. Dumais, and J. Huang. Large-scale analysis of individual and task differences in search result page examination strategies. In *Proc. WSDM*, pages 373–382, 2012.

[7] O. Chapelle and Y. Zhang. A dynamic bayesian network click model for web search ranking. In *Proc. WWW*, pages 1–10, 2009.

[8] E. Cutrell and Z. Guan. What are you looking for?: an eye-tracking study of information usage in web search. In *Proc. CHI*, pages 407–416, 2007.

[9] S. Dumais, G. Buscher, and E. Cutrell. Individual differences in gaze patterns for web search. In *Proc. IIiX*, pages 185–194, 2010.

[10] C. L. Folk, R. W. Remington, and J. H. Wright. The structure of attentional control: contingent attentional capture by apparent motion, abrupt onset, and color. *Journal of Experimental Psychology: Human perception and performance*, 20(2):317, 1994.

[11] Q. Guo and E. Agichtein. Towards predicting web searcher gaze position from mouse movements. In *Proc. CHI Extended Abstracts*, pages 3601–3606, 2010.

[12] D. W. Hansen and Q. Ji. In the eye of the beholder: A survey of models for eyes and gaze. *IEEE TPAMI*, 32(3):478–500, 2010.

[13] D. Hauger, A. Paramythis, and S. Weibelzahl. Using browser interaction data to determine page reading behavior. In *User Modeling, Adaption and Personalization*, pages 147–158. Springer, 2011.

[14] J. Hong, J. Ng, S. Lederer, and J. Landay. Privacy risk models for designing privacy-sensitive ubiquitous computing systems. In *Proc. DIS*, pages 91–100, 2004.

[15] J. Huang, R. W. White, and G. Buscher. User see, user point: Gaze and cursor alignment in web search. In *Proc. CHI*, pages 1341–1350, 2012.

[16] J. Huang, R. W. White, and S. Dumais. No clicks, no problem: using cursor movements to understand and improve search. In *Proc. CHI*, pages 1225–1234, 2011.

[17] M. X. Huang, T. C. Kwok, G. Ngai, S. C. Chan, and H. V. Leong. Building a personalized, auto-calibrating eye tracker from user interactions. In *Proc. CHI*, pages 5169–5179, 2016.

[18] T. Joachims, L. Granka, B. Pan, H. Hembrooke, and G. Gay. Accurately interpreting clickthrough data as implicit feedback. In *Proc. SIGIR*, pages 154–161, 2005.

[19] T. Joachims, L. Granka, B. Pan, H. Hembrooke, F. Radlinski, and G. Gay. Evaluating the accuracy of implicit feedback from clicks and query reformulations in web search. *ACM TOIS*, 25(2):7, 2007.

[20] B. Kules, R. Capra, M. Banta, and T. Sierra. What do exploratory searchers look at in a faceted search interface? In *Proc. JCDL*, pages 313–322, 2009.

[21] D. Lagun and E. Agichtein. Viewser: Enabling large-scale remote user studies of web search examination and interaction. In *Proc. SIGIR*, pages 365–374, 2011.

[22] D. Lagun and E. Agichtein. Inferring searcher attention by jointly modeling user interactions and content salience. In *Proc. SIGIR*, pages 483–492, 2015.

[23] Y. Liu, Z. Liu, K. Zhou, M. Wang, H. Luan, C. Wang, M. Zhang, and S. Ma. Predicting search user examination with visual saliency. In *Proc. SIGIR*, pages 619–628, 2016.

[24] Y. Liu, C. Wang, K. Zhou, J. Nie, M. Zhang, and S. Ma. From skimming to reading: A two-stage examination model for web search. In *Proc. CIKM*, pages 849–858, 2014.

[25] A. Mathias. clmtrackr: Javascript library for precise tracking of facial features via Constrained Local Models. https://github.com/auduno/clmtrackr, 2014. [Online; accessed 2016-05-08].

[26] V. Navalpakkam, L. Jentzsch, R. Sayres, S. Ravi, A. Ahmed, and A. Smola. Measurement and modeling of eye-mouse behavior in the presence of nonlinear page layouts. In *Proc. WWW*, pages 953–964, 2013.

[27] A. Papoutsaki, P. Sangkloy, J. Laskey, N. Daskalova, J. Huang, and J. Hays. Webgazer: Scalable webcam eye tracking using user interactions. In *Proc. IJCAI*, pages 3839–3845, 2016.

[28] K. Rodden, X. Fu, A. Aula, and I. Spiro. Eye-mouse coordination patterns on web search results pages. In *Proc. CHI Extended Abstracts*, pages 2997–3002, 2008.

[29] R. Srikant, S. Basu, N. Wang, and D. Pregibon. User browsing models: relevance versus examination. In *Proc. SIGKDD*, pages 223–232, 2010.

[30] Y. Sugano, Y. Matsushita, and Y. Sato. Calibration-free gaze sensing using saliency maps. In *Proc. CVPR*, pages 2667–2674, 2010.

[31] A. Wallar, A. Sazonovs, C. Poellabauer, and P. Flynn. Camgaze.js: Browser-based Eye Tracking and Gaze Prediction using JavaScript. http://aw204.host.cs.st-andrews.ac.uk/camgaze.js, 2014. [Online; accessed 2015-03-12].

[32] P. Xu, K. A. Ehinger, Y. Zhang, A. Finkelstein, S. R. Kulkarni, and J. Xiao. Turkergaze: Crowdsourcing saliency with webcam based eye tracking. *arXiv preprint arXiv:1504.06755*, 2015.

[33] P. Xu, Y. Sugano, and A. Bulling. Spatio-temporal modeling and prediction of visual attention in graphical user interfaces. In *Proc. CHI*, pages 3299–3310, 2016.

[34] P. Zielinski. Opengazer: open-source gaze tracker for ordinary webcams. http://www.inference.phy.cam.ac.uk/opengazer, 2007. [Online; accessed 2014-08-24].

Asking "Good" Questions: Questionnaire Design and Analysis in Interactive Information Retrieval Research

Heather L. O'Brien
School of Library, Archival and Information Studies
University of British Columbia
Vancouver, British Columbia, Canada
1-604-827-5842
h.obrien@ubc.ca

Lori McCay-Peet
School of Information Management
Dalhousie University
Halifax, Nova Scotia, Canada
1-902-494-6119
mccay@dal.ca

ABSTRACT

Asking questions is a central element of Interactive Information Retrieval (IIR) studies, yet the challenges associated with asking "good" questions is are rarely discussed. This perspectives paper examines the development, evaluation, and application of questionnaires in IIR research. The authors draw upon prior literature and their own research to explore how to best construct and extract meaning from questionnaires. Since building IIR knowledge and theories requires the employment of valid, reliable, dimensional, and sensitive self-report measures, this paper's contribution is an overview of best practices for developing, administering, and analyzing questionaires.

CCS Concepts

• **General and reference ~ Measurement** • **General and reference ~ Evaluation** • **Human-centered computing ~ HCI design and evaluation methods**

Keywords

Self-report measures; Questionnaires; Psychometric scales; Measurement; Evaluation; Reliability; Validity; Interactive information retrieval

1. INTRODUCTION

Self-report measures are commonly used in Interactive Information Retrieval (IIR) research. We *ask questions* to capture users' affective (e.g., frustration, satisfaction) and cognitive (e.g., complexity, ease of use) perceptions of information tasks and systems. Questionnaires and psychometric scales may be used to differentiate users on the basis of specific qualities, such as age, cognitive style, or reading aptitude, enabling the exploration of how such qualities impact IIR behaviors (*How does self-efficacy impact search strategy selection?*). Finally, self-reports may be used to make sense of behavioral or neurophysiological data (*How does self-reported interest correlate with gaze patterns?*).

CHIIR '17, March 07 - 11, 2017, Oslo, Norway

ACM 978-1-4503-4677-1/17/03...$15.00 DOI: http://dx.doi.org/10.1145/3020165.3020167

Despite the versatility and extensive use of self-report measures, they tend to be given "short shrift". Firstly, researchers may consider self-report measures "subjective" and therefore less robust than "objective," quantifiable measures, such as number of mouse clicks, page visits, etc. Secondly, researchers may not investigate the rigor of questionnaires and scales before adopting them, nor during the analysis of the data they have collected. In addition, descriptive statistics and reliability and validity tests particular to the questionnaires and scales used are not systematically reported. As a result, the robustness of many commonly used IIR self-report measures is unknown. Thirdly, instruments may be misused because researchers lack sufficient knowledge to implement and analyze them. All of these issues perpetuate the notion that self-reports are not an effective way to collect useful IIR data.

We focus on *asking questions* as a fundamental component of IIR research design and analysis. We do not claim that self-reports are the only measures of importance in IIR studies. Most experts agree that including multiple measures in a research study is advisable to capture multifaceted constructs and to ensure that the results are reflective of the phenomenon of interest [20][24]. However, the measures selected must be complementary. There is a risk in using one type of measure, whether subjective or objective. For instance, patterns of mouse clicks may be interpreted very differently independently versus in the context of an exit interview. We see self-report measures, including questionnaires, as part of a suite of IIR tools that can be "profitably thought of as one prong of a multifaceted data collection strategy" [24] (p. 221).

Overall, this paper makes three important contributions to the CHIIR community:

- Firstly, we aim to facilitate dialog amongst IIR researchers that to date has occured through backchannels. We (the authors) continually field queries about how to use and meaningfully interpret the experiential questionnaires we developed. There is an onus on us as creators to provide documentation for and continuously improve upon our questionnaires. However, others must be aware of the methodological issues associated with such measures to make effective decisions as peer reviewers and when adopting them for use in their own work.
- Our second goal is to enhance the quality of self-report measures used in IIR research by emphasizing the need to consider the fit of self-report instruments to phenomena of interest, and the quality of the questionnaires or scales available. It could also lead to better empirical and reporting practices that would allow self-report measures to be evaluated over time and across studies and settings.

- Finally, while questionnaire development and evaluation are challenging, lengthy processes, the validation of constructs in IIR research is critical to theory development—good theory cannot be built on a house of cards. By providing an overview of current best practices in the field, we offer a means to build and enrich IIR knowledge and theory.

Through the use of relevant examples, we 1) examine the development and evaluation of questionnaires and psychometric scales, with particular emphasis on reliability and validity; and 2) recommend best practices for their selection and use. We build on the work of Kelly [21] [23] here to expose the potential pitfalls of how self-report measures are used and reported on in IIR. Our work is distinguished from Kelly in that she and colleagues have looked at evaluation issues more broadly at the experimental level, and we have focused specifically on questionnaires in order to illuminate the special considerations involved in developing, evaluating, adopting, and reporting on these specific measures.

2. BACKGROUND

2.1 Terminology

Self-report measures, including questionnaires and psychometric scales, capture "a respondent's direct appraisal of his or her standing with respect to a target construct or behavior" and may be gathered directly through interviews, or indirectly through online surveys; self-reports may be highly or loosely structured [24]. Questionnaires, "a formulated series of questions by which information is sought from a selected group" [44], capture perceptions of an experience at a particular point in time. Psychometric scales, by comparison, are psychological tests designed to measure innate and acquired qualities such as "mental capacity, thought processes, aspects of personality" [43].

While questionnaires are more common in IIR research than psychometric scales, they may be used in a complimentary capacity. For example, Heinström [16] used the NEO Five-Factor Inventory, a psychometric scale that measures five "core dimensions" of personality (e.g., extraversion, openness to experience) with the Approaches and Study Skills Inventory for Students (ASSIST). While closed-ended questionnaires and psychometric scales are fundamentally different in terms of what they measure, both require thoughtful, rigorous development and use similar statistical methods to evaluate their reliability and validity. For the sake of simplicity, we will use the term *questionnaire* in this paper, unless we need to semantically distinguish questionnaires and psychometric scales.

2.2 Questionnaires in IIR Research

Kelly [21] acknowledges the long-standing use of questionnaires in IIR evaluation, and distinguishes five types:

- demographic (e.g., sex, age);
- pre-task (e.g., prior knowledge of the system or topic);
- post-task (e.g., task satisfaction);
- post-system (e.g., overall experience of interacting with an information system); and
- exit (e.g, cross-system comparisons of ease of use or preference) (p. 94).

These types demonstrate that self-reports may be solicited before, during, and after an experiment or field study and serve different purposes. Each requires careful attention in terms of what is being asked, and how it contributes to the overarching research goals. In other words, researchers must attend not only consider the results or outcome of the study (i.e., the acceptance or rejection of the study's hypotheses), but the quality of the instruments used to measure the variables of interest [20](p. 206). Crowdsourcing has been used, for example, extensively to conduct relevance assessments. While its low cost and speed and ease of implementation make it desirable, drawbacks such as poor replicability have been noted and ways to improve quality of research design suggested [1].

Questionnaires may be used to collect specific IIR measures. We focus on what Kelly labels *usability* and *contextual* measures. Usability measures capture participants' "attitudes and feelings about the system and their interactions with it" [21] (p. 100). Contextual measures refer to those used to assess "the information seeking situation" (e.g., task type), or "those used to categorize subjects" (i.e., individual differences, such as search expertise, learning style, personality) [21] (p. 100). Kelly concedes that *usability* as a category is limited, in part due to terminology: "usability" does not encompass the range of phenomenon that can be explored in IIR (e.g., usefulness, satisfaction, mental load) and its use in IIR is not congruent with the ISO definition of usability, i.e., effectiveness, efficiency and satisfaction [21][23].

However, Kelly [21] also critiques the ways in which usability measures are treated in IIR studies.

> *In many cases, researchers do not provide any conceptual or operational definitions of usability and instead lump all self-report data together and call it usability data. Referring to all self-report data as usability data overly restricts the types of questions that can be asked and does not encourage much thought about the nature of the data that is collected* (p. 116).

Kelly's concerns are further substantiated in later work with Sugimoto [23]. They conducted a systematic review of 127 IIR articles published between 1967-2006. Among other factors, Kelly and Sugimoto [23] examined measurement practices and observed that measures were generally not well described in the papers, and that usability measures in particular were "the poorest" (p. 760). The majority of usability measures featured in the articles were self-reports trying to assess such varied constructs as ease of use, understandability, general and search results satisfaction, and perceive time to perform a search task. The authors pointed out that the lack of description made the reuse and evaluation of these measures impossible "because [descriptions] are tied directly to the quality of the questions asked and the choices and scales provided. Questions might be biased, loaded, or poorly worded; scale labels might be confusing or not represent a continuum" (p. 760). While the usability measures were interpretable, they were further limited by the seemingly "ad hoc" manner in which they were developed. Further, the robustness of the measures was not addressed and therefore "questionable" [23] (p. 761).

Kelly and Sugimoto [23] raise two key issues that reinforce the motivation of this perspectives paper. First, self-report measures are not being used effectively in IIR research. This is supported by the inadequate reporting processes that caused Kelly and Sugimoto to wonder whether "these aspects were perhaps not taken seriously by many researchers" (p. 760). Secondly, the use of usability measures in IIR appears to be growing over time compared to other types measures, yet the scholarship on user-centered research methods is sparse.

At the same time, there is emerging interest in the creation and critical evaluation of instruments to assess *contextual* (e.g., self-efficacy [9], search expertise [5]), and *usability* (e.g., serendipity [30][31], engagement [35][36]) aspects of IIR. However, compared to other fields, such as psychology, education, and management, IIR research lacks sustained scholarship on self-report measures. This limits the ability to compare the use of measures across populations, though such appraisals would be beneficial. For example, substantiating the link between specific self-report measures and behavioural patterns would allow researchers to better assess constructs such as user engagement in online search environments where it is impossible to ask searchers about their experiences, but where there is an abundance of interaction data to draw upon [1][25]. Thus, our emphasis is on how to ask "good" questions and work within the constraints of different settings to measure what we think we are measuring.

3. EVALUATING QUESTIONNAIRES

Common methodological challenges associated with self-reports (e.g., demand effects, acquiescence/naysaying, end-aversion bias, social desirability) are well documented threats to internal validity [21] (for an excellent discussion of these issues and other limitations of self-report measures, see [20][22][24]). However, self-report data "are used frequently, often provide valid data, and are often used to complement other types of assessment" [24] (p. 222). In the IIR context, Kelly [21] astutely points out that it is not the type of measure that is at issue, but rather the lack of investment in the evaluation of self-report measures, specifically questionnaires and scales:

> *While there are some items and scales that appear in many studies and could be characterized as a core question set, most of these items have not undergone any significant validity and reliability testing. They have become the* core by default [emphasis ours] *rather than because of their specific properties* (p. 179).

The reliability and validity of all measures used in a research study is essential; questionnaires are no exception. Evaluating questionnaires requires different techniques, sample sizes, and statistical analyses than, for example, log data.

Stages of questionnaire development

Stage/Goal	Method
Conceptualization Understand construct, related constructs, and key attributes; define construct; identify dimensions	• Review of the literature • Interviews with subject matter experts (SMEs) or representatives of population to gain understanding of construct
Develop questionnaire Identify items to represent construct and its dimension(s)	• Review of the literature • Interviews, focus groups, or surveys to get input from SMEs or representatives of population
Assess content validity Ensure items represent different aspects of construct's content domain and together represent the domain of the construct	• Evaluation of representativeness of questionnaire by SMEs or non-SMEs
Refine questionnaire, assess construct validity and reliability Reduce number of items in questionnaire, ensure questionnaire is measuring what it is intended to measure	• Use questionnaire in survey; apply statistical techniques such as exploratory and confirmatory factor analysis, multiple regression, and structural equation modelling

Figure 1 Stages of questionnaire development

In this section, we discuss reliability and validity with respect to questionnaires, and consider two additional criteria: dimensionality, which pertains to whether more than one facet of a construct is being captured by a questionnaire, and measurement sensitivity, or how well the measure can detect differences in populations or settings. Figure 1 illustrates the goals of each stage of questionnaire development and possible methods used. There are different methods for executing each stage, and the researcher must decide how to best reach each goal [26][45]. In the following sections we discuss the stages of questionnaire development, followed by two examples to illustrate different approaches to the process.

3.1 Reliability

Reliability speaks to measurement quality, and may refer to either a questionnaire's consistency in measuring a construct, or the repeatability of the research design. Reliability is essentially "an attempt to hit the bull's eye" [48] (p. 117): when darts are scattered across a dartboard, reliability is low, i.e., the darts did not find a *single* mark. Similarly, when data are not consistent, the measure has not effectively captured a single construct, and there is no discernable pattern. On the other hand, when darts converge on the dartboard—when data consistently point to a single conclusion—high reliability is assumed. Several factors may affect the reliability of questionnaires in IIR research in particular: 1) questionnaire attributes, and 2) study implementation.

3.1.1 Questionnaire attributes.

A number of attributes may affect reliability including wording and length. The wording of questions may introduce problems of reliability if they introduce social desirability bias [33]. For instance, asking a "threatening question" may lead to a decline in reported frequency [33] of a specific behavior if they perceive they will be judged negatively. Brevity is also important in questionnaire design. Individual questions should be brief to improve reliability [16] and, regarding questionnaire length, "a few reliable variables give a more meaningful solution than a large number of less reliable variables" [51] (p. 11). Cronbach's alpha (α) provides a tool for assessing the internal consistency of summated questionnaires and is the most commonly used approach for testing reliability. Cronbach's alpha is a way in which to identify those items or questions that may be removed to improve reliability through item-to-item correlation tests [26].

3.1.2 Study implementation.

Systematic error may be introduced during questionnaire implementation, compromising reliability. For example, in studies in which participants are asked to compare systems, they may respond more favourably to the novel system to please the researcher. This again illustrates social desirability bias [33], a problem that has been noted in IIR research [21]. In this case, systematic error may be reduced through self-administered questionnaires, which may ensure a level of distance between the researcher and participant [33]. Common IIR study designs that put the researcher and participant in close proximity can make anonymity difficult. However, other methods including batch-mode studies, in which many participants are run through the study at the same time, and web-administered questionnaires, may reduce social desirability bias and thus systematic error, though these approaches may introduce other reliability risks [21].

3.2 Validity

While reliability is an important aspect of measurement, its primary limitation should be noted. To return to the dartboard analogy, high reliability only requires the darts to converge on the same spot—they may miss the bull's eye entirely! While the measurement may be reliable, consistently delivering the same results and thus illustrating the measurement of a single construct, it may not be measuring the construct the researcher theorized it would measure. Validity needs to be considered [48].

High validity is achieved when there is consistency in measurement *and* when the construct of interest is captured by the questionnaire. It has been argued that while IIR measures have face validity, that is, they make sense to the researcher, most do not have demonstrated validity (e.g., content validity) [21]. Construct validity, which encompasses a number of types of validity, "must be investigated whenever no criterion or universe of content is accepted as entirely adequate to define the quality to be measured" [13] (p. 282). In other words, it is not enough to declare that a particular measurement tool assesses usability, usefulness, etc.: a test must prove that it measures what it purports to measure. Unfortunately there is no single empirical test for construct validity. Rather, construct validation is an iterative and unending process punctuated by critical reviews. Psychological phenomena (e.g., emotion, cognition, perception) are difficult if not impossible to observe and their definitions (and subsequently their measurements) are uncertain. Construct validation does, however, allow researchers to become more confident in the veracity of constructs, and is essential in each phase of the research process, from theory development to empirical observation to theory revision.

3.3 Dimensionality

Dimensionality refers to "whether there are multiple sub-dimensions of the focal construct" [26] (p. 300). Questionnaires may be *uni-* or *multidimensional* depending on the presence of one or more aspects, attributes, or sub-dimensions. In this section we provide examples of both types of questionnaires and why this distinction is important for IIR research.

The System Usability Scale (SUS) [11][12] is a ten-item *unidimensional* questionnaire that measures perceived system usability and learnability. Ten items are used to calculate a score between 0 and 100; scores can be plotted as percentile rankings to assess a system's usability or how it compares to others. While unidimensional instruments are straightforward, they may be overly simplistic. Brinkman, Haakma, and Bouwhuis [10] developed a component-based usability questionnaire to fill a perceived gap that "existing usability questionnaires regard the system as a single entity and provide information only on this level" (p. 121). Brooke [12] acknowledged that the SUS provides a snapshot of perceived usability at a specific point in time, and does not guide system developers to improve the usability of systems. Thus, unidimensional questionnaires may be limited in the depth at which they represent complex constructs, which has implications for using the resulting data or scores in meaningful ways. The issue of unidimensionality may be particularly salient in multi-faceted information retrieval interactions.

One example of a *multidimensional* questionnaire is the Cognitive Absorption Scale (CAS) [4], which purports to measure cognitive absorption (CA), "a state of deep involvement with software" (p. 673) and is comprised of five sub-dimensions: temporal dissociation, focused immersion, heightened enjoyment, control, and curiosity. The CAS contains three-five items for each of its sub-dimensions. In the case of multidimensional instruments, more than one sub-dimension is significant to the meaning of the overarching or "focal" construct, and the nature of the relationships between sub-dimensions and the focal construct may be additive or multiplicative [26]. For instance, if CA is enhanced when an individual experiences increased temporal dissociation *or* focused immersion *or* enjoyment *or* control *or* curiosity, then CA is a "union" of its subdimensions. However, if CA is truly a product or intersection of its subdimensions, then we would need a *minimal level* of temporal dissociation *and* focused immersion *and* heightened enjoyment *and* control *and* curiosity for it to manifest [26].

The additive versus multiplicative relationship between sub-dimensions is important for IIR researchers wishing to use a multidimensional scale. Time constraints or concerns over participant fatigue may cause researchers to consider using only some sub-dimensions, but this decision may have implications for whether the focal construct is actually being measured in the study. Returning to the usability example, if we adopted a multidimensional usability questionnaire with three sub-dimensions (efficiency, effectiveness, and satisfaction), but elected to use only the satisfaction items, then we are not actually measuring usability, because usability is the sum of its three components.

3.4 Measurement Sensitivity

IIR researchers may want to determine the generalizability of their data to the broader population from which a sample is drawn or to other search systems. In the case of questionnaires, measurement sensitivity is "the capacity of a measure to reflect systematic variation, change, or differences in response to an experimental manipulation, intervention, or different group composition" [20] (pp. 209-210). To illustrate, if we tested two systems, one with high and one with low search response latency, we would expect to find differences in users' perceptions of the system; for example, if SUS scores for system A and B were significantly different, then we would conclude that the SUS was a sensitive measure.

Measurement sensitivity can be difficult to gauge *a priori*, because it is influenced by other aspects of the study, such as the size and strength of between-group differences and of the manipulation [20]. Returning to the above example of search latency, Arapakis and colleagues [3] tested search results latencies of 0, 750, 1250 or 1750 milliseconds (ms). They found that latencies of up to 500 ms were not detectable by users, but "after a certain threshold (1000 ms), the users could feel the added delay with very high likelihood" (p. 111). Therefore, if only latencies of low (0 and 500 ms) *or* high (1250 and 1750 ms) were tested, then it is unlikely that the researchers would have detected differences in their dependent variables (focused attention, system usability, and positive and negative affect), as the former range (0-500 ms) was below the threshold of detectable difference and the latter (1250-1750 ms) was above.

4. EXAMPLES

Reliability, validity, dimensionality, and sensitivity are important aspects of questionnaire evaluation, and can be approached in different ways. In this section we use two experiential questionnaires to illustrate the development and evaluation process.

4.1 Serendipitous Digital Environment Scale

Serendipity is defined as "an unexpected experience prompted by an individual's valuable interaction with ideas, information, objects, or phenomena" ([29], p. 1474). The *serendipitous digital environment scale (SDE)* is a multidimensional questionnaire designed to measure how well a digital environment, e.g., social media site, mobile application, etc., facilitates serendipity [31]. Its development was motivated at the beginning of McCay-Peet's [27] dissertation work with the rise of personalization and, consequently, "filter bubbles" [40] which appeared to threaten serendipity in digital environments. Moreover, while mobile apps, recommender systems, and search engines were being developed to support serendipity, there were few measurement tools to assess their "serendipitousness". Specifically, there was no self-report tool designed to elicit feedback from users, those in the best position to judge the serendipitousness of their experiences with various digital information environments.

The SDE is comprised of four dimensions or subscales: 1) enables connections; 2) highlights triggers; 3) trigger rich; and 4) leads to the unexpected. Each subscale has three to five items for a total of 15 items. Items include, for example, "I can see connections between topics in [X]," and "I bump into unexpected content in [X]." [X] in each case is replaced by the name of the digital information environment being examined (e.g., the mobile app, search engine). Responses to the items are rated on a five-point agreement scale (strongly disagree, disagree, neither agree nor disagree, agree, strongly agree).

The SDE was developed using qualitative and quantitative research methods: interviews, expert review, and online surveys. These varied approaches enabled the validity and reliability of the scale to be tested at all stages of construction. In the conceptualization stage, interviews with 12 knowledge workers with serendipitous experiences related to work or research were used to define the construct of serendipity and to identify key elements of the serendipity process and facets or sub-dimensions of serendipitous environments [29]. These findings were integrated with prior research findings. This stage grounded the development of the scale.

Second, an expert review with eight international experts in the content domain of serendipity and related constructs was used to hone the sub-dimensions and pool of items for the proposed scale [30]. This stage was primarily used as a way to guide scale item development and improve the resulting scale's content validity, but was also an opportunity to enhance the construct validity of the scale, as experts were asked if any important dimensions were missing. Third, an online survey, completed by 107 university students, applied the "ANOVA approach" [18] to test the content validity of the scale [30]. Essentionally, students were asked to rate the extent to which items of the preliminary scale reflected the content domain they were intended to capture.

Finally, an online survey of 289 professionals, academics, and students engaged in thesis work was used to refine and test the construct validity of the scale [31]. Principal components analysis (PCA) was used to hone and improve the reliability of the scale which was reduced from 37 to 15 items. A "Perception of Serendipity Scale" comprised of definitions of serendipity and the related construct of information encountering (e.g., "I encounter useful information, ideas, or resources that I am not looking for when I use [X]" (adapted from [15]) was used as a global or direct measure of serendipity and relationships to contextual measures often associated with serendipity were tested (openness to experience, extraversion, locus of control, creative work environment). Through multiple regression analyses, the global measure was used to test whether dimensions or factors of the SDE (e.g., enables connnections) were related to perceptions of its serendipitousness as they were intended; in other words, whether the measure was "hitting the bull's eye" (construct validity).

Ultimately, results indicated that three of the dimensions (enables connections, trigger rich, leads to the unexpected) were significantly related to perceptions of serendipity while, interestingly, the contextual variables had no significant relationship [31]. The SDE is relatively new and research is currently underway to explore how its dimensions may be operationalized for user experience (UX) designers and to test the scale in specific digital environments (e.g., Twitter).

4.2 User Engagement Scale

The User Engagement Scale (UES) is a 31-item, multi-dimensional questionnaire designed to measure user engagement in digital environments. While research on user engagement is now abundant in many digital domains including search, there was scant work in the area a decade ago; what research did exist was in many ways, exemplary and foundational, but was limited to educational multimedia and conducted in the early- to mid-90s. (For more information about the history and development of self-report measures of user engagement please see Chapter 2 in [25]) Further, user engagement has proven an elusive construct to define, and hence, measure. O'Brien's [35] dissertation work set out to answer the questions, *What is user engagement?* [39] and *How do we measure it?* [38].

Like the SDE, the UES was developed using both qualitative and quantitative methods. After a systematic literature review of user engagement and related constructs and theories in several disciplines, O'Brien [35] proposed that engagement consisted of a number of attributes: challenge, positive affect, endurability, aesthetic and sensory appeal, attention, feedback, variety/novelty, interactivity, and perceived user control. These attributes informed semi-structured interviews with gamers, web searchers, online shoppers, and online learners. The interviews were used to examine the manifestation of the various attributes in users' experiences and to determine if there were other attributes that had not come to light in prior literature. At the conclusion of this research stage, it was hypothesized that "engagement is a quality of user experiences with technology that is characterized by challenge, aesthetic and sensory appeal, feedback, novelty, interactivity, perceived control and time, awareness, motivation, interest, and affect" [39] (p. 949).

In stage two of the UES's development, items were derived from the aforementioned interviews and existing measures for each of the identified attributes. The resulting 400+ items were assessed for validity by an independent researcher who was provided with the defintitions of the attributes and their corresponding items to assess fit. This resulted in a smaller pool of items that was administered to over 400 online shoppers. Reliability assessment and exploratory factor analysis (EFA) was used to eliminate unreliable items and examine the dimensionality of the items. The outcome of this survey was a 49 item questionnaire with items loading on six factors: perceived usability, aesthetic appeal, novelty, felt involvement, focused attention, and endurability (overall feelings about the experience). These 49 items were administered in another online survey with 800+ shoppers. Structural equation modeling was used to confirm the six-factor structure of the scale (confirmatory factor analysis or CFA) and the relationships between the dimensions (path analysis); the scale was further reduced to 31-items [35][38].

Since its development, the UES has been used in over 50 research studies. Recently O'Brien [37] surveyed this work, which crossed several digital domains, including education, marketing, search, haptic, and game applications. It was observed that the UES has, in general, been reliable, valid, and sensitive in different contexts, but has shown it's limitations. In a few studies, it failed to detect differences between systems or correlate with specific behavioral measures. Most notably, its dimensionality has been questioned, i.e., studies have found four factors rather than six. However, O'Brien noted the lack of description in how people adopted the measure. It was often unclear what items or sub-dimensions of the UES were used and there was a lack of reporting of basic descriptive data. Echoing earlier findings [23], she concluded that "it is difficult to create a cohesive picture of measurement when instruments are used only in part or studies lack a rationale for why specific [items/sub-dimensions] were chosen" [37] (p. 48).

O'Brien [36][37] also noted the continuous challenge of defining user engagement consistently—and beyond its attributes—and that a vital stage of the evaluation process is absent for the UES: the development of norms "to aid in the interpretation of scores on the scale" [26] (p. 325). While O'Brien has been examining ranges (low, medium, high scores) and mean/median averages within her own studies, user ratings at a broader level (like the aforementioned SUS) is unknown. Thus other researchers would have a difficult time ascertaining if UES scores were low or high compared to other samples. Norming the UES is further complicated by the fact that norms change over time [26], especially in dynamic fields such as IIR, and the aforementioned reporting issues for the UES [37].

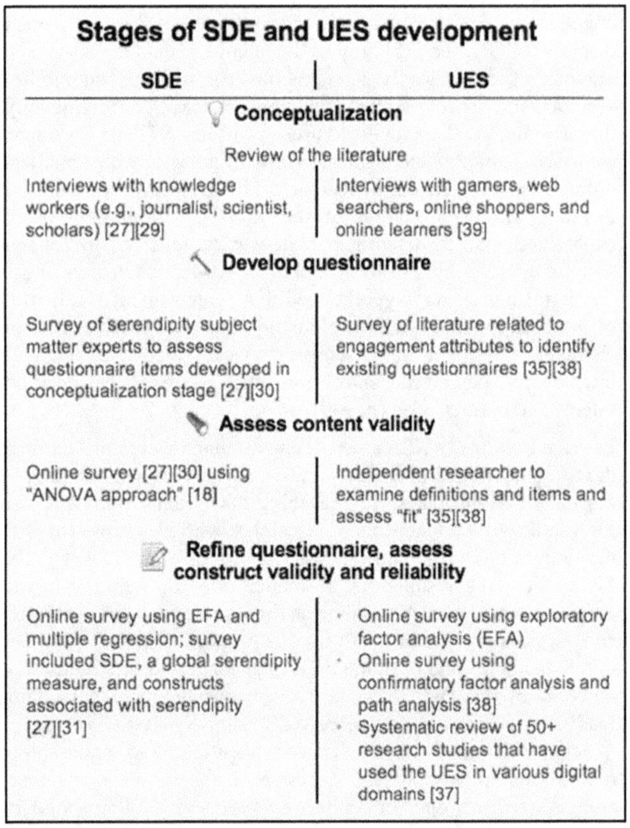

Figure 2 Comparison of Methods Used in Stages of the Serendipitous Digital Environment (SDE) Scale and the User Engagement Scale (UES) Development

4.3 Summary

Both the Serendipitous Digital Environment (SDE) scale and the User Engagement Scale (UES) converge and diverge in their development and evaluation processes. Figure 2 summarizes the stages introduced in Figure 1 and how each was approached by the developers of the SDE and UES.

Developing measures for abstract constructs such as serendipity and engagement has been challenging and time consuming. With few established questionnaires in IIR, authors of both the SDE and UES turned to the questionnaire development literature in other disciplines for direction and to find commonalities that could inform their approach. While this was useful, it was sometimes difficult to bridge work outside of the discipline to the IIR context. In addition to methodological literature, it was necessary to conduct research that would help ground decisions made in the scale development process. This was accomplished through interviews that enabled the identification of key elements of the serendipity process (e.g., trigger, connection, unexpected thread) [29] or engagement attributes [39], which were reflected in the development of the dimensions of each scale.

Both authors parsed characteristics of serendipitous digital environments or attributes of user engagement to provide tools for understanding what makes specific digital environments more or less serendipitous or engaging. The ultimate goal of both questionnaires was to utilize them in the development of system requirements or heuristics, akin to how usability has been operationalized by Nielsen [34] and others. This goal has been front of mind at each stage of the scale development process to ensure construct validity, but operationalizing characteristics of serendipitous environments or user engagement is challenging: the formula for serendipity and engagement is not exact. Some researchers [19][50] have suggested that certain system features can precipitate different qualities of UE (e.g., pictures of people capture users' attention), but such recommendations cannot be applied in a blanket fashion. User experience is a complex interaction of users' motivation, mood, expectations, and abilities, systems, and tasks, and may also be affected by domain, e.g., game versus search applications.

Scale development does not come to an end once the questionnaire is published. In the case of the SDE and UES, each author continues to document their questionnaires' uses and limitations, and to further refine and test them for the purpose of informing theory and application. For those wishing to use these and similar questionnaires, it must be acknowledged that questionnaire development and evaluation is an ongoing process, and that a "perfect measure" does not exist. These examples highlight the longitudinal and varied work required to bring a questionnaire to fruition and continue to improve upon it, as well as the different considerations, steps taken, and decisions made along the way.

5. SELECTING QUESTIONNAIRES

The majority of IIR researchers will not be developing their own questionnaires, but will be looking to adopt and adapt existing meaures to suit their own contexts of use. We now turn our attention to the selection of questionnaires drawing upon previous discussions about reliability, validity, dimensionality, and measurement sensitivity.

5.1 Defining Phenomenon of Interest

The most important question that a researcher must ask is "what do I want to measure?" The issues raised earlier regarding usability measures in IIR [21][23] indicate that our community may not be spending sufficient time on this step. It is not enough to say that we want to know what searchers thought about interacting with a sytem; are we referring to ease of use, task satisfaction, or some other aspect of experience? In addition, we need to take a more nuanced view of the phenomenon of interest. For example, the challenge users experience during a search session could be negative (taxing, frustrating) or positive (engaging), so simply asking them if they felt challenged fails to accurately capture their experience.

It is useful to begin with a definition of the phenomenon of interest (when one exists). This allows the researcher to then evaluate questionnaires and other measures in terms of whether they actually measure the construct. If we adopt the ISO definition of usability, for instance, then we are specifically looking for a measure that includes efficiency, effectiveness and satisfaction. It is not adequate to adopt a measure simply because it has been used by other researchers in the past [20] [21]. With a firm sense of the phemonon of interest, the researcher can then move on to locating potential measures.

5.2 Finding questionnaires

A new measure does not and should not be developed for every research project. There are numerous questionnaires and scales in existence that have been carefully developed. Due to the multidisciplinary nature of IIR, a number of questionnaires from cognate fields, e.g., psychology, education, and management information systems, may be utilized. These questionnaires may be developed and reported in other research studies or in the form of a standardized instrument. The former has the advantage of enabling comparisons across different research studies and settings, but only if the measures and results are adequately reported. Further, Kazdin [20] notes "much research is conducted in a tradition of weak or narrow assessment with little innovation to push or elaborate the limits of a construct" (p. 213).

Standardized instruments are useful because of the amount of work that has been invested by other researchers, and,

> *That work facilitates interpretation of the measure...In all of these circumstances, the investigator need not worry about defending the measure or providing support for its construct validity in light of the prior work that has been completed* [20] (p. 214).

There are a number of possible approaches to finding standardized instruments [14]. *Mental Measurements Yearbook* is a research database of over 3,000 current and commercially available testing instruments in psychology, education, business, and leadership [32]. Other, broader searches in IIR-related databases (e.g., ACM), domain-specific journals that relate to the construct of interest (e.g., cognition, personality), or ones focused on measurement may also prove fruitful. Some libraries have online guides for finding scales in databases, e.g., [8][46][52]. These libguides provide lists of databases and outline approaches to finding relevant surveys and questionnaires best used in searches in the various databases (e.g., keywords to use).

Finding a questionnaire that measures the construct of interest in IIR research does not guarantee success. The questionnaire may not be an appropriate measure to use for a number of reasons including, e.g., validity, reliability, the population for which it was designed, language, ease of use, and cost [52]. The questionnaire needs to be evaluated for suitability across a variety of criteria.

5.3 Selecting questionnaires

Kazdin [20] frames the selection of a questionnaire as "auditioning possible measures" (p. 2016) and, as previously noted, popularity or frequency of use are not sufficient criteria to use in the evaluation of a measure. Bawden and Robinson [6], for instance, examined individual differences research in information behavior studies, specifically singling out the Minnesota Multiphasic Personality Inventory (MMPI) as a flawed instrument, yet noted its inadequacies were not regularly attended to by those adopting it. Kazdin encourages researchers to ask: "What exactly has been shown to relate to the measure? What is the evidence that this measure I am considering captures or encompasses the characteristic I want to assess?" (p. 207).

Published studies may not explicitly state that a measure has good construct validity, but may present the findings in such a way that the researcher can determine this. In other words, a self-report instrument should "generate data that behave as they should, given current theories about important behavioral, psychological, and social outcomes that should be linked to that instrument" [24] (p. 221). For example, an IIR researcher might be interested in whether searchers experience negative cognitive load when using an experimental IR system and select the NASA-Task Load Index (TLX). The TLX includes six sub-scales: mental demands, physical demands, temporal demands, own performance, effort and frustration. The researcher might look at other studies that have used the entire measure or its sub-scales to consider their relationship to other variables. For example, perhaps several studies have found a correlation between "physical demands" and number of mouse clicks and pages visited, or an association between "effort and frustration" and the Positive and Negative Affect Scale (PANAS). Such relationship patterns would demonstrate that these two TLX sub-scales relate to other measures as we would expect. If we saw that "temporal demands" varied as a result of whether previous experiments included time constraints then we would be more cautious, since it may be the context of the study, rather than task or system variables, that contributed to participants' responses.

We would also want to consider how other people performed using the measure, and whether the sampled populations are similar to our own. If we are interested in looking at the search strategies of adults over the age of 50, then hundreds of studies with university students may provide little substantiation that a measure will be useful for our purposes. Kazdin also notes that we must also keep in mind previously mentioned methodological issues of demand effects, acquiescence/naysaying, end-aversion bias, social desirability [20][22][24][33] when considering a questionnaire's validity. Moreover, language is often a key factor in questionnaire selection. It may be the case that an existing measure was developed in one language or for a particular cultural group, but the researcher wants to apply it to a different population. Translated or adapted questionnaires may be available for more established questionaires (e.g., [6]).

Lastly, as the UES and SDE examples have shown, factor analysis or principal components analysis are often used in the evaluation of questionnaires. Factor or component labels are chosen to reflect the sub-set of items within a specific factor/component, and these may be indicative of the construct's sub-dimensions, or distinct constructs, depending on whether relationships amongst the factors have been demonstrated, e.g., path analysis. It is also useful to note that factor/components analysis can be performed and interpreted in different ways. There are instances, for example, when it may be preferable to examine the structure matrix over the pattern matrix and to allow items to load on multiple factors [51]. In addition, exploratory factor analysis is a reductionist technique, and it may be more appropriate to use confirmatory factor analysis with an established questionnaire [37]. In short, "factors are not 'in' a measure—they reflect how a particular sample responded to the measure" [20] (p. 208), and thus the results of factor analysis must be replicated to determine whether item groupings are consistent across different studies and populations.

6. USING QUESTIONNAIRES

6.1 Adapting or adopting questionnaires?

In some cases, researchers may adopt instruments but elect to modify or tailor them [23]. Such tailoring may be minor, e.g., changing the name of the system in the questionnaire to reflect the system being investigated in the current study. For example, the SUS item, "I thought the system was easy to use" might be modified to "I thought the library catalogue was easy to use." However, if we rephrased the same SUS item to read, "I thought this search task was easy to perform" then we have changed the nature of what is being measured (system versus task) and the action of interest (use versus perform). Again, it is important to be mindful of the research undertaken to develop the original questionnaire. Changing the wording of questions may change what the measure is now measuring. Removing questions may result in an insufficient number of items to capture a construct. Fewer items can also create less variability in scale scores, making it difficult to detect differences amongst groups or conditions. This can lead to *ceiling* or *floor effects,* defined as "the limited range of possible scores at the higher or lower end of the scale that could make the measure unable to identify real differences that might be found without the scale's limited range" [20] (p. 210).

Modifications may be necessary, but over-tailoring may affect the ability to compare questionnaire data across studies, and create challenges for assessing generalizability [23]. It is also important to remember that even if a measure is "tried and true," the researcher must assess its validity and reliability anew when employing it in a new setting or tailoring it [20]:

> *As a general rule, when one tinkers with the content or format of a measure, some evidence is needed within the study to show that the measure continues to assess the construct of interest and behaves psychometrically in a defensible fashion* [20] (p. 215).

Selecting only a few items of a questionnaire for use in a study should also not be confused with *brief measures*, which tend to be shortened versions of established questionnaires. Brief measures are subjected to the same rigour (e.g., validity, reliability) as regular measures [20]. Likewise, adding new items to a questionnaire may seem like a good idea, but these items will have "face validity only—an unacceptable indefensible criterion from the standpoint of methodology" ([20], p. 220).

In addition to changing questionnaire items, researchers may also be tempted to change the rating scale used in the original scale, and this deserves some consideration. Preston and Coleman [42] report that internal consistency and test-retest reliability is lowest for scales with 2, 3 and 4-point rating scales, and the most reliable scores are obtained when scales have 7-10 response categories. Furthermore, fewer response categories may save participants time, but are actually least preferred by respondents because they do not give people sufficient range to express feelings or attitudes [42]. Seven is the optimal number of response categories, but five categories are most typically used. Preston and Colemon reason this is supported by long-standing psychology research on short term memory and information processing capacity (i.e., 7 +/- 2). However, these authors note that selecting the number of response categories is also driven by a study's needs and constraints, e.g., fewer categories when time is limited; more categories in earlier stages of scale development when the researcher wants to examine the face validity of the items [42].

Some flexibility is necessary. While maintaining original questions is important, it shouldn't be at the expense of comprehensibility or the phenomenon of interest of the current study. The choice may come down to not using the measure at all or adapting it. It may be that some dimensions of a measure make sense for a study, but others do not (see for example [28]). But it should be documented what changes were made and why.

6.2 Questionnaire analysis

In most cases, developers of questionnaires will provide enough information to allow other researchers to use the questionnaire (e.g., items, instructions provided to participants, question format) and analyse its results. Particularly for well-developed scales that have been around for awhile, such as the PANAS [53], there may be instuctions for both how to calculate *and* interpret the scores. At minimum, researchers need to be aware of how to prepare the data for analysis and what type of analysis is most appropriate given the nature of the questionnaire and the study design.

For example, a combination of negative and positive items in a questionnaire is sometimes used to ensure that people are continuing to *read* the items and not just select the same response for all questions. To prepare for analysis, researchers need to consider whether there are items that need to be reverse scored (e.g., response ratings of 1 become 5, 2 becomes 4, etc. for a 5-point rating scale) and how to transform the data accordingly before beginning the analysis. Many of the UES' perceived usability items contain negative items that require this reverse scoring treatment.

The researcher must also decide on an appropriate statistical technique. As previously mentioned, if the researcher is using an established questionnaire, confirmatory factor analysis may be appropriate to test whether the sample responded in a similar manner to the items as samples from prior research, but multivariate analysis options should be explored in advance (see [51]). Moreover, once data has been prepared for analysis, consideration must be given to how to calculate scores. For example, it may be recommended to calculate the mean of each of the dimensions if it is a multidimensional scale (e.g., [31] [36]).

6.3 Questionnaire reporting

It has been noted in IIR and beyond that inadequate reporting of the results of self-report measures is problematic for being able to assess measurement use and quality, perform meta-analyses to compare measures across studies and populations, and objectively evaluate the findings of research studies [20][23]. Kazdin [20] addressed the severity of poor or absent reporting practices:

> *This is not merely a reporting issue; it can mean there is no clear assurance that the constructs the authors discuss were in fact suitably assessed by the measures. This is not minor—interpretation of any findings depends on being confident about what was actually measured and making the case to the reader (and even before that, to oneself)* (p. 209).

Kelly and Sugimoto [23] acknowledged that the varied backgrounds of IIR researchers may be the reason that standard reporting practices have not emerged in IIR, but this is not a reason *not* to develop standard report practices going forward. They state that this will make meta-analysis, "a very useful method for systematically and reliably synthesizing research results across a body of literature" possible, and will contribute to theory development (p. 767).

Limitations of the research should be clearly noted. For example, analyses using multivariate statistical techniques generally require a significant number of cases within the data set. If sample size is smaller than recommended in the literature, interpretation of the results should be cautious and the limitations of the study clearly stated. While there is little agreement on optimal sample size, some benchmarks have be suggested depending on, for example, the number of items in the questionnaire (see [51]). Moreover, in some cases, it may not be possible, due to time, sample, or design constraints, to perform tests of reliability, validity, dimensionality and sensitivity. At the very least, however, researchers can report what items/sub-dimensions of a questionnaire were used and why, and what the means/standard deviations of test scores were to assist other researchers – and the questionnaire developers – in assessing the strengths and weaknesses of the tool in a given study.

7. CONCLUSION

This perspectives paper is an important constribution to the CHIIR conference and community, and a call to action to ask questions more clearly, consistently and transparently. We have demonstrated that questionnaires and psychometric scales can be equally, if not more, complex that objective measures.

> *The value and role of self-reports in the assessment of any specific construct is best evaluated on a domain-by-domain and study-by-study basis. Universal recommendations, even within a specific area, are unwise because various contextual factors can influence the validity and utility of self-reports. Thus, it is incumbent upon the users of self-report instruments to document that their particular measure behaves as it should, given current theories about the construct it measures* [24] (p. 222).

Thus, self-report measures are not "plug and play" and involve deep and detailed consideration in their construction and deployment. The researcher must, like an abstract painter, understand the rules in order to bend them, and, like a scientist, follow a systematic development and evaluation process that relies upon evidence-based decision making [41][47].

Fuzzy constructs, such as satisfaction, serendipity, and engagement are challenging to measure, and measures of this kind are best developed from a theoretical perspective where the phenomenon of interest is well-grounded in previous research, and where the measurement can, in turn, inform theory. Indeed construct validity is "basic theory testing," representing "an ongoing process of discovery, pertaining both to theories and the measures that embody them" [49] (p. 405-406). If we think about it in this way, we are not so much trying to find *the* measure. Rather, we recognize that measurement is an imperfect journey where we equip ourselves with the proper tools and knowledge of how to use them, but we cannot necessarily predict the outcome. This is not a matter of not "trusting" the tool, but acknowledging the complexity of human beings, and the contexts in which they use IIR systems.

8. ACKNOWLEDGMENTS

We thank the anonymous peer reviewers and meta-reviewer for their thoughtful feedback on the original version of this paper.

9. REFERENCES [abbreviate titles]

[1] Alonso, O. and Baeza-Yates, R. 2011. Design and implementation of relevance assessments using crowdsourcing. In ECIR 2011, LNCS 611, P. Cough et al. Eds, Springer-Verlag, 153-164.

[2] Arapakis, I., Lalmas, M., and Valkanas, G. 2014a. Understanding within-content engagement through pattern analysis of mouse gestures. In *Proc CIKM* (Shanghai, China, November 3-7, 2014). ACM, New York, NY, 1439-1448.

[3] Arapakis, I. Xiao, B., and Cambazoglu, B.B. 2014b. Impact of response latency on user behavior in web search. In *Proc SIGIR* (Queensland, Australia, July 6-11, 2014). ACM, New York, NY, 103-112.

[4] Agarwal, R. and Karahanna, E. 2000. Time flies when you're having fun: Cognitive absorption and beliefs about information technology usage. *MISQ.* 24, 4, 665-694.

[5] Bailey, E. and Kelly, D. 2016. Developing a measure of search expertise. In *Proc CHIIR* (Chapel Hill, NC, March 13-17, 2016), 237-240. ACM, New York, NY.

[6] Bawden, D. and Robinson, L. 2011. Individual differences in information-related behavior. In *New Directions in Information Behaviour,* A. Spink and J. Heinström, Eds, Emerald Publishing Group, 127-158.

[7] Blažica, B. and Lewis, J.R. 2015. A Slovene translation of the system usability scale: The SUS-SI. *Int J Hum-Comput Int.* 31, 112-117.

[8] Boruff, J. n.d. Finding instruments, measures, scales & tests in education, health, psychology & social work. Retrieved June 15, 2016, from http://libraryguides.mcgill.ca/measures

[9] Brennan, K., Kelly, D., and Zhang, Y. 2016. Factor analysis of a search self-efficacy scale. In *Proc CHIIR* (Chapel Hill, NC, March 13-17, 2016), 241-244. ACM, NY.

[10] Brinkman, W. w., Haakma, R., and Bouwhuis, D. G. 2009. The theoretical foundation and validity of a component-based usability questionnaire. *Behav Inform Technol.* 28, 2, 121-137.

[11] Brooke, J. 1996. SUS: A "quick and dirty" usability scale. In *Usability Evaluation in Industry,* P. W. Jordan, B. Thomas, B. A. Weerdmeester, and A. L. McClelland, Eds. Taylor and Francis, London, 189-94.

[12] Brooke, J. 2013. SUS: A retrospective. *JUS.* 8, 2, 29-40.

[13] Cronbach, L.J. and Meehl, P.E. 1955. Construct validity in psychological tests. *Psychol Bull.* 52, 4, 281-302.

[14] DeVellis, R. F. 2003. *Scale Development: Theory and Applications*. Sage Publications, Thousand Oaks, California.

[15] Erdelez, S. 2005. Information encountering. In *Theories of Information Behavior*, K. E. Fisher, S. Erdelez and L. McKechnie, Eds. Information Today, Medford, NJ, 179-185.

[16] Hamby, T. and Ickes, W. 2015. Do the readability and average item length of personality scales affect their reliability? *J Individ Diff.* 36,, 54-63.

[17] Heinström, J. 2005. Fast surfing, broad scanning and deep diving: The influence of personality and study approach on students' information-seeking behaviour. *J Doc.* 61, 228-247.

[18] Hinkin, T. R. and Tracey, J. B. 1999. An analysis of variance approach to content validation. *Organ Res Methods.* 2, 2, 175-186.

[19] Jacques, R.D. 1996. *The nature of engagement and its role in hypermedia evaluation and design.* Unpublished Doctoral Dissertation, South Bank University, London.

[20] Kazdin, A.E. 2016. Selecting measures for research investigations. In *Methodological issues and strategies in*

clinical research (4th ed.), A. E. Kazdin, Ed. APA, Washington, DC, 205-226.

[21] Kelly, D. 2009. Methods for evaluating interactive information retrieval systems with users. *Foundations and Trends in Information Retrieval.* 3, 1-224.

[22] Kelly, D., Harper, D. J., and Landau, B. 2008. Questionnaire mode effects in interactive information retrieval experiments. *Info Proc Manage.* 44, 122–141.

[23] Kelly, D. and Sugimoto, C.R. 2013. A systematic review of interactive informationr evaluation studies, 1967–2006. *JASIS&T.* 64, 4, 745–770.

[24] Krueger, R. F., and Kling, K. C. 2000. Self-report. In *Encyclopedia of psychology, Vol. 7,* A. E. Kazdin, Ed. APA, Washington, DC, 220-224.

[25] Lalmas, M., O'Brien, H., and Yom-Tov, E. 2014. Measuring user engagement. *Synthesis Lectures on Information Concepts, Retrieval, and Services.* 6, 4, 1-132.

[26] MacKenzie, S. B., Podsakoff, P. M., and Podsakoff, N. P. 2011. Construct measurement and validation procedures in MIS and behavioral research. *MISQ.* 35, 293-334.

[27] McCay-Peet, L. 2013. *Investigating work-related serendipity, what influences it, and how it may be facilitated in digital environments.* http://dalspace.library.dal.ca/handle/10222/42727

[28] McCay-Peet, L., Lalmas, M., and Navalpakkam, V. 2012. On saliency, affect and focused attention. In *Proc of SIGCHI* (Austin, TX, May 5-10, 2012). ACM, New York, 541-550.

[29] McCay-Peet, L. and Toms, E.G. 2015. Investigating serendipity: How it unfolds and what may influence it. *JASIS&T.* 66, 7, 1463-1476.

[30] McCay-Peet, L., Toms, E.G. and Kelloway, E.K. 2014. Development and assessment of the content validity of a scale to measure how well a digital environment facilitates serendipity. *Inform Res.* 19, 3, paper 630.

[31] McCay-Peet, L., Toms, E.G., and Kelloway, E.K. 2015. Examination of relationships among serendipity, the environment, and individual differences. *Inform Process Manag.* 51, 391-412.

[32] *Mental Measurements Yearbook.* n.d. Retrieved from http://buros.org/mental-measurements-yearbook

[33] Nederhof, A.J. 1985. Methods of coping with social desirability bias. *Eur J Soc Psychol.* 15, 3, 263-280.

[34] Nielsen, J. 1995. Ten usability characteristics by Jackob Nielsen. http://www.useit.com/papers/heuristic/

[35] O'Brien, H.L. 2008. *Defining and measuring engagement in user experiences with technology.* (Order No. NR43935). Available from ProQuest Dissertations & Theses Global.

[36] O'Brien, H.L. 2016*a*. Theoretical perspectives on user engagement. In *Why engagement matters: Cross-disciplinary perspectives of user engagement in digital media,* H.L. O'Brien and P. Cairns, P., Eds. Springer International Publishing, 1-26.

[37] O'Brien, H.L. 2016*b*. Translating theory into methodological practice. In *Why engagement matters: Cross-disciplinary perspectives of user engagement in digital media,* H.L. O'Brien and P. Cairns, P., Eds. Springer International Publishing, 27-52.

[38] O'Brien, H.L. and Toms, E.G. 2010. The development and evaluation of a survey to measure user engagement in e-commerce environments. *JASIS&T.* 61, 1, 50-69.

[39] O'Brien, H.L. and Toms, E.G. 2008. What is user engagement? A conceptual framework for defining user engagement with technology. *JASIS&T.* 59, 6, 938-955.

[40] Pariser, E. 2011. *The Filter Bubble: What the Internet is Hiding From You.* Penguin Press, New York.

[41] Payne, S.L. 1951. *The Art of Asking Questions.* Princeton Univ. Press, Princeton, NJ.

[42] Preston, C. C. and Colman, A. M. 2000. Optimal number of response categories in rating scales: Reliability, validity, discriminating power, and respondent preferences. *Acta Psychologica.* 104, 1-15.

[43] "psychometrics, n.". *OED Online.* March 2016. http://www.oed.com/view/Entry/238072?redirectedFrom=psychometrics& (accessed June 01, 2016).

[44] "questionnaire, n.". *OED Online.* March 2016. http://www.oed.com/view/Entry/156364?redirectedFrom=questionnaire& (accessed June 01, 2016).

[45] Radhakrishna, R.B. 2007. Tips for developing and testing questionnaires/instruments. *J Extension. 45.* Available at http://www.joe.org/joe/2007february/tt2.php

[46] Research instruments: Surveys, questionnaires, and other measurement tools. n.d. Retrieved June 15, 2016 from http://researchguides.uvm.edu/researchinstruments

[47] Schaeffer, N. C., & Presser, S. (2003). The science of asking questions. *Annual Review of Sociology.* 29, 1, 65–88. http://doi.org/10.1146/annurev.soc.29.110702.110112

[48] Singleton, R., Straits, B.C., and Straits, M.M. 1993. *Approaches to Social Research.* Oxford UP, New York.

[49] Smith, G.T. 2005. On construct validity: Issues of method and measurement. *Psychol Assessment.* 17, 4, 396-408.

[50] Sutcliffe, A. 2010. *Designing for User Engagement: Aesthetic and Attractive User Interfaces.* Morgan & Claypool Publishers, San Rafael.

[51] Tabachnick, B. G. and Fidell, L. S. 2013. *Using Multivariate Statistics, 6th ed.* Allyn and Bacon, Boston.

[52] Test and Measurement Resources Research Guide. (n.d.). Retrieved June 15, 2016, from https://www.lib.ncsu.edu/guides/tests

[53] Watson, D., and Clark, L. A. 1994. The PANAS-X: Manual for the Positive and Negative Affect Schedule-Expanded Form. The University of Iowa, Ames, Iowa. Retrieved from http://www.midss.org/content/panas-x-manual-positive-and-negative-affect-schedule

Something is Lost, Something is Found: Book Use at the Library Shelves

George Buchanan
University of Melbourne
Parkville, Melbourne
Victoria 3010, Australia
george.buchanan@unimelb.edu.au

Dana McKay
Swinburne University of Technology Library
John Street, Hawthorn
Victoria 3122, Australia
dmckay@swin.edu.au

ABSTRACT

This paper investigates the life of books on physical library shelves. Most existing data on the use of library books uses logs to quantify loans, or user interviews to obtain insights into their use. We deploy a new specialised technique, photographing library shelves systematically over a week-long period, and noting changes to the positions of individual books, and movement over each shelf as a whole. Through this indirect observation, we demonstrate the use of shelved books within, rather than on leaving, the library. We reveal the first insight into within-library book use, and demonstrate that in-library use appears to be more common and over a longer period than previous research suggests.

Keywords

Libraries; information behaviour; information interaction; user study.

1. INTRODUCTION

The behaviour of library users has been studied for many years in order to better understand human information seeking [8; 9]. While (digital) library catalogues have been criticised for poor usability, and a weak fit with user expectations, other aspects of the physical library have maintained a perceived advantage over computer-based seeking.

Two key, if sometimes disputed, areas of advantage to physical libraries are the perceived usability of paper documents, and the ease of browsing wide ranges of books [13; 22; 38; 39]. However, while the emergence of ebooks has led to more detailed study of the reading of both digital and print books, the use of physical library spaces for consulting and retrieving books has received surprisingly scant attention.

This gap is made all the more worth closing, as much of the little material that we have to hand is in fact quite dated. Studies from, for example, 1987 [10], date from the period where most university and public libraries were moving from a card-index to a computerised catalogue. The focus of concern then was to understand how to tailor and improve the digital catalogue, through comprehending its use. That research was certainly fruitful, but the prospect of digital texts supplanting printed books was a distant one.

Today, we have services that comprise a fully digital catalogue with exclusively, or at least predominantly, electronic books. However, what actually occurs at the physical library shelves is little known or understood. While there is clearly the simple physical retrieval of known books—a task readily supplanted effectively by digital delivery—contextual studies have reported indirectly the use of shelves for browsing, selection and reference.

The main resource of knowledge used in previous studies of library behaviour is the library catalogue. Given their digitisation three decades ago, there is great depth to the data available on books taken out of libraries for consultation at home (see for example [20; 21]). In reference libraries, the retrieval of stock from closed stacks is also well-known, but this use sheds necessarily little light on the more flexible tasks available in open-access shelves.

Borrowing records only record the withdrawal of a book for some (usually unknown) reading purpose, its possible later renewal and eventual return. Some researchers, dating from Hancock-Beaulieu onwards, have also followed individual users in the library, or interviewed library users about their behaviour. The goals of this work have varied. Hancock-Beaulieu sought to understand the impact of a digital, versus card, catalogue on user search strategies [9]. The triage of books for selection at the shelf, or the use of texts for a quick reference are given only limited treatment, as these tasks were incidental to the goals of the study.

More recently, researchers have interviewed library readers as to how they do their searching in the library, sometimes supplemented by observing the same users at the shelves [13]. Given the paucity of prior work, the focus of such studies has been on basic elements such as the perceived use of shelves at different heights (e.g. above head-height, at foot level). These studies again reported browsing activity and some at-shelf reference work, but their data, being focused on individuals regarding one event, provides limited reliability in terms of assessing the relative frequency of these activities, compared to "grab-and-go" retrieval.

This paper aims to close that gap—we capture evidence from the shelves of their use, and contrast that data against the contemporaneous borrowing records for the same groups of books. The data demonstrates that significant, currently unrecorded, use of books is made within the library. Furthermore, we contribute a method of indirect observation of users, through the direct observation of the artefact of library shelving, that can be used to gain knowledge both about libraries in general, and the use of individual libraries specifically.

CHIIR '17, March 07 - 11, 2017, Oslo, Norway

ACM 978-1-4503-4677-1/17/03...$15.00
DOI: http://dx.doi.org/10.1145/3020165.3020187

2. BACKGROUND

This section will review some of the methodologies used to understand information use in libraries, then describe the shelves as an information seeking experience.

2.1 Watching Library Users

Observational and ethnographic methods have been used extensively to assess libraries [16]. They have also been used within libraries to understand a range of aspects of information seeking, including serendipity [22], book selection [13] and the influence of digital libraries [1; 40].

These studies have been exploratory in nature and given us insights we simply would not have using other methods; they offer twin advantages of seeing natural user behaviour (such as shelf browsing) and understanding user motivation (such as the use of non-bibliographic cues in book selection [22; 40]). Observational studies are necessarily limited [34], though; to understand the prevalence of specific behaviours we need larger numbers of users than are typically captured by observation. One approach to gaining the large number of users is surveys, another is log analysis of various kinds; the use of these types of studies is addressed in Section 2.2 below.

The study we present in this paper is exploratory in nature and suited to the smaller sample sizes typically seen with ethnographic methods. The problem with this, however, is that the behaviours we are investigating, and the changes they wreak at the shelves, require more than a handful of users to understand. As such, we turned to aggregate observation, most commonly seen in libraries as log analysis.

2.2 Counting Library Use

There is a long trend in libraries to attempt to enumerate use. One of the earliest strategies for such enumeration is the materials availability survey; it asks library visitors whether they found what they came for. This strategy has been used for forty years [15], but has a number of difficulties, particularly in a digital age. This approach does not allow for the use of electronic resources, nor does it take non-specific information needs into account [29]. It is also dependent on the testimony of individual users, which—while it clearly addresses their own experience—is no guarantee of usage, nor does it provide an aggregate view of use.

Early circulation analysis—counting and analysing which books had been loaned and returned—relied on counting by hand, typically using a sample of all books. This method has been used in interesting ways, for example Losee's analysis of borrowing by individuals that shows they borrow books close together [21]. It was not until the advent of digital inventory management that complete sample circulation analysis could take place. This completeness has allowed for some interesting analyses, for example the numerous comparisons between print and ebook circulation [5; 20] and an early market basket analysis of borrowing across subject categories [7]. Circulation analysis, though, has typically been used for collection management (for example [17]) and not for understanding actual user experience. This focus on the collection has changed recently, with a few attempts to understand user behaviour—specifically browsing [31; 32]—being based on circulation data; our study continues in this user focused tradition.

While it is relatively easy to count out-of-library information use, this does not give a full picture of how much information library users are accessing: it is clear from earlier work that many library users read inside the library [3; 4; 13], and (for print books) this is largely invisible to counting exercises. Previous studies have attempted to evaluate this type of use by retrospective analysis of date stamps [11], noting what is re-shelved from trolleys and desks [26], or voluntary reader questionnaires at the shelves [8]. This data, though, is necessarily incomplete. For example, re-shelving data doesn't account for users returning their own books to the shelves, nor do voluntary questionnaires capture more than a fraction of total users. Even so, these studies report 50-60 % of book use happening within libraries and thus invisible to circulation analysis.

Of course with the advent of ebooks, it is possible to count all use—every action can be logged [24]. While use of this capacity has been largely restricted to circulation analysis, some studies have used it to look at reading [27] and book selection [28; 30]. Ebooks, though, have only a single discovery mechanism: search. Search is another aspect of library use that has lent itself well to log analysis, we understand that searchers use short queries, like keyword searching and are often unsuccessful [2; 6; 19; 41]. Search doesn't meet all information needs, though—it is only a small part of human information seeking behaviour [18; 23]. The restriction of ebook access to search is one of the reasons readers have given for avoiding ebooks [28].

Our study uses a counting approach to try to make visible library use that has previously been invisible: in-library use of print books. It also assesses the stability of the shelves as an information interface; while being presented with unexpected finds can lead to a feeling of serendipity [12], unstable or inconsistent interfaces are not known for their usability [35]. This is a novel approach to studying the shelves.

2.3 Shelves Under Study

There are not many studies of how library users approach and use the shelves, but there are a few. The earliest of these is Beaulieu's early work, showing that shelf browsing was an important component of information seeking [9]. In the 90s two observational studies considered how children use the library shelves [33; 37]; they demonstrated that location within the physical structure of the shelves was important to children, but did not note for any participant whether the shelf environment was stable. More recent studies have focused on adults, but they have been observational and used few participants. Like with children, these studies have found that adults focus more on the middle shelves [13]. They also reinforce that shelves are a clear part of the information seeking process, used for browsing and serendipity seeking [1; 22; 40].

Our study takes a different approach—we do not observe users at the shelves, but instead document the traces of their use.

3. METHOD

As noted above, previous work has relied primarily on the use of borrowing logs to establish the level of use of library content. However, for open-access reserve material, or content that is often consulted within the library, this can be an entirely or substantially incomplete picture. While the methods for examining library loan logs are well established, specific methods for examining at-shelf and within-library use are very few.

Ethical considerations are also at play. Techniques that require the participation of library users would of course require informed consent. Obtaining consent from the many users of an individual library, or part of it, would potentially disrupt the work of many, and potentially discourage its use by at least a few.

Indirect observation is a long-standing approach within human-computer interaction and library interaction studies [16], and we adopted this strategy to underpin our work. Shelves were photographed at approximately a metre distance when they were not in use. The capture of the visual data in a concrete form also enabled a detailed and systematic review at a later date, rather than hurriedly attempting to record information manually at the moment of data gathering. This reflects general advantages of indirect observation, but avoiding the mediating effects of the data-capture being performed by users themselves.

Our approach directly captured the artefacts—i.e. the positioning of books—but this only indirectly gathers the intentions of users, if it gathers them at all. However, at this early stage of investigation, we did not know even the frequency of evidence of book use. While the method is limited, it does ensure higher accuracy of the book movement data than more user-focussed alternatives.

We had piloted a photographic method for capturing book movements in the context of bookshops, in response to earlier work that had tracked individual users. This proved fruitful, but the movement of books in shops is only loosely associated with information work of any form, and so we turned the technique to the more task-oriented context of a physical library.

The library that the full study took place in is the main library of Swinburne, a small, research active university in Australia. The predominant users of the library's open-shelf books students; staff mostly using online research resources. The core open-stack collection is held on two floors, adjacent to quiet study areas, including desks, desktop PCs and power-points for laptop use. These areas are primarily intended to support individual work. Other levels of the library provide more open spaces and flexible areas targeted at groupwork.

The study period was set in May 2015, across the third and fourth weeks of the second term of the year's teaching. The semester's teaching concluded at the end of the month, two weeks after the study ended. This avoided the extreme use patterns of both holiday and examination periods.

3.1 Sampling Method

Covering the entirety of a library was impracticable, at least in terms of the subsequent analysis of photographs. Therefore, we instead consulted the library catalogue data, and identified the eight most active blocks of 200 books (in terms of loan activity) by shelf location. We added to these eight, at the request of the University Librarian at our host institution, two blocks. The first was the most active block in a collection purported to be used primarily for browsing, the second was the most active block in a new, purpose bought collection. The shelves are organised using Dewey Decimal Classification, and the classification spans used in this study are given in Table 1.

Focussing on the most frequently used parts of the library increased our chances of observing movement in our week-long capture phase.

In a pilot, we took photographs of shelves four times a day. However, the observed rate of change did not seem to justify this frequency, and in the main study we captured the shelf photographs twice a day—once at 10:30-11:00am, and again at 3:00-3:30pm These times were the beginning and end of peak occupancy time measured by a gate counter in the target library. In addition, an extra opening and closing round were taken at the start of the first day, and end of the last day, and a particular round before the weekend closure that fell in the middle of the study.

The study commenced and finished on a Wednesday (a total of 8 days, 6 working days. We chose to span a weekend in case there was a particular shift in use from Friday to Monday or effect of the weekend. Photographs were checked for clarity at the point of capture, and if they appeared too blurry for use, a second was taken. All photographs were automatically date-stamped.

We used high-resolution digital cameras (10Mp+) with low compression levels. Due to the varying thickness of the books on the shelves, the number of photographs for a given set of 200 books ranged from four to eight photographs. Each individual photograph covered two (or occasionally three) shelves of books. The shelving is in bays, each of which contains six shelves, and each set spanned three or four bays. Every complete survey required up to 120 photographs.

Table 1. Sampled Dewey Decimal Ranges (in descending order of loan frequency)

Seq	Dewey Range		Subject Holdings
1	320-952 WAR	320-994 LUC	Politics (mostly Australian)
2	571-64 BIO	572-8 BRO	Biochemistry
3	300-723 THO	301-0 PAR	Social Sciences (Surveys)
4	658-8 KOT	658-8 SER	Marketing
5	651-74 HAN	657-0 MAR	Management and Accounting
6	523-88-CEP	530-1 CAP	Astronomy
7	629-8 DUK	629-836 NAR	Engineering (electronics)
8	174-4 MUR	174-915 WEL	Occupational Ethics
9	300-711 COM	300-72 PAT	Social Sciences (Research Methods)
10	320-994 MAC	321-8 ROS	Politics

In addition, we photographed the re-shelving trolleys placed around the library for users to place unneeded books for return to the shelves by the library staff. This allowed us to potentially identify books that were removed from the shelves and remained in the library, but were not returned immediately after use. It also allowed us to repeat the analysis performed in earlier work [11]. Furthermore, we surveyed the working spaces on each round, taking photographs when we found abandoned target books.

3.2 Analysis

Following the data capture, we first manually coded each photograph with the Dewey range found on its shelf. Given the short timespan of the study, strategic re-shelving did not occur, and books remained, if in their intended place, at the same location. The sets were each re-inspected and recoded until exhaustion had been reached, and no further movements were discerned.

Three main codes were used for movement:

Removed: a book disappears from view that was present in the previous photograph of the same shelves.

Returned: a book appears that was not present in the previous photograph of the shelves.

Moved: a book that appeared in the last photograph in the sequence is identified in a different location on the same shelves.

In addition, the following codes were used for other changes:

Titled: one or more books are tilted to a different angle than in the previous photograph. This code was *not* applied where the movement was contiguous to the removal, return or movement of a book, as this is often only further evidence of that change.

Slumped: any tilting of books that was immediately next to a removed or returned book.

Pulled: one or more books appear further out from the shelf, or are moved further back on the shelf than previously. We encountered only one case of the latter. Books pulled in this manner are frequently associated with the inspection of book covers in the prior literature.

Out of Order: a book appears in the photograph that is from outside of the Dewey range for that shelf. This is a known phenomenon from previous library observations, but the purpose of it is not well-known.

Across all these codes, a code is only reported when a change occurred on the shelves—hence, an "out-of-order" book will be noted when it appears, or is removed, but was not counted repeatedly between these events to ensure all changes were detected.

Having coded the photographs, we then searched for each Dewey code in turn, creating sequences of photographs of the same location across the study period. For each shelf, we compared the photographs with the preceding and succeeding images. This allowed us to identify movements in books—from removal, through replacing, to tipping and angling. Each movement was then recorded textually, identifying the book(s) affected, the action taken, the time and date of the action, and the shelf location both in terms of Dewey code and relative to its bay. All bays had six shelves, though exact shelf heights and positions varied slightly. The shelf number was taken to start from 1 (at the top of the bay) to 6 (just above floor level).

The library borrowing records for each Dewey sequence were obtained from the library catalogue for the dates studied. Renewals and recall notices, which would not affect the shelving, were excluded, and returns and loans were retained. This borrowing data was then checked against the shelf observation data, to ensure that no loans were overlooked. This check did not reveal any oversights.

Finally, the movement on the shelves was correlated with the borrowing recorded on the same dates, and photographs of re-shelving trolleys were checked for evidence of books taken from the shelves, but not returned to them.

4. RESULTS

Below we give the catalogue borrowing data for the ten sampled ranges for our census date range. Renewals were not observable in the library, and are given to provide context for the overall level of activity in the collection. In addition to those below, there were seven recall requests, for materials currently on loan and not available in the library, and two loans of related software, which are catalogued in the same range, but not available on the shelves. We refer here, as will be the case in the rest of the paper, to only the beginning of each range.

As can be seen, the overall borrowing levels in the week were low, but this is consistent with previous lending data from print libraries [11; 31]. We next aggregated the basic data of actions on the shelves, as described in the Method section above.

Table 2. Sampled Dewey Decimal Ranges : Borrowing activity

Seq	Subject	Loans	Renewals
1	Australian Politics	1	2
2	Biochemistry	0	0
3	Soc. Science #1	0	0
4	Marketing	9	2
5	Management	2	1
6	Astronomy	1	5
7	Engineering	2	1
8	Ethics	0	4
9	Soc. Science #2	3	5
10	Politics	2	1
	Total	20	21

Table 3. Sampled Dewey Decimal Ranges : At-shelf activity

Seq	Topic Set	Removed	Returned
1	Australian Politics	5	3
2	Biochemistry	3	2
3	Soc. Science #1	10	4
4	Marketing	14	19
5	Management	15	15
6	Astronomy	16	2
7	Engineering	8	11
8	Ethics	5	0
9	Soc. Science #2	8	5
10	Politics	5	1
	Total	89	62

As seen in tables 2 and 3, there appears to be an overall activity level of approximately three to four times the borrowing uses noted by the library catalogue. The Pearson's correlation between the recorded borrowing and the overall removal of books from the shelves is 0.436—a modestly strong result, but misleading as in fact any borrowed book is necessarily among those removed from the shelves. Testing for the number of borrowed books versus non-loaned removals reveals a surprising value of $r=-0.15$: in other words there is scarcely any relationship.

To place further confidence in these results, the distribution of non-loan versus loan removals yields $p=0.0038$ ($\chi^2=24.36$, $df=9$). The populations are significantly different from each other. This suggests that books are often removed from the shelves for purposes weakly- or un-related to borrowing.

4.1 Movement of Books

We observed three other phenomena in this study: the shifting of books within the shelves; the location of books removed from the shelves in the return trolleys; and the appearance of alien books out-of-place on the shelves we were observing. We first report the tilting, moving and pulling (outwards, towards the reader) of books on the shelves, seen in Table 4.

Table 4. Sampled Dewey Decimal Ranges : At-shelf activity

Seq	Topic Set	Tilted: Books (incidents)	Moved	Pulled	Out-of-order
1	Australian Politics	3(1)	2	2	1
2	Biochemistry	2(1)	0	2	0
3	Soc. Science #1	27(3)	1	0	0
4	Marketing	23(3)	3	0	1
5	Management	2(2)	5	1	2
6	Astronomy	4(1)	0	1	2
7	Engineering	60(11)	3	1	0
8	Ethics	32(2)	0	1	0
9	Soc. Science #2	15(2)	0	1	0
10	Politics	23(4)	0	1	0
	Total	185(25)	14	10	6

There is extensive tilting of books, though as can be seen in the table, usually several were tilted at once—an average of over seven. Moving of books within a shelf was less frequent, and pulling less so again. In total six books were deposited in our set shelves out-of-order.

The correlation between the loan (and return) rates and these figures is again weak. For example, the correlation between the number of tilted books and loans is 0.107, which is far below the 0.30 threshold normally expected of even a low correlation. Where data is sparse, e.g. in the positioning of out-of-order books, calculating a correlation is ill-advised. Nor is the correlation between removals from the shelf a good predictor of other activity—the correlation between in-library removals and tilting activity being -0.235.

We also considered the location of the books removed from the shelves, but which remained in the library. First, we identified the number returned to their shelf during the survey, which totalled 34 of the 85 books taken from the shelves. Of these, twelve were returned on the same day, eleven within twenty-four hours, and ten were absent for a longer period.

Eight books taken from the shelves were found on the re-shelving trolleys. One was removed and seen on a trolley on two separate occasions (i.e. for a total of 9 incidents involving 8 books). Two were seen on the last day of the survey, one was found on a trolley at the very start, three were involved in a same-day return, and the remaining two were away from their shelves for two days. Trolley books always reappeared at their shelf the same day or, if found at the end of the afternoon, the following morning. This was consistent with local procedure. It is worth noting that one trolley item—the one seen twice—that returned on the same day was then (later) marked out-of-place the same day on another shelf, so it appears it was returned and removed once more.

Trolleys appear to be most associated with same-day returns, with the occasional longer-term absence. Only two next-day or longer items were found on the trolleys—under 10% of those groups. The total count also formed under a quarter of the short-term uses of books within the library. This leaves a substantial fraction of within-library removals where their location is unaccounted for during their absence.

In addition to those that were returned during the survey period, fifty-five were removed and not returned. Of these, twenty were loaned books, but this leaves thirty-five unaccounted for. Twelve were removed on the last day, and would likely appear the following, given the rest of our data; only two were removed at the start of the period and had not reappeared by the end. However, eleven had absent for three days. As a result of casual observation, two sets of these (five books) had been encountered elsewhere in the library, out of place. Both sets were disturbed daily, suggesting that they had not been abandoned, but rather were being hoarded out-of-place. In addition, we observed two astronomy books that had been returned out-of-place in an immediately neighbouring bay.

Figure 1: example movement on the shelves—note previous position of books that appear on the far right

Overall, there were twenty cases where books were removed from their shelves overnight, and were later returned, but were not placed or on moved to re-shelving trolleys in the meantime. We had in addition a further twenty-one that were not returned for at least a day, and were still away from their home shelves at the end of the survey. The working spaces are cleared at the end of the day, so they cannot have been left on benches or desks overnight.

Figure 2: Two 'out-of-order' books placed in a nearby bay

This phenomenon might be mostly explained by the appearance of six "alien" books in our sample shelves, as well as the five wandering books of our sets that were observed on other shelves.

As some informal evidence has suggested, books are placed elsewhere on the shelves of the library. While others may have been randomly abandoned on more distant shelves than was the case with the astronomy books, it seems unlikely that much effort would be expended moving unwanted books a long distance.

As a final note, the eight books found on the trolleys come from across the sampled set, and there is insufficient evidence to draw any sound conclusions on effects from topic etc. However, to provide an overview: three were from the management set, one from biochemistry, one from the social sciences, one from engineering, two from marketing.

Figure 3: A volume present (top left), removed (top right—note the extra label on the second book from left); and on a res-helving trolley (bottom).

As seen in Table 4, six books were deposited on the shelves out of their correction position. We did not count cases where books moved within the same shelf (see the moved total instead).

4.2 Spans of Short-term Use

We also identified the time periods within which use-and-return in the same period covered. Thirty-four books—or over a third of all removals—were cases where books were removed and replaced to their original position in the sample period. These removals were gathered together, and the relative span between removal and replacement was calculated. Twelve were replaced on the same day, eleven on the following day (and within 24 hours), and ten were absent for over 24 hours.

The mean of the observed time between their removal being detected and their return identified was just over 23 hours. The longest period for which a book was absent—a large volume on engineering—was 105 hours. This was neither found nearby its shelves, nor on the re-shelving trolleys across that entire period.

For these calculations we entirely discount the weekend, as no action could occur during the library's closure. Clearly, our sampling method allows a fair degree of error for both times, and a denser sampling rate would increase the accuracy. Any time detected where a book was on a trolley is also discounted.

Thus, a substantial proportion of books were away from their 'home' for extended periods. One book was observed on the workspace of a reader over the three days it was away from its home shelf, without any sign of that shelf being disturbed (which would have been necessary, were that book returned—as did occur when it was eventually replaced). Again, there is suggestive evidence that books may be kept away from their assigned shelf for an extended period when removed by a reader.

4.3 Ebook use

We further investigated the loan activity by identifying the ebook usage from the university ebook collection over the same period. Due to limitations of the system, we cannot separate on-site with off-site use. The ebook borrowing information is presented in table 6, which excludes the ebook loans that took place over the weekend where the library was closed. As can readily be seen, most of the activity is found in the 658.8 (Marketing) set. This was also a busy set for in-library use, as already seen in the data.

We analysed the similarities and correlations between ebook and book use in the library. Individual ebook loans are capped at 24 hours—a user who reads the same book across more than that - period creates a new loan for each successive 24 hour period. Therefore, as only a third of the in-library uses, and none of the out-of-library loans fell within 24 hours, we used the number of unique users (per book) as the loan figure for ebooks.

The distribution of online loans versus in-library removals differs across the Dewey topic sets ($p<0.0001$, $\chi^2=42.34$, $df=9$), with the Marketing set being particularly well-used. Similar results are obtained if the loan or book data is used, so the result appears to be robust.

Table 5. Sampled Dewey Decimal Ranges : eBook Borrowing activity (weekdays only)

Seq	Topic Set	Loans	Users	Books
1	Australian Politics	0	0	0
2	Biochemistry	6	4	1
3	Soc. Science #1	0	0	0
4	Marketing	35	20	15
5	Management	1	1	1
6	Astronomy	1	1	1
7	Engineering	0	0	0
8	Ethics	5	3	3
9	Soc. Science #2	18	10	8
10	Politics	0	0	0
	Total	66	39	29

One can also consider whether there is a correlation between the online use of ebooks and in-library use of books by topic set. We calculated the (Pearson's r) correlation between e-Book users and library loans on one hand, and three sets of book numbers on the other. The three library data sets were out-of-library loans, in-library use, and the combined data. The correlations were r=0.715, r=-0.213 and r=0.315 respectively. What this reveals is that while there is a good correlation between ebook loans and out-of-library book loans, the relationship between in-library use and ebook loans is minimal.

4.4 Shelf Heights

As noted previously, there is evidence that children in particular are prone to using the lowest shelves in the library [33; 37] and some suggestive evidence, and some speculative intuition, has led to the expectation that adults show the same patterns. Our data again provides the potential to test this assumption, as it aggregates over the use of a set of shelves by a number of individuals with, likely, different specific tasks and interests.

The data of the number of tilting and moving actions by shelf height is shown below, in Table 7. As noted in the method section, all the sets of shelves we observed had the same general layout of six shelves in a bay, with only minor variations in shelf height between them. Some sets had empty shelves, and these were all eliminated from the shelf counts given below.

Table 6. Shelf position and user action

Shelf	No. of Shelves	Tilt incidents	Tilted books	Pulled
1 (top)	19	3	10	0
2	20	10	53	5
3	19	6	36	1
4	18	4	33	4
5	20	5	41	2
6 (bottom)	20	2	12	0

We tested the frequencies above against the expected distribution given the number of shelves at each position. While for the number of tilting incidents, we did not find a reliable difference in the distributions ($p=0.185$, $df=5$, $\chi^2=7.98$), there was a significant variation when the number of tilted books was considered ($p<0.0001$, $df=5$, $\chi^2=45.12$). We did not test the movement of books, as the values were too low for a reliable result.

Table 7. Shelf position and user action

Shelf	No. of Shelves	Removals	Returns	Loans
1 (top)	19	9	6	2
2	20	26	18	6
3	19	6	4	1
4	18	16	13	7
5	20	17	17	2
6 (bottom)	20	10	3	2

The activity of removals and returns was also totalled, and we again tested using the chi-square test, yielding $p=0.0011$ and $p=0.0004$ ($df=5$, $\chi^2=20.29,22.58$) respectively. Again, the location of content on the shelf appeared to influence its use.

4.5 Order and Disorder

We noted in Table 4 that 14 books were moved within their assigned shelf, and a further six were deposited out-of-order. In addition, we counted the number of events where shelves were tidied. In total, twenty tidying events were discerned, that included 156 books. As noted in the Method section, we did not count tilting of books as such when it coincided with the removal of a book, as this may be a consequence of the removal, rather than a separate event. We did count those occasions where removing a book led to a tilt-like movement: there were six in total, affecting thirty-one books. These events consistently coincided with the return of books to the shelves—typically those returned from loan. One case was a re-shelving from the trolleys, and one case was both a loan return and a trolley return.

Tidying was accompanied by the return of books to the vertical (from horizontal or titled), and the relocation of books to their correct order in the shelf sequence. This, and the association of returning books from loan or trolleys strongly suggests librarian involvement. In contrast, the vast majority of returns were rather untidy, with books being deposited slightly out-of-place, on top of other books, or otherwise incongruously. The movement in Figure 1, for example, is consistent with the re-shelving normally seen during the study.

One potential criticism of shelf access is that readers may fail to find their required book due to it being on loan. During the period being studied, this particular library did not exhaust its supply of multiple holdings, and only one recall was issued for a book that was not already available on the shelves (and that a specialist single holding on Einstein's relationship with South America). For our data, therefore, the negative impact of non-availability of a text is unlikely to have been an issue. Overall availability of titles was maintained at over 99% across the period.

5. DISCUSSION

As noted in the introduction, the study of user activity at the library shelves is of recent research interest. While claims have been repeatedly made for serendipitous discovery, browsing and simply retrieval at open-stack shelves, most of the available evidence of library user activity has tracked loans, when books are removed from the building.

Our chosen method does not enable us to investigate incidents of serendipitous discovery, or other primarily cognitive work. Thankfully, recent observational research has started to address that particular issue [4; 13].

What our technique does permit us to identify in an unprecedented level is the aggregate effect of user activity at the shelves, independent of books being withdrawn from the library.

5.1 Volume of Within-Library 'Loans'

Prior data in of within-library borrowing of books from the shelves is scant, and in the vast majority of cases predates the introduction of digital library catalogues in the [8; 11]. At that time, the best evidence suggested that the predominant use of books is outside the library. Harris, for example, reported minimal use of books for study within the library building, running at close to 10% of all book use [11]. Our data demonstrates that in contrast to this prior data, a substantial volume of information work is (at least now) conducted within the library itself. In contrast to twenty loans, we saw evidence of almost 90 uses within the library.

As we only sampled twice a day for most of the survey, it is likely that our data still under-reports in-library use, particularly for shorter uses of books. We saw at least one case of a book being moved that was suggestive of it having been used more extensively than simply lifted from the shelves and briefly opened. Nonetheless, the picture our data provides is sharply different to the prior literature. Nor is it simply a matter of scale—the within-library use of books showed no correlation with library loans, and so simple multiplication of loans to extrapolate overall activity is likely to lead to erroneous conclusions, at least within a particular topic.

One baseline in our data was the relative use of re-shelving locations in the library, as this was precisely what both Harris [11] and McGrath [26] used in 1971. While occasionally books are littered on other places, there were few occasions where we encountered abandoned books on the many desks and benches provided for reader use. These were recorded in the same manner as the trolleys, but were very few. While we knew of over eighty books removed from the shelves, only eight, or under 10%, were located on the re-shelving areas at any point. Thus, over 90% of book use appears to be driven by readers removing and returning books themselves, without librarian involvement.

Harris [11] reported reshelving activity to be c. 10% of the level of loan activity. We found a higher proportion (c. 2:1 rather than 10:1), but our smaller sample doesn't readily allow for strong conclusions to be drawn on a comparison. What we can assert is that reshelving is a very small proportion of overall internal circulation, and this probably explains Harris' much lower assessment of within-library use.

Fussler and Simon's highly cited (1961) work [8] used an entirely different method than Harris' focus on reshelving of books. However as those authors themselves noted, their use of self-reporting questionnaires at the shelves was extremely vulnerable to under-reporting. Their data would suggest an approximately equal balance of use within- and outside-the library. Again, our data suggests a much higher level of in-library use than their research appeared to capture.

It is worth noting that in recent years, academic and public libraries have sought to increase their utility as working spaces, rather than as repositories. Plausibly, this is a factor that may have also caused a shift in behaviour from data gathered in the early 1960s and 1970s. However, this is difficult to assess without concrete data to corroborate it.

5.2 Duration of within-library use

Unfortunately, no prior data that we could locate shed light on the duration of absence from the shelves. While Fussler and Simon obtained self-reported data at the time of removal [8], and Harris detected the point of re-shelving [11], neither consistently identified both the time of removal or return. Fussler and Simon did capture instantaneous use, as they enquired about reader's first actions with the book. However, they did not enquire as to the duration of in-library use. Thus, neither study could capture longer-term within-library use, given their limitations.

The most striking aspect of our data was the volume of book removal from the shelves for prolonged periods. This provides an important picture of information use that is absent from the previous literature.

Only a third of the books where we could detect removal and return reappeared on the same day. Almost identical proportions reappeared on the next day, and at a later point in time. While we cannot be sure of the whereabouts of these items, the presence of alien books in the observed locations, plus the detection of books removed from our sets in other locations, and in use over contiguous days, may suggest that the informally reported deliberate misplacing of books in a library for personal storage may be in fact be more ubiquitous than the scant evidence to date (e.g. [14]) might have suggested.

5.3 Readers at the Shelves

Beyond the aggregate picture, our data provides some evidence for assessing what is actually done by users at or near library shelves. Previous literature [3; 4; 13], suggests that users both browse and use books for brief reference at the shelves. Browsing itself may not require the user to touch the books or shelves, but reading book cover blurbs, sometimes even titles, and certainly internal content necessarily require the reader to at least partially take a book from the shelf.

The primary purposes of library shelves are to provide storage and enable retrieval [36]. However, the total activity we observed is only mildly correlated with what has been dubbed 'grab-and-go' retrieval [3]. Our data shows that books are regularly moved or disturbed without being taken from the library or the shelf for several hours. The prior data that suggested the primary use of libraries was as a retrieval mechanism for work outside them is therefore either dated or simply incorrect. What evidence is there of other activity?

Triage activity—choosing from a number of candidate books—in theory requires the reader to engage with the content and metadata of the candidates. Naturally, in a physical library, this is found in the book titles and names on the spines, blurb and further information on the front and rear of the book, and in the content of the book itself. Accessing anything bar the basic title-and-author data placed on the spine is likely to require manipulation of the shelves and their contents. Again, there is minimal existing data on this, and our results give the initial baseline for this value.

We detected twenty-five incidents of one or more books being tilted, likely as a consequence of a book being inspected either on- or off- the shelf. In addition, we found ten cases of books being pulled (or in one case "pushed"). None of these cases were associated with the removal of a book from the shelves for a prolonged period—though quite probably some of the few pulled books were both taken down and placed carefully back in place.

Overall, there is plentiful indirect evidence of triage—and possibly browsing—activity, though it should be borne in mind that other short-term uses, e.g. simply seeking a text for quick reference, will likely produce similar patterns of disturbance.

Shelf height has been long raised as an issue in the use of library content [8] However, the historic data is strongly influenced by the overarching concern of making more effective use of physical library space, and the available sequencing details of the shelf heights (e.g. [8]) is very limited, as we lack any idea of the total height or layout of the storage being studied—eight or nine shelves being typical in that period, but being almost unknown using modern shelving units.

What our data demonstrates more explicitly is that there is a peak at around shoulder height, and another at what approximates to kneeling head-height, or standing waist-height. This *likely* corresponds with one of the peaks reported historically. The main survey—Fussler and Simon's—relied on a questionnaire placed at around standing height, so a match with that height could be caused by several different factors [8]. Furthermore, they only used shelf number, when the number of shelves in a bay varied. This led, by their own admission, to marked and confounding effects in their data. These two effects may also explain the relatively low response rate for the lower shelves reported in that study.

Added to this, our data demonstrates that, again, loan use is at best weakly correlated with in-library use, and this applies as much to the effect of shelf height as any other factor.

5.4 Order and Disorder

Those book returns that we could attribute to loan activity were normally associated with the locations being tidied, underlining the likelihood of librarians being responsible for the tidying of shelves. The shelves were regularly disrupted and re-arranged. Occasionally 'alien' books were found in existing locations, and over 150 books were tilted at one or more points in the study. This level of activity is far beyond the sparse loan activity of libraries in general, but also far above the limited loan activity recorded for our target areas across the study period.

Our data may have the limitation of occurring in a relatively optimal situation. While concerns have been raised about the non-availability of books in traditional libraries (due to a lack of holding, or exhaustion of supply by demand), this is unlikely to have been a problem in our case. It may be that the context studied here was not representative of the general experience of the use of physical libraries, if availability is lower.

5.5 Loans, Removals and Ebook Use

We also compared the activity of physical book use with the use of electronic books at the same institution. This data reinforced previous findings that levels of electronic book use varies between disciplines [5]. The triangulation of our users' behaviour against prior work helps support our new findings. What the data revealed for the first time was that while the rate of loans outside the library correlate well with ebook loans, they have little or—more likely—no relationship with the level of within-library use of books, both off- and on- the shelves.

In various parts of information work, developers of new systems have compared their proposed solution with known patterns of prior behaviour. Providing naturalistic and effective trials of physical versus digital media is often noted as problematic, even by leading researchers [25] Our data would suggest caution in using library loan data, despite its previous endorsements [26] as a benchmark of overall use, but we can provide some indication of the current relationship between loan and overall activity.

5.6 Future Work

Our method is new, but it complements existing techniques and supports many earlier findings.

One concern or limitation is that without knowing the choices and compromises being made by users, we may draw false conclusions based on current behaviour. It may be that the use of print media is a side-effect of it being the preferred format for book selection [13]. Qualitative investigation of what library users are doing, particularly in terms of their user journey from the shelves to any following work in the library building. Better understanding the user needs that lead to short-term interactions with library books can inform library ebook acquisition policies and the design of future electronic systems.

The lack of cognitive insight from an artefact-focussed method is also a key limitation. There is a slight body of recent research on what users do in the library with books, but more is needed if we are to understand their current patterns. Browsing at shelves [13] has been relatively well addressed, and studies of work outside the library have also started to emerge [4]. Recent studies of individual and group work in libraries [31; 32] have underlined the common use of books in individual academic work. However, the coverage of information work over time, rather than momentarily, or the interplay between book selection and use is extraordinarily scant. A contrast of our data with earlier work [8; 11; 26] suggests that work is more commonly extended than data gathered at-shelf revealed, and similar omissions are likely to plague on recent observational work that again focussed on the shelves themselves [13]. We need to investigate what happens afterwards, in or out of the library or office.

Digital systems can clearly deliver books to readers' desks, but the underestimation of print use in libraries has led to the supposition that ebook systems were (comparatively) more effective than they are. This demonstrates a large gap in capability that we have suspected but not proven until this point.

6. CONCLUSIONS

Previous research had suggested that use of books inside physical libraries was limited [11; 26]. Due to the lack of availability of other information, loan data has served as the benchmark for the use of print libraries. Our data demonstrates that this assumption is unreliable, and needs to be approached with caution. Ebook use seems well correlated with loan data, but weakly correlated with in-library use. While triage activity [24] in the library may account for some of the gap, its brevity means it is unlikely to explain the long uses that we frequently detected. It seems that while digital systems successfully deliver material for use—at least for some work –there remains an advantage to print that has not yet been closed.

We have shown for the first time that books are often absent for extended periods from their assigned shelves, even in a well-maintained environment is. It seems likely that readers hoard books in out-of-order places to secure access to them. Further knowledge of these prolonged absences is needed to complete our picture of work in the library.

7. ACKNOWLEDGMENTS

Our thanks to Swinburne University of Technology for providing access to the library.

8. REFERENCES

[1] Blandford, A., Rimmer, J., and Warwick, C., 2006. Experiences of the Library in the Digital Age. In *Proc. CCCDT 06* (Tavros, Greece), Foundation of the Hellenic World.

[2] Borgman, C.L., 1996. Why are online catalogs *still* hard to use? *JASIS* 47, 7, 493-503. DOI= http://doi.org/10.1002/(SICI)1097-4571(199607)47:7<493::AID-ASI3>3.0.CO;2-P.

[3] Buchanan, G., Cunningham, S.J., Blandford, A., Rimmer, J., and Warwick, C., 2005. Information Seeking by Humanities Scholars. In *Proc. ECDL 2005* (Vienna, Austria), Springer, 218-229. DOI= http://doi.org/10.1007/11551362_20.

[4] Buchanan, G., McKay, D., and Levitt, J., 2015. Where My Books Go: Choice and Place in Digital Reading. In *Proc. JCDL 15* (Knoxville, TN), ACM, 17-26. DOI= http://doi.org/10.1145/2756406.2756917.

[5] Christianson, M., 2005. Patterns of use of electronic books. *Libr Collect Acquis* 29, 4, 351-363. DOI= http://doi.org/10.1080/14649055.2005.10766084.

[6] Cooper, M.D., 2001. Usage patterns of a web-based library catalog. *JASIST* 52, 2, 137-148. DOI= http://doi.org/10.1002/1097-4571(2000)9999:9999<::aid-asi1547>3.0.co;2-e.

[7] Cunningham, S.J. and Frank, E., 1999. Market basket analysis of library circulation data. In *Proc. ICONIP 99*, 825-830. DOI= http://doi.org/10.1109/ICONIP.1999.845702.

[8] Fussler, H.H. and Simon, J.L., 1969. *Patterns in the use of books in large research libraries*. University of Chicago Press, Chicago, IL.

[9] Hancock-Beaulieu, M., 1993. Evaluating the impact of an online library catalogue on subject searching at the catalogue and at the shelves. *J Doc* 46, 4, 318-338. DOI= http://doi.org/10.1108/eb026863.

[10] Hancock-Beaulieu, M., 1987. Subject Searching Behaviour at the Library Catalogue and at the Shelves: Implications for Online Interactive Catalogues. *J Doc* 43, 4, 303-321.

[11] Harris, C., 1977. A comparison of issues and in-library use of books. *Aslib Proceedings* 29, 3, 118-126. DOI= http://doi.org/10.1108/eb050585.

[12] Herlocker, J.L., Konstan, J.A., Terveen, L.G., and Riedl, J.T., 2004. Evaluating collaborative filtering recommender systems. *ToIS* 22, 1, 5-53. DOI= http://doi.org/10.1145/963770.963772.

[13] Hinze, A., McKay, D., Vanderschantz, N., Timpany, C., and Cunningham, S.J., 2012. Book selection behavior in the physical library: implications for ebook collections. In *Proc. JCDL '12* (Washington, DC), ACM, 305-314. DOI= http://doi.org/10.1145/2232817.2232874.

[14] Jamali, H.R., Nicholas, D., and Rowlands, I., 2009. Scholarly e-books: the views of 16,000 academics: Results from the JISC National E-Book Observatory. *Aslib Proceedings* 61, 1, 33-47.

[15] Kantor, P.B., 1976. Availability analysis. *JASIST* 27, 5, 311-319. DOI= http://doi.org/10.1002/asi.4630270507.

[16] Khoo, M., Rozaklis, L., and Hall, C., 2012. A survey of the use of ethnographic methods in the study of libraries and library users. *Libr. Inf. Sci. Res.* 34, 2, 82-91. DOI= http://doi.org/10.1016/j.lisr.2011.07.010.

[17] Knievel, J.E., Wicht, H., and Connaway, L.S., 2006. Use of circulation statistics and interlibrary loan data in collection management. *C&RL* 67, 1, 35-49.

[18] Kuhlthau, C.C., 1991. Inside the Search Process: Information Seeking from the User's Perspective. *JASIST* 42, 5, 361-371. DOI= http://doi.org/10.1002/(SICI)1097-4571(199106)42:5<361::AID-ASI6>3.0.CO;2-#.

[19] Lau, E.P. and Goh, D.H.-L., 2006. In search of query patterns: A case study of a university OPAC. *Inform Process Manag* 42, 5, 1316-1329. DOI= http://doi.org/10.1016/j.ipm.2006.02.003.

[20] Littman, J. and Connaway, L.S., 2004. A Circulation Analysis of Print Books and E-Books in an Academic Research Library. *Libr Resour Tech Serv* 48, 256-262.

[21] Losee, R.M., 1993. The relative shelf location of circulated books: A study of classification, users, and browsing. *Libr Resour Tech Serv* 37, 2, 197-209.

[22] Makri, S., Blandford, A., Gow, J., Rimmer, J., Warwick, C., and Buchanan, G., 2007. A library or just another information resource? A case study of users' mental models of traditional and digital libraries. *JASIST* 58, 3, 433-445. DOI= http://doi.org/10.1002/asi.20510.

[23] Marchionini, G., 1997. *Information Seeking in Electronic Environments*. Cambridge University Press, Cambridge, UK.

[24] Marshall, C.C., 2010. *Reading and Writing the Electronic Book*. Morgan & Claypool, Chapel Hill, NC.

[25] Marshall, C.C., Price, M., Golovchinsky, G., and Schilit, B.N., 1999. Introducing a digital library reading appliance into a reading group. In, *Proc DL00* ACM, 77-84.

[26] McGrath, W.E., 1971. Correlating the Subjects of Books Taken Out Of and Books Used Within an Open-Stack Library. *C&RL* 32, 4, 280-285.

[27] McKay, D., 2011. A jump to the left (and then a step to the right): reading practices within academic ebooks. In *Proc. OzCHI 11* (Canberra, Australia), ACM, 202-210. DOI= http://doi.org/10.1145/2071536.2071569.

[28] McKay, D., Buchanan, G., Vanderschantz, N., Timpany, C., Cunningham, S.J., and Hinze, A., 2012. Judging a book by its cover: interface elements that affect reader selection of ebooks. In *Proc. OzCHI 12* (Melbourne, Australia), ACM, 381-390. DOI= http://doi.org/10.1145/2414536.2414597.

[29] McKay, D. and Hardy, G., 2011. Can they find it? Yes they can (maybe): Results of a materials availability survey. In (Sydney, Australia), ALIA.

[30] McKay, D., Hinze, A., Heese, R., Vanderschantz, N., Timpany, C., and Cunningham, S.J., 2012. An Exploration of ebook Selection Behavior in Academic Library Collections. In *Proc. TPDL '12* (Paphos, Cyprus), Springer, 13-24. DOI= http://doi.org/10.1007/978-3-642-33290-6_2.

[31] McKay, D., Smith, W., and Chang, S., 2014. Lend me some sugar: Borrowing rates of neighbouring books as evidence for browsing. In *Proc. DL 2014* (London, UK), 145-154. DOI= http://doi.org/10.1109/JCDL.2014.6970161.

[32] McKay, D., Smith, W., and Chang, S., 2015. Down the Superhighway in a Single Tome: Examining the Impact of Book Format on Borrowing Interactions. In *Proc. OZCHI 16* (Melbourne, Australia), ACM, 517-525. DOI= http://doi.org/10.1145/2838739.2838766.

[33] Moore, P., 1995. Information Problem Solving: A Wider View of Library Skills. *Contemporary Educational Psychology* 20, 1, 1-31. DOI= http://doi.org/10.1006/ceps.1995.1001.

[34] Neuman, W.L., 2006. *Social research methods: Qualitative and quantitative approaches*. Pearson, New York.

[35] Nielsen, J. and Molich, R., 1990. Heuristic Evaluation of User Interfaces. In (Seattle, Washington, United States), ACM. DOI= http://doi.org/10.1145/97243.97281.

[36] Petroski, H., 2010. *The Book on the Bookshelf.* Vintage, London UK.

[37] Reutzel, D.R. and Gali, K., 1998. The Art of Children's Book Selection: A Labyrinth Unexplored. *Reading Psychology* 19, 1, 3-50. DOI= http://doi.org/10.1080/0270271980190101.

[38] Shibata, H. and Takano, K., 2014. Reading from paper versus reading from a touch-based tablet device in proofreading. In *Proc. DL 14* (London, United Kingdom), IEEE Press, 433-434.

[39] Shibata, H., Takano, K., Omura, K., and Tano, S.i., 2015. Page Navigation on Paper Books and Electronic Media in Reading to Answer Questions. In *Proc. OZCHI 15* (Parkville, VIC, Australia), ACM, 526-534. DOI= http://doi.org/10.1145/2838739.2838747.

[40] Stelmaszewska, H. and Blandford, A., 2004. From physical to digital: a case study of computer scientists' behaviour in physical libraries. *IJDL* 4, 2, 82-92. DOI= http://doi.org/10.1007/s00799-003-0072-6.

[41] Warren, P., 2001. Why They Still Cannot Use Their Library Catalogues. In (Krakow, Poland), Poland Cracow University of Economics

Manoeuvres in the Dark: Design Implications of the Physical Mechanics of Library Shelf Browsing

Dana McKay
University of Melbourne
Parkville, VIC 3010
Australia
danamckay@gmail.com

Shanton Chang
University of Melbourne
Parkville, VIC 3010
Australia
shanton.chang@unimelb.edu.au

Wally Smith
University of Melbourne
Parkville, VIC 3010
Australia
wsmith@unimelb.edu.au

ABSTRACT
Library shelf browsing is a much-loved but little-understood form of information seeking. Attempts have been made to replicate or replace it online, however they have not typically been based on a principled understanding of the goals and behaviours of readers. This paper addresses the behaviour of readers, presenting an empirical examination of the mechanics of library shelf browsing. We note some previously undescribed behaviours, such as placemarking, and some hitherto unknown details such as the large number of books browsers consider. We situate our findings in the literature, and use them to drive design recommendations.

Keywords
Browsing; libraries; books; interface design; observation

1. INTRODUCTION
Ebooks have a number of advantages over their print counterparts: their content is searchable; readers can squeeze many of them onto a single, lightweight device; and even when contained within a library they are accessible anywhere and anytime [28; 34; 45; 51]. Combined with rapid improvements in the reading experience of ebooks [48], these factors are likely the catalyst for the explosion in personal use of ebooks [16], and their widespread acquisition by public and academic libraries [11; 18; 34].

Ebooks have one significant failing in comparison with their print counterparts, however: currently no system exists that provides the rich, broad experience of browsing the shelves. There is little scope for serendipitous discovery, and outside a few experimental systems, options for collection understanding are poor. These difficulties demonstrably affect borrowing patterns in comparison with print [40], and some commentators fear that they will go on to affect the breadth and depth of scholarship in general [9; 42].

Browsing is not just part of human information seeking behaviour generally [23; 33], it is also a widely used and deeply valued part of library information seeking [4; 22; 30; 50; 55]. Despite the known drawbacks of the shelves (for example missing or checked out books [4]) some readers value the shelf browsing experience so highly that they reject ebooks [19; 30]. The rise of ebooks creates a new limitation to shelf-based information seeking: much of a collection will be invisible to readers at the shelves. It is thus both timely and important that adequate online browsing tools are developed.

CHIIR '17, March 07 - 11, 2017, Oslo, Norway

ACM 978-1-4503-4677-1/17/03...$15.00
DOI: http://dx.doi.org/10.1145/3020165.3020179

There are a number of tools to facilitate online book browsing in early development (for example [20; 22; 47; 59]—for more on this see Section 2.3). None of these tools, however, has been based on a principled understanding of what readers' goals and behaviours are when they browse. This is perhaps due to a lack of detailed research on how readers actually physically interact with book collections on shelves. It is this latter gap that we aim to address in this paper. We are specifically investigating natural browsing behaviour, and what physical actions readers take when they browse. By understanding the mechanics of browsing we hope to drive system design; by supporting natural behaviour we can build a better online experience.

The remainder of the paper will be divided up as follows: first we provide a literature background, next we give a detailed account of our method. We then provide results and the design recommendations that arise from our findings, then discuss these in relation to the existing literature. Finally we draw conclusions and provide avenues for future work.

2. BACKGROUND
In this section we provide the literature background on information seeking browsing. We give a definition of browsing in Section 2.1. We then demonstrate the gaps in other studies of the use of library shelves in Section.2.2, and online browsing systems in Section 2.3, demonstrating where our study fits in.

2.1 Browsing and Information Behaviour
While it is easy to assume that search has solved the information problems of the world, browsing is a clear part of information seeking behaviour according to the predominant models [14; 23; 33; 41]. Search is highly effective for readers who have a specific item in mind, but information needs do not spring into our minds as fully formed queries [5; 46]. Stumbling toward the point where we know we have an information need [23], understanding the options available to us [33], looking for non-specific information [41]; looking in a non-specific undirected way [41] or seeking inspiration in the form or serendipity [14; 30]; all are the province of browsing. Search caters to only a small part of the information seeking process under any circumstances, not just in libraries—yet it is the predominant information interaction paradigm online. This is an untenable situation for those information seekers who don't have a clear information need; Borgman's 1996 assertion that search—and library search in particular—'is difficult because it requires you to describe information you don't have' remains true today [5].

Bates is widely acknowledged as an authority on online browsing. In 2007 she asserted that browsing is a part of the human condition in a paper that draws on disciplines as diverse as neurobiology and information science [2]. Her paper defines browsing as: seeing a large, varied scene glimpsing and sequentially examining objects of interest and selecting or rejecting them for use; our paper uses this definition. As noted in [22] library shelves are a near-ideal browsing engine according to this definition. Our study took place at the library shelves, drawing on a long tradition of investigating physical information seeking to drive online design [8; 10; 31; 55].

2.2 Library Shelf Studies

There are many studies of readers at the library shelves, however—as we will show—none focus on the physical interactions browsers have with shelves.

The earliest study addressing shelf use is Beaulieu's 1993 work [17] on the changes to library information seeking wrought by the introduction of an online catalogue. This study followed 100 users and noted that shelf browsing was an important driver of book choice, with over half of all searchers selecting a second book by browsing. This study did not, however, examine the physical mechanics of browsing.

In 1997 another study [53] examined what happened in a library when the shelves are rearranged; unsurprisingly rearrangement was shown to affect borrowing, but again this study did not address the physical activities within browsing and shelf use.

Early studies reporting on the mechanics of shelf browsing were on children; Moore noted that children did not browse in depth and considered eye level shelves most frequently in 1995 [43]. Reutzel and Gali examined physical browsing in children [49], and came up with a description of physical actions that bears some similarity to the one presented here. Children's information seeking, though, is necessarily different from that of adults [6]. Moreover, the information landscape has changed significantly in the past twenty years with the introduction of ebooks, new generation library search and even some online browsing tools.

Beginning ten years ago there were a number of observational studies on or including how readers approached the library shelves [4; 19; 30; 55], usually in the context of some other aspect of information seeking (for example the impact of online systems or serendipity). These studies identified a number of drawbacks to the physical shelves, including lost or misshelved books. They also identified a range of book features that contribute to book selection including bibliographic features such as title and author, but also including non-bibliographic features such as book size and cover. These studies also identified a near-universal fondness for shelf browsing that can result in the rejection of ebooks.

More recently a single study has had an exploratory look at the mechanics of shelf browsing [19], and attempted to apply Reutzel and Gali's framework to adult browsing. This paper, however, examined the selection process for only a single book per participant, missing much of the richness of a complete browsing experience. Furthermore the assumption that adult behaviour will mirror that of children is inherent in the analytical approach of that paper; that assumption may prove to be flawed. Finally Hinze et al do not address design implications of their findings. While their paper is an excellent first look at browsing in adults, it does not look in as much depth as the work we present here.

Our own earlier work has used log analysis to support the case for shelf browsing affecting borrowing [35; 39; 40]; Losee has also made this case [26]. Another study [37], drawing on questions asked in the library stacks, identifies stack layout as a barrier to information seeking. Interview and survey studies such as [29; 50; 52] about library information seeking often result in mentions of the library stacks, too. None of these, however, include the depth of information on physical browsing needed to drive new design.

We extend the work described here by focusing on natural browsing and book selection, examining the whole selection process (rather than just a part of it) by looking particularly at physical interactions with books and shelves and by using our findings to make design recommendations.

2.3 Existing Browsing Systems

Recent years have seen an increased interest in providing browsing or serendipitous discovery in the online library. Many of these approaches use either small [20] or large scale replicas [22] of the shelves, an approach that offers many of the drawbacks of library shelves without the advantages of physical affordance.

One alternative approach [59] used book size, cover colour and publication year to create novel serendipitous discovery approaches. The use of book size and cover is particularly savvy as these features are non-bibliographic cues that already drive decision-making. This system was presented at the library shelves on bespoke hardware, user testing is ongoing. Another approach, Bookfish [47] allows readers to select books using sliders to locate them on a number of dichotomous continuums. Readers are presented with 12 books that best match their criteria.

Commercial systems are also being trialled; Whichbook[1] is similar to Bookfish in its approach. A system at developed at UTS[2] and Ex Libris' discovery tool[3] each present a limited (3 book default) simulation of the library shelves in tandem with individual results.

These systems have been built to take into account considerations beyond keyword search, to look at exploration or even to build in some serendipity. None of them, however, has been grounded in a principled and thorough understanding of reader motivations and intentions in browsing, nor the physical process used to do it. This paper addresses the latter gap in the literature.

3. METHOD

This section describes our research method, which is based on a situated observational approach analysed with techniques drawn from grounded theory. This approach was chosen to allow us to build theory in a relatively sparse research space, and in turn to drive design based on this theory [1]. Section 3.1 describes our data gathering method and Section 3.2 explains our data analysis.

3.1 Data Gathering

We drew our participants from two libraries; this gave us a more diverse participant pool and avoided conclusions based on the peculiarities of layout in any given library. The first site is the main campus library of Swinburne, a small, research active university in Australia. Books are arranged by Dewey Decimal Classification (DDC) and spread over five distinct geographical areas on three floors of the library. The second library, State Library of Victoria (SLV) is a public research library with a large open collection. While there are several different collections in this library, all observations took place in two of these. The first is the main collection, which is spread down two sides of the lower level of a large airy room, and continues around the edge of a mezzanine gallery; the second is the arts collection in a small, single level room. Again, books are arranged by DDC. In each library, we continued our observations until we had reached saturation—no new behaviours were being seen [44]. This

[1] www.wwhichbookom

[2] http://www.lib.uts.edu.au/news/92740/another-new-way-to-browse-librarys-collection

[3] http://initiatives.exlibrisgroup.com/2015/04/the-virtual-bookshelf.html

resulted in 15 observations at Swinburne, all during term time, and 16 at SLV, 15 in the main collection and one in the arts room. These numbers are larger than many studies of this type [4; 30; 55], and commensurate with the most comparable [19].

32 readers were approached as they neared the shelves and asked if they minded us observing their book selection; only one (male, at the university site) refused. Participants were all over 18 years of age (as required by the ethics process), 23 out of 31 were students (14 of 15 at Swinburne and 7 of 16 at SLV). 16 participants were male, 15 female. Participants selected books on a wide range of topics, and topic was not observed to have any effect on behaviour.

All observations were conducted by a single researcher. During observations, participants were followed until they indicated they were finished book seeking. During book seeking they were questioned about any aspects of their behaviour the observer wished to clarify. Upon completion of book seeking the observer conducted a brief semi-structured interview about their book seeking intentions and purpose, whether they had searched online prior to approaching the shelves, and whether the books they had selected were what they had hoped to find. This approach has been used in a number of studies before ours [4; 19; 30; 55], though none have both approached readers at the shelves and followed them throughout their book selection process. The data gathered consisted of tallies of certain behaviours (such as the number of books touched) and handwritten notes on observations and interviews. Immediately after each observation the observer wrote a detailed narrative (akin to the serendipity stories in [29]) to record events in sequence and provide detailed accounts of the observations. Narratives and tallies were later transcribed to a spreadsheet for analysis. Results presented in this paper are based on all observations, rather than a selected sample.

3.2 Analysis

Our analysis was conducted in two phases. In the first phase two researchers analysed the data using inductive techniques drawn from grounded theory [1; 44] until consensus was formed. The major difference between our approach and grounded theory is that—due to the availability of the second researcher—data was not analysed concurrently with collection, but rather after collection. The use of a second researcher reduces the impact of the first researcher's biases and preconceptions. The second phase of research used the classification scheme formed in the first to count behaviours.

Two researchers examined the narrative data independently and each devised a classification scheme. The schemes were discussed and (as they were very similar) merged. Narratives were then classified per the resultant scheme, which had 12 classes with between two and nine codes each. The work in this paper addresses the seven classes that reflect readers' physical actions in choosing books, and as such reflects primarily observational data. The interview data is largely used to identify search behaviour prior to readers entering the stacks—particularly for the identification of grab-and-go readers (see Section 4.2) Table 1 illustrates the classification scheme used in this paper; interview data is denoted (I), observational data (O).

After determining the classification scheme, researchers independently classified the data, and results were discussed and compared. Density was found to be both inconsistently applied and difficult to apply well, a few other aspects of the data were noted as interesting but unclassified. Disagreements were primarily resolved by clarifying nuances in the data. The coding scheme was amended accordingly and the data reclassified.

Table 1: Classification scheme. Definitions given in Section 4.

Class	Codes	Inter-rater agreement (%)
Search	None (*I*)	100
	On another occasion (*I*)	100
	During session at shelves (*O*)	75
	During session away from shelves (*O*)	68
	Prior to session themselves (*I*)	90
	Prior to session someone else (*I*)	100
Physical Range	Target book (*O*)	100
	Small (*O*)	100
	Medium (*O*)	80
	Wide (*O*)	88
	Very wide (*O*)	100
Density	Target book (*O*)	100
	Local (*O*)	83
	Exhaustive (*O*)	100
	Intermediate (*O*)	92
	Scattershot (*O*)	92
Stack Actions	Reading signs (*O*)	100
	Moving along stacks (*O*)	85
	Vertical movement (*O*)	93
	Step back (*O*)	100
	Scanning (*O*)	100
	Rechecking (*O*)	100
	Turn (*O*)	75
	Head tilt (*O*)	100
Shelf Actions	Running finger along shelves (*O*)	100
	Flipping books along shelves (*O*)	83
	Half pull (*O*)	100
	Complete pull (*O*)	100
	Placemarking (*O*)	100
Book selection criteria	Known item (*I*)	100
	Title (*O*)	87
	Author (*O*)	100
	Table of Contents (*O*)	100
	Index (*O*)	100
	Publication date (*I*)	100
	Cover (*O*)	86
	Blurb/back cover (*O*)	80
	Content (*O*)	100
Triage location	At shelves (*O*)	100
	Away from shelves (*O*)	100
Tools	Note surface	100
	Camera	100

Upon reclassification all classes but density and shelf actions had inter-rater agreement of greater than 90%; those classes reached 83% and 87% respectively. While individual codes within the search class have agreement lower than 80%, these codes were applied infrequently; the disparity represents disagreement over only a single observation in each case.

4. RESULTS

This section begins with a description of readers who—in our observations—did not browse, so as to exclude them from further discussion (Section 4.1). We go on to provide numerical descriptions of some behaviours (Section 4.2). The middle of this section (sections 4.3-4.10) is structured according to the coding scheme shown above, one section for each classification. While it is unusual to include analysis in a results section, we will include the design recommendations arising from our observations within our results that the rationale for each recommendation is clear. In section 4.11 we present a summary of design recommendations, summarizing the physical interactions they support. Finally in section 4.12 we acknowledge the limitations of this study.

To adequately describe the behaviour of users at the shelves, we need to use some library terms for the shelves (see Figure 1). Briefly a **shelf** is a single shelf in a single bay one one shelving unit, typically holding 40-70 books. A **bay** is a horizontal division within a shelving unit used so that readers can scan a classification without moving along the shelves; bays can hold up to 700 books. A **stack** is a shelving unit.

Figure 1: Library shelf terminology

4.1 Grab-and-go: Readers Who Don't Browse

While we will not delve too much into the intentions of the readers we observed in this paper, there was one group that was less interesting for understanding browsing: the readers who had a target book in mind, selected it, and immediately left the shelves. These readers invariably had a range and density covering only their target books, and selected books on a known item basis. This type of reader is aptly termed 'grab and go' in [8], and in an online environment would be better served by an effective keyword search than any browsing facility. These readers account for 9 observations, 7 at the university library and 2 in the research library. This leaves 22 observations in our analysis.

4.2 Counted Behaviours

For each reader we recorded a tally of the number of books they touched, the number of books removed from the shelves, the number of books they selected ad removed from the shelves for later use, and the number of shelves and bays they examined. For grab-and-go readers the number in each case should be 1, however we saw these readers examine as many as 24 shelves, sometimes spread over a large area in the library. This is further evidence for supporting this type of information seeking with search; requiring these users to cover such a range of ground is simply wasting their time. As such grab and go readers are excluded from the tallies the numbers shown in Table 2.

Table 2 demonstrates that that browsing may be extremely cursory, as little as a glance over a single bay without examining any items in detail, or it may well be extensive covering many hundreds of books; examination of a single shelf amounts to approximately 60 books [35]. Loizides points out in his work on triage (the process of selecting and rejecting candidate documents) that choosing not to examine something is an implicit value judgement [25], an assertion that also applies here.

Table 2: Browsing interactions by the numbers

	Mean	Median	Min	Max
Books touched	6.05	4	1	19
Books moved from shelves	3.41	2	0	15
Books selected	1.77	1	0	6
Shelves examined	7.05	5	0	30
Bays examined	3.86	3	1	18

Currently available browsing interfaces do not afford the rapid visual scanning of large numbers of books seen in our study; this is a feature that must be offered to adequately support browsing.

We also recorded for each reader whether they selected any books—selecting any book can be considered an indicator of success. In total, only four readers left the shelves empty handed

4.3 The Presence or Absence of Search

We noted for each reader whether they had engaged in any form of catalogue search in conjunction with their browsing. This might be search before approaching the stacks, possibly assisted by someone else (usually a librarian), or while they were using the stacks, or on another occasion of library use or not at all.

All grab-and-go readers had searched before entering the stacks, some of them repeated their search in the stacks on a device carried with them to remind themselves of a call number. For this group these interactions merely represent a circuitous path, and retrieval would be best at the time of search.

Three readers had **not engaged in search at all**. Two of those readers were looking for something to occupy their time and had time to browse extensively, the third knew where to look on the shelves for the information she sought. This approach demonstrates a need for browsing systems that allow readers to access information without searching first.

Two readers had searched **on another occasion** and were returning to known areas in the shelves. Browsing systems must support readers in returning to areas of interest on subsequent information seeking occasions. .

Four readers searched **during their information seeking session**. In three cases this was because a primary browsing strategy had failed to yield results, and in the fourth the reader was looking for further information (he had also searched before entering the stacks). Two of these readers left the stacks to approach a catalogue, two searched within the stacks (one on a phone, one on a laptop). Leaving the stacks was inconvenient and driven by catalogue location, rather than a deliberate strategy. This behaviour speaks to the oft-noted requirement that search and browse be easily interleaved [23; 33; 38]; not a new finding but one supported by our work.

Eleven readers had **searched prior to entering the shelves**. This search-then-browse pattern is the primary model of library information seeking and—while it may not necessarily hold in a good online system—must be supported. Given the number of books browsers are scanning over, though (as seen in Section 4.2), presenting a set of ten or even fifty search results is not enough to meet the needs of this group.

Three users had enlisted the help of **someone else to search before they entered the shelves**. One of these had also tried searching himself, and enlisted help when his own attempts were ineffective. Another was wandering lost because he could not read the handwriting of the librarian who had written down the call number for him. These interactions speak to the need for any online system to support novice and unconfident users. Ideally this support would not require expert intervention—keyword search should be effective enough to return results readily (catalogue search is often poor and perceived as such [13; 21; 24]). In some cases, though, readers will require expert help and the system should support them in accessing it. Again, these are not new findings—the poor user experience of catalogues has been addressed repeatedly over many years [5; 27; 54] and expert help has long been posited as a solution to this [10; 46]. Nevertheless, these requirements remain as important today as they were 20 years ago.

4.4 Physical Range

We coded each observation according to the range covered by the reader within the library. This range was sometimes as narrow as a single bay, and sometimes so wide as to encompass different locations within the library.

Four readers browsed a **small** range of books, less than one bay. These readers tended to have fairly targeted information needs, and were often selecting a single book from a range of close alternatives. These readers would be well served by search that returned semantically similar results, or by very targeted browsing such as that offered by UTS and Ex Libris (see Section 2.3)

Four readers browsed a **medium** range of books, more than one bay but less than one stack. In each case these readers had a clear, well defined topic in mind (for example chemistry or international relations). Three were looking for study related information in a hurry, one was working on a targeted question. This suggests that an ideal browsing system will make it possible to quickly scan the material on a single, coherent topic,

Five readers browsed a **wide** range of books, covering more than one stack in a single area of the library. This group was largely similar to the medium group, demonstrating a clear design requirement to cover all of a topic quickly.

Eight browsers worked over a **very wide** range, examining books in disparate sections of the library. In four cases this was because these readers were somewhat lost and had examined one area by mistake. In the other four cases, however it was a deliberate strategy to select books that were geographically distant but topically similar. One of these in particular was notable—she closely examined one small group of books, then crossed the floor of the library without hesitation to examine another small group, investigating two clear small target clusters.

Related books shelved apart is a known problem in any classification scheme (see [26] and [7] for a discussion of this). Online browsing, however, has the chance to ameliorate this problem: where print books can be presented in only a single, fixed arrangement online shelves can be rearranged at will. There is clearly a need for systems that allow readers to cluster books according to topic boundaries that scan classification schemes.

4.5 Density

Within a physical range readers examined shelves more or less closely.

Three readers browsed **exhaustively**, systematically looking at every book within their range—amounting in all three cases to well over 300 books. Two of these readers had already decided which books they wanted to borrow, and were "just checking" to ensure they had not missed anything. One of these moved along the shelves (crossing bays rather than following Dewey order) running his finger along the shelves to visually placemark; once he had exhausted the books in call number 658 he noted he was "surprised there were so many". These readers need to be supported with a detailed view of closely related books that can be examined quickly and sequentially in some way.

Five readers browsed **locally**—exhaustively within one or more small ranges with gaps between these areas of close examination These users would likely be well served by something like the Ex Libris Shelf View mentioned in Section 2.3 provided it met their other browsing needs (for example not needing to search).

Two readers were **scattershot** in their approach, examining shelves unsystematically and missing large areas. One of these readers was lost, the other was looking for leisure reading. This approach speaks to the need to be able to skip sections of books, but also assess many books rapidly, as at the shelves

The remaining 12 readers browsed with **intermediate density**, doing some close browsing and some scanning. This approach speaks to the need to zoom in and out while browsing, switching readily from close examination to more cursory scanning.

4.6 Stack Actions

Readers engaged in a number of physical actions that did not result in them touching bookshelves, we termed these stack actions. Most browsers performed more than one stack action; possible actions taken are described below.

The stack action conducted furthest from books was **reading signs**. These signs were located at the end of stacks and intended and used for wayfinding, so that readers did not have to delve into stacks to locate a relevant are of the library. One reader noted her frustration at how poor the signs were, complaining "these shelves aren't sorted in groups". Three users engaged the use of signs; these readers could be served in an online collection by providing a high level overview of the collection and allowing them to navigate to the correct section by drilling down.

Three readers actively **stood back** from the shelves, moving away from them to broaden their view during information seeking. These readers would be best served by the ability to take a wide or overview-like view while browsing.

One of the most common shelf actions was to **move horizontally along the shelves** one or more bays; this was done by nine of 22 readers who did any browsing at all. This demonstrates the vast coverage of a large number of books rapidly that browsing can support; this is a key requirement of online browsing systems that has not yet been met.

Another very common action was **vertical** movement over one or more bays—looking (and in one case climbing on a stool) to see over eye level, or squatting or kneeling to see books below eye level. 12 readers in our study engaged in vertical movement. [19; 49]. The fact that more readers moved vertically than along the shelves speaks to the importance of relevance—shelves are more closely related semantically vertically within a bay than horizontally between bays. While convenience is important, readers are prepared to endure minor physical discomfort to select books. It is an advantage of online spaces that they can essentially remove the inconvenience of non-eye-level shelves; it is a testament to the power of browsing that these shelves are examined at all.

Four readers in our study **turned** to look at the shelves behind them, and not always at the end of a stack. In the middle of a stack in a large collection, the books on the shelves behind a reader are likely to be related to the ones in front of them, but fairly distantly. The bays on either side of a reader offer more closely related books. This speaks of readers either being in slightly the wrong place, or looking for inspiration; online systems need to support larger jumps within an ordered set of books.

Visible **visual scanning** of shelves was relatively common, seen in 6 of 21 browsers. This is an interesting behaviour, as readers' gaze seems to pass over books so quickly as to not be able to take in much detail. This is related to the earlier noted requirement for assessing many books very quickly. It remains unclear, though, what features readers are looking for when they do this.

Two readers returned to an area they had previously visited to **recheck** what was on offer. There are two possible reasons for this—being unsure of what has previously been checked, or confirming that all useful books have been gleaned from an area. It may be useful to design systems to allow readers to see that they have previously checked an area over, and also to see where, if anywhere, they have selected books.

The precursor to engaging physically with the shelves was a reader **head tilt**, seen in three readers (also noted in [49]). This is because titles and call numbers are often printed ay 90 degrees to a spine when the book is standing upright; reading this information is the first relevance assessment many readers will make. Ensuring titles are legible is a key component of online browsing; allowing browsers to access them horizontally with ease would be a useful system feature.

4.7 Shelf Actions

Shelf actions are those where readers touch either the shelves or the books and typically demonstrated a closer level of interest in the content of the shelves than stack actions. While some of the actions here reflect those described in [49], many do not and to our knowledge have not been described elsewhere in the literature. Like stack actions, a number of participants engaged in more than one of these.

The least engaged of all shelf actions was readers **running their fingers** along the shelves as a visual marker as they scanned. This was seen in 5 of 21 browsers, and suggests a need for a similar placemarking technique in online systems.

The next level of engagement was to **flip books along the shelves**, like flicking through CDs in a retail CD rack. This action, seen in four interactions, allowed readers to rapidly and quickly glance at covers without removing books from the shelves. It could be facilitated by a swipe or coverpop style interface.

Longer investigations of covers without committing to a book by removing it from the shelves were achieved by the '**half pull**' [49]. This was seen in a much smaller proportion of our readers than Reutzel and Gali's [49]or Hinze et al.'s [19], only two out of 21 browsers. Whether, given its rarity, this is something that needs to be supported online remains an open question. The seamlessness of interaction in moving from a head tilt to taking a book off the shelves has been noted before [19], we confirm this finding and reiterate the need for seamlessness online.

The final stage before selecting a book was the **complete pull**, removing it from the shelves to assess relevance. We only recorded this action for books that were subsequently returned to the shelves, as selected books are recorded elsewhere. Seven readers returned rejected books to the shelves meaning it must be possible to triage books easily and readily online.

The final shelf action we noted was **placemarking**, where readers used a book, pen, object or finger to mark where on the shelves they were "up to" while they triaged books. This behaviour was the deliberate creation of a visual reminder to make it easier to return to browsing, and it was seen in four observations. It should be possible to engage in an analogous action online.

4.8 Triage Location

Triage is the process of evaluating individual documents in a small candidate group to select relevant ones for later use. All but one reader **triaged books at the shelves**, with remaining alternative books clearly visually present. This behaviour was notable both for its near unanimity (only one reader **triaged away from the shelves**) and its stark contrast to existing information systems. Current systems near-inevitably require readers to click away from a search result list to examine a book in any depth counter to their behaviour if given a choice. A good information seeking support system would allow users to retain visuals on options while triaging individual items.

4.9 Book Selection Criteria

The vast majority of book evaluations involved more than one feature of a book; system design must present more than a simple list of titles.

Many of the selection criteria, including **title** (9 observations), **author** (2 observations), **table of contents** (7 readers), **index** (4 readers) and **date** (3 readers) have been seen in previous literature [3; 32; 55; 56]. Date was only used to filter out recent books; one reader was looking for information on a technology topic where only the latest would do, another was working on an assignment and had been told that he could only use references from the past five years. In contrast with the readers seen in [8], our participants seemed comfortable using the copyright page in books to assess this kind of information. These features should clearly be readily accessible when readers make decisions about individual books.

It was notable that we saw much less use of cues like book size and dust than other studies report [4; 30; 55], however our participants did use other reported non-bibliographic cues including **cover** (5 readers), **blurb** (4 readers) and **content** (3 readers). These cues have also been seen in previous work [12; 19; 36; 52; 55]. Nine readers in total (out of 21 browsers) used some kind of non-bibliographic data in their decision making What is abundantly apparent—as other studies have identified—is how poorly library search systems support reader decision making. They do not offer this information readily, if at all, and it is key to the provision of an adequate browsing experience.

Overall ten readers opened the books they were assessing when making their selections; this is in stark contrast with [8] where almost none of the observed bookshop customers opened a book. It is not clear why this is the case—particularly given that the bookshop study observed purchases of non-fiction books, similar to those used by our participants—but it is clear that readers need the option to open books when assessing them online.

What is interesting about these criteria is that we asked each reader who selected a book from the shelf—even if they later returned it—what made them choose that particular book rather than its near neighbours. One answered that 'that was a very good question' and many others answered that it was cover or title, even when they chose books so quickly that it seems unlikely that either titles or spines (which is all of the cover that was visible in most cases) had had time to really register. What is actually happening here, cognitively, remains work for a future study.

4.10 Tools

While most readers did not use any physical equipment to support their browsing (not even the lists seen in [19]) some did. One of the most surprising aspects of tool use is how rarely digital tools featured, other than the laptop used to search at the shelves (see Section 4.3) phones were the only digital tools seen, whether used as a note surface or a camera.

By far the most common (nine readers) was a **note surface** such as a notebook, scrap of paper, or even the reader's hand on which one or more call numbers was recorded. Given that call numbers are an addressing mechanism [57] they should not really be needed in a supportive online system, where readers should navigate intuitively and using plain language descriptions rather than opaque, long and difficult to understand call numbers [15].

Two readers used a **camera** to document things they wished to save for later. One of these was a call number, but another reader photographed the cover of a book so she could come back to it noting that she did not have time to read more than one book that day (and she was in the research library, so she could not check books out for later use). A lightweight capture method is a necessity in a well-designed information seeking system.

4.11 A Summary of Design Recommendations

This section has presented a large range of behaviour with design recommendations throughout; we reiterate the recommendations here. We recognize the difficulty in separating which behaviours are a result of the constraints of the physical environment, and which are intrinsic to browsing. Nonetheless we have attempted to evaluate these recommendations against the issue of physical constraints and provide only recommendations that will improve browsing experiences online. Our recommendations are:

- **Display a large range of books for browsing:** Our readers examined an astonishingly large range and density of books while moving among the shelves; this finding has not (to our knowledge) been noted in any other study. In a well-designed browsing engine it must be possible to scan many hundreds of books very rapidly, just as it is in the shelves.
- **Enable multiple points of access to the collection:** Browsers access the collection in many ways: in addition to the traditional search-first approach many readers treated the shelves as a walk-up-and-use interface. Both approaches must be supported online. Readers must also be able to readily return to sections of the collection they have browsed on previous occasions—another form of placemarking. Finally readers must be able to access groups of books that would not typically be shelved together. These relationships could be derived from known issues with classification schemes (for example HCI being spread amongst computing, design, ad psychology), or could be based on borrowing data, akin to Amazon's 'customers who bought...' feature.
- **Support zooming capability:** Zooming behaviour was seen in the shelf actions of standing back then refocusing on books, and in the scattershot approach taken by many readers. Support for zooming is thus a key requirement of online browsing. Equally, a well-designed browsing system must support users in moving around a bit—rapidly accessing books some semantic distance from where they are (like turning around in the shelves) or accessing related books in a distant part of the subject hierarchy.
- **Seamless transitions:** The transition from shelf to book must be seamless and (possibly) touch-based. Other work [19] has noted how deftly readers move from standing back to evaluating a candidate book and back again; this study identified a similar pattern.
- **Placemarking:** This study demonstrates a need for visible (and perhaps tangible) placemarking while browsing. Finger running, flipping and actual placemarking all appeared frequently; visual markers could also help readers identify what they have seen when rechecking shelves.
- **Visual alternatives during triage:** Nearly all of our participants triaged books at the shelves; retaining visual access to alternative books is necessary for good browsing.
- **Access to book information:** While not novel our findings about book selection criteria—title, date, author, table of contents, index, cover, blurb and content show that many library systems are not offering what readers need. An ideal information seeking system would provide not just the basics of title and author, but also non-bibliographic details such as blurb, table of contents and cover.

Finally, this study reiterated the importance of browsing: readers accessed material on inconvenient shelves and browsed in the vast majority of our observations. The search systems readers have used for so long are not enough on their own to meet reader needs in increasingly online libraries.

4.12 Limitations

Like any study, this study has a number of limitations. Firstly, while data was gathered on several weekdays at both sites, none was gathered outside normal business hours. As such means we may underreport browsing (as demonstrated by our previous work [35]). Secondly while observation is an excellent technique for understanding complex behaviour [44], it has the potential to change participant behaviour [10]. We have tried to limit this effect by situating this study in a suite of work that includes other techniques, such as log analysis [35; 39; 40], and by reporting only behaviour repeated between participants. Thirdly, this study addresses behaviour in research libraries; readers may well behave differently in public libraries, particularly looking for fiction. Extending Vakkari's existing work on fiction (e.g. [52]) remains an interesting avenue for future work. Fourthly we aimed to extend earlier work [19; 49] by observing the entire book selection process. Only 8 participants (26%) selected more than one book, however, meaning often we observed little more than earlier authors. Nonetheless, our work is the first to analyse book seeking by adults from the formative perspective [49] took with children. Finally for space reasons this paper reports only individual actions; future work will take a 'session view' of book seeking to address interactions between these actions.

5. DISCUSSION

In this section we first outline our contribution to the literature on information seeking, then address our findings in terms of search and browse systems specifically.

5.1 Information Seeking and the Mechanics of Browsing

While browsing is mentioned in major models of information seeking [23; 33], little work has gone into depth on what browsing actually looks like. Models of information seeking that include less-directed approaches to information seeking tend to focus on passive discovery [41] and serendipity [14].

While serendipity is closely related to shelf browsing, it does not encompass all aspects of it; browsing includes active information seeking where serendipity—by definition—is a happy accident, and occurs when information seekers are not looking. We know that plenty of serendipity happens at the shelves [9; 14; 30; 55]. We also know that precursors for serendipitous discovery generally are likely to facilitate positive shelf browsing experiences [9]. Like information seeking, though there are clear models for serendipity based on empirical work [29]. Browsing, thus far, has not been subject to the same kind of empirical research and modelling.

Two previous studies have begun the work of modelling browsing in children [49], and extending that approach to adults [19] however the interactions observed in these studies were brief and focused on a single book. The work presented in this paper followed interactions over a longer period and took a formative approach and as such contributes novel understandings.

Our work has confirmed some previous findings, such as the potential benefits afforded by rearranging the shelves and the criteria by which readers choose books, however there are novel findings as well. One such finding is the ebb and flow of focus at the shelves, with readers being intermittently more and less fine-grained in their examination. Another is the propensity to placemark when browsing, possibly to narrow visual focus to just a few items rather than a whole shelf or stack. The major contribution of this paper, though, is an exhaustive catalogue of physical interactions undertaken while browsing at the library shelves which—when combined with an understanding of readers' goals and motivations—could give us the underpinnings of an empirical model of browsing.

5.2 What About Search?

One of the most striking findings of this study is how successful readers were in locating at least something while browsing. Studies of library search show 50% of readers (or more) having difficulty locating items that meet their needs [5; 24; 58] during library search, whereas our study shows a success rate of around 87%. It is hard to untangle this from search success, of course, because the majority of information seekers seen at the shelves (80% in our study) have already conducted a search at some point. Even these readers, though, show success rates of 76% at the shelves—so having a single specific item in mind does not preclude success, even where that item is not available. It thus seems likely that most readers provided with enough interaction options and the guidance to locate a relevant pool of items will find something of value.

One reason for the high proportion of readers who search before entering the stacks (80% in our study) is that it is difficult to identify a relevant pool of options in a library without the use of search. If readers were presented with a way to access library books without search up front—such as structured subject hierarchies, for example—how many of them would take it?

We have seen in the past that even those readers who do search often select more books than they identify in search when presented with the cornucopia of riches offered at the library shelves [4; 17; 30; 55]. When we examine the preconditions for serendipity, such as openness to new ideas and a rich environment of triggers [31], it is hardly surprising that this is the case; the shelves (as noted by others [22]) provide an ideal serendipity engine. Our study, demonstrating significant physical movement and large numbers of books scanned shows that environment can—and should—be very rich indeed. This is in stark contrast to library search results, which show fifty or so at most, and (again, in contrast to our findings) require readers to move away from their options to assess individual items.

In sum, no matter how good search gets it simply will not be a complete answer to the question of how readers might locate books online. Our findings point to several possible improvements, such as allowing access to cover, blurb and full text and making it possible to evaluate individual books with other results still visible, but search alone cannot replace the experience of browsing the library shelves.

5.3 Comparing Existing Browsing Systems

It is clear that the novel browsing systems we described in Section 2.3 are meeting readers needs for browsing with variable degrees of success. Bookfish and Whichbook are based on the need to rearrange the shelves according to user interest so no-one has to cross the floor of a library. All the systems we mentioned offer readers the chance to view covers of books when they are assessing them, one [59] even offers readers the chance to browse based on cover features. That same system offers readers many points of access into the collection it presents; while their options are not searching, browsing and reading the signs readers have choices. The two library-based commercial systems (UTS' and Ex Libris') offer readers the opportunity to interleave search and browse without having to 'leave the stacks', but do require readers to begin information seeking by searching.

There are two areas where none of the novel browsing systems are supporting readers: visual placemarking as they browse, and zooming in and out rapidly over the collection. The ability to placemark was identified through a range of actions—flipping books along a shelf, running a finger along a shelf, and physically placing books in gaps on the shelves to hold places. Similarly a range of actions, such as scattershot browsing, turning in the stacks and stepping back away from the shelves demonstrate a need to zoom in and out. How best to facilitate these behaviours is a novel question for interaction design.

6. CONCLUSIONS AND FUTURE WORK

In this paper we have presented an observational study of natural browsing behaviour that generates a number of new findings. We have also translated these findings into design recommendations.

One of the most surprising findings in this paper is the volume of content readers scan when browsing—often many hundreds of books. While some of them do this systematically, the majority move in and out of close examination mode, turning around in the shelves to look behind them at distantly related books and moving more or less rapidly past sections of the shelves. How best to support this behaviour in an online environment—likely on a small screen remains a question for future work.

It is widely realized that browsing is important and much loved by readers, but is surprising how successful our participants were—87% of browsers left the shelves with one or more books. This is astonishing: other work in this area has shown a success rate of around 50% [17].

Many of the findings in this paper reinforce earlier work; it is not news, for example, that readers would like to interleave search and browse, nor are the elements of books used in decision making new findings. It is certainly not news that browsing is important at all. This study lends weight to all of those arguments, though, and further begs the question why these needs are not being met in online systems. What would actually meet these needs is outside the scope of this paper and therefore future work, but our understanding of the physical mechanics of browsing could—and should—support future system design in this area.

Our study reflects the hierarchical engagement model shown in [49] and supported in [19]. It further demonstrates that this model is iterative with readers examining shelves more and less closely, and moving over a range of books.

Finally, our study demonstrates a new interaction not noted in previous studies of browsing: physical placemarking by running fingers along the shelves, putting books in empty spaces and flipping books along shelves. This is clearly an important behavioural component of browsing, and not a single current system offers anything to support it.

While we have made some recommendations for system design in this paper, quite what a system that supports all these interactions might look like is unclear. Equally, while we have addressed the physical actions of readers in this study, we have not considered their underlying intentions and mental models. System design and understanding the cognitive underpinnings of the actions we have identified remain future work.

7. ACKNOWLEDEGMENTS

The authors thank Ben Conyers (SLV) and Kim Tairi (Swinburne) for facilitating data gathering. Thanks to George Buchanan for assistance with data analysis. Further thanks to SIGIR's travel grants program for travel support to the conference.

8. REFERENCES

[1] Adams, A., Lunt, P., and Cairns, P., 2008. A Qualitative Approach to HCI Research. In *Research Methods for Human Computer Interaction*, P. Cairns and A.L. Cox Eds. Cambridge University Press, Cambridge, UK, 138-157.

[2] Bates, M.J., 2007. What is browsing--really? A model drawing from behavioural science research. *Inform Res 12*.

[3] Berg, S.A., Hoffmann, K., and Dawson, D., 2010. Not on the Same Page: Undergraduates' Information Retrieval in Electronic and Print Books. *J Acad Libr 36*, 6, 518-525. DOI= http://doi.org/10.1016/j.acalib.2010.08.008.

[4] Blandford, A., Rimmer, J., and Warwick, C., 2006. Experiences of the Library in the Digital Age. In *Proc CCCDT 06* (Tavros, Greece), FOHW.

[5] Borgman, C.L., 1996. Why are online catalogs *still* hard to use? *JASIS 47*, 7, 493-503. DOI= http://doi.org/10.1002/(SICI)1097-4571(199607)47:7<493::AID-ASI3>3.0.CO;2-P.

[6] Borgman, C.L., Hirsh, S.G., Walter, V.A., and Gallagher, A.L., 1995. Children's searching behavior on browsing and keyword online catalogs: The Science Library Catalog project. *JASIS 46*, 9, 663-684. DOI= http://doi.org/10.1002/(sici)1097-4571(199510)46:9<663::aid-asi4>3.0.co;2-2.

[7] Bowker, G.C. and Star, S.L., 2000. *Sorting things out: classification and its consequences*. MIT Press, Boston, MA.

[8] Buchanan, G. and Mckay, D., 2011. In the Bookshop: Examining Popular Search Strategies. In *Proc JCDL 11* (Ottawa, Canada), ACM, 269-278. DOI= http://doi.org/10.1145/1998076.1998127.

[9] Cooksey, E.B., 2004. Too Important to Be Left to Chance—Serendipity and the Digital Library. *Sci & Tech Lib 25*, 1-2, 23-32. DOI= http://doi.org/10.1300/J122v25n01_03.

[10] Crabtree, A., Twidale, M.B., O'brien, J., and Nichols, D.M., 1997. Talking in the Library: Implications for the Design of Digital Libraries. In *Proc DL97* (Philadelphia, PA), ACM, 221-228. DOI= http://doi.org/10.1145/263690.263824.

[11] Cummings, I., 2011. Kansas libraries lead way in e-book access. In *Kansan.com* http://www.kansan.com/news/2011/nov/01/kansas-libraries-lead-way-e-book-access/?news

[12] Cunningham, S.J., 2011. How children find books for leisure reading: implications for the digital library. In *Proc JCDL 11* (Ottawa, Canada), ACM, 431-432. DOI= http://doi.org/10.1145/1998076.1998170.

[13] Fast, K.V. and Campbell, D.G., 2004. "I still like Google" University student perceptions of searching OPACs and the web. *ASIST Proceedings 41*, 1, 138-146.

[14] Foster, A. and Ford, N., 2003. Serendipity and information seeking: An empirical study. *J Doc 59*, 3, 321-340. DOI= http://doi.org/10.1108/00220410310472518.

[15] Gorman, M., 1981. The Longer the Number the Smaller the Spine. *Amer Libr 12*, 8, 498.

[16] Hamblen, 2011. Amazon: E-books now outsell print books. In *Computerworld*. http://www.computerworld.com/s/article/9216869/Amazon_E_books_now_outsell_print_books

[17] Hancock-Beaulieu, M., 1993. Evaluating the impact of an online library catalogue on subject searching at the catalogue and at the shelves. *J Doc 46*, 4, 318-338. DOI= http://doi.org/10.1108/eb026863.

[18] Hardy, G. and Davies, T., 2007. Letting the patrons choose: using EBL as a method for unmediated acquisition of ebook materials. In *Proc InfoOnline* (Sydney, Australia), ALIA.

[19] Hinze, A., Mckay, D., Vanderschantz, N., Timpany, C., and Cunningham, S.J., 2012. Book selection behavior in the physical library: implications for ebook collections. In *Proc JCDL '12* (Washington, DC), ACM, 305-314. DOI= http://doi.org/10.1145/2232817.2232874.

[20] Jervis, M. and Masoodian, M., 2013. Visualization of physical library shelves to facilitate collection management and retrieval. In *Proc EICS 13* (London, UK), ACM, 133-138. DOI= http://doi.org/10.1145/2480296.2480321.

[21] Khoo, M. and Hall, C., 2012. What would 'Google' Do? Users' Mental Models of a Digital Library Search Engine. In *Proc TPDL 12* (Paphos, Cyprus), Springer, 1-12. DOI= http://doi.org/10.1007/978-3-642-33290-6_1.

[22] Kleiner, E., Rädle, R., and Reiterer, H., 2013. Blended shelf: reality-based presentation and exploration of library collections. In *Proc CHI 13* (Paris, France), ACM, 577-582. DOI= http://doi.org/10.1145/2468356.2468458.

[23] Kuhlthau, C.C., 1991. Inside the Search Process: Information Seeking from the User's Perspective. *JASIST 42*, 5, 361-371. DOI= http://doi.org/10.1002/(SICI)1097-4571(199106)42:5<361::AID-ASI6>3.0.CO;2-#.

[24] Lau, E.P. and Goh, D.H.-L., 2006. In search of query patterns: A case study of a university OPAC. *Inform Process Manag 42*, 5, 1316-1329. DOI= http://doi.org/10.1016/j.ipm.2006.02.003.

[25] Loizides, F. and Buchanan, G., 2013. Towards a Framework for Human (Manual) Information Retrieval. In *Proc IRFC 13* (Limassol, Cyprus), Springer Berlin Heidelberg, 87-98. DOI= http://doi.org/10.1007/978-3-642-41057-4_10.

[26] Losee, R.M., 1993. The relative shelf location of circulated books: A study of classification, users, and browsing. *Libr Resour Tech Serv 37*, 2, 197-209.

[27] Lown, C., Sierra, T., and Boyer, J., 2012. How Users Search the Library from a Single Search Box. *Coll Res Libr* (Jan 9).

[28] Macfayden, H., 2011. The Reader's Devices: The affordances of ebook readers. *Dalhousie J Interdisc Manag 7*, 1. DOI= http://doi.org/10.1007/s00779-002-0211-x.

[29] Makri, S. and Blandford, A., 2012. Coming across information serendipitously: Part 1 – A process model. *J Doc 68*, 5, 685-704. DOI= http://doi.org/10.1108/00220411211256030.

[30] Makri, S., Blandford, A., Gow, J., Rimmer, J., Warwick, C., and Buchanan, G., 2007. A library or just another information resource? A case study of users' mental models of traditional and digital libraries. *JASIST 58*, 3, 433-445. DOI= http://doi.org/10.1002/asi.20510.

[31] Makri, S., Blandford, A., Woods, M., Sharples, S., and Maxwell, D., 2014. "Making my own luck": Serendipity strategies and how to support them in digital information environments. *JASIST 65*, 11, 2179-2194. DOI= http://doi.org/10.1002/asi.23200.

[32] Malama, C., Landoni, M., and Wilson, R., 2004. Fiction Electronic Books: A Usability Study. In *Proc ECDL 04* (Bath, UK), Springer, 69-79. DOI= http://doi.org/10.1007/978-3-540-30230-8_7.

[33] Marchionini, G., 1997. *Information Seeking in Electronic Environments*. Cambridge University Press, Cambridge, UK.

[34] Marshall, C.C., 2010. *Reading and Writing the Electronic Book*. Morgan & Claypool, Chapel Hill, NC.

[35] Mckay, D., Buchanan, G., and Chang, S., 2015. Tyranny of Distance: Understanding Academic Library Browsing by Refining the Neighbour Effect. In *Proc TPDL 15* (Poznan, Poland), Springer, 280-294. DOI= http://doi.org/10.1007/978-3-319-24592-8_21.

[36] Mckay, D., Buchanan, G., Vanderschantz, N., Timpany, C., Cunningham, S.J., and Hinze, A., 2012. Judging a book by its cover: interface elements that affect reader selection of ebooks. In *Proc OzCHI 12* (Melbourne, Australia), ACM, 381-390. DOI= http://doi.org/10.1145/2414536.2414597.

[37] Mckay, D. and Conyers, B., 2010. Where the streets have no name: how library users get lost in the stacks. In *Proc CHINZ 10* (Auckland, New Zealand), ACM, 77-80. DOI= http://doi.org/10.1145/1832838.1832852.

[38] Mckay, D. and Cunningham, S.J., 2003. Browsing a Digital Library: A New Approach for the New Zealand Digital Library. In *Proc ICADL 03* (Kuala Lumpur), Springer, 329-339. DOI= http://doi.org/10.1007/978-3-540-24594-0_34.

[39] Mckay, D., Smith, W., and Chang, S., 2014. Lend me some sugar: Borrowing rates of neighbouring books as evidence for browsing. In *Proc DL 2014* (London, UK), 145-154. DOI= http://doi.org/10.1109/JCDL.2014.6970161.

[40] Mckay, D., Smith, W., and Chang, S., 2015. Down the Superhighway in a Single Tome: Examining the Impact of Book Format on Borrowing Interactions. In *Proc OZCHI 16* (Melbourne, Australia), ACM, 517-525. DOI= http://doi.org/10.1145/2838739.2838766.

[41] Mckenzie, P.J., 2003. A model of information practices in accounts of everyday-life information seeking. *J Doc 59*, 1, 19-40. DOI= http://doi.org/10.1108/00220410310457993.

[42] Megarrity, L., 2010. Books Matter: The Place of Traditional Books in Tomorrow's Library. *ALJ 59*, 1/2, 6-11.

[43] Moore, P., 1995. Information Problem Solving: A Wider View of Library Skills. *Contemp Educ Psych 20*, 1, 1-31. DOI= http://doi.org/10.1006/ceps.1995.1001.

[44] Neuman, W.L., 2006. *Social research methods: Qualitative and quantitative approaches*. Pearson, New York.

[45] Nicholas, D., Rowlands, I., and Jamali, H.R., 2010. E-textbook use, information seeking behaviour and its impact: Case study business and management. *J Inf Sci 36*, 2, 263-280. DOI= http://doi.org/10.1177/0165551510363660.

[46] Nordlie, R., 1999. "User Revealment"— A Comparison of Initial Queries and Ensuing Question Development in Online Searching and in Human Reference Interactions. In *Proc SIGIR '99* (Berkeley, CA), ACM, 11-18. DOI= http://doi.org/10.1145/312624.312618.

[47] Pearce, J. and Chang, S., 2014. Exploration without Keywords: The Bookfish Case. In *Proc OzCHI 2014* (Sydney, Australia), ACM, 76-79. DOI= http://doi.org/10.1145/2686612.2686639.

[48] Pearson, J., Buchanan, G., and Thimbleby, H., 2010. HCI design principles for ereaders. In *Proc Booksonline 10* (Toronto, Canada), ACM. DOI= http://doi.org/10.1145/1871854.1871860.

[49] Reutzel, D.R. and Gali, K., 1998. The Art of Children's Book Selection: A Labyrinth Unexplored. *Reading Psychology 19*, 1, 3-50. DOI= http://doi.org/10.1080/0270271980190101.

[50] Rowlands, I. and Nicholas, D., 2008. Understanding Information Behaviour: How Do Students and Faculty Find Books? *J Acad Libr 34*, 1, 3-15. DOI= http://doi.org/10.1016/j.acalib.2007.11.005.

[51] Rowlands, I., Nicholas, D., Jamali, H.R., and Huntington, P., 2007. What do faculty and students really think about e-books? *Aslib Proceedings 59*, 6, 489-511. DOI= http://doi.org/10.1108/00012530710839588.

[52] Saarinen, K. and Vakkari, P., 2013. A sign of a good book: readers' methods of accessing fiction in the public library. *J Doc. 69*, 5, 736-754. DOI= http://doi.org/10.1108/JD-04-2012-0041.

[53] Saarti, J., 1997. Feeding with the spoon, or the effects of shelf classification of fiction on the loaning of fiction. *Inform Serv Use 17*, 2/3, 159. DOI= http://doi.org/10.3233/ISU-1997-172-312.

[54] Sadeh, T., 2007. User Experience in the Library. *New Library World 109*, 1/2, 7-24.

[55] Stelmaszewska, H. and Blandford, A., 2004. From physical to digital: a case study of computer scientists' behaviour in physical libraries. *IJDL 4*, 2, 82-92. DOI= http://doi.org/10.1007/s00799-003-0072-6.

[56] Stieve, T. and Schoen, D., 2006. Undergraduate Students' Book Selection: A Study of Factors in the Decision-Making Process. *J Acad Libr 32*, 6, 599-608. DOI= http://doi.org/10.1016/j.acalib.2006.09.001.

[57] Svenonius, E., 2000. *The Intellectual Foundation of Information Organization*. MIT Press, Boston, MA.

[58] Swanson, T.A. and Green, J., 2011. Why We Are Not Google: Lessons from a Library Web site Usability Study. *J Acad Libr 37*, 3, 222-229.

[59] Thudt, A., Hinrichs, U., and Carpendale, S., 2012. The bohemian bookshelf: supporting serendipitous book discoveries through information visualization. In *Proc CHI 12* (Austin, TX), ACM, 1461-1470. DOI= http://doi.org/10.1145/2207676.2208607.

Visual Re-Ranking for Multi-Aspect Information Retrieval

Khalil Klouche[1,3], Tuukka Ruotsalo[2], Luana Micallef[2]
Salvatore Andolina[2], Giulio Jacucci[1,2]
[1]Helsinki Institute for Information Technology HIIT, Department of Computer Science,
University of Helsinki, PO Box 68, 00014 University of Helsinki, Finland
[2]Helsinki Institute for Information Technology HIIT, Aalto University,
PO Box 15600, 00076 Aalto, Finland
[3]Aalto University, School of Arts, Design and Architecture, Media Lab Helsinki,
Hämeentie 135 c, 00560 Helsinki, Finland
[1]first.last@helsinki.fi, [2]first.last@aalto.fi

ABSTRACT

We present visual re-ranking, an interactive visualization technique for multi-aspect information retrieval. In multi-aspect search, the information need of the user consists of more than one aspect or query simultaneously. While visualization and interactive search user interface techniques for improving user interpretation of search results have been proposed, the current research lacks understanding on how useful these are for the user: whether they lead to quantifiable benefits in perceiving the result space and allow faster, and more precise retrieval. Our technique visualizes relevance and document density on a two-dimensional map with respect to the query phrases. Pointing to a location on the map specifies a weight distribution of the relevance to each of the query phrases, according to which search results are re-ranked. User experiments compared our technique to a uni-dimensional search interface with typed query and ranked result list, in perception and retrieval tasks. Visual re-ranking yielded improved accuracy in perception, higher precision in retrieval and overall faster task execution. Our findings demonstrate the utility of visual re-ranking, and can help designing search user interfaces that support multi-aspect search.

Keywords

Information visualization; information retrieval; multi-aspect search; multi-dimensional ranking

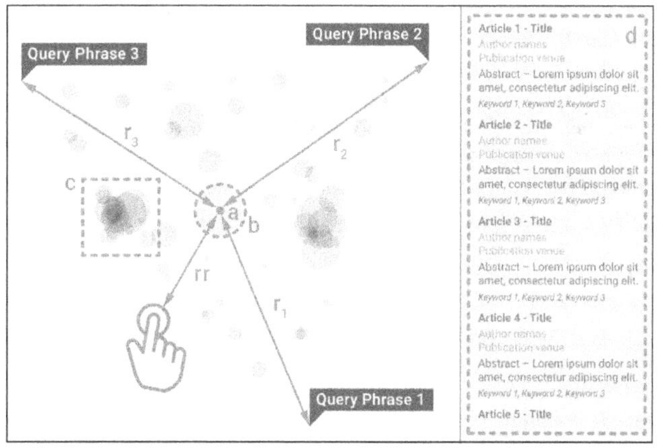

Figure 1: Interactive relevance map visualization. (a) Position of a document marker is computed as a weighted linear combination of relevance to individual query phrases $r1, r2, r3$. (b) Radius of a document marker encodes the overall relevance of the corresponding document to all query phrases. (c) Opacity encodes the density of document mass in a certain position of the 2D plane. (d) The result list can be re-ranked by relevance and the distance to the selected position rr.

1. INTRODUCTION

Multi-aspect search refers to activities in which the information need of the user consists of more than one aspect or query simultaneously. Such situation arises in contexts such as exploratory search, item selection and multi-criteria decision making. In exploratory search activities, the user's goal is not clearly defined, and the information space is usually unfamiliar to the user. In such scenarios, the user might start from a small set of notions, with the intent of learning and making sense of the related document space. In this case, conventional result lists offer little insight of the data and nothing indicates how the given results relate to the multiple aspects of the query. For example, a user looking for recent literature on physiological measurements might want to search for aspects such as 'Electroencephalography', 'Electrodermal Activity', 'Electromyography' and quickly be able to assess how the result space is distributed and how the retrieved documents relate to each aspect.

Item or product selection is currently widely supported by faceted search and search result clustering. Such systems are widespread in e-commerce and library catalogs. These techniques allow the user to investigate the results through the use of multiple filters, but they offer limited support for perceiving the result space and weighting the aspects accordingly. Conventional query-based search tools usually visualize results as a one-dimensional ranked list, and offer limited support for multi-aspect retrieval. Another example is multi-criteria decision making, a well researched process that often requires multi-aspect search [8]. Take the example of a user looking online for a new car. Usual faceted tools allow her to select filters to narrow down the offering: e.g., a manufacturer, a price range, a fuel type. Such criteria require the user to have

CHIIR '17, March 07-11, 2017, Oslo, Norway

 ISBN 978-1-4503-4677-1/17/03...$15.00

DOI: http://dx.doi.org/10.1145/3020165.3020174

a specific goal in mind, whereas a typical user would be inclined to come up with more vague criteria such as: *good gas-mileage* (no specific threshold in mind), *family-friendly*, and/or *fun to drive*. Such criteria are not binary, and the user can expect to find on the market several satisfying solution with different tradeoffs, instead of one ideal car. On the other hand, looking for such criteria using one single unified query on a conventional search engine returns a list of results that does not reflect the user's preferences and does not allow for conscious tradeoffs.

In all these cases, the user should be able to quickly assess distribution of the results with respect to how they relate to each researched aspect, and then be able to rapidly inspect them, which is possible if the user 1) perceives the distribution to understand which parts of the result space contain interesting information (i.e. what are the tradeoffs between the query phrases) and 2) is able to determine the tradeoff rapidly using the visualization.

We present a visual re-ranking technique that uses multi-dimensional ranking and two-dimensional interactive visualization. Inspired by earlier work on visual information retrieval and seeking [33, 2], the technique allows the user to perceive the relevance distribution with respect to multiple query phrases by using a *relevance map* visualization. A novel feature of this technique is that it allows the user to investigate specific areas on the map by re-ranking the results through pointing at the map. The method estimates document relevance with respect to user-specified query phrases in a multi-dimensional space in which the query phrases define the dimensionality. The method then computes a layout for the documents on a two-dimensional plane where relative distances of document markers to each query phrases are defined by their respective relevance, overall relevance of each document is visualized as the radius, and higher document density translates in darker areas. (see Figure 1). The visualization allows the user to perceive how the result space is populated with respect to both density and relevance to some query phrases.

Rather than relying only on a one-dimensional ranking algorithm to select the documents most relevant to a query, the role of the system is to organize and present information about many documents and multi-dimensional query phrases in a way that makes comparison possible. Re-ranking by pointing allows users to rank documents with respect to relative relevance weights to the query phrases. For example, expressing that a user wants the ranking to be based a little on both query phrases *interaction* and *interfaces*, but mainly on the phrase *design* can be done simply by pointing to an area on the map that is inside a triangle of the query phrases but closer to the concept *design*.

The approach was evaluated in a controlled laboratory study with 20 participants performing two tasks: perception and retrieval. In the perception task, participants were asked to find out how a document space was populated and organized with respect to specific topics, such as whether there was more research about *interaction* or *design*. In the retrieval task, the participants were asked to find documents with varying relevance to several topics, such as a document that was mainly related to design, but slightly related to interaction and interfaces.

Our results show significant improvement in task completion time as well as improved accuracy in perception, and improvement in task completion time in retrieval, without compromising effectiveness measured as the quality of the task outcome. These results suggest that relevance mapping and re-ranking is effective in cases when the initial one-dimensional result list is not enough for the user to analyze the information.

The contributions of this paper are: (1) We present a visual re-ranking approach to multi-aspect information retrieval in which users can perceive the result space and rapidly re-rank the result list by pointing to the visualization. (2) We demonstrate that users can complete perception and re-ranking tasks significantly faster without compromising the effectiveness. (3) While different approaches for search result visualization have been proposed in the past, up to our knowledge, this is the first study that empirically verifies the benefits of interactive visualization for multi-aspect information retrieval.

2. RELATED WORK

2.1 Visual Information Retrieval and Seeking

Information spaces can be huge and thus hard to comprehend. However, visualizing the space and allowing the user to directly interact with and manipulate objects in the space facilitates comprehension. For instance, when the results of actions are shown immediately and when typing is replaced with pointing or selecting, exploration and retention increase while errors decrease [46]. For information seeking, the following visualization and interaction features are of particular importance [43]: (a) dynamic querying for rapid browsing and filtering to view how results change; (b) a starfield display for the immediate, continuous, scalable display of result sets as different queries are processed; (c) tight coupling of queries to easily use the output of one query as input to another [1]. For instance, a user study indicates that dynamic querying significantly improves user response time and enthusiasm. Using such techniques, systems like FilmFinder [1] support querying over multiple varying attributes such as time, while showing the changing query results in the context of the overall data. User studies also indicate that user interfaces that show the result list together with an overview of the result categories encourage a deeper and more extensive exploration of the information space [25], especially when the system allows relevance feedback to be given on such categories to direct the exploration [40, 39].

2.2 Document Collection Visualization

Various visualizations have been proposed for large document collections [24]. Most of these techniques adopt the visual information seeking mantra [44] to provide an overview at first and details only on demand. The documents are often visualized on a 2D plane, in the form of a map based on a similarity metric. Higher-level entities, such as topics, are also displayed on the map for immediate and better understanding of the document space organization.

Document Atlas [12] uses Latent Semantic Indexing and multi-dimensional scaling (MDS) to extract semantic concepts from the text and position the documents with respect to the concepts. Document densities around concepts are visualized as a heat map. On mouse hover, common keywords in the area are listed, and on zoom in, more details are shown.

Self-Organizing Maps have also been used by systems like WEBSOM [20] and Lin's maps [26] to position the documents on the 2D plane. WEBSOM also suggests areas in the map that could be relevant to the user's search query. Lin's maps are further split up into regions whose area indicates the number of documents with specific related terms.

Other techniques visualize the documents as glyphs to indicate additional inter-document relationships and metadata on the map (e.g., [38, 29]). Various metaphors have also been adopted; examples include the terrain metaphor, in which dense regions in the map are seen as mountains with valleys in between [9, 49]; the galaxy metaphor, in which documents are seen as stars in different constellations (document clusters) [16]; and the physical metaphor, in which documents are considered to be moving particles and the inter-particle forces move similar documents closer to each other and dissimilar documents apart [10]. Visualizations with two dimensions and meaningful axes (e.g., categories vs. hierarchies [45], query results vs. query index [6, 23], production vs. popularity [1]) have also been proposed.

These visualizations provide an overview of the entire document collection, but they do not allow the user to direct and focus the exploration as required. A user-driven rather than a data-driven technique could be more helpful when searching for documents relevant to multiple keywords. To that end, such a technique should visualize the ranking of documents with respect to multiple keywords so the user can easily judge the relevance of documents to each of the keywords of interest [33]. However, most of the current techniques only visualize whether a document is relevant or not to a keyword using set visualizations [4], without showing the document's degree of relevance to each keyword.

2.3 Multi-Aspect Search

In multi-aspect search the information need of the user consists of more than one aspect or query simultaneously. As a consequence, an item in a collection needs to be ranked differently based on its multiple attributes. The Graphics, Ranking, and Interaction for Discovery (GRID) principles and the corresponding rank-by-feature framework state that interactive exploration of multi-dimensional data can be facilitated by first analyzing one- and two-dimensional distributions and then by exploring relationships between the dimensions, using multi-dimensional rankings to set hypotheses and statistics to confirm them [41]. However, comparing, analyzing and relating different ranks is difficult and requires an interactive visualization that supports the various requirements identified by Gratz et al. [13].

Multi aspect search support is provided in Song et al. [47], with the proposal of a strategy for multi-aspect oriented query summarization task. The approach is based on a composite query strategy, where a set of component queries are used as data sources for the original query. Similarly Kang et al. [19] propose a multi-aspect relevance formulation, but in the context of vertical search.

LineUp [13] is an interactive visualization that uses bar charts to support the ranking of objects with respect to multiple heterogeneous attributes. Stepping Stones [11] visualizes search results for a pair of queries, using a graph to show relationships between the two sets of results. Sparkler [14] allows to visually compare results sets for different queries on the same topic.Tilebars [15] visualizes the frequency of different words in various sections of documents as a heat map and ranks the documents accordingly. Similarly, HotMap uses a two-dimensional grid layout to augment a conventional list of search results with colors indicating how hot (relevant) specific search terms are with respect to the document [18]. Ranking cube [50] is a novel rank-aware cube structure that is capable of simultaneously handling ranked queries and multi-dimensional selections. RankExplorer [42] uses stack graphs for time-series data. Techniques for incomplete and partial data have also been proposed [22]. TreeJuxtaposer [31] was primarily devised to compare rankings.

For document collections, the vector space model could be used, such that each document and search query is a vector in a multi-dimensional space, each axis is a term, and the document position is determined by the frequencies of each term in that document (e.g., [36]). Visualizations of such a model could aid understanding of the document space, but more research is required, particularly for user-driven approaches that allow the user to specify the dimensions of interest [33].

2.4 User-driven Visualization

VIBE [33] is one of the most well-known user-driven multi-dimensional ranking visualization for large document collections. To indicate the subspace of interest, the user first enters two or more query terms, known as "points of interest" (POIs). POIs are then shown (as circles) on a 2D plane, together with documents (as rectangles) related to at least one POI, forming a map. The position of each rectangle indicates the relevance of the corresponding document to each of the POIs. The size of a rectangle indicates the relevance of that document to the search query. Citation details of documents selected from the map are listed; clicking on an item in the list opens the full document. Any time a POI is added, removed or moved, the map is updated accordingly. However, regions of the map with numerous close-by documents are not easily detectable because the rectangles are not color filled; using semi-transparent color filled shapes reduces overplotting [28] and facilitates perceptual ordering of different regions in the map by their density [27]. Also, documents are not re-ranked as the user navigates over the map.

Variants of VIBE include: WebVIBE [30], in which POIs act like magnets that attract documents containing related terms; VR-VIBE [7], which visualizes the space in 3D (for more space to view documents between POIs) and depicts relevance by color; and Adaptive VIBE [3], in which POIs are query terms (as in VIBE) but also user profile terms that are automatically extracted from user notes.

Similar to VIBE, GUIDO [32], DARE [53] and TOFIR [52] also allow users to specify POIs and display documents based on their relevance to the POIs. However, in GUIDO each POI is an axis (not an icon on a 2D plane) and documents are positioned based on their absolute rather than relative distances from the POIs. In DARE and TOFIR, relevance to POIs is indicated by both distance and angle.

Other user-driven systems, like combinFormation [21], TopicShop [5] and InfoCrystal [48], retrieve and display search results related to user-defined keywords but do not visualize the results' multi-dimensional ranks. Similarly, HotMap [18] supports a weighted re-ranking of the search results, but without leveraging a graphical interactive approach for specifying the weights. WordBars [17] also supports re-ranking of the search results, but uses additional terms extracted from the search results rather than relying on the query terms.

While similar techniques of mapping data to 2D visualization for better user interpretation have been proposed, the current research lacks understanding on (1) how useful these are for the user and (2) whether they lead to quantifiable benefits in specific tasks related to search activity. This work is the first to demonstrate a technique where the visualization can be effectively used for re-ranking search results. It is also the first that empirically verifies that users perceive the document space faster and are able to execute retrieval faster without compromising the quality of retrieved information.

3. RELEVANCE MAPPING

The method for relevance mapping is first illustrated with an overview from the user perspective. Then the computation of the layout and document visualization is explained.

3.1 Overview

Figure 2 shows an example of the relevance map visualization. Here, a user investigates a document space delimited by three query phrases with corresponding markers on the map: *design*, *interaction* and *interface*. A fourth query marker, *exploration*, is greyed out because it has been disabled to permit a temporary focus on the three remaining query markers. The user has positioned the

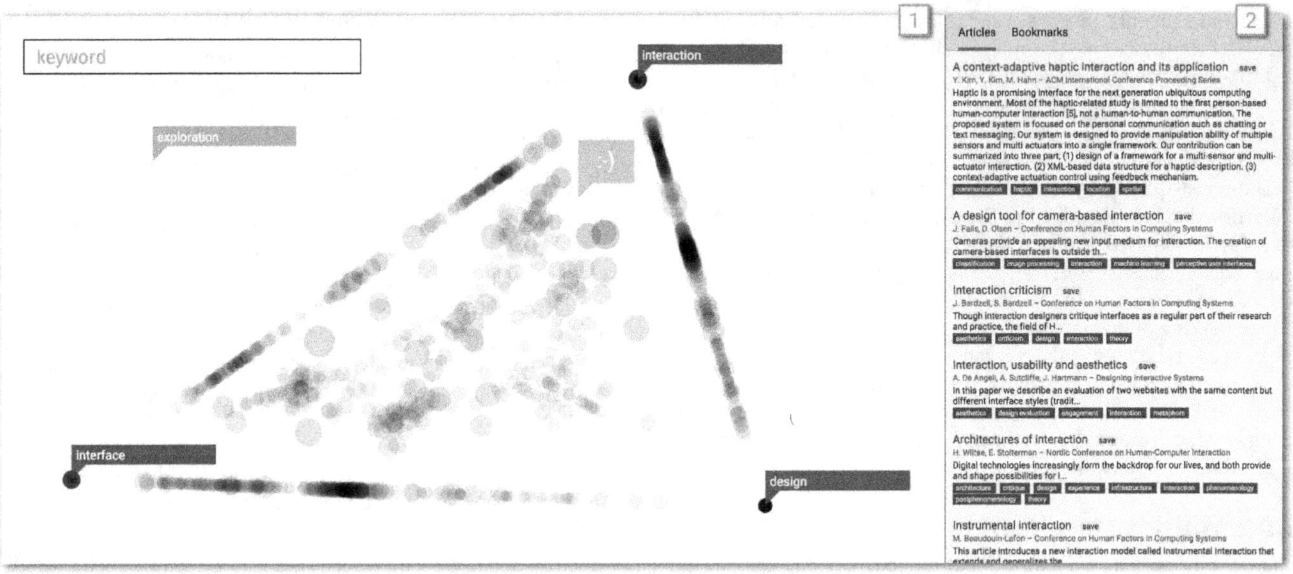

Figure 2: The relevance map (1) displays documents in relation to multiple query phrases, displayed as red text labels. Here, a fourth query phrase is greyed out (disabled). The exploration cursor (in blue) is located at the user-specified position to be used for the re-ranking. Red document markers indicate the position of articles currently on display in the result list (2).

pointer (blue flag with a smiley face) close to *interaction* to investigate a collection of documents highly related to *interaction* and more loosely related to *interface* and *design*. As a result, the list shows articles ranked with a specific focus on the selected area.

Query markers are created by inputting keywords in the query box in the top left. Each query marker can be activated or disabled by clicking it. Documents returned by the system are visualized on the map as semi-opaque dots scattered between the query markers with respect to their individual relevance. The overall relevance of a document is indicated by the radius of the dot. The partial opacity translates overlapping into a darkened tint that cues the user on the number of document markers in any given area. Query markers can be moved/dragged around on the map, which updates the position of the document markers. The position of the pointer can be positioned by dragging or tapping on the map. Any change in the pointer position or query marker organization triggers a re-ranking of documents based on their overall relevance and proximity to the pointer.

The ranked articles appear in a conventional one-dimensional list layout in the result list (2). Documents being displayed in the result list are shown as red dots on the map. The result list is scrollable. Each document is displayed with its title, authors, publication venue, abstract and keywords. Abstracts are first shown partially but can be displayed in full at a click or a tap. Keywords are interactive, as they can be added to the map as new query markers on a tap.

3.2 Layout

The data used to compute the relevance map layout consists of a set of m query phrases $q_{1...m} \in Q$, a set of k documents $d_{1...k} \in D$ and relevance estimates $r_{1...k} \in R$ for each of the k documents according to each of the m query phrases.

Each query marker and each document marker has a position on the plane, pos_{q_x}, pos_{q_y} and pos_{d_x}, pos_{d_y} respectively. The position of each query phrase marker is defined by the user by moving it to the desired position on the plane. The position of each of the document markers is computed as a weighted linear combination of the relevance scores to each query phrase and the relative position of the query marker. Intuitively, document markers are positioned proportional to their relevance to each of the query phrases. Formally, the position of an jth document marker on dimension dim is:

$$pos_{d_{j_{dim}}} = \frac{\sum_{i}^{|Q|} r_{q_i d_j} \cdot pos_{q_{dim}}}{|Q|} \quad (1)$$

so that $pos_{d_{i_{dim}}}$ is the coordinate of document d_i with respect to dimension dim. On a two-dimensional plane dim can be x or y. The relevance estimation $r_{q_i d_j}$ of a document to a query phrase is explained in the next section.

3.3 Document Marker Visualization

The radius of the document marker is directly the relevance $r_{q_i d_j}$. That is, the size of the dot is defined by the relevance.

The opacity of overlapping document markers is used to visualize the density of the document mass in a particular position on the plane. We use a standard computation of opacity [35] in which opacity of o of a pixel on the plane is computed as:

$$o = 1 - (1 - f)^n \quad (2)$$

where n is the number of overlapping layers and f is a constant setting of an opacity effect of an individual layer and was set to $f = 0.95$.

4. RELEVANCE ESTIMATION

The relevance estimation used in ranking and computing the document marker layout and size are explained in this section.

4.1 Relevance Estimation

Given the document collection and a set of query phrases that specify the multiple dimensions to be used in ranking and visualization, the relevance estimation method results in a set of probabilities $r_{1...k} \in R$ for each document d of k documents in the collection according to each query phrase $q_{1...m} \in Q$.

To estimate the probabilities from the query phrases Q and documents D, we utilize the language modeling approach of information retrieval [34]. We use a multinomial unigram language model. The vector Q of query phrases is treated as a sample of a desired document, and document d_j is ranked according to a query phrase q_i by the probability that q_i would be generated by the respective language model M_{d_j} for the document; with the maximum likelihood estimation we get

$$P(q|M_{d_j}) = \prod_{i=1}^{m} \hat{P}_{mle}(q_i|M_{d_j})^{w_i}, \quad (3)$$

where w_i is the weight of each of the query phrases and is set as $w_i = \frac{1}{|Q|}$ as default. In case of interactive re-ranking w_i is weighted based on user interactions as explained in the next section.

To estimate the relevance $r_{q_{i}d_j}$ of an individual document d_j with respect to an individual dimension defined by each query phrase q_i and avoid zero probabilities, we then compute a smoothed relevance estimate by using Bayesian Dirichlet smoothing for the language model so that

$$r_{q_{i}d_j} = P_{mle}(q_i|M_{d_j}) = \frac{c(q_i|d_j) + \mu p(q_i|C)}{\sum_k c(q|d_j) + \mu}, \quad (4)$$

where $c(d_i|d_j)$ is the count of a query phrase q_i in document d_j, $p(q_i|C)$ is the occurrence probability (proportion) of a query phrase q_i in the whole document collection, and the parameter μ is set to 2000 as suggested in the literature [51].

4.2 Ranking

Given the probability estimates for each of the documents, we apply a probability ranking principle [37] to rank the documents in descending order of their probabilities for the query phrases. These are then used to compute the total ordering of the document list. The top-k ranking computation remains efficient by making use of priority queue with complexity log(k) of k search results with presorted inverted index.

The user can interactively re-rank the result list by selecting a point on the relevance map. The point for the desired re-ranking is defined by its two-dimensional coordinates rr_x and rr_y with respect to the two-dimensional coordinates of the query markers $pos_{q_{ix}}$ and $pos_{q_{iy}}$ for the $i = 1 \ldots |Q|$ query phrases.

The re-rank weighting for an ith query marker is computed as the Euclidean distance between the $pos_{q_{ix}}$ and $pos_{q_{iy}}$ and the rr_x and rr_y. Formally,

$$w_i = \frac{\sqrt{(pos_{q_{ix}} - rr_x)^2 + (pos_{q_{ix}} - rr_y)^2}}{\sum_i^{|Q|} q_i}, \quad (5)$$

The re-ranking of the documents is then computed using these distances by Formula 3 by setting the weight w_i accordingly. Intuitively, the distance from the query marker is used as the importance of the query phrase in the ranking of the documents.

5. EXPERIMENTS

The current research lacks understanding on the end-user benefits of interactive visualization in multi-aspect search scenarios. The perceived simplicity and overall familiarity of well-studied conventional search system interfaces – like the current de-facto search interface with typed query and a ranked result list – have not been challenged in experiments that measure the quantifiable benefits of task completion time and effectiveness.

We conducted a controlled laboratory experiment in which the relevance mapping and re-ranking were compared to a conventional ranked list visualization in two basic tasks that searchers have to perform when using an information retrieval system: perception and retrieval.

The perception task sought understanding on the benefits of the visualization in perceiving the distribution and density of resulting documents with respect to the multi-aspect query phrases. The retrieval task sought understanding on the benefits of the visualization in re-ranking the results according to a user specified distribution over the importance of the different query phrases (see Figures 3*b*,3c_1, and 3c_2). The benefits were measured with respect to task completion time and effectiveness (quality of the perception or retrieval). The following subsections explain the details of the experiments.

5.1 Hypotheses

The study tested the following four hypotheses:

- *H*1: Efficient perception hypothesis: The relevance map allows faster perception of the result set.
- *H*2: Efficient retrieval hypothesis: The relevance map allows faster retrieval of relevant information.
- *H*3: Effective perception hypothesis: The relevance map allows more accurate perception of the result set.
- *H*4: Effective retrieval hypothesis: The relevance map allows retrieval of more highly relevant information.

5.2 Experimental Design

The experiment used a 2×2 within-subjects design with two search tasks and two systems. The conditions were counterbalanced by varying the order of the systems and tasks.

5.3 Baseline

A baseline system, shown in Figure 3*a*, was implemented to enable comparability and as to ensure that the evaluation revealed the effects solely on the features enabling relevance mapping and re-ranking. The baseline used the same data collection as well as the same document ranking model. All retrieved information in the baseline system was displayed with a ranked list layout. The baseline did not feature a relevance map, and the ranking was based on a single query at a time. The baseline was using the same hardware, i.e. a multi-touch-enabled desktop computer with a physical keyboard.

5.4 Tasks

The experiment consisted of two tasks, perception and retrieval, which are explained below and exemplified in Figures 3*b*,3c_1, and 3c_2. Both tasks used a common set of four topics, either (1) interaction, tabletop, tangible, and prototyping, or (2) surfaces, exploration, visualization, and sound. The two set of topics were formed by two researchers who were experts on human-computer interaction. The same researchers were then asked to assess the task outcomes of the participants.

5.4.1 *Perception Task*

The perception task aimed to measure task completion time and effectiveness, to help understand how a document space is populated and organized with respect to specific query topics. Participants were asked the two following questions: (1) "Out of the 4 topics provided, which 2 topics are related to the highest amount of

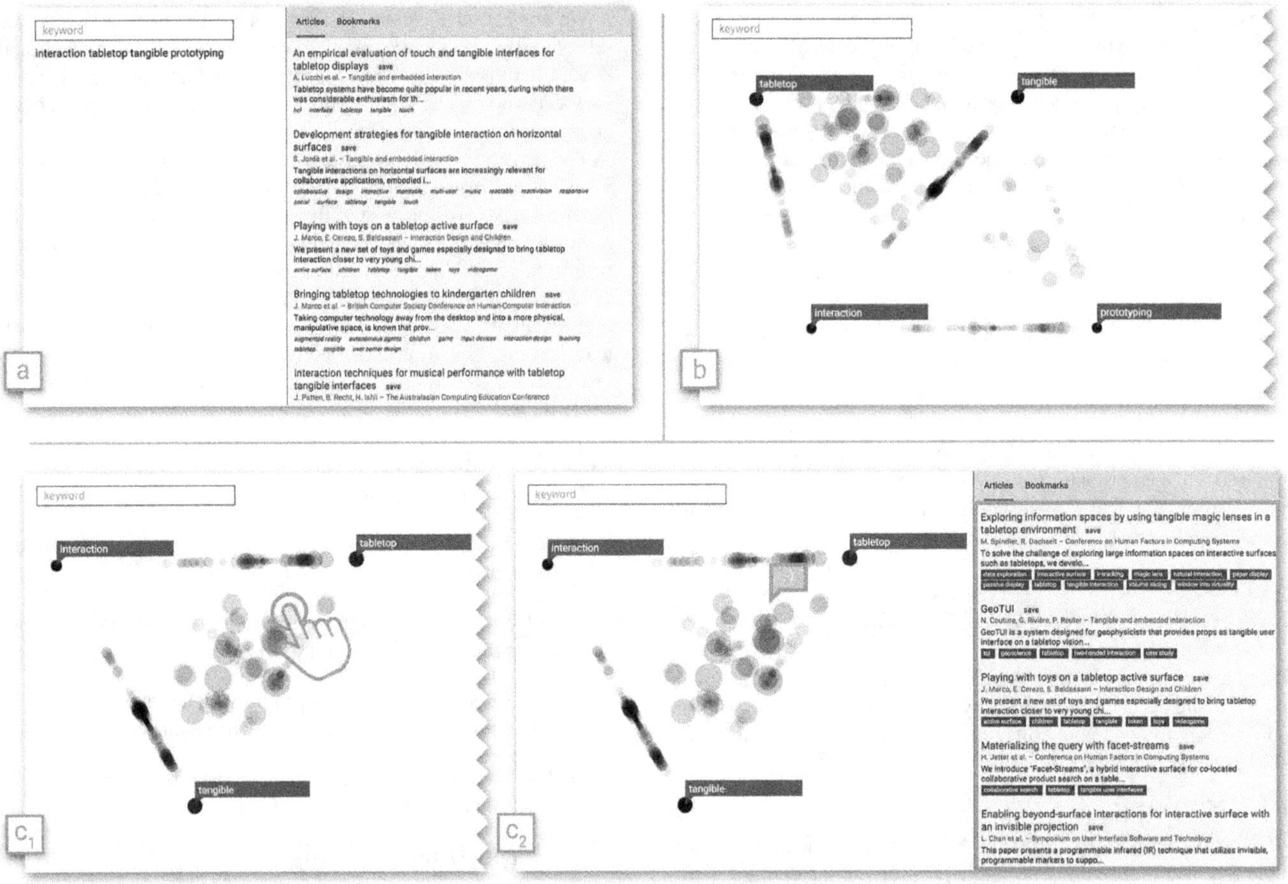

Figure 3: In the perception task, participants must identify the two and three keywords out of four that are the most related to relevant information. In the baseline (a), they must skim through the ranked list of results to infer the most prevalent keywords from the top articles. Using the relevance map, they must interpret the distribution of document markers. In the retrieval task, participants must find an article that shows a high relevance to one keyword (say, *tabletop*), and a lesser relevance with two other keywords (say, *tangible* and *interaction*). Using the baseline (a), they must query the three keywords, then find a fitting article in the result list. Using the relevance map, they point (by tapping on the touch-enabled monitor) at an area between the three keywords (c1), somewhere closer to *tabletop* than *tangible* or *interaction*, which triggers a re-ranking of retrieved articles based on the selected position (c2). The participant should be able to select one of the top articles as a fitting task outcome.

relevant documents?", and (2) "Out of the 4 topics provided, which 3 topics are related to the highest number of relevant documents?".

An example visualization from which the user had to select the topics is shown in Figure 3*b*. In that case, we can see that the space delimited by *tabletop*, *tangible*, and *interaction* is the most densely populated through sheer amount of document markers, making them part of the answer. To find the two keywords, they must then compare pair-wise document density by focusing on the edges between query phrase markers, with a slight but noticeable lead in density (encoded as darkness) between *tangible* and *interaction*.

5.4.2 Retrieval Task

The retrieval task aimed to measure task completion time and effectiveness in finding documents with varying multi-dimensional relevance toward several topics. Participants were given the following instruction: "Find one article that is highly relevant to 'Topic A' and slightly related to 'Topic B' and 'Topic C'.". The task was then repeated one more time with a different topic priority: "Find one paper that is highly relevant to 'Topic B' and slightly related to 'Topic A' and 'Topic C'."

An example sequence of a visualization, user pointing to the visualization to re-rank the document list from which the user had to select the documents is shown in Figures 3c_1 and 3c_2.

5.5 Measures

We used two performance measures: task completion time and effectiveness. *Task Completion Time* measured the time required to complete the task. *Effectiveness* measured the quality of the task outcome.

5.5.1 Task Completion Time

Task completion time was computed directly as the duration in seconds from the beginning of the task to the completion of the task.

5.5.2 Effectiveness

Effectiveness was computed differently for the two tasks and the corresponding ground truths for the task outcomes were defined differently.

In the perception task, effectiveness was measured as the accuracy of the participants answer. The ground truth was available from the relevance estimation and was computed as a sum of the relevance scores associated to each query phrase representing the topic. The topics were then ordered based on the sum of relevance scores and the top 2 and top 3 topics corresponding to the task description were selected as the ground truth to which each answer was then compared. Accuracy was computed for each answer, resulting in a grade of 1 for a match, 0 for a mismatch, and – in the case two topics selected out of four – 0.5 for a partial match. Each participant having returned two answers, effectiveness was then measured as the mean of both grades.

In the retrieval task, effectiveness was measured as precision on the documents selected by the participants. All documents chosen by any of the participants in any of the two system conditions were pooled. Two experts then assessed the actual relevance of each document to each topic. The experts being authors of the experiment design and having themselves devised the topics, potential bias in the assessment was addressed by following a strict double-blind procedure (i.e. experts had no knowledge of the participant, the system or concurrent assessment) and balancing the use of each set of topics across both conditions. The experts assigned for each document a grade between 0 (non-relevant) and 5 (highly relevant) to each of the topics, which were then averaged (mean) into a final grade. The topic defined as highly relevant was given a double coefficient so that the final grade reflected the weighted aspect of the task. The final grade indicated the expert opinion on how relevant the document was for the task. The inter-annotator agreement between the experts was measured by using Cohen's Kappa for two raters who provided three relevance assessments per document. Agreement was found to be substantial (Kappa = 0.684, Z = 7.04, $p < 0.001$), indicating that the expert assessments were consistent.

Additionally, we collected the position in the result list of each document returned by each participant, to better understand the reranking/scrolling tradeoff.

5.6 Data logging and data collection

For the purpose of the task completion time measurement, we recorded (1) the task duration from the start button press to the end button press. For the purpose of the effectiveness measurement, we recorded (2) bookmarked documents. After completion of both tasks in both conditions, participants were given a questionnaire to collect data on their age, gender, academic background and research experience.

We used a document set including all articles available at the Digital Library of the Association of Computing Machinery (ACM) as of the end of 2011. The information about each document consists of its title, abstract, author names, publication year, and publication venue. Articles with missing information in the metadata were excluded during the indexing phase, resulting in a database with over 320,000 documents. Both the baseline and the proposed system used the same document set and the users were presented with the top 2000 documents.

5.7 Participants

Twenty researchers in computer science (40% females) from two universities, ranging in age from 21 to 36 years old and from 1 to 8 years in research experience, volunteered to participate in the experiment. The participants were all compensated with a movie voucher that they received at the end of the experiment. All participants were assigned the same experimental tasks on both systems with systematic varying order between the systems. In this experiment, informed consent was obtained from all participants.

5.8 Apparatus

Participants performed the experiment on a desktop computer with a 27" multi-touch-enabled capacitive monitor (Dell XPS27). The computer was running Microsoft Windows 8 and both systems – being Web based – were used on a Chrome Web browser version 45.0.2454.85 m. A physical keyboard was provided for text input, whereas pointing, dragging and scrolling were performed through touch interaction. The search engine implementing the relevance estimation method was running on a virtual server and the document index was implemented as an in-memory inverted index allowing very fast response times with an average latency of less than one second.

5.9 Procedure

The tasks were described on individual instruction sheets that incorporated one of the two sets of keywords, to which we will refer as the task versions. The duration of the tasks was not constrained. To avoid introduction of confounding variables, we counterbalanced the tasks by systematically changing the order of the systems, the order of the task versions, and which task version was allocated to each system.

Considering the novelty aspect of the visualization, a training version of the tasks was devised, allowing participants to use both system with comparable proficiency. Training tasks had to be done using each system, right before the main task, using a separate set of four keywords: *creativity*, *collaboration*, *children* and *robotics*. The training started with the participant receiving a tutorial on how to use the system, then, while performing the training task, she could ask questions about either the task or the system. As soon as the training task was completed and the participant had no more questions, the participants started the actual experiment.

Participants were asked to underline the chosen answers on the instruction sheet. In the retrieval task, we asked the participants to bookmark the chosen articles. A Start/Submit button was added to both systems in the upper right corner. To be able to use each system, participants had to tap Start when ready to perform each task and Submit when they had completed it.

6. RESULTS

The results of the experiment regarding performance are shown in Table 1 and illustrated in Figure 4 with respect to the selected measures: task completion time and effectiveness, and reported according to both tasks, perception and retrieval. The mean position of selected articles in the result list is also illustrated in Figure 4. The results are discussed in detail in the following sections.

6.1 Task Completion Time

Significant differences were found between the systems in both tasks, which are discussed as follows.

6.1.1 Perception Task

The results of the perception task show that participants spent substantially less time completing the perception task when using the relevance map than when using the baseline system. The mean task duration for the relevance map was 84.23 seconds, while the mean task duration for the baseline system was 177.72 seconds. The differences between the systems were found statistically significant (Wilcoxon pair-matching ranked-sign test: $Z = 3.27$; $p < 0.001$). In conclusion, the relevance map shows 111% improvement, and was therefore more efficient for the perception task, confirming $H1$.

	Task Completion Time					Effectiveness				
	Baseline (B)		Map (M)		B vs. M	Baseline (B)		Map (M)		B vs. M
	M	SD	M	SD	Wilcoxon Test	M	SD	M	SD	Wilcoxon Test
Perception	177.72	116.20	**84.23**	39.38	**p < 0.001**	0.75	0.23	**0.89**	0.17	**p = 0.013**
Retrieval	137.53	101.66	**80.93**	70.65	**p < 0.001**	0.70	0.13	0.71	0.12	p = 0.95

Table 1: Task completion time and effectiveness results for both tasks. Task completion time is reported as a duration of the task averaged over participants. Effectiveness in the perception task is reported by mean quality of topics averaged over participants, and effectiveness in the retrieval task by mean quality of documents averaged over participants. Results showing significant improvement over the baseline are shown in bold.

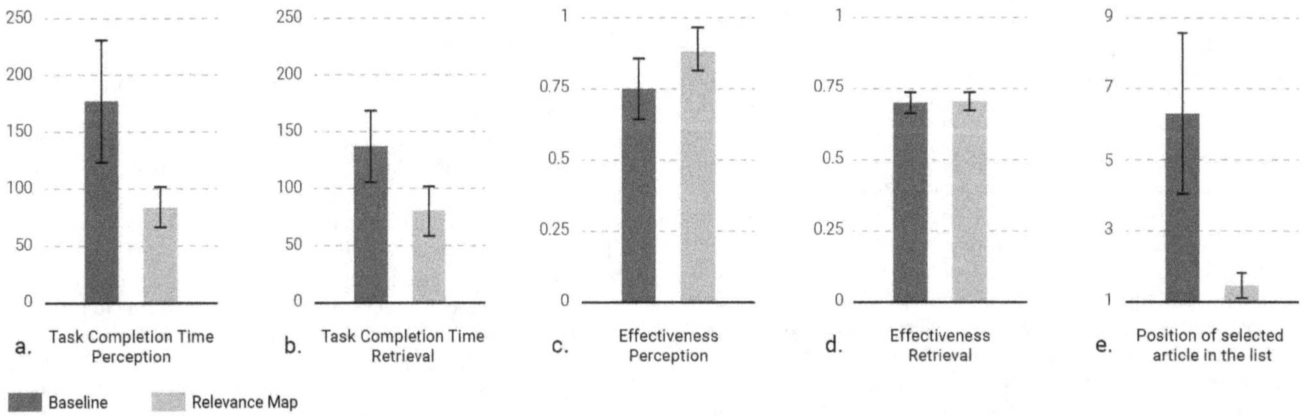

Figure 4: Results from the performance measures displayed for both systems with confidence intervals for: (a) task completion time in the perception task and (b) task completion time in the retrieval task with the mean duration (lower is better), (c) effectiveness in the perception task with the mean topic quality, and (d) effectiveness in the retrieval task with the mean document quality (higher is better). (e) Mean position in the result list of selected articles in the retrieval task.

6.1.2 Retrieval Task

In the retrieval task, participants spent substantially less time completing the task when using the relevance map than when using the baseline system. The mean task duration for the relevance map was 80.93 seconds, while the mean task duration for the baseline system was 137.53 seconds. The differences between the systems were found to be statistically significant (Wilcoxon pair-matching ranked-sign test: $Z = 3.87$; $p < 0.001$). In conclusion, relevance map shows 70% improvement and was therefore more efficient for the retrieval task, confirming *H*2.

Using the relevance map, participants selected articles close to the top in the result list, with a mean position of 1.48 (SD = 1.20), while the mean position of the selected article for the baseline system was 6.33 (SD = 7.20). The differences between the systems were found statistically significant (Wilcoxon pair-matching ranked-sign test: $Z = 4.77$; $p < 0.001$).

6.2 Effectiveness

6.2.1 Perception Task

In the perception task, the effectiveness as measured by the accuracy of the topics selected by the participants on the relevance map is 0.89, while accuracy on the baseline system is 0.75. The differences between the systems were found to be statistically significant (Wilcoxon pair-matching ranked-sign test: $Z = -2.46$; $p = 0.013$). In conclusion, relevance map was more effective for the perception task, confirming *H*3.

6.2.2 Retrieval Task

No statistically significant difference in the relevance of retrieved documents was found in the retrieval task (Wilcoxon pair-matching ranked-sign test: $Z = -0.07$ and $p = 0.95$). The fourth chart in figure 4 shows very similar results for both systems. This result fails to confirm *H*4, but it shows that the improvement in task completion time observed in the retrieval task did not impair the quality of the retrieved documents.

7. DISCUSSION

The results of the experiments show significant improvements in task completion time in both perception and retrieval, without compromising effectiveness. These results confirm hypotheses *H*1, *H*2 and *H*3.

In the perception task, participants were able to use the relevance map visualization to make decisions with greater accuracy, 111% faster. The visualization allowed the participants to understand more accurately the distribution of information with respects to the multiple aspects of the query.

In the retrieval task, documents fitting complex criteria were retrieved 70% faster using re-ranking through interaction with the relevance map. While finding documents with different relevance to several topics requires users to go through long lists of results and assess the relevance of individual documents, our proposed method for re-ranking through pointing at the map successfully narrows down the top results to documents that fit the criteria.

The quality of the task outcome was the same in both conditions in the retrieval task, which failed to confirm hypothesis *H*4. A possible reason for equal performance is the absence of strict time constraints for participants to complete the tasks. It is possible that a constrained time to complete the task would have negatively impacted the quality of the task outcome for the baseline, as the participants would not have been able to carefully examine the list to find a fitting article, but would have been forced to skim, resulting in possibly lower quality of selected topics and articles.

While our results show substantial improvements over the baseline, there is a tradeoff between the perceived simplicity of a result list and the added visual complexity of a relevance map. Interaction-wise, a result list is explored by scrolling, while a relevance map requires more complex behavior, justifying the use of a training session and tutorial. In the context of the present experiment, the necessity for a tutorial introduces a risk of influencing participants towards optimal behaviors that may outperform self-devised strategies. While our results suggest that the design of such visual interfaces can make both retrieval and perception faster, simpler interfaces may be more effective when the cost of interactions is higher, e.g. smaller devices and mobile scenarios.

We see further research directions to be addressed. First, different task complexity could be investigated and open-ended tasks explored, in which users would have more control over the search process. Second, more realistic search situations outside of our present laboratory experiment could be exploited to investigate interaction with relevance mapping and re-ranking functionality in situations in which users would have the possibility to try their own areas of interest and determine whether the suggestion effectively met their preferences and expectations.

8. CONCLUSION

Conventional systems for information retrieval are not designed to provide important insights of the data, such as relevance distribution of the results with respect to the user's query phrases. In this paper, we introduced visual re-ranking, an interactive visualization technique for multi-aspect information retrieval that helps overcome such limitations. The method proved successful in substantially improving performance over complex analytical tasks. Evaluation showed that users are able to make sense of the relevance map and take advantage of the re-ranking interaction to lower the time required to make analytic decisions or retrieve documents based on complex criteria. These results suggest that the conventional one-dimensional ranked list of results may not be enough for complex search-related tasks that go beyond simple fact finding.

9. ACKNOWLEDGMENTS

This research was partially funded by the European Commission through the FP7 Project MindSee 611570 and the Academy of Finland (Multivire, 255725, 278090 and 305739). The data used in the experiments is derived from the ACM Digital Library.

10. REFERENCES

[1] C. Ahlberg and B. Shneiderman. Visual information seeking: Tight coupling of dynamic query filters with starfield displays. In *Proc. CHI'94*, pages 313–317. ACM, 1994.

[2] C. Ahlberg, C. Williamson, and B. Shneiderman. Dynamic queries for information exploration: An implementation and evaluation. In *Proc. CHI'92*, pages 619–626. ACM, 1992.

[3] J.-W. Ahn and P. Brusilovsky. Adaptive visualization of search results: Bringing user models to visual analytics. *Information Visualization*, 8(3):167–179, 2009.

[4] B. Alsallakh, L. Micallef, W. Aigner, H. Hauser, S. Miksch, and P. Rodgers. Visualizing sets and set-typed data: State-of-the-art and future challenges. In *EuroVis– State of The Art Reports*, pages 1–21. Eurographics, 2014.

[5] B. Amento, W. Hill, L. Terveen, D. Hix, and P. Ju. An empirical evaluation of user interfaces for topic management of web sites. In *Proc. CHI'99*, pages 552–559. ACM, 1999.

[6] S. Andolina, K. Klouche, J. Peltonen, M. Hoque, T. Ruotsalo, D. Cabral, A. Klami, D. Głowacka, P. Floréen, and G. Jacucci. Intentstreams: smart parallel search streams for branching exploratory search. In *Proc. IUI'15*, pages 300–305. ACM, 2015.

[7] S. Benford, D. Snowdon, C. Greenhalgh, R. Ingram, I. Knox, and C. Brown. Vr-vibe: A virtual environment for co-operative information retrieval. In *Computer Graphics Forum*, volume 14, pages 349–360. Wiley, 1995.

[8] P. P. Bonissone, R. Subbu, and J. Lizzi. Multicriteria decision making (MCDM): a framework for research and applications. *Computational Intelligence Magazine*, 4(3):48–61, 2009.

[9] K. W. Boyack, B. N. Wylie, and G. S. Davidson. Domain visualization using VxInsight® for science and technology management. *JASIST*, 53(9):764–774, 2002.

[10] M. Chalmers and P. Chitson. Bead: Explorations in information visualization. In *Proc. SIGIR'92*, pages 330–337. ACM, 1992.

[11] F. Das-Neves, E. A. Fox, and X. Yu. Connecting topics in document collections with stepping stones and pathways. In *Proc. CIKM'05*, pages 91–98. ACM, 2005.

[12] B. Fortuna, M. Grobelnik, and D. Mladenic. Visualization of text document corpus. *Informatica*, 29(4):497–502, 2005.

[13] S. Gratzl, A. Lex, N. Gehlenborg, H. Pfister, and M. Streit. Lineup: Visual analysis of multi-attribute rankings. *TVCG*, 19(12):2277–2286, Dec 2013.

[14] S. Havre, E. Hetzler, K. Perrine, E. Jurrus, and N. Miller. Interactive visualization of multiple query results. In *Information Visualization*, page 105. IEEE, 2001.

[15] M. A. Hearst. Tilebars: Visualization of term distribution information in full text information access. In *Proc. CHI'95*, pages 59–66. ACM, 1995.

[16] E. Hetzler and A. Turner. Analysis experiences using information visualization. *IEEE CG&A*, 24(5):22–26, 2004.

[17] O. Hoeber and X. D. Yang. Interactive web information retrieval using wordbars. In *International Conference on Web Intelligence*, pages 875–882. IEEE, 2006.

[18] O. Hoeber and X. D. Yang. The visual exploration of web search results using hotmap. In *Proc. IV'06*, pages 157–165. IEEE Computer Society, 2006.

[19] C. Kang, X. Wang, Y. Chang, and B. Tseng. Learning to rank with multi-aspect relevance for vertical search. In *Proc. WSDM'12*, pages 453–462. ACM, 2012.

[20] S. Kaski, T. Honkela, K. Lagus, and T. Kohonen. WEBSOM–self-organizing maps of document collections. *Neurocomputing*, 21(1):101–117, 1998.

[21] A. Kerne, E. Koh, B. Dworaczyk, J. M. Mistrot, H. Choi, S. M. Smith, R. Graeber, D. Caruso, A. Webb, R. Hill, and J. Albea. combinformation: A mixed-initiative system for representing collections as compositions of image and text surrogates. In *Proc. JCDL'06*, pages 11–20. ACM, 2006.

[22] P. Kidwell, G. Lebanon, and W. S. Cleveland. Visualizing incomplete and partially ranked data. volume 14, pages 1356–1363. IEEE, 2008.

[23] K. Klouche, T. Ruotsalo, D. Cabral, S. Andolina, A. Bellucci, and G. Jacucci. Designing for exploratory search on touch devices. In *Proc. CHI'15*, pages 4189–4198. ACM, 2015.

[24] K. Kucher and A. Kerren. Text visualization techniques: Taxonomy, visual survey, and community insights. In *PacificVis'15*, pages 117–121. IEEE Computer Society, 2015.

[25] B. Kules and B. Shneiderman. Users can change their web search tactics: Design guidelines for categorized overviews. *IPM*, 44(2):463–484, 2008.

[26] X. Lin. Map displays for information retrieval. *JASIS*, 48(1):40–54, 1997.

[27] J. Mackinlay. Automating the design of graphical presentations of relational information. *TOG*, 5(2):110–141, 1986.

[28] J. Matejka, F. Anderson, and G. Fitzmaurice. Dynamic opacity optimization for scatter plots. In *Proc. CHI'15*, pages 2707–2710. ACM, 2015.

[29] N. E. Miller, P. C. Wong, M. Brewster, and H. Foote. Topic islands tm-a wavelet-based text visualization system. In *Proc. VIS*, pages 189–196. IEEE, 1998.

[30] E. Morse and M. Lewis. Why information retrieval visualizations sometimes fail. In *Proc. IEEE SMC'97*, volume 2, pages 1680–1685, Oct 1997.

[31] T. Munzner, F. Guimbretière, S. Tasiran, L. Zhang, and Y. Zhou. TreeJuxtaposer: scalable tree comparison using focus + context with guaranteed visibility. *TOG*, 22(3):453–462, 2003.

[32] A. Nuchprayoon and R. R. Korfhage. Guido, a visual tool for retrieving documents. In *Proc. VL/HCC'94*, pages 64–71. IEEE, 1994.

[33] K. A. Olsen, R. R. Korfhage, K. M. Sochats, M. B. Spring, and J. G. Williams. Visualization of a document collection: The VIBE system. *IPM*, 29(1):69–81, 1993.

[34] J. M. Ponte and W. B. Croft. A language modeling approach to information retrieval. In *Proc. SIGIR'98*, pages 275–281. ACM, 1998.

[35] T. Porter and T. Duff. Compositing digital images. In *Proc. SIGGRAPH'84*, pages 253–259. ACM, 1984.

[36] V. V. Raghavan and S. M. Wong. A critical analysis of vector space model for information retrieval. *JASIS*, 37(5):279–287, 1986.

[37] S. E. Robertson. Readings in information retrieval. chapter The Probability Ranking Principle in IR, pages 281–286. Morgan Kaufmann Publishers Inc., 1997.

[38] R. M. Rohrer, D. S. Ebert, and J. L. Sibert. The shape of Shakespeare: visualizing text using implicit surfaces. In *Proc. InfoVis*, pages 121–129. IEEE, 1998.

[39] T. Ruotsalo, G. Jacucci, P. Myllymäki, and S. Kaski. Interactive intent modeling: Information discovery beyond search. *Communications of the ACM*, 58(1):86–92, 2015.

[40] T. Ruotsalo, J. Peltonen, M. Eugster, D. Głowacka, K. Konyushkova, K. Athukorala, I. Kosunen, A. Reijonen, P. Myllymäki, G. Jacucci, et al. Directing exploratory search with interactive intent modeling. In *Proc. CIKM'13*, pages 1759–1764. ACM, 2013.

[41] J. Seo and B. Shneiderman. A rank-by-feature framework for interactive exploration of multidimensional data. *Information Visualization*, 4(2):96–113, 2005.

[42] C. Shi, W. Cui, S. Liu, P. Xu, W. Chen, and H. Qu. RankExplorer: Visualization of ranking changes in large time series data. *TVCG*, 18(12):2669–2678, 2012.

[43] B. Shneiderman. Dynamic queries for visual information seeking. *Software*, 11(6):70–77, Nov 1994.

[44] B. Shneiderman. The eyes have it: A task by data type taxonomy for information visualizations. In *Proc. VL/HCC'96*, pages 336–343. IEEE, 1996.

[45] B. Shneiderman, D. Feldman, A. Rose, and X. F. Grau. Visualizing digital library search results with categorical and hierarchical axes. In *Proc. DL'00*, pages 57–66. ACM, 2000.

[46] B. Shneiderman, C. Plaisant, M. Cohen, and S. Jacobs. *Designing the User Interface: Strategies for Effective Human-Computer Interaction*. Addison-Wesley Publishing Company, 5th edition, 2009.

[47] W. Song, Q. Yu, Z. Xu, T. Liu, S. Li, and J.-R. Wen. Multi-aspect query summarization by composite query. In *Proc. SIGIR'12*, pages 325–334. ACM, 2012.

[48] A. Spoerri. InfoCrystal: A visual tool for information retrieval & management. In *Proc. CIKM'93*, pages 11–20. ACM, 1993.

[49] J. Wise, J. J. Thomas, K. Pennock, D. Lantrip, M. Pottier, A. Schur, V. Crow, et al. Visualizing the non-visual: spatial analysis and interaction with information from text documents. In *Proc. Information Visualization*, pages 51–58. IEEE, 1995.

[50] D. Xin, J. Han, H. Cheng, and X. Li. Answering top-k queries with multi-dimensional selections: The ranking cube approach. In *Proc. VLDB'06*, pages 463–474. VLDB, 2006.

[51] C. Zhai and J. Lafferty. A study of smoothing methods for language models applied to information retrieval. *TOIS*, 22(2):179–214, 2004.

[52] J. Zhang. Tofir: A tool of facilitating information retrieval–introduce a visual retrieval model. *IPM*, 37(4):639–657, 2001.

[53] J. Zhang and R. R. Korfhage. Dare: Distance and angle retrieval environment: A tale of the two measures. *JASIS*, 50(9):779–787, 1999.

User Behaviour and Task Characteristics: A Field Study of Daily Information Behaviour

Jiyin He
Centrum Wiskunde & Informatica
Science Park 123
1098XG Amsterdam
j.he@cwi.nl

Emine Yilmaz
University College London
66-72 Gower Street
London WC1E 6EA
emine.yilmaz@ucl.ac.uk

ABSTRACT

Previous studies investigating task based search often take the form of lab studies or large scale log analysis. In lab studies, users typically perform a designed task under a controlled environment, which may not reflect their natural behaviour. While log analysis allows the observation of users' natural search behaviour, often strong assumptions need to be made in order to associate the unobserved underlying user tasks with log signals.

We describe a field study during which we log participants' daily search and browsing activities for 5 days, and users are asked to self-annotate their search logs with the tasks they conducted as well as to describe the task characteristics according to a conceptual task classification scheme. This provides us with a more realistic and comprehensive view on how user tasks are associated with logged interactions than seen in previous log- or lab-based studies; and allows us to explore the complex interactions between task characteristics and their presence in naturalistic tasks which has not been studied previously.

We find a higher number of queries, longer timespan, as well as more task switches than reported in previous log based studies; and 41% of our tasks are zero-query tasks implying that large amounts of user task activities remain unobserved when only focused on query logs. Further, tasks sharing similar descriptions can vary greatly in their characteristics, suggesting that when supporting users with their tasks, it is important to know not only the task they are engaged with but also the context of the user in the task.

Keywords

Task-based search, field study, search log analysis

1. INTRODUCTION

Users of search systems often have a specific task in mind, ranging from simple fact look-up to complex quests, e.g., organising a wedding. User interactions with systems during tasks are recorded in logs, however, logs do not typically capture information about which interactions belong to which tasks; nor the specific characteristics, e.g., difficulty, of a task. Therefore little is known about when users start, stop, switch, or resume tasks, and in order for systems to better support users' information seeking processes in a task-aware manner, it is necessary to understand the relation between task characteristics, how they affect users' behaviour, and how this is reflected in logs.

Tasks in search have received increasing attention as a factor affecting user search behavior and satisfaction [15]. Early work in task-based search has focused on conceptualising tasks in the context of information seeking [5, 6, 15, 29] and characterising tasks along several dimensions [22]. The resulting conceptual models and classifications of tasks have provided a theoretical framework for the discussion of tasks and task characteristics.

To study specific characteristics (aspects) of tasks, lab user studies observe user behaviour during artificial tasks in a controlled setting. Analyses of interaction logs combined with interviews, questionnaires, or think aloud observations have provided rich contextual information about the relation between users' behavior and specific task characteristics. However, findings are limited to the tasks designed by the experimenters and the time spent in the lab, which may not necessarily reflect users' natural behaviour. Alternatively, field studies observe user behavior when engaging with tasks in a naturalistic setting [17]. However, these studies often focus on a single type of task, e.g. a course project [4].

Finally, large scale log analysis allows observing and identifying activity patterns of users naturally engaging in tasks at scale. However, the actual tasks users engage in are unobserved and strong assumptions need to be made by the analyst to associate tasks and log signals. Further, current log-based studies are typically focused on the level of "search tasks", e.g., by defining user tasks as topically coherent query sequences [13, 16, 21, 24]; few studies go beyond search tasks to consider tasks at a level of information seeking tasks (e.g., [2]) or work tasks [5].

In this study, we combine the log analysis and field study approaches to gain insights in the relation between users' searching and browsing behaviour and their tasks in a naturalistic setting. With user consent, we install a browser plug-in on participants' computer and record their daily searching and browsing activities for 5 days. Each day users are asked to annotate their own logs with the tasks they engaged in. This results in a data set that provides a more accurate view on how user tasks are associated with interactions recorded in search logs than seen in previous studies. By further asking participants to characterise their tasks according to the conceptual classification scheme of task facets and attributes [22], we obtain a holistic view of the relation between user tasks and task characteristics that was previously not possible due to the limitations of both in-lab user studies and log analysis.

We relate and contrast our results to some of the assumptions and observations made in previous log based studies on short term tasks, seeking answers to the research question (Section 4):

CHIIR '17, March 07 - 11, 2017, Oslo, Norway

ISBN 978-1-4503-4677-1/17/03...$15.00

DOI: http://dx.doi.org/10.1145/3020165.3020188

RQ1 From a user annotated search log with records of rich types of interactions, do we observe similar statistics of task sessions as those observed from an expert annotated "query-only" log?

Further, by performing an exploratory analysis of the interactions between a wide range of task characteristics and their presence in users' naturalistic tasks, we discuss (in Section 5)

RQ2 How do task characteristics relate to each other? and how do these characteristics co-occur within actual Web user tasks?

Our contributions are as follows. In terms of methodology, we contribute an alternative approach to study the tasks underlying users' daily online activities, enabling insights that were not possible before. With this approach, (i) we add to the existing log-based studies with new insights obtained with logs that contain rich types of interactions and accurate task annotations; and (ii) we add to the existing results of in-lab/field studies by analysing a comprehensive set of task characteristics not limited to specific task designs and characteristics. Further, we discuss the implications of these results for future log based studies and in-lab experiment designs.

2. RELATED WORK

Recent studies on task-based information retrieval generally fall into three categories: lab user studies, large scale log analyses, and field studies. Below, we review and discuss findings from work within each category as well as how these relate to our work.

Lab studies. Lab user studies provide experimenters with control over the experimental setting and have often been employed to gain a better understanding of how different task characteristics affect users' information seeking behaviours. In these studies users typically perform tasks that are carefully designed by the experimenter so that the tasks carry the characteristics of interest. For example, Liu et al. [23] studied the associations between measures of user search behaviours with task characteristics along four dimensions: task complexity, product, goals, and levels. In a journalism scenario, four search tasks were designed to reflect varying conditions in these dimensions.

Task complexity is a frequently studied dimension. In a study of factual information finding tasks with varying complexity, Gwizdka and Spence [12] found that task difficulty is correlated with the number of unique pages visited, time spent on each page, deviation from the optimal path, and the linearity of the navigation path. Task complexity was found to affect the relative importance of these factors, and to affect user perceived task difficulty.

Based on education theory Kelly et al. [19] proposed a framework for the design of tasks with varying levels of cognitive complexity to support design and evaluation of IIR experiments. By examing behavioural and self-reported user data from a lab study, they found that cognitively more complex tasks require significantly more search activity from participants, but participants do not perceive cognitive complex tasks as more difficult, and were satisfied with their performance across tasks.

In a large scale user study of struggling behaviour during search, Aula et al. [1] found that users tend to formulate more diverse queries, use more advanced operators and spend longer time on the search result pages as compared to the successful tasks.

While carefully designed tasks performed in a lab setting allows testing specific hypotheses under controlled conditions, it also limits the generalizability of the findings towards users' search behaviour in a naturalistic setting. For example, it is difficult to observe interactions between tasks such as the multi-tasking behaviour of users, which are prevalent in online search [13, 20, 24, 28] or tasks that take longer than a typical lab study session. Moreover, while it is possible to control a particular aspect of the designed tasks, it is almost impossible to control multiple task characteristics simultaneously and design their ways of interactions that naturally occur in reality. In our study we monitor users remotely and we do not ask users to engage in specific tasks in order to observe users' natural search behavior.

Large scale log analysis. As an alternative to lab user studies, analyses of large scale search logs—typically containing user search queries and activities on the search result page—allow making observations of users' natural search behaviour.

One of the first challenges here is the identification of the user tasks from the search logs. Jones and Klinkner [16] argued that traditional time-out based search session segmentation is not sufficient as a criterion for identifying sessions of user tasks. Based on annotations from external assessors[1] classifiers were trained to identify task (mission) boundaries between consecutive query pairs.

A number of studies have focussed on improving the recall in task identification by tackling semantic relations between queries, task interleaving, and session boundary detection. Lucchese et al. [24] studied two unsupervised methods to identify task sessions from query logs: a time-based thresholding heuristic method, and a clustering based method. Similar to [24], Li et al. [21] proposed an algorithm that combines topic models with Hawkes processes to identify search tasks from query logs, based on the assumption that queries belonging to the same tasks are temporally close and topically coherent. Hagen et al. [13] proposed a 2-stage method that identifies search missions from query logs in 6 steps. Unlike [24] which focused on identifying task sessions, this study considers interleaved task sessions that belong to the same mission. To verify the algorithms, a sample of query logs from a commercial search system were annotated by external annotators [13, 24].

In a different setup, Kotov et al. [20] proposed a classification based method to (1) identify related queries from previous sessions for a given query, and (2) to predict whether a user will return to the same task in the future for a given multi-query task. User searching and browsing episodes were recorded with a browser plug-in. For ground-truth collection, automatic labelling of search tasks was followed by a manual correction process. In a related study, Awadallah et al. [2] proposed a method to mine search tasks from search logs. An association graph was constructed to connect multiple tasks and used to recommend a set of interesting and diverse tasks to support searchers during complex search tasks.

Although significant advances have been made in terms of task detection in logs, a limitation of this type of work is that external annotators need to create ground truth data to allow training and evaluation. Further, often strong assumptions are made in order to select a subset of data, e.g., sessions with a certain length [25] or users that visited a particular site [9], for annotators to process. However, Russell et al. [26] noted in a study where self-labelled task sessions were compared to labels provided by external annotators: *"the most accurate labelling of search task session data is done by the searchers themselves, and that it is very difficult for an external observer or automatic classifier to infer where the task boundaries are or what the actual user task goal is."*

Mechanical Turk has been proposed as a middle ground between log and lab studies [32]. However, existing crowdsourcing platforms do not overcome the limitations of experimenters designing tasks for workers and imposing time (or monetary) constraints on performing tasks, making such a set up unsuitable for our purposes.

[1]We refer to annotators or assessors other than the user him/herself as "external" annotators.

In our study we ask participants to annotate their own search logs in order to obtain both naturalistic observations of search behaviour as well as accurate task labels associated with the behaviour.

Field studies. In addition to lab studies and log analysis, field or longitudinal studies are another approach often employed in investigating user information seeking behaviour. These studies typically focus on a specific task in a particular setting. For instance, the change of user search terms and tactics during the writing of a research proposal [30], or users' use and preferences of different search interfaces [4] and query reformulation patterns [14] during a study course.

In a longitudinal study of users' online information seeking behaviour, Kelly and Belkin [18] found that document display times differ significantly according to specific tasks and specific users. A following up study concludes that tailoring display time thresholds based on task information improves implicit relevance feedback [31]. Greifeneder [11] studied effect of distraction on users' task completion behaviours in a naturalistic environment and made observations contradictory to previous findings from in-lab studies. In the mobile context, Church et al. [7] conducted a large scale study over a three month period, aimed at a comprehensive understanding of people's daily information needs, and how these needs are addressed and influenced by contextual, techonological, and demograhpical factors.

In a study closely related to ours [17], the Web usage activities of 21 participants were logged, and participants were asked to categorise their Web usage into 5 categories: fact finding, information gathering, browsing, and transactions. Analyses show that user behaviour differs between task types in terms of measures such as dwell time, number of pages viewed, and user browser activities.

We take a similar field study and diary based approach. The differences being: (1) instead of categorising tasks into 5 general types, we study task characteristics in greater detail by following the faceted task categorisation scheme introduced by Li and Belkin [22]; (2) while Kellar et al. [17] has focused on users' Web usage activities, we focus on users' search and browsing behaviour during information seeking tasks and relate our findings to some of the recent lab and log studies discussed above.

Theoretical perspectives. Apart from empirical studies, a large body of work in information studies addresses task-based information seeking from a theoretical perspective. These studies provide various alternative frameworks for the characterisation of different types of search and work tasks.

Different perspectives of tasks and consideration of different levels of task granularity have led to different definitions of tasks [5, 15, 29]. Byström and Hansen [5] suggest that tasks can be studied at three levels: work tasks, information seeking tasks, and information search tasks, with the latter being sub-tasks of the former. In the context of this study, the user tasks we investigate can be seen as somewhere in between the level of work tasks and information seeking tasks, which may be further divided into smaller information search tasks, e.g., through searching in different types of information, subject topics, and sources.

Other theoretical frameworks categorise tasks based on characteristics. Li and Belkin [22] reviewed and compared several task categorisation schemes, and proposed a faceted task classification framework, which applies to work tasks as well as search tasks. In this study, we follow this classification scheme for the purpose of characterising the user tasks identified from the user logs.

In addition, log-based studies often have their own working definitions regarding task and task search sessions, making a direct comparison of their observations difficult. We therefore conduct a conceptual comparison of these different concepts from three representative studies [13, 16, 24] (Section 4), based on which we discuss and contrast our observations to those reported previously.

3. USER STUDY

3.1 Study procedure

The study consisted of three stages as detailed below.

Introduction session (30 min). In this session, participants were invited to the lab brining in their own laptops. We explained the procedure of the study and installed the logger on the participant's laptop. The participant was asked to fill in a pre-questionnaire to collect demographic information. A training session was then provided to familiarise participants with the logging software and the annotation tool used to annotate their logs with task labels.

Diary study (5 days). After the introduction session, participants were told to go home and use their computers as usual. Meanwhile, the logger automatically recorded their online searching and browsing activities. By the end of each day, the participants were asked to review their logs in order to: (1) remove any log entries that they did not wish to share, and (2) to associate each search/browsing event with the task they were engaged in. Allowing participants to review the information that is being shared improves a bond of trust between experimenter and participant and improves the chances of participants completing the study [27]. Participants could review and annotate their logs at any time during the experiment period. Kellar et al. [17] found in their field study that there is equal user preference between real time and delayed annotation.

De-brief session (30 min). After 5 days, participants were invited back to the lab for a debrief session. In this session, participants were asked to select 5 to 10 tasks of their choice, and to describe the characteristics of these tasks by filling in a post questionnaire.

3.2 The logger

We log both search and browsing activities of the participants. To this end, we developed a Chrome extension that records events triggered by browser operations, and information attached to these events such as user input. Four types of events are recorded (see below), each associated with a timestamp, a URL, and a tab ID. Participants can submit a blacklist of URLs or URL prefixes to prevent events with matching URLs to be recorded.

Search events. In terms of search events, we recorded participants' activities with three major search engines: Google, Bing, and Yahoo. Related information includes: the query issued, the type of vertical (e.g. image, news, etc.), and the engine used. We consider the events triggered by issuing a query or switching between verticals as an individual "search event". Of course, users can perform search in other sites such as in an organisation's intranet or dedicated domain like Amazon. However, it is not always possible to recognise search events from each of those sites due to their diverse interface designs. Therefore, in this study we focused on Web search activities, with the belief that the majority happen with the three major Web search engines.

Link click events. We identify two types of link clicks: clicks on a result in a SERP, and clicks on a regular page leading to an external or internal target page. Information related to click events includes the clicked anchor text and the linked target page URL.

Tab events. We also record user operations on tabs, including: open-a-new-tab, close-a-tab, switch-to-a-tab, open-a-link-in-new-tab, as well as the tab-loading status. This information helps us to determine for example whether a user has "viewed" a page or the dwell time a user has been on a page. For instance sometimes users

Task characteristics	Description	Values
Frequency (FQ)	How frequent would you say the following task have occurred? (Not limited to the experiment period, think about e.g. in the last year).	(1) One-time task—Routine tasks (5)
Length (TL)	How quickly do you think the following task can be finished?	(1) Very quick (< 1 day)—long term ($\geq$ 1 month) (5)
Stage (STG)	To what extend did you manage to complete the task so far?	(1) Just started—(Almost) finished (5)
Cognitive level (CL)	Different tasks involve cognitive activities of different levels of complexity. At which level would you rate the activities involved to complete the following task?	(1) Remember; (2) Understand; (3) Apply; (4) Analyse; (5) Evaluate; (6) Create. (For each option, we provided explanations following [19]).
Collaboration (COL)	To what extend would you say you were responsible for the task?	(1) Solely responsible—Collaborates with many people (5)
Importance (IMP)	How would you rate the importance of the task?	(1) Unimportant—Extremely important (5)
Urgency (UR)	How would you rate the urgency of the task?	(1) Not urgent—Extremely urgent (5)
Difficulty (DIF)	How do you feel about the difficulty of the task? (e.g. difficult to find relevant information, or requires great effort in thinking/understanding).	(1) Easy—Extremely difficult (5)
Complexity (COM)	How do you feel about the complexity of the task? (e.g. it may involve many steps or subtasks in order to complete the task).	(1) Simple—Extremely complex (5)
Knowledge of topic (KT)	How would you rate your knowledge on the topic of the task?	(1) No knowledge—Highly knowledgeable (5)
Knowledge of procedure (KP)	How would you rate your knowledge on the procedure to complete the task?	(1) No knowledge—Highly knowledgeable (5)
Satisfaction (SAT)	Were you satisfied with the process of information seeking activities for completing the task?	(1) Unsatisfied, unable to find the information needed—Very satisfied, could find needed information easily (5)

Table 1: The characteristics of user tasks enquired in the post-questionnaire.

open links in new tabs, but stay on the original page and would not see the content of the linked page.

Navigation events. Navigation events contain information about how users arrive at a page, e.g. via link, via direct URL input, by form submission, or by forward/backward navigation. We keep this information to enrich the context of the rest of the logged events. For instance, it allows us to observe how much time the user has spent on a page based on the switches between different tabs.

3.3 Log review and task annotation

Annotation tool. To facilitate the diary study, we developed an online annotation tool. Figure 1 shows the annotation interface.

Participants review their log entries in the log review panel (1) and remove any items that they would not like to be recorded. In order to improve the readability of the log, only two types of events are shown to the participants: search queries and visited pages. Once a query or page visit is marked to be removed, related events with the same URL and tab ID are also removed from the log.

To annotate log entries with tasks, participants first need to enter a list of tasks in the task editing area (2), which works like a to-do list. The tasks entered by participants show up automatically as candidate labels under each log entry. Participants can then indicate the task that is associated with a given log entry by clicking the corresponding label. Participants can edit the task list before or during the annotation process.

To speed up the annotation process, participants can use the batch operation toolbar (3) to search and filter entries, and to batch remove and label selected entries. With batch operations it typically takes about 15 to 30 minutes for a participant to annotate a one-day log. Participants can review their annotation progress in the progress bar by selecting the corresponding date (4).

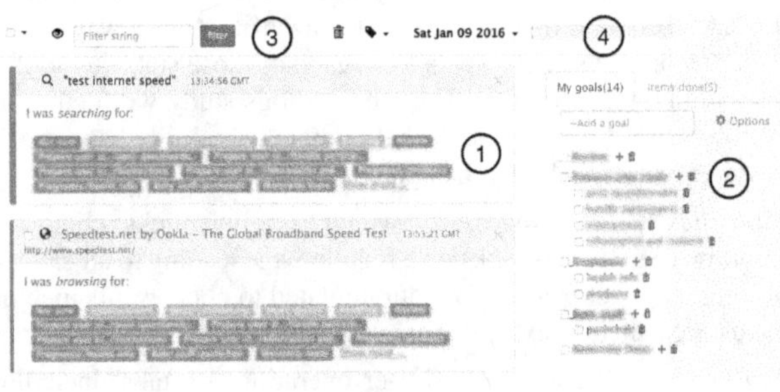

Figure 1: Annotation tool for diary study: (1) log review; (2) task list; (3) batch annotation tool bar; (4) progress bar. Items in task list and candidate task labels are blurred out for privacy reasons.

Annotation instructions. To encourage participants to think of the notion of "tasks" at a level comparable to that are typically considered in the literature, in the introduction session we asked the participants to think of 3 to 5 tasks they plan to conduct, or have been recently engaged with and will continue to conduct in the next few days; we further gave example tasks such as "planning a vacation", "write a report".

On the other hand, not all search/browsing activities can be categorised to a specific named task. Apart from participant specified tasks, we also provide pre-defined task labels for typical online activities not always considered as a work task or search task, including: Emailing (001), Social networking (002), Entertainment (003), and News update (004), as well as a "Not sure" label (000) in case participants do not remember what they were doing.

3.4 Task characteristics

Questionnaire. The classification scheme by Li and Belkin [22] provides us with a rather comprehensive list of both objective and subjective properties that can be used to characterise an information task. Following this scheme, we translated the identified facets and attributes of tasks into a post-questionnaire.

In order to reduce participants' effort both in understanding and in making answers, we made the following adaptations to this classification scheme: (1) We excluded attributes that can be derived from the log directly, e.g. whether a task contains multiple subtasks/goals. (2) After pilot testing we excluded questions that participants feel difficult to interpret and answer. In particular, we replaced the "product" facet and the "objective complexity" attribute from Li and Belkin [22]'s scheme by the 6-level cognitive task complexity framework proposed by Kelly et al. [19], as this framework provides clear instructions for participants to categorise the cognitive activities involved for a task. Also, the outcome of these cognitive activities resembles the task outcomes described by the "product" facet, but with more consistent categories. In total we derived 12 questions (see Table 1).

Participant instructions. Participants were asked to rate their answers or perceptions of these characteristics on a 1-5 point Likert style item (1 - 6 levels in the case of rating the cognitive complexity levels). In all cases, the ratings can be treated as ordinal variables.

To limit participants' effort, they are asked to select 5 - 10 tasks of their choice and only answer questions for these selected tasks.

According to Li and Belkin [22], the first 5 characteristics (FQ—COL) are objective, while the latter 7 (IMP—SAT) are subjective. In order to help participants to answer these objective questions in a comparable manner, we provided detailed definitions for the options (see Table 1), and provided further explanation when needed.

3.5 Data obtained

We recruited participants by distributing flyers on the university campus. Participants volunteered to take part in the study and were told that they are free to quit at any moment. Each participant was paid an Amazon voucher worth 20 pounds for participating.

A total of 23 participants completed the study, including 13 males and 10 females; and 11 are between 18 - 24 years old, and 12 are between 25 - 34 years old. Participants also self-rated their experience of using search engines on a 1-5 scale (median = 5, IQR = 1.0). In addition, as people often use multiple devices, it is likely that what we observe during the study is only a sample of users' actual information seeking activities if participants spend most of their time searching on other devices such as mobiles. Among the 23 participants, 18 (78 %) indicated that they always or mostly search with their laptop computer, while 5 (22 %) indicated that about half of their search happens with mobiles/tablets.

There are 289 user defined tasks, i.e., which excludes tasks that were annotated with general labels such as "emailing" as defined in Section 3.3. Among those 17 have subtasks. Further, 135 tasks were selected by participants to provide characteristics using the post-questionnaire. In total, 2566 queries and $32,902$ page visits were annotated, where 1768 queries and $17,313$ page visits were annotated with user defined tasks.

4. USER TASK ACTIVITIES IN LOGS

A key differences between our study and previous studies on search log analysis of user tasks is that, we analyse a log that contains rich types of user activities annotated by task doers, as compared to a *query-only* log annotated by experimenters. In this section we investigate whether, and if so how, tasks annotated by users themselves leads to new observations in the scope of tasks and observed statistics in log analysis (**Q1**).

We chose three studies for this investigation, namely Jones and Klinkner [16], Lucchese et al. [24], and Hagen et al. [13], for the following reasons. (i) All studies describe tasks in terms of search sessions, and reported a number of common measures to characterise user task behaviours. (ii) They all used human external assessors to annotate tasks in search logs—in particular, [16] attempted to recreate the user experience for the external annotators. Both factors make these studies more comparable among each other, as compared to, e.g. studies using alternative annotation methods.

We start with a conceptual exploration of the notion "task" as defined in these studies, followed by an empirical comparison of the observations made from these studies. On the one hand, this helps position our work in the literature and provides context for our findings, as in, to which extend our "tasks" correspond to the tasks discussed in previous studies. On the other hand, this provides implications for reading the conclusions drawn from previous studies as well as the hypotheses considered and assumptions made when training and validating various task identification algorithms.

4.1 Task & sessions: a conceptual exploration

Each of the studies defined a set of concepts to operationalize user tasks in terms of various types of search session. While these concepts share similarity across studies, different terminology has

Concepts	Physical session	Logical session	(Complex) task
Definition	All user queries or activities within a time window.	Consecutive queries belonging to the same task [13].	A set of related information needs span over one or more logical sessions.
Terminology			
Jones [16]	session	goal	mission
Lucchese [24]	time-gap session	task session	–
Hagen [13]	physical session	logical session	mission
Ours	physical session	logical/subtask	task

Table 2: A mapping between concepts as used in the literature.

been used. (Explained below.) In Table 2 we attempt to provide a loose mapping between the concepts defined in different studies.

Physical session. Physical sessions are typically defined by a timeout threshold on user inactivities. For instance [24] set a threshold of 26 minutes and [13] set a threshold of 90 minutes on time-gaps between queries, with the assumption that users are likely to switch tasks after a long pause. Like [13], we take a conservative threshold of 90 minutes as threshold to determine physical sessions, simply assuming that users have left the session (to do something else) after such a long inactivity.

Logical session. Although named differently, in all three studies, a logical session consists of queries related to a same information need. However, each study has a slightly different version of this concept. In [13] it consists of consecutive queries, and in [24] nonconsecutive queries, within a physical session. The related concept "goal" in [16], however, consists of queries that are neither consecutive nor within the same physical session. In our study, we refer "logical session" to consecutive queries related to the same task within a physical session (cf. [13]). The notion of "goal" in [16] is similar to our notion of "subtask". However, our "subtask" does not necessarily represent an *atomic* information need [16], as it can still be a complex information need. For example, one of our participants wrote "plan vacation trip Christmas" as the main task, and "find out how to go from Denmark to Norway" as one of the subtasks, which is a rather open question.

(Complex) task. This concept corresponds to the notion of "mission" in both [16] and [13], and we simply refer to it as "task". It does not correspond to a concept in [24], as the "task-session" defined in [24] does not go beyond a physical session. In practice, we see that while physical sessions do not always represent units of user tasks, both logical sessions and subtasks (or goals as defined in [16]) are units that constitute a complex task. While logical sessions can be directly observed from a user annotated log, in our study very few participants actually decided to detail the subtasks (only 17 out of 289 tasks have subtasks specified).

4.2 Task and sessions: empirical analysis

When analysing user task behaviour in search logs, all three studies reported the following measures: the number of queries issued and the timespan over task sessions, as well as the relation between physical sessions and user tasks. In this section, we report analyses over the same set of variables and seek to answer RQ1.

4.2.1 Task session statistics

We measure the number of queries issued and the timespan at two levels, namely the logical session level and the task level. We filter out logical sessions that have a duration of 0 seconds (e.g. the user closed a tab related to a task when working on another task) as in such cases the user was not really working on the related task. We compute a task session as the collection of all logical sessions with the label of that task. Table 3 lists the result of these measures, as compared to those reported in the previous studies.

Dataset	per Logical sessions		per Tasks	
	# queries	timespan	# queries	timespan
Jones [16]	–	–	2 (md)	38 secs (md)
Lucchese [24]	2.57 (m)	–	–	–
Hagen [13]	–	–	6.42(m)	–
Ours (all)	0 (md)	12.9 secs (md)	1 (md)	10.5 mins (md)
	0.28 (m)	112 secs (m)	6.79 (m)	44.8 mins (m)
Ours (queries)	1 (md)	19.3 secs (md)	4 (md)	15.7 mins (md)
	1.66 (m)	134 secs (m)	11.5 (m)	57.9 mins(m)

Table 3: A comparative view of user task behaviour at the level of logical sessions and tasks. (md) refers to median, and (m) refers to mean. Ours (queries) refers to statistics computed over our data excluding zero-query sessions/tasks.

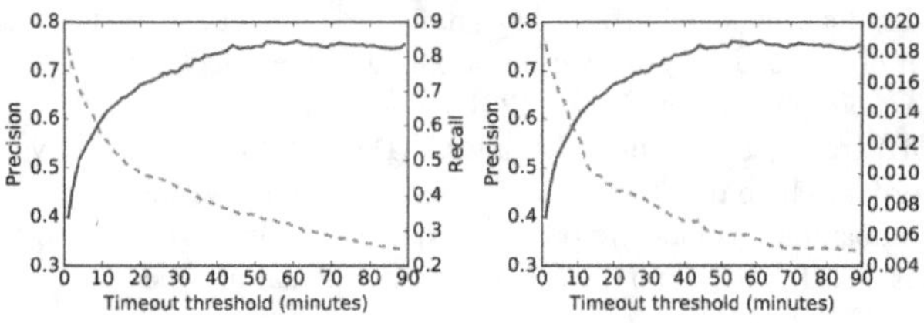

(a) Query based task boundaries (b) Event based task boundaries

Figure 2: Precision (blue solid line) and Recall (red dashed line) of time-out based task boundary identification.

Number of queries. One immediate observation from Table 3 is that our median number of queries per logical session is 0. Indeed, a further examination shows that 82% of the logical sessions, and 41% of the user tasks, do not contain query requests. Unlike our annotation which includes user activities other than query requests, analysis of the three previous studies are based on *query logs*, hence the effect of zero-query sessions would not have been observed.

Looking at logical sessions and tasks that do contain query requests, we see that in terms of logical sessions, the average number of queries (1.66) is lower than that of the task sessions reported in [24] (2.57). In terms of tasks, the median (4) and mean (11.5) number of queries per task are relatively high compared to those reported previously (median 2 [16] and mean 6.42 [13]). This implies that users may do more task switching than one would think, i.e. a task may contain many logical sessions (meaning tasks are being interrupted a lot) while each session contains few queries.

Timespan. We compute the timespan of a task as the sum of the duration of all logical sessions of this task. While there is no report on timespan of logical sessions for a direct comparison, we see that at task level, our observed task duration is much higher than what was reported previously (38 secs [16]). In fact, the task (mission) duration reported by Jones and Klinkner [16] is more comparable to the timespan of our logical sessions.

That our data show both more queries and longer timespan at the task level may be due to two reasons: (1) we have observations over a longer period (5 days), compared to 3 days reported in [16]; and (2) our data contains more than just querying activities, which contributes to the accumulated observed time spent on a task.

Task revisits. A common observation among the three studies is that, tasks (or goals and missions) are interleaved. Jones and Klinkner [16] reported 17% of the missions were revisited, and Hagen et al. [13] reported each task contains 2.09 logical sessions on average. In our data, we see that on average each task contains 23.9 logical sessions (median of 8.0), and among those 86% have more than one logical session (i.e. task was interrupted and revisited). Part of the difference in observation is due to the fact that our data contains task activities other than query events. If we only consider logical sessions with queries—as with a query log, we see that on average a task contains 6.9 logical sessions (median of 2.0), and about 68% of them were interrupted and revisited.

4.2.2 Physical sessions and task boundaries

When analysing physical sessions in relation to tasks, the main focus of the previous studies were whether a time-out threshold on gaps between user queries would signify switches of user tasks. Using the concepts discussed previously, it is equivalent to examine how well physical sessions (i.e. time-out based segmentation of logs) matches the logical sessions (i.e. task annotation based segmentation of logs). Although all studies have shown that applying a diverse set of features and learning algorithms can significantly improve the boundary detection accuracy, time-out remains an important feature, e.g. it alone achieves a F1-score of 0.65 [16].

Following [16], we create physical sessions by applying varying time-out thresholds on time gaps between *user queries*, and inspect the precision and recall of each threshold in correctly identifying task boundaries. In terms of ground truth of task boundaries, previous studies were all focused on logical sessions that purely consist of queries. However, we have already seen that users switch tasks in between queries. We therefore also compare the segmentation results to *event-based* logical sessions that include queries as well as other user activities.

To compute precision and recall, we need to determine when a task boundary is correctly identified. When comparing against a query-based ground truth, we consider a boundary between two consecutive queries correct if the two queries belong to two different tasks. However, when computing recall using the event-based ground truth, we do not require an exact match of task boundaries. For example in an event sequence $q_1, e_1, ...e_i, q_2$, it may happen that the time-out threshold identifies that q_1 and q_2 are task boundaries, while the actual task switch happens at event $e \in e_1, ..., e_i$. We consider the task boundary between two consecutive queries correct if the two queries indeed belong to two different tasks and there is no more than 1 task switch on the other events between the two queries. This way we avoid over-counting failures to detect task boundaries.

Figure Fig. 2a and Fig. 2b show the effectiveness of thresholds on time-out between queries, compared against query-based and event-based ground truth, respectively. In terms of precision (obviously, the two setups should have the same precision), we see that our data generally agrees with what was reported in [16]. That is, as the threshold varies, the maximum precision can be achieved is in the range of 70% to 80%; and above certain threshold values e.g. 30 mins, there is no obvious change. While Jones and Klinkner [16] did not report recall, we see from Fig. 2a that reasonable recall values can be achieved; further, at a threshold of 5 minutes a maximum F1 score can be achieved at 0.59 (cf.0.65 [16]). The optimal threshold, as we have seen, differs from study to study (e.g. 26 minutes by [24] and 13 minutes by [16]). This can be both a result of differences in the logs (e.g. differences in how people use a particular search engine), as well as an artefact of how these studies pre-process the log—for instance in [24] annotators discarded queries that they considered as meaningless. Nevertheless, across all these studies, including ours, the achievable accuracy of time-out based task boundary identification is in a similar range.

On the other hand, from Fig. 2b we see that when comparing the query-based physical sessions to the event-based ground truth, recall significantly drops to the range below 0.02. That is, there is a majority of task switches happening in between queries that are missed out if we only look at queries to identify task switches.

Having observed that many task switches happen with user ac-

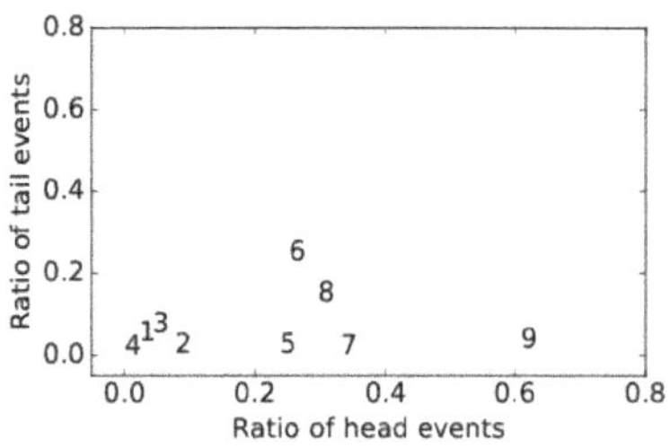

id	event type	% M
1	form submit	94.3
2	for/backward	91.9
3	link click	90.0
4	pagination	100
5	query	75.7
6	tab close	51.6
7	tab new	66.7
8	tab switch	57.3
9	go to url	37.3

Figure 3: Percentage of an event type being the head or tail of a logical session. Legend on the right side also lists the percentage of an event type being neither heads or tail (% M).

tivities other than querying, we further look into what other events may signify task switches. To this end, we compute the percentage that an event type is at the head (the first event), the tail (the last event), and in the middle of a logical session. Fig. 3 shows the result. Event types 1–4 allocated in the lower left corner of the plot are events that rarely occur as the boundary of a logical session (i.e. switch of task): >90% of the times they occur in the middle of a logical session. Indeed activities such as link clicks and paginations are most likely performed during a task. Event types 5–8 (issuing a query and various tab operations) are, however, more evenly distributed as being boundary- or non-boundary-events. In particular, events like issuing a new query (5) and opening a new tab (7) are more likely to signify a start of a new task than ending a task. In addition, when users directly go to a page by typing in the URL (9), it is quite likely to start a new task (about 60%).

5. TASK CHARACTERISTICS AND USER ACTIVITIES

While user activities can often be directly observed from logs, task characteristics are usually unavailable to search systems. Lab studies have therefore focussed on studying the relation between user activities and tasks designed to have specific characteristics. However, in labs studies typically a limited number of task characteristics is controlled for and a small set of tasks is employed. Therefore, we lack a holistic view of *how task characteristics relate to each other* and *how these characteristics co-occur within actual Web user tasks.* The naturalistic setup and the explicitly annotated task characteristics obtained in our study allow us to gain insights into the relations between task characteristics as well as to provide examples of tasks in which these characteristics naturally occur (**Q2**). We present our findings below.

5.1 Interactions between task characteristics

5.1.1 Clustered task characteristics

A correlation analysis provides insights in the degree of association between variables. Here we apply correlation analysis to the task characteristics of the 135 tasks that users annotated. We measure the correlation between two task characteristics using Kendall's τ.

Table 4 presents the correlations between the task characteristics. To facilitate the discussion, we cluster the characteristics. These clusters represent groups of task characteristics that often co-occur with a task. We employ Affinity Propagation [10] as the clustering method, given that it automatically searches for the appropriate number of clusters; and the absolute values of the correlation coefficients between two characteristics as the measure of similarity.

Table 5 shows the groups of task characteristics with strong mutual correlations. We observe that each group has a certain "theme".

Group	Member characteristics
1	CL, COM, DIF, TL, SAT
2	COL, KT, KP
3	IMP, STG, UG
4	FQ

Table 5: Clusters of task characteristics.

Group 1 consists of variables relating to task complexity (CL, COM), difficulty (DIF), expected length (TL), and user satisfaction (SAT). A set of variables that are often discussed together in studies (e.g., [19]). Group 2 concerns the knowledge of users (KT, KP), and collaborations on tasks (COL). Group 3 features the importance (IMP) and urgency (UR) aspects of the tasks, and their relation with task stages (STG). We discuss each group in more detail next.

G1: CL, COM, DIF, TL, SAT. Figure 4a shows the mutual correlation between the G1 variables. We observe that the level of cognitive complexity (CL), user perceived task complexity (COM), task difficulty (DIF), and expected task length (TL) have a significant positive correlation with each other. Further, user perceived satisfaction (SAT) has a significant negative correlation with the above four variables, indicating that the more difficult/complex/lengthy a task is, the less likely that the user is satisfied.

Interestingly, the observations here are somewhat contradictory to those reported by Kelly et al. [19], where users do not perceive a cognitively complex task more difficult or complex, and that users were equality happy with their performance across tasks of different CL levels. One possible explanation is that while tasks used in [19] were designed to control for levels of cognitive complexity, they were not necessarily controlled in terms of difficulty/complexity. Given the small sample of designed tasks it may not have been possible to detect variations across levels of difficulty.

G2: COL, KT, KP. We see (Figure 4b) that a user's knowledge of a task topic (KT) and task procedure (KP) has a significant positive correlation—which aligns with our intuition. Further, the level of task collaboration (COL) has a negative correlation with both KT and KP, i.e., the more collaboration is involved in a task, the less knowledge the user has about the topic or the procedure of the task.

G3: IMP, STG, UR. In Figure 4c we observe that user perceived task urgency (UR) has a significant positive correlation with user perceived task importance (IMP), as well as the task stage (STG). That is, the more important a task is, or the more advanced stage the task is at, the more urgent the user feels about the task.

5.1.2 Between group correlations

We now continue to examine the correlations between variables from different clusters, as illustrated in Figure 5.

G1 - G2. From Figure 5a we see that both user knowledge of task topic (KT) and procedure (KP) have a significant negative correlation with perceived task complexity (COM), difficulty (DIF), expected task length (TL), and level of cognitive complexity (CL); but a significant positive correlation with their task satisfaction (SAT). These correlations feel intuitively right: the more users knows about the task (KT, KP), the less they perceive the task as difficulty/complex, and the more they are likely to be satisfied with the task.

Further, there is a significant positive correlation between task collaboration (COL) and perceived task difficult (DIF), complexity (COM), and length (TL), i.e., the more collaboration is involved in a task, the more likely that the task is perceived as complex/difficult.

G1 - G3. Between G1 and G3 (shown in Figure 5b), we observe that task stage (STG) has a significant negative correlation with all

	CL	COL	COM	DIF	FQ	IMP	KP	KT	SAT	STG	TL	UR
CL	--	0.01	**0.43****	**0.49****	-0.07	**0.30****	**-0.21****	**-0.18****	**-0.26****	**-0.19****	**0.47****	0.10
COL	0.01	--	**0.23****	**0.14***	-0.08	**-0.13***	**-0.29****	**-0.12***	-0.07	**-0.14***	**0.20****	-0.10
COM	**0.43****	**0.23****	--	**0.69****	-0.07	**0.37****	**-0.35****	**-0.25****	**-0.34****	**-0.15***	**0.40****	**0.24****
DIF	**0.49****	**0.14***	**0.69****	--	-0.10	**0.28****	**-0.37****	**-0.24****	**-0.35****	**-0.19****	**0.46****	**0.14***
FQ	-0.07	-0.08	-0.07	-0.10	--	**0.12***	**0.19****	**0.24****	**0.18****	0.05	-0.05	0.01
IMP	**0.30****	**-0.13***	**0.37****	**0.28****	**0.12***	--	-0.08	0.03	0.00	0.04	0.11	**0.47****
KP	**-0.21****	**-0.29****	**-0.35****	**-0.37****	**0.19****	-0.08	--	**0.45****	**0.33****	**0.13***	**-0.23****	-0.09
KT	**-0.18****	**-0.12***	**-0.25****	**-0.24****	**0.24****	0.03	**0.45****	--	**0.34****	0.09	**-0.22****	-0.00
SAT	**-0.26****	-0.07	**-0.34****	**-0.35****	**0.18****	0.00	**0.33****	**0.34****	--	**0.21****	**-0.20****	0.06
STG	**-0.19****	**-0.14***	**-0.15***	**-0.19****	0.05	0.04	**0.13***	0.09	**0.21****	--	**-0.44****	**0.21****
TL	**0.47****	**0.20****	**0.40****	**0.46****	-0.05	0.11	**-0.23****	**-0.22****	**-0.20****	**-0.44****	--	-0.00
UR	0.10	-0.10	**0.24****	**0.14***	0.01	**0.47****	-0.09	-0.00	0.06	**0.21****	-0.00	--

Table 4: Correlation (Kendall's τ) between task characteristics. *: p-value < 0.05; **: p-value < 0.01.

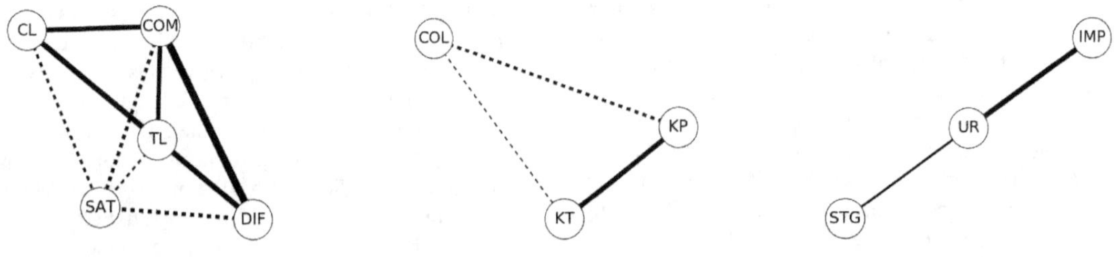

(a) G1: CL, COM, DIF, TL, SAT (b) G2: COL, KT, KP (c) G3: IMP, STG, UG

Figure 4: Illustration of the mutual correlation between the variables within a cluster. Solid edges indicate a significant positive correlation ($p < 0.05$); dashed edges indicate a significant negative correlation. The width of edges are proportional to the correlation coefficient τ.

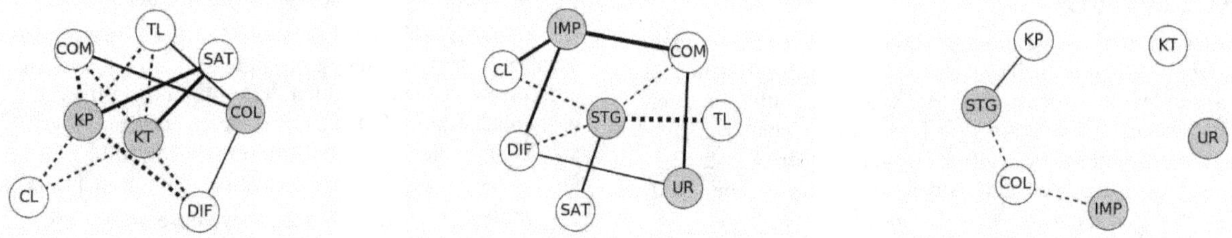

(a) G1 - G2; dark nodes are from Group 2 (b) G1 - G3; dark nodes are from Group 3 (c) G2 - G3: dark nodes are from Group 3

Figure 5: Illustration of the mutual correlation between the variables from two cluster. Solid edges indicate a significant positive correlation ($p < 0.05$); dashed edges indicate a significant negative correlation. The width of edges are proportional to the correlation coefficient τ.

the difficulty/complex variables (CL, COM, DIF, TL), but a significant positive correlation with task satisfaction (SAT). That is, the more advanced stage the user is at a task, the more likely he/she is satisfied with the task, and the less he/she find the task complex/difficult.

Both task urgency (UR) and importance (IMP) have a significant positive correlation with the perceived task complexity (COM) and difficulty (DIF). In addition, IMP is also positively correlated with the level of cognitive complexity (CL) which means that the higher the level of cognitive complexity of a task is, the more likely users perceive it as important.

G2 - G3. Figure 5c shows the correlation between variables from group 2 and 3. We see that task stage (STG) has a significant positive correlation with users' knowledge of task procedure (KP)—the more advanced the stage the user is at in a task, the more likely that the user has knowledge of the task procedure.

Task collaboration (COL) has a negative correlation with both task importance (IMP) and task stage (STG). While one can imagine that the more collaboration is involved, the less importance the individual user may feel towards the task, the correlation between STG and COL is rather surprising. It suggests that less collaboration is involved at advanced stages of a task.

G4 - G1, G2, G3. Finally, we also observe (Table 4, column 5) that there is a positive correlation between task frequency (FQ) from group 4, and task importance (IMP), users' knowledge (KT and KP), and task satisfaction (SAT). That is, frequently performed tasks tend to be important, and users are more likely to have more knowledge about the task and to be satisfied.

5.2 Task characteristics in naturalistic user tasks: a case with cognitive complexity

To study user behaviour in context of certain types of tasks, in lab studies users are typically given one or more tasks which are designed with the desired characteristics. However, the design process is far from trivial. For instance Kelly et al. [19] proposed a framework to design search tasks of different levels of cognitive complexity and reported observations of user behaviours and perceptions in relation to the resulting tasks. We add to this framework with concrete examples of tasks that, from a user's personal perception, fall into one of the six categories of cognitive complexity.

Task anonymisation and abstraction. Since many of the user tasks share the same topic, e.g. look for jobs, we aggregated these tasks into a single topic. To avoid over-interpreting users' intent and activities, we perform the abstraction only for obvious cases, e.g. when the topic or its synonyms were mentioned in the task description. We then show tasks within popular topics distributed over different cognitive complexity levels, and the typical topics at each level. We anonymised the task examples by masking the identifiable information in the task description with "X".

Discussion. We list the top 8 most frequent topics (shared by at least 5 tasks) and their cognitive complexity levels, and one example task for each topic and cognitive complexity level (Table 6).

We see that each of the popular task topics spans over multiple cognitive complexity levels. In particular, tasks related to travel planning and job hunting almost cover all levels. This suggests that when people describe their tasks, although sometimes it seems that they are doing the same thing, the actual intention and activities involved can be very different. Indeed, a close check on the logged queries of "travel planning/booking" tasks reveals that in some cases users explored different touristic options, and in other cases users were just checking some facts such as currency rates.

The diversity of cognitive levels within a task topic certainly contributes to the difficulty of categorisation of tasks by external annotators, cf. [26]. We also considered to abstract the tasks using a taxonomy of Web activities, e.g., the taxonomy defined by Russell et al. [26] or the approach by Dumais [8] which uses a verb and topic to describe a task. The main problem we encountered is that it is almost unavoidable that we need to guess the intent of the user with these taxonomies, as shown in the above "travel planning" example. In fact, this observation is also reflected in Dumais [8]'s taxonomy, where tasks such as "plan travel" are mapped to both "Explore/Learn" and "Locate/Acquire" categories of Russell et al. [26]'s taxonomy and to "informational" and "transactional" categories in Broder [3]'s taxonomy. In addition, users may have mixed activities of multiple categories. For example a user was writing a report, and her log shows that she was both searching information related to the research topic (*Explore/Learn* [26]), and looking up latex commands (*find-simple* [26]).

Further, we see that different cognitive complexity levels are not evenly distributed across task topics. This suggests that some task topics are more likely to involve certain levels of cognitive complexity than others. For example, tasks related to writing, doing projects, programming and research tend to involve higher levels of cognitive complexity—which makes sense. Meanwhile tasks such as travel planning and shopping can be both low (as a simple booking/purchasing action) and high (by comparing, evaluating, and analysing different options). Sometimes a task and the associated cognitive complexity are surprising. For example, one user annotated watching online videos as "analyse" for the task "binge watching"—it seems that he/she was carefully researching a number of TV series before deciding to watch them.

6. DISCUSSION AND CONCLUSIONS

We conducted a diary style field study focusing on the tasks user engage in while searching and browsing online. We examined statistics of users' task activities in their search logs, correlations between task characteristics, and task characteristics of naturalistic user tasks. Here, we conclude our study by summarising and discussing the implications of our observations.

User tasks in search logs. We started this analysis with a comparison of the concepts used to describe task search sessions defined in three closely related studies that all aimed to identify task sessions from query logs (Section 4). We find that search sessions can be described at three levels: physical, logical, and task. However, each study we examined has a slightly different definition of these concepts, which makes a direct comparison of the observations made from these studies difficult. We hope that our review of these concepts will provide guidance for future work on task identification.

We continued with an empirical comparison of the statistics obtained from our self-annotated search log to that reported from these studies (RQ1). The main messages can be summarised as follows. (i) We have observed 41% zero-query tasks and 82% zero-query logical sessions, which implies that a large number of user task activities remain unobserved if we only focus on search queries. (ii) When restricting the analysis to only the queries in our log, we observed a higher number of queries and timespan per task compared to those reported in previous studies. This could be both an artefact of the differences in the log samples of different studies, as well as the way the logs were annotated (e.g. self vs external annotators). However, since the three studies we compared reported statistics in different measures (e.g. mean vs. median) and at different session levels, it is hard to verify if there were consistent results. However, our results suggest that tasks can require more queries and take longer than previously thought. (iii) Finally, we find that the canonical time-out for physical sessions is reasonably accurate in detecting task boundaries between queries within user defined tasks. However, in order to capture task switches in-between queries, activities other than queries need to be considered.

Task characteristics and user activities. Previous lab studies have investigated task characteristics with tasks specifically designed to address a single or a limited set of task dimensions. With designed tasks, however, it is difficult to investigate how different dimensions interact and how these occur in the daily information tasks. With the logs obtained in out naturalistic setup and explicitly annotated with task characteristics, we were able to perform an exploratory analysis and provide a comprehensive view of how task characteristics interact with each other and how they relate to user online activities (RQ2).

We identified groups of task characteristics that have strong mutual correlation. This has implications for task designs for lab studies. For instance, task collaboration is seen related to complex/difficult tasks, implying that studies of complex/difficult tasks may need to consider collaboration as an additional variable.

We further illustrated that tasks that share similar descriptions can vary greatly in their characteristics (cognitive complexity as an example). This supports the observation that it is very difficult for external annotators to classify user tasks or activities with a taxonomy [26]. This also has implications for studies that aimed at identifying user tasks from search logs in order to support their tasks. For example, we need to know not only what task the user is engaged with, but also *what status* the task is in, e.g., in terms of complexity and difficulty for the user, which would require different types of support.

Acknowledgements. This research was supported by the Dutch Technol-

Topics	Remember	Understand	Apply	Analyse	Evaluate	Create	Tot
Shopping	**10 (56%)** "Amazon-Heater"	– –	2 (11%) "sort out X lights"	3 (17%) "Baby products"	3 (17%) "buy contact lenses"	– –	18 (13%)
Writing	1 (9%) "compile X paper	– –	2 (18%) "Complete X tutorial	– –	**4 (36%)** "X Essay"	**4(36%)** "X paper"	11 (8%)
Travel	**3 (30%)** "weekend travel"	1 (10%) "X trip"	1 (10%) "Book trip to X"	1 (10%) "Flight home"	2 (20%) "book tickets for X "	2 (20%) "Plan trip for X"	10 (7%)
Job	1 (14%) "Look for jobs"	– –	1 (14%) "Tutor jobs"	1 (14%) "Internship applications"	**3 (43%)** "job hunt"	1 (14%) "Finding job"	7 (5%)
Project	– –	1 (17%) "Project management	**2 (33%)** " X project"	1 (17%) "X proj"	**2 (33%)** "research project-X	– –	6 (4%)
Research	– –	– –	**3 (50%)** "Research"	1 (17%) "...research for X"	1 (17%) "X research"	1 (17%) "X study"	6 (4%)
Program- ming	– –	1 (20%) "test X interface"	– –	**3 (60%)** "port X to java"	1 (20%) "...interface for X"	– –	5 (3%)
Watch X	2 (40%) "Youtube/streaming"	– –	– –	**3 (60%)** "Binge watch X"	– –	– –	5 (3%)
Other	21 "check location of X"	10 "stock knowledge	17 "Find solutions to X"	5 "learn about X"	9 "buy flat"	5 "study X"	67 (49%)
Total	38	13	28	18	25	13	135

Table 6: Example tasks at each cognitive complexity level. Each cell contains the counts of tasks within a topic at a CL level, and its percentage w.r.t the total number of tasks at that level. Boldface shows the most frequent CL level assigned to tasks within a topic.

ogy Foundation (STW) under project nr. 13675.

7. REFERENCES

[1] A. Aula, R. M. Khan, and Z. Guan. How does search behavior change as search becomes more difficult? In *SIGCHI'10*, pages 35–44. ACM, 2010.

[2] A. H. Awadallah, R. W. White, P. Pantel, S. T. Dumais, and Y.-M. Wang. Supporting complex search tasks. In *CIKM'14*, pages 1–10, 2014.

[3] A. Broder. A taxonomy of web search. In *ACM Sigir forum*, volume 36, pages 3–10. ACM, 2002.

[4] M. Bron, J. Van Gorp, F. Nack, L. B. Baltussen, and M. de Rijke. Aggregated search interface preferences in multi-session search tasks. In *SIGIR'13*, pages 123–132. ACM, 2013.

[5] K. Byström and P. Hansen. Conceptual framework for tasks in information studies. *JASIST*, 56(10):1050–1061, 2005.

[6] K. Byström and K. Järvelin. Task complexity affects information seeking and use. *IP&M*, 31(2):191–213, 1995.

[7] K. Church, M. Cherubini, and N. Oliver. A large-scale study of daily information needs captured in situ. *ACM TOCHI*, 21(2):10, 2014.

[8] S. Dumais. Task-based search: a search engine perspective. In *NSF Workshop on Task-Based Search*, page 1, 2013.

[9] C. Eickhoff, J. Teevan, R. White, and S. Dumais. Lessons from the journey: a query log analysis of within-session learning. In *WSDM'14*, pages 223–232. ACM, 2014.

[10] B. J. Frey and D. Dueck. Clustering by passing messages between data points. *science*, 315(5814):972–976, 2007.

[11] E. Greifeneder. The effects of distraction on task completion scores in a natural environment test setting. *JASIST*, 2015.

[12] J. Gwizdka and I. Spence. What can searching behavior tell us about the difficulty of information tasks. *A study of Web navigation. ASIST*, 6, 2006.

[13] M. Hagen, J. Gomoll, A. Beyer, and B. Stein. From search session detection to search mission detection. In *OAIR'13*, pages 85–92, 2013.

[14] J. He, M. Bron, and A. P. de Vries. Characterizing stages of a multi-session complex search task through direct and indirect query modifications. In *SIGIR'13*, pages 897–900. ACM, 2013.

[15] K. Järvelin and P. Ingwersen. Information seeking research needs extension towards tasks and technology. *Information Research*, 10 (1), 2004.

[16] R. Jones and K. L. Klinkner. Beyond the session timeout: automatic hierarchical segmentation of search topics in query logs. In *CIKM'08*, pages 699–708. ACM, 2008.

[17] M. Kellar, C. Watters, and M. Shepherd. A field study characterizing web-based information-seeking tasks. *JASIST*, 58(7):999–1018, 2007.

[18] D. Kelly and N. J. Belkin. Display time as implicit feedback: understanding task effects. In *SIGIR'04*, pages 377–384. ACM, 2004.

[19] D. Kelly, J. Arguello, A. Edwards, and W.-c. Wu. Development and evaluation of search tasks for iir experiments using a cognitive complexity framework. In *ICTIR'15*, pages 101–110. ACM, 2015.

[20] A. Kotov, P. N. Bennett, R. W. White, S. T. Dumais, and J. Teevan. Modeling and analysis of cross-session search tasks. In *SIGIR'11*, pages 5–14. ACM, 2011.

[21] L. Li, H. Deng, A. Dong, Y. Chang, and H. Zha. Identifying and labeling search tasks via query-based hawkes processes. In *SIGKDD'14*, pages 731–740. ACM, 2014.

[22] Y. Li and N. J. Belkin. A faceted approach to conceptualizing tasks in information seeking. *IP&M*, 44(6):1822–1837, 2008.

[23] J. Liu, M. J. Cole, C. Liu, R. Bierig, J. Gwizdka, N. J. Belkin, J. Zhang, and X. Zhang. Search behaviors in different task types. In *JCDL'10*, pages 69–78. ACM, 2010.

[24] C. Lucchese, S. Orlando, R. Perego, F. Silvestri, and G. Tolomei. Identifying task-based sessions in search engine query logs. In *WSDM'11*, pages 277–286. ACM, 2011.

[25] D. Odijk, R. W. White, A. Hassan Awadallah, and S. T. Dumais. Struggling and success in web search. In *CIKM'15*, pages 1551–1560. ACM, 2015.

[26] D. M. Russell, D. Tang, M. Kellar, and R. Jeffries. Task behaviors during web search: The difficulty of assigning labels. In *System Sciences, 2009. HICSS'09.*, pages 1–5. IEEE, 2009.

[27] C. L. Smith. Conditions of trust for completely-remote methods: A proposal for collaboration. In *HCIR*, 2012.

[28] A. Spink, M. Park, B. J. Jansen, and J. Pedersen. Multitasking during web search sessions. *IP&M*, 42(1):264–275, 2006.

[29] P. Vakkari. Task-based information searching. *Annual review of information science and technology*, 37(1):413–464, 2003.

[30] P. Vakkari, M. Pennanen, and S. Serola. Changes of search terms and tactics while writing a research proposal: A longitudinal case study. *IP&M*, 39(3):445–463, 2003.

[31] R. W. White and D. Kelly. A study on the effects of personalization and task information on implicit feedback performance. In *CIKM'06*, pages 297–306. ACM, 2006.

[32] G. Zuccon, T. Leelanupab, S. Whiting, E. Yilmaz, J. M. Jose, and L. Azzopardi. Crowdsourcing interactions: using crowdsourcing for evaluating interactive information retrieval systems. *Information retrieval*, 16(2):267–305, 2013.

Evaluating the Value of Lensing Wikipedia During the Information Seeking Process

Orland Hoeber
University of Regina
Regina, SK, Canada
orland.hoeber@uregina.ca

Anoop Sarkar
Simon Fraser University
Burnaby, BC, Canada
anoop@sfu.ca

Andrei Vacariu
Simon Fraser University
Burnaby, BC, Canada
avacariu@sfu.ca

Max Whitney
Simon Fraser University
Burnaby, BC, Canada
mwhitney@sfu.ca

Manali Gaikwad
University of Regina
Regina, SK, Canada
gaikwadm@uregina.ca

Gursimran Kaur
University of Regina
Regina, SK, Canada
gil202g@uregina.ca

ABSTRACT

While Wikipedia is an excellent source of information about entities, discovering relationships among them is not well-supported by its search features. Lensing Wikipedia was designed as an alternate search and summarization interface, providing a set of filtering, visualization, and exploration tools that enable searching among the connections between people, organizations, and locations. In this paper, we present the results of a user study on how these features are used in each of Vakkari's stages of information seeking (pre-focus, focus formulation, and post-focus), and the participants perceptions of the utility of these features to their overall information-seeking goals. Participants primarily used input and control features during the pre-focus stage, informational and personalization features during the focus formulation stage, and personalization features during the post-focus stage. Findings from this study contribute to understanding how people use advanced search, summarization, and visualization tools to aid their information seeking tasks.

CCS Concepts

•Information systems → Search interfaces; •Human-centered computing → Empirical studies in HCI;

Keywords

Wikipedia search; User study; Information seeking

1. INTRODUCTION

Discovering relationships between entities within complex document collections such as Wikipedia can be a difficult and cognitively taxing activity. For example, suppose a student wishes to study the relationship between Charlemagne and Pope Adrian I for a class report. Doing so within a simple search interface, such as that provided by Wikipedia, requires the searcher to formulate their information needs and devise queries, evaluate the relevance of documents, view and evaluate the information within the selected documents, synthesize what they have learned, and prepare an assessment of what has been discovered. Lensing Wikipedia provides a series of search and summarization features that are designed to enable searchers to discover and explore among such relationships [27]. Following the taxonomy proposed by Wilson [34] these features can be classified as being input, control, informational, or personalization. The goal of this study is to assess how these different types of features are used during each of Vakkari's stages of information seeking [31] (pre-focus, focus formulation, and post-focus), how the participants perceive the usefulness of the features, and their overall satisfaction with Lensing Wikipedia.

Knowing which features are used during each of the stages of the information seeking process will not only contribute to a better understanding of how to support search within digital encyclopedias, but will also allow us to refine Lensing Wikipedia. In particular, features that are not useful may be removed in order to avoid interface complexity. Those features that are useful may then be re-ordered to more closely follow the information seeking stages. If we are able to detect the searcher changing from one stage to another, Lensing Wikipedia may be able to dynamically adjust the availability of features based on the type of task the searcher is expected to perform.

The remainder of this paper is organized as follows. Section 2 provides a review of the recent literature on searching within Wikipedia, as well as an overview of the information seeking literature that informed the design of this study. Section 3 provides brief explanation of the core features of Lensing Wikipedia. The user study methodology, design, analysis methods, and results are provided in Section 4. The paper concludes with a summary of the primary contributions and future work in Section 5.

CHIIR '17, March 07-11, 2017, Oslo, Norway

DOI: http://dx.doi.org/10.1145/3020165.3020178

2. LITERATURE REVIEW

2.1 Wikipedia Search and Exploration

The default search interface in Wikipedia matches the user-supplied query against the titles of the articles. For instance, a search for "Napoleon" will directly lead to the wiki/Napoleon page, but does not show alternatives such as wiki/Napoleon_III. The information in the text of the page itself is ignored in such a search interface. Although there is an advanced search feature that matches the contents of the page, it follows the traditional query box and search results list paradigm, requiring the searchers to consider each search result one-by-one.

A visual approach to displaying the full text search results was adopted in [30], in which a visual clustering of Wikipedia articles was created using a vector-space model over the bag of words in the Wikipedia articles. While such an approach may help a searcher to identify groups of related documents, it does not enable the searcher to identify the relationships among the entities in these clusters.

Apart from the titles of pages, there is a wealth of structured information in most Wikipedia pages in the form of infoboxes and Wikipedia Categories. The structured information in Wikipedia has been an important topic of research in the semantic web community and in the knowledge-base construction community. Two major projects in this area are DBPedia [4, 23, 32] and YAGO [29, 16], both of which create entity based knowledge bases from Wikipedia.

The information in infoboxes extracted in DBPedia lends itself to a faceted search interface such as the one that was explored by Hahn et al. [12]. A similar approach has leveraged user queries to support facet construction [36]. Others have sought to take advantage of how information is structured within Wikipedia articles to enhance the search process. For example, Vispedia [8] allows searchers to select a table of data, apply a visualization technique to the data (e.g., timeline), and subsequently use that to enable interactive querying to supplement the visualization.

The geo-location of pages can also be exploited and combined with the YAGO database to provide map based browsing of Wikipedia articles [15]. It also provides graph-based visualizations based on typed links between entities in the YAGO knowledge base.

In all of these approaches, the information encoded within the text of the Wikipedia articles themselves are largely ignored. Our goal with Lensing Wikipedia is to use natural language processing to extract information from the textual descriptions about entities, which are grounded in a specific time and location, and expose this information to searchers through an interactive visual interface.

2.2 Information Seeking

Although some have been advocating for the importance of considering searchers' interactions with information retrieval systems as a central concern for many years [2], support for the study of interactive information retrieval has only recently made its way to the forefront of information retrieval research [3]. The goal among such research is to study how search systems can support people in fulfilling their information seeking tasks and goals. What has become clear is the value of the search interface in allowing searchers to effectively undertake their information seeking processes.

The importance of the search interface is exemplified by the inclusion of chapters on this topic within current information retrieval textbooks [14, 34], and books dedicated solely to the design and study of search interfaces [13]. These works generally focus on discussing the accepted models of information seeking, surveying current trends in search interface design, providing best-practices advice, and advocating for careful evaluations of new interfaces.

When designing new search interfaces, it is helpful to consider the type of interaction that the user needs to perform, and only add new interaction methods that support specific information seeking tasks. Wilson provided a useful taxonomy in which interactive features may be classified as *input*, *control*, *informational*, and *personalization* [34]. Input features are those that allow a searcher to provide input into the search process (e.g., query box, facets). Control features are those that allow a searcher to manipulate how the search results are shown (e.g., custom sort, filters). Informational features are those that present information to the searcher (e.g., search results list, visualizations). Personalization features are those that allow a searcher to build a view that is unique to their specific needs (e.g., rejecting irrelevant search results, saving results to evaluate later).

Building upon an exhaustive list of information seeking tasks that one may undertake when seeking to resolve an information seeking problem (initiation, selection, exploration, formulation, collection, and presentation [20]), Vakkari developed a three-stage model of information seeking [31]. The *pre-focus* stage deals with the initiation of the search and undertaking a broad exploration of the topic. In the *focus formulation* stage, searchers refine their goals and explore these in detail. During the *post-focus* stage, searchers collect, synthesize, and present the results of their search. While this model was developed in the context of fulfilling information seeking goals that are complex in nature and are performed over multiple search sessions, it has been used to study single-session search activities as well [17].

In this paper, we have drawn inspiration for the organization of our study from Huurdeman et al. [17]. They developed a custom search interface that included a number of lightweight interactive features designed to aid the searcher, and evaluated it in the context of situated work tasks that guide the searchers through Vakkari's three stages of information seeking. Measuring both active use (interface logging) and passive use (eye tracking), they found that certain types of interface features are more useful during certain stages, and less useful during others (e.g., control features are more useful during the early stages, whereas personalization features are more useful during the late stages).

3. LENSING WIKIPEDIA

We employ a "machine reading" approach to the creation of a knowledge base from Wikipedia natural language text. Previous work has focused on extracting semantic relations between entities [24] observed in a large number of instances by parsing the text. Some construct a rich ontology (e.g., NELL [7] and PROSPERA [25]), or simply deal with token-level facts (e.g., TextRunner [1, 22]). In all of these approaches, each semantic relation extracted has to occur frequently in the collection.

In our approach, information is extracted from every clause in every sentence in the data set. We aggregate information from multiple sentences, using a natural language processing approach commonly called *Semantic Role Labeling* (SRL) [10]. SRL is used to extract predicate argument structures from text to automatically populate a predicate-centric ontology for a domain. A predicate argument structure looks for a predicate (an action or a state commonly instantiated by a verb) and the arguments of the predicate (the entities, typically noun phrases). We use supervised machine learning to train a SRL parser.

We choose a subset of Wikipedia that focuses on events about human history, because it contains facts about events, very few opinions, and almost no sentiment. The sentences describe who did what to whom, when, and where, as represented in the predicate-argument structure. At the time of the crawl, English Wikipedia contained about 2600 URLs (from 1500 BCE to 2016 CE), which are natural language summaries of important events in each year or decade in human history. We followed all these Wikipedia URLs and obtained about 41,000 events, with each event described by one to several sentences. The result is 83,000 predicate argument structures discovered through SRL. Using methods from [35] we combine the information extracted from the natural language text with other structured information in Wikipedia such as dates and geo-location information.

3.1 Semantic Roles

For SRL, we used supervised machine learning to train a parser capable of taking natural language sentences and returning predicate-argument structures [10, 21], using the human annotated corpus called the Proposition Bank (PropBank) [26].

For example, in the sentence "The House of York defeats the House of Lancaster" we identify *defeat* as the predicate with arguments *The House of York* (*arg0*) and *the House of Lancaster* (*arg1*), where (*arg0* and *arg1*) are the abstract semantic roles. These abstract roles are then converted into human readable types (*arg0: 'entity victorious'* and *arg1: 'entity defeated'*) using information in PropBank. This is done using machine learning of the mapping between abstract semantic role labels and verbose descriptions such as *'entity victorious'*. The verbose label depends on identifying the sense of the verb. For instance, arg0 for 'get' might be labeled as 'receiver', but the right label could also be 'instigator' for another sense of the verb (get across). We explored many machine learning approaches to solve this task, and our best result could find verbose labels with 92% accuracy [27] on unseen test data.

These verbose labels are crucial in Lensing Wikipedia because they provide a lightweight ontology (or useful types). For instance, we could search for all entities that match "buyer" or "entity defeated" types. These predicate-centric types are often more useful than the types from Freebase [5] which need further disambiguation to be applied correctly to the entities and events in our data.

3.2 Entity Extraction

We also perform named entity extraction from text data, using Wikipedia hyperlinks and named entity recognition (NER). Lensing Wikipedia focuses on *Person* and *Location* as named entity types. We used Stanford NER [9] to detect candidate entities along with their types. Each candidate entity is then verified by linking that entity mention to an article in Wikipedia. In addition to entities recognized by NER, we take advantage of hyperlinks embedded in the event's texts. Using NER and Wikipedia hyperlinks, we identify mentions in the text with Wikipedia URLs and then verify the entity type (person, geographic location, or NIL). For this we use the Wikipedia categories associated with the URL. Wikipedia categories are organized as a hierarchical ontology, but they are not anchored in general conceptual classes like entity types (e.g., person). We use the category labels and infoboxes to verify entity mentions as the correct entity type (person, location) (e.g., categories like *Category:y_births* where y is a year, are associated with entity type *person*).

3.3 Temporal and Geographical Identification

From the SRL output and the entities identified and linked with Wikipedia URLs, we extract temporal information such as the date the event occurred. For event geo-location, we used the information in the Wikipedia URLs to obtain latitude and longitude information. Having geo-location information, we are able to extract the current country(ies) where the event happened by reverse geocoding using the Google Geocoding API [11].

3.4 Search Interface

To show the effectiveness of this knowledge base to represent the underlying data, we created an interactive search interface called *Lensing Wikipedia*. The system consists of five core interface elements, organized on separate tabs: facets, storyline, timeline, comparison, and map (see Figure 1). In addition, as the queries are dynamically generated using these features, a search results list is created consisting of information extracted from the Wikipedia articles. Clicking on any links within this list will open the associated Wikipedia page in a new browser tab, allowing the searcher to keep relevant documents open while returning to the Lensing Wikipedia interface. A free-form note-taking feature is provided to allow searchers to document information relevant to their search.

Within the facets tab, the information regarding the extracted entities and their roles in the history of events are provided as the primary mechanism for constructing a query. The faceted classification allows users to explore among a collection of information by interactively applying multiple filters. While faceted browsing has been applied for closed domains with structured data (e.g., Nobel prize winners, and recipes [28]), to our knowledge this is the first time faceted browsing has been implemented for an open domain data set where the facets are generated from unstructured data.

The storyline tab provides a representation of the relationships between a selected entity and other entities within the knowledge base. For example, if Napoleon is selected, all other entities of this same type (person) that co-occur within the knowledge base are depicted within a flow-based visualization. The interaction between two or more entities are identified using vertical bars.

The timeline tab shows when in the full history of events the currently selected events have occurred. Using stacked views, the searcher can zoom into a specific temporal range, yet remain aware of when this exists in the full history of events in Wikipedia.

The comparison tab illustrates the number of events over time for the selected entity and other significant related entities. This can be used to show how the interaction between sets of entities overlap in time.

The map tab leverages the extracted geo-location data, situating the events on an interactive map. Variably sized discs are used to represent the number of events in the specific location. In order to show where the entities' events have occurred, numerical values are provided on the map.

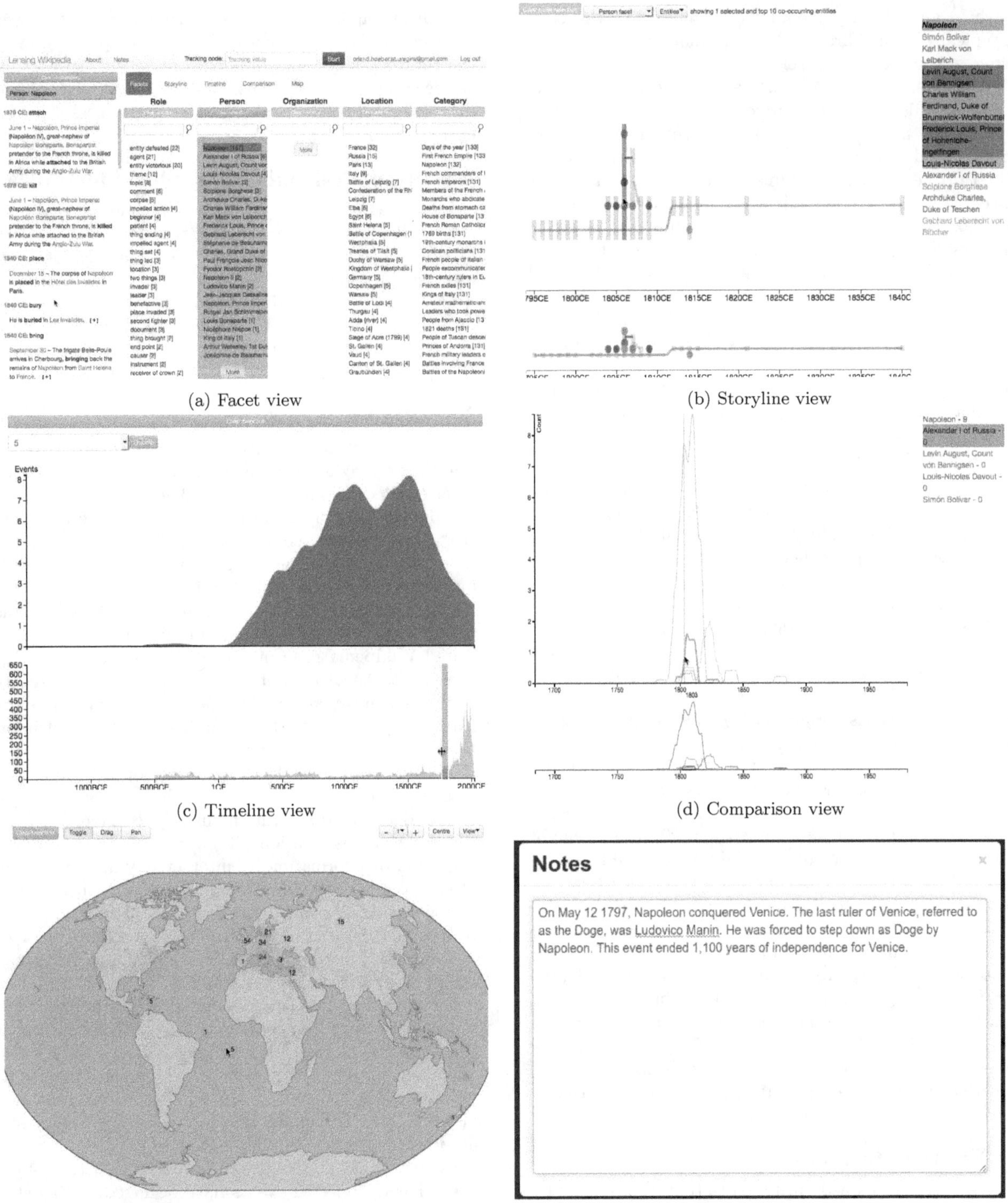

(a) Facet view (b) Storyline view (c) Timeline view (d) Comparison view (e) Map view (f) Notes input

Figure 1: Views available in Lensing Wikipedia.

4. USER STUDY

While a researcher may be well-intentioned in the design and development of novel features to support interactive information retrieval, the actual usefulness of such features remains unknown until the interface is properly evaluated. Such evaluations will often take the form of user studies, where the goal is to study searchers' behaviours and experiences as they use the software, with particular focus on how they interact with the interface and the information provided [18]. Furthermore, the searchers' impressions of the usefulness of a search interface is a fundamentally important measure for evaluating information retrieval performance [3].

Studying a search interface in the context of the breadth of strategies, behaviours, and complex search activities [19] is necessary when the search interface is designed for general use. However, when the search interface is designed for a specific search context, the evaluation can be more focused. In the case of Lensing Wikipedia, the interface was designed to support exploring among the relationships between entities, which is used as the motivating information seeking activities in the study design. By evaluating the software in the context for which it was designed, we can answer the question: what value does it provide in supporting the intended tasks?

Rather than evaluating each feature of Lensing Wikipedia in isolation, we take a holistic view in the evaluation. Following the IIR evaluation model [6], specific situated work tasks in the context of defined information seeking activities were provided to each participant, which focus on the issue of discovering information about connections between entities. In particular, we have prepared these situated work tasks in the context of a student writing an outline for a history course report centred on specified historical figures.

To guide the analysis of Lensing Wikipedia and evaluate the support it provides for the information seeking activities, we have classified its features according to Wilson's taxonomy [34] (see Table 1). The tasks are structured to follow Vakkari's stages of information seeking [31]. This provides an organizational structure for the discussion regarding which types of features are useful during which stages of the information seeking process.

4.1 Methodology

The specific methodology for the evaluation was designed to answer the following four research questions:

RQ1: How does the search stage influence the use of the different types of Lensing Wikipedia features?

RQ2: How much knowledge was gained as a result of undertaking the information seeking activities using Lensing Wikipedia?

RQ3: How useful do the searchers perceive the Lensing Wikipedia features for fulfilling their overall information seeking goal?

RQ4: How satisfied were the searchers in using Lensing Wikipedia?

Participants for this study were recruited from the first author's University population. Because of the importance of being able to effectively read and write in English, the participant recruitment process included an online screening component where we collected self-reported English language proficiency details, along with history knowledge and Wikipedia search expertise. All participants with good or excellent English skills, reasonably good knowledge of history, and some experience with using Wikipedia were invited to continue participation in the study (n=14).

Table 1: A summary of the feature interaction types in Lensing Wikipedia.

Interaction Type	Lensing Wikipedia Features
Input	facets tab
Control	remove constraints
Informational	storyline tab timeline tab comparison tab map tab follow link
Personalization	return to document edit notes

Each study session began with an overview of the study procedures and a confirmation of informed consent to continue with the study. A 10-minute training video was shown to the participant to introduce each of the core features of the software, after which the researcher answered any questions the participants may have had. The participant was then introduced to the software setup and specific study procedures. On a 27-inch display, Lensing Wikipedia was provided in a window that took 2/3 of the screen width. The remaining 1/3 of the screen was filled with an online questionnaire that lead the participant through the procedures of the study, the specific steps of the information seeking tasks, and the post-study questionnaire. Two printed pages were provided: a brief description of the Lensing Wikipedia features, and an overview of the study procedures.

Three information seeking activities were assigned to the participant, focusing on using Lensing Wikipedia to explore and study the relationships between a historical figure and other important people in history that they discover. The first two historical figures were randomly assigned between "John, King of England" and "Franklin D. Roosevelt". The third activity allowed the participant to choose their own historical figure upon which to base their search. Note that the training video focused on a similar activity centred around "Napoleon". Participants were given specific instructions that guided them through the information seeking process (see Figure 2).

At the beginning of each of the three information seeking activities, participants were asked to rate their level of prior knowledge on the topic. While using Lensing Wikipedia, all interactions with the software were logged. As the participants completed each stage of the process, they were asked to notify the researcher and explicitly indicate within the interface movement to the next stage of the process. At the end of each activity, participants were asked to rate how much they learned about the topic.

After all activities were complete, a post-study questionnaire was administered. A set of questions were provided regarding the perceived usefulness of each core feature of Lensing Wikipedia (facets, storyline, timeline, comparison, and map tabs), along with other supporting features (modify constraints, follow link, return to document, and edit notes). The participants were then asked three questions regarding the overall usefulness of Lensing Wikipedia (based on the Technology Acceptance Model instrument [33]) and one question regarding their satisfaction with Lensing Wikipedia for the tasks.

The study took approximately 1.5 hours. Each participant was given a $10 gift-card for their time and effort. In order to inspire the participants to take the assigned activities and tasks seriously and do their best work, a further incentive of a $50 gift card was given to the participant who provided the best essay outline for each of the three activities. These incentives were indicated in the informed consent.

4.2 Analysis

Because of the subtle differences between each of the assigned information seeking activities, we analyzed and present

Introduction: For a history course, you have been given an assignment to write a short 2-page essay about the relationship between [primary person] and some other important person in history. Today, you have given yourself the goals of (1) finding a small set of important people related to [primary person], (2) narrowing this down to one person and studying the relationship between these two people that will be the focus of your paper, and (3) producing a list of sources to support the writing of your essay.

Stage 1 (pre-focus): Using Lensing Wikipedia, search within Wikipedia to find three people that had significant interactions or relationships with [primary person]. Feel free to use any feature of Lensing Wikipedia and the browser that you feel will help you with this activity. A list of features and their primary purpose is provided to help you learn what each feature is for. Document the names of these individuals in the space provided, as well as your ideas about the essay you will write.

Stage 2 (focus formulation): Select one of the people you have identified in the previous step, and use Lensing Wikipedia to learn about the relationship between these two individuals. Feel free to use any feature of Lensing Wikipedia and the browser that you feel will help you with this activity. Document the name of the individual that will be the focus of your paper, along your notes on the relationship, when it took place, and any other information you feel is relevant.

Stage 3 (post-focus): Your goal now is to collect and organize the source material that will help you with writing the short essay. Find five articles that you think will be useful, copy their URLs in the space provided, and then write a short summary of what is in each that is relevant to your paper. Finally, write a short (200 word) outline for your essay.

Figure 2: Instructions given to participants.

each separately. The average amount of time and average number of interactions are presented in graphical format using standard error about the mean as a measure of variability in the data. These are organized by the information seeking stage, allowing the reader to observe the pattern of feature use across the stages. Statistical analyses of the data were performed, using ANOVA to determine if there is a statistically significant difference in the feature use between each stage.

In order to compare the prior knowledge and the knowledge gained during each activity, the responses were aggregated by task and stacked. Similarly, the usefulness of each feature, as reported by the participants at the end of the study, was aggregated and presented in graphical format using a stacked bar chart. Likewise, the overall perceived usefulness measures and level of satisfaction are presented in a similar manner. These provide a summary of the perceptions of the participants regarding their knowledge gained and the value of Lensing Wikipedia

4.3 Results

4.3.1 Feature Use in Each Information Seeking Stage

For each of the three activities, the amount of time and the number of interactions with the core interface features were analyzed across each of the three information seeking stages. Figures 3, 4, and 5 show the average values of these measures, with error bars representing the error about the mean. One can see a general pattern emerging: during the pre-focus stage (light colour in the figures), participants spent time using the facets tab (input) to explore among the relationships and removed constraints (control) that were added during the interactive exploration process. There was some use of the storyline and comparison tabs (informational), but these were minimal in comparison to the facets tab. Some time was also spent with the notes (personalization), but these consisted of many short interactions as the searchers entered brief information relevant to the task.

Things changed somewhat in the focus formulation stage (mid-weight colour in the figures). Here we can see that participants spent less time with the facets tab (input) than in the previous stage, and made more use of the storyline tab (informational). The other tabs that were similar in informational nature (timeline, comparison, and map tabs) were used somewhat, in what we characterize as experimentation (many interactions, but little time spent using the features). In this stage, we notice that participants followed the most links (informational) and spent time with these documents judging their relevance. More time was spent editing the notes (personalization), as participants added more information to aid their decision-making process.

In the post-focus stage (dark colour in the figures), it is no surprise that the participants spent the majority of their time editing the notes (personalization) and returning to previously opened documents (personalization). The high number of interactions with these features was an indication of the participants flipping back and forth between these views. Some supplemental exploration of the data was also performed (facets and storyline tabs, removing constraints, and following links). Post-hoc analysis of the logs revealed that this was often done near the end of the stage, presumably as a method to verify what was written and to ensure completeness.

While the pattern is generally consistent between the first two assigned activities, things were somewhat different with the third self-selected activity. Since this activity was chosen by the participants, they had a strong interest in fulfilling the information seeking goals. They appeared to make quicker decisions regarding relevance during the pre-focus stage, evidence of which can be seen in similar number of pre-focus interactions with the input (facets tab), control (remove constraints), and informational (storyline tab) features as in the first two activities, yet much less time spent with these feature. The focus formulation stage took much less time than with the assigned activities, with much attention given to following links (informational). The post-focus stage was consistent with the other activities, following a pattern of returning to previously opened documents (personalization) and editing the notes (personalization). However, less time was spent with the previously opened documents than in the two assigned activities.

We conducted the statistical analysis on the features that were used regularly by all participants in the study, exclud-

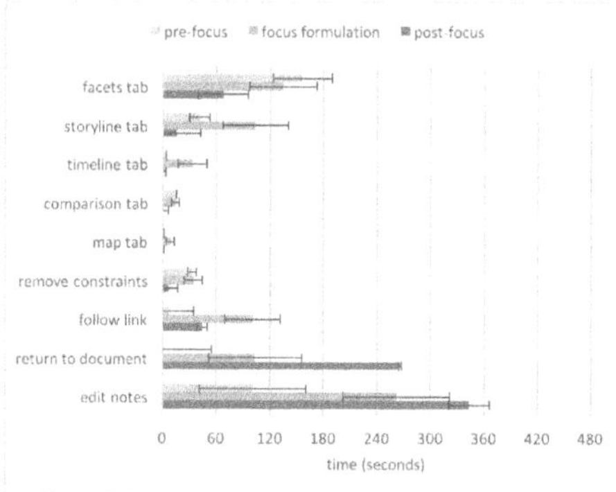

(a) Time spent using each feature.

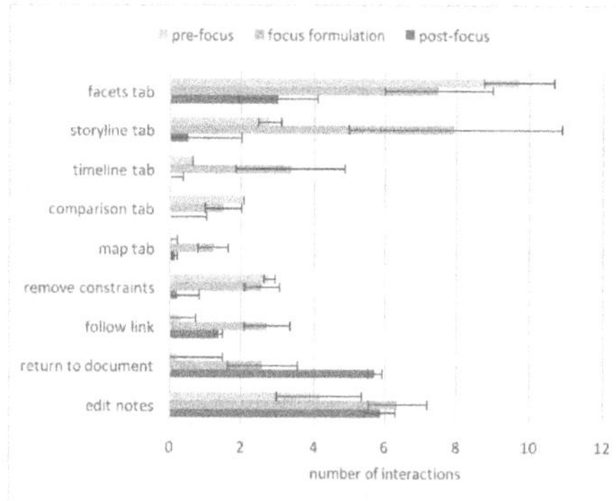

(b) Frequency of interaction with each feature.

Figure 3: The use of the core features during the "John, King of England" activity.

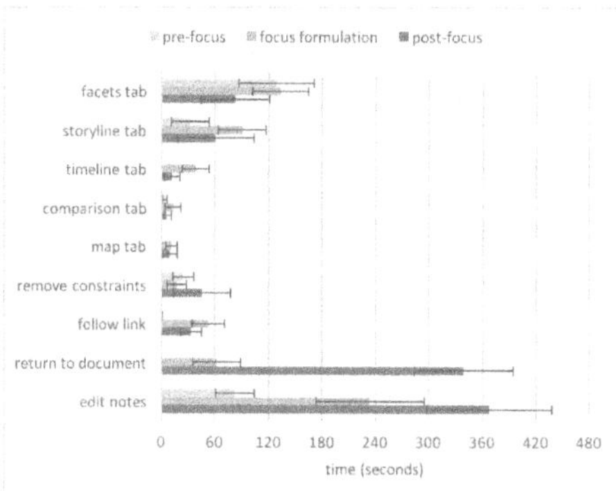

(a) Time spent using each feature.

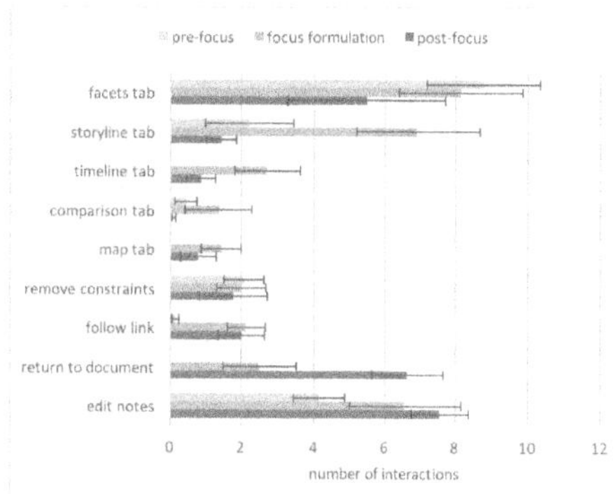

(b) Frequency of interaction with each feature.

Figure 4: The use of the core features during the "Franklin D. Roosevelt" activity.

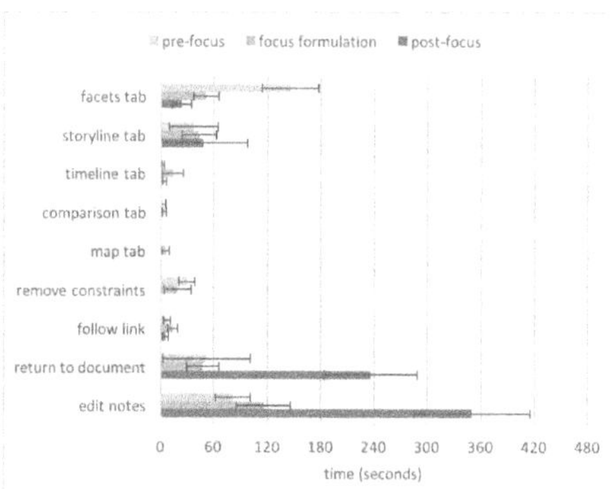

(a) Time spent using each feature.

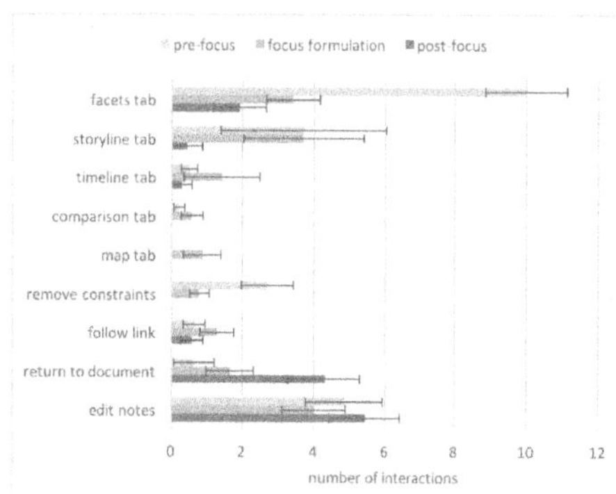

(b) Frequency of interaction with each feature.

Figure 5: The use of the core features during the participant-selected activity.

ing the timeline, comparison, and map tabs due to insufficient data on their use. Table 2 summarizes this analysis, with statistically significant results in bold. While there was some variability regarding the input (facets tab) and control (remove constraints) features, there are three noteworthy aspects of this statistical analysis.

For the assigned tasks, we found a consistent pattern of participants following links (informational) during the focus formulation stage. During the pre-focus stage, participants were able to discover the information they needed from within the Lensing Wikipedia interface, and did not follow many links. During the post-focus stage, few links were followed and instead participants returned to documents found in the focus formulation stage. This finding validates some important features of Lensing Wikipedia: showing snippets that describe the extracted relationships from the Wikipedia articles helps searchers to make decisions during the pre-focus stage; providing links to the source documents helps searchers to find specific information that is needed in the focus formulation stage, and opening links in browser tabs allows searchers to return to previously found documents during the post-focus stage.

Table 2: Statistical analysis (ANOVA) of the time and frequency of feature use across the stages of the information seeking process.

Feature	Task	Time Spent Using the Feature	Frequency of Interaction
facets tab	John, King of England	$F(2, 39) = 1.944, p = 0.157$	**$F(2, 39) = 8.190, p < 0.005$**
	Franklin D. Roosevelt	$F(2, 39) = 0.564, p = 0.573$	$F(2, 39) = 0.887, p = 0.420$
	Participant's Selection	**$F(2, 39) = 9.361, p < 0.005$**	**$F(2, 39) = 23.167, p < 0.001$**
storyline tab	John, King of England	$F(2, 39) = 2.811, p = 0.072$	**$F(2, 39) = 3.900, p < 0.05$**
	Franklin D. Roosevelt	$F(2, 39) = 0.867, p = 0.428$	**$F(2, 39) = 5.600, p < 0.05$**
	Participant's Selection	$F(2, 39) = 0.030, p = 0.970$	$F(2, 39) = 1.281, p = 0.239$
remove constraints	John, King of England	$F(2, 39) = 3.215, p = 0.051$	**$F(2, 39) = 9.911, p < 0.005$**
	Franklin D. Roosevelt	$F(2, 39) = 0.501, p = 0.610$	$F(2, 39) = 0.038, p = 0.963$
	Participant's Selection	$F(2, 39) = 2.239, p = 0.121$	**$F(2, 39) = 9.752, p < 0.005$**
follow link	John, King of England	**$F(2, 39) = 3.760, p < 0.05$**	**$F(2, 39) = 7.563, p < 0.005$**
	Franklin D. Roosevelt	**$F(2, 39) = 4.632, p < 0.05$**	**$F(2, 39) = 5.172, p < 0.05$**
	Participant's Selection	$F(2, 39) = 0.846, p = 0.437$	$F(2, 39) = 1.090, p = 0.346$
return to document	John, King of England	**$F(2, 39) = 9.593, p < 0.001$**	**$F(2, 39) = 8.909, p < 0.001$**
	Franklin D. Roosevelt	**$F(2, 39) = 25.976, p < 0.001$**	**$F(2, 39) = 16.490, p < 0.001$**
	Participant's Selection	**$F(2, 39) = 6.353, p < 0.005$**	**$F(2, 39) = 6.020, p < 0.05$**
edit notes	John, King of England	**$F(2, 39) = 5.971, p < 0.05$**	$F(2, 39) = 1.767, p = 0.184$
	Franklin D. Roosevelt	**$F(2, 39) = 6.747, p < 0.005$**	$F(2, 39) = 2.577, p = 0.089$
	Participant's Selection	**$F(2, 39) = 11.720, p < 0.001$**	$F(2, 39) = 0.531, p = 0.592$

Contrary to the two assigned tasks, for the participant-selected tasks we found statistically significant differences in which stage participants used the facets tab (input), and no statistically significant differences in when links were followed (informational). For these tasks, participants used the facets tab much more in the pre-focus stage than the other two, and followed links throughout all three stages. What this tells us is that when searchers seek information that is of personal interest, they may be able to quickly and easily narrow down the search results during the pre-focus stage to the information they need for the later stages, follow the relevant links to load the required documents, and not find it necessary to continue to explore during the focus formulation stage or verify completeness during the post-focus stage.

The personalization features of returning to documents and editing notes followed a consistent pattern across all tasks. Participants spent significantly more time viewing documents they previously clicked on during the post-focus stage, and undertook this action significantly more frequently. Similarly, they spent significantly more time editing their notes during this stage, although the number of times they opened the notes was not significantly different across the stages. This finding highlights the need to make it easy for searchers who are in the post-focus stage to easily change between reading previously found documents and writing their notes about the information they discover.

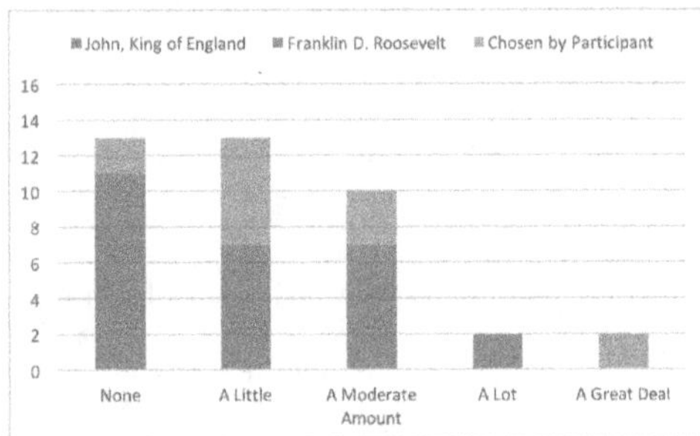

(a) Prior knowledge.

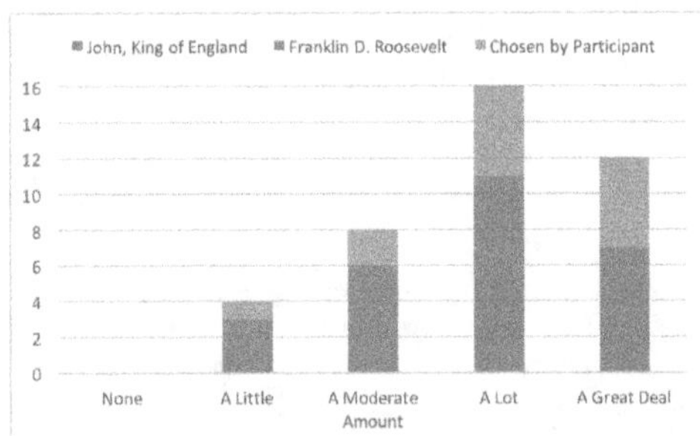

(b) Knowledge gained.

Figure 6: Amount of knowledge participants reported to have had before and gained during the three activities.

4.3.2 Perceived Knowledge Gained

Before and after each activity, participants self-reported how much prior knowledge they had on the historical figure in question, and how much knowledge they gained as a result of using Lensing Wikipedia to fulfil the information seeking goal. Figure 6a shows that most participants had a low to moderate amount of prior knowledge, and Figure 6b shows that most participants reported having learned a moderate amount, a lot, or a great deal. Of special note is the amount of knowledge the participants gained in their self-selected activity. Even though this may be attributed to their growing confidence with using Lensing Wikipedia (this activity was always performed last), we consider it an indicator of the success that searchers experienced using Lensing Wikipedia.

4.3.3 Perceived Usefulness of Features

While there were a core set of features that were consistently reported as being useful by the participants, there was also a set that had mixed reactions (see Figure 7a). Virtually all participants reported positively regarding the usefulness of the facets tab, the ability to remove constraints, following links, returning to documents, and editing notes. This is consistent with the time spent using these features and the frequency of interaction.

The informational features (storyline, timeline, comparison, and map tabs) were perceived by some participants as useful, and by others as not useful. Some participants did not bother to use these features, others used them briefly and then reverted to the more familiar facets tab, and the remainder made an honest effort to use these features to learn about the information presented in them. Of these, the storyline, comparison, and map tabs showed promise and could prove to be more useful with additional refinement and training.

4.3.4 Perceived Overall Usefulness & Satisfaction

Overall, participants in this study reported positive perceptions of usefulness of Lensing Wikipedia, and were satisfied with using it to fulfill their information seeking goals (see Figure 7b). In fact, over half of the participants strongly agreed that Lensing Wikipedia enhanced their effectiveness and was useful for the task. There was general agreement of being satisfied, with the caveat of one participant being neutral and another disagreeing. We observed within the usage logs the difficulties these two participants experienced in finding information about their self-selected historical figures, which was due to limited information in Wikipedia, rather than the features of Lensing Wikipedia.

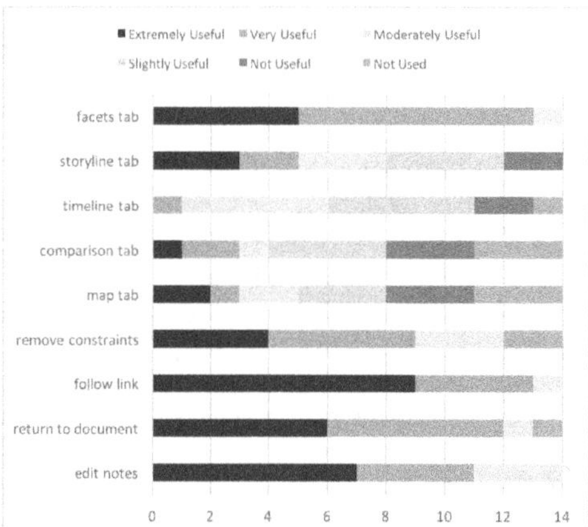

(a) Feature-level usefulness.

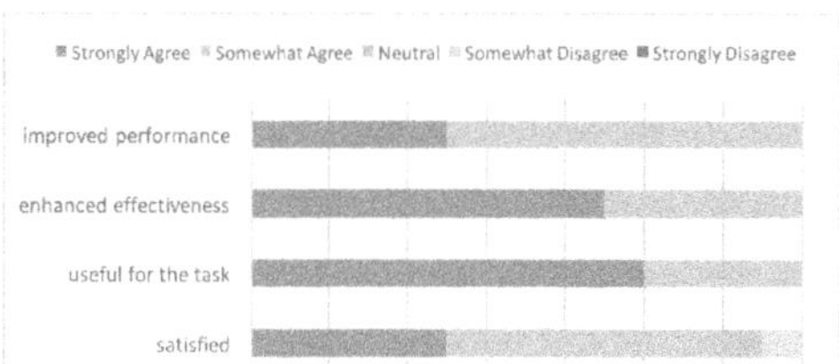

(b) Overall usefulness and satisfaction.

Figure 7: Responses to questionnaires regarding the feature-level usefulness and overall usefulness and satisfaction with using Lensing Wikipedia.

5. CONCLUSIONS & FUTURE WORK

This study illustrated the utility of the features of Lensing Wikipedia through the three information seeking stages. During the pre-focus stage, participants primarily used the input and control features; during the focus formulation stage, they primarily used the informational and personalization features; and during the post-focus stage, they used the personalization features almost exclusively. The findings are consistent with that of other similar studies [17]. Of note was the difference we found between the assigned and self-selected search activities. Participants self-reported positive knowledge gain, and generally high degrees of usefulness and satisfaction.

Findings from this study contribute to understanding how people use advanced search tools to aid their information seeking tasks, and will be used to further refine the features of Lensing Wikipedia before releasing it as a public service. In particular, we plan to group features that are used together within the three separate information seeking stages, and to re-evaluate the utility of the less-used visualization features. Efforts will be made to combine the storyline, timeline, comparison, and map tabs, thereby providing a unified view of the information that may be helpful for a searcher to "see" the story.

6. REFERENCES

[1] M. Banko, M. J. Cafarella, S. Soderland, M. Broadhead, and O. Etzioni. Open information extraction from the web. In *Proceedings of the International Joint Conference on Artifical Intelligence*, pages 2670–2676, 2007.

[2] N. Belkin. Intelligent information retrieval: Whose intelligence? In *Proceedings of the International Symposium for Information Science*, pages 25–31, 1996.

[3] N. J. Belkin. People, interacting with information. *ACM SIGIR Forum*, 49(2):13–27, 2015.

[4] C. Bizer, J. Lehmann, G. Kobilarov, S. Auer, C. Becker, R. Cyganiak, and S. Hellmann. DBpedia - a crystallization point for the web of data. *Web Semantics: Science, Services and Agents on the World Wide Web*, 7(3):154–165, 2009.

[5] K. Bollacker, C. Evans, P. Paritosh, T. Sturge, and J. Taylor. Freebase: a collaboratively created graph database for structuring human knowledge. In *Proceedings of the ACM SIGMOD International Conference on Management of Data*, pages 1247–1250, 2008.

[6] P. Borland. The IIR evaluation model: A framework for evaluation of interactive information retrieval systems. *Information Research*, 8(3), 2003.

[7] A. Carlson, J. Betteridge, B. Kisiel, B. Settles, E. R. Hruschka Jr., and T. M. Mitchell. Toward an architecture for never-ending language learning. In *Proceedings of the Conference on Artificial Intelligence*, pages 1306–1313, 2010.

[8] B. Chan, L. Wu, J. Talbot, M. Cammarano, and P. Hanrahan. Vispedia: Interactive visual exploration of Wikipedia data via search-based integration. *IEEE Transactions on Visualization and Computer Graphics*, 14(6):1213–1220, 2008.

[9] J. R. Finkel, T. Grenager, and C. Manning.

Incorporating non-local information into information extraction systems by Gibbs sampling. In *Proceedings of the Annual Meeting on Association for Computational Linguistics*, pages 363–370, 2005.

[10] D. Gildea and D. Jurafsky. Automatic labeling of semantic roles. *Computational Linguistics*, 28(3):245–288, 2002.

[11] Google Developers. Google geocoding. https://developers.google.com/maps/documentation/geocoding/.

[12] R. Hahn, C. Bizer, C. Sahnwaldt, C. Herta, S. Robinson, M. Bürgle, H. Düwiger, and U. Scheel. Faceted Wikipedia search. In *Proceedings of the International Conference on Business Information Systems*, pages 1–11, 2010.

[13] M. Hearst. *Search User Interfaces.* Cambridge University Press, Cambridge, UK, 2009.

[14] M. Hearst. User interfaces for search. In R. Baeza-Yates and B. Ribeiro-Neto, editors, *Modern Information Retrieval: The Concepts and Technology Behind Search*, pages 21–55. Addison-Wesley Professional, 2nd edition, 2011.

[15] J. Hoffart, F. M. Suchanek, K. Berberich, E. Lewis-Kelham, G. de Melo, and G. Weikum. YAGO2: Exploring and querying world knowledge in time, space, context, and many languages. In *Proceedings of the International World Wide Web Conference*, pages 229–232, 2011.

[16] J. Hoffart, F. M. Suchanek, K. Berberich, and G. Weikum. YAGO2: a spatially and temporally enhanced knowledge base from Wikipedia. *Artificial. Intelligence*, 194:28–61, 2013.

[17] H. C. Huurdeman, M. L. Wilson, and J. Kamps. Active and passive utility of search interface features in different information seeking task stages. In *Proceedings of the ACM SIGIR Conference on Human Information Interaction and Retrieval*, pages 3–12, 2016.

[18] D. Kelly. Methods for evaluating interactive information retrieval systems with users. *Foundations and Trends in Information Retrieval*, 3(1-2):1–224, 2009.

[19] D. Kelly, S. Dumais, and J. O. Pedersen. Evaulation challenges and directions for information-seeking support systems. *IEEE Computer*, 42(3):60–66, 2009.

[20] C. C. Kuhlthau. Inside the search process: Information seeking from the user's perspective. *Journal of the American Society for Information Science*, 42(5):361–371, 1991.

[21] Y. Liu and A. Sarkar. Experimental evaluation of LTAG-based features for semantic role labeling. In *Proceedings of the Conference on Empirical Methods on Natural Language Processing and Computational Natural Language Learning*, pages 590–599, 2007.

[22] Mausam, M. Schmitz, S. Soderland, R. Bart, and O. Etzioni. Open language learning for information extraction. In *Proceedings of the Joint Conference on Empirical Methods in Natural Language Processing and Computational Natural Language Learning*, pages 523–534, 2012.

[23] P. N. Mendes, M. Jakob, and C. Bizer. DBpedia: A multilingual cross-domain knowledge base. In *Proceedings of the International Conference on Language Resources and Evaluation*, pages 1813–1817, 2012.

[24] T. M. Mitchell, J. Betteridge, A. Carlson, E. R. Hruschka Jr., and R. C. Wang. Populating the semantic web by macro-reading Internet text. In *Proceedings of the International Semantic Web Conference*, pages 998–1002, 2009.

[25] N. Nakashole, M. Theobald, and G. Weikum. Scalable knowledge harvesting with high precision and high recall. In *Proceedings of the ACM International Conference on Web Search and Data Mining*, pages 227–236, 2011.

[26] M. Palmer, D. Gildea, and P. Kingsbury. The proposition bank: An annotated corpus of semantic roles. *Computational Linguistics*, 31(1):71–106, 2005.

[27] M. Siahbani, R. Vadlapudi, M. Whitney, and A. Sarkar. Knowledge base population and visualization using an ontology based on semantic roles. In *Proceedings of the Workshop on Automated Knowledge Base Construction*, pages 85–90, 2013.

[28] E. Stoica, M. A. Hearst, and M. Richardson. Automating creation of hierarchical faceted metadata structures. In *In Proceedings of the Human Language Technology Conference*, pages 244–251, 2007.

[29] F. M. Suchanek, G. Kasneci, and G. Weikum. YAGO: A core of semantic knowledge. In *Proceedings of the International World Wide Web Conference*, pages 697–706, 2007.

[30] J. Szymański. Self–organizing map representation for clustering Wikipedia search results. In *Proceedings of the International Conference on Intelligent Information and Database Systems*, pages 140–149, 2011.

[31] P. Vakkari. Task-based information searching. *Annual Review of Information Science and Technology*, 37(1):413–464, 2003.

[32] M. van Erp, P. N. Mendes, H. Paulheim, F. Ilievski, J. Plu, G. Rizzo, and J. Waitelonis. Evaluating entity linking: An analysis of current benchmark datasets and a roadmap for doing a better job. In *Proceedings of the International Conference on Language Resources and Evaluation*, pages 4373–4379, 2016.

[33] V. Venkatesh and F. D. Davis. A theoretical extension of the technology acceptance model: Four longitudinal field studies. *Management Science*, 46(2):186–204, 2000.

[34] M. L. Wilson. Interfaces for information retrieval. In I. Ruthvan and D. Kelly, editors, *Interactive Information Seeking, Behaviour and Retrieval.* Facet Publishing, 2011.

[35] F. Wu and D. S. Weld. Open information extraction using Wikipedia. In *Proceedings of the Annual Meeting of the Association for Computational Linguistics*, pages 118–127, 2010.

[36] N. Yan, C. Li, S. B. Roy, R. Ramegowda, and G. Das. Facetedpedia: Enabling query-dependent faceted search for Wikipedia. In *Proceedings of the ACM International Conference on Information and Knowledge Management*, pages 1927–1928, 2010.

Exploration or Fact-Finding: Inferring User's Search Activity Just in Time

Michael Kotzyba
DKE Group
Otto von Guericke University
Magdeburg, Germany
michael.kotzyba@ovgu.de

Tatiana Gossen
DKE Group
Otto von Guericke University
Magdeburg, Germany
tatiana.gossen@ovgu.de

Johannes Schwerdt
DKE Group
Otto von Guericke University
Magdeburg, Germany
johannes.schwerdt@ovgu.de

Andreas Nürnberger
DKE Group
Otto von Guericke University
Magdeburg, Germany
andreas.nuernberger@ovgu.de

ABSTRACT

Being able to differentiate between search activities a user is currently engaged in is crucial for adaptive information retrieval systems in order to provide appropriate support to the user in time. In this paper, we conduct an investigation into modeling two kinds of search activities: exploratory activities and fact-finding activities during web search. Specifically, we consider the case where a user is conducting consecutive fact-finding searches on multiple topics. This information behavior is also known as multitasking search. The goal of our research is to build models of users' web information-seeking behavior in order to differentiate between search activities caused by exploratory search tasks and consecutive fact-finding search tasks while users are still searching. In order to build search process models, we have designed and conducted a user study where the participants interact with a common web search engine. Based on the gathered log data, we built search models based on (Hidden) Markov Models and analyze the results. Our results yield to classification rates between 73.6% and 92.1% using different Markov Models and different data configurations. Furthermore, even with interaction sequences of a limited length, the models reach a classification rate of 85.6% within the first four interactions and about 89% with 30 and more interactions. Using a reduced data set the models still reach an accuracy of 87.7%. That is, within a single session the trained models can be used to detect the search activity to provide appropriate user support.

Keywords

Exploratory Search; Fact-Finding Search; Multitasking Search; User Study; Modeling; Recognition

CHIIR '17, March 07 - 11, 2017, Oslo, Norway

ISBN 978-1-4503-4677-1/17/03...$15.00

DOI: http://dx.doi.org/10.1145/3020165.3020180

1. INTRODUCTION

Literature shows two broad categories of search activities (also called modes) that can be differentiated: lookup and exploratory search [14]. During lookup search (also referred to as fact-finding) users have a precise goal of finding specific factual information to answer a well-specified question. Exploratory search expands fact-finding by using techniques of learning and investigating, e.g. knowledge acquisition, comparison, analyses, planning etc. [14]. According to Gossen et al. [6], *"exploratory search is a highly dynamic process of a user to interact with an information space in order to satisfy an information need that requires learning about structure and/or content of the information space"*. Furthermore, exploratory search is often characterized as open-ended, multifaceted search with unclear goals [21, 22]. In exploratory search, the acts of searching, browsing and navigation are often more important than the actual find. That is, success in exploratory search does not necessarily mean to find a certain piece of information, but to learn, to investigate and to conceptualize about an initial information need by building up a personal mental model.

Current (web) search engines are quite successful in finding facts in relevant websites or documents if the user is able to specify his or her information need precisely. However search engines still lack sufficient methods to support users who are not familiar with the search domain and hence need to explore the domain. In order to support exploratory search tasks novel search user interfaces (SUIs) have been proposed, e.g. [15, 16], that go beyond conventional interaction techniques and list result visualization allowing users to interact with an information space in a more dynamic way. Furthermore, Huurdeman and Kamps [10] investigate different exploratory features of a user interface, e.g. rapid query refinement, histories/workspaces/progress, and suggest that there are differences in the interaction flow with search user interface features depending on the stage of an exploratory search. Not only the SUIs, but also retrieval algorithms should provide mechanisms to support exploratory search tasks, e.g. ensuring a diversity of search results to cover as many different aspects of the query topic as possible [21]. Therefore, to better support searchers, it is important to be able to differentiate what categories of search activities they are engaged in: lookup search activity or exploratory search activity. Furthermore, if the users current search activity is recognized, not only the selection of search results but also the support provided by the SUIs can be improved.

In this paper, we aim at distinguishing between user's search modes during the search session, which is necessary to provide users with appropriate support at the time of the search. This problem was already mentioned by Belkin in 2008 [4] but is still not sufficiently solved. While it is more simple to consider a user who is performing an exploratory search and distinguish it from a user who is performing a single fact-finding search (which is shorter in nature than an exploratory one [2]), in reality the chance is high that users would carry out multiple searches. Thus, it is not clear when one search ends and another begins. Therefore, we take a step further and consider a user who is successively conducting fact-finding searches on multiple topics. This behavior is also known as multitasking search [19]. Multitasking search sessions are longer than single topic sessions which makes it more challenging to distinguish between them and exploratory search sessions. That is, the goal is to develop a user search behavior model that is able to distinguish between multitasking and exploratory search sessions.

In summary, our contributions include:

- A user study where we collected search behavior data of users solving both consecutive fact-finding tasks on multiple topics and exploratory search tasks on a single topic respectively.
- A user search behavior model that captures natural user's behavior in terms of their interactions, either a multitasking search (consecutive fact-finding) or an exploratory search, with a standard search engine and a web browser.
- Experiments with techniques to recognize user's search mode during the search session. Specifically, we investigated the minimal number of interactions required to classify the search activity with a high accuracy.

The structure of the paper is as follows. In Sect. 2 we describe existing scientific work related to our topic. The description of our user study that was conducted to gather behavioral data is explained in Sect. 3. Based on the gathered data, models of users' search beahavior are built in Sect. 4. We use those models to make inference of users' search mode and analyze the results in Sect. 5. We conclude this investigation in Sect. 6 where we summarize our work and provide possible further research directions.

2. RELATED WORK

2.1 Factual and Exploratory Search

Fact-finding and exploratory search can be intrgrated into the broader field of information-seeking. Research related to this field focuses on the users' behavioral perspective. Kuhlthau [11] proposed an information-seeking model with six stages and corresponding search activities in terms of a so called information search process (ISP). The stages are: Initiation, Selection, Exploration, Formulation, Collection, and Presentation. The model describes information acquisition in relation to user's feelings, thoughts and actions and hence has a strong phenomenological aspect. In the Selection and Exploration stages the user identifies (first) relevant search domains that apparently lead to success but he or she still lacks of knowledge to specify the precise information need and therefore investigates general, broad topics. This stages are strongly related to exploratory search activities. In the Formulation and Collection stages the user is confident, has a focused perspective of the topic (i.e. has domain knowledge) and can clearly gather relevant information. Hence in this stages fact-finding search activities are performed. In [17] the authors proposed an approach to clearly distinguish between the six stages of the ISP over two search sessions for individuals. However, for collaborative information-seeking the distinction between Exploration, Formulation and Collection stages was vague [17]. In contrast to their work, we investigate the classification of search activities within a single session and furthermore analyze the minimal number of interactions to classify this activities.

Further research to investigate differences in information-seeking behavior was done by Marchionini [13]. He investigated the differences between user's search behavior caused by "open", i.e. imprecise, tasks where the information need can not be specified precisely and "closed", i.e. precise, tasks that lead to a clear derivable information need. In his studies Marchionini was able to show that especially novices need more time and have more difficulties to specify the queries for "open" tasks. Focusing on easy and difficult closed tasks, Aula et al. [3] presented the results of a large-scale study with the goal to detect the task difficulty based on the information search behavior. In their work Aula et al. described what kind of strategies users apply if they had difficulties to solve the tasks. For example, users increase the number of queries, view more results or spend more time on result pages. Liu et al. [12] investigated the influence of tasks with different difficulty levels and different types on the user behavior as well. Their findings show that dwell time alone is not a reliable measure for prediction whether users are performing difficult tasks. Hassan et al. [9] investigated user behavior if they experienced difficulties during the search and if users are exploring. The authors highlight the need for advanced methods to distinguish between the users situation. Athukorala et al. [2] conducted a user study with 32 computer science researchers and explored different parameters that can help to distinguish exploratory from lookup tasks. They found that the length of the first query is shorter in exploratory tasks. In exploratory tasks users spend more time reading the documents and scroll significantly deeper than in lookup tasks. The findings of Athukorala et al. [2] are, however, limited to information search related to the machine learning domain in scientific documents when using a search engine they designed (e.g. 40 search results are displayed per page).

The results of the investigations above point out the need for appropriate user support in relation to the current search activity. A search system that is able to distinguish between fact-finding and exploratory search can provide enhanced methods for an adaptive user support. Finally a comprehensive literature review about exploratory search and related studies is given in [18].

2.2 Modeling and Prediction

In order to model users interactions Markov Models were commonly applied in Information Retrieval, however, in settings different to ours. For example, Tran and Fuhr [20] modeled Amazon book search using Markov Chains with four states - search query, search results, book information and shopping cart. Hassan et al. [8] proposed modeling user search behavior using a Markov Model with transition times and showed that this approach performs significantly more accurate than traditional relevance-based models for predicting user search goal success. Ageev et al. [1] applied different Markov Model approaches to predict user's success for fact-finding search tasks. Cole et al. [5] used Markov Models to study interaction patters for complex search tasks. They used users' interaction and gaze data and showed that those two data types can be used independently to distinguish between the search tasks. Yue et al. [24] used Hidden Markov Models to compare collaborative and individual exploratory searches.

Besides Markov Models, machine learning approaches have been used in order to make predictions of user's success in search. Shah et al. [18] applied Support Vector Machines to forecast how well users will perform in the later stages of exploratory search process based on the actions they are currently performing. Athukorala et al. [2] used Random Forests, a machine learning method for classification, to distinguish exploratory from lookup searches after the search is done. Thus, the question remains how well the system can distinguish between the search modes while users are still searching? To the best of our knowledge, there exist no previous work about user's search mode (exploration vs. consecutive fact-finding) identification during the search session. In addition most of related work investigates search activities in specific domains and/or with specific search systems. In this work users searched for multiple topics with a common web search engine.

3. ACQUIRING SEARCH BEHAVIOR DATA

In order to build users' search models, we first acquired search behavior data by conducting a user study in form of a questionnaire and a lab experiment. With the questionnaire we gathered users' demographic data and their experience with search engines. The lab experiment was designed for users to perform multiple search tasks. Two of them were exploratory tasks (*Expl*) and twelve were fact-finding tasks (*Fact*) with varying complexity summarized to a multitasking search. The purpose was to record a sufficient number of interactions for both search activities. Each participant had at most 40 minutes to perform both exploratory tasks (20 minutes per task) and at most 20 minutes to solve up to twelve factual tasks. Thus, each experimental search session was limited to one hour per participant. We used a Latin Square study design to vary the order of tasks between participants with three task blocks:

- Design 1: $Fact$, $Expl_1$, $Expl_2$
- Design 2: $Expl_1$, $Expl_2$, $Fact$
- Design 3: $Expl_2$, $Fact$, $Expl_1$

The twelve tasks within the *Fact* block were randomized. We decided to conduct two exploratory tasks to avoid biases regarding the search task topic in the model generation

The experiment was carried out using the *Firefox* browser. We used the *Google* search engine to perform the search. We recorded users' interactions using a logger developed in our research group as a browser add-on. It enables recording

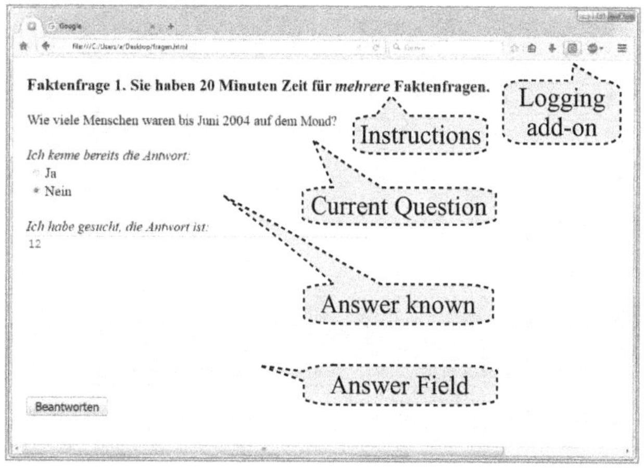

Figure 1: Opened quiz tab during a fact-finding search in the prepared Firefox. The used elements are described via the dotted balloons.

user interactions with the search engine (e.g. result clicks, durations and the search engine result page (SERP) number) and with the browser (scrolling, tab and window activation).

The task assignment was programmed as a quiz which was placed in the first tab (also called quiz tab) of the browser and fixed. The interface, i.e. the quiz tab, is illustrated in Fig. 1. For each task the participants were asked to identify if they already knew the answer (*Fact*) or how much expertise they had (*Expl*). The users had to search for the answer using the search engine even if they knew the answer. We explained that the quality/correctness of the answer is a priority over the number of tasks solved and did not mentioned that the *Fact* block has twelve tasks. We believe that this would result in a more natural search behavior. Once a participant submitted an answer, they got the next question and could not correct this answer later. Since all questions were from different domains and the users should always search only for the current task, it was not necessary to allow a correction of a previous answer. We logged the users' subjective knowledge, the answers and the time they spent with a question. After each participant, the browser history was deleted to avoid highlighting of previously clicked search results and personalization.

3.1 Search Tasks and Participants

We designed twelve fact-finding tasks with two levels of complexity. There were six tasks in each category. Search tasks are considered to be *simple* if the answer to the task can be found in (or derived from) the search result or result snippet on the first SERP using search queries emerged from the task formulation. A task is *difficult*, if all the snippets for the search queries emerged from the task formulation are equally non-informative, so that a user has to evaluate many documents to find the answer or at least read one long document and derive an answer. Table 1 shows all search tasks for each category. One reason to use this categorization was that fact-finding tasks can have, by their nature, different complexity. A further reason was that fact-finding search sessions including difficult tasks may be harder to separate from exploratory search sessions. All tasks have been pretested by two people.

Table 1: Complexity levels and corresponding fact-finding tasks (translated from German).

Level	Task description
Simple	*In what year did the Google search engine went online for the first time?*
Simple	*How old is Mickey Mouse today?*
Simple	*According to current information, how many rooms are in the Buckingham Palace in London?*
Simple	*What are sciaphobs afraid of?*
Simple	*How many men were on the moon until June 2004?*
Simple	*What is the name of the largest passenger aircraft?*
Difficult	*In what period of the Paleozoic era the first reptiles appeared?*
Difficult	*What percentage of German men aged between 70 and 79 suffer from diabetes (data for the year 2011)?*
Difficult	*Which word is coded in Morse code as "–. – . – – – – – – . – .."?*
Difficult	*Which actor won the same year the Golden Raspberry Award for Worst Actor, Worst Supporting Actor and Worst Supporting Actress?*
Difficult	*What is the largest known planet in the binary star system Kepler-47?*
Difficult	*How many years passed between the first flight of the Kitty Hawk Flyers and Neil Armstrong's moon landing?*

For the design of exploratory tasks we considered the attributes described in [22] such as the tasks have

- learning and investigation as goals,
- general, ill-structured and open-ended problems and,
- an involved uncertainty.

We had two exploratory tasks (assigned in German):

[Expl$_1$, adapted from [7]] *Your friends are planning to build a new house and have heard that using solar energy panels for heating can save a lot of money. Since they do not know anything about home heating and the issues involved, they have asked for your help. You are uncertain as well, and do some research to identify some issues that need to be considered in deciding between more conventional methods of home heating and solar panels. Afterwards you want to discuss this topic with your friends and, therefore, make some notes.*

[Expl$_2$, adapted from [23]] *You are flying to Moscow next month. During the travel arrangements you learn that body scanners are being used in many airports as part of routine security procedures. You start thinking about health issues related to their use. Your friends want to calm you down and say that people are exposed to different kind of radiation every day. You want to learn more and start a research to gather a range of information about radiation and health. Afterwards you want to discuss this topic with your friends and, therefore, make some notes.*

Table 2: Time distribution (average *Avg* and standard deviation *SD*) for the three task blocks. *Fact* block had up to twelve factual tasks.

Block	Time, Avg in sec.	Time, SD in sec.
Fact	1177	59
$Expl_1$	1029	194
$Expl_2$	901	319

19 users participated in our study (13 men and 6 women). The majority of the them (14) had a computer science background (PhD students). They were recruited via mailing lists. The study took place in our lab. All the participants use the Internet on the daily basis (several times), use it to search for information and search with *Google*. 17 participants use the Internet for work. All but two of the participants did not know any answers to the factual tasks before the search. Each of those two participants only knew the answer to the (easy) question relating to the largest passenger aircraft. For the exploratory tasks, the participants had to indicate how familiar they were with the topic using a 5-point Likert scale from 1 (Expert) to 5 (Not familiar). The participants had only little information about the topics for both exploratory tasks ($Expl_1$: $median = 4$, $Avg = 4$; $Expl_2$: $median = 5$, $Avg = 4$). They knew less about the topic of the second exploratory task $Expl_2$. Overall, the participants had comparable pre-conditions for the search induced by the fact-finding and exploratory tasks.

Participants spent on average 128 seconds ($min = 18$, $max = 693$, $median = 93$) to answer a factual question. It took them on average 2.6 times longer to answer difficult questions (in sec.: $Avg = 184$, $min = 43$, $max = 693$, $median = 147$) than easy ones (in sec.: $Avg = 69$, $min = 18$, $max = 229$, $median = 51$). On average, the participants answered to 8.8 factual questions ($min = 4$, $max = 12$, $SD = 2.6$). 80% of the answers were correct. The participants made more errors answering difficult questions (28.6% errors) than easy ones (10% errors). The time distribution for the three task blocks is shown in Table 2.

4. MODELING USER'S SEARCH MODE

In order to model user's search, we use and train (*Hidden*) *Markov Models* with different parameters. After defining the models we discuss how the trained models are used to classify a given sequence of user interactions in Sect. 5.

4.1 Modeling the Search Session

User search sessions (*Fact*, $Expl_1$ or $Expl_2$) can be thought of as a sequence of interactions with a search engine and a web browser. Each interaction is represented as a *discrete state*. In this paper, we consider the following four searcher's states:

- *Query* - A searcher is formulating a search query. Searchers can enter a query themselves and also use the *Google*'s query autocomplete suggestions.
- *SERP* - A searcher is examining a search engine result page after the query is submitted.
- *Page* - A searcher is viewing a web page as result of a SERP or a web page found by navigating from an other web page using hyperlinks.

- *Main* - A searcher is viewing the first tab in the browser (the quiz tab) to read, answer or make notes for the current question.

Hence, our data set $\overline{\underline{S}}$ consists of N search sessions indexed by $\underline{S}^i$ with the length L^i and each session comprises a sequence of visited states from the *state space: Query, SERP, Page* and *Main*. That is, $\overline{\underline{S}} := (\underline{S}^1, ..., \underline{S}^N)$ with $\underline{S}^i := (S_1^i, ..., S_{L^i}^i)^T$ and $S_j^i \in \{Query, SERP, Page, Main\}$.

4.2 Markov Models

We assume an independent and identical distribution for all search sessions. The sequence of states for each individual search session forms the following *joint distribution* which will be transformed without loss of generality using the *product rule*:

$$\begin{aligned} P(\overline{\underline{S}}) &= \prod_{i=1}^{N} P(\underline{S}^i) = \prod_{i=1}^{N} P(S_1^i, ..., S_{L_i}^i) \\ &= \prod_{i=1}^{N} P(S_1^i) \cdot \prod_{l=2}^{L^i} P(S_l^i | S_1^i, ..., S_{l-1}^i) \end{aligned} \tag{1}$$

We assume the *Markov assumption* on the conditional distributions. From this it follows that each observation is independent of all previous observations given the most recent. The *Markov Model* directly approximates the *joint distribution* (1).

$$\begin{aligned} P(\underline{S}) &= P(S_1) \cdot \prod_{l=2}^{L} P(S_l | S_1, ..., S_{l-1}) \\ &= P(S_1) \cdot \prod_{l=2}^{L} P(S_l | S_{l-1}) \end{aligned} \tag{2}$$

$P(S_1)$ is the *start probability* of state S_1 and $P(S_l|S_{l-1})$ is the *transition probability* from state S_{l-1} to state S_l. Given a training set comprising of samples representing different search activities we can learn the generative model θ^C for each search activity $C \in \{Fact, Expl\}$. Using the *Bayes Theorem* in combination with the sequence model (2) we are able to apply a probabilistic classifier.

$$\begin{aligned} P(\theta^C | \underline{S}) &= \frac{P(\underline{S}|\theta^C) \cdot P(\theta^C)}{P(\underline{S})} \\ &= \frac{P(\underline{S}|\theta^C) \cdot P(\theta^C)}{\sum_{C'} P(\underline{S}|\theta^{C'}) \cdot P(\theta^{C'})} \end{aligned} \tag{3}$$

$P(\underline{S}|\theta^C)$ is the *likelihood* of the search session given strategy C and $P(\theta^C)$ is the *prior* associated to model θ^C.

4.3 Hidden Markov Models

In addition to *Markov Models* we use *Hidden Markov Models* (HMM) as they are well suited for sequence analysis tasks. HMM make it possible to consider not only the state transition probabilities but also the features associated with each state. In a HMM each interaction is represented as a *discrete state*, which consists of measurable *observations*. In this paper, we concetrate on duration time and scrolling time as measurable observations. The study of Athukorala et al. [2] indicate that these parameters might help to distinguish between lookup and exploratory tasks.

Extending the state sequence $\underline{S}$ we take advantage from the features $\underline{X}$ associated to each state. This will form the combined dataset $\overline{\underline{Z}}$ containing paired sequences $\underline{Z}^i$ of all N searches: $\overline{\underline{Z}} := (\underline{Z}^1, ..., \underline{Z}^N)$ with $\underline{Z}^i := (\underline{X}^i, \underline{S}^i)$. That is, for each search sequence $\underline{S}^i := (S_1^i, ..., S_{L^i}^i)^T$ an associated sequence of feature $\underline{X}^i := (X_1^i, ..., X_{L^i}^i)^T$ is given. Both sequences $\underline{S}^i$ and $\underline{X}^i$ have the length L_i. Analogue to the *Markov Models* we can form the *joint distribution* for $\overline{\underline{Z}}$:

$$P(\overline{\underline{Z}}) = \prod_{i=1}^{N} P(Z_1^i) \cdot \prod_{l=2}^{L^i} P(Z_l^i | Z_{l-1}^i) \tag{4}$$

We assume a HMM on the distribution (4). This implies that the sequence of states follows the *Markov Chain* (2) and the duration/scrolling time in each state i is independent of all states except state i.

$$\begin{aligned} P(\underline{Z}) &= P(\underline{X}, \underline{S}) \\ &= P(S_1) \cdot P(X_1|S_1) \cdot \prod_{l=2}^{L} P(S_l|S_{l-1}) \cdot P(X_l|S_l) \end{aligned} \tag{5}$$

The emission of features (e.g. duration time) is modeled naive with *Exponential Distributions*. We can learn the generative model θ^C for each search activity $C \in \{Fact, Expl\}$. Using the *Bayes Theorem* analogue to (3) we are able to apply a probabilistic classifier.

5. INFERRING USER'S SEARCH MODE

In this section we describe the gathered log data and the experiments to classify the user's search activity using the models defined in Sect. 4. In total, we have recorded user interactions that correspond to 4022 transitions (2130 *Fact* and 1892 *Expl*) in 19 fact-finding and 2x19=38 exploratory search sessions. For the fact-finding sessions this results in the median of 111 interactions with a 25-% and 75-%-quantil of 93 and 122 interactions. In contrast the exploratory search results in a median of 50 and quantils of 34 and 65 interactions respectively. That is, considering the average time spend on the task blocks *Fact* and *Expl* (cf. Tab. 2), in *Fact* each 10.6th second and in *Expl* each 19.3th second an interaction was made.

We structured our approach in 6 consecutive sub tasks. First we characterize a trained *Markov Model* to give a detailed analysis to its real life interpretation. To verify the models applicability we use cross validation to identify its prediction accuracy. Further on, we incorporated additional features to our model and examine the influence to the classification rate. Different model complexities were trained and the optimal settings were selected. We analyzed the interaction of minimal session length and model prediction. Conclusively, to increase the generalizability of our findings we remove artifacts associated to our experimental design, namely the state *main*.

Experiment 1: To get first insights into the differences of fact-finding and exploratory search activities we derive a first order *Markov Model* with all transition probabilities for each search activity, cf. Fig. 2. Besides the obvious transitions, a self reference on the *SERP* state means the click on the next (or previous) search engine result page. When

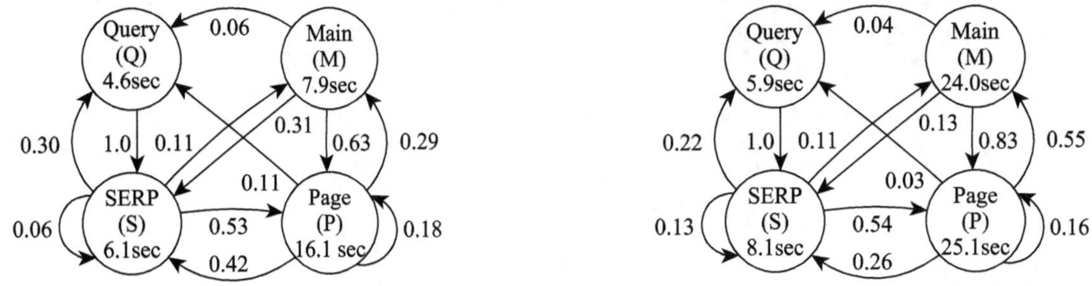

(a) *Fact*; Typical example sequence $\underline{S}^i$: M-Q-S-P-S-Q-S-P-M(Answer)-S-Q-S-Q-S-P-M(Answer)-...

(b) *Expl*; Typical example sequence $\underline{S}^i$: M-Q-S-P-M-P-M-P-M-P-S-Q-S-P-M-P-S-Q-S-P-M-...

Figure 2: First order Markov Models for fact-finding search (a) and exploratory search (b) with their corresponding transition probabilities, average durations and for illustration a typical example sequence $\underline{S}^i$.

comparing the transition probabilities for *Fact* and *Expl* it stands out that users tend to click twice as much on a further SERP in *Expl*, i.e. users examine the result pages more exhaustive. This can indicate a higher complexity for the users to estimate relevant results for the current search query. Interestingly, the probability to go a step back from the *Page* to the *SERP* state and further to the query state is higher in *Fact* than in *Expl*. This could have been due to the time restrictions on each task block (20 min) in our study design: The users need more time on web pages in *Expl* (see below) and, therefore, have less chance to go back and initiate a new search. However, the majority of the users spent less than 20 minutes solving the exploratory tasks. Thus, this assumption does not hold. A more plausible reason is user's ambition to perform best: Even though the study supervisor explicitly informed the participants that the number of solved tasks has no priority, it is possible that the users still tried to solve as many fact-finding tasks as possible and hence formulated more queries in *Fact*. A further interesting difference is the strong interaction between a web page and the quiz tab (*Main*) in *Expl*. Here the users more often switch to the quiz tab to collect/note pieces of information to solve the exploratory task. In *Fact* users mostly reached the *Main* status (only) to submit the answer for the current task, read the next question and seldom made notes. This behavior is also reflected by a selection of typical example sequences in Fig. 2. The reason for the low transition probabilities from the *Main* to the *Query* state is that users rather tend to select an previously used SERP and type in a new query instead of first opening a new (blank) start page and than type the query.

Besides the transition probabilities we also derived and accumulated the durations users spend on several states, cf. states in Fig. 2. When comparing the mean state durations of *Fact* and *Expl* it stands out that the users spend more time in every state of *Expl*. While query formulation and interaction with the *SERP* only take slightly more time, the time spent on web pages and the quiz tab is considerably higher. A possible reason for this difference is that users who are searching for a specific, well-formulated fact only need to fast-scan a web page to estimate, whether the sought information is present or not. During an exploratory search it may be unclear, what information is useful and hence more time is necessary to examine a web page and actually read the text. This confirms the results of Athukorala et al. [2] that users spend more time reading documents, respectively web pages, in exploratory search. Fig. 3 provides a more detailed illustration of the state durations including the exponential distributions with its characteristic parameter lambda.

Experiment 2: To analyze the predictive power of the proposed model we trained Markov Models (cf. Sect. 4) for each search activity using a 5-fold cross validation with 2000 repetitions. That is, for each of the both search activities *Fact* and *Expl* we randomly divide the dataset $\underline{S}$ in a training and test partition. The size of the training set is approximately 4/5 of the data set, i.e. 15 of 19 search sessions of consecutive fact-findings tasks from *Fact* and 30 of 38 search sessions of exploratory search tasks from *Expl*. The training partition is used to learn the two models θ^{Fact} and θ^{Exlp}. Afterwards, the remaining search sessions from the test partition and the trained models are used in the classifier, cf. Eq. 3. According to the two classes in our data set the prior $P(\theta^C)$ was set to the relative class sizes respectively. The whole procedure is repeated 2000 times and afterwards the median for the classification results is calculated, cf. Table 3. According to the table the classification rate is 73.6%.

Experiment 3: As mentioned in the previous section, the results of Athukorala et al. [2] indicate that the parameters state duration and scrolling time might help to distinguish between lookup and exploratory tasks. To incorporate this parameters we use Hidden Markov Models (cf. Sect. 4). In Table 4 the classification results using the scrolling time vs. state duration time are depicted. Using the feature scrolling, the classification rate for *Fact* is nearly identical to Experiment 2 and for *Expl* only one search session more

Table 3: Confusion Matrix for Markov Model according to Experiment 2

	Real Class	
	Fact	Expl
Classified as Fact	13	9
Classified as Expl	6	29
	19	38

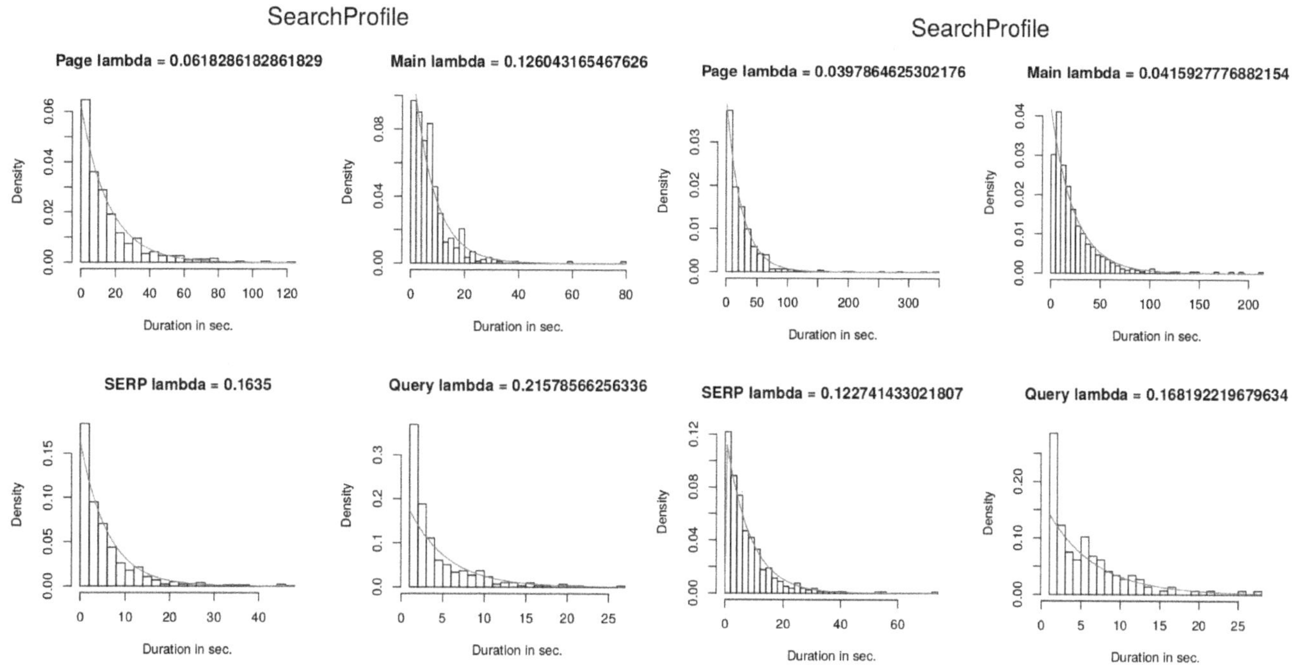

(a) *Fact* (b) *Expl*

Figure 3: Histogram of the empirical state durations with the estimated Exponential Distribution in red for Fact (a) and Expl (b).

is classified correctly and leads to a total classification rate of 75.4%. Using the feature state duration, the total classification rate is increased to 89.4% with 16 right *Fact* and 35 right *Expl* session. If both features are used simultaneously, the classification rate drops down to a value comparable to using only scrolling as feature. A reason for this is that in the models both features are considered independent. But actually the time for scrolling is always contained in the state duration time and therefore the features are correlated. The violation of this independence assumption might lead to the increased classification errors.

Experiment 4: All previous experiments considered (Hidden) Markov Models using the first order, i.e. the probability to reach a state only depends on its direct predecessor state, cf. Fig. 2. To increase the prediction accuracy of Markov Models, it is possible to extend the models by considering the state history up to a specific length, i.e. to increase the model order. The choice of the order depends strongly on the size of data because the higher the order, the longer the necessary interaction sequences and the lower the probability that these interaction sequences are present in a sufficient number in the data set. In Fig. 4 an accuracy comparison of different orders using a simple Maximum Likelihood (ML) estimator and a more advanced Maximum Aposteriori (MAP) estimator is illustrated. The models used in this comparison are the same models as used in Experiment 3 with the state duration feature only. The classification rate for the first order is comparable for ML and MAP, namely on 89.4%. For model orders greater than one the accuracy differs in comparison of the distinct estimation methods. The accuracy for the Maximum Likelihood estimator decreases with each order. The reason for this is the lack of long interaction sequences in the data set. For the Maximum Aposteriori estimator we can observe a similar behavior but with a less crucial effect on the accuracy. The second order model has the highest accuracy with 92.1% in average with a relatively small variance. The diagram in Fig. 4 implies that order two is the best choice for our data set. Using the methods Bayesian model selection, Akaike information criterion and Bayesian information criterion, the choice for order two is confirmed.

Table 4: Confusion Matrix for Hidden Markov Model according to Experiment 3

	Real Class			
	Scrolling		Duration	
	Fact	Expl	Fact	Expl
Classified as Fact	13	8	16	3
Classified as Expl	6	30	3	35
	19	38	19	38

Experiment 5: Additionally, we investigate the minimal interaction sequence length that still leads to high classification rates. In the previous experiments we considered the interaction sequences always in full length. Now we cut the end of each sequence and only consider a certain number on interactions beginning at the first sequence interaction. This will allow us to make an estimate of the minimal interaction length for when the classifier will reach an accurate prediction. As before we continue the optimization process and use for these experiments the models derived in Experiment 4, i.e. HMM with state duration as feature and Markov order two (and for comparison order one, three and four). In Fig. 5 the accuracies for different sequence lengths are illustrated. For the minimal sequence length of one each model makes

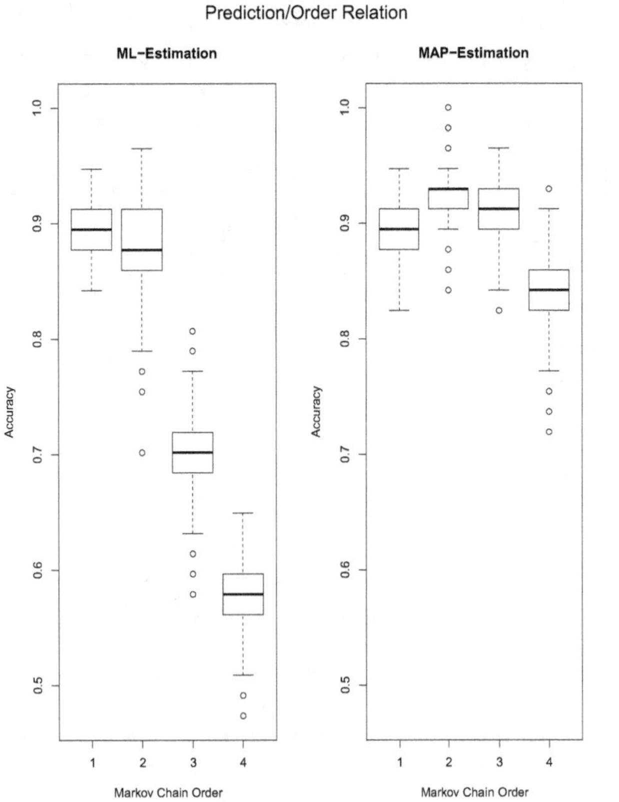

Figure 4: Accuracy comparison of different Markov Model orders using a Maximum Likelihood (ML) and a Maximum Aposteriori (MAP) estimator

predictions on the rate of the prior. Each search starts on the same state *main* and only the duration time holds aspects for classification. While the HMM of order one reaches the maximum of 89.9% accuracy fast within the 4 interactions there is a clear drop off under 80% within the following sequence interactions. Not until 30 interactions the accuracy recovers at a rate of about 85% again. In comparison the HMM of order two reaches an accuracy of 85.6% within the first 4 interactions but without such a crucial drop off in the following predictions. A convergence to stable prediction is reached on 30 interactions on a rate of ca. 89%. HMM's of higher orders suffer from the overfitting problem and produces less accurate results. The drop off is observable even though less crucial than in the case of the HMM of order one. Although the predictive power of the models is slightly reduce in the beginning of the search sessions Experiment 5 indicate that the model is capable to discriminate the search strategy early on within the search session.

Experiment 6: To conduct the user study and gather the interaction data we decided to enable the users to read and process all tasks digital via the web browser (in the question tab). This decision has several advantages. Users do not need to switch between different media (sheet of paper and screen), they can copy paste question fragments directly to the query field (as normal) and can copy paste information from web pages directly to the answer field in the quiz tab. Last but not least for future investigations with eye tracker data the users focus for the whole study

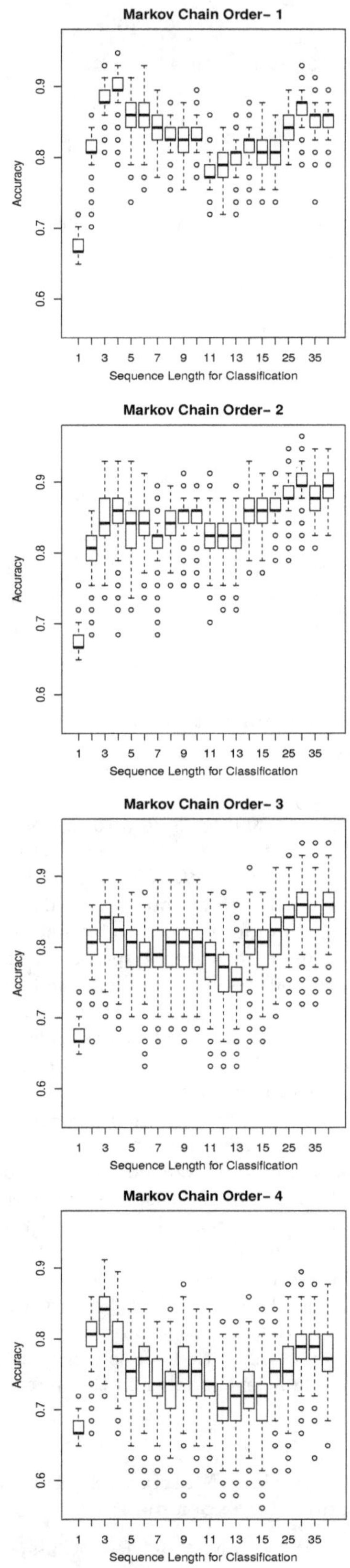

Figure 5: Accuracy comparison for the Markov Model orders one to four using different interaction sequence length; Note the scale switch at the 15th interaction

Table 5: Confusion Matrix for Hidden Markov Model according to Experiment 6

	Real Class	
	Fact	Expl
Classified as Fact	17	5
Classified as Expl	2	33
	19	38

on the screen and hence also gaze data for question reading and answering can be analyzed. Nevertheless the quiz tab is an artifact of the user study and influences a natural interaction with a search system. Thus for Experiment 6 we erased the *main* state from all search sessions and trained the HMM of order two with state durations to receive more realistic results. If the *main* state was between two different other states, the *main* state and its associated feature values (duration and scrolling) could be erased easy. For example P-M-S becomes to P-S (cf. notation in Fig. 2). If *main* was between the same state, the *main* state and its associated feature values were erased and the features for the remaining state were accumulated, e.g. P-M-P becomes to P.

The results are depicted in Table 5. While the classification rate for *Fact* is further increased to 17 (of 19), the rate for *Expl* is decreased to 33. This can be explained by the (previously mentioned) strong interaction between *Page* and *Main* in *Expl* that is now reduced to *Page* (with longer durations). That is, the search sessions for *Expl* become more similar to *Fact* and cause miss classifications. The total classification rate according to Tab. 5 is 87.7%.

6. CONCLUSIONS AND FUTURE WORK

We conducted an investigation into modeling two kinds of web search activities: consecutive fact-finding tasks on multiple topics and exploratory tasks. We designed and carried out a user study to obtain the training data. All assigned tasks were from multiple topics to ensure that the data set is domain independent. We built interaction models based on (Hidden) Markov Models that captures a natural users' behavior in terms of their interactions with a standard search engine (*Google*) and a web browser. We analyzed users' behavior when performing different kinds of search activities. Our findings are consistent with previous evidence [2] that users spend more time reading the documents and scroll more during the search induced by exploratory tasks in comparison to fact-finding tasks. In addition, our findings enrich and supplement the previous results by providing more detailed information about the whole picture of user's interactions, i.e. interaction probabilities and time spent performing different actions during both exploratory and fact-finding search using a common web search engine. The experiments to infer the user's search mode yield classification results between 73.6% and 92.1% for different model and data configurations. That is, within a single session the trained models are able to detect the search activity just in time. Embedding this approach into an adaptive information retrieval systems allows to provide a search activity dependent user support by e.g. ensuring a diversity of search results and providing appropriate suggestions for SUIs.

For future work the contribution of additional recorded modalities such as gaze data (cf. Cole et al. [5]) or users facial expressions to increase the classification rates will be investigated. After investigating the classification of users current search activity there are still many questions how to use this knowledge in a way that users can be supported appropriatley during their search and exploration. Furthermore, the influence of user group specific characteristics can be helpful to estimate the user's current needs and preferred search support.

7. ACKNOWLEDGMENTS

This work was supported by the Transregional Collaborative Research Centre SFB/TRR 62 "A Companion-Technology for Cognitive Technical Systems" funded by the German Research Foundation (DFG). In addition, we would link to thank our research assistants Tetiana Lavynska and Jan-Ole Perschewski for supporting us with the log data preparation.

8. REFERENCES

[1] M. Ageev, Q. Guo, D. Lagun, and E. Agichtein. Find it if you can: a game for modeling different types of web search success using interaction data. In *Proceedings of the 34th international ACM SIGIR conference on Research and development in Information Retrieval*, pages 345–354. ACM, 2011.

[2] K. Athukorala, D. Głowacka, G. Jacucci, A. Oulasvirta, and J. Vreeken. Is exploratory search different? a comparison of information search behavior for exploratory and lookup tasks. *Journal of the Association for Information Science and Technology*, 2015.

[3] A. Aula, R. M. Khan, and Z. Guan. How does search behavior change as search becomes more difficult? In *Proceedings of the SIGCHI Conference on Human Factors in Computing Systems*, CHI '10, pages 35–44, New York, NY, USA, 2010. ACM.

[4] N. J. Belkin. Some(what) grand challenges for information retrieval. *SIGIR Forum*, 42(1):47–54, June 2008.

[5] M. J. Cole, C. Hendahewa, N. J. Belkin, and C. Shah. Discrimination between tasks with user activity patterns during information search. In *Proceedings of the 37th international ACM SIGIR conference on Research & development in information retrieval*, pages 567–576. ACM, 2014.

[6] T. Gossen, M. Nitsche, S. Haun, and A. Nürnberger. Data exploration for bisociative knowledge discovery: A brief overview of tools and evaluation methods. In *Bisociative Knowledge Discovery*, pages 287–300. Springer, 2012.

[7] J. Gwizdka and I. Lopatovska. The role of subjective factors in the information search process. *Journal of the American Society for Information Science and Technology*, 60(12):2452–2464, 2009.

[8] A. Hassan, R. Jones, and K. L. Klinkner. Beyond dcg: user behavior as a predictor of a successful search. In *Proceedings of the third ACM international conference on Web search and data mining*, pages 221–230. ACM, 2010.

[9] A. Hassan, R. W. White, S. T. Dumais, and Y.-M. Wang. Struggling or exploring?: Disambiguating long search sessions. In *Proceedings of the 7th ACM International Conference on Web Search and Data*

Mining, WSDM '14, pages 53–62, New York, NY, USA, 2014. ACM.

[10] H. C. Huurdeman and J. Kamps. From multistage information-seeking models to multistage search systems. In *Proceedings of the 5th Information Interaction in Context Symposium*, pages 145–154. ACM, 2014.

[11] C. C. Kuhlthau. Inside the search process: Information seeking from the user's perspective. *Journal of the American Society for Information Science*, 42(5):361–371, 1991.

[12] J. Liu, C. Liu, J. Gwizdka, and N. J. Belkin. Can search systems detect users' task difficulty?: Some behavioral signals. In *Proceedings of the 33rd International ACM SIGIR Conference on Research and Development in Information Retrieval*, SIGIR '10, pages 845–846, New York, NY, USA, 2010. ACM.

[13] G. Marchionini. Information-seeking strategies of novices using a full-text electronic encyclopedia. *Journal of the American Society for Information Science*, 40(1):54, 1989.

[14] G. Marchionini. Exploratory search: from finding to understanding. *Communications of the ACM*, 49(4):41–46, 2006.

[15] M. Nitsche and A. Nürnberger. Trailblazing information: an exploratory search user interface. In *Human Interface and the Management of Information. Information and Interaction Design*, pages 230–239. Springer, 2013.

[16] T. Ruotsalo, J. Peltonen, M. Eugster, D. Głowacka, K. Konyushkova, K. Athukorala, I. Kosunen, A. Reijonen, P. Myllymäki, G. Jacucci, et al. Directing exploratory search with interactive intent modeling. In *Proceedings of the 22nd ACM international conference on Conference on information & knowledge management*, pages 1759–1764. ACM, 2013.

[17] C. Shah and R. GonzÃąlez-IbÃąÃśez. Exploring information seeking processes in collaborative search tasks. *Proceedings of the American Society for Information Science and Technology*, 47(1):1–7, 2010.

[18] C. Shah, C. Hendahewa, and R. González-Ibáñez. Rain or shine? forecasting search process performance in exploratory search tasks. *Journal of the Association for Information Science and Technology*, 2015.

[19] A. Spink, M. Park, B. J. Jansen, and J. Pedersen. Multitasking during web search sessions. *Information Processing & Management*, 42(1):264–275, 2006.

[20] V. T. Tran and N. Fuhr. Using eye-tracking with dynamic areas of interest for analyzing interactive information retrieval. In *Proceedings of the 35th international ACM SIGIR conference on Research and development in information retrieval*, pages 1165–1166. ACM, 2012.

[21] R. W. White and R. A. Roth. Exploratory search: Beyond the query-response paradigm. *Synthesis Lectures on Information Concepts, Retrieval, and Services*, 1(1):1–98, 2009.

[22] B. M. Wildemuth and L. Freund. Assigning search tasks designed to elicit exploratory search behaviors. In *Proceedings of the Symposium on Human-Computer Interaction and Information Retrieval*, page 4. ACM, 2012.

[23] W.-C. Wu, D. Kelly, and K. Huang. User evaluation of query quality. In *Proceedings of the 35th international ACM SIGIR conference on Research and development in information retrieval*, pages 215–224. ACM, 2012.

[24] Z. Yue, S. Han, and D. He. Modeling search processes using hidden states in collaborative exploratory web search. In *Proceedings of the 17th ACM conference on Computer supported cooperative work & social computing*, pages 820–830. ACM, 2014.

What Snippet Size is Needed in Mobile Web Search?

Jaewon Kim[†], Paul Thomas[§†], Ramesh Sankaranarayana[†], Tom Gedeon[†], Hwan-Jin Yoon[¶]

[†]Research School of Computer Science, [¶]Statistical Consulting Unit
The Australian National University
Canberra, Australia
{jaewon.kim, ramesh.sankaranarayana, tom.gedeon, hwan-jin.yoon}@anu.edu.au

[§]Microsoft
Canberra, Australia
pathom@microsoft.com

ABSTRACT

A snippet (content summary for a web page) is one of the main elements in a search result page. Search engines have been improved to reduce users' effort in web search, e.g., providing flexible snippet sizes by considering the purpose of the search and suggesting predicted answers. In most cases, search engines for mobile devices present two or three lines of snippet for each result link. Some studies suggest that long snippets provide a better search experience on desktop screens, but this may not be true for mobile devices because of the smaller screen.

We conducted a user study to investigate what size of snippet is appropriate for mobile devices. Our findings suggest that users with long snippets on mobile devices exhibit longer search times with no better search accuracy for informational tasks. This is caused by the longer reading time, frequent scrolling with bigger viewport movements, and greater time consumption for searching and reading one result. The overall findings suggest that, unlike desktop users, mobile users are best served by snippets of two to three lines.

CCS Concepts

•Information systems → Search interfaces; Web search engines; •Human-centered computing → *Touch screens; Laboratory experiments;*

Keywords

Mobile web search; snippet length; search engine result page

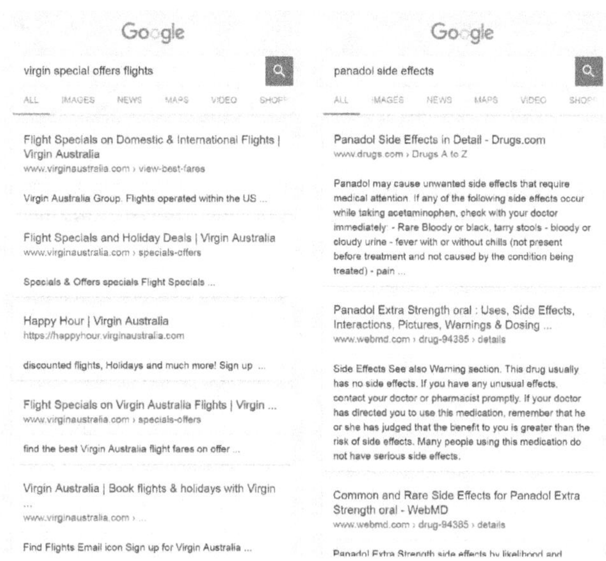

Figure 1: Examples of initial SERPs with short (left) and long (right) snippets.

1. INTRODUCTION

Web searching is a major activity on mobile devices [1] and its usage is increasing [24]. Most search engines display *search engine result pages* (SERPs) with several result links, which mainly contain the title, URL, and *snippet* (also known as the summary, caption, or document surrogate). The snippet occupies a larger space in each result, compared to the title and URL.

Current commercial mobile search engines often provide a knowledge graph (KG) to present relevant long information or an instant answer (IA) for popular user queries. Some search engines control the snippet length by predicting the users' goals through analysing the queries. In addition, some mobile SERPs provide a few lines of snippet for each result link that can be expanded to six or more lines by using the 'view more' buttons. The above ideas and technologies are clearly implemented to reduce user effort to reach some particular bit of information or destination web site, and for a better search experience.

Although search engines have been developed with the above-mentioned technologies, most search engines for mobile devices typically provide two or three lines of snippet for a result link; the information in the snippets does not seem to differ from the displays in desktop monitors. Furthermore, when the KG and IA are not relevant, the effect is

CHIIR '17, March 07-11, 2017, Oslo, Norway

 ISBN 978-1-4503-4677-1/17/03...$15.00

DOI: http://dx.doi.org/10.1145/3020165.3020173

worse user satisfaction with increased search times for users on mobile devices [17].

Some studies have investigated the effect of snippet lengths on desktop screens [4, 13, 21]. Some of their results suggest that long snippets are more useful for finding a particular piece of information [4], and that snippets are currently too short to provide sufficient information in many cases [13].

Several studies [11, 14, 16, 22] have suggested that search behaviour can vary by screen size. Therefore, the appropriate snippet length for a mobile device may be different from that of a desktop machine. We conducted an experiment to investigate the effect of snippet length on a mobile device with three different lengths (see Figure 1 for examples of short and long snippets) and two different task-types.

Considering the results from previous studies regarding snippet lengths on desktop screens, we formulated three hypotheses prior to conducting the experiment. First, although there might be some difference due to the smaller screen, we imagined that long snippets would have a positive effect in the search time when looking for a particular piece of information, similar to the results in the previous study [4]:

- H1. For finding a particular piece of information, users will take less search time with long snippets, and need more time with short snippets.

Second, we expected that the users would focus on different elements in the same way they do on a desktop screen [4]:

- H2. Among the title, URL, and snippet, users will consider the snippet as the most important element for finding a particular bit of information, and the URL for reaching a requested web page.

Third, even though we guessed that the search time would be reduced with long snippets, the user satisfaction might differ because of the small screen and familiarity with the snippet length of current search engines:

- H3. Users will express better satisfaction with medium snippets for finding a particular piece of information, and with short snippets for reaching a requested web page.

2. BACKGROUND

We introduce three necessary general lines of background knowledge. The first concerns *reading and scanning SERPs*, the second is related to *search behaviour by snippet length*, and the third addresses *mobile web search*.

2.1 Reading and scanning SERPs

Eye-tracking is a popular method of investigating user interaction in web search, which provides information on the user's gaze, e.g., user attention, saccade, and pupil dilation [12, 23]. Although much work has examined user interaction with web searches using gaze data, we would like to mention some studies related to general search behaviours, which are helpful for reading this paper.

A few studies have investigated broad scanning patterns on SERPs, e.g., the areas that attract searchers' attention and the sequence of the interest. Hotchkiss et al. [9] found that users make a "golden triangle" pattern: the most popular area in first time visits to a SERP, and suggest that considering this pattern is important for SERP design, because a user's interest is dramatically reduced outside of the golden triangle. The result of another study [20] indicates that users exhibit an "F-shaped pattern" while searching, i.e., they scan one vertical stripe followed by two horizontal stripes. This study suggests some guidelines for better web page design, e.g., the most important things should be stated within the first two paragraphs.

Some studies investigated users' scanning patterns involved in their first click decision. Granka et al. [8] focused on how users explore the result links in SERPs above and below the selected link. Their finding suggests that ranks one and two receive most of the user's attention, similar to the results of Hotchkiss [9] and Nielsen [20]. They also found that users tend to scan the links above the selected link. However users often use different patterns near the page fold with some further observation below the selected link.

A study by Joachims et al. [10] presented results similar to the findings of Granka et al. [8] and additionally suggested that users are affected by rank order, after analysing the effects of three different manipulated rank orders (normal, swapped, and reversed). The results of both studies broadly indicate that users read the search results with a top-to-bottom scanning pattern, although Thomas et al. [28] found that some users began their exploration from a different position rather than the top rank on SERPs.

A few studies examined search behaviours according to the user's goals in web search. Broder [3] classified task types into *informational*, *navigational*, and *transactional* web searches with purposes of finding particular information, reaching a specific website, and performing some web-activity, e.g., an online purchase, respectively.

Lorigo et al. [18] conducted an experiment to investigate user behaviours with the informational and navigational tasks. Their findings suggest that users take more time to complete informational tasks. Both informational and navigational tasks have been commonly used (e.g., [8, 10, 14]), and the task types are one main consideration in this study.

In addition, Lorigo et al. defined a *compressed sequence* and a *minimal scanpath* using the fixation sequence. The original scanpath is the sequence of all fixations on a SERP. We can extract the compressed sequence by aggregating consecutive fixations on the same object, and the minimal scanpath can be obtained by removing the previous visits from the compressed sequence. For example, if we assumed that the original scanpath is 2-2-2-1-1-2-3-3-2-4-4, the compressed sequence would be 2-1-2-3-2-4 (length: 6), and the minimal scanpath would be 2-1-3-4 (length: 4). Both the compressed sequence and minimal scanpath have been adopted by several studies to investigate users' search strategies. In this paper, they are valuable measurements for analysing the sequence of movements in user attention.

2.2 Search behaviour by snippet length

Some researchers studied the effects of snippets in SERPs. Paek et al. [21] conducted a user study to compare the usability and user preferences regarding different methods of displaying snippet information, e.g., *normal view*: the full web page was shown by clicking the title; *instant view*: an expanded snippet was additionally displayed by a mouse click; and *dynamic view*: an effect similar to the instant view by mouse hovering over a particular result. They found that the instant view exhibited faster task completion than the normal view, and about half of the participants preferred the instant view.

A study by Cutrell and Guan [4] focused on the effects of snippet length. They examined search behaviours with three different snippet lengths on a desktop screen (short, medium, and long). Their findings indicated that users tend to spend less search time with the long snippets for informational tasks, whereas the long snippets for navigational tasks required more time. They also found that long snippets for informational tasks led the user to look at fewer links; however the opposite pattern was observed for navigational tasks.

Kaisser et al. [13] conducted two experiments to estimate the preferred snippet length according to answer type (e.g., person, time, and place), and to compare the results of the preferred snippet length to users' preferences in a user study to investigate whether the preferred snippet length could be predicted. Their results suggested that the preferred snippet length depends on the answer type, and users tend to express better satisfaction with the estimated preferred snippet length. Overall their findings indicate that longer snippets may be more useful if the snippets are relevant for the query.

2.3 Mobile web search

Several studies of mobile web search provide reasons for investigating the effect of snippet length on mobile devices. A few studies evaluated the search performance and behaviour between mobile devices and desktop monitors. Jones et al. [11] investigated the search performance of a mobile phone, a personal digital assistant (PDA), and a desktop monitor. Their findings indicated that small screens lead to worse search speed and accuracy. In addition, Kim et al. [14] examined user performance and behaviour on small and large screens for mobile devices and desktop monitors using an eye tracker. They found that users with a small screen were slower to complete tasks due to more reading time, having more difficulty extracting information and displaying less eye movement.

Some studies focused on search behaviour with small screens. Raptis et al. [22] conducted a user study to investigate the effects of three different mobile device screen sizes (3.5, 4.3, and 5.3 inches). They evaluated three variables: perceived usability, task completion times (for efficiency), and task completion rates (for effectiveness). They found that users with the smallest screen needed more time to complete tasks, although no effect was found related to the perceived usability and task completion rate.

Recently, Kim et al. [16] investigated search performance, behaviour, and user satisfaction on three sizes of mobile phone screens (3.6 inches for early smartphones, 4.7 inches for recent smartphones and 5.5 inches for phablets). They saw different behaviours on each screen size, that is, the small size: a higher chance of scrolling with the worst user satisfaction; the medium size: fast information extraction with some hesitation before selecting a link; and the large size: less eye movements on top links.

The above work on user interaction in mobile web search broadly suggest that search behaviour can differ according to screen size, and search engines should consider the difference, which supports the need for this study.

Table 1: Examples of task descriptions and queries.

Informational
• Panadol is a brand of pain reliever. What are some side-effects of Panadol? Is a rash one of them? (panadol side effects) • You are interested in some facts about the Golden Gate bridge in U.S. In what year was the bridge construction completed? (golden gate bridge) • Which two countries played for the 4th match in the Cricket World Cup 2011? (cricket world cup 2011 dates)
Navigational
•You are interested in shoes from Adidas. Find the official Adidas homepage.(adidas shoes [country]) • Find the web page where you can apply for a saving account on the Citibank website. (citibank new account) • You bought a laptop from Sony and something doesn't work as expected. Find the page for Sony technical support.(sony laptop technical support)

3. USER STUDY

This section describes the experimental design and the procedure.

3.1 Participants

We recruited 30 participants with varying backgrounds, e.g., chemistry, biology, computer science, education, history, and law, from inside and outside a university campus. We excluded six of them due to low eye gaze tracker calibration accuracy, leaving us with 24 participants (13 male) aged 22–42 (mean: 29.4, standard deviation (SD): 5.7).

Using 7-point Likert-scale questions (1: completely unfamiliar/bad, 7: completely familiar/good), participants were asked how familiar they were with search engines and how good they were at using mobile devices. The participants marked high scores for both the first (mean: 6.25, SD: 0.6) and second (mean: 5.79, SD: 1.0) questions. That is, most participants considered themselves familiar with search engines and good at using mobile devices.

3.2 Tasks

Each participant completed twelve tasks (six each of informational and navigational tasks; see Table 1 for examples of the tasks) which were derived from those of Dumais et al. [6]. The task categories varied, e.g., chemistry, sports, travel, history, and law, and the tasks were simple. Every task had at least two relevant links within the top three ranks, and included a correct answer/destination web page.

We extracted the SERP rank orders with titles and URLs from one of the most popular mobile search engines (Google). However, we generated the different snippet lengths using Nutch for crawling and Solr for snippets with the Lucene library [27] using the highlight function, because we were unable to find a search engine that provided long snippets (six or more lines) when we designed the experiment[1]. Each task had 10 search result links with titles, URLs and snippets.

We prepared three different snippet lengths: short with one line, medium with two or three lines, and long with six

[1]Yandex recently introduced longer snippets with 'read more' buttons if the users want to see more than the typical snippet lines. This is not available via an API at the time of writing.

to seven lines as shown in the short and long snippet examples in Figure 1. With the snippet length manipulation, the initial SERPs displayed 5.0 (4.6–5.4), 3.7 (3.4–3.9), and 2.4 (2.3–2.7) result links above the page fold with short, medium and long snippets, respectively. The long snippet includes the medium snippet, and the short snippet is part of the medium snippet.

3.3 Design and procedure

In this experiment, we adopted a within-subject design to investigate the effect of the two main treatments: task type (2) × snippet length (3). Each participant completed 12 tasks, including six tasks for each task type, and two of the six tasks included the same type of snippet length (i.e., a set of 'SSMMLL' for informational and navigational tasks. S, M, and L denote short, medium, and long, respectively). To minimize the carry-over effect, we randomized the task order within each task type. In addition, the orders for task type and snippet length were counter-balanced, and every task was evenly shown with the three different snippet sizes across the participants.

After they agreed and signed the consent form, we showed them three sample tasks with each snippet length to familiarize them with solving the tasks. We then calibrated their gaze recording using a 9-point procedure, and the task lists were shown on the screen.

When the participants clicked the first task on the list, the description and initial query for the task were displayed. After this, the participants could proceed to the first SERP. Once they announced the desired information or reached the requested web page, we considered the task to be completed. After each task, the participants were asked about their satisfaction with the snippet length using a 7-point Likert scale (1: completely dissatisfied, 7: completely satisfied). The cycle was continued to the last (12th) task.

At the end of the experiment, participants were asked to fill out a post-experiment questionnaire, which included basic information, such as age, background, familiarity with search engines and using mobile devices, their preferred snippet length, and their thoughts about the most important SERP element (title, URL, or snippet) for each task type. Our participants spent about 25–30 minutes in the laboratory room to complete everything from the welcome introduction to filling out the questionnaire.

3.4 Apparatus

We adopted an iPhone 6 plus (5.5 inches with a 1080×1920 pixel resolution) for the experiment, which has a popular screen size [19]. The mobile phone was connected to the main system as a secondary monitor using the Twomon software [5] and search results were displayed through Internet Explorer. To collect the gaze data, we used Facelab 5 [26], and we analyzed the data using Eyeworks [7].

4. RESULTS

We obtained data from 288 tasks (144 tasks for each task type, and 48 tasks for each snippet length within each task type). We focused on the effects both by task types (*informational tasks* (ITs) and *navigational tasks* (NTs)) and snippet length (short, medium and long).

To investigate the hypotheses, we measured search time for H1, user attention for H2, and user satisfaction for H2 and H3. We explored search behaviour, e.g., scroll rates, with viewport movements and scanpath, as introduced in Section 2. In further investigation, we analysed how search behaviour was related to search performance and user attention.

We adopted several analysis techniques. First, we employed analysis of variance (ANOVA) for continuous data, e.g., search time and fixation duration, with a log-transformation $log(x+1)$ to maintain the normality assumption. Second, we adopted generalized linear mixed models (GLMMs) [2] with a binomial distribution and a logit link function for binary data, and a Poisson distribution and logarithm link function for countable data. Third, for the score data from the 7-point Likert scale, we used a linear mixed model (LMM) [30]. Finally, linear regression [25] was adopted to analyse the relationships between two dependent variables (e.g., scanpath and search time).

We acknowledge that there may be individual differences in our participants' familiarity with web search engines and mobile devices. To consider the individual difference, we used a block structure (subject) for ANOVA, and adopted a GLMM and LMM instead of a generalized linear model (GLM) and a linear model (LM) because observed random effects between subjects (σ_s^2) were greater than standard errors (SEs) in all variables.

All analyses were conducted using the GenStat statistical package [29].

4.1 Search performance and user attention

To test H1, we first adopted *task completion duration* (the total time required to complete a task) as search time; this is the same approach as in Cutrell and Guan's study [4]. Only task type significantly affected task completion duration ($F_{(1,259)} = 172.22$, $p < 0.001$). As can be seen in Table 2, the time spent for ITs was almost twice that for NTs (36–41 s for ITs vs 18–21 s for NTs) and participants exhibited no difference on time spent by snippet length. However, because each task included several relevant links on a SERP, the time spent on the linked web pages varied considerably according to the design for either a full site or a mobile-friendly version. The effect of different resolutions among web pages is beyond the search engine's control. Therefore we considered the *time to first click* as the main search time in this study instead of task completion duration, and compared search time to search behaviour. Note that the time to first click is very similar to the task completion duration minus the time spent on web documents, because participants needed only one click to reach the answer for most of the tasks (overall 94%).

We also found significant effects due to task type, snippet length and their interaction on time to first click ($F_{(1,259)} = 32.58$, $p < 0.001$, $F_{(2,259)} = 5.63$, $p < 0.01$, and $F_{(2,259)} = 3.36$, $p < 0.05$, respectively). This indicates that participants with ITs needed more time to decide (mean 18.9 s vs 13.6 s, for averages of ITs and NTs, respectively), and long snippets led participants to stay longer on the SERPs (mean 14.6 s, 15 s, and 19.3 s, for short, medium, and long, respectively). The effect of the interaction of the two treatments seems to be caused by long snippets for ITs (about 8 s higher, as shown in Table 2). As can be seen in Figure 2, participants with ITs exhibited the highest time consumption with long snippets, although the time spent for NTs does not follow this pattern.

We calculated search accuracy as another search perfor-

Table 2: Search performance, behaviour, and satisfaction for each task type, broken down by snippet length.

		ITs			NTs			*p*-value		
		S	M	L	S	M	L	Task type	Snippet length	Interaction
Search performance	Task completion duration [s]	36.37	41.20	40.98	18.89	20.43	21.10	***	0.24	0.80
	Time to first click [s]	16.24	16.35	24.03	12.90	13.69	14.47	***	**	*
	Search accuracy	0.85	0.85	0.94	1.00	0.98	1.00	*	0.22	0.97
Fixation duration	Total [s]	7.71	7.98	11.69	6.71	6.87	6.98	***	0.06	*
	On titles [s]	4.20	3.48	3.60	3.65	3.60	2.79	0.15	*	0.24
	On URLs [s]	1.55	1.44	1.41	1.68	1.30	1.41	0.42	0.29	0.92
	On snippets [s]	1.96	3.06	6.68	1.38	1.97	2.79	***	***	**
	per link [s]	1.85	2.52	3.56	1.92	2.51	2.66	*	***	*
Search behaviour	Scroll rate	0.29	0.21	0.46	0.17	0.13	0.25	**	**	0.89
	Viewport movement (pixel)	540	675	1148	640	422	1021	0.20	**	0.72
	Compressed sequence length	9.56	7.50	8.27	7.13	6.42	5.75	***	0.12	0.61
	Minimal scanpath length	4.17	3.23	3.13	3.46	2.79	2.50	***	***	0.81
	Revisit	5.40	4.27	5.15	3.67	3.63	3.25	**	0.66	0.60
User satisfaction	7-point Likert scale	4.46	5.35	4.67	5.25	5.21	4.23	0.60	***	***

*Significant at 0.05 level. ** Significant at 0.01 level. *** Significant at 0.001 level.
Note: ITs and NTs denote informational and navigational tasks, and S, M, and L denote short, medium and long snippets, respectively.

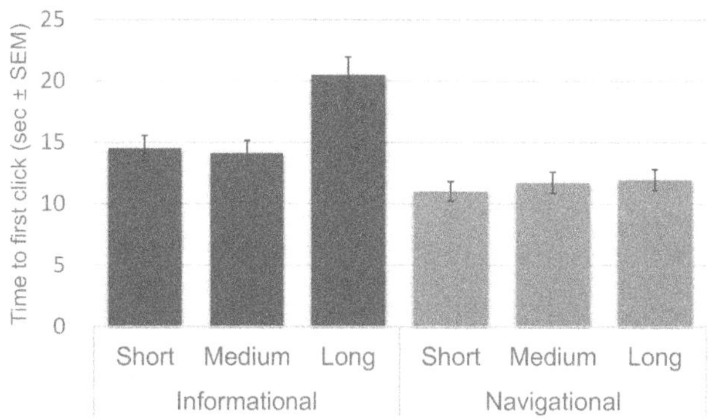

Figure 2: Search time (time to first click). Note that numbers on each y-axis are the values after back-transformation.

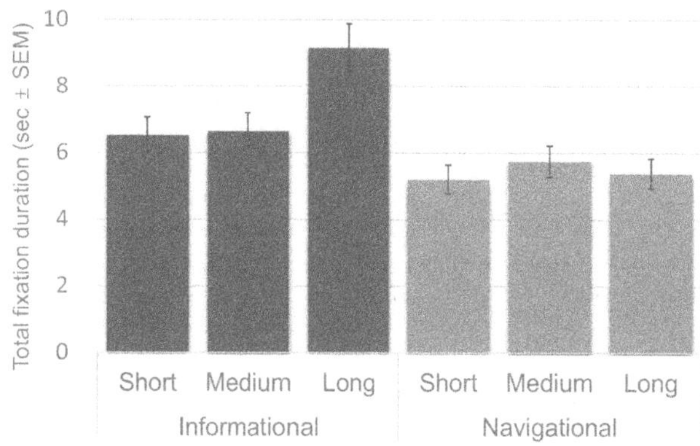

Figure 3: Total fixation duration. Note that numbers on each y-axis are the values after back-transformation.

mance measurement. Each SERP in our tasks included several relevant links with correct answers, unlike the tasks in Cutrell and Guan's study [4], which only contained one best answer. In this paper, therefore, we defined accuracy as the proportion of reaching the correct answer on the first attempt.

A significant difference can be observed in search accuracy between the task types ($\sigma_s^2 = 0.464$, $\chi^2 = 5.10$, df $= 1$, $p < 0.05$). This indicates that navigational tasks are easier to complete. However, even though we considered the chance at the first attempt, the rates are very high for both task types (the lowest is 85%). In addition, the mean rate for long snippets for ITs is higher than with other snippets (about 9%). However, this result is not statistically significant and does not seem to explain the reason for the longest time spent with long snippets for ITs. Although long snippets might lead to better correct answer rates if the tasks are more difficult than ours, our results suggest that participants with long snippets for ITs did not exhibit better search accuracy, despite spending more time.

To test H2 and further investigate the influences on search time, we measured fixation duration to examine how much effort participants expended to extract the information [12, 23]. Considering the screen size and the distance between participants and the screen, fixations were recorded if a gaze lasted at least 100 ms within a 70 pixel diameter region using algorithms in the Eyeworks software, and we assigned areas of interest (AOIs) to titles, URLs and snippets in each result link.

We adopted ANOVA to compare the user's attention on titles, URLs, and snippets, and the total duration of the three elements. The task type and the interaction between task type and snippet length had significant effects on total fixation duration ($F_{(1,259)} = 20.86$, $p < 0.001$ and $F_{(2,259)} = 3.27$, $p < 0.05$, respectively). As shown in Table 2, ITs with long snippets received about 4 s more attention than the other snippets. With the interaction of task type and snippet length, the pattern shown in Figure 3, for each task type, and broken down by snippet length, is very similar to the pattern for search time (see Figure 2). Using linear regression, we ran further investigations for the relation between total fixation duration and search time and, we found that the relation was clearly positive (common slope: 0.73, SE: 0.29). This suggests that the increase in search time is mainly explained by an increase in time spent reading.

Before moving our focus to user attention on each element, we thought it would be helpful to confirm the difference of the proportion of total fixation duration of each element, to

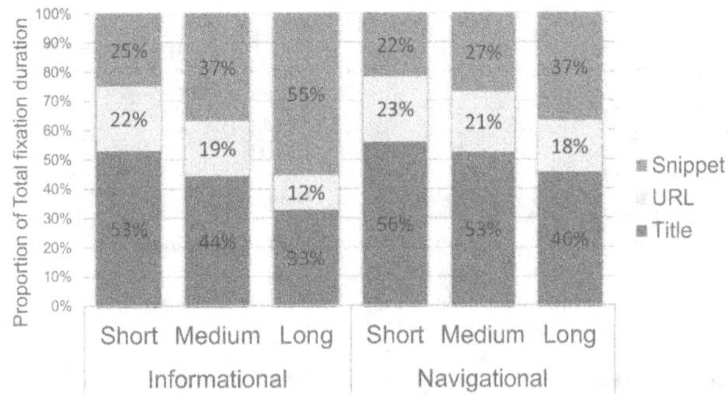

Figure 4: Proportion of total fixation duration for each element of SERPs.

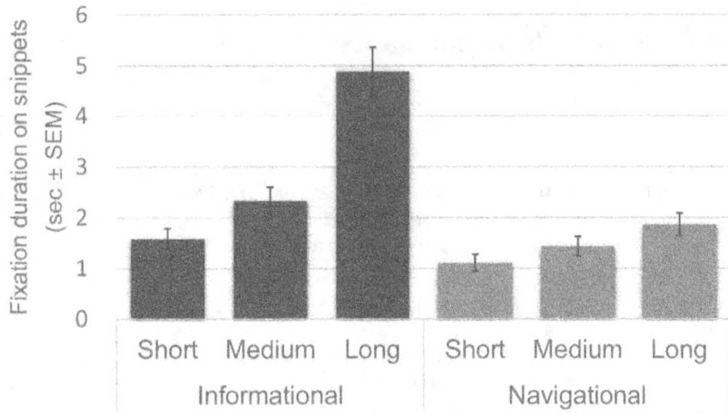

Figure 5: Fixation duration on snippets. Note that the numbers on each y-axis are the values after back-transformation.

better understand overall user attention and also make it possible to test H2.

Figure 4 illustrates how participants distributed their interests for each SERP element according to task type and snippet length. As a general pattern, participants exhibited similar attention for both task types: as the snippet size increased, the title and URL received smaller proportions of attention, whereas the participants tended to look more at snippets. Although participants with NTs also exhibited this pattern, it was clearer for ITs: the proportions of reading the title and URL for ITs were reduced by almost half (from 53.0% and 22.2% to 32.8% and 11.9% for the title and URL, respectively).

Considering the result of total fixation duration (the longer reading time with long snippets for ITs), one possible inference is that participants with long snippets applied additional effort to snippets for ITs, rather than that the proportions of reading the title and URL were absorbed into the snippet reading time. We investigated the inference by analysing user attention on each element.

Fixation duration on the title exhibited a significant difference according to snippet length ($F_{(2,259)} = 3.23$, $p < 0.05$). Although participants paid less attention to the title with long snippets across both task types, as expected from the difference in the proportion of user attention on the title, the maximum difference within each task type was less than 1 s as shown in Table 2. In addition, participants did not exhibit any difference in attention on the URL due to both variables. We now expect that the inference is true: the longest total fixation duration with long snippets for ITs is due to the different fixation duration on snippets, because the difference in proportions of reading both the title and URL had little (about 1 s on the title) or no effect.

Fixation duration on the snippet was affected by task type, snippet length, and their interaction ($F_{(1,259)} = 41.08$, $p < 0.001$, $F_{(2,259)} = 26.54$, $p < 0.001$, and $F_{(2,259)} = 6.06$, $p < 0.01$, respectively). As we inferred, Figure 5 shows that medium snippets for ITs led participants to pay more attention to the snippet than the short snippets did (1.96 s vs 3.06 s in Table 2) and long snippets for ITs resulted in the most attention (6.68 s in Table 2). The pattern for navigational tasks looked similar but the difference observed between short and long snippets was only about 1.4 s, which is not as large as the effect with ITs. Considering the effect due to task type, this result also suggests that the subjects did not need to read the NT snippets as much as they needed to read IT snippets.

Although there was a little difference in user attention on the title (less than 1 s), the above user-attention results on each element suggested that participants basically read the title and URL with some duration across all snippet lengths; then, they paid more attention to the snippet if its length was longer. This pattern was especially strong for ITs.

Aggregating the search-performance results, ITs caused a longer search time than NTs, and participants with long snippets for the ITs required more time, whereas they exhibited no difference by snippet length for NTs. In addition, they exhibited very high accuracy rates without the effect of snippet length. When we considered user attention, we confirmed that the different reading time for snippets is an important component of the biggest cost for search time with long snippets for ITs.

Considering several different conditions (e.g., tasks, participants, and measurements for search time) between our experiment and Cutrell and Guan's experiment [4], we cannot compare the results directly. However, our findings suggest at least that the long snippet does not improve search speed for ITs, unlike the result on a desktop monitor [4]. Therefore, our result does not support H1. In addition, we expected that we could test H2 (user preference among title, URL, and snippet for both task types) with the results of the proportion of fixation duration on each element. However, because the proportions varied according to snippet length, we could not judge whether our results supported H2 or not. This test is revisited in Section 4.3 with the user-preference results in the post-experiment questionnaire.

4.2 Search behaviour

We confirmed that fixation duration is one main contributor to the difference in search time. However, the common slope for the relation between search time and total fixation duration is 0.73, which indicates that the difference in search time is not entirely explained by the time spent reading. In this section, we explore scanning behaviours such as scrolling and the scanpath, and investigate some relations between the behaviour and the search time to determine what else caused the longer search time with long snippets for ITs.

Scroll action. Once users scroll a page, they tend to read a few more results over the page fold [8, 10], and this may cause an additional cost beyond the page fold. Using a

GLMM, we found significant effects due to task type and snippet length on scroll rate ($\sigma_s^2 = 0.387$, $\chi^2 = 7.36$, df = 1, $p < 0.01$ and $\chi^2 = 4.85$, df = 2, $p < 0.01$, respectively). As can be seen in Table 2, participants exhibited different scrolling habits and tended to scroll more often for ITs (14% higher).

The main reason for the difference due to snippet length was the high chance of scrolling with long snippets for both task types. Although snippet length caused a similar pattern in both task types, the difference between the medium and long snippets for ITs appears larger (25% and 12% for ITs and NTs, respectively) and this frequent chance of scrolling seems to be related to the searching and reading time.

Using an LMM, we confirmed the effect of scrolling (scrolled vs. non-scrolled) on search time: scrolling significantly affected search time ($\sigma_s^2 = 0.011$, $\chi^2 = 112.57$, df = 1, $p < 0.001$) without any interaction with task type or snippet length. This result means that participant scrolling led to an increased search time (mean: from 12.93 s to 26.11 s).

With the result of how often users scrolled, we also wondered how far the participants moved the viewport to look at further results beyond the page fold once they had scrolled, because participants with long snippets needed to scroll more to see another link. Based on an LMM and using a log-transformation for the normality assumption, a significant snippet length effect could be observed in viewport movement ($\sigma_s^2 = 0.078$, $\chi^2 = 5.71$, df = 2, $p < 0.01$). As shown in Table 2, the long snippet brought more viewport movement for both task types.

Both results regarding scrolling indicate that the higher chance of scrolling (46%) with bigger viewport movements is another contributor for longer search times with long snippets for ITs.

Scanpath. Scanpath presents the sequence of movements in user attention. Based on a GLMM, we analysed some scanpath measurements, e.g., compressed sequence and minimal scanpath lengths. As introduced in Section 2.1, compressed sequence (how many links a user looked at, including repeat visits) and minimal scanpath (how many different links a user looked at, removing repeated visits from the compressed sequence) were commonly adopted [6, 14, 16, 18] to investigate users' scanning strategy.

Only task type effect was observed on compressed sequence length ($\sigma_s^2 = 0.088$, $\chi^2 = 10.73$, df = 1, $p < 0.001$). This indicates that the subjects tended to visit more links (including revisits) for ITs. Because this length consists of the actual number of links the users looked at and revisits into the links, we could investigate this further by analysing minimal scanpath length.

We also found significant task type and snippet length effects on minimal scanpath length ($\sigma_s^2 = 0.046$, $\chi^2 = 15.53$, df = 1, $p < 0.001$ and $\chi^2 = 16.70$, df = 2, $p < 0.001$, respectively). This means that participants looked at more links with short snippets for both task types (maximum about one link), whereas they exhibited no difference between medium and long snippets (3.1–3.3 links for ITs, 2.5–2.8 links for NTs).

However, when we considered the numbers of result links displayed on the initial SERPs with each snippet length (averages: 5.0, 3.7, and 2.4 links; see Figure 1 for examples of short and long snippets), the mean minimal scanpath lengths for long snippets (3.13 and 2.5) appeared somewhat

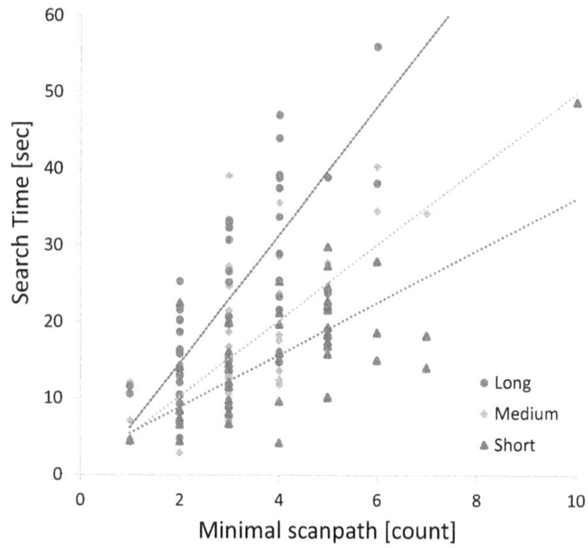

Figure 6: Relationship between minimal scanpath (scanned links) [count] and search time (elapsed time to first click) [sec]. When a participant looks at three links, this leads to about 12.3, 15.2, and 23.0 s spent with short, medium, and long snippets, respectively. The slopes (SEs) are 8.38 (0.66), 4.95 (0.78), and 3.41 (0.62) with p < 0.001 for short, medium, and long snippets, respectively.

high to explain the effect without scrolling, especially for ITs. As we confirmed the relationship between scrolling and search time, we also wondered how the number of scanned links affected search time. Therefore, we investigated the relationship between minimal scanpath (how many links a participant looked at) and the search time (time to first click) for ITs.

Figure 6 uses linear regression to show the relationship. When the minimal scanpath was one, users spent the same amount of time with each snippet length. However, as the length of minimal scanpath increased, users with longer snippets needed to spend more time. This suggests that participants with long snippets scanned slightly less/similar numbers of links compared to those with short and medium snippets; however, the number of scanned links with long snippets required a larger time cost, possibly because of the higher scroll rate.

Relations between search behaviours. With the results of compressed sequences and minimal scanpaths, we can measure two interesting search behaviours. First, using the difference between minimal scanpath and compressed sequence, we can extract the number of links the participants revisited. Revisit count exhibited a significant difference according to snippet length ($\sigma_s^2 = 0.144$, $\chi^2 = 7.85$, df = 1, $p < 0.01$). Although the revisit counts differed between task types (about 1.5 links more on average for ITs), the participants exhibited no different revisit patterns across the snippet length for either task types; even the number of revisited links with long snippets in ITs (5.15) is larger than the count for medium snippets (4.27). If we take the revisit counts as a proxy for users' hesitating, the participant tended to similarly hesitate with the different snippet lengths before

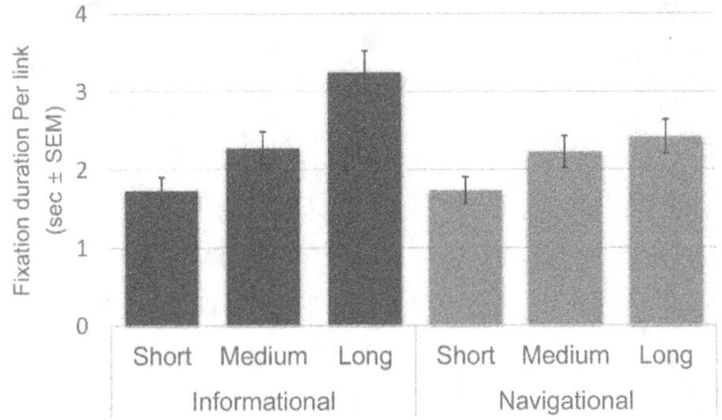

Figure 7: Fixation duration per link. Note that numbers on each y-axis are the values after back-transformation.

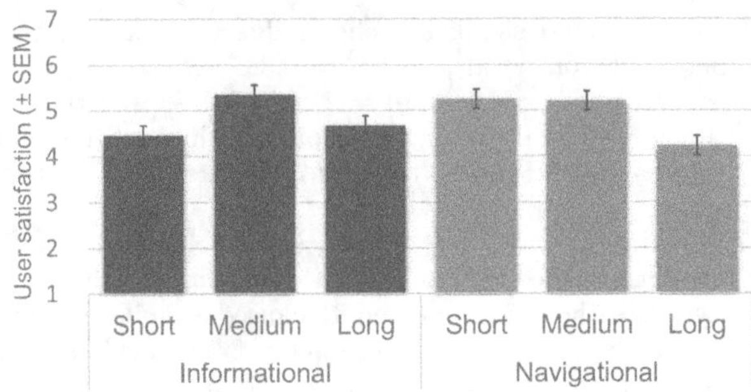

Figure 8: User satisfaction: 7-points Likert scale.

deciding where to click on SERPs, despite those with long snippets needing more effort to move their eye gaze to other links (and possibly scroll).

Second, connecting minimal scanpath to the fixation duration, we could extract fixation duration per link which means how much effort users made to read a link. We found significant effects due to task type, snippet length and their interaction on fixation duration per link ($F_{(1,259)} = 4.59$, $p < 0.05$, $F_{(2,259)} = 27.70$, $p < 0.001$ and $F_{(2,259)} = 3.68$, $p < 0.05$, respectively). As can be seen in Table 2, the participants exhibited slightly less reading time for each scanned link for NTs (2.65 s vs 2.36 s, for ITs and NTs, respectively), and they also spent different amounts of time reading with the three different snippet lengths. As shown in Figure 7, participants needed more time to extract information from one link as snippet length increased (1.85 s, 2,52 s, and 3.56 s from short to long snippets), this pattern was observed between short and medium snippets for NTs.

This explains the relation between the number of scanned links (minimal scanpath) and the reading time. The search time in Figure 6 includes both reading time and other actions (e.g. scrolling). Therefore, we could not examine whether the participants also needed to spend different times reading each link according to snippet length. With this figure, we can confirm that the long snippets for ITs caused both longer reading and search time per link.

In this sub-section, we found that participants with long snippets scrolled more frequently with bigger viewport movements, and that they needed more effort with long snippets to both search and read one link with similar or slightly fewer numbers of looks at links per task, and with similar hesitation in choosing a link. We confirmed that the above two results were related to search time, and these were other reasons for the greater time consumption with long snippets for ITs.

4.3 User preference and post-experiment questionnaire

In a qualitative analysis, user satisfaction is one of the most important factors in designing user interfaces, including SERPs design. As mentioned in Section 3.3, participants were required to score their satisfaction after each task using a 7-point Likert scale regarding the snippet length. Table 2 shows that there were significant effects due to snippet length and the interaction of task type and snippet length on user satisfaction ($\sigma_s^2 = 0.447$, $\chi^2 = 12.93$, df $= 2$, $p < 0.001$ and $\chi^2 = 7.68$, df $= 2$, $p < 0.001$, respectively). The overall satisfaction was affected by snippet length, however the patterns differed according to task type.

Figure 8 shows that participants with ITs marked the highest scores (5.35) for the medium snippets (no difference between short and long snippets, with scores of 4.46 and 4.67, respectively), and they expressed the worst satisfaction on the long snippets for NTs (4.23). In other words, participants preferred the medium snippet for ITs, and disliked long snippets for NTs. Unfortunately, it is complicated to find a relationship between user satisfaction and search performance.

After the experiment, participants were asked to choose the most important element among the title, URL, and snippet for deciding about each task type. They also needed to fill out their preference about snippet length for the task types, along with the reasons for their preference.

For ITs, sixteen participants replied that the snippet was the most important element. Six of the remainder replied that they mainly looked at the title when choosing (one of them also chose the snippet as well). Only three participants considered the URL as the most valuable element for ITs. Similar to the user satisfaction results, the participants' overall preferred IT snippet length was the medium snippet (medium: 18, long: 5, and short: 1). Participants' opinions, such as those below, reflected our observations of searching and reading time:

"6–7 lines [of snippet] were useful, but I could not concentrate."

"Long [snippet] takes more time to read and short [snippets] sometimes does not contain enough information."

For NTs, eleven participants replied that the title was the most important component, and 14 subjects said the URL was the most useful factor (one user chose both). However, no one chose 'snippet'. Participants preferred one or 2–3 (short or medium) line snippets for NTs to six or more lines (long snippets). Thirteen of the subjects expressed that short snippets were the best, the remainder (11) replied that medium snippets were suitable for NTs. No one chose the long snippets for NTs. This also matches the user satisfaction results: long snippets were worst and medium or short were better for NTs.

"Firstly, I use the URL to specify the website and I use snippets to support my thought. 2-3 lines [of snippet] are enough to check some basic information."

"One line is too short, and I don't need long sentences [for NTs]."

"[I need one line because,] the title and URL are enough to reach the particular web page."

In addition, we asked participants about the quality of the query and the task difficulty; i.e., if the cached queries were relevant and how difficult the tasks were. With a 7-point Likert scale (1: completely different/difficult, 7: completely same/easy), the participants scored 6.4 (SD: 0.6) for similarity between the cached queries and their own if they could make them up (they could re-check all descriptions and queries before they marked the scores), and gave 6.25 (SD: 0.8) points for task difficulty. Therefore we could confirm that we prepared appropriate queries for the tasks, and the tasks were simple.

We could not confirm whether our results supported H2 by analysing the proportion of fixation duration on each element, because it varied by snippet length. According to the user preference results for SERP elements, almost consistent with H2, users considered that the most valuable component was the snippet for ITs, and the title and URL for NTs. Regarding H3, although it was not 100% consistent, participants were satisfied with the medium snippets for ITs, and with short and medium snippets for NTs. Therefore our results broadly supported H3.

5. DISCUSSION

For each result, we have discussed the meanings of explicit and implicit data for search performance, behaviour, and user preference. In this section, we summarize our discussion and address several limitations in this experiment that we should consider.

First, our search performance results show that navigational tasks are easier than informational tasks, similar to the results from previous studies (e.g. [4, 14]). We also found a snippet-length effect: i.e., participants with long snippets for ITs exhibited longer search time with no difference in search accuracy. This result on a mobile device differed from the results on a desktop [4]: long snippets reduced search time, although we could not compare directly.

When we investigated user attention, we found one reason for the longer time consumption because of the long snippets: participants' attention on SERPs formed a pattern very similar to search time across the snippet length and task types. Furthermore, we finally confirmed that the longer reading time with the long snippets mainly came from the longer user attention on the snippets. Further analysis is required to investigate the reason why users read the long snippets.

Second, we analysed search behaviour to investigate how participants reacted differently to SERPs with different snippet sizes, and to see if there was another factor that affected search time. Our findings suggested that the higher scrolling frequency with more viewport movements to see additional links beyond the page fold was another reason for the worse search time for long IT snippets, even when participants could reach a relevant link without scrolling.

We also confirmed that participants with long snippets scanned similar (or slightly different) numbers of links with similar hesitation before deciding on the SERPs, although the long snippets clearly required more time for searching and reading each link. The combination of scrolling and scanning behaviour was another reason for the long search times with long snippets for ITs. In addition, the difference in search time between both task types seemed to come from obvious differences in scroll rates and scanpath: less chance of scrolling and fewer scanned links. For users' better search experience, horizontal pagination [15] may help reduce the effect of scrolling, and highlighting the query words in the snippets may reduce hesitation behavior on SERPs.

Third, our findings displayed similar results in both post-task and experiment questionnaires. For ITs, our participants expressed that the snippet was the most important element, but they preferred two or three line snippets. For NTs, they considered the URL and title as more valuable than the snippet, and no one wanted long snippets (over six lines). In addition, our participants expressed the view that the prepared queries were very appropriate for each tasks and the tasks were quite easy to solve. This results seems that they might be "trained" through their everyday searches with the snippet length provided by current search engines.

5.1 Limitations

We acknowledge that our experiment had several limitations, which might affect our results. First, we recruited participants from a particular pool, although the age range was wide and they had varying backgrounds. Therefore, our results cannot represent the search behaviour of all users in the world.

Second, one disadvantage of the laboratory study was that our participants could not move while conducting the experiment. They were asked to sit on a chair and not make big movements to ensure accuracy for our gaze recording. We know this condition is different from actual searching on mobile devices.

Third, the tasks had similar difficulties including at least two relevant results within the top three links, and we counter-balanced the task distribution across the participants. Moreover our participants confirmed that the quality of tasks was very appropriate. However, we recognize that different task difficulties and/or lower quality of queries might lead to different user interaction.

Fourth, even though the mobile device in our experiment had a popular screen size [19], the screen size is a major factor in displaying different snippet lengths. The number of links shown in SERPs should differ according to screen size [16, 22], and this could cause different results.

Fifth, we extracted snippets using Nutch and Solr/Lucene. Therefore the quality of snippets may differ from snippets extracted by other search engines.

6. CONCLUSIONS AND FUTURE WORK

The purpose of this study was to investigate user interaction according to different snippet lengths with both informational and navigational task types. Considering the limitations, we concluded that if we provide users with long snippets for mobile searches, instead of the typical two or three snippet lines, it will take longer because they will read the snippets.

In addition, even if a relevant link is on the top page, users will frequently want to read more to check further links over the page fold, and the cost of scrolling and reading far outweighs the benefit (no better chance of reaching a correct answer), especially for finding a particular piece of information. Most importantly, users would not be satisfied with the long snippets and would finally want to read two–three lines for ITs and one–three lines for NTs.

Unlike the effect of long snippets for desktop screens, the long snippets did not seem to be useful for mobile devices. Overall, although users might become accustomed to searching with the typical snippet size, our results suggested that mobile users are best served by snippets of two to three lines.

The limitations indicated that the screen size and task difficulty might cause other effects, and the function for expanding snippets (e.g., Yandex mobile search engine) appears to improve search performance and user satisfaction. Therefore, our future work will include extending this investigation with various levels of task difficulty on several different screen sizes of mobile devices, and evaluating the usability of expandable snippets.

7. REFERENCES

[1] Adwords. Building for the next moment, 2015. Retrieved from http://adwords.blogspot.com.au/2015/05/building-for-next-moment.html.

[2] N. E. Breslow and D. G. Clayton. Approximate inference in generalized linear mixed models. *Journal of the American Statistical Association*, 88(421):9–25, 1993.

[3] A. Broder. A taxonomy of web search. *ACM SIGIR Forum*, 36(2):3–10, 2002.

[4] E. Cutrell and Z. Guan. What are you looking for?: An eye-tracking study of information usage in web search. In *Proceedings of the SIGCHI conference*, pages 407–416. ACM, 2007.

[5] Devguru. Twomon USB. Retrieved from http://devguru.co.kr/easynlight-en/.

[6] S. Dumais, G. Buscher, and E. Cutrell. Individual differences in gaze patterns for web search. In *Proceedings of the third symposium on Information interaction in context*, pages 185–194. ACM, 2010.

[7] Eyetracking. Eyeworks. Retrieved from http://www.eyetracking.com/Software/EyeWorks.

[8] L. A. Granka, T. Joachims, and G. Gay. Eye-tracking analysis of user behavior in WWW search. In *Proceedings of the 27th annual international ACM SIGIR conference*, pages 478–479. ACM, 2004.

[9] G. Hotchkiss, S. Alston, and G. Edwards. Eye tracking study. *Research white paper, Enquiro Search Solutions Inc*, 2005.

[10] T. Joachims, L. Granka, B. Pan, H. Hembrooke, and G. Gay. Accurately interpreting clickthrough data as implicit feedback. In *Proceedings of the 28th annual international ACM SIGIR conference*, pages 154–161. ACM, 2005.

[11] M. Jones, G. Buchanan, and H. Thimbleby. Improving web search on small screen devices. *Interacting with Computers*, 15(4):479–495, 2003.

[12] M. A. Just and P. A. Carpenter. Eye fixations and cognitive processes. *Cognitive Psychology*, 8(4):441–480, 1976.

[13] M. Kaisser, M. A. Hearst, and J. B. Lowe. Improving search results quality by customizing summary lengths. In *ACL*, pages 701–709, 2008.

[14] J. Kim, P. Thomas, R. Sankaranarayana, T. Gedeon, and H.-J. Yoon. Eye-tracking analysis of user behavior and performance in web search on large and small screens. *Journal of the Association for Information Science and Technology*, 66(3):526–544, 2015.

[15] J. Kim, P. Thomas, R. Sankaranarayana, T. Gedeon, and H.-J. Yoon. Pagination versus scrolling in mobile web search. In *Proceedings of the 25th ACM International on Conference on Information and Knowledge Management*, pages 751–760. ACM, 2016.

[16] J. Kim, P. Thomas, R. Sankaranarayana, T. Gedeon, and H.-J. Yoon. Understanding eye movements on mobile devices for better presentation of search results. *Journal of the Association for Information Science and Technology*, 2016.

[17] D. Lagun, C.-H. Hsieh, D. Webster, and V. Navalpakkam. Towards better measurement of attention and satisfaction in mobile search. In *Proceedings of the 37th international ACM SIGIR conference*, pages 113–122. ACM, 2014.

[18] L. Lorigo, B. Pan, H. Hembrooke, T. Joachims, L. Granka, and G. Gay. The influence of task and gender on search and evaluation behavior using Google. *Information Processing & Management*, 42(4):1123–1131, 2006.

[19] Mobile Marketing. Majority of mobile web browsing on smartphones bigger than 5 inches, 2015. Retrieved from http://mobilemarketingmagazine.com/54708-2/.

[20] J. Nielsen. F-shaped pattern for reading web content. *Jakob Nielsen's Alertbox*, 17, 2006.

[21] T. Paek, S. Dumais, and R. Logan. Wavelens: A new view onto internet search results. In *Proceedings of the SIGCHI conference*, pages 727–734. ACM, 2004.

[22] D. Raptis, N. Tselios, J. Kjeldskov, and M. B. Skov. Does size matter?: Investigating the impact of mobile phone screen size on users' perceived usability, effectiveness and efficiency. In *Proceedings of the 15th international conference on Human-computer interaction with mobile devices and services*, pages 127–136. ACM, 2013.

[23] K. Rayner. Eye movements in reading and information processing: 20 years of research. *Psychological Bulletin*, 124(3):372, 1998.

[24] Search Engine Land. Worldwide, more than half of Google's searches happen on mobile, 2015. Retrieved from http://searchengineland.com/half-of-google-search-is-mobile-232994.

[25] S. Searle. *Linear Models*. Wiley Classics Library. Wiley, 1997.

[26] Seeingmachines. Facelab5. Retrieved from http://www.seeingmachines.com/.

[27] The Apache Software Foundation. Nutch and Solr/Lucene. Retrieved from http://www.apache.org/.

[28] P. Thomas, F. Scholer, and A. Moffat. What users do: The eyes have it. In *Asia Information Retrieval Symposium*, pages 416–427. Springer, 2013.

[29] VSN International. Genstat for Windows 17th edition., 2014. VSN International, Hemel Hempstead, UK. Web page: www.vsni.co.uk.

[30] B. T. West, K. B. Welch, and A. T. Galecki. *Linear mixed models: A practical guide using statistical software*. CRC Press, 2014.

Structure-Aware Visualization of Text Corpora

Jaspreet Singh
L3S Research Center
Hannover, Germany
singh@L3S.de

Sergej Zerr
University of Southampton
Southampton, UK
s.zerr@soton.ac.uk

Stefan Siersdorfer
Hannover, Germany
siersdorfer@outlook.de

ABSTRACT

Trying to comprehend the structure and content of large text corpora can be a daunting and often time consuming task. In this paper, we introduce a novel tool that exploits the structural properties for extracting and visualizing the underlying topics in a given dataset. To this end, we make use of a combination of latent topic analysis, discriminative feature selection applied on top of the category structure of corpora, and various ranking methods in order to extract the most representative topics for a given corpus. The visual moniker to depict the outcome of these methods can be chosen based on the context. Such visual representations can be useful for depicting trends, identifying "hot" topics, and discovering interesting patterns in the underlying data. As applications, we create example representations for a variety of corpora obtained from conference proceedings, movie summaries, and newsgroup postings. Our user experiments demonstrate the viability of our approach, with a flower-like visualization inspired by the "wheel of emotion", for generating high quality representative topics and for unearthing hidden structures and connections in large document corpora.

1. INTRODUCTION

Today's web contains a vast amount of text corpora such as collections of blogs, newsgroup postings, proceedings of scientific conferences, and data from different social media platforms. Web search engines also often return over a million web pages even for specific queries. These datasets can be extremely large and often cover a wide range of facets and topics. Historians, social scientists, and journalists frequently face the challenge of analyzing such corpora; obtaining a good overview of the data often serves as a starting point for deeper analyses.

Analytic tools like [1, 21] focus on data exploration and trend discovery whilst tag clouds have become a popular overview tool for web data and other document collections. On the Web, the latter were initially introduced by the social photo sharing platform Flickr to show the most popular tags used in the community. Tag clouds visualize tags in different sizes which typically correspond to term frequencies, and arrange them in various graphical layouts. This type of visualization soon spread throughout the Web 2.0 sphere, and is nowadays also used to visualize other text corpora [24].

CHIIR '17, March 07-11, 2017, Oslo, Norway

DOI: http://dx.doi.org/10.1145/3020165.3020182

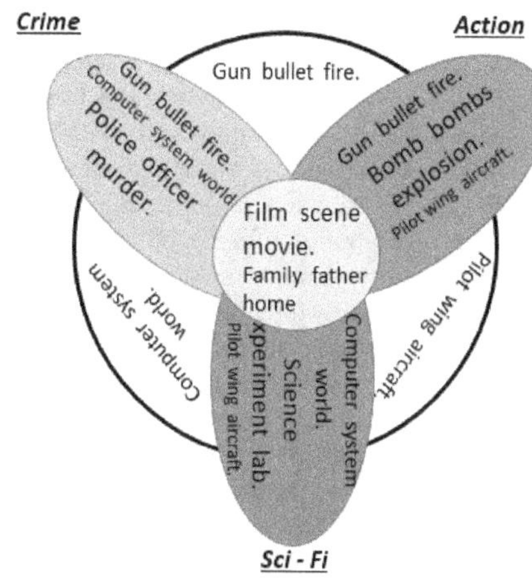

Figure 1: Stylized representation of TopicFlower for a dataset of movies with 3 categories (see Figure. 3 for more detailed real world examples).

Content analysis and overview tools, like tag clouds, often depend on unsupervised techniques like clustering, LDA and word2vec to first find a more compact representation of the information space. Next depending on the scenario and typicalities of the corpus, an appropriate visualization is chosen, which imposes certain structural constrainsts. Finally the tool must automatically select the best information to fit in the chosen visualization. Tag clouds can provide a compact and meaningful overview of a data set, and, by exposing the most frequently occurring words, can enable users to form an impression of the underlying information and to gain additional insights. Advancements made in semantic analysis and topic modeling lead to an increasing popularity of *topics*, represented through key terms, for describing and analyzing datasets [11]. Typically such tag and topic clouds ignore the underlying structure of the described collection, though.

Let us consider large document collections that exhibit some kind of explicit or implicit category structure. For instance, web repositories are often subdivided into different thematic categories, newsgroups are structured into different subtopics and scientific papers can be both categorized by research areas and the time of publication. Current tag and topic clouds are not tailored to inherently deal with corpora containing such category structure. Tag clouds look at the corpus on a term level and are not concerned with the organization of the documents in the dataset. Sticking with tag clouds one could argue that we just have to generate tag clouds for each category in order to obtain a sufficient visual overview. However, this is where the tag cloud's bias towards the most frequent tags/terms becomes an inherent weakness. The more documents we have in the dataset the more likely it is that the terms within the dataset reflect the domain in general if we just consider raw frequency. Analysts, however, need to be able to find topics that discern each category rather than just representing generic domain information.

For text corpora with flat categorization, we propose the usage of a flower-like visualization (sketched in Figure 1) inspired by the manually generated "wheel of emotions" described in [33]. Corpora with richer categorization structure, like hierarchies, can be visualized by more complex graphs but in this paper we focus on the simpler use case. The flower moniker allows us effectively to distribute terms or topics mined from the corpus with respect to the categories. Similar to tag clouds we focus on the textual content of the data set rather than statistics like number of documents per category. Our visualization, named TopicFlower, is content centric rather than document centric, and guided by the structure of the data set. The flower representation captures many interesting aspects of text collections such as central topics, relatedness of categories, and connecting topics; at the same time this moniker avoids exposing the user to plethoric information such as the precise volumes of sub-corpora, the similarity between all possible pairs of categories, and the exact distribution of topics. Our example in Figure 1 shows a stylized illustration of a TopicFlower (see Figure 3 in Section 4.2 for real automatically generated visualizations). The corpus in the example contains three categories corresponding to movie genres and forming the petals of the flower: "Crime", "Action", and "Sci-Fi". Each petal contains a number of characteristic topics. In addition, connecting topics between adjacent categories are provided in between the petals. The center of the flower shows topics that are representative for the corpus as a whole.

In order to generate a TopicFlower, we first extract topics from the entire dataset using latent topic modeling (LDA) [4]. Note, other text clustering and summarization techniques can also be used but we focus on LDA in this work. Such latent topics can be represented as a list of characteristic terms. Topics with high probability that are rather evenly distributed accross categories can be seen as the most generic for the domain of the whole corpus, and provide us with a broad picture - they are placed in the middle. The petals of the flower represent the categories and are ordered according to estimated semantic similarity. Petals contain topics that are more specific for a given category, and the space between the petals contains the topics connecting adjacent categories. Our method for generating such flowers does not depend on a specific dataset or domain. In a comprehensive user study we show the efficacy of using a combination of discriminative analysis and LDA for identifying the representative topics for a given category and connecting topics between categories. We also test whether the most uniformly distributed topics are adequate to describe a corpus in general. Finally, we conduct additional studies to reveal the ability of the TopicFlower to help users discerning more insights when compared to current tag/topic clouds.

The rest of this paper is organized as follows: In Section 2, we describe related work on cluster labeling, self-organizing maps, tag clouds, and representations based on topics. Section 3 introduces our methods and steps involved in generating TopicFlower representations from corpora. In Section 4 we show examples of automatically generated representations for various datasets, evaluate the individual steps of our methods, and compare them to other baseline approaches and state-of-the-art methods for term based summarization of corpora. Finally, we conclude and point out directions for future work in Section 5.

2. RELATED WORK

Cluster Labeling. Cluster labeling [27] deals with assigning a concise label for a set of objects or documents with similar properties. Centroid based techniques select terms, phrases, or titles that are most similar to the majority of the documents in such sets. When multiple clusters have to be labeled, information theoretic measures can be used to select labels, that uniquely differentiate a given cluster from other clusters in the collection [27]. In addition, external knowledge such as information extracted from Wikipedia can be exploited to obtain descriptive cluster labels [5]. However, current works on cluster labeling do not take into account latent topic structures and connections between clusters, as well as the combined visualization of these aspects.

Self Organizing Maps. Self-organizing maps (SOMs) were originally developed by Kohonen [19] who employed a neural network based algorithm to spatially represent documents or other data instances in a corpus (with points in the map corresponding to individual instances). SOMs serve as a succinct representation of the organization of data sets based on a selected set of features. Points in the map close to each other are also closely related semantically [25]. SOMs have been widely used as an IR tool and for exploring documents on the Web [18, 21, 20]. In this paper, we focus on summarizing content and identifying connections between categories of structured corpora, rather than on computing spacial representations of instances.

Tag clouds. Tag clouds are a simple method for providing visual summaries and for exploring data [37]. They illustrate the content using a cloud of words where the font size varies according to the importance of the word - with "importance" being typically estimated by term frequencies. Skoutas et al. [38] explore different alternatives to the frequency based approach, including diversification and rank aggregation. Their results show that considering raw term frequency is one of the better approaches in terms of tag coverage, overlap, and selectivity. Numerous studies have looked at improving tag clouds by altering their layout. For instance, Schrammel et al [36] found in their experiments that ordering the tags based on semantic similarity was more useful than other layouts. Hearst et al [16] study the actual efficacy of a tag cloud as a data analysis tool. An important conclusion within the scope of this paper is that many users perceive tag clouds as less useful as an analysis tool due to the bias of tag clouds towards the most popular terms. In [8] multiple parallel tag clouds are built to provide a more comprehensive overview of a faceted dataset - in that specific work to highlight the differences between the facets of a court hearings data set. The corpus representation method presented in this paper goes beyond the described term-based cloud representations by providing additional context information through identification of more general (latent) topics for categories in a structured corpus and through visualization of connections between categories.

Representations based on topic models. Techniques like Latent Dirichlet Analysis (LDA) [4] can be employed for uncovering the latent semantics of corpora. Hierarchical LDA [2] is a generalization of LDA that models hierarchies of topics. Although our TopicFlower representation also includes hierarchies (where topics can be considered as facets of categories), in this paper, we focus on the distribution of topics among the categories rather than hierarchical structures within the topic model itself.

A major trend has been to study the evolution of topics over time. In [3] the temporal evolution of individual topics is taken into ac-

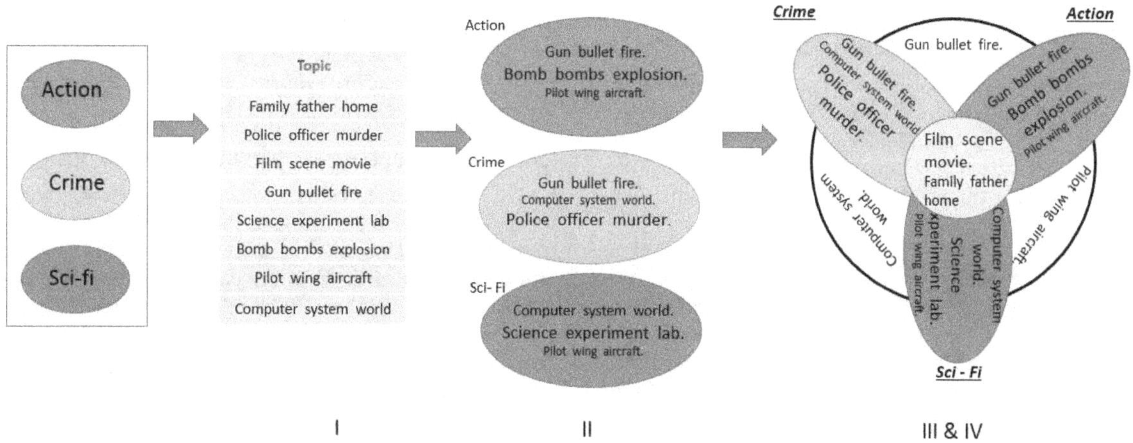

Figure 2: TopicFlower generation: (I): Extract topics using LDA. (II): Select most representative topics. (III) & (IV): Select connecting topics and most general topics.

count for adjusting term probabilities over time. However, temporal structures are not used for computing a selection of topics that are typical for a given time period. Work on interactive user interfaces includes applications such as [26] where a continuous histogram shows the variation in topic probability over time in the corpus, but, again these works do not identify the typicality of topics. In [17] the authors visualize the relation between documents and topics in a corpus, where topics correspond to points in the 2D space and documents are also embedded in 2D space, with distances between documents and topics reflecting the probabilities of the topics in the documents. In contrast to our approach this method does not take into account the category structure of corpora. Browsable topic views such as [10, 6, 12] attempt to visually summarize corpora using latent topics by depicting the probability distributions of documents over topics, and by providing an interactive interface for exploration. Another highly scalable and efficient method for generating summaries is the selection of example documents that represent the entire corpus using parametric embedding [7], where the difference between topics represents the number of topics instead of number of words shared. Again the focus of those works is on the relation between topics and documents, whereas we choose to provide an overview over the content represented as topics in relation to the existing structure within the dataset. Certain approaches tend to be more domain specific such as Themail [40] for analyzing the content in email conversations and TileBars [15] for studying the results of an information retrieval task. In contrast, we aim at building a general framework to visually analyze text corpora of any application domain. Additionally, TopicFlower is not query driven like tools such as [35]. Instead we mine insights purely from the collection without any external stimulus.

To the best of our knowledge, we are the first to make use of the category structure of data using latent topics in combination with discriminative analysis for generating thematic representations of document corpora. The advantage is that latent topics provide more context than terms (e.g. in tag clouds) and that we also leverage the existing structure of the dataset to provide the user with an insightful overview of the content of datasets containing categories.

3. TOPICFLOWER COMPUTATION

In this section we explain the construction of the corpus representation in TopicFlower as depicted in Figure 1. We choose to visualize the corpus as a flower because the central axis of such a representation gives us the possibility to effectively represent general topics. A general topic is a topic contained with high probability in all categories. Aligning the general topics in the center and not individually for each category reduces redundancy in the information displayed and allows us to utilize the available space more effectively. Figure 2 illustrates the computational steps involved: (I) We first compute latent topics using Latent Dirichlet Allocation. (II) For each category in the corpus we identify the most typical of these latent topics. (III) In order to obtain the order of the petals in the flower we estimate the most similar categories. (IV) For the adjacent categories we compute a list of representative connecting topics; in addition, we extract the most general topics for the center of the TopicFlower.

3.1 Topic Computation

Instead of representing topics in datasets by individual terms as in classical tag clouds, we employ latent topic analysis - a powerful tool, that provides us with a broader context on the underlying topics of a dataset. For this step, we use Latent Dirichlet Allocation [4], which additionally allows for a probabilistic assignment of different topics to a single document.

Latent Dirichlet allocation (LDA) identifies a given number of $|Z|$ topics within a corpus. Being the most important parameter for LDA, this number determines the granularity of the resulting topics. In order to find the latent topics, LDA relies on probabilistic modeling. This process can be described as determining a mixture of topics z for each document d in the corpus, i.e., $P(z|d)$, where each topic is described by terms w following another probability distribution, i.e., $P(w|z)$.

This can be formalized as

$$P(w_i|d) = \sum_{j=1}^{|Z|} P(w_i|z_j)P(z_j|d), \tag{1}$$

where $P(w_i|d)$ is the probability of the ith n-gram for a given document d, $P(w_i|z_j)$ is the probability of w_i within latent topic z_j, and $P(z_j|d)$ is the probability of picking a term from topic z_j in the document. We make use of Gibbs Sampling [13] for computing the topic model(For basic LDA computation we used MALLET [28]).

In our experiments we used between 3 and 6 most probable terms for representing a latent topic. By applying LDA we are able to represent topics as a list of terms with a probability for each term indicating the membership degree for the topic. Furthermore, for each document in our corpus we can determine through topic probabilities $P(z_j|d_i)$ to which topics it belongs and to which degree. As illustrative examples for latent topics obtained for our datasets (cf. Section 4) we just mention "user touch device interaction input" in the context of a computer science dataset or "ship crew pirates captain boat" in the context of a movie dataset.

3.2 Representative Topics for Categories

In this work we consider corpora containing documents from different categories. Examples of corpora that we will study in more detail in Section 4 include movie descriptions (with categories corresponding to genres), newsgroup postings (with categories corresponding to different types of newsgroups) and conference data (with temporal categories corresponding to publication years). Finding representative topics for these categories is a key step for providing the user with a bird's eye view of such corpora. In order to identify these topics we generalize a method based on an information theoretic measure, which was previously employed in the context of the finding discriminative terms for text classification. Pointwise Mutual Information (PMI) is an information theoretic measure to compute the mutual dependence between two random variables. Mutual information has been used in the past to do feature selection for text categorization [42, 44] and for exploiting the occurrence of emoticons in blogs to build an emotion lexicon [41]. In our case, we are interested in the dependence between the occurrence of a term w and the membership to a category c of a corpus. In its general form, pointwise mutual information is defined as[1]

$$PMI(w,c) = P(w,c)\log\left(\frac{P(w,c)}{P(w)\cdot P(c)}\right) \tag{2}$$

where w is a term, c is a category in the corpus, and $P(w,c)$ is the probability that term w occurs in a document of category c. $P(w)$ is computed using maximum likelihood estimation, which returns the document frequency in this case; $P(c)$ is estimated analogously using the class frequency.

In order to account for different degrees of topic membership, we incorporate the topic probability of a document and its rating class probability into the pointwise mutual information computation (Eq. 2). To this end, we extend pointwise mutual information as follows:

$$PMI(z_i,c) = \frac{1}{n}\sum_{j=1}^{n} p(z_i|d_j)\cdot I(c,d_j) \tag{3}$$

$$\cdot \log\left[\frac{\frac{1}{n}\sum_{j=1}^{n}(p(z_i|d_j)\cdot I(c,d_j))}{\frac{1}{n}\sum_{j=1}^{n} p(z_i|d_j)\cdot\frac{1}{n}\sum_{j=1}^{n} I(c,d_j)}\right]$$

where n is the number of documents in the corpus, and $I(c,d_j)$ is an indicator function with value 1 if document d_j is contained in category c and 0 otherwise. Note that this can be seen as a generalization of equation 2: The expression $p(z_i|d_j)\cdot I(c,d_j)$ weights documents in category c by their probability for latent topic z_i (instead of hard binary checks for term occurrence). For presenting a category c in our visualization we chose the top-k latent topics with highest PMI scores (with k=6 in our specific implementation). Note that the actual size n of an individual category does not affect the PMI score because we average over $p(z_i|d_j)$ for all documents d_j in category c. Examples for characteristic latent topics for a movie dataset used for our evaluation (cf. Section 4) were "vampire blood coffin" for the category "Horror" and "army soldiers men" for category "War".

3.3 Connecting Topics between Categories

Categories are represented as petals in our flower, with adjacent petals corresponding to the categories with highest similarity. The arrangement is similar to the wheel of emotion [33] where similar emotions are placed adjacent to each other. Examples for related categories are "War" and "Action" in the movie dataset. The arrangement allows us to explore relations between categories; those are further specified by connecting topics between adjacent petals.

For estimating the similarity between two categories c_i and c_j we consider the average Jaccard similarity JSC between all pairs (d_k, d_l) of documents d_k from c_i and d_l from c_j. We chose Jaccard similarity because the average pairwise similarity can be efficiently computed even for very large corpora [9]. We obtain an optimal ordering of categories for a given dataset by selecting the order of categories that maximizes the average Jaccard similarity over all adjacent pairs. Having obtained the order of categories in the flower, we now describe two different methods for identifying connecting topics of adjacent categories in the flower.

Method A: Mutual Information. In order to find the most connecting topics we apply a similar concept as described in Section 3.2. For each pair of adjacent categories c_i and c_j, we first merge their sets of documents and then apply equation 3 to the merged category. Ordering the resulting latent topics by their MI values provides us with candidates for connecting topics. However, if merged categories are highly unbalanced, topics from larger categories might contribute disproportionately to the connecting topics.

Method B: Rank Combination. To address the issue of unbalanced category sizes, we employ a method based on rank combination for identifying connecting topics. To this end, we first compute two *separate* topic rankings for adjacent categories c_i and c_j using equation 3 and then combine these rankings. Let $r(c_i, z_k)$ and $r(c_j, z_k)$ be the resulting rank of topic i and j respectively and $|Z|$ be the overall number of latent topics. We assign the score $s(c_i, z_k) = |Z| + 1 - r(c_i, z_k)$ to topic z_k and for category c_i (i.e. higher ranks correspond to higher scores), and compute a combined score $s(z_k)$ for latent topic z_k as follows:

$$s(z_k) = 2\frac{s(c_i,z_k)+s(c_j,z_k)}{s(c_i,z_k)\cdot s(c_j,z_k)} \tag{4}$$

i.e. we compute the harmonic mean of the scores. Note that in this way we avoid getting high scores for latent topics with a high rank for one category but a low rank for the other. Also note, that the resulting scores are independent of the category sizes. For each pair of adjacent categories in the flower we consider the latent topics with highest combined score (in our experiments we chose the top-5) as connecting topics.

3.4 General Topics

The general idea of a structured dataset can be usually described through a small number of common topics related to all underlying categories. To this end, we visualize the most general topics in the center of the flower (top-4 topics in our qualitative study and exam-

[1]In some works the weighting factor $P(w,c)$ is ignored.

ple TopicFlowers - Figure 3). In the following, we introduce two approaches for the identification of top-k general topics. The first is a simplistic approach to adopt $P(z_j)$ directly from the generated topic model. This approach however does not take into account the specific distributions of topic probabilities across the categories. To address this issue we devised a second approach for putting higher weight on topics whose probability distribution is closer to uniform across all categories. Finally, we re-rank the top-k "even" topics by their initial probability $P(z_j)$.

We employ an evenness index for measuring the uniformness of the topic distributions. As an example, if the conditional probability of a topic z_j given a category c_i, $P(z_j|c_i)$, is close to $1/|C|$ (where C is the set of categories in the given dataset) for every category $c \in C$ then the topic z_j should obtain a high evenness index. In our approach, we employ Pielou's evenness index [32] which is used extensively in the ecological sciences to determine the uniformity of the distribution of groups of species in an ecosystem. In our case, given a dataset composed of a set of categories C and a set of latent topics Z, the evenness index is computed for each topic $z \in Z$ across all categories $c \in C$ using Pielou's classical formula: $E = \frac{H'}{H'_{max}}$, where H' is the value derived from Shannon's Diversity Index and H'_{max} is the maximum value of H', equal to: $-\sum \frac{1}{S} \ln \frac{1}{S} = \ln S$. S is the number of species which in our case is the number of categories $|C|$ for a given dataset. The formula for Shannon's diversity index is as follows: $H' = -\sum p_i \, ln \, p_i$, where p_i is the proportion of the ith species in the ecosystem. In our case we consider p_i as the proportion of a topic z_j in category c_i which directly corresponds to $P(z_j|c_i)$.

We compute the evenness index E_j for all topics $z_j \in Z$, and rank the topics according to these values, ensuring that topics that are just specific for a limited number of categories are ranked lower. Finally, we take the top-k most even topics and re-rank them by the initial probabilities ($P(z_j)$). Using this two step approach we derive a set of evenly distributed and highly probable topics for the dataset to display in the center of the TopicFlower.

4. EVALUATION

The objective of our experimental evaluation was twofold: (1) to evaluate the individual steps described in Section 3 for computing the TopicFlower representation of corpora - this includes evaluating (a) the quality of topics assigned to different categories in our corpora and to the center of the flower and (b) the quality of the connecting topics identified for neighbor categories in the flower; (2) to compare our TopicFlower with baseline approaches and existing methods for term and topic based representations of corpora.

4.1 Data and Setup

Our aim was to build a data visualization tool that provides a quick overview of the structure and topical content for a wide range of document corpora. Different corpora can vary largely in structure and content, and insights deduced from the visualization might depend on the expertise of users. In order to cover as many aspects as possible, we carried out experiments on four real-world corpora with different properties (see Table 1 for a summary):

Movies: We first decided to collect documents from the movie domain as it requires no particular user expertise to understand its topics. From the Wikipedia movies-by-genre lists we extracted all available movies belonging to one or more of 10 main genres such as "Action", "Comedy" and "Drama", amounting to 11,070 movie descriptions. The number of movies in the different categories ranges from 656 to 2,364. From each of the movie pages we only considered the content of the sections "Plot" or "Description" and omitted the surrounding meta data information.

Name	Structure	Expertise required	#Cats	#Docs
Movies	Genres	No	10	11070
Newsgroups	News Topics	No	7	19,997
CS Pubs	CS Areas	Yes	6	2957
WWW-Temp	Years	Yes	6	1687

Table 1: Experimental datasets along with their properties

Newsgroups: The 20-Newsgroups dataset was originally collected by K. Lang [23]. It consists of 19,997 newsgroup postings and is usually divided into 6 categories for supervised learning. However, we considered the following 7 categories covering different areas: "alt" - atheism, "comp"- computer hardware and software, "misc"- things for sale, "rec" - baseball, hockey, cars, and bikes, "sci" - cryptography, medicine, space, and electronics, "soc" - Christianity, and "talk" - religion, politics, guns, and the middle east. The number of postings for these categories vary from 997 to 5,000. We considered only the "raw" content of the postings, i.e. from each posting we removed metadata such as sender and recipient of the article as well as topic labels.

CS Pubs: We collected scientific publications within the Computer Science domain as a dataset that requires high user expertise. We gathered 2,957 scientific documents from proceedings of the conferences in the following areas: "Databases" (VLDB, EDBT), "Data Mining" (KDD,ICDM), "E-Learning" (ECTEL, ICWL), "IR" (SIGIR,ECIR), "Multimedia" (ACM MM, ICMR), "CH Interfaces" (CHI, IUI), and "Web Science" (WWW, HYPERTEXT). The number of publications for these categories vary from 179 to 905. We limited our selection to conferences that took place in the years 2011 and 2012 and publications with more than four pages. As our focus in this work is on topic-related textual content, we removed references and acknowledgment sections.

WWW-Temp: Besides categories and genres our approach can be also applied to entirely different types of partitions, for instance based on time periods. As an example, we collected conference proceedings from the ACM WWW conferences in the time period between 2001 and 2012, capturing the evolution of expert knowledge in the context of the World Wide Web. We grouped the resulting 1,687 documents by pairs of consecutive years and obtained the following six categories: "2001-2002", "2003-2004",..., and "2011-2012". The number of publications for these temporal categories vary from 139 to 637. [2]

Setup. In order to reduce the influence of noise in our algorithms we performed different document preprocessing steps for all of the datasets. To this end, we reduced the vocabulary size by using the StanfordNLP part-of-speech tagger Tagger [39] for extracting and keeping only nouns from the original documents. In addition, we split each document into paragraphs as they are more topically focused compared to whole documents. We computed the latent topics using the ParallelTopicModel of the Mallet topic modeling toolkit [28]. Mallet offers a parallel implementation of LDA [29] along with a SparseLDA sampling scheme and data structure [43]. One of the input parameters required by Mallet is the number of topics, k, in the dataset. Lower values of k result in more general topics, while higher values result in more specific topics. We generated models for 50, 100, 200, 500 and 1000 topics, and identified $k = 200$ as a reasonable number for all datasets. We used 4 threads and 1000 iterations to compute the experimental topic set for each corpus.

[2]Note that there exists work on modeling the temporal evolution of individual topics [3]. In contrast, our objective is to identify the most relevant topics for given time intervals. However, our approach could be easily extended using such alternative topic models.

When computing characteristic, connecting and general topics we use all documents available in a dataset.Note that our approach can also handle unbalanced categories, since the PMI score of a topic in a category (shown in equation 3) is independent of the category size. The participants of our studies for assessing different aspects of the generated representations consisted of undergraduate and graduate students from the Computer Science department for the "WWW-Temp" and "CS Pubs" datasets and students from all disciplines for the other datasets.

4.2 Examples for Generated TopicFlowers

Figure 3 shows automatically generated topic flowers for the "Movie" corpus and for the "WWW-Temp" corpus (for space reasons depicted in a slightly different layout than previous stylized illustrations in this paper). Topics are represented by a text line containing the top-3 terms as scored by LDA. Font sizes of topic terms correspond to their representativeness for the categories. The center of the figure contains a polygon with the most probable (general) topics for the corpus. Each category is represented by a labeled ellipse. Categories with higher similarity score are situated visually closer to each other, and connecting topics are placed between adjacent categories. Since "WWW-Temp" has time based categories the link between 2012 and 2001 is omitted for that dataset.

The flower representation of the movie dataset (cf. Figure 3a) reveals many category specific topics such as "ranch gene cattle" and "horse cattle man" for the Western genre, "band song music" for Musicals, and "king palace process" for Adventure movies. Western and War are connected through the topic "officer war soldier" which might be related to battles between colonists and indians; for Crime and Drama "drug dealer police" and "police murder killer" were found as connecting topics, possibly corresponding to dramatic experiences in the context of criminal activities. The most dominant topic in the flower center is the generic topic "film scene movie" which nicely summarizes the overall scope of the dataset.

For the "WWW-Temp" dataset our algorithm was able to put the petals in almost natural temporal order from 2001 to 2012 (only www09-10 and www11-12 are swapped) as displayed in Figure 3b. We observe that the articles in WWW01-02 mainly deal with "traditional" Web related topics such as "page web site" or "proxy object policy". For WWW03-04 the uprising P2P trend is, for instance, identified as a prominent topic ("peer network node"). The years 2009 and 2010 saw a large increase in studies and applications in the context of the Social Web ("network user friend"), and in recent years microblogging became a popular technique ("user account tweet"). We can also observe that especially earlier conferences in the years 2001-2005 are connected through XML related topics such as "xml parser validation" and "xml document schema". Finally, the center of the flower contains general topics such as "web system information" related to the WWW domain as well the generic scientific topic "section paper work".

4.3 Evaluation of Topic Generation Methods

In this section we describe the results of our evaluation for the individual steps from Section 3; to this end, we conducted a number of user based studies. The experiments for representative, connective and general topics were conducted for the *Movies*, *Newsgroups* and, *CS Pubs* datasets. The participants of the study consisted of 19 undergraduate students of Computer Science and other disciplines, and 6 graduate students of Computer Science. The topic distributions within the "Movies" and "Newsgroups" datasets were evaluated by all of the participants; the graduate Computer Science students additionally evaluated the "CS Pubs" dataset of scientific publications. Participants spent approximately 2 hours on average to complete the study and answered over 6900 questions in total. Note that for large scale corpora which do not require specific expertise, crowdsourcing could be employed as an alternate method of evaluation.

Evaluation of characteristic topics. In order to examine the viability of topics for representing categories in the TopicFlower, for each of the categories we selected two sets of topics from those generated by LDA. The first set contained top-6 topics as selected by our method. The second consisted of the same number of uniformly sampled topics. The topic sets were merged, put into random order, and presented to the users. Users were asked to assess the relevance of the topics for the categories on a 5-point Likert scale corresponding to the options "strongly agree", "agree", "disagree", "strongly disagree" and "don't know" as answer to the following question: "Do you think the topics given below are representative for the given category?".

Table 2 shows the mean ratings for top-6 topics (mean(TP)) and other topics (mean(FP)) along with the results of t-tests conducted to compare these means (test statistics t, degrees of freedom d.f. and, power values P). For the experiments on characteristic topics for categories all of the results were statistically significant on a 95% confidence level. We also computed the inter-rater agreement using Fleiss' Kappa [14], a statistical measure of agreement between individuals for qualitative ratings. Note that according to Fleiss' definition, $\kappa < 0$ corresponds to no agreement, $\kappa = 0$ to agreement by chance, and $0 < \kappa \leq 1$ to agreement beyond chance. To obtain a complete inter-rater matrix we selected a subset of 103 categories and 18 users where each user rated each category. We measured κ on this set and obtained a moderate agreement of 0.51.

The results shown confirm our hypothesis that topics in the flower are suitable for representing categories. As an example, for the "Movies" corpus the mean user rating for highest scored topics for the categories in the flower was 3.2 in contrast to a mean of 2.0 for other topics for both topic sets, with statistical significance shown by the t-test.

Evaluation of connecting topics. We performed a similar study to evaluate connecting topics (located in between the petals of the flower). For assessing the connectivity of topics we asked our participants "Do you think the topics given below are representative for the intersection of the given category pair?"; We used the same 5-point scale as before. Analogous to our previous experiments, topics were partly chosen by our algorithms and partly uniformly sampled. While the score difference for connecting topics stays statistically significant within a confidence interval of 95% (cf. Table 2), the raters only achieved a slight agreement of $\kappa = 0.21$ for this experiment.

Evaluation of general topics. To evaluate the general topics, we employed a pairwise topic comparison study where users were asked to determine which topic of a given pair can be considered as the more general one. We asked our participants 'Which of the given topics is more general for the current dataset?'. Each pair presented to the user consisted of a topic selected using evenness index and a randomly selected topic. The order of topics within a pair was also randomized. We used the top 10 topics selected by our approach to compare with 10 uniformly sampled topics from the rest. User judgments were then translated to the 5 point scale to make it comparable in Table 2 without any loss. Users preferred our approach to identify general topics with an average score difference of 1.4 (statistically significant within 95% confidence interval). Raters in this study were in moderate agreement with a score $\kappa = 0.39$.

(a) Visualization of the "Movie" dataset - topics are connected to genres

(b) Visualization of the "WWW-Temp" dataset - topics are connected to 2 years periods

Figure 3: Generated visualizations of topics and categories/time intervals for the "Movie" and "WWW-Temp" datasets.

4.4 Evaluation of the Visualization

In order to evaluate our TopicFlower based visualization for a categorically structured dataset we designed an "insight" based study. In the literature on visualization an *insight* is defined as "an individual observation about the data by the participant or a unit of discovery" [22]. Insight based evaluation is one of the seven scenarios for information visualization evaluation described in [22], and has been shown to be suitable for modeling real world scenar-

Dataset	Experiment type	mean(TP)	mean(FP)	significant	d.f.	t-value	P-value
Movies	category	3.2	2.0	yes	2755	33.62	2.89×10^{-180}
	connection	2.8	2.0	yes	1074	17.09	2.25×10^{-52}
	general	3.5	1.5	yes	2188	44.35	1.1×10^{-246}
Newsgroups	category	3.1	2.1	yes	1531	20.98	2.13×10^{-77}
	connection	2.6	2.1	yes	656	8.07	1.49×10^{-14}
	general	2.9	2.1	yes	524	6.69	1.37×10^{-10}
CS pubs	category	3.1	2.6	yes	906	11.15	8.25×10^{-26}
	connection	2.5	2.1	yes	352	4.91	2.11×10^{-6}
	general	3.3	1.7	yes	898	19.77	5.03×10^{-63}

Table 2: Evaluation results for characteristic, connecting and general topics of the categories

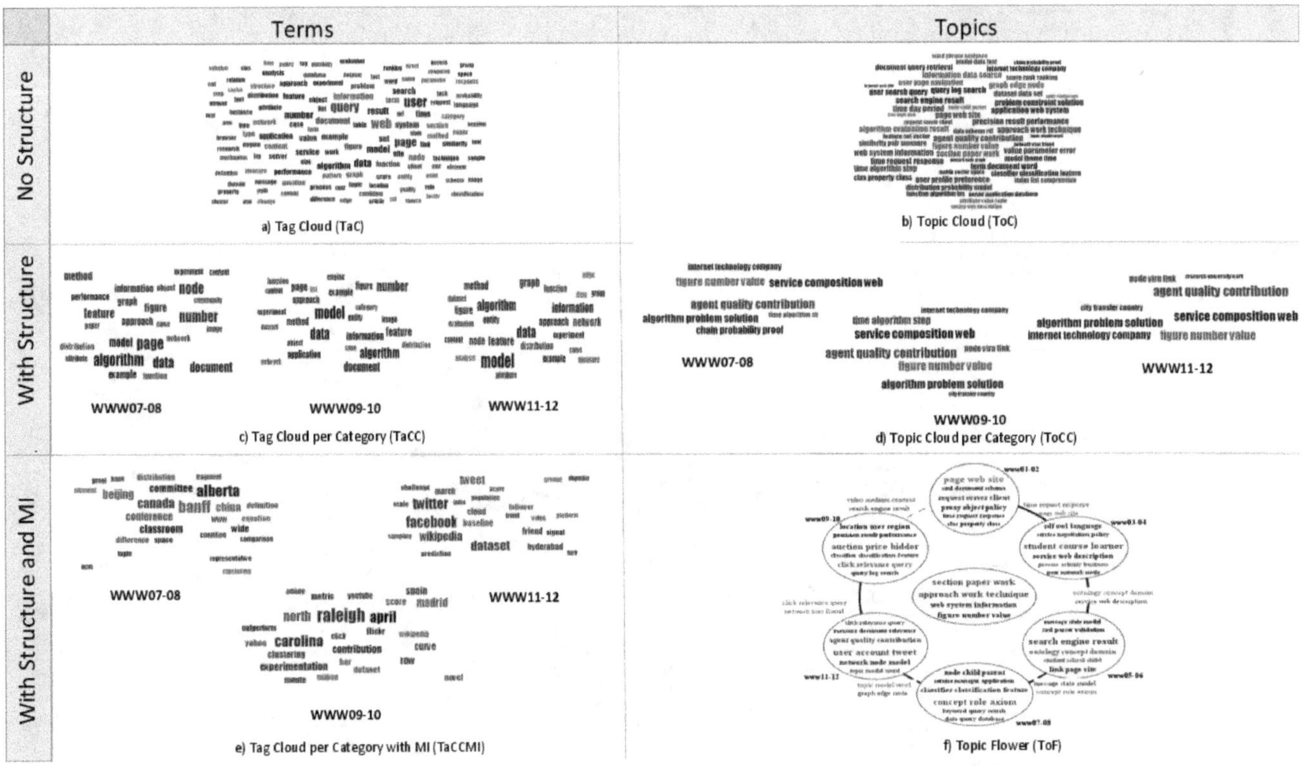

Figure 4: Methods for term/topic-based summarization of corpora with or without structure.

ios [30]. Instead of giving users a predefined task, they are asked to explore the visualization and describe as many observations as they can. The objective of such a study is to let users interact with different visualizations and compare the number of observations.

Methodology for evaluation. Our evaluation is similar to the one performed in [34]. We asked 10 researchers in the area of Web Mining and Retrieval as well as 20 people consisting of students and researchers to list their insights gained from various visualizations of "WWW-Temp" and "Movie" corpora, respectively. To this end, we chose to study the effect of one independent variable: the type of visualization, on a single dependent variable: the number of insights gained in a fixed period of time. The entire study was divided into 3 steps: a preliminary step to determine what the participants consider as insights for a given dataset, the second step to count the number of insights gained by each participant for each visualization and the final step, where we asked participants to rank their favorite visualizations based on utility for exploration.

The different types of compared visualizations are illustrated in Figure 4 on the example of the "WWW-Temp" dataset. Starting from the traditional tag cloud, we explored two "dimensions" of information: Moving from left to right (from "Tags" to "Topics") adds additional context in form of topics; moving from top to bottom (from "No structure" to "Structure and MI") takes into account information about the corpora structure, where the categories are handled independently. Finally, for the visualisations in the bottom row we used mutual information theory to select elements, representative for each category. In order to keep visualizations comparable we fixed the number of terms in each representation (300 for the "Movies" and 150 for the "WWW" datasets). This results in the following six visualizations:

- *Tag Cloud (TaC)*: A simple tag cloud, consisting of the most frequent words within the dataset excluding stop words of the English language.
- *Topic Cloud (ToC)*: A topic cloud consisting of the most probable topics for the dataset. Each topic is represented by its 5 most representative words.

- *Tag Cloud per Category (TaCC)*: A set of tags clouds, with clouds being separately computed for each category as a set of the most frequent words.
- *Topic Cloud per Category (ToCC)*: Analogous to TaCC but with topics instead of terms.
- *Tag Cloud per Category with MI (TaCCMI)*: Analogous to TaCC but with the most representative (instead of most frequent) terms per category (selected using MI).
- *TopicFlower (ToF)*: Our TopicFlower representation combines both topic and category structure as depicted in Figure 3. We displayed 5 representative topics for each of the categories. Each pair of adjacent categories was connected by 3 topics. In addition, the 4 most general topics were presented in the flower center.

Results and lessons learned. As mentioned earlier, there were 3 steps in each study. In this section we describe the results from each step for the "WWW-Temp" and "Movies" dataset.

Step 1. Describing insights: In this preliminary step we described the "WWW-Temp" dataset to computer science researchers and the "Movies" dataset to all participants. We then asked participants to identify observations they expected to be made using a term based visualization. For the "WWW-Temp" dataset we obtained five possible types of observations, namely:

- The important topics in the WWW conference over the last 10 years.
- The important topics in different years.
- The recent important topics.
- The topics that used to be more popular in the past than now.
- Trends: how topics in the conference changed over time.

Each interesting topic discovered using a particular visualization would correspond to an "insight" gained in step 2. We did not discriminate between the types of insights when counting. Similarly for the "Movies" dataset we identified a list of possible insight types and consider each one of them to be equally important. Some of the the insight types identified were:

- The important topics covered by movies in each genre.
- The topics covered by all movie genres.
- The most similar genres.

Step 2 Counting insights: Next, for each participant we showed the 6 visualizations in random order for 2 minutes each. We found that topic importance is a very subjective concept. It can be influenced by a number of different factors such as user expertise and interest in particular areas. Overall, 20 users were able to extract 488 insights from the Movie dataset and 10 experts extracted 298 insights from the "WWW-Temp" dataset (insights from different visualizations for a dataset may partially overlap). We observed that generally a higher portion of interesting topics was typically extracted from the TopicFlower when compared to other visualizations. The number of insights found per participant in a given time period, ranged from 0 to 23 due to their difference in learning pace. In order to compare user output, we replaced the absolute number of extracted insights with their proportion and averaged the results over all users. For the "Movies" dataset on average 20% of the insights per participant were obtained from each of the MI based visualizations (TaCCMI & ToF) and from each of the other visualizations 13-15%. For the "WWW-Temp" datasets topic based visualizations (Topic Cloud and TopicFlower) gained 19-21% and the rest were distributed in the range 11-17%. Overall, the TopicFlower turned out to be constantly among the winners and collected around 20% of all insights across 6 visualizations in both datasets.

Step 3. Subjective ranking: In the final step each participant was asked to identify the top three (of the six presented) visualizations according to perceived usefulness in real exploratory scenarios. The participants were further encouraged to explain their choice. Both TaCC and TopicFlower were considered as the most useful visualizations, while simple term and tag clouds were perceived as "too general". TopicFlower was considered the winner in 6 of the 9 cases (and as the second best by two other participants) for the Movie dataset. In contrast, the next best visualization Tag Cloud, was considered a winner only by two participants. In the movie dataset TopicFlower was prioritized by 9 participants (and as the second and third best by five other participants). In contrast, coming next, the MI based tag cloud representation attracted only four participants (and was the second best option for 5 others).

We also obtained "think aloud" feedback during the evaluation sessions. Insights found in the topic flower representation relate both to transitions between topics such as the *tendency from an infrastructure oriented view of the Web towards a user centric perspective* as well as topics that provide a better context than just individual keywords in tag clouds (e.g. *social network analysis* represented through the term combination "user network friend" in 2009/2010). Generally topic based visualizations were considered as "textually overloaded" and 2-3 words were suggested as an optimal number for topic labels. For the tag cloud the "largest" words were considered too general. For the tag cloud by category (TaCC) participants criticized the low diversity of the words (The union of the top 5 terms from each of the 6 categories consists of only 13 words). Overall the participants perceived the TopicFlower as the most useful visualization although it requires slightly more time to understand and get used to compared to a simple tag cloud or tag cloud by category.

5. CONCLUSIONS AND FUTURE WORK

In this paper, we have taken preliminary steps to show that category structure in corpora can be leveraged for generating overviews that go beyond traditional tag clouds. More specifically, in what is a novel combination of latent topic analysis, discriminative analysis, and rank aggregation we identified both category specific and general topics as well as connections between categories in the corpora. The visual moniker of our method is the TopicFlower inspired by cyclic diagrams such as the "wheel of emotions". The evaluation of individual components of the flower and their overall arrangement shows the viability of our methods for illustrating the topical structure of categorical datasets and discovering insights such as representative topics as well as trends and connections between categories. We also aim to extend the TopicFlower by integrating different data browsing and exploration functionalities. The discovery of documents using topics has been discussed in the literature but it would be interesting to see how the flower influences the decision making process in this context. Finally, we believe that the proposed techniques have direct applications for visualizing and summarizing information in digital libraries and Web archives as rich categorical and temporal structures are omnipresent in these domains.

6. ACKNOWLEDGMENTS

This work is funded by the ERC under the grant 339233 (ALEXANDRIA).

7. REFERENCES

[1] U. Anthony, T. Martin, and H. Heike. *Graphics of Large Datasets: Visualizing a Million.*

[2] D. M. Blei, T. L. Griffiths, and M. I. Jordan. The nested chinese restaurant process and bayesian nonparametric inference of topic hierarchies. In *Proceedings of,* NCR 2010.

[3] D. M. Blei and J. D. Lafferty. Dynamic topic models. In *Proceedings of* ACM ICML 2006.

[4] D. M. Blei, A. Y. Ng, and M. I. Jordan. Latent dirichlet allocation. In *The Journal of machine Learning research,* 2003.

[5] D. Carmel, H. Roitman, and N. Zwerdling. Enhancing cluster labeling using wikipedia. In *Proceedings of* SIGIR 2009.

[6] A. J.-B. Chaney and D. M. Blei. Visualizing topic models. In *Proceedings of* ICWSM 2012.

[7] Y. Chen, L. Wang, M. Dong, and J. Hua. Exemplar-based visualization of large document corpus. In *Visualization and Computer Graphics, IEEE Transactions,* 2009.

[8] C. Collins, F. B. Viegas, and M. Wattenberg. Parallel tag clouds to explore and analyze faceted text corpora. In *VAST 2009,* IEEE Symposium.

[9] F. Deng, S. Siersdorfer, and S. Zerr. Efficient jaccard-based diversity analysis of large document collections. In *Proceedings of* CIKM 2012.

[10] W. Dou, X. Wang, R. Chang, and W. Ribarsky. Paralleltopics: A probabilistic approach to exploring document collections. In *Proceedings of* IEEE VAST, 2011.

[11] B. Fortuna, D. Mladenić, and M. Grobelnik. In *Visualization of text document corpus.* 2005.

[12] M. Gardner, J. Lutes, J. Lund, D. Hansen, J. andWalker, E. Ringger, and K. Deppi. The topic browser: An interactive tool for browsing topic models. In *Proceedings of* NIPS 2010.

[13] T. L. Griffiths and M. Steyvers. Finding scientific topics. In *National Proceedings of AcadSci USA,* 2004.

[14] K. Gwet. *Handbook of Inter-Rater Reliability* In *Advanced Analytics, LLC,* 2012.

[15] M. A. Hearst. Tilebars: visualization of term distribution information in full text information access. In *Proceedings of* SIGCHI 1995.

[16] M. A. Hearst and D. Rosner. Tag clouds: Data analysis tool or social signaller? In *Proceedings of the Hawaii International Conference on System Sciences.* IEEE, 2008.

[17] T. Iwata, T. Yamada, and N. Ueda. Probabilistic latent semantic visualization: topic model for visualizing documents. In *Proceedings of* SIGKDD 2008.

[18] S. Kaski. Data exploration using self-organizing maps. In *Acta Polytechnica Scandinavica, Mathematics, Computing and Management in Engineering Series* 1997.

[19] T. Kohonen. The self-organizing map. In *Proceedings of the IEEE,* 78(9):1464–1480, 1990.

[20] T. Kohonen. Exploration of very large databases by self-organizing maps. In *International Conference on Neural Networks,* 1997.

[21] T. Kohonen. Self-organization of very large document collections: State of the art. In *Proceedings of* ICANN 1998.

[22] H. Lam, E. Bertini, P. Isenberg, C. Plaisant, and S. Carpendale. Empirical studies in information visualization: Seven scenarios. In *IEEE Trans. Vis. Comput. Graph.,* 2012.

[23] K. Lang. Newsweeder: Learning to filter netnews. In *in Proceedings of* ML 1995.

[24] B. Lee, N. H. Riche, A. K. Karlson, and S. Carpendale. Sparkclouds: Visualizing trends in tag clouds. In *IEEE Transactions on Visualization and Computer Graphics,* 2010.

[25] X. Lin, D. Soergel, and G. Marchionini. A self-organizing semantic map for information retrieval. In *Proceedings of* SIGIR 1991.

[26] S. Liu, M. X. Zhou, S. Pan, W. Qian, W. Cai, and X. Lian. Interactive, topic-based visual text summarization and analysis. In *Proceedings of* CIKM 2009.

[27] C. D. Manning, P. Raghavan, and H. Schütze. *Introduction to Information Retrieval.* In *Cambridge University Press,* 2008.

[28] A. K. McCallum. Mallet: A machine learning for language toolkit. http://www.mallet.cs.umass.edu, 2002.

[29] D. Newman, A. U. Asuncion, P. Smyth, and M. Welling. Distributed algorithms for topic models. In *Journal of Machine Learning Research,* 2009.

[30] C. North, P. Saraiya, and K. Duca. A comparison of benchmark task and insight evaluation methods for information visualization. In *Information Visualization* 2011.

[31] W. Parrott. *Emotions in social psychology: Essential readings.* In *Psychology Press,* 2001.

[32] E. Pielou. The measurement of diversity in different types of biological collections. In *Journal of theoretical biology,* 1966.

[33] R. Plutchik. Emotions: A general psychoevolutionary theory. In *Approaches to Emotion,* 1984.

[34] P. Saraiya, C. North, V. Lam, and K. A. Duca. An insight-based longitudinal study of visual analytics. In *IEEE Transactions on Visualization and Computer Graphics,* 2006.

[35] D. Shahaf, Y. Jaewon, S. Caroline, J. Jeff, H. Wang and J.Leskovec. Information cartography: creating zoomable, large-scale maps of information In *Proceedings of ACM SIGKDD,* 2013.

[36] J. Schrammel, M. Leitner, and M. Tscheligi. Semantically structured tag clouds: an empirical evaluation of clustered presentation approaches. In *Proceedings of,* SIGCHI 2009.

[37] J. Sinclair and M. Cardew-Hall. The folksonomy tag cloud: when is it useful? In *Journal of Information Science,* 2008.

[38] D. Skoutas and M. Alrifai. Tag clouds revisited. In *Proceedings of* CIKM 2011.

[39] K. Toutanova, D. Klein, C. D. Manning, and Y. Singer. Feature-rich part-of-speech tagging with a cyclic dependency network. In *Proceedings of* NAACL 2003.

[40] F. B. Viégas, S. Golder, and J. Donath. Visualizing email content: portraying relationships from conversational histories. In *Proceedings of* SIGCHI 2006.

[41] F.-J. Yang. An overview of intelligent tutoring systems. In *Proceedings of* IC-AI 2007.

[42] Y. Yang and J. O. Pedersen. A comparative study on feature selection in text categorization. In *Proceedings of* ML 1997.

[43] L. Yao, D. Mimno, and A. McCallum. Efficient methods for topic model inference on streaming document collections. In *Proceedings of* SIGKDD 2009.

[44] Z. Zheng, X. Wu, and R. Srihari. Feature selection for text categorization on imbalanced data. In *SIGKDD Explor. Newsletter,* 2004.

A Theoretical Framework for Conversational Search

Filip Radlinski*
filiprad@microsoft.com
Microsoft, United Kingdom

Nick Craswell
nickcr@microsoft.com
Microsoft, United States

ABSTRACT

This paper studies conversational approaches to information retrieval, presenting a theory and model of information interaction in a chat setting. In particular, we consider the question of what properties would be desirable for a conversational information retrieval system so that the system can allow users to answer a variety of information needs in a natural and efficient manner. We study past work on human conversations, and propose a small set of properties that taken together could measure the extent to which a system is conversational. Following this, we present a theoretical model of a conversational system that implements the properties. We describe how this system could be implemented, making the action space of an conversational search agent explicit. Our analysis of this model shows that while theoretical, the model could be practically implemented to satisfy the desirable properties presented. In doing so, we show that the properties are also feasible.

Keywords: Conversational Search, Chatbot, Personal Agent

1. INTRODUCTION

Recent progress in Machine Learning has brought tremendous improvements in natural language dialogs between humans and conversational agents. This has led to a plethora of commercial conversational agents (also called *chat bots* or simply *bots*) that are able to answer user requests from ordering pizza to suggesting holiday destinations. Such systems are *conversational* in that they assist users using a dialog interaction, be it in written or spoken form, usually with a rich human-like vocabulary.

To build an information retrieval system with a conversational user interface, it is useful to define a computational model that describes the process of conversational search. The model should allow the user to make a natural language request, akin to a traditional information retrieval query. It should allow the system to propose search results, but also ask the user for clarification if necessary. It should allow the user to give feedback on the system's results and suggestions, including negative feedback. Over time, the process should allow the system to build a cumulative picture of the user's information need based on their query statements and other relevance feedback.

We observe that conversational search is in keeping with trends in the design of computing devices and interfaces [15]. Modern devices with small or no screen may provide responses via small on-screen cards and speech synthesis, so succinct conversational responses are appropriate. With speech recognition accuracy also improving due to progress in machine learning, the popularity of speech-based search input is also growing[1]. Such a growth in natural language dialog between users and search systems may even lead to the dominant interaction model of one-shot keyword queries being displaced with conversational systems.

To build a computational model for conversational search it is important to define which steps are allowable during a conversation: The types of statements that can be made by the system and by the user. The system must build a model of the user's information need over the course of the conversation, such that he or she does not need to repeat important aspects of the information need. Cumulative clarifications should tend to move the process closer to success. To make the conversation more flexible and natural, ideally most conversational steps that humans would take should be interpretable by the system and also potentially generated by the system. For example, in a real conversation about restaurants a person might ask "*Do you like sushi? I went to a great place yesterday*" or perhaps ask key questions such as "*Are you looking for somewhere fancy?*" In certain contexts the question may not directly appear to be about food, such as "*How much time do you have?*" People take into account what they know about the other person from past conversations and other aspects of context, and even ask for direct feedback "*What did you think of the restaurant that I suggested to you last week?*"

Many conversational search tasks are similar: People offer a reference point, or a key choice, to elicit the information they consider most important for separating the sorts of places that they might recommend. In the restaurant domain, people very rarely enumerate the types of cuisines or ask for a specific limit on the number of miles you are willing to travel. The same applies in other domains, such as when searching personal photo collections – a particular photo may serve as a reference point from which the target may for instance be earlier/later, in a different location, but with the same people.

In the field of spoken dialog systems, approaches already exist allowing conversational slot filling of a structured query within a schema (e.g. [44]). This allows users to book a ticket for a certain concert on a certain night, or set a certain reminder message to

*Now at Google UK.

CHIIR '17, March 07 - 11, 2017, Oslo, Norway

ISBN 978-1-4503-4677-1/17/03...$15.00

DOI: http://dx.doi.org/10.1145/3020165.3020183

[1]http://www.prnewswire.com/news-releases/teens-use-voice-search-most-even-in-bathroom-googles-mobile-voice-study-finds-279106351.html

appear on their mobile device at a certain time. By contrast, in other conversational search scenarios there may not be a fixed schema or the underlying data may not be structured as a database. In those cases rather than slot filling it may be beneficial to use a more free-form conversation that nevertheless builds its understanding over the user's needs over multiple rounds of conversation and may provide responses as well as ask clarifying questions.

We hypothesize that two aspects of conversations are particularly pertinent to search settings. First, users often do not know how to describe their information need – be it for a recommendation, or information regarding a new topic. Part of the role of the conversation is to elicit the actual need from the user by helping them formulate it clearly [24]. Second, for many tasks particularly suited to multi-turn conversational interactions, a *set* of results interact to produce a single item response which satisfies the need. For instance, when selecting a product to purchase, it is often driven by a preference among available options [13]. On the other hand, in some settings the solution is by its very nature a set, as in when deciding upon a holiday destination which requires travel, accommodation and dining requirements to be satisfied [21].

This paper presents a formalism that allows for richer sharing of initiative, and longer-term adaptation and personalization. Our goal is to capture the desirable properties of conversation specifically from an *information retrieval* perspective. Intuitively, the setting is that a conversational agent (assistant) has been asked satisfy an information need. At each point in time, the agent can perform one of a fixed set of actions, to which the user responds, with a back-and-forth. Mixed initiative and memory are key parts of this model. Our key contributions are

1. We suggest a formal definition of a conversation from an information retrieval perspective, showing why each property is desirable.
2. We propose a theoretical model of conversations that allows agents to satisfy the formal properties, demonstrating that the definition is also practical.

2. RELATED WORK

Human conversations have been studied for decades, and conversational research can be understood in relation to a number of existing research areas. We present an overview of the space to place our work in context. We start with conversations as applied to information retrieval, then discuss the broader literature regarding the essence of conversations.

2.1 Search and Recommender Systems

In traditional ad hoc search, the system allows the user to provide a natural language request (query) describing results that they want. A minimal response from the system is a ranked list of results (akin to "try looking at these") and a search box that remains available (the system allowing the user to "tell me what you want"). Systems may also correct the user's query ("did you mean?"), suggest other queries ("try these related searches") or provide faceted browsing in the results ("refine by") [43]. In that sense the user is having a conversation with a system that is providing a variety of responses, and many results at once are bundled into a single search engine results page.

During such a conversation, even if the user's search task does not change their understanding of the task, their query vocabulary may change and they may apply a variety of search strategies [2]. In some systems the retrieval response is based only on the user's most recent query, but other systems can take into account past queries and other context [4, 22]. In that sense modern contextual information retrieval systems already allow some co-active development, where both the system and the human user develop their understanding over time. However, real conversations may have mixed initiative [37], where control of the conversation passes from one side to the other via assertions, commands, questions and prompts. For instance, Dredze et al. [14] showed how in the context of email search an agent may propose pertinent ways to select subsets of the result set by adding key-value pairs to the query.

Already over two decades ago, Belkin et al. [3] considered conversational information retrieval by characterizing information-seeking strategies. They proposed scripts that can be followed by a system for different types of retrieval tasks, using case-based reasoning to select next steps and offer users choices. This differs from our work, as we assume a simpler conversational interface (such as a chat) where users enter text in response to agent actions also consisting of simple statements. The users may or may not respond directly to the system's requests. Also, we model the retrieval problem as one where the system reasons about items that can be retrieved, rather than over the space of possible user intents.

Conversational agents for more advanced multi-turn tasks have been proposed continuously since then, for instance recent work to isolate and resolve technical issues typically handled by a help desk [42]. This differs from our work, as we address the task of information retrieval rather than guiding a process by which a problem may be resolved. While a related informational goal could be to identify an instruction document, our goal is a characterization of a more general class of conversations.

In a spoken conversation or on a device with a small screen, it also becomes important for the search system to chose one response or a small number of responses, rather than bundling a large number of results and suggestions into a results page. For example, if the user's query was ambiguous it may be optimal to show search results for just one intent and query suggestions for another [19]. If we consider the query suggestion to be a clarifying question, then showing such a suggestion prominently allows for a greater reward later by incurring an initially costly question. The idea of reinforcement learning, to optimally plan for a delayed reward rather than greedily always choosing the maximum immediate reward, is also explored under the card model of information retrieval [45]. These are important steps towards a mixed initiative conversational search system, although still with traditional system responses such as results and query suggestions.

Methods for conversational recommendation have also been proposed. Recently, Christakopoulou et al. [9] studied whether to ask absolute or relative questions, comparing the utility of each for learning about users. They also asked questions contextually, based on what is already known. Much earlier, Linden et al. [21] proposed a conversational travel agent that allows the user to find an optimal or near-optimal trip by presenting the user with examples that characterize the solution space and allowing the user to express and modify their criteria. A key method for expressing such updates is critiquing, which gives feedback on facets of importance – such as airline, price or departure time of a flight – with respect to the options already presented. In general a critique can be directed at a particular attribute of a particular item, for example "like this one but cheaper" [23]. Another form of critiquing is at the item level, dating to the Rocchio relevance feedback algorithm where users of a search system may annotate results as relevant or not to refine the search query [29]. A critique differs in that it explains how a result could be modified to improve its utility to the user.

We note that in human conversation critiquing also happens, but it is not limited to a pre-defined set of facets. An ideal conversational information retrieval system might allow free form critiquing of suggested results in natural language. To enable free-form queries and critiques, the information retrieval system could build its models based on the language modeling approach to information retrieval. However, more advanced forms of reasoning may be required, particularly when the user answers a question or refers to other parts of the conversation, suggesting the use of more sophisticated natural language technology. Despite this, today most end-to-end conversational systems based on deep neural networks lack the ability to explicitly focus on a search task, rather giving generic contextual responses (for example, [31]). Memory networks have proved very effective at complex question answering scenarios, able to provide correct answers given complex pieces of information and potentially a large knowledge base [33]. However, they are unable to request clarification of the task at hand when the solution is uncertain.

2.2 Spoken Dialog Systems

Spoken dialog system research enables a flexible conversation to take place including corrections and clarifications, usually in a closed domain such as setting a reminder or booking tickets (for instance, [44]). In an early system, Paek and Horvitz modeled spoken conversations using a Bayesian network that tracks confidence from the level of the audio signal obtained from the user through to predicting the user's goal with appropriate back-off depending on detected failure modes [26]. More recently, Chen et al. [8] have studied how a system can estimate the user's intent within a particular conversation step. In a simpler task, the Dialog State Tracking Challenge has pushed forward the ability of systems to fill known slots for the task of bus travel planning (e.g. [16]). Yet such a slot-driven approach differs from human recommendation where it is rarely important to fill all slots [9].

Co-reference resolution can successfully track references to entities across spoken queries[2], yet back references to preferences expressed in a search scenario have not been explored to the best of our knowledge. Further, these systems do not involve mixed initiative, with the system simply keeping up with the human. Even in closed domain dialog systems, additional work is needed to make the turn-taking behavior of the system more flexible and efficient [27]. In a more open domain, Jiang et al. recently studied the most popular commercial personal agent systems capable of multi-turn task solving. They identified a set of actions that agents tend to perform, albeit at a high level [17]. Such an agent performs a mix of slot filling and information tasks, although in many cases for an information retrieval task it resorts to a traditional search engine results page.

2.3 The Human Perspective

Finally we turn to work studying conversations as performed by people. Perhaps among the most famous attempts to replicate conversations, Eliza was one of the first chat bots, replying to user statements consistently with how a therapist may engage a patient [39]. The algorithm rephrased statements made by the patient, reformulating them as questions back to the patient. More recently, deep learning systems have attempted to build contextualized chit chat systems, for instance as a Twitter bot that responds to context [31]. We consider what roles conversations per se appear to play as part of information exchange.

Conversations as Revealment

One significant role of conversation from an information retrieval perspective is to allow the two parties to reach an understanding as to what is required by the user, and what the answerer knows. Before Web search became prevalent, as much information retrieval occurred in libraries, it was noted that the role of librarians was to help users to express their information needs. In particular, [24] studied how librarians assist in this task. The author found that the method of the librarians wasn't as important as that the conversation was happening. This suggests that automated conversational systems may also be effective even if using very different techniques.

Initiative and Engaging Behavior

A number of authors have studied how a "virtual human" should behave [6, 38]. For instance Traum et al. describe desirable aspects of a system conversing with humans, such as being real-time and incremental as utterances are formed over time [36]. Similarly there has been extensive work on multi-modal systems, expressing emotion and so forth. These aspects are beyond the scope of our work, as we restrict ourselves to chat type interfaces. Additionally, our focus is to consider conditions on *what* needs to be possible to be said rather than *how* the information should be conveyed.

One of the key aspects of human conversations is initiative. A number of authors have considered what constitutes initiative in dialog systems [1, 10, 25]. Of key interest to us is *mixed initiative*: At different times in the conversation, the human or the agent may take initiative. We use a generic definition of mixed initiative compared to past work, defining it as both the human and the system having initiative at different points in time. For instance, the agent may take initiative to clarify or elicit information from the user whenever appropriate, while allowing the user to drive the conversation at other times.

Trust and Moral Character

A final important concept in agents emulating human behavior is one of *moral character* [18]. Any agent taking part in a conversation conveys a personality, and inherently builds a relationship with the user (for instance, trust with regards to what happens to information shared by the person with the agent). However, this aspect of conversational behavior is outside the scope of our work and is not a goal of the conversational model.

It is also the case that when provided information (such as advice or recommendations), the source matters to people – it has been established that different sources have different influence on purchase decisions [30]. Effectiveness of a conversational system would likely depend on the system saying *why* it made a specific recommendations [35]. As with moral character, we do not address this question in this work.

3. CONVERSATIONS FOR SEARCH

In this section we consider the properties of conversations, proposing aspects that are applicable to search.

3.1 What is a Conversation?

The Oxford English Dictionary defines a conversation as *a talk, especially an informal one, between two or more people, in which news and ideas are exchanged.* While broad, this provides some guidance in information retrieval settings. In particular, we note that information is *exchanged*, suggesting symmetry where initiative may belong to both sides at different point in the conversation (rather than say a lecture). Hence we postulate that a conversational search system is a mixed-initiative system.

We may also classify conversations by their outcomes. Often, a conversation may be an end in itself. We do not consider this type of conversation here as it does not involve information retrieval. Similarly, conversations may have as a goal to assist a person to follow a known sequence of steps. Once more, this type of conversation falls

[2]http://searchengineland.com/googles-impressive-conversational-search-goes-live-on-chrome-160445

beyond the scope of this work. We focus on conversations that aim to elicit user preferences, and identify target information.

As a third aspect, we postulate that there is an element of memory: The conversation is a unit, and earlier statements can be referenced later in the conversation. Indeed, it should be possible to reference earlier statements in earlier conversations. A first consequence of the ability to index earlier statements is the existence of repair mechanisms, for instance the ability to clarify with *"what I meant is..."* [34, chapter 7]. More importantly in a search setting, memory allows information to be elicited from the user in a piecemeal fashion, maintaining simple steps that can together describe an arbitrarily complex information need. Indeed, it has been shown that loss of context is a common reason for user frustration with conversational systems [20]. It is important to note that memory thus plays two roles:

1. The systems remembers what was previously said by the user or the system to assist in resolving the user's information need.

2. It is possible for the user to explicitly reference past information, for example to indicate what statements are not correct or should be "forgotten".

Finally, the conversation should be adaptive, with neither participant following a script, but rather adapting to the current context. This expands upon common definitions of personalization, while avoiding the challenge of sessions. In particular, a conversational search agent is essentially fulfilling a long-term task, which may otherwise have consisted of many sessions in the traditional search engine sense. The abstraction will prove useful below.

Taken together, these properties lead to the following definition:

DEFINITION 1. *A* **conversational search system** *is a system for retrieving information that permits a mixed-initiative back and forth between a user and agent, where the agent's actions are chosen in response to a model of current user needs within the current conversation, using both short- and long-term knowledge of the user.*

Further, the system has the following five properties, which we term the RRIMS properties:

User **R**evealment The system helps the user express (potentially discover) their true information need, and possibly also long-term preferences.

System **R**evealment The system reveals to the user its capabilities and corpus, building the user's expectations of what it can and cannot do.

Mixed **I**nitiative The system and user both can take initiative as appropriate.

Memory The user can reference past statements, which implicitly also remain true unless contradicted.

Set Retrieval The system can reason about the utility of sets of complementary items.

3.2 When should search involve conversation?

The appropriateness of a conversation for a search task is largely driven by the complexity of the task. The simplest search settings, where the user enters a single query and they expect to immediately identify relevant results clearly does not call for a back-and-forth with a search agent.

The next more complex type of tasks require *memoryless refinement*: The user learns the right terms to describe their information need by iterating with a search system. If each step is only informed by the results from the previous iteration, this does not require memory nor agent initiative. In such a setting a more complex model may in fact reduce user utility and does not call for conversational approaches to search.

However, consider these more complex scenarios where a conversation is more likely to be appropriate:

Faceted Elicitation

The user is searching for an item with rich attributes that can be individually specified, but are much simpler to provide piecewise. For instance, it may be possible to describe a difficult to find email such as *I'm looking for an email that contains a link to a research paper that I got from a student who emailed me right after SIGIR last year. I can't remember the student's name, but I had never heard from her before.*

The user is selecting among items based on facets – but cannot be expected to know how to reference these directly as this would involve memorizing a complex query language. As part of the search, the user is identifying aspects that can be used to describe a relevant item. In contrast to memoryless refinement, here the user may need to learn about a facet before returning to the top level of the search process with a tag describing how this facet can be satisfied. For instance, consider a similar case where the user is selecting a vacuum cleaner to purchase. Here, as an aside, the user may need to learn about relevant attributes such as how loud a given number of decibels really is, and then returning to his main task.

Multi-Item Elicitation

The user is searching for a single item supported by a set of nearby items. For instance, a photo which can only be described by the properties of other photos taken earlier such as *the photo Alice took of me right after I took her picture a few months ago.* In this case, the system may need to learn who *Alice* is.

While the search is for an item that has an easy to establish relevance, the user's only known description of this item (i.e. query) depends on other items, which may themselves need to be found. Then, the search system must estimate the relevance of the whole set of items.

Multi-Item Faceted Elicitation

In this setting, the user is searching for a set of items directly. Importantly, not only must the system estimate the utility of each single item, it must combine the utilities of multiple items to reach an assessment of an entire set.

For instance, planning a vacation where the results consist of a hotel, travel arrangements, restaurant plans, places to see, and so forth. During the conversation, the agent elicits users to describe relevant aspects of different destinations, hotels, transport options and attractions. Then, it must elicit information from the user to learn how to combine the utilities of a whole set of items to reach a final decision about a holiday as a package.

It is this last setting in which we hypothesize that conversational approaches to search have the highest usefulness.

Bounding Choices / Building Expectations

Simultaneously, a conversational interface may simplify the problem of need elicitation by providing users with *bounded choices.* It may be easier for a user to clarify their needs given precise choices rather than expecting them to come up with particular terms. Similarly, choices can be bounded by allowing the user to understand complex features available in a search system, as examples of how a need can be presented are given.

For instance users engage with facets for email search much more often when these are suggested contextually, rather than relying on the user to generate the relevant terms [14]. Similarly, expert search users are much more likely to use advanced operators [40], presumably as less expert users are unaware of the options available.

This concept of bounding choices can also be considered as revealment from the side of the system, showing the user examples of the possibilities the system offers.

3.3 Learning, curiosity and serendipity

During any search interaction, the agent may acquire knowledge that is useful to answer the user's current information need, while also building a model to improve personalization in future. For instance, an example in the previous section required the agent to learn to identify Alice in a query. This knowledge would allow the agent to answer future queries that refer to Alice without requiring the label to be provided anew.

It is worth noting that there are also cases where the agent may provide the user with long-term utility at a cost in the current query, perhaps by eliciting information that happens to be related but not directly relevant. For instance, consider a user who searches for a restaurant recommendation and specifies that it should be vegetarian. The agent may clarify if the requirement is simply for the current query, or indicates that the user always requires vegetarian restaurants. Similarly, in a photo search scenario, the agent may elicit a name that can be applied to a face common in candidate photos.

We do not exclude such scenarios from expectations of a conversational agents, although such actions return to issues of trust and moral character, and thus further treatment of them are beyond the scope of the current work.

4. CONVERSATIONAL SEARCH MODEL

For our model, we assume there is a user searching for information, and a system or agent that is assisting the user. Search is performed over a well-defined corpus C, where the user it looking for an item $i \in C$ (which may not be unique) that contains the information needed. Such needed items are said to be of high utility to the user. Within a conversation, the system must estimate the utility of each item, which we write u_i. We note that the agent may have a prior estimate of utility over items $\hat{u}_i$ before the user has specified anything, based on long-term knowledge, although do not further consider how this prior utility is maintained.

4.1 Interaction Approaches

In each back and forth step in a conversation, the system provides some information to the user, and the user responds. Depending on what is provided, and what the response is, we find ourselves in different conversation settings seen in prior work. Existing approaches of which we are aware are summarized in Figure 1.

From the system perspective, our model provides for three basic types of information that the system may provide to the user. We term these *actions* that the system may perform. In increasing specificity, these are *nothing*, *a partial item* and *a complete item*. In particular, an item may be partially described in many ways. In the simplest case, the system may select a specific item feature to focus on, such as the concept of `price` in a product search scenario. Alternatively, the system may provide a suggested value of each field, e.g. `price between $50 and $100`. Finally, the system may present a cluster of items, for instance a grouping of products that are somehow similar; this can be through of as a dynamic field having been created for say "electronic gadgets that make good gifts for a teenager".

Conversely, the user may be expected to provide (equivalently, the system may understand user statements that provide), feedback of different types. The simplest design would be for the user to provide either a binary or ordinal score in response to a question, or a preference given two or more choices. A more sophisticated feedback from the user would be a critique [23, 28] that indicates in what way the item or partial item presented by the system does not represent the user's information need. The most detailed level of feedback a user may provide would be free text. Clearly, the meaning of the user's feedback is only well defined given a specific question.

Considering previous work, we note that each prior system typically falls into a single cell as indicated in the Figure. We now describe each of the labeled cells in turn. This will describe the basis of the richer action space model we propose in this paper.

Null System - Free Text User

This is the starting point for most information retrieval systems such as Web search engines, and often for conversational systems where the user may specify many possible requests (such as commercial intelligent agents including Cortana and Siri). The user is simply presented with a search box into which any query can be entered.

Partial Item System - Pref/Rating User

A user may be presented with partial information about matching items in various ways. The most common approach is for a conversational system to confirm a slot that has been inferred, such as "you are looking for an Italian restaurant, correct?" (see, for example [17]). Some systems may also cluster items, asking for a preference. For instance, it might ask "would you prefer to a fancy restaurant, or an inexpensive one?". A third interaction mode, where a preference is elicited over a set of (feature,value) pairs would for instance "would you prefer a laptop with a 12 inch screen for $1000, or a laptop with a 14 inch screen for $1200". Note that all of these interaction modes – as well as critiques and free text entry discussed below – may also be considered "faceted search".

Partial Item System - Critique User

When the user may provide a richer answer than a simple score or preference, this presents a more powerful information retrieval paradigm. In the simplest case, fielded search provides users with a selection of known fields and users may select or specify ranges for any property they desire. This is common in online shopping scenarios, where often the allowed field values are pre-specified. In other settings a user is presented with specific individual facet values. Some commercial intelligent agents allow users to clarify in this way, rather requiring a simple yes/no. For instance, in response to a prompt "you are looking for an Italian restaurant, correct?", the user may reply "no, I'm looking for an Indian restaurant."

Partial Item System - Free Text User

When a system asks a user to fill in a particular aspect of an information need, this is usually referred to as slot filling. For instance, many recommendation systems work in this way. As an example, systems taking part in the Dialog State Tracking Challenge [41] require users to specify travel details to complete a structured query over a public transit schedule.

Complete Item System - Pref/Rating User

Classic approaches to recommendation often request ratings of items to learn a user model for further recommendations. These may be absolute rating requests ("how much did you enjoy the movie Kill Bill?") or preference requests ("did you enjoy Kill Bill or Pride and

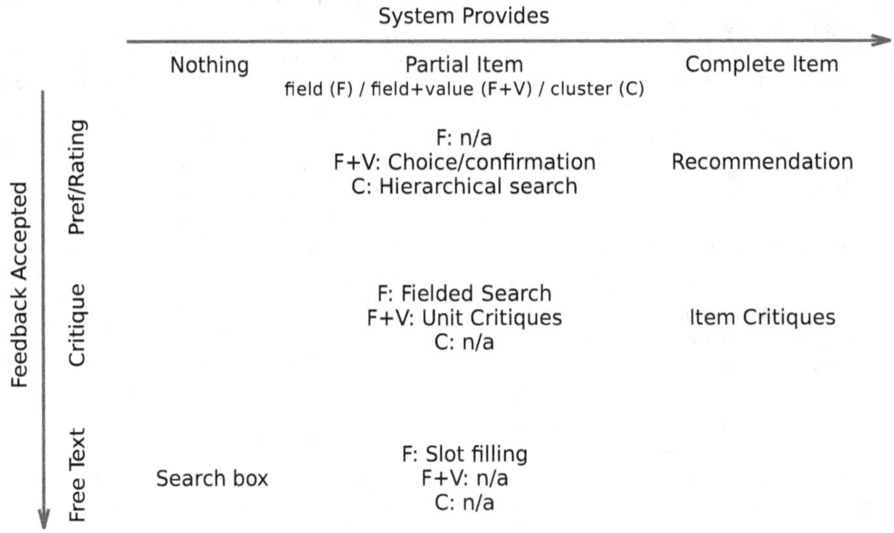

Figure 1: Conversation action space, as matched to previous names from past work. The system may provide three types of feedback, and expect three types of responses in return. In each cell, we describe related work that falls into the appropriate category. We also note that many of the partial item field (F) or field+value (F+V) interaction approaches are often considered variants of faceted search.

Prejudice more?"). For example, Christakopoulou et al. [9] describe such a system in the restaurant domain.

Complete Item System - Critique User

In this case, a system may select a given item, then allow the user to refine their information need anchoring of the properties of the item. For instance, Reilly et al. [28] describe a system where users are presented with an item and possible ways the information need can be refined. Users may select a pre-defined rich critique that allows the system to move closer to the user's goals. Su et al. [32] describe a more sophisticated restaurant recommendation system, where queries are matched to a complete item, which can then be refined or further metadata can be requested.

We also propose an extension to the critique model to allow the agent to learn about the collection directly from user feedback. For example, suppose the agent has been asked to recommend a movie. Given a movie, the user might respond with a critique "that movie is too gory". This can inform the agent about the existence of the concept "gory", which may not have been known to the agent previously. Once given a name and one example, the agent may learn to model it through further interactions with this and other users.

4.2 Interaction Choice

Based on the above variety of existing user/system interaction models, we can now formally model a conversation as a back-and-forth, where the user and agent take turns. For convenience, the conversation always starts with the agent. Each time it is the agent's turn, it will (1) select an action to perform and (2) request for the user to provide a specific type of response. Specifically, the actions available to the agent are:

- $a_\emptyset$ The null action – provide nothing, user is requested for free text describing the information need.
- a_p^1 System provides a single partial item/cluster. User is requested to provide a rating, critique, or free text.
- a_p^{2+} System provides two or a small number of partial items, requesting a preference, critique, or free text.
- a_i^1 System provides a single complete item. User is requested to provide a rating, critique, or free text.
- a_i^{2+} System provides two or a small number of complete items. User is requested to provide a preference, critique, or free text.

The user responses are of the following types:

- r_r A rating of the current item/partial item.
- r_p A preference among the presented items/partial items.
- r_{np} A lack of preference, either $\emptyset$ indicating that none of the option is suitable, or $\star$ indicating that all options are equally suitable.
- r_c A critique of the current item/partial item, indicating how the current item/partial item could be modified to be of higher relevance to the user.
- r_t Unstructured text describing their information need.

4.3 Action Selection

As described at the start of Section 4, the system maintains a distribution over utility values u_i for each item $i \in C$. The goal in an information retrieval setting is to find an item with maximal utility. Thus, a conversational search algorithm must select actions to maximize user satisfaction while tracking expectations over user responses. The motivation behind the above model is that the choice available to the system is simple enough that the utility of each action and response request can be estimated, yet provides the richness necessary for a true conversational retrieval system.

Specific satisfaction metrics that can be optimized are beyond the scope of this work, given the large amount of past work on this topic (see recent work by Kiseleva et al. [20] for an overview). However, we will describe an example algorithm for this selection process in the analysis of our model below.

5. ANALYSIS

We finally present an analysis of the conversational model. In particular we assess four natural analysis questions: Are the criteria suggested for conversations both necessary and sufficient? Are the system action and user response spaces sufficiently rich? How can the system select among the possible actions? How can the system correctly interpret user feedback in this rich environment? We discuss each in turn.

5.1 Are the conversational properties presented both necessary and sufficient?

The goal of the conversational model presented in this work is to allow efficient and effective conversational information retrieval without more complexity than necessary. Thus the first research question we must address considers what kinds of tasks and can be solved with the properties presented. While showing that a wide variety of previously studied information retrieval tasks can be addressed, we argue that each of the properties presented is also necessary.

Example application 1: Basic information retrieval.

We start by considering a standard information retrieval task. We take the first topic from the most recent TREC Web Track [11]:

```
Topic ID: 251
Query:  Identifying spider bites
Description:  Find data on how to identify
spider bites.
```

While the task description is a short query, it suggests the user may need to identify a *specific* spider bite. As the variety of spiders is large, this need would likely be satisfied best in a conversation where the user and the system exchange information to assist the user in narrowing down the candidate set of all possible spiders into the most likely one(s). During this process, the system needs to remember what information the user has already provided, to allow the user to answer individual questions one at a time. It may also be the case that the user needs to revisit or alter answers by referring to past statements. For instance, the user may incorrectly answer one of the questions and not realize until later in the conversation.

Being able to satisfy such needs illustrates the importance of user revealment, as well as memory in the conversational search setting.

Example application 2: Personal information search.

We consider a second information retrieval setting with increasing research attention – search over personal information. This may involve searching for personal emails (e.g. [5]), documents (e.g. [12]) or over personal records that allow a user to investigate for instance where a particular event took place [7]. Such search tasks involve heterogeneous items with rich metadata, where a user may remember a variety of contextual information. An effective conversational retrieval system must aid the user in specifying such information, without requiring the user to remember a complex query language.

In this setting, mixed initiative is particularly valuable, where a system may prompt the user with information that the user may remember. This in turn may lead the user to recall other pertinent information the he or she wishes to provide. Traditional search interfaces for personal information of this nature tend to present rich user interfaces [5, 7, 12]. A mixed initiative system can present users with choices when appropriate to refine the search space, yet allow the user to describe their information need in free text when this is the optimal strategy. Additionally, the value of system revealment and memory is clear.

Example application 3: Product recommendation.

A common information retrieval task is product selection given a general information need. For instance, consider a new parent who must purchase a stroller for the first time. The parent may be unaware of the qualities of such a product without having previously engaged in this task. In an offline recommendation setting, the parent visits a retailer, and an assistant will describe the range of products available, how they differ and elicit the information from the parent as to which features are important, and ultimately guide the parent to suitable choices.

In a conversational search setting, the agent must similarly reveal to the user characteristics of the available search space, knowledge of which features exist in the corpus of items, and assist the user in expressing their information need suitably. Thus this example illustrates particularly the necessity for system and user revealment.

Example application 4: Travel planning.

In some settings, search involves heterogeneous items that give rise to two distinct types of user utility: A given item has a utility to the user, while a set of items is needed to answer the user's information yet has a different type of utility.

One common example is travel planning (see for example [21]), where travel and accommodation are both necessary yet each have their own utilities (cost, convenience, brand, etc), while the combination is the ultimate user's need and has its own utility to the user. For example, even an otherwise perfect inexpensive five star hotel is likely to have low utility for a cost-conscious traveler if it can only be reached by private helicopter on the intended travel date. Other distinct aspect to travel plans – including attractions and restaurants further complicate the retrieval setting, giving rise to distinct item-based and set utility functions.

While in the previous example total cost might be considered a strong indicator of utility for both an item and a set of items, in related settings these utilities may be quite different. For instance, consider an itinerary within a city: The user may have preferences about what types of attractions they prefer to visit, giving rise to an item utility. However for a complete itinerary the user may also value diversity, so as not to spend the entire day visiting only attractions of one type.

Summary.

As we have seen, each of the properties presented – User Revealment, System Revealement, Mixed Initiative, Memory and Set Retrieval – are natural for at least one of the example applications. These applications typify the settings in which information retrieval systems are commonly used, and this in which conversational information retrieval should be possible. As such, we argue that the proposed properties are both necessary, as well as being sufficient to enable many common information retrieval tasks.

5.2 Are the system and user action spaces sufficiently rich?

After presenting the desirable properties for a conversational IR system, we presented a model in Section 4. We now analyze to what extent this model satisfies the desired properties.

User Revealment.

During search, a common strategy to assist users to refine their information needs is to present alternatives within the space of extant items. As such, the action spaces a_p^{2+} and a_i^{2+} provide efficient ways for the user to identify alternative items, as well as dimensions on which the items differ, and ambiguities within the information need described so far.

For instance, when searching for a suitable product in a class where the user is unfamiliar (say, the first time a new parent must purchase a stroller), choices help the user reveal the relevant features to the user.

System Revealment.

Free-form text entry systems are known to have low discoverability (e.g. [40]). By presenting users with confirmations (a_p^1) and requesting a rating (r_r) or critique (r_c) as well as partial item choices a_p^{2+}, the system both demonstrates the ways in which it can partition and refine the search space, as well as common properties of the corpus available.

Set Retrieval.

In modeling partial item presentation as clusters, the model allows for retrieval of sets of items. For instance, taking a travel set retrieval scenario, the system may assist the user in identifying high utility items of various types, then subsequently present sets of complementary items as candidate solutions to the user's information need (for instance, inviting critiques of proposed combinations). We note that as seen in Figure 1, to the best of our knowledge such structured set-based retrieval has not been previously studied in a conversational setting, rather relying on a rich user interface.

Memory.

As previously noted, we postulated that memory plays two distinct roles in a conversational search setting: (1) the system recalling past statements by default, and (2) the ability to reference explicitly to past statements (for instance to indicate that they are no longer correct). The first is addressed in the model implicitly, as a conversation is designed to be a continuous process, thus a continuation of a conversation implicitly requires the continuation of a user's information need and thus all earlier conversational steps.

The second is addressed in the requirement that the model allows the user to always enter free text (r_t). While a weaker constraint on the implementation, this possibility – assuming the user text is interpreted correctly by the system – allows the user to refer to a previous statement to override it specifically. However, the details of how this could be implemented is left as future work.

Mixed Initiative.

In providing the system a number of alternative interaction modes, from a basic free-text ($a_\emptyset$) to structured and preference-based (a_p, a_i), the system is designed to choose the right level of initiative for an information task. In allowing the user to always return unstructured text (r_t), the user can at any time take the initiative from the system.

5.3 Could a system optimally select the next action from the search space?

Given the choices of actions, the system must have a model allowing it to decide which action it is to take at any given point in time. It must (1) select an action in a given context, and (2) interpret the user's response given the previous conversational history. We focus on the action selection process here, arguing that a system could reasonably implement the model presented while leaving the practical details as an open challenge for future work.

In our model, the system maintains a distribution over utility values u_i for each item $i \in C$. As the goal in an information retrieval setting is to find an item with maximal utility, the action must be selected so as to maximize how efficiently this is achieved. While a number of algorithms may be optimal with different implementations of the model, here we present one possible implementation to demonstrate feasibility. Other approaches may be more efficient or lead to better user experiences. One of the goals of this paper is to inspire such approaches, hence we leave them as future work. Rather, we argue here that our model is suitable for describing a conversational information retrieval system.

For each action the system may take, if the user response comes from a known distribution, we can infer the update to the utility of each item. Specifically, suppose that for each item the system has an estimate of utility u_i, as well as an estimate of the uncertainty of the utility σ_i. If the system were to take some action a, and observe response r, the system can predict the update of the item utility and uncertainty (for instance, [9] propose a specific virtual-update multi-armed bandit algorithm for this purpose). Summing over all items and possible user responses, the utility of a system action can be computed as the expected reduction in uncertainty about which items have highest utility. This is more difficult in cases where the distribution over user responses is unknown, such as where the user is requested to provide free text. Here, the utility must be estimated based on prior observations of the system when such an action was requested. A deployed conversational system may estimate the expected utility gain of such open-ended requests, and use this for selecting when to perform such actions.

While the above addresses the system-side utility of an action, a second aspect of question utility is that of the cost a system action incurs upon the user. For instance, a question that has high utility in terms of uncertainty reduction may be difficult for a user to answer. This cost needs to be estimated by the system when selecting actions. A simple approach would be to assume a fixed cost for users to respond to any action. This assumption is commonly used by recommendation system where users are requested to label particular examples as part of the learning process. An alternative would be for a conversational system to observe how long it takes a user to respond to a given type of action, and/or how often the user response is not of the requested type for the given system action.

Finally, in the more complex case of set retrieval, the goal of the user is to find a suitable set of items rather than a single item. In this case, once the system has been able to identify items of high utility, it must learn a combined utility function. The form of this utility function would depend on the particular type of information need being addressed. For instance, in a travel planning scenario there may be complex constraints (e.g. only one hotel is needed at a time, the hotel must be near an airport to which there is a suitable flight, and so forth). While the action space is sufficiently rich to allow the system to propose tradeoffs between combinations, we believe that the details of the utility function learning needs to be addressed in a task-by-task manner.

5.4 How can the system interpret user feedback?

Finally, we consider the question of whether our conversational model allows a system to interpret user feedback effectively.

The model is for the system to take an action a at each turn, requesting the user for a specific response. If the user response is of the expected type, the system will clearly be able to interpret it. However, we have also shown it important that the model allows the user to ignore the system's action (question) and provide alternative feedback, as in a real conversation. In this way, the user would be taking his or her own initiative, for instance if the agent is not providing useful information.

One way to reduce the likelihood of unexpected feedback is to explicitly model common conversational outcomes. For instance, our model specifies one of the possible preference answers is r_{np} – that there is no preference among options being presented (with the uniform label still being positive or negative). This was noted by [9] that such feedback is particularly useful in some settings.

While "unexpected" answers are thus the most problematic, we believe that our model provides the right amount of structure to facilitate interpretability. If the user chooses to provide alternative free-text feedback, interpretation of this feedback is relatively limited given the conversational context. Future success of conversational systems adhering to our general model will hinge on how often users choose to (or need to) revert to other answer types, and how well the system captures such deviations. A system that supports memory is also more robust to errors.

Therefore we claim that our model provides a suitable framework for effectively interpreting user feedback.

6. CONCLUSIONS AND FUTURE WORK

In this paper, we have described the characteristics of a conversational information retrieval system. These characteristics are based on a broad overview of previous work on human conversations. What have argued that the properties of conversations described are both necessary and sufficient to allow a rich variety of information retrieval tasks to be naturally performed using a conversational interface. We consider the primary contribution of these properties to provide a framework for design and evaluation of future conversational information retrieval systems. In allowing approaches to be compared, the types of tasks that such systems can address, and the way in which they differ from human-level conversations can be more easily characterized.

In doing so, we also discussed when conversational approaches appear most valuable for information retrieval, illustrating with a number of tasks that appear to be well suited to chat-based search.

Following this presentation, we presented a theoretical model that satisfies the conversational properties. While theoretical, the model provides the framework for a conversational search system that appears practical in implementation. The model is a generalization of many specialized systems that have previously been implemented, and have been shown to be effective by previous authors. However, none of the previous systems satisfy all the proposed properties of a conversational information retrieval system. We view the contribution of this model as a proposed structure that can be employed towards obtaining true conversational information retrieval. Implementing the model proposed is the most important future extension of this work.

It is further worth considering limitations in the characterization of conversational information retrieval. It may be the case that some of the properties presented can be replaced with others that serve similar function but lead to higher user satisfaction through more natural interaction. The properties described reflect previous findings of human conversations, thus it may be the case that automatic conversational system do not need to reflect human level conversation to be widely useful for information retrieval. In particular, we have chosen to represent knowledge about the corpus as a utility function defined over items and sets of items. It is possible that such a utility function may not exist, or may be too complex to model in relatively short interactions. Incorporating prior knowledge about global utility and popularity may allow the conversational properties to be refined.

Acknowledgments

The authors would like to thank Cecily Morrison and Alex Taylor for insightful discussions about the nature of (human) conversations. We also thank Paul Thomas for useful feedback on related work, and the anonymous reviewers for helpful comments.

References

[1] J. Allen, C. I. Guinn, and E. Horvtz. Mixed-initiative interaction. *IEEE Intelligent Systems and their Applications*, 14(5):14–23, 1999.

[2] M. J. Bates. The design of browsing and berrypicking techniques for the online search interface. *Online review*, 13(5):407–424, 1989.

[3] N. J. Belkin, C. Cool, A. Stein, and U. Thiel. Cases, scripts, and information seeking strategies: on the design of interactive information retrieval systems. *Expert Systems with Applications*, 9:379–395, 1995.

[4] P. N. Bennett, R. W. White, W. Chu, S. T. Dumais, P. Bailey, F. Borisyuk, and X. Cui. Modeling the impact of short- and long-term behavior on search personalization. In *Proceedings of the ACM SIGIR International Conference on Research and Development in Information Retrieval (SIGIR)*, 2012.

[5] D. Carmel, G. Halawi, L. Lewin-Eytan, Y. Maarek, and A. Raviv. Rank by time or by relevance?: Revisiting email search. In *Proceedings of ACM Conference on Information and Knowledge Management (CIKM)*, pages 283–292, 2015.

[6] J. Cassell. More than just another pretty face: Embodied conversational interface agents. *Communications of the ACM*, 4(43):70–78, 2000.

[7] Y. Chen and G. J. F. Jones. Are episodic context features helpful for refinding tasks? lessons learnt from a case study with lifelogs. In *Proceedings of the Information Interaction in Context Symposium (IIiX)*, 2014.

[8] Y.-N. Chen, D. Hakkani-Tur, and X. He. Zero-shot learning of intent embeddings for expansion by convolutional deep structured semantic models. In *Proceedings of the International Conference on Acoustics, Speech, and Signal Processing (ICASSP)*, March 2016.

[9] K. Christakopoulou, F. Radlinski, and K. Hofmann. Towards conversational recommender systems. In *Proceedings of the ACM SIGKDD International Conference on Knowledge Discovery and Data Mining (KDD)*, 2016.

[10] J. Chu-Carroll and M. K. Brown. An evidential model for tracking initiative in collaborative dialogue interactions. In S. Haller, A. Kobsa, and S. McRoy, editors, *Computational Models of Mixed-Initiative Interaction*, pages 49–87. Springer, 1999.

[11] K. Collins-Thompson, C. Macdonald, P. Bennett, and E. M. Voorhees. TREC 2014 web track overview. *NIST Special Publication 500-308: The Twenty-Third Text REtrieval Conference Proceedings (TREC)*, 2014.

[12] E. Cutrell, S. T. Dumais, and J. Teevan. Searching to eliminate personal information management. *Communications of the ACM*, 49(1):58–64, 2006.

[13] R. Dhar. Consumer preference for a no-choice option. *Journal of Consumer Research*, 24(2):215–231, 1997.

[14] M. Dredze, B. N. Schilit, and P. Norvig. Suggesting email view filters for triage and search. In *Proceedings of the International Joint Conference on Artificial Intelligence (IJCAI)*, 2009.

[15] M. A. Hearst. 'natural' search user interfaces. *Communications of the ACM*, 54(11):60–67, 2011.

[16] M. Henderson, B. Thomson, and S. J. Young. Deep neural network approach for the dialog state tracking challenge. In *Proceedings of the Annual SIGdial Meeting on Discourse and Dialogue (SIGDIAL)*, 2013.

[17] J. Jiang, A. H. Awadallah, R. Jones, U. Ozertem, I. Zitouni, R. G. Kulkarni, and O. Z. Khan. Automatic online evaluation of intelligent assistants. In *Proceedings of the International World Wide Web Conference (WWW)*, 2015.

[18] D. G. Johnson and T. M. Powers. Computers as surrogate agents. In J. van den Hoven and J. Weckert, editors, *Information Technology and Moral Philosophy*, chapter 13. Cambridge University Press, 2008.

[19] M. P. Kato and K. Tanaka. To suggest, or not to suggest for queries with diverse intents: Optimizing search result presentation. In *Proceedings of the ACM International Conference on Web Search and Data Mining (WSDM)*, pages 133–142. ACM, 2016.

[20] J. Kiseleva, K. Williams, J. Jiang, A. H. Awadallah, A. C. Crook, I. Zitouni, and T. Anastasakos. Understanding user satisfaction with intelligent assistants. In *Proceedings of the ACM SIGIR Conference on Human Information Interaction and Retrieval (CHIIR)*, 2016.

[21] G. Linden, S. Hanks, and N. Lesh. Interactive assessment of user preference models: The automated travel assistant. In *User Modeling*, pages 67–78. Springer, 1997.

[22] N. Matthijs and F. Radlinski. Personalizing web search using long term browsing history. In *Proceedings of the ACM International Conference on Web Search and Data Mining (WSDM)*, pages 25–34, 2011.

[23] K. McCarthy, Y. Salem, and B. Smyth. Experience-based critiquing: Reusing critiquing experiences to improve conversational recommendation. In *Proceedings of the International Conference on Case-Based Reasoning*, pages 480–494. Springer, 2010.

[24] R. Nordlie. "user revealment" – a comparison of initial queries and ensuing question development in online searching and in human reference interactions. In *Proceedings of the ACM SIGIR International Conference on Research and Development in Information Retrieval (SIGIR)*, pages 11–18, 1999.

[25] D. G. Novick and S. Sutton. What is mixed-initiative interaction. In *Procedings of the AAAI Spring Symposium on Computational Models for Mixed Initiative Interaction*, pages 114–116, 1997.

[26] T. Paek and E. Horvitz. Conversation as action under uncertainty. In *Proceedings of the Conference on Uncertainty in Artificial Intelligence (UAI)*, pages 455–464, 2000.

[27] A. Raux and M. Eskenazi. Optimizing the turn-taking behavior of task-oriented spoken dialog systems. *ACM Transactions on Speech Language Processing*, 9(1):1:1–1:23, May 2012.

[28] J. Reilly, K. McCarthy, L. McGinty, and B. Smyth. Incremental critiquing. In *Proceedings of the SGAI International Conference on Innovative Techniques and Applications of Artificial Intelligence*, 2004.

[29] J. J. Rocchio. Relevance feedback in information retrieval. In G. Salton, editor, *The SMART Retrieval System - Experiments in Automatic Document Processing*. Prentice Hall, Englewood, Cliffs, New Jersey, 1971.

[30] S. Senecal and J. Nantel. The influence of online product recommendations on consumers' online choices. *Journal of Retailing*, 80:159–169, 2004.

[31] A. Sordoni, M. Galley, M. Auli, C. Brockett, Y. Ji, M. Mitchell, J.-Y. Nie, J. Gao, and B. Dolan. A neural network approach to context-sensitive generation of conversational responses. In *Proceedings of the Conference of the North American Chapter of the Association for Computational Linguistics – Human Language Technologies (NAACL-HLT)*, June 2015.

[32] P.-H. Su, M. Gašić, N. Mrkšić, L. Rojas-Barahona, S. Ultes, D. Vandyke, T.-H. Wen, and S. Young. On-line active reward learning for policy optimisation in spoken dialogue systems. In *Proceedings of the Annual Meeting of the Association for Computational Linguistics (ACL)*, 2016.

[33] S. Sukhbaatar, a. szlam, J. Weston, and R. Fergus. End-to-end memory networks. In *Proceedings of the International Conference on Advances in Neural Information Processing Systems (NIPS)*, pages 2440–2448, 2015.

[34] P. ten Have. *Doing Conversation Analysis: A Practical Guide*. SAGE Publications Ltd, 2007.

[35] N. Tintarev and J. Masthoff. Effective explanations of recommendations: user-centered design. In *Proceedings of the ACM conference on Recommender Systems (RecSys)*, pages 153–156, 2007.

[36] D. Traum, D. DeValut, J. Lee, Z. Wang, and S. Marsella. Incremental dialogue understanding and feedback for multiparty, multimodal conversation. In *Proceedings of Intelligent Virtual Agents (IVA)*, pages 275–288, 2012.

[37] M. Walker and S. Whittaker. Mixed initiative in dialogue: An investigation into discourse segmentation. In *Proceedings of the Annual Meeting of the Association for Computational Linguistics (ACL)*, pages 70–78, 1990.

[38] Z. Wang, J. Lee, and S. Marsella. Towards more comprehensive listening behavior: Beyond the bobble head. In *Proceedings of Intelligent Virtual Agents (IVA)*, pages 216–227, 2011.

[39] J. Weizenbaum. ELIZA – a computer program for the study of natural language communication between man and machine. *Communications of the ACM*, 9:36–45, January 1966.

[40] R. W. White and D. Morris. Investigating the querying and browsing behavior of advanced search engine users. In *Proceedings of the ACM SIGIR International Conference on Research and Development in Information Retrieval (SIGIR)*, 2007.

[41] J. Williams, A. Raux, D. Ramachadran, and A. Black. The dialog state tracking challenge. In *Proceedings of the Annual SIGdial Meeting on Discourse and Dialogue (SIGDIAL)*, 2013.

[42] K. Yao and G. Zweig. Attention with intention for neural network conversation model. In *NIPS Workshop on Machine Learning for Spoken Language Understanding and Interaction*, 2015.

[43] K.-P. Yee, K. Swearingen, K. Li, and M. Hearst. Faceted metadata for image search and browsing. In *Proceedings of the SIGCHI Conference on Human Factors in Computing Systems (CHI)*, pages 401–408. ACM, 2003.

[44] S. Young, M. Gašić, B. Thomson, and J. D. Williams. Pomdp-based statistical spoken dialog systems: A review. *Proceedings of the IEEE*, 101(5):1160–1179, 2013.

[45] Y. Zhang and C. Zhai. A sequential decision formulation of the interface card model for interactive ir. In *Proceedings of the ACM SIGIR International Conference on Research and Development in Information Retrieval (SIGIR)*, pages 85–94. ACM, 2016.

Investigating Users' Time Perception during Web Search

Cheng Luo[†],Xue Li[†], Yiqun Liu[†]*, Tetsuya Sakai[◇], Fan Zhang[†], Min Zhang[†], Shaoping Ma[†]
[†]Tsinghua National Laboratory for Information Science and Technology, Department of Computer Science and Technology, Tsinghua University, Beijing 100084, China
[◇]Waseda University
yiqunliu@tsinghua.edu.cn

ABSTRACT

Due to the tremendous economic value of search result pages, search engine companies have invested a lot to improve their quality. Recently, much effort has been made to directly model key aspects of users' interactions with search system, for example, *Benefit* and *Cost*. Time has been widely adopted in both of the two aspects since benefit and cost must be expressed in meaningful units in practical application. Psychological studies have demonstrated that the subjectively perceived time might be different from the objective time measured by timing device and the time perception process of human beings is affected by some psychological factors, such as motivation and interest, which are closely related to the search process. Considering that time is usually used to describe the subject experience of search users, it is necessary to investigate the difference between perceived time and objective time in search process. In psychology, there is a temporal illusion effect named *Vierordt's law*, i.e. shorter intervals tend to be overestimated while longer intervals tend to be underestimated. In this work, we carefully designed a lab-study to examine the impact of duration length on user's time perception in the context of search. Experimental results show that Vierordt's law is consistently observed in Web search environment. This work could help us to correct the estimation of users' perceived time and provide insights about the mechanism of satisfaction.

Keywords

Interactive Information Retrieval; Time Perception; Search Evaluation

1. INTRODUCTION

Search engines have become one of the most important tools to access Web resources for many years. Due to the tremendous economic value of search engine result pages, search engine companies put great effort to improve their quality. Thus search effectiveness evaluation has attracted a lot of attention from both industry and academia.

Beyond traditional Cranfield evaluation paradigm based on test collections, query set, relevance judgments and metrics [14], recently much effort has been made to directly model key aspects of users' interaction with the search system [12]. Several theories have been proposed to glean insights and generate hypothesis about users' behavior [5], for example, Information Foraging Theory [52], Interactive Probability Ranking Principle [28] and Search Economic Theory [4]. The concepts of *Benefit* and *Cost* sit at the center of all these theories. Time is widely adopted in both of the two aspects, because benefit and cost must be expressed in meaningful units in practical calculation. Search cost is often measured by the time of a series of actions, such as formulating queries, examining snippets, clicks on results and etc. Search benefit might be measured in Time Well Spent (TWS), i.e. the time spent viewing relevant material [13]. Temporal information is also incorporated into traditional evaluation metrics. Time is either explicitly used as a parameter of decay function (for example, in Time Biased Gain [54], and Expected Latency-discounted Gain [3]) or implicitly encoded in other measures such as the length of text read by user in U-measure [53].

To summarize, time plays an important role in varying perspectives of search evaluation. We find that the time in most existing works is the *objective* time measured by clock instead of the *subjective* time perceived by human beings. However, we argue that it is more intuitive to adopt perceived time while time is serving as an estimation of effort, because effort itself represents the exertion of mental power and is highly likely to be subjective. Time perception is the subjective experience of time, which is measured by someone's own perception of durations of the indefinite and unfolding of events [30]. A number of researches have established that the perception of temporal information is influenced by both psychological factors (for example, attention [55], complexity [35] and emotion [22]) and physical factors (for example, body temperature [58] and age [21]). Although many of these factors are also regarded as important research issues in IR community, their effects on perceived time have not received much attention.

To the best of our knowledge, only a small number of studies have investigated the difference between objective time and perceived time in Web search scenario. Luo et al. showed that high level of Temporal Relevance [47] and irrelevant document [46] would make the users overestimate

*Corresponding Author

CHIIR '17, March 07-11, 2017, Oslo, Norway

DOI: http://dx.doi.org/10.1145/3020165.3020184

the durations than usual. Czerwinski et al. [18] found that the perceived duration of an uncompleted task would be overestimated, while the duration on a task completed successfully would be underestimated in various application scenarios (also known as Zeigarnik effect [59]). Although these studies shed some light on time perception in Web search environment, it is not clear whether some other fundamental factors would affect the time perception.

In this paper, we investigate users' time perception in the context of search. In psychology, there is a long standing theory named *Vierordt's law* proposed by Karl von Vierordt [25], which states that "short" intervals of time tend to be overestimated while "long" intervals of time tend to be underestimated. We wonder whether Vierordt's law exists in Web search, i.e. whether and how the absolute dwell time length would influence the users' time perception. Based on existing study [33], relatively long dwell intervals are usually assumed to be more likely to accompany relevant materials and users' satisfaction than short ones. Considering that satisfaction would affect user's attention and interest, which have potential effects on time perception, we further explore whether the impact of object interval length exists under varying satisfaction conditions.

To answer these questions, we conducted a controlled user study with 50 participants. The participants were instructed to complete several search tasks and report their perceived durations afterwards. Experimental analysis indicates that in Web search, the perceived time was affected by the absolute duration length as Vierordt's law states and this effect exists consistently across different users' satisfaction. The findings of this work suggests that when using time as an estimation of users' effort, we should adopt the user perceived time by making an adjustment based on duration length. What's more important, the users' perceived time would provide insights about the mechanism of information need fulfillment in the search process.

To summarize, the contributions of this paper are stated as follows: (1) We carefully designed a experimental framework to investigate the users' time perception in Web search environment. (2) We analyzed the impact of different factors on time perception and found that the perceived time was affected by absolute duration length as in Vierordt's law: long durations tend to be underestimated and short durations tend to be overestimated. (3) Differences in dwell time usually coincide with differences in user satisfaction. We examined the influence of absolute duration length under different satisfaction conditions. Experimental results show that the influence exists consistently.

2. RELATED WORK

2.1 Time in Web Search

Time and temporal information is widely used in multiple perspectives of IR researches.

In **Search Intent Understanding**, the queries which have temporally dependent intents are usually recognized as *time-sensitive* queries [20], whose best search results change with time, for example "presidential elections" or "CHIIR conference". The temporal aspects are identified [6, 51, 32] and integrated into the overall ranking mechanism to improve the freshness and relevance of search results [49, 24, 19, 40, 11]. From the aspect of time urgency, some queries are *time-critical*, where users have urgent information needs in the context of an acute problem, for example, "stroke in woman" [50]. Crescenzi et al. showed that time pressure would lead to changes in user behavior [17, 16]. Mishra et al. proposed a model to predict urgent information needs with features including user behavior [50]. On the opposite side of time-critical query, Teevan et al. explored "slow search", a class of search where traditional speed requirements are relaxed in favor of a high quality search experience [56].

In **User Behavior Analysis**, a number of temporal measurements have been proposed as users' implicit feedback [9]. For example, *time-between-clicks* is an estimation of users' dwell time on landing page. It is widely used in multiple applications: satisfaction prediction [42], search success evaluation [33], result usefulness [44] and task difficulty prediction [45].

In **Search Evaluation**, time is taken into consideration in both offline and online evaluation methods. In offline evaluation, time is either explicitly used as the parameter in decay function (for example, Time Biased Gain [54] and Expected Latency-discounted Gain [3]) or implicitly encoded in other measures, such as examination depth in Precision and Recall, and the length of trailtext in U-measure [53]. Recently, some researchers have focused on directly modeling essential aspects of users' interactions, for example, benefit and cost. Time is often used as an estimation of users' search cost in practical computation of corresponding theories, for example, Information Foraging Theory [52], Interactive Probability Ranking Principle [28] and Search Economic Theory [4]. It is intuitive that the more time a user spent on a specific action (examine a snippet, read a document and etc.) usually indicates the more cognitive resources he/she has invested. Similar to system-centric evaluation methods, time is also encoded in other measures like the number of queries in a session [38]. For benefits, Time Well Spent (TWS) [13], expressed as the total time spent on relevant material, measures the utility users have gained in search.

2.2 Time Perception in Psychology

Time perception, referred to as the subjective experience of the objective duration has been carefully studied for decades in the fields of psychology and neuroscience [8, 27]. While time itself is objective, the perceived succession and duration of time is subjective.

Based on phenomenological and experimental data, huge amount of efforts has been invested to explore what the human being is able to know about time through perception and estimation of durations. The experiments are usually adopted in two paradigms: *prospective* timing and *retrospective* timing [7]. It is called prospective when a participant is aware of the necessity to judge the experience of time before the duration. Otherwise, it is called retrospective. Dan Zakay [60] summarized several models of time perception theory and proposed that time perception is manipulated by the following factors: non-temporal information processing load (simple or complex stimuli), type of judgment (absolute or relative), and experimental paradigm (prospective or retrospective).

Time perception would be affected by both psychological (interestingness, attention, cognitive load etc.) and physical factors (body temperature, drug usage, etc.) [55]. Some of these concepts have also attracted the IR community. For example, the cognitive complexity of search tasks for interactive IR experiments has been explored by Kelly et al. [41]. User would be more engaged in interesting tasks and they spent longer completing these tasks [23]. However, in Web search environment, how these factors would affect the users' perception of time has not received much attention. A laboratory study conducted by Luo et al. [47] shows that in high temporal relevance situations, users would tend to overestimate the duration length than usual. They also found that on document level, search users tend to shorten their perceived time on relevant documents [46].

Although these studies opened the door to time perception in Web search environment, it is an open question as whether and how some more central factors, for example, the user satisfaction and dwell time length would affect the perceived time of users.

Time perception is a subjective feeling about the duration of the indefinite and continuous unfolding of events [30]. That is to say, there is not a straightforward way to measure the perceived time. In experimental psychology, several methods have been developed to assess estimations of the perceived time. The first method named *Verbal Estimation* requires the participants to provide a verbal estimation of a duration using temporal units, such as minute and second. In the second method *Reproduction*, the participant is first shown a duration and then asked to reproduce the interval by some operations, for example, push and hold a button for some time. Similar to Reproduction, in the third method *Production*, the participant is required to produce an interval according to a duration in temporal units. The last method *Comparison* presents two durations and requires the participants to make a judgment about which one is longer.

3. METHOD

To investigate the perceived time of users in search tasks, we designed and conducted a laboratory user study with several tasks. Although the controlled experiment had a smaller scale comparing with search log analysis, it enabled us to control variabilities and to collect users' perceived time with effective psychological methods.

3.1 Scenario, Tasks and System

In our user study, the participants need to perform 9 ad-hoc search tasks in our experimental search system. The first task is for instruction and training, while the remaining ones are for formal experiments. For each task, the participants need to read the *task description* and then search for relevant information with a predefined *query* in our system. Then they were instructed to estimate how long they have spent in the searching process. Throughout the experiment, a participant completed several questionnaires including a demographic questionnaire, pre/post-search questionnaires and an exit questionnaire.

We created 9 informational search tasks which are similar with the topics of TREC Session Track[1]. Several criteria were taken into consideration when organizing these tasks: Firstly, the tasks should be of varying levels of cognitive complexity. Cognitive complexity refers to the amount of learning and cognitive effort required to complete the search. Based on psychological theory [35], cognitive complexity might have an effect on time perception. Following previous

[1]http://trec.nist.gov/data/session.html

Table 1: An Example of the Search Tasks

#	Topic	Cognitive Complexity	Goal	Product
1	Science	Remember	Clear	Factual
The Halo Effect is a very interesting psychological effect, please search for some information about this effect, and find an appropriate example from our daily lives.				
Query	Halo Effect			

Interactive IR researches [10, 36, 41], our tasks vary across four domains (psychology, culture, healthcare and science) and across four levels of cognitive complexity according to the taxonomy of learning proposed by Anderson and Krathwohl [1]: (1) *Remember*: recalling relevant knowledge from long-term memory; (2) *Understand*: constructing meaning through summarizing and explaining; (3) *Analyze*: breaking material into constituent parts and determining how the parts relate to each other, and (4) *Evaluate*: making judgments through checking and critiquing. In the eight tasks for formal experiment, for each level of cognitive complexity, we have two tasks.

Secondly, we consider the goal of the tasks, which is associated with interactive search behavior [37]. Li and Belkin [43] identified a variety of generic facets of tasks in information seeking, such as Source of task, Action, Goal, Product and etc. We follow Jiang and Ni's experimental design and consider two characteristics of search tasks [39]: the goal of a search task is either clear or amorphous (`goal`); the product of a search task is either factual information, or enhanced intellectual understanding of the user (`product`). In our experiment, all of the tasks have a clear goal, because we have to make sure that the tasks are clearly stated and all the participants can interpreted the task descriptions in the same way. For task product, we have 4 intellectual tasks and 4 factual tasks. In Jiang and Ni's work [39], they also take the user's self-rated familiarity (`familiarity`) into consideration, we investigate this in our pre-task questionnaire.

For each search task, we provided a predefined query to perform search in our system. Although the fixed query might threaten the ecological validity of our experiment, it would make sure that all the participants were presented with identical Search Engine Result Page (SERP) for each task. An example of the tasks is shown in Table 1.

To simulate a real Web search environment, we developed an experimental search system, which is very similar with general Web search engines. When the user begins search, our system will provide ten search results, which are manipulated (as described in Section 3.4) based on SERPs crawled from a commercial search engine. We removed all the query suggestions, sponsored results, ads and vertical results to prevent potential distraction. For the purpose of variabilities controlling, query reformulation and pagination are not supported in this experiment. All the users' interactions including clicks, scrolling, tab switching and mouse movements are logged in the back-end database using an injected Javascript script.

After the setup of the experimental system, the authors of this paper double-checked the tasks carefully to make sure: (1) The tasks and topics are geared towards our participants, i.e. university students. (2) The manipulated search results could provide enough information to fulfill the information needs proposed in task descriptions.

3.2 Study Participants

In our experiments, we recruited 50 undergraduate students from a university located in China. The average age of the participants was 20.02 (SD=2.00) and 32 of them were female. A variety of majors were represented across the natural sciences (N=10), social sciences (N=8), arts (N=4), and engineering (N=28). All of the participants searched at least 1 to 3 times per day. 37 of the 50 participants reported at least 4 to 6 searches per day. The participants reported a high level of familiarity with search engine (4.88/7, SD=1.17). They were informed in advance that they would be paid $15 for the participation. The experiments actually lasted about 60 minutes and the participants all signed a post facto participation form revealing the content of the experiment.

3.3 Experiment Procedure

The experiments were performed in a quiet room to avoid external disturbance. The participants were asked to take off their watches and turn off any device which would provide temporal information. They were also asked to remove all jewelry or anything which might be a distraction during the experiment.

The study used the following protocol as shown in Figure 1. (I) Firstly, the participants need to complete a demographic questionnaire, which is about their age, gender, and familiarity with search engine. (II) The participants then received instruction via a video on screen. In the video, we introduced the procedure of the experiment and completed the training task as an example. More specifically, the participants were instructed as follows: *"First, please read the task description and make sure you have understood the information needs, then you will see a search result page. Please find relevant information as you are using search engine in a natural manner."*. The participants were not informed about the purpose of our experiment. They were instructed to estimate the durations spent on searching after each task. After instruction, the participants would go through the training task to get familiar with the procedure and the experimental system. (III) For each formal task, the participants were first shown the task description, then a pre-task questionnaire (III-a) was used to investigate their familiarity, interest, expected difficulty and understanding about the topic. Once they finished the questionnaire, they would enter the SERP (III-b), which had ten search results presented as a commercial search engine. While no task time limits were imposed, the search process ended when the participants felt satisfied or hopeless, or just finished examining all the ten results. Then the participants were redirected to another page in which they reported their minimal/maximal estimations (III-c) to the nearest 10 seconds about the dwell time on the SERP. This estimation method is following Grondin et al.'s approach [31] about multi-minute intervals estimations. The participants were then asked to report their perceived quality of search results, perceived difficulty, consciousness of time elapsing, and perceived urgency (III-d). As suggested by Mao et al. [48], the participants were asked to summarize their outcome after each task. This would encourage the participants to concentrate on the search process to find useful information. The answer would be recorded by voice instead of keyboard, which would reduce their efforts as much as possible.

Finally, after the participants completed the search tasks, they were directed to an exit-questionnaire (IV), which investigates their overall experience during all the formal tasks. The exit-questionnaire is about their average interests, consciousness of quality manipulation, fatigue and confidence of time estimations.

For all the questions in pre/post-task questionnaires and exit-questionnaires, participants were asked to respond their agreement on 7-point Likert scale (from strong disagreement to strong agreement) to the predefined statements such as: "You felt tired after all the tasks were completed" as in Arapakis et al.'s experiment [2]. Moreover, we conducted a pilot experiment to confirm that the tasks and procedures are appropriate and the manipulation of search results is effective.

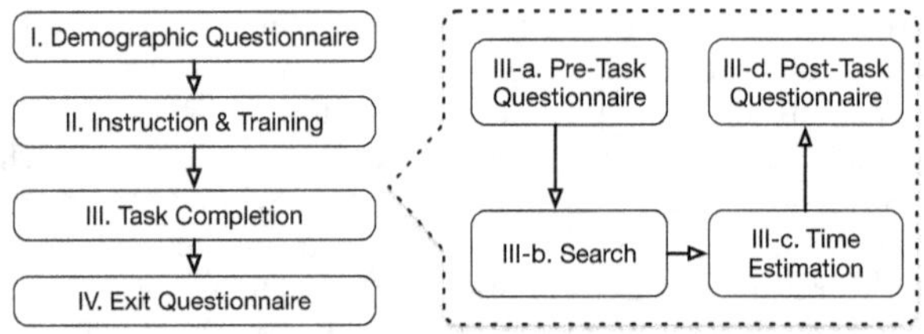

Figure 1: Procedure of the Experiment

3.4 Experiment Design

In this work, we focus on the impact of objective duration length on users' perceived time. However, as we know, the dwell time of a search session is a user's reaction towards many factors, such as system effectiveness and result presentation. It is also affected by some subjective factors, e.g. reading speed and cognitive ability.

Another factor accompanying dwell time is user's satisfaction. There are a number of studies using dwell time as a feature to predict users' satisfaction [34, 38]. According to psychological studies [22, 30], satisfaction would have an impact on users' motivation and emotional states, which further leads to illusions of perceived time. However, there is not a certain relationship between dwell time and satisfaction. For example in Table 2, a search session with long dwell time could be a complex information needs solved by several relevant documents or a struggling process with several irrelevant documents. On the other hand, a session with short dwell time may be an information need resolved by a high quality document ranked at top position or an early abandonment on a disappointed SERP.

In our experiment, the two factors which may influence users' time perception, absolute dwell time length and satisfaction are nested together to some degree. Therefore, to tackle this problem, we attempted to present SERPs of varying qualities in different tasks. Following Smucker et al. [54], we manipulated the precision of the SERPs. More specifically, for each task, there are two different SERPs as follows:

Poor Quality: three of the ten search results are relevant (Precision=0.3) while none of the top five ones is relevant.

High Quality: seven of the ten search results are relevant (Precision=0.7) while none of the top five ones is irrelevant.

The SERPs are manipulated from two aspects: the quantity and position of relevant results. Comparing with

Table 2: **Example of Sessions with Long/Short Dwell Time under Different Satisfaction Conditions (SAT/DISSAT)**

	Long Dwell Time	Short Dwell Time
SAT	The user viewed a few relevant results to resolve a complex problem. For example, "history of WW2".	The user was satisfied by a top relevant result. For example, "NYC Weather".
DISSAT	The user examined several results however few of them were relevant. For example, "inline bug in C program".	The user felt disappointed by the SERP and gave up this query.

High Quality SERPs, the Poor Quality SERPs have fewer relevant results, which are presented at lower positions.

For a specific search task, we first crawled the top search results of the predefined query from a commercial search engine. Then the binary relevance score (relevant, irrelevant) of each search result is judged by three professional assessors. We only kept the results for which the assessors reached an agreement, i.e. all of the assessors labelled the search results as relevant or irrelevant. At last, we sequentially selected 10 search results to fill the slots on Poor Quality SERPs and High Quality SERPs and made sure that the quantity and position of relevant results meet our definitions.

In the user study, participants search for relevant information for 9 tasks. The first one is for training purpose and we presented High Quality to make sure all the participants received identical instruction. For the remaining 8 tasks, we randomly assigned 4 of them to High Quality group and the other 4 tasks to Poor Quality group. We rotated the sequence of 8 formal tasks using Latin Square to avoid presentation order bias. For each task, the participants in the two groups are balanced, i.e. half of the participants were presented with High Quality SERPs while the other half were presented with Poor Quality SERPs.

4. DATA

4.1 Users' Perceived Satisfaction v.s. Manipulated SERP Quality

The participants were not informed of the purpose and the manipulation of our experiments. We begin our analysis by examining the perceived satisfaction under SERPs of varying qualities.

Recall that in post-task questionnaire, participants were asked to report their agreement about "You are satisfied with the search results about this topic" on a 7-point scale (1 to 7, from strong disagreement to strong agreement). To fold the users' satisfaction ratings into binary categories (SAT, DISSAT), we arbitrarily used 4 as the threshold of satisfaction, i.e. for a specific topic and SERP, if a user gives a rating which is equal or greater than 4, we think that it is a satisfied search.

We assume that users would be satisfied with High Quality SERPs and dissatisfied with Poor Quality SERPs. Then we can measure the consistency of users' perceived satisfaction and SERP quality by calculating the accuracy. More specifically,

$$accuracy = \frac{\#SAT\_on\_HQ + \#DISSAT\_on\_PQ}{\#Tasks} \quad (1)$$

The results are shown in Figure 2. We can see that for most of the users (46/50), the accuracy is above 60%, except for participant #4 (50.0%), #23 (50.0%), #24 (50.0%) and #27 (25.0%). There might be various reasons which lead to these divergences. First, the participant may have misunderstood the feedback mechanism. For example, #27 gave relatively high ratings (7, 5, 5 and 3) on Poor Quality SERPs and low ratings (3, 2, 2 and 5) on High Quality SERPs. Second, the users may have various levels of satisfaction even on SERPs with identical content, because their expectations about the performance of the search engine are also varying with individuals [57]. In our experiment, participant #4, #23 and #24 gave ratings which are greater than 4 for all of the search sessions. Third, it is possible that the participants would make mistakes due to fatigue or distraction during the experiment. We remove the data of these 4 participants in the further analysis to reduce potential noise.

4.2 Average Dwell Time on Different SERPs

The average dwell time on different SERPs of each task is presented in Figure 3 and the error bars indicate the corresponding standard deviations.

Figure 3 illustrates that for most of the tasks, the average dwell time on the High Quality and Poor Quality SERPs are very close. This observation is possible against the intuition that users should spent longer time on High Quality SERPs, because there are more relevant results and the durations on relevant results are usually longer [26]. A potential reason is that dwell time on SERP level is affected by multiple factors. Although previous studies found that users spend longer on relevant documents, in practical search scenario, on a High Quality SERP, a user may leave earlier since he/she may be satisfied by a relevant result ranked at top positions while on a Poor Quality SERP, users may have to examine more results, which also leads to long durations. We conducted a two-sided t-test and found only the difference on Task #6 is significant (t-stat=−2.130, p-value=0.038, df=43.90, ES=0.642). The Task #6 requires the participants to investigate the ranking of movie box office value in 2015. We found that on the High Quality SERP, most participants were satisfied by the first relevant result.

4.3 Feedbacks

We grouped the response to the items on the pre/post-task questionnaire as follows. We put the search sessions in which the High Quality SERPs were presented into the "HQ Group", and then placed the remaining ones into "PQ Group". For the questions which were reported on a 7-point Likert scale, we converted the responses to numeric values from 1 to 7. We also calculated the average dwell time length and perceived time length of different groups. A two-sided t-test was conducted to examine whether the difference between two groups is significant. The results are presented in Table 3.

We can see that for pre-task questionnaire, the responses from both groups are quite similar. The participants reported moderate level of *familiarity with the topic* and relatively high level of *interest in the topics*. They

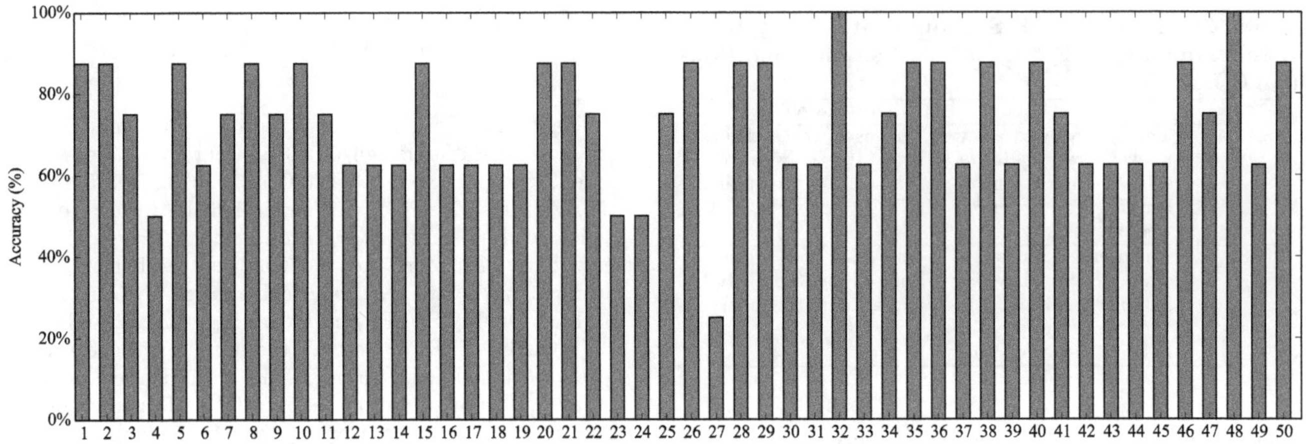

Figure 2: Consistency between Users' Satisfaction and SERP Quality

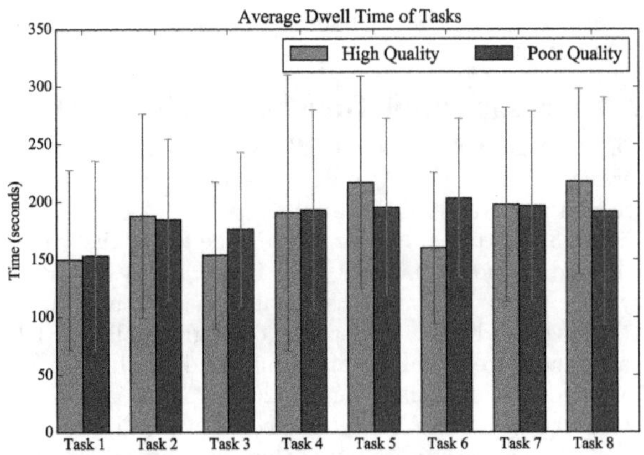

Figure 3: Average Dwell time on High Quality/Poor Quality SERPs of Different Tasks

were very confident that they had fully understood the information needs of the tasks (*understanding about info. need*). The expected search difficulty in HQ Group (Mean=3.705, SD=1.599) is slightly higher than that in PQ Group (Mean=3.577, SD=1.690) but the difference is not statistically significant. It is not surprising that none of the items in pre-task questionnaire is significantly different between two groups since the participants were not aware of the purpose and the manipulation of the experiment.

In the post-task questionnaire, the participants perceived significantly higher satisfaction in HQ Group (Mean=5.325, SD=1.410) than in PQ Group (Mean=3.397, SD=1.721). This shows that our SERP manipulation effectively affects users' satisfaction. They also felt that it is much easier to find relevant information in HQ Group (Mean=2.635, SD=1.422) than in PQ Group (Mean=3.748, SD=1.700). The participants from both HQ Group and PQ Group reported that they are aware of the elapsing of time when conducting the search tasks. They also perceived a relatively high level of time pressure. Although we did not give any time limit in the experiment, the participants might feel some pressure because that they were required to report their perceived time after each task.

Table 3: Statistics of Participants' feedback in Questionnaire and Behavior (** indicates significant at $p<0.01$; * indicates significant at $p<0.05$)

	HQ Group	PQ Group
	Pre-task Questionnaire	
Familiarity with the topic	3.920(1.703)	3.829(1.804)
Interest in the topic	5.150(1.614)	5.166(1.625)
Understanding about info. need	6.305(0.879)	6.351(0.685)
Expected search difficulty	3.705(1.599)	3.577(1.690)
	Post-task Questionnaire	
Perceived Satisfaction**	5.325(1.410)	3.397(1.721)
Perceived search difficulty**	2.635(1.422)	3.748(1.700)
Awareness of time*	6.095(0.752)	5.970(0.789)
Perceived time pressure	4.910(1.030)	4.930(0.948)
	Behavior	
Dwell time length (seconds)	182.985(87.372)	184.804(80.214)
Perceived time length (seconds)	163.925(75.334)	165.954(74.576)

The dwell/perceived time length in HQ Group and PQ Group is quite close. This is consistent with our observations on each task (Figure 3). It should be noted that the variations of dwell time is quite large, which allows us to observe the influence of dwell time length on time perception.

5. EXPERIMENTAL RESULTS

This section discusses the following research questions:

RQ1: How can we measure the relationship between users' dwell time and perceived time?

RQ2: What is the relationship between the absolute dwell time and the user's perceived time? Does Vierordt's law exist in Web search?

RQ3: Does the relationship between the absolute dwell time and the user's perceived time differ under different user satisfaction conditions?

5.1 Measuring the Relationship between Dwell Time and Perceived Time

In our experiment, the participants provided minimal/maximal estimations about how long they had spent on search in temporal units. Following Grondin et al.'s approach [31], we use the mean of minimal and maximal duration length as their estimations. To measure the relationship between perceived time and actual time (**RQ1**), we first define a measure named *P-rate*. For a specific user u in task t, the *P-rate* (u, t) is defined as:

$$P\text{-}rate(u,t) = \log \frac{perceived\ time}{dwell\ time} \tag{2}$$

where *perceived time* and *dwell time* denotes the perceived duration length and actual duration length respectively. *P-rate* is defined as a logarithm function to ensure that the absolute value represents the difference between perceived time and dwell time and the signal(+/-) reflects whether the perceived time is shorter or longer.

P-rate reflects the ratio between the perceived time and actual dwell time. The perceived time is normalized by the actual dwell time since we are focusing on whether the perceived duration is overestimated or underestimated comparing with the actual duration length. For a specific search session, *P-rate* < 0 means that the perceived time is shorter than the dwell time, i.e. the duration length is underestimated. On the opposite side, *P-rate* > 0 indicates that the perceived time is longer than dwell time and the duration length is overestimated.

The distribution of *P-rate* on dwell time is shown in Figure 4. Each point in the figure denotes a certain search session. An intuitive observation is that the *P-rate* correlates negatively with dwell time length. Most of the points whose *P-rate* is positive appear at the positions where dwell time is shorter than 200 seconds, which means that the overestimated sessions usually have a relatively short dwell time. For almost all the points whose dwell time is longer than 300 seconds, the *P-rate* is negative, i.e. the long durations tend to be underestimated. We would to examine the effect of dwell time on *P-rate* with regression analysis in Section 5.2.

5.2 Impacts of Different Factors on Time Perception

To investigate the impact of absolute dwell time length on *P-rate* (**RQ2**), we ran a regression analysis to analyze the effect of duration length by controlling different factors following Crescenzi et al. [15] . We developed several linear regression models with different factors. More specifically,

- **Model 1** dependent variable: *P-rate*; independent variable: absolute dwell time length.
- **Model 2** dependent variable: *P-rate*; independent variables: absolute dwell time and the factors reported in pre-task questionnaire.

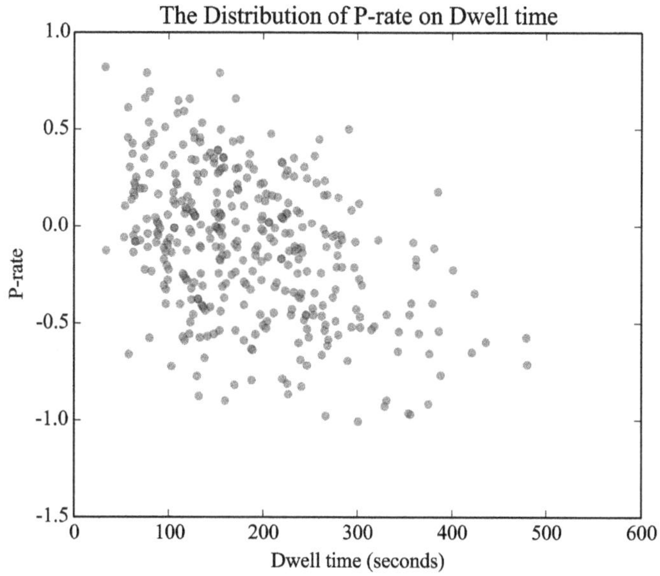

Figure 4: The Distribution of *P-rate* on Dwell Time

- **Model 3** dependent variable: *P-rate*; independent variables: absolute dwell time, the factors reported in pre-task questionnaire and the information of tasks and participants.

In Model 1, we focus on the effect of absolute dwell time length while in Model 2 more factors reported in pre-task questionnaire are taken into consideration. We did not involve factors which were reported in the post-task questionnaire since these factors are probably dependent on the dwell time length. In Model 3, we further took several the task and participant specific factors into consideration to capture the potential variability: participants (one per participant), task cognitive complexity (4 levels, remember, understand, analyze and evaluate respectively), task goal (2 levels, clear or amorphous) and task product (2 levels, factual or intellectual).

Table 4 displays the regression coefficients (β) and intercepts (constant). In Model 1, we can see that the dwell time length is a significant predictor of *P-rate*. With each additional unit (seconds) of dwell time, the *P-rate* would decrease 0.0018. Although the effect looks slightly weak, based on the fact that the dwell time ranges from tens to hundreds of seconds and the *P-rate* is defined as a logarithm function, the effect of absolute dwell time is statistically significant ($p < 0.001$) and cannot be ignored.

In Model 2, we added several factors which were reported by the participants in pre-task questionnaire: familiarity with the topic, interests in the topic, understanding about the information need and the expected difficulty. The dwell time length is still statistically significant ($p < 0.001$). The other factors presents statistically insignificant correlations with *P-rate*. We did not found interaction effect between dwell time length and these factors.

In Model 3, the dwell time shows similar effect with that in Model 1 & 2. The participant presents a coefficient varying from -0.4436 to 0.5467. Among all the 46 participants, 18 bring significant ($p < 0.05$) impact on *P-rate*. This finding is in line with previous psychological studies [30],

Table 4: Regression Models for *P-rate* with Different Strategies (*** indicates $p < 0.001$ and * indicates $p < 0.05$)

Variables	Model 1	Model 2	Model 3
Absolute dwell time length	-0.0018^{***}	-0.0018^{***}	-0.0015^{***}
Familiarity with the topic		-0.0119	-0.0098
Interests in the topic		0.0010	0.0015
Understanding about info. need		-0.0130	-0.0116
Expected search difficulty		-0.0049	0.0058
Participant			-0.4436 to 0.5467
Task Cognitive Complexity			0.0223^{*}
Task Goal			-0.0224
Task Product			-0.0451
Constant	0.2359^{***}	0.3785^{*}	0.1717^{*}
R-squared	0.3776	0.3828	0.6857

time perception is a subject cognitive process of human beings and highly affected by individual factors. For the task based factors, only cognitive complexity has a significant ($p < 0.05$) influence on *P-rate*. With each additional unit of cognitive complexity, the model predicts that *P-rate* will increase by 0.0223. When the task becomes more complex, the user tends to overestimate perceived time. This phenomenon may also be supported by some theories in psychology. When the task become more complex, users would have lower motivation since he/she has to invest more cognitive resource and mental power. Psychological studies find that motivation causes the time to be underestimated during pleasant experiences and overestimated during struggling experiences [29].

We can see that in Model 1, dwell time length explained a sizeable proportion of the variance in *P-rate*, in Model 1, $R^2 = 0.3776$, F(1,365)=80.01, $p < 0.001$.

5.3 Vierordt's law in Time Perception

In psychological studies about time perception, there is a long standing temporal illusion named *Vierordt's law* [25], which states that human beings tend to overestimate short durations and underestimate long durations. We want to investigate whether Vierordt's law works in the Web search environment.

In our experiments, we can see that when the dwell time is relative short, the *P-rate* tends to be positive. According to the definition of *P-rate*, it indicates that the perceived time is longer than the dwell time, i.e. the dwell time is overestimated. Based on the regression analysis, *P-rate* correlates negatively with dwell time length. As dwell time grows, *P-rate* decreases and becomes negative. That is to say, when the duration is relative long, $\frac{perceived\ time}{dwell\ time}$ decreases and goes below 1, i.e comparing with the absolute dwell time, the perceived time is underestimated.

To examine whether this effect is consistent across search sessions with different length, we split the search sessions into several parts according to the dwell time length and ran regression analysis on each part.

Table 5: Regression Models for *P-rate* on Search Sessions with Different Lengths (*** indicates $p < 0.001$, ** indicates $p < 0.01$ and * indicates $p < 0.05$)

Variables	Short	Middle	Long
Absolute dwell time length	-0.0058^{***}	-0.0013^{**}	-0.0014
Constant	0.5382^{**}	0.1632^{*}	-0.3280
R-squared	0.4776	0.2828	0.0480

The search sessions were divided into the following groups:

- **Short Group (N=60):** dwell time is shorter than 100 seconds.
- **Middle Group (N= 272):** dwell time is longer than 100 seconds and shorter than 300 seconds.
- **Long Group (N=36):** dwell time is longer than 300 seconds.

We conducted regression analysis on all the three groups and the results are presented in Table 5. We can see that the absolute dwell time length presents a negative effect across all the three groups. On the Short Group, the effect is much more stronger than that on the Middle and Long Groups. Comparing with the *Underestimation of Long Dwell Time*, the *Overestimation of Short Dwell Time* is more substantial and statistically significant. The effect on the Long Group is not statistically significant, a potential implication is that the data in Long Group is too sparse.

In summary, we find that the absolute dwell time has a substantial effect on the *P-rate*. When the dwell time is relatively short, *P-rate* is positive, i.e. user tends to overestimate the duration. As time grows, *P-rate* decreases and becomes negative, which indicates user underestimates the duration.

Our experimental results are consistent with Vierordt's law. This would help us to better understand the cost model of users in Web search, e.g. we can estimate the perceived time based on the duration length to better users' effort during Web search.

5.4 Impact of Dwell Time Length Under Different Satisfaction Conditions

As we mentioned before, satisfaction is another factor which may influence the perceived time. We want to investigate whether the effect of dwell time length is consistent across different satisfaction conditions. To this end, we split the search sessions into two groups according to the self-reported satisfaction of users: **Satisfied Group** (perceived satisfaction$\geq$4) and **Dissatisfied Group** (perceived satisfaction<4). Since satisfaction may have an impact on perceived time by affecting motivation and emotional states, the user perceived satisfaction may be more appropriate than the predefined SERP quality.

We ran a regression analysis on each group and the coefficients (β) and intercepts (constant) were shown in Table 6. The dwell time length presents a negative and significant correlation on both the two groups. As discussed in Section 5.3, we can conclude that Vierordt's law was consistently observed under different satisfaction conditions.

Table 6: Regression Models for *P-rate* on Search Sessions Under Different Satisfaction Conditions (*** indicates $p < 0.001$ and * indicates $p < 0.05$)

Variables	Satisfied	Dissatisfied
Absolute dwell time length	-0.0022^{***}	-0.0012^{***}
Constant	0.3079^{***}	0.1127^{*}
R-squared	0.3601	0.3828

On Satisfied Group, the effect of dwell time length was slightly stronger than on the Dissatisfied Group. This result suggests that when users' satisfaction might be another factor which will influence the time perception in Web search.

6. CONCLUSION AND FUTURE WORK

In this work, we investigated the subjective perception of time in the context of Web search. Based on a controlled user experiment, this paper provides insights on the impact of dwell time length on perceived time. We found that Vierordt's law had a consistent and significant effect on users' perceived time under varying satisfaction conditions: participants tend to underestimation relatively long durations and overestimate short durations. The findings in this paper may help us better understand the time perception mechanism and cost model of Web search users. In the future work, we would like to explore adopting the perceived time in existing evaluation framework.

Our study has a few limitations. Our experiment was conducted in a lab environment in which participants have to feedback their perceived time explicitly. This is different from a natural environment. Time perception is a subjective mental activity. When a person is using a search engine, many factors (presentation, response latency etc.) would influence the time perception process. In this experiment, we tried our best to control these factors and findings in this work may provide guidance for further experimental design in a more practical environment.

7. ACKNOWLEDGMENTS

This work was supported by Natural Science Foundation (61622208, 61532011, 61472206) of China and National Key Basic Research Program (2015CB358700).

8. REFERENCES

[1] L. Anderson, D. Krathwohl, and B. Bloom. *A taxonomy for learning, teaching, and assessing: a revision of Bloom's taxonomy of educational objectives.* Longman, 2001.

[2] I. Arapakis, X. Bai, and B. B. Cambazoglu. Impact of response latency on user behavior in web search. In *SIGIR '14*.

[3] J. A. Aslam, M. Ekstrand-Abueg, V. Pavlu, F. Diaz, and T. Sakai. Trec 2013 temporal summarization. In *TREC '13*.

[4] L. Azzopardi. The economics in interactive information retrieval. In *SIGIR '11*.

[5] L. Azzopardi and G. Zuccon. An analysis of theories of search and search behavior. In *ICTIR '15*, pages 81–90. ACM, 2015.

[6] K. Berberich, S. Bedathur, O. Alonso, and G. Weikum. A language modeling approach for temporal information needs. In *ECIR '10*.

[7] R. A. Block and D. Zakay. Prospective and retrospective duration judgments: A meta-analytic review. *Psychonomic bulletin & review*, 4(2):184–197, 1997.

[8] R. A. Block and D. Zakay. Psychological time at the millennium: Some past, present, future, and interdisciplinary issues. *Time: Perspectives at the millennium (The study of time X)*, 2001.

[9] A. Borisov, I. Markov, M. de Rijke, and P. Serdyukov. A context-aware time model for web search.

[10] R. Capra, J. Arguello, A. Crescenzi, and E. Vardell. Differences in the use of search assistance for tasks of varying complexity. In *SIGIR '15*.

[11] S. Cheng, A. Arvanitis, and V. Hristidis. How fresh do you want your search results? In *CIKM'2013*.

[12] C. L. Clarke, M. D. Smucker, and E. Yilmaz. Ir evaluation: Modeling user behavior for measuring effectiveness. In *SIGIR '15*.

[13] C. L. A. Clarke and M. D. Smucker. Time well spent. In *IIiX '14*.

[14] C. W. Cleverdon and M. Keen. Aslib cranfield research project-factors determining the performance of indexing systems; volume 2, test results. 1966.

[15] A. Crescenzi, R. Capra, and J. Arguello. Time pressure, user satisfaction and task difficulty. In *Proceedings of the 76th ASIS&T Annual Meeting: Beyond the Cloud: Rethinking Information Boundaries*, ASIST '13, pages 122:1–122:4, Silver Springs, MD, USA, 2013. American Society for Information Science.

[16] A. Crescenzi, D. Kelly, and L. Azzopardi. Impacts of time constraints and system delays on user experience. In *CHIIR'2016*.

[17] A. Crescenzi, D. Kelly, and L. Azzopardi. Time pressure and system delays in information search. In *SIGIR'2015*.

[18] M. Czerwinski, E. Horvitz, and E. Cutrell. Subjective duration assessment: An implicit probe for software usability. In *IHM-HCI'2001*.

[19] N. Dai, M. Shokouhi, and B. D. Davison. Learning to rank for freshness and relevance. In *Proceedings of the 34th international ACM SIGIR conference on Research and development in Information Retrieval*, pages 95–104. ACM, 2011.

[20] W. Dakka, L. Gravano, and P. G. Ipeirotis. Answering general time sensitive queries. In *Proceedings of the 17th ACM Conference on Information and Knowledge Management*, CIKM '08, pages 1437–1438, New York, NY, USA, 2008. ACM.

[21] J.-C. Dreher, A. Meyer-Lindenberg, P. Kohn, and K. F. Berman. Age-related changes in midbrain dopaminergic regulation of the human reward system. *Proceedings of the National Academy of Sciences*, 105(39):15106–15111, 2008.

[22] S. Droit-Volet, S. L. Fayolle, and S. Gil. Emotion and time perception: effects of film-induced mood. *Frontiers in integrative neuroscience*, 5, 2011.

[23] A. Edwards and D. Kelly. How does interest in a work task impact search behavior and engagement? In *CHIIR '16*, pages 249–252. ACM, 2016.

[24] M. Efron and G. Golovchinsky. Estimation methods for ranking recent information. In *SIGIR '11*.

[25] C. Fortin and R. Rousseau. Interference from short-term memory processing on encoding and reproducing brief durations. *Psychological Research*, 61(4):269–276, 1998.

[26] S. Fox, K. Karnawat, M. Mydland, S. Dumais, and T. White. Evaluating implicit measures to improve web search. *ACM Transactions on Information Systems (TOIS)*, 23(2):147–168, 2005.

[27] P. Fraisse. Perception and estimation of time. *Annual review of psychology*, 35(1):1–37, 1984.

[28] N. Fuhr. A probability ranking principle for interactive information retrieval. *Information Retrieval*, 11(3):251–265, 2008.

[29] P. A. Gable and B. D. Poole. Time flies when you're having approach-motivated fun effects of motivational intensity on time perception. *Psychological science*, page 0956797611435817, 2012.

[30] S. Grondin. *Psychology of time*. Emerald Group Publishing, 2008.

[31] S. Grondin and M. Plourde. Judging multi-minute intervals retrospectively. *The Quarterly Journal of Experimental Psychology*, 60(9):1303–1312, 2007.

[32] D. Gupta and K. Berberich. Identifying time intervals of interest to queries. In *CIKM '14*.

[33] A. Hassan. A semi-supervised approach to modeling web search satisfaction. In *SIGIR '12*.

[34] A. Hassan and R. W. White. Personalized models of search satisfaction. In *CIKM'13*.

[35] R. E. Hicks, G. W. Miller, G. Gaes, and K. Bierman. Concurrent processing demands and the experience of time-in-passing. *The American Journal of Psychology*, pages 431–446, 1977.

[36] B. J. Jansen, D. Booth, and B. Smith. Using the taxonomy of cognitive learning to model online searching. *Information Processing & Management*, 45(6):643–663, 2009.

[37] K. Järvelin, P. Vakkari, P. Arvola, F. Baskaya, A. Järvelin, J. Kekäläinen, H. Keskustalo, S. Kumpulainen, M. Saastamoinen, R. Savolainen, et al. Task-based information interaction evaluation: The viewpoint of program theory. *ACM Trans. Inf. Syst.*, 33(1):3:1–3:30, Mar. 2015.

[38] J. Jiang, A. Hassan Awadallah, X. Shi, and R. W. White. Understanding and predicting graded search satisfaction. In *WSDM '15*.

[39] J. Jiang and C. Ni. What affects word changes in query reformulation during a task-based search session? In *CHIIR '16*.

[40] N. Kanhabua and K. Nørvåg. Learning to rank search results for time-sensitive queries. In *CIKM'2012*.

[41] D. Kelly, J. Arguello, A. Edwards, and W.-c. Wu. Development and evaluation of search tasks for iir experiments using a cognitive complexity framework. In *ICTIR '15*.

[42] Y. Kim, A. Hassan, R. W. White, and I. Zitouni. Modeling dwell time to predict click-level satisfaction. In *WSDM '14*.

[43] Y. Li and N. J. Belkin. A faceted approach to conceptualizing tasks in information seeking. *Information Processing & Management*, 44(6):1822 – 1837, 2008.

[44] C. Liu, J. Liu, N. Belkin, M. Cole, and J. Gwizdka. Using dwell time as an implicit measure of usefulness in different task types. *Proceedings of the American Society for Information Science and Technology*, 48(1):1–4, 2011.

[45] J. Liu, C. Liu, M. Cole, N. J. Belkin, and X. Zhang. Exploring and predicting search task difficulty. In *CIKM '12*.

[46] C. Luo, Y. Liu, T. Sakai, K. Zhou, F. Zhang, X. Li, and S. Ma. Does document relevance affect the searcher's perception of time? In *WSDM'17*.

[47] C. Luo, F. Zhang, X. Li, Y. Liu, M. Zhang, S. Ma, and D. Yang. Manipulating time perception of web search users. In *CHIIR '16*.

[48] J. Mao, Y. Liu, K. Zhou, J.-Y. Nie, J. Song, M. Zhang, S. Ma, J. Sun, and H. Luo. When does relevance mean usefulness and user satisfaction in web search?

[49] D. Metzler, R. Jones, F. Peng, and R. Zhang. Improving search relevance for implicitly temporal queries. In *SIGIR'09*.

[50] N. Mishra, R. W. White, S. Ieong, and E. Horvitz. Time-critical search. In *SIGIR'2014*.

[51] M.-H. Peetz, E. Meij, and M. de Rijke. Using temporal bursts for query modeling. *Information Retrieval*, 17(1):74–108, 2014.

[52] P. Pirolli and S. Card. Information foraging. *Psychological review*, 106(4):643, 1999.

[53] T. Sakai and Z. Dou. Summaries, ranked retrieval and sessions: A unified framework for information access evaluation. In *SIGIR '13*.

[54] M. D. Smucker and C. L. Clarke. Time-based calibration of effectiveness measures. In *SIGIR '12*.

[55] M. Sucala, B. Scheckner, and D. David. Psychological time: interval length judgments and subjective passage of time judgments. *Current psychology letters. Behaviour, brain & cognition*, 26(2, 2010), 2011.

[56] J. Teevan, K. Collins-Thompson, R. W. White, S. T. Dumais, and Y. Kim. Slow search: Information retrieval without time constraints. In *HCIR'2013*.

[57] D. K. Tse and P. C. Wilton. Models of consumer satisfaction formation: An extension. *Journal of marketing research*, pages 204–212, 1988.

[58] J. H. Wearden and I. S. Penton-Voak. Feeling the heat: Body temperature and the rate of subjective time, revisited. *The Quarterly Journal of Experimental Psychology*, 48(2):129–141, 1995.

[59] B. B. Weybrew. The zeigarnik phenomenon revisited: Implications for enhancement of morale. *Perceptual and Motor Skills*, 58(1):223–226, 1984.

[60] D. Zakay. Relative and absolute duration judgments under prospective and retrospective paradigms. *Perception & psychophysics*, 54(5):656–664, 1993.

Understanding Ephemeral State of Relevance

Jiepu Jiang[†], Daqing He[‡], Diane Kelly[§], James Allan[†]
[†] Center for Intelligent Information Retrieval (CIIR), University of Massachusetts Amherst
[‡] School of Information Sciences, University of Pittsburgh
[§] School of Information Sciences, University of Tennessee, Knoxville
jpjiang@cs.umass.edu, dah44@pitt.edu, dianek@utk.edu, allan@cs.umass.edu

ABSTRACT

Despite its dynamic nature, relevance is often measured in a context-independent manner in information retrieval practice. We look into this discrepancy. We propose a contextual relevance/usefulness measurement called *ephemeral state of relevance* (ESR), which is defined as the amount of useful information a user acquired from a clicked result as assessed just after examining the result during an interactive search session. We collect ESR and context-independent usefulness judgments through a laboratory user study and compare the two. We examine factors related to both judgments and examine their differences.

Our study demonstrates a few advantages of ESR: it captures users' real-time state of mind and perceptions; it measures how much useful information the user is able to acquire from a result rather than how much there is in the result; it better reflects users' needs and criteria of useful results during a session, highlighting novelty as a salient factor. However, we also find that users may not be able to correctly assess the credibility of information during a session, which may reduce the reliability of the collected ESR judgments.

We evaluate ESR, context-independent usefulness judgments, and TREC-style topical relevance judgments by correlating with user experience in a session. The results demonstrate that switching the judgment criterion from topical relevance to usefulness is fruitful, but moving from context-independent judgments to contextual ones has only limited advantages with respect to its cost and complexity. Our study enriches current understanding on the dynamics of relevance in a search session and identifies both opportunities and challenges for collecting contextual relevance judgments.

Keywords

Relevance judgment; usefulness; user experience; web search.

1. INTRODUCTION

Relevance is a key notion in information retrieval. Most search systems are designed and trained to rank results by relevance, and almost all offline methods for evaluating search systems are based on relevance judgments. Previous studies had numerous discussions on the notion of relevance [5, 26, 27, 28] and its measurement [35, 36, 37]. Most of these studies acknowledged that relevance depends on not only topic aboutness but also many other factors such as novelty, understandability, reliability, search task, search context, users' interaction with the search results, and so on.

However, in practice, relevance is usually assessed by external annotators, without genuine search context, and primarily focusing on topical relevance. A typical example is the TREC ad hoc tracks [34] and web tracks [9], where external assessors judged a preassigned set of documents one after another, using criteria focusing on topical relevance.

In this paper, we propose a relevance judgment measurement called *ephemeral state of relevance* (ESR), which is defined as the perceived amount of useful information a user acquired from a clicked result just after the user finished examining the result during a search session. Particularly, ESR has the following characteristics:

- ESR is assessed by real searchers in real time under a real search context.
- ESR is assessed by the criterion of being useful to the problem at hand.
- ESR distinguishes between the relevance contained in a result and the relevance acquired by a user.

In order to obtain data for studying ESR, we conducted a laboratory user study including 28 participants' ESR judgments on 736 clicked search results in 112 search sessions. We answer the following questions in the rest of the article:

- *What contributes to ESR judgments?* We examine the influence of topicality, novelty, understandability, reliability, and effort factors on ESR judgments in Section 5, along with a wide range of other factors as controls, including user background, search task attributes, and user behavior signals.
- *How do ESR and context-independent usefulness judgments differ from each other?* To examine the influence of context on relevance/usefulness judgments, we also collected users' usefulness judgments in a context-independent setting after a search session. Section 5 also analyzes the influencing factors for the context-independent usefulness judgments and compares with those for ESR.

CHIIR '17, March 07-11, 2017, Oslo, Norway
© 2017 ACM. ISBN 978-1-4503-4677-1/17/03...$15.00
DOI: http://dx.doi.org/10.1145/3020165.3020176

- *How well do ESR judgments correlate with users' search experience?* Section 7 evaluates ESR, static usefulness judgments, and TREC-style topical relevance judgments by correlating with user experience in a session.

2. RELATED WORK

Many articles reviewed the concept and dynamics of relevance [5, 27, 28]. Due to the limited space, we only summarize a few most important understandings of relevance that are related to our study: relevance is not only topic aboutness or relatedness; relevance can be subjective and needs to be assessed by users themselves; relevance and relevance judgments are influenced by context; relevance is time-dependent during a search process; "relevance is derived" and users need to interact with a search result to acquire relevant information. The de facto standard of relevance judgments in information retrieval practice, however, still largely focuses on topical relevance. A typical example is the criteria of the TREC web tracks 2009–2014 [9].

Recently, Belkin et al. [3, 4, 8] proposed to adopt usefulness as the criterion for evaluating interactive information retrieval systems. They [4, 8] proposed an evaluation model for interactive search systems based on three levels of usefulness regarding "the entire information seeking episode", "each interaction", and "system support", respectively. However, studies comparing usefulness and other search result judgment measures (such as topical relevance) are very limited. In a recent study, Mao et al. [24] measured searchers' judgments on the usefulness of search results and compared with topical relevance judgments by external annotators. However, the measured usefulness does not take into account real search context, and they had not excluded the influence of the difference between searchers and external annotators. The contextual judgment we measured in this paper (ESR) can be considered as a specific case of the usefulness of "each interaction" in Belkin et al.'s model, where the interaction is a visit to a search result. We compare the ESR judgments with a static usefulness judgments collected in a setting similar to Mao et al.'s study [24] to examine the influence of context on search result usefulness judgments.

We examine factors related to ESR judgments. The examined factors are based on previous studies of factors for relevance judgments. Xu et al. [35] examined five factors related to relevance judgments, including topicality, novelty, understandability, reliability, and scope. Except for scope, Xu et al. [35] found that the other four factors significantly contribute to relevance judgments. We suspect that usefulness judgments may also relate to the four factors. Many other factors [30, 31] may also relate to relevance judgments, but we do not examine them, such as to reduce the total number of judgments collected after a click activity.

We also examined the difference of users' perceptions on understandability and reliability during and after a search session as factors for the difference between contextual and contextual-independent usefulness judgments. A few previous studies also reported similar findings [29, 32], but they all examined very long search process (may last several months). In contrast, we examine the factors within a relatively short session (about 10 minutes).

3. EPHEMERAL STATE OF RELEVANCE

This paper studies a contextual relevance measurement called ephemeral state of relevance (ESR). We introduce the notion in this section and propose a few related hypotheses.

3.1 Definition

Without loss of generality, we define the *ephemeral state of relevance* (ESR) of an information object (such as a search result) as the amount of useful information a user would acquire from the object by interacting with it under a natural condition at a particular moment of a search process. More specifically, its working definition in this paper, for the purpose of measurement, is the perceived amount of useful information a user acquired from a clicked result right after the user finished examining the result during a search session.

We consider ESR as a "snapshot" of the *situational relevance* by Saracevic:

> *"Situational relevance or utility: Relation between the situation, task, or problem at hand, and information objects (retrieved or in the systems file, or even in existence). Usefulness in decision making, appropriateness of information in resolution of a problem, reduction of uncertainty, and the like are criteria by which situational relevance is inferred. This may be extended to involve general social and cultural factors as well."* [28]

We also consider ESR as a particular implementation of Belkin et al.'s evaluation model [4, 8], where the second level measures the usefulness regarding "each interaction". In the case of ESR, the interaction being evaluated is a click on a search result.

ESR has the following characteristics:

- The criterion for assessing ESR is to be useful regarding the problem at hand. *Relevance* and *usefulness* are interchangeable in the context of ESR.

- ESR depends on the result, the user, the search task, and the time of a search process (a search session). Not only ESR but also the state of the user and the search task are time-dependent. Users may have both cognitive and affective changes during a search process [18], and the search task at hand may also evolve during a search session. Thus, ESR captures not only the dynamics of search result relevance, but also the state of the user and the search task in a search session.

- ESR measures the effectiveness of the interaction for acquiring relevant/useful information from a result. It is not an attribute of the result. For example, users do not necessarily read the whole result document in order to obtain all the information. They may skip reading a result if it costs too much effort to locate or understand the information they need. Thus, ESR measures not only how much useful information the result contains, but also how much the users are willing to acquire from the result in the particular search context.

- As its name denotes, ESR slips away soon and cannot be restored, because both the state of the user and the problem at hand are changing. ESR needs to be assessed by the user just-in-time in a search process.

We call ESR a *contextual* relevance/usefulness judgment measure because users assess ESR in real search context. ESR takes into account factors such as the status and background of the user, the search task, the time of a session, previously viewed results, the easiness to understand the content of the result, the effort spent on the result, and so on. In contrast, we call relevance/usefulness judgments that do not involve a search context *static* or *context-independent* relevance judgments. A typical example is the TREC approach for relevance judgments [9], where annotators are requested to judge a preassigned set of results one after another, without a real search context. ESR has many theoretical advantages, which may make it a more accurate measure than static relevance judgments in IR system design and evaluation. However, we also note that it requires a more complex setting (and possibly a higher cost) to collect ESR judgments. Thus, it requires a comprehensive analysis regarding both the pros and cons of ESR judgments. The purposes of this study are:

- to understand factors contributing to ESR and its differences to context-independent judgments;
- to evaluate ESR as a relevance judgment measure and to examine its advantages and limitations.

3.2 Hypotheses

After reviewing previous studies, we come to a few initial hypotheses regarding ESR:

- **H1** – ESR relates to users' perceptions on the topicality, novelty, understandability, and reliability of the search result at the time of assessing ESR. H1 is based on Xu et al.'s [35] and Zhang et al.'s studies [37].
- **H2** – ESR relates to the effort spent on the result, since it measures the amount of acquired useful information.
- **H3** – ESR relates to the user and the search task. H3 is based on previous studies that show user background and and search task influence user behavior patterns in a session [7, 15, 20, 22, 23]. We suspect ESR is also related to user background and search task.
- **H4** – ESR differs from context-independent usefulness judgments. We believe context influences the state of the user and the search task in a session and consequently makes contextual and context-independent usefulness judgments different.

We designed and conducted a user study (§ 4) to collect data to examine these hypotheses.

4. USER STUDY

We conducted a laboratory user study to collect the data. The participants worked on preassigned tasks in an experimental search system. The tasks range from locating facts to exploratory ones. For each task, the participant needed to perform a 10-minute interactive search session to fulfill the goal of the task. We recorded participants' search behaviors and collected their judgments on the clicked results and their search experience in a session.

4.1 Experiment Design

Each participant completed four tasks of different types. The tasks were developed by the TREC session tracks [6]. They were categorized into four types by the targeted task product and goal based on Li and Belkin's faceted classification scheme [19]. The targeted product of a task is either *factual* (to locate facts) or *intellectual* (to enhance the user's understanding of a problem or topic). The goal of a task is either *specific* (well-defined and fully developed) or *amorphous* (an ill-defined or unclear goal that may evolve along with the user's exploration).

We divided the participants into groups of four. Participants in the same group finished the same four tasks (one task for each type), but with a different sequence (rotated using a Latin square). We assigned different tasks to each group, which was to increase task diversity and reduce the concern regarding task parity in experiment design [17].

For each task, the participants went through two stages:

- **Search stage (10 minutes)**. The participants needed to perform an interactive search session for 10 minutes to fulfill the task goal. They could issue and reformulate any queries and click on any results. After clicking on a result's link, the participants switched to the result webpage in a new browser tab. When the participants had finished examining the result and turned back to the SERP, they needed to complete some judgments on the clicked results (called **post-click judgments**) before they could resume the search session.
- **Judgment stage (about 10 minutes)**. The participants rated their search experience in the session and finished additional judgments on each clicked result (called **post-session judgments**). We will introduce details of the judgments in Section 4.2.

The interface of the experimental search system is similar to popular search engines. It redirected users' queries to Google and returned filtered Google results. The system only showed ordinary "10-blue links", vertical results (except image verticals), and related queries. We removed other SERP elements such as ads, direct answers, and entity information to simplify the user study. The system displayed search results in the same way they would appear on Google. The main difference between the experimental search system and Google in SERP design was that our system showed task description on the top of a SERP. We made this change to help participants recall the task requirements.

In total, the experiment took a participant about 100 minutes to complete. First, we required the participants to work on a training task for 10 minutes. Then, the participants worked on four formal tasks (about 20 minutes for each task). We also required the participants to take a 5-minute break after they finished two formal tasks.

4.2 User Judgments

We collected users' judgments on the clicked results and the search sessions to verify the hypotheses in Section 3.2. Table 1 shows the questions for collecting users' judgments.

We collected three relevance/usefulness judgments:

- **ESR** is a contextual usefulness judgment assessed during a search session just after a user finished examining

Table 1: Questions for collecting post-click and post-session search result judgments and users' experience in a session.

Post-click Judgments

Ephemeral State of Relevance (**ESR**)	How much useful information did you get from this webpage? From 1 (none) to 7 (a lot of).
Novelty (**Nov.**)	How much new information did you get from this webpage? From 1 (none) to 7 (a lot of)
Effort (**Effort**)	How much effort did you spend on this webpage? From 1 (none) to 7 (a lot of).
Understandability (**Under.**)	How difficult is it for you to follow the content of this webpage? From 1 (very difficult) to 7 (very easy).
Reliability (**Relia.**)	How trustworthy is the information in this webpage? From 1 (not at all trustworthy) to 7 (very trustworthy).

Post-session Judgments

Topical Relevance (**TRel.**)	How relevant is this webpage? • *Key* (3): this page or site is dedicated to the topic; authoritative and comprehensive; it is worthy of being a top result in a web search engine. • *Highly Relevant* (2): the content of this page provides substantial information on the topic. • *Relevant* (1): the content of this page provides some information on the topic, which may be minimal. • *Not Relevant* or *Spam* (0).
Usefulness (**Usef.**)	How much useful information does this webpage provide for the task? From 1 (none) to 7 (a lot of).
Understandability (**Under.ps**)	How difficult is it for you to follow the content of this webpage? From 1 (very difficult) to 7 (very easy).
Reliability (**Relia.ps**)	How trustworthy is the information in this webpage? From 1 (not at all trustworthy) to 7 (very trustworthy).

Search Experience Measures

Satisfaction	How satisfied was your search experience? From 1 (very unsatisfied) to 7 (very satisfied).
Frustration	How frustrated were you with this task? From 1 (not frustrated) to 7 (very frustrated).
System Helpfulness	How well did the system help you in this task? From 1 (very badly) to 7 (very well).
Goal Success	How well did you fulfill the goal of this task? From 1 (very badly) to 7 (very well).
Session Effort	How much effort did this task take? From 1 (minimum) to 7 (a lot of).
Task Difficulty	How diffcult was this task? From 1 (very easy) to 7 (very difficult).

a clicked result. The wording of the question emphasizes the *acquired* amount of useful information (... *did you get* ...).

- Usefulness (**Usef.**) is a context-independent usefulness judgment collected after a search session terminated. The wording of the question is similar to that for ESR, but puts an emphasis on the amount of useful information the result contains (... *does this webpage provide for the task* ...).

- Topical relevance (**TRel.**) is a context-independent relevance judgment using the same criteria of the TREC web tracks [9], which uses topic aboutness as the main criterion. Table 1 shows the question and options for TRel. judgments.

In the search stage, we instructed the participants to examine results as they would normally do when using a search engine in their daily lives. For example, they did not need to fully read the content and they could abandon examining a result. Particularly, they were instructed that during post-click judgments, they should not revisit the results for the purpose of answering the judgment questions. This is to make sure that the post-click judgments only measure the utility of the latest search result examination activity.

In the judgment stage, we asked the participants to read the results in a better detail to finish the post-session judgments. The system also required the participants to revisit each clicked result and spend at least 30 seconds before they could submit their post-session judgments.

In addition to ESR, the post-click judgments also include users' perceptions on the novelty (**Nov.**), understandability (**Under.**), and reliability (**Relia.**) of the results, and their **effort** spent on the clicked results. In the post-session judgments, we collected understandability (**Under.ps**) and reliability (**Relia.ps**) judgments again to examine changes in users' perceptions. We did not collect novelty judgments again because participants of a pilot study reported confusions on the criteria of assessing novelty in the post-session judgments. Except TRel., the participants answered questions using a 7-point Likert scale.

In the judgment stage, participants also rated their search experience in the session using a 7-point Likert scale. We collected six search experience measures, including satisfaction [14], frustration [10], system helpfulness, goal success [13], session effort, and task difficulty [21].

4.3 Collected Data

We recruited 28 participants through flyers posted on the campuses of two universities in the United States. We required the participants to be English native speakers to exclude the influence of language fluency on relevance judgments [12]. All participants were college or graduate students studying different majors. 16 of them are female. They were reimbursed $15 per hour.

We collected 112 sessions by 28 participants on 28 tasks. Each participant worked on four tasks and each task was performed by four participants. The collected dataset includes judgments on 736 clicked results (6.6 results per session).

5. WHAT AFFECTS ESR JUDGMENTS?

This section studies factors related to the ESR judgments using multilevel regression analysis (§ 5.1). We also examine factors related to the static usefulness judgments (Usef.) and compare with those for ESR.

5.1 Multilevel Regression

We examine two regression models M1 and M2, where the dependent variables (DVs) are ESR and Usef. judgments, respectively. M1 and M2 include the same set of independent variables (IVs):

- Our main purpose is to examine the impacts of other judgments in Table 1 on ESR and Usef. judgments.

- User background information (collected from an entry survey): including gender (*Male* or *Female*), age (four levels; 0 for *18–24*, 1 for *25–30*, 2 for *31–40*, and 3 for

Table 2: Pearson's correlation matrix of variables.

	ESR	Novelty	Effort	Under.	Relia.	TRel.	Usef.	Under.ps
Novelty	0.70							
Effort	0.25	0.27						
Understandability	0.26	0.20	−0.36					
Reliability	0.47	0.43	0.11	0.28				
Topical Relevance	0.65	0.49	0.18	0.19	0.45			
Usefulness (post-session)	0.75	0.56	0.18	0.24	0.47	0.83		
Understandability (post-session)	0.27	0.23	−0.30	0.72	0.28	0.25	0.31	
Reliability (post-session)	0.45	0.42	0.09	0.23	0.82	0.51	0.54	0.30

Light , dark , and darker shadings indicate the correlation is significant at 0.05, 0.01, and 0.001 levels.

Table 3: Multilevel (hierarchical) regression analysis – ESR judgments as dependent variable (M1) and post-session usefulness judgments (Usef.) as dependent variable (M2). Independent variables without † are controls.

	Independent Variable	**Standardized Coefficients Beta** M1 (ESR)	M2 (Usef.)
	(Constant)	-	-
	Gender: *Male*	−0.05	−0.05
	Age	−0.02	0.01
	Highest degree: *Graduate*	0.03	0.03
	Search engine expertise	0.05	0.03
	Product: *Factual*	0.09	0.02
	Goal: *Specific*	0.06	0.03
	Topic familiarity	0.06	−0.00
	Time spent in the session	0.06	0.01
	Number of past queries	−0.03	−0.05
	Number of past clicks	0.01	0.03
	Dwell time (log)	0.08	0.07
†	Topical Relevance	0.33	0.67
†	Novelty	0.48	0.16
†	Understandability	0.10	0.02
†	Reliability	0.09	−0.04
†	Effort	0.07	0.02
†	Understandability (post-session)	0.01	0.06
†	Reliability (post-session)	−0.04	0.11
	Adjusted R^2	**0.639**	**0.741**

Light , dark , and darker shadings indicate the coefficient is significant at 0.05, 0.01, and 0.001 levels, respectively.

Over 40), highest degree obtained or expected (*Undergraduate* or *Graduate*), and the expertise of using web search engines rated using a Likert scale from 1 (*very badly*) to 5 (*very well*).

- Task attributes (assigned or collected before each session): product (*Factual* or *Intellectual*), goal (*Specific* or *Amorphous*), and user's familiarity with the topic of the task rated using a Likert scale from 1 (*very unfamiliar*) to 7 (*very familiar*).
- Search behavior related to a click: the total time spent in the current session while clicking, the number of past queries and clicks in the session, and the dwell time on the clicked result (in logarithm).

We conduct multilevel regression analysis [11, 16] because the collected observations are nested—each session can have many clicks, and each user performed four sessions. In such a case, some observations share the same contexts at the session or user levels, violating the independence assumption for regular regression analysis. Multilevel models address these issues. We construct models with three levels: Level 1 includes other judgments and search behavior, Level 2 includes task attributes, and Level 3 includes user background information. We perform analysis using SPSS 24.

We examine multicollinearity between variables using variance inflation factor (VIF). The IVs of both models satisfy VIF < 4. The VIF values are below the commonly suggested threshold (4–10) for concerns on multicollinearity issues [25].

Table 3 reports the standardized coefficients (β) of IVs in M1 and M2. Positive and negative β values indicate positive and negative relationships, respectively, between the IV and the DV. The absolute value of the standardized coefficient β is often interpreted as the impact of the independent variable on the variance of the dependent variable (normalized by the standard deviation of variables)—the magnitude of change in the DV (relative to its standard deviation) caused by one-unit change in the IV (relative to the IV's standard deviation) while other variables being equal. We also report the bivariate correlation (Pearson's r) of the collected search results judgments in Table 2 for reference.

5.2 Topical Relevance and Novelty

Topical relevance and novelty are the two most important factors for both ESR and context-independent usefulness judgments (Usef.). However, novelty shows a much greater impact on ESR judgments compared with its effect on the collected Usef. judgments.

Novelty shows a significant positive effect on ESR judgments in model M1 ($\beta = 0.48$, $p < 0.001$). According to the standardized coefficients, novelty has the most salient impact on ESR judgments among the examined independent variables. Topical relevance also has a significant positive effect on ESR judgments ($\beta = 0.33$, $p < 0.001$), which is the second strongest in model M1. In contrast, model M2 shows that topical relevance is the most significant factor affecting context-independent usefulness judgments (Usef.) ($\beta = 0.67$, $p < 0.001$). Although the second most important variable in M2, novelty exhibits a much weaker impact on the Usef. judgments ($\beta = 0.16$, $p < 0.001$) compared with its influence on ESR judgments.

While confirming the central place of topical relevance and novelty in both contextual and context-independent usefulness judgments (ESR and Usef.), results also disclose the different contribution of the two factors in the two usefulness judgment settings. Compared with its impact on context-independent usefulness judgments (Usef.), novelty plays a more important role in determining the actual perceived amount of useful information acquired from a clicked result assessed in a contextual setting (ESR). This suggests that conventional context-independent relevance/usefulness judgments [9, 24, 34] may have the risk to overlook the novelty of search results.

However, we note the reported results are based on judgments collected for the clicked results from the top-ranked entries returned by a search engine (Google). Therefore, we are cautious regarding the seemingly most important role of novelty in determining ESR judgments. The top-ranked results from a search engine are mostly topically relevant, which may reduce the importance of topical relevance among the retrieved entries. In addition, users' click decisions and bias may also influence the representativeness of the clicked results, making it difficult to assess the importance of the factors sorely based on data collected from our study.

5.3 Understandability

We collected users' understandability judgments twice in the experiment (post-click and post-session). The two judgments have a strong correlation ($r = 0.72$, $p < 0.001$), but they also have differences in 38% of the results. The mean absolute difference of the two ratings is 0.63 (in a 7-point scale). This indicates that users' perceptions on the understandability of a result indeed undergo some changes during a 10-minute search session.

Model M1 shows that ESR only relates to the contextual (post-click) understandability judgments but not the context-independent (post-session) ones. Although ESR has a weak positive linear correlation with both understandability judgments ($r = 0.26$ and 0.27, respectively), only the post-click judgments show a significant positive effect in M1 ($\beta = 0.10$, $p < 0.01$). The post-session judgments do not show any significant effect in M1 at 0.05 level, suggesting that it provides little value in addition to the post-click judgments for explaining the variance of the ESR judgments. Similarly, model M2 shows that Usef. judgments only relates to the context-independent understandability judgments but not the contextual ones.

The relationship between ESR and the two understandability judgments discloses a potential advantage of ESR—it takes into account a user's ability to understand at a particular time of a search session. As a user's understanding varies over time, the user may prefer results with different understandability levels at different stages of a session, e.g., a user may expect to read easy-to-understand introductory texts such as a Wikipedia entry at the beginning of a session. Collecting ESR judgments potentially makes it possible to account for such issues in system design and evaluation.

5.4 Reliability

We also collected users' reliability judgments twice. The two reliability judgments have a strong correlation ($r = 0.82$, $p < 0.001$), but they are also different in 43% of the clicked results. The mean absolute difference of the two reliability judgments is 0.60 (in a 7-point scale). This suggests that users' perceptions on the reliability of a search result also undergo some changes in a 10-minute search session.

Similar to the findings regarding understandability judgments, ESR also only relates to post-click reliability judgments but not the post-session ones. Although ESR shows a moderate correlation with both reliability judgments ($r = 0.47$ and 0.45, respectively), only the post-click reliability judgments have a significant positive effect on users' ESR judgments ($\beta = 0.09$, $p < 0.05$).

ESR seems to account for users' perceptions on the reliability of search results at the time they examined the results. However, we believe this brings in a risk of performing ESR judgments. Unlike the subjective nature of understandability, the reliability of a result is a rather objective existence. It is reasonable to believe that after a search session's exploration, searchers may have acquired more knowledge to assess the reliability of results with better accuracy in post-session judgments. The post-click reliability judgments may be less accurate than the post-session ones, since a user may fail to accurately assess the reliability of a result during a search session due to the limited knowledge on the task. As a significant factor for ESR judgments, the possibly defective contextual (post-click) reliability judgments may consequently reduce the quality of the ESR judgments as well.

5.5 Effort

ESR judgments also relate to the effort spent on the results in a positive way, partly confirming that ESR captures users' interaction for acquiring useful information from the results. Effort exhibits a significant positive effect on ESR ($\beta = 0.07$, $p < 0.05$). Also, there is a weak positive linear correlation between ESR and effort ($r = 0.25$, $p < 0.001$).

However, despite its statistically significant effect in M1, effort only seems to have a small practical contribution for explaining the variance of the ESR judgments compared with other variables. We suspect a possible reason is that the connection between ESR and effort is more complex than simply a linear relationship. Section 6 analyzes this issue in detail.

It is also worth mention that the significant effect of effort is observed with many other variables as controls. Previous studies often connect effort with dwell time and understandability [2, 33]. We indeed observed some correlation of effort with both dwell time ($r = 0.33$, $p < 0.001$) and understandability judgments ($r = -0.36$, $p < 0.001$). Despite these connections, both effort judgments and the other two variables show significant effects on ESR judgments, suggesting a non-replacable value of effort judgments in addition to time and understandability for explaining ESR judgments. This also suggests that the effort spent on a clicked result relates to factors other than dwell time and understandability.

5.6 Control Variables

We included a wide variety of variables as controls in the regression models. Results suggest that in addition to the collected search result judgments, ESR also significantly relates to gender, the expertise of using search engines, task attributes, and the dwell time on the clicked result.

Among the examined user background variables, gender and the expertise of using web search engines show significant effects on the ESR judgments, while age and the highest obtained or expected degree do not. Results suggest that male participants rated the ESR of the clicked results lower than female participants ($\beta = -0.05$, $p < 0.05$). The expertise of using search engines has a positive effect on the ESR of the clicked results ($\beta = 0.05$, $p < 0.05$), probably because it is easier for experienced searchers to find useful results.

All the three examined task attributes show significant effects on the ESR judgments. Searching in a session targeting a *factual* product (compared with one for an *intellectual* product) has a significant positive effect on ESR judgments

($\beta = 0.09$, $p < 0.001$). Searching in a session with a *specific* goal (compared with an *amorphous* one) also shows a significant positive effect on ESR ($\beta = 0.06$, $p < 0.01$). In addition, users' familiarity with the task topic also has a significant positive effect on ESR judgments ($\beta = 0.06$, $p < 0.01$). However, it is difficult to interpret why task attributes influence ESR judgments sorely based on regression analysis. A possible explanation is that task attributes are linked to search task difficulty and performance, such that users can more effectively find useful results in certain sessions (such as sessions dealing with simple tasks). However, it may also come from factors such as users' different criteria of assessing usefulness in different types of sessions and so on. We believe it requires further investigation to fully understand these issues.

5.7 ESR vs. Usef. Judgments

Model M2 examines factors for the context-independent usefulness (Usef.) judgments. In contrast to ESR, Usef. relates to a substantially different set of variables and by different strengths. A comparison between M1 and M2 discloses many differences between the contextual and context-independent usefulness judgments (ESR and Usef.):

- Usef. judgments relate to topical relevance by a greater extent than ESR judgments do (as discussed in § 5.2).
- ESR captures users' real time perceptions on the understandability and reliability of the results when they examined the results in a search session, while Usef. only significantly relates to those after a search session while users performed the Usef. judgments.
- ESR is significantly influenced by the attributes of the search task while Usef. judgments are not.
- Usef. judgments do not account for the actual effort spent in a session for acquiring relevant/useful information from the result but ESR judgments do.
- ESR is significantly related to the expertise of using search engine while Usef. judgments are not.

To sum up, the differences of M1 and M2 confirm that the ESR judgments collected in a contextual setting capture more contextual factors than the Usef. judgments collected in a context-independent setting. This suggests that by collecting context-independent relevance/usefulness judgments, we may fail to capture factors such as search task, users' actual interaction with the result, users' cognitive state in a session, and so on.

5.8 Summary

To summarize, the regression analysis performed in this section confirms our hypotheses H1–H4.

- **H1** – Similar to previous studies on factors for relevance judgments [35, 37], we found that ESR judgments also significantly relate to topicality, novelty, understandability, and reliability. Particularly, ESR depends on users' real time perceptions on the understandability and reliability of the results at the time of examining the results, confirming that ESR indeed captures users' changing state of mind in a search session.
- **H2** – ESR judgments are significantly affected by the effort spent on the results, indicating that ESR depends on users' actual interaction with the results for acquiring relevant/useful information.
- **H3** – ESR judgments significantly relate to two user background variables and three search task attributes, suggesting that we may expect certain variation of ESR judgments from different users and in different types of tasks.
- **H4** – Results confirm that ESR and Usef. judgments are different in many aspects. Particularly, Usef. only significantly relates to topicality, novelty, users' perceptions on understandability and reliability in post-session judgments, and gender.

6. ESR, EFFORT, AND INTERACTION

Section 5 examined the relationship between ESR and other variables using linear models. However, a deeper analysis shows that the regression models concealed complex and non-linear relationships of the variables.

This section examines the ESR of and the effort spent on the results with different understandability and reliability levels (based on post-click judgments). We group results into five levels to make the sample size of each group as close as possible (although group size still varies a lot due to the skewed distribution of users' judgments). The five understandability levels are 1–2 ($N = 45$), 3–4 ($N = 69$), 5 ($N = 84$), 6 ($N = 137$), and 7 ($N = 401$). The five reliability levels are 1–3 ($N = 117$), 4 ($N = 112$), 5 ($N = 152$), 6 ($N = 154$), and 7 ($N = 201$). Figure 1 plots the results.

ESR, Effort, and Understandability – Users acquired a lot of useful information (mean ESR = 4.87) with only a small amount of effort (mean effort = 1.93) from the results with the highest level of understandability (7). While encountering results that are more difficult to understand (Under. = 6 and 5), users spent significantly greater effort (mean effort = 3.01 and 3.49), and they were still able to acquire a similar amount of useful information (mean ESR = 5.04 and 4.92). When the results are even more difficult to understand (Under. =3–4), the trend of spending more effort stopped (mean effort = 3.54), and the acquired amount of useful information also declined significantly (mean ESR = 3.91). When the results are extremely difficult to understand (Under =1–2), users started to abandon examining results, spending fewer effort (mean effort = 3.16) and acquiring very limited amount of useful information (mean ESR = 2.67).

ESR, Effort, and Reliability – We also observed a similar pattern on results with different reliability levels. Users acquired a lot of useful information (mean ESR = 5.36 and 5.45) with a small amount of effort (mean effort = 2.57 and 2.42) from the results with the two highest reliability levels (Relia. =7 and 6). When the results provide less reliable information (Relia. = 5 and 4), users spent significantly greater effort (mean effort = 2.86 and 2.86), but started to acquire a significantly fewer amount of useful information (mean ESR = 5.01 and 4.04). They abandoned examining results when the reliability level is very low (1–3), spending the least amount of effort (mean effort = 1.90) and acquiring very limited useful information (mean ESR = 2.69).

The empirical findings in Figure 1 discloses that the process of examining search results and acquiring useful infor-

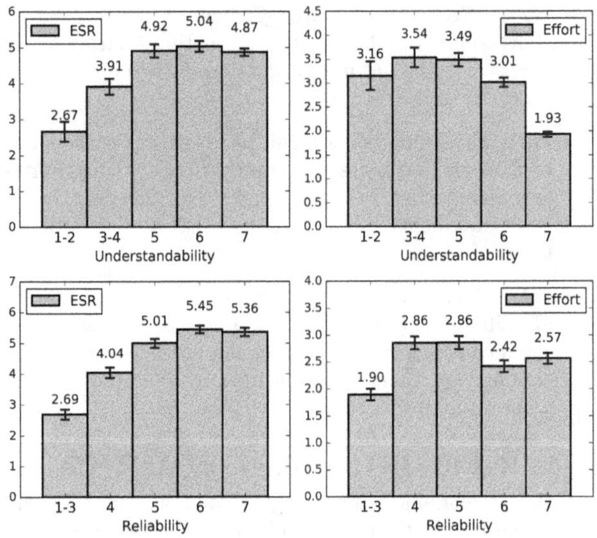

Figure 1: Mean ESR and effort (the error bars are standard error) for results with different novelty, understandability, and reliability levels (in post-examination judgments).

mation involves complex interaction and decisions. We propose a hypothesis for this process as in Figure 2:

- The acquired amount of useful information and the effort spent on a result depend on not only how much useful information the result contains but also the efficiency of acquiring useful information from the result, which further depends on both the result itself and the user.
- When the efficiency of acquiring useful information (x-axis) declines, users will first try to spend more effort (red lines) to compensate the limited efficiency, such that the amount of useful information acquired from the result (the blue line) still maintains at a relatively high level. However, when the efficiency is very low, users will abandon examining the result to avoid wasting effort or due to too much effort spent.
- The efficiency of acquiring useful information from a result correlates with factors such as the understandability and reliability of the results. For example, users need to spend more effort if the result is difficult to understand. They also need to spend more effort on the less reliable results such as to assess the credibility of information.

The empirical observations in Figure 1 fit well with the hypothesis. Here we do not have the resource to fully verify this hypothesis, but we believe it offers a new understanding to users' interaction with the search results. Nevertheless, results in Figure 1 demonstrate that the process of acquiring useful information from the search results involve complex interactions, which is also an expected advantage of ESR over static relevance/usefulness judgments.

7. ESR AND USER EXPERIENCE

The main purpose of performing relevance judgment is to collect ground truth data to optimize and evaluate search

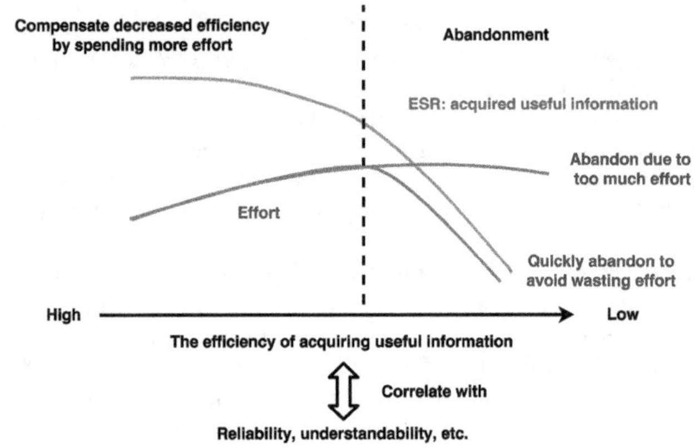

Figure 2: A hypothetical relationship between the amount of acquired useful information (ESR), the effort spent on the result, and the efficiency of acquring useful information.

Table 4: Pearson's correlation between user experience measures and the mean value of the clicked results' judgments.

User Experience	mean ESR	mean Usef.	mean TRel.
Satisfaction	**0.50**	0.48	0.44
Frustration	−0.37	**−0.41**	−0.30
System Helpfulness	**0.40**	0.38	0.31
Goal Success	**0.51**	0.49	0.37
Session Effort	**−0.42**	**−0.42**	−0.33
Task Difficulty	**−0.46**	−0.43	−0.36

All correlations are significant at least at 0.01 level.

systems. A good measure for relevance judgment should be able to identify high-quality results, such that presenting the results to users leads to a satisfactory search experience.

This section compares ESR, Usef., and TRel. judgments for their abilities to correlate with users' search experience. We assume the quality of the clicked results in a session is a factor for the user's experience in that session. For each session, we use the mean ESR, Usef., and TRel. of the clicked results as indicators for that session's search experience. We correlate the mean values of the judgments with users' perceptions on six search experience measures in the collected 112 search sessions. Table 4 reports the results.

Although ESR has many theoretical advantages, Table 4 shows that the collected ESR and Usef. judgments have only slight differences in terms of correlating with the six user experience measures. Mean ESR of results has slightly stronger correlations with satisfaction, system helpfulness, goal success, and task difficulty, while mean Usef. has a slightly stronger correlation with frustration. The differences in correlation values do not exceed 0.04, suggesting that whether to offer high ESR results or high Usef. ones may not differ much in terms of correlating with user experience in a session. However, we also note that our results are based on short sessions (10 minutes). We expect that in longer search processes, ESR and Usef. judgments may have greater differences.

The limited practical advantage of ESR compared with Usef. judgments in terms of correlating with user experience is not unexplainable. First, the collected ESR and Usef. judgments do not vary greatly ($r = 0.75$). Second, as we discussed in Section 5.4, users may not have enough knowledge to correctly assess the credibility of information during a search session, which may consequently reduce the quality of the collected ESR judgments.

Considering that it requires a more complex setting (and probably a higher cost) to collect ESR judgments, collecting context-independent usefulness judgments seems a more practical choice. Table 4 shows a clear difference between TRel. and Usef. in terms of correlating with the six user experience measures (0.04–0.14). This suggests that, even in a context-independent setting, using usefulness as the criterion for assessing search results better correlate with users' search experience in a session.

8. DISCUSSION AND CONCLUSIONS

A key challenge of information retrieval is to determine which result is relevant and what accounts for a relevant result. We examined the long-lasting discrepancy between theoretical discussions of relevance and the actual measurement of relevance in IR practice. We proposed a contextual relevance measurement called *ephemeral state of relevance* (ESR), which is tightly connected to Saracevic's situational relevance [27, 28] and Belkin et al.'s evaluation model [3, 8]. We designed an experiment to collect ESR judgments. We compared this contextual judgments with context-independent ones, examined factors related to both, and looked into their differences. Our work makes the following contribution:

First, we successfully designed and collected contextual relevance judgments, confirming that it is possible to measure search result relevance/usefulness in a contextual and interactive manner. Numerous results verified that the collected ESR judgments indeed have the characteristics we expected, suggesting that our measurement of ESR is successful for its purpose. The experiment design also sheds lights on further studies with a similar purpose.

Second, through a thorough analysis of the related factors, our study offers new understandings on both contextual (ESR) and context-independent relevance/usefulness judgments. We note a few findings of particular importance:

- Similar to static relevance judgments, ESR judgments are also influenced by the four relevance judgment factors identified in previous studies (topicality, novelty, understandability, and reliability).
- ESR and static usefulness judgments weigh the four factors differently—ESR puts a higher weight on novelty, but Usef. puts a higher one on topicality. This shows different needs of searchers on search result at different periods and for different types of judgments.
- The state of mind of a user is changing over time, and such changes affect relevance judgments over time as well. Users' perceptions on understandability and reliability during and after a session are different, but both ESR and static usefulness judgments are only influenced by users' perceptions at the moment they performed the judgments.
- The acquired amount of useful information is affected by the effort spent on the results—it depends on not only how much the result contains, but also how much cost the user paid.

Third, this is the first study exploring the relationship between the acquired useful information, the effort spent, and the efficiency of acquiring useful information from the results. While encountering results from which it is difficult to acquire useful information (such as those with limited understandability and reliability), users would first spend more effort to compensate for the limited efficiency of acquiring useful information; but the users would also abandon examining the results if the efficiency declines below a threshold, acquiring limited useful information but costing only a small amount of effort as well. These observations complement understandings on the dynamics of user interaction at a search result level, while many previous studies stay at the session and SERP levels [1].

Last, we offer practical suggestions on the choice of relevance judgment measures by correlating different relevance judgments with user experience in a session—we show that switching the judgment criterion from topical relevance to usefulness is fruitful, while moving from context-independent judgments to contextual ones seems to have only limited improvements (in terms of correlating with user experience). Given what we now know, it seems more practical to simply collect usefulness judgments in a context-independent manner due to its reasonable correlation with user experience and low complexity in collection.

To conclude, our study uncovers the advantages and limitations for both contextual (ESR) and context-independent (static) relevance/usefulness judgments. The results demonstrate several advantages of ESR judgments compared with context-independent relevance/usefulness judgments:

- ESR judgments are closer to users' needs on the search results in a search session. As our results show, users' criteria for ESR judgments are different from those for static judgments in that ESR puts a higher weight on novelty. Using ESR judgments for system design and evaluation can better capture such needs of users.
- ESR captures the user's real-time state of mind when they examine the search results, which are subject to change during a search session. Using ESR judgments for IR system development can better capture such changes.
- ESR measures not only how much useful information a result contains but also how much the user is able or willing to acquire from the result. As we showed, users do not acquire all information from results. IR systems using ESR judgments can more accurately assess the influence of the results to the searchers.

Despite ESR's having several interesting characteristics, the results in this paper suggest that a few practical issues need to be solved to make ESR a practical and useful measurement. Results also shed light on a few important areas of applications in the future:

- Collecting ESR judgments requires a more complex experimental setting (and very likely also a higher cost) than that for collecting static judgments. Thus, an important area of application in the future is to develop prediction models for ESR judgments based on implicit feedback signals (such as dwell time) and static relevance/usefulness judgments. Such techniques may reduce the high complexity of collecting ESR judgments.
- The procedure of collecting ESR judgments brings in a selection bias—we can only collect judgments for

the clicked results, because ESR needs to be judged in a natural setting to preserve a genuine context. In contrast, static judgments fit well with the standard test collection development procedures such as pooling. The ESR prediction models discussed above may also solve the selection bias issues—as long as we can predict ESR reasonably well without click-related features (such as dwell time), we can apply the model to predict ESR judgments for the unclicked results.

- Capturing users' real-time states of mind in judgments is not always ideal, because searchers may not have the ability to correctly assess the results. As the study shows, users may overestimate or underestimate the reliability of a search result. Thus, we believe it will also be helpful to develop techniques to rectify ESR judgments by setting off users' inaccurate perceptions of results during a session.

Of course, our study also has a few limitations. First, our analysis is only based on data collected from a laboratory user study, which may not entirely represent real search scenarios. It is also worth noting that the adopted tasks in our study are more complex than regular web search information needs (such as navigational search). Second, we restrict our user study to relatively short search sessions (about 10 minutes), while real-world search process can be much longer and more complex (such as involving multiple sessions). We expect a greater difference between ESR and static judgments in such cases. We leave these issues for future work.

9. REFERENCES

[1] L. Azzopardi. Modelling interaction with economic models of search. In *SIGIR '14*, pages 3–12, 2014.

[2] L. Azzopardi and G. Zuccon. An analysis of the cost and benefit of search interactions. In *ICTIR '16*, pages 59–68, 2016.

[3] N. J. Belkin. Salton award lecture: People, interacting with information. In *SIGIR '15*, pages 1–2, 2015.

[4] N. J. Belkin, M. J. Cole, and J. Liu. A model for evaluation of interactive information retrieval. In *Proceedings of the SIGIR 2009 Workshop on the Future of IR Evaluation*, 2009.

[5] P. Borlund. The concept of relevance in IR. *J. Am. Soc. Inf. Sci. Technol.*, 54(10):913–925, 2003.

[6] B. Carterette, P. Clough, M. Hall, E. Kanoulas, and M. Sanderson. Evaluating retrieval over sessions: The TREC session track 2011-2014. In *SIGIR '16*, pages 685–688, 2016.

[7] M. J. Cole, J. Gwizdka, C. Liu, R. Bierig, N. J. Belkin, and X. Zhang. Task and user effects on reading patterns in information search. *Interact. Comput.*, 23(4):346–362, 2011.

[8] M. J. Cole, J. Liu, N. J. Belkin, R. Bierig, J. Gwizdka, C. Liu, J. Zhang, and X. Zhang. Usefulness as the criterion for evaluation of interactive information retrieval. In *HCIR '09*, 2009.

[9] K. Collins-Thompson, C. Macdonald, P. Bennett, F. Diaz, and E. Voorhees. TREC 2014 web track overview. In *TREC 2014*.

[10] H. A. Feild, J. Allan, and R. Jones. Predicting searcher frustration. In *SIGIR '10*, pages 34–41, 2010.

[11] A. Gelman and J. Hill. *Data analysis using regression and multilevel/hierarchical models.* Cambridge University, 2006.

[12] P. Hansen and J. Karlgren. Effects of foreign language and task scenario on relevance assessment. *J. Doc.*, 61(5):623–639, 2005.

[13] A. Hassan, R. Jones, and K. L. Klinkner. Beyond DCG: User behavior as a predictor of a successful search. In *WSDM '10*, pages 221–230, 2010.

[14] J. Jiang, A. Hassan Awadallah, X. Shi, and R. W. White. Understanding and predicting graded search satisfaction. In *WSDM '15*, pages 57–66, 2015.

[15] J. Jiang, D. He, and J. Allan. Searching, browsing, and clicking in a search session: Changes in user behavior by task and over time. In *SIGIR '14*, pages 607–616, 2014.

[16] J. Jiang and C. Ni. What affects word changes in query reformulation during a task-based search session? In *CHIIR '16*, pages 111–120, 2016.

[17] D. Kelly, J. Arguello, A. Edwards, and W.-c. Wu. Development and evaluation of search tasks for IIR experiments using a cognitive complexity framework. In *ICTIR '15*, pages 101–110, 2015.

[18] C. C. Kuhlthau. Inside the search process: Information seeking from the user's perspective. *J. Am. Soc. Inf. Sci.*, 42(5):361–371, 1991.

[19] Y. Li and N. J. Belkin. A faceted approach to conceptualizing tasks in information seeking. *Inf. Process. Manage.*, 44(6):1822–1837, 2008.

[20] C. Liu, N. J. Belkin, and M. J. Cole. Personalization of search results using interaction behaviors in search sessions. In *SIGIR '12*, pages 205–214, 2012.

[21] C. Liu, J. Liu, and N. J. Belkin. Predicting search task difficulty at different search stages. In *CIKM '14*, pages 569–578, 2014.

[22] J. Liu and N. J. Belkin. Personalizing information retrieval for multi-session tasks: The roles of task stage and task type. In *SIGIR '10*, pages 26–33, 2010.

[23] J. Liu, M. J. Cole, C. Liu, R. Bierig, J. Gwizdka, N. J. Belkin, J. Zhang, and X. Zhang. Search behaviors in different task types. In *JCDL '10*, pages 69–78, 2010.

[24] J. Mao, Y. Liu, K. Zhou, J.-Y. Nie, J. Song, M. Zhang, S. Ma, J. Sun, and H. Luo. When does relevance mean usefulness and user satisfaction in web search? In *SIGIR '16*, pages 463–472, 2016.

[25] S. Menard. *Applied Logistic Regression Analysis.* Sage, 1997.

[26] S. Mizzaro. Relevance: The whole history. *J. Am. Soc. Inf. Sci.*, 48(9):810–832, 1997.

[27] T. Saracevic. Relevance reconsidered. In *CoLIS 2*, pages 201–218, 1996.

[28] T. Saracevic. Relevance: A review of the literature and a framework for thinking on the notion in information science. part II: Nature and manifestations of relevance. *J. Am. Soc. Inf. Sci. Technol.*, 58(13):1915–1933, 2007.

[29] R. Tang and P. Solomon. Use of relevance criteria across stages of document evaluation: On the complementarity of experimental and naturalistic studies. *J. Am. Soc. Inf. Sci. Technol.*, 52(8):676–685, 2001.

[30] A. Tombros, I. Ruthven, and J. M. Jose. How users assess web pages for information seeking. *J. Am. Soc. Inf. Sci. Technol.*, 56(4):327–344, 2005.

[31] E. G. Toms, H. L. O'Brien, R. Kopak, and L. Freund. Searching for relevance in the relevance of search. In *CoLIS '05*, pages 59–78, 2005.

[32] P. Vakkari and N. Hakala. Changes in relevance criteria and problem stages in task performance. *J. Doc.*, 56(5):540–562, 2000.

[33] M. Verma, E. Yilmaz, and N. Craswell. On obtaining effort based judgements for information retrieval. In *WSDM '16*, pages 277–286, 2016.

[34] E. Voorhees and D. Harman. Overview of the fifth Text REtrieval Conference (TREC-5). In *TREC-5.*

[35] Y. Xu and Z. Chen. Relevance judgment: What do information users consider beyond topicality? *J. Am. Soc. Inf. Sci. Technol.*, 57(7):961–973, 2006.

[36] Y. Xu and D. Wang. Order effect in relevance judgment. *J. Am. Soc. Inf. Sci. Technol.*, 59(8):1264–1275, 2008.

[37] Y. Zhang, J. Zhang, M. Lease, and J. Gwizdka. Multidimensional relevance modeling via psychometrics and crowdsourcing. In *SIGIR '14*, pages 435–444, 2014.

The Tetris Model of Resolving Information Needs within the Information Seeking Process

Max L. Wilson
Mixed Reality Lab, School of Computer Science
University of Nottingham
Nottingham, UK
max.wilson@nottingham.ac.uk

ABSTRACT

Theoretical abstractions, of many different aspects of search, have played a crucial role in driving research into human information seeking and retrieval forward. From models of the Information Seeking Process, to how we perceive search systems, these models help us to 1) conceptually formalise and separate aspects of the model's focus, 2) communicate more clearly about these aspects, 3) create hypotheses for subsequent research, and 4) produce implications for future systems. Implicit in these four aspects is that models and theories should have a focus and a purpose. After clarifying the relationships between models, theories, and meta-theories, this perspectives paper introduces the Tetris Model of Resolving Information Needs within the Information Seeking Process, the purpose of which is to better represent the behaviours around the Human Computer Interaction with Information Retrieval, which are often confounded within stage-based models of the Information Seeking Process. In particular, the possible sequence of actions performed by a searcher are typically linearly aligned from left-to-right, and thus imply a temporal progression. The differing focus of the Tetris model is to better capture the temporal experience of searching, by removing the implied progression of left-to-right. The aim of this perspectives paper, therefore, is to introduce this new Tetris Model, such that it can be used to formalise people's interactive experiences in a new way, so that we can more clearly communicate about them, create hypotheses from the model, and consider novel design implications based upon it.

CCS Concepts

•Information systems → Users and interactive retrieval;

Keywords

Information Seeking Process; Information Need; Theory; Model

1. INTRODUCTION

There have been many theories and models of information retrieval, information seeking, and information behaviour (including, in fact, a model of how these three are related [58]. The focus of one book, for example, was purley to catalogue the many theories from Information Science into one publication [17]. These theories and models play a crucial role in research, allowing us to 1) communicate more clearly about search (e.g. [31]), 2) formalise our understanding (e.g. [8]), 3) create hypotheses or explain research findings (as surveyed by Pettigrew & McLechnie [35]), and 4) produce implications for design (e.g. [6, 20, 56]). Many of the theories mentioned in this paper have been produced by people in our community, but its also an acceptable practice to consider whether theories from outside of our research area may also help us to develop new understandings or explanations for observed results (e.g. [6]).

By their vary nature, models are reductionist abstractions of the reality we are observing or recording. We typically categorise possible behaviours into reasonable numbers of major groups [9], such that we can examine them separately, but not have to do so for an infinite number of situations. We might also define typical relationships between categorisations [31], so that systems can expect what users might do next. Whatever the aim of the model or theory, and regardless of what they are trying to communicate, they help us to understand something a little better, but necessarily the level of abstraction means that they cannot encapsulate all of the reality. This also means, however, that having theories and producing models means that we can critique them [22] (although these can lead to some rather interesting and very public debates [7, 23]).

One common (but inevitable) limitation to models of the Information Seeking Process (ISP), is that in defining the possible stages that users can go through, they cannot so easily define the actual process likely to be experienced by the searcher. Perhaps most evident in this is the well known and popular model of the ISP produced by Marchionini [31] in Figure 1. Marchionini's figure is typically cited for the key stages, shown left-to-right, that a user would go through. Most interesting for this paper, about Marchionini's figure however, is the sheer number of back-arrows (its perhaps an interesting challenge to find a pair of boxes that are *not* connected by a back arrow). While Marchionini's ISP model is highly effective at conveying the key stages a searcher *must* progress through, its left-to-right presentation implies a temporal progression that a searcher *will* progress through; the back-arrows are there of course to highlight that its not *normal* to go straight in that order, but that other paths are possible, if not more normal.

The aim of this paper is to introduce a the Tetris Model of Resolving Information Needs within the ISP, with the aim of specifically modeling the search process, as experienced by a searcher resolving an information need. This new model does not represent the stages or categorise the possible behaviours, but instead complements these by representing the motivations of a searcher as they move between them. Below, I first set the scene by discussing the exact nature

CHIIR '17, March 7–11, 2017, Oslo, Norway.

ISBN 978-1-4503-4677-1/17/03...$15.00

DOI: http://dx.doi.org/10.1145/3020165.3020169

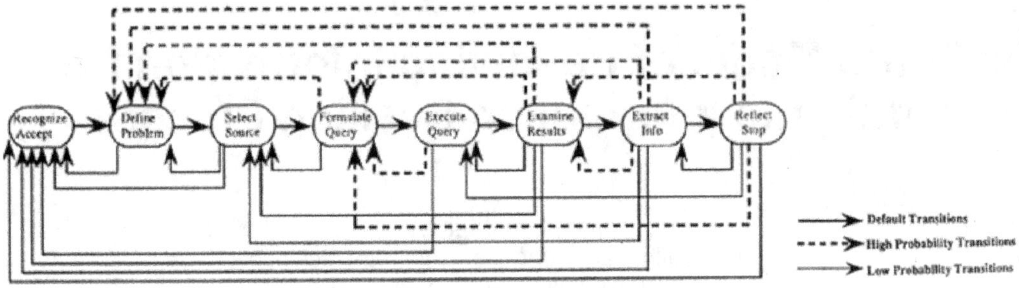

Figure 1: The Information Seeking Process provided by Marchionini, from [31]

of theories, models, and frameworks, before surveying a range of different theories in our research community. I then present the Tetris model, before concluding with a discussion of what it can tell us about search, whilst considering what it cannot tell us.

2. RELATED WORK

I have not, so far, been especially clear on the use of *theories* and *models*, or indeed how they relate to *principles*, *metatheories* and *frameworks*, if not many more similar terms. In honesty, nor do I wish to go into these in depth, which could be an academic endeavor of its own. To set a cursory pretext, however, a theory, in general, is a perhaps complex but particular principle that we believe to hold true across many circumstances; Information Theory [44], Activity Theory [28], and Information Foraging Theory [36] are a few examples. Information Foraging Theory, for example, explains how information is found in much the same way that animals forage for food, involving several principles such as an effort vs cost tradeoff. Whether or not the creators of a theory are explicitly aware of it, theories typically come from a certain pespective on interpreting the real world; Hjørland discusses meta-theoretical perspectives in more detail for a reader that would like a philosphical challenge [21]. Models (in our discipline at least), however, are usually smaller specific abstractions used within theories to represent a point. Typically tabular or graphical, models encapsulate an idea into a single metaphor or representation such that they can be portrayed, discussed, and even tested. In more algorithmic parts of Computer Science and Information Retrieval, models are often explicitly implemented to show that they produce more accurate results (e.g. tfidf [46], BM25 [40], language models [37] etc.) In Human-Computer Interaction with Information Retrieval (HCIR), we are more likely to create conceptual models of human behaviours, and create experiments or build systems to support them [9]. Finally, frameworks are typically an application of a theory or model that somebody takes as a guide to frame their work. One might take the principles of Activity Theory as a framework for designing future research (e.g. [28]), or likewise might use Information Foraging Theory to design a new search user interface widget [49]. Similarly, Wilson et al [57] used Belkin's model of search situations [9] and Bates' taxonomy of tactics [2] as a framework for predicting user interaction with search user interfaces. In practice, these terminologies are often used informally or incorrectly within literature, and the boundaries between can become arguable; it is not the aim of this perspective paper to discuss these concepts in detail nor the correct use of them.

2.1 Models of Interactive Information Retrieval

There are of course both many models and theories that could be discussed, and many ways to approach them. Bigger surveys of theories [17] and their uses in research [35] have been produced. In this paper, I will review a few that are most relevant to the Tetris Model of the ISP being presented here.

2.1.1 Levels of Granularity

Search can be modelled at very tiny levels of Information Retrieval actions, and at very grand levels of process. A key set of theories has been to break categorise and separate the levels being discussed into: Information Behaviour, Information Seeking Behaviour, and Information Search Behaviour [58]. The benefit of separating these levels, is that other models can be specific about which granularity they are concerned with. Jarvelin & Ingwersen used similar levels to describe how each level motivates the levels within, and to specify which evaluation criteria should be used to measure success at each level [25]. Elsweiler et al considered that their model worked only for work contexts and further extended their model to describe the difference between work behaviours at each level and casual behaviours at each level [15]. Overall, its common for theories and models to be focusing on one these levels, if not describing the relationship between them. Research into creating realistic Work Tasks [10], for example, focuses on the need for information retrieval to be motivated by real information seeking tasks, which are in turn realistically motivated by how the result of seeking will be actually used in a Work Task.

2.1.2 Information Behaviour

At a very high level, information seeking is considered as only one of many information behaviours. Godbold [19] produced a model that highlighted that informaiton behaviour also includes creating information, avoiding informaiton, destroying information and much more. A nice example outside of information seeking is information encountering [16], which describes how people might encounter information without trying to find it. Formalisations of the reasons that Information Behaviour exists, include Dervin's model of the sensemaking gap [12], which highlights a few points including the existance of a gap, the need to take action to cross it, and the cost involved in doing so. Belkin's formalisation of the Anomalous State of Knolwedge [8] further describes the implciations of knowledge gaps and the motivations to resolve them as information needs. Another of Wilson's models encapsulates each of these in a little more detail, highlighting activating mechanisms for e.g. choosing to seek information [58]. Each of these models aim to convey some important aspect of the reasons why we search (or not) for information, to help us make predictions about human behaviour, or to interpret the outcomes of information seeking with more clarity.

2.1.3 Information Search Process

Perhaps most common and well known are three models of the Information Seeking Process (ISP). Marchionini's model (Figure 1), for example, highlights the key stages that a user progresses through [31] but using finer-grained language that implies stages of a smaller information retrieval process. In a similar way, Ellis [14] describes some of the key activities that searchers embark on during an ISP, including: Chaining, Browsing, Monitoring, Differentiating, Extracting and Varifying. With a different aim to convey the user motivations and emotions, and describing larger endeavours into researching, Kuhlthau's model highlights a series of major phases that searchers go through [27]: Initiation of project, Selection of topic, Exploration of ideas, Formulation of the key information needs, Collection of results relating to them, and Presentation of what they have found. Her model highlights levels of e.g. anxiety and clarity as they move through these stages. Whether explicitly mentioned or not, knowing such emotions and phases has inspired much subsequent work on estimating frustration in search [34] and to support confidence in the trustworthyness of search results [43].

As mentioned above, without taking away from the value that these well known models provide, they (like all models) have limitations in what they convey. In particular, these examples imply a linear left-to-right progression and the back-arrows in Marchionini's model are an attempt to compensate for this implication. Instead, Spink visualises information seeking as a sequence of information retrieval cycles rather than a linear progression of one retrieval episode [47], where each cycle involves both the use of a search tactic, and the relevant judgement of what is found. Taking the non-linear concept further, Bates' Berrypicking Model is a well known example that specifically highlights that we collect information from many different places as we exploring information, especially when browsing [3]. Bate's model aimed to convey that resolving an information need is often achieved by collecting and piecing together separate bits of information found in those multiple locations. Likewise, Forster's nonlinear model conceptualises this as searcher having a paint pallette, using information seeking activities as necessary to achieve the bigger picture they are looking for [18].

Other models focus differently on the type of searching situation that develops these information seeking episodes. Marchionini more recently identified many types of search episode, but broke them down into three major categories: *Lookup*, *Learn*, and *Investigate* [32], with the aim of highlighting that they can be treated differently. Belkin broke down seeking into 16 situations, based on four binary dimensions including problem clarity and knowledge of the target result [9], before using them as a framework to build a system to handle them each differently. It could be said that the left-to-right stages describe a straightforward *lookup*, and that all the back-arrows describe all the deviations that we largely describe as Exploratory Search [52]. In order to model all the types of situations that Exploratory Search tasks might involve, Wildemuth & Freund modeled a strong set of dimensions that can be used as a framework for designing tasks for experiments [54].

2.1.4 *Aspects of the Search Process*

A final set of key models break down the different aspects, or factors, that are at play during search. Saracevic identified several key layers involved in searching, from both the user side and the system side [42]. A user has motivations, strategies to use, and actions to achieve them, where as a system has the document collection, the algorithm to retreive them, and the interface to present them. Bates later broke these down into many more levels [5], having already highlighted that the amount of automation in a system could be studied at each level [4]. Jarvelin and Ingwersen identify 9 key aspects to any searching situation: including the data, the algorithms, the user interface, the dimensions of the searcher themselves, the tasks, and indeed the searchers perceptions of the tasks [25]. Ingwersen also produced a useful cognitive model (perhaps best represented with the clouds in [24]) that focused specifically on this issue of perception, highlighting that information seeking behaviour depends on what they know about the possible results, what they know about how the retrieval algorithm works, what they know about the user interface features, and so on.

Figure 2: Example Tetris interface. Unedited image ©joefoodie, taken from: `https://flic.kr/p/AQDh2`

2.2 Summary

There are many more models and theories that could be described that relate to HCIR, but there are two key takeaways from those noted above: 1) models are created to convey a particular understanding: the factors that affect user behaviour, the aspects of retrieval system, the users perception of those aspects, the levels of searching behaviour, the evaluation criteria for levels of searching behaviour, and so on. 2) that there is a gap in explaining how information needs, the retrieval of both known and unknown information, and the resolution of information needs, all relate to each other through the ISP. The aim of the Tetris Model of ISP, described below, is to model how these issues relate, and help elaborate on why and when e.g. users take the back-arrows in Marcionini's model.

3. THE TETRIS MODEL

The aim of this section is to propose that the aim of the game of Tetris, perhaps taken (for now) without the fun-creating aspects of time pressure, is a valuable model for understanding how searchers resolve information needs during the Information Seeking Process (ISP). In particular, the aim is to remove the notion of progressing from left-to-right through stages, in order to tie progess to the resolution of information needs instead.

3.1 A Recap of Tetris

The aim of the game, shown in Figure 2, is to fit the descending pieces, of varying shape, together so that they create one or more complete lines across the width of the screen. When a complete line has been created, the line is removed from the game and the score is increased. In order to better fit these pieces together, users are able to rotate the descending objects and move them left and right as necessary. To make this game fun and challenging, the rate at which pieces descend increases, so that the user has less time to a) work out where to place the piece, and b) move and orientate the piece accordingly.

We are not the first to consider Tetris within academic purposes. Kirsh and Maglio [26], for example, have studied the difference between epistemic and pragmatic actions performed by users, as the speed of the game increases, to learn more about perception and reaction protocols. Further, Veksler and Gray used a Tetris-based task set to measure learning [50].

3.2 Introducing the Tetris Model

As an overview of how we use this Tetris analogy, the game window itself is considered to be a working space for an information need. The pieces already at the bottom of the game window, making up incomplete horizontal lines, represent a *current information need* or Anomalous State of Knowledge [8]. The depth of the incomplete horizontal lines represents the depth or complexity of the current information need, and determines the amount of information needed to resolve the information need (perhaps demanding more exploratory learning and investigating). Being aware of these unresolved lines is paralleled to recognising that you have an information need; something captured in many models. Arriving, descending pieces in the game are considered as *new pieces of information* that the user finds from searching, or simply encounters [16]. The user is hoping that these new bits of information found will resolve an information need, fitting into their gaps in knowledge, but may not fit completely (patrially resolving the information need), or may not fit at all (perhaps creating new information gaps). Any completed lines of the game are resolved information needs, and thus removed from the working space, and a score value incremented, which represents the cumulative amount of knowledge a searcher has about this topic.

In this model, we consider *progress* as resolving gaps in knowledge (completing lines), rather than by going through a series of stages. At this point, we are ignoring the time pressure that adds the 'fun' to Tetris, but highlight that progress is not going through a series of stages, but in resolving information needs. We are also breaching the randomness of pieces entering a game of Tetris, considering that although users could incidentally encounter information, they might purposefully look for the *right* pieces.

The different stages, captured in other ISP Models, that searches may be in are identified by the state of the game. If a new piece of information arrives into an empty window, then a user has a new information need to resolve (typically the first stage of every ISP model). If the user chooses to begin a new information seeking episode, they are trying to clear that new piece of information from the board. As the user can see what information need they have, they can construct an idea of what remaining pieces they would like to find and encounter. As the user analyses search results, new pieces arrive in the window of the game, and hopefully help to resolve the information need. As the pieces arrive, the user has to analyse how and where they fit into their developing knowledge on the topic. These new pieces, however, may not directly resolve the need, and deepen the number of lines that need resolving, causing the searcher to reformulate their information needs. As the pieces do fit together, however, the user is able to reflect on the state of the game. When the lines have been cleared, the user can consider that they have resolved their information need.

3.3 Applications of the Tetris Model

In the following subsections, I further explain the Tetris Model, beginning with three diverse examples that represent different complexities of information needs, taken from the broad categories described by Marchionini [32]: Lookup, Learn, and Investigate.

3.3.1 Lookup Example

A simple lookup has been shown to be a regular part of everyday life, when a simple problem is identified (caused by the arrival of new piece of information), described easily, found quickly, and therefore resolved with ease. This scenario, portrayed in Figure 3.a), can be represented easily by the first three pieces of a game each being made up of simple bits of information. Each block can be laid side by side, horizontally, so that they make up an entire line and the problem is removed. That is, the original problem, the first piece, was simple and, given the empty game window, created a shallow information need. Equally, the searcher came across the appropriate information to resolve the need easily. The newly found information fits simply, without further deepening the information need, and the line (or information need) is resolved. Overall the IS episode was quickly resolved and the screen, until a new problem piece arrives, is entirely empty.

3.3.2 Learning Example

In learning examples, an original information need may appear to be relatively simple, such as needing to buy a camera. The next piece found, however, indicates that more is to be learned before a final camera can be chosen, such as the difference between metering modes and ISO capabilities. The new pieces of information confound the chance of resolving the problem in a single line, and deepen the problem space to a number of Tetris lines (Figure 3.b). Consequently, more information must be sought to resolve any or, hopefully, all of the lines. It is possible, however, for this deepened information need to be completely solved with a single final piece, by clearing several lines at once (Figure 3.c). Alternatively, each of the lines may be resolved one at a time with successive pieces.

3.3.3 Investigate

Investigating is represented by tasks such as planning, analysis, synthesis, and evaluation, where the complexity lies in the initial problem pieces, such as a multi-faceted problem, or a poorly defined information need. If the initial problem piece has a complex shape (Figure 3.d), then the information need can only be resolved by several pieces. The depth of the problem, unlike Learning examples, is controlled by the complexity of the earlier rather than the later pieces. This does not exclude, however, the later pieces from increasing the complexity of the problem, as investigating may often include learning (Figure 3.e).

3.4 Taking the Model Further

One value of the Tetris Model, is that it can be extended to describe much larger and/or complex sessions. As another example of the versatility of modelling the ISP with a Tetris analogy, life-long learning can even be captured by the Tetris Model. There may be some topics that people spend their entire lives learning about, such as the focus of an academic career, or a personal interest or hobby. During the large period of time, people may engage in lookups, learning exercises and investigations, where each one resolves something they did not understand before, or discovers new pieces of information. Realistically, we process many bits of information as we search, and by resolving one information need, there may always be unresolved blocks that represent information that has not been explained or investigated (Figure 3.f). Here, we can imagine that users pause the game until such time that they wish to engage in information seeking to either resolve new information needs, or the leftover blocks from a previous information seeking session. In Tetris, users' unresolved lines might be occluded by new pieces of information (e.g. Figure 2 above). The searcher may have to clear several lines and resolve several information seeking problems be-

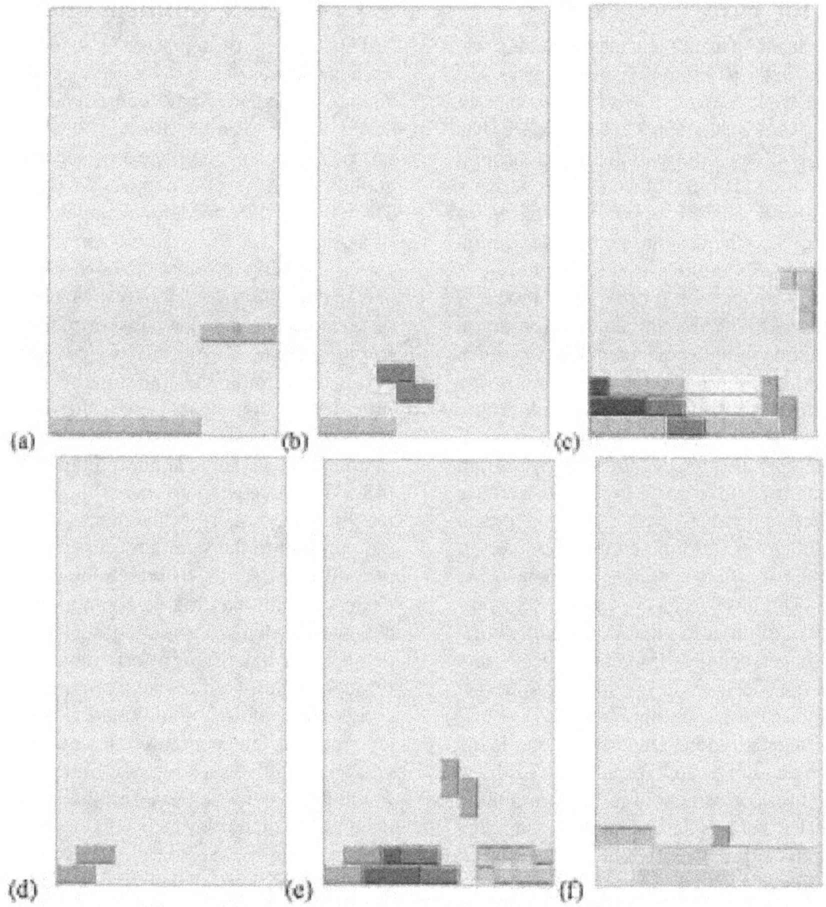

Figure 3: Example information seeking states, where (a) is a simple lookup task resolved easily; (b) is a learning example where the information need was deepend by the second bit of information; (c) presents a deep information need being eventually solved with one piece; (d) shows a more complex initial information need for investigation; (e) shows an investigation need getting even deeper; and (f) represents excess information found that is surplus to solving the information need.

fore one day resolving something that they did not complete before. This may occur when new pieces of information need to be checked, or first understood before the original problem can be resolved.

4. DISCUSSION

In this section, I reflect on the advantages, limitations, and possible uses of this model in terms of the four values that models can provide, as noted in the introduction: 1) formalising our understanding of the search process, 2) commuicating about the search process, 3) creating hypotheses for future research, and 4) drawing implications for design.

4.1 Formalising and Communicating

An important concern for any new model is what is its focus and thus what novel insight does it provide. The main insight provided by the Tetris model is in tying the progression of a search episode, and the complexity of the behaviour in the search episode, to the depth and complexity of an information need, rather than in the progression through certain behaviours. This is particularly important because, as a community, we are grappling with the Exploratory Search agenda, to design support for more complex searching to resolve more complex information needs. In particular, research into Exploratory Search in our community often conflates various scenarios and task factors [54], where one study might set a task involving comparison, and another simply sets a task focused on multi-part problem, but both call them 'an exloratory search task'. The Tetris Model may help to facilitate the discussion of these different types of tasks more clearly in a way that would be harder to do with stage-based models.

There is a general consensus within research that the ISP involves a start goal, whether it be broad or focused, and an endpoint where all or part of the goal has been achieved. Unlike most models of the ISP, the Tetris Model tries to integrate information need into the process of searching. Further, search is often considered to occur within one IS episode [9], or across multiple search episodes [30]. In the Tetris model, the start and completion of an ISP is not represented by an axis or a direction. Instead, the status of the Tetris working space, the complexity of the unresolved lines (the information need), and the value of newly arriving pieces of information, all determine which of the stages of Marchionini's model, for example, the searcher is in and which (back-)arrows they follow. Unlike stage-based models, the Tetris Model can accomodate these across multiple sessions. The Tetris Model, therefore connects ISP models with information need models and behavioural models together in a new way that helps us to understand the search process in more detail, and communicate more effectively about how they relate.

4.2 Opportunities for Future Research

In contrast to the life-long learning example, there are topics that individuals have learned about in the past, but have many blocks still to resolve. If the user is not actively seeking, one way or another, in those topic areas, then these games can be considered on pause. Unpausing may, therefore, occur as new information arrived through passive information encountering [16], or if the searcher actively engages in a new search episode. There is opportunity, based on this model, to further explore research questions about a) activation causes, b) search resumption, and c) multi-session searching.

Conversely, one open research question for the Tetris model is to decide if users are able to fail ISP-Tetris for certain information problems, as they reach maxima in their understanding of topics. In Tetris, failing is indicated by the stack of unresolved, incomplete, lines filling the available vertical space allocated to the game. Although a maximum vertical space doesnt have a direct parallel in our understanding of the cognitive aspects of search, we can draw parallels with when searchers give up on their task, because it seems unresolvable. Perhaps individuals who fail to understand hard problems have reached their vertical limit on reasonable effort to resolve complex gaps in their knowledge, despite having resolved some set of lines in the past. This gives us an opportunity to, again, consider surprise discovery of information that does suddenly resolve a knowledge gap and make a complex information need seem achievable [11]. Similarly, the model gives us opportunity to further consider the role of effort and satisficing during search [51].

One interesting area of research into information seeking is the role that existing knowledge plays on search formulation [53] and on relevance judgements and the correctness of found information [41]. The interesting research questions lie around the impact that incomplete prior knowledge has on assessing whether new information correctly resolves an information need. Answer correctness, or a measure of an answers strength, is often used in studies of searching behaviour, whilst also trying to measure pre- and post-search knowledge on a topic [55]. The Tetris Model may help to draw new finer-grained questions about the sequence in which information is found during search.

One final element of the Tetris game that is not covered by this model, is that of the increasing speed at which pieces descend as time progresses. This element of speed is added to the game to introduce both challenge and enjoyment. In real life, however, information seeking is often performed under time pressures such as deadlines or medical emergencies. Similarly, many user studies impose an element of time on their information seeking tasks. Users are often timed as they carry out the tasks, and most analyses assume that improvements in task completion time make their system better. In some respects this is true, if the system in question is producing pieces that will fit together nicely to resolve a problem, then they have supported the users by not accidentally deepening the information need. If the original challenge is more exploratory or investigative, however, then time pressure may make it harder for searchers to fit new pieces in with the unresolved lines. Indeed, many studies involving exploratory search tasks explicitly remove time pressure in order to measure value gain from the system, and are even investigating the benefits of slower search response times providing better and more relevant information to fill information needs [48]. Consequently, time and effort tradeoffs are a current concern in information retrieval research [45, 1], and aspects like hover time and dwell time are examined for what the imply about relevance of results [29]. So although, in general, we have not included time pressure in the Tetris Model, there are interesting questions about the implications of time than can be explored in future research.

4.3 Possible Implications for Design

This concept of depth for an information need, rather than sequenctial stages, is a fairly novel way of thinking about the ISP, and so may immediately have consequences for new designs of search systems. For example, the model poses the question of whether, instead of tracking the stage at which a user is currently at, a system could track the level of depth and detail that the user is currently at. There is very little need, for example, to provide a growing overview of a domain if the user simply performs a short look-up. A space for synthesising information, however, would be very useful as the users information need deepens. Marchionini and White [33] report on previous research that has shown, for example, that automatically trying to create a synthesised view of a domain allowed users to perform Learning and Investigative tasks significantly faster, but provided no significant benefit for look-up tasks. Research has also shown, however, that shown at the wrong time, search user interface features can actually impede straight forward searching [13]. Google appears to share this sentiment, by typically placing recommended query refinements *after* the first ten results rather than upfront in the search process. Some interfaces exist that support different depths of search, however they have typically been designed from the progressive models. We have yet to see, to the authors knowledge, a system designed specifically from the view of depth or complexity of information need, rather than progression through stages. One research opportunity above is to examine the consequence of finding information before earlier information gaps are resolved. Early research, for example, has examined showing you what you've seen already [38], what new information can be found [49], and whether information can be presented in order of need rather than relevance [39]. Each of these are interesting approaches that could be developed further by considering the design of a search user interface from the point of view of the information need, depth and complexity.

4.4 Limitations of the Model

There are, as with any model, limitations to what the Tetris Model captures and represent. As noted above, it does not capture the activities that searchers may perform like ISP models from Marchionini and Ellis, just the reason for trying to find information and effect of having found information. This is of particular importance, because in real life, new information does not arrive to us randomly, but we take actions (captured in other ISP models) to influence the information we encounter. We aim, as it were, to find a square piece when we have a square hole in our knowledge. Further, when we search, or enounter information, we are likely to come across information we already know. The description of the model above implies that arriving, descending pieces are *new* pieces of information; the model therefore does not capture or represent what happens when we encounter information that we already know. We may also encounter information that we do not need, and these do not necessarily deepen our Information Need. Together, these aspects mean that the random allocation of incoming pieces in the game does not clearly represent what determines the information we encounter, but it is true that we may not find the information we hoped for, and will likely enounter many other pieces of information along the way. The Tetris analogy also implies that we have to resolve higher lines before we can resolve lower information needs, but this is not enforced in real life.

5. CONCLUSIONS

This perspectives paper has introduced the Tetris Model that describes how the process of Information Seeking relates to and is affected by the depth and complexity of an information need, and the relevance and utility of the information found or encountered to resolve it. Unlike most models of Information Seeking, which usually try to reduce the process to a single progression across stages, the Tetris model describes a progression separately from spatial presentation, implying that progression is instead temporal and about resolving gaps in knowledge. This means that the Tetris Model directly captures the freeflowing movement between defining an information need, searching for more information, and integrating this into existing knowledge. Further, by making the depth of the problem analogous to the current depth of the unresolved lines in the game, the model allows for any new information in the process to both resolve and/or deepen the problem. The examples of lookup, learning, and investigating above have shown the versatility of the Tetris model for describing diverse searching scenarios. Further, the discussion has identified its potential strengths, as well as how these strengths might be used to direct future research and support the design of future search interfaces.

As identified in the introduction, the purpose of any model is to help us structure what we do know, communicate effectively, hypothesise about research, and draw new implications for, in this case, how people resolve information needs within the Information Seeking Process. In turn these new avenues of research can support or strengthen our models, through identifying and resolving limitations, so that they may again inform new ideas. My hope is that the Tetris Model described above helps to formalise our communities understanding of the search process, especially in regards to Human-Computer Intreaction with Information Retrieval (HCIR) around dynamic Exploratory Search conditions.

6. ACKNOWLEDGEMENTS

Thank you to everyone that over time has given me comments on this idea, and encouraged me to submit this paper.

Data access statement: There is no dataset underlying this model.

7. REFERENCES

[1] L. Azzopardi, D. Kelly, and K. Brennan. How query cost affects search behavior. In *Proceedings of the 36th international ACM SIGIR conference on Research and development in information retrieval*, pages 23–32. ACM, 2013.

[2] M. J. Bates. Information search tactics. *Journal of the American Society for information Science*, 30(4):205–214, 1979.

[3] M. J. Bates. The design of browsing and berrypicking techniques for the online search interface. *Online review*, 13(5):407–424, 1989.

[4] M. J. Bates. Where should the person stop and the information search interface start? *Information Processing & Management*, 26(5):575–591, 1990.

[5] M. J. Bates. The cascade of interactions in the digital library interface. *Information Processing & Management*, 38(3):381–400, 2002.

[6] M. J. Bates. What is browsing-really? a model drawing from behavioural science research, 2007.

[7] M. J. Bates. Birger hjørland's manichean misconstruction of marcia bates' work. *Journal of the American Society for Information Science and Technology*, 62(10):2038–2044, 2011.

[8] N. J. Belkin. Anomalous states of knowledge as a basis for information-retrieval. *Canadian Journal of Information Science-Revue Canadienne Des Sciences De L Information*, 5(MAY):133–143, 1980.

[9] N. J. Belkin, C. Cool, A. Stein, and U. Thiel. Cases, scripts, and information-seeking strategies: On the design of interactive information retrieval systems. *Expert systems with applications*, 9(3):379–395, 1995.

[10] P. Borlund. The iir evaluation model: a framework for evaluation of interactive information retrieval systems. *Information research*, 8(3), 2003.

[11] L. S. Connaway, T. J. Dickey, and M. L. Radford. âĂIJif it is too inconvenient i'm not going after it:âĂİ convenience as a critical factor in information-seeking behaviors. *Library & Information Science Research*, 33(3):179–190, 2011.

[12] B. Dervin, L. Foreman-Wernet, and E. Lauterbach. *Sense-making methodology reader: Selected writings of Brenda Dervin*. Hampton Pr, 2003.

[13] A. Diriye, A. Blandford, and A. Tombros. Exploring the impact of search interface features on search tasks. In *International Conference on Theory and Practice of Digital Libraries*, pages 184–195. Springer, 2010.

[14] D. Ellis. A behavioural model for information retrieval system design. *Journal of information science*, 15(4-5):237–247, 1989.

[15] D. Elsweiler, M. L. Wilson, and B. Kirkegaard Lunn. Chapter 9 understanding casualleisure information behaviour. *New Directions in Information Behaviour, Emerald Group Publishing, Bingley*, pages 211–241, 2011.

[16] S. Erdelez. Information encountering: a conceptual framework for accidental information discovery. In *Proceedings of an international conference on Information seeking in context*, pages 412–421. Taylor Graham Publishing, 1997.

[17] K. E. Fisher and L. McKechnie. *Theories of information behavior*. Information Today, Inc., 2005.

[18] A. Foster. A nonlinear model of information-seeking behavior. *Journal of the American society for information science and technology*, 55(3):228–237, 2004.

[19] N. Godbold. Beyond information seeking: towards a general model of information behaviour. *Information research*, 11(4):9, 2005.

[20] M. Hearst. *Search user interfaces*. Cambridge University Press, 2009.

[21] B. Hjørland. Theory and metatheory of information science: a new interpretation. *Journal of documentation*, 54(5):606–621, 1998.

[22] B. Hjørland. The importance of theories of knowledge: Browsing as an example. *Journal of the American Society for Information Science and Technology*, 62(3):594–603, 2011.

[23] B. Hjørland. Theoretical clarity is not'manicheanism': A reply to marcia bates. *Journal of information science*, page 0165551511423169, 2011.

[24] P. Ingwersen and K. Järvelin. *The turn: Integration of information seeking and retrieval in context*, volume 18. Springer Science & Business Media, 2006.

[25] K. Järvelin and P. Ingwersen. Information seeking research needs extension towards tasks and technology. *Information Research: An International Electronic Journal*, 10(1):n1, 2004.

[26] D. Kirsh and P. Maglio. Reaction and reflection in tetris. 1992.

[27] C. C. Kuhlthau. Inside the search process: Information seeking from the user's perspective. *Journal of the American society for information science*, 42(5):361, 1991.

[28] K. Kuutti. Activity theory as a potential framework for human-computer interaction research. *Context and*

consciousness: Activity theory and human-computer interaction, pages 17–44, 1996.

[29] C. Liu, R. W. White, and S. Dumais. Understanding web browsing behaviors through weibull analysis of dwell time. In *Proceedings of the 33rd international ACM SIGIR conference on Research and development in information retrieval*, pages 379–386. ACM, 2010.

[30] B. Mackay and C. Watters. Exploring multi-session web tasks. In *Proceedings of the SIGCHI Conference on Human Factors in Computing Systems*, pages 1187–1196. ACM, 2008.

[31] G. Marchionini. *Information seeking in electronic environments*. Cambridge university press, 1995.

[32] G. Marchionini. Exploratory search: from finding to understanding. *Communications of the ACM*, 49(4):41–46, 2006.

[33] G. Marchionini and R. White. Find what you need, understand what you find. *International Journal of Human [# x02013] Computer Interaction*, 23(3):205–237, 2007.

[34] A. Marcovitz and Y. Levy. Frustration in protein–dna binding influences conformational switching and target search kinetics. *Proceedings of the National Academy of Sciences*, 108(44):17957–17962, 2011.

[35] K. E. Pettigrew and L. E. McKechnie. The use of theory in information science research. *Journal of the American Society for Information Science and Technology*, 52(1):62–73, 2001.

[36] P. Pirolli and S. Card. Information foraging in information access environments. In *Proceedings of the SIGCHI conference on Human factors in computing systems*, pages 51–58. ACM Press/Addison-Wesley Publishing Co., 1995.

[37] J. M. Ponte and W. B. Croft. A language modeling approach to information retrieval. In *Proceedings of the 21st annual international ACM SIGIR conference on Research and development in information retrieval*, pages 275–281. ACM, 1998.

[38] P. Qvarfordt, S. Tretter, G. Golovchinsky, and T. Dunnigan. Searchpanel: framing complex search needs. In *Proceedings of the 37th international ACM SIGIR conference on Research & development in information retrieval*, pages 495–504. ACM, 2014.

[39] K. Raman, P. N. Bennett, and K. Collins-Thompson. Toward whole-session relevance: exploring intrinsic diversity in web search. In *Proceedings of the 36th international ACM SIGIR conference on Research and development in information retrieval*, pages 463–472. ACM, 2013.

[40] S. E. Robertson, S. Walker, S. Jones, M. M. Hancock-Beaulieu, M. Gatford, et al. Okapi at trec-3. *NIST SPECIAL PUBLICATION SP*, 109:109, 1995.

[41] I. Ruthven, M. Baillie, and D. Elsweiler. The relative effects of knowledge, interest and confidence in assessing relevance. *Journal of Documentation*, 63(4):482–504, 2007.

[42] T. Saracevic. The stratified model of information retrieval interaction: Extension and applications. In *Proceedings of the Annual Meeting-American Society for Information Science*, volume 34, pages 313–327. LEARNED INFORMATION (EUROPE) LTD, 1997.

[43] J. Schwarz and M. Morris. Augmenting web pages and search results to support credibility assessment. In *Proceedings of the SIGCHI Conference on Human Factors in Computing Systems*, pages 1245–1254. ACM, 2011.

[44] C. E. Shannon and W. Weaver. *A mathematical theory of communication*. University of Illinois Press, 1949.

[45] M. D. Smucker and C. L. Clarke. Modeling user variance in time-biased gain. In *Proceedings of the Symposium on Human-Computer Interaction and Information Retrieval*, page 3. ACM, 2012.

[46] K. Sparck Jones. A statistical interpretation of term specificity and its application in retrieval. *Journal of documentation*, 28(1):11–21, 1972.

[47] A. Spink. Study of interactive feedback during mediated information retrieval. *Journal of the American Society for Information Science*, 48(5):382–394, 1997.

[48] J. Teevan, K. Collins-Thompson, R. W. White, S. T. Dumais, and Y. Kim. Slow search: Information retrieval without time constraints. In *Proceedings of the Symposium on Human-Computer Interaction and Information Retrieval*, page 1. ACM, 2013.

[49] K. Umemoto, T. Yamamoto, and K. Tanaka. Scentbar: A query suggestion interface visualizing the amount of missed relevant information for intrinsically diverse search. In *Proceedings of the 39th International ACM SIGIR Conference on Research and Development in Information Retrieval*, SIGIR '16, pages 405–414, New York, NY, USA, 2016. ACM.

[50] V. D. Veksler and W. D. Gray. State definition in the tetris task: Designing a hybrid model of cognition. In *ICCM*, pages 394–395, 2004.

[51] C. Warwick, J. Rimmer, A. Blandford, J. Gow, and G. Buchanan. Cognitive economy and satisficing in information seeking: A longitudinal study of undergraduate information behavior. *Journal of the American Society for Information Science and Technology*, 60(12):2402–2415, 2009.

[52] R. W. White and R. A. Roth. Exploratory search: Beyond the query-response paradigm. *Synthesis Lectures on Information Concepts, Retrieval, and Services*, 1(1):1–98, 2009.

[53] B. M. Wildemuth. The effects of domain knowledge on search tactic formulation. *Journal of the american society for information science and technology*, 55(3):246–258, 2004.

[54] B. M. Wildemuth and L. Freund. Assigning search tasks designed to elicit exploratory search behaviors. In *Proceedings of the Symposium on Human-Computer Interaction and Information Retrieval*, page 4. ACM, 2012.

[55] M. J. Wilson and M. L. Wilson. A comparison of techniques for measuring sensemaking and learning within participant-generated summaries. *Journal of the American Society for Information Science and Technology*, 64(2):291–306, 2013.

[56] M. L. Wilson. Search user interface design. *Synthesis lectures on information concepts, retrieval, and services*, 3(3):1–143, 2011.

[57] M. L. Wilson, m. c. schraefel, and R. W. White. Evaluating advanced search interfaces using established information-seeking models. *Journal of the American Society for information Science and Technology*, 60(7):1407–1422, July 2009.

[58] T. D. Wilson. Models in information behaviour research. *Journal of documentation*, 55(3):249–270, 1999.

Fresh and Diverse Social Signals: Any Impacts on Search?

Ismail Badache
LSIS UMR 7296 CNRS
University of Aix-Marseille
Marseille, France
Ismail.Badache@lsis.org

Mohand Boughanem
IRIT UMR 5505 CNRS
University of Toulouse III
Toulouse, France
Mohand.Boughanem@irit.fr

ABSTRACT

In this paper, we extensively study the impact of social signals (users' actions) obtained from several social networks on search ranking task. Social signals associated with web resources (documents) can be considered as an additional information that can play a vital role to estimate a priori importance of these resources. Particularly, we are interested in the freshness of signals and their diversity. We hypothesize that the moment (the date) when the user actions occur and the diversity of actions may impact the search performance. We propose to model these heterogeneous social features as document prior. We evaluate the effectiveness of our approach by carrying out extensive experiments on two different INEX datasets, namely SBS and IMDb, enriched with several social signals collected from social networks. Our experimental results consistently demonstrate the interest of integrating fresh and diverse signals in the retrieval process.

Categories and Subject Descriptors

H.3.3 [**Information Storage and Retrieval**]: Information Search and Retrieval, *Social Search Process*

Keywords

Social signals; Social networks; Signals diversity; Freshness

1. INTRODUCTION

The majority of information retrieval (IR) systems exploit two classes of features to rank documents in response to user's query. The first class, the most used one, is query-dependent, which includes features corresponding to particular statistics of query terms such as term frequency, and term distribution within a document or in the collection of documents. The second class, referred to as documents prior, corresponds to query-independent features such as the number of incoming links to a document [26], PageRank [9], topical locality [15], presence of URL [35], document authors [27] and social signals [25].

CHIIR '17, March 07-11, 2017, Oslo, Norway

DOI: http://dx.doi.org/10.1145/3020165.3020177

Among these features, social signals such as (*like*, *+1*, *share*, *tweet*, *comment*) are probably one of the most interesting sources of evidence to measure document prior. Indeed, different web pages use social network buttons which allow users to express their support by (*like*, *+1*), *recommend* content [1], *comment* or *rate* a resource, send a *tweet* mentioning a resource, etc. In 2016, some statistics show that among 3.7 billion Internet users 76% are registered on at least one social network[1]. Such significant statistics have attracted researcher to study the degree of activity of those users. For instance, on Facebook, every 60 seconds there are about 50,000 posts with more than 2.3 million of *like* performed on different documents. All these social signals are valuable to improve document relevance ranking in conventional text search.

Most of existing approaches [11, 12, 22, 25] exploit these signals to estimate the document prior by simply considering the quantity (the number) of signals related to a resource, or the polarity for some specific signals. In this paper, we hypothesize that the time (age) of signals (when they occur), signals diversity on a resource, and the resource age may affect on the prior estimation. Therefore, we assume firstly, that fresh (recent) user actions may indicate some recent interests toward the resource. Secondly, the number of signals on a resource depends on the resource age. In general, an old resource may have much more signals than a recent one. Thirdly, we consider that signals diversity can be seen as a clue showing the degree of interest toward a resource, beyond a given social network or a community.

Note that some works have already investigated the temporality of social signals and their diversity associated to web resources in poster papers [6, 5]. They only described some preliminary results and they did not deeply evaluate and analyze the results. This paper extends significantly their work in the following additional aspects:

- exploiting additional signals namely, multi-valued signal such as *rating* (number of *rating* and *rating* value),
- evaluating the impact of freshness of signals,
- evaluating the signals normalization with resource age,
- evaluating jointly the impact of diversity and freshness of signals on IR process.
- conducting new and extensive experiments on a standard collection, namely INEX SBS,
- comparing the signals and identifying those that are important to improve IR.

[1] www.blogdumoderateur.com/chiffres-internet-2016-une-minute/

The research questions addressed in this paper are summarized as follows:

- What is the effect of the freshness of each action of the same type of signal (e.g. age of each action of *rating*) on IR system performance?
- What are the best temporal-dependent signals that can enhance a search?
- What is the impact of signals' diversity on IR process?

The remaining part is organized as follows. Section 2 reviews some related work. Section 3 describes our social approach. In section 4, we evaluate the effectiveness of our suggested approach and discuss the results. Finally, we conclude the paper with mentioning some future directions.

2. BACKGROUND AND RELATED WORK

In this section, we report related work that has leveraged social signals to measure a priori relevance of a resource. We distinguish those they do not take into account time when exploiting the social signals and those they do.

2.1 Time-Independent Signals Approaches

Some works focus on analyzing different statistical patterns of UGC (user generated content) such as YouTube videos [13], or on how to improve IR effectiveness by exploiting these UGC, particularly users' actions, with their underlying social network [7, 11, 12, 22, 23, 25].

Cheng et al. [13] presented a detailed investigation of characteristics of YouTube videos such as number of *views*, *comment*, number of *like* and number of *dislike*. This work does not exploit the potential of these studied features in retrieval process. In the last years, some works have concentrated on studying the richness and the possible use of these user-generated characteristics in search. *Chelaru et al.* [11, 12] studied the impact of social signals (*like*, *dislike*, *comment*, etc) on the effectiveness of search on YouTube. They showed that, although the basic criteria using the similarity of query with video title and annotations are effective for video search, social criteria are also useful and have improved the ranking of search results for 48% queries. They also evaluated the impact of social feedback on YouTube videos retrieval by using the state-of-the-art learning to rank approaches with a greedy feature selection algorithm.

Other studies are interested in exploiting social features to improve IR on the web and on the social networks. *Karweg et al.* [22] proposed an approach that combines topical score and social score based on two factors: (i) the engagement intensity, which specifies how strongly a user has interacted with a document using social services; for example, both *clicking* on a link and *recommending* a restaurant to a friend are interactions/engagements; (ii) the trust degree which determines how intense the relation between the user and other individuals registered on the same social network based on the *popularity* feature, using PageRank algorithm. They showed that the ranking improves as long as the searcher adds more friends, or his friends create more content over time. They found that social results are available for most queries and usually lead to more satisfying results. Similarly, *Khodaei and Shahabi* [25] proposed a ranking approach exploiting several social factors including the relationships between document owners and querying user, the importance of each user and user action (*playcount*: number of times a user listens to a track on lastfm) performed on web documents. They have conducted an extensive experiments on "lastfm" dataset. They showed a significant improvement of socio-textual ranking compared to the textual only and social only approaches.

Some prior studies tackled the *popularity* prediction of online content. We here briefly review some of them including social media signals to compute a "document prior" or, rather, a *popularity* for web content estimation (e.g. news article, tweet, etc). For example, *Borghol et al.* [7] analyzed differences among YouTube videos that have essentially the same content (clones) but different *popularity* using a multilinear regression model. This *popularity* is estimated based on *view* count, uploader's *followers* count, number of *comments*, *likes* and *favourite* events and average *rating*. *Bandari et al.* [3] and *Hong et al.* [19] exploited textual features extracted from messages (e.g., *hashtags* or *URLs*), the topic of the message, and user related features (e.g., number of *followers*) to predict the *popularity* of news and tweets. More specifically, *Hong et al.* [19] used *retweets* as a measure of *popularity* of *tweet* and then applied machine-learning techniques to predict how often new messages will be re-tweeted. In their work, different features have been used, including the content of messages, temporal information, metadata of messages and users, and the user's social graph. *Castillo et al.* [10] proposed a linear regression model to predict the total number of visits to a news article, using social media reactions. Unlike news, tweets, and videos, tips are associated with specific venues, and tend to be much less ephemeral as they remain associated with the venue (and thus visible to users) for a longer time. Thus, the *popularity* of a tip may be affected by features of the target venue as well.

Finally, there are other studies initiated by Microsoft Bing researchers [28, 33], which show the usefulness of different social contents generated by the network of user friends on Facebook. *Kazai and Milic-Frayling* [23] incorporated different types of social approval *votes* for book search using external resources that refer to books in the corpus, such as lists from libraries and publishers, and lists of bestsellers and award winning books. They defined a set of features to compute the social static rank and then train a neural network to integrate it with full-text search. They observed the effect of individual features with showing that the representations of the general consumer appeal tend to be more effective. Also, they found that social approval *votes* can improve a BM25F baseline that indexes both full-text and MARC[2] records. *Pantel et al.* [29] studied the leverage of social annotations on the quality of search results. They observed that the social annotations can benefit web search in two aspects: (i) the annotations are usually good summaries of corresponding web pages; (ii) the annotations indicate the *interest* and *popularity* of web pages. They also considered the type of social data (e.g., *like, share*) that can affect the user's choice. It was found that the user can benefit from such information in different ways such as a) personalized search results, b) participation in the activities of friends, and c) ranking results. These approaches exploit social signals of the experimental dataset, whereas our approach utilizes external signals from multiple social networks.

2.2 Time-Aware Social Signals Approaches

While considerable work has been done in the context of temporal query classification, there is still lack of studies that would analyze users' actions in temporal search from

[2]http://www.loc.gov/marc/

diverse viewpoints. Majority of existing works do not consider the time of action in the search process.

The works that are most related to our approach include [16, 21, 24], which attempt to improve ranking in web search. The approaches put forward by *Dong et al.* [16] and *Inagaki et al.* [21] used user click feedback features to identify how document relevance varies over time. More precisely, *Dong et al.* [16] incorporated fresh URLs extracted from Twitter into a general web search system. Using the labeled *<query,url>* training data pairs, a machine-learning ranking algorithm can predict the appropriate ranking of the search results for unseen queries. *Inagaki et al.* [21] proposed to exploit the temporal click, called ClickBuzz, which captures the interest of document over time. This method helps to exploit the user feedback to improve machine learning recency ranking by favoring URLs that have recent interest for the user's recency-sensitive query. The use of ClickBuzz in the ranking models leads mainly to an improvement in NDCG. *Khodaei and Alonso* [24] considered that the great mass of user-generated content in social networks provides an opportunity to examine how users produce and consume this type of content over time. They categorized the social interests of users into five classes: "recent", "ongoing", "seasonal", "past" and "random" and then analyze Twitter as well as Facebook data on social activities of users. They also discussed three different solutions where these time-sensitive signals can be applied: a) personalized IR; b) IR based on friends; and c) collective IR.

Another work presented by *Yuan et al.* [38] related to [19], and also heavily relies on temporal features to predict who will retweet a tweet. They investigated the dynamics of dyadic friend relationships through online social interactions, in terms of a variety of aspects, such as *reciprocity, temporality,* and *contextuality.* They propose a model to predict *repliers* and *retweeters* given a particular tweet posted at a certain time in a microblog-based social network. More specifically, they used learning-to-rank approach to train a ranker that considers user-level and tweet-level features (*like sentiment, self-disclosure,* and *responsiveness*) to address these dynamics. In the prediction phase, a tweet posted by a user is deemed a query and the predicted *repliers/retweeters* are retrieved using the learned ranker. *Borisov et al.* [8] was among the first to propose that time elapsed between a pair of user actions depends on the context of behaviors. They further construct a context-aware model to predict time between user actions in contexts. Their work shows that the dwell time of user clicks is affected by many different factors and incorporating such information may help the behavior model to better correlate with users' practical actions.

In this paper, we exploit novel social characteristics based on the same principle that some related work. However, unlike previous work [3, 7, 11, 12, 19, 23, 25], that attempt to improve a search on specific social networks (e.g. YouTube, Twitter) by exploiting their own signals, our work specifically focuses on, firstly, exploiting various signals from different sources as document priors to enhance Web IR. Secondly, considering *diversity* of signals as an additional factors in the estimation of the resource relevance. We note that in related work diversity has been applied only to the textual content of the document [2, 32]. Thirdly, evaluating the impact of the *freshness* of signals on the search performance by using their *creation date.* Fourthly, normalizing the distribution of signals on the resource using the *age of the resource.* Furthermore, we evaluated jointly the impact of *diversity* and *freshness* of signals on IR performance.

In addition, different to the approaches presented in [22, 29, 38], our approach does not take into account the user aspect, as well as we do not use a linear combination. However, we incorporate social signals and their different aspects (*freshness, diversity* and signal normalization with *resource age*) into a language model that provides a theoretical founded way to take into account the notion of a prior probability of a document. Finally our approach is completely unsupervised, and it is evaluated on different types of test data (Social Book Search and Internet Movie Database).

3. SOCIAL IR APPROACH

Our approach consists of exploiting social signals as a priori knowledge to be taken into account in retrieval model. We rely on language model to combine topical relevance of a given resource to a query and its importance modeled as a prior probability.

3.1 Notation

Social information that we exploit within the framework of our model can be represented by 5-tuple <U, R, A, T, SN> where *U, R, A, T, SN* are finite sets of instances: *Users, Resources, Actions, Times* and *Social Networks.*

Resources. We consider a collection $C=\{D_1, D_2,...D_n\}$ of n documents. Each document (resource) D can be a web page, video or other type of web resources. We assume that resource D can be represented both by a set of textual keywords $D_w=\{w_1, w_2,...w_z\}$ and a set of social actions A performed on this resource, $D_a=\{a_1, a_2,...a_m\}$.

Actions. We consider a set $A=\{a_1, a_2,...a_m\}$ of m actions (signals) that users can perform on resources. These actions represent the relation between users $U=\{u_1, u_2,...u_h\}$ and resources C. For instance, on Facebook, users can perform the following actions: *like, share.*

Time. T represents two types of temporal dimensions:

1. The history of social action, let $T_{a_i}=\{t_{1,a_i}, t_{2,a_i},..t_{k,a_i}\}$ a set of k moments (date) at which action a_i was produced. A moment t_{k,a_i} represents the datetime of action a_i.
2. Age of resource, let $T_d=\{t_{D_1}, t_{D_2},..t_{D_n}\}$ a set of n dates at which each resource D was published. t_D is the publication date of the resource D, date is provided in datetime format.

3.2 Query Likelihood and Document Prior

We exploit language models (LM) [31] to estimate the relevance of document to a query. The language modeling approach computes the probability $P(D|Q)$ of a document D being generated by query Q as follows:

$$P(D|Q) \overset{\text{rank}}{=} P(D) \cdot P(Q|D) = P(D) \cdot \prod_{w_i \in Q} P(w_i|D) \quad (1)$$

$P(D)$ is a document prior, i.e. query-independent feature representing the probability of seeing the document. The document prior is useful for representing and incorporating other sources of evidence in the retrieval process. w_i represents words of query Q. Estimating $P(w_i|D)$ can be performed using different models (Jelineck Mercer, Dirichlet). The main contribution in this paper is how to estimate $P(D)$ by exploiting social signals.

3.3 Document Prior

Document prior $P(D)$ can be estimated by considering different assumptions. First, each action can be considered individually. In this case, we got as much probabilities as actions. Each $P(D)$ measures the impact of a given action relatively to the other actions in the document or in a set of documents. Second, we compute the joint effect of a set (group) of observed actions in a document, where each document is associated with one probability. In our case, we assume that the signals are independent. Therefore, the general formula is:

$$P(D) = \prod_{a_i \in A} P(a_i) \tag{2}$$

The set of actions A can be associated to a given group of signals. For instance, signals from a given social network (e.g. *TotalFacebook* which includes *like*, *share* and *comment*), or signals of the same type, or all signals. $P(a_i)$ estimation depends on the type of signal a_i: "mono-valued signals" such as *like*, *share* and *tweet* or "multi-valued signals" such as *rating*.

3.3.1 Mono-valued signals

In this case, the $P(a_i)$ is estimated using maximum-likelihood:

$$P(a_i) = \frac{Count(a_i, D)}{Count(a_\bullet, D)} \tag{3}$$

To avoid zero-valued probability, we smooth $P(a_i)$ by collection C using Dirichlet [39]. The formula becomes as follows:

$$P(a_i) = \frac{Count(a_i, D) + \mu \cdot P(a_i|C)}{Count(a_\bullet, D) + \mu} \tag{4}$$

$P(a_i|C)$ is estimated by using maximum-likelihood:

$$P(a_i|C) = \frac{Count(a_i, C)}{Count(a_\bullet, C)} \tag{5}$$

Where:

- $Count(a_i, Y)$ represents the number of actions a_i performed on Y (Y is either the document D or the Collection C).
- $Count(a_\bullet, Y)$ is the total number of actions performed on Y.

3.3.2 Multi-valued signals (rating)

Rating cannot be treated by a simple counting of actions as described above. *Rating* is a point in a range of values. For instance, values between 1 and 5 where 3 means "acceptable" and 5 "outstanding", and depends on the number of users who rate the document.

For this purpose, we use the Bayesian Average (BA) of the *ratings* [36] as a document prior, which takes into account the number of users that have rated the document and the rating value. Hereby, the BA of a document is computed as follows:

$$BA(D) = \frac{avg(r) \cdot |r| + \sum_{D' \in C} avg(r') \cdot |r'|}{|r| + \sum_{D' \in C} |r'|} \tag{6}$$

Where:

- $r = \{r_i\}$ is a set of *ratings* values associated to document D. r_i is the ith *rating* given by user i to D.
- *avg* is the average value of *ratings* r associated to D.
- r' is the set of *ratings* in the collection C.

We note that considering logarithmic priors helps to compress the score range and thereby reduces the impact of the priors on the global score.

$$P(a_i|a_i = rating) = \frac{\log(1 + BA(D))}{\log(1 + \sum_{D' \in C} BA(D'))} \tag{7}$$

For documents with no *ratings*, this would result zero probability. In order to avoid this problem, we use the Add-One smoothing method:

$$P(a_i|a_i = rating) = \frac{1 + \log(1 + BA(D))}{1 + \log(1 + \sum_{D' \in C} BA(D'))} \tag{8}$$

Remark: we believe that this simple counting of signals may boost old resources compared to recent ones, because resources with long life on the web has much more chance to get more signals than recent ones. We need therefore to normalize the counts by the age of the resource. In addition, we assume that resources that have recent signals are more likely to interest the user. We propose to estimate the social importance of a resource by exploiting the moment when the interaction (signal) has occurred and the publication date of the resource. We take the same general model as described above. Also, we propose to take into account the temporal aspect, the time of the actions and the age of the resources. We describe in the following, how these two temporal aspects are considered.

3.4 Time-Based Document Prior

We assume that the resources associated with fresh signals (recent) should be favored (promoted) over those that are associated with old signals. Whenever a signal occurs, it is associated with its date of occurrence. We propose to associate to each action a temporal weight related to the time when it was associated to a resource. The corresponding formula is as follows:

$$Count_{t_a}(t_{j,a_i}, D) = \sum_{j=1}^{k} f(t_{j,a_i}, D) \tag{9}$$

The importance of signal at a given time can be estimated in different ways. A simple way is to take the inverse distance between actual date and the date of action, or an exponential weighting that further promotes the "recent" signals against the "old" signals:

$$f(t_{j,a_i}, D) = \exp\left(-\frac{\| t_{actual} - t_{j,a_i} \|^2}{2\sigma^2}\right) \tag{10}$$

We use formula 10 where $f(t_{j,a_i}, D)$ represents the signal-time function, estimated by using a Gaussian kernel [34]. This function calculates the temporal distance between the actual date t_{actual} and the date of the action t_{j,a_i}. $\sigma \in \mathbb{R}^+$ is the Gaussian kernel parameter.

The prior probability $P(D)$ is estimated using formula 4 but by replacing $Count()$ by $Count_{t_a}()$. We note that if the date of signal is ignored $f(t_{j,a_i}, D) = 1\ \forall t_{j,a_i}$.

Regarding the *rating*, we consider the time when the vote occurred. We use the similar principle as above, the temporal *rating* is defined by using the Gaussian kernel as follows:

$$r_t = r_i \cdot \exp\left(-\frac{\| t_{actual} - t_{r_i} \|^2}{2\sigma^2}\right) \tag{11}$$

Where: $r_t = \{r_{t_i}\}$ is a set of temporal *ratings* associated to D. r_{t_i} is the ith *rating* biased by it creation date t_{r_i} given by the user i to D.

We note that we estimate $P(a_i|a_i = rating)$ by using the formula 8, with replacing r by r_t in formula 6.

3.5 Signal Normalization with Resource Age

The priors we defined are proportional to the quantity of signals associated to a resource. This may lead to an undesirable effect where old resources will naturally have much more signals than new ones. This will promote old resources. To cope with this issue, we propose to normalize the distribution of social signals associated with a resource through resource publication date. Different functions can be used to estimate the normalization factor that takes into account the age of the resource. We used the Gaussian formula which will boost recent resource. The formula is the following:

$$A(D) = \exp\left(-\frac{\| t_{actual} - t_D \|^2}{2\sigma^2}\right) \quad (12)$$

The counting function $Count_{t_D}(a_i, D)$ and the $BA(D)$ will be normalized as follows:

$$Count_{t_D}(a_i, D) = Count(a_i, D) \cdot A(D) \quad (13)$$

$$BA_{T_D}(D) = BA(D) \cdot A(D) \quad (14)$$

The prior probability $P(a_i)$ based on normalization factor is estimated using formula 4, by replacing $Count()$ by $Count_{t_D}()$ for document and $Count_{t_C}()$ for collection, and for $P(a_i|a_i = rating)$ using the formula 8, with replacing $BA(D)$ by $BA_{T_D}(D)$.

3.6 Diversity of Social Signals

The diversity of signals associated with a resource reflects the variety of social communities which interact with this resource. It is important to mention that users are from heterogeneous social network and do not have the same social signals buttons. These diverse signals from different origins that judge the resource, can be play a role to cope the risk of manipulation and blind-following on the positive or negative judgment of content. For example, LinkedIn users do not see what Facebook users think about the same resource.

We believe that the diversity of signals on a resource is a clue that may indicate an interest toward a social network or a community. Diversity and quantitative distribution of social signals in a resource may be considered as factors of significance, i.e., a resource dominated by a single signal should be disadvantaged against a resource with an equitable distribution of the signals. Therefore, we propose to integrate signals diversity factor in the search model. We propose to evaluate this diversity by using diversity index of Shannon-Wiener [30], an entropy. It is given by the following formula:

$$Diversity(D) = -\sum_{i=1}^{m} P(a_i) \cdot log(P(a_i)) \quad (15)$$

Where $P(a_i)$ can be estimated as above (with or without considering *resource age*), and m represents the total number of signals.

The Shannon index is often accompanied by Pielou evenness index [30]:

$$Diversity^{Equit}(D) = \frac{Diversity(D)}{MAX(Diversity(D))} \quad (16)$$

Where:

$$MAX(Diversity(D)) = log(m) \quad (17)$$

The priori probability $P(D)$ is estimated using the formula 4 multiplied by the diversity factor as follows:

$$P(D) = \left(\prod_{a_i \in A} P(a_i)\right) \cdot Diversity^{Equit}(D) \quad (18)$$

4. EXPERIMENTAL EVALUATION

To evaluate our approach, we conducted a series of experiments on two datasets, SBS (Social Book Search) and IMDb (Internet Movie Database).We compared our approach which takes into account diversity and temporality of signals, with the baseline formed by only a textual model or simply counting of signals. Our goals in these experiments are:

1. to evaluate the impact of temporally-aware signals.
2. to evaluate the impact of signals diversity.

4.1 Description of Test Datasets

We used the collections SBS[3] and IMDb[4] documents provided by INEX. Each document describes a book on SBS and movie on IMDb. It is represented by a set of metadata, which has been indexed according to keywords extracted from fields (e.g. *title*, *actors* for IMDb and *book*, *summary* for SBS). For each document, we collected specific social signals via their corresponding API of 6 social networks listed in Table 3. We chose 30 and 208 topics with their relevance judgments provided by INEX IMDb 2011 and SBS 2015, respectively. In our study, we focused on the effectiveness of the top 1000 results.

Tables 1 and 2 show an example of social data of SBS and IMDb document. For instance, in Table 1, the IMDb document having Id=*tt1922777* was shared for the last time on Facebook at *2014-09-29T02:49:01* and published for the first time at *2011-05-07T19:00:57*. While, in Table 2 which contains SBS document, we have additional information compared to IMDb documents, the date of each *rating* associated with a document. For example, the SBS document having Id=*0553583859*, its first two *ratings* occurred on *1999-12-15* and *2000-01-04*.

Table 3 presents the social signals that we take into account in our experimentation.

Unfortunately, until now, Facebook does not allow the extraction of the dates of the various actions through its API. We have only the date of each *rating* from Amazon/LT.

Therefore, we represent the results using the formula 9 biased (taking account of the time) only by the date of *ratings*.

4.2 Results and Discussions

We conducted experiments with models based only on textual content of documents (Lucene Solr model, BM25 and Hiemstra language model without prior), as well as approaches combining textual content and social characteristics with taking into account their temporal aspect and diversity. We note that the best value of μ (smoothing parameter used in Dirichlet) belongs to the intervals: $\mu \in [90, 100]$ for IMDb and $\mu \in [2400, 2500]$ for SBS.

[3]http://social-book-search.humanities.uva.nl/#/data
[4]https://inex.mmci.uni-saarland.de/tracks/dc/2011/

Table 1: Instance of IMDb document with social data

	Facebook			Google+	Delicious	Twitter	LinkedIn
Id	Like	Share	Comment	+1	Bookmark	Tweet	Share
tt1922777	14763	13881	22914	341	12	2859	14
	Facebook						
Id	Last Share		Last Comment		Publication Date		
tt1922777	2014-09-29T02:49:01		2014-09-28T00:41:01		2011-05-07T19:00:57		

Table 2: Instance of SBS document with social data

	Facebook					
Id	Like	Share	Comment	Last Share	Last Comment	Publication Date
0553583859	137	60	17	2014-03-10T32:01:32	2014-03-18T00:01:43	2008-12-14T02:13:22
	Amazon/LibraryThing					
Id	Tag	Rating		Rating Date		
0553583859	13	4		1999-12-15		
		3		2000-01-04		

Table 3: Exploited social signals According Dataset

Social signals	Sources	Dataset
Number of *Comment*	Facebook	SBS, IMDb
Number of *Tweet*	Twitter	IMDb
Number of *Share(LIn)*	LinkedIn	IMDb
Number of *Share*	Facebook	SBS, IMDb
Number of *Reviews*	Amazon/LT	SBS
Number of *Tags*	Amazon/LT	SBS
Number of *Like*	Facebook	SBS, IMDb
Number of *Mention* +1	Google+	IMDb
Number of *Bookmark*	Delicious	IMDb
Number of *Ratings*	Amazon/LT	SBS

Remark: we have already shown taking into account these signals regardless of temporal aspect and diversity improves the IR performance, compared to baseline (based only on the topical relevance) [4] (Baseline (B) in Tables 4 and 5).

We can clearly notice in Tables 4 and 5 that considering signals separately or grouped (*All Criteria*) improve significantly the results. Furthermore, the obtained results using signals awarded first place in the INEX 2015 Social Book Search Competition[5]. This work is conducted in collaboration with *blinded* [20].

The different results are listed in tables 4, 5, 6 and 7 in terms of precision@k with $k \in \{10, 20\}$, nDCG and MAP. Baseline (A) represents textual models (BM25, Lucene Solr model and Hiemstra language model without prior), Baseline (B) represents configurations which do not take into account time in the priors estimation, and Baseline (C) represents configurations without considering signals diversity.

In order to check the significance of the results compared to the baseline, we conducted the Student's t-test [17] and the normality test [14]. We attached * (strong significance against Baseline (A), (B) and (C)) and ** (very strong significance against Baseline (A), (B) and (C)) to the performance number of each row in the tables when *p-value*$<$*0.05* and *p-value*$<$*0.01* confidence level, respectively. We discuss in the following the results of each configuration we investigated.

We evaluated our approach using different configurations, taking into account social signals as priors with: 1) their creation date, 2) publication date of the resource, and 3) the diversity of signals within a resource.

4.2.1 Impact of the "Time-Dependent Signal"

Table 4 lists the results obtained by integrating the date of the signal (the moment when a signal occurs). As aforementioned, the results obtained concern only the *rating* on the SBS. Table 4 show that the nDCG, precision@k and MAP are generally better compared to those obtained when the action time is ignored (Baseline (B) in Table 4). We record an improvement rate of 42.75% for *rating* compared to the run *BA_Rating* without considering time. These results are statistically significant.

[5]http://social-book-search.humanities.uva.nl/#/results15

Table 4: Results of P@k, nDCG and MAP for SBS

Models	P@10	P@20	nDCG	MAP
Baseline (A) : Without Priors				
BM25	0.0601	0.0517	0.1581	0.0517
Lucene Solr	0.0528	0.0487	0.1300	0.0463
ML.Hiemstra	0.0607	0.0559	0.1620	0.0527
Baseline (B) : Without Considering Time				
Like	0.0857	0.0689	0.1864	0.0741
Share	0.0901	0.0711	0.1900	0.0872
Comment	0.0799	0.0678	0.1807	0.0701
TotalFacebook	0.0958	0.0810	0.1937	0.0892
BA_Rating	0.0730	0.0559	0.1748	0.0620
Log_Tag	0.0770	0.0531	0.1742	0.0610
All Criteria	0.0973	0.0787	0.1981	0.0900
(a) With Considering Action Date T_a				
BA_Rating^{T_a}	0.0941**	0.0732**	0.1904**	0.0885**
(b) With Considering Publication Date T_D				
Like^{T_D}	0.0891*	0.0708*	0.1900*	0.0873*
Share^{T_D}	0.0917*	0.0796*	0.1947*	0.0903*
Comment^{T_D}	0.0881*	0.0711*	0.1882*	0.0777*
TotalFacebook^{T_D}	0.0957**	0.0873**	0.1959**	0.0928**
BA_Rating^{T_D}	0.0790*	0.0695*	0.1808*	0.0685*
Log_Tag^{T_D}	0.0782*	0.0599*	0.1771*	0.0666*
All Criteria^{T_D}	0.1078**	0.0973**	0.2080**	0.0986**

Table 5: Results of P@k, nDCG and MAP for IMDb

Models	P@10	P@20	nDCG	MAP
Baseline (A) : Without Priors				
BM25	0.3500	0.3371	0.4113	0.2068
Lucene Solr	0.3411	0.3122	0.3919	0.1782
ML.Hiemstra	0.3700	0.3403	0.4325	0.2402
Baseline (B) : Without Considering Time				
Like	0.3938	0.3620	0.5130	0.2832
Share	0.4061	0.3649	0.5262	0.2905
Comment	0.3857	0.3551	0.5121	0.2813
TotalFacebook	0.4209	0.4102	0.5681	0.3125
Tweet	0.3879	0.3512	0.4769	0.2735
+1	0.3826	0.3468	0.5017	0.2704
Bookmark	0.3730	0.3414	0.4621	0.2600
Share (LIn)	0.3739	0.3432	0.4566	0.2515
All Criteria	0.4408	0.4262	0.5974	0.3300
(b) With Considering Publication Date T_D				
Like^{T_D}	0.4091*	0.3620*	0.5308*	0.2907*
Share^{T_D}	0.4177*	0.3721*	0.5544*	0.2989*
Comment^{T_D}	0.3912*	0.3683*	0.5285*	0.2874*
TotalFacebook^{T_D}	0.4302	0.4258	0.5827	0.3200
Tweet^{T_D}	0.3918*	0.3579*	0.4903*	0.2779*
+1^{T_D}	0.3900	0.3511	0.5246	0.2748
Bookmark^{T_D}	0.3732	0.3427	0.4671	0.2618
Share^{T_D} (LIn)	0.3762	0.3449	0.4606	0.2542
All Criteria^{T_D}	0.4484*	0.4305*	0.6200*	0.3366*

We can explain these results as follows, for example, in the context of IMDb, searching for the name of an actor (e.g. topic number 2013106: *Paul Verhoeven Arnold Schwarzenegger*) the user might expect the most recent movies for the particular actor and social signals could help to discover them. However, we have not really evaluated the real impact of our proposal with respect to all the signals (except for the *rating*). But the results obtained by the $rating^{T_a}$ configuration, for which all conditions were satisfied are encouraging.

These results support our hypothesis, that states that the resources associated with fresh signals should be favored in comparison with those associated with old signals.

4.2.2 Impact of "Resource Age"

The results presented in part (b): *With Considering Publication Date* T_D of Tables 4 and 5, respectively, show that the nDCG and the precision are better compared to those obtained when the publication date of the resource is ignored (Baseline (A) and (B)). All signals either taken separately or grouped (according to their social networks (*TotalFacebook*), or all criteria) seem to take advantage from this normalization. These results seem to be correlated with the quantity of signals associated to the resource. For instance, the results for *share*, *like* and *comment* by considering the date are significantly better than those without considering date, in both collections. Indeed, we notice that the average number of *share* and *like* per resource are 362 and 360, respectively. Whereas the average number of *bookmark* is 13. The best results are obtained when combining all criteria (named *All* $Criteria^{T_D}$ in Tables 4 and 5), with a rate of improvement in terms of nDCG 4% on IMDb and 5% on SBS, compared to *All Criteria* where the time is ignored. Indeed, the resource that generates a social activity of 100 actions of *like* in one hour does not have the same importance and the same temporal interest for the users compared to a resource that gathered 100 of actions of *like* during a week.

4.2.3 Impact of "Diversity"

Tables 6 and 7 list the results when considering *TotalFacebook* and *All Criteria* with and without diversity. For both collections, the nDCG and the precisions are generally better where diversity is considered.

Table 6: Results of P@k, nDCG and MAP for IMDb

Models	P@10	P@20	nDCG	MAP
Baseline (C): Without Considering Diversity				
TotalFacebook	0.4209	0.4102	0.5681	0.3125
All Criteria	0.4408	0.4262	0.5974	0.3300
With Considering Diversity *Div*				
$TotalFacebook^{Div}$	0.4227*	0.4187*	0.5713*	0.3167*
$All\ Criteria^{Div}$	0.4463*	0.4318*	0.6174*	0.3325*

Table 7: Results of P@k, nDCG and MAP for SBS

Models	P@10	P@20	nDCG	MAP
Baseline (C): Without Considering Diversity				
TotalFacebook	0.0958	0.0810	0.1937	0.0892
All Criteria	0.0973	0.0787	0.1981	0.0900
With Considering Diversity *Div*				
$TotalFacebook^{Div}$	0.0960*	0.0840*	0.1945*	0.0907*
$All\ Criteria^{Div}$	0.1011*	0.0915*	0.2031*	0.0952*

The best results are obtained by combining all social criteria $All\ Criteria^{Div}$. This later, is better than both *TotalFacebook* and *All Criteria* without diversity factor. Taken into account all criteria (signals) coming from different social networks give more social credibility through the multitude of approval sources. Even though the quantity of signals coming from the other sources namely, LinkedIn, Google+, Delicious, are very low (in average 13, 29, 67 actions per resource, respectively) compared to those coming from Facebook (in average 360 per action and per resource), we notice that adding these sources improves significantly the results for both collections (P@10 is improved of 5% compared to $TotalFacebook^{Div}$ for both collections). Indeed, if many users of different social communities found that a resource is useful, then it is more likely that other users will find it useful too.

4.2.4 Impact of "Diversity" and "Resource Age"

Tables 8 and 9 summarize the results obtained when taking into account the diversity and signals normalization with a resource age. We list only the configurations that consider the grouped signals, the only ones for which diversity has meaning. We attached * (strong significance against the corresponding configurations which do not consider the publication date of the resource T_D and diversity *Div*).

Table 8: Results of P@k, nDCG and MAP for IMDb

Models	P@10	P@20	nDCG	MAP
Diversity and Document Publication Date T_D				
$TotalFacebook^{Div}_{T_D}$	0.4417*	0.4289*	0.5966*	0.3273*
$All\ Criteria^{Div}_{T_D}$	0.4568*	0.4334*	0.6311*	0.3427*

Table 9: Results of P@k, nDCG and MAP for SBS

Models	P@10	P@20	nDCG	MAP
Diversity and Document Publication Date T_D				
$TotalFacebook^{Div}_{T_D}$	0.0978*	0.0868*	0.1970*	0.0932*
$All\ Criteria^{Div}_{T_D}$	0.1092*	0.0988*	0.2095*	0.0997*

Comparing the results listed in Tables 8 and 9 with those obtained in the above (Tables 4, 5, 6 and 7), we notice that the diversity combined with the age of the resource factor improves the results on the two datasets. It seems that this combination takes cumulative advantage from both criteria, Diversity and Age of the resource, since this combination outperforms the results obtained by each criteria taken separately. Indeed, the resource that records a high diversity of signals during two days has not the same importance compared to a resource that records signals diversity during two weeks. In addition, a resource containing a high frequency of a variety of signals mean that the crowd judgment of this resource is more significant than a resource dominated by a single signal. A resource with a high signal diversity implies a high spread of this resource in several social networking communities.

We note that our method of combining diversity with the date of the action does not improve the results, therefore we have not presented the results of this configuration.

4.3 Diversity Distribution on Documents

In order to have a view on the distribution of diversity of social signals within documents, we have taken all documents returned by IMDb and SBS topics and then we have calculated the diversity score for each document. Then, we associated the relevance judgments provided by Qrels of INEX with each document. We represented the overlapping between the relevance and signals diversity through figures 1 and 2.

Figure 1: Signals diversity with respect to the relevance of IMDb documents

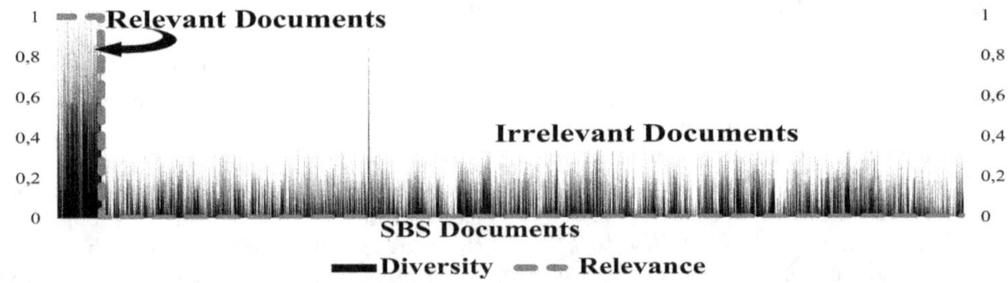

Figure 2: Signals diversity with respect to the relevance of SBS documents

Figures 1 and 2 show the scores of signals diversity for each document. In order to better differentiate between the relevant documents and the irrelevant ones, we sorted the documents according to their relevance. We note that the majority of relevant documents (returned) are delimited by the red rectangle in figures 1 and 2. They have the higher signals diversity scores compared to irrelevant documents, except one segment of irrelevant documents on SBS that shows high scores. We conclude that the diversity of signals obtains its best scores with the relevant documents.

4.4 Features Selection Algorithms Study

The problem of the described methods is in giving all signals same importance since we only count its frequency. However, it is obvious that signals are different. For instance a *like* signal designs a kind of positive vote for a given resource, whereas a *comment* might be positive or negative, in our case we only count this signal.

To better understand the importance of each signal, the real impact of social signals, we used the feature selection algorithms applied on both collections (IMDb and SBS). Feature selection algorithms [18] aim at identifying and eliminating as many irrelevant and redundant information as possible. Our goal is to determine the best time-dependent signals that can be effectively exploited in IR, as well as to verify if the results obtained previously (prior probability of the document) are consistent. We used Weka[6] for this experiment. It is a powerful open-source Java-based learning tool that brings together a large number of algorithms for selecting attributes.

We proceeded as follows, the top 1000 resources for each topic (30 IMDb topics and 208 SBS topics) were extracted using Lucene Solr model (using only text-based retrieval). Then, the scores (probability) of all criteria (signals) are calculated for each resource. We identify relevant resources and irrelevant according to the Qrels. The set obtained contains 30000 IMDb documents and 115248 SBS documents composed of:

- 2765 relevant documents and 27235 irrelevant documents for IMDb.
- 2953 relevant documents and 112295 irrelevant documents for SBS.

We observed that the classes of these sets are unbalanced. This occurs when there are many more instances in one class than others in a training collection. In this case, a classifier usually tends to predict samples from the majority class and completely ignore the minority class [37]. For this reason, we applied an approach to subsampling (reducing the number of samples that have the majority class) to generate a balanced collection composed of:

- 2765 relevant documents and 2765 irrelevant documents for IMDb.
- 2953 relevant documents and 2953 irrelevant documents for SBS.

Irrelevant documents for this study were selected randomly. Finally, we applied the attribute selection algorithms on the two sets obtained, for 5 iterations of cross-validation. **Remark**: these algorithms operate differently, some return an importance ranking of attributes, while others return the number of times that a given attribute has been selected by an algorithm in a cross-validation.

Tables 10 and 11 list the number of times (*folds number*: this value is between 0 and 5) that a given signal has been selected by an algorithm (9 signals were evaluated), and the rank of the signal (selected in order of preference) compared to other signals. Regarding the SBS, the value of *rank* is between 1 and 8, with 8 the number of evaluated criteria. For IMDb, the value of *rank* is between 1 and 9. For example, in Table 11 *tweet* has been selected 5 times by the algorithm *CfsSubsetEval* (numbered A_i=1), 3 times by *WrapperSubsetEval* and has been ranked 5th among the 9 criteria by the algorithm *ChiSquaredAttributeEval*. We discuss the results in the following.

- **Impact of signals biased by age of document** : according to Tables 10 and 11 (columns corresponding to Publication date of document T_D), we note that

[6]http://www.cs.waikato.ac.nz/ml

Table 10: Selection of temporally dependent signals with attribute selection algorithms (Applied on SBS)

			Publication date of document T_D					Date of action T_a		
A_i	Algorithms	Metric	Comment	Share	Tag	Like	Rating	Comment	Share	Rating
1	CfsSubsetEval	[folds number]	5	5	2	5	2	3	5	5
2	WrapperSubsetEval	[folds number]	1	5	2	4	4	4	5	5
3	ConsistencySubsetEval	[folds number]	4	5	3	5	4	4	5	5
4	FilteredSubsetEval	[folds number]	4	5	2	5	2	3	5	5
		Average	3.5	5	2.25	4.75	3	3.5	5	5
5	ChiSquaredAttributeEval	[rank]	5	2	8	4	7	6	3	1
6	FilteredAttributeEval	[rank]	6	3	8	4	7	5	1	2
7	GainRatioAttributeEval	[rank]	6	1	8	4	7	5	3	2
8	InfoGainAttributeEval	[rank]	5	1	7	4	8	6	3	2
9	OneRAttributeEval	[rank]	6	3	7	4	8	5	2	1
10	ReliefFAttributeEval	[rank]	5	2	8	4	7	6	3	1
11	SVMAttributeEval	[rank]	5	2	8	4	7	6	3	1
12	SymetricalUncertEval	[rank]	5	2	8	4	7	6	3	1
		Average	5.375	2	7.75	4	7.25	5.625	2.625	1.375

Table 11: Selection of temporally dependent signals with attribute selection algorithms (applied on IMDb)

		Publication date of document T_D							Date of action T_a	
A_i	Metric	Comment	Tweet	Share(LIn)	Share	Like	+1	Bookmark	Share	Comment
1	[folds number]	5	5	0	5	5	3	0	5	5
2	[folds number]	3	3	2	5	5	3	2	5	2
3	[folds number]	5	5	5	5	5	5	4	5	5
4	[folds number]	5	5	0	5	5	3	0	5	5
	Average	4.5	4.5	1.75	5	5	3.25	1.5	5	4.25
5	[rank]	4	5	8	1	2	6	9	3	7
6	[rank]	5	4	8	1	2	6	9	3	7
7	[rank]	5	4	8	2	1	6	9	3	7
8	[rank]	4	5	8	2	1	6	9	3	7
9	[rank]	4	5	8	2	1	6	9	3	7
10	[rank]	5	4	8	1	2	6	9	3	7
11	[rank]	5	4	8	1	2	6	9	3	7
12	[rank]	5	4	8	1	2	6	9	3	7
	Average	4.625	4.375	8	1.375	1.625	6	9	3	7

the biased signals by the document age: *Share*(LIn), *Bookmark*, *Tag* and *Rating* are weakly favored by the selection algorithms with average ranks of 8, 9, 7.75, 7.25, respectively, and average selection of 1.75, 1.5, 2.25, 3, respectively. While in Table 11, the action +1 is moderately favored (with average ranks of 6 and average selection of 3.25). However, they are all selected by each algorithm except *Share*(LIn) and *Bookmark* in Table 11, which have not been selected by both algorithms *CfsSubsetEval* and *FilteredSubsetEval*. Indeed, this is an indication about their weak impact. The Facebook signals: *Like* and *Share* are the highest ranked (with averages ranks: 1.6 and 1.3, respectively) compared to other signals; they are strongly validated during the 5-fold cross-validation. The signals *Comment* and *Tweet* are in second place; they are often selected over the 5-fold cross-validation.

- **Impact of signals biased by their date** : regarding signals biased by their creation date, we remark through Table 10 that *Rating* is the best signal compared to all other signals. It is selected in 5 iterations of cross-validation by all algorithms and ranked first. One of the reasons of these results returns to the efficiency of exploitation of the dates of each action *Rating*. Consequently, our hypothesis is completely verified. We also note that *Share* comes in second position followed by *Comment* (with average ranks of 5.6 on SBS and 7 on IMDb). We recall that for these two signals, we have only used the date of the last action.

By comparing these results with the results appearing in Tables 4 and 5, we notice that the same factors of relevance highlighted by the model based on prior probability are highlighted by the study with attribute selection techniques. Social signals considered with their temporality, ($Rating^{T_a}$ and $Share^{T_D}$), which provide the best results (statistically significant) are the most favored and the highest ranked by the different selection algorithms. Finally, our study confirms the interest of the temporal dimension of social signals used to improve IR: relevant resources have a high number of social actions but also the recent interactions, and this number is proportional to the life of the resource on the web.

5. CONCLUSION

Previous work showed the impact of the signals without considering time. This paper focuses on studying the impact of *freshness* and *diversity* of signals associated with a resource on search. We have proposed to estimate the prior probability of document by considering these factors. The experiments conducted on IMDb and SBS datasets reveal that taking into account signals *diversity* and temporal aspects (*signal date, resource age*) in textual model improve the quality of search results. We used also feature selection algorithms to identify the best time-aware social signals for this task of IR.

For future work, we plan to address some limitations of the current study. We plan to study the importance of social networks and social actors of these signals and their impact on the relevance. This requires tracking users' personal profiles as well as those of their followers and those of users they *share, like, rate, tweet*, etc. We intend to collect these data in the future to evaluate the user preferences, compared to social neighbors, to solve the personalized search. User-centric data would likely help us for better understanding the temporal interests of users. Moreover, considering the polarity (positive, negative, neutral) of the textual content of the signals in search. This is even with these simple elements, the results encourage us to invest more this track.

6. REFERENCES

[1] O. Alonso and V. Kandylas. A study on placement of social buttons in web pages. *arXiv*, 2014.

[2] A. Angel and N. Koudas. Efficient diversity-aware search. In *SIGMOD*, pages 781–792, 2011.

[3] Roja B., Sitaram A., and Bernardo A.H. The pulse of news in social media: Forecasting popularity. In *ICWSM*, 2012.

[4] I. Badache and M. Boughanem. Social priors to estimate relevance of a resource. In *IIiX*, pages 106–114, 2014.

[5] I. Badache and M. Boughanem. Document priors based on time-sensitive social signals. In *European Conference on IR*, pages 617–622, 2015.

[6] I. Badache and M. Boughanem. A priori relevance based on quality and diversity of social signals. In *SIGIR*, pages 731–734, 2015.

[7] Y. Borghol, S. Ardon, N. Carlsson, D. Eager, and A. Mahanti. The untold story of the clones: content-agnostic factors that impact youtube video popularity. In *SIGKDD*, pages 1186–1194, 2012.

[8] A. Borisov, I. Markov, M. de Rijke, and P. Serdyukov. A context-aware time model for web search. In *SIGIR*.

[9] S. Brin and L. Page. The anatomy of a large-scale hypertextual web search engine. In *WWW*, pages 107–117, 1998.

[10] C. Castillo, M. El-Haddad, J. Pfeffer, and M. Stempeck. Characterizing the life cycle of online news stories using social media reactions. In *CSCW*, pages 211–223, 2014.

[11] S. Chelaru, C. Orellana-Rodriguez, and I. S. Altingovde. Can social features help learning to rank youtube videos? In *WISE*, pages 552–566, 2012.

[12] S. Chelaru, C. Orellana-Rodriguez, and I. S. Altingovde. How useful is social feedback for learning to rank youtube videos? *World Wide Web*, 2013.

[13] X. Cheng, C. Dale, and J. Liu. Statistics and social network of youtube videos. In *IWQoS Workshop*, pages 229–238, 2008.

[14] Ralph B. D'Agostino. Tests for the normal distribution. *Goodness-of-fit techniques*, 68:576, 1986.

[15] B.D. Davison. Topical locality in the web. In *SIGIR*, pages 272–279, 2000.

[16] A. Dong, R. Zhang, P. Kolari, J. Bai, F. Diaz, Y. Chang, Z. Zheng, and H. Zha. Time is of the essence: improving recency ranking using twitter data. In *WWW*, pages 331–340, 2010.

[17] William Sealy Gosset. The probable error of a mean. *Biometrika*, 6:1–25, 1908.

[18] Mark A. Hall and G. Holmes. Benchmarking attribute selection techniques for discrete class data mining. *IEEE Trans. on Knowl. and Data Eng.*, 15(6):1437–1447, 2003.

[19] L. Hong, O. Dan, and B. Davison. Predicting popular messages in twitter. In *WWW*, pages 57–58, 2011.

[20] M. Imhof, I. Badache, and M. Boughanem. Multimodal social book search. In *CLEF*, 2015.

[21] Y. Inagaki, N. Sadagopan, G. Dupret, A. Dong, C. Liao, Y. Chang, and Z. Zheng. Session based click features for recency ranking. In *AAAI Press*, 2010.

[22] B. Karweg, C. Huetter, and K. Böhm. Evolving social search based on bookmarks and status messages from social networks. In *CIKM*, pages 1825–1834, 2011.

[23] G. Kazai and N. Milic-Frayling. Effects of social approval votes on search performance. In *ITNG*, pages 1554–1559, 2009.

[24] A. Khodaei and O. Alonso. Temporally-aware signals for social search. In *SIGIR Workshop TAIA*, 2012.

[25] A. Khodaei and C. Shahabi. Social-textual search and ranking. In *CrowdSearch*, pages 3–8, 2012.

[26] W. Kraaij, T. Westerveld, and D. Hiemstra. The importance of prior probabilities for entry page search. In *SIGIR*, pages 27–34, 2002.

[27] C. Macdonald and I. Ounis. Voting for candidates: adapting data fusion techniques for an expert search task. In *CIKM*, pages 387–396, 2006.

[28] M. R. Morris and J. Teevan. Exploring the complementary roles of social networks and search engines. In *HCIC Workshop*, pages 1–10, 2012.

[29] P. Pantel, M. Gamon, O. Alonso, and K. Haas. Social annotations: Utility and prediction modeling. In *SIGIR*, pages 285–294, 2012.

[30] E.C. Pielou. Shannon's formula as a measure of specific diversity: its use and misuse. *American Naturalist*, pages 463–465, 1966.

[31] Jay M. Ponte and W. Bruce Croft. A language modeling approach to information retrieval. In *SIGIR*, pages 275–281, 1998.

[32] L. Qin, Jeffrey X. Y., and L. Chang. Diversifying top-k results. *VLDB Endowment*, 5(11):1124–1135, 2012.

[33] M. Raza. A new level of social search: Discovering the user's opinion before he make one. In *Microsoft Research*, pages 1–6, 2011.

[34] J-P Vert, K. Tsuda, and B. Schölkopf. A primer on kernel methods. *Kernel Methods in Computational Biology*, pages 35–70, 2004.

[35] T. Westerveld, W. Kraaij, and D. Hiemstra. Retrieving web pages using content, links, urls and anchors. 2002.

[36] Xiao Y. and Zhaoxin Z. Combining prestige and relevance ranking for personalized recommendation. In *CIKM*, pages 1877–1880, 2013.

[37] S-J. Yen and Y-S. Lee. Under-sampling approaches for improving prediction of the minority class in an imbalanced dataset. In *Intelligent Control and Automation*, volume 344, pages 731–740, 2006.

[38] N.J. Yuan, Y. Zhong, F. Zhang, X. Xie, C-Y. Lin, and Y. Rui. Who will reply to/retweet this tweet?: The dynamics of intimacy from online social interactions. In *WSDM*, pages 3–12, 2016.

[39] C. Zhai and J. Lafferty. A study of smoothing methods for language models applied to information retrieval. *ACM Trans. Inf. Syst.*, 22(2):179–214, 2004.

Bad Users or Bad Content? Breaking the Vicious Cycle by Finding Struggling Students in Community Question-Answering

Long T. Le
Department of Computer Science
Rutgers University
longtle@cs.rutgers.edu

Chirag Shah
School of Communication and Information
Rutgers University
chirags@rutgers.edu

Erik Choi
Brainly
erik.choi@brainly.com

ABSTRACT

Community Question Answering (CQA) services have become popular methods to seek and share information. In CQA, users with an information need, or askers, post a question that community members can answer. This question-answering process allows both askers and answerers to learn through the exchange of information. CQA services have also been widely used in the education domain, as some of such services are designed specifically for students' information seeking. However, due to insufficient knowledge, lack of experience, and other reasons, students often struggle in producing quality or even appropriate content. This low quality production causes their content to be flagged or deleted, further discouraging them from participating in the CQA process and instigating a vicious cycle of bad users and bad content. In an effort to break this cycle, the work reported here focuses on identifying users whose postings demonstrate a high deletion rate with a presumption that the *bad* content is an indication of a struggling student rather than a malicious user. In this work, experiments are conducted on a large student-oriented online CQA community to understand struggling students' behaviors. A framework is proposed to find these users based solely on their activities. Finally, community feedback (i.e. human judgment) such as moderator evaluation or community votes for good content is used to detect these users in the early stages of their respective struggles. To evaluate this framework, we used data from Brainly, a large educational CQA service that is used in two different markets with more than 3.7 million users and 10.7 million answers. The results show that the human judgment feature identifies early-stage struggling users with high accuracy. Identifying these struggling users (students) could help educators to determine suitable ways to help their students instead of presuming them to be *bad* users and cutting them off from the community.

1. INTRODUCTION

With the emergence of the Web and more specifically Web 2.0, a vast number of users have used interactive online communities in order to seek and share information. Examples of these online community platforms include social networks, wikis, blogs, and community question-answering (CQA) sites. These platforms provide an unprecedented opportunity for users to enrich their minds and share knowledge. One popular way to ask a question is through CQA, where users often desire more personalized answers. CQA also takes advantage of *Wisdom of the Crowd*, or the idea that everyone knows something [30]. Users can contribute to the community by asking questions, giving answers, and voting for high-quality posts.

Many initial CQA venues, such as Yahoo! Answers and AnswerBag, were developed to support general-purpose questions. Other CQA platforms focus on more specific topics; for example, Stack Overflow supports issues related to computer programming. Recently, CQA has evolved to support online learning. Some small-scale CQAs were introduced in order to support small groups of university students [2], [28]. These educational CQA sites include Chegg[1], Piazza[2], and Brainly[3]. Brainly, for instance, specializes in online learning for primary and secondary students, helping them interact with each other by asking and answering questions related to school subjects (e.g., English, Mathematics, Biology, Physics, Chemistry, etc.) [7]. Although most CQAs are publicly available and any student is welcome to join for educational purposes, a majority of new CQA users may be fully or partially unaware of these sites' community norms. These norms constitute user behaviors that govern how to appropriately ask and answer a question in order to satisfy an asker's information need. Misunderstanding these norms may affect a user's ability to post appropriate and mutually beneficial answers to a CQA community. Though users who struggle to understand community norms but continue to answer questions differ from online lurkers who most likely consume content without creating it [29], they both need guidance in order to create appropriate answers and participate in healthy question-answering activities. Thus, the main research objective of the current study is to understand characteristics of those struggling CQA users and investigate a series of features that indicate their behaviors. To do so, we propose a framework to automatically identify struggling users based on their question-answering activities. We also attempt to investigate the feasibility of detecting struggling users in the early stages of their problems by using community feedback. Community feedback is the feedback from other users to the quality of answers such as other users vote for best answers or moderators delete bad quality answers. Understanding struggling users and identifying them in the early stages

CHIIR '17, March 07 - 11, 2017, Oslo, Norway

ISBN 978-1-4503-4677-1/17/03...$15.00

DOI: http://dx.doi.org/10.1145/3020165.3020181

[1] https://chegg.com/study/qa

[2] https://piazza.com/

[3] http://brainly.com

of their CQA activities may help create appropriate user guidelines that demonstrate how students can properly seek and share information within an online education community in order to increase or improve their knowledge.

In the current study for identifying struggling users, we attempt to examine Brainly, one of the largest CQA services specifically targeted towards education. Brainly is an online social learning network for students and educators with millions of active users. It has approximately 60 million monthly unique visitors as of January 2016 and is available in 35 countries, including the United States, Poland, Russia, Turkey, Brazil, France, Indonesia, and more.

Our specific contributions with this work are as follows.

- Conducting an empirical study centered on struggling users to see how their actions differ from user norms.
- Proposing a framework to find the struggling users based solely on their online activity.
- Proposing a framework to detect the struggling users in their early stages through their online activity and community feedback (i.e. human judgment on the quality of answers). Early detection can help us outline suitable actions to help these users.
- Examining the importance of features in detecting struggling users. These show that some early community feedback is important.

2. BACKGROUND AND RELATED WORKS

2.1 Community Question-Answering (CQA)

The emergence of the Web, and specifically Web 2.0 technologies, have changed the way that users look for information in virtual environments. Search engines allow users to quickly find information, but they do not satisfy needs that require more personalized answers. These needs led to the development of Community Question-Answering (CQA) platforms, which have become popular places for Internet users to look for more personalized answers to their questions. Some popular CQAs, such as Yahoo! Answers and Stack Overflow, attract millions of users, and CQA takes advantage of *Wisdom of the Crowd*, or the idea that everyone knows something [30]. In CQA, any user can join and become a part of the community by asking questions, giving answers, making comments, and voting for appropriate and thorough posts. In order to ensure content quality, a small number of users are promoted to moderators, and the majority of the community's activities are curated by those moderators.

The popularity and success of CQA have attracted academic research interests. Previous works have investigated user interest and motivation for participating in CQA [24, 33]. Using the popular Yahoo! Answers, Adamic et al. [1] studied the characteristics of CQA participants. The authors analyzed questions and clustered them based on their contents. The results identified diverse user types. The study revealed that a majority of users is only interested in a small number of topics, while other users have a broad interest. The work also showed that it is possible to automatically select questions' best answers via some basic features, such as a post's length and the past answers given by its author.

Moreover, as answer quality is among the most critical factors for a CQA site's success, previous work showed that it is possible to automatically examine answer quality based on users' past history [26, 31, 11]. Shah et al. [27] discovered that questions remain unanswered in CQA when they are fact-based. This work also explored why fact-based questions often fail to attract an answer. Automatically determining a posts' quality can significantly reduce the work CQA can require of human judgment. Le et al. [17] used different group of features to evaluate the quality of educational answers automatically. Teevan et al. [32] discovered that questions' punctuation, length and scope affect the quantity, quality, and speed of answers in CQA.

2.2 CQA for Online Learning

Early-developed CQA platforms, such as Yahoo! Answers and WikiAnswers, support general-purpose activities. Later forums such as Stack Overflow center around narrower topics and attract more focused communities. Recently, CQA has been deployed in education. Some small-scale CQA tools were developed to support small groups of university students [2], [28]. Some larger educational CQAs are becoming popular; these include Chegg, Piazza, and Brainly. Brainly specializes in online learning for students through asking and answering activities in 16 main school subjects (e.g., English, Mathematics, Biology, Physics, etc.) [7].

Educational CQA not only provides a platform to support questioning and answering, but can also test a student's knowledge based on the content they generate. A student can learn from others' answers, and can also learn through their own answering activities, as helping others allows them to test whether they understand a question and its topic.

2.3 User Behavior in an Online Community

An online community's success greatly depends on its users because community content and activities are primarily based on users' activities. Thus, user behavior attracts a great deal of research interest. A community's size–especially the ratio of answered to unanswered questions–is a large component of its overall effectiveness. [34]. Dumais et al. [8] studied users' behaviors based on the log of activity and suggested suitable methods to design the system to collect search data. They also discussed the challenges of using real users' activity logs. Users make diverse contributions in CQA. Le and Shah [16] showed that a small number of users contribute heavily to their community and are crucial to its health. This observation motivated these researchers to develop a framework in which they integrated various features to detect top contributors in their early stages of site use. Contrastingly, "the lurker" is prevalent in many online communities. Gong et al. [9] profiled lurkers in an online social network. Compared to other users, lurkers maintain far fewer social connections. The work found that popular global events will break lurkers' silence. It is not clear why these users are lurkers or why active users become lurkers.

The ability to detect an untruthful contribution is also an important task [23, 31]. Pelleg et al. [23] studied truthfulness in CQA sites. This research examined whether users provide truthful information about themselves on CQA sites, and found that askers generally provide accurate personal information, even when they post sensitive questions. Tan et al. [31] proposed a new method called CQAL to automatically predict the quality of a post in a social knowledge base. On these platforms, such as Wikipedia or Freebase, users can edit articles. These contributions might contain inaccurate information and detract from other users' experiences with these sites. Some signals that help determine truthfulness include user contribution history, the features of each subject, and user expertise. Determining question and answer quality will ultimately prove essential when analyzing questioning and answering behaviors in CQA.

All communities want to attract new members, but existing members who leave a community are a prevalent issue. Understanding when and why users leave a particular community provides a overview of the community's health [21], [19], [25]. These works used user behavior *ego-nets* to predict behavior and activity patterns. Pal et al. [22] provided an overview of user evolution in CQA, which included various users' in-site activities and their effects. Antisocial users also indicate community health. Cheng et al. [6] examined antisocial behavior in online postings. Research shows that it is significantly different from other kinds of behavior. For example, antisocial users compose their posts differently than others, or display a more negative sentiment. Deleting these users forms a bimodal distribution which is very high or very low. User experience with online activity also attracts interest from the research community [20], [13]. Scholars showed that user engagement is complex. Furthermore, click patterns, dwell times, and keyboard actions correlate with user engagement. Mao et al. [18] predicted users' engagement with volunteer crowd-sourcing. The study showed that the average number of tasks was the strongest predictor of future engagement with online crowd-sourcing.

In our work, we focus on investigating struggling users who want to contribute to a CQA community, but may be unable to participate in an acceptable way. To the best of our knowledge, our work is the first study in struggling users in educational CQA.

3. DATASETS AND CHARACTERIZATION OF THE DATA

Overview: In this study, we use data provided by Brainly.com. This is an online Q&A for students and educators with millions of active users. Here, we use data from two markets: the United States (US) and Poland (PL). US is an emerging market that started in 2013 while PL is a well-established market that began in 2009. Table 1 describes some characteristics of these data sets. Brainly requires high quality answers. Thus, moderators delete incorrect answers, incomplete answers, or spam posts. A small fraction of highly experienced users are promoted to be the moderators. The moderators not only have experience, but also have a history of significantly contributing to the community. In terms of assuring answer quality, moderators are able to delete wrong, poor, and spam answers with additional explanations to answerers; approve appropriate answers; warn and ban users who behave against policies; and participate in the forum to share their experiences with content moderation. There are 207 active moderators in US and 377 active moderators in PL who voluntarily curate content on a daily basis. Moderators also evaluate the majority of new material. The posts in Brainly are divided into three levels (grades): primary, secondary, and high school. Brainly also integrates social networking into the platform, as it allows users to make "friends" and exchange ideas.

Table 1: Description about data.

Site	Period	# of Users	# of Answers
US	Nov '13 to Dec '15	800 K	700 K
PL	Mar '09 to Dec '15	2.9 M	10 M

Figure 1 plots the distribution of the number of answers given by each user. This follows the power law with some very active users. Answering questions is a popular way for users to earn higher scores and increase their ranking in the community. Giving many answers shows that an active user is willing to devote their time to helping others.

4. EXAMINING STRUGGLING USERS

To understand struggling users based on their online activities, we first show that these users exist in the community and display

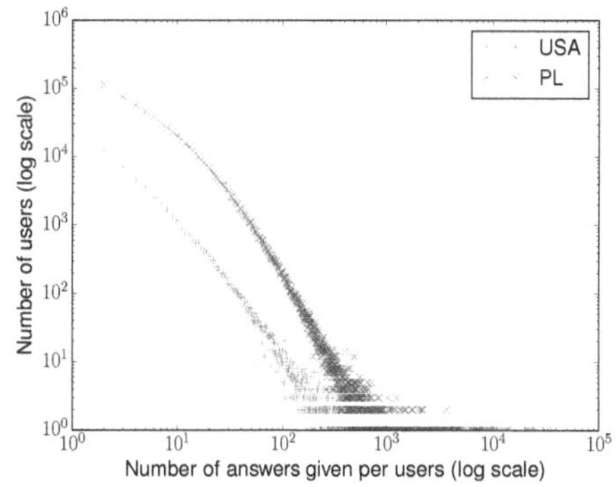

Figure 1: Distribution of number of answers given by each user. A small fraction of users answer many questions while many users answer a small number of questions.

behaviors that deviate from established community norms.

4.1 Definition of Struggling Users

In our work, we are focused on active users who have a limited ability to make meaningful contributions. We define struggling users as those who actively provide low-quality answers to other users' questions. In particular, struggling users generate at least X posts, with a ratio of deletion of at least Y percent. The value depends on the requirement of the site. In this study, we work directly with Brainly's data analysis and business intelligence team to determine the threshold. The Brainly data analysis team suggests $X = 10$ and $Y = 0.7$. We also extensively evaluate our method with a wide threshold range to show its efficacy. Our method works well with different thresholds.

4.2 Existence of Struggling Users

We examine the proportion of active users who are struggling within the community. We consider struggling users to be those who have the majority of their answering contributions deleted. Figure 2 plots the histogram of the deletion rate of different types of users. We plot the histogram of the deletion rates for the general population, as well as users with at least 10 and at least 20 answers. We see that some users have a higher deletion rate.

Figure 2 describes the percentage of struggling users in our data sets. We see that there are quite a few users who want to learn and contribute to the community, but cannot provide sufficient answers. These users might need significant help, making it important to detect and assist them. For example, 7.7% and 13.9% of active users in US and PL markets have a deletion rate higher than 70%. This is a large number of users equivalent to 28,364 individuals in PL's market alone. The number of struggling users will increase when the site becomes more popular. As Brainly focuses on education, it attracts a student user population whose learning process is of particular importance.

4.3 Social Connections of Struggling Users

We examine whether there is any difference between the social connections of struggling users and those of normal users. To encourage users to exchange information, Brainly includes a social network-like structure in its architecture. We graphically represent these social connections. Each user is a node, and each friendship is an edge in the graph. The number of edges, a user's clustering coefficient, and a user's egonet (or friends of friends) represent some

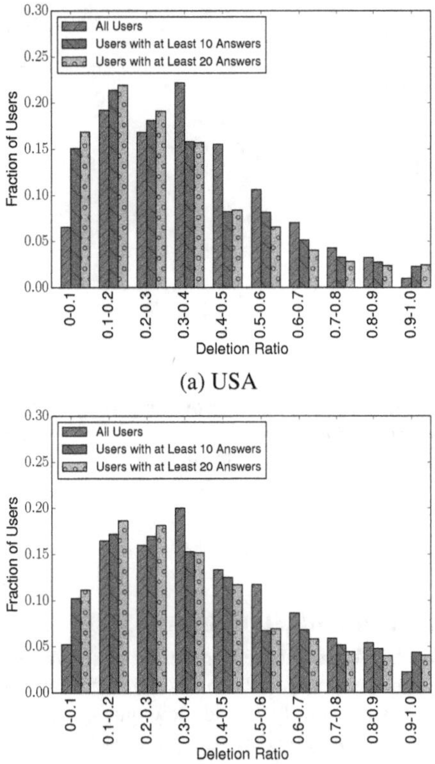

(a) USA

(b) PL

Figure 2: Deletion Rate. Histogram of deletion rate in two markets. Percentage of users with deletion rate higher than 0.7 is the sum of the last three bars (0.7-0.8, 0-8-0.9 and 0.9-1).

features that demonstrate a user's social connections. For example, the clustering coefficient (CC_i) of a node measures how closely a user's neighbors form a clique–or cluster together–and is defined as:

$$CC_i = \frac{\#\ of\ triangles\ connected\ i}{\#\ of\ connected\ triples\ centered\ on\ i} \tag{1}$$

The higher clustering coefficient means that this user and their friends form a stronger connection. For example, a fully connected graph has (CC_i) equals to 1, and a star graph has (CC_i) equals to 0. We denote $d_i = |N(i)|$ as the number of friends of users i, while $|N(i)|$ denotes i's set of neighbors. The average degree of neighborhood is defined as

$$\bar{d}_N(i) = \frac{1}{d_i} \times \sum\nolimits_{j \in N_i} d_j \tag{2}$$

We also use a node's egonet features. A node's egonet is the subgraph created by the node and its neighbors. Egonet features include its size, number of outgoing edges, and number of neighbors.

We use these features because they incorporate four social theories: Social Capital, Structural Hole, Balance, and Social Exchange [3]. The capacity of social connection plays important role in information propagation [10, 15]. Furthermore, these features can be calculated locally which is scalable for large networks.

Table 2 summarizes the social connection features of normal users and struggling users. In general, struggling users have fewer social connections compared to normal users. Several reasons could explain this deficiency. For example, it is possible that users who provide low quality answers are less attractive to others. We perform t-tests on these two user groups. The degree and the clustering coefficient are significantly different with $p = 0.01$. A student might want to connect with someone who gives high quality answers. Thus, they are less likely to connect with struggling users. Alternatively, struggling users may not know how to enrich their social connections. In the case that struggling users do not know how to connect with good peer users, a recommendation from a new friend could help.

Table 2: Comparing the social connections between normal and struggling users. The table presents the mean values and standard error mean in the parentheses. Struggling users have fewer social connections than normal users.

Features	USA		PL	
	Normal	Struggling	Normal	Struggling
Degree	9.09 (0.41)	7.5 (1.07)	6.5 (0.08)	4.3 (0.10)
Degree_Adj	80.3 (1.60)	78.6 (1.41)	65.7 (0.3)	60.9 (0.6)
CC	0.13 (.003)	0.14 (.012)	0.04 (.002)	0.03 (.001)
CC_Adj	0.03 (.001)	0.02 (.0005)	0.09 (.002)	0.12 (.004)
Ego	25.8 (2.59)	14.2 (2.37)	14.6 (0.74)	4.5 (0.58)
Ego_Out	618.2 (19.7)	517.5 (29.6)	573.3 (7.9)	311.7 (11.2)

4.4 Reasons for Struggling Users

Fractions of deleted answers on Brainly receive comments from moderators. The site wants to enhance its users' experiences by asking the moderators to explain why posts may be inappropriate and should be deleted. In theory, moderators' responses will help answerers to improve their subsequent posts. Avoiding repetitive mistakes betters the entire community's experience. Some popular reasons for deleting answers are listed in Table 3. There are many reasons answers are considered incorrect. In the majority of cases, posts are deleted due to answerers' insufficient knowledge. In some cases, an answer might be considered low quality due to improper grammar, language, and other details.

4.5 Time to Answer Question

In the majority of tasks, greater enthusiasm and effort lead to better results. We want to see this happen in educational CQA. We measure the average time that users take to answer a question. We also measure answer length. Table 4 shows that, compared to struggling users, normal users spend much more time and effort on their answers. Additionally, answers provided by struggling users display a shorter length than those provided by the general population. We perform t-tests on normal and struggling users. The average length of answer and average time spent per answer are significantly different with p = 0.01. The statistics show that struggling users should put more effort into crafting high quality answers.

4.6 Difference Between Level of Education

Users with varying levels of education may not be equally capable of expressing answers. We examine whether there are differences among users from primary, secondary and high school levels. Figure 3 describes the percentage of struggling students based on their respective levels of education. The percentage of struggling primary students is higher than secondary and high school students, likely because primary students lack the ability to clearly express

Table 3: **Popular reasons for deleting answers. Answers are deleted for diverse reasons. Plagiarism, for instance, indicates the answerer copied and pasted from other information sources without paraphrasing.**

Reason	Example
The answer contains mistakes	Q: How do I solve 24-4*3? A:Answer=60. 24-4=20. 20 x 3=60
The answer is uninformative and does not show any work	Q: The total cost of renting a car is $30.00 for each day,the car is rented + 28.5 c for each mile What is the total cost of renting the car for5 days and driving 350 miles?? A: I believe the total cost is 265.5$
The answer is pointless/meaningless	Q: When was Central Intelligence Agency founded? A: It needs to have more topic or it cant be understood or else it would be a pleasure to help you.
The answer is too vague	Q: Simplify the expression $(2x-1)(x^2+3x-2)$ A: Your answer is going to be $2x^3+5x^2-7x+2$
The answer is incomplete	Q: How to estimate 5.804+126.009+56.2345? A: You round to the nearest thousandth
The answer contains linguistic errors or grammatical errors	Q: What color is given for desert in map? A: The answer is (BEROWN) .
The answer is plagiarized	Q: Why shouldn't we bath after having lunch or dinner? A: Following ingestion food the splanchnic circulation or blood circulation to the viscera or the different parts and organs concerned with food ...

their ideas. Fortunately, when detected and assisted at their primary (young) age, these users can significantly improve their capability.

4.7 Activeness of Struggling Users

As we mentioned, we only studied users who generated a certain amount of answers. In particular, we examined users who had at least ten posts. Among these users, we found that struggling users answered 33 questions in the US data set, and 25 questions in the PL data set. These values are lower compared to normal active users, but still high. They suggest that some struggling users want to participate in the community, but their limitations prevent them from making quality contributions.

Table 4: Comparing the effort put into creating an answer. The table presents the mean values and standard error mean in the parentheses. Struggling users spent less time and effort when providing an answer compared to normal users.

Features	USA		PL	
	Normal	Struggling	Normal	Struggling
Avg Time (sec)	80.4 (0.8)	42.2 (1.3)	171.4 (0.3)	79.5 (0.4)
Avg Length	119.9 (0.9)	94.8 (1.2)	367.7 (0.6)	321.1 (1.2)

4.8 Readability of Answers

To determine the quality of struggling users' written text, we measure its readability based on two popular indexes: automated readability index (ARI), and Flesch reading ease score of answer (FRES) [12]. The ARI measures what grade level should understand the text, which is measured by

$$\alpha * \frac{\#\, of\ characters}{\#\, of\ words} + \beta * \frac{\#\, of\ words}{\#\, of\ sentences} - \gamma \qquad (3)$$

where α, β, γ are 4.71, 0.5, 21.43 respectively based on empirical study.

The FRES index measures the readability of the document. FRES index is calculated as

$$\alpha' - \beta' * \frac{\#\, of\ words}{\#\, of\ sentences} - \gamma' * \frac{\#\, of\ syllables}{\#\, of\ words} \qquad (4)$$

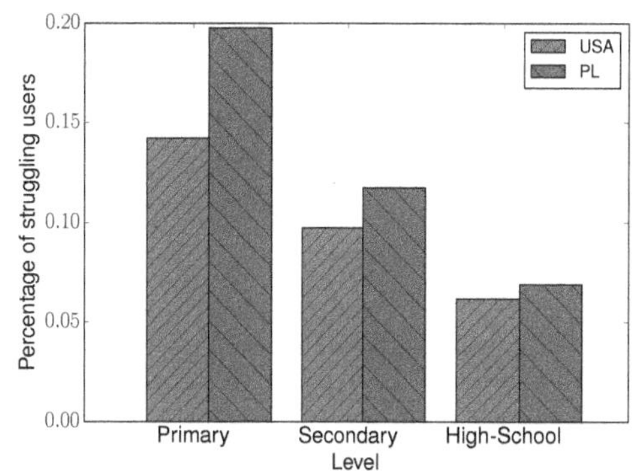

Figure 3: Percentage of struggling users with different education levels. Many primary school students struggled to provide good quality answers.

Again, α', β', γ' are calculated based on empirical study and are equal to 206.8, 1.01, 84.6 respectively. Higher FRES scores indicate the text is easier to understand.

The average FRES value for normal users is 64.1(0.4) while the FRES value of struggling users is 39.1(1.5). This reveals that it is more difficult to read the answers given by struggling users, which explains why some of their posts are deleted. But the distribution of the FRES value varies widely between struggling users. Many struggling users compose easy-to-read posts that provide incorrect information. This observation bolsters the claim that posts are deleted for a diverse array of reasons.

5. DETECTING STRUGGLING USERS WITHOUT HUMAN JUDGMENT

In the CQA community, a small number of high profile users are authorized to examine answer quality. As the community develops, users generate more content, and this places a growing burden on moderators. In this section, we examine whether it is possible to automatically detect struggling users without any human judgment. Human judgment is the actions by moderator or other users such as voting for the best answers or bad answers. The formal definition is: *"Given a user and all of their posts, can we predict, without any human judgment, whether this user has struggled with the site?"*.

Finding these users is a classification problem, which includes extracting features, building the classifier and applying the model automatically.

5.1 Features Extraction

We identified a list of features based on our observations to extract struggling users. Table 5 lists the features used in our study. They are divided into four groups: *Personal Features*, *Community Features*, *Textual Features*, and *Contextual Features*. The *Personal Features* include the number of answers given by the users, users' grade level, users' lifetime site presence, and how much time users spend on the site. The *Community Features* include users' social connections, as described in the previous section. The *Textual Features* include the ARI and FRES index, answers' average length, and features to represent the format of users' writing, such as whether their text is well formatted or whether it contains latex typing. The *Contextual Features* include the time to answer or typing speed.

These features are based on users' activities. We excluded features generated by moderators or other human judgment. The purpose is to examine whether we can automatically evaluate the users.

Table 5: Lists of features are classified into four groups: Personal, Community, Textual, and Contextual. Features' abbreviations are in brackets.

Personal Features
Number of answers given (n_answers)
Grade level of users (u_grade)
Lifetime of users (life_time)
Time spent with the site (spent_time)
Community Features
Number of friends in community (friends_count)
Clustering Coefficient in friendship network (cc)
Average degree of neighborhood (deg_adj)
Average CC of friends (cc_adj)
Size of ego-network of friendship (ego)
Number of outgoing edges in ego-network (ego_out)
Number of neighbors in ego-network (ego_adj)
Textual features
The avg. length of answer (length)
The avg. readability of answer (ari)
The avg. Flesch Reading Ease Score of answer (fres)
The format of answer (well_format)
Using advance math typing: latex (contain_tex)
Contextual features
Duration of time taken to answer (time_to_answer)
Typing speed (typing_speed)

5.2 Classification

Since our problem is a typical binary classification problem, any classification method can work with our framework. In this work, we applied different popular classification algorithms, including logistic regression, support vector machine, decision trees and Random Forest [4]. Let $X = x_1, x_2, ..., x_n$ is the list of features such as n_answers, u_grade. The list of classification algorithms is summarized as:

- Logistic regression (log-reg): Log-reg is a generalized linear model with sigmoid function: $P(Y = 1|X = \frac{1}{1+exp(-b)})$, where $b = w_0 + \sum(w_i.x_i)$, w_i are the inferred parameters from regression.
- Support vector machine (SVM) with Radial basis (RBF) kernel. The RBF kernel is defined as $K(x, x') = exp(-\frac{1}{2}||x - x'||)^2$
- Decision trees: The Tree-based method is a nonlinear model that partitions features into smaller sets and fits a simple model into each subset. The decision tree includes two-stage processes: tree growing and tree pruning. These steps stop when a certain depth is reached or each partition has a fixed number of nodes.
- Random Forest (RF): RF is an average model approach. We use a bag of 100 decision trees. Given a sample set, the RF method randomly samples data and builds a decision tree. This step also selects a random subset of features for each tree. The final outcome is based on the average of these decisions.

5.3 Experiment Setup

We perform the prediction on a balanced data set of normal and struggling users by under sampling method to create a balanced data set [5]. We perform 10-fold cross validation in all experiments. We measure the efficacy of our method with importance metrics including accuracy, F1-score, and Receiver Operating Characteristic (ROC).

- Accuracy: The accuracy measures the percentage of struggling users that we can accurately detect. The higher the accuracy, the better the algorithm.
- F1-score: This score considers both precision and recall. The precision is the fraction of instances that are relevant, while recall is the fraction of relevant instances that are retrieved. Given precision and recall, F1-score is calculated as:

$$F1 = 2 * \frac{precision * recall}{precision + recall} \quad (5)$$

- Area Under ROC: This involves measuring the area of the plot with true positive versus false positive rates as the threshold changes from 0 to 1. The higher the value, the better algorithm. A random guess algorithm achieves the value of 0.5, where the true positive rate increases linearly with the false positive rate.

Setting different thresholds: According to our definition, the struggling user makes at least X posts, and the ratio of deletion is at least Y percent. The value depends on the requirement of the site. Even Brainly's analytic teams suggest $X = 10$ and $Y = 0.7$; we evaluate the efficacy of our method with different thresholds. Below is the set of thresholds tested in our method X and Y to show the efficacy of our method.

- $X = \{5, \ 10, \ 15, \ 20\}$
- $Y = \{0.5, \ 0.6, \ 0.7, \ 0.8, \ 0.9\}$

5.4 Results

Figure 4 plots the accuracy and F1-score when we use different number of posts (X) and deletion rate (Y) thresholds by applying Random Forest algorithm. These values show that we do not achieve high performance if we only rely on user activity and do not include community feedback. Our method performs better with higher thresholds X and Y. Higher value X indicates that we can observe more activity and gather more information about the users. Higher threshold Y means that the users are very different from the community norm. For example, users with a deletion rate of 0.9 are very extreme users. In such cases, it is easier to detect these extreme users.

Table 6 describes the accuracy from different classifiers applied in the current study. In both data sets, Random Forest achieves the highest accuracy. Random Forest achieves the highest performance and is a scalable algorithm. In our experiment with a single machine with 2.2 GHz quad-core, 16 GB of RAM, implemented in Python code, it took less than one millisecond to classify each user. Furthermore, the tree can be built separately and is easily computed to be distributed for a larger data set.

Table 6: Comparing different classifiers. We change the thresholds of number of answers and deletion rate as in experiment setting and take the average. The table presents the average accuracy with standard deviation in the parentheses. Random Forest achieves the best accuracy.

Data sets	LogReg	SVM	Decision Trees	RF
USA	70.8 (.042)	74.2 (.028)	68.1 (.039)	**73.7 (.031)**
PL	75.1 (.045)	76.3 (.029)	70.7 (.037)	**78.6 (.035)**

We also measure the Area Under ROC curve to see the trade-off between true positive and false positive rates. The Area Under ROC for US and PL are 0.83 and 0.84, respectively. Again, these values reflect moderate performance value. We need to improve for a real application.

6. DETECTING STRUGGLING USERS AT THEIR EARLY STAGE WITH HUMAN JUDGMENT

In the previous Section, we demonstrate the low accuracy involved in predicting whether a user will struggle. In this Section, we will examine whether it is possible to predict whether users will struggle at an early stage with community feedback. When new answer is generated in CQA, other users can judge the content. Some typical human judgment includes moderator deletes the bad content or other users vote for good content. The formal definition is *"Given a user with his T posts and human feedback, can we predict whether this user will struggle with the site in the future?"*.

Since the moderator judges user answers, we can get some early feedback on answer quality. We use the same features as Table 5 in Section 5. We add new features, including: *del_ratio* represents the percentage of the first T answers that are deleted, and *n_best_answers* represents the number of answers that are selected as the best answer. Other features, such as readability or answer length, are similar to those in the previous section, but we only calculate the features based on the first T answers.

6.1 Experiment Set Up

We observe the community behavior and feedback on the first $X/2$ posts of each user and predict whether these users will struggle in the long term. Higher value X means we observe more activities. We also add two new features– *del_ratio* and *n_best_answers* –in the *Community Features* group. Other settings are similar to the previous task. We also try different thresholds including the number of post X and the deletion rate Y to show the efficacy of our method.

6.2 Results

Figure 5 plots the accuracy of our method. The new features, *n_deletion* and *n_best*, significantly increase the accuracy. For brevity, we do not report the F1-score, which is is similar to the accuracy. Results demonstrate that our method achieves high accuracy and F1-score in both US and PL data sets, which are both at 90% for high deletion rate threshold. These key performance metrics predict struggling users more accurately than those that measure all posts without human judgment. Furthermore, two new features significantly increase the accuracy. We will discuss the importance of each feature separately in a later part of this paper.

When using Random Forest, our method's Area Under ROC is 0.93 and 0.94, respectively. These are very high performance metrics reiterated by Accuracy and F1-score. We see that some community feedback helps us significantly increase the system's performance. Furthermore, we only need feedback on a user's few initial posts to make the framework perform well, which could significantly reduce the moderator's workload.

6.3 Experiment Results Discussion

6.3.1 *Feature Importance*

We measure the importance of each feature in our prediction framework. There are multiple ways to measure the importance of each feature. The general idea is to measure how a particular feature's removal affects the framework's overall accuracy. In the bagging method, we use a permutation test to remove the features and measure the accuracy of out-out-bag (OOB) samples. The important features will decrease the accuracy more than others.

Figure 6 measures the importance of each feature in our study. In both scenarios, the average time users spend on an answer and the average length of an answer are important features. When detecting early-stage struggling users, human judgment is vital. In Figure 6b, the deletion ratio has a higher value than other features. Thus, we can achieve better performance with some human judgment in our framework.

6.4 Feature Selection

We use a small number of features in our study. Thus, feature selection does not improve performance; even some features, such as using latex, are not powerful. Furthermore, the main result presented in this work is achieved via Random Forest. When building each tree of the random forest, the algorithm already randomly selects some features. This suggests that performing feature selection is unnecessary.

6.5 Setting the Threshold

In the real system, we might choose a different threshold to identify the users who may need guidance to create appropriate answers. If we want to detect the majority of struggling users, we might need to accept a higher error rate. If we want a very low error rate, we would detect fewer struggling users. The curve in Figure 7 plots the True Positive rate against the False Positive rate. We first observe the high Area ROC in both data sets. Secondly, we can detect the majority of struggling users with the small False Positive Rate. For example, if we want to identify 80% of struggling users (True Positive Rate = 0.8), the error rate is very small. In this case, the False Positive Rate is 0.03 and 0.05, respectively. Thus, the framework is quite promising in a real system.

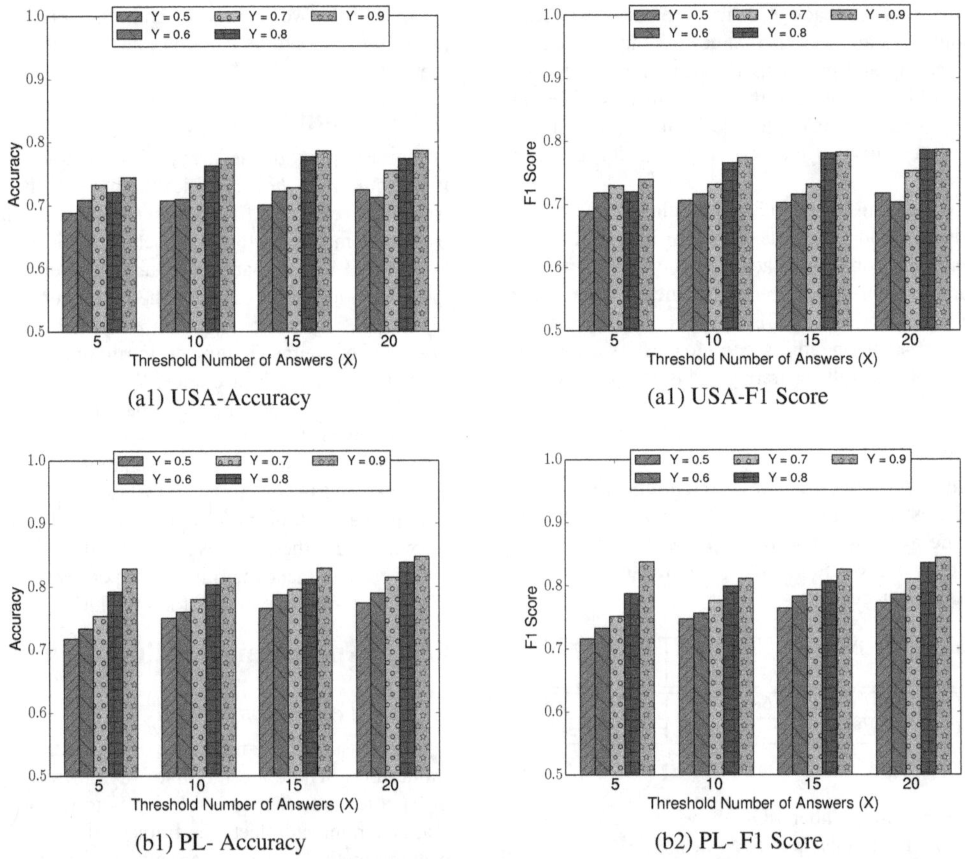

(a1) USA-Accuracy (a1) USA-F1 Score

(b1) PL- Accuracy (b2) PL- F1 Score

Figure 4: Accuracy and F1 Score. The accuracy and F1 Score of detecting struggling users without human judgment. The Figures present the results when applying Random Forest with all Features. The performance is moderate without human judgment.

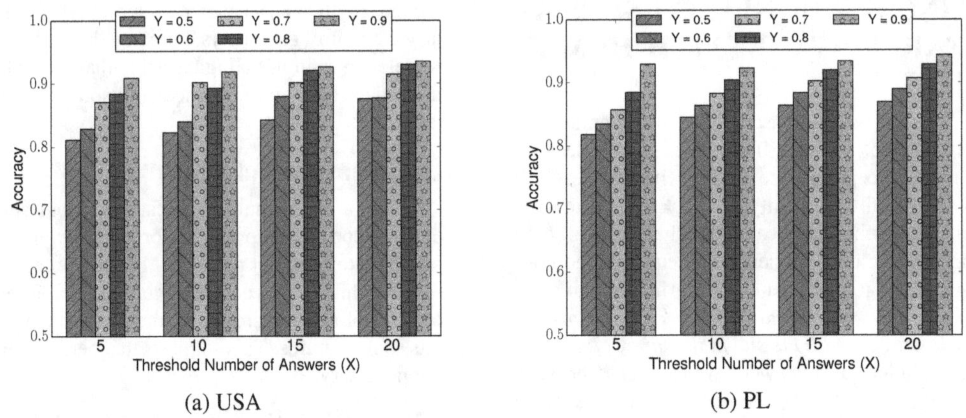

(a) USA (b) PL

Figure 5: Accuracy. The accuracy of detecting struggling users in the early stage. The Figures present the results when applying Random Forest with all Features. Our method is robust to a different threshold of X and Y. Our method performs better with higher value X and Y. Users with higher deletion rate Y are different from the community norm.

7. DISCUSSION

CQA has become an important knowledge-sharing avenue. Education is also an important field, and one in which society has always held a vested interest. Our findings show that many users are struggling within online CQA communities that are geared towards students. These struggling users should not be neglected, especially because they hail from educational institutions. These users could be detected with high accuracy if there is some help from the CQA community. In the current system, all feedback must come from moderators, who must exert an undue amount of human effort to properly assist struggling users. Furthermore, detecting late-stage struggling users comes with a high cost in terms of those users and

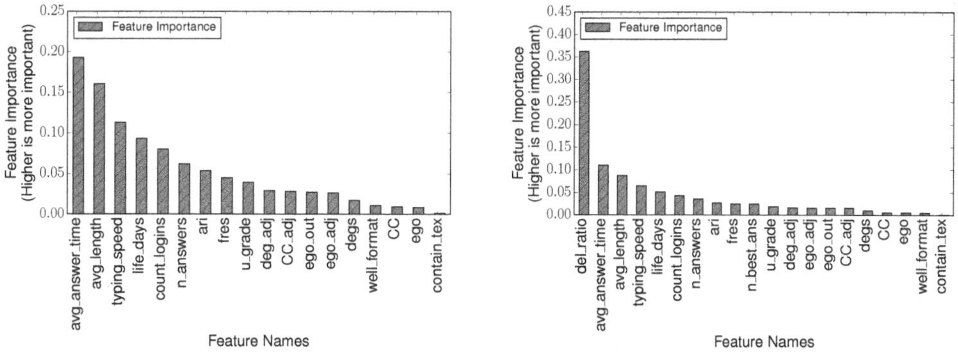

(a) Without Human Judgment

(b) With Human Judgment in the Early Stage

Figure 6: Measure the importance of each feature. Average answer time and the average length of answers are important features. Furthermore, the deletion ratio in the case of human judgment is a vital feature.

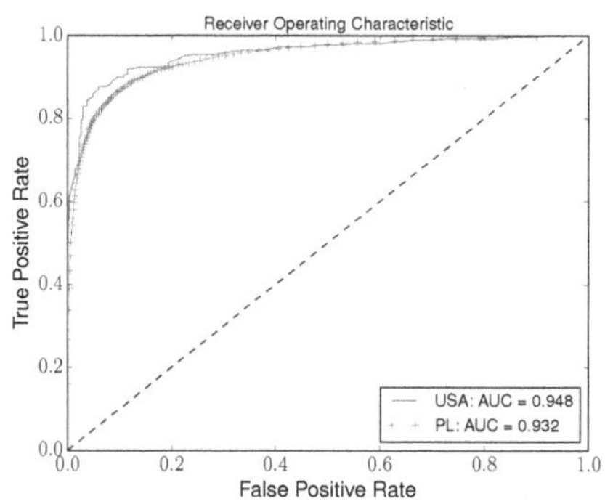

Figure 7: Plotting of ROC to select the suitable threshold. We can detect the majority of struggling users with minuscule error rate.

their wider online community; the users could be frustrated and leave the community. Furthermore, it might be too difficult to fix their knowledge gaps if they are discovered too late. Our work shows that it is possible to find struggling users in their early stage with some community feedback.

Our study has some limitations, which can be addressed in future research. First, we do not discern the reason that users are struggling in the community. Providing users with automatic, concrete feedback could improve their performance and allow them to quickly transcend their shortcomings. Second, it would be highly beneficial to directly interact with struggling users to determine how to best assist them. Observing the effect of such an early interaction would be valuable. In our future work, we hope to resolve these limitations.

8. CONCLUSION

The current work focuses on struggling users in community question answering (CQA). Some students are found to be struggling within education-oriented CQA sites, such as Brainly. These struggling users want to participate in the community, but are unable to produce acceptable answers due to their inexperience and lack of knowledge. While these characteristics may be undesirable outside of an educational context, here they are to be expected and should be addressed to enhance students' learning experience. It follows that flagging these users simply because they are producing *bad* content may not be the best course of action. Instead, if we could use this information to identify such users and recognize that their behavior could indicate a learning-related problem and opportunity, we could help them become better users and better students. In order to identify and eventually assist these individuals, the current study compares their behavior to that of regular active CQA users. Our study reveals that struggling users want to participate in their community, but often do not possess the proper skills or attention to detail that are necessary to make valuable contributions.

Currently, in Brainly and other CQA sites, only moderators judge user performance, and this gives them an unfairly heavy workload. We show that it is possible to detect struggling users without any human judgment with moderate accuracy. However, detecting struggling users without human judgment may come too late, as many users leave the community if they are dissatisfied with their respective performances. Our framework shows that it is more accurate and effective to detect struggling users in their early stage with initial community feedback. Furthermore, using early community feedback can significantly reduce a moderator's workload.

Understanding struggling users' behavior can help us design CQA sites that better help these users. This applies to general CQA as well as educational CQA. However, detecting early-stage struggling users is particularly important in the realm of education since educators can effectively intervene and assist if they know which students are struggling. Detecting struggling users in their early stage ensures that we have enough resources and time to intervene [14]. Although the work in this paper is limited to educational CQA, the framework – including feature extraction, classifier, and evaluation – could apply to other general and topical CQA sites.

In future work, we hope to not only detect struggling users, but also to understand the more specific reasons behind their difficulties. At the moment, the CQA system still needs some input from its moderators, and automatic feedback remains the ultimate goal. To achieve automatic feedback, we might need a more complex taxonomy to analyze user-generated content. Furthermore, finding struggling users is also an important task in other domains such as search or information seeking. If we can detect struggling users in their early stage, suitable action could be taken to help them, including early intervention or content recommendation. The findings from this study give us an approach to detect such users.

9. ACKNOWLEDGEMENTS

The work reported here is in part funded by the US Institute of Museum and Library Services (IMLS) National Leadership Grant #LG-81-16-0025. A portion of this work was possible due to funds and data access provided by Brainly.

10. REFERENCES

[1] L. A. Adamic, J. Zhang, E. Bakshy, and M. S. Ackerman. Knowledge sharing and yahoo answers: Everyone knows something. In *WWW*, pages 665–674, 2008.

[2] C. Aritajati and N. H. Narayanan. Facilitating students' collaboration and learning in a question and answer system. In *CSCW Companion*, pages 101–106, 2013.

[3] M. Berlingerio, D. Koutra, T. Eliassi-Rad, and C. Faloutsos. Network similarity via multiple social theories. In *ASONAM*, pages 1439–1440, 2013.

[4] C. M. Bishop. *Pattern Recognition and Machine Learning (Information Science and Statistics)*. Springer, 2006.

[5] N. V. Chawla. Data mining for imbalanced datasets: An overview. In *The Data Mining and Knowledge Discovery Handbook*, pages 853–867. Springer, 2005.

[6] J. Cheng, C. Danescu-Niculescu-Mizil, and J. Leskovec. Antisocial behavior in online discussion communities. In *ICWSM*, pages 140–149, 2015.

[7] E. Choi, M. Borkowski, J. Zakoian, K. Sagan, K. Scholla, C. Ponti, M. Labedz, and M. Bielski. Utilizing content moderators to investigate critical factors for assessing the quality of answers on brainly, social learning Q&A platform for students: a pilot study. In *ASIST*, pages 69:1–69:4, 2015.

[8] S. Dumais, R. Jeffries, D. M. Russell, D. Tang, and J. Teevan. Understanding user behavior through log data and analysis. In *Ways of Knowing in HCI*, pages 349–372. Springer New York, 2014.

[9] W. Gong, E.-P. Lim, and F. Zhu. Characterizing silent users in social media communities. In *ICWSM*, pages 140–149, 2015.

[10] A. Goyal, F. Bonchi, L. V. S. Lakshmanan, and S. Venkatasubramanian. On minimizing budget and time in influence propagation over social networks. *Social Netw. Analys. Mining*, 3(2):179–192, 2013.

[11] H. J. Jung and M. Lease. Modeling temporal crowd work quality with limited supervision. In *HCOMP*, pages 83–91, 2015.

[12] J. P. Kincaid, R. P. Fishburne, R. L. Rogers, and B. S. Chissom. Derivation of New Readability Formulas (Automated Readability Index, Fog Count and Flesch Reading Ease Formula) for Navy Enlisted Personnel. Technical report, Naval Air Station Memphis, 1975.

[13] J. Kiseleva, K. Williams, J. Jiang, A. Hassan Awadallah, A. C. Crook, I. Zitouni, and T. Anastasakos. Understanding user satisfaction with intelligent assistants. In *CHIIR*, pages 121–130, 2016.

[14] H. Lakkaraju, E. Aguiar, C. Shan, D. Miller, N. Bhanpuri, R. Ghani, and K. L. Addison. A machine learning framework to identify students at risk of adverse academic outcomes. In *KDD*, pages 1909–1918, 2015.

[15] L. T. Le, T. Eliassi-Rad, and H. Tong. MET: A fast algorithm for minimizing propagation in large graphs with small eigen-gaps. In *SDM*, pages 694–702, 2015.

[16] L. T. Le and C. Shah. Retrieving rising stars in focused community question-answering. In *ACIIDS*, pages 25–36, 2016.

[17] L. T. Le, C. Shah, and E. Choi. Evaluating the quality of educational answers in community question-answering. In *JCDL*, pages 25–36, 2016.

[18] A. Mao, E. Kamar, and E. Horvitz. Why stop now? predicting worker engagement in online crowdsourcing. In *HCOMP*, pages 103–111, 2013.

[19] B. Ngonmang, E. Viennet, and M. Tchuente. Churn prediction in a real online social network using local community analysis. In *ASONAM*, pages 282–288, 2012.

[20] H. L. O'Brien, L. Freund, and R. Kopak. Investigating the role of user engagement in digital reading environments. In *CHIIR*, pages 71–80, 2016.

[21] R. J. Oentaryo, E.-P. Lim, D. Lo, F. Zhu, and P. K. Prasetyo. Collective churn prediction in social network. In *ASONAM*, pages 210–214, 2012.

[22] A. Pal, S. Chang, and J. A. Konstan. Evolution of experts in question answering communities. In *ICWSM*, pages 274–281, 2012.

[23] D. Pelleg, E. Yom-Tov, and Y. Maarek. Can you believe an anonymous contributor? on truthfulness in yahoo! answers. In *SOCIALCOM-PASSAT*, pages 411–420, 2012.

[24] J. Preece, B. Nonnecke, and D. Andrews. The top five reasons for lurking: improving community experiences for everyone. *Computers in Human Behavior*, 20(2):201 – 223, 2004.

[25] Y. Richter, E. Yom-Tov, and N. Slonim. Predicting customer churn in mobile networks through analysis of social groups. In *SDM*, pages 732–741, 2010.

[26] C. Shah and J. Pomerantz. Evaluating and predicting answer quality in community qa. In *SIGIR*, pages 411–418, 2010.

[27] C. Shah, M. Radford, L. Connaway, E. Choi, and V. Kitzie. How much change do you get from 40$? analyzing and addressing failed questions on social Q&A. In *ASIST*, pages 1–10, 2012.

[28] I. Srba and M. Bielikova. Askalot: Community question answering as a means for knowledge sharing in an educational organization. In *CSCW Companion*, pages 179–182, 2015.

[29] R. P. M. L. Sun, L. Understanding lurkers in online communities: a literature review. *Computers in Human Behavior*, 38:110–117, 2014.

[30] J. Surowiecki. *The Wisdom of Crowds*. Anchor, 2005.

[31] C. H. Tan, E. Agichtein, P. Ipeirotis, and E. Gabrilovich. Trust, but verify: Predicting contribution quality for knowledge base construction and curation. In *WSDM*, pages 553–562, 2014.

[32] J. Teevan, M. R. Morris, and K. Panovich. Factors affecting response quantity, quality, and speed for questions asked via social network status messages. In *ICWSM*, pages 600–603, 2011.

[33] G. Wang, K. Gill, M. Mohanlal, H. Zheng, and B. Y. Zhao. Wisdom in the social crowd: An analysis of quora. In *WWW*, pages 1341–1352, 2013.

[34] R. W. White, M. Richardson, and Y. Liu. Effects of community size and contact rate in synchronous social Q&A. In *CHI*, pages 2837–2846, 2011.

Making Sense of Conflicting Science Information: Exploring Bias in the Search Engine Result Page

Alamir Novin
University of British Columbia
1961 East Mall, Vancouver, BC, Canada
alamir.novin@ubc.ca

Eric Meyers
University of British Columbia
1961 East Mall, Vancouver, BC, Canada
eric.meyers@ubc.ca

ABSTRACT

Currently, there is widespread media coverage about the problems with 'fake news' that appears in social media, but the effects of biased information that appears in search engine results is also increasing. The authors argue that the search engine results page (SERP) exposes three important types of bias: source bias, algorithmic bias, and cognitive bias. To explore the relationship between these three types of bias, we conducted a mixed methods study with sixty participants (plus fourteen in a pilot to make a total of seventy-four participants). Within a library setting, participants were provided with mock search engine pages that presented order-controlled sources on a science controversy. Participants were then asked to rank the sources' usefulness and then summarize the controversy. We found that participants ranked the usefulness of sources depending on its presentation within a SERP. In turn, this also influenced how the participants summarized the topic. We attribute the differences in the participants' writings to the cognitive biases that affect a user's judgment when selecting sources on a SERP. We identify four main cognitive biases that a SERP can evoke in students: Priming, Anchoring, Framing, and the Availability Heuristic. While policing information quality is a quixotic task, changes can be made to both SERPs and a user's decision-making when selecting sources. As bias emerges both on the system side and the user side of search, we suggest a two-fold solution is required to address these challenges.

1. INTRODUCTION

Did Facebook's 'fake news' affect policy? Did Google's results influence the Brexit vote? Recent scholarship indicates that our opinions can be influenced by the manner in which news aggregators and search interfaces present information on everyday topics, from politics to fashion to science [1]–[3]. Information presentation likely affects the quality of thinking and knowledge creation, particularly when study respondents demonstrate and report relying heavily on the authority of search engines [3], [4].

According to the National Science Board, the public's primary form of science education is via the medium of search engines [5]. However, while the Internet increases the public's access to scientific information, it also increases access to misinformation [5]. Therefore, it is worth questioning the level of critical thinking that people apply when selecting sources on a search engine results page (SERP) [6], [7]. In this study, we pose the question: How do search engine results influence the way students conceptualize a science topic about which they have little prior knowledge?

CHIIR '17, March 07 - 11, 2017, Oslo, Norway

ACM 978-1-4503-4677-1/17/03…$15.00
DOI: http://dx.doi.org/10.1145/3020165.3020185

While search engines appear to fulfill a public good, as they provide a seemingly "free" service to users of the Internet, they are neither "objective" nor are they disinterested in what the searcher selects. For example, Google's search engine algorithm presents a hierarchical list of what is deemed to be the most important sources. However, the list itself may be limited by the way search engines qualify relevance over other contextual factors [8], [9]. The presentation of a hierarchical list visually removes all intellectual relationships between each item in the list [10] and the algorithm behind Google's document ordering is ambiguous to even Google's search engine developers themselves [11]. Whether the top result on Google is there because it is the most relevant, useful, popular, current, or even the most hyperlinked is unknown to users. As a result, users remain unaware of the hidden biases in search engines [12].

We argue that search results are a fruitful venue for examining the intersection of several types of bias: the influence of search engine design (algorithmic bias); the influence of document design and the persuasive nature of content organization (source bias), and the way visual and contextual cues affect human thinking (cognitive bias). In addition, we theorize that a user's unawareness of algorithmic bias increases their susceptibility to cognitive bias, which increases the influence that source bias may have.

Using a *population-based survey experiment* [13] with sixty participants, this study explored the intersectional nature of cognitive bias by asking post-secondary students to use and rank alternative perspectives in an order-controlled mock SERP. We found that students' understanding of a topic, as expressed in their written summaries, depended on how information was presented in a SERP. In a post-hoc analysis, the authors identify four possible types of cognitive biases that influenced student learning: Priming, Anchoring, Framing, and the Availability Heuristic. For students who are relying on search engines as a learning intervention, the search system must present diversity and a user must understand how to select amongst multiple perspectives to minimize the influence of intersecting biases.

2. THEORETICAL FRAMEWORK

2.1 Information, Bias, and the Public

It has been almost a hundred years since the often-called "Lippmann-Dewey debate" [14]–[17] covered the issue of how the public can detangle the bias in sources of information and the biases in the structures of institutions. While Walter Lippmann argued for the values of expertise that could limit the biases of public opinion by scientifically measuring the objective elements in information and creating a "system of records" [17], John

Dewey suggested that democratic processes would remove those biases when the public has greater means to participate via dialogue [16]. Lippmann recognized the bias that exists in media sources, but made an exception for "the exact sciences" since he felt science's quest for objectivity minimized bias [17]. Scholars argue that a similar belief in the objectivity of the sciences still thrives today amongst the public and many academics [18]–[22]. However, Dewey was critical about the management of multiple perspectives found in public discourse [16]. Democracy is an ongoing practice and the management of information can be biased by ideological forces and scientific information is not any different [16]. Other scholars have also taken Dewey's position, arguing that scientific sources can be tainted by the personal agendas of fringe scientists, non-scientific agenda-building by the media, and corporate science organizations that seek monetary gains at the expense of scientific accuracy [19], [23]–[28]. Most notably, Bowker and Star found Dewey's criticisms of information management in the biases of classification systems on diseases and race [29].

While the Lippmann-Dewey debate was focused on traditional media, we seek to update this conversation for the 21st Century. The Internet provides greater access to the "system of records" Lippmann advocated for [14], but it also brought the bias that appears in many blogs and news websites we might consider source bias [30], [31]. While Dewey defended the importance of dialogue in the public, a SERP may be at risk of promoting the most popular ideas in a community over pluralism. He was also concerned with the management of public information, which we can relate to the algorithmic bias that appears in a search engine. There is a common misconception that search engines are objective, but humans may code their biases into the algorithms [30], [31],[32]. Specifically, the authors are concerned with how the algorithm prioritizes which document genres to present on an interface and in which document order.

If this research can contribute to the unresolved Lippmann-Dewey debate, it would add that our individual parsing techniques for searching and retrieving information also contributes a cognitive bias. Cognitive biases occur when the mental operations that mediate an individual's judgment are misapplied [33], [34]. The errors in judgment are often motivated by an individual's wish to minimize cognitive effort [35]. For example, individuals researching a topic often only seek information that confirms their bias while disregarding information that challenges it [36]. Peter C. Wason found students were more prone to exhibiting cognitive biases with abstract problem-tasks than tasks with greater context [37]. Familiarity with the problem-task also plays a role [35]. A SERP provides more familiarity than Wason's selection task to users, but without enough context for users to understand the relationship between different sources. Therefore, we question whether this lack of context in Google's SERP influences the deductive reasoning of students selecting amongst sources of information.

2.2 Prior Work on Search Engine Results

People value highly ranked search results on a SERP [38]–[41] over lower ranking results [1] and often do not look below the third result [42]. Despite the high value placed on the top results, there are no standard qualifiers to identify 'relevant' information [43]. Raya Fidel notes that information retrieval models often falsely assume that agents behave rationally, wanting all the "relevant" documents and none of the "irrelevant" ones [42]. To counter this assumption, Fidel highlights research that shows only some documents may be used by agents conducting searches instead of all the relevant ones [42]. She also brings attention to research that finds irrelevant documents may also be seen as useful [42]. If only *some* documents are selected by an agent, then how does the agent select which documents to use? Studies suggest that people will rely on their prior knowledge and select documents that confirm their biases [44], [45]. Currently, students often trust lists produced by search algorithms over their own analytical skills [4]. However, users themselves are not sure how a SERPs ranking system works [12], just like most Google developers [46]. This is concerning because people are more vulnerable to bias when they are unaware of how it might influence them [35], [47], [48]. For example, even the order in which search results are listed can influence our opinions and decisions [1]–[3]. Cognitive biases become especially troublesome in search queries dealing with controversial science topics where conflicting information may be retrieved [49], whereby non-experts either ignore or reinterpret information that conflicts with their queries' assumptions [50]. Salmerón, Kammerer, and García-Carrión observed that a SERP's order of conflicting sources on a scientific topic affected a users' judgement of its relevancy, but that the usage of the information was dependent on their level of prior-knowledge of the scientific topic [51]. Furthermore, they conclude that their finding demonstrates the importance of researching not only how users search for information, but also how they use it too [51].

Scholars, notably Nick Belkin, have expounded on this concept of *usefulness* as a more appropriate indicator than relevance [1], [52], [53]. Usefulness refers to whether a document is perceived as important for the completion of a task and whether it was used to achieve an outcome [54]. Similarly, Donald O. Case argues that over the last sixty-years our measures for understanding information use have increased, but more research should consider the final outcomes [55]. This type of research is often difficult to carry out due to limitations on measuring the influence that one source of information has on a final outcome [56].

To expand on the arguments by Case on the influence information has on an outcome, it is worth questioning how a SERP itself influences a user's perception of usefulness. While Google is often credited for its minimalist SERP interface [57], it does not mean that less subtle influences do not exist. For a decade now, Google's goal during its "Evolution of Search" is to disperse information with minimal effort from their users [58], but as the next section shows, cognitive biases also work best when cognitive effort is minimized [35]. The authors theorize that a user's unawareness of algorithmic biases will increase their chances of exhibiting cognitive bias, which also raises the influence that a source bias may have.

2.3 Cognitive Bias: Your Brain on SERP

To understand the role of bias in constructing meaning from search engines, we draw on research in cognitive science, particularly in judgment and decision making. Cognitive biases and heuristics affect the way people perceive and process new information about a topic – particularly when the learner has to process conflicting or non-intuitive information [59]. Some scholars identify as many as 53 different kinds of cognitive biases that contribute to difficulties in inferential thinking [60] (see also [35] for a survey of the literature). However, research groups found only *some* of the main cognitive biases are experimentally reproducible [61]. Instead of testing for all 53 biases, the authors experimented with two document variables (document order and document genre) and its effect on the participants' psychological construct on a topic. We then matched them with the cognitive biases that provided the best explanation for our observations. In our post-hoc analysis, we identified four cognitive biases that occur in a loosely chronological order when a user reads a SERP [Figure 1]: From a user's initial viewing of a SERP, whereby 1) *Priming* effects occur; to reading the top result on a SERP that evokes 2) *Anchoring*; to the next few SERP results that may cause 3) *Framing*; and then finally the engagement or avoidance of other sources dependent on 4) the *Availability Heuristic.*

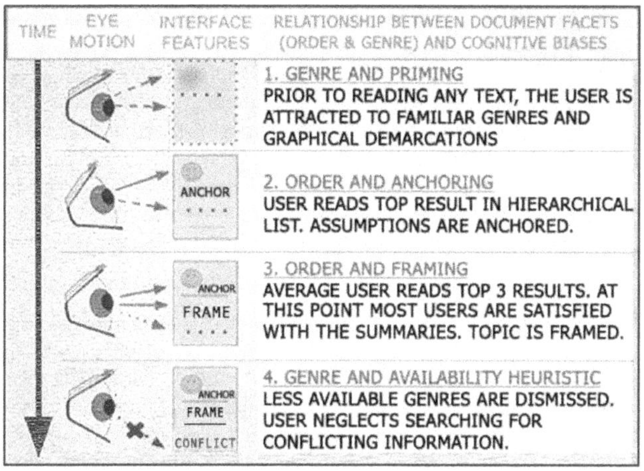

Figure 1 The relationship between time, eye motion, the interface, document facets, and their effects on cognitive bias.

2.3.1 Priming effects

A priming effect in user interfaces occurs when the repeated use of a layout automatically directs our eyes to information [62]. This creates a cognitive bias whereby we are influenced by certain cues [63]. Search engines will very frequently show Wikipedia results because the expectation by users is that it will assist users with quickly solving queries [64], [65]. Similarly, scholars have observed that Google's algorithm is biased towards mainstream information that users will find familiar [66]–[71]. While efficient, users may skip over unfamiliar document genres. For example, a parent trying to find a link between vaccines and autism may skip a source to a health journal debunking the link due to its visual cues, such as the parent's prior experience with journals behind pay-walls or incomprehensible scientific jargon.

2.3.2 Anchoring Effects

Anchoring occurs when we are biased towards the first value we perceive in a set of data [59]. The first result in a SERP can affect the user's impression of the importance of the next result [72]. For example, if the first result in a SERP presents a medical condition as severe, it will affect the participants impression of its overall severity even when the other search results downplay the severity [72]. Even though users are unaware of the relationship between results [12], the top result can affect the level of critical thinking that is applied to all other search results that follow.

2.3.3 Framing Effect

The framing effect is a cognitive bias that occurs when peoples' choices are influenced by the manner information is presented [73]. Framing is not about unavailable information, but about whether the presentation makes us care about competing views and how [74]. The visualization of information can create a narrative that runs parallel to the framing studies in rhetorical political messaging [75]. One form of visualization in a SERP is the document genre (e.g., blog, journal article, news report, encyclopedia, etc.). The document genre of a source's text works as a framing device [76]. A SERP provides multiple document genres for a user with minimal ordering.

2.3.4 Availability Heuristic

An availability heuristic bias occurs when a person's estimate is influenced by the ease of a person's access to information over subsequent information [59]. For example, when people scan a list they place greater attention on the first few results — those which are easiest to access [59]. Similarly, *document ordering* effects are observable after the first five results [77]. When dealing with a controversial topic, non-experts may have difficulty determining which sources of information are authoritative when popular, but questionable, information is presented first. Furthermore, the effort to "optimize" search results can affect the presentation order of politically-charged topics.

In summary, these constructs represent kinds of cognitive short cuts, techniques that we employ, either consciously or not, to ease our cognitive load when resolving information problems. These factors contribute to judgment errors in information seeking, but can also affect the extent to which new information leads to the development or revision of conceptual structures.

3. Methods

3.1 Methodological Framework

Current research in information search and retrieval is interested in studying more complete models of information use, from the interactions users have with systems [8], the usefulness of its information [54], its influences [55], and the outcome of the retrieval [78]. Researching these factors requires tailoring the work task to the information environment and participants [78]. Pia Borlund provides the following example, which applies to our study: "if the evaluation takes place by involvement of university students then the simulated work task situation should be to describe a situation they can relate to, and report on how the situation was simulated" [78]. In addition, to create such a situation, the task should be piloted and the final report should explain how the situation was simulated [78]. Thus, this study conducted a population-based survey experiment, whereby participants are randomly assigned to an experiment that takes place outside of a lab and within the population itself [13]. Diana C. Mutz argues the main advantage of choosing this method is that "theories can be tested on samples that are representative of the populations to which they are said to apply" [13]. Therefore, we chose the common area of a university library to study whether cognitive bias theories influence the information search and retrieval processes of students researching.

To measure the usefulness of information a quantitative and qualitative approach should be applied [55]. Mixed methods can increase the responsiveness of participants in an otherwise complex research activity that is asking for a significant amount of effort [79]. Creswell identifies this application of a mixed-methods approach as an Explanatory Sequential Design, whereby a quantitative data collection and analysis is used to inform the mixing of a qualitative data collection and analysis [80]. This mixed methods design may be best suited to draw inferences to explain the observed data.

To investigate user interactions with cognitive biases when selecting different perspectives on a science controversy, it is important to choose a topic for the SERP that is easy to grasp and that participants have little prior knowledge of or opinions about.

One subject that meets this criteria is biofuels [81]–[86]. Biofuels are organic matter, which are used as an alternative to unrenewable fuels. They are generally viewed positively due to their renewable nature and both the USA and Canada invest billions of dollars in developing the technology [87]. One scientific controversy with biofuels is known as the "food vs. fuel" debate. We found that querying for "Biofuels" would consistently lead to a Google SERP page that explicitly mentioned the controversy. However, we also found the Biofuel Wikipedia page would also consistently appear near the top of the SERP. Given Wikipedia's reputation this may be a pragmatic choice, but a closer investigation of Wikipedia's biofuel page reveals that the issues with biofuels are relegated to a hyperlink near the latter half of the Wikipedia page. Users would have to click through it to access a second Wikipedia page entitled "Issues with Biofuels." Google's algorithm did not include the second Wikipedia page in their SERP unless we specifically queried for biofuels issues. The study experimented with including sources that raised these issues with biofuels in different document genres and document orders in a mock-SERP [Figure 2].

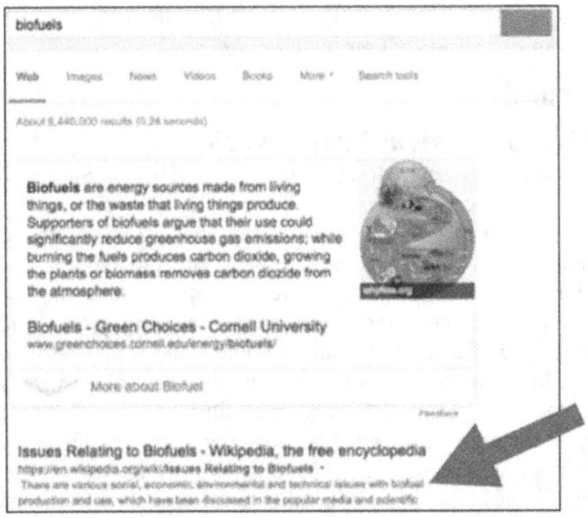

Figure 2 [Screen-capture] The original SERP query for "biofuels" did not show the second result: "Issues Relating to Biofuels" (arrow). We included it in the mock-SERP's HTML.

In a similar study to our own, Salmerón et al., [51] found that document-order affected how students perceived the relevancy of conflicting information on a science topic in a SERP. Interestingly, when students were deciding whether the website should be bookmarked their judgement of its relevance changed. However, as Salmerón et al., [51] acknowledge, this still does not determine whether these new judgements will affect how the information will be *used* by the student in a task. In this study, by analyzing the students' search result evaluations before and after reading the webpages we can first compare this direct change in judgement. Therefore, to compare the change in judgement to the actual usage of information we asked participants to use any of the sources for a final write-up and then analyzed which sources were used. For example, when a student first visits a SERP on biofuels with conflicting results they might judge that a website promoting corn biofuels is more relevant than a website that focuses on the "food-vs-fuel" debate. However, after reading larger excerpts of both websites they may change their mind about the relevancy because they might judge that the "food-vs-fuel" website supports their criticisms of corn biofuels well. This change in judgement is important, but it still does not determine which websites will be *used* by the student. Therefore, we asked participants for a final write-up summarizing the topic to see which websites are used and how the controversial biofuel information is acknowledged.

Beyond simply acknowledging controversial information, we were interested in the *reconciliation of conflicting information.* We define *conflicting* information as sources that counterpoint or negate an explicit or implicit assumption in a query (i.e., it provides the "other side" of the story). Therefore, in the mock-SERP we included a *conflicting* source of information on the topic of corn biofuels—"Advanced Biofuels." By definition, Advanced Biofuels aim to minimize the "Food vs. Fuel" concerns by deriving fuel from non-food biological-sources, such as algae. In summary, our SERP held conflicting narratives that contextualized the topic of the advantages of plant biofuels. The first narrative acknowledged the controversy that 1) biofuels can drive up the price of food. The second narrative conflicted with the first, proposing that 2) algae biofuels resolve the "food vs. fuel" debate and thus may be the more advanced biofuel.

3.2 Procedure

Prior to the actual experiment, a pilot test was conducted. The pilot recruited fourteen participants through convenience sampling to test the experiment's mock-SERP. Each participant was provided with a laptop where the mock-SERP appeared as a Google webpage. They would interact with the mock-SERP webpage by reading (or scrolling) through the results and clicking on the ones that they found useful. For the pilot, participants were asked to "think out-loud" as they scored the usefulness of the six search results. Participants in the pilot were also interviewed to understand why they scored certain articles as more or less useful. Next, they were asked to summarize the topic. Finally, the participants were asked whether any part of the experiment required clarification. The pilot informed our assumptions and allowed us to tweak our mock-SERP. From the pilot study, two main findings informed the eventual *population-based survey experiment*: 1) Participants rely heavily on top search results and they 2) overlook comprehensive discussions (i.e., multiple perspectives). The survey-experiment was then tweaked to focus its measure on how document order and document genre influenced the participants' interaction with the SERP.

For the population-based survey experiment, two laptops were setup on a table in the common area of a university library with a sign calling for participation. As the library requested, students were not approached unless they inquired about our sign. Sixty students were recruited for this study. Their age range was 18-34, gender distribution was 45% female and 55% male, and 91% of participants had little to no knowledge of the topic prior to their participation. Despite their little knowledge on the topic, participants were also asked if they could express any personal opinions on biofuels and none mentioned any strong sentiments about the topic. When asked to list any prior knowledge on the topic of biofuels only one participant mentioned that they were aware of biofuels other than corn.

The experiment was conducted in four stages that paralleled the pilot. In Stage 1, participants were provided a laptop with the same mock-Google SERP page. Participants were asked to read the SERP and score each search result (six in total) based on their usefulness. Unlike the pilot, this was not a think-out-loud process – to protect the anonymity of the participants. The result with conflicting information (i.e., on algae biofuels) appeared in either a different document genre or in a different document order. There were three different possible document orders for the SERP, whereby the conflicting information either appeared at the 1) top (first result), 2) middle (third result), or 3) bottom (last result) of the search page. Via a double-blind procedure, a computer randomly assigned students to one of these different SERP arrangements. Students were not instructed to read from top to bottom. In Stage 2, all the students wrote their own summary of the scientific topic as though it were intended to be read by a colleague. In Stage 3, students revisited the SERP's summaries for each of the search results, but read longer abstracts for each page, extended from 25 words to 150 words. In Stage 4, participants were then re-shown their prior summary and asked if there was any information they wished to add to their prior summaries. Our survey system allowed us to see the changes made in both the usefulness scores and the summary of results.

The data analysis on document genre and document order was conducted in the following manner:

3.2.1 Method for Data Analysis on Document Genre and Document Order:

Data Analysis on Document Genre:

Scoring of Sources: Participants were presented with the following document genres: Scholarly articles, News articles, Wikipedia (as a familiar source) and non-familiar sources that summarize biofuels. They were then asked to first score the usefulness of the results in a SERP. *Prior* to reading longer excerpts of the articles, students were then asked to summarize the SERP using only the information they recalled.

Textual-Analysis of Write-Up: We conducted a textual analysis of participant responses to see how the document genre affected the participants' write-ups. The two narratives on biofuels were that 1) corn biofuels can drive up the price of food and 2) algae can be a more sustainable alternative in the future. Both narratives existed in the SERP at the same time, but different groups of participants were presented with the second narrative in different document genres. We then used an automated textual analysis tool, provided by FluidSurveys, to highlight the word frequencies for each group of participants. We were interested in whether the write-up of participants used a narrative that correlated with the document genres of the information that was presented.

Data Analysis on Document Order:

Textual-Analysis of Write-Up: After students were asked to summarize the topic of biofuels, a textual analysis identified whether they mentioned a controversy. We compared whether the conflicting information at the top of a SERP is correlated with whether participants mention the controversy by using a chi-square test for independence. The hypothesis is that conflicting information at the top of a SERP is correlated with whether a controversy is mentioned. The null hypothesis is that there is no correlation.

Scoring of Sources: We presented participants with a source that was challenging because it was both scientific in language and appeared at the bottom of the SERP. Theoretically, for its usefulness to be recognized users had to re-adjust their assumptions that were implicitly accumulated from prior sources. To test this, after their initial scoring we asked participants to read longer excerpts of the sources on a SERP. We then asked the participants to score the usefulness of these results as well.

4. FINDINGS

Document Genre Effects on Scoring:

When participants were asked to score the usefulness of the results in a SERP, familiarity with Wikipedia was an influencer because it was consistently scored as more useful than others [Figure 3]. As Participant 77 explained, they used "the perceived neutrality of Wikipedia links as a basis" for such assignments. As we will expand on in our discussion, this perspective of Wikipedia is generally reasonable, but the issue is that Wikipedia was not neutral in its presentation of the topic of biofuels.

However, when the source was a scholarly article on biofuels (i.e., with an academic document genre) and was presented at the top of the SERP, the majority of participants skipped it. As Participant 3 explained: "I was hit with the scientific jargon too immediately [...] all the biofuel information became too jarring so I moved on to the other sources." When the participant was questioned if they felt the need to return to the source, they responded that the other sources provided enough information for them not to feel the need to do so. The preference for Wikipedia over the academic article may indicate priming effects are causing cognitive bias.

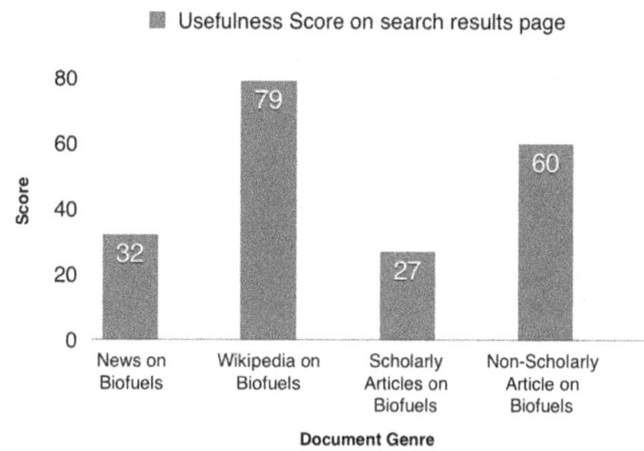

Figure 3 Scores on usefulness of Wikipedia article on "Biofuels" in comparison to other sources (reported in percentages).

Textual-Analysis of Document Genre Effects on Write-Up:

A textual analysis of participant responses found that if sources on corn biofuels and its controversies were placed alongside a source on algae biofuels that was in an academic-genre, then students would focus their write-ups mostly on the food controversy. Using an automated textual analysis for word frequency, the three key terms "food price", "production", and "land" were mentioned frequently. However, if the sources on corn biofuels and its controversies was placed alongside sources on algae biofuels that had a more common document genre, students would shift their focus on how scientists were addressing the food controversy. In this case, the key terms "new" "generation", "focus", and the perspective of "scientists" were mentioned most frequently.

For example, participants who were provided the algae biofuels alongside the food controversy would include statements, such as: *"Scientists are becoming aware of the food issues and have come up with other ways to obtain biofuels. There are 4 'generations' of biofuels each with different types of materials used. Algae seems to be a promising source of biofuels."* (Participant 2). These types of statements were less likely to appear when the sources on biofuel algae was in an academic document genre. In addition, we found the answers to be more comprehensive because participants would contextualize their summary of biofuels by first 1) explaining what biofuels are, then 2) explaining the controversy of biofuels that are derived from corn, and finally 3) explaining the potential of algae biofuels. Whereas groups who had the algae sources appear at the bottom of the SERP would not include this third component in their summary. As we will explain in the Discussions section the differences in contextual narratives between the two groups may indicate framing effects are causing cognitive bias.

Textual-Analysis of Document Order Effects on Write-Up:

We found that the higher an article on the biofuel controversy was presented to participants, the more likely they were to mention the biofuel controversies in their write-up. When the top result on a SERP was a source that explicitly mentioned the biofuel controversy, 73% of the participants mentioned the controversy in their write-ups. However, if the same source was elsewhere inthe SERP, only 41% of students would mention the controversy, respectively. For example, when Participant 42 had the controversy mentioned at the top they wrote: "*Biofuels are basically fuels that comes from starch based plants such as corn or soy. However, because of this it takes up farmland which raises food prices. This can be really devastating to poor countries/those in poverty because they cannot afford the food.*" In contrast, most participants who did not have the controversy mentioned at the top of the SERP did not mention the controversy.

A Pearson chi-square test was performed to analyze whether a topic's position on the results list was related to students mentioning the topic in their explanations. A relationship was found between whether a group had a controversial topic anchored at the top of a SERP and the number of participants that mention the controversy in their write up, X2 (1, N = 42) = 4.1067, p =0.043. The association between rows (groups) and columns (outcomes) is statistically significant [Table 1].

When the controversial source appeared at the top of the search results, students were more likely to incorporate this information in their written responses, as opposed to the controversial information appearing lower in the search results page. As we will explain in the Discussions section the differences between the two groups may indicate anchoring effects are causing cognitive bias.

Table 1 Chi square comparison of write-ups between group with anchored results vs. groups without.

	Number of participants that mention controversy in their write-up	Number of participants that do not mention controversy in their write-up	Total
Group with Controversy Anchored at top	11	4	15
Groups without Controversy Anchored at top	11	16	27
Total	22	20	42

Document Order Effects on Scoring:

We presented participants with a source with an academic document genre that was challenging because it was scientific in language and low-ranking on the SERP. When users were presented with the source on the SERP the users did not view the information as useful and gave it a very low score [Figure 4]. However, when participants were asked to read a large excerpt of the same result, its usefulness received a much higher score [Figure 4]. As we will explain in the Discussions section this increase in score may be due to a participant's initial reluctance to apply cognitive effort on a scholarly source at the bottom of a SERP and the availability-heuristic may be causing a cognitive bias.

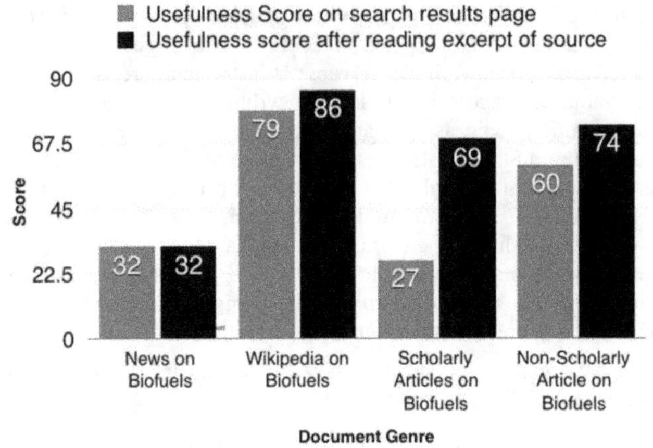

Figure 4 Comparison between score of SERP results before and after reading excerpts of the sources.

5. DISCUSSION

The Lippmann-Dewey debate addressed the entanglement between public information, biased opinions in media, and democracy. As mentioned, the Internet is the machine that has brought us both the access to the system of records Lippmann advocated for to combat source bias (i.e., bias in the sources provided by a search engine) and the public's capability to dispute those records as Dewey advocated for in order to minimize algorithmic bias (i.e., the search engine's management of sources). This research can contribute to the unresolved Lippmann-Dewey debate by adding that our individual parsing techniques for searching and retrieving information contains cognitive biases in itself.

While prior studies mostly observed confirmation-bias in a user's search, we were interested in which cognitive biases emerge when a user has little prior knowledge of a controversy and thus little knowledge to "confirm"). We identified four cognitive biases that can emerge from how a SERP manages document genres and the document order. We list the cognitive biases in the loosely chronological order that they occur, from a user's initial viewing of a SERP, whereby 1) Priming effects occur; to reading the top result on a SERP that evokes 2) Anchoring; to the next few SERP results that may cause 3) Framing; and then finally the engagement or avoidance of other sources dependent on the 4) Availability Heuristic [Figure 1]. In response, we suggest four strategies users can use to identify and contextualize the biases.

5.1 Priming:

Immediately upon visiting a SERP, priming can occur, whereby users are visually drawn to familiar features on a SERP. Priming features include Google presenting the top result in a demarcated box accompanied by a thumbnail illustration of a biofuel cycle [Figure 2]. Prior research using eye-tracking has found that users will often be drawn to this area of a SERP [88]. Users will also be drawn to images before even reading any information [88]. Features such as the "I'm Feeling Lucky" button and Google's "Answer Box" (i.e., when the top result on Google provides an answer so that users do not need to leave the SERP) provide aesthetically pleasing answers when compared to the other low ranking sources. This becomes problematic when the aesthetically pleasing answer singles out a perspective over equally valuable perspectives. Similarly, users are also automatically drawn to the familiarity of Wikipedia. Our study found that users consistently rate Wikipedia as highly useful [Figure 3]. On the other hand, we observed that a source with an unfamiliar document genre for non-experts that is positioned at the top would receive an opposite reaction [Figure 3]. When a SERP presents an academic journal with little context at the top, users may skip the entry, instead choosing sources that do provide responses with a familiar genre for non-experts. This is problematic because participants skipped sources based on their document genre that were otherwise useful. It was only after participants were asked to engage with the unfamiliar document genre by actively reading through the content that the users began to rank the usefulness of the source higher [Figure 4].

In response, the authors suggest that SERPs can visually identify conflicting information more explicitly by drawing a user's attention to more perspectives on a topic. One strategy users can use to mitigate cognitive bias is to compensate for this priming effect by actively searching for information that conflicts, counter-points, or even contradicts search results. This approach is grounded in Karl Popper's arguments for how researchers should falsify their hypotheses [89]. If we can draw a parallel between a user searching a query and how scientists should research a hypothesis, then a pragmatic implementation would be that users should question their own query to consider whether any implicit biases exist – with the goal of finding results that provide the colloquial 'other side of a story.'

5.2 Anchoring

Generally, hierarchical lists emphasize the top result over other results [90]. This is problematic with science controversies where the top result might emphasize a particular view in a debate over equally valuable perspectives. This was the case with the SERP page on biofuels, whereby users placed a high level of trust in the top result. In our study, we found that when the top SERP result focused heavily on corn biofuels, users would fail to mention its controversial aspects. Similarly, the algae biofuel research that aims to address the controversy in their write-ups was also rarely mentioned. This suggests that students trusted the top result to give the general idea of what biofuels were and neglected adjusting this perspective for any conflicting sources. These ordering effects are due to Google presenting results in a hierarchical list, which causes students to access information in a top-down manner. In addition, the relationship between the first and every subsequent result is not made clear to users. The design forces users to apply an anchor-and-adjusting heuristic iteratively with information until they are satisfied with the answer. One method users can employ to minimize the effect of anchoring is to maintain standards for the document genre of information they will retrieve, while still investigating multiple sources. This method is parallel to how researchers should create a plan of how they will collect data before being influenced by the first few results or cherry-picking data [91], [92]. Similarly, users should set criteria for the type of sources that are sought and in which sequence sources will be retrieved (e.g., first retrieving Wikipedia articles, then moving on to academic sources, and then checking news media). By setting out to first investigate information by a sequence of document genres, users will break up the effects of document order. More importantly, they will maintain a path for retrieving information that will not be satisfied by the first few answers in a SERP.

5.3 Framing

SERPs may attribute conflicting results with irrelevant ones and rank them lower. However, this frames a debate by narrowing the multiple perspectives that can contextualize it. As our study found, the genre in which diverse sources of information in a SERP are presented will affect whether multiple perspectives are represented in a user's output. A document genre may make itself seem esoteric and not intended for a certain audience. However, by placing value on the task of acquiring multiple perspectives on a topic, we might transfer value on a document's alternative genre rather than avoid it.

Expanding the frames set around a debate is a difficult task. However, when users limit their scope of a topic to the top three results on a SERP [42], the variety of perspectives is narrowed. While Wikipedia has earned its reputation as a respectable source, that does not imply that it will always be the more comprehensive or least biased source. For example, during our research we found that querying for "Biofuels" would consistently lead to the Biofuel Wikipedia page appearing near the top of the SERP, but not to the Wikipedia page on the "issues" related to biofuels. Although humans naturally wish to minimize cognitive work, valuing the representation of multiple perspectives can cause a user to pause and reevaluate the strengths and weaknesses in their own query.

In addition, greater transparency is required in SERPs so that users can understand the relationships between multiple sources. By being able to examine the strength of these relationships (i.e., why certain sources appear next to each other in a list) users may be able to determine the parameters surrounding their query.

5.4 Availability Heuristic

Our human tendency to favor simple language and our ease of recall on the prior sources of a topic can cause useful sources to seem like anomalies. As our study found, a source that seems out of place for users will not be seen as useful [Figure 4]. It is only after users were asked to read a longer excerpt of the source, that its usefulness score increased. A challenge for SERPs is how to convey the usefulness of a resource that can re-adjust the assumptions that we implicitly accumulate from prior sources. While search engines are designed to demarcate quick and easy answers, they may inadvertently mask alternative perspectives that provide the correct context.

One way to broaden our scope of a topic is to first scan the landscape of debate before delving in depth into a topic. A quick scan of a SERP's page may increase our chance of not missing alternative perspectives. This suggested strategy becomes increasingly challenging when Google's designers have repeatedly claimed that its goal is to provide "seamless" single-source *answers* to complex queries [11], [46], [58]. Google's goal makes the reductionist assumption that underlying every human query is an essential truth waiting to be uncovered by an algorithm. This line of thought runs parallel with Lippmann's reductionist views on "public opinions" [17] and we therefore invoke Dewey's objections to reductionist views on "the public and its problems" [16]: Science controversies require various perspectives to be weighted and the source of the 'controversy' itself often involves external sociological or cultural actors. In addition, a *socio-cultural* perspective situates our learning in more common everyday scenarios [93].

Recently, scholars have expounded on the numerous benefits of collaborative searching, including its potential to provide multiple perspectives on controversial topics. A variety of online documents can be retrieved by individual students, but student collaboration can synthesize perspectives and make better inferences [94]. Whereas Internet search engine designs were based on idealized views that information searches are conducted in isolation [95], scholars are observing that the search process is rarely a solitary activity and is intertwined with the communication and collaboration that takes place in everyday life [96]–[100]. Collaborative sense-making can assist students with understanding complex science topics [101], [102]. The social engagement with controversial information is why collaborative searching shows some promise. While this area of research has not come up with an ideal method of conducting collaborative searching to minimize cognitive biases, we suggest searching with colleagues or sharing results may assist in the discovery of multiple perspectives on findings. Aside from the benefit of a wider range of useful results, future studies may investigate whether a wider range of search strategies employed by collaborators can minimize cognitive bias.

There are several important limitations to this work. First, the pilot and main study were conducted with a student population that may not represent the broader public. Second, the small number of participants in the pilot and main study (14 and 60 respectively), limit the power of the analysis. Although we chose biofuels because it was a topic that fit within our purpose and methodology, we acknowledge that biofuels may not be motivating as a search and learning topic for all individuals. Third, none of our suggested solutions have been tested since they were not part of our initial study design. Fourth, to control for the diversity in website interfaces, participants were provided with only textual excerpts of webpages, but users might browse the actual webpages differently. Future studies should consider whether our suggestions for searching work. Nonetheless, this study paves the way for additional analyses of how search engine result pages interact with learning tasks to influence how individuals develop their understanding of science topics.

6. CONCLUSION

Search engines are the "go to" strategy for finding information on the Internet, yet they harbor several challenging features we must confront, both in terms of pedagogy and policy. Their function is opaque to the user, and may present challenges to understanding content we are just beginning to comprehend. This work found that students need to consider the role of multiple, systemic and personal biases in the presentation and processing of scientific information. A user's unawareness of algorithmic bias increases their susceptibility to cognitive bias, which increases the influence that source bias may have. Specifically, they are susceptible to four cognitive biases that emerge from the following heuristics when selecting sources on a SERP: Priming, Anchoring, Framing, and the Availability Heuristic.

As users continue to rely on digital information to participate in the public sphere, including information that informs decisions of personal and public importance, we need to understand how these biases may intersect to shape the way individual and public opinion is constructed and used.

7. REFERENCES

[1] N. J. Belkin, M. Cole, and J. Liu, "A model for evaluation of interactive information retrieval," presented at the Proceedings of the SIGIR 2009 Workshop on the Future of IR Evaluation, 2009, pp. 7–8.

[2] R. Epstein and R. E. Robertson, "The search engine manipulation effect (SEME) and its possible impact on the outcomes of elections," *Proc. Natl. Acad. Sci.*, p. 201419828, Aug. 2015.

[3] E. Hargittai, "Digital Na(t)ives? Variation in Internet Skills and Uses among Members of the 'Net Generation,'" *Sociol. Inq.*, vol. 80, no. 1, pp. 92–113, Feb. 2010.

[4] E. M. Meyers, "Access denied: how students resolve information needs when an ideal document is restricted," in *Proceedings of the 2012 iConference*, 2012, pp. 629–631.

[5] "National Science Board (2014) Science and Engineering Indicators." National Science Foundation, Arlington, VA., 2014.

[6] Q. Guo, R. W. White, S. T. Dumais, J. Wang, and B. Anderson, "Predicting query performance using query, result, and user interaction features," presented at the Adaptivity, Personalization and Fusion of Heterogeneous Information, 2010, pp. 198–201.

[7] N. Höchstötter and D. Lewandowski, "What users see–Structures in search engine results pages," *Inf. Sci.*, vol. 179, no. 12, pp. 1796–1812, 2009.

[8] D. Kelly, "Methods for evaluating interactive information retrieval systems with users," *Found. Trends Inf. Retr.*, vol. 3, no. 1—2, pp. 1–224, 2009.

[9] A. Shiri and L. Zvyagintseva, "Dynamic Query Suggestion in Web Search Engines: A Comparative Examination," presented at the Proceedings of the Annual Conference of CAIS/Actes du congrès annuel de l'ACSI, 2014.

[10] E. R. Tufte, *Beautiful evidence*. Cheshire, Conn: Graphics Press, 2006.

[11] R. Cellan-Jones, "Six searches that show the power of Google," Apr. 2016.

[12] S. Gerhart, "Do Web search engines suppress controversy?," *First Monday*, vol. 9, no. 1, 2004.

[13] D. C. Mutz, *Population-based survey experiments*. Princeton University Press, 2011.

[14] M. Schudson, "The' Lippmann-Dewey Debate' and the Invention of Walter Lippmann as an Anti-Democrat 1985-1996," *Int. J. Commun.*, vol. 2, p. 12, 2008.

[15] J. W. Carey, *Communication as Culture: Essays on Media and Society*. Psychology Press, 1989.

[16] J. Dewey and M. L. Rogers, *The public and its problems: An essay in political inquiry*. Penn State Press, 2012.

[17] W. Lippmann, *Public opinion*. Transaction Publishers, 1946.

[18] E. Amend and D. Barney, "Getting It Right: Canadian Conservatives and the' War on Science'.," *Can. J. Commun.*, vol. 41, no. 1, 2016.

[19] S. Dunwoody, "Science journalism," *Handb. Public Commun. Sci. Technol.*, pp. 15–26, 2008.

[20] E. Segev and A. J. Sharon, "Temporal patterns of scientific information-seeking on Google and Wikipedia," *Public Underst. Sci.*, p. 963662516648565, 2016.

[21] B. Latour, *Science in action: How to follow scientists and engineers through society*. Harvard university press, 1987.

[22] L. Daston and P. Galison, "The Image of Objectivity," *Representations*, no. 40, pp. 81–128, Oct. 1992.

[23] T. Bubela *et al.*, "Science communication reconsidered," *Nat. Biotechnol.*, vol. 27, no. 6, pp. 514–518, 2009.

[24] L. D. Carsten and D. L. Illman, "Perceptions of accuracy in science writing," *Prof. Commun. IEEE Trans. On*, vol. 45, no. 3, pp. 153–156, 2002.

[25] S. Dunwoody and M. Ryan, "Scientific barriers to the popularization of science in the mass media," *J. Commun.*, vol. 35, no. 1, pp. 26–42, 1985.

[26] McComas and Simone, "Media Coverage of Conflict Science Communication," *Vol 24 No*, vol. 24, no. 4, Jun. 2003.

[27] D. Nelkin, *Selling Science - How the Press Covers Science and Technology*. New York: W.H. Freeman and Company, 1987.

[28] D. A. Scheufele, "Science communication as political communication," *Proc. Natl. Acad. Sci.*, vol. 111, no. Supplement_4, pp. 13585–13592, Sep. 2014.

[29] G. C. Bowker and S. L. Star, *Sorting things out classification and its consequences*. Cambridge, Mass.: MIT Press, 1999.

[30] E. Morozov, *The net delusion: the dark side of internet freedom*, 1. ed. New York, NY: Public Affairs, 2011.

[31] B. J. Fogg, *Persuasive Technology: Using Computers to Change what We Think and Do*. Morgan Kaufmann, 2003.

[32] B. Friedman and H. Nissenbaum, "Bias in computer systems," *ACM Trans. Inf. Syst. TOIS*, vol. 14, no. 3, pp. 330–347, 1996.

[33] D. Kahneman and A. Tversky, "Subjective probability: A judgment of representativeness," *Cognit. Psychol.*, vol. 3, no. 3, pp. 430–454, 1972.

[34] D. Kahneman and A. Tversky, "On the reality of cognitive illusions.," 1996.

[35] D. Kahneman, *Thinking, fast and slow*. 2013.

[36] S. Lewandowsky, U. K. H. Ecker, C. M. Seifert, N. Schwarz, and J. Cook, "Misinformation and Its Correction: Continued Influence and Successful Debiasing," *Psychol. Sci. Public Interest*, vol. 13, no. 3, pp. 106–131, Dec. 2012.

[37] P. C. Wason and D. Shapiro, "Natural and contrived experience in a reasoning problem," *Q. J. Exp. Psychol.*, vol. 23, no. 1, pp. 63–71, Feb. 1971.

[38] C. Behnert and D. Lewandowski, "Ranking Search Results in Library Information Systems — Considering Ranking Approaches Adapted From Web Search Engines," *J. Acad. Librariansh.*, vol. 41, no. 6, pp. 725–735, Nov. 2015.

[39] L. Lorigo *et al.*, "Eye tracking and online search: Lessons learned and challenges ahead," *J. Am. Soc. Inf. Sci. Technol.*, vol. 59, no. 7, pp. 1041–1052, 2008.

[40] B. Pan, H. Hembrooke, T. Joachims, L. Lorigo, G. Gay, and L. Granka, "In google we trust: Users' decisions on rank, position, and relevance," *J. Comput. Commun.*, vol. 12, no. 3, pp. 801–823, 2007.

[41] T. Joachims, L. Granka, B. Pan, H. Hembrooke, F. Radlinski, and G. Gay, "Evaluating the accuracy of implicit feedback from clicks and query reformulations in web search," *ACM Trans. Inf. Syst. TOIS*, vol. 25, no. 2, p. 7, 2007.

[42] R. Fidel, *Human information interaction: an ecological approach to information behavior*. MIT Press, 2012.

[43] D. O. Case, *Looking for Information: A Survey of Research on Information Seeking, Needs and Behavior*. Emerald Group Publishing, 2012.

[44] G. B. Chapman and E. J. Johnson, "Incorporating the irrelevant: Anchors in judgments of belief and value," *Heuristics Biases Psychol. Intuitive Judgm.*, pp. 120–138, 2002.

[45] J. S. B. T. Evans and D. E. Over, *Rationality and Reasoning*. Psychology Press, 2013.

[46] R. Cellan-Jones, "The Force of Google," *BBC Radio 4*, May-2016.

[47] R. B. Zajonc, "Mere exposure: A gateway to the subliminal," *Curr. Dir. Psychol. Sci.*, vol. 10, no. 6, pp. 224–228, 2001.

[48] J. A. Bargh, P. M. Gollwitzer, A. Lee-Chai, K. Barndollar, and R. Trötschel, "The automated will: nonconscious activation and pursuit of behavioral goals.," *J. Pers. Soc. Psychol.*, vol. 81, no. 6, p. 1014, 2001.

[49] C. R. Mynatt, M. E. Doherty, and R. D. Tweney, "Confirmation bias in a simulated research environment: An experimental study of scientific inference," *Q. J. Exp. Psychol.*, vol. 29, no. 1, pp. 85–95, Feb. 1977.

[50] C. A. Chinn, "Factors that Influence," presented at the Proceedings of the Fifteenth Annual Conference of the Cognitive Science Society: June 18 to 21, 1993, Institute of Cognitive Science, University of Colorado-Boulder, 1993, vol. 15, p. 318.

[51] L. Salmerón, Y. Kammerer, and P. García-Carrión, "Searching the Web for conflicting topics: Page and user factors," *Comput. Hum. Behav.*, vol. 29, no. 6, pp. 2161–2171, Nov. 2013.

[52] E. Agichtein, E. Brill, and S. Dumais, "Improving web search ranking by incorporating user behavior information," presented at the Proceedings of the 29th annual international ACM SIGIR conference on Research and development in information retrieval, 2006, pp. 19–26.

[53] J. Liu and N. J. Belkin, "Personalizing information retrieval for multi-session tasks: Examining the roles of task stage, task type, and topic knowledge on the interpretation of dwell time as an indicator of document usefulness," *J. Assoc. Inf. Sci. Technol.*, vol. 66, no. 1, pp. 58–81, 2015.

[54] N. J. Belkin, M. Cole, and J. Liu, "A model for evaluation of interactive information retrieval," presented at the Proceedings of the SIGIR 2009 Workshop on the Future of IR Evaluation, 2009, pp. 7–8.

[55] D. Case, "Sixty years of measuring the use of information and its sources: from consultation to application," *Libr. Digit. Age LIDA Proc.*, vol. 13, 2014.

[56] D. O. Case and L. G. O'Connor, "What's the use? Measuring the frequency of studies of information outcomes: Journal of the Association for Information Science and Technology," *J. Assoc. Inf. Sci. Technol.*, vol. 67, no. 3, pp. 649–661, Mar. 2016.

[57] B. Pan, H. Hembrooke, T. Joachims, L. Lorigo, G. Gay, and L. Granka, "In Google We Trust: Users' Decisions on Rank, Position, and Relevance," *J. Comput.-Mediat. Commun.*, vol. 12, no. 3, pp. 801–823, Apr. 2007.

[58] Google, *The Evolution of Search*. 2011.

[59] A. Tversky and D. Kahneman, "Judgment under uncertainty: Heuristics and biases," *science*, vol. 185, no. 4157, pp. 1124–1131, 1974.

[60] M. Hilbert, "Toward a synthesis of cognitive biases: How noisy information processing can bias human decision making.," *Psychol. Bull.*, vol. 138, no. 2, pp. 211–237, 2012.

[61] E. Yong, "Psychologists strike a blow for reproducibility," *Nature*, Nov. 2013.

[62] C. Ware, *Information visualization: perception for design*, Third edition. Waltham, MA: Morgan Kaufmann, 2013.

[63] D. Kahneman, A. Treisman, and B. J. Gibbs, "The reviewing of object files: Object-specific integration of information," *Cognit. Psychol.*, vol. 24, no. 2, pp. 175–219, Apr. 1992.

[64] N. Höchstötter and D. Lewandowski, "What users see – Structures in search engine results pages," *Inf. Sci.*, vol. 179, no. 12, pp. 1796–1812, May 2009.

[65] M. R. Laurent and T. J. Vickers, "Seeking health information online: does Wikipedia matter?," *J. Am. Med. Inform. Assoc.*, vol. 16, no. 4, pp. 471–479, 2009.

[66] J. Braun and T. Gillespie, "Hosting the public discourse, hosting the public: When online news and social media converge," *Journal. Pract.*, vol. 5, no. 4, pp. 383–398, 2011.

[67] A. Diaz, "Through the Google Goggles: Sociopolitical Bias in Search Engine Design," in *Web search:*

multidisciplinary perspectives, A. Spink and M. Zimmer, Eds. Berlin: Springer, 2008, pp. 11–34.

[68] T. Gillespie, "The politics of 'platforms,'" *New Media Soc.*, vol. 12, no. 3, pp. 347–364, May 2010.

[69] T. Harper, "The big data public and its problems: Big data and the structural transformation of the public sphere," *New Media Soc.*, p. 1461444816642167, 2016.

[70] P. Ladwig, A. A. Anderson, D. Brossard, D. A. Scheufele, and B. Shaw, "Narrowing the nano discourse?," *Mater. Today*, vol. 13, no. 5, pp. 52–54, 2010.

[71] B. Rieder and G. Sire, "Conflicts of interest and incentives to bias: A microeconomic critique of Google's tangled position on the Web," *New Media Soc.*, p. 1461444813481195, 2013.

[72] C. Lauckner and G. Hsieh, "The presentation of health-related search results and its impact on negative emotional outcomes," in *Proceedings of the SIGCHI Conference on Human Factors in Computing Systems*, 2013, pp. 333–342.

[73] D. Kahneman, "Maps of bounded rationality: A perspective on intuitive judgment and choice," *Nobel Prize Lect.*, vol. 8, pp. 351–401, 2002.

[74] D. A. Scheufele and D. Tewksbury, "Framing, Agenda Setting, and Priming: The Evolution of Three Media Effects Models," *J. Commun.*, vol. 57, no. 1, pp. 9–20, Mar. 2007.

[75] J. Hullman and N. Diakopoulos, "Visualization rhetoric: Framing effects in narrative visualization," *IEEE Trans. Vis. Comput. Graph.*, vol. 17, no. 12, pp. 2231–2240, 2011.

[76] R. Bauman, "Genre," *J. Linguist. Anthropol.*, vol. 9, no. 1/2, pp. 84–87, 1999.

[77] Y.-C. Huang, H.-H. Chen, M.-L. Yeh, and Y.-C. Chung, "Case studies combined with or without concept maps improve critical thinking in hospital-based nurses: A randomized-controlled trial," *Int. J. Nurs. Stud.*, vol. 49, no. 6, pp. 747–754, 2012.

[78] P. Borlund, "Interactive Information Retrieval: An Introduction," *J. Inf. Sci. Theory Pract.*, vol. 1, no. 3, pp. 12–32, Sep. 2013.

[79] K. B. Rasmussen, "General Approaches to Data Quality and Internet-generated Data," in *The Sage Handbook of online Research Methods*, Fielding, Lee, and Blank, Eds. Sage, 2008.

[80] J. Creswell, *Research Design - Qualitative, Quantitative, and Mixed Methods Approach*, vol. 3. Sage, 2014.

[81] M. A. Carriquiry, X. Du, and G. R. Timilsina, "Second generation biofuels: Economics and policies," *Spec. Sect. Renew. Energy Policy Dev.*, vol. 39, no. 7, pp. 4222–4234, Jul. 2011.

[82] A. B. Delshad, L. Raymond, V. Sawicki, and D. T. Wegener, "Public attitudes toward political and technological options for biofuels," *Energy Policy*, vol. 38, no. 7, pp. 3414–3425, Jul. 2010.

[83] H. Longstaff, D. M. Secko, G. Capurro, P. Hanney, and T. McIntyre, "Fostering citizen deliberations on the social acceptability of renewable fuels policy: The case of advanced lignocellulosic biofuels in Canada," *Biomass Bioenergy*, vol. 74, pp. 103–112, Mar. 2015.

[84] T. E. McKone *et al.*, "Grand Challenges for Life-Cycle Assessment of Biofuels," *Env. Sci Technol*, vol. 45, no. 5, pp. 1751–1756, 2011.

[85] D. M. Secko and E. Einsiedel, "The biofuels quadrilemma, public perceptions and policy," *Biofuels*, vol. 5, no. 3, pp. 207–209, May 2014.

[86] D. Smith, "BFN Annual Report 2015," 2015. [Online]. Available: http://www.biofuelnet.ca/wp-content/uploads/2013/02/BFN-2015-Annual-Report_11.10.15_web.pdf. [Accessed: 25-Oct-2015].

[87] National Resources Canada, "Biodiesel - Government Programs and Regulations | Natural Resources Canada," 2015. [Online]. Available: http://www.nrcan.gc.ca/energy/alternative-fuels/fuel-facts/biodiesel/3515. [Accessed: 06-Mar-2016].

[88] G. Hotchkiss, T. Sherman, R. Tobin, C. Bates, and K. Brown, "Search engine results: 2010," *Enq. Search Solut.*, pp. 1–61, 2010.

[89] K. Popper, *Realism and the aim of science: From the postscript to the logic of scientific discovery.* Routledge, 2013.

[90] J. Wood, D. Badawood, J. Dykes, and A. Slingsby, "BallotMaps: Detecting name bias in alphabetically ordered ballot papers," *IEEE Trans. Vis. Comput. Graph.*, vol. 17, no. 12, pp. 2384–2391, 2011.

[91] E.-J. Wagenmakers, R. Wetzels, D. Borsboom, H. L. J. van der Maas, and R. A. Kievit, "An Agenda for Purely Confirmatory Research," *Perspect. Psychol. Sci.*, vol. 7, no. 6, pp. 632–638, Nov. 2012.

[92] M. L. Berger, M. Mamdani, D. Atkins, and M. L. Johnson, "Good Research Practices for Comparative Effectiveness Research: Defining, Reporting and Interpreting Nonrandomized Studies of Treatment Effects Using Secondary Data Sources: The ISPOR Good Research Practices for Retrospective Database Analysis Task Force Report—Part I," *Value Health*, vol. 12, no. 8, pp. 1044–1052, Nov. 2009.

[93] A. Collins, J. Greeno, L. Resnick, B. Berliner, and R. Calfee, "Cognition and learning," *B Berl. R Calfee Handb. Educ. Psychol. N. Y. Simon Shuster MacMillan*, 1992.

[94] E. M. Meyers, "Losses and gains in collaborative search: Insights from the Middle School Classroom," *GROUP'10 Novemb. 7–12 2010 Sanibel Isl. FL USA*, 2010.

[95] D. M. Levy and C. C. Marshall, "Going digital: a look at assumptions underlying digital libraries," *Commun. ACM*, vol. 38, no. 4, pp. 77–84, Apr. 1995.

[96] P. Dillenbourg and M. Baker, "Negotiation spaces in human-computer collaborative learning," in *Proceedings of the International Conference on Cooperative Systems*, 1996, pp. 12–14.

[97] J. Foster, Ed., *Collaborative information behavior: user engagement and communication sharing.* Hershey PA: Information Science Reference, 2010.

[98] P. Hansen, C. Shah, and C.-P. Klas, Eds., *Collaborative Information Seeking.* Cham: Springer International Publishing, 2015.

[99] M. R. Morris, "Collaborative search revisited," in *Proceedings of the 2013 conference on Computer supported cooperative work*, 2013, pp. 1181–1192.

[100] M. B. Twidale, D. M. Nichols, and C. D. Paice, "Browsing is a collaborative process," *Inf. Process. Manag.*, vol. 33, no. 6, pp. 761–783, 1997.

[101] J. D. Novak and A. J. Cañas, "The theory underlying concept maps and how to construct and use them," *Fla. Inst. Hum. Mach. Cogn.*, vol. 2008, 2008.

[102] J. D. Novak, *Learning how to learn.* Cambridge [Cambridgeshire] ; New York: Cambridge University Press, 1984.

Learning From the News: The Role of Topic, Multimedia and Interest in Knowledge Retention

Heather O'Brien
School of Library, Archival and Information Studies
University of British Columbia
Vancouver, Canada
1-604-827-5842
h.obrien@ubc.ca

Jocelyn McKay
School of Library, Archival and Information Studies
University of British Columbia
Vancouver, Canada
1-604-827-5842
jocelyn.d.mckay@gmail.com

Jacob Vangeest
School of Library, Archival and Information Studies
University of British Columbia
Vancouver, Canada
1-604-827-5842
jvangeest@gmail.com

ABSTRACT

We conducted a study to examine how people interact with and learn from human-interest news stories. Participants engaged with news stories and completed knowledge retention tests to evaluate their ability to remember the content. We analyzed how the stories and the way in which they were presented (audio, video, text) related to knowledge retention. Results demonstrated a complex interaction between topic and knowledge retention, where participants obtained higher scores for the least preferred story. We explored these findings with respect to participants' demographics and user experience.

CCS Concepts

• ***Human-centered computing~User studies*** • ***Human-centered computing~Empirical studies in HCI***

Keywords

Information interaction; learning; multimedia; online news

1. INTRODUCTION

Information seeking is comprised of several iterative stages: defining an information need, choosing a source, querying, examining and assessing search results, extracting information, and determining when one has 'enough' information – or has had enough of the search process [19]. Over the past decades studies have investigated how searchers translate (or fail to translate) information needs into queries [5], adopt specific strategies to accomplish different tasks [18], and assess the relevance of search results [26]. Extraction, "working through material in relevant sources" [6] (p. 480) and information use tend to be less studied, but are nonetheless essential for understanding and measuring information interaction outcomes [3]. Rather than focusing on the whole search process, we isolated the less studied stages of extraction and use, focusing on the way in which news content delivery affects the basic learning outcome of remembering.

Content and its presentation (e.g., media, interactivity) are closely coupled in digital environments, and impact users' experiences and capacity to extract and meaningfully use or learn from information, [9; 16; 24]. Information content evokes affective responses in searchers, and is strongly tied to interest [2; 21]. Interest and other personal qualities of searchers, such as prior knowledge, motivation, and expectations, are strong predictors of information extraction and use, along with tasks, systems, domains, and settings. These "information seeking factors are not mutually exclusive…[but] linked by relationships that vary in complexity and importance [19] (pp. 48).

In this study, we explored the relationship amongst information seeking factors and learning at the point of information extraction and use. We presented two human-interest news stories in audio, video, or text formats, and measured learning at a basic level of knowledge retention. This paper outlines the study and its findings, which suggest that the news stories, rather than how they were delivered, resulted in greater knowledge retention scores.

2. PRIOR RESEARCH

Extraction consists of a host of activities, including "reading, scanning, listening, classifying, copying, and storing information" [19] (pp. 57). Users extract information using strategies, such as restating information in their own words, copying or annotating text, etc. In doing so, information is incorporated into their existing knowledge base and changes how they evaluate new information [19], i.e., learning. Extraction is inextricably linked with information use, which may be conceptual (intangible) or instrumental (tangible) [3].

There is longstanding agreement that information use is understudied in interactive information retrieval [3; 27]. Vakkari [27], drawing upon papers accepted at the International Information Seeking in Context (ISIC) Conference in 1997, noted that work was concentrated on information needs and seeking, with much less emphasis on use. This illustrated "gap" in information seeking research was in spite of the "growing interest in relating information needs and seeking to the outcomes of the work roles or tasks" (pp. 461). Almost two decades later, Case and O'Connor's [3] systematic review suggests there are still limitations in understanding how extracted information is used. Conceptual or intangible use ("in head") is difficult to capture, and though bibliometrics and social media/web analytics provide some indication of what people do with information, ascertaining "meaningful use" remains a challenge. For example, citing research may be more "ritualistic" than "a meaningful application of the contents" [3] (p. 657), and social media activities may or may not represent meaningful information exchange. The

CHIIR '17, March 07 - 11, 2017, Oslo, Norway

ACM 978-1-4503-4677-1/17/03…$15.00
DOI: http://dx.doi.org/10.1145/3020165.3020166

resurgence of interest in IIR on searching as learning[1] indicates that the community is invested in understanding how people seek, extract, and use information for the purpose of learning.

This paper focuses on conceptual use, operationalized here as short-term recall, to understand the effects of media format on knowledge retention. Two human interest news stories of equal readability and sentiment were selected to reduce the influence of content characteristics on participants' ability to extract information, as it was hypothesized that media would have a greater impact on recall. Actual findings were counter to these predictions, and thus personal interest in the news stories and demographic variables were examined to make sense of these contrary results.

2.1 Learning

The ability to understand or make sense of information is an important goal of information seeking [20]. There is general agreement that learning involves cognitive, affective and behavioral elements [12], though much work in information interaction has focused on cognitive learning, specifically Bloom's Taxonomy (remembering, understanding, applying, analyzing, evaluating, and creating) [1]. Jansen, Booth and Smith [14] found that tasks designed to activate lower (remembering, understanding) and higher (evaluating, creating) levels of learning resulted in shorter queries than middle levels (applying, analyzing), which also required more search time.

Building on Jansen et al. [14], Kelly, Arguello, Edwards and Woo [15] categorized twenty tasks according to Bloom's taxonomy and examined the relationship between learning tasks, cognitive complexity, and search behavior. More complex learning tasks required more time and consisted of more interactions (e.g., SERP clicks), but were not associated with higher difficulty or lower satisfaction. The researchers observed that users' initial perceptions of task difficulty shaped their perceived difficulty as they progressed, amplifying negative emotions when the task was found to more challenging than expected. Though they did not measure cognitive learning outcomes in the study, their findings underscored the role of affect on the completion of cognitive "searching as learning" tasks. This would suggest that user perceptions of and reactions to information tasks impacts user satisfaction, and potentially tangible outcomes such as learning. Thus, exploring what shapes the user experience is important for understanding if, how, and to what extent information is used.

2.2 User Experience

User experience (UX) "is rooted in how people perceive, act upon, and feel about" their digitally mediated interactions with the world [23] (p. 73). Whether focused on the design of digital applications or on the subjective experience of the user, UX acknowledges that interactions with technology hinge upon more than usability; rather they are the complex interplay of user, system, and contextual factors. In this study we concentrated specifically on how information is delivered (i.e., format) and users' reactions to content.

Colbert and Boodoo [4] concluded that poorly presented content interfered with information extraction and use in an online experiment. They compared behavioral patterns of visitors to two websites that differed only in their adherence to guidelines for writing web content. People spent more time interacting with and were more apt to return to the compliant website. The authors reasoned that participants who were led to the non-compliant version evaluated its presentation of information (e.g., ineffective use of lists or images, large amounts of text, or confusing wording) negatively, and therefore its information less credible.

Hong [13] found that the decision to interact further with content was contingent upon the way in which it was framed. She exposed participants to one of two versions of a health message about the relationship between diet and eye health: promotional ("...diets rich in fruits and vegetables may create better eyesight, including improved night vision"), and preventive ("...diets rich in fruits and vegetables may reduce the risk of developing eyesight problems, including cataract"). Participants were then invited to interact with promotional (i.e., create more energy, improve digestive health, and strengthen bones) and preventative (i.e., reduce risk of cancer, lower blood pressure, prevent heart disease) taglines to explore further content. Participants' behaviors were guided by whether subsequent content matched the orientation of the condition to which they were assigned. In other words, those assigned to the promotional message chose promotional taglines, and those who encountered the preventative message were more apt to select preventative taglines.

Research has also shown that user interactions with content are driven by interest. McCay-Peet, Lalmas and Navalpakkum [21] found that the visual saliency of news headlines, based on cues such as color, size, and placement on the screen, increased participants' search task efficiency, but, in some cases, participants wanted to pursue content that was personally interesting but not task relevant. Interest was also a defining component of Arapakis, Lalmas, Cambazoglu, Marcos, and Jose's [2] online news study. They analyzed 13,000 news articles to select 18 articles that varied in interest (high, low) and polarity (positive, negative) and employed these in a user study. Arapakis et al. [2] found that affect, interest, and curiosity were positively associated with sentiment, but more so when news content became more negative. They concluded that both cognitive (interest) and affective (polarity) content elements affected the user experience.

In addition to interest, user interactions with content during information seeking an be affected by user individual differences, such as age, gender, prior knowledge, expertise, level of education, and cognitive and affective variables. For example, Ford et al. [9] demonstrated that searchers enact information processing strategies, whereby they search for information in a particular and consistent manner, and that these strategies affect information retrieval success.

User experience can also be influenced by how information is packaged. In a study that linked aspects of content and its presentation, Koehler, Yadav, Phillips and Cavazos-Kottke [17] experimented with four content genres (human interest story, informative or persuasive story, poem, and scholarly lecture) across two media formats (video and text). The researchers were interested in how the representational affordances of various media types affected learning outcomes, as well as how story type influenced user-media interactions. Koehler and colleagues [17] found that when people interacted with content in video format, they perceived the information as more factual, the author as more authoritative, and that they had learned more.

Koehler et al.'s [17] study suggested that "modality interactivity" is important for helping people "access the core message that the

[1] Recent activities include the the Special Issue of the *Journal of Information Science* (vol. 42) published in February 2016, and the IIiX 2014 (http://www.diigubc.ca/IIIXSAL/) and SIGIR 2016 (http://chauff.github.io/sal2016/) workshops.

medium aims to deliver, rather than merely increase[ing] navigational activity" [24] (p. 214). In a study that used an informational website to deliver anti-smoking messages, Oh and Sundar [24] showed that the level of modality interactivity increased users' cognitive absorption, favorable attitudes toward the website and its messages, and led to more positive interface assessments. However, high modality interactivity "significantly reduced the amount of message-related thoughts after browsing" (p. 227), suggesting that positive engagement with the site may not have led to learning.

Recent work by Freund and colleagues [10] investigated how people interacted with and comprehended reading materials (journal article, webpage, blog). They presented the materials in plain text or "in context" (with design, graphical and paratextual cues) and varied the interactivity of the reading environment (no interactivity, reading tools for annotating and highlighting text). Participants in the plain text, non-interactive condition achieved the highest comprehension scores, while those in the in-context, non-interactive condition had the lowest scores. This was surprising as "structural features [of texts] such as headings and outlines...can aid in extracting relevant information [19] (p. 58). Participants in the two interactive conditions achieved similar comprehension scores, suggesting that the ability to annotate or highlight text was linked to understanding more than in-context presentation.

In summary, user experience is impacted by information quality [4], framing [13], and sentiment [2], as well as topical interest [2; 21]. Genre, media format, and interactivity can affect user experience and searchers' ability to extract information from content [9; 17; 24]. How such content and media characteristics impact learning is inconclusive, since positive user experiences may not be indicative of information extraction and use [24]. Information interaction research suggests that different levels of cognitive learning, operationalized through search tasks, result in different search behaviors that are associated with cognitive complexity, perceived challenge and affect.

3. CURRENT STUDY

This study isolated select content and media characteristics to examine their relationship to learning, operationalized at Bloom's basic level of remembering. We asked participants to interact with two different news stories that were comparable in terms of genre, readability, and sentiment, but topically different. We anticipated that there would be no differences in knowledge retention between the two stories. We measured interest, curiosity, and participants' behavioral intentions to link to related content or share the stories with others to understand what effect topic might have on UX.

In terms of media characteristics, we manipulated only the format in which the stories were delivered. News and information platforms deliver content in a variety of media (video, infographics, text) and include interactive functions, e.g., links to share information through social media channels, features to rate or comment publically on content. We expected that video, which is more interactive and multi-sensory than audio and text, would result in greater recall and recognition. Our rationale for this was situated in dual coding theory, which proposes that verbal (language-specialized) and nonverbal (symbolic or imagery) information is represented and processed by different cognitive sub-systems that function independently, but are also interconnected and trigger each other [25] (pp. 53-54, 62). In other words, information that activates both sub-systems (e.g., text and images, video and audio) results in deeper information processing.

Holding content characteristics of genre, sentiment, and readability constant allowed us to investigate topic effects, while manipulating only media format enabled us to separate format and interactivity to examine effects of information delivery on knowledge retention. Quantitative and qualitative data collected in the study were drawn upon in this paper to make sense of the user experience at the point of information extraction, and its relationship to participants' ability to remember the content with which they interacted.[2]

4. Method

4.1 Participants

Seventy-eight people (F=50, M=27, no response=1) took part in this study. Recruitment took place at a university through email lists, posters, and a website advertising research studies. Interested individuals contacted the researchers via email to arrange a session. The majority of participants were students (88.5%) under the age of 30 (74.7%; 31-40, 24.3%) who had completed high school and were pursuing or had completed some form of post-secondary education. Non-students included two research assistants and two sales or marketing staff, as well as one housewife, security guard/tennis instructor, customer service representative, programmer, administrator, and library staff member; one person did not specify their current employment. The participants were avid news readers and interacted with news daily (n=38), several times a week (n=23), or on a weekly (n=15) or monthly (n=2) basis.

4.2 News media

Two human-interest news stories were selected for this study. Only one genre was examined in this study to afford greater experimental control of story type; it was reasoned that this would allow clear observations of media and topic effects.

The stories were available from a news provider in audio, video, and transcript-style text formats. A narrative-style version of each story was created that each contained one image. We did not alter the order of story ideas. The stories were different topically, but in pre-testing the video versions of the stories, users rated them similarly in terms of interest (story 1: 6/7; story 2: 5/7) and positive sentiment (5/7). The stories also varied in duration: the video and audio versions of story 1 (mining) (9 minutes, 54 seconds) were longer than story 2 (farming) (6 minutes, 26 seconds). The narrative versions were 1336 words (story 1), and 981 words (story 2). However, both stories had similar Flesch-Kincaid Reading Ease scores (story 1=62.4; story 2= 63.3) and Flesch-Kincaid Grade Levels (story 1=8.7; story 2=8.6) (readability-score.com). Our texts were comparable to other popular press materials, e.g., Reader's Digest has a reading ease

[2] Study results are reported in two additional publications:

A more extensive analysis of the individual and situational nature of participants' interest in the news items by story and media format appears in the 2016 short paper: "What makes online news interesting? Personal and situational interest and the effect on behavioral intentions" in *Proceedings of the Association of Information Science and Information Technology*. 53: 1–6.

The quantitative findings depicting the effects of story and media on user engagement and knowledge retention are examined in-depth in "Antecedents and Learning Outcomes of Online News Engagement" to appear in *The Journal of the Association for Information Science and Technology*.

score of 65 [8]. Readability is based on the average number of syllables per word and average number of words per sentence. Longer sentences and words with more syllables are more complex and require more reading skill [7]. Readability assessments are not the same as reader perceptions of text difficulty.

4.3 Measures

We used a variety of measures to record participants' characteristics and their experiences interacting with news stories in this study. Here we report only on the instruments corresponding to variables examined in this paper.

Demographic questionnaire. We gathered information about participants' demographics including gender, age, occupation (student/non-student), and highest level of education obtained. We also asked about the frequency and format in which they typically interacted with news.

User experience. Participants were asked to indicate their post-task levels of interest and curiosity about each story, and whether they would link to additional materials on the same topic or recommend the story to others. These four items, collected after each story, were measured using a seven-point rating scale. We also conducted semi-structured interviews with approximately half (n=41) of our participants to gather their perceptions of interacting with the stories. Individuals were asked about their interaction with each story, how the format in which they interacted with the stories compared to their typical news reading behavior, and the overall quality of the news experience; probes were used to solicit elaborations on responses as needed.

Knowledge retention. The lead author and a graduate research assistant (GRA) created ten short answer and multiple-choice questions per story. Two other GRAs interacted with each story, and responded to and assessed the questions. Questions were revised and retested with a convenience sample to ensure equal distribution of short answer and multiple-choice items, and of user perceived easy, medium, and difficult questions per story.

4.4 Procedure

The experimental study took place on a university campus. All materials were delivered through a laptop with a 15-inch monitor; a mouse and headphones were attached for participants use. An experimental system was created to deliver the study questionnaires and tasks. After participants completed the electronic consent form, the system randomly assigned them to one of four media conditions (video, audio, transcript-style text, or narrative text), and presented one of the two stories; story presentation was counterbalanced to prevent order effects. The system saved all data entered by participants and stored it on a university server backed up daily on a local external hard drive.

An experimental protocol was adhered to for all sessions to ensure consistency across sessions, as three GRAs assisted with the study. At the beginning of the experiment, the GRA opened the experimental system and led the participant through the informed consent process. Once they had the opportunity to read and ask questions about the study, participants were asked to click the "continue" button at the bottom of the screen to signify their consent to proceed. The GRA then followed a standard script, telling participants that the study materials, including the stories and questionnaires with which they would interact, would be presented on the laptop; participants were instructed not to hit the back button in the experimental system. The GRA explained they would be asked to answer questions about their experiences interacting with the stories and about the events depicted in the stories. Participants were encouraged to, "do your best to answer the questions, but please do not worry if you cannot answer them all." The GRA stayed in the room to assist participants as needed.

Participants first completed the demographic questionnaire, which was followed by the human-interest news stories presented in counterbalanced order. The stories were incorporated into the experimental system via a link to the original news website; the set up used a frame to ensure that participants did not leave or close the experimental system.

After interacting with each story, participants completed a questionnaire about their interest in, curiosity about, and behavioral intentions regarding the stories. In addition to the rating scale for these questions, an open-ended text box encouraged participants to explain their responses. Next, participants completed the knowledge retention test. This pattern of interacting with the story and answering questions was repeated for each story. A concluding page thanked participants, reiterated contact information for the principle investigator, and asked participants to inform the GRA that they had finished. Participants took, on average, 35 minutes, 42 seconds to complete this portion of the study. Half of the sample (n=41) was then interviewed post-session. We interviewed the first people to take part and skipped or added additional interviews sequentially to ensure adequate representation across all media conditions. There were 9 video, 12 transcript, 9 audio, and 10 narrative interviews. Upon completion of the study, participants were thanked for their time and paid an honorarium.

4.5 Data Screening and Preparation

GRAs took note of any anomalies that occurred during the study, and these notes were used to identify potential issues in data collection for subsequent analysis. Two participants encountered difficulties with the experimental system, i.e., one was assigned to a different media format for each story, and one person's session was interrupted when the browser unexpectedly closed. An additional person was observed to "cheat", that is, return to the stories to answer the knowledge retention questions at the end; and one person had previously encountered the stories. Data for these individuals was removed leaving 78 valid cases.

Data was downloaded from the experimental system database in .csv format. Quantitative data, e.g., demographics and questionnaire items, were analyzed using SPSS statistical software. Open-ended items in the post-task questionnaires and post-session interviews were transcribed and explored qualitatively using NVivo software. Interviews were brief and were coded thematically based on the semi-structured questions we asked. We were interested in looking at this data according to what participants said about the stories, media, their overall experience, and whether they would want to find out more about the topic; another category was created for comments related specifically to learning or remembering content from the stories. We examined the interviews according to these broad areas, noting the participant ID, media condition, and specific story during the coding process. In this study, we report only on quantitative and qualitative data that is directly related to the research questions.

4.5.1 Knowledge retention test scores

We created knowledge retention scores for each story based on an answer key; multiple-choice questions were straightforward (i.e., correct or incorrect); short answer questions were more nuanced. Two coders independently evaluated participants' responses to the questions, scoring answers as 1 for "correct," 0.5 for a "partially correct" or 0 "incorrect". We used percent agreement to calculate the inter-coder reliability, though we realize there is a risk of over-estimating the level of agreement using this method. For story 1, the percent agreement was 80.73% (126 disagreements, 654 agreements) and 94.3% for story 2 (42 disagreements/738 agreement). The coders then compared the number of agreements and disagreements between them and provided a rationale for the discrepancies. The lead author reviewed the coders' rationales and made a decision confirming either coder A or B's initial assessment. A score was then calculated per participant per story.

We examined *z*-scores to identify outliers in the data; only one value for story two was above 3 (z=3.13). However, the Shapiro Wilk test was significant for both story 1 (W=0.932(78), p=0.000) and 2 (W=0.954(78), p=0.007), and therefore the assumption of normality was not met; the scores for both stories were negatively skewed. Thus, we proceeded with our analysis using non-parametric tests.

5. RESULTS

We report the relationship between knowledge retention scores and story and media format, and look at these findings with respect to participants' interest in the stories and demographic characteristics. The quantitative data is complemented by insights gained from open-ended post-task questionnaire responses (n=78) and post-session interviews (n=41). The qualitative data is not analyzed in-depth in this report but is used to aid in the interpretation of the quantitative findings.

5.1 Story and media format

First, we examined whether there was an effect of story or multimedia condition on knowledge retention test scores. Table 1 shows the means and standard deviations for overall and story specific knowledge retention scores by media condition. The Wilcoxon paired sign rank test demonstrated that participants had higher knowledge test scores for the mining story (M=6.55, SD=1.96) compared to the farming story (M=6.04, SD=1.60), $Z(77)$=-2.44, p=0.015. Second, the Kruskal-Wallis Test showed that media format did not influence knowledge retention ($x^2(3)$=6.487, p=0.09). Those in the narrative and video conditions achieved similar overall knowledge retention scores, while those in the audio condition obtained the lowest scores.

Table 1: Descriptive statistics for story and condition by knowledge retention scores

Media Condition	*N*	Overall Knowledge Retention M(SD)	Story 1 (Mining) M(SD)	Story 2 (Farming) M(SD)
Audio	40	11.5(2.65)	5.85(1.77)	5.65(1.34)
Transcript	38	12.36(3.47)	6.77(2.08)	5.58(1.77)
Video	40	13.26(3.16)	7(1.73)	6.26(1.86)
Narrative	42	13.26(2.52)	6.64(2.19)	6.61(1.29)
		Total by Story	6.55(1.96)	6.04(1.6)

When we looked at knowledge retention scores for each story by media condition, there were no significant differences for either story 1 (mining) ($x^2(3)$=4.43, p=0.218), or story 2 (farming) ($x^2(3)$=6.73, p=0.08) according to the Kruskall-Wallis Test. Though not significant, it is interesting to note that those in the audio condition had the lowest test scores for story 1 and transcript text was lowest for story 2. For story 1, video was highest, followed by transcript and narrative text, while for story 2, narrative was highest, followed by video and audio.

Our analysis showed that the stories participants interacted with had an impact on their ability to recall information, but that media condition did not; therefore neither prediction was supported. Though not statistically significant, mean scores varied as a product of the media condition to which people were assigned on a story-by-story basis. While those in the narrative condition achieved comparable knowledge retention scores across both stories, participants in the video and transcript conditions achieved higher scores for story 1 than story 2. Audio participants had lower scores than those in other conditions, but they achieved slightly higher scores for story 2 than story 1. These patterns were not due to order effects because the stories were counterbalanced as part of the study design. However, other factors related to content presentation could have been at play. For example, some participants described editorial mistakes, tone, language, flow, and density of information as negative factors of story presentation.

During the post-task interviews, participants highlighted the importance of visuals in understanding a story's content. One participant (P17, transcript) stated they needed visuals to better connect to the people in the story, while many others voiced a desire to see wells being drilled for farmers (story 2), or the mines where the minerals came from (story 1). For both stories, participants in the audio condition scored lower than those who interacted with video and narrative text, which both contained images.

Another possible reason for lower achievement in the audio format may be the lack of "navigational control" experienced by audio participants (e.g., P6, P7). Unlike the narrative format in which a reader may reread a particularly difficult or interesting paragraph, refinding information in an audio or video clip is more challenging, especially if there are limited navigation affordances. This was illustrated by a video participant (P12):

> *If it was text you could simply go two paragraphs above and look it up and it's hard to search for specific information in video. Right, so you have to guess at which point, in the story is it a minute and a half for the story and then it's you know, I don't think it's as easy to navigate the story.*

One participant revealed that their lack of interest in the story combined with the audio format required them to pay extra attention, and that this resulted in them forgetting details (such as speaker names) of the story (P35, audio). Conversely, participants interacting with the narrative format appreciated the navigational control they had when rereading sections they did not understand or had never encountered before the study (P60, narrative).

Given these results, coupled with the significant effect of story on knowledge retention reported earlier, there may be an undetected interaction effect between story and media condition. Despite comparable reading ease and grade level scores for both stories (see "News media" section), other qualities of the stories – whether length or topic – led to different knowledge retention scores.

5.2 User experience of interacting with the news stories

After each news story, participants were asked to rate their interactions according to interest, curiosity, desire to link to further content on the topic, and likelihood to recommend the story to others. There were no missing values with the exception of one question (likelihood to recommend) for story 2 only. Table 2 shows the mean (standard deviations) for each of these post-task questions, based on a 7-point rating scale, for each story. Story 2 (farming) was rated, on average, higher on all questions. A Wilcoxon paired sign rank test revealed this difference was significant for self-reported interest, curiosity, and willingness to recommend the stories to others, but not for participants' intentions to link to related content.

Table 2. Descriptive statistics for post-task user experience questions by story

	No. responses	**Story 1: Mining *M(SD)***	**Story 2: Farming *M(SD)***	***Z(p)***
Interest	78	4.56 (1.82)	5.23 (1.28)	-2.404 (0.016)*
Curiosity	78	4.71 (1.71)	5.33 (1.33)	-2.585 (0.010)*
Link to content	77	3.65 (2.02)	3.94 (1.97)	-0.865 (0.387)
Recommend to others	78	3.35 (2.06)	4.12 (1.86)	-2.661 (0.008)*

**Significant at $p<0.05$*

We examined users' perceptions of their experiences in relation to their knowledge retention scores for each story using the Spearman's rank correlation coefficient or Spearman's rho. For story 1 (mining), there was a positive association between knowledge retention scores and interest (*rho*=0.306, *p*=0.006) and curiosity (*rho*=0.282, *p*=0.012), but not willingness to link to related content (*rho*=0.091, *p*=0.428) or recommend to family and friends (*rho*=0.216, *p*=0.058); though the latter is not statistically significant, there is a weak correlation present. For story 2, there were no significant correlations between knowledge retention and interest (*rho*=0.152, *p*=0.184), curiosity (*rho*=0.075, *p*=0.516), desire to link to related content (*rho*=0.182, *p*=0.101) or willingness to share (*rho*=0.182, *p*=0.113).

Overall, participants rated story 1 (mining) less positively than story 2 (farming), and stated that they would be less willing to share it with others or to look for further content on the topic. Behavioral intention to share the stories with others or to link to further content was not significantly related to knowledge retention for either story, but interest and curiosity were related to higher knowledge retention scores for story 1 (mining). The post-session interviews indicated that participants were interested in the people in the story, the relevance of the content to their own lives, or their ability to connect the story to their own experiences. Those who were disinterested in story 1 (mining) found it difficult to relate to the content because it was about a distant country, lacked focus on people, and was perceived as disconnected from the participants' own lived experience.

Participants rated their experiences with the news stories before completing the knowledge test, so perceptions of interest were not based on how well they perceived they did on the knowledge retention test. The positive correlation between knowledge retention scores and user experience for story 1 suggests that those who enjoyed the story most did better on the knowledge retention test, and those who did not enjoy the story did worse; interest did not affect participants' ability to remember details about story 2.

5.3 Demographic characteristics

To understand if individual differences had any bearing on knowledge retention scores, we examined demographic variables including gender, occupation, age, education level, and the typical ways in which participants interacted with news and their news reading frequency. Overall, there were no significant effects of gender (*U*=958, *p*=309) or occupation (*U*=201.5, *p*=0.087), according to the Mann- Whitney U test on the overall knowledge retention test scores. Knowledge retention was also not related to education level ($x^2(5)$=6.183, *p*=0.289) or age ($x^2(3)$=4.486, *p*=0.223) according to the Kruskall Wallis test.

When we examined the demographic data based on story, we observed some differences for occupation, but not for gender, education, or age. Students had higher knowledge retention scores than non-students for story 1 (mining). Students' mean scores were also higher for story 2 (farming), but this difference was not significant (Table 3). This finding should be interpreted with caution due to the low number of non-students in the sample (11.5%), but one reason for the difference could be that students are immersed in an environment where they regularly need to read and retain knowledge, e.g., to pass a quiz, and thus may invoke different strategies for interacting with content – even when it is not explicitly linked with an academic purpose or performance; the experimental setting may have activated this behavior.

Table 3: Mean rank of knowledge retention test scores by occupation

	N	**Story 1 (Mining)**	**Story 2 (Farming)**
Student	69	41.43	40.53
Non-student	9	24.72	31.61
Mann-Whitney U		**177.5, *p*=0.036**	239.5, *p*=0.257

How people typically interacted with news did not impact overall knowledge retention ($x^2(2)$=0.813, *p*=0.666). Story 1 (mining) knowledge retention scores were highest for those who read print and online news, followed by those who read web news only, and then print, ($x^2(2)$=0.583, *p*=0.747). This pattern was different for story 2 (farming): web only news readers had the highest knowledge retention scores, followed by the print only and then print/web news readers ($x^2(2)$=2.151, *p*=0.341) (Table 4). These patterns were not statistically significant.

Table 4: Mean rank of knowledge test scores by typical news reading format

	N	**Story 1 (Mining)**	**Story 2 (Farming)**	**Overall Mean Rank**
Print	3	32.67	40.00	32.17
Web	30	38.05	44.08	42.02
Print & Web	45	40.92	36.41	38.31

Qualitatively participants commented that they were not accustomed to interacting with video news stories (P30, video), and that watching a video was less efficient than reading a news story: "[you] could probably get more information and background into an article that you know could be read in the same period of time it took to watch the video" (P24, video). However, participants interacting with web-based news may engage with news in its more traditional text format rather than listening or viewing news. Therefore, future studies should ask more fine-grained questions about news interactions rather than whether people access news in print or online.

Based on the Kruskall-Wallis test, there were significant differences in knowledge retention scores based on news reading frequency ($x^2(3)$=13.001, *p*=0.005). As shown in Table 5, those who read news several times per week had the highest mean rank knowledge retention scores for both stories, followed by the weekly, daily, and, finally, monthly news readers. This pattern was the same for both stories and was significant for story 1 ($x^2(3)=12.322, p=0.006$), but not story 2 ($x^2(3)=7.095, p=0.069$).

Table 5: Mean rank of knowledge test scores by typical news reading frequency

	N	Story 1 (Mining)	Story 2 (Farming)	Mean Rank
Daily	38	33.74	37.54	33.89
Several times/ week	23	49.54	44.52	49.85
Weekly	15	43.33	41.67	42.83
Monthly	2	4.75	2.75	2

6. DISCUSSION

We examined how people interact with and extract information from multimedia content. We explored differences in knowledge retention scored by story and media format, and how short-term recall was related to user experience (i.e., interest in and behavioral intention toward the news stories) demographic variables, and news reading habits. We found that people had higher knowledge retention scores for story 1 (mining) even though story 2 (farming) was more preferred, as measured through participants' interest, curiosity, and willingness to recommend ratings. However, media format did not affect knowledge retention. Few demographic variables influenced retention.

6.1 Media Format, Story and Knowledge Retention

In the current study participants using the video format scored the highest out of all formats for story 1, and second highest for story 2 (though not statistically significant). Koehler et al. [17] proposed that, according to dual coding theory, video should provide the greatest learning benefits given "there is little competition for resources when presenting visual and auditory information together" (pp. 250). Like Koehler et al., we failed to find a significant effect of media on recall. In the current study, narrative participants' scores were also high, and relatively stable across both stories. They were provided with one still image, yet it is difficult to say whether this visual was sufficient to enhance their representation and processing capacity. One study participant believed that the act of reading was directly and positively related to comprehension: "you are probably more bound to remember things… if you've read them" (P10, video). Our questions about typical news reading behaviors focused on web, print or web and print interactions, rather than multimedia interactions. Thus, participants in this study may be habituated to reading news despite new modes of news presentation, and this may have resulted in positive outcomes for the narrative group and minimized any gains for video participants.

Audio and transcript text, which relied on either the symbolic or language sub-systems, faired the poorest in terms of recall outcomes. Many participants in the audio and transcript text conditions relayed the need for visuals to enhance their understanding of the stories, and, further, that format was a major deterrent for engagement. Interestingly, these participants were primarily those interacting with the transcript format. For example, P16 stated that although they were interested in story 2, the fact that the content was "filled with grammatical mistakes or strange contextual ramblings" made them want to "jump to another website" for information on the topic. This aligns with Colbert and Boodoo's [4] finding that users prefer web content to follow particular writing guidelines and has implications for website designers and content writers. The transcript text was, although accurate, perplexing for users and atypical of most news and general web interactions. The audio participants relied exclusively on the language sub-system and thus this media may have been more cognitively taxing. One caveat is that our news interactions were passive in nature. Koehler et al [17] argued that learning "depends far more on an interaction between the content and style of the presentation than on the medium itself" (p. 270). While other studies have included forms of modality interactivity, they have failed to link media interactivity with learning [24], or concluded that interactivity can be useful for comprehending information when people cannot strip away the contextual elements of the interface [10], as is the case for most web and database systems. Looking at media with respect to active and passive content delivery may lead to more insights into the affects of media format on information extraction and use.

6.2 User Experience and Demographics

Our findings demonstrate the complexity and interconnectivity of factors affecting user experience with news stories and knowledge retention, specifically interest in content and select individual differences. We found that students had higher knowledge retention scores than non-students, and that the frequency and format in which participants interacted with news also affected information recall. This speaks to the role of prior knowledge, which is not only declarative (topic-based) but also procedural and habitual (applied) in nature. However, it is essential to note that additional individual differences should have been measured in this study, such as cognitive ability, to offer more concrete explanations of why topic and not media led to different knowledge retention outcomes.

Of note in this study was that daily news readers did not have the highest mean rank recall scores. Thus, while interacting with news on a regular basis (i.e., several times per week, weekly) played a role in knowledge retention, this relationship was not linear. Recent Pew research reported that 63% of Americans surveyed used Facebook and Twitter to consume national, international, business, sports, and other news. Although growth in social media news consumption has been consistent across demographic groups, younger users (under 35) are more likely to view news via these platforms [22]. Given the young age of our participants, and that news is consumed through a variety of news and social media sources, those who interacted with news most frequently (daily) may focus less attention on individual news stories to cope with the steady stream of information; those who interact weekly/several times a week may be more selective in what they read and more likely to engage more deeply. However, these ideas need verification.

In addition to participants' news reading habits, their perceptions of the stories and their interactions with them provide further evidence that cognitive and affective factors are related to learning outcomes [11]. The current study sample was larger than our pre-test sample (*n=6*), and while we found similar interest and sentiment ratings for both stories amongst pilot participants, story 1 (mining) was more polarizing in terms of perceived interest in the main study. Story 2 (farming) was significantly more interesting, and participants expressed more curiosity about it and willingness to share it with others or link to further content on the topic compared to story 1. Overall, we saw an interesting paradox where participants preferred story 2 (farming) to story 1 (mining), but actually achieved higher average knowledge retention scores for the *less preferred* story. However, interest and curiosity were only related to knowledge outcomes for story 1. One explanation for these findings could be that story 1 was perceived to be more difficult for some. Although reading ease and grade level were equivocal for the two stories, we did not measure users' perceptions of difficulty. There were an equal number of knowledge retention questions per story, but story 1 was longer and thus contained more content. The length of story 1 may have made it more cognitively complex, and, for those who lacked interest in the story (e.g. could not relate to it), this may have negatively affected their perceptions of effort [15] and subsequent ability to derive meaning from the story.

However, we cannot say whether interest affected people's willingness to interact with the story, or whether interacting with the story created or deterred interest, resulting in more or less positive learning outcomes. Yet, the substantial role of interest in this study corresponds to other work linking interest and affect [2; 21]. Many participants in our study pointed to the human element in the stories, but particularly story 2 (farming). The inability to relate to story 1, due to its geographical setting, emphasis on technology rather than people, and perceived distance from participants' daily lives, produced disinterest in some participants, and this was directly related to knowledge retention scores.

6.2.1 Limitations

A limitation of this study is that it used static news experiences, limited to two stories, focusing on users' interactions with content and media rather than investigating a multi-stage search process. However, in a dynamic search process it would be difficult to distinguish the effects of content and media on the user experience and learning. The experimental design used in this study afforded us the ability to isolate and systematically investigate our variables of interest, and to learn more about the extraction phase of information retrieval and its relationship to participants' ability to remember story content.

We operationalized learning at a very basic level of Bloom's taxonomy: remembering, as measured using a knowledge retention test. It can be argued as to whether or not our measure was optimal, given that we did not systematically assess prior knowledge of the story topics [27], and many researchers have stressed the need to go beyond recall and recognition as an outcome of searching as learning [10; 28]. These arguments are rooted in the fact that searching involves acts of information acquisition, but also comprehension, interpretation, and comparison [20] and results in changes within learners [14].

Recent attempts to measure learning have tried to be more encompassing than simply the number of recalled facts. Wilson and Wilson [28] developed measures based on the usefulness of recalled facts, participants' ability to incorporate facts into intelligent statements, and their use of facts to raise further questions about the content within participant-generated summary statements. Freund et al. [10] used Kintsch's Construction–Integration (C-I) Model [16] to develop instruments (true and false, sentence verification, and summary statements) to measure comprehension with reading materials. Both studies reported successful implementation of their measures. Wilson and Wilson [28] found significant differences between pre- and post-task summaries for all of their measures, but the length of the summaries and participants' prior knowledge affected the results, while Freund et al. [10] found significant differences in participants' ability to decode and recall content, but they did not demonstrate more global processing of the material. Freund et al. [10] noted that assessing comprehension was the "major challenge in conducting [their] study, and it is one that must be faced by the information retrieval community given that learning is an important outcome of search" (p. 90). As work in this area increases, we look forward to replicating this study with more sophisticated, theoretically derived measures of learning and to study information extraction and use over a longer period of time.

7. Conclusion

Although there were non-significant different learning outcomes for participants according to the media format to which they were assigned, the stories themselves generated the most significant differences in knowledge retention scores. Interestingly, the most interesting story (farming) had lower average knowledge test scores than the less interesting, longer, and, perhaps more challenging story (mining). We suggest that participants' level of interest in story 1 affected their learning outcomes (positively and negatively), emphasizing the role of cognitive and affective responses to content in learning, and suggesting that media may be less significant in the extraction and use of information than the content itself. This has implications for the way in which content is delivered to information consumers, and suggests that the format and interactivity of media may affect user experience but not other important outcomes such as the ability to recall content.

While we cannot control the personal characteristics that people bring to information interactions (e.g., prior knowledge, habitual interaction modes), we can focus on ways to generate situational interest during the extraction process to promote knowledge gains. Our qualitative data suggest that content factors other than media may be more influential, which bears further investigation. These findings have implications for the design of information systems. Given the differences in knowledge retention by media condition, we need to understand why participants' performance was stable for the narrative condition, but varied for the video, audio and transcript conditions. This could be achieved by measuring other content factors beyond readability (as we did in this study) and individual differences, testing active versus passive information extraction, and deploying more sophisticated measures of learning outcomes to understand the relationship between user perceptions and information complexity.

8. ACKNOWLEDGMENTS

This study was supported by the Social Sciences and Humanities Research Council of Canada and the UBC Hampton Research Fund. Thank you to research assistants Devin Soper, Tammi Mercado, Jack Hallin and Zoe MacDougall.

9. REFERENCES

[1] Anderson, L. W., Krathwohl, D. R., & Bloom, B. S. (Eds.). (2001). *A Taxonomy for Learning, Teaching, and Assessing: A Revision of Bloom's Taxonomy of Educational Objectives.* New York, NY: Longman.

[2] Arapakis, I., Lalmas, M., Cambazoglu, B., Marcos, M.-C. & Jose, J.M. (2014). User engagement in online news: Under the scope of sentiment, interest, affect, and gaze. *Journal of the American Society for Information Science and Technology*, *65*(10), 1988-2005.

[3] Case, D.O. & O'Connor, L.G. (2016). What's the use? Measuring the frequency of studies of information outcomes. *Journal of the Association of Information Science & Technology, 67*(3), 649-661.

[4] Colbert, M. & Boodoo, A. (2011) Does 'Letting Go of the Words' increase engagement: A traffic study. In *Extended*

Abstracts on Human Factors in Computing Systems (pp. 655–67). ACM.

[5] Cole, C. (2012). *Information Need: A Theory Connecting Information Search to Knowledge Formation.* Medford, NJ: Information Today.

[6] Ellis, D. (1993). Modeling the information-seeking patterns of academic researchers: A grounded theory approach. *The Library Quarterly, 63*(4), 469-486.

[7] Farrall, M. L. (2012). *Reading Assessment: Linking Language, Literacy, and Cognition.* Somerset, NJ: John Wiley & Sons. Retrieved from http://www.ebrary.com

[8] Flesch, R. *How to write plain English.* University of Canterbury. Retrieved 11 February 2016 from http://www.mang.canterbury.ac.nz/writing_guide/writing/flesch.shtml

[9] Ford, N., Miller, D., & Moss, N. (2001). The role of individual differences in Internet searching: An empirical study. *Journal of the American Society for Information Science and Technology, 52*(12), 1049–1066.

[10] Freund, L., Kopak, R. & O'Brien, H.L. (2016). The effects of textual environment on reading comprehension: Implications for searching as learning. *Journal of Information Science, 42*(1) 79–93.

[11] Graesser, A., & D'Mello, S. K. (2011). Theoretical perspectives on affect and deep learning. In R. A. Calvo & S. K. D'Mello (Eds.), *New Perspectives on Affect and Learning Technologies* (pp. 11–21). New York: Springer.

[12] Hess, J. A. (2015). Editor's introduction: What exactly are we studying? *Communication Education, 64*(4), 491–493.

[13] Hong, T. (2012). Internet health search: When process complements goals. *Journal of the American Society for Information Science and Technology, 63*(11), 2283-2293.

[14] Jansen, B. J., Booth, D., & Smith, B. (2009). Using the taxonomy of cognitive learning to model online searching. *Information Processing & Management, 45*(6), 643–663.

[15] Kelly, D., Arguello, J., Edwards, A., & Wu, W. (2015). Development and evaluation of search tasks for IIR experiments using a cognitive complexity framework. In *Proceedings of the 2015 International Conference on The Theory of Information Retrieval* (pp. 101–110). ACM.

[16] Kintsch W. (1998). *Comprehension: A Paradigm for Cognition.* Cambridge, MA: Cambridge University Press.

[17] Koehler, M.J., Yadav, A., Phillips, M. & Cavazos-Kottke, S. (2005). What is video good for? Examining how media and story genre interact. *Journal of Educational Multimedia and Hypermedia, 14*(3), 249–72.

[18] Liu, J., Cole, M. J., Liu, C., Bierig, R., Gwizdka, J., Belkin, N. J., ... & Zhang, X. (2010). Search behaviors in different task types. In *Proceedings of the 10th annual joint conference on Digital libraries* (pp. 69-78). ACM.

[19] Marchionini, G. (1995). *Information Seeking in Electronic Environments.* Cambridge, MA: Cambridge University Press.

[20] Marchionini, G. (2006). Exploratory search: From finding to understanding. *Communications of the ACM, 49*(4), 41–46.

[21] McCay-Peet, L., Lalmas, M. & Navalpakkam, V. (2012). On saliency, affect and focused attention. In *Proceedings of Conference on Human Factors in Computing Systems* (pp. 541-550). ACM.

[22] Mitchell, A., Barthel, M., Shearer, E., et al. (July 14, 2015). The evolving role of news on Twitter and Facebook. Pew Research Centre. Retrieved April 4, 2016, from http://www.journalism.org/files/2015/07/Twitter-and-News-Survey-Report-FINAL2.pdf

[23] O'Brien, H.L. (2011). Weaving the threads of experience into human information interaction (HII): Probing user experience (UX) for new directions in information behaviour. In A. Spink & J. Heinström *New directions in information behaviour* (pp. 69-92). Emerald Publishing.

[24] Oh, J. & Sundar, S.S. (2015). How does interactivity persuade? An experimental test of interactivity on cognitive absorption, elaboration, and attitudes. *Journal of Communication, 65*(2), 213–36.

[25] Paivio, A (1990). *Mental representations: a dual coding approach.* Oxford. England: Oxford University Press.

[26] Saracevic, T. (2007). Relevance: A review of the literature and a framework for thinking on the notion in information science. Part III: Behavior and effects of relevance. *Journal of the American Society for Information Science and Technology, 58*(13), 2126-2144.

[27] Vakkari, P. (1997). Information seeking in context: a changing and challenging metatheory. In P. Vakkari, R. Savolainen, & B. Dervin, *Information seeking in context* (pp. 452-646). London: Graham Taylor.

[28] Wilson, M.J. & Wilson, M.L. (2013). A comparison of techniques for measuring sensemaking and learning within participant-generated summaries. *Journal of the American Society for Information Science and Technology, 64*(2), 291-306.

Self-Es: The Role of Emails-to-Self in Personal Information Management

Horațiu Bota*
School of Computing Science
University of Glasgow
h.bota.1@research.gla.ac.uk

Paul N. Bennett,
Ahmed Hassan Awadallah,
Susan T. Dumais
Microsoft Research
Redmond, WA
{pauben, hassanam, sdumais}@microsoft.com

ABSTRACT

Email has been central to online communication for the past two decades. Through constant use, new information flows are being defined around users' interactions with emails. Alongside traditional messages, the email inbox is an always-available repository of to-do lists, reminders, files and notes. In this paper, we investigate the use of self-addressed emails (*self-Es*) as an information management tool, by analysing both: (i) responses to a survey about email use; and (ii) a collection of user donated self-addressed emails. Our results show that sending self-Es is a frequent behaviour among the users we questioned. In addition, we find that to-dos and reminders are the most popular type of information contained in emails-to-self. Our findings have direct implications for the development of systems that support novel interactions with information flows centred around email.

Keywords

Personal information management; email search.

1. INTRODUCTION

While email has taken a central role in communication, research has primarily focused on the role of email as a *person-to-person* communication tool. However, another phenomenon has occasionally been noted in research [18]: many users often send emails to themselves, where the user sending the mail is the single and only recipient of the mail. For brevity we term such an email a *self-E*[1] (e.g. see Figure 1). For example Bellotti et al.[1] describes such emails as being used as a repository of "to-do" and "to read" items. Shokouhi *et al.* [6] mentions the use for long-term archiving of information; they also note that users have reported difficulty when searching for such mails since common search filters also return results where the user has included themselves in the to/cc with other additional recipients. In this paper, we focus solely on email as a person-to-*self* communication tool via analysis of self-Es.

From: Alex A. Author <a.a.author@acm.org>
To: Alex A. Author <a.a.author@acm.org>
Cc: –
Bcc: –
Subject: after vacation
Sent: Fri 9/2/2016 2:40 PM

\+ Set meeting with Sara
\+ Check whether John resolved the dependency
\+ Ask Pat to pushback timeline

Figure 1: A (hypothetical) example of a self-E. Self-Es are emails where the *only* recipient is the sender. We separate this from the case where the sender may cc himself/herself in addition to others.

Given that a user who sends a self-E is the only recipient of the email, such emails raise interesting questions in *personal* information management. In order to assist the user in taking action on such emails, we must first understand the types of information managed in such a way and then identify likely actions. For example, if a self-E is a "to-do" item such as "write the report", the system can offer to set a reminder. If the item contains driving directions, it may be ranked preferentially on a mobile device. If the item contains meeting notes, then it might be ranked highly based on similarity with a user's calendar to surface at an appropriate time. If the message is sent immediately before a weekend or vacation, the system may surface it to the top when the user returns. Likewise, other user assistance or filtering might be appropriate depending on whether the email contains receipts, images, attachments or keywords such as "test", etc.

However, before such user aids can be designed we must first understand the spectrum of intents users have when sending a self-E. In this paper, we provide the first such characterization using three data sources: (1) we conduct a survey of self-E behaviour and intents; (2) we analyze self-E behaviour in a publicly available email corpus; (3)

*Work performed while at Microsoft Research.
[1]Not to be confused with a selfie photograph!

CHIIR '17, March 07-11, 2017, Oslo, Norway
© 2017 ACM. ISBN 978-1-4503-4677-1/17/03...$15.00
DOI: http://dx.doi.org/10.1145/3020165.3020189

we analyze self-Es that were contributed and labeled by the original senders. In addition, we characterize the frequency of such intents and build classifiers to predict a common intent in self-Es: reminder or to-do intent. The research questions we want to address through our analysis are:

(RQ1): **How many email users send self-Es? How often?** In particular, we want to find out the proportion of users that engages in self-E behaviour and how frequently they send emails to themselves.

(RQ2): **Why do users email themselves?** We want to discover what user tasks drive self-E behaviour, and the types of information contained by emails-to-self.

(RQ3): **Can reminder intent be detected in self-Es?** Specifically, can we use email classification techniques to detect self-Es that serve as reminders or to-do items?

2. RELATED WORK

Email has been central to on-line communication for the past two decades. Because of its central role in communication, extensive effort has been allocated to understanding user interactions with email [5, 18, 19]. Extending these efforts, our work brings together two central areas of research on email: (i) information and task management in email and (ii) email classification.

2.1 Information management in email

Email is a critical tool for communication and collaboration. Whittaker and Sidner [19] studied how users manage their email. They used the term *email overload* to refer to the phenomenon whereby users are overwhelmed by email. They show that even though email was designed for communication, it is actually being used for other tasks, like task management (e.g., preserving task context and monitoring task progress) and organizing longer term information (personal archiving). More recent work has shown that users receive and retain more email [8] reinforcing email's role as a digital archive.

Prior work investigated the use of email for task management [18]. The authors discuss how people not only use emails to communicate about tasks but also send themselves email to put messages in the inbox as reminders and links to useful information. An in-depth look at email as a task management tool is provided in Bellotti et al.[1], in which the authors report on a multi-phase study of email users.

Our work is similar to this line of research in that we focus on email usage for task management. Our work extends this line of work by focusing on characterizing and understanding the different intents of self-addressed emails. The characterization is done using multiple data sources including surveys, emails in a publicly available dataset and emails labelled and contributed by the original sender.

2.2 Email classification

Carvalho and Cohen [5] considered classification of email messages into a set of "speech acts" in email, such as a request or a commitment. They showed that using text features and correlation among email messages in the same thread can improve email-act classification. Sappelli et al. [15] proposed a taxonomy of tasks that are expressed through email messages. They manually annotated two email datasets and evaluated the validity of the dimensions in the taxonomy in addition to investigating the potential for automatic e-mail classification.

Corston-Oliver et al. [17] developed a system for automatically identifying action items in email messages. They used the system to produce a task-focused summary of a message that consists of a list of action items extracted from the message. Bennett and Carbonell [2] also studied the task of action item detection in email. They report that using enriched feature sets, such as n-grams, and contextual cues improves performance by up to 10% over bag-of-word features. Shen et al. [16] predicted tasks associated with an incoming email by leveraging email sender, recipients, and distinct subject words. They found the body words to not provide additional prediction value.

Prior research has also looked into grouping emails into a set of activities. Kushmerick and Lau [10] formalized e-commerce activities as finite-state automata, where transitions among states represent messages sent between participants. Dredze et al. [7] used user generated activity labels and classified emails into activities using overlapping participants and content similarity. Qadir et al. [14] introduced a latent activity model for workplace emails. They posed the problem as probabilistic inference in graphical models that jointly capture the interplay between latent activities and the email contexts they govern, such as the recipients, subject and body.

Similar to this line of work, we also build email classification models. Our work is different in that we focus on predicting a common intent in self-Es: reminder or to-do intent. This is one of the most commonly expressed intents in self-addressed emails and identifying it can enable interesting user assistance scenarios. Additionally, since emails-to-self need not follow communication conventions as those emails sent to others (e.g., they may be brief and lack textual context cues), it is an interesting question if they can be automatically classified.

3. DATA AND METHODS

To conduct our analysis, we make use of three complementary sources of data. First, we consider the information available via a public email corpus named "Avocado" . This helps ground our research in a corpus that others can easily access for reproducibility and helps us with an initial perspective on self-E behaviour. However, given the emails in the corpus are from approximately 15 years ago, it is possible that email behaviours have changed. Therefore, we also conducted an email survey and acquired donations of recent self-addressed emails to understand self-E behaviour in a more modern setting and collect explicit intent labels from our study participants – labels which can help us probe self-E motivations more deeply. In this section, we describe the basic characteristics of these data sources. In Section 4, we discuss the implications of each for our research questions on self-E behaviour and intents.

3.1 Avocado

Our first source of data to understand self-E behaviour is a publicly available email corpus. The Avocado Research Email Collection [13] consists of emails from 279 accounts of a now defunct technology company, referred to as "Avocado", that was active in the early 2000s. From this collection, we selected all accounts that belonged to individual people; that is, the accounts were neither shared accounts

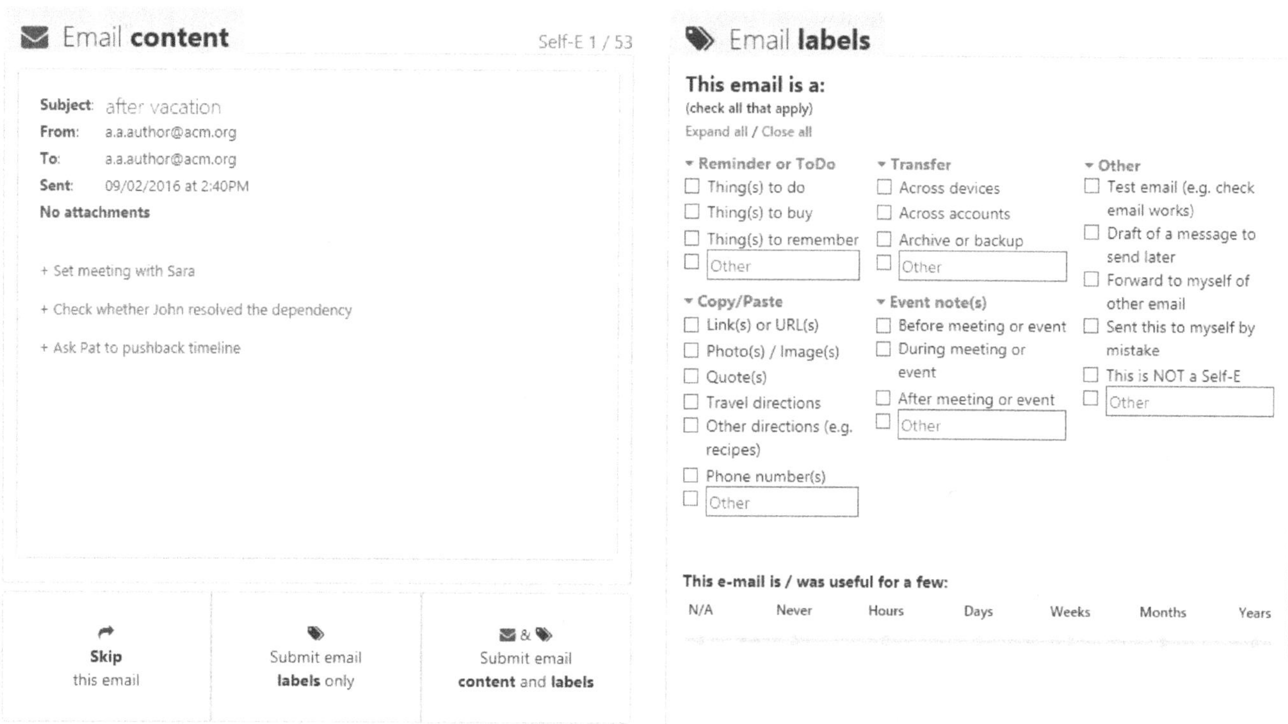

Figure 2: Part of the labelling interface we used to collect self-E donations from users in our organisation. Email content and details are displayed in the panel on the left, email labels are displayed in the panel on the right.

nor system accounts (such as mailing lists or conference room accounts). To ensure a sufficient sample size of email activity, from the accounts that belonged to individual people, we selected all those accounts that were active for at least 50 calendar days, where activity is determined by having at least one email of any type sent or received on a given day. These criteria resulted in 88 email accounts belonging to individual people with sufficient overall email activity. For these accounts, we analysed their entire sent folders for self-E behaviour. Those folders contain 110K (one hundred ten thousand) emails sent to any address(es) by these 88 users.

3.2 Survey

As mentioned above, given that most emails in the Avocado collection were sent roughly 15 years ago, it is possible that e-mail behaviour has changed in the interim. As a more current way of identifying the information needs that underlie self-E behaviour, we conducted a survey to look at both self-E and general email practices. Our main objective was to uncover the types of information that users include in their self-addressed emails. The survey was distributed to a random set of employees within Microsoft who were based in the USA, and responses were received from a total of 238 people: 73.7% ($n = 160$) male, 86.6% ($n = 206$) between 25 and 54 years of age, 77.7% ($n = 174$) had a bachelor's degree or higher. Our respondents held various positions in our organisation, with the two largest groups being "Software Developer" (29.4%, $n = 64$) and "Program Manager" (22.9%, $n = 50$) – other occupations including human resources, sales, marketing and design professionals.

Our survey was structured into four separate sections: in the first section, we asked our respondents to report on general aspects of their use of email, such as the number of accounts they use for personal and work email, the number of emails they send daily from their accounts, and their usage of email management tools (e.g. email folders, marking items read or unread, zero inbox). In the second section, we asked our respondents to think back on the last self-addressed email they sent, and describe, in as much detail as possible, the intent behind their most recent self-E, the task that their self-E helped with and the context they were in when they sent it. In the third section, we asked respondents to report on their general self-E behaviour, how often they send themselves emails, and with what intent. Lastly, we asked a series of demographic questions which were optional. Throughout our survey, we collected intent labels by displaying a set of predefined labels to our respondents, as well as allowing free-form text input for user-defined labels. The predefined labels we used were broken down into five high-level categories, with each category containing several subcategories, as shown in Table 1. The intent categories were initially developed by manually inspecting self-Es we identified in Avocado; we defined the final set of intent categories and subcategories after several iterations in which we tested our survey design, using small samples of respondents – results from those pilot iterations are not included in the analysis we present here.

3.3 Labelling tool

Finally, part of our effort to understand self-E behaviour was concerned with creating a current collection of self-addressed emails. Similar to the survey described in Section 3.2, this has the advantage of measuring current practice.

Intent category	Intent subcategory
Reminder or ToDo	Thing(s) to do Thing(s) to buy Thing(s) to remember Other [free-form text input]
Transfer	Across devices Across accounts Archive or backup Other [free-form text input]
Copy/Paste	Link(s) or URL(s) Photo(s) or Image(s) Quote(s) Travel directions Other directions (e.g. recipes) Phone number(s) Other [free-form text input]
Event note(s)	Before meeting or event During meeting or event After meeting or event Other [free-form text input]
Other	Test email (e.g. check email is working) Draft of a message to send later Forward to myself of another email Sent this to myself by mistake This is NOT a Self-E Other [free-form text input]

Table 1: Pre-defined intent labels (categories and subcategories) used for our survey and our labelling tool.

In addition, compared to working with Avocado data, this approach has the advantage that the sender of the email can label their own intent in sending themself a self-E; compared to the survey, the advantage is that this approach does not rely on user memory which might be subject to biases as to the types of self-Es that are recalled. Although privacy concerns prevent us from sharing the self-Es we collected with the external research community, we expect those that reproduce our methodology, in a similar context as ours, will find results consistent with our corpus.

To build this collection, we developed a Web application that allowed users in our organisation to quickly find, label and donate their recent self-Es. The application integrated with the single sign-on mechanism available in our organisation, and after user login, it automatically searched the user's sent item folder of their work email account for self-addressed mail, retrieving their most recent self-Es. The interface, shown in Figure 2, displayed email properties, together with email content and attachments. Users were able to label individual self-Es using the same pre-defined intent categories used in our survey (and discussed in the previous section). In addition to intent labels, they were able to report how long the displayed self-E was useful to them, using a set of pre-defined labels, in order of increasing duration from a *"Few hours"* to a *"Few years"*. In the following sections we refer to these duration labels as self-E lifetime.

Given the privacy concerns that surround sharing email with third parties, in addition to allowing users to donate self-Es and labels, we allowed our users to skip emails they did not want to share or to label self-Es and donate only the labels, without actual self-E content. For all donations, even skipped self-Es, we logged email meta-data, such as email sent date and time, number of characters in subject or body, and the number of attachments. In total, we collected 1274 self-Es, from 101 unique users: 813 with content and labels, 230 with labels only and 231 with just meta-data. The maximum number of donations per user was 88, and the minimum 1; overall, the mean number of contributed self-Es per user was 12.61, with a standard deviation of 13.84.

To have participants use our self-E collection tool, we used the same methodology as for our survey and sent email invitations internally to a random sample of our organisational address book. Please note that there was no overlap between respondents to our survey and users who donated emails using our labelling tool. That is, users who responded to our survey were not invited to use the labelling tool and vice-versa. The data collected using these two methods (survey and labelling tool) represent complementary perspectives on self-E behaviour.

4. RESULTS

4.1 How many users send self-Es?

To answer our first research question (RQ1), we examine all three of our data sources. In particular, we focus on answering this question by characterizing both the percentage of users who email themselves and how often users email themselves.

To estimate the percentage of users who email themselves, we begin by examining the view offered via the set of 88 active users in Avocado. Overall, 81% ($n = 71$) of these users had at least one self-addressed email in their sent folder, with the mean proportion of self-Es in the 110K total sent mails of these users being close to 1%. Thus, we can conclude that the vast majority of users engage in self-E behaviour with an overall prevalence that is small as a percentage but still significant in terms of overall quantity.

Figure 3 shows the cumulative distribution of self-Es in our sample. Examining it, we find that for 25% of the email accounts we analysed, more than 1% of all outgoing email is self-addressed. This can be seen in Figure 3 by noting that the black dashed line crosses the 1% line at 75% (i.e. 25% of users surpass this level of activity). This indicates that there is a reasonable percentage of users (1 in 4) that engage in this behaviour with a higher frequency than average and the mean is not simply dominated by a few outliers.

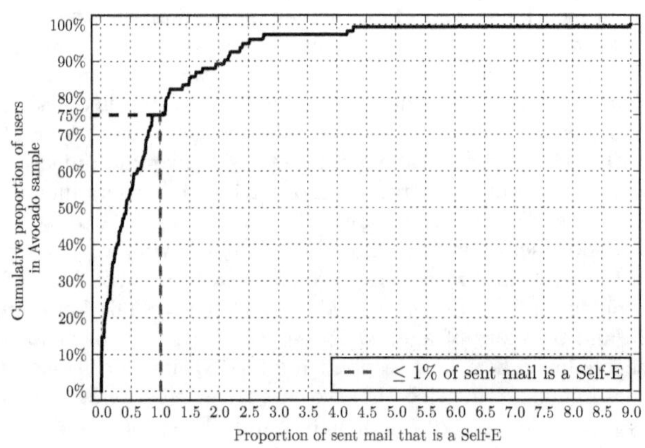

Figure 3: Cumulative distribution of proportion of self-Es per user in our sample of the Avocado email corpus

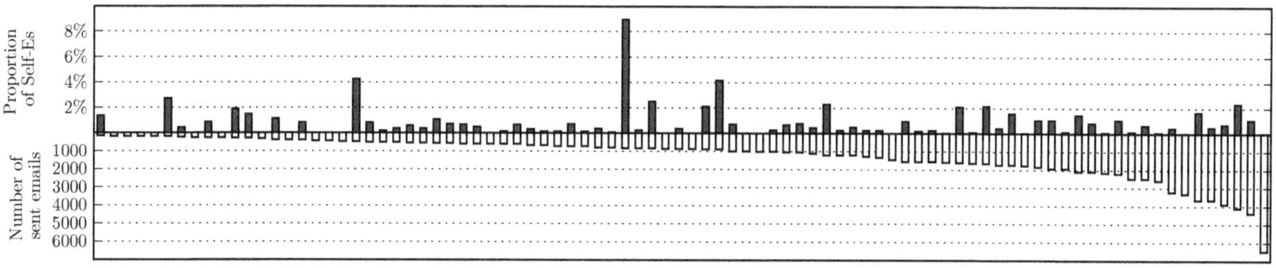

Figure 4: Per user proportion of self-Es in sent mail and sent mail volume in the Avocado corpus. Each pair of bars represents one user in the sample we analysed. The figure is sorted by sent mail volume from the least (*left*) to the most (*right*).

We visualize per user self-E frequency in greater detail in Figure 4. This figure plots both self-E proportion of sent mail and sent mail volume for each of the 88 users. Observe the variation in the height of the dark bars; there is clearly high variance across users with regard to the proportion of sent emails that are self-Es. Furthermore, some users engage in the behaviour more heavily. For example, note in the figure that for one account (who had a total sent mail volume of roughly 1000 mails), more than 8% of all outgoing emails were self-Es! Thus, some small number of users demonstrate this behaviour at a much higher prevalence.

One of the limitations in using the Avocado corpus for self-E analysis is that email habits and practices may have changed since the time period represented by emails in the corpus – approximately 15 years ago. As discussed above, we therefore supplement our understanding from this publicly available corpus by both conducting a survey and collecting email donations. The remainder of the paper focuses on these sources of data.

With regard to the survey, respondents reported whether they sent emails to themselves, how often, and with what intent. Figure 6a shows that almost all respondents to our survey (92%, $n = 219$) have sent at least one email to themselves. In addition, we asked whether they save information that is useful only to themselves in their email accounts, with 81.1% ($n = 193$) reporting that they habitually save useful information in their email. Figure 5 shows that the majority preferred method of saving useful information in email accounts is sending self-Es, namely 71.4% of respondents ($n = 170$) reporting that they regularly save information in their email accounts by sending self-Es.

Overall, our findings show that self-E behaviour is frequent among users of email, ranging from 81% of users in the Avocado email collection to 92% of respondents to our survey having sent at least one self-E. Even more, for those who use email to manage useful information other than traditional email messages, self-addressed emails are preferred over other methods of storing information in email accounts, which suggests that for a large proportion of email users, self-E behaviour has become integrated into general workflows.

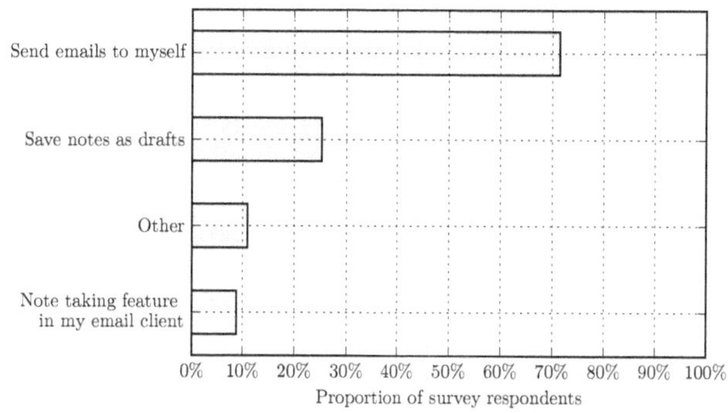

Figure 5: Survey: How do you save information that is useful only to you in your email account?

How often do users send self-Es?

In addition to measuring the proportion of users with self-E behaviour and proportion relative to all sent mail, another of our aims was to understand how often users send themselves emails. To this end, we asked our survey participants who reported having sent at least one self-E ($n = 219$) to describe how long ago they sent this self-E (figure 6b) and how often they send self-Es in general (figure 6c). The majority of answers reported recent self-Es having been sent: either on the same day as the survey (*"Today"* 13.7%, $n = 30$) or a few days before the survey (*"Few days ago"* 48.9%, $n = 107$); less than 12% of respondents reported their most recent self-E as having been sent a *"Few months ago"* or earlier. With regard to general self-E behaviour, our survey answers suggest that the majority of respondents that reported having sent at least one self-E, send themselves emails *"Several times per month"* (37.4%, $n = 82$) or *"Several times per week"* (24.7%, $n = 54$).

To examine how often users send self-Es using the donated self-Es described in Section 3.3, for each user we estimate the average rate of self-Es by dividing the number of self-Es they donated by the duration in weeks between their most recent self-E donated to us, and their oldest self-E, as determined by email sent date. Figure 7 shows the distribution of the average number of self-Es per user, with approximately 65% of users sending one or more self-Es per week. This is in general agreement with the survey data where 62.6% reported their last self-E was within a week and 32.4% reported a frequency of at least two self-Es per week. Thus multiple data sources indicate that although the proportion of sent mails may be small, sending self-Es is a regular weekly habit for the majority of users – and can even be a daily habit for some users. This is supported both by 7.7% ($n = 17$)

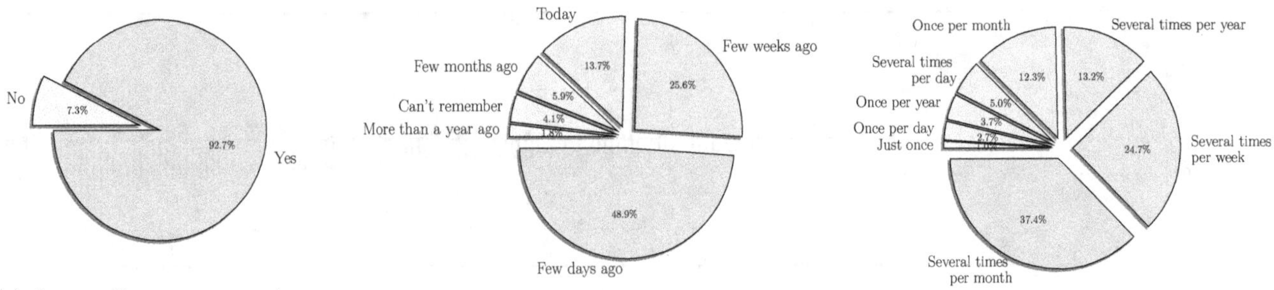

(a) Survey: Have you ever sent an email to yourself, and only yourself, containing information that is useful to you?

(b) Survey: Approximately how long ago did you send yourself your most recent Self-E?

(c) Survey: How often do you send yourself self-Es?

Figure 6: Proportion and recency of sending self-Es in a survey of 238 people at a large technology corporation.

of survey respondents who reported sending self-Es once or several times per day, as well as the information in figure 7 which shows that roughly 8% of email donors have an average weekly self-E rate of 8 or more self-Es. This highlights, from different perspectives, a substantial population of users that is active daily in their interaction with self-Es.

4.2 Why do users email themselves?

Next, we turn to our second research question (RQ2), why do users email themselves? In particular, we wanted to understand the tasks and information needs that drive self-E behaviour. In both our survey and our self-E labelling tool, we asked participants to describe the intents behind their self-Es. In our survey, we asked respondents to describe the intent behind (i) their most recent self-E and (ii) the intents behind their self-Es in general. In our labelling tool, participants were able to directly attach intent labels to their own self-Es. In both the survey and labeling tool, we allowed users to select multiple intents from a set of predefined labels (e.g., "Things to do", "Things to buy") but also allowed them to define their own intent labels as well. Since multiple labels were allowed for the same self-E, when we normalize by the number of total labels (greater than or equal to the number of mails), we refer to it as a percentage of labels (sums to 1 across intent labels). When we normalize by the number of mails we refer to it as a percentage of mails (sums to more than 1 across intent labels).

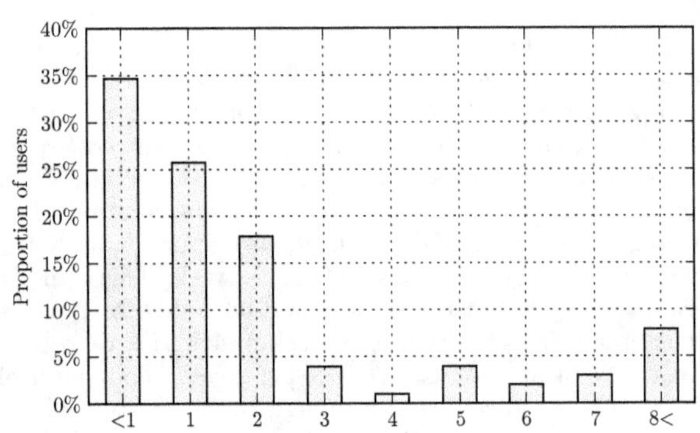

Figure 7: Average number of self-Es per week

Figure 8 shows the percentage of intent labels from the labelling tool (on the *left*) as well as the absolute differences from this distribution, observed in our two survey questions regarding self-E intent (on the *right*). When the survey differences are above zero, it means that survey respondents report a higher percentage of those intent labels than observed when donations are collected. Likewise below zero, it means that survey users report a lower percentage of those intent labels when compared to donations. These differences may be explained by a tendency to have a bias toward certain intents in memory when asked to recall a specific instance – while this aspect bears further investigation, we note that the relative ranking of the intent categories is consistent for both survey and donations: figure 9 shows the proportion of intent labels in both collected self-Es and survey answers, ranked by frequency in the donated self-E collection.

In particular, the most popular intents, for both labelled self-Es and survey answers, are *"Things to do / remember"*, *"File transfer across devices"* and *"Link(s) or URL(s)"*, with *"Things to do / remember"* being the most popular overall. Within the donations, approximately 37% of the labels are *"Reminder or ToDo"* category, and as a percentage of mails, 53% of all donated self-Es had some form of reminder or to-do intent label attached. Among the *"Other"* categories of intent labels, which were free-form text, users reported sending themselves test emails, passwords, photos of receipts, code snippets or mistakenly sending themselves emails. Overall, these distributions emphasize that while "Reminders or To-Dos" form an important large subclass of self-Es they are still only slightly more than half of self-Es and that the remainder captures a rich set of other information management practices where the appropriate automated user assistance may differ by intent.

What types of tasks drive self-Es?

To further understand both the breadth and complexity of self-E intents, one of the questions in our survey asked respondents to describe their most recent self-E in as much detail as possible, including information about why they sent the email to themselves, as well as the context they were in. In this section, we reproduce some of the answers to that question, in order to better illustrate the tasks and intents that appear to drive self-E behaviour, as described by the respondents to our survey. As discussed in the previous section, task management, in particular reminders and to-dos,

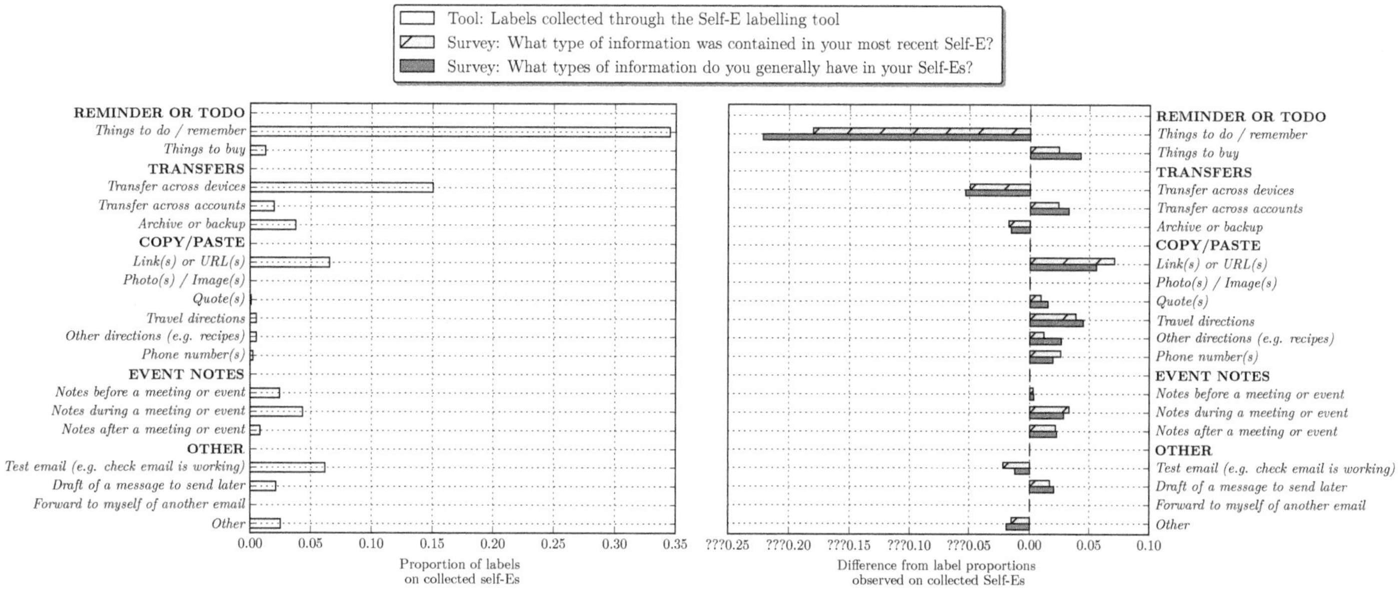

Figure 8: *Self-e* intent labels based on donated emails (left) and survey answers (right)

drives a large proportion of self-E behaviour; in the words of our survey respondents:

1. [My recent self-E contained] *A bullet-pointed list of ideas, tasks and reminders that I sent myself from my phone so that I remembered to break those out into Outlook tasks and later.*
2. *I always send mail to myself when I have some information that I need to save for later use and I am not sure where will I be when I will need to use this information. This mostly happens for personal scenarios and rarely for work scenarios.*
3. *I copied an image from a web site to remind myself of a To Do in a week's time. The To Do is to purchase something, which has a validity date on it and doesn't become valid for another week. I had just arrived back home from vacation and was checking my email when I logged this as a To Do.*
4. *I leverage flagged email option to maintain my TODO list. If I need to add a task for myself by myself, I send an email to myself. I like one place to track every thing whether it is email, follow up or tasks. In my role and most of the management role, email or sometime calendar activities is the main task tracker.*

It is interesting to note that users have integrated some self-E intents with existing information management tools (e.g. *"Outlook tasks"*, *"flagged email"*) and extend their usefulness. In addition, the answers we received describe self-Es as a tool for cross-boundary self-communication: whether across devices (e.g. *"sent myself from my phone"* [to Outlook]), across spaces (e.g. *"not sure where I will be"*) or across time (e.g. *"To Do in a week's time"*). This suggests the ubiquity of email, combined with its familiarity of use, could be further leveraged to develop novel email client features which further support self-E intents.

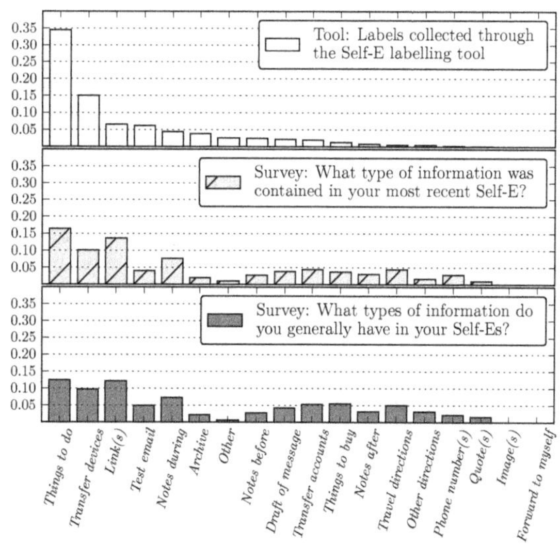

Figure 9: Absolute proportion of *Self-e* intent labels in donated emails (top) and survey answers (middle and bottom). Ordered by label frequency in donated emails (top). Label names are truncated.

How long are self-Es useful after being sent?

In addition to intent labels, we asked our participants to attach lifetime labels to the self-Es they donated. Specifically, users were asked to answer the following question: "How long is or was this self-e useful for you?", using a set of predefined answers as lifetime labels for the self-Es they donated. Self-E lifetime is interesting to explore because it has implications for search or the proactive display of self-Es. For example, knowing how long a self-E is useful can be used to keep that self-E displayed at the top of email stacks, or in task management interfaces, only for the duration of their usefulness. Figure 10 shows the distribution of duration labels over intent labels (each row sums to 100%).

It is interesting to note that both *"Reminders and ToDos"* and *"Copy/Paste"* self-E lifetimes have heavier distribution tails, with these types of self-Es being useful up to a few weeks or months. This suggests they are partially used as archiving devices for various pieces of information. If an email client enhanced these types of self-E with appropriate meta-data – e.g. indicating a significant portion of a self-E's text originated from a copy/paste operation – later rank operations might be able to promote such self-Es in response to user searches, since their longer lifetimes imply they are more likely to be searched for in the future.

Overall, the majority of self-Es have relatively short lifetimes, from a few hours to a few days, which suggests that most self-Es, across intents, are used for immediate or short-running tasks, rather than longer-running ones. In contrast to the other categories of intents, the "Other" self-Es that were labelled as never useful were mostly *"Test emails"* to check email delivery or correct email formatting; even though these emails achieve their purpose, they are generally perceived as never useful. As mentioned above, this has implications for email client design, suggesting that features centred around emails-to-self should be aware of self-E pro-actively rank or display self-Es based on their age and intent.

4.3 Can reminder intent be detected in self-Es?

Given how frequent the *"Reminders or ToDo"* intent is among the emails we collected, we set out to build a classifier that detects reminder self-Es. In particular, we wanted to classify self-Es under the broad category of *"Reminder or ToDo"* items, and not its subclasses (*"Things to do"*, *"Things to remember"* or *"Things to buy"*). From a systems perspective, being able to detect a user's need to be reminded of a to-do self-E can be leveraged for proactive notifications or better email search results. From a research point of view, identifying intent within less formally composed emails is an interesting and challenging problem. Even though others have looked at predicting "to-do" intent in email [16], prior work has focused on detecting "to-do" intent in general *person-to-person* email, which tends to follow

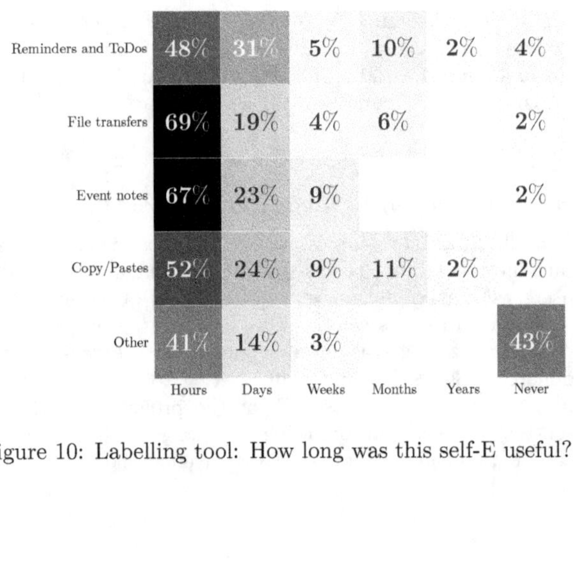

Figure 10: Labelling tool: How long was this self-E useful?

Feature set	Mean accuracy	
	Flat	Stacked
All features	0.651 (±0.046)	0.786 (±0.041)
Content features only	0.606 (±0.067)	0.747 (±0.048)
Metadata features only	0.619 (±0.074)	0.641 (±0.057)

Table 2: Mean classification accuracy and standard deviation over 5 fold cross-validation. For the stacked approach, "All features" significantly improves classification accuracy over both "Content features only" ($t(8) = 2.709, p < 0.05$) and "Metadata features only" ($t(8) = 9.006, p < 0.01$) – determined using an unpaired, one-tail t-test, corrected for multiple comparisons. For the flat approach, there are no significant differences between feature sets.

more formal conversational conventions (e.g. *"Will send you the PDF tonight"*) as opposed to self-Es (e.g. *"PDF Alex"*).

Because we wanted to use text-based features for our classification approach, we use only the donated self-Es that include both content and labels ($n = 813$ emails). The self-Es donated with content *and* labels included 48% ($n = 388$) *"Reminder or ToDo"* self-Es and a roughly equal proportion of other categories (52%, $n = 425$). Thus, our data set is nearly naturally balanced. We report accuracy and area under the ROC curve. We note that random performance would achieve 52% accuracy and 0.5 area under the ROC curve.

We experimented with different feature sets: (i) bag-of-words representation of self-E subject and body, which we refer to as content features, (ii) features extracted from email metadata and header properties, such as the number and type of attachments, sent date and time (e.g. sent in the morning, sent in the weekend), which we refer to as metadata features and (iii) a combination of the previous, which we refer to as mixed features. For our text features, we used simple term frequency.

We could have simply learned a binary classifier by treating all labels that are not "Reminder or ToDo" as negatives. This approach yielded an accuracy better than random using all features (65.1% ± 4.6%) but we desired to do better possibly by leveraging the other labels beyond simply treating them as negatives. To do so, we could have used a structured prediction approach [9, 11] to jointly predict all labels even though our only true target was the "Reminder or ToDo" class. Instead, we leveraged information from the other labels by initially predicting each of the other high-level self-E intent categories (*"Transfers"*, *"Copy/Paste"*, *"Event Notes"*, and *"Other"*) and using those predictions as features to the final classifier on *"Reminder or ToDo"* prediction. By using nested cross-validation on the training set, we ensure the training data is kept free of bias and we never train on the test data.

This is similar to the refined expert approach of Bennett & Nguyen [3] where a stacking approach [4, 20] is extended with related predictions and draws from the multi-task learning literature [12] where learning a set of related tasks may simplify learning the final target. Table 2 shows the mean accuracy (and standard deviation) of our classifier over

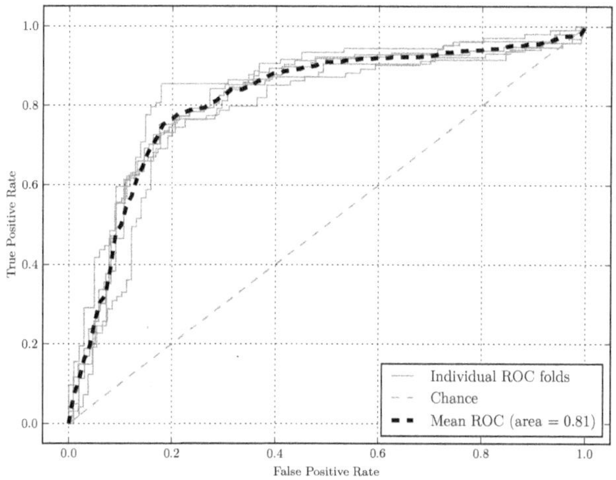

Figure 11: "Reminder or ToDo" intent classifier, using the stacked approach: ROC over 5 fold cross-validation using "All features".

stratified[2] five-fold cross-validation using both the simple (flat) approach and the stacked approach with predictions for each of the related tasks. Note that predicting the related targets using "All features" set yields a significant gain relative to simple binary prediction (78.6% accuracy versus 65.1%; statistical significance determined using an unpaired, one-tail t-test on classifier accuracy scores over 5 random folds of the data: $t(8) = 5.396$, $p < 0.01$). This indicates that there is utility in collecting the other labels even if "Reminder or ToDo" is the final target. Furthermore, comparing the feature sets reported in the table, we see that the content features provide the most value. However, using both content and meta-data features improves beyond content alone.

Finally, figure 11 displays the receiver operating characteristic (ROC) curves for each of the folds using all features, as well as the mean ROC curve, and the area under the curve (see legend). Overall, our classifier performs well, with a mean accuracy of 78.6% self-Es being correctly identified as *"Reminder or ToDo"* items or not. Best performance, in terms of accuracy, is achieved when using both text and email features. Given the small amount of data we had access to, this is an encouraging first step in classifying reminder-oriented self-Es, and we speculate that more data would significantly improve this classification approach.

5. CONCLUSIONS

In order to assist users in taking action on self-addressed emails, we must first understand the types of information managed through self-Es, and identify likely actions users take on this type of mail. Understanding the intent behind self-Es can allow systems to pro-actively support user interaction with self-addressed emails. In this paper we present the first complete characterization of email as a person-to-self communication device. Especially in the context of task management, other authors [1, 6, 18] have noted the use of emails to oneself (and only oneself) before. However, the literature was lacking a characterization of the proportion of users that engage in this self-E behaviour, the frequency with which they do it, and the full spectrum of the types of intents captured by such self-Es. Our analysis from several data sources suggests that the vast majority of users, 81% to 92%, engage in this behaviour at some time and that 32.4% to 40% of users send two or more self-Es per week. Furthermore, sending self-Es is a part of regular behavior for a substantial percentage of users, with approximately 8% of users sending self-Es on a daily basis, on average. Even though in terms of sent mail, self-Es form just 1% of all sent mails, they are part of a regular weekly pattern for the majority of users and are used at least monthly by around 3 out of 4 users.

Furthermore, our analysis illustrated that while the *"Reminder or ToDo"* intent is most common, self-Es actually have a broad spectrum of intents. Given this variety, providing the appropriate support may be different depending on self-E intent. For example, pro-actively surfacing *"Reminder or ToDo"* self-Es in a few days after they are sent to ensure they are not lost in a sudden inbox surge of mails from others may be the best support. In addition, *"Copy/Paste"* intents which constitute verbatim information such as URLs, images, quotes, travel directions, other directions, and phone numbers tend to have a longer lifespan than most other types of self-Es, which implies they are also more likely than other self-Es to be searched for in the future. Augmenting self-Es with longer lifespan with metadata – for instance, in the case of *"Copy/Paste"* self-Es, explicitly flagging copy/paste content – could enable search to distinguish these intents from other self-Es and promote them in searches.

Finally, given past work on extracting "ToDos", reminders or action items from mails to others, it is an interesting question of whether "Reminder or ToDo" intent self-Es can be distinguished from other types of intent. This may be an especially challenging problem since self-Es may be briefer and lack formal grammar and conventions that help distinguish such speech acts in mails to others. We demonstrate that using features of the email body, meta-data and predictions of belonging to other self-E intents that we can distinguish this special class of self-Es well above random. This bodes well for future technology that aims to support "Reminder or ToDo" intents specifically.

[2]Each fold preserved the proportion of samples for each class.

6. REFERENCES

[1] V. Bellotti, N. Ducheneaut, M. Howard, and I. Smith. Taking email to task: The design and evaluation of a task management centered email tool. In *Proceedings of the SIGCHI Conference on Human Factors in Computing Systems*, CHI '03, pages 345–352, New York, NY, USA, 2003. ACM.

[2] P. N. Bennett and J. Carbonell. Detecting action-items in e-mail. In *Proceedings of the 28th Annual International ACM SIGIR Conference on Research and Development in Information Retrieval*, SIGIR '05, pages 585–586, New York, NY, USA, 2005. ACM.

[3] P. N. Bennett and N. Nguyen. Refined experts: Improving classification in large taxonomies. In *Proceedings of the 32nd International ACM SIGIR Conference on Research and Development in Information Retrieval*, SIGIR '09, pages 11–18, New York, NY, USA, 2009. ACM.

[4] L. Breiman. Stacked regressions. *Machine Learning*, 24(1):49–64, 1996.

[5] V. R. Carvalho and W. W. Cohen. On the collective classification of email "speech acts". In *Proceedings of the 28th Annual International ACM SIGIR Conference on Research and Development in Information Retrieval*, SIGIR '05, pages 345–352, New York, NY, USA, 2005. ACM.

[6] M. E. Cecchinato, A. Sellen, M. Shokouhi, and G. Smyth. Finding email in a multi-account, multi-device world. In *Proceedings of the 2016 CHI Conference on Human Factors in Computing Systems*, CHI '16, pages 1200–1210, New York, NY, USA, 2016. ACM.

[7] M. Dredze, H. M. Wallach, D. Puller, and F. Pereira. Generating summary keywords for emails using topics. In *Proceedings of the 13th International Conference on Intelligent User Interfaces*, IUI '08, pages 199–206, New York, NY, USA, 2008. ACM.

[8] B. V. Hanrahan, M. A. Pérez-Quiñones, and D. Martin. Attending to email. *Interacting with Computers*, 2014.

[9] T. Joachims, T. Hofmann, Y. Yue, and C.-N. Yu. Predicting structured objects with support vector machines. *Communications of the ACM, Research Highlight*, 52(11):97–104, November 2009.

[10] N. Kushmerick and T. Lau. Automated email activity management: An unsupervised learning approach. In *Proceedings of the 10th International Conference on Intelligent User Interfaces*, IUI '05, pages 67–74, New York, NY, USA, 2005. ACM.

[11] J. D. Lafferty, A. McCallum, and F. C. N. Pereira. Conditional random fields: Probabilistic models for segmenting and labeling sequence data. In *Proceedings of the 18th International Conference on Machine Learning*, ICML '01, pages 282–289, San Francisco, CA, USA, 2001. Morgan Kaufmann Publishers Inc.

[12] R. Michalski and G. Tecuci, editors. *Machine Learning: A Multistrategy Approach*, volume IV. Morgan Kaufmann Publishers, Inc., 1994.

[13] D. Oard. Avocado research email collection. *Philadelphia: Linguistic Data Consortium*, 2015.

[14] A. Qadir, M. Gamon, P. Pantel, and A. H. Awadallah. Activity modeling in email. In *Proceedings of the 2016 Conference of the North American Chapter of the Association for Computational Linguistics: Human Language Technologies*, pages 1452–1462, San Diego, California, June 2016. Association for Computational Linguistics.

[15] M. Sappelli, G. Pasi, S. Verberne, M. de Boer, and W. Kraaij. Assessing e-mail intent and tasks in e-mail messages. *Inf. Sci.*, 358(C):1–17, Sept. 2016.

[16] J. Shen, L. Li, T. G. Dietterich, and J. L. Herlocker. A hybrid learning system for recognizing user tasks from desktop activities and email messages. In *Proceedings of the 11th International Conference on Intelligent User Interfaces*, IUI '06, pages 86–92, New York, NY, USA, 2006. ACM.

[17] M. G. R. C. Simon H. Corston-Oliver, Eric Ringger. Task-focused summarization of email. Association for Computational Linguistics, July 2004.

[18] S. Whittaker, V. Bellotti, and J. Gwizdka. Email in personal information management. *Commun. ACM*, 49(1):68–73, Jan. 2006.

[19] S. Whittaker and C. Sidner. Email overload: Exploring personal information management of email. In *Proceedings of the SIGCHI Conference on Human Factors in Computing Systems*, CHI '96, pages 276–283, New York, NY, USA, 1996. ACM.

[20] D. H. Wolpert. Stacked generalization. *Neural networks*, 5(2):241–259, 1992.

Large-Scale Analysis of Email Search and Organizational Strategies

Kanika Narang
Department of Computer Science
University of Illinois at Urbana-Champaign
Urbana, IL USA
knarang2@illinois.edu

Susan T. Dumais
Nick Craswell
Dan Liebling
Microsoft Research
Redmond, WA USA
{sdumais, nickcr, danl}
@microsoft.com

Qingyao Ai
College of Information and Computer Sciences
University of Massachusetts Amherst
Amherst, MA USA
aiqy@cs.umass.edu

ABSTRACT

Email continues to be an important form of communication as well as a way to manage tasks and archive personal information. As the volume of email grows, organizing and finding relevant email remains challenging. In this paper, we present a large-scale log analysis of the activities that people perform on email messages (accessing external information via links or attachments, responding to messages, and organizing messages), their search behavior, and their organizational practices in a popular web email client.

First, we characterize general email activities as well as activities associated with search. We find that within search sessions, people are more likely to access information and respond to messages but less likely to organize. Second, we examine the relationship between characteristics of a person's mailbox and their search and organizational practices. People with larger mailboxes tend to organize more, respond a little more, and access information less. People with larger mailboxes and folder structures search more, but the number of folders has less influence on search. Third, we extend previous work on email organization (e.g., *filers* vs. *pilers*; *cleaners* vs. *keepers*) by examining the extent to which these strategies are evident in our large-scale analysis and influence email activities and search. People who rely heavily on one organizational strategy tend to use others less. People who organize less tend to search more. Finally, we describe how these insights can influence the design of email search.

Categories and Subject Descriptors

H.3.3 [Information Storage and Retrieval]: Information Search and Retrieval – *Search process.*

Keywords

Email search; Email management strategies.

CHIIR '17, March 07-11, 2017, Oslo, Norway
© 2017 ACM. ISBN 978-1-4503-4677-1/17/03…$15.00
DOI: http://dx.doi.org/10.1145/3020165.3020175

1. INTRODUCTION

Twenty years ago, Whittaker and Sidner [29] coined the term *email overload* to describe the fact that although email was designed for asynchronous communication, it was being used for multiple purposes including task management and personal archiving. The annual volume of email continues to increase around 5% per year [25], but organizational affordances in email systems have not evolved substantially. Some automation helps by classifying spam emails and estimating message priorities. Users are still left to devise and implement their own organization systems using a small set of features: deleting, filing into folders, flagging, toggling the read/unread state, and tagging. Search scales more efficiently for large quantities of email, but email search is much less studied than web search.

Most prior work on email interactions and organizational strategies involves small-scale diary studies, surveys, or logs obtained from limited deployments [3][5][13]. While informative, these studies cannot capture the broad variety of user activity. To do so requires large-scale log analyses of *in situ* email interactions. Such logs provide a picture of what happens across a wide range of individuals with different volumes of email and different email management strategies. Thus, large-scale investigation allows us to validate and extend taxonomies and hypotheses developed in earlier research.

Recently there have been a few large-scale log studies of email use. Research from Yahoo! looked at email interaction for personal web email accounts. These accounts contain a large amount of machine-generated content, so their research focus has been on automatically categorizing machine-generated emails into a small number of folders [1][12] and predicting what actions people will take on emails [7]. In the work presented in this paper, we focus on work ("enterprise") email accounts. Work email is less dominated by automatically generated commercial mail [12], and involves more email organization and keeping behaviors than is evident in personal accounts [4].

In this paper, we present a large-scale log analysis of hundreds of thousands of anonymized users of a popular web email client. Because of our interest in search, we only consider users who searched at least once during a one-week observation period. We characterize general patterns of email interaction as well as interactions that occur in search sessions. We also examine the relationship between characteristics of people's mailboxes (e.g., size, volume of email, and number of folders) and their actions and search activity. Finally, we extend prior work on email organization by examining the relationship between different organizational strategies and actions that people take on email messages and their search activity at scale.

2. RELATED WORK

Several areas of prior work are relevant to the results presented in this paper, including research on email management practices and log studies of email activities including search.

Email management practices. For several decades, email has been one of the most common communication and personal information management technologies. Although it was originally developed to support asynchronous communication, it quickly became used for task management and personal archives as well [13][29]. Several early email studies examined how people organized and managed their email. In their study of 18 Lotus Notes users, Whittaker and Sidner [29] coined the term "email overload" and identified three common strategies for mitigating overload. **No Filers, Filers, and Spring Cleaners**. *No filers* (sometimes referred to as *pilers*) forego using folders relying instead on browsing or search. *Frequent filers* minimize the number of messages in their inbox by putting emails in folders, and *spring cleaners* organize their mail only occasionally. A decade later, Fisher et al. [11] found that these strategies were still evident using a sample of 600 Microsoft Outlook users. More recently, Grevet et al. [13] revisited these previous findings with a qualitative study of Google Gmail users and found that email overload was still prevalent, now encompassing both work and personal settings. Bälter [2] used a keystroke-level analysis to model the time required to file and retrieve email for frequent filers, spring cleaners, and folderless spring cleaners. Gwizdka [16] identified two additional email management practices, **Cleaners and Keepers**, based on clustering responses to a questionnaire about email practices. Dabbish and Kraut [6] showed that people who kept their inboxes small were less stressed. This finding was also corroborated for academics [3].

The previously mentioned email management practices depend on techniques such as filing or deleting to keep inboxes small. There are also **Information Highlighting** techniques that can visually highlight items, rather than removing them, to make them easier to find when scanning a folder or search results. Gwizdka [14], for example, showed how a graphical task view could be used to support people in completing pending tasks. Although not as sophisticated as this, most email clients, including the one we studied, allow people to make specific messages visible, e.g., by flagging or categorizing, or by simply marking as unread. Such techniques provide a way of organizing messages by visual, sometimes searchable, properties.

Email usage at scale. Most of the results described in the previous section were based on small samples and used qualitative methods such as interviews, diaries or questionnaires, but recently there have been larger-scale studies of people who use popular web email systems. For example, Kalman and Ravid [19] conducted a longitudinal study of the inbox-management strategies of several thousand people using an Outlook add-in. They showed that people have a more diverse repertoire of inbox management behaviors than posited by earlier taxonomies. They developed the Inbox Cleaning Index (ICI) to characterize how the volume of messages in people's inboxes varies over time. In studies of a Yahoo! email users, Koren et al. [21] and Grbovic et al. [12] showed that 70% of Yahoo! web mail users did not define any folders and 90% of the rest did not actually use folders that they created. They argued that search is an increasingly important alternative to human-generated folders and tags. Grbovic et al. [12] found that a large proportion of non-spam email was machine generated (e.g., including e-tickets, confirmations and invoices, newsletters) and they developed automatic classifiers to organize machine-generated email into five categories. In a similar way, Di Castro et al. [7] developed a learning framework to predict the most common email actions, which in their study were read, reply, and delete. Whittaker et al. [28] examined the relationship between email management strategies and subsequent retrieval strategies for re-finding. They noticed that some users expended preparatory effort of creating complex folder structures to promote re-finding while others were more opportunistic and used search and threading to reduce the need to file manually. In a log study of 345 users, they found that people who create complex folder structures did indeed rely on them for retrieval, but that search and threading provided more effective finding. Elsweiler and colleagues [9][10][17] also studied re-finding behavior in email through a series of quantitative and qualitative studies. They found that orienteering is a common strategy used for re-finding emails. Users tend to search with short queries and navigate through their results for cues to find their intended email. They further proposed query similarity and query overlap to be good indicators of re-finding intents of users.

Email practices in personal vs. work settings. Individuals often have multiple email accounts (e.g., work and one or more personal accounts) and multiple devices (e.g., desktop computers, laptops, and phone) from which people interact with email. Smith et al. [27] were the first to point to a tension between work and personal email. They found that in 2003, 54% of their participants had two accounts. A decade later, Capra et al. [3] surveyed 600 university employees and found that 84% of them had separate accounts to help manage boundaries between work and personal life. These two types of accounts had different characteristics; respondents reported more frequent use of keeping behaviors and larger inboxes in their work accounts. However, there were some consistencies as well, indicating that personal preferences or prior experiences also play a role in email management practices. Grevet et al. [13] studied people who used Google's Gmail for either personal or work purposes. In contrast to Capra, they found that inboxes in personal Gmail accounts were generally larger. Cecchinato et al. [5] used a diary study to understand email management and search strategies. They found that people manage their personal and work accounts differently, and use different retrieval strategies. Work accounts were more structured and email was generally retrieved through the folder structure, whereas people had fewer folders in personal accounts and relied more on search to find email.

The research presented in this paper differs from previous work in several ways. We use large-scale log analysis to analyze interaction patterns in work (enterprise) email accounts. We examine the prevalence of email search and the activities that people take on messages following searches. We examine how characteristics of mailboxes (size, volume of incoming messages, and the number of folders) are related to people's interaction with email messages and searching. We also compare people with different email organizational strategies, again looking at differences in email activities and search. The results complement and extend previous smaller-scale and qualitative studies.

3. METHODOLOGY

We now describe how we performed our analysis. We discuss the dataset and formalize the problem. We then define the different measures we use, including behavioral interactions, mailbox characteristics, and organizational strategies.

3.1 Dataset

We sampled one week of interaction log data from Microsoft's web email service. The interaction logs contain message- and search-oriented activities with timestamps and other metadata; section 3.2.1 details the types of activities. We did not have access to any kind of email content or search queries. We focused on corporate email accounts, which were identified by a property in the logs. Because we are interested in email search, we include only users who issued at least one query during the week. To reduce variability, we further include only users in the United States, and remove people who had fewer than 10 or more than 10,000 email activities during the one-week period. The resulting dataset contained 283,000 distinct users and 145.8 million email activities.

The web email system we studied uses a standard email interface. A folder list is shown on the left side, a list of messages is shown in the middle, and the full text of the selected message is shown on the right. The snippet for each message includes the sender's name, the subject, the first few words of the email, and metadata such as the time. Selecting a result opens the full text of the message in the reading pane on the right side. The search box is located on the top left of the page. The results of a search are presented in the same fashion as the list of message described above, and the left pane contains matching folders and options for further refining the query. Exiting the search returns the user to the default folder list and view.

3.2 Measures

In email and web search, people seek to find and re-find information mediated by the IR affordances of the system. In web search, selecting a result link is the most common action. Email search provides a richer set of actions on the messages than are available in web search. For example, a message may be deleted, replied to, forwarded, or filed. We aggregate these actions across users to create behavior-based measures of email interaction.

3.2.1 Activities

We consider thirteen individual activities which are grouped into four broader classes as shown in Table 1. The classes correspond to higher-level tasks that a user performs when interacting with email – selecting messages, accessing external content, responding to messages, and organizing messages.

Class	Included activities
Select	SelectMessage
Access Content	ClickLink, OpenAttachment
Respond	Forward
	Reply+ (Reply and ReplyAll)
Organize	Delete
	Move
	Mark+ (Flag, FlagClear, FlagComplete, MarkAsRead, MarkAsUnread)

Table 1. Classes of message-related activities. We consider thirteen individual activities, grouped into four higher-level classes of email tasks (Select, Access, Respond, Organize).

SelectMessage occurs when a message is selected and its content is shown in the reading pane and allows other actions to be performed on the message. Two actions are used to access external content. ClickLink refers to selecting a link embedded in an email while OpenAttachment is the explicit user action of opening the attachment in an email. Three actions (Reply, ReplyAll and Forward) are used to respond to email messages. And, seven actions (Delete, Move to Folders, Mark As Read or Unread, Flag, Flag Clear or Complete) are used to organized emails in various ways.

SelectMessage is by far the most common activity, accounting for approximately 75% of email activities. This is because selecting a message is necessary to read a message and to perform subsequent actions such as replying or deleting. We remove SelectMessage from the activities considered since we are interested in the actions that people explicitly perform on selected messages.

In order to summarize the actions that people take on selected messages, we compute the distribution of activity types. Specifically, we compute the proportion of total email activities that each activity accounts for aggregated over the whole dataset. We report proportions rather than absolute counts of activities to accommodate a wide variation in the total amount of email interaction that we see across individuals. For example, if one person deletes 4 of the 10 email messages they receive and another person deletes 400 of 1,000 messages they receive, they both delete 40% of their incoming emails.

3.2.2 Search Sessions

In web search, a collection of temporally related queries and result clicks are grouped into a "search session." Analogously, in email, a search session begins with a query and is followed by zero or more additional queries and message-oriented activities. These activities include selecting a result message, opening an attachment, forwarding, replying, deleting, moving to a folder, flagging etc. (as shown in Table 1). The email search session terminates under one of following two conditions: (1) the searcher explicitly closes the search query box in the UI, or (2) there are no searches or message-related activities for ten minutes. This timeout is similar to what is used in web search and handles cases where a person stops interacting with the mail client for a long period of time.

Figure 1 provides a schematic of the relationship between activity within search sessions and non-search email activity. When people interact with their email, there is a steady stream of message-related activity, denoted a in the figure. We are interested in the subset of this stream that comprises search sessions. Search sessions begin with a search query (denoted Q), include one or more subsequent activities or queries, and end with a time-out (denoted —) or an explicit exit from search (denoted X). All activities that occur within search sessions are called search activities. And, all activities which do not occur in search sessions are called non-search activities.

In our dataset, there are 479,000 search sessions which contain 1.9 million searches. In Section 4.1.1, we examine email activities within search sessions (search activities), and in Section 4.1.2 we compare email activities that occur in search sessions with those that do not (non-search activities).

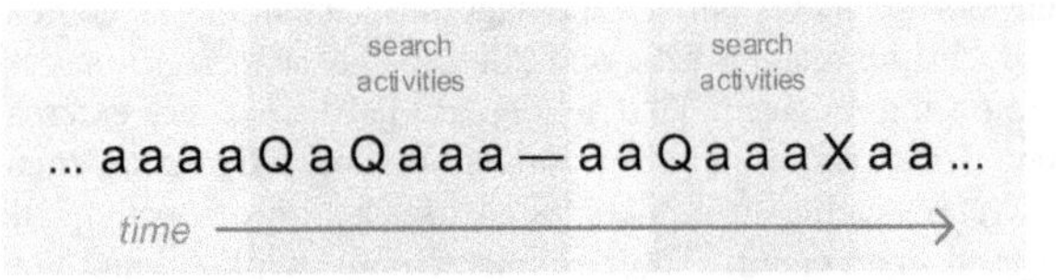

Figure 1. Schematic of search and non-search activities. In a timeline of email activities (labeled a), a search session (highlighted in blue) starts with a query Q and terminates with either a timeout (—) or an explicit closing of the query box (X). Non-search activities are highlighted in yellow.

3.2.3 Mailbox Characteristics

Prior literature suggests a relationship between mailbox size and feelings of email overload and stress [2][6][29].

The actions that people take on their email message and how often they search for messages may also be related to characteristics of their mailboxes. In our analysis, we consider three characteristics of people's mailboxes – the number of items they have in their mailbox (#Items), the number of emails they received during the week of our analysis (#IncomingMessages), and the number of folders they have (#Folders). #IncomingMessages measures email volume over a short, fixed period of time. #Items measures cumulative amount of email kept over the longer term; it includes items in the Inbox and folders but not in the deleted folder. #Folders reflects the number of folders that people use to organize their email.

We rank people by these mailbox characteristics (e.g., #Items), and group them into deciles each containing 10% of the users. (We describe in more detail how we spilt distributions into quantiles in the next section.) We then examine how these mailbox characteristics are associated with people's organizational activities (Delete, Move, Mark+) and search behavior. This allows us to answer questions like: *Do people who have small mailboxes Delete more often than those who have larger mailboxes?*

3.2.4 Organizational Strategies

Prior small-scale qualitative and laboratory studies of email have identified several strategies that people employ in organizing their email [9][13][16][29]. We are interested in whether we can identify behavioral patterns associated with these strategies using large-scale log analyses of *in situ* email interactions.

As an initial step, we identify email activities that are likely associated with three organizational strategies for managing email.

- Delete: Deleting emails distinguishes between Cleaners vs. Keepers [16].
- Move: Moving emails to folders reflects distinction between Filers vs. No-Filers [9][13][29].
- Mark+: Marking emails as unread or adding flags enables quick visual scanning or task reminding [14].

We first identify people who frequently use an activity such as Delete, then compare their email interaction and search patterns with others who use that activity infrequently. To do this, we compute the proportion of each person's email interactions that involve the activity of interest, that is, for a user's set of activities A with class i:

$$Proportion = |A_i| \div \sum_j |Aj|$$

For this analysis, we first remove users who never use an activity, then split the frequency distribution into 33% quantiles. Each quantile contains the same number of users. We consider people in the bottom 33% quantile to be "Low" activity users, and the top 33% to be "High" activity users. Figure 2 illustrates this partitioning with a hypothetical activity distribution for one activity, say *Activity A*. The distribution shows the percent of total activities that are Activity A (x-axis) and the number of people who have that percent of activity (y-axis). The distribution is divided into terciles with Low and High highlighted in blue and green respectively. We compare the High and Low terciles because they represent the two extremes in usage of the activity of interest.

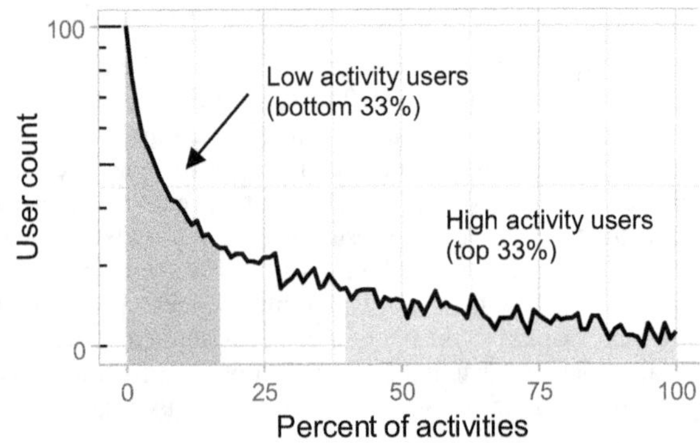

Figure 2. Illustrative activity distribution for organizational strategies. The distribution is divided into terciles, and Low (blue) and High (green) groups are identified.

Once the High and Low groups have been identified, we can compare the distributions of the remaining message-related activities for people in the two groups. In addition, we examine how frequently these groups search. This enables us to answer questions like: *Do people who Delete (or Move or Mark+) more search less?*

We also consider people who never used a particular activity separately; we refer to these people as "Zero" activity users. This group is interesting but difficult to interpret since people who never use an activity may simply not know about it or they may know about it but choose not to use it. In addition, while there are same number of people in the High and Low quantile group by construction, there are different numbers of people in the Zero group. There are very few people who do not use Delete; conversely, the vast majority of people never use Move and Mark+.

4. RESULTS

We first present results that summarize general email and email search activity (section 4.1). We then examine differences in the distributions of email activities and search as a function of characteristics of a person's email store (section 4.2) and of their organizational strategies (section 4.3).

4.1 General Email and Email Search Activity

4.1.1 Search Activities

In web search, the action that people perform on search results is simply to click a link to get to the corresponding page. In email search, however, there is much broader set of activities that people can perform on messages, as described in Section 3.2.1.

Figure 3 shows the distribution of activities that occur on selected messages in search sessions (search) as well as in general interaction with email (non-search). The distribution is computed over all search and non-search activities respectively.

In search sessions (blue histograms), we see that the two most common activities are OpenAttachment (39%) and Delete (26%). ClickLink is also a common activity (6%), as are Reply+/Forward (23% combined). It is not surprising that people search to access content and to respond to email. The prevalence of organizational activities (Delete, Move and Mark+, 32% combined) is more surprising. This indicates that people sometimes search to identify messages in order to clean up or organize their mailboxes. This is a kind of search intent that has not previously been reported in other domains. The majority of these organizational actions were to Delete messages (26%). And, in aggregate, the other organizational activities Moving (4%) and Marking (2%) messages were somewhat more common than Click Link (5%) and a little less common than Forward (8%).

Activities may be common in search sessions, in part, because they are common in general. Thus, it is also interesting to consider activities that occur outside search sessions, and compare these non-search activities to search activities. In non-search activities (red histograms) Delete (42%) and OpenAttachment (15%) are the two most common activities. Other organizational activities, Move and Mark+ (13% and 9% respectively), are also common as is Reply+ (13%). As people go about interacting with incoming email, they access information (mostly attachments) and respond to email, but most of their activities are devoted to organization, whether deleting, filing or marking.

It is interesting to compare the proportion of activities in search vs. non-search settings. We do so in the next section by showing the ratio of search vs. non-search activities.

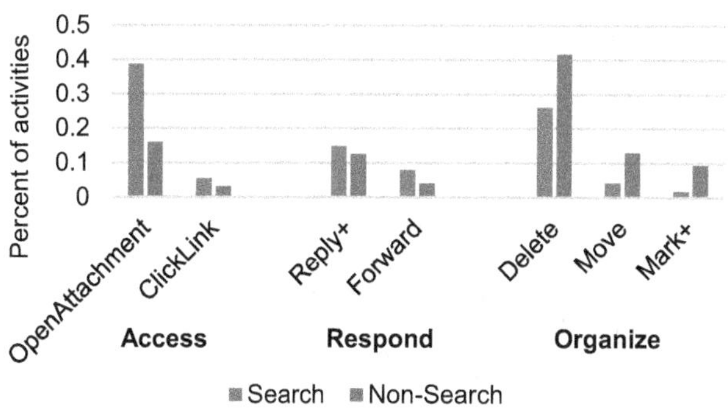

Figure 3. Distribution of activities within (blue) and outside (red) of search sessions

4.1.2 Search vs. Non-Search Activities

Figure 4 shows the ratio of the proportions of search to non-search activities, grouped by activity classes from section 3.2.1. A ratio larger than 1 indicates that the activity is proportionally more likely to occur in search sessions. For example, OpenAttachment is 2.4 times more likely to occur in a search session than outside one. ClickLink, Forward and Reply+ are also more common after a search. Thus, it appears that people search when they want to access information in attachments or links, and when they want to respond to or forward email. Furthermore, search is performed to Forward emails more than it is to Reply+ to them. A ratio less than 1 indicates that the activity is proportionally more likely to

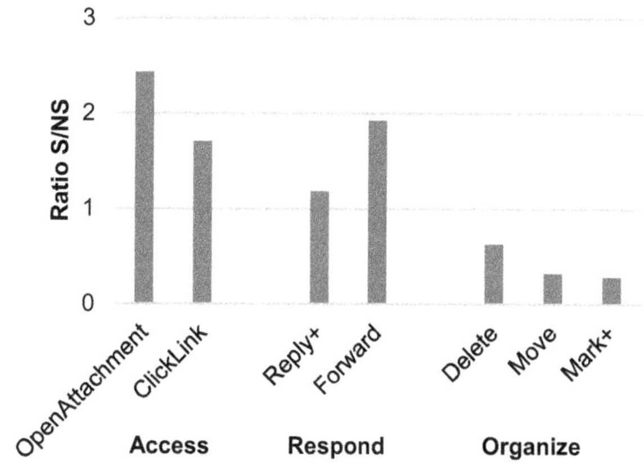

Figure 4. Ratio of activities in Search vs. Non-Search context. A ratio larger than 1 indicates that the activity is proportionally more likely in search sessions than in general email interaction, and a ratio less than 1 in indicates that the activity is proportionally more likely in general email interaction.

occur in general email interaction. Organizational activities (Delete, Move and Mark+) are much more common in general email interaction than after a search. People are less likely to search in order to organize their email than they are to do so in the normal course of going through their Inbox. Although we were surprised to find that Delete was a common activity in search sessions (26% of activities), it is even more common in non-search interactions (41% of activities).

In summary, Delete and OpenAttachment are the two most common activities on email messages, both in general interaction and after searches. However, in search sessions opening an attachment is more common than deleting, and the opposite is true in general interaction. When we compare activities in search sessions to general email activities, we find that people are more likely to use search to access external information via links or attachments or to find messages to respond to them. Conversely, the general organizational activities of deleting, filing and marking are more prevalent in non-search activities.

We now look at how the distribution of activities on email messages varies as a function of characteristics of mailboxes and people's organizational activities. We also look at the prevalence of search for people with different amounts of email and different strategies for organizing email.

4.2 Mailbox Characteristics

In this section, we examine the relationship between different mailbox characteristics (#Items, #IncomingMessages, #Folders) and activities on messages and searches.

4.2.1 Activity Distribution

Figure 5 shows the amount of total email activity as a function of deciles for #Items, #Incoming Messages and #Folders. Due to data publishing constraints, we show relative rather than absolute numbers.

Not surprisingly, people who have more Items in their mailbox, more Incoming Messages, or more Folders also have more overall email activities. The slopes for #Items and #Incoming Messages (blue and red curves, which overlap almost completely) are steeper than that for #Folders (green curve). As the number of incoming messages increases, simply selecting each message will add to

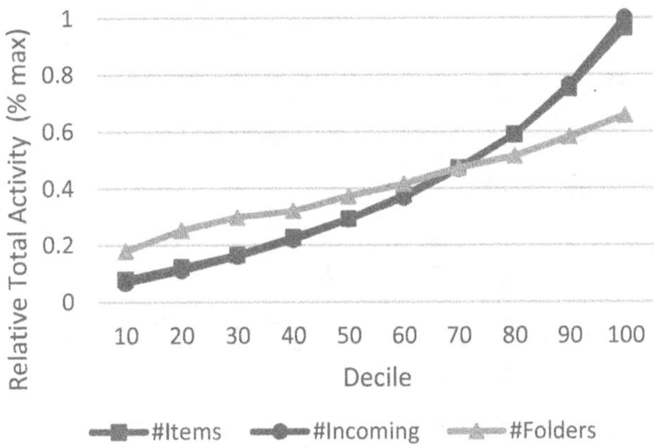

Figure 5. Total activity by mailbox feature deciles. Total email activity is normalized by the max activity. Total Activity increases sharply as mailbox size (#Items, #Incoming) increases, and increases more slowly as the number of folders (#Folders) increases.

the total activity. The fact that activity does not rise as quickly for people with more folders suggests that the number of folders and the number of incoming messages are not perfectly correlated.

We now examine in more detail the relationship between different types of activities and mailbox characteristics. Figure 6 shows the proportion of activities of different types (Access, Respond, Organize) as a function of the number of items in a person's mailbox (#Items). The activity distributions #Incoming Messages and #Folders are similar, so we omit them for space reasons.

As mailbox size increases, people are much more likely to organize by deleting, moving or marking (blue curve). They are also more likely to respond to email (red curve), although the slope is much shallower and the overall amount of responding activity is low relative to organizing activity. Accessing external information via clicking a link or opening an attachment (green curve) declines as the number of items increases.

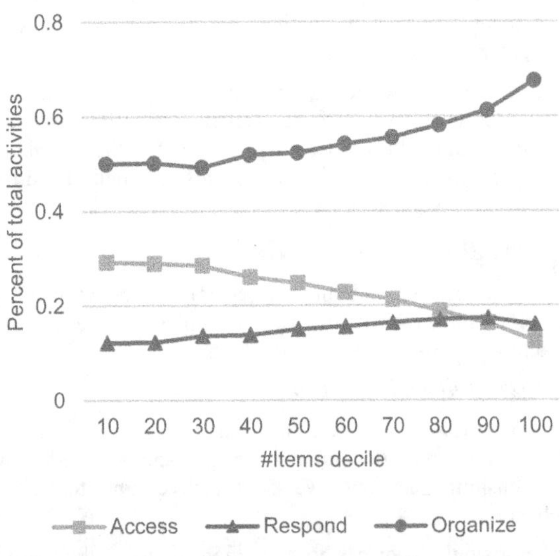

Figure 6. Activity Type × #Items Deciles. Breakdown of total activities into Access, Respond and Organize activities. Organize and Respond both increase with #Items, but Access decreases.

4.2.2 *Search Activity*

Figure 7 shows the search queries as a function of deciles for #Items, #Incoming Messages and #Folders. We cannot report absolute search volume, so we normalize the counts to the maximum in any of the conditions. People with more items in their mailbox, and more incoming messages search more than those with smaller mailboxes. As the amount of information in the Inbox increases, search becomes a more important way of finding information. On the other hand, the number of Folders that people have does not influence the amount of searching as much; there is some increase in the lower deciles but the amount of search plateaus. This may be because people who have many folders navigate to those folders rather than using search to find information (see also Whittaker et al. [28]). In the email client that we studied, search operates over all folders as well as the Inbox so there is no need to navigate to folders. People may not know that search can be used across folders, or they may simply prefer browsing within folders especially when they have invested time in creating many folders.

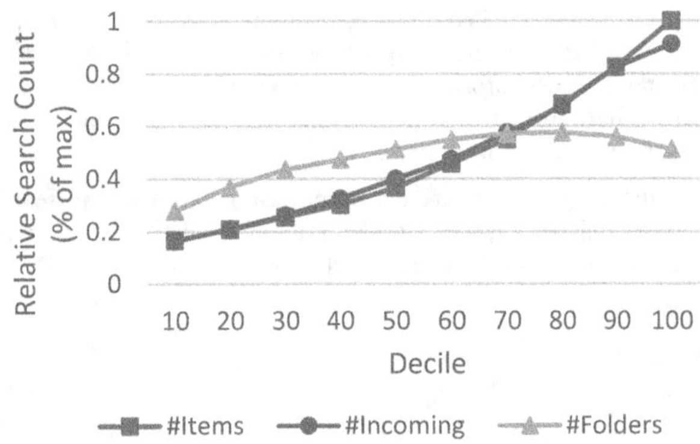

Figure 7. Search count by mailbox feature deciles. Search count is normalized by the max searching in any condition. Number of searches increases sharply as mailbox size increases (#Items, #Incoming), and increases more slowly as the number of folders increases (#Folders).

In summary, we observe that as mailbox size increases (#Items, #Incoming Messages), email interaction and search both increase. Much of the increase arises from more organization of email through deleting, moving or marking. In addition, people with larger mailboxes spend somewhat more time responding to mail. People with more folders, have somewhat more overall activity and search more often, but the relationship is not as strong.

4.3 Organizational Strategies

As described in Section 3.2.4 we consider three strategies that people commonly use to organize their email and their associated actions. Specifically, we look at Delete (Cleaners vs. Keepers), Move (Filers vs. No-Filers), and Mark/Flag (Visual vs. Not). For each, we compare people who use the feature frequently (High), infrequently (Low), and never (Zero). We now summarize the activity and search patterns associated with these different organizational strategies.

		Usage of Delete				Usage of Move				Usage of Mark+			
		High	Low	Zero	Ratio H/L	High	Low	Zero	Ratio H/L	High	Low	Zero	Ratio H/L
Access Content	OpenAttach...	26.9%	25.3%	36.8%	1.06	18.8%	13.9%	20.3%	1.35	19.5%	14.3%	18.6%	1.36
	ClickLink	8.6%	3.3%	8.0%	2.59	3.1%	2.7%	4.0%	1.15	3.2%	2.7%	3.9%	1.21
Respond	Reply+	23.2%	17.8%	12.2%	1.30	17.2%	11.7%	13.4%	1.47	17.4%	11.4%	11.9%	1.53
	Forward	7.9%	6.0%	4.4%	1.32	5.9%	4.2%	4.5%	1.42	5.7%	4.1%	4.1%	1.41
Organize	Delete	-	-	-	-	35.2%	51.9%	40.3%	0.68	26.3%	47.9%	44.7%	0.55
	Move	16.1%	19.1%	7.9%	0.84	-	-	-	-	20.1%	14.4%	8.9%	1.39
	Mark+	8.1%	18.1%	11.1%	0.45	14.4%	10.1%	8.5%	1.43	-	-	-	-
Search	Search	9.2%	10.4%	19.6%	0.89	5.3%	5.6%	9.0%	0.95	7.7%	5.3%	7.9%	1.46

Table 2. Activity distributions including search, with ratios of high to low activity use. High Delete users use other organizational activities relatively less frequently, while High Move and High Mark+ users delete relatively less. Access and Respond activities are more common for High vs. Low organizers of all types. Patterns for Zero users vary, because few people never delete, but many people never Move or Mark.

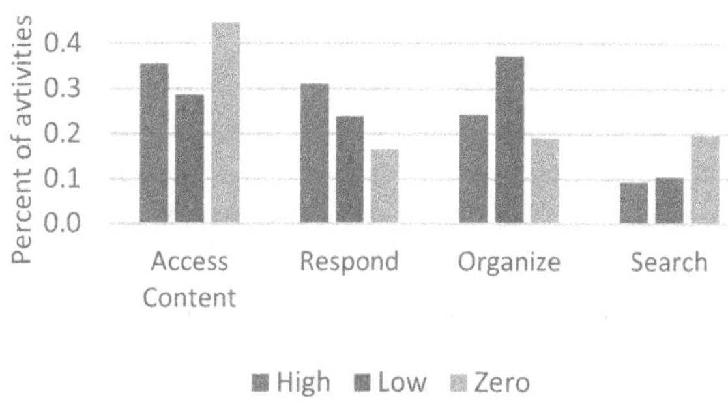

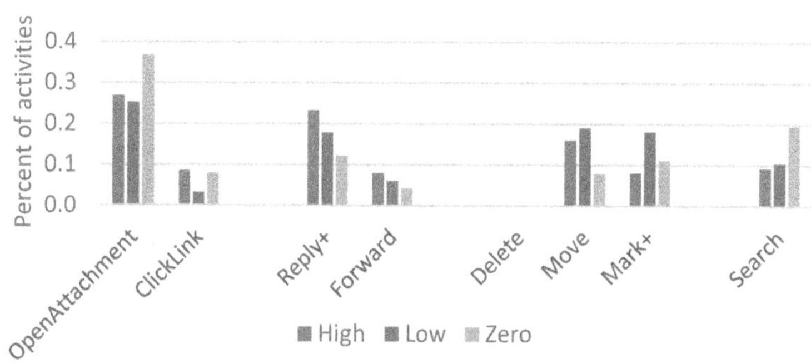

Figure 8. Histograms of the Delete data in Table 2. The left figure aggregates activities from detail in the right figure into activity classes. Searches increase, and Respond activities decrease with Delete use. Organization is more common with low Delete, accessing content more common for people who never delete.

4.3.1 Activity Distribution

Table 2 shows the proportion of each activity for High, Low and Zero people for each of the organizational strategies (Delete, Move, Mark+). The table also shows the ratio of activities for High vs. Low users which makes it easier to compare the proportions of each activity across these two groups.

High vs. Low Deleters (Cleaners vs. Keepers). We start by considering the first four columns representing people who use Delete with different proportions. Figure 8 shows these results graphically. High Deleters use other organizational strategies (Move and Mark+) less often than Low Deleters. This suggests that different organizational strategies are complementary; people who use one frequently tend not to use others as much. Indeed, only 7% of people who are High Deleters are also High Movers and only 6% of High Deleters are also High Markers. It is interesting that Low Deleters mark twice as much as High Deleters, perhaps because they don't delete much and need to rely on other techniques to support their ability to get back to email. High Deleters access content and respond to mail more that Low Deleters, perhaps indicating that they spend more time in email.

While it is straightforward to compare High with Low Deleters, it is more challenging to compare either with Zero Deleters. By definition, one third of the people are High and one third are Low Deleters. There are, however, very few people who did not delete any email during the one-week period. And, these people differ in other ways, notably they have fewer email activities in general. With this caveat in mind, we find that Zero Deleters do not spend much time organizing. In addition, they access more content (via links or attachments) but respond (reply or forward) less, which suggested that they are using email more to get to information than to communicate with others.

High vs. Low Movers (Filers vs. No-Filers). We now consider the middle four columns representing people who use Move differentially. High Movers delete proportionally less often than Low Movers, suggesting again that these two strategies are complementary. As noted above, only 6% of people are both High Deleters and High Movers. High Movers mark items more than Low Movers, and about 12% of people are both High Movers and

High Markers. This may be because High Movers keep their inboxes small (by filing a lot), thus visually highlighting items may be more useful to them. Overall, about 50% of their activities involve organization. High Movers access content and respond to mail more than Low Movers, perhaps indicating that they spend more time in email.

High vs. Low Markers. Finally, we consider the last four columns representing people who use Mark+ with different frequency. High Markers delete much less and move more than Low Markers. Overall, they devote fewer of their email activities to organization. High Markers access content and respond more than Low Markers.

Move and Mark+ are not common activities, so the Zero Move and Zero Mark+ groups represent a large portion of the users in our sample. Thus, their behavior mirrors aggregate email activity that we described earlier.

4.3.2 *Search Activity*

Search activity is shown in the bottom row of Table 2. For Delete and Move, there is a clear trend between the amount of organizational activity and the amount of searching. The more people delete or move, the less they search. For people who never delete, searches compose almost 20% of their activities. This is perhaps what Google was envisioning when they released the original version of Gmail without a delete option.

For Mark+ activity, there is no relationship between marking and searching. If anything, the more people mark items, the more they search. We believe that marking is used more for task management than to make items in search results more visible.

In summary, we extend previous work on email organization by examining the extent to which these strategies are seen in large-scale logs and how they influence email activities and search. People use different strategies to organize their emails and these strategies are generally complementary. For instance, people who delete their email a lot tend to not use folders for organization and vice versa. We also find that people who organize less tend to search more. Finally, spending time in organizing email indicates a higher level of engagement with email. People who organize more (i.e., High Deleters, Movers and Markers) also access content and respond to their emails more than low organizers.

5. DISCUSSION AND FUTURE WORK

In this paper, we used a large-scale log analysis of *in situ* email interactions to study how people interact with email messages in general, the organizational strategies they use, and their search activity.

We first compared email activities in search and non-search context. In a non-search contexts, organizational activities are prevalent. Delete is by far the most common activity accounting for 42% of all activities; and other organizational activities (Move 13% and Mark+ 9%) are also common. Within search sessions, people are proportionally more likely to access information and respond to messages than they are in non-search contexts. Accessing external content via attachments or link clicks is 2.1 times as common in search sessions (44% vs. 19%), and responding to emails via reply+ or forward is 1.6 times as common in search sessions (23% vs. 15%). The prevalence of using search to access external content suggests that search snippets could be enhanced by highlighting the names of attachments or the anchor text of links.

We also examined the relationship between characteristics of a person's mailbox and their email activities and searches. People with larger mailboxes (measured by #Items and #Incoming Messages) have more total activities and conduct more searches than those with smaller mailboxes. The difference in search reflects how more information stored increases difficulty of re-finding. People with more folders (#Folders) show much smaller increases in the email activity and number of searches. People who have many folders seem to rely on their folder structure rather than search for re-finding information. They may not realize that search works across folders, or they may simply want to use the folders that they have invested in developing as Whittaker et al. [28] observed.

Finally, we extended previous work on email organization by examining the extent to which different organizational strategies are seen in large-scale logs, and the relationship between organizational strategies and email activities and search. We used the Delete activity to distinguish between cleaners and keepers, the Move activity to distinguish between filers and pilers, and various Mark activities to identify people who might use visual features to quickly find items. People who use one organizational strategy heavily tend to use others less. In addition, people who organize less tend to search more.

The analysis we presented in this paper is just a first step toward understanding email organization and search practices in situ and at scale. We see several directions for future work. First, we would like to examine techniques for determining the success of email searches. In the context of web search, models have been developed to link implicit interaction (such as dwell time) with search success and it would be interesting to do similarly in email where we also have actions performed on results. Second, we would like to examine re-finding that occurs in ways other than search. Many email messages are retrieved by simply scanning through the inbox and we have not taken this into account in our current analyses. Finally, we would like to extend our analyses to include personal as well as work email, and to explore how email interaction pattern depend on the device being used. In particular, differences in interaction patterns on desktop and mobile clients could reveal the kinds of task that people tend to perform on each (e.g., quick triage vs. more complex information gathering and analysis) and used to optimize the email interface on different devices.

6. REFERENCES

[1] N. Ailon, Z.S. Karnin, E. Liberty and Y. Maarek. Threading machine generated email. In *Proceedings of WSDM 2013*. 405-414.

[2] O. Bälter. Keystroke level analysis of email message organization. In *Proceedings of CHI 2000*, 105-112.

[3] R. Capra, J. Khanova and S. Ramdeen. Work and email e-mail use by university employees: PIM practices across domain boundaries. *JASIST, 64(5)*, 2013, 1029-1044.

[4] D. Carmel, G. Halawai, L. Lewin-Eyan, Y. Maarek and A. Raviv. Rank by time or by relevance? In *Proceedings of CIKM 2015*, 283-292.

[5] M.E. Cecchinato, A. Sellen, M. Shokouhi and G. Smyth. Finding email in a multi-account, multi-device world. In *Proceedings of CHI 2016*, 1200-1210.

[6] L. A. Dabbish and R. E. Kraut. Email overload at work: An analysis of factors associated with email strain. In *Proceedings CSCW 2006*, 431-440.

[7] D. Di Castro, Z. Karnin, L. Lewin-Eytan and Y. Maarek. You've got mail, and here is what you can do with it! Ana-

lyzing and predicting actions on email messages. In *Proceedings of WSDM 2016*, 307-316.

[8] S. Dumais, E. Cutrell, J. J. Cadiz, G. Jancke, R. Sarin and D. C. Robbins. Stuff I've Seen: A system for personal information retrieval and re-use. In *Proceedings of SIGIR 2003*, 72-79.

[9] D. Elsweiler and I. Ruthven. Towards task-based personal information management evaluations. In *Proceedings of SIGIR 2007*, 23-30.

[10] D. Elsweiler, M. Harvey and M. Hacker. Understanding Refinding Behavior in Naturalistic Email Interaction Logs. In *Proceedings of SIGIR 2011*, 35-44.

[11] D. Fisher, A. Brush, E. Gleave and M. A. Smith. Revisiting Whittaker & Sidner's email overload ten years later. In *Proceedings of CSCW 2006*, 309-312.

[12] M. Grbovic, G. Halawi, Z. Karni and Y. Maarek. How many folders do you really need?: Classifying email into a handful of categories. In *Proceedings of CIKM 2014*, 869-878.

[13] C. Grevet, D. Choi, D. Kumar and E. Gilbert. Overload is overloaded: email in the age of Gmail. In *Proceedings of CHI 2014*, 793-802.

[14] J. Gwizdka. TaskView: Design and evaluation of a task-based email interface. In *Proceedings of CASCON 2002*, 136-145.

[15] J. Gwizdka. Reinventing the inbox: Supporting the management of pending tasks in email. In *Proceedings of CHI 2002*, 550-551.

[16] J. Gwizdka. Email task management styles: the cleaners and the keepers. In *Proceedings of CHI 2004*, 1235-1238.

[17] M. Harvey and D. Elsweiler. Exploring query patterns in email search. In *Proceedings of ECIR 2012*, 25-36.

[18] S. Henderson and A. Srinivasan. Filing, piling and structuring: Strategies for personal document management. In *Proceedings of HICSS 2011*, 468-477.

[19] A. Jerejian, C. Reid and C. Rees. The contribution of email volume, email management strategies and propensity to worry in predicting email stress among academics. *Computers in Human Behavior, 29(3)*, 2013, 991-996.

[20] Y.M. Kalman and G. Rivaid. Filing, piling, and everything in between: The dynamics of e-mail inbox management. *JASIST, 66 (12)*, 2015, 2540-2552.

[21] Y. Koren, E. Liberty, Y. Maarek and R. Sandler. Automatically tagging email by leveraging other users' folders. In *Proceedings SIGKDD 2011*, 913-921.

[22] A. Krishnan and S. Jones. TimeSpace: Activity-based temporal visualisation of personal information spaces. In *Proceedings of Personal and Ubiquitous Computing, 9*, 2005, 46-65.

[23] P. Kristen and R. Lee. Email and the internet are the dominant technological tools in American workplaces. *Pew Research Center*, December 2014.

[24] A. Qadir, M. Gamon, P. Pantel and A. H. Awadallah. Activity modeling in email. In *Proceedings of NAACL-HLT 2016*, 1452-1462.

[25] S. Radicati and Q. Hoang. Email statistics report 2012-2016. *The Radicati Group, Inc.*

[26] M. Sappelli, G. Pasi, S. Verberne, M. de Boer and W. Kraaij. Assessing e-mail intent and tasks in e-mail messages. *Information Sciences, 358*, 2016, 1-17.

[27] H. Smith, Y. Rogers and M. Underwood. Managing personal and work email in the same box: Overcoming the tensions through new metaphors. In *Proceedings of HOIT 2003.*

[28] S. Whittaker, T. Matthews, J. Cerruti, H. Badenes and J. Tang. Am I wasting my time organizing email?: A study of email re-finding. In *Proceedings of CHI 2011*, 3449-3458.

[29] S. Whittaker and C. Sidner. Email overload: exploring personal information management of email. In *Proceedings of CHI 1996*, 276-283.

An Interface for Supporting Asynchronous Multi-Level Collaborative Information Retrieval

Nyi Nyi Htun
SEBE
Glasgow Caledonian University
Glasgow, G4 0BA, Scotland, UK
nyinyi.htun@gcu.ac.uk

Martin Halvey
Department of CIS
University of Strathclyde
Glasgow, G1 1XQ, Scotland, UK
martin.halvey@strath.ac.uk

Lynne Baillie
Department of CS
Heriot-Watt University
Edinburgh, EH14 4AS, Scotland, UK
l.baillie@hw.ac.uk

ABSTRACT

A great deal of research into Collaborative Information Retrieval (CIR) has assumed that search team members have the same level of unrestricted access to information. However, case studies and observations from different domains including government, healthcare and legal, have suggested that CIR sometimes involves people with unequal access to information. This type of scenario has been referred to as Multi-Level CIR (MLCIR). In addition to supporting collaboration, MLCIR systems must ensure that there is no unintended disclosure of sensitive information, this is an under investigated area of research. In this paper we present results of an evaluation of an interface we have designed for MLCIR scenarios. Pairs of participants used the interface under 3 different information access scenarios for a variety of search tasks. These scenarios included 1 CIR and 2 MLCIR scenarios, namely: full access (FA), document removal (DR) and term blacklisting (TR). Design interviews were conducted post evaluation to obtain qualitative feedback from participants. Evaluation results showed that our interface performed well for both DR and FA scenarios but for TR, team members with less access had a negative influence on their partner's search performance, demonstrating insights into how different MLCIR scenarios should be supported. Design interview results showed that our interface helped the participants to reformulate their queries, understand their partner's performance, reduce duplicated work and review their team's search history without disclosing sensitive information.

Keywords

information retrieval; asynchronous collaboration; information access; interface design; non-uniform access

1. INTRODUCTION

Collaborative Information Retrieval (CIR) involves people with shared information needs working together to search for information. A great deal of research in CIR, e.g. [12, 23, 34, 35], has focused on supporting seamless collaboration between searchers and enhancing overall search performance by means of different types of interface components and/or algorithms. A common assumption in CIR is that search team members have equal and unrestricted access to the same information. However, some analysis [2, 3, 13, 18] has shown that this may not always be the case for a variety of reasons including security, privacy concerns, etc. In such cases, despite unequal access and shareability, collaborative information search activities may need to be carried out to achieve outcomes [13]. This type of scenario is referred to as Multi-Level Collaborative Information Retrieval (MLCIR), a phrase first coined by Handel and Wang [13]. In their paper Handel and Wang [13] presented a number of case studies and examples from healthcare, business and government domains. One example involved a signal intelligence specialist and a human intelligence specialist working together to understand a new threat. Since they have non-uniform access to underlying information such as intelligence databases, the two specialists may have differing knowledge and may not be able to share any or part of it to one another. Nevertheless, the two specialists must work together to understand the threat. This example demonstrates the challenges of having non-uniform access in CIR.

A number of other researchers have also observed MLCIR scenarios in domains such as healthcare [18], crisis management [3] and legal search [2]. Findings from their observations provided insights of how non-uniform information access and organisational hierarchies can negatively impact collaboration. However, these findings [2, 3, 18] including those of Handel and Wang [13] have been based on observations and experience, and did not provide a systematic and reusable solution to solve the problems with MLCIR. To address this shortcoming, Htun et al. [16] conducted a simulated evaluation using a number of MLCIR scenarios. However, their work did not go as far as a user evaluation.

To address this gap, using details from observations [2, 3, 13, 18] and design suggestions from previous literature, e.g. [1, 8, 11, 15, 23, 30], we designed a new interface for MLCIR. Previous literature [13] suggested that the majority of MLCIR scenarios involve asynchronous collaborations, thus we designed the interface to support asynchronous collaboration on MLCIR. It should be noted that whilst there are similarities between CIR and MLCIR, the fundamental difference between the two is concerned with information flow, security and shareability. Thus, not all CIR interface components and concepts may be directly applicable to MLCIR which is something we investigate in this paper. To evaluate the use of our interface for MLCIR and the applicability of interface components we had, pairs of participants search the web using our MLCIR interface under 3 different information access scenarios for asynchronous collaboration tasks. The information access scenarios included 1 CIR scenario, and 2 MLCIR scenarios that were highlighted by Handel and Wang [13]. A number of existing evaluation metrics [28, 33], and questionnaires [6, 14] were used to assess search outcomes, participants' perceptions and usability of the interface. Design interviews were conducted post evaluation to obtain qualitative feedback. The research questions we attempt to address through this evaluation are:

RQ1: How does support for CIR concepts impact *search outcomes* in MLCIR scenarios?

RQ2: How does support for CIR concepts impact *user perception* in MLCIR scenarios?

CHIIR '17, March 07-11, 2017, Oslo, Norway
© 2017 ACM. ISBN 978-1-4503-4677-1/17/03…$15.00
DOI: http://dx.doi.org/10.1145/3020165.3020172

RQ3: How are the interface components that support CIR concepts *used by participants* on MLCIR?

RQ4: What is the overall *utility* of the interface and how can the *design of the interface* be improved for MLCIR?

The remainder of the paper is organised as follows. In Section 2, we discuss related work regarding CIR and MLCIR. In Section 3, we present our MLCIR interface and an example usage scenario. In Section 4, we describe our experimental setup. In Section 5, we present the results of our study. In Section 6, we discuss those results, providing design recommendations based on our findings from the study. Finally, we conclude this paper in Section 7.

2. RELATED WORK

2.1 Collaborative Information Retrieval

Large numbers of people often engage in collaborative search activities [21, 22]. Working in collaboration for activities such as fact-finding and exploratory search is beneficial compared to individual search [26, 35]. However, collaborative search activities that involve information sharing via conventional communication channels e.g. email, telephone, etc. are often inefficient due to duplication of effort and difficulty in remote collaboration [22]. As a result, a lot of research has been conducted to provide efficient and practical systems to support CIR [1, 8, 12, 23]. Alongside CIR, there has also been research on Collaborative Information Seeking (CIS) e.g. [11, 20, 25, 27]. According to Shah [27] CIS is "a process of information seeking that is defined explicitly among the participants, interactive, and mutually beneficial" (pp. 14) whereas Foster [7] defined CIR as "the study of the systems and practices that enable individuals to collaborate during the seeking, searching, and retrieval of information" (pp. 329).

According to Golovchinsky et al. [10], collaborative search systems can be categorised by four dimensions: intent (explicit or implicit), depth of mediation, concurrency (synchronous or asynchronous) and location (co-located or remote). In explicit collaboration, searchers' intention is explicitly to collaborate for resolving their shared information need. Collaboration is considered implicit when searchers have no intention to collaborate but their behaviour and search results are used by the system to inform new search results of other searchers. Depth of mediation refers to the involvement of algorithmic layers to assist in collaboration. Concurrency of collaboration is asynchronous when a search team performs their search activities at different times whereas in synchronous collaboration, team members perform search activities at the same time. In asynchronous collaboration, only "those who search later can benefit from the work of earlier collaborators" [10] pp. 2. Searchers can also be co-located or remotely located.

Existing collaborative search systems vary in different dimensions. Examples include SearchTogether [23], CoSearch [1], Coagmento [11], ViGOR [12] and Físchlár-DiamondTouch [32]. SearchTogether [23] allows asynchronous collaboration for web search by enabling storage of all objects and actions performed at the end of a search session, this is provided through features like instant messaging and split-screen search. CoSearch [1] is designed for synchronous and co-located web search. It is aimed at allowing collaboration over multiple devices e.g. shared computers and mobile devices. Coagmento [11], a system designed for CIS, exists as a Firefox plug-in and an Android app, and allows asynchronous and remote collaboration on both computers and mobile devices. Coagmento 2.0 [20] was recently introduced with a number of improvements to the previous version [11] including new features such as tagging, filtering the tags and searching the tags. Whilst SearchTogether, CoSearch and Coagmento support text retrieval e.g. webpages, there has also been research conducted into multimedia retrieval. For example, Halvey et al. [12] developed a collaborative video retrieval system called ViGOR, which allows asynchronous and distributed collaboration. Smeaton et al. [32] developed a synchronous and co-located video retrieval system for multi-user, touch sensitive tabletops.

MLCIR examples, as discussed by Handel and Wang [13], contain explicit and remote collaborations, and the need for a highly dedicated algorithmic layer to control information flow, access and shareability. In terms of concurrency, however, both synchronous and asynchronous collaboration may take place. Since the majority of MLCIR examples [13] involve asynchronous collaboration, we designed our interface for supporting asynchronous MLCIR. Some CIR systems (e.g. [12, 23]) employed a number of different concepts for supporting collaboration; these concepts include: awareness, division of labour and persistence. Awareness provides the ability to understand individual team members' actions, search processes and search results reducing the need for lengthy communications. Division of labour enables team members to share certain work-load reducing duplicated work. Persistence of data provides the ability to save search sessions for later use and to conduct asynchronous collaborative search. We believe that some CIR concepts could be adopted for implementing an MLCIR system. However, nuanced difference between CIR and MLCIR means that it may not be easy for certain concepts to be directly applied to MLCIR, e.g. the awareness concept in CIR systems may allow searchers to share search results within a team without restrictions, which for MLCIR systems must be modified.

2.2 Multi-Level Collaborative Information Retrieval

MLCIR issues are often visible in organisations that deal with sensitive information since such organisations do not want any unnecessary information contamination or disclosure of sensitive information within or outside of the organisation. Handel and Wang [13] present a number of industrial case studies in domains such as healthcare, business and government, and discuss challenges that may arise due to non-uniform information access. Other researchers such as Karunakaran and Reddy [18], Attfield et al. [2], and Bjurling and Hansen [3] have also begun to study difficulties and complexities that arise in different domains. Karunakaran and Reddy [18] describe a number of case studies in the healthcare domain, and discuss frequent occurrences of non-uniform knowledge distribution and miscommunication. Attfield et al. [2] present a case study of a large London law firm, and discuss difficulties and complexities that arose in a group-based awareness system. Bjurling and Hansen [3] observed a Swedish crisis management system and discuss inefficiencies in the collaborative network due to different interpretations and sharing of information. However, these research studies do not provide explicit solutions for MLCIR. To quantify the impact of non-uniform information access in CIR, Htun et al. [16] conducted a simulated evaluation using a number of MLCIR scenarios that were highlighted by Handel and Wang [13]. They found that there is a level of tolerance to removing access from document collection. Although in general there was a negative impact, Htun et al. [16] argued that non-uniform information access may not always result in a negative impact on performance. However, since their work was based on simulation, Htun et al. could not provide user-centred design recommendations for MLCIR interfaces. Besides, we believe that for collaborative search, humans can compensate for each other in ways that cannot be easily simulated.

From CIR and CIS perspectives, researchers such as Pickens et al. [24], Shah et al. [31] and Soulier et al. [33], etc. have begun to study different roles in collaborative search activities and proposed a number of different algorithms to enhance search performance based on these roles. These research studies are closely related to MLCIR since MLCIR is also concerned with team members with different roles and different access to information. Pickens et al. [24] introduced an algorithm to support different roles: "miner and prospector" for collaborative search. Pickens et al. demonstrated that the algorithm allowed a team of searchers to find relevant information more efficiently and effectively, and to find relevant information that cannot be found while working individually. Shah et al. [31] introduced a different set of roles: "gatherer and surveyor", and demonstrated similar effectiveness as Pickens et al.'s [24] "miner and prospector" role. Soulier et al. [33] introduced a number of algorithms that monitor users' actions and automatically suggest appropriate roles to optimise CIR performance. More recently, Tamine and Soulier [36] conducted a user study to investigate the impact of role assignment in CIR and found that roles limited the precision of the search results. Despite a great deal of research into different roles in CIR, their primary focus has been on division of labour aspect of CIR [19] instead of solving the problems with MLCIR which are rather concerned with information security, flow, access and shareability between collaborators [13].

To the best of our knowledge, no previous research studies have examined existing CIR concepts and components to provide a systematic and reusable solution for MLCIR. To address this shortcoming, using details from observations [2, 3, 13, 18] and design suggestions from previous literature, e.g. [1, 8, 11, 15, 23, 30], we implemented an MLCIR interface that supports asynchronous collaboration and evaluated the interface using pairs of users.

3. MLCIR INTERFACE

3.1 Interface Description

Figure 3 highlights the MLCIR interface that is evaluated in this paper. The interface was implemented using Google Web Toolkit[1] and Bing search API[2]. The interface contains 3 main components: search (Figure 3: 2), query history (Figure 3: 1) and result history (Figure 3: 3). Rationale for these components emerged from a series of user studies we had conducted [15]. The search component (i.e. Figure 3: 2) contains a search box and search button (i.e. Figure 3: g), a toolbar (i.e. Figure 3: h), a result sort function (i.e. Figure 3: j), and a result area with viewed, relevant and bookmarked labels (i.e. Figure 3: i). Results are fetched using the Bing search API in JSON format. The interface ensured that the webpages that are blocked or the webpages that contain blacklisted terms (see Section 4.1 for details) do not appear in the search results of team members who do not have full access to information. Clicking on a search result opens up a new tab within the browser window to display the full webpage (see Figure 1). The clicked result is then highlighted and marked as "viewed" (i.e. Figure 3: i). Users can then mark the page as relevant and/or bookmark the page if relevancy is uncertain, using the toolbar (i.e. Figure 3: h). The respective buttons in the toolbar can be clicked again to undo relevant or bookmark. Results can be sorted by using the result sort function (i.e. Figure 3: j) which allows sorting by a number of criteria: default, viewed, relevant and bookmarked. Under each result (i.e. Figure 3: i), users can see whether a particular result has been viewed, marked as relevant and/or bookmarked; these result properties are identified by team members' names and colours. A similar design was used in SearchTogether [23], where team members and result properties were identified with profile pictures and icons as shown in Figure 2.

Figure 1. Full webpages are displayed in new tabs

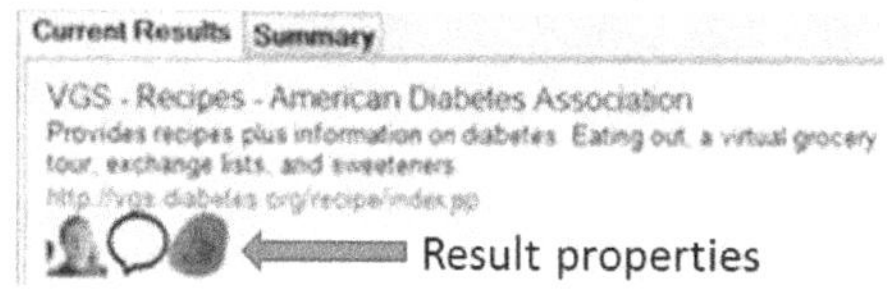

Figure 2. Result section of SearchTogether [23]

The query history component (i.e. Figure 3: 1) contains a history of team's search queries (i.e. Figure 3: a), query properties (i.e. Figure 3: b, c, d, e) and a sort function (i.e. Figure 3: f). Queries between a pair of users are separated using different boxes, names and colours as shown in Figure 3: a. The approach of identifying team members with different colours and names has been used in previous collaborative search systems: CoSearch [1] and Coagmento [11]. Both team members can see every query submitted by the team and can simply click the queries to re-submit. The search component then checks for blocked webpages and blacklisted terms before displaying the results. Query properties namely: number of viewed documents/webpages (VD), number of relevant documents/webpages (RD), number of bookmarked documents/webpages (BD) and time spent on query (TS) are displayed next to each query as shown in Figure 3: b, c, d, e respectively. A search system implemented by Freyne et al [8] augmented search result properties such as: popularity, time spent, etc. next to each search result. Unlike Freyne et al.'s [8] interface, our interface augments query properties instead of result properties. Query history can be sorted based on query properties by using the toggle buttons as shown in Figure 3: f.

The result history component (i.e. Figure 3: 3) contains a history of viewed, relevant and bookmarked results separated into different tabs. The tabs display titles of the respective webpages (i.e. Figure 3: k) together with relevant and bookmark toggle buttons (i.e. Figure 3: l). A mouse hover on any of the title in the result history displays a tooltip with the related query that was used to obtain the respective webpage. Clicking on the title opens up a new tab within the same browser window to display the full webpage (see Figure 1). The relevant and bookmark toggle buttons (i.e. Figure 3: l) have the same functionality as those from the toolbar (i.e. Figure 3: h). The interface ensures that the webpages that are blocked or the webpages that contain blacklisted terms do not appear in the result history of team members who do not have full access to information.

3.2 Example Usage Scenario

This example is based on an MLCIR scenario postulated by Handel and Wang [13], and involves a pair of users, a company employee and a customer, working together to troubleshoot a problem. The customer has access to the company's website whereas the employee has access to the website and the internal database. Depending on the type of results e.g. those that contain information about other customers, the employee may not be able to share certain results with the customer. Using our MLCIR interface, the customer starts his/her search session as s/he normally

[1] http://www.gwtproject.org

[2] https://datamarket.azure.com/dataset/bing/search

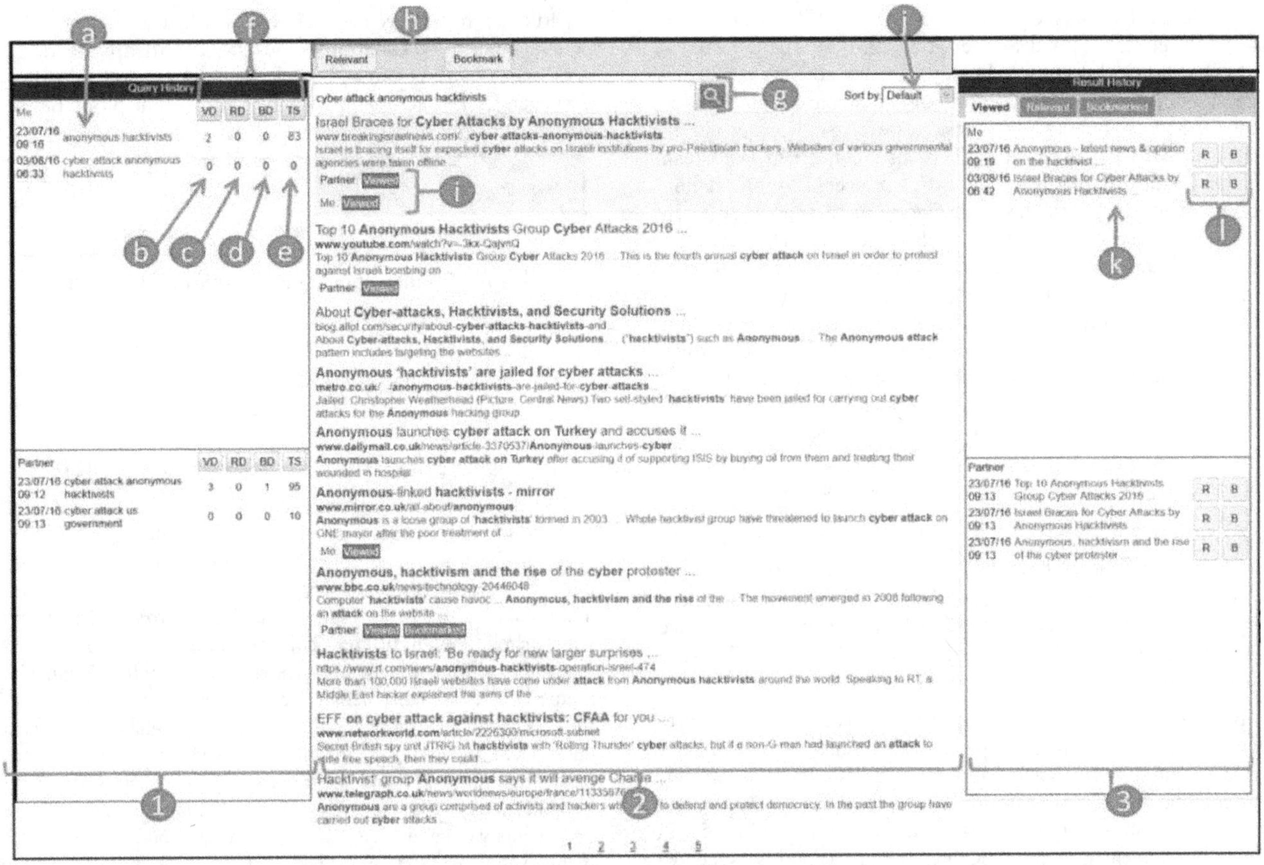

Figure 3. The interface utilised in the study: 1) query history component, 2) search component, 3) result history component, a) query, b) number of viewed documents/webpages, c) number of relevant documents/webpages, d) number of bookmarked documents/webpages, e) time spent on query, f) query sort function, g) search box and button, h) toolbar, i) viewed, relevant, bookmarked labels, j) result sort function, k) titles of saved webpages, l) relevant and bookmark toggle buttons.

would to find troubleshooting documents across the company's website. The customer may not find any relevant information because of their access level, bad search queries or information overloading. The customer finishes the search session after a while. The employee later browses the customer's previous search session and continues searching. The employee looks at the customer's query history and sees an overview of how many different results were seen, marked as relevant and bookmarked, and how long the customer spent on each query. If, for instance, the customer spent a long time in a particularly set of queries and viewed relatively higher number of results but did not find any relevant ones, the employee may be able to look further into such queries and help the customer find relevant results. Similarly, using the result history component, the employee may decide to look at the relevant and bookmarked results and help the customer find similar results. The employee may find both overlapping and different results from the customer. The results that are marked as "viewed" only may be skipped and the results they are also marked as "relevant" or "bookmarked" may be reviewed. The employee may also find the results that contain sensitive information, but may or may not notice it and continues his/her search session anyway. Luckily, the backend of the interface scans through every result and ensures that the results that contain sensitive information (i.e. blacklisted words) or the results that exist only in the internal database (i.e. blacklisted documents) are not displayed in the customer's side. This way, the employee can help the customer find the relevant results without the overhead of inadvertently disclosing sensitive information. The search sessions are saved to allow asynchronous collaboration, thus both the customer and the employee can resume their search session at any time. The customer may later review the employee's search session, reformulate his/her previous queries and find relevant results in the website this time. Throughout this scenario, the customer and the employee did not need to discuss their access and limitation, their results or even their search queries.

4. EXPERIMENTAL SETUP

4.1 Information Access Scenarios

For this evaluation we selected 3 information access scenarios informed by literature [13, 16]. 2 of which were non-uniform access scenarios namely: *document removal* and *term blacklisting,* and the third scenario being a *full access* scenario (see Table 1). In the *document removal* scenario, access to documents is removed for one team member of a pair, simulating team members with access to different databases [13]. In the *term blacklisting* scenario, the most likely search terms are blacklisted for one team member of a pair so that the team member does not find results if s/he submits the blacklisted search terms, simulating restriction of documents at the paragraph level [13]. The *full access* scenario represents the case where all team members have equal and unrestricted access to all documents in a collection, representing the more traditional CIR scenario. These 3 information access scenarios allowed us to compare search outcomes of our interface between CIR (full access) and MLCIR (document removal and term blacklisting) scenarios. During the evaluation, pairs of participants performed search in all 3 information access scenarios. To avoid order effects, the order in which the information access scenarios are presented was rotated using Latin square counterbalancing.

Prior to the study, 6 participants (4 from our research group) were asked to provide at least 20 queries for each of our search tasks (see Section 4.2). This generated a pool of the most likely queries for each task with 85 to 97 unique terms per task. Next, all the queries from this query pool were submitted to the Bing Search API[3]. We then selected at random 25 results from the top 50 for each task. For the document removal scenario (i.e. DR in Table 1), this set of 25 results was used to block the results for one member of a search team (teams were pairs). For the term blacklisting scenario (i.e. TR in Table 1), the top 10 most frequent terms in the query pool for each task was used to blacklist the queries for one member of a search team (teams were pairs). Thus, in the TR scenario all the webpages that contain any of the blacklisted terms are blocked for one member. To the best of our knowledge, no previous research studies have provided guidelines for the DR and TR scenarios based on the web. We believe that our approach of selecting the documents and terms for DR and TR was moderate and served as a starting point for evaluation of our interface. Each non-uniform access scenario had a team member with less access (i.e. either blacklisted terms or blacklisted results) and the other team member with full access. Access within a pair of participants was rotated so that each participant had a chance to experience having full access and non-full access in either the DR or TR scenario.

Table 1. Information access scenarios utilised in this study

Code	Access Scenario	Access removed for a member
DR	Document removal scenario	Random 25 out of top 50 most likely result removed
TR	Term blacklisting scenario	Top 10 most likely terms removed
FA	Full access scenario	-

4.2 Search Tasks

Table 2. Example search task

Cyber-Attack
You are a central intelligence agent working with a national security agent to understand cyber-attacks, that were targeted at the US government facilities (including websites and computers), by the Anonymous hacktivists within the last 10 years. Thus, you and your partner need to search through any available documents to be able to analyse the attacks. However, you will be searching at a different time from your partner (i.e. before or after your partner). You and your partner may or may not have equal access to underlying information.
Search and visit any documents you think are relevant. Once you find an interesting document, either mark it as relevant or bookmark it if you are unsure at the moment. Your main goal is to find as many relevant documents as possible. Your work must help your partner to continue searching.
You should search for the following information: **what were the reasons for the attacks in the last 10 years** and **how the US government responded to the attacks**.

Using the method of Borlund [4], 3 simulated work tasks were created based on the real-life MLCIR examples highlighted by Handel and Wang [13]. The 3 tasks were about: 1) cyber-attack, 2) crime investigation and 3) new robotic technology. An example of cyber-attack task can be found in Table 2. The tasks also informed the participants to find as many relevant documents as possible for their team. Since team members in MLCIR scenarios are unaware of their access, limitation and information shareability [13], we believed this strategy was appropriate. During the evaluation, participants performed all 3 search tasks. Tasks and information access scenarios were rotated between a pair of participants to simulate asynchronous collaboration. Both participants started with different tasks and information access scenarios (i.e. without partner's query and search history), and later continued searching the remaining tasks and information access scenarios following their partner's previous search session.

4.3 Participants

20 participants (10 pairs) were recruited from personal contacts, research group and university contacts for this study. This participant pool size is similar to previous experiments [8, 17, 23, 24]. Participants were assigned partners for the study based on their availability. 8 pairs of the participants knew each other prior to the study and signed up together. Each participant received a £10 Amazon voucher on completion of the study; they were informed of this while being recruited. 8 females and 12 males participated in the study. The average age of the participants was 26.9 (S.D ± 4.08), ranging from 19 to 33. Of all participants, 1 reported spending less than 6 hours per week using search engines, 3 reported 6 to 10 hours per week, 1 reported 11 to 15 hours per week, 4 reported 16 to 20 hours per week and 11 reported more than 20 hours per week. 15 participants reported that they had taken part in a collaborative search at least once using search systems like Google, Bing and Google Scholar, and tools such as social media and phones to share information.

4.4 Study Procedure

Once the participants signed up to participate in the study, they were assigned into pairs based on their availability. Once a pair of participants was assigned into an appropriate timeslot, an email containing an information sheet, a consent form and a demographic questionnaire was sent to each of them. Prior to arriving for the study, the participants were asked to read the information sheet, sign the consent form and send back a digital copy, and then complete the demographic questionnaire.

Upon arrival participants were welcomed, and introduced if they did not know each other prior to the study. The participants were then informed of the information access scenarios, search tasks and interface. They were not told which team member had more (or less) access to underlying information, nor the order of the information access scenarios presented. This was to eliminate the possibility of any bias that could occur when answering post-task questionnaires. For the rest of the procedure, we followed a similar approach to previous research studies [17, 23, 24, 28]. The participants were provided with a short demonstration of the interface and were allowed a maximum of 5 minutes to practice using the search system. The participants were then placed in the same room in front of two separate computers facing away from each other. They were instructed not to communicate directly and to pretend that they were not in the same room. If the participants did not have any questions, each was provided with a search task (see Section 4.2 for the tasks). To simulate asynchronous collaboration, both participants started with different search tasks and information access scenarios, and later continued the previous search sessions of each other. A maximum of 3 minutes was allocated to read their respective search task. A copy of the task was provided to both participants throughout the search session so that they can refer to the task if necessary. A maximum of 15 minutes

[3] https://datamarket.azure.com/dataset/bing/search

was allocated for each task. Upon completion of each task, each participant was provided with a post-task questionnaire. A maximum of 3 minutes was allocated to complete the questionnaire. The questionnaire included a NASA TLX questionnaire [14], and 3 additional 5-point Likert scale questions to assess participants' 1) perception of their access level, 2) interest in the task and 3) familiarity with the task. Once participants completed the post-task questionnaire, they repeated the same steps for the remaining 2 search sessions using different information access scenarios and search tasks. Upon completion of all 3 search sessions, each participant was provided with a System Usability Scale [6]. A maximum of 2 minutes was allocated to answer the SUS questionnaire. Finally, a design interview was conducted with both participants (see Section 4.6). The main researcher asked a series of open ended questions and took notes of participants' responses. The responses were also recorded on an audio recorder, which were later transcribed for analysis. During the interview, participants were also provided with printouts of the interview questions and interface components, as well as empty sheets of paper so that the participants could reference, annotate and sketch while answering the questions. The total length of each study was 90 minutes.

4.5 Evaluation Metrics

To measure search outcomes (RQ1), we adopted some evaluation metrics proposed by Shah and González-Ibáñez [28] for CIS: *recall*, *precision*, *f-measure*, *coverage*, *relevant coverage*, *unique coverage* and *unique relevant coverage*. Following the approach of Shah and González-Ibáñez [28], we first created a pool of all webpages discovered by all of the participants. Next, a pool of relevant webpages was created by combining all the webpages that were marked as relevant by participants. Shah and González-Ibáñez [28] created the pool of relevant webpages by combining all the webpages that were either bookmarked or from where text snippets were collected. For us, since our interface had a relevant function, we used the relevant webpages instead. *Coverage* is the number of distinct webpages discovered by a pair of participants or by an individual participant. *Relevant coverage* is the number of webpages in the *coverage* that intersect with the pool of relevant webpages. *Recall* is *relevant coverage*/pool of relevant webpages. *Precision* is *relevant coverage*/*coverage*. *F-measure* is a harmonic mean of *recall* and *precision* which is represented by the formula: $\frac{2 \,.\, precision \,.\, recall}{(precision + recall)}$. *Unique coverage* is the number of distinct webpages discovered by a pair of participants only in a given case (e.g. only in the DR scenario) and not in any others, or by individuals in a given access (e.g. full access within the DR scenario) and not in the other. *Unique relevant coverage* is the number of webpages in the *unique coverage* that intersect with the pool of relevant webpages. Other evaluation metrics adopted for this study include those proposed by Soulier et al. [33] for CIR: *number of queries* and *average query length*. *Number of queries* is the total number of queries submitted by a pair of participants or by an individual participant. *Average query length* is the average number of words within the *number of queries*. NASA Task Load Index [14] and 3 addition questions were used to answer our second research question (RQ2). Feedback from design interview and System Usability Scale [6] were used to answer our third (RQ3) and fourth (RQ4) research questions.

4.6 Design Interview

The purpose of the design interview was to understand in detail how the interface had an impact on participants during search sessions. It was also designed to capture suggestions from participants so that the interface can be further improved. The design interview consisted of 3 sections. In section 1, participant pairs were asked a series of questions related to the query history component. In section 2, the pairs were asked a series of questions related to the search component. In section 3, the pairs were asked a series of questions related to the result history component. In all 3 sections, we asked the pairs how the component impacted their search sessions, which parts of the components were most/least useful and how the component could be improved. Participants' responses were analysed using the Constant Comparative Method [9], a data analysis method of the Grounded Theory approach.

5. RESULTS

Statistical comparisons were made between the 3 information access scenarios and between individuals with full access and non-full access within the document removal and term blacklisting scenarios. Dependent variables included all the metrics presented in Section 4.5. For comparison between the information access scenarios, since data was paired, one-way repeated measures ANOVA was used for normally distributed data and Friedman and Wilcoxon Sign-Rank tests were used for non-normally distributed data. For comparison between individuals with full and non-full access within the DR and TR scenarios, since data was unpaired, one-way between groups ANOVA was used for normally distributed data and Mann-Whitney U test was used to non-normally distributed data. Results are presented in the following sub-sections. For reasons of space, some results with non-significant differences are not presented.

5.1 Search Performance

Statistical analysis showed that *recall*, *precision* and *f-measure* values differed significantly between the information access scenarios ($F(2,18) = 24.56$, $p<0.001$, $F(2,18) = 15.31$, $p<0.001$ and $F(2,18) = 24.22$, $p<0.001$ respectively). Post hoc analysis, using a Bonferroni corrected alpha, showed that the term blacklisting (TR) scenario had significantly lower *recall*, *precision* and *f-measure* than both document removal (DR) scenario ($p=0.001$, $p=0.001$ and $p<0.001$ respectively) and full access (FA) scenario ($p<0.001$, $p=0.001$ and $p<0.001$ respectively) (see Table 3). There was no significant difference between the DR and FA scenarios. Looking at individual search performance for the DR scenario, no significant performance difference was found between individuals with full access and non-full access. However, for the TR scenario, individuals with full access had significantly higher *recall* ($F(1, 11.307) = 10.952$, $p = 0.007$), *precision* ($F(1, 12.23) = 13.287$, $p = 0.003$) and *f-measure* ($F(1, 11.572) = 12.886$, $p = 0.004$) than individuals with non-full access (see Table 3). It appears that the TR scenario (i.e. blacklisting 10 most likely terms) had a significant negative impact on search performance than the DR scenario (i.e. removing random 25 out of top 50 most likely results). Surprisingly, individuals with full access in the TR scenario had less than half *recall*, *precision* and *f-measure* than those with full access in the DR scenario (see Table 3). While one would expect similar search performance between individuals with full access within the TR and DR scenarios, it appears that those with full access within the TR scenario were negatively influenced by their partner with non-full access.

5.2 Coverage

The 3 information access scenarios had significantly different *coverage* ($F(2,18) = 14.53$, $p<0.001$), *relevant coverage* ($F(2,18) = 18.91$, $p<0.001$), *unique coverage* ($F(2,18) = 14.6$, $p<0.001$) and *unique relevant coverage* ($F(2,18) = 18.78$, $p<0.001$). Post hoc analysis with a Bonferroni correction showed that the term blacklisting (TR) scenario had significantly higher *coverage* and *unique coverage* than the document removal (DR) scenario ($p=0.01$ and $p=0.01$ respectively) and the full access (FA) scenario ($p=0.002$

Table 3. Search performance metrics comparison between the information access scenarios, and between full and non-full access within TR. Bold and underline = statistically different pairs (p < .05). S.D = standard deviation.

		DR	TR	FA	DR		TR	
					Full	Non-full	Full	Non-full
recall	Mean	**0.226**	**0.068**	0.232	0.125	0.129	**0.059**	**0.018**
	S.D	0.095	0.034	0.068	0.058	0.071	0.037	0.013
precision	Mean	**0.186**	**0.030**	0.203	0.198	0.176	**0.053**	**0.016**
	S.D	0.078	0.014	0.088	0.091	0.099	0.030	0.013
f-measure	Mean	**0.197**	**0.040**	0.204	0.150	0.143	**0.053**	**0.016**
	S.D	0.073	0.017	0.060	0.070	0.071	0.031	0.012

Table 4. Coverage metrics comparison between the information access scenarios, and between full and non-full access within TR. Bold and underline = statistically different pairs (p < .05). S.D = standard deviation.

		DR	TR	FA	DR		TR	
					Full	Non-full	Full	Non-full
coverage	Mean	**128.500**	**236.900**	137.700	66.500	69.700	117.600	136.800
	S.D	36.136	85.448	69.746	19.873	36.670	54.923	65.824
relevant coverage	Mean	**23.200**	**6.800**	24.000	13.100	12.900	**5.800**	**1.900**
	S.D	10.130	3.584	8.206	7.078	7.218	3.882	1.663
unique coverage	Mean	**128.100**	**236.500**	137.500	58.800	62.000	100.100	119.300
	S.D	36.260	85.373	69.535	22.968	32.653	45.369	62.118
unique relevant coverage	Mean	**23.200**	**6.800**	24.100	10.300	10.100	**4.900**	**1.000**
	S.D	10.130	3.584	8.399	7.088	6.315	3.247	1.333

and p=0.002 respectively) (see Table 4). It appears that blacklisting search terms forced the participants to discover a great number of diverse results. In terms of *relevant coverage* and *unique relevant coverage*, the TR scenario had significantly lower values in comparison with both DR (p<0.001 and p<0.001 respectively) and FA (p=0.001 and p=0.001 respectively) scenarios (see Table 4). Thus, in terms of discovering relevant results, teams within the TR scenario performed badly which confirms the findings presented in Section 5.1. Looking at individuals' coverage for the TR scenario, individuals with full access had significantly better *relevant coverage* (F(1, 12.2) = 8.53, p=0.013) and *unique relevant coverage* (U = 14.5, p=0.006) than those with non-full access (see Table 4). For the DR scenario, no significant difference was found between full and non-full access. Interestingly, individuals with full access within the TR scenario had almost double the *coverage* and *unique coverage* than those with full access within the DR scenario (see Table 4). In contrast for *relevant coverage* and *unique relevant coverage*, the opposite effect was found; this phenomenon was also discovered for *recall*, *precision* and *f-measure*. This shows the influence of the poorly performing partner on a team.

5.3 Query Submission

Participants submitted a significantly higher *number of queries* in the TR scenario in comparison with both DR (Z = -2.803, p=0.005) and FA (Z = -2.82, p=0.005) scenarios (see Table 5). Individuals with non-full access in the TR scenario submitted a significantly higher *number of queries* (F(1, 18) = 8.98, p=0.008) than those with full access (see Table 5). *Average query length* was not different between the information access scenarios nor between individuals. Individuals with full access within the TR scenario submitted almost double the amount of queries than those with full access within the DR scenario. We observed that blacklisting search terms for one team member resulted in both team members submitting a large amount of queries, thereby also discovering more results as presented in Section 5.2. To understand search term diversity between individuals, we further analysed the number of unique terms submitted by individuals in a given access (e.g. full access within the document removal scenario) and not in the other. *Term diversity* was significantly higher for individuals with non-full access than those with full access within the TR scenario (see Table 5). No significant difference was found between full and non-full access for the DR scenario.

5.4 Participants' Perceptions

Participants' perceptions were measured using the NASA TLX and 3 additional 5-point Likert scale questions which assessed 1) *perception of access level*, 2) *interest* in the task and 3) *familiarly* with the task. Statistical analysis showed significant differences between the information access scenarios for 3 of the NASA TLX scale questions: *performance* ($\chi2(2)$ = 16.64, p<0.001), *effort* (F(2,38) = 8.01, p=0.001) and *frustration* (F(2,38) = 10.94, p<0.001). Post hoc analysis using Bonferroni correction showed that *performance* score for the term blacklisting (TR) scenario was significantly lower than the document removal (DR) scenario (Z = -3.705, p<0.001) and the full access (FA) scenario (Z = -3.124, p=0.002) (see Table 6). The *performance* score of individuals with full access and non-full access also showed that it was lower for those with non-full access (U = 21.5, p=0.03). Unsurprisingly, the scores for *effort* and *frustration* were significantly higher for the TR scenario in comparison with the DR scenario (p=0.014 and p=0.001 respectively) and the FA scenario (p=0.015 and p=0.005 respectively). However, no significant difference was found for the *effort* and *frustration* scores between individuals. Statistical analysis also showed that one of the 3 additional questions: *perception of access level* was statistically different between the information access scenarios ($\chi2(2)$ = 7.03, p=0.03). Post hoc analysis using Bonferroni correction showed that the FA scenario had a significantly higher score than the TR scenario (Z = -2.726, p=0.006) which was expected (see Table 6). Interesting, looking at individuals with full access and non-full access, it was found that the *perception of access* score was higher for individuals with non-full access than those with full access within the DR scenario (F(1, 18) = 6, p=0.025) (see Table 6); no significant difference was found within the TR scenario. To obtain a usability rating of the interface, we administered the System Usability Scale (SUS) after the participants had completed all the search sessions. The average SUS score of the interface across all the participants was 70.75 (SD ±15.793) which is above average (68 is average [5]).

Table 5. Query submission metrics comparison between the information access scenarios, and between full and non-full access within TR. Bold and underline = statistically different pairs (p < .05). S.D = standard deviation.

		DR	TR	FA	DR		TR	
					Full	Non-full	Full	Non-full
number of queries	Mean	**11.100**	**26.600**	10.700	6.100	5.200	**11.300**	**17.800**
	S.D	4.677	6.293	5.100	3.213	2.394	3.945	5.613
term diversity (words that are unique in a given access)	Mean	-	-	-	9.600	7.900	**8.500**	**14.500**
	S.D	-	-	-	6.398	5.216	5.339	6.433

Table 6. Participants' perception metrics comparison between the information access scenarios and between full and non-full access within DR and TR. Bold and underline = statistically different pairs (p < .05). S.D = standard deviation. For *performance*, *effort* and *frustration*, the lower the better. For *perception of access*, 0 = strongly disagree and 5 = strong agree to the statement of having higher access than partner.

		DR	TR	FA	DR		TR	
					Full	Non-full	Full	Non-full
performance	Mean	**7.750**	**14.950**	8.900	7.900	7.600	**12.600**	**17.300**
	S.D	4.363	4.763	5.330	4.122	4.812	5.060	3.164
effort	Mean	**9.750**	**13.500**	9.900	9.900	9.600	13.600	13.400
	S.D	3.972	2.782	4.471	3.071	4.881	2.591	3.098
frustration	Mean	**7.200**	**12.250**	7.900	6.800	7.600	10.800	13.700
	S.D	4.851	5.169	5.119	4.614	5.296	3.853	6.075
perception of access	Mean	3.000	**2.250**	**3.350**	**2.500**	**3.500**	2.300	2.200
	S.D	1.026	1.209	0.988	0.972	0.850	1.252	1.229

5.5 Design Interview

Analysis of design interview transcripts using Constant Comparative Method [9] resulted in 5 main themes: query reformulation, knowledge of partner's performance, reducing duplicated work, reviewing search results and improvements. Details of these themes are presented in the following sub-sections.

5.5.1 Query Reformulation

We found that the query history and result history components were used by most participants to reformulate their queries. 15 (75%) of the participants reported that they used the query history component. For example, one participant explained: "*When I got stuck was when I really looked at what my partner has searched. Looking at my partner's queries helped me overcome not being able to find anything*" (P8). All 15 (75%) participants also mentioned that they used a combination of at least two of the four query properties (i.e. number of viewed results, relevant results and bookmarked results, and time spent) to determine a useful query. 4 (20%) of the participants reported that they also used the relevant results from the result history component for query formulation. For example, one participant mentioned: "*[The relevant tab] is very similar to how the query history affected my search. This came in handy if I was struggling to find the results.*" (P15).

5.5.2 Knowledge of Partner's performance

It appears that the query properties in the history component were able to provide the participants with an overview of their partner's search performance. 14 (70%) of the participants explained that they mostly used the number of viewed results, relevant results and time spent to check search performance of their partner. That way, they were able to focus on a certain direction of search. For example, one participant explained: "*I could find out how many relevant results [my partner] found and how long [my partner] spent on a particular search word. So I can either try to avoid it or go deeper into it.*" (P12)

5.5.3 Reducing Duplicated Work

It appears that being able to see whether a search result was seen, marked as relevant and/or bookmarked by a partner helped reduce duplicated work. 16 (80%) of the participants reported that they skipped the results that were only marked as "viewed" and not as "relevant" and/or "bookmarked". For example, one participant mentioned: "*The 'viewed' labels helped me. And just being able to see it at a glance that my partner has looked that these webpages already and if it says "viewed" not relevant, not bookmarked, I wouldn't really bother to look at it.*" (P7). This is most likely because the participants believed that a particular result is unimportant if their partner had looked at it but did not mark it as relevant or did not bookmark it.

5.5.4 Reviewing Search Results

Having access to a persistent result history gave the participants an overview of their search session and allowed them to refine search results. 15 (75%) of the participants reported using the result history to review their team's search results either to confirm or to explore further. For example, one participant noted: "*...like you can look back through what you have searched and decide if you now want to make something relevant or now you want to bookmark something.*" (P8). It should be noted, though, that the result history displayed only the results that were not blacklisted and did not contain blacklisted terms.

6. DISCUSSION

In relation to our first research question (RQ1): "How does support for CIR concepts impact *search outcomes* in MLCIR scenarios?", we found that the term blacklisting scenario had a significant negative impact on team search performance compared to the document removal and full access scenarios. Teams within the document removal scenario performed as well as those within the full access scenario. It means that our interface can close the performance gap for the document removal scenario, but not for the term blacklisting scenario at our current removal/blacklisting level. We also found that in the term blacklisting scenario, users submitted a large amount of diverse queries compared to the rest of the information access scenarios. This in turn led to discovering a large amount of diverse results. For recall-oriented search tasks, discovering a large amount of diverse results could be considered a good thing. However, in our case we observed that the individuals whose search terms were blacklisted had a negative influence on their partner who had full access. Because of this, individuals with full access within the term blacklisting scenario performed poorly compared to those with full access within the document removal scenario. Arguably, being aware of their partner's search queries and results may have caused the individuals with full access to hinder their search performance.

In relation to our second research question (RQ2): "How does support for CIR concepts impact *user perception* in MLCIR scenarios?", we found that the participants had a significantly negative response to the questions assessing their performance, effort and frustration for the term blacklisting scenario in comparison with the document removal and full access scenarios. This is related to a finding discussed for our first research question (RQ1). Due to the negative impact of the term blacklisting scenario on search performance, it appears that the participants had to put more effort to find relevant results and hence were more frustrated. Surprisingly, we found that the individuals with non-full access within the document removal scenario thought they had higher access than those with full access. It appears that users' perception of access and performance are not affected by our document removal scenario.

In relation to our third research question (RQ3): "How are the interface components that support CIR concepts *used by participants* on MLCIR?", here we discuss findings from the design interview. First, we found that the query history and result history components were used by participants to reformulate their search queries. For the query history component, it was found that the query properties (i.e. number of viewed results, relevant results and bookmarked results, and time spent) played an important role since most participants mentioned that they used the properties to determine a useful query. For the result history, relevant results were used in query formulation perhaps because the participants believed that relevant results contain keywords that are related to the search topic. Second, we found that the query properties in the query history component were used by participants to understand search performance of their partner. Understanding partner's performance enabled the participants to focus on a certain direction of search. Third, it was found that understanding the search results that were viewed, marked as relevant and bookmarked allowed the participants to reduce duplicated work. In our interface, we used a number of labels to show this information in the search results (e.g. Figure 3: j). Fourth, we found that the participants used the result history component to review and refine their team's search results. Note that the findings we discussed for this research question are not the explicit findings for asynchronous MLCIR only. A number of studies in both CIR and CIS [17, 23, 29], have used similar interface components and presented similar findings. Yet because of the differences between CIR/CIS and MLCIR, not all such findings could be applied to MLCIR. Our findings confirm reusability and demonstrate broader applicability of some existing components for designing MLCIR systems. To understand whether the participants used our interface differently between traditional CIR and MLCIR conditions, we further analysed the number of clicks on queries in the query history component, number of times the query history was sorted, number of times results were sorted, and number of clicks on results in the result history component. No differences were found between traditional CIR and MLCIR conditions.

In relation to our fourth research question (RQ4): "What is the overall *utility* of the interface and how can the *design of the interface* be improved for MLCIR?", the overall SUS score of the interface was 70.75, which is above average (68 being the average [5]). For the second part of the research question, we discuss findings from the design interview. One participant suggested linking the query properties and the result history so that one can, for instance, click on the *number of relevant documents* query property (Figure 3: d) to see what these documents are as in the result history (Figure 3: l). 6 (30%) of the participants suggested adding a comment function for search results. For example, a participant described: "*Instead of me going back reading through the whole page, my partner can just say what I need to look here. So, for example, once I bookmark a page, there should be a popup where I can type in.*" (P7). A similar component has been used in SearchTogether [23], where it is referred to as "page-specific metadata". 2 (10%) of the participants suggested that the partner's query history and result history should be displayed above self's query history and result history. This is because during search sessions, users are more likely to be interested in their partner's query and result histories rather than theirs.

While our findings informed new interface components, as well as reusability of some existing components, such findings have fallen into 3 awareness types that were devised by Htun et al. [15] for MLCIR systems; these are: result awareness, team awareness and query awareness. We would like to confirm here that new MLCIR systems could base their design on these 3 awareness types regardless of their domain: healthcare, government, business, etc.

6.1 Limitations

While our evaluation results had shown a number of interesting findings, there are some limitations. First, while our results indicated that the document removal scenario had comparable search performance and collection coverage, it could be due to the amount of documents we blocked (i.e. removing random 25 out of top 50 most likely results). Perhaps blocking more documents may observe a different finding. However, since no previous guidelines existed prior to our study, our approach served as a starting point. Second, since we used a single interface to compare the 3 information access scenarios, the effect of each component could not be compared directly through hypothesis testing. However, findings from the design interview provided a better understanding of the impact of each component during search sessions. Finally, since the search sessions were performed across the open web and we did not have a qrel, we were unable to calculate our evaluation metrics as precisely as using a document collection. However, the method we used to calculate our evaluation metrics has successfully been used by pervious research studies [28, 33].

7. CONCLUSION

This paper presents the first known attempt to evaluate the interface that supports asynchronous collaboration in MLCIR scenarios. We used 3 different information access scenarios highlighted by previous research [13, 16]. These scenarios were: document removal (DR), term blacklisting (TR) and full access (FA). Pairs of participants used the interface across the 3 information access scenarios and tasks, and evaluated the interface. A number of evaluation metrics were used including the CIR and CIS evaluation metrics [28, 33], NASA Task Load Index [14] and System Usability Scale [6]. Design interviews were also conducted post evaluation to understand the participants' experience during search sessions and to obtain design suggestions for further improvement of the interface. Evaluation results showed that the TR scenario had significantly negative impact on team search performance compared to the rest of the information access scenarios. Within the TR scenario, team members whose search terms were blacklisted had a negative influence on their partner who had full access leading both team members towards negative search performance. For our DR scenario, the interface performed as well as for FA, demonstrating that it is possible to close the performance gap when a search team does not have equal access to information. Overall participants rated the usability of the interface as above average. Findings from the design interview showed that using different components of the interface, participants were able to effectively reformulate their queries, obtain knowledge of their partner's performance, reduce duplicated work and easily review their team's search results. A number of design suggestions were also discussed in order to help improve the design of the current interface. In summary, we demonstrated and evaluated the first known interface to support asynchronous collaboration in MLCR scenarios. We showed that our interface has the ability to provide important information for users without disclosing sensitive information during asynchronous collaboration. Besides, we provided important new design suggestions and showed reusability of certain CIR components and concepts for MLCIR interfaces, something that has never been done before. We believe that the findings, interface and design suggestions observed and demonstrated in this paper will serve as the guidelines for further investigations into MLCIR.

8. REFERENCES

[1] Amershi, S. and Morris, M. R.: CoSearch: a system for co-located collaborative web search. *ACM SIGCHI 2008*, 1647-1656.

[2] Attfield, S., Blandford, A., Makri, S.: Social and interactional practices for disseminating current awareness information in an organisational setting. *IPM*, 46(6), 2010, 632-645.

[3] Bjurling, B., Hansen, P.: Contracts for Information Sharing in Collaborative Networks. *ISCRAM 2010*, 1-5.

[4] Borlund, P.: The IIR evaluation model: a framework for evaluation of interactive information retrieval systems. *Information research*, 8(3), 2003, Key: citeulike:1188067.

[5] Brooke, J.: SUS: a retrospective. *Journal of usability studies*, 8(2), 2013, 29-40.

[6] Brooke, J.: SUS-A quick and dirty usability scale. *Usability evaluation in industry*, 189(194), 1996, 4-7.

[7] Foster, J.: Collaborative information seeking and retrieval. *Annual review of information science and technology*, 40(1), 2006, 329-356.

[8] Freyne, J., Farzan, R., Brusilovsky, P., Smyth, B. and Coyle, M.: Collecting community wisdom: integrating social search & social navigation. *ACM IUI 2007*, 52-61.

[9] Glaser, B. G., Strauss, A. L. and Strutzel, E.: The Discovery of Grounded Theory; Strategies for Qualitative Research. *Nursing Research*, 17(4), 1968, 364

[10] Golovchinsky, G., Pickens, J. and Back, M.: A taxonomy of collaboration in online information seeking. *arXiv preprint*, arXiv:0908.0704, 2009.

[11] González-Ibáñez, R. and Shah, C.: Coagmento: A system for supporting collaborative information seeking. *ASIS&T*, 48(1), 2011, 1-4.

[12] Halvey, M., Vallet, D., Hannah, D., Feng, Y., Jose, J. M.: An asynchronous collaborative search system for online video search. *IPM*, 46(6), 2010, 733-748.

[13] Handel, M. J., Wang, E. Y.: I can't tell you what i found: problems in multi-level collaborative information retrieval. *ACM CIR 2011*, 1-6.

[14] Hart, S. G. and Staveland, L. E.: Development of NASA-TLX (Task Load Index): Results of empirical and theoretical research. *Advances in psychology*, 52, 1988, 139-183.

[15] Htun, N. N., Halvey, M. and Baillie, L.: How Can We Better Support Users with Non-Uniform Information Access in Collaborative Information Retrieval? *ACM CHIIR 2017*. DOI: http://dx.doi.org/10.1145/3020165.3020171.

[16] Htun, N. N., Halvey, M. and Baillie, L.: Towards Quantifying the Impact of Non-Uniform Information Access in Collaborative Information Retrieval. *ACM SIGIR 2015*, 843-846.

[17] Joho, H., Hannah, D., Jose, J. M.: Comparing collaborative and independent search in a recall-oriented task. *ACM IIiX 2008*, 89-96.

[18] Karunakaran, A., Reddy, M.: The Role of Narratives in Collaborative Information Seeking. *ACM GROUP 2012*, 273–276.

[19] Kelly, R. and Payne, S.: Division of labour in collaborative information seeking: Current approaches and future directions. *Workshop on Collaborative Information Seeking, held at ACM CSCW 2013*.

[20] Mitsui, M. and Shah, C.: Coagmento 2.0: A System for Capturing Individual and Group Information Seeking Behavior. *ACM JCDL 2016*, 233-234.

[21] Morris, M. R.: Collaborative search revisited. *ACM CSCW 2013*, 1181-1192.

[22] Morris, M. R.: A survey of collaborative web search practices. *ACM CHI 2008*, 1657-1660.

[23] Morris, M. R., Horvitz, E.: SearchTogether: an interface for collaborative web search. *ACM UIST 2007*, 3-12.

[24] Pickens, J., Golovchinsky, G., Shah, C., Qvarfordt, P., Back, M.: Algorithmic mediation for collaborative exploratory search. *ACM SIGIR 2008*, 315-322.

[25] Shah, C.: Collaborative Information Seeking: From 'What?'and 'Why?'to 'How?'and 'So What?'. *Collaborative Information Seeking*, 2015, 3-16. DOI: 10.1007/978-3-319-18988-8_1

[26] Shah, C.: *Collaborative information seeking: The art and science of making the whole greater than the sum of all* (Vol. 34). Springer Science & Business Media, 2012.

[27] Shah, C.: Collaborative information seeking: A literature review. Advances in librarianship, 32(2010), 2010, 3-33.

[28] Shah, C., González-Ibáñez, R.: Evaluating the synergic effect of collaboration in information seeking. *ACM SIGIR 2011*, 913-922.

[29] Shah, C. and Marchionini, G.: Awareness in collaborative information seeking. ASIS&T 61(10), 2010, 1970-1986.

[30] Shah, C., Marchionini, G. and Kelly, D.: Learning design principles for a collaborative information seeking system. *ACM CHI EA 2009*, 3419-3424.

[31] Shah, C., Pickens, J. and Golovchinsky, G.: Role-based results redistribution for collaborative information retrieval. *IPM*, 46(6), 2010, 773-781.

[32] Smeaton, A. F., Lee, H., Foley, C. and McGivney, S.: Collaborative video searching on a tabletop. *Multimedia Systems*, 12(4), 2007, 375-391.

[33] Soulier, L., Shah, C. and Tamine, L.: User-driven system-mediated collaborative information retrieval. *ACM SIGIR 2014*, 485-494.

[34] Soulier, L., Tamine, L. and Shah, C.: MineRank: Leveraging users' latent roles for unsupervised collaborative information retrieval. *IPM*, 52(6), 2016, 1122–1141.

[35] Tamine, L. and Soulier, L.: Collaborative Information Retrieval: Concepts, Models and Evaluation. *ECIR 2016*, 885-888.

[36] Tamine, L. and Soulier, L.: Understanding the Impact of the Role Factor in Collaborative Information Retrieval. *ACM CIKM 2015*, 43-52.

How Can We Better Support Users with Non-Uniform Information Access in Collaborative Information Retrieval?

Nyi Nyi Htun
SEBE
Glasgow Caledonian University
Glasgow, G4 0BA, Scotland, UK
nyinyi.htun@gcu.ac.uk

Martin Halvey
Department of CIS
University of Strathclyde
Glasgow, G1 1XQ, Scotland, UK
martin.halvey@strath.ac.uk

Lynne Baillie
Department of CS
Heriot-Watt University
Edinburgh, EH14 4AS, Scotland, UK
l.baillie@hw.ac.uk

ABSTRACT

The majority of research in Collaborative Information Retrieval (CIR) has assumed that collaborating team members have uniform information access. However, practice and research has shown that there may not always be uniform information access among team members, e.g. in healthcare, government, etc. To the best of our knowledge, there has not been a controlled user evaluation to measure the impact of non-uniform information access on CIR outcomes. To address this shortcoming, we conducted a controlled user evaluation using 2 non-uniform access scenarios (document removal and term blacklisting) and 1 full and uniform access scenario. Following this, a design interview was undertaken to provide interface design suggestions. Evaluation results show that neither of the 2 non-uniform access scenarios had a significant negative impact on collaborative and individual search outcomes. Design interview results suggested that awareness of team's query history and intersecting viewed/judged documents could potentially help users share their expertise without disclosing sensitive information. Based on our results we provide important design recommendations to better support users with non-uniform information access in CIR.

CCS Concepts

• **Information systems~Collaborative search** • *Information systems~Search interfaces* • Information systems~Retrieval effectiveness • Information systems~Presentation of retrieval results

Keywords

collaborative information retrieval; multi-level collaboration; information access; interface design; non-uniform access

1. INTRODUCTION

Although search is often considered a solitary activity, there are many situations that call for people with shared information needs to work together to search for information and judge documents [10]. This is known as Collaborative Information Retrieval (CIR). A great deal of research in CIR [2, 11, 12, 22, 23] has utilised concepts like awareness, division of labour and persistence to enhance the collaboration experience and outcomes for users. However, much of this research has assumed that all members of a collaborative search team have equal access to the underlying information, and that they can share any information with each other without restriction, e.g. [2, 22, 23]. In reality, there are a number of societal, legal or security reasons that may prevent a searcher from sharing information within or outside of a group. An example might be a finance manager and a production manager in a manufacturing company who are working together to identify a problem. Regardless of their differing access to underlying information such as employee records, production-line etc. the two managers must collaborate somehow to achieve a successful outcome. This type of scenario is referred to as Multi-Level Collaborative Information Retrieval (MLCIR) [13]. Whilst MLCIR shares a large number of characteristics with CIR, unlike traditional CIR, MLCIR is also concerned with information flow, security and shareability as well as supporting collaboration.

Some researchers have observed real life MLCIR scenarios and begun to examine MLCIR in areas like legal search [3], crisis management [4] and healthcare [19]. From their observations, these researchers provide insights into how non-uniform information access can negatively impact CIR outcomes. Handel and Wang [13] also presented a number of case studies in healthcare, business and government domains, and explicitly discussed the challenges in MLCIR scenarios. However, this previous work [3, 4, 13, 19] was observational and did not provide empirically based solutions to support users in MLCIR scenarios. As an early attempt to quantify the impact of non-uniform information access in CIR, Htun et al. [15] conducted a simulated evaluation. However, this work did not go as far as a user evaluation. To the best of our knowledge, there has not yet been a controlled user evaluation to assess the impact of non-uniform information access on CIR outcomes. To address this shortcoming, we conducted a user study where we investigated the impact of different information access scenarios; namely: document removal, term blacklisting and full access. The document removal and term blacklisting scenarios are based on real-life MLCIR examples [13]. After being exposed to different information access scenarios in a controlled experiment, we conducted a design interview with our participants to obtain feedback to assist with future development of MLCIR systems. The research questions we attempt to address in this study are:

RQ1: What are the effects of non-uniform information access scenarios on collaborative search outcomes?

RQ2: What are the effects of non-uniform information access scenarios on individual search outcomes?

RQ3: How can MLCIR interfaces be designed so that they are usable and useful for the end users?

The remainder of the paper is organised as follows: in Section 2, we discuss related work regarding CIR and MLCIR. In Section 3, we describe our experimental setup. In Section 4, we present the results of our study. In Section 5, we discuss findings and design recommendations based on the evaluation results and feedback

CHIIR '17, March 07-11, 2017, Oslo, Norway
© 2017 ACM. ISBN 978-1-4503-4677-1/17/03...$15.00
DOI: http://dx.doi.org/10.1145/3020165.3020171

from the design interview. Finally, we provide some conclusions and discuss possible future work in Section 6.

2. RELATED WORK

2.1 Collaborative Information Retrieval

A large number of people often engage in collaborative search activities [21]. Working in collaboration can not only be beneficial for recall-oriented search tasks [25], but also reduces the workload of team members [7]. However, collaborative search activities that involve information sharing via conventional communication channels e.g. email, telephone, etc. are often inefficient [21]. This is mainly because team members do not have an efficient way to obtain awareness, communicate and divide labour for the search task. Also, it is often essential for team members to be able to retain discovered content for later use [21]; this is referred to as "persistence of data" [12, 22, 23]. As such, a great deal of research has been conducted in CIR in order to enhance communication and collaboration capabilities of users [2, 8, 11, 12, 22, 23].

According to Golovchinsky et al. [10], CIR systems range from purely user interface level to algorithmic mediation. In UI-only mediated systems, collaboration is supported only at the user interface level whereas algorithmic mediation search systems employ an algorithmic layer to present results differently to different users. There are also systems that allow collaboration via communication only e.g. instant messaging, voice chat, video conferencing, etc. However, previous research has argued that CIR systems must provide more than just communication [11, 22]. Example systems for UI-level mediation include SearchTogether [22], CoSearch [2], Coagmento [11], WeSearch [23], ViGOR [12] and Físchlár-DiamondTouch [27]. SearchTogether [22] allows asynchronous collaboration for web search by enabling storage of all objects and actions performed at the end of a search session. SearchTogether also allows remote collaboration by providing features like instant messaging and split-screen search. CoSearch [2] is designed for synchronous and co-located web search. It is aimed at allowing collaboration over multiple devices e.g. shared computers and Bluetooth enabled mobile devices. Coagmento [11] was developed as a Firefox plug-in and an Android app to allow asynchronous and remote collaboration on both computers and mobile devices. WeSearch [23] is a system specifically designed for tabletops, and allows co-located web search for up to four people. Whilst SearchTogether, CoSearch, Coagmento and WeSearch support text retrieval e.g. webpages, there has also been research conducted into multimedia CIR. For example, Halvey et al. [12] developed a collaborative video retrieval system called ViGOR, which allows asynchronous and distributed collaboration. Smeaton et al. [27] developed a synchronous and co-located video retrieval system for a multi-user, touch sensitive tabletops named Físchlár.

Algorithmic mediation is widely used in recommender systems (e.g. Amazon shopping recommendations [20]). Such systems have an algorithmic layer for processing users' search behaviour to reorder new search results. In a study conducted by Pickens et al. [24], it was shown that algorithmic mediation can yield better results for recall oriented tasks compared to the UI-only mediated CIR systems. Other examples of algorithmic mediated CIR systems include I-SPY [28] and Cerchiamo [9]. I-SPY [28] is a community-based web search engine which takes advantage of past search behaviour to re-rank future search results in a way that recognises the implicit preferences of communities of searchers. Cerchiamo [9] is an algorithmically mediated synchronous collaborative search system that can allocate roles to users and then split up work based on the roles. Algorithmic mediation often attempts to leverage different roles within a search team. A common assumption within CIR is that different roles can have a positive impact on search outcomes, e.g. Golovchinsky et al. [9] and Pickens et al. [24]. This may not be the case in MLCIR; in some cases, users with differing roles may not be able to share certain information with each other [13], which could have a negative impact on CIR outcomes. More recently, Tamine and Soulier [30] conducted a user study to investigate how role assignment could impact CIR and found that assigning roles to the users could limit the precision of search results, demonstrating that in normal CIR scenarios that an assignment of roles is not always beneficial. Whilst they investigated roles, Tamine and Soulier did not consider how non-uniform information access might exist between the different roles within a team.

2.2 Multi-Level Collaborative Information Retrieval

MLCIR is a complex problem and has multifaceted constraints with regards to information accessibility and shareability [13]. MLCIR in organisations can be difficult to manage as sometimes organisations do not want any unnecessary information contamination or disclosure of sensitive information within or outside of the organisation. In an attempt to gain a better understanding of these problems and difficulties with collaboration in information-sensitive environments, some researchers have begun to investigate a range of real life scenarios. Attfield et al. [3] studied a large London law firm and discussed difficulties and complexities that may arise in a group-based awareness system, and also provided design recommendations for future developments. Karunakaran and Reddy [18] gathered critical-incident self-reports of 307 employees working in various organisations, and studied barriers that exist in collaborative information seeking. Their study found that these barriers exist due to factors like organisational setting, lack of technologies, individual perceptions, and lack of efficient communication in teams. Karunakaran and Reddy [19] also presented case studies in the healthcare domain, and discussed the frequent occurrence of non-uniform knowledge distribution and miscommunication. Bjurling and Hansen [4] looked at a Swedish crisis management system and described how different interpretations and sharing of information could lead to inefficient outcomes in a collaborative network.

In order to investigate the impact of non-uniform information access scenarios in collaborative search, Htun et al. [15] conducted a simulated evaluation using a number of established MLCIR scenarios and found that there is a level of tolerance to removing access to a document collection. Although in general there was a negative impact, Htun et al. argued that non-uniform information access may not always result in a negative impact on performance. However, their findings were based on simulated users and did not go as far as a user evaluation. Handel and Wang [13] put forward a number of design considerations for MLCIR systems, but their suggestions were not based on an empirical evaluation but were rather based on Handel and Wang's experience in Boeing and use cases from different domains. Besides, a fundamental difference in assumption between CIR and MLCIR means that not every CIR component and concept may be directly applicable to MLCIR, e.g. most components in CIR systems [12, 22] may allow users to share search results within their team without restrictions, which for MLCIR systems should be modified. To the best of our knowledge, no user evaluations have been conducted to examine the impact of MLCIR and to provide user-centred design recommendations for future development of MLCIR systems. In order to address this shortcoming, we conducted a controlled user evaluation using three different information access scenarios and pairs of participants. To be able to provide user-centred design recommendations, we undertook a design interview post evaluation using the same pairs of participants.

3. EXPERIMENTAL SETUP

3.1 Document Collection and Search Tasks

For information sources for our evaluation, there were 2 alternative options available: using the web (similar to [2, 22, 25]) or test collections (similar to [16, 26]). As our intention in this study was to remove access to documents and terms from the information source, utilising a test collection was more practical. Besides, this approach lets us precisely calculate traditional Information Retrieval (IR) evaluation metrics such as *precision*, *recall* and *f-measure*. We used the TREC HARD 2005 [1] test collection (which uses AQUAINT corpus), which has also been utilised by a number of other researchers for CIR evaluations [6, 15-17]. The AQUAINT corpus contains a total of 1,033,461 documents (about 3 GB) of newswire text data written in English which were acquired from three news services: the Xinhua News Service (People's Republic of China), the New York Times News Service and the Associated Press Worldstream News Service.

Table 1. Summary of our 10 candidate topics

Topic ID	Title
303	Hubble telescope achievements
363	transportation tunnel disasters
383	mental illness drugs
393	mercy killing
397	automobile recalls
448	ship losses
625	arrests bombing WTC
651	U.S. ethnic population
658	teenage pregnancy
689	family-planning aid

In term of search tasks, there are two alternative options available: using a task that is of mutual interest to the participants (similar to [2, 22]) or using tasks that are selected by the researchers (similar to [12, 25]). The TREC HARD 2005 has a total of 50 test topics[1], from which we selected 10 topics; the same topics have been used by Joho et al. [16] and Htun et al. [15] for their respective simulated evaluations of collaborative search performance (the 10 topics are presented in Table 1). Joho et al. [17] also generated a query pool which contains a list of query terms that are likely to be submitted by users for the 10 topics. We were provided with this query pool and utilised this to blacklist search terms for users (see Section 3.2 for details); this was another reason for selecting these 10 topics. Also by using 10 topics, rather than 3 for example, as we have 3 information access scenarios (see Section 3.2), we had a broad selection of topics for users which cover different parts of the TREC HARD 2005 collection. During the evaluation, we randomly selected from the 10 candidate topics and presented these to the participants for each scenario (see Section 3.4 for the study procedure).

[1] http://trec.nist.gov/data/hard/05/05.50.topics.txt

3.2 Information Access Scenarios and Combinations

For their simulated evaluation, Htun et al. [15] devised 4 non-uniform information access scenarios based on Handel and Wang's [13] observations of MLCIR. These 4 scenarios were 1) document removal, 2) random term blacklisting, 3) term blacklisting based on the most frequent terms in a query pool, and 4) term blacklisting based on the most frequent terms in the collection. The document removal scenario represents the case where access to documents in the collection is removed for some team members. For instance, such a scenario may occur when team members have access to different databases [13]. The term blacklisting scenarios represent the cases where individual team members do not find results if they search using certain blacklisted search terms. For instance, such a scenario may occur when documents are classified at the paragraph level [13]. For this study, we selected 2 out of the 4 scenarios from Htun et al. [15] which we believe are the most practical in real life. These 2 scenarios are: 1) document removal and 2) term blacklisting based on the most frequent terms in a query pool (i.e. the most likely search terms) (see Table 2). We believe these 2 scenarios are practical in real life because the MLCIR cases that involve users with access to different databases and blacklisting the most likely search terms are highly probable [13]. In addition to these 2 non-uniform access scenarios, we also included a full access scenario which represents the case where both team members have equal and unrestricted access to the collection. This scenario was considered as an upper bound to compare search performance with the 2 non-uniform access scenarios and is the norm for most CIR evaluation [16, 17, 25]. During the study, pairs of participants were presented with all 3 information access scenarios. To avoid order effects, the order in which the scenarios were presented was rotated using a Latin Square counterbalancing measure.

Table 2. Information access scenarios and access combinations

Code	Information access scenario	Access combination
DR	Document removal: remove access to documents from collection	100%-60%
TR	Term blacklisting: remove access to most frequent terms in query pool	100%-70%
FA	Full access	100%-100%

For the 2 non-uniform access scenarios, Htun et al. [15] also formulated 55 combinations of access for a pair of simulated users with access level to the collection ranging from 10% up to 100% e.g. 10%-10%, 20%-10%, 20%-20%, 30%-10%..., and 100%-100%. Based on Htun et al.'s [15] simulated evaluation, we selected an access combination for each of the non-uniform access scenarios, where search performance began to deteriorate significantly in comparison to the full access combination; these access combinations are: 100%-60% for document removal scenario and 100%-70% for the term blacklisting scenario. Thus, for the document removal scenario (i.e. DR in Table 2), while full access to the collection (i.e. 100%) is available for one team member, 40% of the documents in the collection are randomly removed for the other. In other words, for the second team member, the index was created using 60% of randomly selected documents from the collection (i.e. 620077 documents), at which point search performance significantly deteriorated according to the previous simulation [15]. For the term blacklisting scenario (i.e. TR in Table 2), while full access (i.e. 100%) is available for one team member, 30% of the most frequent terms in the query pool is blacklisted for the other (thus represented as 70% in Table 2) which means the latter team member does not find results if (s)he submits those blacklisted terms. Please note that although it is represented as 70%, team members in the TR scenario had access to any terms from the collection except for the blacklisted ones. One average, there were about 4 blacklisted terms per topic. For the full access scenario (i.e. FA in Table 2), full access is available for both participants. To avoid order effects, full access and non-full access between a pair of team members were rotated for the non-uniform access scenarios. In other words, each team member had a chance to experience having full access and non-full access once each in the 2 non-uniform access scenarios.

3.3 Participants

A total of twenty participants (ten pairs) were recruited for this study from personal contacts, research group and university contacts. This participant pool size is similar to previous experiments in CIR [8, 17, 22, 24]. Participants were assigned partners for the study based on their available timeslots. There were 9 females and 11 males. The average age of participants was 28 ($\sigma = 4.6$), ranging from 22 to 44. Of the twenty participants, 3 used search systems for more than 20 hours per week, 5 between 16 to 20 hours, 5 between 11 to 15 hours, 2 between 6 to 10 hours and 5 less than 6 hours. 14 of the participants reported that they had been involved in a collaborative search at least once. The majority of their collaborative search experiences consisted of working together either with friends, colleagues or a partner mainly using Google, Google Scholar or Google Maps. Each participant received a £10 Amazon voucher for participation.

3.4 Study Procedure

Figure 1 highlights the steps involved in our study. Before the study began, an email containing an information sheet and a link to a demographic questionnaire was sent to individual participants. They were instructed to complete the questionnaire prior to arriving for the study.

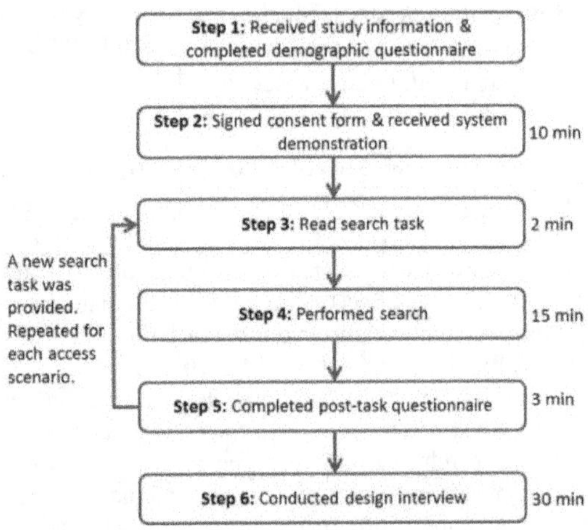

Figure 1. Study procedure

When a pair of participants arrived for the study, they were welcomed, asked to sign a consent form and given a demonstration of the search system. Participants were informed about the information access scenarios but were not told which team member had more (or less) access, nor the order of the information access scenarios presented. They were also instructed not to communicate with each other during the study and to pretend that they were in different rooms. This was to restrain discussion of results and search strategies which could violate the evaluation of MLCIR scenarios. In practice users in MLCIR may not be able to discuss search strategies, documents they can/cannot access or even the results found [13]. A similar approach was used in previous CIR evaluations [17, 22, 25]. Participants were also informed that their goal for each task was to find as many relevant documents as possible for their team. Since team members in MLCIR examples are unaware of their access, limitation and information shareability [13], we believed this strategy was appropriate. They were then given a few minutes to practice searching with the search system.

After practicing with the system, to begin a search session for the first information access scenario, both participants were provided with the same search task randomly selected from the 10 candidate topics (see Table 1). They were allocated 2 minutes to read and familiarise themselves with the task. Participants then performed the search synchronously for a maximum of 15 minutes using different computers in the same room facing opposite directions. This step was followed by a post-task questionnaire. The questionnaire was designed to assess individual participants' perception of the tasks, search performance and interface components (see Table 6). The questionnaire was in the form of 5-point Likert scales and the answers ranged from 1 (strongly disagree) to 3 (neither) to 5 (strongly agree). Once the participants completed the post-task questionnaire, the scenario was changed and the participants were provided with a new randomly selected search task. The same steps were repeated for the remaining scenarios (see Figure 1). A number of previous research in CIR, e.g. [17, 22, 24, 25], used a similar procedure successfully. When all 3 scenarios were completed, a design interview was conducted with both participants. They were briefly reminded about the non-uniform information access scenarios before asking interview questions. A detailed explanation of the design interview is presented in Section 3.6.

3.5 System Description

Although there has been a great deal of research into CIR, there are no user-centred design recommendations relating to MLCIR that we are aware of. Thus, we designed a relatively simple collaborative search system that allows a pair of users to search for and judge documents synchronously. We took our system as a starting point to enable us to empirically evaluate non-uniform information access in CIR which has not been evaluated before. Shah et al. [26] suggested that in order to ensure successful collaboration, the system must have an effective method of communication, an ability to see everyone's actions, a way to distribute tasks and aggregate information, and a mechanism to record user interactions, processes, and results. However, as highlighted by Handel and Wang [13], users in MLCIR scenarios may not be able to discuss search strategies, documents they can/cannot access, or even the results found. To that end, for this study we implemented a system that would not allow direct communication and sharing of results, but that offers an ability to see the query history of the team and documents viewed or judged by the team (see Figure 2). The system was implemented using the Google Web toolkit[2] and the Terrier toolkit[3]. The system consists of 3 main components:

Search component (Figure 2(1)): The search component contains: query-box (Figure 2(a)), search button (Figure 2(b)), result-list (Figure 2(c)) and result-detail (Figure 2(d)). The search

[2] http://gwtproject.org

[3] http://terrier.org

Figure 2. Search system utilised in this study: 1) search component, 2) query history component, 3) viewed/relevant component, a) query-box, b) search-button, c) result-list pane, d) result-detail panel, e) relevant label and f) viewed label

component is the main part of the search system; it allows users to enter queries and results are displayed in the result panels. A number of sample search results are presented in the result-list panel (Figure 2(c)). Clicking on any row in the result-list panel displays full text of the respective document in the result-detail panel below (Figure 2(d)) where users can mark the document as relevant, or un-do the relevant marking. The system ensured that only the documents that are not blocked or the documents that do not contain blacklisted terms appeared in the search results.

Query history component (Figure 2(2)**):** This is provided to enable the participants to gain an awareness of the queries issued by the team. We considered using Integrated Messaging in order to allow communication between the team members. However, in this study, since we wanted to control any discussion of results during the search, we decided to exclude it. Also it has been found that query history is an important component for effective collaborative search [26] and is preferred more by users than text and verbal communication channels [17]. We believed that a query history component may be suitable for non-uniform access scenarios since it provides users with query awareness without the need for direct communication. A list of sample queries entered by the team is shown in Figure 2(2). Queries are displayed in the same way to both team members. There is no information contamination because if the person with lower access submits a blacklisted term, (s)he will not receive any results, and it will not be clear whether this is due to blacklisting or because there are no relevant documents in the collection for that particular query. This is in line with an MLCIR case that was highlighted by Handel and Wang [13]. Some previous CIR systems, e.g. [17, 22, 26], also utilised a query history component successfully.

Viewed/Relevant component (Figure 2(3)**):** This is provided to allow the participants to gain awareness of the documents in their search results that are judged as relevant and/or viewed by the team. Similar to the query history component, this component allows users to obtain awareness of the documents viewed and judged by the team without the need for direct communication. Once a team member views a document (i.e. by clicking a row in the result-list (Figure 2(c))), it is marked as viewed and denoted with the "Viewed" label in the result-list (Figure 2(f)). If the document is marked as relevant by the team member, it is then denoted with the "Relevant" label (Figure 2(e)). Thus, both team members are able to see whether certain documents in their respective result-lists have been viewed or judged as relevant by the team. Previous CIR systems, e.g. [17, 26], also utilised similar components successfully.

3.6 Design Interview

Although a number of design considerations were proposed for MLCIR based on observations [13], none are based on a user-centred design evaluation. Therefore, in order to obtain the participants' feedback about the current search system, and to provide design recommendations for future development of systems that support users in MLCIR scenarios, we conducted a design interview with pairs of participants after the search sessions. The design interview was divided into 2 sections. In the first section, the pairs were asked a series of questions related to their experience with the current search system. We asked the pairs in what way each component (e.g. search component) was easy and difficult to interact with, in what way each component increased or decreased their collaboration capabilities, and how each component could be improved (see Figure 2 for the components). In the second section, the pairs were asked to suggest new components and/or functions that could be added to the current search system in order to improve their collaboration capabilities under non-uniform access. They were also provided with screenshots of the current system and blank sheets of paper to annotate and sketch their design ideas. Throughout the interview, the researcher took notes of participants' responses, and also recorded their responses on an audio recorder, which was later transcribed for analysis.

3.7 Evaluation Metrics

The search system recorded a log of the participants' interactions with the system. This log was used to calculate a number of evaluation metrics in order to compare teams' search outcomes between the information access scenarios (i.e. *DR*, *TR* and *FA*), and to compare individuals' search outcomes between full access and non-full access within the *DR* and *TR* scenarios. We used traditional IR evaluation metrics: *recall*, *precision* and *f-measure*, and also adopted some of the CIR evaluation metrics proposed by Shah and González-Ibáñez [25]: *coverage*, *relevant coverage*, *unique coverage* and *unique relevant coverage*. *Recall* is the number of true positive documents amongst all the documents judged by users divided by the number of relevant documents in the TREC HARD 2005 qrel[4]. *Precision* is the number of true positive documents amongst all the documents judged by the users divided by the number of all of the documents judged by users as relevant. *F-measure* is a harmonic mean of *recall* and *precision* represented by the formula: (2*precision*recall)/(precision+recall). *Coverage* is the number of distinct documents viewed by participants. *Relevant coverage* is the number of documents in the *coverage* that are actually relevant (i.e. true positive). *Unique coverage* is the number of distinct documents viewed by participants only in a given access scenario (e.g. *FA*) and not in any others, or only at a given access level (e.g. full access) and not in the other. *Unique relevant coverage* is the number of documents in the *unique coverage* that are actually relevant. Other CIR evaluation metrics we adopted for this study include those proposed by Soulier et al. [29]: *number of queries* and *query length*. *Number of queries* is the total number of queries submitted by participants. *Query length* represents the average number of terms within the total queries submitted.

In addition, post-task questionnaires were administered to assess individual participants' perception of the tasks, search performance and interface components (see Table 6 for questions). The questionnaire was in the form of 5-point Likert scales and the answers ranged from 1 (strongly disagree) to 3 (neither) to 5 (strongly agree).

4. RESULTS

We compared collaborative search outcomes between the information access scenarios (i.e. *DR*, *TR* & *FA*) and individual search outcomes between full access and non-full access within the *DR* and *TR* scenarios. To compare between the information access scenarios, we used one-way repeated measures ANOVA for normally distributed data, and Friedman and Wilcoxon Sign-Rank tests for non-normally distributed data since the participants within each group were subjected to all three information access scenarios (i.e. data is paired). To compare between full access and non-full access, as data is unpaired we used one-way between groups ANOVA for normally distributed data, and Mann-Whitney U test for non-normally distributed data.

[4] http://trec.nist.gov/data/hard/05/TREC2005.qrels.txt

4.1 Search Performance

Recall, *precision* and *f-measure* were not significantly different between teams within 3 the information access scenarios (RQ1) or between individuals with within the DR and TR scenarios (RQ2). A summary is given in Table 3. It appears that the non-uniform information access scenarios we utilised did not have a negative impact on search performance. This was not expected since Htun et al.'s [15] simulated evaluation showed a negative impact on search performance for the same access combinations we used. We discuss this further in Section 5. We also found that despite the low *recall*, participants were able to judge the documents accurately hence the *precision* was high in most cases (see Table 3). To understand the *best possible recall* that the participants could have achieved, we further analysed a new metric calculated as *relevant coverage* divided by the number of relevant documents in the qrel for a given task. As shown in Table 3, the distribution between *recall* and *best possible recall* was close to each other, demonstrating the participants' high judgement accuracy again.

Table 3. Search performance metrics between individuals within the DR and TR scenarios. S.D = standard deviation.

		DR		TR	
		Full	Non-full	Full	Non-full
Recall	Mean	0.013	0.036	0.044	0.043
	S.D	0.019	0.037	0.057	0.072
Best possible recall	Mean	0.018	0.054	0.047	0.055
	S.D	0.029	0.062	0.059	0.082
Precision	Mean	0.344	0.540	0.458	0.328
	S.D	0.410	0.473	0.431	0.304
F-measure	Mean	0.024	0.066	0.077	0.072
	S.D	0.035	0.067	0.097	0.113

4.2 Query Submission

Number of queries and *query length* [29] showed that in terms of query submission there was no significant difference between teams within the information access scenarios (RQ1) or between individuals within the *DR* and *TR* scenarios (RQ2). This suggests that the participants submitted a similar number of queries and average query words across all search sessions (see Table 4). To understand this further, we also analysed *term diversity* and *term overlap* between the individuals within the DR and TR scenarios, and *average blacklisted terms* between the individuals within the TR scenario. *Term diversity* is the number of terms submitted by individuals in a particular access (e.g. full access within the TR scenario). In contrast, *term overlap* is the number of terms submitted by individuals in both full access and non-full access. *Average blacklisted terms* is the average number of terms submitted by individuals that intersect with the blacklisted terms. In general, the participants submitted twice as many diverse terms as the overlapping ones (see Table 4) suggesting that the participants actively tried to avoid duplicated work. Looking at *query length* and *average blacklisted terms*, we found that roughly 20% of the submitted terms were blacklisted.

Table 4. Query submission metrics between individuals within the DR and TR scenarios. S.D = standard deviation.

		DR		TR	
		Full	Non-full	Full	Non-full
Number of queries	Mean	13.800	11.100	11.900	10.000
	S.D	9.102	6.790	7.141	5.600
Query length	Mean	3.736	3.785	3.500	3.873
	S.D	1.485	1.494	1.976	1.909
Term diversity	Mean	12.600	11.400	11.600	8.300
	S.D	9.766	8.435	10.035	6.447
Term overlap	Mean	6.300	6.300	5.700	5.700
	S.D	2.710	2.710	2.263	2.263
Average blacklisted terms	Mean	-	-	-	0.789
	S.D	-	-	-	0.601

4.3 Collection Coverage

For *coverage*, *relevant coverage*, *unique coverage* and *unique relevant coverage* [25], no significant difference was found between the information access scenarios (RQ1) and between individuals with full access and non-full access within *DR* and *TR* (RQ2) (see Table 5 for result summary). This again suggests that the non-uniform information access scenarios we utilised did not have a negative impact on collection coverage.

Table 5. Collection coverage metrics between individuals within the DR and TR scenarios. S.D = standard deviation.

		DR		TR	
		Full	Non-full	Full	Non-full
Coverage	Mean	23.400	22.400	18.400	28.700
	S.D	13.277	13.040	11.078	16.627
Relevant coverage	Mean	2.000	5.400	4.800	5.600
	S.D	3.400	5.700	5.453	7.516
Unique coverage	Mean	22.600	21.600	17.500	27.800
	S.D	13.866	12.668	10.659	17.165
Unique relevant coverage	Mean	1.800	5.200	4.400	5.200
	S.D	3.155	5.534	5.254	7.495
Relevant documents marked	Mean	4.200	4.200	5.900	9.400
	S.D	5.116	4.467	7.141	10.091

Coverage and *unique coverage* were similar in all cases suggesting that the participants mostly looked at the new documents that were not already viewed. *Relevant coverage* and *unique relevant coverage* were also similar because of the way they were calculated. Looking at the ratio between *coverage* and *relevant coverage*, we found that only about 18% of all the documents viewed by participants were actually relevant. We further looked at the number of *relevant documents marked* by the participants and found that it was very similar to the number of *relevant coverage* (see Table 5). Since the *precision* was high (see Table 3), we can conclude that the participants judged the documents quite accurately.

4.4 Participants' Perceptions

The participants' perceptions of search tasks, search performance and interface components were captured by post-task questionnaires (see Table 6 for questions, and Tables 7 and 8 for result summary). Questions Q1-Q3 measured participants' perceptions of search tasks. Q4 - Q8 measured participants' perceptions of search performance. Questions Q9-Q11 measured participants' perceptions of certain interface components of our current system. Statistical analysis results showed that none of the questions had significantly different scores between the information access scenarios (RQ1) and between individuals with full access and non-full access within the DR and TR scenarios (RQ2). Looking at the results from Tables 7 and 8, we found that participants generally thought the search tasks were easy to understand (Q1) and interesting (Q2). Participants neither agreed nor disagreed with the questions regarding task familiarity (Q3), result satisfaction (Q4) and perception of judging more documents than partner (Q7). Question regarding relevant documents found (Q5) had relatively low score. This may partly be because the candidate topics we utilised only have 86 to 152 relevant documents out of over a million documents in the AQUAINT corpus [16]. Participants were generally confident with the documents they judged (Q6) and thought that their teams performed well in judging documents (Q8). The scores for query history (Q9) and viewed/relevant components (Q10 & Q11) were generally high.

Table 6. Post-task questionnaire questions. Q1-Q3 = assessment of search tasks. Q4-Q8 = assessment of search performance. Q9-Q11 = assessment of interface components.

Q1	The description and narrative of this task were easy to understand.
Q2	The topic of this task is very interesting.
Q3	I was quite familiar with the topic of this task.
Q4	I am satisfied with the documents obtained for my queries for this task.
Q5	I found a lot of relevant documents in the result for this task.
Q6	I am confident with the documents I judged for this task.
Q7	I think I judged more documents than my partner for this task.
Q8	I think my team did a great job in judging documents for this task.
Q9	I think the 'query history' component increased my performance for this task.
Q10	I think being able to know the documents that have already been viewed increased my performance for this task.
Q11	I think being able to know the documents that have already been judged increased my performance for this task.

4.5 Design Interview

A thematic analysis [5] of the transcribed data resulted in 4 main themes: search component, team member awareness, query awareness and result awareness. We present these themes in detail in the following sub-sections. Overall, we obtained 15 design suggestions from the participants: 2 suggestions for the search component, 4 suggestions regarding team member awareness, 5 suggestions regarding query awareness and 4 suggestions regarding result awareness.

4.5.1 Search Component

With regards to the search component, 6 (30%) of the participants suggested adding options to be able to narrow down search results and/or to manipulate the queries. For example, one participant said, *"I'd also like a function to narrow down the results, like from 1000 documents to 500 documents."* (P11). Another participant mentioned, *"I think it'd be great if you could specify exclusion/inclusion criteria in a query, like what keyword to include and what keyword to exclude."* (P12). In order to narrow down the search results, we could consider adding a filter function

Table 7. Mean, standard deviation and median of post-task questionnaire result between the 3 information access scenarios (see Table 6 for the questions). 1 = strongly disagree, 3 = neither, 5 = strongly agree. Q1 to Q3 = assessment of search tasks. Q4 to Q8 = assessment of search performance. Q9 to Q11 = assessment of interface components.

		Q1	Q2	Q3	Q4	Q5	Q6	Q7	Q8	Q9	Q10	Q11
DR	Mean	4.3	3.6	2.8	3	2.3	3.7	3	3.4	3.7	4	4
	S.D	0.9	0.9	1.4	1.3	1.2	0.9	1.5	0.9	0.8	0.9	0.8
	Median	4	4	3	3	2	3.5	3	3	4	4	4
TR	Mean	4.6	4	3.4	3.1	3	3.6	3.1	3.6	3.7	4	4.1
	S.D	0.5	1	1.4	1.4	1.7	1.4	1.1	0.9	1.2	0.8	0.9
	Median	5	4	3.5	4	3	4	3	4	4	4	4
FA	Mean	4.3	3.5	3	2.8	2.7	3.8	2.9	3.4	3.5	4.1	4.2
	S.D	1.1	1.2	1.5	1.3	1.3	1.2	1	1	0.8	0.8	0.9
	Median	5	4	3.5	3	2.5	4	3	4	4	4	4

Table 8. Mean, standard deviation (S.D) and median of post-task questionnaire result between individuals with full access and non-full access (see Table 6 for the questions). 1 = strongly disagree, 3 = neither, 5 = strongly agree. Q1 to Q3 = assessment of search tasks. Q4 to Q8 = assessment of search performance. Q9 to Q11 = assessment of interface components.

			Q1	Q2	Q3	Q4	Q5	Q6	Q7	Q8	Q9	Q10	Q11
DR	Full	Mean	4.5	3.4	3	3.2	2.4	3.8	3.3	3.1	3.8	4.1	3.9
		S.D	0.5	1.1	1.4	1.3	1.4	0.8	1.6	1	0.6	0.7	0.6
		Median	4.5	3.5	3.5	3	2	4	3	3	4	4	4
	Non-full	Mean	4	3.7	2.6	2.7	2.2	3.5	2.6	3.6	3.5	3.9	4
		S.D	1.1	0.8	1.4	1.3	1.1	1	1.3	0.7	1	1	0.9
		Median	4	4	2.5	2.5	2	3	3	3.5	4	4	4
TR	Full	Mean	4.5	3.9	3.3	2.5	2.5	3.3	2.7	3.5	3.3	3.9	4.1
		S.D	0.5	1	1.3	1.6	1.7	1.7	1.3	0.9	1.5	1	1.3
		Median	4.5	4	4	2	2	4	2.5	3.5	2.5	4	4.5
	Non-full	Mean	4.7	4.1	3.4	3.6	3.5	3.8	3.4	3.7	4	4	4
		S.D	0.5	1	1.5	1	1.7	1	1	1	0.7	0.5	0.5
		Median	5	4	3	4	4	4	3.5	4	4	4	4

such as filter by date, etc. For the latter, we could consider allowing the use of inclusion/exclusion keywords such as AND, OR, etc. Although these components are not new for IR and CIR systems, they could be as effectively used in MLCIR systems too. However, to be able to take advantage of these functions, we believe that users may require certain expertise or training.

4.5.2 Team Member Awareness

It appears that users in MLCIR could benefit from being able to easily identify team members and their actions. For the query history component, 12 (60%) of the participants suggested differentiating queries submitted by each person either with different colours (7 participants) or by separating them into a different list (5 participants). For the viewed/relevant component, 13 (65%) of the participants suggested differentiating documents viewed/judged by each person. Amongst them, 5 participants suggested the use of a different colour for each person and 2 participants suggested the use of text such as "by A" or "by B" whilst 4 participants suggested the use of both approaches and 2 suggested no particular approach. One of the participants who suggested both approaches commented: "*When there's more than two people, using names instead of colour would be much better.*" (P19). A previous collaborative search system, CoSearch [2] used both colours and names to identify each person. SearchTogether [22] used profile pictures and names for the same purpose. We wish to suggest here that MLCIR systems could also adopt a similar approach to provide team member awareness.

4.5.3 Query Awareness

11 (55%) participants mentioned that being aware of their partners' queries had given them an idea of what might be a good new query. One participant explained: "*I didn't know much about [a topic], so I looked at [partner's] search history and tried to search for similar keywords.*" (P17). This means that query awareness could help users share their expertise without the necessity to disclose sensitive information. Participants also suggested a number of improvements regarding query awareness. 5 (25%) of the participants suggested that the query history component should display the number of viewed and relevant documents found for a particular query. In addition to this, 2 (10%) of the participants added that effectiveness of a query could be displayed using "hot and cold icons" next to the queries in the query history component (see Figure 3 for an illustration by a participant).

Figure 3. Illustration of hot and cold icons in the query history component (P1)

Such icons may help to identify the effectiveness of a query quickly. Moreover, displaying the time spent on an individual query was suggested by 8 (40%) of the participants. For example, one participant explained: "*The time you spent on the query is an indication of how successful your query is.*" (P13). While this explanation is correct to some extent, the time spent alone cannot always indicate the success of a query. In practice, a combination of different query properties should be used. Displaying query popularity (i.e. the number of times a query has been used) was also suggested by 2 (10%) of the participants. In addition, one of the participants suggested adding a function to sort the query history according to time issued and also according to the effectiveness. Overall, query properties such as query effectiveness, query popularity and time spent on query, as well as a query sorting function maybe important for users to able to obtain better query awareness and to work effectively in non-uniform access scenarios.

4.5.4 Result Awareness

3 (15%) of the participants mentioned that being aware of their partners' judged documents could help them double-check whether the documents are actually relevant. In addition, 2 (10%) other participants noted that being aware of their partners' judged documents could give them an idea of what might be a related new query. One participant explained: "*...if I know that this document is relevant, then I can read it and can go on to another keyword which is related to that document.*" (P18). Therefore, similar to query awareness, being aware of a partner's judged documents could help users share their expertise without the necessity to disclose sensitive information. Participants also suggested a number of improvements with regards to results awareness. 9 (45%) of the participants thought that their viewed and/or judged documents should be easily accessible. 3 (15%) of the participants suggested displaying a list of relevant documents whereas 6 (30%) other participants suggested displaying two different lists for both viewed and relevant documents. Moreover, it was suggested by 6 (30%) of the participants that the results should also be sortable based on their viewed and relevant properties. In addition, 4 (20%) of the participants suggested adding a favourite function that would allow them to keep the documents they want to read later. A favourite function has been implemented previously by Shah et al. [26] and Freyne et al. [8] in their respective systems. MLCIR systems could adopt a similar function to provide users with an option to bookmark documents.

5. DISCUSSION

In relation to our first research question (RQ1): "What are the effects of non-uniform information access scenarios on collaborative search outcomes?" it was found that neither of the two non-uniform access scenarios we investigated had a significant negative impact on search performance or collection coverage. While one might expect a decrease in search performance and collection coverage for non-uniform access scenarios compared to full access scenario, the performance was unchanged. This is different from the findings of Htun et al.'s [15] simulated evaluation where search performance deteriorated significantly at the access combinations 100%-60% for the document removal scenario (*DR*) and 100%-70% for the term blacklisting scenario (*TR*). This difference could be because we used human participants in our study, and humans can compensate for each other in ways that cannot be easily simulated.

In relation to our second research question (RQ2): "What are the effects of non-uniform information access scenarios on individual search outcomes?" we found that the individuals with non-full access performed as well as those with full access for both DR and TR scenarios. It appears that even removing 40% of the documents from the collection (i.e. for DR) and removing 30% of the most likely search terms (i.e. for TR) did not have a negative impact on individuals' search outcomes. In terms of query submission, individual participants submitted a similar number of queries and average words. It appears that since the participants were unaware of their access, they carried on regardless.

In relation to our third research question (RQ3): "How can MLCIR interfaces be designed so that they are usable and useful for the end users?" we discuss our findings from the design interview. In general, our findings 1) confirm the potential of the application of some existing CIR design suggestions to MLCIR, and 2) provide important new design suggestions for MLCIR systems. Awareness seems to play a potentially large role in MLCIR systems, perhaps because being aware of a team member's queries and judged documents could help users share their expertise without disclosing sensitive information. This confirms that whilst awareness has been an important concept in CIR, it may be applicable in MLCIR too. However, MLCIR systems must ensure that providing awareness for users does not compromise any sensitive information. With this in mind, we discuss potential interface components for MLCIR systems. MLCIR systems could provide query properties such as effectiveness, popularity and time spent, and also allow for sorting of queries according to their properties. We believe that these query properties could be implemented by adding different icons and a tooltip function in the query history component. A similar approach has been utilised by Freyne et al. [8] in an attempt to integrate search and browsing functionality. It has also been shown that looking at high-quality query examples can help users create queries that are highly effective [14]. Whilst icons could provide quick access to query properties, the tooltip function could provide further information such as number of viewed/relevant documents, number of times submitted, etc. Handel and Wang [13] highlighted that MLCIR could impact negatively on collaboration since team members are unaware of individual's access limitation. To address this, we believe MLCIR systems could display each team member's blacklisted keywords to those with higher access where appropriate. Thus, team members with higher access can compensate for those with lower access. In addition, like certain CIR systems [11, 22], we believe MLCIR systems could provide easy access to viewed/judged documents of team members. This can be implemented by adding separate lists for viewed and judged documents. However, the system must ensure that these lists do not accidently disclose unnecessary information by regularly checking for blacklisted terms and/or documents for every team member. The systems could also allow sorting of search results by means of their viewed and relevant properties. Moreover, during the search, it is important for users to be able to easily identify each team member's role and their actions. Thus, individual team members could be differentiated using different colours and/or names similar to [2, 22].

5.1 Limitation

Whilst utilising the TREC HARD 2005 collection [1] and its 10 test topics (see Table 1) allowed us to perform a controlled user-evaluation, perhaps our evaluation results could be slightly different for another document collection. However, the TREC HARD 2005 collection [1] is well known and has been utilised widely for various CIR evaluations [6, 15-17].

6. CONCLUSION AND FUTURE WORK

In this paper, we presented a user study of non-uniform information access in CIR, the first such study to the best of our knowledge. For our evaluation, we utilised 2 non-uniform access scenarios (document access removing and search term blacklisting) and 1 full access scenario, together with a collaborative search interface. We compared collaborative search outcomes between the information access scenarios and individual search outcomes between full access and non-full access. Findings from this evaluation suggests that removing 40% of the documents from the collection or removing 30% of the most likely search terms did not have a negative impact on search outcomes. Finally, we discussed design recommendations for the development of new interface components that support MLCIR, based on feedback from the design interview. Findings from the design interview suggested that being aware of team members' submitted queries and as well as viewed and judged documents (i.e. of allowed documents) could help users share their expertise without disclosing sensitive information. Also, we suggested that MLCIR systems must be aware of each user's role, action, access and limitation, and must ensure that providing awareness for users does not compromise any sensitive information. In the future, we intend to implement and test the elicited design recommendations through a number of user studies, in particular focusing on query awareness, result awareness and team awareness. Whilst these concepts have been examined for CIR, the nuanced differences with MLCIR mean more research is required for these concepts to be applicable in all CIR scenarios, not just when access to information is equal amongst a team of searchers. Overall, we believe that our paper has contributed to both HCI and IR communities by providing important design recommendations to assist with the future development of systems that better support users in MLCIR scenarios. We also believe that our paper has laid the groundwork for more research into MLCIR, which was initially laid out by Handel and Wang [13], by 1) confirming the potential for application of some existing CIR principles, an important contribution in itself; and 2) by providing new suggestions for developing MLCIR systems based on user feedback and empirical evaluation.

7. ACKNOWLEDGEMENTS

Thank you to Leif Azzopardi for his helpful comments on multiple versions of this paper.

8. REFERENCES

[1] Allan, J.: HARD Track overview in TREC 2005 high accuracy retrieval from documents. *NIST TREC 2005,* 1-17.

[2] Amershi, S. and Morris, M. R.: CoSearch: a system for co-located collaborative web search. *ACM SIGCHI 2008*, 1647-1656.

[3] Attfield, S., Blandford, A., Makri, S.: Social and interactional practices for disseminating current awareness information in an organisational setting. *IPM*, 46(6), 2010, 632-645.

[4] Bjurling, B., Hansen, P.: Contracts for Information Sharing in Collaborative Networks. *ISCRAM 2010*, 1-5.

[5] Braun, V. and Clarke, V.: Using thematic analysis in psychology. *Qualitative research in psychology*, 3(2), 2006, 77-101.

[6] Capra, R., Chen, A. T., Hawthorne, K., Arguello, J., Shaw, L. and Marchionini, G.: Design and evaluation of a system to support collaborative search. *ASIS&T*, 49(1), 2012, 1-10.

[7] Foley, C. and Smeaton, A. F.: Division of labour and sharing of knowledge for synchronous collaborative information retrieval. *IPM*, 46(6), 2010, 762-772.

[8] Freyne, J., Farzan, R., Brusilovsky, P., Smyth, B. and Coyle, M.: Collecting community wisdom: integrating social search & social navigation. *ACM IUI 2007*, 52-61.

[9] Golovchinsky, G., Adcock, J., Pickens, J., Qvarfordt, P. and Back, M.: Cerchiamo: a collaborative exploratory search tool. *ACM CSCW 2008*, 8-12.

[10] Golovchinsky, G., Pickens, J. and Back, M.: A taxonomy of collaboration in online information seeking. *arXiv preprint*, arXiv:0908.0704, 2009.

[11] González-Ibáñez, R. and Shah, C.: Coagmento: A system for supporting collaborative information seeking. *ASIS&T*, 48(1), 2011, 1-4.

[12] Halvey, M., Vallet, D., Hannah, D., Feng, Y., Jose, J. M.: An asynchronous collaborative search system for online video search. *IPM*, 46(6), 2010, 733-748.

[13] Handel, M. J., Wang, E. Y.: I can't tell you what i found: problems in multi-level collaborative information retrieval. *ACM CIR 2011*, 1-6.

[14] Harvey, M., Hauff, C. and Elsweiler, D.: Learning by Example: training users with high-quality query suggestions. *ACM SIGIR 2015*, 133-142.

[15] Htun, N. N., Halvey, M. and Baillie, L.: Towards Quantifying the Impact of Non-Uniform Information Access in Collaborative Information Retrieval. *ACM SIGIR 2015*, 843-846.

[16] Joho, H., Hannah, D., Jose, J. M.: Revisiting IR techniques for collaborative search strategies. *ECIR 2009*, 66-77.

[17] Joho, H., Hannah, D., Jose, J. M.: Comparing collaborative and independent search in a recall-oriented task. *ACM IIiX 2008*, 89-96.

[18] Karunakaran, A., Reddy, M.: Barriers to collaborative information seeking in organizations. *ASIS&T*, 49(1), 2012, 1-10.

[19] Karunakaran, A., Reddy, M.: The Role of Narratives in Collaborative Information Seeking. *ACM GROUP 2012*, 273–276.

[20] Linden, G., Smith, B. and York, J.: Amazon. com recommendations: Item-to-item collaborative filtering. Internet Computing. *IEEE*, 7(1), 2003, 76-80.

[21] Morris, M. R.: Collaborative search revisited. *ACM CSCW 2013*, pp. 1181-1192.

[22] Morris, M. R., Horvitz, E.: SearchTogether: an interface for collaborative web search. *ACM UIST 2007*, 3-12.

[23] Morris, M. R., Lombardo, J. and Wigdor, D.: WeSearch: supporting collaborative search and sensemaking on a tabletop display. *ACM CSCW 2010*, 401-410.

[24] Pickens, J., Golovchinsky, G., Shah, C., Qvarfordt, P., Back, M.: Algorithmic mediation for collaborative exploratory search. *ACM SIGIR 2008*, 315-322.

[25] Shah, C., González-Ibáñez, R.: Evaluating the synergic effect of collaboration in information seeking. *ACM SIGIR 2011*, 913-922.

[26] Shah, C., Marchionini, G. and Kelly, D.: Learning design principles for a collaborative information seeking system. *ACM CHI EA 2009*, 3419-3424.

[27] Smeaton, A. F., Lee, H., Foley, C. and McGivney, S.: Collaborative video searching on a tabletop. *Multimedia Systems*, 12(4), 2007, 375-391.

[28] Smyth, B., Balfe, E., Freyne, J., Briggs, P., Coyle, M. and Boydell, O.: Exploiting query repetition and regularity in an adaptive community-based web search engine. *UMUAI*, 14(5), 2004, 383-423.

[29] Soulier, L., Shah, C. and Tamine, L.: User-driven system-mediated collaborative information retrieval. *ACM SIGIR 2014*, 485-494.

[30] Tamine, L. and Soulier, L.: Understanding the Impact of the Role Factor in Collaborative Information Retrieval. *ACM CIKM 2015*, 43-52.

Information Sharing and Search Collaboration Activities of Health Consumers in South East Asia

Anushia Inthiran
Department of Accounting and Information Systems
University of Canterbury
Christchurch, New Zealand
anushia.inthiran@canterbury.ac.nz

ABSTRACT
Searching for health information is an activity conducted by people from all walks of life. Performing a health search is not a trivial task. A searcher could be overwhelmed by the sheer amount of information available and the need to understand technical and complex details. Performing a health search collaboratively could increase search efficacy. Sharing health information would encourage discourse. Health search collaboration and information sharing activities in developed countries have been analyzed. However, similar information is not available for health consumers from developing countries. In this work in progress paper, we describe search collaboration and information sharing activities of health consumers in South East Asia.

CCS Concepts
• Information systems→Information Retrieval• User and interactive retrieval

Keywords
collaboration, consumers, health, sharing, South East Asia, online

1. INTRODUCTION
Results of a Pew Survey indicate 72% of American Internet users have gone online to look for health information [1]. Majority of online health seekers commenced the search on a search engine [1]. Activities conducted online have evolved from merely searching for information to reading and watching someone else's health experience [1]. An equally important activity that is yet to be at the forefront of health searching is search collaboration and sharing activities. These activities are important. Searching collaboratively could influence search experience. The activity of sharing information could lead to health consumers gaining new information. For example, if a health search is performed in a collaborative manner, a searcher who is more experienced could help a searcher who is less experienced. The less experienced searcher could experience high search efficacy.

Similarly, if information is shared, there will be greater possibility of discussion, debate and ultimately the creation of new knowledge. Some information on sharing and collaboration activities conducted in developed countries is available. Survey results indicate online health consumers who track health indicators share their health tracking records or notes with another person [1]. Health consumers shared questions and concerns relating to treatment options [1], posted their own health related comments [2] and used Twitter for health orientated question and answer tasks [3]. Results of another study indicate 30% of American users have participated in health related group activities [4]. Searching for health information is the second most popular activity performed collaboratively amongst office colleagues [5]. Results of the above mentioned studies indicate American health consumers actively collaborate to search for health information and shared health information via technological methods.

Whilst there is some information on health collaboration and sharing activities from the United States, similar information from developing countries within the South East Asia (SEA) region is not available. However, citizens in SEA are using the Internet to search for health information. Undergraduate students in Thailand use online sources to obtain information on general health, disease and treatment and nutrition [6]. Results of a study conducted in SEA countries of developing economies indicate parents' are motivated to perform an online search for a doctor and non-doctor visit purposes [7]. Specialised search engines and social media services were used to perform an online search [7]. Results of these studies indicate health information searching is gaining ground in SEA. However, what remains unknown is if health information online is shared and if SEA health consumers search collaboratively? Thus, the aim of this study is to describe collaboration and sharing activities conducted by SEA health consumers. Specifically the following questions are tackled: i) Do SEA health consumers share health information?, ii) Do SEA health consumers collaborate when searching for a health task and iii) How are these activities conducted?

2. RELATED WORK
Studies pertaining to collaboration and sharing activities of citizens in SEA are limited. One study indicates only 50% of participants discussed health information found online with the doctor [8]. However, participants who discussed information with the doctor were elementary and guarded in their approach. Additionally, much insight on sharing and collaboration activities can be gleaned from studies conducted in developed countries. Thus, studies conducted in developed countries are used to set the scene. In developed countries, caregivers and patients living with chronic health conditions used Twitter and blog entries to share their personal health experience [1]. In addition, the emergence of consumer led health portals such as PatientsLikeMe and QuitNet allowed for peer communication, exchange of information and provided an avenue for health consumers to obtain social and emotional support [9]. Members of QuitNet regularly came back to the site to share information with newcomers as an act of giving back to society [10]. Exchange of disease specific information on social sites allows for the creation of new sources of information

CHIIR '17, March 07-11, 2017, Oslo, Norway
© 2017 ACM. ISBN 978-1-4503-4677-1/17/03…$15.00
DOI: http://dx.doi.org/10.1145/3020165.3022125

for support and engagement [11]. Whilst these sharing activities are beneficial, there have also been repercussions pertaining to the appropriateness and ethical implications of these activities [10]. In addition, health consumers indicate often making errors in determining what health information should be shared and with whom [12]. As more information is shared, there is a tendency for health consumers to ignore information from accredited sources. Instead, individuals with a particular disease or condition are validated as authoritative sources [13].

Whilst Web 2.0 and social networking applications are commonly used to share information, young adult health searchers did not utilize these platforms. They also did not use dedicated collaborative applications [14]. Though, young adults did share health information with friends and family members [14], this activity took place in a manner where information was summarized and shared via face to face communication or during a phone conversation [14].

Searching collaboratively is a popular mechanism of obtaining information. Results of a study indicate more than half of participants surveyed have performed a collaborative search [5]. Collaborative activities are important in supporting health consumers learn about a health condition [12]. A study of collaborative searching in electronic health records domain indicate users actively collaborate to create search terms and share their search terms with other users [15]. However, there were also 'search term lechers' who utilized others' search terms but did not contribute to any of their own [15].

In developed countries, sharing health information and collaborative health searching activies led to better overall health outcomes, fewer hospitalizations, lower healthcare expensense and greater patient satisfaction [16]. Aspects of clinical care in the SEA region is undergoing positive transformation from industrial age medicine to information age healthcare with the likes of shared decision making and patient centred healthcare [17]. As health literacy in SEA is low [18] it is expected that the activity of sharing and collaboratively searching for health information would improve health literacy. Increasing health literacy would allow SEA citizens to make informed decisions about their health and well being. In addition, many of the economies in SEA are struggling with a relatively underdeveloped public healthcare system [19].

3. METHODOLOGY

A purposeful homogenous sampling technique was used. Participants were recruited via call for participation notices placed in universities and bulletin boards at community centres. Participants contacted the researcher and an appointment was set. Participants must be a citizen of an SEA country, be residing in a SEA country, be of 18 years or older and must have performed a health search (online or offline). Participants must not be working in or have formal academic qualification from the healthcare or allied healthcare sector.

3.1 Data Collection and Procedure

A questionnaire and semi-structured interview was used to collect data. The questionnaire was designed to collect socio-demographic and health search experience details. The semi structured interview questions were mostly designed to be open ended. The English language was the medium used to conduct the interview. Participants had a minimum English qualification at high school level, thus they were comfortable using English as the medium of conversation. The interview was audio recorded and transcribed verbatim. A pilot test was conducted prior to the main experiment. As a result of the pilot test, interview questions were fine-tuned. The main experiment took place after the pilot test. Participants were informed of the purpose of the study via an explanatory statement. Consent was obtained from participants via signing a consent form. The interview was used to collect information for a larger study [7] however, for the purpose of this study we only provide results to the following questions: 1) have you shared health information in the past? Depending on the answer follow up questions were asked: 1i) whom was information shared with? (participants were allowed to provide multiple open ended answers) 1ii) how was the sharing activity conducted? Or 1iii) why was information not shared? The next set of questions was related to collaboration activities: 2. Have you collaborated to perform a health search? Depending on the answer follow up questions were asked 2i) with whom have you collaborated with and 2i) how was this activity conducted or 2ii) why have you not performed a collaborative search? Depending on answers further questions were asked such as if alternative methods were considered for sharing and collaboration. For example, did participants print out material to be shared, if other technology strategies were used to search collaboratively (through automation) or if participants were members of health chat groups and shared information through this channel. The interview pertaining to information sharing and search collaboration activities took an average of 10 minutes.

3.2 Data Analysis

Results from the questionnaire were analyzed using descriptive statistics. Audio recording was transcribed verbatim. The conventional qualitative content analysis technique [22] was used to analyze the recorded interview. To increase internal validity, an independent researcher cross checked the transcription. Steps for qualitative content analysis were followed as recommended by [23].

3.3 Participants

There were 50 participants. The participants' average age was 36 years (SD=4.7). Participants education qualification ranged from a diploma (college degree) to a PhD. Participants had academic qualifications in fields such as business, engineering and information technology. Occupations ranged from administrators, consultants and business owners. On average participants had a general search experience of 15.9 years (SD=4.1). Participants average health search experience is 8 years (SD=2.1). The frequency of performing a health search ranged from as frequent as once a week to as rare as and when necessary. Participants indicate using only online methods to search for health information. Participants comprised of the following nationalities: Malaysian (40%), Indonesian (24%), Thai (20%) and Cambodian (16%).

4. RESULTS

Results of our survey indicate participants shared health information but did not perform collaborative searching. Table 1 provides a summary of results. All 50 participants had shared health information. The participant's partner being husband or wife is the main person information was shared with. This is followed by sharing information with participant's sibling. In the case of sibling participants always shared information with a female sibling; in this case a younger or/and older sister. Participants also shared information with the doctor. In the case of a doctor participant indicate that information was only shared

Table 1. Details of Information Sharing and Search Collaboration Activities

Description \Activity		Information Sharing	Search Collaboration
Activity being performed?		100%	0%
Shared With	Partner Only	10 participants	
	Partner and Siblings	31 participants	
	Sibling Only	1 participant	
	Partner and Doctor	8 participants	
Mechanism	Partner	Email, F2F, Bookmark	
	Sibling	F2F, Phone Conversation	
	Doctor	F2F, Email	

with the family physician and not with any other physician they may encounter during a doctor's visit.

Various methods were used to share health information. The methods used to share information varied based on whom information was shared with. The most common method of sharing information with a partner was via email. Participants would copy the website link and email it to their partner. The next common method of sharing information is by doing so verbally via face to face (F2F) communication. The remaining participants indicate sharing information by bookmarking a site and showing the site to the partner in the comforts of their home. Occasionally, the sharing activity took place in a discursive mode. This means the searcher would have a computer on and the website displayed. The searcher and partner would be involved in active discussion. In other cases, bookmarked sites are shared with the partner (shown on a computer) and the searcher verbally summarizes information on the website. When information is shared with a sibling, it is done verbally via face to face or over a phone conversation. When information is shared with the doctor, it is done verbally via face to face during a consultation session or via email. In some cases, a discursive conversation takes place via exchange of emails between the searcher and the doctor.

Results of this study indicate SEA health consumers do not collaborate when performing a health search. All 50 participants indicate searching alone. We asked participants for reasons as to why they did not collaborate with their partner or sister since information is shared most often with these two categories of people. Most participants indicate that it was easier to allow for one party to search individually and then come together to share and discuss information found. 10 participants indicate that in the past the collaborative search process was dominated by the better searcher. This led to the other partner being left out of the search process and taking on the role of a passive collaborator. It is noted that these 10 participants were female. Thus, the search process was dominated by the male partner. As a result, collaborative searching is no longer performed. Participants were asked of the possibility of collaborating with a sibling. Participants indicate that this was not possible due to geographic distant between them. It is noted that only female participants shared information with a sibling. Male participants shared information with their partner or/and with the doctor.

5. DISCUSSION

Results of this study indicate SEA health consumers share health information but do not perform collaborative searching. Participants in developed countries shared information on social networking sites and on health portals [1,9]. Participants also took it upon themselves to share information as part of social or community service [10]. Results of this study indicate participants did not share information on social networking sites. This indicates participants did not want to share information publicly. Results of this study indicate old technology methods of communication such as email and bookmarks are used as opposed to Web 2.0 applications. In other cases, information sharing activities took place traditionally via verbal face to face communication and phone conversation. Results of this study indicate young adults use traditional and old technology to share information. This is similar to a previous study [14]. Whilst SEA online consumers are active on social media platforms [22] health information is not shared on these platforms.

Participants shared information with their partner, sibling and with the doctor. This indicates participants did not share information with their parents, the extended family, with their children, friends or work colleagues. This indicates that sharing of health information is a private activity with selected family members. It is noted that a female sibling is the only family member with whom information is shared with. This could be attributed to the role of womenfolk in SEA which is to primarily take care of the family whereas men are seen as breadwinners [23]. An aspect that requires further investigation is why information was not shared with participant's mother or mother in law. Both these categories of people are considered influential females in another female's life [23]. Participants also shared information with the doctor. This is an example of good practice where authoritative sources are consulted unlike results of previous studies which indicate the usage of non-authoritative sources [13,11]. Continuous email exchange and discourse with a doctor is a noteworthy activity as it allows for patient-physician decision making and patient-centered healthcare. However, results of a previous study conducted in SEA indicate a large gap in communication between doctor and patient due to patients' unpreparedness for participatory consultation style and adherence to paternalistic communication styles [23]. Results of this study indicate SEA participants are now more open to discussing and sharing information with the doctor.

Results of this study indicate participants do not perform a health search collaboratively. The main reason for this is because of search dominance. Female participants indicate the male partner would dominate the search and therefore reduce the female collaborator to take on a passive role. This could be attributed to the patriarchal role in SEA where it is the role of the men to take charge of decision making [24]. The second reason as to why searching is not conducted collaboratively (with siblings) is due to convenience (geographic distance). This indicates SEA health consumers are not aware of asynchronous methods of search collaboration. Asynchronous methods allow collaborators to search at their own time and space thus minimizing issues with geographic distance.

6. CONCLUSION AND FUTURE WORK

Results of this work in progress study provide insights to information sharing and search collaboration activities of SEA health consumers. Results of this study cannot be generalized to the general population of SEA. Results provide information in relation to health search practices in SEA. Practically, educating SEA health consumers of collaborative technologies would seem beneficial. In future work, it is hoped that other aspects of sharing activities will be scrutinized. For example, what happens when there is a disagreement about information shared and reasons as to why searchers choose to share information with certain people? As well as cultural and gender roles that influence health searching.

7. ACKNOWLEDGMENTS

The author would like to thank all participants for their candor, time and willingness to participate.

8. REFERENCES

[1] Fox, S. (2014). Pew Research Centre, Health Fact Sheet, Retrieved January 25th, 2016 from http://www.pewinternet.org/fact-sheets/health-fact-sheet/ Fox, S. (2014). Pew Research Centre, Health Fact Sheet, Retrieved January 25th, 2016 from http://www.pewinternet.org/fact-sheets/health-fact-sheet/

[2] Fox, S and Jones, S .(2009) The Social Life of health information, Pew Internet, 2009-12

[3] Paul,A.S., Hong, L., and Chi, E.H. (2011). Is Twitter a good place for asking questions? A characterization study, Proc ICWSM.

[4] Johnson, G.J. and Ambrose, P.J. (2006) Neo-tribes: the power and potential of online communities in health care, CACM, 49 (10)pp.107-113

[5] Morris, M.R. (2013). Collaborative Search Revisited, CSCW 2013

[6] Kitikannakorn, N. and Sitthiworanan, C. (2009). Searching for health information on the Internet by undergraduate students in Phitsanulok, Thailand, Vol. 3, pp. 313-318.

[7] Inthiran, A and Soyiri, I. (2015). Searching for health information for my child: A Perspective from South East Asia, International Conference of Asian Digital Libraries, pp.76-81,Seoul, Korea

[8] Inthiran, A (2015). Do I Talk to the Doctor About Information Found Online. An outlook from South East Asia, Consortium of Information Schools Asia Pacific (CiSAP),Workshop, Seoul, Korea

[9] Graham, A.L., Milner, P., Saul, J.E., Pfaff, L. (2008). Online Advertising as a Public Health and Recruitment Tool: Comparison of Different Media Campaigns to Increase Demand for Smoking Cessation Interventions, JMIR, Vol.10 No.5

[10] O'Rouke (2014). Tweeting Cancer, The New Yorker, http://www.newyorker.com/culture/culture-desk/tweeting-cancer

[11] Green, J.A., Choudhry, N.K., Kilabuk, E. and Shrank, W.H. (2011). Online social networking by patients with diabetics: a qualitative evaluation of communication with Facebook. J Gen Internal Medicine, pp.287-292

[12] Hartzler, A., Skeels, M.M., Mukari, M., and Powell, C., Lkasnja, P. and Pratt, W. (2011) Sharing is caring but not error free: transparency of granular controls for personal sharing health information in social networks, Proc AMIA 559

[13] Wilson, J. (1999). Acknowledging the expertise of patients and their organisations, BMJ, 1999.319pp771-774

[14] Zhang, Y (2013). Consumer Health Information Searching Process in Real Life Settings, ASIST 2012

[15] Zheng, K., Mei, Q., and Hanauer, D (2011). Collaborative search in electronic health records, J AM Med Inform Assoc, 2011,18, pp.282-291

[16] Ng, C.J. , Lee, P.Y., Lee, Y.K., Chew, B.Y., Engkasan, J.P., Irmi, Z.I., Hanafi, N.K., and Tong, S.F. (2014). An overview of patient involvement in healthcare decision-making: a situational analysis of the Malaysian context, BMC Health Services Research, Available at http://www.biomedcentral.com/1472-6963/13/408 [Accessed Date: 15th July 2015]

[17] Lee, Y.K., Low, W.Y., Ng, C.J.(2013).Exploring patient values in medical decision making: a qualitative study, PLoS One, Available at http://www.ncbi.nlm.nih.gov/pubmed/24282518 [Accessed Date: 15th July 2015]

[18] Chen, S.F., Tsai, T.S., Wang, M.H. (2013). Health literacy and impact factors of the Southeast Asian immigrant women in Taiwan, Honor Society of Nursing, Sigma Theta Tau International 24th International Nursing Research Congress, Available at http://www.nursinglibrary.org/vhl/bitstream/10755/304306/1/Chen_HealthLiteracy.pdf [Accessed Date: 29th March 2015]

[19] A perspective of future healthcare landscape in ASEAN and Singapore (2015), Deloitte, Available at https://www2.deloitte.com/content/dam/Deloitte/sg/Documents/risk/sea-risk-future-healthcare-thought-leadership-noexp.pdf

[20] Hsiesh, H.F., and Shannon, S.E. (2005). Three approaches to qualitative content analysis, Qualitative Health Research, Vol. 15 Issue 9, pp.1277-1288

[21] Zhang, Y and Wildemuth, B.M. (2005). Qualitative Analysis of Content, Analysis 1 (2):1-12 (2005)

[22] Internet Society South East Asia (d.u). Retrieved January10, 2015 from http://www.scribd.com/doc/111870071/ASEAN-ICT-Masterplan-2015

[23] Carteret, M (2013). Cultural Values of Asian patients and Families, Dimensions of Culture, Cross Cultural Communications for Health Care Professionals, Available at http://www.dimensionsofculture.com/2010/10/cultural-values-of-asian-patients-and-families/ [Accessed Date: 10th July 2015]

[24] Claramita, M., Van Dalen, J., Van der Vleuten, C. (2011). Doctors in a Southeast Asian country communicate sub-optimally regardless of patients' educational background, Patient Education and Counseling, Volume 85, Issue 3, pp.169–174

Query Reformulation Patterns of Mixed Language Queries in Different Search Intents

Hengyi Fu
School of Information, Florida State University
142 Collegiate Loop, Tallahassee, FL 32306
hf13c@my.fsu.edu

ABSTRACT

With the increasing number of multilingual resources on the Internet, cross-language information retrieval has become an important research topic. In cultures where people speak both Chinese and English, using mixed language in oral speaking and web searching is a common phenomenon. While queries are the key element of information retrieval process, mixed-language queries have not yet been adequately studied. This study use query log analysis to examine the query reformulation patterns regarding Chinese-English mixed language queries, and how search intents may affect the query reformulation types users employ. The results can inform IR system designers to enhance cross-language controlled vocabularies and develop discovery platforms for multilingual content, and improve search engines to provide users with more relevant, personalized search results. The findings could also be expanded to other language combinations that would improve search engine designs.

Keywords

Query reformulation; Mixed language queries; cross-language information retrieval; search intents; query log analysis.

1. INTRODUCTION

In Cross-language information retrieval (CLIR), search queries are translated from the source language to the target language, and the original and translated queries are used to retrieve documents in both the source and targeted languages. The assumption behind this mechanism is that queries are *consistently* used in one language. This mechanism works well when the user is monolingual and is looking for information in a certain language. However, the user of a CLIR system may be bilingual to some extent. For example, in regions where people speak both Chinese and English, using mixed language is a common phenomenon. For example, Hong Kong people typically speak Cantonese with English words. When conducting web searches, they often use Chinese-English mixed language queries to approximate their information needs. This phenomenon, called *code-switching*, has become a focus of research in sociology, psycholinguistics, and linguistics [1].

A ***mixed language*** consists of sentences or terms mostly in the primary language with some words in a secondary language. A mixed language query is a search query including words mixed from two or more languages. For example, the query "Caudalie grape water 效果 (effect)" is a Chinese-English mixed language query looking for reviews about a certain skin care product. Research on Chinese search engines shows that using Chinese-English mixed language queries has become more frequent in recent years [2]. However, very few studies have addressed why and how people use mixed language queries in web searches, and what problems may occur when using mixed language queries. In this paper we present results of part of a larger study which examines mixed language query reformulation patterns based on semi-structured interviews and query log content analysis, but focus more on how search intents will affect the query reformulation patterns of mixed language queries. The findings can inform IR system designers to enhance cross-language controlled vocabularies and develop discovery platforms for multilingual content, as well as to improve search engines to provide users with more relevant results regarding mixed-language queries. Although this study deals with one non-English language, the results could be expanded to other language combinations (e.g. English-Korean mixed queries, etc.) that would improve the search engine design.

CHIIR '17, March 07-11, 2017, Oslo, Norway
 ISBN 978-1-4503-4677-1/17/03…$15.00
DOI: http://dx.doi.org/10.1145/3020165.3022126

2. RELATED WORK

2.1 Classification of Query Reformulation Types

Taxonomies of query reformulation types have been developed for different types of searches. [3] constructed conceptual reformulation categories such as *content*, *format*, and *resource*. [4] proposed four query reformulation types within one search task, including *Generalization*, *New*, *Reformulation* and *Specialization*, based on the change of query content and query length, and when identical queries were ignored. This taxonomy was also used by [5][6]. [7] manually classified 1040 query refinements into ten categories, including *Term splitting*, *Term deletion*, *Repetition*, *Term substitution*, *Derived forms of words*, *Spelling corrections*, *Abbreviation Expansion*, *Punctuation changes*, *Case changing*, and *Others*. [8] also constructed a small taxonomy for query refinement prediction, including *Word splitting*, *Word merging*, *Word stemming*, *Expansion*, and *Spelling correction*. [9] developed an extensive taxonomy including twelve query reformulation types. In addition to the three types identified in [4], namely: *Remove words* (generalization), *Add words* (specialization), and *Word substitution* (reformulation), they also proposed other more linguistic-based types including *Word reorder*, *Whitespace and punctuation*, *Url stripping*, *Stemming*, *Acronym*, *Substring*, *Abbreviation*, *Spelling correction*, and *Others*. All these taxonomies were developed using information obtained from logs. [10] conducted client-side controlled experiments to analyze the relationship between search tasks and five query reformulation strategies including *Generalization*, *New*, *Repeat*, *Word substitution*, and *Specialization*. However, all these studies focused on English queries and there are very few studies that have examined the query reformulation types of non-English queries or mixed language queries.

2.2 User Intents in Web Search

Several studies have attempted to classify user queries in terms of users' informational actions with different methods, including queries [11][12][13], clicked URL and subsequent queries [13], live ticker data [14], and user survey [11][15]. [11] manually classified a small set of queries into transactional, navigational, and informational by using a survey of AltaVista users. Navigational queries are used to find a certain webpage the user has already in mind or at least assumes that such a site exists. Typical queries in this category could be searches for a homepage of an organization. With informational queries users want to find information on certain topics. Such queries usually lead to a set of results rather than to just one suitable document. The purpose of transactional queries is to reach a site where a further interaction is necessary. The interaction could be downloading, shopping, or accessing certain databases. All other studies followed Broder's taxonomy of search intent and most of them used English queries except [14][15].

2.3 Analysis of Chinese-English Mixed Language Queries

[16] collected 1,255,633 queries from a Chinese search engine data Timway, and concluded some characteristics identified in the search log, such as search topics and the mean number of queries per sessions, were similar to those in English search engines. [17] reported their research on the character usage of Chinese search logs by examining the distribution of search query terms. They found that users tended to use more diversified terms and that the usage of characters in search queries was quite different from the character usage of general online information in Chinese. They also suggested it would be valuable to investigate the characteristics of mixed queries and their implications in web searching and search engine design. However, none of these studies actually investigated Chinese-English mixed language queries, although [16] observed the code-switching phenomenon and indicated it would be an interesting topic to explore. The only research found related to Chinese-English mixed language queries was conducted by [18]. They concluded that mixed language query searching was primarily caused by: technical terms in computer science, names of magazines and firms, and the fact that some English words do not have a popular Chinese translation. In our previous studies, we reported findings about the context in which users employed Chinese-English mixed language queries and why they preferred those queries based on semi-structured interviews[19], and topic and search intents of mixed language queries based on query log analysis [20].

3. RESEARCH QUESTION

The following research questions are addressed in this paper:

RQ1: What are the query reformulation patterns of Chinese-English mixed language queries in a web search session?

RQ2: Do users' search intents have an influence on the usage of each reformulation type?

4. QUERY LOG CONTENT ANALYSIS

This study examined queries [1] submitted to the Sogou search engine[2], which was established in 2004 and is now one of the most popular search engines in China. The query-log data were collected in June 2012. Each record consists of six fields: timestamp, user ID, cookies, query content, the clicked URL, and the ranking of the clicked URL. The query-log data contain 45,745,985 non-empty queries. One of the researchers developed a C++ program to select and pre-process all the Chinese-English queries that contain both ASCII and double-byte characters. The final dataset has 346,989 Chinese-English mixed-language queries.

This study used *user identification* (a code to identify a particular computer based on the computer's Internet Protocol address) and *cookie* (an anonymous cookie automatically assigned by the Sogou server to identify unique users on a particular computer based on a browser) to determine sessions. The initial query from a unique IP address and cookie always identified a new session. There are 26,255,952 sessions for the 45,745,985 non-empty queries (1.74 query per session), and 154,663 sessions contain Chinese-English mixed language queries.

This study randomly selected 1,000 sessions containing Chinese-English mixed language queries for query reformulation analysis. *Reformulation* here was defined as the query content change between any two consecutive queries in one session. The selected 1,000 sessions contained 2,178 mixed language queries with 856 reformulations. Table 1 shows a selected session containing three mixed language queries and two reformulations. We used an open coding approach to code each reformulation with reference to [9].

Table 1. One session with three queries and two reformulations

User ID	Cookie	Query Content
654654684446723	6EDHG2KB6EF42HG	Miami 餐馆 (Miami restaurant)
654654684446723	6EDHG2KB6EF42HG	Miami 中餐馆 (Miami Chinese restaurant)
654654684446723	6EDHG2KB6EF42HG	Miami 餐馆评价 (Miami Chinese restaurant review)

Table 2. . User behavior following the query Maxwell Render teaching materials

User behavior	Details
query 1	Maxwell Render 教材 (i.e., Maxwell Render teaching materials)
Result click	http://render.haotui.com/forum-16-1.html
Result click	http://wenku.baidu.com/view/05e2c2175527072 2192ef7ed.html
Query 2	Maxwell Render v2.6 安装方法 (i.e., Maxwell Render v2.6 installation tutorial)
Result click	http://www.xuanran.net/article/363.html

We then open-coded the same set of query reformulations into three search intents based on session. If the user modifies the initial query or clicks on more than one result within a session, the last modified query or the last clicked result in this session is used for search intent analysis, because if the initial query has been modified or more than one clicks existed, it would imply that the initial query or earlier clicked result(s) have not satisfied the user

[1] http://www.sogou.com/labs/dl/q-e.html

[2] http://www.sogou.com/

need completely. Table 2 shows two queries (one query reformulation) and three clicked results within one session. In this case, the query reformulation is classified with an ***informational*** intent.

5. FINDINGS AND DISCUSSION

5.1 Query Reformulation Patterns

Among the 1,000 selected sessions, 932 started with a mixed language query and 846 sessions contained only mixed language queries. A total of 437 sessions contained one query (also a mixed language query).

The 856 query reformulations were distributed in 563 sessions. A total of 108 reformulations occurred among mixed language queries and single language queries, and in most cases (89 instances), the mixed language query was modified to a Chinese-only query. For example, the English movie name "Transformers" in the mixed language query was changed to its Chinese translation, making the modified query Chinese-only. This could be based on the perception that Sogou, as a Chinese local search engine, was less likely to index English full-text web pages, thus, changing the mixed language queries to English-only queries cannot improve the coverage and accuracy of returned results.

A total of 748 reformulations were part of the mixed language queries, indicating that the search engine users chose to keep the mixed language query format for their search tasks. Among the 748 reformulations, 542 reformulations changed the Chinese part of the previous query, 156 changed the English part, and 50 changed both the Chinese and English parts simultaneously. Nine query reformulation patterns were identified based on query log:

- **Add words**: occurs when one or more words are added to the first (initial) query. An add words reformulation usually makes the query more specific.
- **Remove words**: occurs when more or more words are deleted from the first query. A remove words reformulation usually makes the query less specific.
- **Word reorder**: occurs when the words in the first (initial) query are reordered but unchanged.
- **Word split/join**: occurs when only whitespace and punctuation are altered in the first query.
- **Word substitution**: occurs when one or more words in the first query are substituted with semantically related words.
- **Word stemming**: A stemming reformulation involves changing the word stems in the first query.
- **Form/Expand acronym**: A form acronym transformation occurs when the second query is an acronym formed from the first query's words. An expanded acronym reformulation occurs when the first query is an acronym and the reformulation is a query consisting of the words that form the acronym.
- **Spelling correction**: occurs when the second query is used to correct the spelling mistakes in the first query.
- **URL stripping**: occurs when the first and second queries are the same after removing ".com", "www.", and "http" from both sides.

Not all reformulation categories were detected in both the Chinese part and the English part modifications. Tables 3 and 4 show the query reformulation categories as well as the percentage of each category. A chi-squared analysis shows that reformulation type has a statistically significant effect on part (English part or Chinese part) χ^2= 84.28, p < .001.

Table 3. Query reformulation categories of the English part in mixed language queries

Changing the English part	Pre. (206 in total)	Example
Add words	22.33%	Windows 7→Windows task manager
Remove words	13.11%	FTP download →FTP
Word reorder	11.65%	GPS phone→ phone GPS
Word substitution	31.07%	Orlando food →Orlando restaurant
Word stemming	4.37%	Python debugging →Python debug
Form/Expand acronym	5.34%	JCPT → Japanese language proficiency test; Computer-aided design→ CAD
Spelling correction	8.74%	Swaravski → Swarovski
URL	3.40%	http www.sohu.com→ sohu

Table 4. Query reformulation categories of the Chinese part in mixed language queries

Changing the Chinese part	Pre. (592 in total)	Example (with English translation)
Add words	28.21%	下载 (download)→ 下载链接 (download link)
Remove words	12.33%	分辨率等参数(resolution and other parameters)→ 分辨率 (resolution)
Word reorder	7.60%	世预赛 (World cup) 转播表 (rebroadcasting schedule) →转播表(rebroadcasting schedule) 世预赛 (World cup)
Word split/join	9.80%	软件破解(software crack)→ 软件 (software) 破解 (crack)
Word substitution	35.64%	安装教程(installation tutorial) → 如何安装 (how to install)
Form/Expand acronym	2.20%	官网 (abbreviation of official site)→ 官方网站 (official site)
Spelling correction	4.22%	配制 (Wrong spelling of configuration)→ 配置 (configuration)

5.2 Search intent effect on query reformulation

Among the 856 query reformulations, 423 are classified as informational, 302 are transactional, and 131 are navigational. Figure 1 shows the frequency of reformation types in three search intents. Since the frequency of each reformulation type was not normally distributed, non-parametric tests were used in examining significance of differences.

We first examined the search intent effect on the usage of reformulation types. Kruskal-Wallis H tests revealed that four reformulation types were used significantly differently in the different search intents, *Words reorder* (H=18.88, p<.01), *Word*

Substitution (H=21.12, p<.01), *Form/Expand acronym* (H=17.43, p<.01), and *URL stripping* (H=23.25, p<.01). No significant difference was found in the usage of other reformulation types.

A post-hoc analysis using Tamhane tests found that users used *Word Substitution* and *Word reorder* in informational search intent significantly more frequently than other search intents (p<.05); and that they used Form/Expand acronym and URL stripping more frequently in transactional and navigational search intents, respectively (p<.05).

Figure 1. The frequency of each reformulation type in three search intents

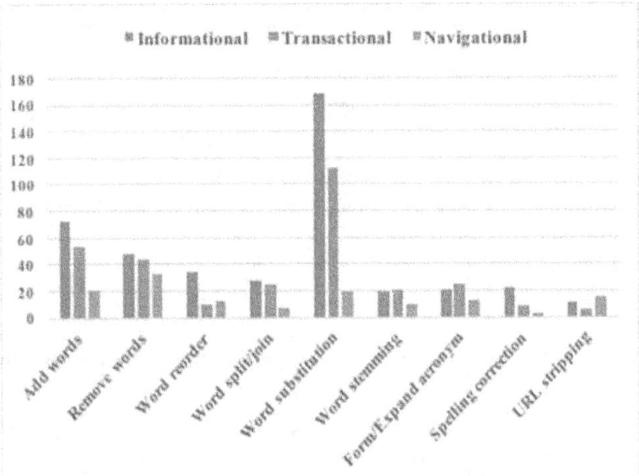

6. CONCLUSION, LIMITATIONS, AND FUTURE WORK

This study reported patterns of Chinese-English mixed language query reformulation and how search intents may affect the usage of different query reformulation types, and the results are likely to inform the development of controlled vocabularies, indexes, and discovery platforms for multilingual content. However, the results of this study may not be generalizable to English native speakers who understand Chinese since the dataset is from a major Chinese search engine. Future research includes examining how other populations (e.g., Chinese learners who use Chinese as a second language) use English-Chinese mixed language queries in web searching, and developing classifiers to automatically detect different query reformulation patterns and analyzing correlations between query reformulation patterns and effectiveness metrics (e.g. user click behavior) to see the effectiveness of different query reformulation patterns regarding Chinese-English mixed language queries. Experiments with question-driven, web-based information search tasks can also be conducted to test the general effectiveness of users' query reformulations in different search intents, and what other factors (e.g. search experience, domain knowledge, etc.) may affect users' query reformulation types in different search intents.

7. REFERENCES

[1] Auer, P. 1998. Code-Switching in conversation: Language, interaction, and identify. Routledge, London.

[2] Chau, M., Fang, X., and Yang, C. C. 2007. Web searching in Chinese: A study of a search engine in Hong Kong. J Am Soc Inf Sci Technol., 58, 7, 1044-1054.

[3] Rieh, S.Y. and Xie, H. 2006. Analysis of multiple query reformulations on the web: the interactive information retrieval context. Inf Process Manag., 42, 3, 751-768.

[4] Lau, T. and Horvitz, E. 1999. Patterns of search: analyzing and modeling Web query refinement. In User Modeling '99, 119-128.

[5] He, D., Göker, A., and Harper, D.J. 2002. Combining evidence for automatic web session identification. Inf Process Manag., 38, 5, 727-742.

[6] Jansen, B. J., Spink, A., Blakely, C., and Koshman, S. 2007. Defining a session on Web search engines: Research Articles. J Am Soc Inf Sci Technol., 58, 6, 862-871.

[7] Bruza, P., and Dennis, S. 1997. Query Reformulation on the Internet: Empirical Data and the Hyperindex Search Engine. In RIAO, 97, 488-499.

[8] Guo, J., Xu, G., Li, H., and Cheng, X. 2008. A unified and discriminative model for query refinement. In SIGIR '08, 379-386.

[9] Huang, J., and Efthimiadis, E. N. 2009. Analyzing and evaluating query reformulation strategies in web search logs. In CIKM'09, 77-86.

[10] Liu, C., Gwizdka, J., Liu, J., Xu, T., and Belkin, N. J. 2010. Analysis and evaluation of query reformulations in different task types. In ASIST'10, 47, 1, 1-9.

[11] Broder, A. 2002. A taxonomy of web search. *SIGIR Forum,* 36, 2, 3-10.

[12] Jansen, B. J., Booth, D. L., and Spink, A. 2008. Determining the informational, navigational, and transactional intent of web queries. *Information Processing and Management,* 44, 3, 1251-1266.

[13] Rose, D., and Levinson, D. 2004. Understanding user goals in web search. In S. Feldman, M. Uretsky, M. Najork, & C. Wills (Eds.), *Proceedings of the 13th International Conference on World Wide Web*, 13–19. New York: ACM Press.

[14] Lewandowski, D. 2006. Query types and search topics of German web search engine users. *Information Services and Use,* 26, 4, 261-269.

[15] Lewandowski, D., Drechsler, J., and Mach, S. 2012. Deriving query intents from web search engine queries. *Journal of the American Society for Information Science and Technology,* 63, 9, 1773-1788.

[16] Chau, M., Fang, X., and Yang, C. C. 2007. Web searching in Chinese: A study of a search engine in Hong Kong. J Am Soc Inf Sci Technol., 58, 7, 1044-1054.

[17] Chau, M., Lu, Y., Fang, X., and Yang, C. C. 2009. Characteristics of character usage in Chinese web searching. Inf Process Manag., 45, 1, 115-130.

[18] Lu, Y., Chau, M., Fang, X., and Yang, C. C. 2006. Analysis of the bilingual queries in a Chinese web search engine. Retrieved June 1, 2014 from http://www.business.hku.hk/~mchau/papers/BilingualQueries_WEB.pdf.

[19] Fu, H., and Wu, S. 2015. Studying Chinese-English mixed language queries from the user perspectives. In JCDL'15, 247-248.

[20] Fu, H., and Wu, S. 2014. Analyzing Chinese-English mixed language queries in a web search engine. In ASIST'14, 51, 1, 1-5.

Automatic Summarization of Domain-specific Forum Threads: Collecting Reference Data

Suzan Verberne
Radboud University
s.verberne@let.ru.nl

Antal van den Bosch
Radboud University
a.vandenbosch@let.ru.nl

Sander Wubben
Tilburg University
s.wubben@uvt.nl

Emiel Krahmer
Tilburg University
E.J.Krahmer@uvt.nl

ABSTRACT

We create and analyze two sets of reference summaries for discussion threads on a patient support forum: expert summaries and crowdsourced, non-expert summaries. Ideally, reference summaries for discussion forum threads are created by expert members of the forum community. When there are few or no expert members available, crowdsourcing the reference summaries is an alternative. In this paper we investigate whether domain-specific forum data requires the hiring of domain experts for creating reference summaries. We analyze the inter-rater agreement for both datasets and we train summarization models using the two types of reference summaries. The inter-rater agreement in crowdsourced reference summaries is low, close to random, while domain experts achieve a considerably higher, fair, agreement. The trained models however are similar to each other. We conclude that it is possible to train an extractive summarization model on crowdsourced data that is similar to an expert model, even if the inter-rater agreement for the crowdsourced data is low.

Keywords

summarization, discussion forums, reference data

1. INTRODUCTION

Discussion forums on the web come in many flavors, each forum covering its own topic and having its own community. The user-generated content on web forums is a valuable source for information. However, in discussion forums where opinions and experiences are shared, it can be difficult to pinpoint the relevant information in a long thread, especially when the forum is accessed on a mobile device.

The Dutch media company Sanoma wants to serve its mobile users better by showing summaries of long discussion threads. The approach we take in this paper is *extractive* summarization [5]: extracting salient units of text from a document and then concatenating them to form a shorter version of the document. In previous work on extractive summarization for discussion threads it was assumed that *posts* are more suitable summarization units than sentences, because selecting sentences from posts would lead to loss of context [1]. However, posts are sometimes long and not all information contained in a post is equally relevant. In this paper we investigate the feasibility of thread summarization at the sentence level: selecting the most relevance sentences from a thread while hiding the less relevant sentences.

For the development and evaluation of automatic summarizers, human reference summaries are required [11]. However, summarization is an inherently subjective task: human summarizers tend to disagree on the information that should be included in the summary. When multiple raters are involved in creating the reference summaries, it is insightful to measure the inter-rater agreement between them. Agreement for extractive summarization – the selection of salient text units from a document – is generally calculated in terms of Cohen's κ [13]. For summaries of newswire texts κ scores between 0.20 and 0.50 have been reported [10], but for the summarization of conversations the agreement tends to be lower: between 0.10 and 0.35 [9, 7, 12].

The case that we study in this paper is that of web forums of patient support groups. Online support groups play an important role in providing patients with informational and emotional support from their peers [4]. The information shared in patient support groups is domain-specific, covering the disease, medications, side effects and coping strategies. Ideally, reference summaries for discussion forum threads are created by active members of the forum community, who are experience experts in the domain of the forum and familiar with the commonalities of the forum community. When there are few or no expert members available, crowdsourcing the reference summaries is an alternative. In this paper we investigate whether domain-specific forum data requires the hiring of domain experts for creating reference summaries, or that crowdsourced reference summaries suffice. We collect two sets of reference summaries for a set of discussion threads from the Facebook group of a patient support community: expert summaries and crowdsourced summaries. We analyze the inter-rater agreement for both datasets, and compare the models trained on both datasets. We address the following research questions:

RQ1 What is the inter-rater agreement for sentence selection from domain-specific discussion forum threads;

CHIIR '17, March 07-11, 2017, Oslo, Norway
© 2017 ACM. ISBN 978-1-4503-4677-1/17/03... $15.00
DOI: http://dx.doi.org/10.1145/3020165.3022127

do domain experts achieve a higher agreement than crowdsourced raters on the task?

RQ2 What are the differences between sentence selection models trained on expert data and crowdsourced datas?

We release the labeled data to be reused by other researchers.[1]

2. RELATED WORK

Over the last decade, some research has been directed at the summarization of forum threads [14, 8, 3]. The most similar to the current work in the context of discussion forum summarization is the work by Bhatia et al. [1], which takes a feature-based approach in selecting the most relevant posts from a thread, arguing that sentence selection would lead to loss of coherence.

The quality of crowdsourced annotations compared to expert annotations has been investigated before in the context of other supervised learning tasks. For the classification of sentiment in political blog snippets it was found that having one individual non-expert annotator leads to a model with poor quality, but using multiple noisy annotations from non-experts can lead to a useful model [6]. For relevance judgments in domain-specific search, crowdsourced judgments give the same results as expert judgments in a global evaluation (ranking of evaluated search engines), but fail in more specific evaluation tasks (distinguish different levels of highly accurate search results) [2].

This paper is the first to analyze the difference between expert annotations and crowd-sourced annotations for the summarization of discussion forum threads, and the first to study the potential of sentence-level summarization of discussion forum threads.

3. METHODOLOGY

3.1 Data

We use data from the Facebook group GIST support international.[2] GIST is a rare form of cancer. We received an export of 3,071 discussion threads from the Facebook group. Threads with more than 26 posts were cut off at 26 by the provider of the data. The average number of posts in a thread after cut-off is 9.5 (median 7). 40% of the threads have more than 10 posts. For our experiment we created a sample of 100 randomly selected threads that have at least 10 posts. We automatically split each post in sentences, using regular expressions and a set of abbreviations in Python. The average number of sentences per post is 2.7 (minimum 1, maximum 18).

3.2 Creating reference summaries

For creating reference summaries, we set up an online thread summarization interface. In this interface the left column of the screen shows the complete thread. When hovering over the text in the posts, separate sentences get highlighted and are clickable. The right column shows an empty table with a placeholder cell for each post and within each post a placeholder `[...]` for each sentence in the post. The subjects were given the following instructions: *"Please select the pieces of text that you think are the most important for the thread. You can either select a post as a whole (by clicking 'select the complete post') or select separate sentence(s) from a post. You can determine the number of selected posts yourself but try to be concise so that the resulting summary does not contain too much redundant information. The selected text together should form an informative summary of the thread."* The subjects also had the possibility to remove sentences or posts from the selection by clicking the selected items.

[1]The data can be downloaded from http://discosumo.ruhosting.nl/

[2]https://www.facebook.com/groups/gistsupport/

Table 1: Sentence features used as independent variables in the regression analysis. Some of the features describe the post in which the sentence occurs.

Name	Description
pos_post	position of post in the thread
pos_sent	position of sentence in the post
cossim_thread	cosine similarity sentence–thread[1]
cossim_openingpost	cosine similarity sentence–opening post[1]
wordcount	word count
ttr	type-token ratio
rel_punctcount	relative punctuation count
avg_wordlength	average word length (# of chars)
author	proportion of posts by author of post

1. tf-idf weighted term vectors

With the annotation interface, we collected two sets of reference summaries:

- **Crowdsourced summaries.** Through the research participation system of our university, we recruited subjects to create reference summaries. The users provided some basic information in the login screen, such as their gender and age. They were then presented with one example thread to get used to the interface. After that, they were presented with a randomly selected thread from our sample. The subjects decided themselves how many threads they wanted to summarize. They were paid a gift certificate. Each thread was shown to 5 different subjects.
- **Expert summaries.** Through the GIST patient community, we recruited 2 experts to create reference summaries. 50 of the 100 threads in our sample were summarized by the experts, using the same instructions and annotation interface as for the crowdsourced summaries.

3.3 Inter-rater agreement

For each thread we computed the agreement between each pair of raters in terms of Cohen's κ.We report the mean κ scores over all threads and all rater pairs.

3.4 Training a model for sentence selection

In order to answer RQ2 we investigated the relationship between sentence features and the selection of sentences using a linear regression analysis. We argue that the number of raters that selected a sentence (the number of 'votes') is an indicator of its relevance: a sentence that is selected by all 5 raters can be expected to be more relevant than a sentence that is selected by only one or two raters. Therefore, we used the number of votes for a sentence as dependent variable in the regression analysis. The sentence features that we used as independent variables are listed in Table 1. We standardized feature values by converting them to their z-value.

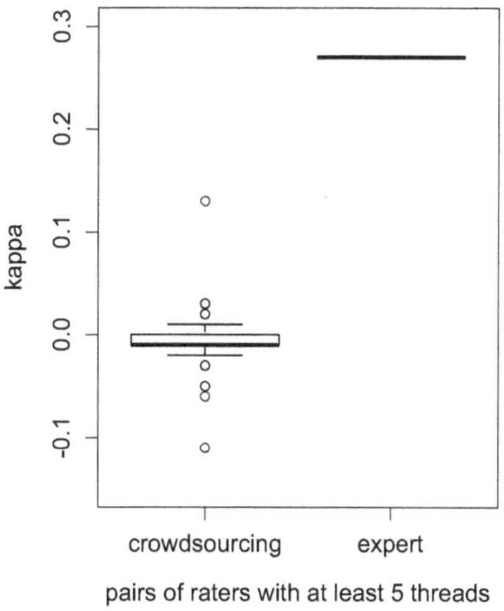

Figure 1: Dispersion of κ scores for the rater pairs with at least 5 common threads (κ scores are averages over the κ scores for individual threads).

4. RESULTS

22 subjects participated in the crowdsourcing study (18 female, average age 23). As quality control for their work, we registered the time they spent on the annotation task. The work of two subjects was disregarded because they completed multiple threads per minute, which would be impossible if they would have taken the task seriously. The median number of items selected in a thread was 7.0 (mean 8.7). The two experts both summarized all 50 threads presented to them. The median number of items selected in a thread was 8.0 (mean 8.0).

We found that for the crowdsourced summaries, the agreement for sentence selection is low: $\kappa = 0.081$. This indicates that the agreement between two raters for selecting sentences from a thread is close to random.[3] The expert agreement is considerably higher: $\kappa = 0.267$, which indicates 'fair agreement'.

We investigated the κ scores of the individual rater pairs in the crowdsourced data to see whether some of the pairs reach the expert agreement level. Figure 1 shows the dispersion of the κ scores for the rater pairs with at least 5 common threads (κ scores are averaged over threads). None of the rater pairs in the crowdsourced data reaches the agreement level of the expert raters. We also investigated the time spent by the individual raters. The mean time spent per thread in the crowdsourced data was 112 seconds while the experts spent 145 seconds on average per thread, which is considerably longer. However, there is no significant correlation between the time spent per thread and the average κ score of an individual rater (Kendall's $\tau = 0.091, p = 0.57$). We also investigated whether relatively more experienced raters reach a higher agreement, but there is no significant correlation between the number of threads summarized and the average κ score of an individual rater (Kendall's $\tau = 0.134, p = 0.41$).

[3]A κ of zero would indicate an agreement level that is not distinguishable from random selection behavior.

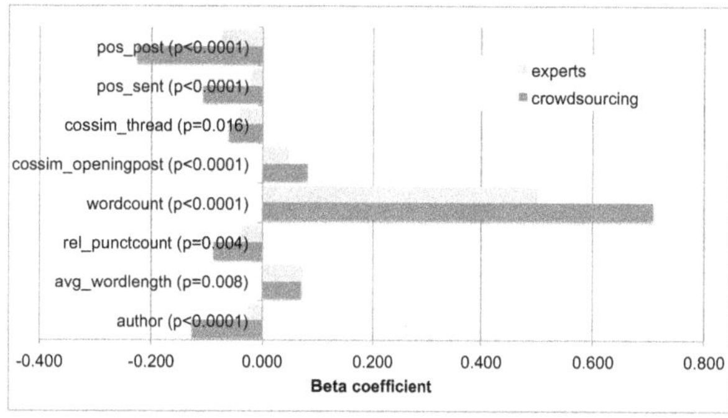

Figure 2: Beta coefficients for sentence features in the LRMs, trained on either the crowdsourced votes or the expert votes. The p-values reported are for the crowdsourced model.

4.1 Characteristics of selected sentences

Using the linear regression model (LRM, see Section 3.4) we studied the relation between the sentence features from Table 1 (used as independent variables in the LRM) and the number of times a sentence was selected by the raters (used as dependent variable in the LRM). In the model trained on the crowdsourced data, all features are significant predictors ($p < 0.05$) except for the type-token ratio. In the expert data, the position of the sentence, the relative punctuation count and the author prominence are not significant either. This is most likely caused by the smaller dataset: 50 threads instead of 100.

Figure 2 shows a direct comparison of the two LRMs in terms of the trained β coefficients for the variables in the two models, indicating the feature weights. The figure shows that the coefficients are similar between the models trained on the expert data and the crowdsourced data: in both models, word count (the number of words in the sentence) is the most important sentence characteristic: longer sentences are selected more often than shorter sentences. The position of the post and the position of the sentence have a negative coefficient, which means that posts in the beginning of the thread and sentences in the beginning of the post are more often selected than posts and sentences further down the thread and the post.

We performed a first evaluation of both models by calculating the correlation (Kendall's τ) between the actual number of votes for a post and the number of votes predicted by either of the models in a cross-data setting: we evaluated the expert model on the crowdsourced data and the crowdsourced model on the expert data. The expert model performs a bit better on the crowdsourced data than vice versa: $\tau = 0.304$ for the expert model while $\tau = 0.234$ for the crowdsourced model (both with $p < 0.0001$). As a comparison, the correlations for random models (randomly assigned vote predictions to sentences) are almost 0 and not significant: $\tau = 0.00139, p = 0.94$ for the expert data and $\tau = -0.00428, p = 0.80$ for the crowdsourced data.

5. CONCLUSION

We found that for the task of selecting relevant sentences in patient forum threads, the inter-rater agreement in crowdsourced data is low, close to random ($\kappa = 0.081$). Domain experts achieve a considerably higher, fair, agreement

($\kappa = 0.267$). None of the rater pairs in the crowdsourced data that have at least five threads in common reach the agreement level of the experts (RQ1). The difference in agreement is not related to time spent on the task or the number of threads summarized by an individual rater.

We trained linear regression models using the two types of reference summaries and a set of sentence features. The models appear to be similar: the characteristics of sentences selected by experts and by crowdsourced raters to be part of the summary are the same: longer sentences are selected more often than shorter sentences and sentences at the beginning of a post and thread are selected more often than sentences later in the post and thread (RQ2).

We conclude that it is possible to train an extractive summarization model on crowdsourced data that is similar to an expert model, even if the inter-rater agreement for the crowdsourced data is low. We speculate that the reasons are: (a) even if two individual raters disagree on the selection of sentences, with five raters per thread the majority opinion is still valuable; (b) the sentence features that we used are generic and robust against noisy selection behavior; (c) the crowdsourced data is bigger than the expert data, which makes it more informative when training the regression model.

One limitation of this work is the low-level nature of the sentence features: we did not include the semantics of the sentences in the model; in future work we will explore more elaborated sentence models. In terms of correlation between the model's predictions and the actual number of votes, the expert model performs a bit better on the crowdsourced data ($\tau = 0.304$) than the crowdsourced model on the expert data ($\tau = 0.234$). In future work, we plan to evaluate the summarization models by running them on unseen forum threads and then showing them to human judges in a blind side-by-side comparison.

With the current data set, we can train robust extractive summarization models by combining the expert and crowdsourced data. This way, we have the reliability of the expert data combined with the size of the crowdsourced data.

Acknowledgments

This work was carried out in the context of the project Discussion Thread Summarization for Mobile Devices (DISCOSUMO), which is financed by the Netherlands Organisation for Scientific Research (NWO), and the project Patient Forum Miner, which was financed by the SIDN Fund. We thank the volunteers of GIST support international for creating the expert reference summaries.

6. REFERENCES

[1] S. Bhatia, P. Biyani, and P. Mitra. Summarizing online forum discussions–can dialog acts of individual messages help? In *Proceedings of the 2014 Conference on Empirical Methods in Natural Language Processing (EMNLP)*, pages 2127–2131. Association for Computational Linguistics, 2014.

[2] P. Clough, M. Sanderson, J. Tang, T. Gollins, and A. Warner. Examining the limits of crowdsourcing for relevance assessment. *IEEE Internet Computing*, 17(4):32–38, 2013.

[3] G. Giannakopoulos, J. Kubina, F. Meade, J. M. Conroy, M. Bowie, J. Steinberger, B. Favre, M. Kabadjov, U. Kruschwitz, and M. Poesio. Multiling 2015: Multilingual summarization of single and multi-documents, on-line fora, and call-center conversations. In *16th Annual Meeting of the Special Interest Group on Discourse and Dialogue*, page 270, 2015.

[4] P. S. Gill and B. Whisnant. A qualitative assessment of an online support community for ovarian cancer patients. *Patient related outcome measures*, 3:51, 2012.

[5] U. Hahn and I. Mani. The challenges of automatic summarization. *Computer*, 33(11):29–36, 2000.

[6] P.-Y. Hsueh, P. Melville, and V. Sindhwani. Data quality from crowdsourcing: a study of annotation selection criteria. In *Proceedings of the NAACL HLT 2009 workshop on active learning for natural language processing*, pages 27–35. Association for Computational Linguistics, 2009.

[7] F. Liu and Y. Liu. Correlation between rouge and human evaluation of extractive meeting summaries. In *Proceedings of the 46th Annual Meeting of the Association for Computational Linguistics on Human Language Technologies: Short Papers*, pages 201–204. Association for Computational Linguistics, 2008.

[8] C. Llewellyn, C. Grover, and J. Oberlander. Summarizing newspaper comments. In *Proceedings of the Eighth International AAAI Conference on Weblogs and Social Media*, pages 599–602, 2014.

[9] M. Marge, S. Banerjee, and A. I. Rudnicky. Using the amazon mechanical turk to transcribe and annotate meeting speech for extractive summarization. In *Proceedings of the NAACL HLT 2010 Workshop on Creating Speech and Language Data with Amazon's Mechanical Turk*, pages 99–107. Association for Computational Linguistics, 2010.

[10] M. Mitray, A. Singhalz, and C. Buckleyyy. Automatic text summarization by paragraph extraction. *Compare*, 22215(22215):26, 1997.

[11] J. L. Neto, A. A. Freitas, and C. A. Kaestner. Automatic text summarization using a machine learning approach. In *Advances in Artificial Intelligence*, pages 205–215. Springer, 2002.

[12] G. Penn and X. Zhu. A critical reassessment of evaluation baselines for speech summarization. In *ACL*, pages 470–478, 2008.

[13] D. R. Radev, S. Teufel, H. Saggion, W. Lam, J. Blitzer, H. Qi, A. Celebi, D. Liu, and E. Drabek. Evaluation challenges in large-scale document summarization. In *Proceedings of the 41st Annual Meeting on Association for Computational Linguistics-Volume 1*, pages 375–382. Association for Computational Linguistics, 2003.

[14] A. S. Tigelaar, R. op den Akker, and D. Hiemstra. Automatic summarisation of discussion fora. *Natural Language Engineering*, 16(02):161–192, 2010.

Accidentally Successful Searching: Users' Perceptions of a Digital Library

Sanna Kumpulainen
Tampere University of Technology
Tampere, Finland
sanna.kumpulainen@tut.fi

Heli Kautonen
Aalto University, School of Science
Helsinki, Finland
heli.kautonen@gmail.com

ABSTRACT

People usually search information by using queries that are targeted to match the wording of the documents in the collections. However, during their search processes they may discover some useful pieces of information they did not expect. Serendipitous searching occurs when people search for information, but during their search process discover unexpected results. One key aspect of serendipity is chance encountering, which means the accidental and unexpected encountering with useful information. In this paper we address to the chance encounters, search success and search interests of information seekers using a national digital library called Finna. This study shows that chance encountering and search success increase with user satisfaction and that digital libraries can support information encountering.

1. INTRODUCTION

Serendipity means making happy and unexpected findings by accident [10]. In the present study, we focus on to what extent the evaluated search service is providing the happy accidents or coincidents called *chance encounters.* We study the chance encounters, user satisfaction and search intents based on a large survey of Finna users.

Finna is a Finnish national digital library search tool providing one access point to the heterogeneous materials of several libraries, archives, and museums in Finland (https://finna.fi/). Finna's potential user base is very wide. Due to its heterogeneous content and wide user base, it is not certain how the service can fulfil the needs of users. This paper aims at fulfilling part of this gap by reporting findings from Finna user survey on the users' perceptions on chance encountering. In this research, we seek to answer the question: *Does Finna support chance encountering?*

We study user patterns, searching in terms of search intents and success, and the chance encounters across the user groups.

2. CHANCE ENCOUNTERS

People may find information even when they are not deliberately seeking any. Serendipitous information discovery comprises two aspects. Firstly, the unknown and unpredictable element that is encountering with some unexpected information. We call accidental information encountering *Chance encounters*.

CHIIR '17, March 07 - 11, 2017, Oslo, Norway

ACM 978-1-4503-4677-1/17/03…$15.00
DOI: http://dx.doi.org/10.1145/3020165.3022124.

Second aspect is the synthetizing of the unexpected information into the existing knowledge structure [2]. In order to fully exploit the happy coincidents during searching, some kind of insight or connections to existing knowledge should be made [8]. However, one may argue that information encountering with search tools does not occur solely by accident, because searching is already taking place and the person is directing the activities towards the finding. Nevertheless, the idea that people encounter something that was unexpected during searching still exists. According to Bawden [3] a prepared mind is favoring serendipitous discovery, and that this precondition helps to perceive the connections due to the exposure to chance encounters.

We focus on the first aspect on serendipitous searching, namely on the respondents' perceptions on the chance encounters. This is understood as a precondition for serendipitous discovery.

3. FINNA

The present study focuses on the user perceptions of the Finna interface. The Finna search interface provides one access point to the heterogeneous materials of several archives, libraries, and museums in Finland. The project for building Finna has been going on for over six years, and the service was first launched to the public in October 2013. The complexity of Finna service is derived both from the wide user base and from the differing cataloguing practices of participating organizations. Furthermore, information needs of different user groups should also be considered, because they may radically vary [1].

Finna user groups has been studied previously by Kautonen [6] and in an in-depth study by Kautonen [5] on one artist's information journey with Finna. It revealed that serendipity played a big role in her work and that Finna offered gaming-like experience that contributed substantially to her work. This study adds to these by studying the perceived change encounters of all user groups.

4. THE SURVEY

The data were collected via an online questionnaire during four weeks in October and December 2014 for the first national Finna user study. The survey was targeted to the users of all Finna's interfaces, i.e., the national Finna.fi and individual organizations' views. The questionnaire module was embedded on the software platform so that it appeared automatically on every interface's view as a pop-up window. Users were given an option to close the pop-up window or to continue with the questionnaire.

National Digital Library Usability Group designed the survey. This group consisted of representatives from organizations who had joined or planned joining Finna. The National Library of Finland coordinated the work, and built the online questionnaire, and collected the data. The participating organizations promoted the questionnaire.

The answers to the questionnaire were collected mostly by multiple choices but there were some open questions that allowed the respondents freely to reflect their opinions. We selected questions from the sections 1., 2. and 4. (See Figure 1.)

Using Finna
- *Why are you using Finna?*
  - I'm searching for certain material
  - I'm searching for information on an interesting topic
  - Just browsing
  - Other reason
- *For what purpose are you searching for information/material?*
  - Work
  - School assignment
  - Studies
  - Hobbies of leisure
  - Something else
  - I'm not searching for particular information/material
- *Did you find what you were looking for?*
  - Yes / No / I wasn't searching for particular information/material
- *Did you find anything else of interest?*
  - Yes /No

Evaluating Finna (1 fully disagree-5 fully agree)
- *Finna is easy to use*
- *Finna is useful*
- *I'm able to find what I'm looking for in Finna*
- *Using Finna saves time*
- *It is enjoyable to use Finna*

Background information
- *How often do you use Finna?*
  - Daily
  - At least once a week
  - A few times a month
  - About once a month
  - Less than once a month
  - I'm using it for the first time
- *Which group do you belong to?*
  - Pupil
  - Student
  - Employee
  - Stay-at-home mother/father
  - Pensioner
  - Other

Figure 1. Selected questions.

5. METHODS

We used Chi Square for testing the statistical significance, because of the non-normal distributions of the data. Nonparametric Spearman's rank correlation coefficient was used to measure the strength of association between the indicators in the User satisfaction variable.

5.1 Variables

The key variables are described briefly below.

Frequency of use is based on the question *How often do you use Finna?* The options *Less than once in a month* and *About once in a month* were collapsed.

Task type variable was created from the question: *For what purpose are you searching for information/material?* Options *School assignment* and *Study* were collapsed into the *Study* category. Also, the options *Something else* and *I'm not searching for particular information/material* were collapsed into the *Other* category.

User satisfaction is a composite variable created by combining the five indicators in the section *Evaluating Finna.* Spearman's rank correlation coefficient shows, that all the indicators of user satisfaction correlate moderately (Table 1). This indicates that the indicators measure the same behavior, and thus support the creation of the composite variable. The values for the composite variable *User satisfaction* were recoded as *Low or Very low*, *Neutral*, *High*, and *Very high.*

Search intent is based on the question: *Why are you using Finna?* Provided options were: *I'm searching for certain material*; *I'm searching for information on an interesting topic; Just browsing*; and, *Other reason*. These were recoded as *Known Item; Topical; Exploratory*; and, *Other*, respectively.

Search success is created from question: *Did you find what you were looking for in Finna?* with the options *Yes, No,* and, *I wasn't searching for particular information/material.* This last option was encoded as *Non-specific.*

Chance encounter is based on question: *Did you find anything else of interest?* Options were *Yes* or *No.* The idea is that they found something else that they were not purposefully seeking for.

User groups were created from the options in question *Which group do you belong to?* We created three groups 1. *Student*; 3. *Employee*; and 3. *Other*. The first group *Student* comprises *Pupil* and *Student* categories from the original options, and similarly, *Stay-at-home mother/father, Pensioner* and *Other* were collapsed into one category *Other.*

6. RESULTS

6.1 Respondents and use patterns

The respondents were all the users of Finna (N=3229). Since the Finna is open to everyone and contains heterogeneous material the potential user population is wide. We used complete-case analysis resulting in a sample size of N=3037.

The size of the user groups varied. *Student* is the largest group (60.7%, n=1842) and is twice as large as the *Employee* group. *Employee* group (32.1%, n=974) consists of researchers, librarian, archivists, journalists and other kinds of knowledge-workers. Smallest group *Other* included e.g. pensioner (7.3%, 221). *Students* visit Finna most often, *Employees* and *Others* groups less (χ^2=(8, N=3037)=339.16, p<.000). 15.4% of all users used Finna for the first time, mostly it was used weekly.

The distributions of task type follow the expected task types of user groups (χ^2=(6, N=3037)=2041.09, p<.000). *Students* use Finna mostly for study purposes (93.2%), *Employees* for working (48.8%) and *Others* (45.2%) for leisure activities. However, *Employees* and *Others* show more varied tasks by reporting that they are using Finna for *Study* tasks with the shares of 19.3% and 17.6%, respectively. Furthermore, while the *Students* use the Finna almost only to study purposes, 22.1% of *Employee* group reported using the tool also for leisure tasks.

6.2 Search success and intents

The overall Search success with Finna was very high. Of all respondents, 76.9% (n=2335) stated that they found what they were searching for. Only 9.7% (n=295) were unsuccessful, and 13.3% were not able to assess whether they were successful or not.

The distribution of all *Search intents* was uneven. Most of the *Search intents* were *Known item* searches (64.4%). The share of *Topical* searches was 16.6% and of *Exploratory* 11.5% of all *Search intents*.

Search success and *Search intents* were also analyzed across the user groups. *Students* were very successful in their searches (χ^2=(4, N=3037)=47.23, p<.000). Most of them reported that they found what they were searching for. The share of successful searches ranged across the groups from group *Other* with 69% success rate to *Students* with 81%. Of all respondents 10% reported that their searches were unsuccessful and 13% were not able to assess success due to the exploratory nature of their searching.

We studied the distribution of *Search intents* across the user groups. Respondents used Finna mainly for *Known item* searches (64%) (χ^2=(6, N=3037)=124.32, p<.000). This was the most common search intent type across all user groups whereas the proportion of topical search intentions ranged from 21.3% (in group *Other)* to 19.6% (group *Employee*). The share of non-directed *Exploratory* search intents ranged from 8.7% *(Students)* to 11.3% (*Employees*). In the group *Other*, there was as many *Topical* as *Exploratory* intents.

Also, we examined the *Search success* across *Search intent* types to find out if some of the *Search intent* types was more successful than the others. Of *Topical* search intents 77.2% (n=389) were successful, whereas *Exploratory* searches were successful only in 35.1% of the searches (n=122) (χ^2=(6, N=3037)= 1055.52, p<.000). The most successful search intent type was *Known item* with success level of 87.8% (n=1663). However, of the *Exploratory* searches, 60.6% (n=211) reported *Non-specific* success, which means that they were not able to assess whether their searching was successful of not. The *Known item* type is closed ended. This means that searcher is able to find a "correct answer" to intents of this kind, but exploration is vaguer, and it is more difficult to assess if the goals of the searching have been reached.

6.3 User satisfaction

User satisfaction is a composite variable created from five separate indicators. Spearman's rank correlation coefficient shows, that all the aspects of user satisfaction (*Ease of Use, Usefulness, Findability, Saving Time, Pleasantness*) correlate moderately. The correlations are shown in Table 1. The correlations indicate that all the aspects measure similar phenomenon, and support combining the aspects into one. *User satisfaction* was analyzed across the *Frequency of use* categories and across the user groups. Firstly, *User satisfaction* was assessed *High* across all *Frequency of use* categories (χ2=(12, N=3037)=111.23, p<.000) and secondly, in all user groups (χ2=(6, N=3037)=23.67, p=.001). Only 3.3% of all users evaluated *User satisfaction Low or very low*, whereas 20.4% evaluated it *Very high* and 19.2% *Neutral*.

Next, we studied how *Search success* varies across *User satisfaction* levels. The share of *Search success* increases significantly with the *User satisfaction*. (χ2=(6, N=3037)=322.121, p<.000). In the cases when *User satisfaction* was assessed low, the proportion of *Search success* was less than half (48.5%), whereas when *User satisfaction* was assessed as *Very High*, the majority of searches was successful (89.7%).

Table 1. Spearman's rank correlation coefficients of the *User satisfaction* indicators.

	Ease Of Use	Usefulness	Findability	Saving Time
Usefulness	.512**			
Findability	.542**	.501**		
Saving Time	.545**	.539**	.555**	
Pleasantness	.680**	.500**	.541**	.688**

** p< .01 (two-tailed)

6.4 Chance encounters

We studied the share of *Chance encounters* across the user groups, *Search success*, *Search intents*, *Task types* and *User satisfaction* levels. Chance encounters were reported by 64.2% (n=1943) of all respondents.

Firstly, we examined the shares across the user groups. The share of *Chance encounters* was 73.3% in the *Employee* group. In the group *Other* up to 76% reported chance encountering, whereas among the *Students* the share was only 57.7% (χ^2=(2, N=3037)=81.83, p<.000).

Secondly, *Chance encounters* were studied across *Search success* categories. The highest proportion of chance encountering (67.7%) occurs in the *Non-specific* search success category (χ^2=(2, N=3037)=8.276, p=0.016). These seem to be the searchers who did not have a well formed, focused search tasks and therefore could not assess the success. Interestingly, unsuccessful searchers reported change encountering (57.2%). These searchers failed to reach their original goal, but nevertheless found something else useful in Finna.

Figure 2 shows the accounts of *Chance encounters* across *Search intents*. Of *Topical* intents, 78% account for chance encounters, and of *Exploratory* searching 72.4%. The k*nown item* and the *Other* intents have slightly smaller shares.

The distribution of chance encounters varies across the motivating tasks. In *Leisure* tasks the share of chance encounters was 20.4% higher and in *Work* tasks the share was 15.6% higher than in *Study* tasks, in which the share was 58.2% (χ^2=(3, N=3037)=85.67, p<.000). If drilling into the positive accounts of Chance encounters (n=1943), the distribution across task types shows that over a half of them (58.2%) occur in *Study* task type.

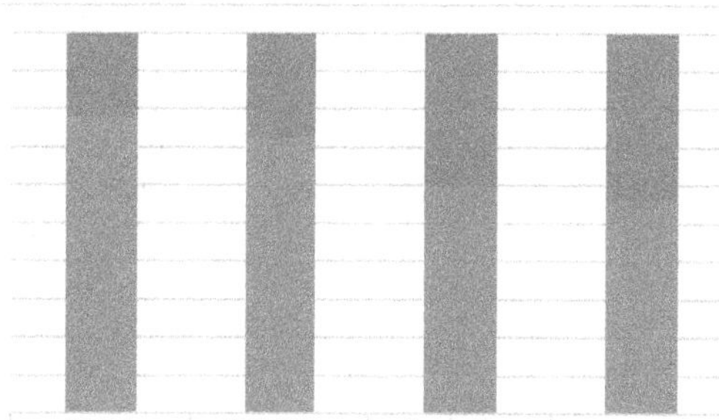

	Topical (n=504)	Exploratory (n=348)	Known item (n=1894)	Other (n=291)
Negative	22.0	27.6	40.1	44.0
Positive	78.0	72.4	59.9	56.0

Figure 2. Chance encounters across Search intents (n=3037; %).

Lastly, we analyzed how the *Chance encounter* is distributed across the varying levels of *User satisfaction*. The proportion of the positive accounts of change encounters increases with the user satisfaction level (see Figure 3.) (χ^2=(4, N=3037)=94.627, p<.000). The share of the positive accounts of chance encounters ranges from 40.6% on the *Low/Very Low* level of the *User satisfaction,* to 73.3% on the *Very high* level. It seems that the chance encountering affects the positive opinions about Finna.

	Low or Very low (n=101)	Neutral (n=584)	High (n=1733)	Very high (n=617)
Negative	59.4	49.0	33.6	26.7
Positive	40.6	51.0	66.4	73.3

Figure 3. Chance encounters across User satisfaction levels. (n=3037; %).

7. DISCUSSION

The study indicates that Finna supports chance encountering by exposing searchers to heterogeneous materials in a digital library. This survey gives a very positive view of the evaluated Finna interface.

Students were the most frequent users of Finna. Almost half of them used it weekly. This huge proportion of frequent users is caused by some university libraries offering a tailored Finna interface to their customers. Students searched Finna almost solely to study purposes. Employees used it for work and for leisure and study activities. Pensioners and others used it mostly for leisure but also for other purposes. This "other" includes also the familiarizing oneself with the service.

All user groups searched mostly for known items. This indicates more OPAC use [7]. The share of known-item searches is in line with earlier findings, that the share of known-item searches is between 33 and 67 percentages [10].

Searchers were mostly successful with their searches. However, in exploratory tasks the success rate was lower. This is due that the searchers were not able to assess the success of the underlying task because their mental model of the task and its goals may be unclear [4, 9]. The known-item searches, which were the most common type, were assessed successful. It is easier to know whether the goal was reached or not in these kinds of close ended tasks. However, this indicates, that at least for the exploratory searching, searchers would benefit from support in conceptual exploration [9].

Chance encounters occurred mostly in exploratory and topical tasks. Searching in exploratory mode is more open minded, cf. [8], and maybe they were aiming to build an understanding about the underlying task [9].

7.1 Limitations

As a web questionnaire suffering from the typical deficiencies related to them we are not sure to what extent the results are generalizable. The population is undefined and the sample may be biased towards a self-selective sample and student population and we do not know the level of non-response. Also, surveys give a flat reflection of the real world. However, despite all the limitations, we believe that the perceptions and opinions of this large group cannot be studied economically otherwise. We selected a web questionnaire by its economic and accessibility reasons.

Surveys and questionnaire studies do not fully reflect the underlying motivations of the searchers. An open-ended question would designate the specific information that was serendipitously discovered. The functionalities of the service that prompt the serendipitous discovery are a possible topic for future research.

8. CONCLUSION

We analyzed a large user survey with over 3000 respondents on their perceptions of a Finnish national digital library Finna. We studied the user patterns, searching and user satisfaction, and to what extent Finna supports chance encountering finding. The service was frequently used and the searches were successful. Both the level chance encountering and search success seemed to increase with user satisfaction rates. Further, this study shows that Finna – and similar digital libraries providing heterogeneous material – can support chance encountering.

9. REFERENCES

[1] Albers, M., & Still, B. (2010). Usability of complex information systems: Evaluation of user interaction. CRC press.

[2] André, P., schraefel, m. c., Teevan, J., & Dumais, S. T. (2009). Discovery is never by chance: Designing for (un) serendipity. In: Proceedings of the Seventh ACM Conference on Creativity and Cognition, 305-314.

[3] Bawden, D. (1986). Information systems and the stimulation of creativity. Journal of Information Science, 12(5), 203-216.

[4] Ingwersen, P., & Järvelin, K. (2005). The turn: Integration of information seeking and retrieval in context. Secaucus, NJ, USA: Springer-Verlag New York, Inc.

[5] Kautonen, H. (2014). Evaluating digital library's service concept and pre-launch implementation. In: Proceedings of AFHE, 111-122.

[6] Kautonen, H. (2015). Playing Dice with a Digital Library: Analysis of an Artist Using a New Information Resource for Her Art Production. In Proceedings of 17th HCI International 2015, Part III., 430-440.

[7] Larson, R. R. (1991). The decline of subject searching: Long-term trends and patterns of index use in an online catalog. Journal of the American Society for Information Science, 42(3), 197-215.

[8] Makri, S., & Blandford, A. (2012). Coming across information serendipitously - part 1: A process model. Journal of Documentation, 68(5), 684-705. doi:10.1108/00220411211256030

[9] Vakkari, P. (2010). Exploratory searching as conceptual exploration. In: Proceedings of HCIR, 24-27.

[10] Wildemuth, B. M., & ONeill, A. L. (1995). The known in known-item searches - empirical support for user-centered design. College & Research Libraries, 56(3), 265-281.

User Click Detection in Ideal Sessions

Mustafa Zengin
Department of Computer and Information Sciences
University of Delaware
Delaware, USA
zengin@udel.edu

Ben Carterette
Department of Computer and Information Sciences
University of Delaware
Delaware, USA
carteret@udel.edu

ABSTRACT

Users interact with search engine result pages in various ways, including their clicks, cursor movements, and page scrolls. Researchers model such user interaction behavior in order to understand users and improve search result presentation. In this paper we propose nine different user click models that take various real life search behavior into account. Our main assumption is that users base their clicks primarily on features of document titles, URLs, and snippets over the entire results page, as well as the queries submitted to the search engine and the documents seen previously in their session history. We evaluate our click models by their effectiveness at predicting actual user clicks using standard classification evaluation measures precision, recall, and area under the ROC curve (AUC). We show that incorporating information about the entire results page gives nearly 40% improvement in precision, and including information about the session history along with it increases precision by up to 43%.

1. INTRODUCTION

User click models have been used widely in information retrieval as a way to improve document ranking (e.g., by inferring document relevance from clicks predicted by a click model), to improve evaluation metrics (e.g., model-based metrics) and to better understand users by inspecting the parameters of click models [6].

Craswell et al. [1] introduced the *cascade model*, the first click model based on position bias, or the fact that the probability of click is influenced by a document's position in the results page. Dupret and Piwowarski [2] introduced the user browsing model (UBM) which makes certain assumptions on users' browsing behavior to estimate the probability a document is seen (or clicked). Chapelle and Zhang [3] introduced the dynamic Bayesian network click model (DBN) for web search ranking by tackling position bias. These studies only made predictions on a single click in the results page; Guo [4] presented the multiple click model which attempts to predict more than one click at a time. Several other methods have been presented based on these methods.

Our approach to this problem is different than these works. Like the first three, we predict a single user click on a snippet. We consider three different main settings: (1) only considering a snippet by itself; (2) considering all snippets on a results page along with the snippet that we make click prediction; and (3) considering the users' session history. The approach is similar to the approach of Carterette et al. [5] in terms of using all snippets on a result page, however in this work we utilize user sessions so that users' cumulated search knowledge up to a certain interaction plays a role on click prediction.

CHIIR '17, March 07-11, 2017, Oslo, Norway

DOI: http://dx.doi.org/10.1145/3020165.3022128

Table 1: Corpus statistics

# sessions	1253
# average number of interactions per session	3.16
# average number of clicks per interaction	0.514
# average number of clicks per session	1.624
# snippets	39570

2. DATA

We use the 2013 and 2014 TREC Session track data for training and testing our models. The TREC Session track data is a large amount of user interaction data which consists of full user search sessions on pre-defined topical information needs. In the context of the track, "session" means a sequence of query reformulations, retrieved results, and user interactions with those results in service of satisfying a specific topical information need [7]. Table 1 summarizes some basic statistics of the data.

3. METHODS

Our main assumption for a proposed click prediction model is that users base their clicks primarily on features of document titles, URLs, and snippets on the current search result page, the queries submitted to the search engine in the history of the users' current session, and the snippets they have seen during the course of their session. Additionally, knowing that other users have seen and/or clicked on the same snippets in their own sessions may influence whether a user clicks on a document in their own session.

Our features are derived from those that have been used in LETOR [10] and other datasets [11] [12] for learning to rank: in particular, retrieval model scores between query and document URL/title/snippet; statistics about query term frequencies (normalized and non-normalized) in document URL/

title/snippet; URL length and depth; number of inlinks and outlinks; spam score as computed by Waterloo's model for web spam [8]; and the Alexa ranking for the domain are all features that are either directly in LETOR data or are similar to other LETOR features that we cannot compute in our own data. Most of the textual features can be computed using our Indri index of ClueWeb12; our index also stores spam scores and inlink counts. The Alexa ranking is available through Alexa's API.

One of the contributions of this work is the extension of many of those features to the *session* context. Since sessions can have varying length, and therefore varying numbers of snippets seen during the course of the session, it is not necessarily straightforward to include features for previously-seen documents (as it is to include features for other documents appear in the same results page). Furthermore, the length of time passed between seeing two snippets may affect the likelihood of a user click as well.

To include features of the session history, we compute all of the textual query-document features listed above for every snippet ranked for every query in the session. We then take the maximum value of the feature over the session history to be included in the model.

Other session-based features such as number of times the snippet has been seen prior to current result page, the distance between the current result page and the result page on which the snippet was most recently clicked, the distance between the current result page and the result page on which the snippet most recently appeared, and the number of times the snippet was clicked in the current session were also calculated. If the snippet has never appeared in any prior interactions, the distance for both click and appearance distances is set to zero.

Finally, we also calculated the number of appearances of and clicks on the target snippet in different sessions on the same topical information need. This information is readily available in the TREC data, though it is not as easily computed in real query logs.

3.1 Models

We test nine different models that offer refinements using incrementally-sized feature sets, laid out in a 3×3 table (Table 5). These models build on each other in two directions: first, using more and more features of a single search result page; second, using more and more features of the session and of other users' activity in similar sessions. For example, M1 only uses features of the snippet for which we are trying to make a prediction—specifically, features in Table 2. M4 builds on that by using features of the target snippet, but also including the same features for the other nine snippets ranked alongside it, while M2 builds on M1 by adding features of the session history, specifically features in Table 3. M7 builds on M4 by including as a feature the same user's click decision on each of the other nine snippets, while M3 builds on M2 by including features of other users' activity in other sessions on the same topic—those in Table 4.

For each of the nine models, we will train a machine-learned model using 0/1 click decisions as the label and a feature vector consisting of one or more of the following feature sets:

1. target result URL/title/snippet. See Table 2 for complete list of features. This set appears in all nine models.

Table 2: List of features. Q stands for query. tf stands for term frequency, sl stands for stream length, T stands for title, SN stands for snippet, WD stands for web document, SE stands for search engine. Q-(Field) stands for the feature is calculated by using the query and the field.

Feature	Notes
covered query term number	Q-(URL,T,SN)
covered query term ratio	Q-(URL,T,SN)
stream length of the field	URL,T,SN
sum of tf of the field	Q-(URL,T,SN)
min of tf of the field	Q-(URL,T,SN)
max of tf of the field	Q-(URL,T,SN)
mean of tf of the field	Q-(URL,T,SN)
variance of tf of the field	Q-(URL,T,SN)
sum of sl normalized tf	Q-(URL,T,SN)
min of sl normalized tf	Q-(URL,T,SN)
max of sl normalized tf	Q-(URL,T,SN)
mean of sl normalized tf	Q-(URL,T,SN)
variance of sl normalized tf	Q-(URL,T,SN)
sum of tf*idf	Q-(URL,T,SN)
min of tf*idf	Q-(URL,T,SN)
max of tf*idf	Q-(URL,T,SN)
mean of tf*idf	Q-(URL,T,SN)
variance of tf*idf	Q-(URL,T,SN)
boolean model	Q-(URL,T,SN)
vector space model	Q-(URL,T,SN)
bm25(okapi) score	Q-SN
LM with Dirichlet smoothing	Q-(URL,T,SN)
LM with Jelinek-Mercer smoothing	Q-(URL,T,SN)
LM with two-stage smoothing	Q-(URL,T,SN)
number of slashes in URL	URL
length of URL	URL
Waterloo spam score	WD
number of inlinks to the web page	WD
alexa ranking of web page	WD
rank of snippet in SERP	SE

Table 3: List of session related features.

Feature	Notes
number of times snippet appears in previous interactions	Session
distance of current interaction to previous interaction that the snippet appeared	Session
number of clicks on the snippet in current session	Session
distance of snippet to its previous click in previous interactions	Session
maximum score of each query dependent feature across previously submitted query in session. For query dependent features check table 2	Session

Table 4: List of features that are retrieved from other user sessions.

Feature	Notes
session appearance count	Other sessions
session click count	Other sessions
same query/different session appearance count	Other sessions
same query/different session click count	Other sessions

Table 5: Nine different click models derived from combining feature sets from two different groups: the search results page and the session history.

ranking features \ session features	none	session history	history + clicks across sessions
target snippet	M1	M2	M3
target snippet + all others	M4	M5	M6
target snippet + all others + clicks	M7	M8	M9

2. other results' URLs/titles/snippets from the same result page (for the fourth to ninth models)

3. other clicks by the same user on other results in the same result page (seventh, eighth and ninth models)

4. historical results' (from earlier in the session) URLs/titles/snippets calculated for corresponding historical queries, along with other information related to previously seen results (for the second, third, fifth, sixth, eight, and ninth models). See Table 3 for complete list of features.

5. User clicks across all topically-related sessions (third, sixth, ninth models). See Table 4 for complete list of features.

4. EXPERIMENTS

We evaluate our click detection models by their effectiveness at predicting actual user clicks, using standard classification evaluation measures like precision, recall, and AUC.

We trained and tested random forest models using all sessions from the TREC 2013 and 2014 Session track. For each ranked result that appears in the Session track data, we have one instance for training/testing: the 0/1 label indicating whether there was a click on that result or not, the features derived from that result, and, depending on the model, other results ranked with it, other results from the session history, or other features of the session. In total there are 39,570 instances in the data, of which 37,535 are no-clicks and 2,035 are clicks. Since the class distribution is so skewed, we rebalanced the training data with SMOTE, which creates artificial data for the under-represented class[9]. We trained and tested using four-fold cross-validation and report micro-averaged evaluation measures aggregated across all four testing splits. Note that only training data, not testing data, in each fold is rebalanced with SMOTE.

Table 6 and Figure 1 summarize performance of the nine models. Table 6 is organized in a way that moving from left to right or top to bottom adds new features to a model, from the current results page or the session, respectively. The top left cell is the baseline. Moving to the right, just adding session related features to the baseline increases AUC by 1.2% and precision by 8.6%, but decreases recall by 5.2%. Using clicks from other sessions along with the session data results in an 6.2% increase in AUC and 24.6% increase in precision, and 4.6% decrease in recall.

Moving down from the top left cell increases precision by 25.1% and AUC by 3.6%. From there, moving right to add session-related features has less influence on the dependence model. Only adding these features increases the precision by 5.5% and AUC by 0.8%, while decreasing recall by 5.4%. Using other click decisions in an interaction has positive influence on all measures.

Finally, moving down to the last row, we see a 2.4% improvement in AUC when we move from M4 to M7. Similar improvements as above are achieved in adding session data to produce the M8 and M9 models. The general tendency of the performances shown on the table demonstrate that moving from top to bottom in models increases AUC and precision, and decreases recall. Moving from left to right mostly increases AUC and precision.

There is clearly benefit in moving in both directions. Result page features alone improve the baseline by up to 39% for precision and 6% for AUC, with a 4% drop in recall. Session features alone can account for up to 25% improvement in precision and 6% in AUC, again with a 4% drop in recall. When both result page features and session features are considered, the improvement over the baseline is 43% for precision and 8% for AUC, though this improvement comes with a 10% drop in recall.

Figure 1 compares the ROC curves for related groups of models. Reading figures from left-to-right/top-to-bottom, we see that adding information about the results page with no session context (going from M1 to M4 to M7) pushes the ROC curve out, and adding that information with session context (M2 to M5 to M8) pushes it out further. When both session context and other sessions are used, the results page does not contribute much to the ROC curve (M3 to M6 to M9).

Similarly, the next figure shows a clear impact from using session history when no information about the results page is used (M1 to M2 to M3). But as more information about the results page is taken into account, the session history seems to provide less impact on the ROC curve (M4 to M5 to M6 and M7 to M8 to M9). Nevertheless, when both are considered together, the gain is clear.

Figure 2 shows mean raw importance of all features for the click class in the independence model that uses session information and clicks across sessions (M3). The top three features in click decisions are the rank of the snippet, the number of clicks on the same snippet in across sessions, and the URL's spam score. Note that session-related features (colored red and yellow) plays a major role in click decisions: the most important session history feature is maximum LM/Jelinek-Mercer score of the URL field, ranked 31st out of 152 features. These features have an overall mean importance of 9.3, compared to 11.8 for query-URL features and 11.6 for query-title features.

5. CONCLUSIONS

We have presented nine different user click models based on increasing information about the overall results page and the session history. We found that a dependency model which uses features of all snippets in a results page is a better click model over one that uses only features of a target document, and furthermore that using features of the session history and of other sessions on the same topic uniformly improve precision and AUC. Still, our predictions frequently do not match reality; we intend to perform a user

Table 6: Precision/recall/AUC of our nine models

ranking features \ session features	none	session history	history + clicks across sessions
target snippet	0.175/0.408/0.753	0.190/0.388/0.762	0.218/0.390/0.800
target snippet + all others	0.219/0.391/0.780	0.231/0.371/0.786	0.249/0.379/0.798
target snippet + all others + clicks	0.243/0.390/0.799	0.252/0.362/0.797	0.251/0.369/0.811

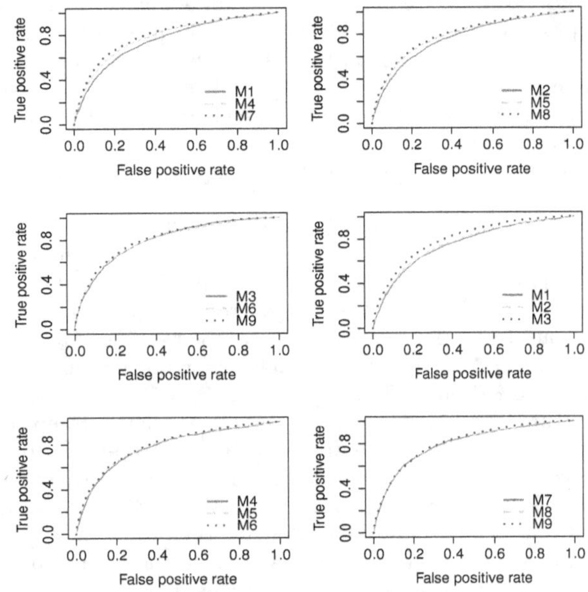

Figure 1: ROC curves for different click detection methods

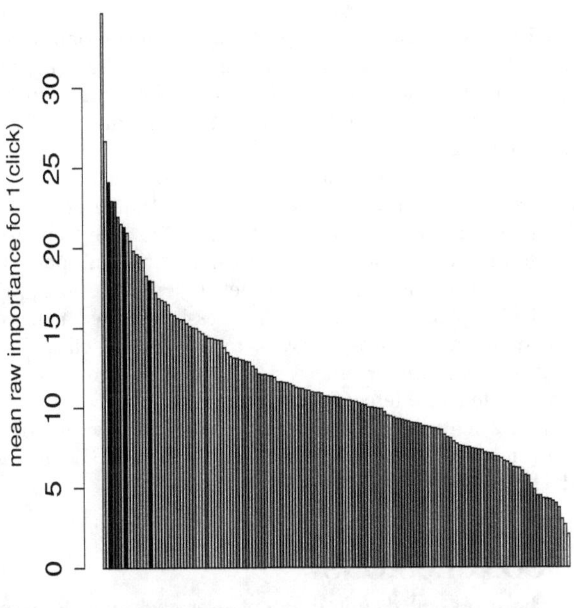

Figure 2: Features ranked by mean raw importance for the positive class for M3. Yellow represents other session related features, green represents query-URL related features, grey represents query-snippet related features, black represents document related features, blue represents URL related features, red represents session related features, purple represents snippet related features, pink represents query-title related features, salmon represents title related features and orange represents search engine related features.

study to further evaluate our predicted clicks in greater detail.

6. REFERENCES

[1] Craswell, N., Zoeter, O., Taylor, M., Ramsey, B. An Experimental Comparison of Click Position-Bias Models. Proc. WSDM, 2008.

[2] Dupret, D., Murdock, V., and Piwowarski, B., Web Search Engine Evaluation Using Clickthrough Data and a User Model. Proc. WWW, 2007.

[3] Chapelle, O., Zhang, Y., A Dynamic Bayesian Network Click Model for Web Search Ranking. Proc. WWW, 2009.

[4] Guo, F., Liu, C., Wang, Y. M. Efficient multiple-click models in web search. Proc. WSDM, 2007.

[5] Carterette, B., Bah, A., Zengin, M. Dynamic Test Collections for Retrieval Evaluation. Proc. ICTIR, 2015.

[6] Chuklin, A., Markov, I., Rijke, M. D. Click Models for Web Search. Synthesis Lectures on Information Concepts, Retrieval, and Services, 7(3), 1-115, 2015.

[7] B. Carterette, E. Kanoulas, P. D. Clough, and M. Hall. Overview of the TREC 2014 Session track. Proc. TREC, 2014

[8] Cormack, G. V., Smucker, M. D., Clarke, C. L. Efficient and effective spam filtering and re-ranking for large web datasets. Information retrieval, 14(5), 441-465, 2011.

[9] Chawla, N. V., Bowyer, K. W., Hall, L. O., Kegelmeyer, W. P. SMOTE: synthetic minority over-sampling technique. Journal of artificial intelligence research, 321-357, 2002.

[10] Liu, T. Y., Xu, J., Qin, T., Xiong, W., Li, H. (2007, July). Letor: Benchmark dataset for research on learning to rank for information retrieval. In Proceedings of SIGIR 2007 workshop on learning to rank for information retrieval (pp. 3-10).

[11] Chapelle, O., Chang, Y. (2011). Yahoo! Learning to Rank Challenge Overview. In Yahoo! Learning to Rank Challenge (pp. 1-24). Chicago

[12] Serdyukov, P., Dupret, G., Craswell, N. (2013, February). WSCD2013: workshop on web search click data 2013. In Proceedings of the sixth ACM international conference on Web search and data mining (pp. 787-788). ACM.

Personalised Query Suggestion for Intranet Search with Temporal User Profiling

Thanh Vu[1], Alistair Willis[1], Udo Kruschwitz[2], and Dawei Song[1,3]
[1] The Open University, Milton Keynes, United Kingdom
[2] University of Essex, Essex, United Kingdom
[3] Tianjin University, Tianjin, P.R.China
{thanh.vu, alistair.willis, dawei.song}@open.ac.uk, udo@essex.ac.uk

ABSTRACT

Recent research has shown the usefulness of using collective user interaction data (e.g., query logs) to recommend query modification suggestions for Intranet search. However, most of the query suggestion approaches for Intranet search follow an "one size fits all" strategy, whereby different users who submit an identical query would get the same query suggestion list. This is problematic, as even with the same query, different users may have different topics of interest, which may change over time in response to the user's interaction with the system.

In this paper, we address the problem by proposing a personalised query suggestion framework for Intranet search. For each search session, we construct two temporal user profiles: a *click user profile* using the user's clicked documents and a *query user profile* using the user's submitted queries. We then use the two profiles to re-rank the non-personalised query suggestion list returned by a state-of-the-art query suggestion method for Intranet search. Experimental results on a large-scale query logs collection show that our personalised framework significantly improves the quality of suggested queries.

Keywords: Interactive IR; Intranet Search; Personalised Query Suggestion; Temporal User Profiles; Learning to Rank;

1. INTRODUCTION

Query suggestion is an important feature in web search engines (e.g., Bing, Google) as well as in domain-specific search engines (e.g., Intranet search) [1]. Query suggestions help users quickly refine the input query to better meet the user's information need by recommending possible terms to modify the original input query.

In this paper, we focus on query suggestion for Intranet search, which is different from web search [6]. Specifically, Intranet search (e.g., university intranets) is *domain-specific* and built to satisfy the user's information need related to a specific domain (e.g., the university's document corpus). Moreover, the Intranet may not be fully indexed and accessible by web search engines. For example, web search engines cannot access and index those Intranet documents which require authorised logins. The searcher, therefore, may need to use an Intranet search engine to locate relevant documents.

Using collective user interaction data (e.g., query logs) for query suggestions has been shown useful for Intranet search [1, 2]. Existing Intranet search approaches appear to follow a "one size fits all" strategy. That is different users who submit the same query receive the same query suggestion list. However, different users may have different topics of interest. Consequently, the users who have submitted the same query may have different search intentions. For example, a sociology student submitting the query "lecture notes" is likely to be more interested in sociology classes than maths classes. Moreover, users' interests and search intentions may be dynamically evolving depending on their interactions with the system (e.g., clicks on documents), and when the interactions are made, during a search session [3].

To address these issues, we propose a unified framework to personalise query suggestions for Intranet search. Specifically, we use the interaction data of each user during a search session to build *user profiles*, which represent the user's topics of interests and may change over time in response to the user's interaction with the system.

It is worth noting that search personalisation (e.g., search result re-ranking, query suggestion, query auto-completion, etc.) has been studied extensively in the context of web search engines [3, 8, 9, 10, 11, 12, 13]. However, little attention has been paid to the same task for Intranet search. Moreover, personalisation methods on web search engines typically construct users' profiles using their click information [3, 10, 11, 12], but less account has been taken of how users modify their queries for building the profiles.

In our proposed framework, we construct two temporal topic-based user profiles for each search session. The first is a *click user profile* based on the clicked documents. The second is a *query user profile* based on the user's query modification history within the search session. We then use the two profiles within a learning-to-rank framework to re-rank suggested queries generated by a non-personalised method for query suggestion on Intranet search [1]. Experimental results show that our approach helps to significantly improve the query suggestion performance.

2. QUERY SUGGESTION FRAMEWORK

2.1 Building Temporal User Profiles

Each search session contains two types of event (i.e., queries and clicks). Given a search session, we propose to build two

CHIIR '17, March 07 - 11, 2017, Oslo, Norway

ISBN 978-1-4503-4677-1/17/03...$15.00
DOI: http://dx.doi.org/10.1145/3020165.3022129

temporal profiles for the specific user. These are a click user profile (denoted as $profile(C)$), built using the user's clicked documents, and a query user profile (denoted as $profile(Q)$), built using the user's submitted queries within the session. Click profile have been extensively used in other search personalisation methods [3]; we expect that the query profile will enrich the representation of the user's search interests.

Since a user's interests and search intentions may change over time, the more recently clicked documents and submitted queries could better represent the user's current interests. In this paper, we propose to use a *decay function* to capture this characteristic as in [3, 12].

2.1.1 Extracting Topics from Clicked Documents

We consider that click information (e.g., clicked documents) is a good indicator of those documents' relevance to the user's interests [7]. To build the user profile, we use the topics discussed in the documents. We first extract clicked documents from the Intranet search's query logs. After that, we employ Latent Dirichlet Allocation (LDA) [4] to automatically extract latent topics (denoted as Z) from the clicked documents (denoted as D). After training an LDA model using the clicked documents, we apply the model to extract topics for the remaining documents in the collection. Finally, each document is described as a multinomial distribution over the topics (denoted as $P(Z|D)$), in which each topic is represented as a multinomial distribution over the entire vocabulary.

2.1.2 Building a Click User Profile

We represent the temporal click user profile as a multinomial distribution over the topics as in [3]. Specifically, the user set is denoted as U. Let u be an instance of U. Let $D_c = \{d_{c_1}, d_{c_2}, ..., d_{c_n}\}$ be the set of clicked documents of the user u in the current search session, we define the click user profile of the user u (given the clicked document set D_c) as a distribution over topics Z (denoted as $P_C(Z|U)$). The probability $p_C(z|u)$ indicates how much the user u is interested in topic $z \in Z$. $p_C(z|u)$ is defined as a mixture of probabilities of z given $d_{c_i} \in D_c$ as follows

$$p_C(z|u) = \sum\nolimits_{d_{c_i} \in D_c} \lambda_i p(z|d_{c_i}) \qquad (1)$$

$\lambda_i = \frac{1}{N}\alpha^{t_{d_{c_i}}-1}$ is the exponential decay function of $t_{d_{c_i}}$, which is the order of the document d_{c_i} clicked by the user u in the search session. $t_{d_{c_i}} = 1$ indicates that d_{c_i} is the most recently clicked document; N is the normalisation factor. α is the decay parameter ($0 \le \alpha \le 1$).

2.1.3 Building a Query User Profile

Let $Q = \{q_1, q_2, , q_m\}$ be the submitted query set of u in the search session. Because the number of Intranet documents is smaller and can be assumed to change less frequently than web search engines', we make the simplifying assumption of describing each query by the set of documents that contain all the query words, denoted as $D_{q_i} = \{d_{i_1}, d_{i_2}, ..., d_{i_k}\}$. Then, each search query q_i (given the document set D_{q_i}) is modelled as a distribution over topics Z (denoted as $P(Z|q_i)$). The probability of a topic $z \in Z$ given $q_i \in Q$ (i.e., $p(z|q_i)$) is defined as a mixture of probabilities of z given a document $d_{i_j} \in D_{q_i}$ as follows

$$p(z|q_i) = \sum\nolimits_{d_{i_j} \in D_{q_i}} \frac{1}{|D_{q_i}|} p(z|d_{i_j}) \qquad (2)$$

$|D_{q_i}|$ is the size of the document set D_{q_i}.

We then model the query user profile of the user u (given the query set Q) as a distribution over topics Z (denoted as $P_Q(Z|u)$). The probability of a topic z given u (i.e., $p_Q(z|u)$) is defined as a mixture of probabilities of z given query $q_i \in Q$ as follows

$$p_Q(z|u) = \sum\nolimits_{q_i \in Q} \lambda_i p(z|q_i) \qquad (3)$$

$p(z|q_i)$ is defined in Equation 2. Similar to the click user profile, $\lambda_i = \frac{1}{M}\alpha^{t_{q_i}-1}$ is the exponential decay function of t_{q_i}, which is the order of the query q_i submitted by the user u in the search session. $t_{q_i} = 1$ indicates that q_i is the most recent query; M is the normalisation factor. α is the decay parameter ($0 \le \alpha \le 1$).

2.2 Re-ranking Suggested Queries

We use the two user profiles in a learning-to-rank mechanism to re-rank the query suggestion list returned by a non-personalised query suggestion method proposed by Adeyanju *et al.* [1], denoted as *Adeyanju's*. Specifically, *Adeyanju's* first constructs a domain knowledge structure in the form of a concept subsumption hierarchy using both the Intranet document collection and collective users' query logs. Next, the suggestion list is generated using the top n terms most relevant to the query in the hierarchy.

For each input query, our re-ranking method is detailed as follows

(1) We generate the top n ranked suggested queries using *Adeyanju's* method. We denote a suggested query as q_s.

(2) We then compute similarity scores between q_s and $profile(C)$, and between q_s and $profile(Q)$. Both the suggested query q_s and a user profile (denoted as pf which is either $profile(C)$ or $profile(Q)$) are modelled as distributions over topics Z (Section 2.1). To measure the similarity between q_s and the user profile pf, we use Jensen-Shannon divergence ($D_{JS}\lfloor.||.\rfloor$), which is a popular method of measuring the divergence (similarity) between two distributions, to measure the similarity between q_s and pf

$$Sim(q_s|pf) = -D_{JS}\lfloor Q||P\rfloor = -(\frac{1}{2}D_{KL}\lfloor Q||M\rfloor + \frac{1}{2}D_{KL}\lfloor P||M\rfloor) \qquad (4)$$

Here, Q and P are distributions over topics of q_s and pf, respectively. $D_{KL}\lfloor.||.\rfloor$ is the Kullback-Leibler divergence and $M = \frac{1}{2}(Q + P)$. We consider the scores as the *personalised features*. We also extract other *non-personalised features* of the input query q and the suggested query q_s. Table 1 shows the features extracted for re-ranking the suggestion list.

Table 1: The personalised query suggestion features

Feature	Description
Personalised Features	
ClickPersonalisedScore	The similarity score between the suggested query and the user click profile
QueryPersonalisedScore	The similarity score between the suggested query and the user query profile
Non-personalised Features	
QueryRank	Rank of the suggested query on the original list
QuerySim	The cosine similarity score between the current query and the previous query
QueryNo	Total number of queries that have been submitted to the Search Engine
SuggestedQueryCosine	The cosine similarity score between the current query and the suggested query
SuggestedQueryJaccard	The Jaccard distance score between the current query and the suggested query
SuggestedQueryEdit	The edit distance between the current query and the suggested query
SuggestedQueryLevenshtein	The Levenshtein distance between the current query and the suggested query
SuggestedQueryPreUsed	Whether the suggested query was used by the user in the same search session?

(3) After extracting the query features, to re-rank the top n suggested queries, we employ LambdaMART [5] to train ranking models. Among many learning-to-rank algorithms, LambdaMART is regarded as one of the best-performing algorithms and has been chosen as the base learning algorithm in various recent approaches to search personalisation [3].

3. EXPERIMENTAL METHODOLOGY

3.1 Evaluation Methodology and Dataset

Evaluation methodology For evaluation, we use *Auto-Eval*, an automated evaluation framework, which measures the performance of query suggestions automatically based on the actual query logs of an Intranet search [2]. For each query *suggestion list*, we assign a positive label for a suggestion if it is an actual *refinement*, which is the next submitted query in the search session, and there is at least one user click on retrieved results after the refinement. In other words, we interpret the user click after a reformulation as the criterion of a relevant suggestion. The remainder of the suggestion list is assigned negative (irrelevant) labels. We use the rank positions of the positively labelled queries as an approximation of the ground truth to evaluate the performance of query suggestions before and after re-ranking.

We also follow the experimental methodology in [1], that is, the model is evaluated continuously at periodic intervals. Specifically, we use the logs in week i for training the re-ranking model and the following week $i+1$ for testing the trained model; where, in our experiments, $1 \leq i \leq w$, the number of weeks in the test period.

Dataset The dataset used in our experiments contains large-scale query logs collected from the search engine installed at the Web site of the University of Essex during the two years covering 1 January 2012 - 31 December 2013. Each log sample contains a session identifier, the event type (i.e., a query or a click), an auto-increment id, the event content (i.e., query text, click URL), and the event time-stamp.

We apply a simple pre-processing step to remove single event search sessions because, with those sessions, it is not possible to determine whether the user found the required information. We also remove those queries whose positive label set is empty from the dataset. We then analyse the remainder of the query logs. Table 2 shows basic statistics.

Table 2: Basic statistics of the evaluation search logs

Item	2012	2013	Total
#search sessions	397,461	338,391	735,804
#events	1,263,179	1,083,992	2,347,171
#events/session	**3.22**	**3.25**	**3.23**
#queries	757,645	659,284	1,416,929
#query/session	**1.91**	**1.95**	**1.93**
#clicked url	505,534	424,708	930,242
#clicks/session	**1.27**	**1.26**	**1.26**

3.2 Experimental Settings

Our personalisation method and baselines We name our proposed re-ranking model as *Ours*. We choose two baselines to compare our work against. The *first baseline* is *Adeyanju's* method [1], which we reimplemented to generate the original suggestion list for *re-ranking*.

We use the session-based approach proposed by Bennett *et al.* [3] as the *second baseline*. Specifically, in the baseline, we use only the click user profile (i.e., $profile(C)$) together with the non-personalised features detailed in Table 1 to re-rank the suggestion list. We name the baseline as *Click*.

It is worth noting that *Adeyanju's* is a non-personalised approach and achieved a good performance of query suggestion on Intranet search [1]. *Click* is a personalised approach and achieved good performances in web search personalisation [3]. Moreover, instead of the session-based approach by Bennett *et al.* [3] as our personalised baseline we could alternatively have used Shokouhi *et al.* [9] or Shokouhi [8].

LDA & LambdaMART We train an LDA model on the clicked documents extracted from the query logs, as detailed in Section 2.1. The number of topics (i.e., 300 in our experiments) is decided by using a held-out validation set which consists of 10% of all clicked documents. The selected number of topics is the one that gives the lowest perplexity value. The decay parameter α for the two user profiles is set to 0.95 as in [3]. The ranking function is learned using LambdaMART [5]. We used the default setting for LambdaMART's prior parameters[1].

Evaluation metrics The evaluation is based on the comparison between our personalised approach and the baselines. We use four evaluation metrics: Mean Average Precision (MAP), Precision (P@k), Mean Reciprocal Rank (MMR), and Normalized Discounted Cumulative Gain (nDCG@k).

4. RESULTS

4.1 Overall Performance

Table 3 shows promising results when user profiles are used to personalise the query suggestion list. We can see that, even using only the click user profile, the *Click* method has led to an improvement of 7.22% on MAP over *Adeyanju's* method. The combination of query and click profiles (i.e., *Ours*) achieves the highest improvement of 10.97% over *Adeyanju's* in terms of MAP score. The improvements indicate that personalisation helps improve the query suggestion performance. The improvements over *Adeyanju's* are all significant (*paired t-test*, $p < 0.01$).

Table 3: Overall performance of the methods. %rel denotes the relative improvement over *Adeyanju's*.

Model	MAP	P@1	P@5	MRR@10	nDCG@5	nDCG@10
Adeyanju's	0.5440	0.4113	0.1823	0.5447	0.5714	0.6000
Click	0.5833	0.4271	0.1981	0.5839	0.6193	0.6583
%rel	*+7.22%*	*+3.84%*	*+8.67%*	*+7.22%*	*+8.38%*	*+9.73%*
Ours	**0.6037**	**0.4526**	**0.2026**	**0.6043**	**0.6413**	**0.678**
%rel	*+10.97%*	*+10.04%*	*+11.14%*	*+10.94%*	*+12.23%*	*+13.02%*

In the comparison between personalisation methods (i.e., *Ours* and *Click*), Table 3 shows that using both the click and query user profiles (i.e., *Ours*) significantly improves the suggestion quality over the *Click* baseline ($p < 0.01$). Interestingly, our method produces a significantly better quality of the first query in the suggestion list with the improvement of 5.97% on P@1 over *Click*. The improvements of *Ours* over *Click* also indicate that the query user profile is important in the query suggestion task, especially for the quality of the first suggested query.

4.2 Performance on Different Query Positions

With more submitted queries and clicked documents, we are able to build richer user profiles. In this experiment, we aim to study whether the position of a query in a search session has any effect on the performance of personalised query suggestion. For each search session, we label queries by their positions during the session. Because there are few sessions containing more than three queries (i.e., 7.65% of sessions in the query logs), we label the first three queries from one to three according to the order of submission in the search session; the remaining queries are labelled as ≥ 4.

It is worth noting that for the first query, we cannot build the click user profile because there is no previously clicked document. However, we can still build the query user profile for the first query. We show the improvement in performance of the personalised methods over *Adeyanju's* in term of MAP

[1]Number of leaves = 10, minimum documents per leaf = 200, number of trees = 100 and learning rate = 0.15

Figure 1: Relative MAP improvements over *Adeyanju's* with different query positions.

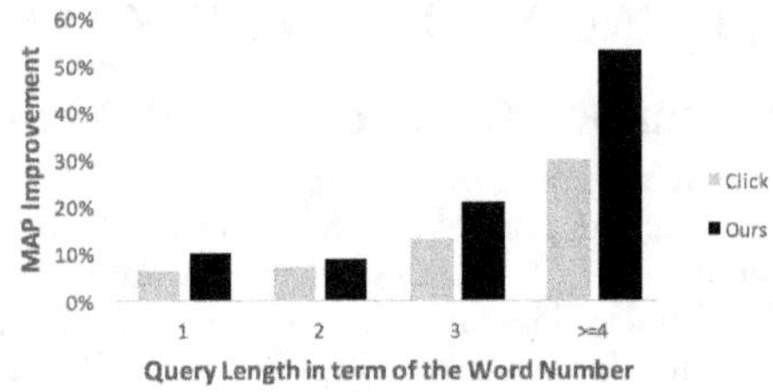

Figure 2: Relative MAP improvements over *Adeyanju's* with different query lengths.

metric with different query positions in Figure 1. Here the statistical significance is verified by t-test ($p < 0.01$). For the first query within a search session, our method, which can use only the query user profile, significantly improves the query suggestion performance over *Adeyanju's*. It again confirms the effectiveness of the query information on personalised query suggestion for Intranet search.

From the second query, we can build both the query and click user profiles. One can see that the higher position of a query is, the larger improvement in performance the personalised query suggestion can be achieved. Specifically, from the query with high positions (i.e., ≥ 4), the improvements of *Click* and *Ours* are 11.37% and 18.22%, respectively. Figure 1 also shows that *Ours* outperforms *Click* significantly with the improvements of at least 3.45% ($p < 0.01$). It indicates that richer user profiles (by observing more clicked documents and submitted queries during the search session) help achieve better query suggestion performances. The findings offer future research directions that use user profiles which go beyond single sessions

4.3 Performance on Different Query Lengths

The query length is defined by the number of words in the query (e.g., the query "University webmail" has the length of 2). The length of a query might give an indication as to how specific the information need of an individual user is (i.e., a longer query can typically be assumed to reflect a more specific information need). In this experiment, we aim to show the impact of personalisation on query suggestion with different query lengths. We label each query by its length, which is the number of words in the query (i.e., from one to three and ≥ 4 words because there are few queries containing more than three words (i.e., 5.7% of queries in the query logs)).

Figure 2 shows the improvement in performance of *Click* and *Ours* over *Adeyanju's* in term of MAP with different query lengths. We see that personalisation methods achieve significantly better performances than the non-personalised method does ($p < 0.01$). Even for short queries (length 1 and 2) which tend to be more generic, the *Click* and *Ours* methods outperform *Adeyanju's* method with the improvement of more than 6.11% and 9.09%, respectively. We see that the longer a query is, the higher improvement personalised methods can achieve. Specifically, with a longer query (i.e., with length ≥ 4), the *Click* and *Ours* methods yield the highest improvements, i.e., 29.82% and 53.85%, respectively. This indicates that a longer query would also get more benefit from personalisation.

Figure 2 also indicates that by combining the query user profile with the click user profile, *Ours* significantly improves the query suggestion performance over *Click* ($p < 0.01$). Moreover, the improvements are larger with the longer queries (i.e., with length ≥ 3). In particular, the improvements of *Ours* over *Click* are 6.7% and 18.2% on the query length 3 and the query length ≥ 4, respectively.

5. CONCLUSIONS

In this paper, we proposed a personalised query suggestion framework and showed how it performed on Intranet search. We built two session-specific temporal user profiles, a query user profile using the submitted queries, and a click user profile using the clicked documents. We then extracted the personalised features using the two profiles and combined them with non-personalised features to learn a ranking model using LamdaMART. Finally, we used the ranking model to re-rank the query suggestion list returned by a state-of-the-art query suggestion approach for Intranet search.

Experimental results on a large-scale query log dataset collected from a university intranet search engine show that personalisation significantly improved the query suggestion performance. Using both the click user profile and query user profile achieved the highest performance indicating that personalised query suggestion for Intranet search should take into account both click and query information. Moreover, the positive impact of personalised query suggestions is more pronounced with longer queries and queries submitted later within a session.

6. REFERENCES

[1] I. A. Adeyanju et al. Adaptation of the concept hierarchy model with search logs for query recommendation on intranets. In *SIGIR'12*, 2012.

[2] M.-D. Albakour et al. Autoeval: An evaluation methodology for evaluating query suggestions using query logs. In *ECIR'11*, 2011.

[3] P. N. Bennett et al. Modeling the impact of short- and long-term behavior on search personalization. In *SIGIR'12*, 2012.

[4] D. M. Blei et al. Latent dirichlet allocation. *J. Mach. Learn. Res.*, 2003.

[5] C. J. C. Burges et al. Learning to rank with non-smooth cost functions. In *NIPS'06*, 2006.

[6] D. Hawking. Enterprise search. In *Modern Information Retrieval, 2nd Ed.* 2010.

[7] T. Joachims et al. Accurately interpreting clickthrough data as implicit feedback. In *SIGIR'05*, 2005.

[8] M. Shokouhi. Learning to personalize query auto-completion. In *SIGIR'13*, 2013.

[9] M. Shokouhi et al. Fighting search engine amnesia: Reranking repeated results. In *SIGIR'13*, 2013.

[10] T. Vu et al. Improving search personalisation with dynamic group formation. In *SIGIR'14*, 2014.

[11] T. Vu et al. Modelling time-aware search tasks for search personalisation. In *WWW'15 Companion*, 2015.

[12] T. Vu et al. Temporal latent topic user profiles for search personalisation. In *ECIR'15*, 2015.

[13] T. Vu et al. Search personalization with embeddings. In *ECIR'17*, 2017.

Goal-Directed Information Seeking in Time-Synchronized and Topic-Linked Records of the Apollo Lunar Missions

Tiffany Jachja
Electrical and Computer Engineering
University of Maryland, College Park
tiffanyjachja@gmail.com

Douglas W. Oard
iSchool and UMIACS
University of Maryland, College Park
oard@umd.edu

ABSTRACT

We live in an era in which ubiquitous networks bring together information from a vast array of sources. The resulting confluence creates new opportunities for providing integrated access. This paper describes the use of a system for exploring the rich recorded legacy of the Apollo missions to the Moon, using the event structure of each mission as an organizing principle. Qualitative analysis of a study with five journalism students indicates that the system is capable of supporting goal-directed information seeking.

1. INTRODUCTION

In a four-year period between 1968 and 1972, 24 people traveled to Earth's moon, twelve of whom walked the surface. Apollo astronauts lived on the surface for a total of nearly two weeks, spending more than 81 hours outside their spacecraft. The Apollo missions remain, to this day, among the most extensively documented events in human history. As is the case for any complex undertaking, many people know a little about what happened and some people know a lot, but nobody knows the whole story. This is why making sense of the historical record requires that we consult multiple sources. As primary sources become increasingly available online, new opportunities emerge to support analysis and synthesis of the historical record. This paper explores two such opportunities: time-synchronized and topic-linked event reconstruction. The Apollo missions offer an outstanding testbed for applying event reconstruction to archival materials for three reasons: (1) several large collections of primary source materials from Apollo are already available online, (2) a substantial subset of this record has sufficiently precise timing information to support straightforward automatic alignment, and (3) the combination of individual records in the form of documents, audio recordings, still images, moving images, and digital data (e.g., trajectory and telemetry data) offers diversity in content. This paper describes our work to date with a substantial subset of those materials.

2. THE APOLLO ARCHIVE EXPLORER

The Apollo program included two crewed spacecraft, the Lunar Module (LM), which was designed to land on the moon, and the Command Module (CM), which remained in lunar orbit awaiting the return of the LM from the surface and then returned the crew to Earth. Each spacecraft had a combined voice and data recorder. NASA made a vast trove of Apollo mission transcripts from those recorders, and from radio communication between the spacecraft and the Mission Control Center, available at the turn of the century [4]. The Apollo astronauts also took about 6,000 still photographs in their 81 hours of moonwalks, for an average rate of about one a minute. The high resolution Hasselblad film cameras that were used to take these photographs were almost always mounted on the astronaut's chest, yielding an unmatched sequence of ego-centric views of lunar surface operations [3]. Fairly precise times have been reconstructed from radio reports and television observations for a substantial number of those photographs. Video from the Apollo missions is available from three sources: Earth-based cameras for launch and splashdown, television sent back during the mission, and 16-mm motion picture film shot during the mission. Maps and other types of cartographic products offer a further perspective on what happened.

This set of content has led to a small cottage industry focused on consolidating media that had initially been separate. One of the most ambitious projects was the Apollo Lunar Surface Journal (ALSJ), an extensively annotated set of hand-corrected transcripts [2]. The ALSJ was later augmented with the Apollo Flight Journal (AFJ) for other portions of the Apollo missions. One limitation of the ALSJ and AFJ is that they are transcript-centric: readers can view linked photographs, maps, or video, or listen to linked audio, but those sources are displayed separately, out of context from the transcript that brought the reader there. An alternative approach is illustrated by the Apollo Archive Explorer (AEX), which we use in this paper [1]. The AEX organizes events temporally on a timeline that represents Ground Elapsed Time (GET), the elapsed time since launch from Earth. The AEX includes the ALSJ and AFJ, scanned transcripts, photographs, audio, video and flight plans, all of which are time-synchronized. While many things can be time-synchronized, some cannot. The NASA Johnson Space Center oral history project has interviewed several hundred people from the Apollo era, and transcripts from almost all of those are available online in PDF format. Topic-linking is an alternative in the case where a source cannot be time-synchronized. These oral history interviews are currently the only topic-linked source in the AEX, although other sources (e.g., technical reports) could also be added.

We started with Version 4.0 of the AEX system [1] and made modifications to simplify the layout for use by novice users, thus creating version 4.1.[1] Figure 1 depicts the user interface of the modified AEX, which is a Java application. The screen is divided into four regions: control (leftmost), two tab-selectable document [2] display zones (middle), and images (rightmost). The control region on the left provides a term-based search capability and a pause button to start and stop the replay. That region also displays the

CHIIR '17, March 07 - 11, 2017, Oslo, Norway

ACM 978-1-4503-4677-1/17/03 $15.00
DOI: http://dx.doi.org/10.1145/3020165.3022130

[1] AEX download: http://www.umiacs.umd.edu/~oard/apollo/aex

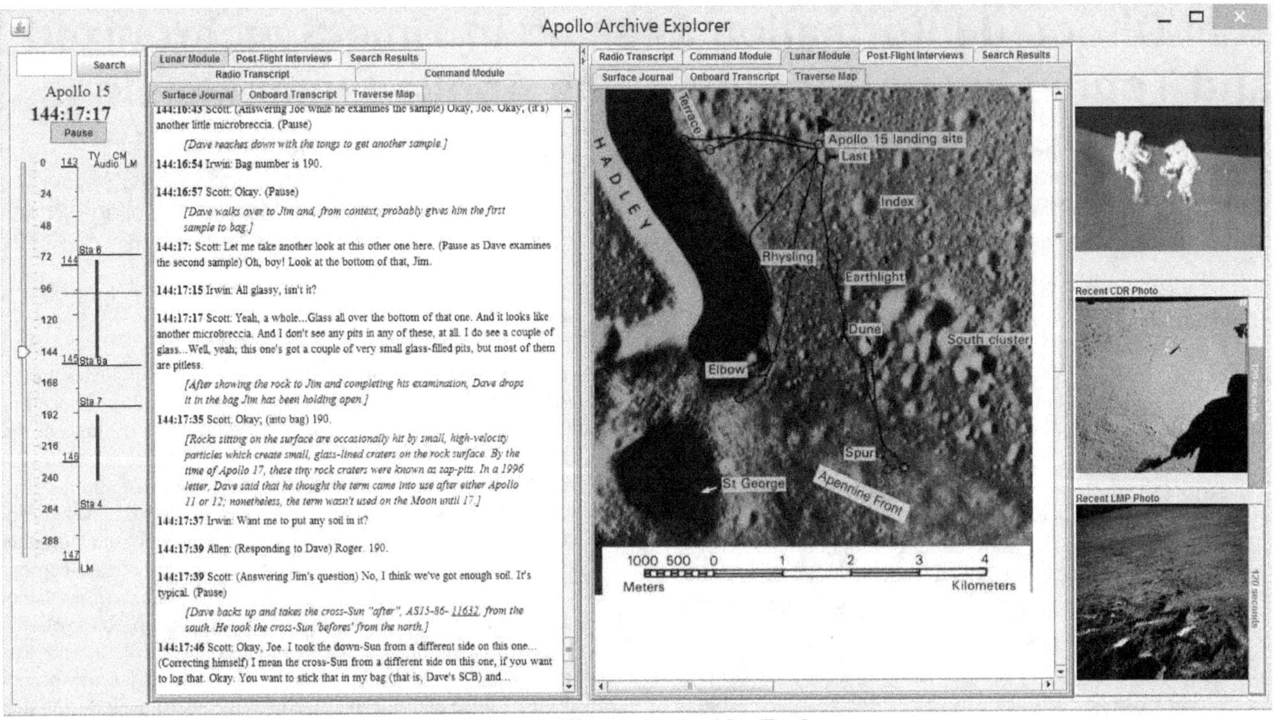

Figure 1. The Apollo Archive Explorer

Apollo lunar landing mission number (currently Apollo 11, 14, 15, 16 or 17), and the Ground Elapsed Time (GET). Below the top row of controls, a major-event timeline is displayed with availability indicators for television (TV), audio (for periods when audio but no video is available), the scanned transcript from the CM recorder (CM), and the scanned transcript from the LM recorder (LM). Clicking in the major event timeline resets the GET to the selected point. The slider bar and the more detailed timeline at the left of the control region work together to allow the user to reset the replay to any time during the mission in one-hour increments. Two document display regions function identically but independently, thus permitting the user to view any selectable content on either side. At most, two levels of tabs are used to control the selection of content for the displays. The top set of tabs can be seen in Figure 1. Selecting the Command Module, Lunar Module or Search Result tab reveals a second set of tabs. As shown for the Lunar Module tab the second set of tabs are for the Surface Journal (the ALSJ, which appears on the left in Figure 1), the Onboard Transcript (from the LM recorder), and the Traverse Map (which appears on the right in Figure 1). On the lowest level, each tab displays some document (or in the case of the traverse map, image), often with added time-specific annotation. For the Surface Journal, the GET of the most recent utterance is highlighted. For scanned transcripts, a bounding box is drawn around the most recent utterance and labeled with the GET. Selecting the traverse map displays the route taken by the astronauts (from post-flight analysis), overlaid with a moving bulls-eye symbol to show their approximate location at the current GET.

3. STUDY DESIGN

To this point, AEX has evolved principally as a platform for experimenting with integration of diverse content. Our ultimate goal has always been to help users to manage complexity, and we are now shifting to a more user-centered design process. For this first user study, we sought to learn how the AEX would actually be used during a focused information seeking task. We chose journalism students as participants because we believed their experience with focused investigation and information seeking would be greater than that of the general population. We recruited five undergraduate students, they were compensated twenty dollars each for their time and participation. Sessions lasted approximately one hour, and participants were tasked with writing brief stories describing specific events.

Apollo Missions Events List

These events occurred during an Apollo Mission to the Moon

1. Proving Galileo's Theory The Hammer And Feather Experiment (Apollo 15)
2. First use of an ultraviolet camera/spectrograph on the Moon (Apollo 16)
3. Alan Shepard hitting 2 golf balls on the Moon (Apollo 14)
4. John Young's Salute On The Moon (Apollo 16)
5. James Irwin and David Scott's discovery of the Genesis Rock (Apollo 15)

Figure 2. Story topics.

As prompts, we wrote one-sentence descriptions for five events as shown in Figure 2. These events were specifically chosen for their potential insight into: (1) the use of time-synchronized sources and (2) the use of topic-linked sources. Our version of the AEX includes many types of time-synchronized sources, but only a single pair of topic-linked sources (from the radio transcript to oral history interviews). Thus, we selected events for which information was available from transcripts, oral history interviews, and at least one other time-synchronized source.

Because of the AEX's complexity, we expected to see substantial learning effects as each user became acquainted with the system. To account for user learning, we asked each participant to perform two tasks. For Task 1, we chose the first event shown in Figure 2, for which the information regarding the event was concentrated at a single point in the mission. Through this first activity, the user could gain experience with time synchronization and topic linking without the need for extensive timeline navigation (this reasoning was not described to participants, however). For Task 2, participants were invited to pick event 2, 3, 4, or 5—if they expressed no preference, an event was chosen for them. These events were designed to be more difficult to summarize, requiring information from multiple sources, or information from different times in a mission.

Participants conducted their session individually. In the first study, both a study conductor (the first author of this paper) and an observer (the second author) were present; for the other sessions a single person (the first author) served both as study conductor and observer. At the start of each session, the participant was shown a seven-minute training video which included screen captures and voice narration. The first half of the video sought to give the participant general knowledge about the Apollo missions to the Moon. The remainder of the video focused on how to use the AEX system, and reviewed each region of the interface separately. The video concluded with an example of how to find information about a specific event. To aid in visualizing the scope of the Apollo program, infographics and images were provided with an outline of the video in a two-page handout. Participants were given this handout at the outset, and could stop the video at any point to ask questions. The study conductor paused the video occasionally to clarify details for participants. Together with the time required to obtain written informed consent, the training phase of each session took about 15 minutes. We allowed at most 15 minutes for the first story generation task and 25 minutes for the second. The two tasks were separated by 5-minute break, and participants could finish either task early if they were satisfied with their story.

We gave participants a written description of their task (to write a brief story), one assigned event (Task 1) and a list of events from which to select (Task 2). Participants were asked to verbalize their thoughts while completing the tasks, and we recorded that audio with their permission. The first author of this paper later transcribed these recordings. The observer (the second author) made notes during the session to record impressions that might not be as well captured by that transcript or the visual screen capture. Because of the complexity of the system and the specialized jargon that might be encountered, participants were invited to ask the study conductor questions for clarification. The study conductor also answered questions concerning the task itself. In a few cases, answers were crafted to highlight sources of information not previously considered by that participant, but such hints were offered in the latter half of the task, and without specificity about what might be found. After completing both tasks, participants completed a questionnaire and a brief semi-structured interview. The questionnaire consisted of six questions to gauge self-reported computer proficiency and prior familiarity with the events, reported on a five-point scale. In the interview, the study conductor asked participants about their search and navigation strategies, opinions about aspects of the AEX system, and about the overall user experience. The questions were tailored to the participant's actions, as observed during the study. Interviews for later participants were also shaped by the interviewer's experience in prior sessions. Together the questionnaire and interview took about 15 minutes.

The primary technique used for analysis was grounded theory [5]. We started with an initial coding frame that included two phases (information seeking and synthesis) and five activities (search, timeline navigation, fact finding, contextualization, and writing). As sessions were completed, we transcribed the user session and coded the observer's notes, the stories created for each event, and the screen capture, initially using that coding frame. As coding proceeded, we evolved the coding frame by identifying actions and sequences of actions that better described the behaviors we observed. For example, we identified problem solving as an additional phase, and learning new terminology as an additional action, with an ordering in which learning new terminology sometimes preceded a refined search. The two authors initially coded parts of one session independently and then met to review and reconcile the resulting coding frames. After arriving at a unified coding frame, the remaining four sessions were conducted and coded by the first author of this paper, further evolving the coding frame as new phenomena were observed. The second author then performed peer review of the resulting coding frame and a sample of coding decisions.

4. FINDINGS

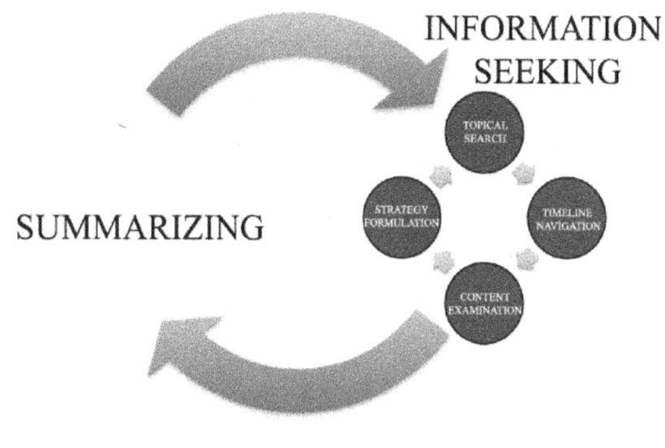

Figure 3. User Activities

As illustrated in Figure 3, we observed two dominant activity phases, information seeking and information synthesis. Within the information seeking phase, we observed four dominant activities: topical search, timeline navigation, content examination, and strategy formulation. Strategy formulation served as a typical entry point, with content examination serving as the exit point. During strategy formulation the user's goal was to figure out how to get to the information that they wanted to see. Often this required getting the AEX to display information from a specific point in the mission (i.e., some specific GET). Although the GET could be set through timeline navigation, at the start of a task our participants did not know where in the mission timeline they might find the event they were looking for, thus they invariably used search to find some content in the temporal vicinity of their event. All of our users had Web search experience and therefore required only a few queries to get to some useful content. Topical search thus emerged as the dominant outcome of strategy formulation. As Table 1 shows, participants were able to find the content they sought for the first task with no more than three queries, and they typically found at least some useful content with their first query. Subsequent queries were used to explore the interviews or to reach other times in the transcripts. Four of the five participants issued markedly more queries for their second task than for their first, reflecting the greater complexity of that second task. This called for experimentation with alternative strategies. Participant 1 (with a single query for each task) was the only exception.

Table 1. Number of queries issued

Participant	*1*	*2*	*3*	*4*	*5*
Task 1	1	1	2	3	3
Task 2	1	6	4	7	5

Three participants stated during the semi-structured interview that search was the most useful AEX system capability. Once a participant had gotten in the neighborhood, the natural next step was to examine some content. Video and photographs were displayed continuously, but tab selection was sometimes needed to get to a specific transcript or journal after first setting the system's GET by selecting a search result. We were surprised to see users making more use of the scanned transcripts than of the ALSJ, despite the fact that the ALSJ includes richer content. The topical search in the present AEX system is based on scanned transcripts, however, and clicking on a search result therefore brings the user to a scanned transcript by default. Users typically did ultimately select the ALSJ at some point, and when they did they often found the extensive commentary in that source to be useful.

When topical search yielded little relevant content, users were seen developing other strategies. As an example, while examining search results for oral history interviews, Participant 3 during the second task, stated that reading questions asked during those interviews helped them determine whether the result was relevant to their event. We observed no productive use of the map showing the path taken during the moonwalks, although none of the tasks were designed specifically to exercise that capability of the system. We did, however, observe that the multimedia content (the audio, video, and photographs) were particularly important to some users. Participant 2 described having multimedia as essential to writing their story. Indeed, when that user found no useful audio or video during the second task, they expressed discomfort and continued using the AEX up to the time limit. This was the only participant to express concern that a report might be incomplete. The same participant explained during the interview that using systems like the AEX allows for a larger amount of information to be conceptualized than if they had to work only with Google or textbooks. In other cases, we found that users were satisfied with only written sources. For example, Participant 1 mentioned that the journals and transcripts were enough to complete both tasks. Notably, that participant did not use all of the time allotted for either task. Another participant stated, "In my research the picture and video function wasn't necessarily a huge aid."

Participants generally found the AEX's time synchronization valuable. At the start of their first task, users were inclined to select the first search result from the radio transcript, they then could navigate to and read the time-synchronized journals. One participant indicated that time synchronization was the most helpful AEX capability, drawing an analogy to the interviews that journalists do: "if you're interviewing five different people in five different places it's hard to line them up and see how they all fit together and so this is nice because everything already is together." Timeline navigation, by contrast, proved to be problematic. A total of four participants tried using timeline navigation, two of whom did not find the timeline navigation process easy to conceptualize, at least in part because the AEX includes separate capabilities for coarse (whole hour) and fine (minute and second) navigation. For example, one participant said: "Getting to an exact time or searching times was not as precise as it could have been."

We found that all participants exhibited similar examination patterns, initially clicking through the tabs for different time-synchronized sources, and only later looking at the oral history interviews. Early participants looked at those interviews only when we reminded them of their availability, emphasis was therefore placed on how to access oral history interviews during training for later participants. The majority of participants used search to find oral history interviews, which was a sensible choice since the content linking capability in the present implementation is constantly searching based on what was said most recently in the linked transcript, and thus the results are only stable when the replay is paused. All participants who searched oral histories at their own initiative did so for both tasks. One participant explained that they found the oral history interviews to be useful because it provided a motive for the event. All users would examine the post-flight interview search results only after including information they had found from images, video (if available), transcripts or journals in their stories. They also quickly demonstrated an understanding of what they were seeing, either through their think-aloud or through their written stories. Often this would occur in a matter of seconds. We observed several participants learning new terms from the content they were examining and then using those terms to search more effectively. This was despite having little prior knowledge to their tasked events. Questionnaire results indicated that every participant reported no prior familiarity with at least one of the events they wrote about. Each participant was also offered the opportunity to do Web searches if they felt that necessary to augment what they were getting from the AEX system, but none chose to do so. A participant inquired only once about event-related content (in that case, asking for the full name of an astronaut).

When working on their second task, for which information was scattered across multiple sources and at different points in the timeline, all participants expressed some confusion or discomfort. However, in all cases participants produced more detailed stories for their second task than their first. They also spent more time on their second task. Three participants worked more quickly than we had allowed for, but Participants 3 and 4 worked up to the time limit, and both expressed a desire for more time in order to add more information to their story. From these and our other results, we conclude that participants were able to master the use of the AEX system in a relatively brief time and that it aided in the synthesis process used to construct their stories.

5. CONCLUSION

From our study, we have learned about how people might use the AEX system, and in particular about which capabilities were most helpful for focused information seeking. In the future we are interested in learning more about how the AEX's content linking capabilities can best be employed. We would also like to extend the range of user and task types, perhaps by initially involving history and communication undergraduates. In terms of system design, our results clearly point to the need for a more intuitive timeline navigation capability. In 1969, few organizations outside NASA could assemble such rich content, but today any of us can use email, Skype, smartphone cameras, and a myriad of other technologies to create similarly rich records. Some of this material can be time synchronized (e.g., [6]), others perhaps topic linked. If we think of Apollo Program's records as a sort of prehistoric lifelogging, then we might even use the AEX to draw some insight from our study of the past into how those in the future might study us.

ACKNOWLEDGMENTS

Material based upon work supported by NSF under Grant 1218159. Findings and conclusions are those of the authors and not NSF.

REFERENCES

[1] D. Oard, J. Malionek (2013) The Apollo Archiver Explorer, JCDL.

[2] G. Heiken, E. Jones (2007) *On the Moon: The Apollo Journals*, Springer Praxis.

[3] G. Kitmacher (n.d.) Astronaut Still Photography during Apollo, NASA. http://history.nasa.gov/apollo_photo.html

[4] G. Swanson (2001) The Story behind the Mercury, Gemini and Apollo Air to Ground Transmissions, *Spaceflight.*

[5] J. Corbin, A. Strauss (1990) *Basics of Qualitative Research: Grounded theory procedures and techniques*, Sage.

[6] Z. Yu, N. Diakopoulos, M. Naaman (2010) The Multiplayer: Multi-perspective Social Video Navigation, UIST.

Towards Identifying User Intentions in Exploratory Search using Gaze and Pupil Tracking

Thomas Low
Otto von Guericke University
Magdeburg, Germany
thomas.low@ovgu.de

Nikola Bubalo
General Psychology
Ulm University, Germany
nikola.bubalo@uni-ulm.de

Tatiana Gossen,
Michael Kotzyba
Otto von Guericke University
Magdeburg, Germany
firstname.lastname@ovgu.de

André Brechmann
Leibniz-Institute for Neurobiology
Magdeburg, Germany
brechmann@lin-magdeburg.de

Anke Huckauf
General Psychology
Ulm University, Germany
anke.huckauf@uni-ulm.de

Andreas Nürnberger
Otto von Guericke University
Magdeburg, Germany
andreas.nuernberger@ovgu.de

ABSTRACT

Exploration in large multimedia collections is challenging because the user often navigates into misleading directions or information areas. The vision of our project is to develop an assistive technology that is able to support the individual user and enhance the efficiency of an ongoing exploratory search. Such a technical search aid should be able to find out about the user's current interests and goals. Respective parameters can be found in the central and in the peripheral nervous system as well as in overt behavior. Therefore, we aim at using eye movements, pupillometry and EEG to assess respective information. Here, we describe the set-up and the first results of a preliminary user study investigating the effects of searching an image collection on eye movements and pupil dilations. First data show that numbers of fixation, fixation durations as well as pupil dilations differ systematically when looking at a subsequently selected target as compared with not selected items. These results support our vision that further research additionally investigating EEG can in fact result in better predicting the searchers goals and next choices.

Keywords

Exploratory Search; Gaze Tracking; Multimedia Retrieval; Pupillometry;

1. INTRODUCTION

Multimedia systems offer a lot of information. However, retrieval of a piece of information can be challenging and/or exhausting and hence exploration in large image collections is not an easy search task. It is a highly dynamic process of a user interacting with an image retrieval system that requires learning about the collection structure and/or content. In addition there is no clear stop criterion at the beginning of the search. The process ends when the user decides that their information need is satisfied [4].

For a user searching a huge multimedia collection, technical assistive systems could aid in improving search efficiency. Users often have no exactly defined target in mind. Instead, they search within a certain field of interest. Here, reducing the amount of possible next actions - ideally only one interaction - would be helpful. In order to suggest such next steps during a search process, the assisting function must be informed about the interests and goals of the searcher. This requires investigating the details of the users' search behavior.

This paper describes the projects vision and first steps and results into the development of such an assistive system, which is investigating user behaviors from a psychological and a neurobiological perspective, and modeling covert and overt reactions for predicting user intentions from a computer science perspective. Before detailing our approach in Section 3, Section 2 provides an overview of suggested approaches using methods such as eye tracking, pupillometry, or EEG. Section 4 describes our setup used to examine gaze parameters during search, and first results concerning gaze and pupil tracking are reported. In the final section, our work is summarized and compared to the related work.

2. RELATED WORK

One important question in exploratory search is which observable variables can be used to anticipate user intentions during the search process and, therefore, help to guide them towards a successful goal fulfillment. Because of the implicit nature of eye control, using gaze data is a promising approach as implicit relevance feedback [11, 12].

Li et al. [8] used fixation duration to identify a users' implicit relevance feedback and with that, improve the performance of content-based image retrieval systems. Their results indicate that eye tracking based relevance feedback improves image retrieval performance.

Golenia et al. [3] combined EEG and eye tracking data in order to disambiguate image search results that are obtained

CHIIR '17, March 07 - 11, 2017, Oslo, Norway

ISBN 978-1-4503-4677-1/17/03...$15.00

DOI: http://dx.doi.org/10.1145/3020165.3022131

using ambiguous textual queries. They were able to make an eye tracking and EEG based prediction that is above chance level.

Nevertheless, there seems to be still one important aspect of information missing. Given that the research described above already utilizes gaze behavior and EEG, one might suggest that information about the activation in the peripheral nervous system might additionally contribute to predicting a user's intention. Therefore, pupil dilation might be an important and available additional source of information. In fact, pupil size differs not only depending on brightness but also depending on cognitive or affective load [13]. Therefore, the pupil size has been suggested as further information channel for gaze-based interaction [1, 2].

Summarizing the research above, the combination of methods such as eye tracking or EEG is a promising approach to improve the search performance and hence the user experience. The optimal way would be to simultaneously observe behavior, central cognitive processes as well as peripheral arousal.

Following Li et al. [8], we decided that gaze might serve as a fruitful tool investigating the users' interests. As a central physiological variable, EEG will be added to our measures to directly observe the user's monitoring process during exploratory search [14]. Here error-related negativity (ERN) potentials will be informative about wrong decisions of subjects and feedback related negativity (FRN) will reflect whether the users expectation on the feedback is met. Moreover, spectral analysis of EEG data may be used to track attentional demand or the users' engagement during the search process [6, 10].

The goal of the current work is to identify which eye tracking parameters are suited for identifying what kind of images a user is interested in while performing an exploratory search. For a well-defined search task in web retrieval Gwizdka and Zhang [5] reported that eye tracking parameters such as fixation durations and pupil diameter differed significantly between observed websites depending on whether they were relevant or irrelevant to the users search objective. We thus aim at enlarging their data to a different scenario of exploratory search.

3. METHOD

We conducted a lab-based experiment in which users were required to navigate through a collection of abstract images in order to find a specified target image. For the study we developed a tool called *NEMP* (*Neighborhood Explorer using MDS and Procrustes Analysis*) which is a web-based tool for navigation in large image collections [9]. *NEMP* projects a set of images to a two-dimensional map and groups them based on their similarities in a high-dimensional feature space through multidimensional scaling (*MDS*) [7]. That means that images, which are more similar to each other are placed closer together. The target image is displayed in the top left corner of the window (see Fig. 1). For users to navigate towards the target image in multiple steps it is not reasonable to show all of the images of the collection at once: It would be difficult for users to analyze such a large amount of information. Therefore, only k images are shown at once. The users can navigate through the images in the collection by selecting one of the images they found to be closest to the target in its feature constellation. This selection triggers a generation of a new map containing the previously selec-

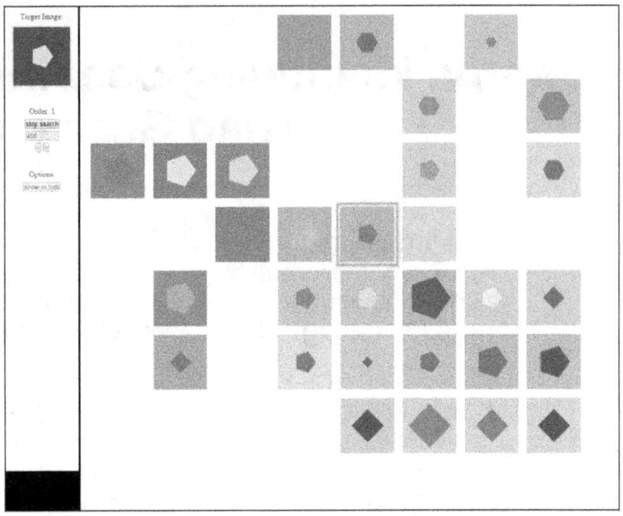

Figure 1: *NEMP* screenshot. 30 polygons are arranged in the map-like interface. The left part of the interface serves to control the user study, i.e. select the target image and the initial view.

ted image in the center, surrounded by $k-1$ images that are most similar to it. This new map is then depicted on the screen. The process is repeated until the user finds and selects the target image. *NEMP* uses a k-nearest neighbors algorithm to determine the set of images to be displayed in the current map. In this study $k = 30$ images were shown to the user at once. The image collection contained 2000 automatically generated regular polygons, which randomly varied in size, number of edges, background and foreground color. We chose artificially generated images instead of real images (e.g. photos) in order to be able to fully model the underlying similarity space. The similarity was measured on the basis of the weighted sum of the similarities of all four features.

Overall, 15 volunteers (mean age 26) participated in the study, of which 10 were male and 5 were female. They were computer science students and reported no color vision deficiencies. The experimental procedure started with the collection of the users' age, sex and profession. Afterwards, users were seated in front of a screen with size of 52 cm (diagonal) at a distance that allowed a comfortable use of the mouse by the user (but not more than 60 cm). The resolution of the screen was 1280x1024 (5:4). The eye tracker bar Tobii Pro X2-60 (gaze sampling frequency: 60Hz, accuracy 0.4°, precision 0.3°, latency < 35 ms) was mounted to the bottom of the screen.

After a short introduction to the setup, the eye tracker was calibrated using the build in calibration procedure and started recording. Users performed one practice trial in order to get acquainted with the task. The practice trial was the same for all users. Consequently, users performed five experimental trials where the order of the same five target polygons was rotated in an ascending order (Latin Square design). The given search tasks simulate an exploratory search, i.e. the participants were free to choose any intermediate direction, the stop criterion was however pre-defined. This trade-off was made in order to ensure comparable searching behavior among the participants. Finally, users were

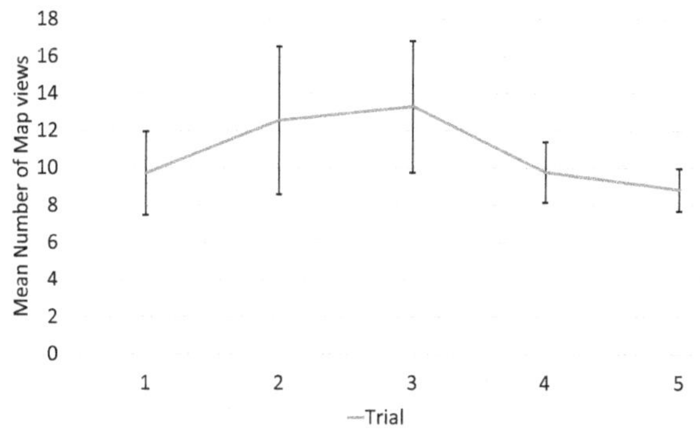

Figure 2: Mean number of maps (± 1 SE) viewed by users separately for each trial in chronological order.

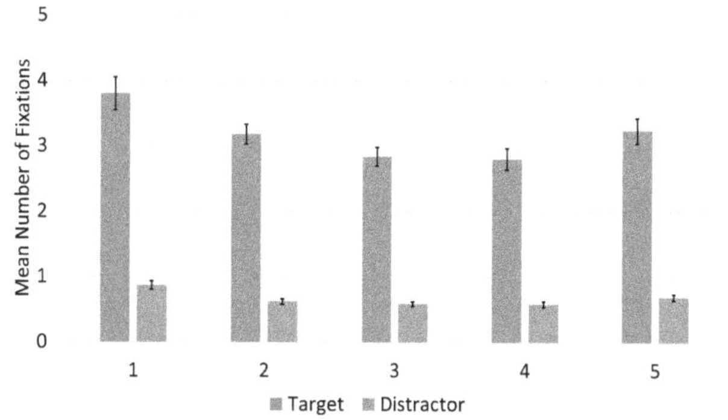

Figure 4: Mean number of fixations (± 1 SE) by users separately for each trial in chronological order.

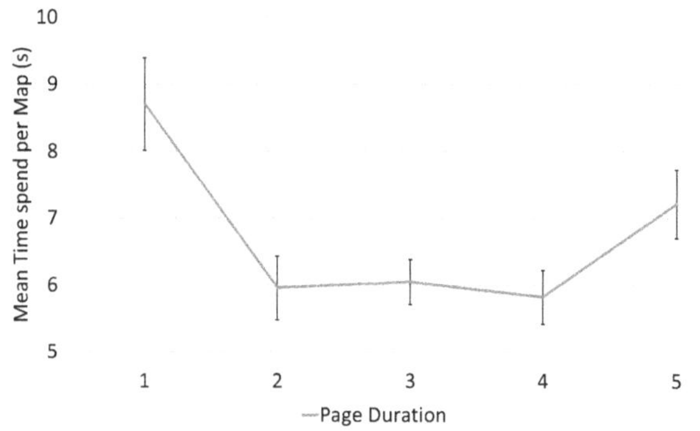

Figure 3: Mean duration spend on maps (± 1 SE) by users separately for each trial in chronological order.

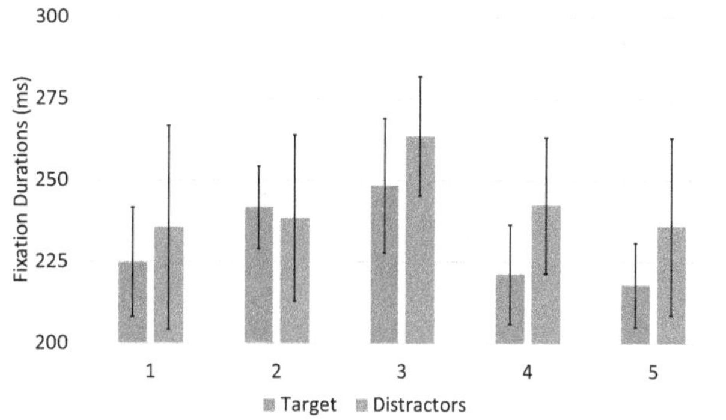

Figure 5: Mean durations of fixations (± 1 SE) by users separately for each trial in chronological order.

required to fill out a short questionnaire inquiring about their subjective user experience with *NEMP*.

4. DATA ANALYSIS AND RESULTS

In mean, our users searched for 10.8 maps before they found the target. The standard deviation (SD) was 10.23 maps. The mean time spend on a map was 6.66 seconds with a SD of 6 seconds. Considering possible learning effects caused by increasing familiarity we analyzed these variables also separately for each trial. The average number of maps visited during a trial initially increased by 28.77% from the first trial (9.73, SE = 2.21) to the second trial (12.53, SE = 3.92) but decreased over the following trials to 91.1% of the initial page visits (see Fig. 2). Multiple comparisons between the trials revealed no significant differences in frequencies ($p < 0.05$) for all comparisons. The average time spend on a map differed significantly between the first trial (8.7 seconds, SD = 8.1) and the remaining trials ($p < 0.05$) which were below 7.3 seconds in average page duration (see Fig. 3).

As a next step, we analyzed the fixations on the polygon stimulus which was chosen on each map as the next polygon of interest and compared their frequency and durations with those fixations placed on the polygons which were not selected. The former will be referred to as the target polygon while the later will be referred to as distractors. On average users fixated the target polygon of a page 3.1 times, with a SD of 1.4. These fixations lasted for 231 milliseconds on average (SD = 58.44). The accumulated number of fixations on distractors averaged to 19.1 (SD = 10.2) which means that a large number of the 29 distractors was not fixated at all. This results in 0.66 fixations per distractor. Fixation durations on distractors were on average 233 milliseconds. As ANOVAs with repeated measures show, users fixated significantly more often ($F(1, 14) = 96.03, p < 0.001, \eta_p^2 = 0.87$) but not longer ($F(1, 13) = 0.48, p = 0.5, \eta_p^2 = 0.04$) onto the respective target than on the individual distractors. All other main and interaction effects were not of significance for both the number of fixations (Trials: $F(4, 56) = 0.6, p = 0.66$; Stimuli * Trials: $F(4, 56) = 0.46, p = 0.77$) and the fixation durations (Trials: $F(4, 52) = 1.62, p = 0.18$; Stimuli * Trials: $F(4, 52) = 0.29, p = 0.88$). Separately for the trials, the average number of fixations on the target stays significantly higher ($p < 0.001$) compared to those on distractors (see Fig. 4 and 5).

Further, pupil sizes were collected during fixations on targets and distractors. There were significant differences in pupil diameter between looking at the target polygon and distractor polygons ($F(1, 13) = 8.67, p = 0.011$). More specifically, average pupil diameters were larger for the target polygons than for the distractors at the third ($p = 0.007$) and fifth trial ($p = 0.015$). Assuming that activation decreases with increasing familiarity one would expect pupil size to decrease with increasing number of trials. This can be observed for both the targets and distractors on a descriptive level. However, looking at the dynamics, pupil diameters were significantly larger ($p < 0.05$) in the fourth and fifth trial compared to the second trial (see Fig. 6).

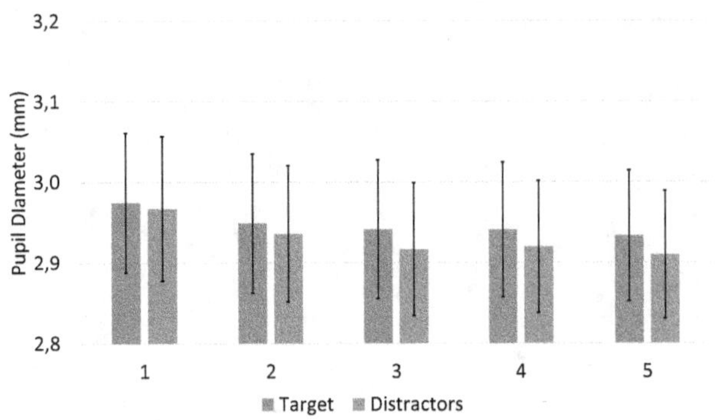

Figure 6: Mean pupil diameter (± 1 SE) for both the target polygon and distractor polygons separately for each trial in chronological order.

5. SUMMARY AND CONCLUSION

In order to identify useful parameters for intention detection in exploratory search tasks, the number of fixations, their durations, and the pupil sizes during fixations were compared between stimuli which were subsequently selected by users (referred to as targets) and those which were not selected (referred to as distractors). Supporting results from well-defined searches [5], we observed differences in all parameters but the fixation duration: In mean, targets were more frequently fixated than distractors. During fixations, pupils were larger suggesting more mental effort. The dynamics for these five trials showed differences from the very first search relative to all others: In the first search, users looked longer onto one map. This resulted in fact in less maps they had to inspect. Hence, although this strategy was shown to be effective, users reduced the amount of time spent on one map, by the cost of needing more maps. That is, obviously, they did not regard this strategy as efficient and thus, changed it. Interestingly, in this first trial, fixation duration on distractors was longer than on the target. Hence, one might assume that users at the beginning thought more about potential targets, whereas in the subsequent trials they decided earlier. Pupil sizes during fixations also demonstrated to be sensitive to intentions: Pupils during fixating a target were larger than during distractor fixations. This difference was of comparable size in all trials. Hence, one might suggest that pupil size increases denote some decision processes. Nevertheless, on should not over-interpret pupil sizes since the absolute sizes were relatively small. Hence, floor effects cannot be ruled out. Taken together, the results show that finding sensitive parameters in exploratory search is possible. Moreover, combining information about fixations and pupillometry seems to be a promising approach for the development of technical assistance in exploratory search. In future research we plan to further analyze correlations between individual features of images and eye tracking data.

6. ACKNOWLEDGMENTS

This work was supported by the Transregional Collaborative Research Centre SFB/TRR 62 "A Companion-Technology for Cognitive Technical Systems" funded by the German Research Foundation.

7. REFERENCES

[1] J. Ehlers, N. Bubalo, M. Loose, and A. Huckauf. Towards voluntary pupil control - training affective strategies? In *Proceedings of the 2nd International Conference on Physiological Computing Systems, PhyCS 2015*, pages 5–12, 2015.

[2] J. Ehlers, C. Strauch, J. Georgi, and A. Huckauf. Pupil size changes as an active information channel for biofeedback applications. *Applied psychophysiology and biofeedback*, pages 1–9, 2016.

[3] J.-E. Golenia, M. Wenzel, and B. Blankertz. Live Demonstrator of EEG and Eye-Tracking Input for Disambiguation of Image Search Results. In *Symbiotic Interaction*, pages 81–86. Springer, 2015.

[4] T. Gossen, M. Nitsche, S. Haun, and A. Nürnberger. Data exploration for bisociative knowledge discovery: A brief overview of tools and evaluation methods. In *Bisociative Knowledge Discovery*, pages 287–300. Springer, 2012.

[5] J. Gwizdka and Y. Zhang. Differences in eye-tracking measures between visits and revisits to relevant and irrelevant Web pages. In *Proceedings of the 38th International ACM SIGIR Conference on Research and Development in Information Retrieval*, pages 811–814. ACM, 2015.

[6] W. Klimesch. EEG alpha and theta oscillations reflect cognitive and memory performance: A review and analysis. *Brain Research Reviews*, 29(2-3):169–195, 1999.

[7] J. B. Kruskal. Nonmetric multidimensional scaling: a numerical method. *Psychometrika*, 29(2):115–129, 1964.

[8] Q. Li, M. Tian, J. Liu, and J. Sun. An implicit relevance feedback method for CBIR with real-time eye tracking. *Multimedia Tools and Applications*, 75(5):2595–2611, 2016.

[9] T. Low, C. Hentschel, S. Stober, H. Sack, and A. Nürnberger. Visual berrypicking in large image collections. In *Proceedings of the 8th Nordic Conference on Human-Computer Interaction: Fun, Fast, Foundational*, NordiCHI '14, pages 1043–1046, New York, NY, USA, 2014. ACM.

[10] J. Macdonald, S. Mathan, and N. Yeung. Trial-by-trial variations in subjective attentional state are reflected in ongoing prestimulus EEG alpha oscillations. *Frontiers in Psychology*, 2(MAY), 2011.

[11] P. Majaranta and A. Bulling. Eye tracking and eye-based human–computer interaction. In *Advances in physiological computing*, pages 39–65. Springer, 2014.

[12] P. Majaranta and K.-J. Räihä. Twenty years of eye typing: systems and design issues. In *Proceedings of the 2002 symposium on Eye tracking research & applications*, pages 15–22. ACM, 2002.

[13] T. Partala and V. Surakka. Pupil size variation as an indication of affective processing. *International journal of human-computer studies*, 59(1):185–198, 2003.

[14] M. Ullsperger, C. Danielmeier, and G. Jocham. Neurophysiology of performance monitoring and adaptive behavior. *Physiological Reviews*, 94(1):35–79, 2014.

'Too Much Serendipity': The Tension between Information Seeking and Encountering at the Library Shelves

Shermaine Waugh
City, University of London
Northampton Square,
London EC1V 0HB, UK
Shermaine.Waugh@city.ac.uk

Dana McKay
University of Melbourne
Parkville, VIC 3010
Australia
danamckay@gmail.com

Stephann Makri
City, University of London
Northampton Square,
London EC1V 0HB, UK
Stephann@city.ac.uk

ABSTRACT
The physical library shelves are regularly the site of serendipitous information discoveries, and are often sought out for this purpose. However, while some drawbacks to the shelves as information gateways have been documented, none to our knowledge relate to their capacity for facilitating serendipity. We present findings from a qualitative study of serendipity at the library shelves. This study uncovered a new drawback that we term the 'seeking-encountering tension'. On one hand, this tension entices people towards the relatively high-risk, high-reward activity of exploring new information avenues discovered serendipitously and, on the other, draws them back towards the relative safety of goal-directed information-seeking. We discuss some of the factors that contribute to this tension, and provide design suggestions for mitigating it. Understanding this tension can inform the design of physical and digital information environments that provide users the agency to switch between more and less focused information-seeking at will.

1. INTRODUCTION
Overabundance of information is a known issue in information-seeking, and providing searchers with too many search results can be as detrimental to finding useful information as providing them with none [2; 9]. It can result in a 'paradox of choice' [2], where obtaining lots of potentially useful results can both facilitate, but also hamper searches—giving rise to 'information pathologies' including information overload, anxiety and avoidance [2].

However, sometimes an overabundance of information can be a good thing, providing the rich environment of triggers necessary for browsing [1] and serendipitous discovery [17]. Both of these approaches are important to information seekers and the human information-seeking process in general [12; 18; 21]. The library is an interesting (and common [10]) site of study of serendipity in the context of information acquisition (termed 'information encountering' by Erdelez [4]). Our study continues in this tradition by examining information encountering at the library shelves.

Information encountering is a source of delight to both public [23] and academic [16] library users. The draw is so strong that many readers cite it as a reason for avoiding ebooks [8]. The library shelves form a type of serendipity engine [11]; semantic arrangement of the shelves facilitates the encountering of related information [24]. Displays and endcaps further allow users to find items of unexpected interest [8; 23]. Savvy users actively leverage the shelves for serendipity, but in early and recent studies (e.g. [7; 11]) around half of participants used the shelves as part of their information seeking, primarily on the understanding that they were likely to find information they had not actively searched for.

CHIIR '17, March 07 - 11, 2017, Oslo, Norway

ACM 978-1-4503-4677-1/17/03…$15.00
DOI: http://dx.doi.org/10.1145/3020165.3022132

The shelves are not without their drawbacks, however. Due to the vagaries of classification schemes, books on a single topic can be spread throughout the library [14]. In addition, the shelves only display physical items, which—with the rise of ebooks—represent a decreasing proportion of what libraries have to offer [22]. While these drawbacks may be opaque to readers, there are others that they understand: readers are aware of (and annoyed by) the number of physical books that go missing, are mis-shelved or merely checked out of the library when they need them [3].

Many of the difficulties of physical shelves could be ameliorated by digital information tools designed to support browsing and information encountering. However, until recently there were very few such tools. While the availability of these tools has increased (e.g.[11; 26]), few have been designed based on an empirical understanding of user needs or behaviour. Studies of library users' behaviour can therefore provide an empirical basis for informing the design of both physical libraries (in terms of how books are classified and showcased) and digital information tools.

We report on an observational study of information encountering in a physical library. We identify a tension information seekers face when browsing the shelves that we term the 'seeking-encountering tension'. This tension, on one hand, entices people towards the relatively high-risk, high-reward activity of exploring new information avenues encountered and, on the other, draws them back towards the relative safety of goal-directed information-seeking. We identify and discuss some of the factors that contribute to the seeking-encountering tension, and provide design suggestions for mitigating it. Throughout this paper, when we refer to 'information-seeking' it is this goal-directed activity we address, rather than the broader human information-seeking process [12; 18]. The broader process often incorporates information encountering [21], and savvy information seekers deliberately pursue encounters when actively searching/browsing [17].

The remainder of this paper consists of our approach, discussed in Section 2; findings in Section 3; discussion and design recommendations in Section 4, and conclusions in Section 5.

2. METHOD
This paper is based on findings from an empirical study of information encountering in physical and digital libraries. While the original study involved both a combined observation and interview component and a survey, we focus only on the observational interviews here, and only in the physical library.

Observation-based approaches have been widely used to investigate information behaviour [3; 10; 16], and have been demonstrated to be valuable, even with a small number of participants [13; 25]. We recruited five participants (four female, one male) from a Library and Information Science Masters student mailing list at City, University of London. LIS students are not typical information seekers [6]: they seek more deeply and reflect more thoughtfully on their information experiences. They are also more familiar with the layout of the library. We sought to specifically exploit these differences to investigate serendipity. We observed these participants conducting an open-ended, naturalistic information task—'find something that appeals to you'—with both the physical and digital versions of the university library. Participants were specifically told to take all the time they needed, and that it didn't matter whether they had a specific or vague idea of what they sought. While we could have opted to observe people already at the shelves, since most students used the library to find specific known items, observing information encounters ad-hoc would have been too time-consuming. Observations were followed by a critical incident-style interview, focusing on participants' recent experiences of serendipity in libraries.

Results were initially analysed using a bottom-up grounded analytical approach based on Grounded Theory methodology, but—due to scheduling constraints—without a cyclic process of data gathering and analysis. The data was then examined by a second researcher who noted the seeking-encountering tension and re-analysed it with this particular theoretical lens. This second analysis was partly inductive and partly deductive, as once the tension was identified, the remainder of the analysis involved looking specifically for findings related to it—how often it occurs, where it occurs and whether there were any common factors in its occurrence. The findings from this analysis are presented here.

3. FINDINGS

This section consists of a description of the seeking-encountering tension and when it occurs, and a discussion of the factors that contribute to this tension.

3.1 The Seeking-Encountering Tension

Participants experienced a tension between information-seeking and encountering when browsing the library shelves; Encountering potentially useful information unexpectedly enticed them to explore the new directions that had presented themselves. This presented both opportunity for new insights, but also the risk of wasting time and effort. Weighing up perceived risk vs. benefits is not straightforward, as the nature and magnitude of the benefits remain unknown until resources have been invested in harvesting them. Therefore, sometimes encounters also drew participants back to the lower-risk activity of goal-directed information-seeking.

On one hand, participants were tempted by the draw and excitement of serendipitous discovery, but on the other felt constrained to focus on goal-directed information-seeking. This is unlikely to have been merely a factor of our task design; 'find something that appeals to you' is particularly broad and non-goal-directed. Indeed, in most cases, participants had a rough idea of a topical area they wanted to browse around, but refrained from looking for specific titles.

Of five participants, four mentioned (either directly or obliquely) that the shelves provided more avenues for exploration than they could pursue. These mentions occurred in a variety of contexts.

P3 stated upfront that they were goal-focused and avoided looking at, much less browsing the library shelves:

'I tend not to interact as much with the physical library space... I find a book that I want...and reserve it or just quickly find out where it is and retrieve it; check it out.'

'I'd go for specific items instead of just wander and browse.'

There was one exception to this—looking for fiction in a public library, when P3 would *'go in and just browse'*.

P1 mentioned disliking *'having too many things thrust on [them] at once'* and noted that they avoid a range of digital information tools (e.g. Twitter) as a result of this. When browsing the shelves, they repeatedly mentioned becoming distracted by encountering information not directly related to their information-seeking goal:

'There's so many things that appeal to me at the same time, but I already put something as my priority...' 'I'm kind of looking for what I want but I keep getting distracted'.

These descriptions are not of information overload (IO)—a negative experience where a person is overwhelmed by the volume of potentially useful information [2], but rather of a seeking-encountering tension—where the 'distraction' may be deemed by the participant as negative, positive or somewhere in-between. P5, for example, gave a fairly negative description of the tension:

'Having too much serendipity when you have a topic in mind, it can be distracting. It can get you off track'.

Similarly, P2 described a specific incident of being distracted by the shelves during a goal-driven search for a known item:

'I searched...and went to go and find the area, and I realised next to it was the thing I had walked past a couple of days earlier.'

While such an encounter might not always be negative, P2 said it was counter to their information-seeking goal at the time:

'I felt I had to be quite efficient with "okay I found this book and I need to use this book to work with"'... 'it was a minibreak in the wrong environment.'

3.2 Factors Contributing to the Tension

All five participants described situations where they would have liked to investigate promising new information, but felt constrained in some way. These factors contribute to the seeking-encountering tension and provide insight into the underlying reasons for it.

Unsurprisingly, a key factor mentioned was **time**; participants were tempted to explore further, but lacked the time to do so:

'If I really had time I'd flip to whatever sections.' (P5)

'Do you like the experience or the option for getting lost?' (Interviewer) *'Not where there is a time limit.'* (P5)

Having a **specific information goal** was a key driver for participants steering themselves back towards goal-directed information-seeking. P5 stated *'I always have a concrete goal'* when asked if they would take the time to wander around. This sentiment was echoed by P1, who commented *'I browse very rarely. I like having a goal'*.

Another factor that contributed to the tension was **self-consciousness** when browsing the shelves. P2 noted the university library was *'a place of study where everyone was working very hard and I should be working hard right now'*; this prevented her from examining a book she had encountered in more detail. This was echoed by P5, who commented that they limit their browsing in the library because

'the 4th floor in particular feels very shhh. Even wearing flip flops makes me self-conscious.'

The need to avoid making noise was also echoed by P1 and P4:

'I think there when you're walking you're making sound and everyone is glaring at you...if you browse willy-nilly in these I think that everyone is looking at me or waiting for you to like "just sit yourself down and not make any noise".' (P1)

'I know I'm making noise by swishing around or pulling books out or when they fall over.' (P4)

The space between the shelves was also mentioned as a factor leading to self-consciousness, as P3 noted:

'The rows are very tight, so if someone else is in that row you don't want to bump into them.'

While these descriptions do not speak to the seeking-encountering tension specifically, they do highlight circumstances where participants noticed information or a section of the library they would have liked to have examined in more detail, but felt constrained - whether by the ingrained need to have a pre-defined goal, space limitations, or the fear of disturbing others.

Another factor that contributed to the tension was **visual distraction**. P5, for example commented *'what's with the pictures? What the f*** is this?'* when attempting to assess a shelf of books on writing skills and noticing a cover depicting blueberries. P4 noted that *'it was hard to get a picture of what it [a book] was about'* from the cover. In this case, the perceived contradiction between the imagery used on the cover and the book's content were at odds to an extent that posed a distraction to the task at hand.

The **physicality** of books was also noted by one participant as a factor limiting the examination of encountered information:

'I often get books out but because they're so heavy I can only take a few out at a time. I have to stagger it.' (P4)

The **wide availability of information sources** was also noted. For example, P1 stated that, in the past, fewer digital sources were available and it was more difficult to explore them than it is today:

*'Searching...browsing... changed a lot since I was younger. When I was younger we didn't have a lot of online resources we just had a library and the browsing system was the ****tiest.'*

Wider availability of sources can provide more potential information avenues to explore and easier browsing can facilitate their exploration. However, sometimes participants did not actually want to explore information sources, but instead wanted to go right to a small set of useful items – as explained by P1:

'In the back of my head I know what I really want to look at, but I don't really know how to get there in terms of topic areas or what I'm supposed to search...'

This is not simply an example of a preference for directed seeking over encountering, but an instance of the seeking-encountering tension—where the participant felt they needed to be more goal-directed, but only had a vague idea of what they were looking for.

The same participant, when asked how serendipity might be facilitated online, stated *'you might [be] forced into it'*. This highlights that while serendipity itself is an inherently positive phenomenon [17], there are some negative implications of serendipitous information encounters, for example particular, being 'forced' into exploration to the detriment of an existing information-seeking goal. Whether a serendipitous information encounter is seen as positive or negative overall may be dependent on the perceived value of the 'distraction' in comparison with the perceived value of pursing the existing goal.

The factors that contribute to the seeking-encountering tension are varied. How to ameliorate it is discussed in the next section.

4. DISCUSSION AND DESIGN ISSUES

The seeking-encountering tension is, in many ways, the negative (or 'dark') side of serendipity. Serendipity requires an open mind, time to reflect, and a trigger-rich environment [17], features which can all contribute to the seeking-encountering tension. Information encountering can be considered a mixed blessing for exploratory search and browsing in general: on one hand, it can tempt information seekers to explore, on the other it can create a degree of chaos, encouraging information avoidance—where potentially useful information sources are ignored due to overload [2].

We know browsing the shelves is more likely to occur when readers have more time [19], and our study demonstrates tension when readers feel time poor. The necessity to invest time to create value from potentially serendipitous experiences and the risk of this investment not paying off has been previously noted [15], but not in the specific context of information acquisition.

Some of the factors contributing to the seeking-encountering tension offer lessons for physical library design: browsing is clearly limited in silent environments and those where shelves are close together (this latter has been noted in retail environments [27], but not libraries before). Some factors, such as book weight (also observed before [8]), noise and self-consciousness could be immediately ameliorated by moving the browsing activity online. We have not yet developed technology, though, that offers a browsing experience that is comparable to the physical, particularly for serendipitous discovery [5; 8; 16]. Thus at present it would be more useful to design physical library spaces in light of these factors, e.g. by separating reading and browsing areas to reduce noise-related **self-consciousness** and offering digital check-out of physical books to counter weight and other **physicality** issues.

The main challenge posed by our findings, is how best to provide users of both physical and digital information environments with just the right amount of opportunity for information encountering. For some, this will be zero—they will know what they want and not be open to other options [22]. For others this might include a huge variety of material [20]. For all, the 'right' amount is likely to vary based on many internal and external factors—including information goals, attitudes and time pressures. In digital environments, design options include ways to zoom in and out over collections, and ways to provide users with agency to expand search result sets at will to related and partly-related items (e.g. a 'serendipity slider'). Designers might also make pursuing new information avenues less risky by providing ways to facilitate rapid and efficient scanning and information extraction from the **wide variety of information sources** available – e.g. integrated reading support, content overviews and ways to move between summary and detailed information. These interventions also aim to counter the **time** barrier faced by our participants. It is also possible to employ positive **visual distraction** (e.g. by providing image-based previews of visual content). Offering timely opportunities for deviation from an existing **specific information goal** may also be useful—either once the goal has been successfully achieved, or when the information-seeker has reached a dead end. Supporting the easy postponement of the examination of encountered information may help in this regard. While potentially useful, these ideas are early and unformed and require further investigation.

5. CONCLUSION

We have presented a new drawback to the library shelves as information gateways: a tension between information-seeking and encountering. This tension is characterised by the temptation to explore information beyond an original goal versus the urge to return to this goal. We have also presented a number of factors that contribute to the seeking-encountering tension, such as perceived time pressure, self-consciousness and visual overload. An understanding of this tension can inform the design of physical and digital information environments that provide opportunity for serendipity without causing negative distraction. We have made some general design suggestions for achieving this, including providing environments that support users in switching dynamically between information-seeking and encountering. How best to integrate these suggestions into physical and digital environments remains an issue for future work.

6. REFERENCES

[1] Bates, M.J., 2007. What is browsing--really? A model drawing from behavioural science research. *Inform Res 12*.

[2] Bawden, D. and Robinson, L., 2009. The dark side of information: overload, anxiety and other paradoxes and pathologies. *J Inf Sci 35*, 2 (April 1, 2009), 180-191. DOI= http://dx.doi.org/10.1177/0165551508095781.

[3] Blandford, A., Rimmer, J., and Warwick, C., 2006. Experiences of the Library in the Digital Age. In *Proc CCCDT 06* (Tavros, Greece), FOHW.

[4] Erdelez, S., 2005. Information Encountering. In *Theories of information behavior*, K.E. Fisher and L. Mckechnie Eds. Information Today, Inc., Medford NJ, 179-184.

[5] Foster, A. and Ford, N., 2003. Serendipity and information seeking: An empirical study. *J Doc 59*, 3, 321-340. DOI= http://dx.doi.org/10.1108/00220410310472518.

[6] Gross, J. and Sheridan, L., 2011. Web scale discovery: the user experience. *New Library World 112*, 5, 236-247. DOI= http://dx.doi.org/10.1108/03074801111136275.

[7] Hancock-Beaulieu, M., 1993. Evaluating the impact of an online library catalogue on subject searching at the catalogue and at the shelves. *J Doc 46*, 4, 318-338. DOI= http://dx.doi.org/10.1108/eb026863.

[8] Hinze, A., Mckay, D., Vanderschantz, N., Timpany, C., and Cunningham, S.J., 2012. Book selection behavior in the physical library: implications for ebook collections. In *Proc JCDL '12* (Washington, DC), ACM, 305-314. DOI= http://dx.doi.org/10.1145/2232817.2232874.

[9] Khoo, M. and Hall, C., 2012. What would 'Google' Do? Users' Mental Models of a Digital Library Search Engine. In *Proc TPDL 12* (Paphos, Cyprus), Springer, 1-12. DOI= http://dx.doi.org/10.1007/978-3-642-33290-6_1.

[10] Khoo, M., Rozaklis, L., and Hall, C., 2012. A survey of the use of ethnographic methods in the study of libraries and library users. *Libr. Inf. Sci. Res. 34*, 2 (4//), 82-91. DOI= http://dx.doi.org/10.1016/j.lisr.2011.07.010.

[11] Kleiner, E., Rädle, R., and Reiterer, H., 2013. Blended shelf: reality-based presentation and exploration of library collections. In *Proc CHI 13* (Paris, France), ACM, 577-582. DOI= http://dx.doi.org/10.1145/2468356.2468458.

[12] Kuhlthau, C.C., 1991. Inside the Search Process: Information Seeking from the User's Perspective. *JASIST 42*, 5, 361-371. DOI= http://dx.doi.org/10.1002/(SICI)1097-4571(199106)42:5<361::AID-ASI6>3.0.CO;2-#.

[13] Kuhlthau, C.C., 1999. The role of experience in the information search process of an early career information worker: Perceptions of uncertainty, complexity, construction, and sources. *JASIST 50*, 5, 399-412. DOI= http://dx.doi.org/10.1002/(SICI)1097-4571(1999)50:5<399::AID-ASI3>3.0.CO;2-L.

[14] Losee, R.M., 1993. The relative shelf location of circulated books: A study of classification, users, and browsing. *Libr Resour Tech Serv 37*, 2, 197-209.

[15] Makri, S. and Blandford, A., 2012. Coming across information serendipitously: Part 1 – A process model. *J Doc 68*, 5, 685-704. DOI= http://dx.doi.org/10.1108/00220411211256030.

[16] Makri, S., Blandford, A., Gow, J., Rimmer, J., Warwick, C., and Buchanan, G., 2007. A library or just another information resource? A case study of users' mental models of traditional and digital libraries. *JASIST 58*, 3, 433-445. DOI= http://dx.doi.org/10.1002/asi.20510.

[17] Makri, S., Blandford, A., Woods, M., Sharples, S., and Maxwell, D., 2014. "Making my own luck": Serendipity strategies and how to support them in digital information environments. *JASIST 65*, 11, 2179-2194. DOI= http://dx.doi.org/10.1002/asi.23200.

[18] Marchionini, G., 1997. *Information Seeking in Electronic Environments*. Cambridge University Press, Cambridge, UK.

[19] Mckay, D., Buchanan, G., and Chang, S., 2015. Tyranny of Distance: Understanding Academic Library Browsing by Refining the Neighbour Effect. In *Proc TPDL 15* (Poznan, Poland), Springer, 280-294. DOI= http://dx.doi.org/10.1007/978-3-319-24592-8_21.

[20] Mckay, D. and Conyers, B., 2010. Where the streets have no name: how library users get lost in the stacks. In *Proc CHINZ 10* (Auckland, New Zealand), ACM, 77-80. DOI= http://dx.doi.org/10.1145/1832838.1832852.

[21] Mckenzie, P.J., 2003. A model of information practices in accounts of everyday-life information seeking. *J Doc 59*, 1, 19-40. DOI= http://dx.doi.org/10.1108/00220410310457993.

[22] Rowlands, I. and Nicholas, D., 2008. Understanding Information Behaviour: How Do Students and Faculty Find Books? *J Acad Libr 34*, 1, 3-15. DOI= http://dx.doi.org/10.1016/j.acalib.2007.11.005.

[23] Saarinen, K. and Vakkari, P., 2013. A sign of a good book: readers' methods of accessing fiction in the public library. *J Doc. 69*, 5, 736-754. DOI= http://dx.doi.org/10.1108/JD-04-2012-0041.

[24] Svenonius, E., 2000. *The Intellectual Foundation of Information Organization*. MIT Press, Boston, MA.

[25] Tang, R. and Solomon, P., 1998. Toward an understanding of the dynamics of relevance judgment: An analysis of one person's search behavior. *IP&M 34*, 2 (1998/03/01), 237-256. DOI= http://dx.doi.org/http://dx.doi.org/10.1016/S0306-4573(97)00081-2.

[26] Thudt, A., Hinrichs, U., and Carpendale, S., 2012. The bohemian bookshelf: supporting serendipitous book discoveries through information visualization. In *Proc CHI 12* (Austin, TX), ACM, 1461-1470. DOI= http://dx.doi.org/10.1145/2207676.2208607.

[27] Underhill, P., 1999. *Why We Buy: The Science of Shopping*. Simon and Schuster, New York.

Strangers in a Strange Land: A Study of Second Language Speakers Searching for e-Services

David Brazier
Computer and Information Sciences
Northumbria University
Newcastle upon Tyne, England
d.brazier@northumbria.ac.uk

Morgan Harvey
Computer and Information Sciences
Northumbria University
Newcastle upon Tyne, England
morgan.harvey@northumbria.ac.uk

ABSTRACT

While the recent trend of digitisation of government and related services offers many advantages, it could introduce problems for those who are less information literate or who have particular issues searching for and understanding the necessary content. In this study ten participants, who speak English as a second language, were given four search tasks designed to reflect actual information seeking situations. They completed pre- and post-search questionnaires to identify the relevancy of the task, their English language ability and search experience.

Our results suggest that, despite a perception that they performed to the best of their abilities, were bookmarking relevant documents and that the given tasks were easy, the students were actually often choosing documents that are only partially or tangentially relevant. The repercussions of this discrepancy are clear and suggest that much more assistance is needed before such services can be made 'digital by default'.

Keywords

information behaviour; search; user studies; e-services; information literacy

1. INTRODUCTION

The digitisation of services and dissemination of Internet-based technologies have resulted in initiatives, such as the UK government's 'digital by default', whereby public sector services are transitioned onto electronic systems (e-services). For the average user, for whom Internet technologies have become an everyday tool, this will come as no great burden; however, information and digital divides place importance on the IT literacy and abilities of the user [4].

For users of such systems whose first language is not English, searching for information in a non-native language could raise numerous problems surrounding: knowledge of content in a unfamiliar culture and setting; language use, where variations in meaning can significantly change search results and awareness of the reliability of sources. Users may have previously relied on face to face encounters with staff or the knowledge and experience of friends, family or community members when their own was lacking. However, situations where these social groups may not be attainable or knowledge and experience is just as lacking can have dire repercussions for some members of society who already face significant barriers [10].

CHIIR '17, March 07 - 11, 2017, Oslo, Norway

ISBN 978-1-4503-4677-1/17/03... $15.00

DOI: http://dx.doi.org/10.1145/3020165.3022136

2. RELATED WORK

A number of studies have looked at multilingual online searching with research focusing on web content (or lack thereof) in the user's native language [2] and language proficiency as major contributors to the user's decision to search in a non-native language, notably when English is that language [2, 3, 11]. Research within the field goes some way to disclosing the search behaviours of multilingual searchers but focuses predominately on "why" rather than "how" they search and how well they perform [12].

In a study of refugee use of government services Lloyd et al. [10] found that information poverty was a product of the social exclusion of the participants as a result of barriers e-services can erect. With this in mind, this paper is motivated by the findings of Rozsa et al. [12] and Lloyd et al. [10] in observing the online search behaviours of non-native users of UK governmental e-services. It acknowledges the participants use of such services as they are now digitised (the 'why') and looks to compare the search behaviours of users whose first language is not English (the 'how').

3. METHODOLOGY

Identification of the types of services such users would use was made by the author in an (as yet) unpublished study in which 7 international PhD students at a UK university, 6 of whom also took part in the study described in this work, were recruited and were tasked with identifying: what a government service entailed; which would be deemed most useful (to the group); and the information needs, information sources and skills that would be required to successfully utilise the e-service. The findings from this study helped shape the task scenarios detailed within this paper.

The 10 study participants were all international PhD students from a large UK university who spoke English as a second language (fluent 80%, competent 20%). All participants were from different countries across Europe (20%), Asia (70%) and Africa (10%) with a total of 11 languages spoken natively, and 15 languages in total up to a competent level. 40% of the participants were female with an average age of 31 (*SD = 3.56*) and 60% were male with an average age of 31.5 (*SD = 3.33*). Each was remunerated for their participation with a £10 Amazon voucher.

There were a total of three sessions with two sessions of three students and one of four as dictated by participant and technical equipment availability. Each session followed the same process of each participant filling in a demographic questionnaire which collected information on their area of study; age; gender; nationality; language(s) spoken and proficiency; IT use; search engine use in English and their native tongue; search engine competency and preference and their own UK governmental service awareness. The participants were then asked to perform four search tasks. Using the Chrome browser, each participant was asked to use the Google Search Engine to start each task but were not limited to the search results page.

Each task was allotted ten minutes for completion with up to five minutes for the participants to read the task and complete the pre- and post-questionnaires. This allowed for no more than one hour in total. Tasks were distributed to participants using a Latin square design to account for task fatigue and potential learning effects [9].

3.1 Tasks

The search tasks were defined based on the results of the previously mentioned short study and are designed to reflect actual information seeking situations in an attempt to be relevant and a more interesting search experience for the participants [6].

1. *Your friend from Peru and their family (2 members) are coming to visit you for 6 months while you are in the UK. Develop a list of instructions to help them apply for the necessary visas.*

2. *A family member is coming to the UK to live and wants information on housing. They have heard there are a number of options and have asked you for advice. Identify the options available to them and recommend which they should choose. Give reasons to support your recommendation.*

3. *Your friend just got back from a trip abroad and suddenly developed a high fever. A dry cough, chills, and breathing difficulties soon followed. What could they have? They have no insurance and have asked your advice on what to do. Provide them with recommended actions.*

4. *Your elderly neighbours have heard about the UK governmen'ts 'digital by default' initiative and are concerned about whether this will affect them and their friends at the local community centre. They have asked you to find out more about it. Use your best judgement to highlight what would impact them with reasons for your choices.*

All 4 tasks were assessed by the participants as being relevant or partially relevant to them with task 1 receiving the highest average relevance score and task 4 the lowest.

Prior to beginning each task, participants were asked to fill in a pre-task questionnaire [6] (see Table 1) to gauge their domain knowledge, interest in the topic and the perceived difficulty of the task using a five point Likert scale where 1 is "Not at all" and 5 is "Very".

Q1	I have searched about this topic before
Q2	I know about this topic
Q3	I am interested in this topic
Q4	It will be difficult to find information about this topic

Table 1: Pre-task questions.

As mentioned prior, the participants' activities were logged with video and audio data recorded and they were asked to bookmark any website (document) deemed relevant to the task. At the end of each task the participant was also required to complete a post-task questionnaire [1, 5, 6, 8, 9] with responses on a five point Likert scale where 1 is "Not at all confident" and 5 is "Very confident". Examples can be seen in Table 2.

Q3	The task was relevant to me
Q6	I performed the task to the best of my ability
Q7	I found the task difficult
Q8	I'm confident the content I found satisfied the task
Q10	I'm confident I identified relevant websites
Q11	I'm confident in my ability to read the website content
Q12	I am confident in my ability to understand the content of the websites I visited

Table 2: Selected post-task questions.

Afterwards participants were invited to take part in a semi-structured group discussion to examine their searching experiences and to highlight any issues or concerns and offer suggestions or solutions to any of the points that arose. Findings from these discussions are not included in this paper due to space limitations.

To determine the relevance of the bookmarks logged by the participants, all bookmarks were assessed by two IR researchers using a voting strategy and given scores between 1 and 4, where 1 is not relevant, 2 is tangentially relevant, 3 is partially relevant and 4 is totally relevant. Any bookmarks not assigned the same score by the two assessors in the first round were discussed and a single score was agreed, although this only occurred for a very small number of cases.

4. RESULTS

In total participants created 267 bookmarks, with an approximately equal split between governmental and non- governmental resources. Table 3 shows the total number of bookmarked URLs that participants deemed relevant to the tasks and whether they were from governmental sources and the mean relevance score. Of all the URLs bookmarked only 60.7% were either partially or totally relevant, with 30.7% tangentially relevant and 8.5% non-relevant and there were no significant differences between the median number of bookmarks per task with each task receiving 8 or 9 per participant on average. Surprisingly, there was little difference in terms of relevance between governmental and non-governmental resources. This was mostly due to some participants bookmarking internal policy documents or documents discussing best practices for civil servant software engineers which were deemed to be only tangentially relevant and unlikely to be of help in the given contexts.

Bookmark	No.	Relevance
Governmental:	141	2.91
non-Governmental:	129	2.92

Table 3: Bookmark types

English proficiency was self-assessed with 80% of the participants declaring themselves fluent and 20% competent with all participants using IT daily and formulating queries (on search engines) in English on a daily basis (90%) or a few times a week (10%). When judging their own abilities in formulating queries in English, identifying relevant search results and information on websites, 8 out of 10 were either confident or very confident in their abilities with the remaining 2 stating they were "slightly confident". Half of the participants had used UK government e-services previously, 30% hadn't and 20% were unsure what was meant by the term.

As shown in Table 4, there was considerable variation in performance by different users with the bookmarks of 5 participants being only relevant in 50% or less of cases. There was also variation in the numbers of pages bookmarked; one participant only bookmarked 3 per task on average with the majority bookmarking 5 or more. Participant J acknowledged their limited bookmarks for the 3rd task as in a real scenario they would not risk the health of another by self diagnosing, and would instead only refer that person to a health professional in the first instance.

User	Precision	Bookmarks/task
A	0.81	6
B	0.74	11
C	0.50	7
D	0.43	10
E	0.44	9
F	0.43	9
G	1.00	6
H	1.00	3
I	0.80	5
J	0.49	9

Table 4: User performance.

When comparing the performance of the participants against the perceived task difficulty (pre-task question 4) they were unable to successfully predict how well they would perform (Figure 1 and Table 5), in fact it appears that they performed best in cases where they expected to perform poorly! In spite of this, there is some correlation, albeit not significant (0.26, p-value = 0.11), between their post-task assessment of difficulty and their pre-task prediction of the same. This suggests that they were unlikely to dramatically change their perception of a task's difficulty after having actually performed that task.

Confidence in their own abilities was in evidence throughout the study and, even in the case of the few who doubted their abilities in the pre-study questionnaire, the level of confidence was predominately in the confident to very confident response levels. As shown in Table 6 and Figure 2, responses to the post-task questions on self-perceived performance (Q6), confidence in having completed the task well (Q8) and of having identified relevant websites (Q10) were

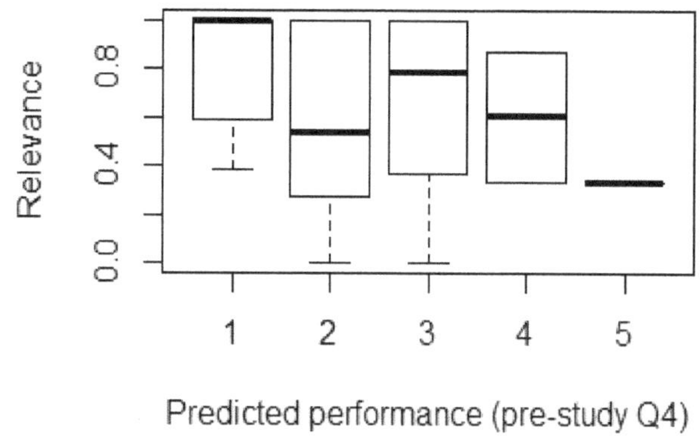

Figure 1: Performance by expected task difficulty.

Pre-study Q4	Relevance	Count
1	1.00	7
2	0.53	18
3	0.79	12
4	0.60	2
5	0.33	1

Table 5: User performance vs expected task difficulty.

overwhelmingly positive. This was also the case with regards to understanding what they had read during the task (Q11) and on the websites bookmarked (Q12). This is further reflected in their categorisation of task difficulty (Q7), where the median response was 2 (not difficult). This confidence is in stark contrast to their overall performance, which was generally quite poor.

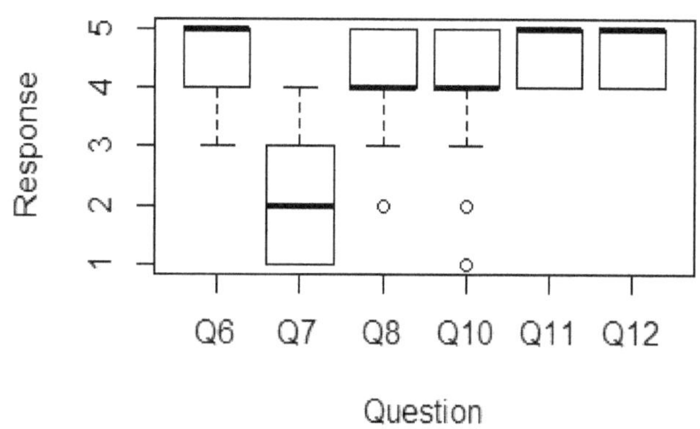

Figure 2: Confidence in abilities and task difficulty.

Further to their views of their abilities, the post-task review of their perceived performance in comparison to their actual performance shows participants were not able to correctly determine how well they had performed. The majority of responses were in the confident to very confident range while precision was actually lower than for the less confident ratings ($p < 0.76$) as shown in Table 7.

Response	Q6	Q7	Q8	Q10	Q11	Q12
1	0	14	0	1	0	0
2	0	10	3	1	0	0
3	4	9	3	1	0	0
4	7	7	18	21	17	16
5	29	0	16	16	23	24

Table 6: Confidence in abilities and task difficulty.

Response	Performance		Count	
	Q8	*Q10*	*Q8*	*Q10*
1	0	1.0	0	1
2	1.0	0.22	3	1
3	1.0	1.0	3	1
4	0.61	0.63	18	21
5	0.69	0.69	16	16

Table 7: Confidence in content that satisfied the task (Q8) and confidence in relevant websites from search results (Q10) versus performance.

5. CONCLUSIONS AND FUTURE WORK

In this work we have investigated the problem of people needing to search for, and assess, documents in a non-native language. Two factors contribute to this becoming an ever more common situation: the increasing numbers of people working and studying abroad as well as those who arrive in countries as refugees; and the push by many governments and organisations to move to fully-digital systems, the so-called 'digital by default' or 'e-government' movements.

The results of our 10-participant user study suggest that this situation may result in people overestimating their abilities and assessing non-relevant sources as being relevant and helpful. Our participants found the tasks to be relevant, assessed their English-language searching and reading abilities to be good and, having completed each task, were confident in their search and bookmarking performance. In spite of this, almost half of the documents they selected were assessed by native speakers to be either non-relevant or only tangentially relevant. The potential repercussions of this, had these situation been real, could be quite costly. Is this due to cultural differences, domain knowledge, or do they rely too much on government/non-government materials? Understanding why these issues arise may inform development of systems and techniques to mitigate these problems, perhaps by "training" users to search better via instruction or "learning by example" [7].

This paper only touches on the findings of this study, with work ongoing into the investigation of the online search behaviours of users who speak English as a second language. In future work we intend to use the various sources of data collected (including screen capture) to investigate the search behaviours and strategies participants employed. Using appropriate software we can mark all of the actions performed by participants during the sessions and calculate metrics such as the time taken to generate queries, the number of query reformulations, query terms used, the amount of time spent on SERPs and how and where the bookmarked documents were actually found. We intend to run the same study with native speakers to determine whether their performance is indeed better, as one would expect and hope, and compare them with the non-native speakers.

6. REFERENCES

[1] D. Bell and I. Ruthven. Searcher's assessments of task complexity for web searching. In *Advances in Information Retrieval*, pages 57–71, Berlin Heidelberg, April 2004. Springer.

[2] B. Berendt and A. Kralisch. A user-centric approach to identifying best deployment strategies for language tools: the impact of content and access language on web user behaviour and attitudes. *Information Retrieval*, 12(3):380–399, 2009.

[3] T. Bogers, M. Gäde, M. Hall, and M. Skov. Analyzing the influence of language proficiency on interactive book search behavior. *iSchools*, 2016.

[4] P. Chu, E. Jozsa, A. Komlodi, and K. Hercegfi. An exploratory study on search behavior in different languages. In *Proceedings of the 4th Information Interaction in Context Symposium*, pages 318–321. ACM, 2012.

[5] K. Collins-Thompson, S. Rieh, C. Haynes, and R. Syed. Assessing learning outcomes in web search: A comparison of tasks and query strategies. In *Proc. of the 2016 ACM on Conference on Human Information Interaction and Retrieval*, pages 163–172. ACM, March 2016.

[6] A. Edwards and D. Kelly. How does interest in a work task impact search behavior and engagement? In *Proc. of the 2016 ACM on Conference on Human Information Interaction and Retrieval*, pages 249–252. ACM, March 2016.

[7] M. Harvey, C. Hauff, and D. Elsweiler. Learning by example: training users with high-quality query suggestions. In *Proceedings of the 38th International ACM SIGIR Conference on Research and Development in Information Retrieval*, pages 133–142. ACM, 2015.

[8] B. Johnston and S. Webber. Information literacy in higher education: a review and case study. *ACM Trans. Program. Lang. Syst.*, 15(5):795–825, November 2003.

[9] D. Kelly, J. Arguello, A. Edwards, and W. Wu. Development and evaluation of search tasks for iir experiments using a cognitive complexity framework. In *Proc. of the 2015 International Conference on The Theory of Information Retrieval*, pages 101–110. ACM, September 2015.

[10] A. Lloyd, M. A. Kennan, K. M. Thompson, and A. Qayyum. Connecting with new information landscapes: information literacy practices of refugees. *Journal of Documentation.*, 69(1):121–144, 2013.

[11] J. Marlow, P. Clough, J. Recuero, and J. Artiles. Exploring the effects of language skills on multilingual web search. In *Advances in Information Retrieval*, pages 249–252, Berlin Heidelberg, March 2016. Springer.

[12] G. Rózsa, A. Komlodi, and P. Chu. Online searching in english as a foreign language. In *Proceedings of the 24th International Conference on World Wide Web Companion*, pages 875–880. International World Wide Web Conferences Steering Committee, 2015.

Visual Analysis of Dyslexia on Search

A. MacFarlane,
G. Buchanan
Centre for HCI Design
City, University of London
Northampton Square,
London EC1V 0HB
{andym, George.Buchanan.1}
@city.ac.uk

A. Al-Wabil
Ideation Lab, School of Engineering
MIT
Cambridge, MA. USA

Areej@mit.edu

G. Andrienko, N. Andrienko
giCentre
City, University of London
Northampton Square
London EC1V 0HB
{Gennady.Andrienko.1,
Natalia.Andrienko.1}@city.ac.uk

ABSTRACT

A key problem in the field of search interfaces is dyslexic users interaction with the UI. Dyslexia is a widespread specific learning difficult (SpLD) (10% of any population is estimated to have this cognitive disability) which is under researched in the field of information retrieval. The focus here is an analysis of the User Interface (UI) for search, using visual analytical methods on eye tracking data to examine the difference between control and dyslexic searchers. We use a number of visual analytic methods including path similarity analysis (PSA) and clustering of time intervals to demonstrate both similarities and differences between the user groups. Observations of videos are used to augment the visualizations. Results demonstrate a clear difference between the user groups, and a clear memory effect on the user of search interfaces is shown – this is a key contribution of this paper. We examine the results using of theories of dyslexia, contributing also to the field of dyslexia and search.

CCS Concepts

• Information systems→ Information Retrieval→ Users and interactive retrieval→ Search interfaces • Human-centered computing→ Visualization→ Visual analytics.

Keywords

Information Retrieval; Visual Analysis; Dyslexia.

1. INTRODUCTION

In an initial study [1] it was demonstrated that there is some evidence of a difference between the information search behavior of dyslexic users and the rest of the population. This paper examines further data collected during this pilot study, namely eye tracking data (not examined in that paper). The purpose of this paper is to augment this research by looking at interaction with the interface itself. The reader is referred to that paper for further detail on issues to do with dyslexia, but Webster's Dictionary definition is: "A learning disorder marked by impairment of the ability to recognize and comprehend written words". The other main focus of the paper, eye tracking in information processing, has generated significant interest over the part 20 or more years [2]. This technique focuses on a number of different variables, the most prominent being saccades with a given duration (rapid movements of the eyes, sometimes with very high velocities) and fixations (a period of relative stillness for the eyes of around 200/300ms). These in themselves can be useful (with some caveats), but they can be used to create scanpaths (a pattern of perception, made up a saccades and fixation sequence). In this paper we use eye tracking techniques in order to augment the information gathered in [1]. The key motivation for the work is to examine the impact of dyslexia on the user of the search interface, in order to provide information on UI designs which better suit those users and hopefully provide better designs for all users – an idea put forward by Shneiderman [3].

The paper is structured as follows. Firstly related work is outlined, including a brief description of the outcomes of the pilot study. The research aims are declared, and participants and methodology used in order to achieve these aims are detailed. The experimental results are detailed, and the implications of these results are then addressed in the summary and conclusions section.

2. RELATED WORK

The key prior study for this paper is the work done by the same team [1]. That paper found differences between dyslexic and control users in a number of different areas, including the number of documents read (dyslexic users read on average 16.2 documents less than control users) and the number of iterations per session (3.8 for dyslexic users and 6.8 for controls). That study provided evidence that there may be some important differences between the two groups of users. Further work [4] found that there was a significant difference between dyslexia and control users on documents judged irrelevant, and demonstrated a memory effect with users with better short term memory being correlated with judging more documents irrelevant – controls having better short term memory than dyslexic users.

With regard to eye tracking there have been a variety of studies both in HCI and IR which are relevant to this paper. Rayner [2] provides a detailed overview on research in the area, while Poole and Ball [5] give a more focused review in the context of HCI.

There have been a number of studies using eye tracking for measuring the effect of dyslexia on the web. The goals of that research has emphasized one of navigation structures, reading or directed search. Collectively, this provides insight into the visual aspects of search.

Al-Wabil [6] conducted a study on the effect of dyslexia on Web navigation. Several areas were investigated in that study. A preliminary investigation established the barriers to web access for this group, and used eye-tracking methodology to investigate differences in visual attention differences between control and dyslexic users. Experiments showed the problems when faced by dyslexic users when navigating web structures. They took longer to complete tasks and experienced more disorientation on such structures than control users. A further experiment found a difference in scanpaths between controls and dyslexic users when

CHIIR '17, March 07-11, 2017, Oslo, Norway
© 2017 ACM. ISBN 978-1-4503-4677-1/17/03…$15.00
DOI: http://dx.doi.org/10.1145/3020165.3022134

viewing text-heavy pages. This has implications for the visual inspection of retrieved documents.

Berget et al [7,8] have investigated the use of icons (visual content) to examine the impact on searching visual and textual content using eye-tracking data. No significant difference was found on visual tasks using icons, however dyslexic users performed significantly slower on textual tasks, mostly due to longer fixations [7]. Longer fixations were also evident in visual tasks [8] that imply a higher cognitive load on search tasks as a whole. Dyslexic users also demonstrated more fixations than controls on dual-modality task together with longer scanpaths when inspecting results lists. Other work by the same authors [9] demonstrated that dyslexic users fixation on the screen was less than controls whilst they were typing queries.

3. RESEARCH AIMS AND QUESTIONS

The primary aim of the work is to examine the difference between control and dyslexic users' interaction with search interfaces whilst resolving their information needs. The motivation for the work is to provide more information on how dyslexic users utilize interfaces, so that we can design UI's to better meet their needs. In order to do this we undertake a visual analysis of their search behavior by examining visual stress and eye tracking data. The objectives are as follows:

- Using eye-tracking data, establish what is the general pattern of interaction with the search interface.
- Using eye tracking data, identify the difference between user types when using the search interface
- Using qualitative data with observations, refine the implications drawn from the quantitative data.

4. PARTICPANTS AND METHODS

We briefly describe the participants of the study in section 4.1, screening methods used prior to the search session in 4.2, and then eye tracking data and observation data in 4.3.

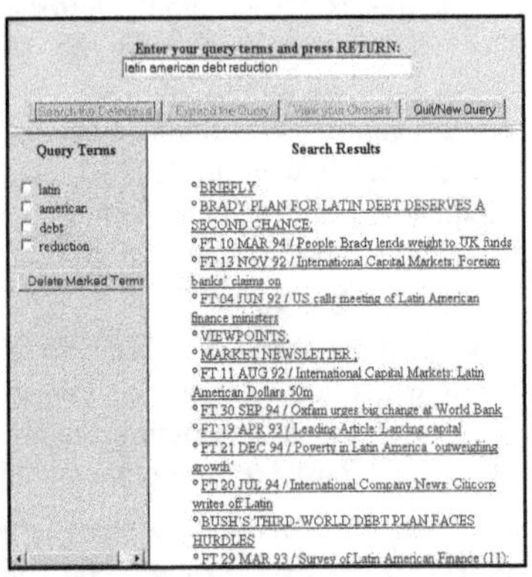

Figure 1. OKAPI PhP. Search interface.

4.1 Participants and experimental setup

A detailed description of the participants and the experimental setup can be found in [1]. We recruited a total of 10 participants for the study, 5 control users and 5 dyslexic users. However one set of eye tracking data of a dyslexic user was not saved due to technical issues, so the data for 9 participants only are recorded. The procedure was approved by the University Ethics committee.

As visual stress can be a significant issue for some dyslexic users, we used Lucid software [10] to screen the participants prior to the experiment. This software establishes the sensitivity to visual stress using a word game, and measuring the disruption to performance in the game by visually stressful stimuli. The word game consists of a task requiring the use to find a word in a grid of letters – the user is presented with N word searches is sequence mixing the stressful and non-stressful items.

There was no evidence of susceptibility to visual stress bar two dyslexic users who did not complete the test. Eligibility criteria for dyslexic participants was a diagnosis of dyslexia by an educational psychologist. This status was confirmed by reviewing a copy of the educational psychologist report that participants provided.

We used the Okapi retrieval system for our experiments, utilizing a PhP web interface developed for conducting user experiments (see fig 1). The UI had a query pane at the top (which was used only once), a term pane on the left (which the user used to refine their queries after the first iteration) and a document/results set pane on the right. The participant monitor was placed on stand to raise it to the level of participants' eyes. Eye movements were recorded using Tobii's X50 commercial eye tracker. The Okapi interface was displayed on a 15 inch flat panel monitor with a resolution of 1024 x 768 pixels. Users were given one TREC topic and asked to search a TREC collection of documents in a limited 30 minute period – more details can be found in [1].

4.2 Search time data collection - Eye tracking data and Observations

Tobii eye tracking software collects a significant amount of data in image form (Gaze Plots and Heat Maps) and text form (x,y co-ordinates of fixations etc.). Unfortunately, as images of Gaza Plots and Heat Maps produced for individual interaction with pages, and pages viewed by users would differ considerably (i.e. viewing widely different results lists and documents), we could not sensibly use the images for analysis. However the text data collected was used to generate the following data for analysis (see Table 1).

Table 1 – Eye Tracking Data

Fixations	Accumulated no of x,y position in pixels of a fixation on the UI
Track Length	Length of moves from one fixation to the next in pixels.
Duration	Duration of the fixation in ms.

Subjects were also videoed while searching and these were viewed afterward in order more closely inspect users searching behaviour. The video shows the users eye tracking movement on the search interface together with an insert showing the user. Audio was also used to record any interactions with the researcher.

4.3 Visual Analytic Methods

The method used to analyze the eye tracking data is explained in more detail elsewhere [11], to produce a number of visualizations including distribution of point, Voronoi tessellation, and histograms for the frequency distribution of move directions. In order to undertake the analysis of movements of lengths and directions, further data was produced from the basic data in table 1 (see table 2).

The system is primarily intended for analysis of geographic data, where the Y-axis is oriented upwards. The direction 0° corresponds to North, 90° to East, and so on. In the map display, we can turn the drawing upside down, to make it correspond to the screen coordinate system, where the Y-axis is oriented downwards. However, this does not affect the computation of the movement directions. Therefore, for the screen coordinate system,

0° corresponds to the direction down, 45° to down right, 90° to right, 135° to up right, 180° to up, 225° to up left, 270° to left, and 315° to down left. Hence, directions 45-65° correspond to movements down right (i.e., from UL to LR), and directions 225-245° to movements up left (i.e., from LR to UL).

Table 2 Analysis of movement lengths and directions

#moves	Total no of saccades.
#moves length >=50	No of saccades with length >= 50 pixels.
Duration	Duration of the fixation in ms.
% Total	% of # saccades length >=50
#moves between clusters	Total number of saccades between clusters
%Cluster moves	% of total saccades which are between clusters
Length	Mean, standard deviation, median and max statistics.

5. EXPERIMENTAL RESULTS

We report the data collected and its handling in section 5.1, visual analysis of the eye tracking data for user interaction patterns is provided in section 5.2 contrasting the interaction patterns of control and dyslexic users with observations of videos discussed in section 5.3.

Table 3 – Eye tracking statistics

Statistic	Users	#Fixations	Track Length	Duration (ms)
Total	*Control*	355079	46243097	8935820
	Dyslexic	254195	34953261	6412348
	All	609274	81196358	15348168
Average	*Control*	71016	9248619	1787164
	Dyslexic	63549	8738315	1603087
	All	67697	9021818	1705352
SD	*Control*	*19293*	3674753	221093
	Dyslexic	22730	2146656	323857
	All	19883	2924430	270526

5.1 Data collected

A total of 774,695 records were collected by the eye tracking software from all 9 users. Of these 5,312 records have no coordinates and 160,109 have identical coordinates (-1024,-768) were interpreted as errors and removed from the data leaving a total of 609,274 points from which to build the eye trajectories. Statistics per user type a provided in Table 3. Note that the averages for all statistics on dyslexic users interaction are less than controls, but standard deviations are greater for the former apart for track length.

5.2 User interaction patterns on UI

From Figure 2, two large and dense clusters of the fixations can be observed. The main clusters differ in spatial extents but have very similar internal structures. Each cluster consists of sub-clusters separated by vertical and horizontal gaps. To investigate this further we created a Voroni tessellation of moves between the clusters (see fig 3) summarizing the movements from the trajectories into moves (or flows) between the cells. It is clear that the main flows are between the right parts of the two main clusters. There are also smaller flows between the left parts of the main clusters. However, there were very few or no movements between the left and right parts within the clusters and between the left part of one cluster and the right part of the other cluster.

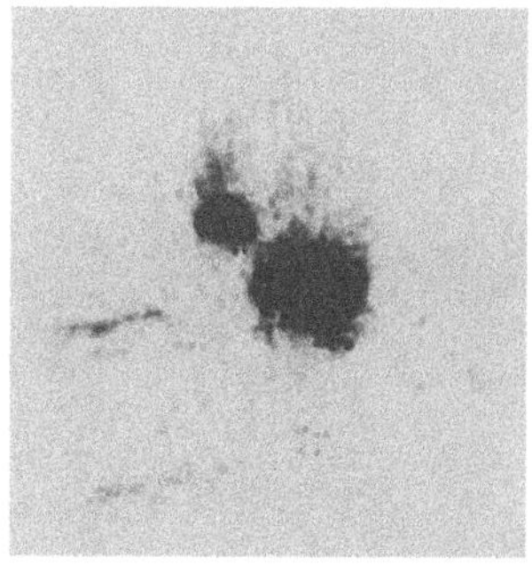

Figure 2 – Distribution of points from eye tracks

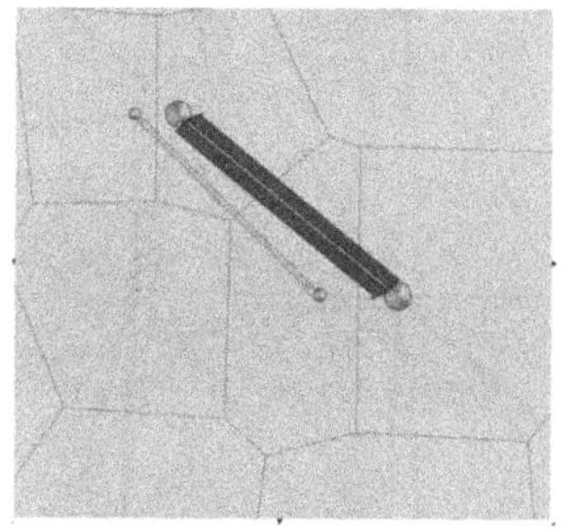

Figure 3 – Voronoi tessellation of moves between clusters

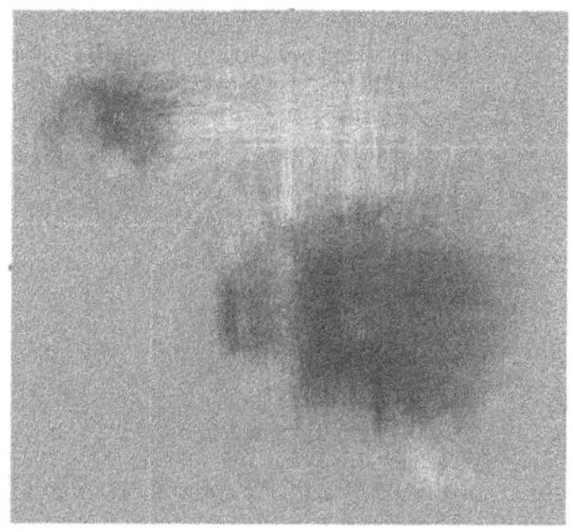

Figure 4 – Distributions of points with trajectory segments between two main clusters removed

In order to investigate this phenomenon we examined the points in the cluster by removing the trajectory segments from the two clusters identified see fig 4. This shows a clearer pattern of interactions within the clusters, showing horizontal and vertical moves. The upper cluster is the results list, which tends to be horizontal, the lower cluster is document views with both horizontal and vertical moves. This interaction occurs after the first iteration, the initial query was set for the experiment and no further interaction was possible with the query pane, hence the concentration of user eye movements in the results list/document view pane (see figure 1).

5.3 Contrast between Dyslexic and Control user interaction patterns

We further used the revised data in Fig 4 to investigate the difference between the two types of users, by producing histograms of moves in terms of degrees (0 to 360°) – see figures 5 and 6.

For the control user group (Fig 5), we see a clear prevalence of horizontal movements (directions around 90° and 270°), more to the right (90°) than to the left (270°). The frequencies of the vertical movements (around 0°=360° and around 180°) are not much higher than for diagonal movements. For the dyslexic user group, we see high frequencies of both horizontal and vertical movements. The frequencies of the vertical movements are almost as high as for the horizontal movements and much higher than for the diagonal movements. The basic difference between the user groups is that control users look more left to right, whereas dyslexic users often look down (0°=360°) and up (180°), e.g. between search result items, or to a previous point in a displayed document more often than is seen in the control group.

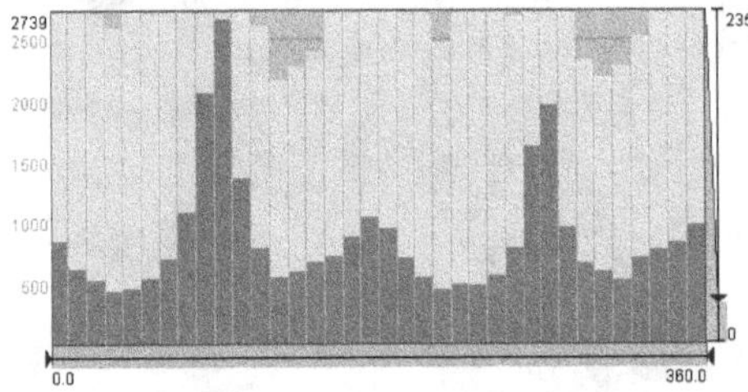

Figure 5 – Control group frequency distribution of moves

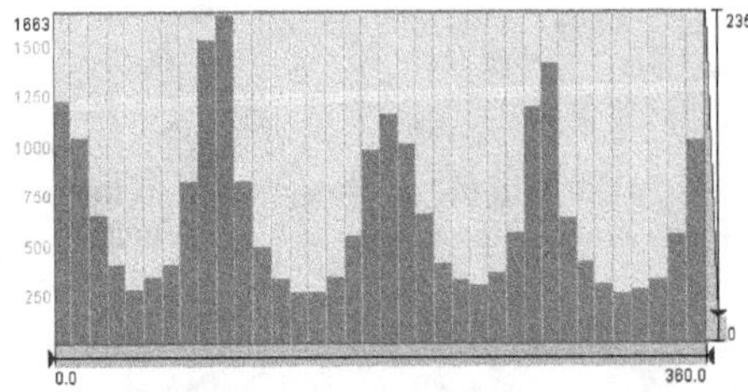

Figure 6 – Dyslexic group frequency distribution of moves

This is an interesting phenomena and an important result. The previous results produced in [4] demonstrated that there was clear evidence of the impact of poor short-term memory of dyslexic users on their interaction with search. We hypothesise that the phenomena found here is a further manifestation of this previous finding. Visual re-scanning is likely to occur because dyslexic users forget information they have already read and subsequently have to back-backtrack to an earlier point in the document (e.g. to the top) and begin reading again in order to remind themselves. This is all the more likely as short-term memory is biased towards recency – i.e. what is most recently encountered is most likely to be retained, and what is least recently is most likely to be forgotten. Furthermore, backtracking is a commonly reported phenomenon in the eye-tracking of dyslexic users [12].

Looking at the videos it was clear that whilst control users tended to view documents linearly with little backtracking, dyslexic users tended to look up again in documents to look over text they had already viewed. The results list interaction for both groups was more complex with backtracking evident in both. It was also clear that most of the attention of interest was on the results list/document pane, with very little left right movement between this pane and the Term pane. When using the Term pane users tended to focus their attention largely on the terms displayed.

6. SUMMARY AND CONCLUSION

We present a small scale study of the use of visual analytic methods on eye tracking data to establish general patterns of interaction on a search UI, and in particular to identify the differences between control and dyslexic users on that interface. The results provide some interesting patterns of usage on the Okapi interface. The general pattern of interaction shows two distinct clusters of interest by the users of the results list/document pane, due to the restriction on interaction method allowing us to concentrate on the textually heavy part of the interface. This allowed us to focus on the issue of most concern when establishing the differences between control and dyslexic users – the latter having specific problems with reading and remembering text. The key result of the paper is that there is an indication of a strong difference between the two cohorts, with dyslexic users showing more inclination to look up and down in the UI than the control users, confirmed by both eye tracking data and video inspection. This is a good indication of short term memory problems, and is in accord with prior research on backtracking, a more common phenomenon in users with dyslexia. Further research will focus on how this evidence will be used to design interfaces for both user groups.

7. REFERENCES

[1] MacFarlane, A., Al-Wabil, A. Marshall, C.R., Albrair, A, Jones, S.A & Zaphris, P. 2010. The effect of dyslexia on information retrieval: A pilot study. JDoc, 66(3), 307-326.

[2] Rayner, K. 1998. Eye movements in reading and Information Processing: 20 Years of Research. Psychological Bulletin, 124 (3),272-422.

[3] Shneiderman, B. 2000. Universal Usability. *Comms. ACM*, 43(5), May, 84-91. DOI=10.1145/332833.332843.

[4] MacFarlane, A, Albrair, A., Marshall, C. R. and Buchanan, G. 2012. Phonological working memory impacts on information searching: An investigation of dyslexia. In *Proceedings of the 4th Information Interaction in Context Symposium*, pp. 27-34. ACM.

[5] Poole, A. & Ball, L. J. 2005. Eye Tracking in Human-Computer Interaction and Usability Research: Current Status and Future Prospects. In Ghaoui, Claude (Ed.). Encyclopedia of Human Computer Interaction. Idea Group.

[6] Al-Wabil, A. 2009. *The effect of dyslexia on Web Navigation*, PhD thesis, April. City University London.

[7] Berget, G. and Sandnes, F.E. 2015. The effect of dyslexia on searching visual and textual content: Are icons really useful? In Universal Access In Human-Computer Interaction: 9th International Conference on Access to Learning, Health and Well-being (Los Angeles, CA, USA), August 2-7, 2015. LNCS 9177. Springer-Verlag, Berlin. 616-625. DOI= 10.1007/978-3-319-20684-4_59.

[8] Berget, G, Mulvey, F., and Sandnes, F.E. 2016. Is Visual content in textual search interfaces beneficial to dyslexic users? I. J. Human-Computer Studies 92 (August 2016), 17-29. DOI=10.1016/j.ijhcs.2016.04.006.

[9] Berget, G. and Sandnes, F.E. 2015. Do Autocomplete Functions Reduce the impact of Dyslexia on Information-Searching Behaviour? The case of Google. J. Assn. Info. Sci. Tech. 151-159. . DOI=10.1002/asi.23572.

[10] Lucid Stress Screening Software (ViSS). 2016. http://www.lucid-research.com/p/128/lucid-viss.

[11] Andrienko, G., Andrienko, N., Burch, M. & Weiskopf. 2012. Visual analytics methodology for eye movement studies. IEEE Trans. Viz. Comp. Graphics, 18 (2), 2889-2898.

[12] Rello, L. and Ballesteros, M. 2015. Detecting readers with dyslexia using machine learning with eye tracking measures. In *Proceedings of the 12th Web for All Conference* (W4A '15). ACM, New York, NY, USA, Article 16 , 8 pages. DOI: http://dx.doi.org/10.1145/2745555.274664.

Relationships between Age, Domain Knowledge and Prior Knowledge Pre-activation on Information Searching

Mylène Sanchiz
Cognition, Language, Ergonomics Lab (UMR CNRS 5263), University of Toulouse, 5 allées A. Machados
31058 Toulouse Cedex, France
mylene.sanchiz@univ-tlse2.fr

Aline Chevalier
Cognition, Language, Ergonomics Lab (UMR CNRS 5263), University of Toulouse, 5 allées A. Machados
31058 Toulouse Cedex, France
aline.chevalier@univ-tlse2.fr

Wai-Tat Fu
Cascade Lab
University of Illinois at Urbana-Champaign
Urbana, IL 61801, USA
wfu@illinois.edu

Franck Amadieu
Cognition, Language, Ergonomics Lab (UMR CNRS 5263), University of Toulouse, 5 allées A. Machados
31058 Toulouse Cedex, France
amadieu@univ-tlse2.fr

ABSTRACT
This study investigated the effects of age, prior domain knowledge and prior knowledge semantic pre-activation task on information searching. Results showed that the age-related differences were observed for the fantastic movies domain (for which older adults had significantly lower prior knowledge), whereas the effects of age were not replicated in the health domain (for which older adults had equal knowledge with young adults?). Semantic pre-activation of prior knowledge in the health domain was correlated to more analytic strategies when processing the search engine pages and when navigating.

CCS Concepts
H.3.3 [**Information Search and Retrieval**]: Search Process, Selection Process

H.5.2 [**User Interfaces**]: User/Machine Systems: Human factors, Human Information Processing, User-centered design

Keywords
Information searching, aging, domain knowledge, prior knowledge activation, web navigation.

1. INTRODUCTION
As older adults are one of the most growing population of users on Internet, web accessibility for seniors has become a burning challenge. Searching for information requires a series of cognitive processes to interact with a search engine (to formulate queries and evaluate the search engine results) and with websites (to select websites and navigate between several webpages). Previous works have shown that older adults experience several difficulties. When interacting with a search engine: older adults are slower [1], they have difficulties selecting a webpage to open up [2] and tend to exploit the queries they produce (i.e. older adults tend to maximize the use of each query by opening up more links per query as compared to young adults [3,4]. When interacting with websites: older adults tend to delay the decision to switch to another webpage [4] and they tend to feel more disoriented than young adults [5].

CHIIR '17, March 07-11, 2017, Oslo, Norway
© 2017 ACM. ISBN 978-1-4503-4677-1/17/03…$15.00
DOI: http://dx.doi.org/10.1145/3020165.3022135

Most of the difficulties older adults encounter can be accounted for by the age-related decline of cognitive abilities such as flexibility, or processing speed [6, 7]. However prior works have shown that crystallized abilities, such as prior domain knowledge (i.e. knowledge about the search topic) can improve information searching strategies [8, 9]. Prior knowledge can improve the evaluation of the search engine results [9], the selection of relevant websites to be visited [10] and the processing of websites' content [10]. Using prior domain knowledge while searching for information on Internet requires users to: (i) activate in working memory the semantic and the lexical representations of concepts (i.e. the meaning and spelling) [11], and (ii) make inferences (i.e. semantic connections) between concepts. These processes require extra cognitive resources and might represent a challenge for older users. Indeed, working memory might be overloaded with the amount of information to process. In addition concept lexical activation tends to decrease with age, causing older adults to feel the *word-on-the-tip-of-the-tong* effect [11]. Hence, older adults' difficulties to access lexical representations of concepts may impact the production of relevant queries and inferences. To overcome this difficulty, the present experiment examined the impact of the semantic pre-activation of prior knowledge before searching on internet. The goal of the semantic pre-activation is to strengthen the activation of prior domain knowledge related to the search problems to be performed and especially supports the activation of lexical representation of concepts by older adults. Focusing on semantic processing and generating keywords should strengthen the connections between concepts in memory and support the search engine results pages (SERPs) evaluation and the integration of new information. Based on these elements, the present work investigated:

(i) To what extend are the age-related differences observed in search engine processes and navigation persistent in different knowledge domains?
(ii) How do prior knowledge and semantic pre-activation moderate the effect of age on information searching?

2. METHOD
2.1 Participants
44 volunteered participated for a 8$ per hour reward: 26 young adults (M_{age} = 22.12, SD = 3.96, 5 males and 21 females, from 18 to 32 years) and 22 older adults (M_{age} = 65.27, SD = 4.77, 5 males and 17 females, from 60 to 77 years). Participants were all English speakers and were recruited via emails or on the University of Illinois at Urbana-Champaign. Older adults were all retired and in good health (Mini Mental State Examination (MMSE) [15]: M =

28.03 SD = 1.10). Both age groups declared spending approximately the same amount of time on the Internet per week (M_{young} = 29.85 SD = 12.23 and M_{older} = 23.63 SD = 20.05, $t(46)$ = 1.32, p =.19).

2.2 Design

2.2.1 Protocol

The experiment was conducted on a 16 inches laptop, running Windows 7 and Google Chrome web browser. Log files were recorded using Chrome History View. A few days before the experiment, participants completed an on-line questionnaire (Qualtrics) assessing internet familiarity and prior knowledge. Each MCQ (fantastic movies and health) consisted in 10 questions (4 possible answers and "I don't know"). After settling on the computer, participants completed a cognitive flexibility test (Trail Making Test [14]) and the 6 information search problems. Half of the participants completed the semantic pre-activation task before searching on the Internet, the other half performed the search problems by searching on the Internet immediately. If participants knew the answer, they were instructed to switch to the next search problem (data were not considered in the analyses). Eventually, older participants took the MMSE [13].

2.2.2 Material

6 search problems were designed (see Table 1 below). The fantastic movies domain tackled famous movies of the genre (such as *Star wars*) whereas the health domain tackled healthy and unhealthy body functioning. The fantastic movie domain was selected because it was more in favor of young adults (i.e. older adults were expected to have lower prior knowledge). The search problem statements required participants to infer relevant keywords (i.e. relevant keywords were switched with semantically ambiguous synonyms in the search problem statements), and to navigate on website(s) via Google.

Table 1. Search problem statements of all search problems (bold concepts are the concepts cued in the semantic pre-activation task, participants did not see bold characters).

Health	Fantastic movies
1.How does the human **body protection system** protects the body from **attacks** such as the **flu** 2. What **substance** produced by the body allows an individual to **store an excess of nutrients** in the body 3. You have heard nearby two colleagues of yours debate on which action tints **blood**. "I wonder what **action tints** blood", asked the first one. "I think it's due to an **excess of glucoses** said the second one.	1. What is the name of Luke **Skywalker's means of transportation** that he used when he destroyed the **Death Star** in **Star Wars**? 2. Which group of fantastic heroes is composed of **4 creatures** specialized in **martial arts,** who live in **New York's underground,** and were heroes of several movies and TV series. 3. Two friends are trying to recall the name of a famous event in which a captain led an army to save the **sieged people** of Rohan in the **Lord of the Rings**. "I bet it's when **Captain Boromir** died", said the first one. "I don't know… not sure"

Semantic pre-activation task:
Participants in the experimental condition first read the search problem statement (one at a time), then we presented three concepts extracted from the search problem statements (in bold letters in Table 1). For each concept presented, written instructions required participants to produce three different keywords semantically related that might be helpful to search on the Internet afterwards. Depending on their prior knowledge, participants could produce semantically specific keywords (such as "*spaceship*" for "*means of transportation*"), or semantically more general keywords (such as "*plane*").

2.2.3 Measures and data analysis

Three independent variables were manipulated: age (between-subjects), domain knowledge (within-subjects) and the semantic pre-activation of prior knowledge (between-subject).

Dependent variables
(i)Performance was assessed through the number of correct answers found and the Task Completion Speed (TCS) [15]. The TCS took into account the number of successfully completed search problems and the time taken to complete them.

(ii)Search engine processing was assessed through the time spent analyzing the SERPs and the number of SERPs consulted.

(iii)Navigation was measured through the mean number of SERPs consulted per search problem and the percentage of time spent exploring/exploiting navigational paths. In line with prior work [5], the number of different websites visited (accessed from the SERPs) and the total number of web pages visited were calculated. The number of new websites opened from the SERP corresponded to exploration (i.e. participants opened up new websites to start new search paths). In contrast, exploitation corresponded to the number of webpages visited within each website opened (i.e. how deep participants processed the search paths initiated once they were on a website). Eventually we calculated the percentage of time spent exploring the navigational paths initiated in order to analyze the navigational strategies of users.

3. RESULTS

After analyzing users' cognitive abilities, multiple hierarchical regression analyses were conducted to investigate the relationships between age, prior domain knowledge, and prior knowledge pre-activation on search performance, search engine processing and web navigation. Age was entered as a dummy variable in the first step of the model. Semantic pre-activation (as a dummy variable) and the interaction between age and prior domain knowledge were entered in the second step. Because of the age differences on prior knowledge (see Table 2 below), analyses were conducted in the two domains separately.

3.1 Users profile: cognitive abilities and prior knowledge

As presented in Table 2 below, t tests analyses showed no age differences on cognitive flexibility ($t(46)$= -.64, p = n.s.) and prior health knowledge ($t(46)$= .17, p = n.s.). However, older adults had significantly lower fantastic movies prior knowledge than young adults ($t(46)$= 2.49, p < .02).

Table 2. Descriptive statistics of cognitive abilities (*p <.05).

Measures	Young adults	Older adults
Cognitive flexibility: TMT (in seconds)	56.78 (38.63)*	62.65 (20.33)
Health prior knowledge (% correct answers)	37.31 (19.29)	36.36 (18.13)
Fantastic movies prior knowledge (% correct answers)	53.46 (2.12)*	38.18 (21.30)

3.2 Fantastic movies domain

3.2.1 Performance

Results showed that the effect of age alone was a better predictor than our model of the Task Completion Speed (TCS) ($R^{2\ adjusted} = .23$, $F(1,47) = 15.002$, $p < .001$) and the number of correct answers found ($R^{2\ adjusted} = .09$, $F(1,47) = 5.89$, $p = .02$) (though our model was significant on the number of correct answers, age was the only significant factor). Older adults took longer to complete the search problems and found fewer correct answers than young ones (respectively $M_{\%\ answers\ found} = 48.86$ $SD = 22.24$ for older adults and $M_{\%\ answers\ found} = 68.27$ $SD = 31.27$ for young ones) (see Table 3).

Table 3: multiple hierarchical **regression analyses of TCS and number of correct answers found**

	Task Completion Speed		Correct answers	
	Model 1	Model 2	Model 1	Model 2
R^2	0.25	0.26	.11	.12
$R^{2\ adjusted}$	0.23	0.21	.09	.06
F value	15.002***	5.15**	5.89*	1.95

(***$p < .001$, *$p < .01$, *$p < .05$)

3.2.2 Search engine processing

Results showed that age alone was a better predictor of the time spent on the SERPs ($R^{2\ adjusted} = .16$, $F(1,47) = 9.46$, $p < .01$): older adults spent significantly more time on the SERPS than young ones. However, neither age ($R^{2\ adjusted} = .02$, $F(1,47) = 1.89$, $p =$ n.s.) nor our model ($R^{2\ adjusted} = -.02$, $F(1,47 = .75$, $p =$ n.s) were significant on the number of SERPs consulted (see Table 3 below).

Table 3: regression analyses of time spent on SERPs, number of SERPs and % of exploration (fantastic movies domain)

	Time spent on SERPS		Number of SERPS		% exploration	
	Model 1	Model 2	Model 1	Model 2	Model 1	Model 2
R^2	.18	.16	.04	.05	.08	.11
$R^{2\ adjusted}$	.21	.15	.02	-.02	.06	.05
F value	9.46**	3.60*	1.89	.75	3.73^	1.74

(***$p < .001$, *$p < .01$, *$p < .05$, ^ $p = .06$)

3.2.3 Navigation

Results (see Table 3 above) showed that age alone was also marginally significant on the percentage of time spent exploring the navigational paths (rather than exploiting them in more depth ($F(1,47) = 3.73$, $p = .06$; $M_{\%\ exploring} = 55.79$ $SD = 26.91$ for older adults and $M_{\%\ exploring} = 43.01$ $SD = 17.26$ for young ones).

3.3 Intermediate conclusion

Results found in the fantastic movies domain replicated known results (Dommes et al., 2011) about the impact of age on information searching. In the fantastic movies domain, for which older adults had significantly lower prior knowledge (see Table 1 above), older adults were slower, found fewer correct answers and spent longer time analyzing the SERPs than young ones.

3.4 Health domain

3.4.1 Performance

Results showed that our model was a better predictor of the TCS than age alone (see Table 4 below). Yet, older adults still had poorer TCS than young ones ($t(45) = -1.95$, B = -.30, $p < .06$). A simple Slop Technique was used to visualize the significant ageXprior knowledge interaction on the TCS. Results suggested that the more prior knowledge older adults had, the faster they completed the search problems, whereas prior knowledge had no effect for young participants.

Table 4: multiple hierarchical regression analyses of TCS and number of correct answers found

	Task Completion Speed		Correct answers	
Model	$R^{2\ adjusted} = .11$, $F(1,47) = 2.77$, $p = .05$		$R^{2\ adjusted} = .21$, $F(1,47) = 5.20$, $p = .004$	
Factors	*F*	η^2_p	*F*	η^2_p
Age	-1.95	-.30	-3.04	-.43*
Pre-activation	-1.42	-.20	-1.91	-.25
Age*prior knowledge	2.28	.35*	2.83	.40*

(*$p < .05$)

Results also showed that our model could account for the number of correct answers found. Age was still significant ($t(47) = -3.04$, B = -.43, $p < .01$): older adults found fewer correct answers than young ones. The simple Slop Technique used to visualize the ageXprior knowledge interaction ($t(47) = 2.83$, B = .40, $p < .01$) suggested that the more prior knowledge older adults had, the more correct answers they found.

3.4.2 Search engine processing

Table 5: regression analyses of time spent on SERPs, number of SERPs consulted and % of exploration (health domain)

	Time spent on SERPs		Number of SERPs		% exploration	
Model	$R^{2\ adjusted} = .09$, $F(1,47) = 2.59$, $p = .06$		$R^{2\ adjusted} = .16$, $F(1,47) = 4.07$, $p = .01$		$R^{2\ adjusted} = .09$, $F(1,47) = 2.58$, $p = .06$	
Main factors	*F*	η^2_p	*F*	η^2_p	*F*	η^2_p
Age	1.75	.25	-2.09	-.29*	-1.09	-.16
Pre-activation	2.14	.30*	2.18	.29*	-2.19	-.31*
Age*prior knowledge	.86	.13	.91	.13	-1.47	-.21

(*$p < .05$)

The model was a better predictor of the time spent on SERPs and the number of SERPs consulted than age alone (see Table 5 above). Participants who completed the semantic pre-activation task spent longer time on Google ($t(44) = 2.14$, B= .30, $p < .04$) and visited a greater number of SERPs ($t(44) = 2.18$, B = .29, $p = .03$). Older adults also consulted fewer SERPS than young ones ($t(44) = -2.09$, B = -.29, $p = .04$).

3.4.3 Navigation

Results showed that the model marginally reached significance on the percentage of time spent exploring navigational paths (see Table 5 above). Semantic prior knowledge pre-activation reduced the percentage of time spent exploring navigational paths ($t(44) = -2.19$, B = -.31, $p = .03$) (and consequently increased the percentage of time spent exploiting them).

3.5 Intermediate conclusion

Results showed that in the health domain, age alone could not account for the differences found between young and older adults. The interaction between age and prior domain knowledge was associated with better search performance. Prior knowledge pre-activation led to deeper processing of the SERPs (longer time and greater number) and exploiting navigational strategies (i.e. fewer navigational paths but processed more deeply). In contrast with the patterns found in the fantastic movies domain, the model including prior knowledge and its semantic pre-activation was significant for most of the dependent variables investigated in the health domain. This tends to show that in a knowledge domain for which older adults have enough prior knowledge (i.e. no age-related differences were found on health prior knowledge as compared to the fantastic movies domain), the impact of age can be moderated.

4. CONCLUSION

The current study examined the role of age, prior domain knowledge and its semantic pre-activation on information searching. In line with prior works, older adults were outperformed by young ones and had difficulties evaluating the SERPs (longer time) and navigating. Indeed, older adults spent a larger percentage of time exploring different navigational paths (rather than processing them in more depth). This may show that older adults had difficulties elaborating relevant navigational paths or evaluating the relevance of the navigational paths elaborated. However, these results were not replicated in the health domain and the effect of age disappeared for most of the dependent variables investigated. As older adults had similar amount of prior health knowledge than young ones (whereas in the fantastic movies domain older adults had significantly lower prior knowledge), results tend to show that the effect of age was coped with by the role of prior domain knowledge and knowledge pre-activation. Analyses showed that pre-activating prior knowledge before information searching fostered deeper and analytic processing of the SERPs (i.e. longer time on SERPs and more SERPs visited) and deeper navigational strategies (i.e. users explored less and exploited the navigational paths elaborated/processed more webpages once they opened up a website from Google). In other words, pre-activating prior knowledge supported the use of top-down strategies: users probably spent more time processing information, making inferences, evaluating sources…

5. IMPLICATIONS

The present experiment aimed at investigating how prior domain knowledge could represent a useful cognitive leverage for older users. Results did show that prior knowledge tended to cope with older adults' difficulties. In addition, semantic pre-activation of concepts might be an interesting way to enrich information searching tool for older users. In line with prior works [4], as older adults tend to rely more on top-down processes (i.e. they visit fewer links and they take longer time to decide which link to open up); pre-activating prior knowledge via information searching tool might support older users' search engine processing and navigation strategies. Further works should investigate the best way to pre-activate prior knowledge. Indeed, generating keywords might have been difficult for users (qualitative analyses showed that most users produced several keywords for each target concept, but not necessarily relevant ones to search for information on the internet).

6. REFERENCES

[1] Chevalier, A., Dommes, A., & Marquié, J.C. Strategy and accuracy during information search on the Web: Effects of age and complexity of the search questions. *Computers in Human Behavior,* 53 (2015), 305–315.

[2] Sharit, J., Taha, J., Berkowsky, R. W., Profita, H., & Czaja, S. J. (2015). Online information search performance and search strategies in a health problem-solving scenario. *Journal of Cognitive Engineering and Decision Making*, *9*(3), 211-228.

[3] Chin, J. and Fu, W-T. (2010). Interactive effects of age and interface differences on search strategies and performance. *ACM Press*, 403–412.

[4] Chin, J., Anderson, E., Chin, C. & Fu, W-T. (2015). Age differences in information search: An exploration-exploitation tradeoff model. *Proceedings of the 59th Annual Meeting of the Human Factors and Ergonomics Society 2015*, Los Angeles, CA: Human Factors and Ergonomics Society.

[5] Wagner, N., Hassanein, K., & Head, M. (2014). The impact of age on website usability. *Computers in Human Behavior*, *37*, 270-282.

[6] Dommes, A., Chevalier, A., & Lia, S. The role of cognitive flexibility and vocabulary abilities of younger and older users in searching for information on the web. *Applied Cognitive Psychology*, 25, 5 (2011), 717–726.

[7] Salthouse, T. (2012). Consequences of age-related cognitive declines. *Annual review of psychology*, *63*, 201

[8] Hölscher, C., & Strube, G. (2000).Web search behavior of Internet experts and newbies. *Computer Networks*, 33, 337–346.

[9] Monchaux, S., Amadieu, F., Chevalier, A., & Mariné, C. (2015). Query strategies during information searching: Effects of prior domain knowledge and complexity of the information problems to be solved. *Information Processing & Management*, *51*(5), 557-569.

[10] Wildemuth, B. M. (2004). The effects of domain knowledge on search tactic formulation. *Journal of the American Society for Information Science and Technology*, *55*(3), 246-258.

[11] Dorot, D., & Mathey, S. (2013). Accès aux représentations sémantiques et phonologiques chez des adultes jeunes et âgés: une étude des mots sur le bout de la langue. *Psychologie Française*, *58*(1), 1-16.

[12] Taconnat, L., Froger, C., Sacher, M., & Isingrini, M. (2008). Generation and associative encoding in young and old adults: The effect of the strength of association between cues and targets on a cued recall task. *Experimental Psychology*, *55*(1), 23-30.

[13] Folstein, M. F., Folstein, S. E., & McHugh, P. R. (1975). "Mini-mental state": a practical method for grading the cognitive state of patients for the clinician *Journal of Psychiatric Research*, *12*(3), 189-198.

[14] Spreen, O., & Strauss, E. (1998). *A compendium of neuropsychological tests: Administration, norms, and commentary*. Oxford University Press.

[15] Aula, A., & Nordhausen, K. (2006). Modeling successful performance in Web searching. *Journal of the American Society for Information Science and Technology*, *57*(12), 1678-1693

Perceptions of the Effect of Fragmented Attention on Mobile Web Search Tasks

Morgan Harvey
CIS Department
Northumbria University
Newcastle upon Tyne, UK
morgan.harvey@northumbria.ac.uk

Matt Pointon
CIS Department
Northumbria University
Newcastle upon Tyne, UK
m.pointon@northumbria.ac.uk

ABSTRACT

Mobile devices are rapidly becoming our main method of accessing the Internet and are frequently used to perform on-the-go search tasks. The use of such devices in situations where attention must be divided, such as when walking, are common and research suggests that this increases cognitive load and, therefore, may have an impact on performance.

In this work we conducted a laboratory experiment with both phone and tablet devices with the aim of evaluating common mobile situations that cause; fragmented attention, impact search performance and impact on user perception. To do this the distraction level was varied by simulating 3 everyday situations: 1) walking quickly (on a treadmill), 2) navigating a pre-defined route and 3) sitting still (which was used as the baseline condition). The results showed that different experimental conditions had a number of different effects on the participants' perceptions of their own search performance, how hurried they felt and how engaged they were in the tasks.

Keywords

mobile search; fragmented attention; search experience; cognition; user study; experimentation

1. INTRODUCTION

Two-thirds of Americans own a smart phone device, 97% of whom use them to access the Internet. These devices "serve as an essential connection to the broader world of online information" [13] and are used by around half of all users for everyday Information Retrieval (IR) tasks such as searching for real estate, jobs and getting information about health problems and government services [13]. People use mobile devices to search the web almost as frequently as desktop and laptop computers and often do this on public transport, while walking from place to place [4, 8, 11] or in social contexts where the presence of others can act as a distraction [2]. Interaction with such devices is commonly achieved via touch screens upon which relatively small "soft buttons" are drawn for users to select items and input text. While these buttons may be easy to accurately press in an *ideal environment*, such as when seated, such small and non-tactile targets may be much more difficult to interact with in other situations [1].

Indeed, distractions during walking, driving, and other real-world interactions can preoccupy users [10], reducing their effectiveness in interacting with the UI [8, 1], resulting in a larger number of misspelled queries and an attempt by users to shorten queries when searching [12, 11]. Walking whilst using a mobile device requires both cognitive and motor abilities and users must divide their attention between the two tasks [6]. This means either an increase in cognitive load, a decrease in pace, a decrease in task performance or a combination of these [7].

A large body of work has investigated how fragmented attention affects user input on mobile devices. Early work investigated how attention is diverted from the interface when following a pre-defined, but otherwise uncontrolled, route through a city and found significant impairment when compared with a "non-social laboratory condition" [10]. In a more controlled set of experiments, Lin et al. [8] demonstrated that error rates of stylus input significantly increased as the amount of distraction, and thus degree of attention fragmentation, increased. Similar effects were demonstrated for touch-based input, with error rates increasing with walking speed [9]. Delays and time pressures, which may be induced by increased levels of distraction and input error rate, have a significant impact on search behaviour and objective performance [3]. Large-scale analysis of mobile search logs [5] has shown that the significant increase in time cost for mobile searches deters some types of search behaviour, such as exploratory search, and causes search sessions to be considerably shorter than in desktop search.

In contrast to previous work, we intend to focus on how different levels of fragmented attention impact on user performance on specific search tasks and on the participants' perceptions of this impact. Does the change in context have an effect on user *behaviour* and is this something that users themselves are aware of? To ensure repeatability, our study is conducted in a lab with simulated contexts, including on a treadmill and navigating an obstacle course. As people frequently also use tablets to access the web on the go, we conduct experiments with both tablet and phone devices.

Our main research questions are:

CHIIR '17, March 07 - 11, 2017, Oslo, Norway

ISBN 978-1-4503-4677-1/17/03...$15.00

DOI: http://dx.doi.org/10.1145/3020165.3022136

- Do common mobile situations that cause fragmented attention have an impact on search performance and how do users perceive this?
- Do these perceptions differ as the task becomes more difficult/attention becomes more fragmented?
- What effect, if any, do the different environments have on user search behaviour?

2. METHOD

We conducted a laboratory experiment with 19 participants drawn from a large European University (a mixture of academic staff, support staff and post-graduate students), of whom 10 were male and who had a modal age range between 25 and 30. There were two independent variables: the type of *device* (tablet or phone) and the level of *distraction*. The distraction level was varied by simulating 2 everyday situations experienced by mobile device users: walking quickly on a treadmill and navigating an environment with obstacles (a pre-defined obstacle course), as well as a baseline condition in which the participant was seated. Distraction level was a between-subjects variable, while device type was within-subjects.

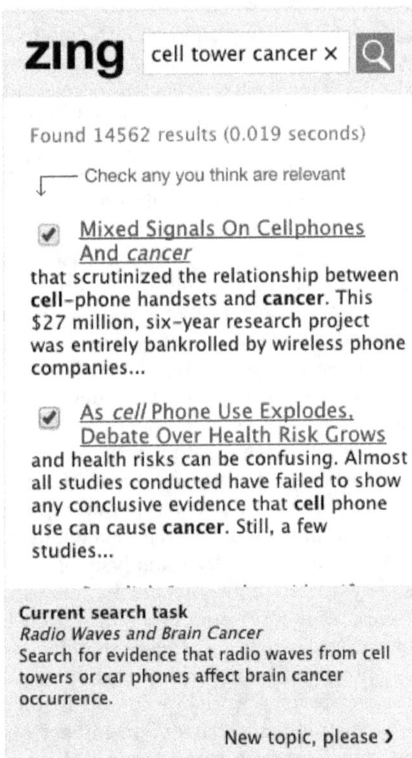

Figure 1: zing search interface on an Apple iPhone 5. Checkboxes used to indicate relevance.

We developed a simple mobile search interface named *zing*, shown in Figure 1, which mimics a standard SE interface by showing 10 links in descending order of relevance together with snippets for each. The interface allowed participants to enter search terms and indicate (via checkboxes) which documents they thought were relevant. It showed the current task (TREC topic) at the bottom of the screen and allowed participants to progress to the next topic at any time. The interface also prompted users to fill in pre- and post-topic questionnaires to survey their perceptions about the task and their self-assessed post-task performance, satisfaction, perceived time pressure and focus/involvement on the task. Half of the participants completed their first 2 topics on a phone, moving on to the tablet for their final 2 topics, while the other half began with the tablet.

We used a standard test collection: AQUAINT[1] together with the 50 TREC 2005 Robust track topics, of which 4[2] were randomly chosen from a subset of those which are neither too difficult nor too easy. Indexing and searching was provided by Apache SOLR[3]. Each participant was given the same 4 topics (tasks) in a random order with a per-task time limit of 15 minutes and alternated between the two *device* conditions. Participants were asked to imagine they wanted to learn more about the subject of each topic for a short report and were requested to select 3-5 documents they thought were relevant. Participant actions and behaviour was recorded by means of a GoPro camera worn on the head, a wide-angle view of the obstacle course and by recording all interactions with the touchscreen and interface (Figure 2).

Figure 2: Example of data recorded via the cameras and screen recording software. Note that information from all 3 sources is temporally synced.

3. RESULTS

3.1 Pre-study questionnaire

Before being told anything about the experiment, participants were asked to fill in a short pre-study questionnaire asking them about their use of mobile devices and search engines as well as how difficult they would expect it to be to search on a phone or a tablet in various contexts.

All but 1 participant uses a mobile device several times a day, 14 use it at least once per day whilst walking and all but 3 use it to search the web on a daily basis. Participants generally expected that using both devices whilst walking on a treadmill would be more difficult than sitting still and navigating an obstacle course even more so (median responses: "very easy," "difficult" and "difficult" respectively) . As participant age increased, the expected difficulty

[1]We removed duplicate documents in a pre-processing step, to provide a better and more familiar user experience.
[2]Topics 362, 367, 404 and 638.
[3]http://lucene.apache.org/solr/

of using a tablet on a treadmill (R-squared: 0.2359, p-value: 0.02) and when navigating an obstacle course (R-squared: 0.124, p-value: 0.077) increased, however this was not the case for phones or for use when sitting still. The more confident people were at using search engines in general, the easier they expected the task to be on the treadmill (p-value: 0.018) and obstacle course (p-value: 0.017), however this did not seem to be the case for sitting still.

3.2 Pre-task perception

Before each task (topic), participants filled in a questionnaire about their prior knowledge of the topic, their interest in it and how difficult they expected the task to be (overall difficulty, difficulty in finding relevant documents, and difficulty in knowing when to finish). There was little variation in the responses between the topics with most people stating that they had fairly little prior knowledge and were moderately interested in the topics. There was only a single instance where a participant was unsure of how to complete the task and in only 14% of cases was a topic deemed to be either very difficult or very easy. As expected, responses to all 3 questions on perceived task difficulty were all significantly correlated with each other (pairwise correlations: Q4-Q5=0.63, Q4-Q6=0.33, Q5-Q6=0.3).

Condition	Sitting	Obstacles	Treadmill
Overall difficulty	2.3	3.0	3.6
Finding rel. docs.	2.5	2.5	3.0
When to finish	2.9	3.2	3.9

Table 1: Mean responses about task difficulty from pre-task questionnaires by condition.

It seems that participants took experimental condition into account when estimating the difficulty of tasks as there were differences in the perceived difficulty of tasks, as shown in Table 1. Those who knew they would be sitting still expected the tasks to be significantly easier than those who were navigating the obstacle course and both thought it would be significantly easier than those on the treadmill. Those who were sitting still and those on the obstacle course thought finding relevant documents would be equally easy, however those on the treadmill expected this to be significantly more difficult. There were no significant differences in perceived task clarity between any of the groups, although those in the baseline group did claim to know more about the topic a priori than those in the other groups.

3.3 Post-task perception

#	Question
Q1	I felt hurried or rushed when completing this task
Q2	It was important to complete this task quickly
Q3	Overall, I thought this was a difficult task
Q4	I am satisfied with steps I took to find information
Q5	I forgot my immediate surroundings during the task
Q6	I was so involved that I ignored everything around me
Q7	I was so involved that I lost track of time
Q8	I was was absorbed in my search task

Table 2: Selected post-task questions.

Immediately after each task participants filled in a post-task questionnaire (see Table 2 for questions). There were significant differences in terms of perceived difficulty between the 4 topics with 2 topics scoring a median Q3 agreement of 2, one at 3 and the most difficult scoring 4. There were, however, no significant differences between the 4 topics for the other questions. Women reported feeling significantly more hurried or rushed (Q2), less absorbed in the task (Q8) and felt less like they lost track of time (Q7).

Condition	Sitting	Obstacles	Treadmill
Q1	2.28 †	2.54 †	3.29
Q2	2.6 *†	3.21	3.32
Q3	2.52 †	3.0	3.32
Q4	3.8 †	3.33	2.93
Q5	3.44 *	2.58 †	3.43 *
Q6	3.2	2.54 †	3.43 *
Q7	2.9	3.2	3.9
Q8	3.8	3.17	3.79

Table 3: Mean responses from post-task questionnaires by condition. * = sig. diff. with Obstacles; † = sig. diff. with Treadmil

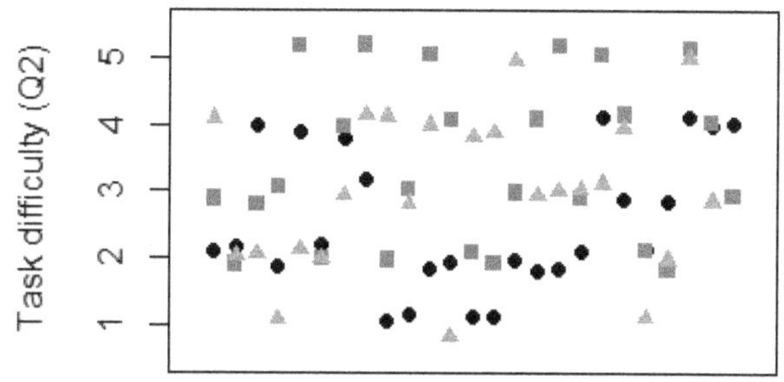

Figure 3: Perceived post-task difficulty by condition. • = sitting; ▲ = obstacle course; ■ = treadmill

As shown in Table 3, the different experimental conditions had a number of different effects on the participants' perceptions. Those on the treadmill felt significantly more rushed than in the other two conditions (Q1) and those sitting still felt significantly less pressure to complete the tasks quickly than the other 2 groups (Q2). It appears that those sitting still generally found the tasks easiest (Q3) - significantly more so than those in the treadmill group - and were more satisfied with the steps they took to find relevant information (Q4). Those sitting and on the treadmill were significantly more likely to forget their immediate surroundings than those on the obstacle course (Q5) and felt more involved in the task (Q6). Although differences were not significant, there was a trend that those on the treadmill felt more involved in the task to the point where they lost track of time (Q7) and those on the obstacle course felt less absorbed in the search tasks (Q8).

4. DISCUSSION AND CONCLUSIONS

In this work we conducted a laboratory experiment with both phone and tablet devices with the aim of evaluating common mobile situations that cause; fragmented attention, impact search performance and impact on user perception. To do this the distraction level was varied by simulating 3 everyday situations: walking quickly (on a treadmill), navigating a pre-defined route and a sitting still (which was used as the baseline condition).

Our pre-study questionnaire showed that participants expected using both devices whilst walking on a treadmill would be more difficult than sitting still and navigating an obstacle course. The older a participant was, the greater the expected difficulty of using a tablet on a treadmill but this was not the case for phones or when sitting. Perhaps this is because younger people are more familiar with such devices and may have more experience using them in mobile situations.

Participants seemed to take the experimental conditions into account when estimating task difficulty with significant differences in perceived task difficulty. Those who knew they would be sitting still expected the tasks to be easier than the other conditions. Those who were sitting still and those on the obstacle course thought finding relevant documents would be equally easy. It is interesting that people expected the treadmill to be most difficult, despite the fact that it should require more cognitive effort to avoid the obstacles. This may be because these participants have control over the pace at which they are walking, while those on the treadmill are kept at a constant speed by the mechanism. Those on the obstacle course have the possibility to slow down while conducting demanding tasks, such as assessing document relevance, thereby reducing their overall cognitive load [6].

Post-task perception showed that different experimental conditions had a number of different effects on the participants' perceptions. Those on the treadmill felt significantly more rushed than in the other two conditions. Oulasvita et al. [10] pointed to the effect of a situation on the duration of continuous attention, finding that participants in their laboratory experiments were more focused on the tasks compared with participants on a busy street. In this study, those sitting and on the treadmill were significantly more likely to forget their immediate surroundings than those on the obstacle course and more involved in the task. This may be because there is an increased need to attend to the surrounding environment when walking, but with the treadmill this is not the case as the situation does not change [8].

Participants on the obstacle course felt less absorbed in the search tasks. This could be due to the fact that walking while using a cell phone requires "both cognitive and motor abilities and appropriate division of attention to each" [6]. The level of absorption in the search tasks is less due to the participant needing to be aware of their surroundings. The participants are walking and using the device, in doing so they take longer to complete a set route and, therefore, walk more slowly. There are two repercussions to this, they will slow down on the obstacle route (because they have control) and experience increased cognitive load on the treadmill (not being able to adjust their speed) [7].

4.1 Future work

As future research in this area we plan to expand on this work by collecting data from more participants and looking at more objective measures of performance (e.g. total time, number of relevant documents, etc.) to investigate how this varies by condition, by age and by prior experience. We have also been recording GoPro footage of each participant as well as screen recordings of their interactions which we plan to evaluate to identify patterns and behaviours unique to each experimental condition. Using the data from the GoPro we will be able to evaluate the participants' spatial awareness (especially on the predefined route) and their "attention-switches" away from the device in different situations. Using the 3 everyday situations we will be able to assess the levels of immersion with each task and compare the GoPro data to the pre-task perceptions - does their initial thinking match reality?

5. REFERENCES

[1] Andrew Bragdon, Eugene Nelson, Yang Li, and Ken Hinckley, *Experimental analysis of touch-screen gesture designs in mobile environments*, SIG CHI, ACM, 2011, pp. 403–412.

[2] Karen Church and Nuria Oliver, *Understanding mobile web and mobile search use in today's dynamic mobile landscape*, Proceedings of the 13th International Conference on Human Computer Interaction with Mobile Devices and Services, ACM, 2011, pp. 67–76.

[3] Anita Crescenzi, Diane Kelly, and Leif Azzopardi, *Impacts of time constraints and system delays on user experience*, ACM CHI, ACM, 2016, pp. 141–150.

[4] Anne Kaikkonen, *Full or tailored mobile web-where and how do people browse on their mobiles?*, Mobility, ACM, 2008, p. 28.

[5] Maryam Kamvar and Shumeet Baluja, *A large scale study of wireless search behavior: Google mobile search*, Proceedings of the SIGCHI conference on Human Factors in computing systems, ACM, 2006, pp. 701–709.

[6] Eric M Lamberg and Lisa M Muratori, *Cell phones change the way we walk*, Gait & posture **35** (2012), no. 4, 688–690.

[7] Sammy Licence, Robynne Smith, Miranda P McGuigan, and Conrad P Earnest, *Gait pattern alterations during walking, texting and walking and texting during cognitively distractive tasks while negotiating common pedestrian obstacles*, PLoS one **10** (2015), no. 7, e0133281.

[8] Min Lin, Rich Goldman, Kathleen J Price, Andrew Sears, and Julie Jacko, *How do people tap when walking? an empirical investigation of nomadic data entry*, International Journal of human-computer studies **65** (2007), no. 9, 759–769.

[9] Hugo Nicolau and Joaquim Jorge, *Touch typing using thumbs: Understanding the effect of mobility and hand posture*, ACM CHI (New York, NY, USA), CHI '12, ACM, 2012, pp. 2683–2686.

[10] Antti Oulasvirta, Sakari Tamminen, Virpi Roto, and Jaana Kuorelahti, *Interaction in 4-second bursts: the fragmented nature of attentional resources in mobile hci*, ACM CHI, ACM, 2005, pp. 919–928.

[11] R. Schaller, M. Harvey, and D. Elsweiler, *Out and about on museums night: Investigating mobile search behaviour for leisure events*, Searching4Fun WS at ECIR, 2012.

[12] Richard Schaller, Morgan Harvey, and David Elsweiler, *Entertainment on the go: finding things to do and see while visiting distributed events*, IIiX, ACM, 2012, pp. 90–99.

[13] Aaron Smith et al., *Us smartphone use in 2015*, Pew Research Center **1** (2015).

Manipulating the Perception of Credibility in Refugee Related Social Media Posts

Johannes Aigner Amelie Durchardt Thiemo Kersting

Markus Kattenbeck David Elsweiler

Chair for Information Science
University of Regensburg
D-93040 Regensburg
{johannes.aigner,amelie.durchardt,thiemo.kersting}@student.ur.de
{markus.kattenbeck,david.elsweiler}@ur.de

ABSTRACT

This paper describes a controlled web-based study (n=126), investigating whether the perception of the credibility of refugee-related Tweets can be influenced by cues already reported in the literature for social media content generally. We provide empirical evidence that both a Tweet's popularity and the presence of links – even neutral links created by URL shortening services – may increase a user's belief that the Tweet contains credible information. This is important because the propagation of false information relating to refugees on social media sites has been well documented.

Keywords

false information; rumours; perception of information; social media

1. INTRODUCTION

Social media has become a prominent information source for breaking news [18], monitoring events [27], as well as sourcing expert opinions [23] and gossip [27]. Community driven, real time posts mean that this kind of media provides quick access to content inaccessible from other sources [10]. Unfortunately, the way social media content is generated means that not all of the information shared is accurate, representative or complete, with literature reporting large proportions of posts to contain "mindless babble" [16], or include spam [2], rumours [3] or even willful deception [6]. Social media can be used to form and shape user opinions or beliefs altering their viewpoints on a variety of topics, including how brands are perceived [24] and the political decisions people take [17].

This is a prominent issue in the context of the refugee situation in western Europe where extensive propagation of false information has been well documented [28, 7]. Research has demonstrated how information presented about refugees can impact on how refugees are perceived, as well as people's emotions and attitudes towards them [11]. False beliefs can, in turn, alter how people behave towards refugees [25].

Whereas past work has investigated the features of social media posts influencing user credibility judgements generally, in this work we focus on judgements about posts regarding refugees by social-network users located in the South of Germany, an area which has recently experienced a large influx of refugees. By means of a controlled study we show that simple and subtle Tweet manipulations can statistically alter how credible readers perceive Tweets to be.

2. RELATED WORK

Users of social-networks have several means by which they can attain information via these services. Information can be sourced by browsing the timeline i.e. via posts made by contacts in their network [21], by actively searching the database [10], by accessing social media content via search engines [27] or by posting questions for contacts in their network to answer [23].

People are known to be more likely to accept information aligning with their existing viewpoints (confirmation bias) [29] or actions they have taken (selective exposure) [13]. Evidence suggests that the Internet is trusted as a news-source at least as much as traditional media [12], although blogs seem to be viewed as a less credible source [1]. Web page credibility and factors influencing it have been well studied with visual appearance [20], the means of locating the web page [15] and characteristics of the user herself [12] all being shown to be important. More recently similar studies have been published for social media content. Castillo et al. performed a series of investigations with the aim of building classifiers for Tweet credibility [4, 14]. Their work has identified several features of Tweets and Tweet authors, which provide insight into how users will perceive credibility. For example, reputation is important (i.e. who the user is and how well he or she is connected in the network), how a Tweet has been propagated is a cue used (i.e. the number of times a Tweet has been retweeted), as are content based features. Tweets which do not include URLs tend to be judged as

CHIIR '17, March 07 - 11, 2017, Oslo, Norway

ISBN 978-1-4503-4677-1/17/03...$15.00

DOI: http://dx.doi.org/10.1145/3020165.3022137

non-credible, whereas tweets containing negative sentiment words are judged as credible. Insights such as these were able to be used to create a practical and helpful real-time system [14].

Morris et al. [22] complemented this work taking a mixed-methods approach. In a first step they collected qualitative observation data whereby participants described the features of Tweets they felt influenced how the Tweet was perceived. The language used (abbreviated language was deemed untrustworthy), the author's account image, as well as the author's connectedness were all important cues. Follow-up experiments in a controlled setting showed that users are poor judges of credibility and are often biased by information like username. Similarly, topical biases exist with Tweets about science receiving a higher mean credibility rating than those about other topics. This finding shows why it is important to study Tweet perception in specific topics of interest, such as the current refugee crisis.

Elsweiler [9] performed a short survey investigating Facebook users' perception of the prominence of false information in Facebook posts. After browsing their Facebook timelines only about one third of respondents did not believe any of the attended to posts contained false information. Many of the posts respondents believed to contain inaccurate information were political, with right and left-wing comments about the refugee crisis being prominent. Two further notable findings from the survey were that 1) a large percentage of posts perceived to contain false information came from friends and 2) the most common source of false information was an external link contained within the post. Neither of these findings align well with the findings of previous work, which shows that people tend to prefer sourcing information from people they know [23] and where links made social media posts seem more credible [4, 22].

3. EXPERIMENTAL DESIGN

We wish to better understand the impact of various Tweet features on the credibility judgements of refugee Tweets. To this end, we conducted an online experiment similar to [22] whereby several properties of Tweets were altered in order to measure their impact on users' credibility assessments.

The study manipulated 6 Tweet properties, which the literature and our own intuition suggested might influence how Tweets about refugees are perceived (see Table 2). We utilised a within-groups design whereby participants each provided 12 (2×6) credibility judgments. One judgment per Tweet (both with feature and without) was collected for each manipulation strategy. To control learning effects and participant fatigue, as well as to ensure no specific strategy was advantaged due to ordering effects, the Tweets judged were rotated in a balanced manner in blocks of 6 participants (see Table 1). The Tweets shown for a condition-strategy combination were chosen at random from a large pool (described below). Participants were shown each Tweet in isolation and provided credibility ratings on a visual analogue scale with the poles being "not credible at all" (0) to "completely credible" (100). No participant was shown the same Tweet for more than one strategy.

Participants. 126 participants (55 female, $M(age) = 26.45$ years, $range = 15 - 55$ years) were recruited via a social-networking marketing campaign and email mailing lists. The recruitment process led to the enlisting of participants living in the South of Germany which reflects our target population well. All of the participants were social-network users with 70% reporting using social networks on a daily basis.

Part.	Strategy-Condition Order	
1	A1 - B1 - C1 - D1 - E1 - F1	A2 - B2 - C2 - D2 - E2 - F2
2	B2 - C2 - D2 - E2 - F2 - A2	B1 - C1 - D1 - E1 - F1 - A1
3	C1 - D1 - E1 - F1 - A1 - B1	C2 - D2 - E2 - F2 - A2 - B2
4	D2 - E2 - F2 - A2 - B2 - C2	D1 - E1 - F1 - A1 - B1 - C1
5	E1 - F1 - A1 - B1 - C1 - D1	E2 - F2 - A2 - B2 - C2 - D2
6	F2 - A2 - B2 - C2 - D2 - E2	F1 - A1 - B1 - C1 - D1 - E1

Table 1: The ordering of strategy(A-F)-condition(1/2) in blocks of six variants.

Sourcing Tweets. We sourced 18 Tweets according to two main criteria: They had to be 1) topically related to refugees in Germany and 2) contain a statement, which was factually incorrect (we checked this manually), but plausible. The idea here was that content provoking doubt would mean that participants rely more on the cues we were manipulating to make their judgements. Moreover, the selection process was performed in such a way that the statements contained in Tweets were balanced in terms of whether they were positive or negative about refugees. Examples of positive Tweets included news that a group of refugees helped in response to a flood and that refugees and local students had been playing football together and enjoying each other's company. Negative Tweets encompassed reports of violence caused by refugees and aggression against people volunteering to help with the refugees situation.

Manipulating Tweets. Each Tweet was manually edited for every strategy (see Table 2 for an overview) so that a pool of Tweets existed with a version of the Tweet for the strategy and a version without. *Popularity* (A) was induced by assigning high re-tweet and favourites to a Tweet. *Profile pictures* (B) were chosen to be non-controversial images (9 male, 9 female), Tweets in condition 2 featured the default Twitter icon. Tweets in the *Verified Account* (C) strategy featured the Twitter verified account badge, which lets users know that an account of public interest is authentic. This is a verification that the Tweet author is who she says she is and is endorsing the content by not making any attempt to anonymise the post. The *Link* (D) strategy modified Tweets with links in the form of a shortened URL-service. This avoided gaining any reliability clues from a domain name. *Emoticons* (E) were hypothesized to be a negative credibility cue and thus condition 1 was without and condition 2 contained at least one smiley. *Retweeted*(F) Tweets were framed as Twitter does when a Tweet enters a user's timeline because it was retweeted by someone the user follows. The pool consisted of 108 (18×6) tweet-pairs in total.

4. RESULTS

Figure 1 offers means and error bars showing how judgements varied across strategies for each condition. We conducted a two-way repeated measures ANOVA based on the two aforementioned factors (strategy and condition) using *GNU R* [26] and its package *ez* [19]. The results show a significant main effect of condition ($F(1, 125) = 19.07, p =$

Letter	Strategy	Condition 1 changes	Condition 2
A	Popularity	Add large number of retweets and likes.	low/ no RT / likes
B	Profile Pic	Replace default icon by picture of person	default icon
C	Account	Add "Verified Account" next to nickname	not added
D	Link	Add a shortened URL at the bottom of tweet.	no link
E	Emoticons	No emoticons present	emoticons ≥ 1
F	Retweeted	Frame tweet with retweeting person	no frame

Table 2: A description of changes made in each strategy for each condition. Please note: Condition 2 means no cue present.

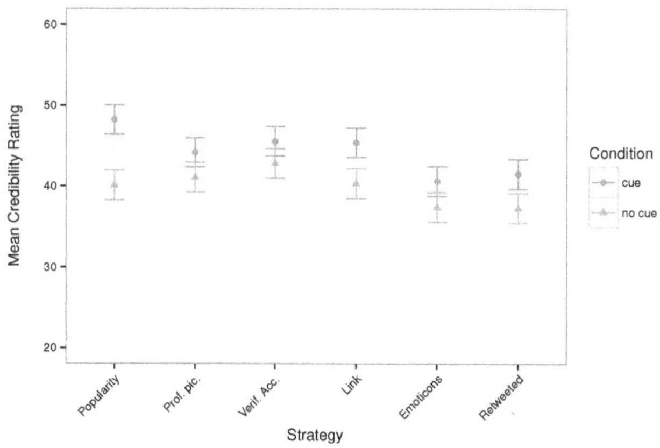

Figure 1: The means and error bars for each condition per strategy.

$2.6e^{-5}$, $\eta^2 = 0.005$), but no significant main effect for strategy or the interaction between these. This shows that it is possible to alter the perceived credibility of Tweets using the manipulations we tested. Pairwise t-tests of conditions per strategy, however, reveal that scores differed only for two strategies (the significance level $\alpha = 0.05$ was Bonferroni-corrected, see [8]). Popular Tweets were given a higher credibility ($M = 48.22$, $SD = 30.75$) than unpopular ones ($M = 40.10$,$SD = 31.02$), $t(125) = 3.56$, $p = 0.00026$, $r = 0.30$. Similarly, Tweets containing a link ($M = 45.38$, $SD = 31.54$) appear to be more trustworthy than those which do not ($M = 40.32$,$SD = 30.48$), $t(125) = 2.48$, $p = 0.00718$, $r = 0.22$. These figures represent a medium sized effect for popularity and a small effect for links according to Cohen's classification [5].

5. DISCUSSION

Our results confirm that it is possible with relatively simple and subtle changes to a Tweet's presentation, to manipulate how the credibility of Tweets relating to the refugee situation in Germany are perceived. While these findings are not surprising given previously published results, they are nevertheless disturbing: Popularity (represented by like and retweet count) does take some effort to manipulate, but it is possible and even likely when one examines the number of likes and retweets factually dubious Tweets receive.

Links created via shortened URL services can, on the other hand, be added with little effort and our findings show these to have a positive effect on user credibility judgements. It is difficult to explain why a neutral shortened external link, which offers no clue as to the source, would increase the credibility-perception of a Tweet. Perhaps this is an automatic, sub-conscious reaction in response to past experiences with social media.

Although reported in earlier studies, we did not find significant effects for profile pic, verified account, and retweets (which also have to do with popularity). This could be because we restricted Tweets to a single, specific topic and these features have less of an influence in this domain. It may also be explained by the presence of other cues in the raw Tweets, for which we did not control (i.e. cues not previously reported in the literature). Examining the judgements for unaltered Tweets (condition 2) shows high variability in the judgements between Tweets. This suggests that other factors may be involved and we plan to examine these Tweets qualitatively to establish other cues, which may be playing a role and can be investigated in future studies. We also observed variability in the judgements for individual Tweets across users. This could mean that individual differences, such as personality, political persuasion or topical knowledge might influence judgements. Future work is required to investigate both intra- and inter-personal factors more carefully. The Tweets judged in our study were all factually incorrect. In future studies we will balance factually incorrect and correct Tweets to examine whether this firstly influences the judgements and secondly to determine how able users are to establish factual accuracy.

The findings should serve as a warning sign both for Twitter users - who should perhaps be made aware of their limitations in judging how credible social media posts are - and for social-network service providers and others such as search engines who distribute content. One option which may wish to be explored based on our findings and the findings of others would be to derive more robust and objective measures of credibility and communicate this to users explicitly.

6. CONCLUSION

In this paper we have presented an initial study investigating user perception of Tweet credibility in the context of Tweets about refugees. We showed empirically that the perception of credibility can be increased by the fact that a URL is present in the Tweet or that the Tweet has been liked or retweeted often by other users. We discussed the findings and suggested other aspects, which could be studied in future work.

7. REFERENCES

[1] *Internet overtakes newspapers as news outlet. http://pewresearch.org/pubs/1066/internetovertakes-newspapers-as-news-source. last accessed on 21.9.2016 2008.*

[2] Fabricio Benevenuto, Gabriel Magno, Tiago Rodrigues, and Virgilio Almeida, *Detecting spammers on twitter*, Collaboration, electronic messaging, anti-abuse and spam conference (CEAS), vol. 6, 2010, p. 12.

[3] Alex Burns and Ben Eltham, *Twitter free iran: an evaluation of twitter's role in public diplomacy and information operations in iran's 2009 election crisis*, Record of the Communications Policy & Research Forum (CPRF) 2009, Network Insight Institute, 2009, pp. 298–310.

[4] Carlos Castillo, Marcelo Mendoza, and Barbara Poblete, *Information credibility on twitter*, Proceedings of the 20th international conference on World wide web, ACM, 2011, pp. 675–684.

[5] Jacob Cohen, *Statistical Power Analysis for the Behavioral Sciences*, 2nd ed., Lawrence Erlbaum Associates, 1988.

[6] David M Cook, Benjamin Waugh, Maldini Abdipanah, Omid Hashemi, and Shaquille Abdul Rahman, *Twitter deception and influence: Issues of identity, slacktivism, and puppetry*, Journal of Information Warfare **13** (2014), no. 1.

[7] Lizzie Dearden, *The fake refugee images that are being used to distort public opinion on asylum seekers*, Independent Newspaper online accessed via http://www.independent.co.uk/news/world/europe/the-fake-refugee-images-that-are-being-used-to-distort-public-opinion-on-asylum-seekers-10503703.html, last accessed 11.09.2016 (2015).

[8] Olive Jean Dunn, *Multiple comparisons among means*, Journal of the American Statistical Association **56** (1961), no. 293, 52–64.

[9] David Elsweiler, *False information in social-media platforms, luddite-technologist accessible via http://davidelsweiler.blogspot.de/2016/01/false-information-in-social-media.html, last accessed 15.09.2016*, (2016).

[10] David Elsweiler and Morgan Harvey, *Engaging and maintaining a sense of being informed: Understanding the tasks motivating twitter search*, Journal of the Association for Information Science and Technology **66** (2015), no. 2, 264–281.

[11] Victoria M Esses, Scott Veenvliet, Gordon Hodson, and Ljiljana Mihic, *Justice, morality, and the dehumanization of refugees*, Social Justice Research **21** (2008), no. 1, 4–25.

[12] Andrew J Flanagin and Miriam J Metzger, *Perceptions of internet information credibility*, Journalism & Mass Communication Quarterly **77** (2000), no. 3, 515–540.

[13] Dieter Frey, *Recent research on selective exposure to information*, Advances in Experimental Social Psychology **19** (1986), 41–80.

[14] Aditi Gupta, Ponnurangam Kumaraguru, Carlos Castillo, and Patrick Meier, *Tweetcred: A real-time web-based system for assessing credibility of content on twitter*, Proc. 6th International Conference on Social Informatics (SocInfo). Barcelona, Spain, 2014.

[15] Eszter Hargittai, Lindsay Fullerton, Ericka Menchen-Trevino, and Kristin Yates Thomas, *Trust online: Young adults' evaluation of web content*, International Journal of Communication **4** (2010), 27.

[16] Jonathan Hurlock and Max L Wilson, *Searching twitter: Separating the tweet from the chaff.*, ICWSM, 2011, pp. 161–168.

[17] Matthew James Kushin and Masahiro Yamamoto, *Did social media really matter? College students' use of online media and political decision making in the 2008 election*, Mass Communication and Society **13** (2010), no. 5, 608–630.

[18] Haewoon Kwak, Changhyun Lee, Hosung Park, and Sue Moon, *What is twitter, a social network or a news media?*, Proceedings of the 19th international conference on World wide web, ACM, 2010, pp. 591–600.

[19] Michael A. Lawrence, *ez: Easy analysis and visualization of factorial experiments*, 2015, R package version 4.3.

[20] Jonathan Lazar, Gabriele Meiselwitz, and Jinjuan Feng, *Understanding web credibility: a synthesis of the research literature*, Now Publishers Inc, 2007.

[21] Florian Meier and David Elsweiler, *Going back in time: An investigation of social media re-finding*, Proceedings of the 39th International ACM SIGIR conference on Research and Development in Information Retrieval, ACM, 2016, pp. 355–364.

[22] Meredith Ringel Morris, Scott Counts, Asta Roseway, Aaron Hoff, and Julia Schwarz, *Tweeting is believing?: understanding microblog credibility perceptions*, Proceedings of the ACM 2012 conference on Computer Supported Cooperative Work, ACM, 2012, pp. 441–450.

[23] Meredith Ringel Morris, Jaime Teevan, and Katrina Panovich, *What do people ask their social networks, and why?: a survey study of status message q&a behavior*, Proceedings of the SIGCHI conference on Human factors in computing systems, ACM, 2010, pp. 1739–1748.

[24] Rebecca Walker Naylor, Cait Poynor Lamberton, and Patricia M West, *Beyond the "like" button: The impact of mere virtual presence on brand evaluations and purchase intentions in social media settings*, Journal of Marketing **76** (2012), no. 6, 105–120.

[25] Anne Pedersen, Susan Watt, and Susan Hansen, *The role of false beliefs in the community's and the federal government's attitudes toward australian asylum seekers*, Australian Journal of Social Issues **41** (2006), no. 1, 105.

[26] R Core Team, *R: A language and environment for statistical computing*, R Foundation for Statistical Computing, Vienna, Austria, 2016.

[27] Jaime Teevan, Daniel Ramage, and Merredith Ringel Morris, *# twittersearch: a comparison of microblog search and web search*, Proceedings of the fourth ACM international conference on Web search and data mining, ACM, 2011, pp. 35–44.

[28] Renate van der Zee, *Rumours and lies: 'the refugee crisis is an information crisis'*, Guardian Online accessed via https://www.theguardian.com/global-development-professionals-network/2016/aug/18/rumours-and-lies-the-refugee-crisis-is-an-information-crisis, last accessed 11.09.2016 (2016).

[29] Ryen White, *Beliefs and biases in web search*, Proceedings of the 36th international ACM SIGIR conference on Research and development in information retrieval, ACM, 2013, pp. 3–12.

Focus Paragraph Detection for Online Zero-Effort Queries

Lessons learned from Eye-Tracking Data

Christin Seifert
Technische Universität
Dresden, Germany
christin.seifert2@tu-dresden.de

Annett Mitschick
Technische Universität
Dresden, Germany
annett.mitschick@tu-dresden.de

Jörg Schlötterer
University of Passau,
Germany
joerg.schloetterer@uni-passau.de

Raimund Dachselt
Technische Universität
Dresden, Germany
dachselt@acm.org

ABSTRACT

In order to realize zero-effort retrieval in a web-context, it is crucial to identify the part of the web page the user is focusing on. In this paper, we investigate the identification of focus paragraphs in web pages. Starting from a naive baseline for paragraph and focus paragraph detection, we conducted an eye-tracking study to evaluate the most promising features. We found that single features (mouse position, paragraph position, mouse activity) are less predictive for gaze which confirms findings from other studies. The results indicate that an algorithm for focus paragraph detection needs to incorporate a weighted combination of those features as well as additional features, e.g. semantic context derived from the user's web history.

Keywords

focus paragraph detection; zero-effort queries; eye tracking

1. INTRODUCTION

Just-in-time retrieval [8], also called zero-effort queries [1] is the idea of retrieving new, relevant information with minimal user effort, ideally in a fully automatic way. Zero-effort retrieval requires i) identification of relevant user context and ii) query construction based on this context. Our goal is to generate zero-effort queries in a web-based setting, i. e., when browsing arbitrary web pages. Conceptually, the ideal relevant textual user context is a paragraph, because each paragraph represents one main idea and the concepts within the paragraph are related to each other and to the main idea (topical coherence) [2]. In particular, on pages that contain diverse topics (in different paragraphs), such as news pages, it is desirable to find the topic (and hence the paragraph) the user is actually interested in.

CHIIR '17, March 07 - 11, 2017, Oslo, Norway

ISBN 978-1-4503-4677-1/17/03...$15.00

DOI: http://dx.doi.org/10.1145/3020165.3022138

This paper investigates the identification of the relevant user context, i. e., the *detection of focus paragraphs* in web pages. We hereby assume that the query construction given a focus paragraph is an independent and/or already optimal process [9]. In this paper we present i) an algorithm for *paragraph detection*, splitting a web page into content-bearing textual parts solely based on structural properties, ii) the results of a first user study on the accuracy of a naive baseline algorithm for *focus paragraph detection*, and iii) the results of an eye-tracking study on the effect of selected layout and interaction features on focus paragraph detection.

2. RELATED WORK

Paragraph detection, i. e., automatic splitting of larger documents into smaller, semantically meaningful parts, has been investigated before [5, 12, 3], but to the best of our knowledge not in the context of real-time processing of general web pages. Web page paragraph detection is especially challenging for two reasons: First, markup tags are used to convey both, semantics and layout information[1]. Second, the storage capabilities and processing power within web browsers are limited, making real-time paragraph detection based on content [5] or visual building blocks [3] intractable. Lagun and Agichtein [7] suggested manually engineered segmentation (i. e. hard-coded) for popular web pages which tend to share the same layout, such as Google search results, and supervised automatic classification based on selected training data for less frequent pages. However, our scenario of zero-effort retrieval on the web requires the paragraph detection to be generally applicable to all kinds of web pages and feasible online.

Previous work on focus detection investigated the correlation between mouse interactions (movements, clicks, text selections) on a web page and gaze with the goal of estimating the reading time spent on single paragraphs in the context of adaptive hypermedia systems. Hauger et al. [4] could predict the focus paragraph with approx. 79 % accuracy a-posteriori. Mouse clicks and text selections were identified as highly indicative for gaze position. Additionally, the authors found that the mean value of vertical eye

[1]Even though semantic elements (like article, section, ...) have been introduced with HTML5 (https://www.w3.org/TR/html5), their use is neither enforced nor guaranteed.

position on web pages is not centered, but slightly shifted towards the top (mean value at pixel position 473 of 996).

The relationship between cursor and gaze has also been investigated for search engine result pages [6]. The authors approximated the x and y position of the gaze separately with a linear model, and achieved a RMSE of approx. 125 pixel in each direction. Their linear model combined the dwell time, the time since a movement, the x-coordinate of the cursor position, and the most likely x-coordinate of the gaze based on future cursor positions (analogous for the y-coordinate). Both authors (as well as [7]) use features that are not applicable because they are not suitable for online processing (future mouse position) or for zero-effort querying (mouse click[2]). Further, a text selection already provides a very specific user context, rendering the paragraph detection unnecessary. While our application scenario is different, we conclude from related work, that i) mouse pointer is a semi-informative feature, ii) frequent mouse usage has to be identified, iii) vertical position seems to be highly indicative.

3. INITIAL SITUATION

In this section we describe the initial situation for our approach, presenting an algorithm for paragraph detection, an initial (naive) solution to determine the focus paragraph, and the results of a first user evaluation.

In order to determine the focus paragraph in a web page, it is necessary i) to split the page into paragraphs and remove non-content elements and ii) to select the paragraph in focus. For the fist step, we utilize the DOM structure of the web page[3]. First, we create a set of candidate paragraphs, composed of nodes that have a textual child node of at least 40 characters. Only the topmost node in a subtree satisfying this criterion is considered, since it already includes all child elements. Next, neighbouring candidates are combined, if they are only separated by text nodes (i. e., there are no other nodes, such as <p> or <br> in between). Finally, the candidate set is filtered by visible paragraphs, which are either combined or contain at least 100 characters and a dot.

A **naive baseline** algorithm for focus paragraph detection is to select the topmost (completely visible) paragraph as focus paragraph and update the selected paragraph only on scroll-events. We used this baseline for two reasons: First, the topmost paragraph is the most likely paragraph to be looked at after following a hyperlink. Second, the topmost area of the page is already excluded by the paragraph detection algorithm if it merely contains navigation elements or advertisements.

In a first study with 77 users[4] we investigated the accuracy of our zero-effort query generation process including the accuracy of the paragraph and focus paragraph detection [10]. The prototype implemented the **naive baseline** for focus paragraph detection. We asked users to correct the focus paragraph if they considered it to be incorrect. This was achieved by simply clicking inside the correct paragraph. In 35% of all cases the focus paragraph was adapted, resulting in an accuracy of 65% for the focus paragraph detection. This accuracy is highly biased, because i) we did not ask whether the paragraph is correct in general, but asked users to correct wrong paragraphs (which took manual effort), ii) we visually outlined the detected paragraph, which might draw the focus of attention, and iii) the detection was embedded in a study with a different focus.

4. IMPROVING FOCUS DETECTION

Although the first study showed an accuracy of the naive baseline algorithm of at least 65%, the study had several limitations as described above. In this section we describe our approach of improving the focus paragraph detection for the context of web-based zero-effort queries using selected features based on related work and the results of an eye-tracking study.

4.1 Feature Selection

We chose to investigate four layout and interaction features in detail (cf. Figure 1): The **paragraph's size** $a = w \cdot h$ as a layout factor should account for the fact that larger areas on the screen have a higher probability of being looked at. The **paragraph's position** d (vertical and horizontal) on the page is included, because it has been identified as predictive for gaze on web pages in a different scenario [4]. We also included the **position of the mouse pointer** relative to the paragraph m, which has shown to be of predictive value if users move their mouse frequently [6]. Thus, we also included a **mouse pointer activity** threshold, indicating whether the mouse is used as aid for cognition [4].

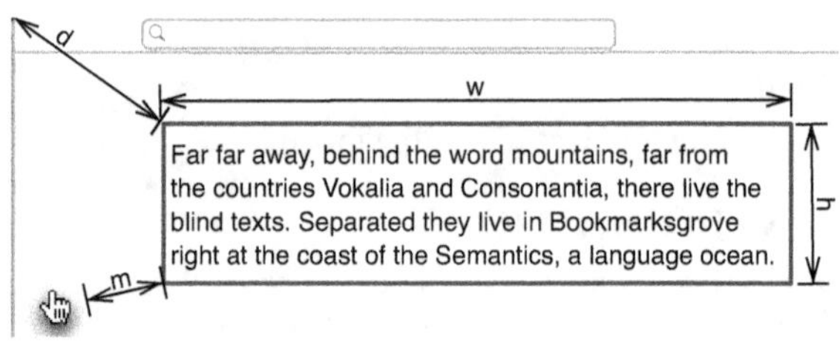

Figure 1: Features for focus paragraph detection

4.2 Eye-Tracking Study

To investigate the applicability of the selected features (paragraph size and position, mouse pointer position and activity) we conducted a user study using an eye-tracker to log the visual focus of users while reading web pages. The initial question was: which feature(s) could improve the accuracy of focus paragraph detection, and to what extend?

4.2.1 Procedure

The user study was conducted in a university lab using a Tobii Pro TX300 eye-tracker (providing a 23″ monitor). Twelve participants volunteered (2 female; age between 21 and 51; mostly students and staff from the local university), four needed a vision aid and used it during the experiment. Each session lasted around 30 minutes. First, the participants had to fill out a questionnaire about their web browsing and retrieval experiences and skills, and their knowledge

[2] A click typically corresponds to following a hyperlink, thus changing the page content. We regard clicks to the non-linked space as feature of user control, explicitly marking the paragraph as focused and hence not applicable to the automatic detection.

[3] The source code is available as part of the c4 framework https://github.com/eexcess/c4#paragraphdetection

[4] A detailed description of the study setup is available at https://github.com/schloett/p2q

and interest in 8 predefined topics such as geography, history, politics, etc. From these topics we later picked 2 or 3 for the session tasks (depending on the user's rating, preferring topics where the user indicated high interest and low or medium prior knowledge). The participants were given basic information about the setup of the study (accompanied by an individual calibration of the eye tracker), but no further details about the purpose. So all subjects knew that their eye movements were tracked and logged, but did not know what exactly we were interested in. Afterwards, the participants were given three questions within the scope of the selected topic and a Wikipedia article[5] in a full-screen browser window on the Tobii monitor (full-HD). The article directly provided the answers to the questions or links to other relevant articles. The task was to read the relevant Wikipedia articles (without time limit) until one felt to be able to answer the questions. We were able to do at least 2 iterations (topics) with each subject.

We tracked and logged coordinates and time stamp of gaze and mouse pointer positions on the screen with 50 Hz, the URL and content of the visited web page including position and layout of all detected paragraphs and detected focus paragraphs (naive algorithm), as well as scrolling and mouse click activities (cf. Figure 2 for some examples). The subjects were instructed not to use the browser's full text search functionality to highlight keywords, so that they were forced to read larger parts of the text to find relevant information.

4.2.2 Results

In order to investigate the relevance and impact of layout and interaction features for focus paragraph detection, we analyzed the logged data as follows: First of all, we evaluated the performance of the naive focus paragraph detection approach by counting the number of gaze events which were targeted at a point within the bounding box of a focus paragraph candidate. To compensate inaccuracies of the eye-tracker[6] we extended the area of the bounding box by 10 pixels in each direction. Furthermore we smoothed the samples using a weighted average filter and removed short fixations (<100 ms), which are usually a result of noise but are especially dispensable in our case as we are interested in sequences of focused reading (at least 100 ms up to 500 ms fixation duration [11]). We learned that an average of 36.63 % (SD 12.93 %) of the gaze events targeted to the screen did not hit a paragraph candidate at all. This is due to the fact that elements like images, headlines, formulas, table of contents, etc. do not provide sufficient textual content to construct the search context for a query formulation, and are thus ignored by the algorithm (as described above). Taking this into account, we only considered gaze events within the set of paragraph candidates. This resulted in an average success rate of 40.71 % (SD 18.27 %) for the naive baseline algorithm. We found that the lowest accuracy (9.5 %) was achieved when the subject was reading thoroughly through large parts of text without any mouse interaction or scrolling, which would trigger the reallocation of the focus. The best result (87.9 %) was achieved when the subject used anchor links within the document to directly jump to a paragraph and read it.

[5]Please note that all participants shared the same native language, in which all reading material was provided.

[6]According to Tobii the TX300 has an average accuracy of 0.4° and a precision of 0.14° [13].

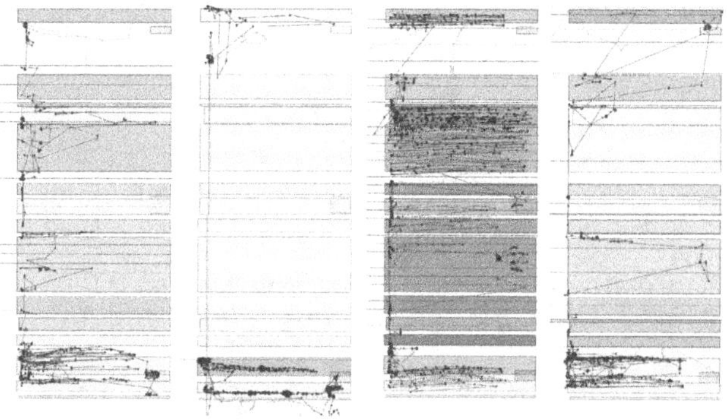

Figure 2: Four participants reading the same web page: gaze hits (blue), assumed focus paragraphs (green), vertical scrolling position (red) and mouse activity (orange)

Next, we investigated the influence of the paragraph's size. We calculated the ratio between the size of the actual read paragraph (fixation duration of at least 3 seconds) and the size of the largest visible paragraph on the screen. The average ratio was 0.56 (SD = 0.35), which means that the mean size of a focused paragraph was about a half of the size of the largest visible paragraph. Only an average of 33 % of the gaze events hit the largest visible paragraph in each case.

After that we focused on the influence of the vertical position of the paragraph on the screen[7]. Regarding the overall vertical distribution of gaze hits on the screen we found that gaze is primarily directed to the upper half of the screen (mean value at 402 of 1080 pixels from the top). We used the frequency values (see Figure 3) to weight the visible paragraphs according to their vertical position when rerunning the focus paragraph detection based on the logs. In this experiment we achieved an average success rate of 41.59 % (SD 16.65 %), which is only slightly better than the baseline algorithm. According to expectations, this approach performed better in cases of thoroughly reading of long text passages.

Furthermore, we investigated the relation between gaze events and simultaneous mouse pointer positions (as one of the feature candidates). As to be seen in Figure 3 the mouse pointer is mainly placed near the vertical center (mean value at 472 pixels of 1080). We calculated a matching between mouse hovering in a vertical distance to the gaze target of under 100 pixels[8] in 38 % of all cases. According to the assumption that the activity of the mouse pointer is an indication for its usage as an aid for cognition [4], we focused on the samples showing high mouse pointer activity. In the selected subset we found a matching in 60 % of the cases.

4.3 Discussion

The results of the study are quite in line with our expectations, regarding the inferior performance of the naive baseline algorithm compared to the results of the first user study. This is mainly due to the limitations of the first study (cf. Section 3) and the difference in measuring the accuracy: while the first study achieved a binary measure through the (indirect) approval or (direct) rejection of the users without

[7]As the majority of the Wikipedia articles used in this study appear in a single-column layout we did not have sufficient data to evaluate the influence of the horizontal position.

[8]The average height of a detected paragraph was 100 pixels.

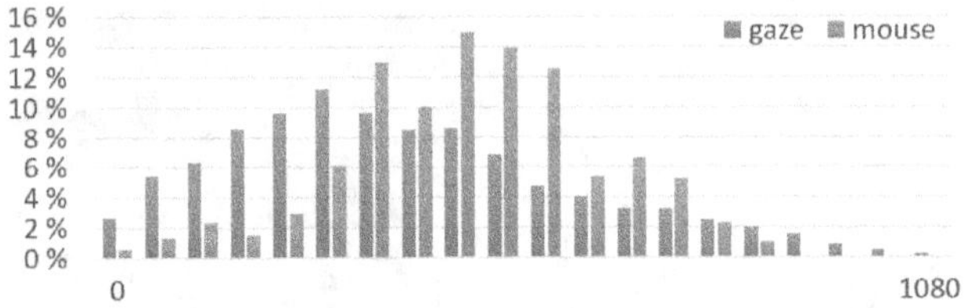

Figure 3: Histogram of the vertical distribution (0=top, 1080=bottom) of gaze (blue) and mouse pointer (red) positions

accounting for dwell time, the eye-tracking study measured gaze hits per paragraph in relation to time. The results confirm former studies [4, 6] concerning the deviation between gaze and mouse positioning, and that the mouse pointer is a semi-informative feature. The approach to use an activity threshold for the mouse pointer increases the accuracy significantly (up to 60 %) but was only applicable in 5 of 25 runs (20 %). The results showed that the relative size of a paragraph on its own is not an informative indicator for it being read. Furthermore, the weighting of the paragraphs according to their vertical positions based on the vertical distribution of gaze hits improved the accuracy only slightly, but seems to be promising in combination with navigational behavior of the users. This leads to the assumption that focus paragraph detection solely based on layout features is not feasible. Instead, future research should be focused on the weighted combination of layout, interaction and semantic features such as content-related background knowledge, browsing and query history, user profiles, etc.

The presented study has some limitations that should be further discussed. First of all, the number of subjects was too small to find similarities between users and derive adequate features in terms of the analysis of typical reading behavior. Second, the subjects knew that their gaze was tracked and logged, which means that we cannot ensure that they acted normally, i. e., performed normal reading behavior, although all of them stated that they did not feel affected by the presence of an eye-tracker. Due to the complexity of the given tasks it is very likely that the participants forgot about the tracking after some minutes. On the other hand, this complexity and a certain pressure to succeed might be the reason that several subjects tended to skim the page to spot relevant keywords instead of attentive reading. We are not sure if this adds to a bias and to what extend.

However, our aim was to get first results as an initial feedback to further improve focus paragraph detection. The insights we gained during the analysis led to promising features that should be taken into consideration.

5. CONCLUSION AND FUTURE WORK

In this paper we presented an approach for paragraph and focus paragraph detection for web-based zero-effort queries. We investigated the influence of layout and interaction features (namely paragraph size and position, and mouse pointer position and activity) with the help of an eye-tracking study. Our analysis showed that the pre-selected features were little informative in general, especially when considered in isolation, but might be effective in combination.

In the experiment we used a Wikipedia test corpus as a proxy for informational pages containing images, navigation elements and a sufficiently complex page structure. While we estimate the approach to be applicable to similar pages, future experiments might be necessary to investigate the applicability of the results to web pages of different types.

To further improve detection accuracy we will i) elaborate on weighting factors and parameters of features in combination, ii) investigate additional features, primarily semantic content features (from browsing/query history, etc.), and iii) investigate personalized focus paragraph detection by providing an initial model to all users, allowing for interactive correction of the detection and integrating the feedback into the model, e. g. to adapt the weights for different features.

6. REFERENCES

[1] J. Allan, B. Croft, A. Moffat, and M. Sanderson. Frontiers, Challenges, and Opportunities for Information Retrieval: Report from SWIRL 2012. *SIGIR Forum*, 46(1):2–32, 2012.

[2] G. Brown and Y. George. *Discourse Analysis.* Cambridge University Press, 1983.

[3] D. Cai, S. Yu, J.-R. Wen, and W.-Y. Ma. Extracting content structure for web pages based on visual representation. In *Proc. Asia-Pacific Web Conference*, pages 406–417, 2003.

[4] D. Hauger, A. Paramythis, and S. Weibelzahl. Using browser interaction data to determine page reading behavior. In *UMAP'11*, pages 147–158, 2011.

[5] M. A. Hearst. Multi-paragraph segmentation of expository text. In *Proc. Annual Meeting on Association for Computational Linguistics*, pages 9–16, 1994.

[6] J. Huang, R. White, and G. Buscher. User see, user point: Gaze and cursor alignment in web search. In *Proc. Conference on Human Factors in Computing Systems*, SIGCHI, pages 1341–1350, 2012.

[7] D. Lagun and E. Agichtein. Inferring searcher attention by jointly modeling user interactions and content salience. In *Proc. Conference on Research and Development in Information Retrieval*, SIGIR '15, pages 483–492, New York, NY, USA, 2015. ACM.

[8] B. J. Rhodes. *Just-In-Time Information Retrieval.* PhD thesis, Massachusetts Institute of Technology, 2000.

[9] J. Schlötterer, C. Seifert, and M. Granitzer. Supporting Web Surfers in Finding Related Material in Digital Library Repositories. In *Proc. Theory and Practice of Digital Libraries*, TPDL, 2016.

[10] C. Seifert, W. Bailer, T. Orgel, L. Gantner, R. Kern, H. Ziak, A. Petit, J. Schlötterer, S. Zwicklbauer, and M. Granitzer. Ubiquitous access to digital cultural heritage. *ACM Journal on Computing and Cultural Heritage (JOCCH)*, 2017. to appear.

[11] S. C. Sereno and K. Rayner. Measuring word recognition in reading: eye movements and event-related potentials. *Trends in Cognitive Sciences*, 7(11):489 – 493, 2003.

[12] C. Sporleder and M. Lapata. Automatic paragraph identification: A study across languages and domains. In *Proc. Conference on Empirical Methods in NLP*, EMNLP, pages 72–79, 2004.

[13] T. Technology. Accuracy and precision test report tx300. Technical report, Tobii Technology AB, 2013.

A Process Model of Scholarly Media Annotation

Liliana Melgar
Univ. of Amsterdam
Netherlands

Marijn Koolen
Huygens/ING
Netherlands

Hugo Huurdeman
Univ. of Oslo
Norway

Jaap Blom
Netherlands Inst. for Sound and Vision, Netherlands

ABSTRACT

Annotation has been identified as one of the "scholarly primitives", and plays a pivotal role in facilitating access to audio-visual (AV) media in a scholarly context. However, there is a lack of understanding of scholars' annotation needs and behavior. This paper is part of a group of studies aiming to understand how to improve annotation support of AV media, in order to facilitate research activities of media scholars and other scholars who make intensive use of AV media. The main findings confirm previous research discerning stages in media scholars' research processes, and indicate a great variety of research activities which occur in a non-linear order. Our studies also show that different annotation activities occur along those stages. The main contribution of this paper is a generic process model capturing AV media annotation, potentially applicable to a variety of research use cases in a scholarly context.

Keywords

time-based media; audio-visual media research; video annotation

1. INTRODUCTION

Scholars in the (Digital) humanities are active and motivated annotators [24]. They annotate all types of media at any level, with many layers of interpretation. Unsworth [21] identified annotating as one of the "scholarly primitives." In the case of audio-visual (AV) or time-based media, manual or semi-automatic annotation of the media content is essential, given the fact that providing fully automated access is more challenging than to textual resources [15]. Scholarly work is also often described as a process [11], where different stages occur over time (e.g., [4]). Providing support to scholarly research requires the analysis of the complex research tasks where knowledge construction is involved. These are not limited to searching and retrieving a list of results, but also other series of scholarly primitives, e.g. classifying, linking [20], comparing, sampling, illustrating, annotating [21], or writing and collaborating [18]. However, little is known about how those complex tasks are performed in the context of scholarly research where AV media is the focal point, for instance, in media and communication studies. In addition, there is a lack of system support for the different methods that this group of researchers uses in different research phases [9]. To understand how annotation should be supported along the research process of media scholars, different investigations are conducted within the CLARIAH project[1], with a focus on research behavior, activities, models, and "tool" analyses. As part of these investigations, this paper presents two user studies about scholars' research processes, with a particular focus on the types of annotation-related activities. The research problem above results in the following research question: *How is annotation of time-based media done in practice by media scholars, and other scholars who make intensive use of AV media, and in which stages of their research process is it used and how?*

The main contributions of this paper consist of (a) extending current research on how to support different stages of the search and research process and (b) identifying the different annotation activities during the research process and the connections between them. Based on our findings and previous research, we propose a generic process model to capture annotation activities across all research stages of the analyzed use cases and highlight the main practical and conceptual implications for future system design.

CHIIR '17, March 07 - 11, 2017, Oslo, Norway

ISBN 978-1-4503-4677-1/17/03...$15.00

DOI: http://dx.doi.org/10.1145/3020165.3022139

2. BACKGROUND RESEARCH

2.1 (Re)search as process

Detailing the process of scholarly research is done either via "prescriptive" models used in textbooks, or discovered via empirical studies of researchers' behavior. Case [3, p. 222] lists a 'classic' view on these stages, which typically start with imagining a research question (1), followed by determining what data are needed and designing a specific study to collect it (2), choosing and implementing research methods (3), analyzing and interpreting observations (4), and considering the overall results (5). The exact nature of these stages, however, is usually not as straightforward, and may vary across disciplines. Media scholars are at the intersection of humanities and social sciences [11]. The research process of social scientists is described in 'prescriptive' models, for instance, Kendall [12], who details a series of "steps" which vary depending on the approach (inductive or deductive). Common steps in the two approaches include: problem definition, literature review, research design, data collection and analysis. In the humanities, on the other hand, the research process cannot necessarily be captured in a sequential model [11]. However, there is current empirical evidence that there are broad phases in the research process of media and communication scholars [2], and of media scholars using web archives [9]. Bron et al. [2] explored this issue by investigating a group of twenty-seven media studies researchers. The authors

[1]CLARIAH is project to develop a Dutch research infrastructure for Digital Humanities, see http://www.clariah.nl/

found common parts in the research processes, summarized in three phases with different associated activities: exploration (studying background material, developing initial research questions, initial information gathering), contextualization (revising research questions, gathering material or selecting data with a focused purpose) and presentation (organizing the data and selecting appropriate evidence to build up a case). Marsden et al. [13] briefly discuss a schematic view of the research process with AV materials in a number of humanities disciplines, which included annotation.

2.2 Annotations and annotation behaviour

The term "annotation" has different meanings to different communities [8]. In the literary tradition, it is used as an equivalent of "glossing.", including "marginalia," or "commonplace books" [26], often used as part of reading activities. Marshall [14] argued the need for annotation tools that support a smooth integration of annotating with reading in a digital environment. In digital humanities, annotation is regarded as one of the "scholarly primitives", which are basic activities or functions common to research across humanities disciplines, over time, and independent of theoretical orientation [21]. Palmer et al. [18] recognized notetaking as one of the cross-cutting primitives. In information processing, the term "annotation" refers to any description that is explicitly used for the purpose of future retrieval [7] (e.g. markup elements or descriptive metadata). Agosti and Ferro [1] and Haslhofer et al. [6] showed how annotations created during reading can be used as metadata. Haslhofer et al. [6], Ruvane [19] and Melgar [15] suggest a holistic view on annotation that is not limited to note-taking, but includes any form of metadata authoring (i.e., indexes, catalog records, tags, keywords, comments, notes), or even the creation of derivative documents or pieces of information derived from the initial information source. These annotations are created by any actor (expert or non-expert both in the domain and the annotation task) in the information interaction continuum, either during reading, information processing, or research. In this scope, it may be possible to study people's "information-annotation behavior" as a form of information use [15]. This broad sense of the term is conveyed in the World Wide Web Consortium (W3C) Annotation Working Group's definition of "annotation" as "any object that is associated with another object by some relationship" [23]. Current work on standards and frameworks for implementing annotation on the web include the W3C candidate recommendation for the Web Annotation Data Model[2] and the "Annotating All Knowledge" coalition[3]. These initiatives do not necessarily focus on the needs of media scholars or annotation of AV-media.

2.3 Media studies research foci and use cases

Humanities scholars are not a homogeneous group [16], and the same can be said about media scholars. Stokes (2003, as cited in [17]) indicates that media and cultural studies focus on three "strands of research": (a) industry (production and distribution of media content), (b) text (style, structure, and meaning of media forms), and, (c) audience (reception of media content). The term "use case" is frequently used in traditional system development [10] . We use the term "research use case" to refer to a type of scholarly research question and possible methods to achieve an answer to it. Research use cases can be grouped into research foci. These foci do not necessarily have epistemological implications for the domain as such, but can guide the design of better systems for supporting specific user groups. Previous work on research behavior of film and television scholars [15] identified different research foci, based on patterns in the types of research questions, data sources needed, and the analysis process. These research foci include:

1. Media aesthetics: the study of media as "texts", e.g. their genres, stylistic features, themes, or narrative structures.

2. Social history of media: the study of patterns of production, distribution, exhibition, or reception of media products (e.g. films, broadcasts, web sites) at a certain moment or place.

3. Aesthetic historiography: a combination of media aesthetics and social media history.

4. Social and cultural history: the intensive use of AV media or web data as sources of historical research.

An analysis of scholarly publications conducted in the beginning of the CLARIAH project further showed three additional foci:

5. Media representations or coverage: the study of coverage, depiction or discussion of specific events, debates, groups of people, or other realities by one specific medium.

6. Trans-media analysis: the comparison of media representations of an issue across different media.

7. Memory studies: the study of the representation of historical events with a focus on how people construct a memory of history.

3. METHOD

This paper is based on two user studies with media scholars in the context of the CLARIAH project. These studies looked at the scholars' research process, with a particular focus on annotation:

A full-day workshop In a hands-on setting, researchers could work with a number of digital tools for searching AV media collections which were going to be part of the infrastructure, including basic and faceted search, tools for temporal analysis, linked data exploration and viewing and annotating video interviews. Five scholars and five information specialists participated, and each media scholar teamed up with an information expert to conduct two simulated research tasks. First, a research focus was assigned to each team. The assigned foci (section 2.3) included: *media aesthetics (1)*, *aesthetic historiography (3)*, *social and cultural history (4)*, *media representations (5)*, and *trans-media analysis (6)*.

Each researcher was familiar and had previous experience with the research focus that was assigned to her. One of the tasks consisted of conducting a research project, from beginning to end, by selecting collections and research tools, but also describing what was needed to conduct the research process at a broader level (e.g., external data, or desired functionalities of the tools). The information expert in the team had to register the steps in a template. Finally, a questionnaire about the two tasks was distributed.

Interviews At a later stage, two of the six experienced media scholars who participated in this workshop, plus a PhD student were interviewed about their research process, this time with a focus on their annotating and analysis activities. These interviews were one-to-one, semi-structured, and lasted between one and three hours. The interviewees' research foci included: *media aesthetics (1)*, *social and cultural history (4)*, and *trans-media analysis (6)*.

The resulting data from both studies consisted of five templates (describing the research questions, "steps", datasets, needed functionalities of tools), and three interviews (audio recordings and summary transcripts). We analyzed the content in two ways: (a) clustering all research activities from both studies following their sequential order, and (b) grouping the activities identified in (a) into categories and research phases, which resulted in the final model.

[2]https://www.w3.org/TR/2016/CR-annotation-model-20161122
[3]https://hypothes.is/annotating-all-knowledge

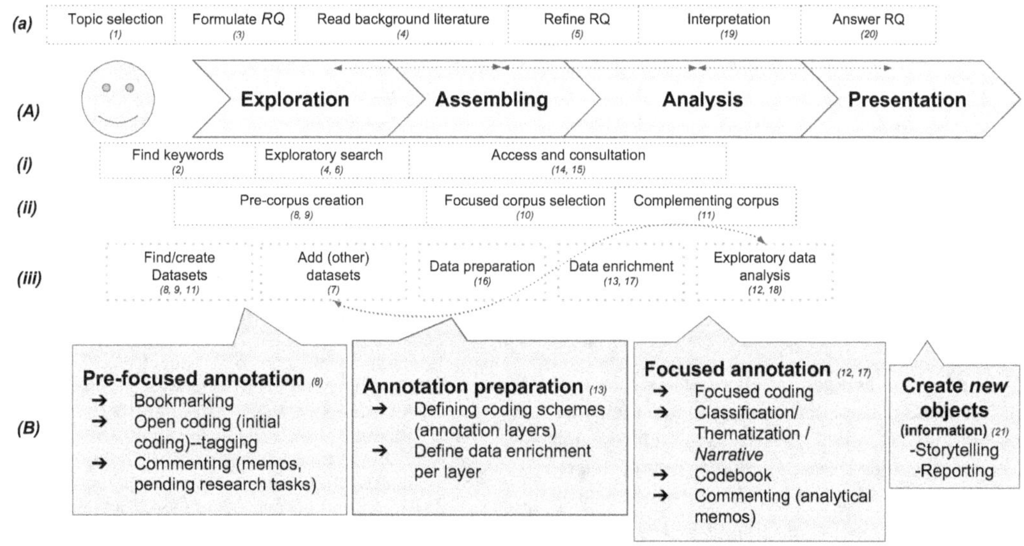

Figure 1: A process model of scholarly media annotation (numbers in parentheses correspond to Table 1)

4. FINDINGS

Annotation activities in media scholarly research Table 1 summarizes the 21 activities identified in our first part of the analysis. We noticed that all participants indicated a number of activities centered on the creation of a corpus and its analysis. In terms of system support, for instance, while exploring a digital collection, scholars indicated the need for support in bookmarking, selecting groups of items after using faceted search or other filtering options, memory features such as query history, selection features for AV media fragments, and the addition of manual annotations, such as comments or tags. During analytic activities, even though the participants used different terms to explain their analysis methods, they often mentioned 'coding' or 'thematization'. In this stage, they also indicated desired functionalities and/or interface features related to refined segmentation, audio transcription, automatic image/audio analysis, fragment summarization, encoding, structuring relationships between coding terms, and linking back to original sources. Some scholars described that the analysis stage included a preparatory phase in which they defined their coding schemes, and/or made their data ready for analysis (e.g, by transcribing it). Our findings also confirmed that media and AV-centered scholars do not annotate time-based media in isolation, but in relation to other media (e.g., scripts, reviews, promotional materials, etc.). We noticed similar annotation activities as those supported by specialized qualitative data analysis software (QDA), see for instance [5]).

Table 2 shows the actual order that was followed by each researcher to accomplish the research project (the numbers refer to the activities in Table 1). This confirms previous studies about the lack of a strict sequence in the research process of humanists, and media and communication scholars (similar to Ellis' study of social scientists, as cited in Case [3, p. 291]). Instead, research activities seem to be recurrent in the different research stages, but with a different degree of refinement. This is especially clear in the case of adding codes or tags to items or fragments, which is more loose in the initial exploratory stage, and more focused in the analysis stage. Likewise, some of the features above were suggested to have different purposes at different moments. For example, in initial research phases, visualization was used for exploratory data analysis. During the analysis, however, visualization was used to facilitate interpretation of the patterns detected in their own corpus.

Table 1: Research activities listed by participants, grouped by research stage

INITIATION/EXPLORATION
(1) Topic selection, (2) Find terms or keywords, (3) Formulate RQ, (4) Search and read background literature, (5) Refine RQ, (6) Explore dataset, (7) Explore other related datasets (aka. 'contextualization')
ASSEMBLING
(8) Pre-corpus identification (identify relevant sources, define "sampling"/selection strategy), (9) Corpus selection (or creation of datasets), (10) Refine corpus (focused selection), (11) Complement corpus (additional data collection, when incomplete)
ANALYSIS
(12) Pre-analysis of initial corpus, (13) Data (corpus) preparation for analysis, (14) 'Contextualize' corpus (find details about the items in a corpus), (15) Access and consultation, (16) Analysis preparation, (17) Analyze corpus, (18) Exploratory data analysis (visualization of own corpus), (19) Interpretation, (20) Answer RQ
PRESENTATION
(21) Present

A model of the annotation process We grouped the 21 activities into categories, depicting them in a graphical conceptual representation, shown in Figure 1. The categories include: the main generic research activities in the research process (a), also represented in (A) in the form of research phases. For representing this part, we departed from the model in [2]. However, in our data we observed that a great proportion of the activities was related to data analysis. Therefore, we extended the original sequence in Bron et al. [2] by adding "analysis" as a separate research phase. We also renamed the "contextualization" phase in Bron et al. [2] to "Assembling" to be more specific. The most important part of the figure, (B), shows the annotation-related activities, which we grouped into phases, from pre-focused annotation to the creation of new information objects. We used the concepts of "pre-focused" and "fo-

Table 2: Order of research activities listed by the participants

Participant	Research focus	Activity order
P1 (workshop)	Aesthetics	1,3,2,8,14,15,17
P2 (workshop)	Media repr.	3,8,4,9,7,10,17, 18,11,18
P3 (workshop)	Trans-media	2,3,9,13,18,16,17
P4 (workshop)	Aesthetic hist.	3,9,4,16,17,7,11,17,18,19,21
P5 (workshop)	Cultural history	8,7,9,12,11,15,17,19,20
P6 (interview)	Aesthetics	3,8,4,15,14,9,10,12,13,(17,18,19)
P7 (interview)	Trans-media	2,3,9,5,10,13,17
P8 (interview)	Memory studies	1,3,9,11,7,12,13,17,18,19,21

cused" from [22] to name the annotation-related stages. Indeed, previous research has found that scholars usually create their own set of semantic categories [25], which correspond to their research questions. We grouped the other research activities in four layers: (i) connected to information seeking and searching (not necessarily system-mediated), (ii) broader stages related to the corpus, and (iii) more specific data processing related activities around the creation and annotation of those corpora.

5. DISCUSSION AND CONCLUSION

The user studies described in this paper confirm that there are discernible, though not strictly sequential, research activities in the research process of media scholars and other AV-centered scholars. In addition, annotation activities seem to have a pivotal supporting function, varying across research stages. Although still in a preliminary stage, the annotation model introduced in this paper contributes to an improved conceptual understanding of information annotating behavior in media research as a process.

These findings have both practical and theoretical implications for future system design applicable to scholarly research. At a practical level, future search systems should offer annotation support. This support can range from basic (e.g. facilitating corpus building), to more complex (e.g. for dynamic analytical activities), or even for the entire research process from corpus creation to data analysis and writing. Most of these tasks are currently supported by separate specialised software, (e.g, QDA packages, or authoring platforms), but the annotations they produce are hardly interoperable. At a theoretical level, the conceptual model presented here has implications for the design of annotation standards and frameworks. For instance, the W3C's Web Annotation Data model, at this point, proposes the concept *motivation* as a way to represent the *intent* behind the creation of an annotation. However, the terms seem to indicate activities, or tasks (i.e. sequences of activities) rather than the actual purpose (e.g., *analysis*). Besides, it does not seem to take into account other ontologies related to research activities (e.g., TaDiRAH) [4]. More research needs to be done to determine whether a phase of the research process should be considered part of the model, or how to handle refinements of annotations for conveying stage-related information. Future work should also provide more details about the requirements for the annotated objects (targets) when there is a need to take into account their structural composition. Finally, because annotations are created by agents with different expertise levels, the Web Annotation Data Model should specify both domain and annotation expertise of the agents involved. This information is essential for supporting collaborative and more varied ways of annotation.

[4]http://tadirah.dariah.eu/vocab/index.php

References

[1] M. Agosti and N. Ferro. *Annotations as Context for Searching Documents*, pages 155–170. Springer Berlin Heidelberg, 2005.

[2] M. Bron, J. Van Gorp, and M. Rijke. Media studies research in the data-driven age: How research questions evolve. *J. Am. Soc. Inf. Sci. Tec.*, 2015.

[3] D. O. Case. *Looking for information: A survey of research on information seeking, needs and behavior*. Emerald Group Publishing, 2016.

[4] C. M. Chu. Literary critics at work and their information needs: A research-phases model. *Libr. Inform. Sci. Res.*, 21(2):247–273, 1999.

[5] G. R. Gibbs. Using Software in Qualitative Analysis. In *The SAGE Handbook of Qualitative Data Analysis*, pages 277–294. SAGE Publications Ltd, 2014.

[6] B. Haslhofer, W. Jochum, R. King, C. Sadilek, and K. Schellner. The LEMO annotation framework: weaving multimedia annotations with the web. *Int. J. on Digital Libraries*, 10(1):15–32, 2009.

[7] L. Hollink. *Semantic annotation for retrieval of visual resources*. Doctoral Dissertation, Vrije Universiteit, 2006.

[8] J. Hunter. Collaborative semantic tagging and annotation systems. *Annu. Rev. Inform. Sci.*, 43(1):1–84, 2009.

[9] H. C. Huurdeman. *Supporting the Complex Dynamics of the Information Seeking Process*. Doctoral thesis, University of Amsterdam, 2017, forthcoming.

[10] I. Jacobson, I. Spence, and B. Kerr. Use-case 2.0. *Commun. ACM*, 59 (5):61–69, 2016.

[11] K. B. Jensen. The complementarity of qualitative and quantitative methodologies in media and communication research. In *A handbook of media and communication research*, pages 283–301. Routledge, London [etc.], 2nd edition, 2012.

[12] D. E. Kendall. *Sociology in our times: the essentials*. Thomson/Wadsworth, Belmont, CA, 2006.

[13] A. Marsden, A. Mackenzie, A. Lindsay, H. Nock, J. Coleman, and G. Kochanski. Tools for searching, annotation and analysis of speech, music, film and video - A survey. *Literary and Linguistic Computing*, 22(4):469–488, 2007.

[14] C. C. Marshall. Annotation: from paper books to the digital library. In *Proceedings of the Second ACM International Conference on Digital Libraries*, pages 131–140. New York: ACM, 1997.

[15] L. Melgar. *From social tagging to polyrepresentation (doctoral thesis). A study of expert annotating behavior of moving images*. University Carlos III of Madrid, 2016.

[16] U. Must. Alone or together: examples from history research. *Scientometrics*, 91(2):527–537, 2012.

[17] J. Noordegraaf. Computational research in media studies: methodological implications. *Kwalon*, 21(1):52–59, 2016.

[18] C. L. Palmer, L. C. Teffeau, and C. M. Pirmann. Scholarly information practices in the online environment: themes from the literature and implications for library service development. Technical report, OCLC Research, 2009.

[19] M. B. Ruvane. Annotation as process: A vital information seeking activity in historical geographic research. In *Proceedings ASIST*, volume 42, 2005.

[20] R. Sanderson, P. Ciccarese, and H. Van de Sompel. Designing the W3C open annotation data model. In *Web Science Proceedings*, pages 366–375, 2013.

[21] J. Unsworth. Scholarly Primitives: what methods do humanities researchers have in common, and how might our tools reflect this? Humanities Computing: formal methods, experimental practice, May 13, 2000, London, UK.

[22] P. Vakkari. A theory of the task-based information retrieval process: a summary and generalisation of a longitudinal study. *J. Doc.*, 57(1): 44–60, 2001.

[23] W3C. Collaboration, knowledge representation and automatability, 1995.

[24] N.-O. Walkowski and E. T. E. Barker. Digital humanists are motivated annotators. In *Digital Humanities 2014, Laussane, Switzerland*, 2014.

[25] S. Westman. Image users' needs and searching behaviour. In *Information Retrieval: Searching in the 21st Century; Human Information Retrieval*, chapter 4, pages 63–83. 2009.

[26] M. Winget. A meditation on social reading and its implications for preservation. *Preservation, Digital Technology & Culture*, 42(1):39–52, 2013.

Web-Retrieval Supported Argument Space Exploration

Marcus Thiel
Otto von Guericke University
Universitätsplatz 2
39106 Magdeburg, Germany
marcus.thiel@ovgu.de

Philipp Ludwig
Otto von Guericke University
Universitätsplatz 2
39106 Magdeburg, Germany
philipp.ludwig@ovgu.de

Till Mossakowski
Otto von Guericke University
Universitätsplatz 2
39106 Magdeburg, Germany
till.mossakowski@ovgu.de

Fabian Neuhaus
Otto von Guericke University
Universitätsplatz 2
39106 Magdeburg, Germany
fabian.neuhaus@ovgu.de

Andreas Nürnberger
Otto von Guericke University
Universitätsplatz 2
39106 Magdeburg, Germany
andreas.nuernberger@ovgu.de

ABSTRACT

Solid decision making should be ideally based on clear arguments that can be justified by trustworthy information sources. However, argument spaces can quickly get quite complex and it is very often hard to trace the line of arguments found in literature or social media such as blogs and forums. In this paper, we propose a framework for a decision supporting interactive information retrieval system using methods for argument exploration based on textual documents. This concept is supported by a prototype that focuses on the actual analysis of the retrieved arguments in order to obtain a justified decision. For that we use a simplified argumentation graph with nodes as arguments and simple attacking and supporting relations. A web-based plausibility value is propagated (using ranked-based argumentation semantics) through the network for estimating the quality of the arguments. This is based on a web search for documents that support these arguments. The final decision can further be supported by chosing certain preferred interpretations of an abstract dialectical framework, leading to an integrated view of searching, creating, analysing and deciding.

1. INTRODUCTION AND MOTIVATION

Many questions do not have clear cut answers. What is the appropriate hight of minimum wage? Should hate speech be protected by freedom of speech? What amount of man-made temperature increase is acceptable? For these kind of questions there is not one objectively correct answer, but people argue for different answers based on their opinions, point of views, and divergent assessments of the available information. Thus, a system would respond to the three questions above with an answer like "8,75 Euro. Yes. 3 degree Celsius." would miss the point. Because a system that assists a user to find an answer to these kind of difficult question does not just need to find facts. Instead it needs to enable the user explore alternative, competing answers as well as a complex network of inter-connected arguments that support and attack the various positions.

Especially due to the uprise of web 2.0 discussion platforms, there is a large body of text containing discussions and arguments available. However, due to the nature of discussions and the way they are represented in online platforms, traditional document retrieval falls short when it comes to answering a specific question a user might have.

To overcome this issue, other means of processing documents and displaying the important information of those items have to be found. Especially interesting in this context are argumentation structures, since they try to reflect the content or topic of the course of arguments on a formal level, in order to be able to reason on them.

In this paper we will propose an information retrieval system that answers a natural language question not just with a list of results, but allows a user to explore a space of arguments for the competing answers. Further, the system is assisting the user by evaluating the relevance of the results concerning the relation of their content to the query.

If for example a user formulates a question like "Is X or Y better?", arguments from the search results for X and Y are extracted – forming the space of arguments – in order to define why X or Y may be superior to the other. The system evaluates the arguments both based on metadata about the arguments and support and attack relations between the arguments. An answer can then suggested given directly with annotated reasons, which are linked to the original sources.

Different approaches for extracting arguments in such a way have been surveyed [?, ?]. Their performance (F-measure) ranges from 15% over 45% to (for very specific tasks) 90%. This clearly shows that automatic argument mining is of quite limited accuracy. Therefore, we propose an interactive tool for argument gathering and the exploration of the obtained argument space. In the following, we first review the state of the art in the representation and reasoning with arguments and discuss approaches for visualization of related graph structures. Based on this we propose a workflow for interactive argument space exploration that is supported by our framework.

CHIIR '17 March 07–11, 2017, Oslo, Norway

DOI: http://dx.doi.org/10.1145/3020165.3022140

2. RELATED WORK

Past research in the field of argumentation evaluation has mostly focused on analyzing argument structures (i.e. graphs of supporting and attacking statements) and creating static visualizations to support the user in understanding elaborate discussions, as for example shown in [?]. However, this approach do not allow to re-organize the representation of argumentations interactively in order to better support the user's individual view during exploring and learning about the course of arguments. This impedes user experience because interpretations of arguments are likely to be subjective. Users should be able to directly influence the created structure, either directly by interacting with the graph or in an indirect way. Especially in a retrieval scenario, where e.g. a researcher might create a formal argumentation structure based on information from multiple documents, any supporting application should be based on an edit-evaluate-reedit loop which allows for quickly revising the argumentation structure. Ideally, this approach will be enhanced by the already known techniques for analyzing argumentation structures to support the user in evaluating the graph and therefore to better understand the actual information and knowledge contained in discussions.

Argumentation frameworks

The study of (possibly contradicting) arguments has been pioneered by Dung [?]. A Dung abstract argumentation framework consists of a set of arguments and a binary attacks relation. Dung gives several semantics to an abstract argumentation framework, among them the grounded, preferred and stable interpretations (extensions in Dung's terminology). Intuitively, the grounded interpretations contains only information which is uncontroversial (i.e. accepted by a skeptical reasoner), while a preferred interpretation is credulous and contains as much information as possible. However, of course this means that generally there are several preferred interpretations that at least partially contradict each other. Stable interpretations are preferred interpretations satisfying some extra condition expressing that there is only limited controversy. Dung [?] argues that there are reasonable abstract argumentation frameworks without stable interpretations, while preferred interpretations always exist.

The argument interchange format (AIF) [?] has become a standard representation formalism and ontology for arguments. AIF graphs feature two types of nodes: I-nodes for propositions, and S-nodes for argumentation schemes (patterns of reasoning). S-nodes can be of type RA (supporting), CA (contradicting) or PA (expressing a preference). As of 2017 the AIFdb database [?] contains 96 public corpora formulated in AIF. While AIF itself concentrates on mere representations, a logical semantics has been given to AIF [?] using Prakken's ASPIC$^+$ frameworks [?, ?]. The semantics of an ASPIC$^+$ structured argumentation framework is defined by translating it to a Dung abstract argumentation framework. Here, the ASPIC$^+$ defeat relation basically represents the attack relation in the Dung semantic.

OVA [?] is an interactive web-based editor for argument gathering from websites. The output is an AIF graph, which can be directly stored in the AIFdb and then evaluated with three different tools. One of them is TOAST [?], which uses the ASPIC$^+$ translation. However, editing and evaluation is separated. We have the feeling that the low quality of many argumentation graphs in the AIFdb is related to this fact. This underlines the need for an integrated environment which allows the user to both retrieve documents (e.g. web pages) which are related to the input query and to update, refine and polish the argumentation structure.

In many cases Dung semantics does not coincide with the user's intuition. E.g., the Language Of Opposition Corpus[1] contains pairs of sentences where the first sentence attacks the second. When evaluating with TOAST, due to the ASPIC$^+$ semantics, in all interpretations, the first sentence is true, and the second false. However, the user might have expected a more symmetric situation, because in many cases, it is not so clear which sentence should be true. But symmetry is only achieved by having both sentences mutually attack each other. Many users will notice this only if an evaluation tool is tightly coupled with the editing process. As a result, user's expectations can be better matched with the semantics of the tool (either by changing the argument graph[2], or the semantics[3]). Our contribution is the provision of an edit-evaluate-reedit loop, all integrated in one application. This will lead to better argumentation graphs.

Visualization methods

In order to understand the argument structure of a discourse, a lot of visualization strategies have been proposed in the past [?]. Beginning from early charts presented by Wigmore in 1931 for evidential reasoning in law cases over to the famous Toulmin's model in 1958 for a formal graphical representation with explicit naming and combination of different parts of an argument. More modern approaches try to either incorporate more knowledge into the argumentation structure or try to be more useable in practice, i.e. being able to represent actual discussions [?]. Online tools such as Rationale[4] usually fall back to simpler graph representations containing mostly supporting and attacking arguments. This leads to a reduced expressiveness, but may make the graph easier to understand. Especially in the context of information retrieval tasks, where users are not expected to have expertise in the field of argumentation theory, easier representations are to be preferred. Gürkan et al. showed that even in very large discussions, users are able to navigate and comprehend the argumentation space when displayed in a structured way [?].

Additionally, in order to be able to grasp the argument structure, it is sensible to let the user interact with the graph. Especially since automatically extracted structures could get quite big, exploration is an essential component. Advances have been made in that field, proposing interactive visualizations of graphs [?]. There are variants, that deal with continous data as nodes in graphs, rendering a multi-partite projection for several contexts [?]. Additionally, an iterative creation of a graph may be helpful in order to support data analysis [?]. The exploration of bigger graphs may also be supported by using degress of interests (or other measures) in order to show subgraph views depending on the context [?]. This can be used to give a filtered view on an argumentation graph by propagating degrees of trust or truth of the single arguments through the network.

[1] http://www.arg.dundee.ac.uk/aif-corpora/looclban

[2] For example, by introducing another attacks relation, such that both arguments attack each other.

[3] For example, in ADFs (see below), also single attacks have a more bidirectional nature.

[4] https://www.rationaleonline.com/

3. CONCEPTUALIZING THE WORKFLOW

Within the scope of this paper, we developed a prototype to sketch the planned workflow of exploring argumentation spaces defined by arguments given in web pages. The conceptual workflow follows the idea to allow a user to formulate a question, e.g. whether aluminum cans, plastic or glass bottles are the most environmentally friendly products, and to extract arguments from relevant documents to answer said question. The search can be done as a web search, though other sources are possible as well. Arguments can be extracted from the web pages of the result set in the context of the topic/question, in order to support a decision and give an answer, that can be explained by the system by providing fitting arguments.

In its current state, the prototype supports the user in extracting the argumentation graph of webpages in a semi-automated way. Figure **??** shows a screenshot of the application, displaying a debate on the Q&A site *StackExchange* as an example. When the user navigates to a webpage like this, arguments can be marked in the text and will be added to the visualization on the left side. At a later state of this work, we plan to enhance the application in such a way that a suggestion of the graph is automatically created by extracting arguments from the text using text-mining approaches, however, at the current state this functionality is not present.

As soon as more than one argument has been added, the user may create edges between two entities to indicate if one argument attacks or supports another one (as indicated in the screenshot by the colors red and green). Furthermore, the prototype allows to add elaborate descriptions for each argument and to remove or alter edges and arguments at a later moment, which represents the edit-evaluate-reedit loop which we introduced in Section **??**.

The user can initiate an evaluation of the graph. An integrated component will translate the graph into an abstract dialectical framework (ADF) [?] representation that currently consists of combining support relations for a node into a disjunction and attack relations into negated arguments in a conjuction. The Diamond software for ADFs is used as a reasoner to compute preferred interpretations for supporting the decision making processes. These interpretations provide information about the degree of truth of each argument (*true*, *false* or *unknown*, shown in green, red or white). Combined with the functionality of the prototype which allows the user to explicitly mark specific arguments as important, this allows the user to gather information regarding the quality of the argumentation structure and the importance of single arguments.

While in the current state of our work the graph is displayed very prominently to the researcher, the vision of the prototype is not about the argumentation graph itself but actual decision making. Therefore, we aim to assign "plausibility" values to the nodes of the graph. These values are intended to automate the workflow steps described above, so that the main focus of the application shifts to actually answering the question asked at the start and less on working with the argumentation graph. The plausibility values are indicated in the screenshot by the thickness of the border of each node.

One of the first steps in implementing this aspect is assigning said plausibility values by performing a websearch for each argument in the graph. We currently use the argument itself as the query and a simple pattern based approach (see [?, ?]) on the top-k results, identifying possible hits and whether they support or attack the argument. We use the amount of results as the ground truth of the argument. Similar approaches have been used in the past, e.g., in the work of De Luca et al. [?]. This is only a very simple solution, which can easily be exchanged in further iterations.

The ground truth value is propagated through the graph via a ranked-based argument semantics that we have developed in [?]. Since the approach only considers attack relations, we adjusted it for support relations. Basically, attack relations decrease the value, whereas support relations increase it. By multiplying these values with 1, -1 or 0 (for true, false or unknown) and summing up, one can transfer them to whole interpretations. The tool always shows the based-rated preferred interpretation.

This concluding step increases the usefulness of the graph further, allowing to gather information regarding the importance of each argument and how they relate to each other. Using this approach we are able to show the user which arguments in the graph are the most important ones and which may have less impact on decision making, not only from a theoretical or logical point of view but also from the perspective of the plausibility of the argument structure with respect to the document collection.

4. CONCLUSION AND OUTLOOK

We presented the workflow of a preliminary prototype along with the concept of exploring argumentation spaces in order to support decision making processes. Based on this workflow, we showed possibilities of interpreting single arguments via a websearch and adding plausibility to the final automatic decisions made by the analysis of the reasoner. Furthermore, abstract dialectical frameworks (ADFs) help in understanding the structure of the argument space.

While currently our tool uses a simplified form of argument graphs with attack and support relations, in the future we intend to fully support the argument interchange format AIF. A challenge will be to develop a semantics of AIF that meets user's expectations – whether it will be the currently dominating ASPIC$^+$ semantics or a semantics based on three-valued ADF interpretations. In a review of AIFdb corpora we noticed that the user's understanding of the semantics of argument graphs seems to deviate from the semantics used by ASPIC$^+$ of ADF. Our approach of integrating manual argument mining with tool-supported evaluation of the argument structure will greatly help here.

When these semantics have been integrated into the prototype, we plan to conduct a study to evaluate how the user, who is looking for arguments for and against a hypothesis, benefits from the structured visualization of the arguments. Furthermore, the workflow will be enhanced with additional features such as automatic extraction of arguments, direct visual comparison of single arguments and their supporting claims and documents, and better measures for propagating the truth values along the graph. This will lead to a more comprehensive estimation of a decision, which could be evaluated in another user study.

5. REFERENCES

[1] F. Bex, S. Modgil, H. Prakken, and C. Reed. On logical specifications of the Argument Interchange Format. *J. Log. Comput.*, 23(5):951–989, 2013.

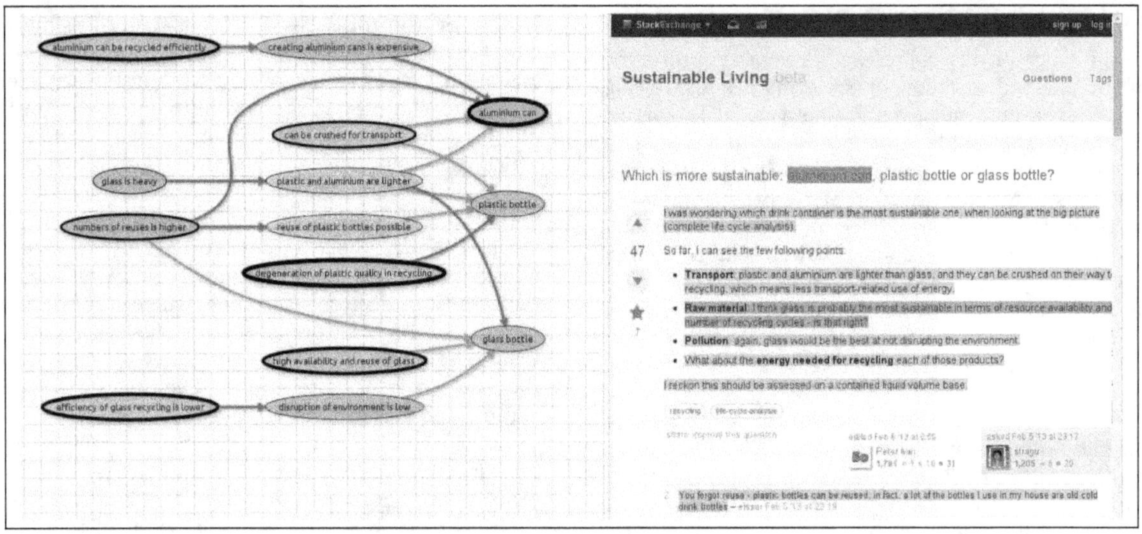

Figure 1: Screenshot of the demo application

[2] G. Brewka, S. Ellmauthaler, H. Strass, J. P. Wallner, and S. Woltran. Abstract Dialectical Frameworks Revisited. In *Proc. of IJCA*, 2013.

[3] S. Buckingham Shum. The Roots of Computer Supported Argument Visualization. In *Visualizing Argumentation: Software Tools for Collaborative and Educational Sense-Making*, pages 3–24, London, 2003.

[4] E. W. De Luca, S. Hauke, A. Nürnberger, and S. Schlechtweg. Using Multilingual Ontologies for Adaptive Web-Based Language Exploration. In *Proc. of SW-EL 06 (part of AH 2006)*, pages 35–44, 2006.

[5] P. M. Dung. On the Acceptability of Arguments and its Fundamental Role in Nonmonotonic Reasoning, Logic Programming and n-Person Games. *Artif. Intell.*, 77(2):321–358, 1995.

[6] O. Etzioni, M. Cafarella, D. Downey, S. Kok, A.-M. Popescu, T. Shaked, S. Soderland, D. S. Weld, and A. Yates. Web-scale information extraction in Knowitall: (preliminary results). In *Proc. of WWW*. ACM, 2004.

[7] A. Gürkan, L. Iandoli, M. Klein, and G. Zollo. Mediating debate through on-line large-scale argumentation: Evidence from the field. *Information Sciences*, 180(19):3686–3702, 2010.

[8] S. Haun, T. Gossen, A. Nürnberger, T. Kötter, K. Thiel, and M. R. Berthold. On the Integration of Graph Exploration and Data Analysis: The Creative Exploration Toolkit. In *Bisociative Knowledge Discovery*, pages 301–312. Springer, 2012.

[9] S. Haun, M. Nitsche, and A. Nürnberger. Interactive Visualization of Continuous Node Features in Graphs. In *Proc. Works. on Explorative Analytics of Information Networks (part of ECML/PKDD)*, pages 98–106, 2009.

[10] M. A. Hearst. Automatic acquisition of hyponyms from large text corpora. In *Proc. of COLING*, 1992.

[11] J. Lawrence, F. Bex, C. Reed, and M. Snaith. AIFdb: Infrastructure for the argument web. In *Proc. of Computational Models of Argument (COMMA)*, 2012.

[12] M. Lippi and P. Torroni. Argumentation Mining: State of the Art and Emerging Trends. *ACM Transactions on Internet Technologies*, 16(2):10:1–10:25, 2016.

[13] S. Modgil and H. Prakken. The $ASPIC^+$ framework for structured argumentation: a tutorial. *Argument & Computation*, 5(1):31–62, 2014.

[14] T. Mossakowski and F. Neuhaus. Bipolar weighted argumentation graphs. http://arxiv.org/abs/1611.08572.

[15] A. Peldszus and M. Stede. From Argument Diagrams to Argumentation Mining in Texts: A Survey. *IJCINI*, 7(1):1–31, 2013.

[16] R. Pienta, J. Abello, M. Kahng, and D. H. Chau. Scalable graph exploration and visualization: Sensemaking challenges and opportunities. In *Proc. Intl. Conf. on Big Data and Smart Comp. (BIGCOMP)*, pages 271–278. IEEE, 2015.

[17] H. Prakken. An abstract framework for argumentation with structured arguments. *Argument & Computation*, 1(2):93–124, 2010.

[18] I. Rahwan and C. Reed. The Argument Interchange Format. In *Argumentation in Artificial Intelligence*, chapter 19, pages 383–402. Springer, 2009.

[19] M. Snaith, J. Lawrence, and C. Reed. Mixed initiative argument in public deliberation. In *Proc. of 4th Intl. Conf. on Online Deliberation*, 2010.

[20] M. Snaith and C. Reed. TOAST: Online $ASPIC^+$ implementation. In *Proc. of Computational Models of Argument (COMMA)*, 2012.

[21] S. W. van den Braak, H. v. Oostendorp, H. Prakken, and G. A. Vreeswijk. A critical review of argument visualization tools: Do users become better reasoners? In *Workshop Notes of the ECAI-06 Workshop on CMNA*, pages 67–75, 2008.

[22] F. van Ham and A. Perer. Search, Show Context, Expand on Demand: Supporting Large Graph Exploration with Degree-of-Interest. *IEEE Trans. on Visual. and Comp. Graphics*, 15(6):953–960, 2009.

Using Topic Models to Assess Document Relevance in Exploratory Search User Studies

Alan Medlar
Institute of Biotechnology
University of Helsinki
Helsinki, Finland
alan.j.medlar@helsinki.fi

Dorota Głowacka
Department of Computer Science
University of Helsinki
Helsinki, Finland
glowacka@cs.helsinki.fi

ABSTRACT

Evaluation is crucial in assessing the effectiveness of new information retrieval and human computer interaction techniques and systems. Relevance judgements are often performed by humans, which makes obtaining them expensive and time consuming. Consequently, relevance judgements are usually performed only on a subset of a given collection of data or experimental results with a focus on the top ranked documents. However, when assessing the performance of exploratory search systems, the diversity or subjective relevance of documents that the user was presented with over a search session are often of more importance than the relative ranking of top documents. In order to perform these types of assessment, all the documents in a given collection need to be judged for relevance. In this paper, we propose an approach based on topic modeling that can greatly accelerate document relevance judgment of an entire document collection with an expert assessor needing to mark only a small subset of documents from a given collection. Experimental results show a substantial overlap between relevance judgments compared to a human assessor.

CCS Concepts

•**Information systems** → **Relevance assessment;** •**Human-centered computing** → *Heuristic evaluations;* •**Computing methodologies** → *Topic modeling;*

Keywords

topic models; relevance assessment; user studies; exploratory search

1. INTRODUCTION

Relevance judgements are a crucial aspect of experiments in Information Retrieval (IR) as well as in Human Computer Interaction (HCI) [18]. However, relevance judgements require the involvement of human assessors, which makes them expensive to obtain. Additionally, obtaining human relevance judgements can be time consuming with multiple assessors going through lists of hundreds or sometimes even thousands of documents. However, in many instances, user studies of information retrieval systems need fast and efficient assessment of the relevance of the obtained results to allow the experimenter to formulate new hypotheses or to allow him to proceed to the next stage of the user study. In this paper, we propose a procedure based on topic models that can greatly speed up the relevance assessment process in IR user studies. The procedure only requires the assessor to indicate which topics, based on the top keywords associated with a given topic, would be relevant for a given query or search area, and to assess the relevance of a small subset of documents from each relevant topic. Following the expert assessment, we fit a logistic regression model using the document probability from the topic model as a predictor of document relevance and use this model to classify all documents shown to the user.

This type of relevance assessment is particularly useful in comparing different exploratory search systems or techniques [14], where the more subjective and loosely understood relevance of a given document with respect to a search query cannot be easily captured by traditional learning to rank methods. For example, even though the query might be "neural networks", documents that cover "deep learning" would be equally relevant to that query. Moreover, in exploratory search systems what often matters is whether the user is presented with a sufficiently diverse set of documents related to the search area or query as opposed to a strict ranking of documents with respect to their relevance to a search query [3, 9, 12]. Using broad groupings of words/terms provided by topic models allows the assessor to easily capture these types of generalisations. Our initial assessment of the proposed method is based on past experimental data and we demonstrate that such classifications are not only highly accurate, but offer "substantial" inter-rater agreement compared with a human assessor.

2. RELATED LITERATURE

Existing methods for IR system assessment are unsuitable for exploratory search systems [21]. They rely heavily on a strict ranking of documents and take into account only a small subset of the entire collection. In exploratory information retrieval systems, the initial ranking of documents is of less importance as the user tries to understand what types of documents a given search system contains or what types of documents would best satisfy their broad search query.

CHIIR '17, March 07-11, 2017, Oslo, Norway

DOI: http://dx.doi.org/10.1145/3020165.3022141

Assessment methods that rely on ranking build experimental test collections through *pooling*, i.e. only a subset, or pool, of the entire document collection is judged for each query [7]. Having enough relevant documents in the pool, it is safe to assume that the unjudged documents are not relevant, leading to a set of judgements that are sufficiently complete and unbiased. This approach is followed in numerous IR evaluation competitions, such as TREC, CLEF or INEX, where for each search task the pool of documents to be judged is constructed by taking the union of the top k documents retrieved by the participating systems [19].

There are a number of studies on how to efficiently scan pools with the objective of extracting a sufficient number of documents as quickly as possible. In the MoveToFront method [8], the runs are prioritised and the top-ranked document from the run with the top priority is judged. If it is relevant, then documents from the same run continue to be examined until a non-relevant document is found, at which point the priority of the current run is reduced and the judgement process moves to the next priority run. Moffat *et al.* [17] proposed a number of methods for ordering judgments based on various weighting schemes to rank documents in each run. Recently, document judging was cast as a multi-armed bandit problem, where the judgement process can be seen as a learning from interaction environment. As the judgements come, the system gradually learns which runs yield the most relevant documents [13].

3. TOPIC MODELS

Topic models are algorithms for discovering the main themes that pervade a large and otherwise unstructured collection of documents [6]. A document is assumed to draw its vocabulary from one or more topics. Topics are represented as probability distributions over the vocabulary, where differing topics give different words high probabilities. A topic related to genetics, for example, would give high probability to the words: "gene" and "phenotype", whereas a similar topic like evolutionary biology would give a higher relative probability to words such as "phylogeny" and "evolution". These topics can also be used to retrieve documents in the same domain as the query – intuitively relevant documents have topic distributions that are likely to have generated the set of words associated with the query. Due to this property, over the last decade there has been an increasing interest in applying topic models in IR for document modeling and query expansion [2, 16, 20, 22]. In this paper, we propose how to use topic models for document relevance judgments.

Statistical or probabilistic topic models are generative processes that specify procedures by which documents are created. There are a range of topic models [5], however, the most widely used is Latent Dirichlet Allocation (LDA) [6], which is also the version of topic models that we used in our experiments. LDA assumes that there are multiple topics in the corpus and a document can have multiple topics. LDA has a more complicated probabilistic procedure of generating a document which captures correlations between words, but not between topics.

4. METHOD DESCRIPTION

The aim of the approach described below is to help researchers to quickly assess experimental results from user studies involving IR systems. The method is particularly useful when analysing how many documents were relevant, i.e. from a particular field of research or topic, in the assessment of an exploratory search system. The method can also help experimenters to select appropriate queries to test their system, especially when dealing with a dataset of documents they are unfamiliar with. Below, we briefly describe how topic models can be used in experimental query selection and/or experimental data analysis as follows:

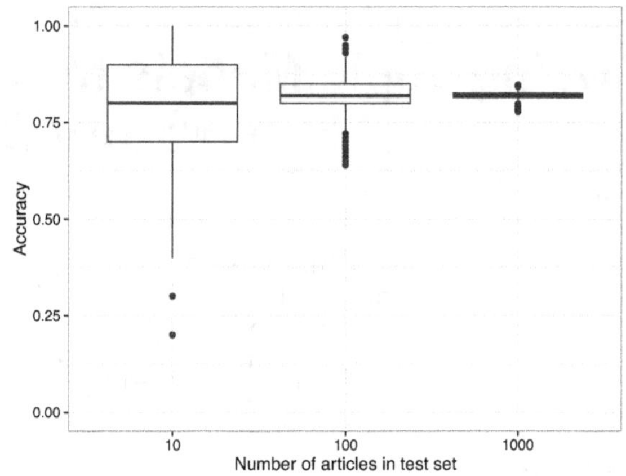

Figure 1: Boxplots showing the distribution of accuracy scores given different sized test sets. Classifying 1000 documents or more consistently produces results close to the long running average.

1) Build topic model: Train a topic model on the complete corpus of documents. As topic models require that the number of topics, k, be pre-specified, several values of k might need to be tried to get clearly defined topics with an expert assessing what value of k provides the best "quality" of topics. The optimal number of topics will be dataset dependent and, as its selection relies on human assessment, highly subjective. We note that automatic methods for determining the optimal number of topics exist [10], however their use is outside of the scope of this work.

2) Identify queries: A subset of topics must be identified by an expert assessor that can be associated with suitable search queries based on the ranked keywords for each topic. For example, a topic with the keywords: "neural", "networks", "brain", "network", "deep", "artificial", "layer", etc, could be labeled with the search query "neural networks".

3) Train classifier: Select a subset of documents from each topic associated with each search query for expert assessment of relevance to that search query. Using these results, we train a logistic regression model using the document probability (from the topic model) as a predictor of its binary relevance (as determined by the expert assessor).

4) Perform experiment: In the experiments themselves search sessions are initiated using a search query identified in step 2, selected by the user or experimenter as needed, and the search proceeds as usual.

5) Assess relevance: After all experiments are complete, we use the logistic regression model to classify all the documents that were shown to the user during a search session by their relevance.

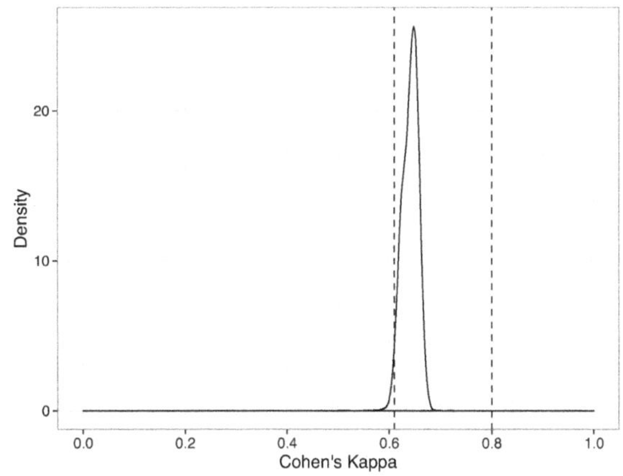

Figure 2: Density of Cohen's Kappa statistic for inter-rater agreement. Vertical dashed lines indicate the range 0.61-0.8, which would indicate "substantial" agreement.

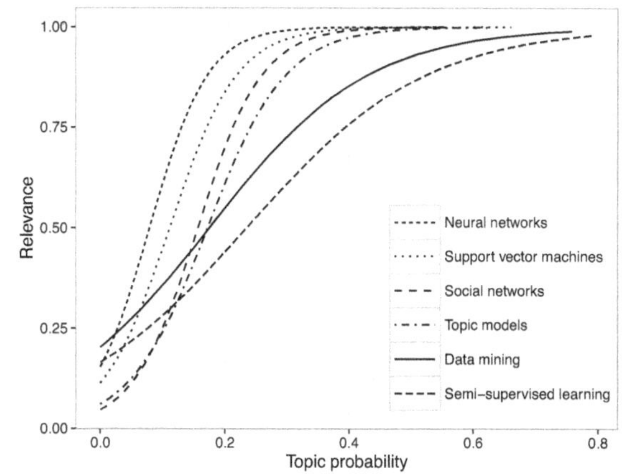

Figure 3: Logistic functions stratified by search query. The gradient increases with the broadness of the search query.

Alternately, if the corpus is large and therefore hard to process, the number of relevant documents is small relative to other topics, or the experiments have already been performed, then the topic model can instead be trained after the experiment using only those documents shown to users, with the rest of the procedure remaining unchanged.

5. EXPERIMENTAL RESULTS

In this section we describe the initial evaluation of the proposed approach.

5.1 Data

To evaluate our approach we took expert assessments from a recent exploratory search study of scientific literature. The study from which we obtained the data consisted of a comparison of lookup searches and exploratory searches [1, 4]. The data for the study was extracted from the arXiv repository of scientific literature comprising documents primarily from physics, mathematics, computer science and quantitative biology (https://arxiv.org/). All the participants of the user study had a background in computer science and so all the search queries focused on this area of research. Upon completion of the experiments, two experts in the area of machine learning and artificial intelligence judged the relevance of all documents with their respective queries. We excluded lookup searches from our assessment as well as searches that were abandoned by users after the first iteration. This left 4722 unique documents shown to users which was used to build a topic model. We experimented with different numbers of topics ranging from 10-200 and found that 50 appeared to work well for this dataset. In order to obtain the topic models, we used MALLET [15] – a popular topic modeling toolkit that contains efficient, sampling-based implementations of LDA.

From this dataset, we identified 6 search queries performed by 9 users for use in our experiments (neural networks, support vector machines, data mining, social networks, semi-supervised learning and topic models). These queries were clearly exploratory [3], mapped well to topics and were well represented in the corpus. The number of documents per search query ranged from 81 – 352. In total the 9 search sessions contained 1181 documents, 585 of which were deemed relevant to the subject of the search by the expert assessors.

5.2 Assessment

To assess our method we performed Monte Carlo cross validation. We wanted to understand, not just the long running accuracy, but also how the variance behaves given different numbers of documents in the test set. In brief, we sampled (without replacement) 100 documents to use as the training set for the logistic regression and, unless stated otherwise, randomly sampled 1000 documents to use as a test set. Based on evaluation using the test set, different metrics were calculated to assess performance. This procedure was repeated 100,000 times.

5.3 Results

The mean accuracy was 82% with mean precision and recall of 86% and 77%, respectively. Recall was comparatively low due to the existence of documents that are relevant, but either do not contain the main keywords of a topic or else belong to multiple topics, diluting the signal. While the accuracy is consistently high, the variance depends on the number of documents being classified, with smaller numbers exhibiting high variance. Figure 1 shows how for 10, 100 and 1000 document sized test sets the accuracy can vary dramatically. For example, the inter-quartile range for accuracy when classifying 10 documents is 70-90% and in 2.2% of experiments the accuracy is 50% or less. For 1000 documents, however, the minimum accuracy is 78%.

In Figure 2, we show the distribution of Cohen's Kappa to assess the inter-rater agreement between our approach and the expert assessor. The mean inter-rater agreement was 0.64, with 97% of the distribution greater than 0.61, which would be considered "substantial" agreement between assessors [11].

Our approach does not use topic as a factor in the logistic regression model, only using the document probability. However, as shown in Figure 3, there is a positive correlation between narrowness of the query and the slope of the logistic function were we to include a topic term in the model. The query "neural networks", for example, has a steeper gradient than "semi-supervised learning" which might involve the use of neural networks and therefore include some of the same keywords. This is suggestive of the limitations of such an approach, with broader topics, for example, entire research domains ("computer science", "culture", etc.), being difficult to capture with current topic modeling approaches.

6. SUMMARY AND CONCLUSIONS

In this paper, we described an approach based on topic models to perform relevance judgments on documents obtained from user studies involving exploratory searches. The approach significantly reduces the time required on the part of a human judgment assessor – instead of going through a list of thousands of documents, the assessor only needs to look at top keywords from each topic and then judge a small sample of documents with a range of probabilities of belonging to the relevant topics. The experimental results show a substantial overlap between a human expert and the topic model based judgments, which points to the applicability of the proposed method in the relevance assessment of experimental data.

Our current approach uses Latent Dirichlet Allocation for topic modeling, however, in the future we plan to experiment with different methods for topic modeling to see whether they would give us higher quality clusters. Currently, we only use topic models to assess the relevance of the displayed documents. We are planning to use topic models to assess the diversity of documents displayed over a search session by looking at which topics all the displayed documents are highly associated with. This approach will also allow us to trace the concept drift over a long search session as the topic membership of the displayed documents may change between search iterations.

Acknowledgements: This work was partly supported by The Finnish Funding Agency for Innovation (under project Re:Know) and by the Academy of Finland (under the Finnish Centre of Excellence in Computational Inference).

7. REFERENCES

[1] K. Ahukorala, A. Medlar, K. Ilves, and D. Głowacka. Balancing exploration and exploitation: Empirical parameterization of exploratory search systems. In *Proc. CIKM*, pages 1703–1706. ACM, 2015.

[2] D. Andrzejewski and D. Buttler. Latent topic feedback for information retrieval. In *Proc. SIGKDD*, pages 600–608. ACM, 2011.

[3] K. Athukorala, D. Głowacka, G. Jacucci, A. Oulasvirta, and J. Vreeken. Is exploratory search different? a comparison of information search behavior for exploratory and lookup tasks. *Journal of the Association for Information Science and Technology*, 2015.

[4] K. Athukorala, A. Medlar, A. Oulasvirta, G. Jacucci, and D. Glowacka. Beyond relevance: Adapting exploration/exploitation in information retrieval. In *Proc. IUI*, pages 359–369. ACM, 2016.

[5] D. M. Blei. Probabilistic topic models. *Communications of the ACM*, 55(4):77–84, 2012.

[6] D. M. Blei, A. Y. Ng, and M. I. Jordan. Latent dirichlet allocation. *JLMR*, 3:993–1022, 2003.

[7] C. Buckley, D. Dimmick, I. Soboroff, and E. Voorhees. Bias and the limits of pooling for large collections. *Information retrieval*, 10(6):491–508, 2007.

[8] G. V. Cormack, C. R. Palmer, and C. L. Clarke. Efficient construction of large test collections. In *Proc. SIGIR*, pages 282–289. ACM, 1998.

[9] D. Głowacka, T. Ruotsalo, K. Konuyshkova, K. Athukorala, S. Kaski, and G. Jacucci. Directing exploratory search: Reinforcement learning from user interactions with keywords. In *Proc. IUI*, pages 117–128. ACM, 2013.

[10] D. Greene, D. O'Callaghan, and P. Cunningham. How many topics? stability analysis for topic models. In *Proc. ECML PKDD*, 2014.

[11] K. L. Gwet. *Handbook of inter-rater reliability: The definitive guide to measuring the extent of agreement among raters.* Advanced Analytics, LLC, 2014.

[12] A. Kangasrääsiö, D. Głowacka, and S. Kaski. Improving controllability and predictability of interactive recommendation interfaces for exploratory search. In *Proc. IUI*, pages 247–251. ACM, 2015.

[13] D. E. Losada, J. Parapar, and Á. Barreiro. Feeling lucky?: multi-armed bandits for ordering judgements in pooling-based evaluation. In *Proc. SAC*, pages 1027–1034. ACM, 2016.

[14] G. Marchionini. Exploratory search: from finding to understanding. *Communications of the ACM*, 49(4):41–46, 2006.

[15] A. K. McCallum. Mallet: A machine learning for language toolkit. http://mallet.cs.umass.edu, 2002.

[16] A. Medlar, K. Ilves, P. Wang, W. Buntine, and D. Głowacka. PULP: A system for exploratory search of scientific literature. In *Proc. SIGIR*, pages 1133–1136. ACM, 2016.

[17] A. Moffat, W. Webber, and J. Zobel. Strategic system comparisons via targeted relevance judgments. In *Proc. SIGIR*, pages 375–382. ACM, 2007.

[18] M. Sanderson and J. Zobel. Information retrieval system evaluation: effort, sensitivity, and reliability. In *Proc. SIGIR*, pages 162–169. ACM, 2005.

[19] E. M. Voorhees, D. K. Harman, et al. *TREC: Experiment and evaluation in information retrieval.* MIT Press, 2005.

[20] X. Wei and W. B. Croft. LDA-based document models for ad-hoc retrieval. In *Proc. SIGIR*. ACM, 2006.

[21] R. W. White, G. Marchionini, and G. Muresan. Evaluating exploratory search systems: Introduction to special topic issue of information processing and management. *Information Processing & Management*, 44(2):433–436, 2008.

[22] X. Yi and J. Allan. A comparative study of utilizing topic models for information retrieval. In *Proc. ECIR*, pages 29–41, 2009.

A Structural Equation Model of Information Retrieval Skills

Emi Ishita
Kyushu University
Fukuoka, Japan, 812-8581
ishita.emi.982@m.kyushu-u.ac.jp

Yosuke Miyata
Teikyo University
Tokyo, Japan, 192-0395
m@miyay.org

Shuichi Ueda
Rikkyo University
Tokyo, Japan, 171-8506
uedas@rikkyo.ac.jp

Keiko Kurata
Keio University
Tokyo, Japan, 108-8345
kei.kurata@keio.jp

ABSTRACT

Identifying factors that influence information retrieval skills can help us to understand search behavior and show what skills are required to conduct efficient and accurate searches. This paper describes a study in which relationship factors that influence the information retrieval skills of a cohort of 1,551 Japanese Internet users are investigated using a combination of survey methods, factor analysis, and structural equation modeling. Our factor analysis confirms the importance of three sub-skill groups that are similar to sub-skill groups that have been previously reported (i.e., formal Internet skills, operational skills, and assessment skills) and indicates the importance of a fourth group (which we call "search strategy skills"). Our structural equation model incorporates two novel factors that have not previously been studied in this context: critical thinking ability, and self-efficacy for the Internet and information retrieval. The results show that critical thinking ability and self-efficacy positively influence the information retrieval skill level, and age is found to be a negative influence. Contrary to previously reported results, little independent effect is seen from educational attainment.

CCS Concepts

• Information systems→Information retrieval • Social and professional topics→User characteristics.

Keywords

Information retrieval skills; critical thinking ability; self-efficacy for the Internet and information retrieval; structural equation model.

1. INTRODUCTION

In traditional information retrieval (IR) systems, users were referred to researchers or specialists regarded as having knowledge about discipline-specific databases and retrieval skills customized for specific IR systems. However, with the spread of the Internet and the popularization of search engines, IR systems have been more common. The general public has become able to obtain a huge variety of information from the Web on a daily basis. A change of Web-based environment for IR might effect a change in IR skills compared with traditional IR skills. It is important to know what skills are required to adapt to a Web-based environment and what factors might affect IR skills. Identifying the structure of IR skills and factors affecting the level of IR skills of the general public helps us to understand search behavior. Moreover, it helps us to know what basic skills are required to conduct efficient and accurate searches on a daily basis. This is also important for explaining the human aspect of IR skills.

We focus on the IR skills of the general Japanese public. IR skills include knowledge about information resources, search strategies, and techniques for using search engines that are required on the Web. When we build IR systems, it is very important to understand users, for example, what skills users already have or what factors affect IR skills. In this study, we propose three hypotheses. These hypotheses include what factors affect IR skills. We develop questions about IR skills and factors that may affect IR skills with a survey of related works. As factors affecting the IR skill level we introduce two new factors that have not been studied by previous researchers: critical thinking ability, and self-efficacy for the Internet and IR. After conducting the questionnaire survey with the general Japanese public, we identify sub-skills that consist of IR skills and factors that may affect IR skills using factor analysis. We then model the relationship between IR skill levels in Japanese people and the factors affecting those levels using structural equation modeling (SEM).

2. RELATED WORK

The IR skills researched in this study are similar to the Internet skills defined in [1]. The authors conducted a series of studies on Internet skills as important skills the general public should have to survive in the digital age. They particularly focused on Internet skills as the capacity to handle the Internet skillfully. They categorized Internet skills into two groups: medium-related (e.g., operational Internet skills and formal Internet skills) and content-related (i.e., information Internet skills and strategic Internet skills). First, they measured or assessed the level of Internet skills of people from the Netherlands. Then they conducted analysis to determine which of the following factors contribute to the level of people's Internet skills: gender, age, educational attainment, Internet experience, and amount of time spent on the Internet. Based on structural equation modeling, their primary results were as follows: (1) educational attainment positively affects the level of both medium- and content-related Internet skills, (2) age has an effect on medium-related skills, and (3) medium-related Internet skills positively affect the level of content-related skills [1]. IR

CHIIR '17, March 07-11, 2017, Oslo, Norway
© 2017 ACM. ISBN 978-1-4503-4677-1/17/03…$15.00
DOI: http://dx.doi.org/10.1145/3020165.3022142

skills and Internet skills are essentially identical; however, IR skills specialize in information search. To measure IR skills, we used the same questions as van Deursen et al. [1] for their study of Internet skills, and added questions about search techniques and information resource knowledge.

We selected critical thinking ability as one of the factors affecting IR skill levels. Wallace and Jefferson [7] stated that "critical thinking skills are essential when conducting information research." Robert and Jonson [6] stated that "critical thinking about information is the essential component in research." We supposed that both critical thinking ability and IR skills are required to conduct research. Moreover, both skills might influence each other. Hirayama and Kusumi [3] developed 18 questions about critical thinking dispositions for a questionnaire survey. These questions included having "the confidence to develop orderly plans to address complex problems" (for the factor of awareness of logical thinking), being "interested in people with different ideas from me" (inquiry-mindedness), usually intending "to make an unbiased judgment" (objectivity), and examining "as many relevant facts and as much evidence as possible when I make a judgment" (evidence-based judgment). Hirayama and Kusumi extracted four factors using exploratory factor analysis.

We also selected self-efficacy as a factor affecting IR skill level. Helsper and Eynon [2] tested a model of digital skill in which they used an overall measure of digital self-efficacy as a confidence indicator. We supposed that self-efficacy for the Internet and IR also has an influence on IR skills.

3. RESEARCH QUESTIONS

Our hypotheses are as follows:

(1) Factors selected by previous studies, especially age and educational attainment, affect the level of a person's IR skills.

(2) Critical thinking ability affects the level of a person's IR skills.

(3) Self-efficacy for the Internet and IR affects the level of a person's IR skills.

4. METHOD

4.1 Procedure

This section explains our questionnaire survey and provides the basic model of IR skills and other factors we developed as a preliminary result. The procedure for our survey was as follows: (1) develop questions about IR skills, (2) develop questions about critical thinking ability and self-efficacy as new factors assumed to affect IR skills, (3) conduct an online questionnaire survey for Japanese people, (4) conduct exploratory factor analysis and identify factors of IR skills and critical thinking ability, and (5) use SEM to model the relationship between IR skills and the factors that influence those skills. The aggregate results of the questionnaire survey was reported in Minami et al. [5].

Questions	I	II	III	IV
Operational skills				
download programs	**0.72**	-0.06	0.06	-0.02
* use file types such as .pdf or .doc when searching	**0.69**	0.1	-0.08	-0.31
save files	**0.68**	-0.09	0.03	0.12
* use the cached button in the browser	**0.61**	0.06	-0.02	-0.07
upload files to another computer	**0.58**	-0.03	-0.01	-0.01
use the refresh button	**0.56**	0	-0.02	0.16
use reference websites	**0.52**	-0.05	0	0.24
Search strategy skills				
* predict the search results before a search	0	**0.75**	-0.08	-0.08
* prepare alternative search queries	-0.01	**0.72**	0	0.02
* prefer efficiency	-0.11	**0.72**	-0.02	0.03
* clearly understand information that I want before the search	0.01	**0.65**	0.04	0
* determine whether a given page is reliable immediately	0.13	**0.56**	0.11	-0.11
* prefer quality	-0.08	**0.55**	-0.03	0.23
* have knowledge that entered terms are not found unless in the database	-0.02	**0.47**	0.04	0.07
* use multiple evaluation criteria for search results	0.11	**0.44**	0	0.11
Formal Internet skills				
feel disoriented	-0.05	-0.05	**0.81**	0.13
find websites to be confusing	-0.01	-0.02	**0.79**	-0.07
navigate without getting lost	0.01	0.01	**0.78**	0.06
experience difficulties with a website's layout	0.07	0.07	**0.72**	-0.09
know exactly where a link will take me	0.05	-0.02	**0.59**	-0.04
Assessment skills				
use information about a specific subject from multiple sites	0.04	-0.01	0.03	**0.69**
examine the results on subsequent result pages	-0.09	-0.04	0.02	**0.66**
* re-search if the results are not sufficient	-0.1	0.03	0	**0.65**
use more than one search keyword	0.07	0.02	0.01	**0.6**
benefit from using the Internet	-0.1	0.06	0.02	**0.57**
make a decision based on retrieved information	0.27	-0.03	0	**0.5**

Table 1 Questions about four factors contributing to IR skills.

4.2 Development of Questions about IR Skills

We used 34 questions regarding IR skills. Among them, 19 questions were selected from the 20 questions used in [1]. One question was eliminated because all the participants in our survey selected the same response. Fifteen other questions were originally developed from textbooks or technical books about IR practices and search engines. The 26 questions shown in Table 1 and another eight questions were used in our questionnaire survey. The questions marked with * were from [1], whereas the remaining questions were developed by us. We asked participants to select one of five options regarding the frequency with which they performed a number of tasks. The five options ranged from "daily/ strongly agree" (5) to "never/strongly disagree" (1).

4.3 Development of Questions about Factors

We selected six factors that were assumed to influence IR skills: critical thinking ability, self-efficacy, age, educational attainment, Internet experience, and frequency of Internet use.

For questions relating to critical thinking ability, we used the 18 questions composed in [3]. They include the following: "I always try to make unbiased judgements (objectivity)," "When I make a conclusion, I stick to concrete evidence that has been presented (evidence-based judgement)," "I am interested in people with different ideas from me (inquiry-mindedness)," and "I try to provide logical explanations so everyone can understand and agree with what I mean (awareness of logical thinking)." We used the same options as those for the questions about IR skills.

We then developed five questions regarding self-efficacy. They include the following: "I have knowledge of IR," "I have knowledge of computers," "I like the Internet," "I like computers, and "I like searching for information." We also used the same options as those for the questions about IR skills.

We selected age, educational attainment, Internet experience, and frequency of Internet use as factors that appear to influence Internet skills, according to [1]. Participants chose from five age brackets: 18–29, 30–39, 40–49, 50–59, and 60+. For participants' educational attainment, they were asked to select from three groups: "pursuing or completed a bachelor's, master's, or doctoral program at a university" (3), "pursuing or completed a diploma program at a two-year college (similar to an associate's degree from a community college)" (2), and "pursuing or completed high school or junior high school" (1). For frequency of Internet use, they chose from three options: "many times a day" (3), "every day" (2), and "one or two times a week" (1). For Internet experience, they had six options: "over 20 years" (6), "less than or equal to 20 years" (5), "less than or equal to 15 years" (4), "less than or equal to 10 years" (3), "less than or equal to five years" (2), and "less than or equal to one year" (1).

4.4 The Questionnaire Survey

We asked an online survey company to conduct our questionnaire survey in August 2014. This survey company holds more than one million panels in Japan. We stopped the survey after obtaining 1,500 participants. In fact, we obtained 1,551 participants who use the Internet for more than email more than once a week. The participants consisted of equal samples of both genders and all five age brackets. We presented the questions about IR skills, critical thinking ability, and self-efficacy to participants in a random order. Although the questions were written in Japanese on the questionnaire, in this paper, we show the questions translated into English.

5. RESULTS

5.1 Exploratory Factor Analysis

We conducted factor analysis to determine the sub-skills structure of IR skills and critical thinking ability. For the analysis, we used Psych package 1.4.8.11 and the fa function in R3.1.1 software. The maximum likelihood method was used for factor extraction.

5.1.1 Sub-skills of IR skills

A screening test was used to determine the number of factors, and then factor analysis of the 34 questions was conducted. The factors whose eigenvalues were less than 1.0 and the questions whose loadings were less than 0.4 for all remaining factors were removed. Factor analysis was then re-conducted for the remaining questions using a promax rotation. The results showed the factor structure had four factors whose eigenvalues were greater than 1.0 for 26 questions. These four factors accounted for 43% of the total variance. All four factors have Cronbach's alpha >0.7.

Table 1 shows the four extracted factors. Factor I consists of five questions regarding operational Internet skills [1]. Two other questions for this factor were developed for our survey. This factor represents skills needed for the operation of search engines or use of computers. We named Factor I "Operational skills." Factor II consists of eight questions, all originally developed for our survey. This factor represents skills regarding what strategy or criteria a user takes before a search. We named this factor "Search strategy skills." Factor III consists of five questions, which were regarding formal Internet skills in [1]. We named this "Formal Internet skills." Factor IV consists of six questions, five from the strategic Internet skills and information Internet skills in [1]. This factor represents the actions we do or take when we see the search results, so we named it "Assessment skills." We call these skills sub-skills consisting of IR skills.

5.1.2 Critical thinking ability

Exploratory factor analysis was also conducted to determine the factor structure of critical thinking ability (18 questions). We applied the same procedure that we used for IR skills. Three questions were removed because of low eigenvalues and loadings. The results show a factor structure with two factors for 15 questions. The two factors accounted for 47% of the total variance. Factor I consists of 11 questions from three factors used in [3]: objectivity, evidence-based judgment, and inquiry-mindedness. We named this factor "Critical thinking disposition". Factor II consists of all four questions for "Awareness of logical thinking" in [3]. We used the same name for Factor II.

5.2 The Model of IR Skills and the Factors

Figure 1 shows the model of IR skills and the factors with standardized path coefficients. The figure shows the standard deviation of each factor. If the path coefficient value is high, the factor affects IR skills. We used the sem function of the lavaan package 0.5.17 in R software. For the evaluation measures, X^2 is 0.00, the Comparative Fit Index (CFI) value is 0.831, Tucker–Lewis Index (TLI) value is 0.822, root mean square error of approximation (RMSEA) value is 0.053, and standardized root mean square residual (SRMR) value is 0.064 (90% confidence interval: 0.052, 0.055). According to Hu and Bentler [4], a model is sufficient even if the RMSEA value exceeds 0.05, if the RMSEA value is less than or equal to 0.06 and the SRMR value is less than or equal to 0.08; thus, our model is acceptable.

A set of four sub-skills, search strategy skill, assessment, operational skill, and formal Internet skill, contribute to IR skills.

Among those four sub-skills, search strategy skills make the most significant contribution to IR skills (with a standardized path coefficient of 0.93), whereas the formal Internet skills defined by van Deursen et al. [1] make only a small contribution (0.26). The model means that when the search strategy skill is high, the level of IR skills increases.

Among the six factors, self-efficacy and critical thinking ability strongly positively affect the level of IR skills (0.55 and 0.50, respectively). This indicates that both hypotheses 2 and 3 were accepted. Age has a weakly negative effect on IR skills (-0.15). This result is similar to that obtained by van Deursen et al. [1]. Educational attainment (0.03), Internet experience (0.09), and frequency of Internet use (-0.05) have little effect on the IR skill level. This indicates that hypothesis 1 was not accepted; that is, improving the self-efficacy level and critical thinking ability level is helpful for the improvement of IR skills.

6. CONCLUSION

The results indicate that IR skills consist of four sub-skills and the search strategy skills make the most significant contribution to IR skills. The structural equation model incorporates two novel factors that have not previously been studied in this context: critical thinking ability, and self-efficacy for the Internet and IR. Critical thinking ability and self-efficacy are found to positively influence the IR skill level, and age is found to be a negative influence. However, contrary to previously reported results, little independent effect is seen from educational attainment in [1]. The model indicates that educational attainment can possibly be replaced by critical thinking ability. We predict that critical thinking ability is improved through education.

In this paper, we modeled all the factors we selected. However, there is much room for improvement of the model, because the model is not sufficient according to the evaluation measures.

7. ACKNOWLEDGMENTS

This work was supported by JSPS KAKENHI Grant-in-Aid Number JP26280121.

8. REFERENCES

[1] van Deursen, A.J.A.M., van Dijk, J.A.G.M., and Peters, O. 2011. Rethinking Internet skills: The contribution of gender, age, education, Internet experience, and hours online to medium- and content-related Internet skills. *Poetics*, 39, 124–144.

[2] Helsper, E.J., and Eynon, R. 2013. Distinct skill pathways to digital engagement. *European Journal of Communication*, 28, 6, 696–713.

[3] Hirayama, R., and Kusumi, T. 2004. Effect of critical thinking disposition on interpretation of controversial issues: Evaluating evidences and drawing conclusions. *Japanese Journal of Educational Psychology*, 52, 186–198 (in Japanese).

[4] Hu, L. and Bentler, P. M. 1999. Cutoff criteria for fit indexes in covariance structure analysis: Conventional criteria versus new alternatives. Structural Equation Modeling. 6, 1-55.

[5] Minami, Y., Iwase, A., Miyata, Y., Ishita, E., Ueda, S., and Kurata, K. 2016. Information retrieval skills in Web environment. *Journal of Japan Society of Library and Information Science*. 62, 3, 163-180 (in Japanese).

[6] Robert, D., and Jonson, A.M. 2011. Focusing on the thinking, not the tools: Incorporating critical thinking into an information literacy module for an introduction to business course. *Journal of Business & Finance Librarianship*. 16, 101–107.

[7] Wallace, D., and Jefferson, R.N. 2013. Developing critical thinking skills for information seeking success. *New Review of Academic Librarianship*, 19, 3, 246–255

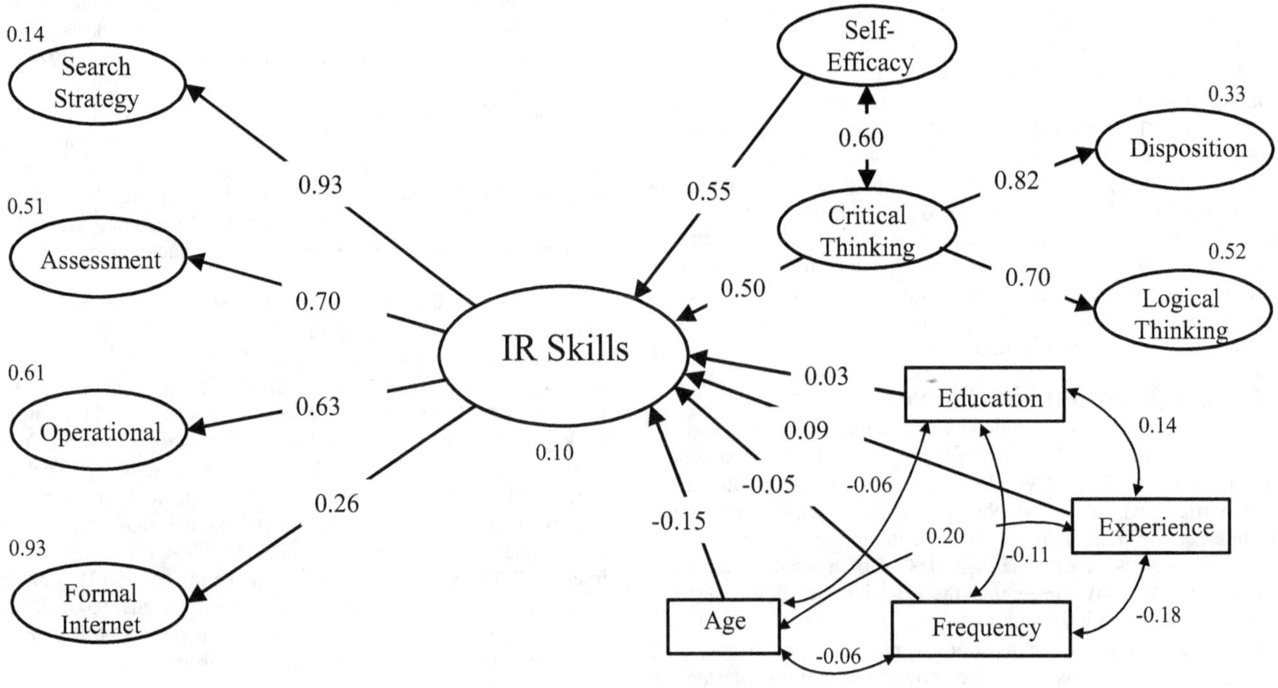

Figure 2. An SEM of IR skills and factors affecting IR skills.

Categorization of Known-Item Search Terms in a TV Archive

Anne-Stine Ruud Husevåg
Department of Archivistics
Library and Information Science
Oslo and Akershus University
College of Applied Science
Oslo, Norway
+47 67 23 82 88
Anne-Stine.Husevag@hioa.no

ABSTRACT

This paper reports on a preliminary explorative study that categorizes search terms provided by 50 users after having watched short clips from TV programs from The Norwegian Broadcasting Corporation archive. The aim of this study is to improve indexing by gaining knowledge about users preferred search terms. One clip is from a news program, and two clips come from a literature program. The search terms are categorized according to The Panofsky-Shatford mode/facet matrix. The study shows that specific search terms like named entities are used the most for both genres, and that generic and abstract terms are more important in the literature clips than the news clip. The search terms provided by users were matched with text from the subtitles from the clip, and the results showed that 17 %, 32 % and 40 % of the terms were found for literature clip 1, literature clip 2 and news clip respectively. The percentage was higher when the terms were matched with subtitles from the whole program, and would have been even higher if additional on-screen text was included.

CCS Concepts

• Information systems~Multimedia information systems • Information systems~Video search • *Information systems~Information retrieval query processing*

Keywords

Multimedia indexing; Metadata; Search term categorization

1. INTRODUCTION

Advances in storage techniques and web access have triggered several digitization efforts and an increase in the amount of digital multimedia objects. The Norwegian Broadcasting Corporation, NRK have multiple projects running that makes old TV material available to the public, and they are continuously uploading content in order to provide access to our visual heritage. These developments have heightened the need for effective indexing and retrieval techniques.

It may take a cataloguer up to three times the length of a TV-program to manually annotate keywords, depending on the genre [1]. Gustman et al. found that the process of creating a three-sentence summary of a clip and any necessary person objects, and then linking appropriate thesaurus descriptors and persons to the clip took about 15 hours for each hour of video [2]. Indexing content is an integral part of any collection of material and vital to the information retrieval process. Indexing multimedia material is a complex process, but automatic processing of text from subtitles (closed captions) is relatively simple, and therefore has a huge potential in terms of future implementation and actual use. Subtitles for the hard of hearing exists for almost all NRK programs, and aim to represent all spoken dialogue, but generally not graphic on-screen texts or sounds like doorbells, phones etc. The subtitles are linked to the timeframe of the broadcast, so it is possible to use a word from the subtitles as a locator to where in the broadcast this word was uttered.

The aim of this research is to explore the actual terms used by users when describing and searching for clips from TV, and compare them with terms found in subtitles. This information could be used to improve term weights in an automatic indexing algorithm. The terms will be categorized according to the Panofsky-Shatford mode/facet matrix [3], a schema already well established for the analysis of levels of meaning in images. The study reported here is a preliminary study in a PhD project that wishes to contribute towards a greater understanding of users' choice of words when searching for a multimedia object, and a better-informed view of how subtitles can contribute to automatic indexing of visually encoded information.

2. THEORETICAL FRAMEWORK

Researchers can use various classification schemes and methods to categorize still and moving images and the terms used to describe and to search for such materials.

The philosophical work of the art historian Erwin Panofsky [4] has become the basis for subject indexing of many visual collections. Panofsky recognized three successive levels of meaning in Renaissance art: the pre-iconographical description, the iconographical analysis and the iconological interpretation. The pre-iconographical level is the most basic level of understanding of identifiable objects, devoid of any added cultural knowledge. The iconographical analysis goes a step further and makes use of cultural and iconographic knowledge. The third level of meaning, the iconological interpretation, looks at art not as an isolated incident, but as the product of a cultural background and historical environment. Panofskys model, as interpreted by Karen Markey [5], [6], Sara Shatford [7], and others, has been influential on many people working to develop systems for subject access to images [8].

Markey [5] redefined the subject matter of an image in terms of primary subject matter and secondary subject matter, where the primary subject matter is a factual description of objects in an

CHIIR '17, March 7–11, 2017, Oslo, Norway.
© 2017 ACM. ISBN 978-1-4503-4677-1/17/03…$15.00.
DOI: http://dx.doi.org/10.1145/3020165.3022143

Table 1. The Panofsky-Shatford mode/facet matrix as presented and used in Armitage and Enser [3].

	Iconography (Specifics)	Pre-iconography (Generics)	Iconology (Abstracts)
Who?	Individually named person, group, thing (S1)	kind of person or thing (G1)	mythical or fictitious being (A1)
What?	individually named event, action (S2)	kind of event , action, condition (G2)	emotion or abstraction (A2)
Where?	individually named geographical location (S3)	kind of place: geographical, architectural (G3)	place symbolised (A3)
When?	linear time: date or period (S4)	cyclical time: season, time of day (G4)	emotion, abstraction symbolised by time (A4)

image, while secondary subject matter focuses on identifying cultural symbols and is based on the prior identification of primary subject matter. She argued that providing access to collections by primary subject matter could ease the task of users since it requires only one level of interpretation, practical experience, and knowledge of the history of style.

Shatford [7] extended Panofskys model and showed its significance for all types of images. Inspired by Panofskys three levels, she categorized the subjects of pictures as Generic of, Specific of and About. The generic level describes general objects and actions, the specific level describes individually named objects and events or what we now often call named entities, and the about level includes emotions, symbols and abstract concepts.

Shatford also added four facets from Ranganathan's categories of subject classification to each level: who, what, where and when. This resulted in a 3x4 matrix for the classification of image descriptions. The so-called Panofsky/Shatford model has become a widespread model for the classification of image descriptions and has been used by several researchers [9], [10].

Armitage and Enser [3] sought to develop a general-purpose categorization of user requests for still and moving visual images. To do this, they derived an analytical tool from the Panofsky-Shatford mode/facet matrix.

Seven picture libraries participated in [3]. Two of the archives in the study, the National Film and Television Archive and the BBC Natural History Unit, consisted of collections of moving imagery. The National Film and Television Archive have a collection similar to NRK, they both supports a wide and general user base interested in the world of film and television. Armitage and Enser found a high incidence of queries that contained elements of both uniqueness and non-uniqueness in their material, and wanted to adopt a more formal facet-based analytic technique. This schema makes it possible to categorize queries that seek very different still and moving image material and it is also applicable to both the image material and the queries that are used to search for that material. This could eventually contribute to a knowledge organization system that enables information retrieval at users' preferred level of specificity and abstraction.

3. DATA COLLECTION TECHNIQUES

A previous search log analysis of logs from NRK revealed that users almost exclusively searched for program titles and names of program hosts and other contributors. This was congruent with the search function at the time of the analysis, and could be a result of the users adapting to the search system, more than a representation of the users information need.

For this paper, information from users is collected through a questionnaire. Users have been recruited among students during their first weeks of library and information science at Oslo University College (22 users) and from a self-recruited sample of Facebook users (28 users). The answers from the students will later be compared with students at different stages in their education. The recruited users are 18-68 years old (avg. 36,6). The goal of the recruitment process was not to find a representative NRK archive user, but to get a rich variety of answers from different people.

Table 2. An example of how search terms are categorized in this study.

	Iconography (Specifics)	Pre-iconography (Generics)	Iconology (Abstracts)
Who?	"Medaljens forside" (book title) (S1)	"bøker" (books) (G1)	
What?			"litteratur" (literature) (A2)
Where?	"Tollbugata" (street name) (S3)	"gatelangs" (along the streets) (G3)	"i sentrum" (at the (city)centre, here used in the meaning centre of attention) (A3)
When?	1990 (S4)		

The users are asked to watch two short clips and then write down the search terms they would have used if they wanted to find this clip again, i.e. a known-item task. In this study there are three different clips, two from a literature program (clip 1 is 2 minutes and 6 seconds, clip 2 is 2 minutes and 45 seconds) and one news story (1 minute 32 seconds). The clips from the literature programs are chosen because they are typical examples from that genre. The researcher have chosen the news clip because its content is similar to the literature clips in terms of naming of specifics, and at the same time serves as a contrast to the culture programmes. The questionnaire is designed so that which two clips and the order in which they are presented to users varies. 37 users have assessed the first literature clip, 39 users have assessed the second literature clip and 20 users have assessed the news clip.

Subtitles for the literature programs have been obtained from NRK. The author has used a PowerShell script to perform a

Table 3. Categorization of terms provided by users for the different clips.

	Iconography (Specifics)				Pre-iconography (Generics)				Iconology (Abstracts)			
Clips	S1 Who?	S2 What?	S3 Where?	S4 When?	G1 Who?	G2 What?	G3 Where?	G4 When?	A1 Who?	A2 What?	A3 Where?	A4 When?
Lit 1	33 %	0 %	27 %	0 %	11 %	1 %	5 %	0 %	0 %	25 %	0 %	0 %
Lit 2	60 %	0 %	2 %	1 %	13 %	11 %	0 %	0 %	0 %	10 %	0 %	0 %
News	61 %	0 %	17 %	1 %	3 %	10 %	0 %	0 %	0 %	7 %	0 %	0 %
Lit 1	59 %				16 %				25 %			
Lit 2	64 %				25 %				11 %			
News	80 %				13 %				7 %			

simple text matching of terms provided by users and the full text in subtitles and transcript.

4. RESULTS

In average the users provided 3,6 search terms for the first literature clip, 4,5 search terms for literature clip 2 and 4,2 search terms for the news clip. The questionnaire asked the users to separate the terms with a comma, and the complete lists were terms with different name forms and spelling all were counted as different terms resulted in 42 terms for literature clip 1, 65 for literature clip 2, and 43 terms for the news clip.

When Armitage and Enser categorized the queries, they categorized the whole query. This resulted in some queries being categorized in several categories, and the sample percentages of the mode/facet categorization were over a hundred percent for some facets. In this paper, phrases and compound terms have been split to get a clearer view of the different categories used. In table 3, we see an overview of the categorization of the different terms provided by the users and a summation of the facets in the different modes.

When we take a closer look at the most used terms, the differences between the different modes get bigger. Figure 1, 2 and 3 show the distribution of popular search terms for the different clips. The news clip have been assessed by fewer users than the literature clips, so terms used by two users or more are included in the chart, compared to terms used by three users or more for the literature clips. Terms used by three users or more for the news clip were only specifics.

In comparison, the distribution for the queries for the National Film and Television Archive studied by Armitage and Enser was 74 % specifics, 26 % generics and 0 % abstracts (rounded down from 0,002463054) [3].

The terms provided by users have been compared with terms in full text. For the two literature programs, the users' terms have been compared with both subtitles from the clip, and the subtitle text for the whole program. The news story is taken from a program where the only introduction is "Good evening", and the different news stories in the program are unrelated. The users' terms for the news story are therefore only compared to the subtitles of the clip.

Table 4. Categorization of terms provided by users for the different clips.

	Lit1	Lit2	News
Number of different search terms	42	65	43
% of used terms in subtitles from clip	17 %	32 %	40 %
% of used terms in subtitles from program	48 %	40 %	-

For literature clip 1, a majority of the users agreed on three terms. The clip shows to men walking around in the city Drammen, talking about famous writers and their connection to different buildings and places in the city. 28 of 37 users used the search term "Drammen", 17 used the last name of the host (his last name is also a part of the title of the program) and 6 used his full name, and 14 used the term "literature", but if we split compound terms, different forms of the term literature is used 28 times. Of the terms used by three or more users, only two were present in the subtitles for the clip: "Drammen" and "literature".

Literature clip 2 is a feature about novels from the corporate world, and one book in particular, a commissioned book about a large Norwegian company. 26 of the 39 users used the name of

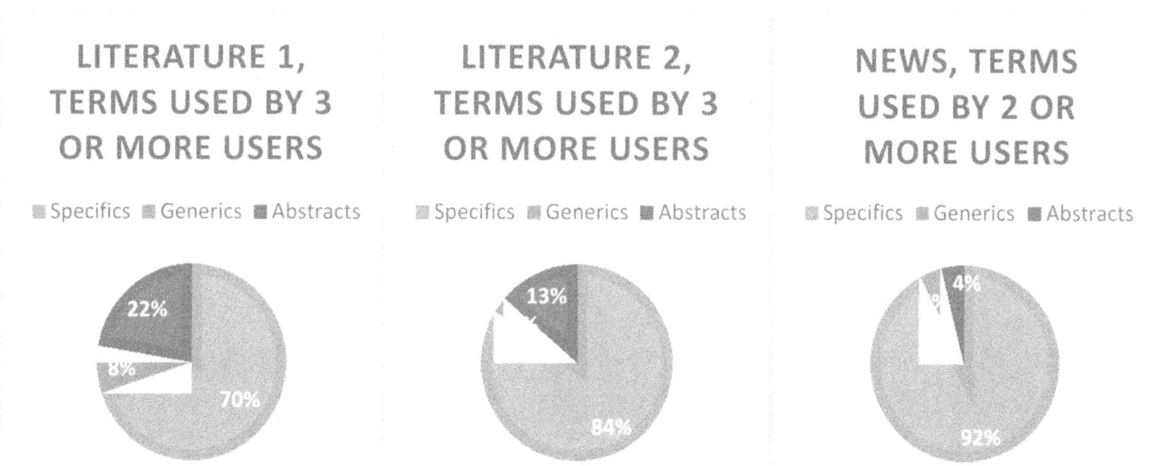

Figure 1, 2, 3 Distribution of search term categories of the most used search terms.

the company as a search term, 25 of the users chose the name of the author of this book as a search term (17 full name, 8 only last name). Both of those names are present in the clips subtitles. 19 use the name of the reporter who has the voice over on the clip (his name is also a part of the name of the clip) (11 full name, 5 only last name). His name is not in the subtitle, but the name of the clip "Skråblikk ved Knut Hoem" (An oblique glance by Knut Hoem) is a digital on-screen graphic. Another popular term among the users is the name of another literature program "Bokstavelig talt" (used by 11 users), a clip inside the clip, from the time the featured book was released. Both this name and the title of the book (used by 7 users) are present in subtitles. Many users tried to express the subject with various combinations of Norwegian terms for essentially three facets: business (finance, industry, corporations), history and literature (fiction, books, novels). Some users also included a variant of the term "Norwegian". Two of the more popular variants are present in the subtitles. "Næringsliv" (could be translated as business and commerce) is used as a single word by 5 users, but it is included as a component in 23 used terms, like "næringslivshistorie" (business history, used by 6) and "roman" (novel), which 3 users have used alone, but it is a component in 12 compound terms.

20 users have provided search terms for the news clip. The news story is about a large building project in downtown Oslo, and politicians who want to stop the project. The building have its own name, "Lambda", which is used by 18 users. 11 of the users use a variant of "the Munch-museum", a museum that is going to move into Lambda when the building is finished. Other popular terms are the name of the exact place where Lambda is being built and the name of the parties the critical politicians are leaders of. All of these are present in the subtitles, but not all spelling variants of "the Munch-museum" will match the text in the subtitles.

5. CONCLUSION

In accordance with earlier research, users in this study largely would have used specifics to search for a recently viewed known-item. This is more evident for the news story than for the literature clips. For the news story, 80 % of the search terms from the users where specifics. All of these are named entities, the majority of these are names of buildings and places. For the two literature clips, 59 % and 64 % of the search terms are specifics, almost exclusively focusing on answering the questions "Who?" and "Where?" from Ranganathan's facets. Generics are much less used, but when used, it is the kind of person, ting, event or action that is of interest to the users. The only facet used in the abstracts category is a general emotion or abstraction, mostly used to categorize fields of study like art, literature and history. Emotions were never used as search terms in this study.

Some of the terms used by users were found in the clips' subtitles (17 % and 32 % for the literature clips, 40 % for the news clip). When the terms provided by users for the literature clips were compared to the subtitles from the whole program, 48 % of the terms were found in literature clip 1 and 40 % were found in literature clip 2.

Popular search terms from users not included in the subtitles were the name of the program, the name of the clip, the TV station, the genre, the host and people talking in the clip. In several cases the names of the people present on screen are not uttered, but displayed as on-screen text, and is therefore not present in the subtitles. For the search terms provided by the 50 users in this study, less than 50 % were found in the subtitles. The subtitle texts for the studied clips and programs could be useful as a supplement to traditional metadata, but the subtitle texts is not sufficient as the only source for textual retrieval of these clips. Recall would improve if it had been possible for users to search in on-screen graphic texts.

6. REFERENCES

[1] Gazendam L., Wartena C., Malaisé V., Schreiber G., Jong A. de, Brugman H. Automatic Annotation Suggestions for Audiovisual Archives: Evaluation Aspects. Interdiscip Sci Rev. 2009 Sep 1;34(2–3):172–88.

[2] Gustman S., Soergel D., Oard D., Byrne W., Picheny M., Ramabhadran B., et al. Supporting access to large digital oral history archives. In: Proceedings of the 2nd ACM/IEEE-CS joint conference on Digital libraries. ACM; 2002. 18–27.

[3] Armitage L. H., Enser P. G. Analysis of user need in image archives. J Inf Sci. 1997;23(4):287–299.

[4] Panofsky E. Studies in iconology: humanistic themes in the art of the Renaissance. New York: Icon Editions; 1972. xliii+262. (Icon editions; vol. 25).

[5] Markey K. Access to iconographic research collections. Libr Trends. 1988;37(2):154–174.

[6] Markey K. Computer-assisted construction of a thematic catalog of primary and secondary subject matter. Vis Resour. 1983;3(1):16–49.

[7] Shatford S. Analyzing the subject of a picture: a theoretical approach. Cat Classif Q. 1986;6(3):39–62.

[8] Collins K. Providing subject access to images: A study of user queries. Am Arch. 1998;61(1):36–55.

[9] Hollink L, Schreiber A. T., Wielinga B. J., Worring M. Classification of user image descriptions. Int J Hum-Comput Stud. 2004 Nov;61(5):601–26.

[10] Benson A. C. Image descriptions and their relational expressions: a review of the literature and the issues. J Doc. 2015 Jan 9;71(1):143–64.

How Do People Interact in Conversational Speech-Only Search Tasks: A Preliminary Analysis

Johanne R. Trippas
johanne.trippas@rmit.edu.au

Damiano Spina
damiano.spina@rmit.edu.au

Lawrence Cavedon
lawrence.cavedon@rmit.edu.au

Mark Sanderson
mark.sanderson@rmit.edu.au

RMIT University, Melbourne, Australia

ABSTRACT

We present preliminary findings from a study of mixed initiative conversational behaviour for informational search in an acoustic setting. The aim of the observational study is to reveal insights into how users would conduct searches over voice where a screen is absent but where users are able to converse interactively with the search system. We conducted a laboratory-based observational study of 13 pairs of participants each completing three search tasks with different cognitive complexity levels. The communication between the pairs was analyzed for interaction patterns used in the search process. This setup mimics the situation of a user interacting with a search system via a speech-only interface.

Keywords

Spoken Conversational Search; Observational Study; Voice Search

1. INTRODUCTION

Speech-based web search is becoming ubiquitous, particularly through the use of mobile devices. However, presenting lists of search results in a speech-only setting presents a number of challenges and simply speaking the textual component of a standard search results list has been shown to be ineffective [7]. Intelligent Assistants such as Siri, Google Now, or Cortana can reply to factoid queries. However, when non-factoid queries are posed the search engine result page (SERP) is still displayed on the screen.

In this paper, we present preliminary results of an empirical laboratory study designed to understand how users search in a setting where all communication is over speech. This study observed pairs of participants speaking in order to accomplish a search goal, allowing us to understand the users' conversational patterns. We used quantitative and qualitative research designs for our analysis. The purpose of this observational study was to explore techniques used by people to search over a speech-only communication setting. Thus this paper presents initial identified interaction themes which inform a coding scheme for user-system conversational speech-only search. These themes contribute to our broader goal which is to understand effective response generation techniques for search tasks with different degrees of complexity. Overall we are interested in how spoken interactive information retrieval (IIR) conversations develop over multiple turns and whether there are recurring patterns in response generating techniques depending on task difficulty.

CHIIR '17, March 07-11, 2017, Oslo, Norway

© 2017 ACM. ISBN 978-1-4503-4677-1/17/03...$15.00

DOI: http://dx.doi.org/10.1145/3020165.3022144

2. METHODOLOGY

A controlled laboratory study was conducted in June 2016 with 30 people of whom 70% were university students (recruited via the RMIT University Behavioural Business Lab, https://orsee.bf.rmit.edu.au). The participants were divided into pairs with two pairs used in the pilot studies (not included in this analysis). The setup was reviewed and approved by RMIT University's Ethics Board (ASEHAPP 08-16). Thus 13 pairs conducted a search where one participant acted as the *User* (participant with the search task) and the other participant acted as the *Retriever* (participant with the search engine); i.e. the User acted as the searcher and Retriever simulated the voice interface. Users and Retrievers did not have access to each others' search task or search engine interface, could not see each other, and could communicate only verbally. Each pair completed three search tasks with different dimensions of Anderson and Krathwol's Taxonomy of Learning [1]. There were nine search tasks in total, rotated using a Latin square design. Retrievers were navigated to use Google but were not stopped if they changed search engine. Retrievers were instructed to type in exactly what they heard Users instruct them to search for.

Each search ended when Users believed they had enough information to answer the backstory or when a 10-minute limit was reached. All participants completed three questionnaires (Pre-test, Post-task and Exit), and an exit interview. Users also completed a Pre-task questionnaire. The complete task took no longer than 90 minutes. No sample search task solution was given to avoid biasing the results.

2.1 Tasks

We describe an evaluation of nine search tasks based on the cognitive complexity framework of the Taxonomy of Learning [1]. The search tasks used in this study were based on TREC Q02, R03, and T04 and described in [2]. The following three of the five cognitive dimensions were used: *Remember* (Retrieving, recognizing, and recalling relevant knowledge from long-term memory); *Understand* (Constructing meaning from oral, written, and graphic messages through interpreting, exemplifying, classifying, summarizing, inferring, comparing, and explaining); and *Analyze* (Breaking material into constituent parts, determining how the parts relate to one another and to an overall structure or purpose through differenti-

Table 1: Examples of task complexity [1] with corresponding title and sample backstory [2] and example user queries.

Complexity	Title (1) and Sample Backstory (2)	Example Queries Submitted by Users
Remember	(1) Where does cinnamon come from? (2) The other day you were eating some spiced biscuits from Europe, when it occurred to you that cinnamon probably isn't native to that part of the world. You would like to know where it comes from.	-Where does cinnamon come from -Which country does cinnamon which country grows the most cinnamon
Understand	(1) Recycle automobile tires (2) You need to buy new tires for your car, and the local dealer has offered to take the old ones for recycling. You didn't know tires could be recycled and you wonder what new uses they are being put to.	-Can you just type in tire uhm... car tire recycling -Uses for old car then the query or... passenger vehicle tyres... (user spells tyres) or... in caps tires... (user spells tires) and I wanna uhm... do a date-range so the data is from a recent 12 months... so uses for old car caps or passenger vehicle or tyres (user spells tyres) caps or tires (user spells tires) and data in the last 12 months that's the query ▼
Analyze	(1) Per capita alcohol consumption (2) You recently attended a big party and woke up with a hangover, and have decided to learn more about the average consumption of alcohol. You are particularly interested in any information that reports per capita consumption, and want to compare across groups, for example at the country, state, or province level.	-What's the average alcohol consumption of an Australian -OK so... uhm... in general I sort of want to try to find out the average consumption of alcohol uhm by... by the country state... for local level... so maybe just start of with type in uhm alcohol consumption by country... tell me if anything related to statistics uhm... about alcohol consumption uhm... between countries ▲

▼denotes teleporting and ▲denotes query babbling (see Section 3.1.1)

ating, organizing, and attributing). The dimensions are ranked in task complexity from Remember (least complex) to Analyze (most complex). Table 1 presents title and backstory examples. Example queries spoken by Users are shown in the last column.

2.2 Annotation and Analysis

Users, Retrievers, and the Retriever's screen were video recorded. The recordings were synchronized and merged. The annotations and transcriptions were created in ELAN.[1] Recordings were analyzed using Thematic analysis to generate themes [3]; search and interaction behaviours were analyzed in terms of words used and time on task. The transcriptions were changed to lower case, and punctuation and extra spacing was removed. The fill-word "uhm" was also removed for analysis purposes. However, we deliberately did not remove any errors, false starts or confirmations since these will likely occur in real case voice search scenarios.[2]

In the context of mixed initiative information retrieval dialogues, researchers have used the *control* and *initiative* terms interchangeably. However, we use the approach of *taking the initiative equals taking the turn* [5]. This means that one turn can consist of multiple moves or communication goals. An annotation schema relevant to our research aims was designed after inspecting the data; the complete data set was then coded using these data-derived *codes* [3]. Thus codes were applied to each turn taken by either User or Retriever and these codes were collated to create *themes*. Themes can consist of *subthemes* which capture specific concepts of that theme [3]. Themes were created independently of the previous turn meaning that each turn may consist of similar themes or subthemes. The first and second authors coded the data set independently. Inter-rater reliability was very high (Cohen's κ =0.88). Thirteen pairs provides data saturation, given that in thematic analysis saturation has been found to occur within 12 interviews [4]. We report our early findings of this inductive analysis of themes and patterns using the identified codes.

[1]http://tla.mpi.nl/tools/tla-tools/elan/

[2]Please contact the first author regarding access to the data.

3. RESULTS

Figure 1 shows the themes identified by the analysis of the coded videos. Turn 1 consists of the initial Information Request from the Users. We have grouped the response generating strategies of Turn 2 into the following themes:

Meta-communication Theme: In this theme Retrievers engaged in communication about the Information Request with Users before accessing the SERP, representing 59% of Turn 2 interactions. This *Meta-communication theme* included the following subthemes: Retrievers ask Users to repeat the Information Request (*Asks to repeat*, 28%); Retrievers formulate the desire for a refinement of the Information Request (*Query Refinement Offer*, 23%); or Retrievers confirm their action (*Confirms*, 8%). The *Query Refinement Offer* subtheme consisted of five different codes: multiple/single explicit or multiple/single implicit query suggestions or Information Request paraphrasing. The majority of *Query Refinement Offers* (75%) were asked before Retrievers accessed the SERP. The *Ask to Repeat* subtheme consisted of utterances where Retrievers specified their desire for an Information Request repeat explicitly ("sorry say that again" or "can you repeat that please") or implicitly (hesitantly started to repeat the Information Request back to the User or informed the User about their predicament without explicitly asking for a repetition of the Information Request). This subtheme also captured the Retrievers' "yes" utterances (*Confirms*).

Search Engine Result Page (SERP) Theme: This theme presented 38.5% of Turn 2 interactions and included three subthemes: Retrievers presented the SERP with/without the source (*SERP Presentation without Modification*, 20.5%); the SERP was synthesized/an overview was given (*SERP Presentation with Modification*, 13%); and SERP overview was given with further search suggestions (*SERP Presentation with Modification and Suggestion*, 5%).

Scanning Document Theme: This theme represented 2.5% of Turn 2 and consists of Retrievers neither initiating meta-communication nor engaging in any SERP presentation activities; instead Retrievers directly accessed a document and presented this to the user.

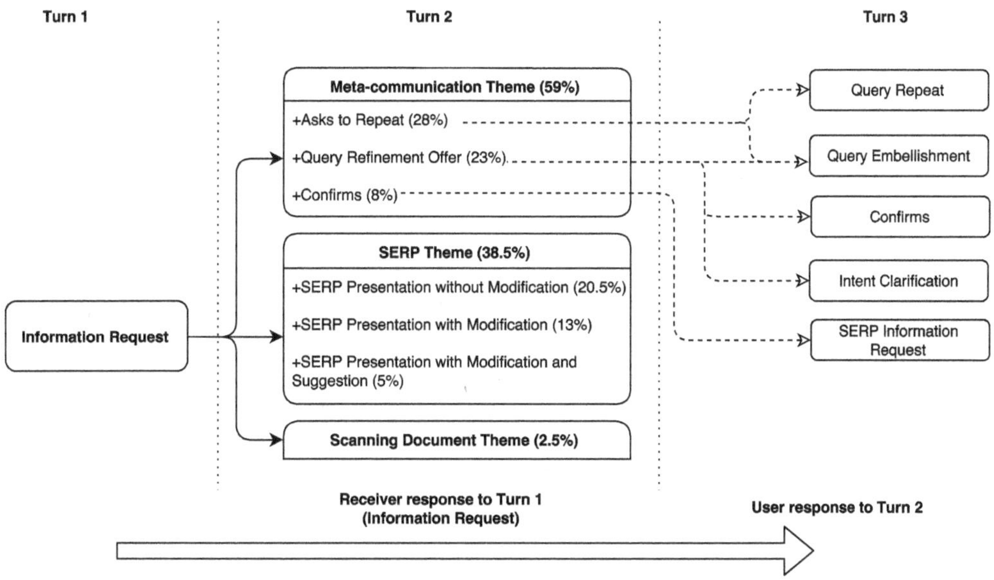

Figure 1: Interaction Theme Map (First three turns).

3.1 Search and Interaction Behaviours

The average length of Information Requests was 14.97 words. However, this length differed depending on the task complexity. As shown in Table 2, the average length of Remember Information Requests was shorter than for the Understand and Analyze categories. However, when non-query related words were stripped from the Information Request there was a higher number of query words in the Remember category. Simultaneously, the average time on search tasks for Remember tasks was nearly half the time as for Understand and Analyze tasks. The table shows a trend to longer Information Requests and time on the search task as the task complexity increases.

Finally, Users spent an average of 7.7 seconds in one turn and Retrievers 14.3 seconds. Table 2 indicates that Retrievers spent less time on Remember tasks than Understand and Analyze tasks. Even though participants received no instructions as to which search engines could be used, several participants were observed accessing Google Scholar. These search engine switches were mostly observed in Understand and Analyze search tasks.

3.1.1 *Information Request Length*

The average number of query terms in all unique queries issued for a task differed depending on the level of task difficulty. We observed two techniques which contributed to the length of the Information Requests. Firstly, we observed Users adopting a technique whereby they did not specify their query but instead discussed their information need. An example query is shown in Table 1 with the ▲notation. Secondly, some Information Requests were submitted using a very detailed and carefully crafted structure in order to capture the complete information request in one turn. An example is shown in Table 1 with the ▼notation. Users who submitted such Information Requests typically received a full SERP list from the Retrievers as search result. Users who started the Information Request with either of these two approaches were more likely to continue with this approach throughout that particular search task.

3.1.2 *Information Request Similarity*

Information Request similarity was measured after stopword removal and stemming between the overlapping Users' Information

Table 2: Search and Interaction Behaviours

Measure	Task complexity		
	Remember	Understand	Analyze
Inf. Req. Length in Words	11.92	16.25	16.77
Avg. Amount of Query Words	3.15	0.84	2.2
Avg. Query Word Similarity	0.88	0.817	0.819
Avg. Time on Task	3.57 min.	7.09 min.	7.34 min.
Avg. User Time on Task	7.20 sec.	7.93 sec.	8.01 sec.
Avg. Retriever Time on Task	9.14 sec.	17.16 sec.	16.69 sec.
Meta-communication Theme	6	8	9
SERP Theme	7	5	3
Scanning Document Theme	0	0	1
Query Refinement Offer Subtheme	1	4	4
Task Stopped by User	11	7	6

Requests words (i.e. query words) and backstory titles. The micro-averaged cosine similarity measure was used and these scores were aggregated according to the task complexity of Remember, Understand and Analyze. The similarity test scores for three types of queries were analyzed using one-way analysis of variance (ANOVA). Test assumptions of normality and homogeneity of variance were satisfactory, and the result was not statistically significant.

3.2 Meta-communication User Responses

As mentioned in Section 3, Retrievers deployed three different response generating strategies on the initial Information Request which we divided into the following themes: *Meta-communication*,

SERP, and *Scanning Document*. The *Meta-communication* theme was most frequently used and therefore is discussed in more detail in this preliminary analysis. Retrievers refined the Information Request within the *Query Refinement Offer* subtheme. Users replied to the *Query Refinement Offer* with one of the following three types of responses: *Confirms* (confirming the proposed *Query Refinement Offer*); *Intent Clarification* (replying to clarify the search intent); or *Query Embellishment* (enrichment of the given query, for example by adding query words).

The *Ask to Repeat* subtheme shared the *Query Embellishment* response with the *Query Refinement Offer* subtheme. However, when Retrievers asked users to repeat their Information Request we noted that Users mostly replied with a *Query Repeat* (a repetition of their Information Request without enrichments).

The *Confirms* subtheme received responses from users such as "so what's the first result that you get…" and "what kind of results come up" and were recorded as *SERP Information Request*.

An example of a *Query Refinement Offer* with *Query Clarification* is shown in Figure 2.

Turn 1: USER	(Information Request)	Effectiveness of new security measures at airports
Turn 2: RETRIEVER	(Query Refinement Offer)	Australia or at the airport
Turn 3: USER	(Intent Clarification)	Put uhm... put international airports

Figure 2: Initial Conversation Example.

4. DISCUSSION & CONCLUSION

We presented on a study designed to explore techniques used in search over a speech-only communication channel. An annotation schema was designed and the observed techniques were classified into three themes: Meta-communication, SERP, and Scanning Document.

Retrievers accessed the *Meta-communication* theme more often as task complexity increased; they specifically asked for more query clarifications. Retrievers presented the SERP without engaging in meta-communication more often as task complexity decreased. We are currently investigating whether differences exist between the Information Requests which received a response from the *Meta-communication* or *SERP* theme. This would allow us to understand when it would be beneficial to engage the user in either of these themes.

The *Query Refinement Offer* subtheme from the *Meta-communication* theme consisted of five response generating techniques: multiple/single explicit or multiple/single implicit Information Request refinements, and paraphrasing of Information Requests. These response generating techniques may be comparable to query disambiguation and refinement techniques such as query auto-completion or expansion techniques in a textual setting.

The subtheme *SERP Presentation with Modification and Suggestion* allowed Retrievers to scan a SERP and synthesize multiple results presenting an overview of that SERP. This technique may prevent users from information overload by filtering out the important facts of multiple results. A similar technique was used by Retrievers synthesizing and aggregating information from documents in order to group and present common information.

Overall, Information Requests became longer in words as the task complexity increased. However, even though Remember Information Requests were the shortest in length, they contained more query words relevant to the backstory title. Nevertheless, the overall similarity of the Information Request query words was similar to the backstory title for all three levels of task complexity. The increase in query words in the Remember tasks may be due to the tasks requiring factoid-style queries [2].

Two techniques which contributed to the Information Request length were observed. Firstly, Users submitted Information Requests by talking about their information need. This technique is similar to *querying by babbling* [6]. Secondly, users submitted very detailed and carefully crafted Information Requests and resembles *teleporting*, i.e. trying to jump directly to the information target [8]. Interestingly, teleporting is also observed among people who use screen readers in order to directly access relevant information without having to go through search results [7].

The average time on task became longer as the task complexity increased. More tasks were stopped by Users in Remember tasks while Understand and Analyze tasks were more likely to continue until the time limit was met.

There are no clear signs that Understand and Analyze tasks resulted in different patterns to each other. However, Remember tasks received enough information to satisfy the Information Request in a much shorter time frame than the Understand and Analyze tasks. The Remember tasks also involved less meta-communication in the first two interactions about the task in order to complete the task.

Independently of task complexity, User–Retriever pairs did not utilize the same response generating themes in each task; that is, pairs utilized a combination of *Meta-communication* or *SERP* themes. No observations of Information Request abandonment were made; however it would be interesting to see whether this is also the case in a non-laboratory setting. We plan to investigate if the guidance of Retrievers or system may lower the abandonment rate.

This initial analysis of search conversations between two people was performed in order to explore conversational search patterns in a speech-only setting. The interaction themes and coding scheme for a conversational speech-only search were identified uncovering two main response generating themes, *Meta-communication* and *SERP*.

As future work, we will test and validate the response generating techniques observed in these themes with Wizard of Oz and crowdsourcing experiments. We will also continue coding the interactions and extend this study. The coding scheme could be used for future crowdsourced classification and for validation of similar experiments. We are ultimately interested in understanding conversation designing effective strategies in a spoken IIR setting.

5. REFERENCES

[1] L. W. Anderson, D. R. Krathwohl, and B. S. Bloom. *A taxonomy for learning, teaching, and assessing: A revision of Bloom's taxonomy of educational objectives*. Longman, New York, 2001.

[2] P. Bailey, A. Moffat, F. Scholer, and P. Thomas. User variability and IR system evaluation. In *Proc. of SIGIR'15*, pages 625–634, 2015.

[3] V. Braun and V. Clarke. *Successful Qualitative Research: A Practical Guide for Beginners*. Sage, 2013.

[4] G. Guest, A. Bunce, and L. Johnson. How many interviews are enough? an experiment with data saturation and variability. *Field Methods*, 18(1):59–82, 2006.

[5] E. Hagen. An approach to mixed initiative spoken information retrieval dialogue. In *Computational Models of Mixed-Initiative Interaction*, pages 351–397. Springer, 1999.

[6] D. W. Oard. Query by babbling: A research agenda. In *Proc. of CIKM'12*, pages 17–21, 2012.

[7] N. G. Sahib, A. Tombros, and T. Stockman. A comparative analysis of the information-seeking behavior of visually impaired and sighted searchers. *JASIST*, 63(2):377–391, 2012.

[8] J. Teevan, C. Alvarado, M. S. Ackerman, and D. R. Karger. The perfect search engine is not enough: a study of orienteering behavior in directed search. In *Proc. of SIGCHI'04*, pages 415–422, 2004.

Discerning the Quality of Questions in Educational Q&A using Textual Features

Manasa Rath
School of Communication and Information
Rutgers University
manasa.rath@rutgers.edu

Long T. Le
Department of Computer Science
Rutgers University
longtle@cs.rutgers.edu

Chirag Shah
School of Communication and Information
Rutgers University
chirags@rutgers.edu

ABSTRACT

In an information seeking episode, attributes such as relevance, quality, and the nature of the information sought/obtained are directly related to the nature and the quality of the query or question that represents an information need. It is, therefore, imperative that we identify potential problems with such representation to make the information seeking outcome and the experience more successful. In this paper, we investigate the question quality for the educational community question answering (CQA) site Brainly by examining 2,000 questions, of which 1,000 were answered and 1,000 were unanswered. Two human assessors rated the quality of each question on a scale from 1-5 based on factors such as ambiguity, poor syntax, lack of information, complexity, inappropriateness, and inconsistency. We then identified different textual features that are needed to detect question quality. A logistic regression classifier was built to categorize question features based on the rating scale and textual features present in the question. The results show higher ROC curves for ambiguity, lack of information, inappropriateness, complexity and excessive information; and lower ROC values for poor syntax and inconsistency among the questions. The findings demonstrate that the classifier failed to perform when faced with ill-framed or inconsistent phrases in a question. The work described here presents a method for identifying high and low quality questions, the knowledge of which could be instrumental in helping reformulate users' questions and present them to a system or a community for more successful processes and outcomes.

Keywords

Community Q&A, question quality, machine learning, logistic regression

1. INTRODUCTION

The popularity of community question answering (CQA) sites has exponentially increased over the past several years. As a result, researchers have built an impressive body of work around CQA-related topics. These include improving users' experience when searching for answers to their information needs [13, 14] and evaluating the quality of answers given by their peers [1]. Research has also examined question askers' motivations in different contexts and situations in online Q&A [4]. Popular CQA sites include Stack Overflow, Yahoo! Answers, and Answerbag. The CQA sites for education provide an excellent platform for users to ask, learn, question and provide information using brief language. Among CQA-related research, scholars have determined why certain questions are answered over others, and what users expect when asking a question. It is now important to develop an automated process to detect and correct poorly received questions that go unanswered.

Studies demonstrate that question quality positively correlates with answer quality [1, 9]. The work in this paper describes whether automatically extracted textual features can approximately predict how humans may assess a question, and whether this approach can aid with question reformulation. In this paper, we first describe how human assessors rated questions. We then explain how we built a classifier based on the question features examined by human subjects. Finally, we discuss the implications of our classifier and how it contributes to a model for automatic question-quality detection.

CHIIR '17, March 07 - 11, 2017, Oslo, Norway

ISBN 978-1-4503-4677-1/17/03...$15.00

DOI: http://dx.doi.org/10.1145/3020165.3022145

2. BACKGROUND

2.1 Question Quality and Types in CQA

CQA services provide a platform on which users can exchange personal information and receive social support. A wide variability exists among the types of answers askers may receive via these channels. In several cases, a question's construction can predict its answers' presence and quality. In some cases, questions asked in Q&A sites can be either informational or conversational. When asking an informational question, a user aims to receive a reply [6]. These questions are usually direct, simple, concise, and precise. An asker may pose a more complex conversational question, on the other hand, if they want to begin a discussion. However, it has also been noted that in some cases users participate to earn points due to their fascination with a site's "reward system" [11]. Belonging to different linguistic, cultural and social backgrounds may compromise perceived question quality. Therefore, on some occasions, questions may lack clarity and/or contain incoherent or awkwardly placed phrases [10]. To determine and improve question quality, various textual features such as word count, misspelled words, and sentence readability need to be taken into account.

2.2 CQA for Education and Learning

Educational Q&A sites have emerged as popular learning platforms for students. They include Chegg[1], Khan Academy[2] and Brainly.[3] In this paper we focus on a data set obtained from Brainly,

[1] https://chegg.com/study/qa

[2] https://khanacademy.org

[3] https://brainly.com

an online CQA site meant for students studying in middle school and high school. Within Brainly, students can ask questions in sixteen different subjects such as Mathematics, History and English. Brainly has spread across 35 countries and 12 languages. It is estimated that Brainly has approximately 60 million monthly users, generates around 100,000 answers a day, and has over 1,000 moderators curating its knowledge base.

2.3 Evaluating the Questions Using Machine Learning Methods

Any community member can generate a CQA site's content, meaning quality is often an issue. It is therefore necessary to automate the process of determining content quality. Existing research used various factors to detect educational answers' worth, and showed that personal features and community features are more robust in detecting valuable content [6]. Other research used askers' history, question length, and topic to predict whether a question would be answered [8]. But an unanswered question can be a good question. There are several reasons that a quality question may go unanswered. For example, other users may be uninformed on a question's topic, or a question may go unseen. In our work, we evaluate the quality of questions in educational CQA by examining a list of different criteria generated by humans. Then, we develop a list of textual features to automatically detect question quality.

3. METHOD

3.1 Defining the Problem

The central inquiry of this investigation is: given a question, can we automatically predict its quality? In this study, we classify questions based on their quality using different human-assessed criteria - such as ambiguity, lack of information, excessive information, poor syntax, etc. - all of which serve as our class labels. Textual features such as total word count, readability scores, and misspelled words help us assess the CQA questions. Here, we train the textual features along with the human ratings on the classifier to categorize each question using seven different class labels, which include ambiguity, lack of information, and poor syntax.

3.2 Obtaining Non-Textual Assessments

A total of 2,000 questions were extracted from Brainly's database in the first week of January, 2016 by writing a SQL query. From this, 1,000 questions were answered and 1,000 questions were unanswered. An equal amount of answered and unanswered questions were considered to remove sampling bias.To obtain the non-textual assessments, two trained coders were asked to evaluate the data set based on the Likert-scale items developed in [10]. The human assessors were asked to read the following explanation of various qualitative labels, then rate each question on a scale from 1-5 (least to most prevalent).

- *Ambiguity (AM)*: The manner in which the question is structured confuses the user and therefore makes it difficult to interpret the meaning of the question.
- *Lack of Information (LI):* The question does not have enough information that could be used to determine its meaning.
- *Poor Syntax (PS):* The spelling, grammar and syntax used in the writing of the question is too poor, and consequently the question is difficult to understand.
- *Complex (C):* The question is too complex, and uses difficult terminologies that cannot be answered in a particular amount of time.
- *Excessive Information (EI):* The question has excessive information that deviates from or decreases interest in the topic.
- *Inappropriate (IA):* The question uses inappropriate language, which may include taboo words, jokes, socially awkward information, and/or follow up information.
- *Inconsistent (IC):* The content of the question is not consistent with the topic, and/or the question includes (an) unrelated topic(s).

The coders were presented with and asked to rate a set of n=100 questions. It was found that the inter-coder reliability value ($\alpha >$ 0.71) was higher than the norm. Given the results, the coders were asked to code the rest of the questions.

3.3 List of Textual Features

We extracted a number of textual features that correspond to the presence of certain interrogative phrases, the number of misspellings, the total number of question marks in an entire query, the automated readability scores, the total number of characters, and the total number of words. The following list elaborates upon what these features mean and/or how they were derived.

- The presence of interrogative words such as "why," "how," "who," "where," and "what" was noted.
- We detected the presence of spelling errors to estimate the number of typos a user made. To do so, we used the Python auto correct packet.
- The presence of a question mark(s) (?) was recorded.
- The Automated Readability Index (ARI) [7] scores estimates the grade level of the user, which could comprehend the question.
- The number of characters in the question – including any special characters – were counted without the white spaces between them.
- The number of words in the question were counted to determine the question's precision or specificity.

The total number of words and characters demonstrated each question's precision. Misspelled words were detected, and suggestions for possible corrections were made. Calculated textual features suggested how each question was constructed. The readability values helped to determine the level of complexity and ambiguity present in a question's content.

3.4 Classification and Prediction Quality

With the combined results of the different textual features and the human ratings, classification of question quality was performed using the Weka v 3.9.0. Our framework works well in different classifiers like Support Vector Machine (SVM), Random Forests (RF), and Simple Logistic Regression (SLR). Here, we present the results for SLR. SLR [2] was used for ten-cross fold-validation to preserve internal validity and robustness of the model. Let $X = x_1, x_2, ..., x_n$ be the list of features. Logistic Regression (log-reg) is a generalized linear model with a sigmoid function: $P(Y = 1|X = \frac{1}{1+exp(-b)})$; where $b = w_o + \sum(w_i.x_i)$ where, w_i are the inferred parameters from regression [2]. A threshold ratings value ranging from 1-5 was set to be 3 for the individual items in every question. If the value of the rating was greater than or equal to 3, the question was labeled "Bad"; otherwise, it was labeled "Good."

Table 1: Confusion matrix for Answered Questions for Ambiguity

	Good	Bad
Good	905	14
Bad	68	13

Table 2: Confusion matrix for Unanswered Questions for Ambiguity

	Good	Bad
Good	211	13
Bad	708	68

The accuracy values were determined for all individual items, such as ambiguity, lack of information, poor syntax, complexity, excessive information, inappropriateness, and inconsistency. The values determined from those results included precision, recall, F-measure, Receiver Operating Characteristic (ROC) curves, and the class (Good or Bad) to which the question belonged. The binary classification of the question using the logistic regression classifier helped to identify a question as "Good" over "Bad".

4. FINDINGS

To evaluate the efficacy of our framework, we examine a few key metrics that include Accuracy, F1 score, and Area under the ROC curve [2]. Accuracy is the percentage of questions classified correctly. The F1 score considers both precision and recall, and can be interpreted as the weighted average of the two. Precision is the fraction of retrieved instances that are relevant, while recall is the fraction of relevant instances that are retrieved (the recall values are not mentioned in Table 3). The F1 score values can be calculated as: $F1 = 2 * \frac{precision*recall}{precision+recall}$.

Table 3: Accuracy results found per class label.

Class Label	Precision	F-measure	ROC Curve
AM Bad	0.762	0.794	0.861
AM Good	0.863	0.833	0.861
LI Bad	0.780	0.781	0.866
LI Good	0.841	0.840	0.866
PS Bad	0.000	0.000	0.498
PS Good	0.999	0.955	0.498
C Bad	0.448	0.830	0.707
C Good	0.721	0.083	0.707
EI Bad	0.902	0.049	0.779
EI Good	0.833	0.948	0.779
IA Bad	0.578	0.281	0.723
IA Good	0.711	0.808	0.723
IC Bad	0.557	0.255	0.684
IC Good	0.683	0.788	0.684

(AM: Ambiguity, LI: Lack of Information, PS: Poor Syntax, C: Complex, EI: Excessive Information, IA: Inappropriate, IC: Inconsistent)

The results indicate significant agreement among the precision values. The most important way to determine the efficiency of the classifier is to examine the ROC curves or Area Under Curve (AUC), which indicate the number of times the classifier will correctly define an instance of "Good" or "Bad" categorization. In the ROC curve, an area of 1 indicates that accuracy is measured perfectly, whereas an area below 0.7 represents a poor performance of the classifier. The AUC values for ambiguity, lack of information, excessive information, and inappropriateness show agreeable values. However, the ROC curve values for poor syntax and incompleteness show poor results.

Table 4: Information Gain values for "Ambiguity".

Textual Features	Ranked Values
Total Characters	0.437
Total Question Marks (?)	0.01243
Interrogative Phrases	0.0124
Readability Scores	0.0075
Total Words	0.0066
Misspelled Words	0.000

The ROC curve values for ambiguity, lack of information, complexity, excessive information, and inappropriateness are decent at > 0.71. However, for poor syntax and incompleteness, the ROC values are lower, possibly because the model fails to detect question quality. This could be the auto-extraction type feature of the question that fails to recognize its special characters, grammatical errors, Internet slang, and/or informal nature. The classes we studied were highly imbalanced because the model we prepared during training is biased towards the more popular classes. This is not an uncommon scenario in data sets that have a skewed distribution of minor categories. The frequency of instances in the "poor syntax" and "inconsistent" categories was very low. As a result, our system failed to retrieve relevant instances for those categories. The precision values reported for most of the items are fairly high, showing much agreement with recall, and thereby sufficient F-measure. Usually, precision gives an idea of the fraction of relevant items retrieved. However, if the overall recall is low, it leads to low values for both true and false positives, thus leading to higher values for precision with lower ROC values. This is observed in the case of the "poor syntax" item for the "Good" class value. Similarly, we see instances where the precision values are slightly high but the ROC values are low. The chi-square statistic was found out for the good and bad questions for both answered and unanswered question. It was found that the difference between the distribution of good and bad questions between answered and unanswered questions was significant ($\chi^2 = 983.38, df = 1, p<0.05$).

Features' importance and features' selection: Considering that we only had six of the textual features present and accounted for, feature selection was not performed. However, in order to determine the amount of information gained from the textual features for a particular class label [5], the textual features were ranked using a ranking filter, and the ranked values were obtained. The results show that certain features such as total characters and the total number of question marks (?) were ranked higher compared to other textual features. The information gain values of the "Ambiguity" class label are mentioned in Table 4. Higher values indicate that a feature has more prediction value.

5. DISCUSSION

Findings based on insufficient ROC values show that the model fails to classify the questions based on poor syntax and inconsistency. Our sample is much smaller compared to the data sets used in other studies, which is a major limitation of this work. We would like to attempt to further experiment and obtain better results for the ROC curve in future research [9, 8]. On the other hand, the experiments described here show that non-textual attributes play a crucial role in determining the question quality. The study here paves a path for future research that involves developing better techniques for parsing the misspellings and grammatical errors present in the questions. Future studies could divide the questions into categories – such as fact-based, opinion-based, and advisory – using the textual features we examined. This division would help to build specific classification models based on the textual features prominent in a particular set of questions. Future work may also include decision trees to individually detect the issues present in a particular class-label. The "poor syntax" and the "inconsistent" ROC values show that these items fail to be classified by our model. We could fix these low ROC curve values using the SMOTEBoost Methodology within the Adaboost procedure to improve the model's construction. Mining in the imbalanced datasets is a prominent problem that scientists are trying to solve [3]. The results also indicate that the unanswered questions have been significantly more (using χ^2 test, $p < 0.05$) misclassified by the classifier for "Ambiguity" than they were for the answered questions (Table 2). However, it would be interesting to see in future research how well the classifier performs in other items for unanswered questions. This demonstrates an important concern with CQA sites: that moderators of some kind should assist question-askers, as ill-framed questions that do not signify any meaning can leave the question unattended. This work also has significant implications for improved question quality, and it would be interesting to note whether answer quality improves along with questions. This would cause human intervention or an auto-completion feature to be introduced in a Q&A site, which could streamline the question-answering process and alleviate tensions within Q&A services.

6. CONCLUSION

Our study addresses an important question held by the CQA community: how can we determine question quality in (educational) CQA? This determination is important, and our study suggests that automated processes can effectively evaluate a question's quality and improve its performance. Revising and improving question quality is immensely important, as this work could facilitate immediate access to virtual learning tools. In the absence of a mechanical learning tool, a CQA site may close. Google Answers, for example, was launched in 2001 and terminated in 2006 [12]. Beyond detecting poor questions, we need a framework for reformulating them. Here, we have shown the construction of a robust model that classifies answered and unanswered questions as "Good" or "Bad." However, our model's performance could be improved in light of future research goals, including wider question reformulation and revision. Helping users form accurate questions would also increase the possibility that they would receive precise and exact answers, which is the aim of educational CQA sites.

Some previous work have involved predicting the quality of question and answers in online communities, but did not provide sufficient details. Those methods typically suggested that a question is "good" or "bad" without examining the nuance behind those labels. To the best of our knowledge, our work is the first to consider the particular factors that make a question "bad" in CQA. It determines certain features that make a question high or low quality. The results presented here demonstrate the potential benefits of giving educational CQA users more detailed feedback and suggestions.

7. ACKNOWLEDGEMENTS

The work reported in this paper is supported by the US Institute of Museum and Library Services (IMLS) grant #LG-81-16-0025. We are also grateful to Brainly for providing us with the data.

8. REFERENCES

[1] E. Agichtein, C. Castillo, D. Donato, A. Gionis, and G. Mishne. Finding high-quality content in social media. In *Proceedings of the 2008 international conference on web search and data mining*, pages 183–194. ACM, 2008.

[2] C. M. Bishop. Pattern recognition. *Machine Learning*, 128, 2006.

[3] N. V. Chawla. Data mining for imbalanced datasets: An overview. In *Data mining and knowledge discovery handbook*, pages 853–867. Springer, 2005.

[4] E. Choi and C. Shah. User motivations for asking questions in online q&a services. *Journal of the Association for Information Science and Technology*, 2015.

[5] W. B. Croft, D. Metzler, and T. Strohmann. *Search engines*. Pearson Education, 2010.

[6] F. M. Harper, D. Moy, and J. A. Konstan. Facts or friends?: distinguishing informational and conversational questions in social q&a sites. In *Proceedings of the SIGCHI Conference on Human Factors in Computing Systems*, pages 759–768. ACM, 2009.

[7] J. P. Kincaid, R. P. Fishburne Jr, R. L. Rogers, and B. S. Chissom. Derivation of new readability formulas (automated readability index, fog count and flesch reading ease formula) for navy enlisted personnel. Technical report, DTIC Document, 1975.

[8] L. T. Le, C. Shah, and E. Choi. Evaluating the quality of educational answers in community question-answering. In *Proceedings of the 16th ACM/IEEE-CS on Joint Conference on Digital Libraries*, pages 129–138. ACM, 2016.

[9] Y. Liu, J. Bian, and E. Agichtein. Predicting information seeker satisfaction in community question answering. In *Proceedings of the 31st annual international ACM SIGIR conference on Research and development in information retrieval*, pages 483–490. ACM, 2008.

[10] C. Shah, M. L. Radford, L. S. Connaway, E. Choi, and V. Kitzie. How much change do you get from 40$?–analyzing and addressing failed questions on social q&a. *Proceedings of the American Society for Information Science and Technology*, 49(1):1–10, 2012.

[11] I. Srba and M. Bielikova. Askalot: community question answering as a means for knowledge sharing in an educational organization. In *Proceedings of the 18th ACM Conference Companion on Computer Supported Cooperative Work & Social Computing*, pages 179–182. ACM, 2015.

[12] G. Wang, K. Gill, M. Mohanlal, H. Zheng, and B. Y. Zhao. Wisdom in the social crowd: an analysis of quora. In *Proceedings of the 22nd international conference on World Wide Web*, pages 1341–1352. ACM, 2013.

[13] X. Xue, J. Jeon, and W. B. Croft. Retrieval models for question and answer archives. In *Proceedings of the 31st annual international ACM SIGIR conference on Research and development in information retrieval*, pages 475–482. ACM, 2008.

[14] J. Zhang, M. S. Ackerman, and L. Adamic. Expertise networks in online communities: structure and algorithms. In *Proceedings of the 16th international conference on World Wide Web*, pages 221–230. ACM, 2007.

Scroll Up or Down? Using Wheel Activity as an Indicator of Browsing Strategy across Different Contextual Factors

Chang Liu
Peking University
5 Yiheyuan Street,
Beijing, China, 100871
imliuc@pku.edu.cn

Jiqun Liu
Rutgers University
4 Huntington Street,
New Brunswick, NJ, 08901
jl2033@scarletmail.rutgers.edu

Yiming Wei
Carnegie Mellon University
5000 Forbes Avenue
Pittsburgh, PA, 15213-3891
yimingw1@andrew.cmu.edu

ABSTRACT

This study used wheel activity as an indicator of users' browsing strategy, and explored the effects of various contextual factors on users' browsing patterns. Users' wheel activities were extracted from a search log in a user experiment, in which forty participants with different backgrounds conducted an online search in various contexts. To statistically test the potential effects of contexts on browsing strategy, we calculated three types of scroll-based variables to capture different types of browsing behaviors, and analyzed the effects of contextual factors via OLS regression analysis. Our results revealed that information understanding type tasks might lead to more proportion of revisit browsing range, while higher pressure level and higher pre-familiarity might lead to larger one-time browsing range; however, time constraint did not influence their browsing strategies. Our study also provided methodological implication for future interactive information retrieval studies by testifying and highlighting the usefulness of users' wheel activities in depicting online browsing patterns.

CCS Concepts

• **Information systems → Information retrieval →** Users and interactive retrieval

KEYWORDS

Wheel activity, browsing behavior, task facet, page type

1. INTRODUCTION

In interactive information retrieval studies, researchers have extracted and examined a series of interaction measures to describe searchers' activities and/or to evaluate search process. The common types of interaction measures include page-related measures (e.g. number of documents visited, number of search results visited, number of documents saved, etc.), query-related measures (e.g. number of queries, average query length, etc.), and time-related measures (e.g. dwell time on content pages on search result pages, etc.). Among these measures, mouse clicks and mouse movements were not frequently examined. Some studies examined the frequency of specific interface functions, by counting the number of mouse clicks on specific functions. Besides clicking, the mouse activities also include cursor movements and wheel activities.

CHIIR '17, March 07-11, 2017, Oslo, Norway
© 2017 ACM. ISBN 978-1-4503-4677-1/17/03…$15.00
DOI: http://dx.doi.org/10.1145/3020165.3022146

Cursor and wheel activities have been examined to describe users' search strategies or to help predict the relevance of a webpage to the user. Huang, White & Dumais [7] examined users' cursor behaviors on search result pages (SERPs), including clicks, cursor movements and hovers, and suggested that hover data can improve the estimation of SERP relevance and cursor trails may help to differentiate between good and bad search abandonment. Buscher, White, Dumais & Huang [2] also used cursor data, together with clicks and scrolling data, to understand users' SERP examination strategies, and identified three types of searchers: economic, exhaustive-active and exhaustive-passive strategies. Among them, economic users conducted fewer scrolls than the other two kinds of users. Besides, some studies have also explored the relationship between the amounts of scrolls on webpages and users' interest to the page as implicit relevance feedback (e.g. [3][6]).

As shown in previous studies, wheel activity has not been a common type of measures to describe users' search interactions; and previous studies often selected single contextual factor, e.g. search result relevance, and then compared the difference between two or more conditions. None studies have fully examined users' wheel activities or how they were affected by contextual factors. The goal of this study is to calculate multiple measures of wheel activities to reflect users' browsing strategies, and to explore how various contextual factors affect users' wheel activities on webpages. For the analysis of wheel activities, three types of indicators were calculated: number of scrolls, range of one-time browsing and proportion of multi-time browsing range. By one-time browsing, we refer to monodirectional browsing behavior which has no "revisited area" on the webpage browsed. Multi-time browsing range refers to the range that was browsed by user(s) more than one time (thus corresponding to the revisiting or scrolling up and down alternately). Correspondingly, given these two basic definitions as starting point, we investigate three research questions: What are the effects of contextual factors on 1) the number of scrolls; 2) one-time browsing behaviors; 3) revisiting behavior in web page browsing?

2. Method

This research used the data collected from a laboratory user experiment in which forty undergraduate students at Peking University participated to search for four search tasks in two time conditions. This section describes the process of experiment and the operationalization of independent and dependent variables.

2.1 Experiment

The user experiment was conducted to examine time constraint effects on search behaviors and strategies, so two time conditions were manipulated for participants to search for tasks: with time constraint (TC) and without time constraint (NTC). In TC condition, time available for subjects to finish a search task was restricted to five minutes; in NTC condition, subjects were told beforehand that they could stop searching whenever they thought enough information had been collected for the task. With respect to search tasks, two types of search tasks were designed according to the first two cognitive process dimensions of the Taxonomy of Learning ([1]): Remember—retrieving, recognizing, and recalling relevant knowledge from long-term memory (so called Fact Finding tasks) and Understanding—constructing meaning from oral, written, and graphic messages through interpreting, exemplifying, classifying, summarizing, inferring, and explaining (so called Information Understanding tasks). Each type of tasks consists of two tasks with different topics, and a detailed description of the research design and the user experiment for the data collection can be found in [8].

2.2 Independent variables

We explored the effects of several contextual factors manipulated or collected in this experiment for analysis. For the facets of tasks, there are task type and time condition, which were described in the previous section. For individual characteristics, the experiment measured subjects' pressure level using Perceived Pressure Scale (PPS) questionnaire [4], as part of the background questionnaire. PPS consisted of 14 items asking subjects to rate their pressure during the past month on a five-point Likert scale. The pressure score for each participant was calculated by adding up their scores in all of the questions. PPS questionnaire has been shown to be a reliable tool to measure the amount of stress and a higher score indicates greater levels of perceived stress. Participants in our study were then divided into two groups (high pressure level and low pressure level, HP and LP) by the median of all participants (pressure score=28).

For combined factors of users and tasks, we considered two variables collected in pre-search questionnaire before each of search tasks: pre-confidence and pre-familiarity. For pre-search confidence, subjects were asked "how familiar are you with the topic of this search task?" and for pre-search confidence, subjects were asked "how much confidence do you have to complete this search task?". The answers to both questions were 5-point Likert scale. In these scales, the larger value means the higher confidence or familiarity.

The type of webpages users were browsing may also influence their browsing strategies. In this study, we focused on three types of webpages: query SERP[1], SERP and content pages. Table 1 is the list of the definition and variable values of all the aforementioned contextual factors.

Table 1 Contextual factors, variables and values

Contextual Factor	Variables	Values
Facets of Task	Task Type	FF=0, IU=1
	Time Condition	NTC=0, TC=1
Individual Characteristics	Pressure level	LP=0, HP=1
Page Type	Query SERP	No=0, Yes=1
	Content page	No=0, Yes=1
Combined Factors of users and tasks	Pre Confidence	5-point Scale
	Pre Familiarity	5-point Scale

Note: if Query SERP =0 and content =0, then the page type = SERP. SERP as dummy variable was excluded into following regression analysis for avoiding collinearity.

Table 2. Types of wheel activities, variables and operational definitions

Types of wheel activity	Variable names	Operational definitions
Number of scrolls	UP	the number of scroll up
	DOWN	the number of scroll down
	SUM	the number of scroll up and down
One-time browsing	Range of one-time browsing (ROB)	$\mid UP - DOWN \mid$
Multi-time browsing	Proportion of multi-time browsing range(POMB)	$1 - \frac{\mid UP - DOWN \mid}{\max(UP, DOWN)}$

2.3 Dependent variables

The experiment recorded searchers' interactions on the computer unobtrusively during search Morae Recorder 3.0[2]. For the analysis in this study, searchers' wheel activities on each webpage were extracted from the search logs. Each scroll recorded in the log represents the same distance, so the number of scrolling reflects the distance of browsing on the page. The wheel activities were classified into three types (as shown in Table 2). Number of scrolls: the variables—UP, DOWN and SUM represent respectively the number of scroll up, scroll down, and all scrolls; One-time browsing: the range of one-time browsing (ROB) on a webpage, calculated as the absolute value of the differences between the values of UP and DOWN; Multi-time browsing: the proportion of multi-time browsing range (POMB) is calculated as the range that the user browsed more than once on the page divided by the max of UP or DOWN.

3. RESULTS

3.1 The effects on the number of scrolls

We first examined the effects of contextual factors on the number of scrolls. The results (shown in the second to the fourth columns in Table 3) demonstrated that the regression models were statistically significant (p<.001 in every regression).

[1] In this study, Query SERP refers to the first time a SERP was shown after the user issued a query; and SERP refers to all the other SERPs that the user visited except Query SERP.

[2] Morae recorder, https://www.techsmith.com/morae.html

Table 3. OLS regression results on wheel activities (coefficients and standard errors)

Variables	UP	DOWN	SUM	ROB	POMB
Task Type	**1.46(.48)****	.40(1.28)	1.86(1.63)	-.68(1.02)	**.05(.02)****
Time Condition	-.59(.56)	-1.94(1.49)	-2.53(1.91)	-1.57(1.19)	.01(.02)
Pressure	**-1.07(.56)***	1.76(1.48)	.70(1.88)	1.25(1.17)	**-.05(.02)***
Query SERP	-1.00(.74)	-.13(1.96)	-1.13(2.50)	-1.21(1.55)	**.11(.03)****
Content page	**1.48(.54)****	**7.59(1.44)****	**9.07(1.83)****	**4.95(1.14)****	**.11(.02)****
Pre Confidence	-.43(.37)	-.87(.99)	-.52(1.27)	.01(.79)	-.02(.01)
Pre Familiarity	.13(.31)	**1.75(.83)***	1.89(1.05)	**1.39(0.66)***	.01(.01)
Constant	4.03(1.50)	.03(3.99)	4.05(5.08)	1.73(3.17)	.16(.05)

Note: Variables with significant coefficients (p<0.05) are highlighted in bold in the cells. * p<0.05; ** p<0.01

In terms of users' scrolling up behavior, task type (p<.01) and the dummy variable of content page (p<.01) were significant predictors, and the signs of coefficients are positive. Therefore, ceteris paribus, users who were searching for information understanding type of search tasks would do more scrolling up than their counterparts dealing with fact finding type of tasks. Similarly, user tended to do more scrolling up when browsing content pages than other pages. Besides, pressure was marginally significant (p=.055), and the coefficient is -1.07, indicating that users with higher pressure may be less patient to do scrolling up on web pages, compared with users with lower pressure level.

For scrolling down activities, users' pre-familiarity of given task (p<.05) and the dummy variable of content page (p<.01) were statistically significant, and the signs of coefficients are positive. Hence, when a user is browsing content page or more familiar with the search task, he or she would engage in more scrolling down activities, and thus browsing more contents.

For the total number of all scrolls, the dummy variable of content page (p<.01) is the only significant predictor, and the signs of coefficient is positive, meaning that users tend to have more scrolls and be more active in browsing when reading content pages than Query SERPs and SERPs.

3.2 The effects on one-time browsing behavior

We then examined the effects of contextual factors one-time browsing range, and the result is shown in the fifth column (ROB) of . For ROB, the regression model was statistically significant (p<.001). The dummy variable of content page (p<.01) and users' pre-familiarity of task (p<.05) were significant predictors, and the signs of coefficients are positive. Thus, ceteris paribus, users with higher level of pre-familiarity on task tend to have larger one-time browsing range than users with lower level of pre-familiarity, and they tend to have larger range of one-time browsing on content pages than on SERPs or Query SERPs.

3.3 The effects on revisiting behavior

We further examined the effects of contextual factors on users' revisiting behavior in webpage browsing, and the result is shown in the last column (POMB) of **Table** 3. The regression model was statistically significant (p<.001). The dummy variable of the content page and query SERP page and task type were significant predictors (p<.01 for these three coefficients), and both signs of the coefficients are positive. That is to say, users reading a content page or query SERP would do more percentage of prudent, multi-time revisiting behavior in web browsing than reading a SERP, ceteris paribus. Users searching for information understanding type of tasks would also have more proportion of multi-time revisiting browsing than in fact finding type of tasks. Pressure was also a significant predictor (p<.05) and the sign of its coefficient is negative. Therefore, users with a higher level of pressure tend to do less revisit than users with a lower pressure level.

4. DISCUSSION

We employed users' wheel activity as an indicator of their browsing strategy. Our results revealed that task type, time condition, page types, individual pressure level and task-individual combined factors had different effects on users' browsing behaviors.

The results demonstrated that task type has positive impact on the number of scrolls (UP, DOWN, SUM) and POMB, but the coefficient for ROB is negative, even though it is not significant. Such results indicate that task type has positive influence on users' the amount of scrolls, especially the revisits behaviors, but has negative influence on the range of one-time browsing. Therefore, users' tend to read the web pages more carefully with more proportion of revisits in information understanding type of tasks than in fact finding tasks. It probably indicates that users often scrolled back and forth to make sure they understand the content when searching for information understanding type of tasks; while in fact finding type of task, users only need to locate the specific facts on the page without much understanding cognitive process.

With respect to the influence of the time condition, it is surprising to see that time condition does not have any significant impact on any of the scroll behaviors. Since one of our previous findings was that users would have significant fewer mouse clicks per page when searching under time constraint than when there was no time constraint [9], we would expect that users would browse less content on each of pages when given time constraint, and would read more content when there was no time constraint. But the non-significant results indicate that users still try to browse similar amount of content on each of the webpages with or without time constraint. In one of our previous study [8], we found there was no significant difference on the mean dwell time on content pages or on SERPs. Combining the results from both studies, it is possible to infer that users did not accelerate their reading speed when giving time constraint. But we should acknowledge that besides wheel scrolls, users could also scroll the webpage using keyboard or by dragging the scrolling bar on the side of the webpage. We should further examine the ways searchers used to scroll the webpage in this experiment.

The pressure level we measured using PPS questionnaire reflected the subjects' pressure level during the past month, and this measure was collected before they conducted search. According to the psychological pressure research, this could belong to the chronic states, which is constant and persisting over an extended period of time ([10]). Therefore, the pressure level in this study could be considered as an internal individual characteristic, and is not caused by contextual factors. The results also showed that the pressure level has significant negative effects on UP and POMB measures, but has positive effects on DOWN, SUM and ROB, although not significant. Such results indicate that users with higher pressure level were less likely to scroll up or revisit the content they have browsed; instead, they would tend to browse more content, rather than revisit. The reason for this might be that people with higher pressure level were more worried and unsure, and they tend to read more content to release their pressure.

As for the effects of page type, we considered three types of Webpages—content page, Query SERPs and SERPs. The results showed whether the page is Query SERP or not had significantly positive effect on POMB, but negative effects on all the other wheel activity variables. Specially, users were more likely to revisit more proportion of content on Query SERP than other pages, but they would have fewer scrolls in total and shorter range of one-time browsing on Query SERP. This is reasonable since searchers need to browse the snippets on Query SERP to decide which page to click from the list. On the other hand, content page has significant positive effects on all the scroll behaviors, so users often read more carefully on content pages than on SERPs or Query SERPs.

It is also interesting to see that users' pre-confidence and pre-familiarity to the search tasks have opposite effects on users' wheel activities. Users' pre-confidence has negative effects on most of the scroll behaviors (UP, DOWN, SUM, POMB), so the more confident users towards the tasks, the less content they would browse. However, pre-familiarity has significantly positive effects on all the scroll behaviors; indicating that the more familiar to the task, the longer range users would browse. The reason of this may be that users who were more familiar with tasks would read the content smoothly and had more interests to read longer, so they kept scrolling down and tried to digest new contents. But searchers with more pre-confidence believe they could accomplish the task easily and they did not read the content as carefully as their counterparts.

5. CONCLUSION

This study examined three groups of users' wheel activities to represent different types of browsing strategies: the amount of scrolls on webpages, the range of one-time browsing, and the proportion of multi-time browsing range; and explored the effects of several contextual factors on these wheel activities. Results demonstrated that information understanding type of tasks might lead to more scrolls and larger revisit browsing range; users' browsing strategy appears to be not sensitive to time constraint than other signals of user behavior; in terms of the impacts of the pressure level, higher pressure may lead to longer one-time browsing range but shorter revisit area; and higher pre-familiarity may lead to longer one-time browsing range. Such results help us understand users' browsing strategies and how they were affected by contextual factors. This study is an exploration of mining wheel activities to depict users' browsing patterns, and found that they are good indicators. We acknowledge that besides wheel scrolls, users could use keyboard or the scrolling bar on the side of the webpage to scroll the page. It is also important to examine how much chance would searchers use wheel to scroll compared with other ways. We should further examine the ways searchers used to scroll the webpage in this experiment. In future studies, we will also explore other measures (speed-related measures) to represent users' browsing strategies, or other interaction variables to depict browsing strategies and explore their relationships with contextual factors. In addition, besides the contextual factors examined this study, future studies should also examine the relationship between browsing behaviors and or scrolling behaviors with document usefulness to explore whether scrolling behaviors would be good indicators of document usefulness.

ACKNOWLEDGMENTS

This work was supported by the NSFC #71303015.

6. REFERENCES

[1] Anderson, L. W. and Krathwohl, D. A. 2001. *A taxonomy for learning, teaching and assessing: A revision of Bloom's taxonomy of educational objectives*. New York: Longman.

[2] Buscher, G., White, R. W., Dumais, S., and Huang, J. 2012. Large-scale analysis of individual and task differences in search result page examination strategies. In *Proceedings of the 5th ACM international conference on Web search and data mining* (Seattle, WA, Feb 08-12, 2012). ACM: New York, NY: 373-382.

[3] Claypool, M., Le, P., Wased, M., and Brown, D. 2001. Implicit interest indicators. *In Proceedings of the 6th International Conference on Intelligent User Interfaces* (pp. 33-40). Santa Fe, New Mexico, United States.

[4] Cohen S., Kamarak T., & Mermelstein R. (1983). A global measure of perceived stress. Journal of health and social behavior, 24, 385–396. http://dx.doi.org/10.2307/2136404

[5] Fox, S., Karnawat, K., Mydland, M., Dumais, S., and White, T. 2005. Evaluating implicit measures to improve web search. *ACM Transactions on Information Systems, 23* (April 2005), 147-168.

[6] Goecks, J., and Shavlik, J. 2000. Learning users' interests by unobtrusively observing their normal behavior. *Proceedings of the 5th International Conference on Intelligent User Interfaces,* (New Orleans, LA, January 09-12, 2000). 129-132.

[7] Huang, J., White, R. W., and Dumais, S. 2011. No clicks, no problem: using cursor movements to understand and improve search. In *Proceedings of the SIGCHI Conference on Human Factors in Computing Systems* (Vancouver, Canada, April 27 -May 02, 2011). ACM, New York, NY, 1225-1234.

[8] Liu, C. & Wei, Y. (2016). The impacts of time constraint on users' search strategy during search process. In Proceedings of the 79th ASIS&T Annual Meeting: Creating Knowledge, Enhancing Lives through Information & Technology (ASIST '16). American Society for Information Science, Silver Springs, MD, USA, Article 51, 9 pages.

[9] Liu, C., & Xu, T. (2016). Preliminary Exploration of the Effect of Time Constraint on Search Interactions on Webpages. Acm/ieee-Cs on Joint Conference on Digital Libraries (pp.265-266). ACM.

[10] Lundberg, U. (2005). Stress hormones in health and illness: the roles of work and gender. Psychoneuroendocrinology, 30(10), 1017-1021.

[11] Rodden, K., Fu, X., Aula, A., and Spiro, I. 2008. Eye-mouse coordination patterns on web search results pages. *In CHI'08 extended abstracts on Human factors in computing systems.* (Florence, Italy, April 05-10, 2008). ACM: New York, NY, 2997-3002.

Evaluation of the Comprehensiveness of Bar Charts with and without Stacking Functionality using Eye-Tracking

Falk Böschen
Kiel University
fboe@informatik.uni-kiel.de

Benjamin Strobel
IPN - Leibniz Institute for Science and Mathematics Education
strobel@ipn.uni-kiel.de

Steffen Goos
Kiel University
stg@informatik.uni-kiel.de

Christoph Liebers
Kiel University
clie@informatik.uni-kiel.de

Bastian Rathje
Kiel University
bar@informatik.uni-kiel.de

Ansgar Scherp
Kiel University and
ZBW - Leibniz Information Centre for Economics
a.scherp@zbw.eu

ABSTRACT

Bar charts are widely used to visualize core results of experiments in research papers or display statistics in news, media, and other reports. However, visualizations like bar charts are mostly manually designed, static presentations of data without the option of adaption to a user's needs. But so far, it is unknown whether interactivity improves the understanding of charts. In this work, we compare static with dynamic bar charts, which offer an interactive stacking option. We assess the efficiency, effectiveness, and satisfaction when answering questions regarding the content of a bar chart. An eye-tracker is used to measure the efficiency. We have conducted a between group experiment with 38 participants. While one group had to solve the aggregation tasks using stackable, i. e., interactive bar charts, the other group was limited to static visualizations. Even though new interactive features require familiarization, we found that the stacking feature significantly helps completing the tasks with respect to efficiency, effectiveness, and satisfaction for bar charts of varying complexity.

Keywords

Interactive Bar Charts; Stacking; User Study; Eye-Tracking

1. INTRODUCTION

Bar charts are commonly used to visualize data in research papers or printed material. With few exceptions, they are static and convey a predefined message. However, the aggregation of multiple values is often necessary for common comparison and aggregation tasks (e. g., to sum up the costs over certain period of time or to compare two periods). In these tasks, it would be helpful to provide the users a possibility to alter the chart by mouse interaction. In our experiment, we introduce the option to interactively aggregate bars as stacks to help users in tasks that require aggregation of data. We use an eye-tracker to measure the efficiency, which is reflected in the number of saccades between areas of interests (e. g., bars and labels). In general, saccades are fast movements of the eye between two fixations. In our analysis, we are specifically interested in eye movements between areas of interests on the bar chart.

We hypothesize that solving aggregation tasks is faster, more precise, and more satisfying when using interactive bar charts than using static charts, regardless of data complexity. Thus, we assess different data complexities in our experiment to examine if interactive bar charts are always an improvement. To test our hypothesis, we have conducted a between-group experiment with 38 participants. Each participant solved the same 10 tasks in random order. We analyze the eye movements as well as the completion time to assess the efficiency. We designed the tasks in such a way that the answer to be provided by the participants is entered as numerical value. Thus, we can compute the effectiveness as the relative deviation of the entered value from the exact value. After the experiment, the participants filled a questionnaire which is used to gain insight about the user satisfaction and validate the experimental setup.

The results of our experiment support our hypothesis. All observed differences are significant, except for the effectiveness in tasks with complex charts. In the following, we briefly present the related research. Subsequently, we describe the apparatus, procedure, tasks, and participants. We present the results and interpret them, before we conclude.

2. RELATED WORK

Most similar to our research is the work by Abell et al. [1], who also investigated some interaction feature on stacked bar charts. In their work, the users could adapt which data row (i. e., bar) of the stacked bar chart is plotted on the x-axis. This allows to interactively align a user selected data row with the base line of the chart to enable easier comparison. Abell et al. conducted a small experiment with 10 participants and were able to identify improvements for three out of five task types (e. g., find min/max, compare sums,

CHIIR '17, March 7–11, 2017, Oslo, Norway.

ISBN 978-1-4503-4677-1/17/03...$15.00

DOI: http://dx.doi.org/10.1145/3020165.3022147

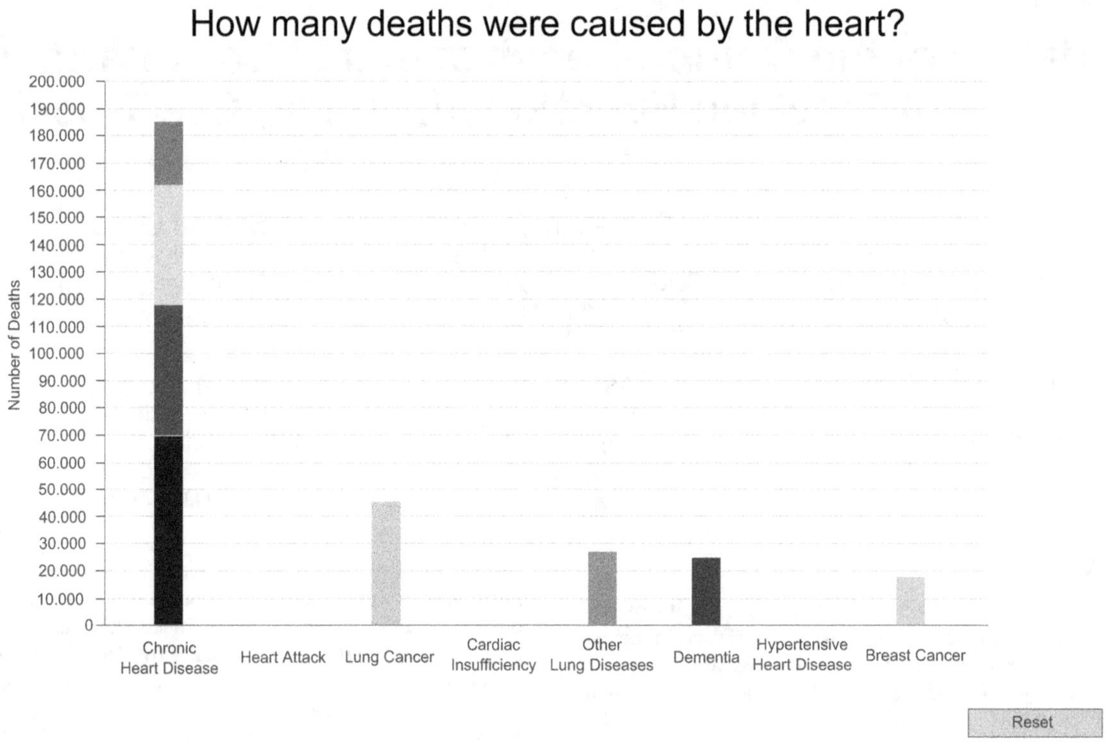

Figure 1: A chart where the bars no. 2, 4, and 7 are stacked onto bar no. 1.

identify trends) when using the interactive chart. The improvement was measured by assessing the number of correct, incorrect, and not-given answers (option "I don't know") per scenario. Furthermore, they investigated the number of interactions in the interactive case as well as the time needed by the participants until they provided the answer. However, they did not perform any significance tests on their results, perhaps due to the small size of 10 participants in their experiment, and they did not use an eye-tracker in their evaluation. Burch et al. [2] investigated the users' behavior by exploring different layouts for hierarchical structures like tree maps. They compared three types: traditional, orthogonal, and radial node-link diagrams. Eye-tracking was used to detect the visual exploration behaviors. They found out that traditional and orthogonal layouts have a significantly better performance. Kim and Lombardino [5] analyzed the influence of the complexity of bar charts on user's comprehension compared with plain text using eye-tracking data. They discovered that providing answers to complex questions using charts is significantly more efficient than text. However, when the complexity of the chart increases, this advantage becomes less apparent. Unlike our work, their experiment did not contain any interactive features.

3. EXPERIMENT

We describe the apparatus, tasks, procedure, and measures. Finally, we report descriptive statistics about our participants.

3.1 Apparatus

The experiment software ran on a notebook with Microsoft Windows 10 to which the Tobii eye-tracker was connected via USB 3.0. The eye-tracker runs with a frequency of 60 hertz. The monitor is a 24" screen with a resolution of 1920x1200 pixels. We used two identical eye-trackers in parallel, distributed among two adjacent rooms with comparable environmental conditions.

3.2 Tasks

We defined 10 aggregation tasks which consist of a bar chart and a question that the participant has to answer by looking at the chart. Each task either requires to report the sum of multiple bars or the difference between two sums of bars. We decided to use real world data and not artificially created data to avoid a potential bias induced by artificial tasks. The data/charts on which each task is based are taken from different German websites that provide statistical data (e. g., Destatis[1]). Five of the tasks (A1) present simple bar charts, while the other five tasks (A2) show complex bar charts. The simple bar charts have two dimensions and eight bars. The complex bar charts have a third dimension, which is defined by additional data rows, and 15 bars. All questions require a numerical value as answer, e. g., the number of deaths caused by a heart illness (see Figure 1).

3.3 Procedure

Before the experiment started, the procedure of the experiment was explained to the participants and they signed an informed consent form. Each participant was pseudo-randomly assigned to either the experimental group (interactive) or control group (static) to assure balanced groups. Afterwards the eye-tracker was calibrated for each partici-

[1]https://www.destatis.de/EN/Homepage.htmls

pant. Then a training task followed so that the participants of both groups could get familiar with the type of questions in the experiment and how to answer them. In addition, participants in the experimental group had time to get familiar with the interactive stacking feature.

Each task consists of three screens. First, the task is displayed. After looking at a synchronization point (red dot) at the top of the screen for two seconds the next screen is loaded. The synchronization point unifies the starting point on the bar chart screen for all participants and thus avoids the so-called center bias, observed in earlier eye-tracking experiments [7]. The second screen shows the bar chart and the participants have to analyze the chart to find the answer to the question. Participants in the experimental group are able to stack bars via drag-and-drop as depicted in Figure 1. The figure shows a user-modified bar chart where the second, fourth, and seventh bar are stacked onto the first bar. Once the answer is found, the participants must press the space bar to access the third screen, where they enter their answer. It is important to note that there are no tool-tips displaying the exact values when hovering over a bar. Thus, the participants have to estimate the value(s) by looking at the charts. After completing a training task, the main experiment started. Each participant completed the ten tasks (5×A1 and 5×A2), one at a time, in random order. Subsequently, the participants filled a questionnaire to collect feedback regarding their perception of the experiment.

3.4 Measures

We measured the effectiveness by calculating the deviation of the answers, provided by the participants, from the ground truth. Since all answers are numerical, but of different scale, we compute the deviation as standard percentage.

We computed two measures for the efficiency: First, we computed the task completion time which is the time the participant spent to solve a task. The second efficiency measure is computed using eye-tracking information, which can be more accurate because it is possible to detect when participants were distracted from the screen. Furthermore, it allows for an in depth analysis of the steps each participant took to solve a task. We decided to assess the eye-tracking information on an area-of-interest (AOI) based approach. Each bar, as well as the axes and labels of the coordinate systems and the question, had its own rectangular AOI. Thus, in the interactive setting we had to keep track of the AOIs that change their coordinates due to the stacking of the bars. The detected fixations on the AOIs where entered in a transition matrix [4] to calculate how efficient a participant was at solving a task. A participant was more efficient if he had less transitions (eye movements between AOIs) per task.

Information about the satisfaction of the participants was collected with a questionnaire based on IsoMetrics [3]. We defined three blocks of five questions. The blocks assess the satisfaction with the visualizations, the tasks, and the interactivity. The questions regarding the interactivity are only answered by participants of the interactive group. All questions are based on an ordinal 5-Point-Likert scale from strongly disagree (−−) to strongly agree (++). We encoded the scale from 1 (−−) to 5 (++) to evaluate the results. In addition, the participants provided information about their age, job, gender, corrective lenses or glasses, and some general feedback.

3.5 Participant Statistics

In total, we had 38 participants in our experiment (9 female). The participants were equally distributed over the two conditions of the between group design (i.e. interactive group and static control group). In terms of visual aids, 12 participants wore glasses and 4 had contact lenses. The average age of the participants of the control group is about 24.84 years and the average age of the participants of the experimental group is about 26.16 years. The participants were recruited in the area of Kiel University with most of them being students (33).

4. RESULTS AND DISCUSSION

Effectiveness: Table 1 shows the average percentage answer deviation (M) and standard deviation (SD) per task for both groups. The answers to the simple tasks in the experimental group deviate on average only about 1.66% from the correct value, while the answers in the control group deviate about 6.67%. Regarding the answers to the complex tasks, the answers of the experimental group differ about 34.51% from the correct value while the answers of the control group differ about 90.62%. Thus, we can see a difference between simple and complex tasks and experimental and control group.

Table 1: Average deviation of the participants' answers per task as percentages

	Interactive		Static	
Task	M	SD	M	SD
A1.1	0.79	0.77	8.50	18.63
A1.2	0.13	0.56	3.98	12.73
A1.3	0.23	0.11	3.24	8.18
A1.4	6.39	20.84	9.11	16.10
A1.5	0.74	1.86	8.53	16.53
A1	1.66	9.47	6.67	14.79
A2.1	14.47	17.31	96.05	215.10
A2.2	17.63	48.63	48.71	91.45
A2.3	61.51	116.80	63.16	96.93
A2.4	71.05	80.09	218.86	365.39
A2.5	7.89	25.07	26.32	38.62
A2	34.51	71.91	90.62	206.85

In order to evaluate the effectiveness, significance tests have been conducted. First, we checked for normal distribution using Shapiro-Wilk, which showed that the data is not normally distributed ($p<.001$). Thus, we used the non-parametric one-sided Wilcoxon Signed Rank Test to see whether there is a significant difference in answer deviation between the test and control group for A1 and A2. We choose $\alpha = .05$. The tasks using simple bar charts showed a significant difference (W=3,456, $p<.003$) and the tasks using complex bar charts differed significantly as well (W=3,722, $p<.02$). We also assessed the significance over both task complexities together and the results also differed significantly (W=14,984, $p<0.002$).

Efficiency: We calculate the efficiency based on the task duration as well as eye-tracking information. Table 2 shows the average task duration for the test and control group on A1, the tasks with simple bar charts, and A2, the tasks with complex bar charts.

Table 2: Average efficiency measure for the test and control group split up by level of complexity (A1 vs. A2) and experiment conditions (interactive vs. static)

		Task Duration		Transitions	
Subset	**n**	**M**	**SD**	**M**	**SD**
Int-A1	95	22.12	9.05	13.31	6.65
Stat-A1	95	39.68	25.52	17.20	10.07
Int-A2	95	43.63	16.43	41.76	19.06
Stat-A2	95	58.60	26.74	53.22	26.64

We can see that the average task duration for the tasks with simple bar charts in the experimental group (M=22.12, SD=9.05) is lower than the average in the control group (M=39.68, SD=25.52). For the tasks with complex bar charts, the average of the experimental group (M=44.63, SD=16.43) is also lower than the average of the control group (M=58.6, SD=26.74). We first conducted a Shapiro-Wilk test, which resulted in detecting a non-normal distribution ($p<.001$). Thus, we used a one-sided Wilcoxon Signed Rank Test to compute the significance of the difference. The results for the tasks with simple bar charts (W=2,409, $p<.001$) as well as the results for the tasks with complex bar charts (W=2,890, $p<.001$) are significant. We conclude that the experimental group is significantly more efficient than the control group based on the task duration.

The assessment of the efficiency using eye-tracking information shows similar results (see Table 2). Here, the average for the experimental group is lower than the average of the control group and for both levels of task complexity. Due to the fact that the data is again not following a normal distribution, a Wilcoxon Signed Ranks Test was used to determine the significance. The results are significant for the tasks with simple bar charts (W=3,540, $p<.005$) as well as for the tasks with complex bar charts (W=3,314, $p<.001$). Thus, we can conclude that the interactive approach is more efficient, regardless of the task complexity.

Satisfaction: Finally, we analyzed the satisfaction based on the answer given by the participants in the questionnaire at the end of the experiment. The answers differed on average only marginally between the experimental group and the control group. The only major difference was in the perception of the task clarity, where the experimental group gave an average rating of about 2.7, while the control groups' rating was on average 3.5. The expected differences with respect to task complexity and problems when solving the tasks could not be observed. However, the opportunity to interact with the bars in terms of stacking was highly rated (M=4.84) and the interaction feature was assessed as intuitive (M=3.79). Furthermore, the participants of the experimental group stated that the tasks would have been too difficult to solve without the interaction (M=3.79).

Discussion: The interactive stacking feature tends to increase the efficiency and effectiveness in task performance regardless of the task complexity. From a cognitive perspective, we assume that the stacking features facilitates cognitive processes that are more difficult and error-prone in static displays such as mental movement of bar elements to estimate the stacked height or the extraction of multiple values and subsequent computation of sums [6]. After stacking multiple bars, participants can rely on perceptual processes to determine the total height rather than depending on computations that are limited by the working memory capacity of the human mind.

Our results further confirm the findings of Kim and Lombardino (see Related Work section) that the efficiency decreases with increasing complexity. This can be observed for the static as well as the interactive condition. The results regarding effectiveness of task A2.5 suggest that the definition of our task complexity should be discussed. Complexity depends on many factors like number of dimensions, label length, or number of digits. We only considered the first for our complexity definition. However, the other two factors seem to be important for the required memory load as well. Thus, they should be investigated in future experiments. Finally, a more detailed assessment of the recorded eye-movements could provide more insights on how the improvement in effectiveness and efficiency was achieved.

5. CONCLUSION

We have reported the results of our eye-tracking experiment with 38 participants to evaluate whether the possibility to modify a bar chart improves its comprehensibility. Our results support our hypothesis that the use of the stacking feature significantly improves the efficiency and effectiveness, independent of the complexity of the bar chart. We observed that the use of the stacking feature is perceived as a benefit, although the task complexity perception did not differ from the one reported by the control group.

Acknowledgement. This research was co-financed by the EU H2020 project MOVING (http://www.moving-project.eu/) under contract no 693092. We thank all participants of our experiment for their input and time.

6. REFERENCES

[1] W. Abell, C. Churcher, and J. Lee. An evaluation of interactive stacked bar charts. *IJCAT*, 34(4):285–290, 2009.

[2] M. Burch, N. Konevtsova, J. Heinrich, M. Hoeferlin, and D. Weiskopf. Evaluation of traditional, orthogonal, and radial tree diagrams by an eye tracking study. *IEEE TVCG*, 17(12):2440–2448, 2011.

[3] G. Gediga, K. Hamborg, and I. Düntsch. The isometrics usability inventory: An operationalization of ISO 9241-10 supporting summative and formative evaluation of software systems. *Behaviour & IT*, 18(3):151–164, 1999.

[4] J. H. Goldberg and X. P. Kotval. Computer interface evaluation using eye movements: methods and constructs. In *International Journal of Industrial Ergonomics*, volume 24, pages 631–645, 1999.

[5] S. Kim and L. J. Lombardino. Comparing graphs and text: Effects of complexity and task. *Journal of Eye Movement Research*, 8(3), 2015.

[6] S. Pinker. A theory of graph comprehension. In R. O. Freedle, editor, *Artificial Intelligence and the Future of Testing*, chapter 4, pages 73–126. Lawrence Erlbaum Associates, Inc, Hillsdale, NJ, England, 1990.

[7] T. Walber, A. Scherp, and S. Staab. Benefiting from users' gaze: selection of image regions from eye tracking information for provided tags. *Multimedia Tools Appl.*, 71(1):363–390, 2014.

I Can and So I Search More: Effects of Memory Span on Search Behavior

Jacek Gwizdka
School of Information, University of Texas at Austin
1616 Guadalupe St, Austin, TX 78701, USA
chiir2017@gwizdka.com

ABSTRACT

Search effort is an important aspect of Interactive Information Retrieval (IIR). Prior findings show that higher cognitive ability searchers tend to perform more actions than lower ability searchers. In an eye-tracking lab study we investigated the effects of working memory (WM) on search effort. The findings show that higher WM searchers perform more actions and that most significant differences are in time spent on reading results pages. We also show that behavior of high and low WM searchers changes differently in the course of a search task performance.

CCS Concepts

• Information systems~Users and interactive retrieval • Human-centered computing~User studies • Human-centered computing~User models • Applied computing~Psychology

Keywords

Web Search; Eye-tracking; Mental Effort; Working Memory Span.

1. INTRODUCTION

Demands imposed on searchers by tasks and IR systems and effort expended by them influence task performance and outcomes. Understanding these effects is important for interactive information retrieval. It can help in evaluating IR systems and in analysis of searchers' behavior. The concern with the effects of effort in search is certainly not new, it can be dated back at least to Zipf's "Principle of Least Effort" [1]. More recently, search effort has been investigated, for example, in relation to effects of system and search interface [2–4], searcher performance on tasks [5], and searchers' cognitive abilities [4, 6, 7]. Effort has been theorized as affecting subjective perception of relevance in communication [8] and empirically shown to differ between judging relevant and irrelevant documents [9, 10].

Investigations of cognitive ability effects found that higher ability searchers tend to do more on their search tasks. In particular, on more complex tasks the difference in search effort between the high and low ability searchers increases [7]. At the same time task outcomes do not necessarily improve for higher ability than for lower ability searchers. There is still no good explanation of these findings. We aim to contribute to better understanding of this phenomenon. In this short paper, we report on effects of working memory capacity on search effort in multi-aspectual search tasks on health-related topics. We conducted an eye-tracking lab study and asked the following research questions:

CHIIR '17, March 07 - 11, 2017, Oslo, Norway

ACM 978-1-4503-4677-1/17/03···$15.00
DOI: http://dx.doi.org/10.1145/3020165.3022148

RQ1: Are search effort variables related to WM levels?

RQ2: Which search effort variables differ significantly for WM levels?

RQ3: How does search effort differ for higher and lower WM searchers in the course of a task?

Our contributions are to investigate differences in effort between searchers at higher and lower levels of WM and to show that their behavior changes differently in the course of a task.

2. RELATED WORK

2.1 Working Memory

Human mental capacity is constrained by a limited capacity of working memory (WM) [11, 12]. This limitation has a profound effect on human information processing and interaction with external world, including information interaction. Therefore, we elected to study effects of individual differences in WM capacity on search behavior. It is worth noting that this memory capacity should not be simple understood as number of "storage slots" [13]. Modern views describe WM as combined focus of attention [14].

2.2 Search Effort

Roots for concern with how much effort humans invest in their actions can be sought in Zipf's [1] and Herb Simon's work [15]. The former proposed that humans choose actions to incur the least effort. The latter proposed "satisficing" as a cognitive strategy applied by humans under conditions when one cannot feasibly search through all available alternatives, hence one is satisfied with a sufficient, but not necessarily optimal choice.

Not surprisingly, IR researchers have been interested in search effort for a long time. Due to imitations of space, we only briefly highlight a few past projects. [5] showed that the amount of effort was a good indicator of user success on search tasks. [2] studied searcher adaptation to poorly performing systems and found that searchers changed their search behaviors between difficult and easy topics in a way that could indicate that users are satisficing. Differences in search effort between different types systems (higher effort invested in searching library database vs. web) were found by [3]. A couple of studies showed that mental effort involved in judging document relevance is lower for irrelevant and higher for relevant documents [9, 10]. At a more general level, borrowing from economic models of human or organizational behavior, [16] argued for the gain and cost of search and associated interactions to be an essential part of theoretical underpinnings of IIR.

Of particular interest to our present focus are past investigations that included cognitive abilities in the study of search behavior. [7] showed that as task complexity increased users high on working memory continued performing more actions, while those low on WM changed their behavior and decreased the number of result documents they opened. However, no significant differences were found in task outcomes. [6] found that searchers high on perceptual speed or on visualization ability entered longer queries, clicked more on search engine result pages (SERPs), viewed more web pages than those low on these abilities.

3. METHOD

A controlled experiment was conducted in Information eXperience lab at University of Texas at Austin (N=30). Due to technical difficulties data for four participants was not recorded correctly and good data is available for 26 participants (16 females; mean participant age 24.5). Participants were pre-screened for their English native level, very good eye-sight (uncorrected 20/20), and non-expert topic familiarity. All participants reported daily Internet use and the majority also considered themselves as proficient in Web search. Each participant performed three search tasks (two assigned tasks and one self-generated) on health-related topics in counterbalanced order (six rotations), plus one training task. The assigned tasks followed a simulated work-task approach that triggers realistic information need for participants [17]. The tasks were designed to be complex and contain multiple facets (Table 1). We report here participant behavior on the two assigned tasks.

Table 1. Assigned search tasks.

Task 1–*Vitamin A: Your teenage cousin has asked your advice in regard to taking vitamin A for health improvement purposes. You have heard conflicting reports about the effects of vitamin A, and you want to explore this topic in order to help your cousin. Specifically, you want to know:* *1) What is the recommended dosage of vitamin A for underweight teenagers?* *2) What are the health benefits of taking vitamin A? Please find at least 3 benefits and 3 disadvantages of vitamin A.* *3) What are the consequences of vitamin A deficiency or excess? Please find 3 consequences of vitamin A deficiency and 3 consequences of its excess.* *4) Please find at least 3 food items that are considered as good sources of vit. A.*
Task 2–*Hypotension: Your friend has hypotension. You are curious about this issue and want to investigate more. Specifically, you want to know: 1) What are the causes of hypotension?* *2) What are the consequences of hypotension?* *3) What are the differences between hypotension and hypertension in terms of symptoms? Please find at least 3 differences in symptoms between them.* *4) What are some medical treatments for hypotension? Which solution would you recommend to your friend if he/she also has a heart condition? Why?*

Participants performed search on publicly available websites and were asked to save relevant web pages and add their typewritten notes describing relevant information they found on a page. At the end of each task they could edit all notes and save them as final notes. Search results were retrieved from Google in real-time in the background by a dedicated proxy server. Architecture of our system is described in [18]. A custom search engine result page (SERP) was used to achieve control over the display of search results and limit the number of results per page to seven to ensure that eye fixations can be accurately tracked on individual search results. Each user session typically lasted from 1.5 to 2 hours. Participants' interactions with the browser and eye gaze were recorded. Eye tracking data was collected using Tobii TX-300 eye-tracker. At the completion of a session, each participant received $25.

3.1 Measures

Measurement of WM capacity is often operationalized as measurement of memory span (MS). We used a standard memory span test from a cognitive lab textbook [19].

Table 2. MS scores overall and for short and long words with comparison to larger populations

Data source	overall mean (SD)	short words mean (SD)	long words mean (SD)
present study	5.45 (0.72)	5.54 (1.14)	4.15 (1.16)
own data from 113 participants	5.47 (0.71)	5.40 (1.15)	4.20 (0.95)
CogLab 2.0 web data from 47199 participants[a]	5.36 (1.26)	5.27 (1.21)	4.24 (1.17)

[a] http://coglab.wadsworth.com/

Due to emphasis on reading and text processing in our tasks, we used mean scores from two subscales that measure memory span for short and long words. This score is our *independent variable*. Our participants' scores are statistically no different from scores of larger populations of (mainly) college students (Table 2). We divided participants into three groups according to their memory span for words score: below 1st quartile (<4.13), in-between, and above 3rd quartile (>5.38). Minimum score was 3 and maximum 7. In our analysis we used data from the bottom and top groups and obtained a well-balanced set of 14 participants (~50% of study participants with good data), 7 in each group: we'll refer to them: H-L WM groups.

There is no common agreement on measures that should be used to comprehensively represent search effort. Researchers used counts of actions along with time spent on search [5] or just counts of selected actions [4]. The observable actions used in these approaches were typically carefully selected to represent cognitive actions. [20] argued for using transitions between search stages (including end of a task) to tap into search effort and demonstrated that the selected search transitions measure some part of effort. Others have used measures external to search interaction, for example performance on a secondary task [21, 22] or physiological signals.

We use counts of actions that we believe require a cognitive assessment (e.g., evaluate SERP, select a result for viewing) or production (e.g., enter a query) from a searcher. Some of the actions are associated with durations of a state to which they lead, we include these durations as well. An additional class of measures is derived from eye-tracking data, they include durations and counts of fixations. We further consider two types of fixations: reading (R) and scanning (S) fixations (see [23] for detail). Longer eye fixation durations generally indicate a higher mental effort [24]. Each of these measures reflects some aspect of search effort – they are our *dependent variables*.

Table 3. List of dependent variable groups

Variable Group	No. of Individual Vars.
number of queries and duration of query entry	2
number and duration of visits to all web pages (all visits)	2
number and duration of visits to SERPs (first and all visits)	4
number and duration of visits to result pages (1st and all visits)	4
number and duration of fixations on all web pages, SERPs, and result pages. For all fixations and for reading and scanning fixations separately (first and all visits)	24
mean result rank clicked on SERPs	1
number of relevant pages saved and length of notes taken	2
final notes on a task: length and coverage of task aspects	2
number of queries and duration of query entry	2
all duration variables divided by a length of a task	16

4. RESULTS

Since our focus is on effects of an individual difference, our unit of analysis is participant. Values presented in this section are averages across the two tasks.

We investigated *RQ1* by performing binary classification of dependent variables with H-L WM groups as predictor using Random Forest (RF) algorithm and obtained 5 incorrectly classified instances (accuracy 64.3%; mean ROC 0.64). We examined differences in dependent variable values between the two predicted classes. One class was characterized by consistently higher values of dependent variables, and thus by higher search effort – we call this *Class "more"*. The other class was characterized by lower search effort – we call this *Class "less"*. As can be seen in Table 4, both *high WM* and *Class "more"* tended to invest more effort in search than *low WM* and *Class "less"*.

Table 4. Selected values for H-L WM groups & classification

Variable	High WM mean (SD)	Low WM mean (SD)	Class "more"	Class "less"
# of visited web pages	30 (12)	25 (13)	32.5 (15)	22 (4.6)
total time on web pages [s]	922 (185)	823 (204)	981 (168)	726 (119)
# of visits to SERPs	14 (8.7)	11 (4.1)	16.6 (9.1)	8 (4.2)
total time on SERPs	150 (96)	120 (65)	184 (93)	65 (25)
# of visits to result pages	16 (6.4)	14.8 (9.4)	16.9 (7)	14 (6.4)
total time on result pages	771 (118)	703 (158)	826 (85)	635 (44)
total R fixation duration on all web pages [s]	**569 (122)***	**424 (101)***	616 (111)	453 (56)
total R fixation duration 1st visits to result pages [s]	**368 (89)***	**240 (80)***	325 (106)	276 (106)
count of R fixations on 1st visits to result pages	**1376(304)***	**911 (341)***	1234 (405)	1023 (393)
# of saved relevant pages	4.9 (1.7)	4.4 (1)	4.7 (1.3)	4.4 (1)
final notes coverage	0.83 (.37)	0.76 (.25)	0.94 (.09)	0.67 (.27)
final notes word length	136 (57)	131 (106)	141 (119)	124 (113)

Significant differences between H-L WM groups: Mann-Whitney test.
*** p <.05; Sig. (2-tailed).**

Due to not normal distribution and inequality of variance in our data, we used non-parametric statistics test (Mann-Whitney) to examine significant differences between H-L WM groups (*RQ2*). Significant differences are highlighted in Table 4. Table 5 lists differences in proportion of task time spent on reading web pages.

Table 5. Total reading fixation durations on visits to specified types of web pages as a proportion of task time [%]

Type of visits to pages	High WM mean (SD)	Low WM mean (SD)	M-W U	p
all web pages	59 (4)	50 (6.7)	5	**.011**
result pages	59 (7.1)	51 (8.7)	10	.073[a]
first visits to result pages	46 (11)	34 (9)	8	**.038**

Significant differences between H-L WM groups: Mann-Whitney test.
[a] Approaching significance

Task outcomes can be assessed by comparing the number of relevant pages saved and by evaluating the coverage of task topic facets in final notes. For both measures, there was no significant difference. However, examination of distribution of final notes coverage scores shows that H-WM participants tended to produce consistently better coverage than L-WM (Figure 1).

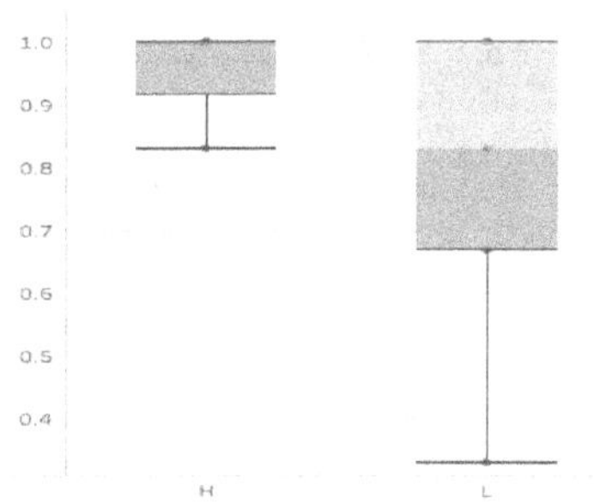

Figure 1. Coverage of topic facets in final notes (H-L WM).

To gain insights into differences in search behavior during the course of each task (*RQ3*) we divided tasks into three phases of equal duration (for each users' task session) and calculated for each of the task phases, the same measures that were presented for the whole task level (shown in Table 4 and Table 5). Figure 2. Reading fixation durations on SERPs and result pages across three task phases (1-3) for H-L WM groups. Figure 2 and Figure 3 show differences between H-WM and L-WM searchers across three task phases for selected measures. Figure 2 shows that H-WM participants spent more time reading SERPs than L-WM (recall from Table 4 that there was no sig difference in task duration between H and L-WM). Initially (first task phase), H- and L-WM users spent about the same amount of time reading result pages, however, in the last task phase (phase 3), L-WM users tended to spend less time on result pages.

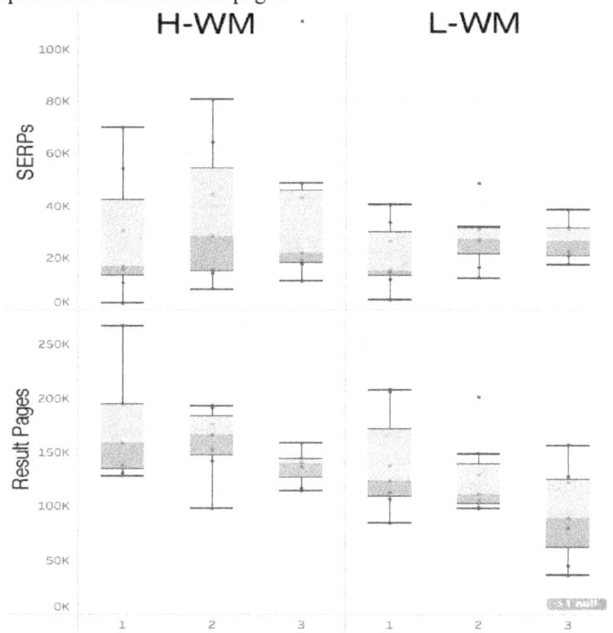

Figure 2. Reading fixation durations on SERPs and result pages across three task phases (1-3) for H-L WM groups.

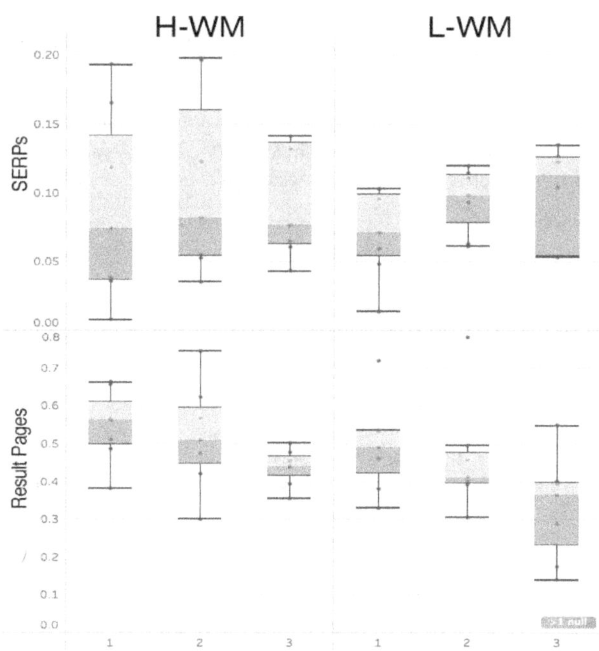

Figure 3. Reading fixation durations on SERPs and result pages as a proportion of each task phase duration for H-L WM groups

Figure 3 shows fixation durations as a proportion of time spent on a task phase. Reading SERPs takes generally less than 20% of time for H-WM, and less than 14% for L-WM searchers. For reading result pages, we first note that differences between H- and L-WM groups are statistically significant at the task level (Table 5). Searchers spent more time reading results pages than SERPs: up to 75% for H-WM and 56% for L-WM searchers (not considering outliers). Interestingly, in the third task phase, time spent reading SERPs overall seems to increase for L-WM, while time their spent reading result pages decreases. For H-WM searchers, we only observe a slight decrease in reading time spent on result pages.

5. DISCUSSION & CONCLUSIONS

Our findings show that searchers in H-WM group perform more actions on search tasks than those in L-WM group (*RQ1*). This generally confirms results form previous work [6, 7]. However, in contrast to [6], searchers low on cognitive ability (L-WM) did not spend more time on tasks; they actually spent less time than H-WM, but the difference is not significant. The differences found between between WM groups and classification groups, indicate that other factors may be needed to fully explain the amount of effort invested by individuals in search tasks. The other factors may include a collection of different cognitive abilities, but also person's interest and prior knowledge. We controlled prior knowledge to some extent by recruiting only participants who self-rated their knowledge of assigned tasks as low and by inviting only participants from a relatively uniform population of undergraduate students in our college. In follow up studies an explicit measurement of a wider range of possible factors should be undertaken.

Availability of eye-tracking data in our study sheds further light on the difference in performance – on the multi-faceted and rather complex tasks, such as those used in our study – searchers in H-WM group tended to read more. This difference is particularly apparent on result pages. Absolute reading time and time relative to the task length are statistically significantly longer for H-W than for L-WM (*RQ2*). The number of relevant pages saved and the final notes typed by participants (Table 4) do not show an advantage for H-MW searchers. However, examination of distributions of task facet coverage (Figure 1), suggests that the lack of statistical difference does not tell the whole story. The H-WM clearly performed more consistently and we could conclude, overall better.

The relative measures (Figure 3) show differences in performance between H- and L-WM groups (*RQ3*). They indicate that in the last phase of search tasks, L-WM searchers tended to read less on results pages, but at the same time they seemed to increase their reading time on SERPs. This could be a results of a satisficing strategy, similar to the one observed in the study reported in [7].

Our work aims to contribute to better understanding of differences in search effort invested by users who are high and low on cognitive abilities. This short paper presents results from an initial data analysis. Our future plans include a more comprehensive analysis and presentation of results, as well as studies in which we will measure a wider battery of cognitive abilities.

6. ACKNOWLEDGMENTS

This research was supported, in part, by IMLS Career award to Jacek Gwizdka # RE-04-11-0062-11.

7. REFERENCES

[1] Zipf, G.K. 1949. *Human behavior and the principle of least effort: an introduction to human ecology*. Addison-Wesley.

[2] Smith, C.& Kantor, P.B. 2008. User Adaptation: Good Results from Poor Systems. *Proceedings of SIGIR'2008*, 147–154.

[3] Rieh, S.Y. et al. 2012. Amount of invested mental effort (AIME) in online searching. *Information Processing & Management*. 48, 6, 1136–1150.

[4] Gwizdka, J. 2009. What a Difference a Tag Cloud Makes: Effects of Tasks and Cognitive Abilities on Search Results Interface Use. *Information Research*. 14, 4.

[5] Bailey, E. and Kelly, D. 2011. Is amount of effort a better predictor of search success than use of specific search tactics? *Proceedings of ASIST'2011*. 48, 1, 1–10.

[6] Brennan, K. et al. 2014. The Effect of Cognitive Abilities on Information Search for Tasks of Varying Levels of Complexity. *Proceedings of IIiX'2014*, 165–174.

[7] Gwizdka, J. 2013. Effects of working memory capacity on users' search effort. *Proceedings of MIDI'2013*, 11:1–11:8.

[8] Wilson, D. & Sperber, D. 2002. Relevance Theory. *Handbook of Pragmatics*. G. Ward & L. Horn, eds. Blackwell.

[9] Villa, R. and Halvey, M. 2013. Is relevance hard work?: evaluating the effort of making relevant assessments. *Proceedings SIGIR'2013*, 765–768.

[10] Gwizdka, J. 2014. Characterizing Relevance with Eye-tracking Measures. *Proceedings of IIiX'2014*, 58–67.

[11] Miller, G. 1956. The magical Number Seven, Plus or Minus Two: Some Limits on Our Capacity for Processing Information. *Psychological Review*. 63, 2, 81–97.

[12] Cowan, N. 2010. The Magical Mystery Four: How is Working Memory Capacity Limited, and Why? *Current directions in psychological science*. 19, 1, 51–57.

[13] Engle, R.W. 2002. Working Memory Capacity as Executive Attention. *Current Directions in Psych. Science*. 11, 1, 19–23.

[14] Baddeley, A. 2012. Working Memory: Theories, Models, and Controversies. *Annual Review of Psychology*. 63, 1, 1–29.

[15] Simon, H.A. 1956. Rational choice and the structure of the environment. *Psychological Review*. 63, 2, 129–138.

[16] Azzopardi, L. 2014. Modelling Interaction with Economic Models of Search. *Proceedings of SIGIR'2014*, 3–12.

[17] Borlund, P. 2003. The IIR evaluation model: A framework for evaluation of interactive information retrieval systems. *Information Research*. 8, 3, paper no. 152.

[18] Wei, X. et al. 2014. YASFIIRE: Yet Another System for IIR Evaluation. *Proceedings of IIiX' 2014*, 316–319.

[19] Francis, G. and Neath, I. 2003. *CogLab on a CD*. Wadsworth Publishing.

[20] Nordlie, R. and Pharo, N. 2013. Search transition as a measure of effort in information retrieval interaction. *Proceedings of ASIST'2013*. 50, 1, 1–7.

[21] Kim, Y.-M. and Rieh, S.Y. 2005. Dual-task performance as a measure of mental effort in searching a library system and the Web. *Proceedings of ASIST'2005*. 42, 1.

[22] Gwizdka, J. 2010. Distribution of cognitive load in Web search. *Journal of the American Society for Information Science and Technology*. 61, 11, 2167–2187.

[23] Cole, M.J. et al. 2011. Task and user effects on reading patterns in information search. *Interacting with Computers*. 23, 4, 346–362.

[24] Rayner, K. et al. 2011. *Psychology of Reading*. Psychology Press.

What Do You Mean Exactly? Analyzing Clarification Questions in CQA

Pavel Braslavski*
Ural Federal University
pbras@yandex.ru

Denis Savenkov
Emory University
dsavenk@emory.edu

Eugene Agichtein
Emory University
eugene@mathcs.emory.edu

Alina Dubatovka
Saint Petersburg University
alina.dubatovka@gmail.com

ABSTRACT

Search as a dialogue is an emerging paradigm that is fueled by the proliferation of mobile devices and technological advances, e.g., in speech recognition and natural language processing. Such an interface allows search systems to engage in a dialogue with users aimed at fulfilling their information needs. One key capability required to make such search dialogues effective is asking *clarification questions* (CLARQ) proactively, when a user's intent is not clear, which could help the system provide more useful responses. With this in mind, we explore the dialogues between the users on a community question answering (CQA) website as a rich repository of information-seeking interactions. In particular, we study the clarification questions asked by CQA users in two different domains, analyze their behavior, and the types of clarification questions asked. Our results suggest that the types of CLARQ are very diverse, while the questions themselves tend to be specific and require both domain- and general knowledge. However, focusing on popular CLARQ types and domains can be fruitful. As a first step towards automatic generation of clarification questions, we explore the problem of predicting the specific subject of a clarification question. Our findings can be useful for future improvements of intelligent dialog search and question answering systems.

1. INTRODUCTION

Proliferation of mobile devices and more "natural" interfaces [4] are changing the way people search for information on the web. Many experts envision that search in the near future will be a dialog between a user and an intelligent assistant, rather than just "ten blue links" in response to a one-shot keyword query.[1] Participants of the SWIRL'2012 workshop foresaw a fusion of traditional IR and QA [1]: "Dialogue would be initiated by the searcher and proactively by the system. The dialogue would be about questions and answers, with the aim of refining the understanding of questions and improving the quality of answers." Today we can witness this trend embodied in such products as Apple Siri, Microsoft Cortana, Google's Allo, and others.

To build a system that can be engaged in a dialog with the user and ask probing questions proactively, the most natural option is to learn from the human interaction data. Community question answering (CQA) sites, such as Yahoo!Answers[2], Quora[3], and Stack Exchange[4], allow users to post questions on various topics to other community members, vote for questions and answers, as well as gain scores for their activities. CQA platforms received a considerable deal of popularity and collected a vast amount of user-generated content.

In this paper, we make the first attempt to examine the clarification questions (CLARQ) that users ask on the Stack Exchange community question answering (CQA) platform. We analyze Stack Exchange data in two domains corresponding to about 300K questions and comments. The contributions of this study are threefold:

- To learn about user behavior associated with CLARQ and about their role in CQA communications. We find that CLARQ are quite common on Stack Exchange, and therefore represent a good source of data for analysis.
- To study the types of CLARQ users asks in different situations. We classify clarification questions into several categories according to their target as well as syntactic patterns, which help define the space of CLARQ for future research;
- To make the first step towards automatic generation of CLARQ: we build a model to predict the subject of a particular popular type of clarification questions, which shows the potential of such approach for future research.

2. RELATED WORK

Several studies paved the way towards conversational answer retrieval and explored various types of clarifications in response to user questions. Kotov and Zhai [6] introduced

*Work was performed while the author was a Fulbright visiting scholar at Emory IRLab.

[1] http://time.com/google-now/

[2] http://answers.yahoo.com

[3] https://www.quora.com/

[4] http://stackexchange.com/

CHIIR '17, March 07 - 11, 2017, Oslo, Norway

ISBN 978-1-4503-4677-1/17/03...$15.00

DOI: http://dx.doi.org/10.1145/3020165.3022149

a concept of *question-guided search*, which can be seen as a variant of query suggestion scenario: in response to initial query the user is presented with a list of natural language questions that reflect possible aspects of the information need behind the query. Tang et al. [12] proposed a method for refinement question generation based on similar questions retrieved from a question archive, a thesaurus and question templates. Sajjad et al. [10] described a framework for search over a collection of items with textual descriptions exemplified with xbox avatar assets. Initially, attribute–value pairs were extracted from crowdsourced descriptions. In online phase intermediate search results are analyzed and yes/no questions about attributes and values are generated sequentially in order to bisect the result set and finally come to the sought item. Gangadharaiah and Narayanaswamy [3] elaborated a similar approach to search results refinement through clarification questions. The authors considered customer support scenario using forum data. Noun phrases, attribute–value pairs, and action tuples are extracted from forum collection in offline phase. In online phase answers to automatically generated questions help reduce the answer candidates set. These works demonstrate successful cases of CLARQ for search tasks. Our study looks into uses of CLARQ in answer seeking dialogs between real users, which could be useful for future improvements of the systems.

Kato et al. [5] investigated clarification questions in context of an enterprise Q&A instant messaging in software domain. Analysis has shown that about one third of all dialogues have clarification requests; 8.2% of all utterances in the log are related to clarifications. The authors developed a question classifier that prompted the asker to provide clarifications in case the request was identified as underspecified. This work is closest to our study: we also analyze human Q&A behavior. However, we deal with a different type of data – CQA archives – and investigate if the resource can be potentially useful for a different application – QA.

The ability to ask clarification questions is one of the key desired components of conversational search systems [9], and can be used for multiple tasks, e.g., to resolve anaphora and coreferences [8]. In spoken dialog systems, clarification questions can be used to resolve speech recognition uncertainty, either of individual words, or of whole utterances [11].

A large body of work deals with community question answering data, data from Stack Exchange sites in particular. For example, Anderson et al. [2] showed that long-term value of a question and its answers on Stack Overflow was positively correlated with the number of comments on the answers and the time for highest-score answer to arrive. Our work complements these studies and focus on clarification comments to gather insights, useful for automatic conversational search system development.

3. DATA

We took two Stack Exchange sites – Home improvements (DIY)[5] and Arqade (GAMES)[6]. These two domains are quite different – the former is devoted to purely practical real-world problems, the latter – to the virtual world of video games. Stack Exchange users can comment on the questions and answers; sometimes it leads to multi-turn forum-like discussions (see Fig. 1). The data dumps provided by Stack Exchange[7] cover a period of 5.5 years – from July 2010 to January 2016.

We define CLARQ in a straightforward manner: sentences in comments to the initial questions ending with question mark, provided by the users different from the asker of the initial question, four words and longer. This heuristic is not perfect, as clarification requests can be formulated as declarative sentence, e.g., *Please provide details...* or question mark can be just missed. At the same time, these interrogative comments may be rhetorical questions, or not on the initial question's subject. Nevertheless, manual inspection showed that this definition of CLARQ is operational and allows extraction of CLARQ with precision acceptable for an exploratory study.

Basic statistics of the two datasets are reported in Table 1.

Figure 1: Screenshot of a DIY question page with threaded conversation in comments

	DIY	*GAMES*
# of questions	20,702	62,511
# of answers	36,580	105,167
# of accepted answers	8,381	40,049
# of comments	87,238	228,074
average question length in words	130.8	86.5
average comment length in words	33.8	25.8
# of comments on questions	37,296	96,247
# of non-asker comments on questions	27,873	72,495
# of comments on questions with '?'	11,040	21,448
CLARQ followed by asker's comments	3,679	8,021
CLARQ followed by post editing	4,270	9,038
CLARQ followed by post editing by asker	1,631	3,772

Table 1: Stack Exchange datasets statistics

4. RESULTS

4.1 User behavior

As Table 1 shows, the presence of CLARQ in CQA is substantial. Many characteristics such as questions/answers, accepted answers/all answers ratios are similar for both domains. Questions and comments in DIY are longer then in GAMES, which is expected: DIY implies richer and more diverse contexts. Askers are engaged in communication even

[5]http://diy.stackexchange.com/

[6]http://gaming.stackexchange.com/

[7]https://archive.org/details/stackexchange

after the initial question is posted: they comment on questions and edit them (however, questions are edited by community members more often). Although there are more comments on questions in DIY, GAMES seem to be somewhat more conversational: askers respond to questions on questions more often. Interestingly, thousands of initial questions are followed by clarifications, and in many cases these are followed by the original question being edited, presumably in response to the clarification request.

Unfortunately, we see that questions followed by CLARQ do not differ much from questions without any comments in length – a simple assumption that CLARQ are targeted at short underspecified questions does not hold. The hypothesis that questions asked by novice, less experienced community members (based on users' ratings) receive more CLARQ is not supported either. We also did not find any topical specificity of questions with CLARQ based on tags.

Figure 2 shows rating distribution of the GAMES users, who ask CLARQ and those who provide accepted answers (i.e., the best answerers in the community). We can observe that distribution for the former group is shifted towards higher scores (DIY exhibits a very similar distribution). However, the users who ask for clarifications provide answers for the initial questions very rarely. This observation suggests that CLARQ in CQA are a form of 'quality control measures' undertaken by most experienced users.

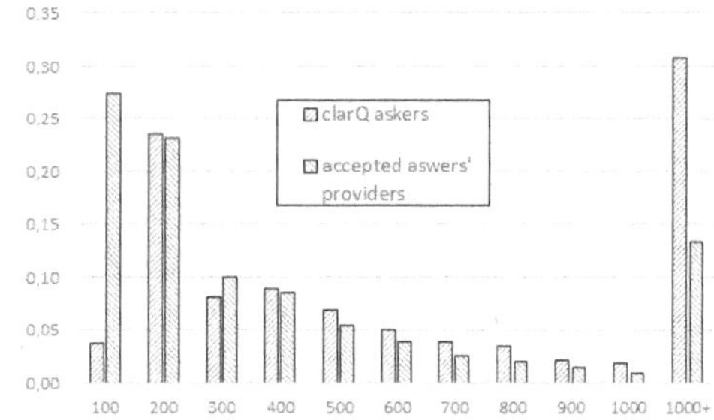

Figure 2: Distribution of users' reputation scores in the groups of accepted answers' providers and commentators on questions (GAMES)

4.2 Question types and patterns

In order to investigate CLARQ breakdown by type, we sampled 294 comments on questions from both domains, and two authors performed manual annotation analogously to [5], see results in Table 2. Comments that are not aimed at clarifying the main question contain rhetorical or humorous questions, questions to previous comments, citations of other questions on the platform, etc. Interestingly, the breakdown of CLARQ by type is roughly the same as in [5].

Further, upon examining the sample we identified a list of common three-word question starting patterns, and calculated their frequency in the whole dataset, see Table 3. As can be seen from the Table 3, some patterns are quite indicative for the clarification type (e.g., *what kind of* corresponds to *More info* category, whereas *have you tried* – to *Experience*). This observation suggests that recognition of clarification question type is a feasible task.

Category	*%*	*Example*
More Info	28.6	What OS are you using?
Check	29.3	Are you on a 64-bit system?
Reason	8.5	What is the reason you want a drip pan?
General	10.2	Can you add more details to this question?
Selection	9.9	Are you using latex or oil based Kilz?
Experience	10.2	Have you tried to update video card drivers?
Not a CLARQ	13.9	Out of curiosity what elo are you?

Table 2: Questions in comments by type. Some comments contain several clarQ of different types, so the sum is more the 100%.

4.3 Clarification subject prediction

As we have shown, there are many different kinds of questions that users ask in comments. Many of them address a certain ambiguity present in questions, e.g., *what kind of* questions inquire about a subtype of a mentioned object. These questions are quite common (Table 3) and have a simple structure, which make them a quite appealing target for automatic question generation. The first step for such question generation is to predict the object to ask about. We collected questions, which received at least one *what (kind|type) of* CLARQ in DIY. From these comments and questions we extracted noun phrases using Stanford CoreNLP parser [7], and kept only those questions that have a common pair of noun phrases in the question and comment. We formulated the task as the noun phrase ranking problem, where the noun phrase from the comment should be placed higher in the list than other noun phrases from the question. Each candidate phrase was represented with the following set of features:

- **prior**: number of times the noun phrase was used in comments (separate from the training and test sets)
- **topicality**: number of occurrences of the phrase in the current question (in title and body together)
- **position**: position of the first occurrence of the noun phrase relative to the beginning of the question
- **entropy**: collection-based statistic, computed using all noun phrases that contain the given noun phrase, which estimates the number of different modifications of the current noun phrase object
- **length**: number of words in the noun phrase

To train the ranking model we used a random forest algorithm implemented in the RankLib library[8]. We optimized DCG@10 and Table 4 summarizes the performance metrics on 10-fold cross validation. As we can see, even with a limited set of features our model was able to place the true subject of a clarification question above other candidates in 35% of the cases. To study the contributions of different feature groups we conducted a series of experiments to train the model with each group of features individually. The results in Table 4 suggest, that the number of occurrences of a phrase and the position of the first occurrence are strong features, and confirms our intuition that CLARQ are usually asked about the main topic of the question. However, some noun phrases are more ambiguous in general, therefore the prior feature also contributed significantly to the quality of the model.

Overall, our experiment showed promising results for predicting the subject for certain type of CLARQ. As a next

[8]https://sourceforge.net/p/lemur/wiki/RankLib

Pattern	DIY	GAMES	Example
have you (tried|considered)	256	1,123	Have you tried reinstalling the game yet?
do you have	592	692	Do you have enough disk space left?
do you mean	248	552	Do you mean a separate tub and shower?
are you sure	206	366	Are you sure you have timber frame construction?
what (is|are) the	558	361	What is the slope of the floor?
what do you	103	284	What do you mean by squeaking?
(are|is) there any	154	147	Are there any airflow ducts in the room already?
can you (post|provide)	204	125	can you post some pictures?
how X (is|are)	290	117	how old is the water heater?
is it a	186	112	is it a constant 18-22 fps?
what (kind|type) of	344	106	What kind of texture is on the wallpaper?
why do you	73	101	Why do you need to run it from the Flash drive?
have you checked	66	98	Have you checked the frequency of the outlets?
is it possible	78	84	Is it possible the tank is just over filling?
do you know	120	64	Do you know the manufacturer of the fixture?

Table 3: Question patterns in comments (sorted by frequency in GAMES)

Model	*P@1*	*MAP*	*RR@10*	*ERR@10*
random	0.077	0.215	0.231	0.015
+ entropy	0.143	0.334	0.350	0.024
+ length	0.148	0.337	0.345	0.024
+ position	0.165	0.335	0.357	0.024
+ prior	0.214	0.402	0.427	0.030
+ topicality	0.319	0.426	0.473	0.032
all features	0.350	0.508	0.549	0.038

Table 4: Performance metrics (P@1 – precision at 1, MAP – mean average precision, RR@10 – reciprocal rank at 10, ERR@10 – expected reciprocal rank) of the ranking model for "ambiguous" noun phrase selection problem

step, our model can be combined with an ambiguity detection classifier, which would trigger clarification as a response from a conversational search agent.

5. DISCUSSION AND FUTURE WORK

As a step towards general-purpose interactive QA system, we analyzed clarification questions asked by CQA users. In particular, we examined user interactions related to CLARQ, as well as the role and place of these questions in CQA. We analyzed a large sample of CLARQ according to their type, and identified most common syntactic patterns in a large collection of CLARQ. Finally, we conducted an experiment aimed at automatically detecting the subject of clarification question of a particular type.

Based on our analyses, we can conclude that CLARQ are common in CQA archives, and introduce a valuable resource for user behavior studies and QA research. Clarification questions asked by community members are an important component in maintaining the quality of user-generated content in CQA. Furthermore, we see that clarification questions are quite diverse in topic and style, are are highly dependent on context and individual characteristics of the users. However, there are several types of questions and syntactic patterns that are common within each domain. As a first step towards automatically generating clarification questions, we show promising results on identifying the subject of CLARQ based on a small set of shallow features. Our findings suggest that CQA data may be useful for research in the field of interactive QA.

There is still a long way to go towards automatic generation of clarification questions. This capability would require identification of user questions which are indeed ambiguous, choosing an aspect and type of clarification, and generating the text. These steps imply naturally an analysis of answer candidates, which was not addressed in the current work. A significant portion of CLARQ deals with properties, attributes, relations and types of the objects mentioned in the initial question. This suggests that domain-specific knowledge-based approach to CLARQ generation can be promising.

These two tasks – the use of candidate answers and knowledge bases – define the directions for future research in the area of clarification questions generation for interactive QA.

6. REFERENCES

[1] J. Allan, B. Croft, A. Moffat, and M. Sanderson. Frontiers, challenges, and opportunities for information retrieval. *SIGIR Forum*, 46(1):2–32, 2012.

[2] A. Anderson et al. Discovering value from community activity on focused question answering sites: a case study of stack overflow. In *KDD'2012*.

[3] R. Gangadharaiah and B. Narayanaswamy. Natural language query refinement for problem resolution from crowdsourced semi-structured data. In *IJCNLP'2013*.

[4] M. A. Hearst. 'Natural' search user interfaces. *CACM*, 54(11), 2011.

[5] M. P. Kato, R. W. White, J. Teevan, and S. T. Dumais. Clarifications and question specificity in synchronous social Q&A. In *CHI'2013 Extended Abstracts*.

[6] A. Kotov and C. Zhai. Towards natural question guided search. In *WWW'2010*.

[7] C. D. Manning et al. The Stanford CoreNLP natural language processing toolkit. In *ACL System Demonstrations'2014*.

[8] S. Quarteroni and S. Manandhar. Designing an interactive open-domain question answering system. *Natural Language Engineering*, 15(01):73–95, 2009.

[9] F. Radlinski and N. Craswell. A theoretical framework for conversational search. In *CHIIR'2017*.

[10] H. Sajjad, P. Pantel, and M. Gamon. Underspecified query refinement via natural language question generation. In *COLING'2012*.

[11] S. Stoyanchev, A. Liu, and J. Hirschberg. Modelling human clarification strategies. In *SIGDIAL'2013*.

[12] Y. Tang, F. Bu, Z. Zheng, and X. Zhu. Towards interactive qa: suggesting refinement for questions. In *SIGIR'2011 Workshop on "entertain me": Supporting Complex Search Tasks*.

Time Limits, Information Search and the Use of Search Assistance

Anita Crescenzi
amcc@email.unc.edu

Rob Capra
rcapra@email.unc.edu

Jaime Arguello
jarguell@email.unc.edu

School of Information and Library Science, University of North Carolina
Chapel Hill, NC, USA

ABSTRACT

In this paper, we analyze the impact of task time limits as described by 24 participants in an experimental study investigating the use of a search assistance tool, the Search Guide (SG), during four search tasks with varying levels of cognitive complexity. Participants were given a 12 minute task time limit and a warning notification when 3 minutes remained. In post-experiment interviews, participants reported two different impacts of the time limit on use of the SG: ten described using the SG as a way to save time given the time limit while five reported less SG use due to uncertainty whether it would contain useful information. Participants also described skimming and reading pages more shallowly, selecting easier to read search results, and bookmarking pages more freely because of the limited time they had to complete the task.

Keywords

time limit; time pressure; information search;

1. INTRODUCTION

Researchers often impose task time limits in interactive information retrieval studies as an experimental manipulation (i.e., to examine its impact on search) or for pragmatic reasons relating to the experimental design (e.g., to allow time to complete multiple tasks within an experimental session or minimize fatigue).

In recent studies, researchers have imposed different task time limits and found significant differences in search behaviors and outcomes [5, 13, 16] and searchers' post-task perceptions of their performance [6, 12, 16]. Research has also found significantly higher levels of perceived time pressure with shorter time limits [5, 6] as well as variability in reported time pressure even when participants were given the same time limit [4]. In addition, time pressure has been found to be higher as participants near the end of their allowed time [6].

CHIIR '17, March 07 - 11, 2017, Oslo, Norway

ISBN 978-1-4503-4677-1/17/03...$15.00

DOI: http://dx.doi.org/10.1145/3020165.3022150

Understanding how and why time constraints influence users' interactions with search systems provides insight into how an important contextual factor [15] impacts search processes and outcomes. There are also important implications for research design and analysis when researchers impose time limits.

Our work extends prior research by examining participants' perceptions of how and why a time limit impacts search behaviors when all participants are given the same time limit. This research was part of a broader lab-based experimental study [2] on the use of a novel search assistance feature, the Search Guide, that provides searchers with access to the search trails followed by previous searchers. In post-experiment interviews with 24 participants, we asked participants if the researcher-imposed 12 minute task time limit and three minute warning notification impacted their use of the Search Guide or their search behaviors during any of the tasks they completed.

In this short paper, we present our results of the influences of the time limit and warning notification on (1) use of the Search Guide and (2) search behaviors and strategies. We also analyze (3) the relationship between task time and perceived time pressure.

2. BACKGROUND

Research has found differences in information search behaviors and outcomes across varying task time limits including less time spent, shallower results inspection [3, 5], faster document inspection [5], and less information collected [13]. Time limits have also been found to influence the viewing of features within documents [14, 16], and the strategies used to allocate attention across a set of documents [18].

Time constraints can also impact participants' perceptions and reflections about their searches and outcomes; time constrained searchers report lower levels of confidence [3, 12] and less satisfaction with search outcomes [6, 16]. Participants with (shorter) time limits have reported higher levels of post-task difficulty and higher levels of reported stress or time pressure while searching [6, 12, 16]. Researchers have found interaction effects of time limits with search results presentation on participants' satisfaction with a selected search result [3], with task type on self-reported knowledge gain [13], and with task completion time on time pressure, task difficulty, search satisfaction, and task time and progress monitoring [6].

Researchers have noted potential effects of time constraints or time pressure as explanations for unanticipated information seeking behaviors including the selection of more convenient and less credible sources [17, 19], not verifying information found [10], and copying and pasting information rather than writing [11].

Time limits may also play a role in the use of novel interface tools or features. In previous studies of novel search assistance features [2, 7], researchers found several reasons for non-use including that participants preferred to search by themselves or they forgot the feature was there. Limited time may present a barrier to use: engaging with a new feature requires time to learn and may involve uncertainty about the benefits. For example, in a study of a search system with novel overview and filtering features, Kules & Shneiderman [9] noted, "the time available was substantial for each session, but not long enough for searchers to completely adapt their tactics" [p. 477].

In the work presented here, we focus on the ways in which participants describe the impact of time limits on their use of a novel search interface feature and their search process and outcomes.

3. METHOD

The research presented here was conducted as part of a broader study to investigate use of a novel search assistance tool called the SearchGuide (SG) [2]. The SG provides users with access to the search trails followed by previous users who searched for information on the same topic. The broader study involved 48 participants; the analysis presented here is from the 24 participants who had the SG available. Participants were all undergraduate students.

Each participant completed four search tasks of different levels of cognitive complexity. The tasks were adapted from Kelly et al. [8] and were based on Anderson and Krathwohl's Taxonomy of Learning [1]. The four task types were: (1) *remember* tasks that involved finding a fact, (2) *understand* tasks that required compiling a list of items, (3) *analyze* tasks that required compiling a list of items and understanding their differences, and (4) *evaluate* tasks that involved compiling a list of items, understanding their differences, and making a recommendation. Task complexity was rotated across participants using a Latin square.

Participants used a search system that was similar to standard web search engines (Figure 1). Participants could see the current task (A), enter queries (B), and click and view results on the search results page (SERP) (C). Web search results were returned using the Bing Search API. A bookmarking feature was added to the web browser toolbar to allow participants to save relevant pages (D). The SG was shown to the right of the web search results (E) and displayed three search trails ("paths") taken by different users who completed the same search task. Each path included the queries that were issued by the other user and for each query, the sequence of search results that the other user clicked and bookmarked. A SG relevant to the current task was shown on every SERP (i.e., after the first query was issued). Participants were shown a brief video introducing the SG features at the start of the study, but they were not instructed to use the SG.

During an experimental session, participants completed four search tasks with pre- and post-task questionnaires and were asked to think-aloud while they conducted their searches. Participants were given up to 12 minutes to work on each task so that all components could be completed within the 1.5 hour experimental session time limit. A pop-up message

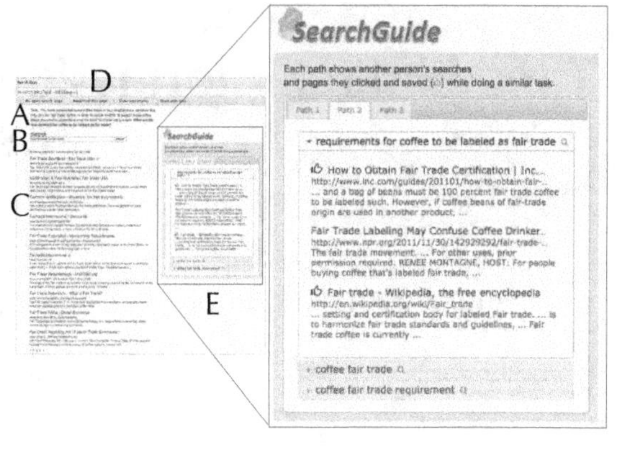

Figure 1: Search Interface and Search Guide

notified participants when three minutes were remaining.

After completing all four tasks, the moderator conducted a retrospective stimulated recall interview about each task and a semi-structured post-experiment interview in which three questions about the tasks (as a group) were asked: Do you think the 12 minute time limit influenced...

- ...how you completed any of the search tasks?
- ...the pages you bookmarked for any of the search tasks?
- ...your use of the SG in any way?[1]

If the participant saw the three minute warning message, the moderator asked similar questions about its effects.

The entire session was recorded using TechSmith Morae screen recording software. We used qualitative analysis techniques with four rounds of coding to analyze participants mentions of the impact of time limits on SG use and task process. Round 1 involved two researchers independently open coding the data and resolving codes to form a set of closed codes. In Round 2 these codes were refined, and in Round 3, two researchers independently coded half the interviews and reviewed the other researchers codes. All disagreements were discussed and resolved by both researchers. One researcher coded the direction of the impact of time limit on SG use in Round 4.

4. RESULTS

4.1 Time Limit and SG Use

We were interested in how the time limit might have influenced participants' decisions to use or not use the SG (i.e., click on it). In post-experiment interviews, a majority of participants (n=15, 63%) said the 12 minute time limit or 3 minute warning influenced their use of the SG.

Positive impact. As shown in Fig. 2, ten participants (42%) said their use of the SG was due in part to the short time limit. All ten clicked on the SG for at least one task (median=3). Participants said they used the SG more because of the time limit or because it was more efficient to use it.

> When I thought that I might not have enough time to finish, I definitely used the Search Guide a little more than I would have if I didn't feel pressured for time. *(p25)*

[1]Inadvertently, one participant was only asked about their use of the SG.

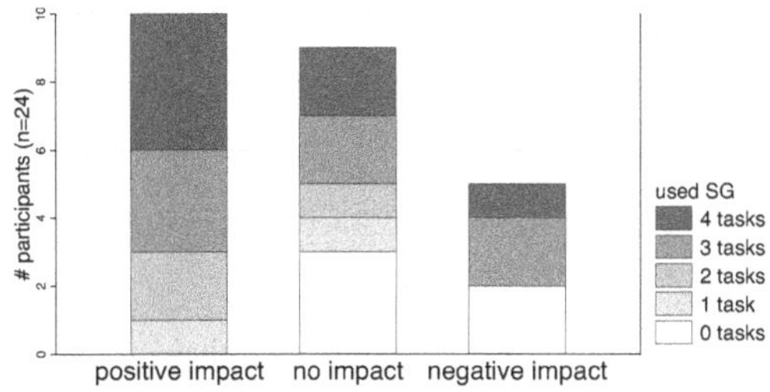

Figure 2: Described time limit impact on SG use

One participant described turning to the SG for a difficult task so that they didn't run out of time.

> When it was the easy questions, the time was like whatever. But when it came time to do like the first one with the farmer, it was like 'go to the Search Guide to find information' because if you don't then you might run out of time. *(p11)*

One participant noted that the 3 minute warning may have triggered them to use the SG to verify what they found.

> it may have...encouraged me to look at the Search Guide just to see what other people searched for as well to see if I was on the same track as they were or if they found something more interesting or more informative. *(p27)*

Negative impact. Five participants (21%) attributed their non-use or low level of use of the SG to the time limit; however, three of the five used the SG for at least three tasks. One described feeling uncertain that they would find useful information in the SG.

> I think the 12 minute made me less likely to use it because if I was rushed and I wasn't sure what I would find in the Search Guide, I might as well just search it myself. *(p13)*

Another participant mentioned that they didn't have time to verify its usefulness during the time allowed.

> Maybe this would be useful but I don't have time to verify that it would be useful in the 12 minutes. *(p19)*

Two participants said they would have used the SG more if they had more time: one who never used the SG and one who used the SG for each task.

> It was kind of a new feature...the search bar looks exactly like Google which I use all the time so I was just more comfortable with that...once I had gotten into the topic, I felt a little more comfortable using a new method-the Search Guide. *(p215)*

4.2 Time Limit and Task Process

In the post-experiment interviews, we asked participants if they thought the time limit influenced how they completed any of the tasks or the pages they bookmarked. Twenty participants (83%) said the time limit influenced how they completed their tasks including when they stopped searching, how they selected and read pages, which pages they bookmarked and changes in their strategy.

Stopping. Several participants described abandoning the task or part of the task early (n=10). Specifically, they said they would have continued working on the task if they had more time (n=6), searched more (n=3), examined more pages (n=2), or bookmarked more pages (n=4).

Selecting and reading pages. Participants described an impact of the time limit on their selection and reading of pages. Twelve participants reported skimming or reading pages shallowly, and two participants described looking for pages that were easy to skim or that would provide background information (e.g., Wikipedia).

> I didn't want to spend a lot of time reading specific details, I was looking for main points. *(p39)*

Two participants described avoiding pages with scholarly or scientific information.

> I only had 12 minutes...I didn't want to spent it trying to decipher this scholarly article. *(p17)*

One participant described deciding to avoid information that was difficult to understand due to the time limit.

Bookmarking. Ten participants described being less selective in their bookmarking as a result of the time limit such as bookmarking with "more leniancy" *(p19)* or being more "bookmark friendly" *(p39)*. One described trying to find "a larger number of lower quality pages instead of that one page that really hit the mark" *(p9)*. Another described less selectivity near the end of the task.

> I bookmarked something like the last minute because you don't have time to go back. It seems like it's alright so you'll be ok. *(p11)*

Strategy. Several participants said the 3 minute warning triggered metacognitive reflection and task strategy shifts.

> When the 3 minute timer came up, I was like what information do I have, what do I need, what can I get in 3 minutes *(p33)*

After the 3 minute warning, participants described verifying that they had nearly completed the task (n=3) and evaluating the information they had already found to determine if there were any gaps (n=5).

> I was using the 'you have 3 minutes left' as a point where like, ok, evaluate all the information gathered, and I used the time before that to gather as much information as possible *(p17)*

No impact. Four participants said that the time limit had no impact on their search process or bookmarking. Of these, three finished the task in under 9 minutes (before the 3 minute warning).

4.3 Time and Time Pressure

As part of our analysis, we looked at task completion time and self-reported time pressure to see how they varied across the 96 search tasks completed by the 24 participants.

Mean task completion time was 7.3 minutes (SD=3.4) with participant means ranging from 4.6-11.5 min. Nineteen participants (79%) received a 3 minute warning on at least one task, and ten participants (42%) received a warning on 2 or more tasks. The 3 minute warning was displayed in 38% of tasks (36 of 96) and it was displayed in significantly fewer of the least cognitively complex tasks ($\chi^2(3)=8.53$, $p<.05$): only 3 (of 24) *remember* tasks compared to 11 each (of 24) of *understand*, *analyse* and *evaluate* tasks.

Overall, participants reported low post-task time pressure (M=1.9, SD=1.2; "How much time pressure did you feel while completing this task?" 1=none, 5=a great deal). Time pressure (>1) was reported in 49 out of 96 tasks by 18 of 24 participants. Time pressure was reported more frequently for cognitively complex tasks: 8 (of 24) *remember*, 9 *analyze*, 14 *understand*, and 18 *evaluate* tasks ($\chi^2(3)$=12.10, p<.01). Six participants described the influence of task complexity (i.e., the number of task components and the clarity of the outcome needed) on time pressure in interviews.

Task completion time was moderately correlated with reported time pressure (r_s=.465, p<.001, n=95). In our interviews, several participants specifically described feeling more time pressure when it took them longer to complete the task.

> ...for the ones where I didn't get the information right away, I was like oh my gosh I'm not learning anything and my time is slowly ticking away ... So I felt pressured then when the information wasn't popping up...when it was just right there, I didn't feel any time pressure. *(p11)*

5. DISCUSSION

We have three main findings from our research. First, the task time limit influenced our participants' decisions to engage and avoid engaging with a novel search assistance feature. Second, participants reported and described adapting their search behaviors due to the task time limit. Finally, time pressure was subjectively experienced even with a consistent time limit and it was correlated with the time spent on the task. Our findings are in line with other research that has found time to be an important situational factor of information search [15].

A majority of our participants said the time limit influenced their use of the SG: ten said they used the SG more and five less or not at all. Novel interface features take cognitive effort and time to learn [9] and may involve uncertainty about the benefits. Several previous studies of novel search assistance features have reported reasons for nonuse including a preference to search on ones' own and the novelty of the interface feature [2, 7, 9]. Our work suggests that time limits may be another reason for nonuse with implications for future research: If a researcher is testing a novel interface feature, a task time limit might impact its use.

Nearly all participants described one or more adaptations to their search process to meet the task goal due to time limits: searchers described stopping their task earlier, skimming or reading pages more shallowly, selecting easier to read pages and information, less selective bookmarking, and changes in their strategy. This is line with previous work on skimming in time-constrained document triage [14] and provides some evidence for an impact of time pressure on source selection criteria as previously suggested [17, 19].

We found time spent on the task and time pressure to be correlated. The variability of reported time pressure across tasks suggests that task characteristics (e.g., cognitive complexity) influence the impact of time limits on time pressure.

Finally, researchers should directly consider the potential impact of task time limits during experimental design and analysis. Task time limits may influence not only the time the participant spends on the task but also the use of novel features, search behavior and searcher perceptions.

6. ACKNOWLEDGEMENTS

The authors thank Emily Vardell, our participants and our reviewers. This work was supported in part by NSF grant IIS-1552587. Any opinions, findings, conclusions, and recommendations expressed in this paper are those of the authors and do not necessarily reflect the views of the NSF.

7. REFERENCES

[1] L. W. Anderson and D. R. Krathwohl. *A Taxonomy for Learning, Teaching, and Assessing.* Longman, New York, 2001.

[2] R. Capra, J. Arguello, A. Crescenzi, and E. Vardell. Differences in the use of search assistance for tasks of varying complexity. In *Proc. SIGIR*, 23–32, 2015.

[3] P. Chiravirakul and S. J. Payne. Choice overload in search engine use? In *Proc. CHI*, 1285–1294, 2014.

[4] A. Crescenzi, R. Capra, and J. Arguello. Time pressure, user satisfaction and task difficulty. *Proc. ASIST*, 50(1):1–4, 2013.

[5] A. Crescenzi, D. Kelly, and L. Azzopardi. Time Pressure and System Delays in Information Search. In *Proc. SIGIR*, 767–770, 2015.

[6] A. Crescenzi, D. Kelly, and L. Azzopardi. Impacts of Time Constraints and System Delays on User Experience. In *Proc. CHIIR*, 141–150, 2016.

[7] B. J. Jansen and M. D. McNeese. Evaluating the effectiveness of and patterns of interactions with automated searching assistance. *JASIST*, 56(14):1480–1503, 2005.

[8] D. Kelly, J. Arguello, A. Edwards, and W.-C. Wu. Development and evaluation of search tasks for IIR experiments using a cognitive complexity framework. In *Proc. ICTIR*, 101–110, 2015.

[9] B. Kules and B. Shneiderman. Users can change their web search tactics: Design guidelines for categorized overviews. *Inf Process Manag*, 44(2):463–484, 2008.

[10] A. W. Lazonder. Minimalist instruction for learning to search the World Wide Web. *Educ Inf Technol*, 6(3):161–176, 2001.

[11] C. Leeder and C. Shah. Library research as collaborative information seeking. *Libr Inf Sci Res*, 38(3):202–211, 2016.

[12] C. Liu, F. Yang, Y. Zhao, Q. Jiang, and L. Zhang. What does time constraint mean to information searchers? *Proc. IIiX*, 227–230, 2014.

[13] C. Liu, L. Zhang, Q. Jiang, F. Yang, and Y. Zhao. The influence of task type on search experience from the perspective of time constraint. In *Proc. ASIST*, 2014.

[14] F. Loizides. Information seekers' visual focus during time constraint document triage. In P. Zaphiris, editor, *Theory Pract Digit Libr*, 25–31. Springer, 2012.

[15] R. Savolainen. Time as a context of information seeking. *Libr Inf Sci Res*, 28(1):110–127, 2006.

[16] A. Tombros, I. Ruthven, and J. M. Jose. How users assess web pages for information seeking. *JASIST*, 56(4):327–344, 2005.

[17] A. Walraven, S. Brand-Gruwel, and H. P. A. Boshuizen. How students evaluate information and sources when searching the World Wide Web for information. *Comput Educ*, 52(1):234–246, 2009.

[18] S. C. Wilkinson, W. Reader, and S. J. Payne. Adaptive browsing: Sensitivity to time pressure and task difficulty. *Int J Hum Comput Stud*, 70(1):14–25, 2012.

[19] Y. C. Xu, B. C. Tan, and L. Yang. Who will you ask? An empirical study of interpersonal task information seeking. *JASIST*, 57(12):1666–1677, 2006.

Investigating Information Seekers' Selection of Interpersonal and Impersonal Sources

Yiwei Wang, Shawon Sarkar, Chirag Shah
School of Communication & Information (SC&I), Rutgers University
4 Huntington St., New Brunswick, NJ 08901, USA
{yw498, ss2577}@scarletmail.rutgers.edu, chirags@rutgers.edu

ABSTRACT

Information source selection is essential to individuals' information seeking behaviors. Existing studies have focused on the criteria seekers employ when choosing information sources, such as sources' accessibility and quality, as well as the contextual factors that shape a seeker's selection. However, existing findings are somewhat conflicting and lack in-depth understanding of the reasons behind individuals' choices. The study reported here invited 53 participants from diverse backgrounds to perform simulated information seeking tasks over a two-day period and to report their experiences and findings in an online logbook. Semi-structured interviews with 23 of them were also conducted in order to examine the issues that arose from the logbooks. Our preliminary findings present several factors associated with participants' choices between impersonal and interpersonal sources. While interpersonal sources are deemed to be more suitable in capturing the context of an information query and providing personalized information, impersonal sources are found to be more accessible under a time constraint while depicting no emotion towards sensitive issues.

Keywords

Information seeking; information seeking sources; information seeking in context

1. INTRODUCTION AND LITERATURE REVIEW

Individuals utilize all types of information sources while fulfilling their information needs. Carriers of information can be impersonal (e.g., online sources, physical documents) or interpersonal (e.g., friends, colleagues) on a variety of online or offline channels. How and why information seekers select sources for information has been a research topic of continued interest. Three main streams of research that display different perspectives emerged from the literature. First, a least effort perspective suggests that seekers predominantly choose easily accessible sources [4]. The second stream is a cost-benefit perspective in which users weigh sources' perceived accessibility (cost) and quality (benefit) when making a decision [21]. There is also a quality-driven perspective that argues that source quality is the dominant factor in source selection [10].

CHIIR '17, March 07 - 11, 2017, Oslo, Norway

ACM 978-1-4503-4677-1/17/03$15.00
DOI: http://dx.doi.org/10.1145/3020165.3022151

While attempting to examine which model is accurate, researchers have discovered that these three models alone may not sufficiently explain seekers' source selection, and have thus introduced a variety of contingency variables (e.g., time pressure, subjective task value) that shape seekers' judgements of source quality and accessibility. Morrison and Vancouver [12] focused on aerospace engineers' personal behavioral changes that affected their information seeking habits. Factoring in participants' need for achievement, perceived quality and accessibility positively affect their likelihood of consulting a source. Woudstra et al. [20] investigated the characteristics of internal interpersonal sources (i.e., coworkers) that influenced financial professionals' choices of whom to ask for information. For instance, under a time constraint, people were willing to take less reliable information offered by more physically accessible sources.

The literature also revealed that people approach impersonal and interpersonal sources differently and have a preference for one over another under certain circumstances. For example, Fidel and Green [3] highlighted the different reasons that engineers chose impersonal or interpersonal sources. While engineers reported using human sources because of familiarity, their top reason for selecting documentary sources was saving time. In Lin et al.'s [7] research on how Chinese business managers evaluate information sources, participants preferred internal over external sources, and personal information sources over impersonal sources. Oeldorf-Hirsch et al. [13] observed that individuals' decisions to use impersonal or interpersonal sources have different consequences in respect to information value, satisfaction, and trust. For example, some people believe information derived from an impersonal source is more useful and trustworthy than information from an interpersonal source. Lu and Yuan [8] concluded that individuals' likelihood of choosing interpersonal sources increases as their information need increases. In short, while human sources may be more knowledgeable and more likely to provide personalized information [5], documentary sources can offer convenient and readily available information [6].

Despite the considerable efforts devoted to research on information source selection, the literature lacks sufficient and in-depth comparison between impersonal and interpersonal sources. Specifically, we have a limited understanding of how and why individuals pick and utilize these two types of sources and how they may complement or replace one another. Also, extant studies dominantly focused on heavy information users (e.g., academic users, engineers) in professional contexts. An investigation of source selection in everyday contexts can be a meaningful addition to the current body of information source literature.

In the study reported here, we collected the information seeking experiences of 53 participants from diverse backgrounds using a combination of semi-structured logbooks and semi-structured interviews. We discuss in this paper a part of our preliminary findings concerning individuals' information source selection.

Compared to many previous studies that employed a survey method to question participants' desired sources, the current study required participants to perform simulated information seeking tasks while writing down their activities, which caused them to authentically judge a number of source characteristics before or during their information seeking episodes. During these episodes, they eventually had to utilize their selected sources. Arguably, this method more accurately captured participants' source selection in real life situations.

2. METHODS

2.1 Participants

53 participants were recruited from Amazon's Mechanical Turk (hereafter MTurk) and participated in the study. MTurk is a crowdsourcing platform for people to post tasks that require human intelligence (e.g., surveys, labeling). In recent years, it has been increasingly used for research studies as it provides access to one of the largest and most diverse participant pools [12]. Only participants residing in the United States were recruited for this study. Among the 53 participants, 27 were female. Ages ranged from 19 to 65 years (mean = 35.8, SD=11). 67.9% had at least a college education. They came from a wide variety of professional or educational backgrounds such as engineering, biology, retailing, painting, and firefighting.

2.2 Tasks

We asked participants to finish four information seeking tasks related to controversial topics or everyday life problems and describe their information seeking experiences in an online logbook. Task topics were inspired by a qualitative survey we conducted on MTurk that examined individuals' information seeking failures [17]. Participant-reported tasks that were rated as *highly difficult* served as the foundation for developing the simulated tasks used in this study. We also followed Wildemuth and Freund's [18] guidelines for designing exploratory search tasks that provide specific contexts and situations while simultaneously allowing for flexible task outcomes and possibilities of multi-staged and multi-faceted information seeking. For tasks 1 and 3, participants were instructed to find at least five arguments that support each side of two controversial topics: illegalizing/legalizing abortion and cellphone is safe/unsafe for human health. For tasks 2 and 4, participants were instructed to seek information regarding two everyday life tasks: purchasing a hybrid car and apartment hunting.

2.3 Logbooks

In their logs, participants should have detailed their information seeking strategies, the difficulties they encountered (if there were any), their findings, and whether they considered each strategy to be successful. For each task, they were required to use at least three different strategies to look for their desired information. At least one strategy should have included interpersonal source(s) (i.e. interacting with people online or offline). Participants could perform their queries and fill in the logbook anytime within the two days that followed their acceptance of the tasks. The system automatically saved their partial responses so they could pause at any time and start at their previous stopping point.

Aiming to understand participants' information seeking experiences, we did not expect them to thoroughly finish each task. They were encouraged to spend up to an hour on each task regardless of how much information they found, and they were free to decide if they found enough information or wanted to give up. MTurk timed the tasks so that a participant would not have access to them after two days. Any unfinished tasks were open for subsequent available participants. Each participant was compensated $15 for finishing the logbook and given the option to sign up for a half-hour follow-up interview with the first author.

2.4 Follow-up Interviews

Semi-structured interviews were conducted to gather in-depth explanations of participants' activities and to answer questions that arose from unclear or incomplete descriptions. Data collected from the logbooks did not always completely capture the dynamic and complex nature of many situations nor sufficiently explain participants' perspectives. For example, one participant complained that a website *"was not organized enough for someone who has no knowledge on cars,"* but did not elaborate further. We were able to learn about how the website was badly organized in the interview. The interviews also provided plenty of informative details not included in logbooks such as the motivations behind certain actions (e.g., why they picked some sources over the other available ones), and thus constructed a more complete picture of participants' experiences than the logbook data alone. 23 participants completed the follow-up interviews through audio chatting via GoToMeeting and were compensated an extra $10. Both stages of the study could be finished remotely (online logbook and audio call) so participants did not have to be physically present. We determined the rate of compensation based on our previous experience with MTurk and a review of research studies that utilized MTurk (e.g., [15]).

2.5 Data Analysis

Participants submitted a total of 636 information seeking episodes. Their selection of information sources (e.g., websites, people), the channels in which they consulted these sources (e.g., face-to-face, phone), the barriers they faced, and the contextual factors that shaped their information seeking approaches were coded using three different coding schemes.

We used Agarwal's [1] classification of source/channel types to categorize the sources and channels employed by participants. This classification considered three dimensions of sources/channels—1) interpersonal-impersonal; 2) physical-electronic; 3) synchronous- asynchronous—that resulted in six types of sources/channels including face-to-face, phone, online chatting/texting, email/online forums, online information, and physical book/manual. We modified the original classification by separating phone and online chat into two categories to achieve a finer-grained distinction.

We utilized a codebook developed from a previous study [17] to categorize individuals' barriers in information seeking, and inductively drew new codes from the data. Our initial codebook consisted of the barriers collected from information seeking literature [2, 9, 14, 16]. For contextual factors that influenced seekers' activities, we modified the intervening variables in Wilson's [19] second model of information seeking behavior. Codes were collapsed into six main categories of contextual factors: characteristics of the sources, demographic variables, knowledge/experience, environmental variables, and factors related to one's social role, as well as physiological, cognitive, and emotional characteristics.

Two coders first coded 20% of the data independently and achieved satisfactory inter-coder reliabilities for all three coding schemes (Cohen's kappa > .75). After resolving the disagreement, each of them then coded half of the rest of the data.

3. RESULTS AND DISCUSSION

All types of impersonal and interpersonal sources listed in Agarwal's [1] classification were uncovered from the data, though the frequencies with which they appeared varied to a great extent. For example, the large majority of participants started with a general Google search, which helped them discover desired online sources. They also utilized search engines to locate other information sources they had in mind (e.g., *"I first googled Craigslist"*). In contrast, only one person reported visiting a physical library and locating books. It is not surprising that participants dominantly chose online sources rather than physical documentary sources. One participant stated that the time limit prevented her from going to the library, which she preferred over the Internet because *"anybody can post anything on the Internet"*. For frequencies of types of sources/channels used, see Table 1&2.

Table 1: Impersonal Sources/Channels

	Web Search Engines	Professional Websites (e.g., Kelley Blue Book)	Pre-posted Entries in Forums, Q&A sites, etc.	Others (e.g. Newspaper, TV)	Not Specified
T1	80	124	10	14	0
T2	78	110	6	0	0
T3	73	108	2	8	3
T4	49	121	1	1	1

Table 2: Interpersonal Sources/Channels

	Phone	Face to Face	Posting on Online Forums, Social Networking Sites	Others (e.g., Email, Chatting)	Not Specified
T1	7	7	11	5	8
T2	20	2	4	7	9
T3	8	3	10	12	5
T4	26	0	4	10	1

All participants utilized both impersonal and interpersonal sources as instructed except one who solely relied on the Web and employed Google to facilitate all of his information seeking episodes. In the interview, he explained that there was "*not really a time that Google can't satisfy me,*" so he did not feel a need to consult human sources. People generally used more impersonal sources than interpersonal sources, probably due to their easy and immediate access to most online sources. The large majority of participants used only one interpersonal source for each task and some went to the same person for multiple tasks.

Our preliminary analysis reveals some intriguing comparisons between impersonal and interpersonal sources. First of all, impersonal sources can be more accessible than interpersonal sources under a time constraint. Impersonal sources, particularly online sources, were mostly accessible instantly and thus demanded less effort than acquiring interpersonal sources, with the exception of some scientific or peer-reviewed research articles that had restricted access. Interpersonal sources, on the contrary, were often not available 24/7, if they were available at all. Professional sources (e.g., realtors, salespeople) were only available during business hours. One major barrier reported by participants was unavailable or unresponsive sources (e.g., "*the LiveHelp Online Chat was offline*"). Although communication and information technology has made interpersonal communication easier than ever and we did not set restrictions on participants' channels of communication (e.g., phone, chatting, posting online), it could still take them quite some time to hear back from other people (e.g., "*I sent an email but it was after hours on Sunday so they didn't reply back to me*").

In some situations, participants were willing to compromise source quality in favor of other considerations such as time and convenience. For example, some participants solicited opinions from parents or spouses knowing these sources were not knowledgeable on given topics, but rather were readily accessible within a given time constraint. (e.g., "*I really didn't learn anything from my wife. Honestly, I didn't expect her to know anything about this topic*"). A few participants who posted in online forums or Facebook groups did receive a decent amount of responses or *"enough to answer the question"*. However, few participants tried this strategy, partly because they assumed that posting online and waiting for responses could be time consuming.

Prompt access to information was extremely important and desired in this study because of the two-day time constraint that ensured participants were unwilling to wait. Also, although participants were not required (or encouraged) to finish all tasks in one sitting, one participant specifically mentioned that he preferred to enter everything into the logbook at once to prevent potential data loss. Therefore, leaving the logbook unfinished while waiting for a response from an interpersonal source was not ideal for some participants. Moreover, they sometimes did not start the tasks right after accepting them, which left even less time for them to finish. Some participants considered waiting to be the hardest part, and reported that the tasks would have been a lot easier if they did not involve interpersonal interaction. Strict time constraints (e.g., work deadlines) can also occur frequently in real life situations. This finding indicates that, under strict time constraints, individuals may prefer impersonal online sources. It mirrors previous studies in which people selected documentary sources to save time (e.g., [3]).

Additionally, locating interpersonal sources is related to an individual's social network. While some participants had trouble finding trusted sources such as friends or acquaintances, some participants were able to consult multiple people on a single topic. For instance, one participant ran ten short interviews (10-15 minutes) with her co-workers during break time at work, which was rare in this study. In contrast, a few participants found it difficult to have a person to talk to: "*The hardest part was trying to get someone to actively talk.*" Comparatively, most documentary sources were available to everyone.

It is also notable that questioning interpersonal sources about controversial topics could generate emotional reactions. Several participants thought the abortion topic was too sensitive to ask family and friends. One had to watch her relative, who had an abortion, cry for an hour. Participants also indicated that they were hesitant to ask about the abortion topic in online forums or social networking sites as it was an "*emotionally charged issue*" and might lead to arguments. In contrast, impersonal sources do not hold emotion towards certain topics, and thus were preferred by participants in controversial topic research.

Interestingly, while human sources can better understand a question's context, the process of explaining the context could be troublesome (e.g., "*[I] had to explain why I was asking*"). Some participants found that people in a chat room did not take the questions seriously: *"there weren't many people online and the ones that were on were too busy goofing off to answer my questions accurately.*" As a result, some participants went through a lot of pain to explain why they needed answers. This finding points out a potential difficulty in real life information seeking involving human sources. Compared to impersonal sources that always provide information regardless of a question's context, interpersonal sources were impeded by their curiosity (e.g., why do you need this information?). While the context is generally believed to be an asset for the delivery of personalized information, it could be undesirable under certain circumstances when individuals need quick answers or prefer to keep it hidden.

Although one type of source was more suitable than the other for some topics or under some circumstances, interpersonal and impersonal sources often complemented one another as well. In some cases, participants turned to interpersonal sources first and thought that the responses were biased towards one side of a controversial topic or incomplete regarding an everyday life problem. They conducted further searches via search engines to cross-reference and verify their initial findings (e.g., "*from taking their opinion, now I can go and verify online.*").

4. CONCLUSION

In this paper, we presented a part of our preliminary results for an information seeking study in which 53 participants spent two days completing four simulated tasks and reported their experiences in an online logbook. Our discussion here concentrates on the comparison between impersonal and interpersonal information sources, particularly how and why individuals choose one type over the other and which source was more suitable in which conditions. Our analysis revealed several interesting factors behind individuals' source selection. First, impersonal sources were more readily available compared to interpersonal sources under a time restriction, and were less influenced by a person's social network. Second, although interpersonal sources possessed a better understanding of the context of a seeker's question, this knowledge might be unnecessary, and could be a barrier to information seeking. We also unexpectedly discovered the emotional issues related to interpersonal sources, as controversial topics could be sensitive or cause unwanted arguments.

These initial findings inspire us to continue our data analysis and offer us an opportunity to seek feedback with this paper. Our next steps will include a more comprehensive analysis of participants' source selection by looking at how they evaluate information sources and the influence of other contextual factors. We also plan to interpret and evaluate their information seeking strategies and look for the connections between tactics and information seeking outcomes. As we move forward on data analysis, we wish to suggest practical implications for assisting in individuals' task-based information seeking.

5. ACKNOWLEDGEMENT

The work reported in this paper is supported by the US Institute of Museum and Library Services (IMLS) grant #LG-81-16-0025.

6. REFERENCES

[1] Agarwal, N.K. 2011. Information source and its relationship with the context of information seeking behavior. In *Proc. of the iConference'11* (Seattle, USA, February 08 – 11, 2011). ACM, New York, NY, 48-55.

[2] Chowdhury, S., Gibb, F., and Landoni, M. 2011. Uncertainty in information seeking and retrieval: A study in an academic environment. *Inform. Process. Manag.* 47, 2 (March 2011), 157-175.

[3] Fidel, R., and Green, M. 2004. The many faces of accessibility: Engineers' perception of information sources. *Inform. Process. Manag.* 40, 3 (May 2004), 563-581.

[4] Hardy, A.P. 1982. The selection of channels when seeking information: Cost/benefit vs least-effort. *Inform. Process. Manag.* 18, 6 (1982), 289-293.

[5] Hertzum, M. 2014. Expertise seeking: A review. *Inform. Process. Manag.* 50, 5 (September 2014), 775-795.

[6] Hirsh, S., and Dinkelacker, J. 2004. Seeking information in order to produce information: An empirical study at Hewlett Packard labs. *JASIST.* 55, 9 (July 2004), 807-817.

[7] Lin, Y., Cole, C., and Dalkir, K. 2014. The relationship between perceived value and information source use during KM strategic decision-making: A study of 17 Chinese business managers. *Inform. Process. Manag.* 50, 1 (January 2014), 156-174.

[8] Lu, L., and Yuan, Y.C. 2011. Shall I Google it or ask the competent villain down the hall? The moderating role of information need in information source selection. *JASIST.* 62, 1 (January 2011), 133-145.

[9] Mansourian, Y., and Ford, N. 2007. Search persistence and failure on the Web: A "bounded rationality" and "satisficing" analysis. *Journal of Documentation.* 63, 5, 680-701.

[10] Marton, C., and Choo, C.W. 2002. A question of quality: The effect of source quality on information seeking by women in it professions. In *Proc. of ASIST* (November 2002), 39, 1, 140-151.

[11] Mason, W., and Suri, S. 2012. Conducting behavioral research on Amazon's Mechanical Turk. *Behavior Research Methods.* 44, 1 (March 2012), 1–23.

[12] Morrison, E. W., and Vancouver, J. B. 2000. Within-person analysis of information seeking: The effects of perceived costs and benefits. *Journal of Management.* 26, 1 (February 2000), 119-137.

[13] Oeldorf-Hirsch, A., Hecht, B., Morris, M.R., Teevan, J., and Gergle, D. 2014. To search or to ask: The routing of information needs between traditional search engines and social networks. In *Proc. of CSCW'14* (Baltimore, MD, USA, February 15 – 19, 2014). ACM, New York, NY, 16-27.

[14] Savolainen, R. 2015. Cognitive barriers to information seeking. *J. Inform. Sci.* 41, 5 (October 2015), 613-623.

[15] Shapiro, D. N., Chandler, J., and Mueller, P.A. 2013. Using Mechanical Turk to study clinical populations. *Clinical Psychological Science.* 1, 2 (2013), 213-220.

[16] Świgoń, M. 2011. Information limits: Definition, typology and types. *Aslib Proceedings.* 63, 4 (2011), 364-379.

[17] Wang, Y., and Shah, C. 2016. Exploring support for the unconquerable barriers in information seeking. In *Proc. of the 79th ASIS&T Annual Meeting* (Copenhagen, Denmark, October 14-18, 2016). ACM, New York, NY.

[18] Wildemuth, B.M., and Freund, L. 2012. Assigning search tasks designed to elicit exploratory search behaviors. In *Proc. of the Symposium on Human-Computer Interaction and Information Retrieval* (Cambridge, MA, USA, October 4 - 5, 2012). ACM, New York, NY.

[19] Wilson, T.D. 1999. Models in information behavior research. *Journal of Documentation.* 55, 3, 249-270.

[20] Woudstra, L., van den Hooff, B., and Schouten, A. 2015. The quality versus accessibility debate revisited: A contingency perspective on human information source selection. *JASIST.* 67, 9 (September 2016), 2060-2071.

[21] Zimmer, J.C., Henry, R.M., and Butler, B.S. 2007. Determinants of the use of relational and nonrelational information sources. *J. Manage. Inform. Syst.* 24, 3, 297-331.

Sketching Dynamic User-Item Interactions for Online Item Recommendation

Takuya Kitazawa
Graduate School of Information Science and Technology
The University of Tokyo, Japan
k.takuti@gmail.com

ABSTRACT

Online recommendation techniques such as incremental matrix factorization have been widely studied to capture users' preferences from real-world dynamic user-item interactions. These recommenders generally take a model-based approach which relies on stochastic gradient descent optimization, but it sometimes shows difficulties on hyperparameter optimization and scalability. In order to work around this difficulty, the author considers a completely different approach based on matrix sketching, which is more mathematically tractable and flexible than the existing techniques. More specifically, this paper proposes a new online item recommender inspired by a matrix-sketching-based streaming anomaly detection framework. We discuss its fruitful properties with particular emphasis on the similarities between item recommendation and anomaly detection. Experimental results demonstrate robustness and flexibility of the proposed framework.

Keywords

Matrix sketching; online learning; implicit feedback

1. INTRODUCTION

On the real-world applications such as online ad and e-commerce, user-item interactions (e.g. click, purchase, rate) are valuable to capture users' preferences, and recommender systems need to tackle an item ranking problem based on such users' implicit feedback. Most importantly, recent studies showed that real-world item recommenders commonly suffer from cold-start persistency, and online updating of a recommendation engine is an effective way to overcome the problem [3]. However, the state-of-the-art techniques are not always practical for the following reasons.

First, most online item recommenders take a model-based approach which can be optimized by stochastic gradient descent, and they usually face the lack of effective ways to find proper hyperparameters in an incremental fashion. To give an example of state-of-the-art incremental matrix factorization (iMF) [6] and incremental factorization machines (iFMs) [3], even if we narrowly find the optima in an initial batch training step, the best values may show poor compatibility with further unforeseen events. Hence, streaming algorithms with less, simpler hyperparameters are preferable in reality.

Moreover, scores computed by the classical item recommenders are unnatural. Since modern recommenders stress "post-processing" such as generating explanation and incorporating into a hybrid recommender, the scores have to be easily interpretable. However, binary prediction $\hat{y}$ obtained from the existing techniques can be less than 0 or greater than 1, and incremental MF and FMs compute item scores by an inelegant heuristic function $|1 - \hat{y}|$.

As the example above shows, the current state-of-the-arts are in some sense inflexible. Therefore, this paper turns to a different direction and seeks a more mathematically tractable approach to propose a robust, flexible recommender that can fully take advantage of intuitive concepts and theoretical guarantees. To the end, we apply an efficient matrix sketching technique to a stream of user-item interactions, and recommend items based on the orthogonal projection. We also discuss how item recommenders resemble anomaly detectors, because our algorithm relies on a streaming anomaly detection framework. The proposed framework is a whole new paradigm of looking at item recommendation.

2. PROBLEM DESCRIPTION

Our goal is to develop a recommender system which works efficiently and effectively in a realistic streaming environment as depicted in Fig. 1.

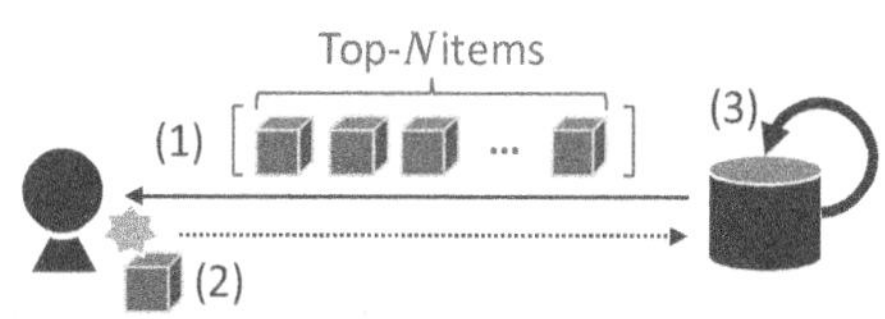

Figure 1: Online item recommender: (1) recommend a top-N list to a user, (2) interact with an item (e.g. click, buy, rate), and (3) update parameters based on the interaction.

More specifically, satisfying the following two properties is a minimum requirement for online item recommenders:

1. **Online-updating.** Algorithms have to be incremental.
2. **Implicit feedback.** Explicit rating is not considered.

In addition, this paper requires the proposed item recommender to hold the following properties:

CHIIR '17, March 07-11, 2017, Oslo, Norway

DOI: http://dx.doi.org/10.1145/3020165.3022152

3. **Feature-expressiveness.** Due to users' rare activity and dynamically changing user/item properties, modern recommenders have to use auxiliary information (e.g. time, demographics) as feature representations.
4. **Usability.** Hyperparameters and item scores should be simple; easy-to-choose integer hyperparameters and easily understandable scores are desired to improve feasibility of a recommender.
5. **Parallelizability.** Modern applications usually stand on distributed systems, so parallelizing and merging recommendation models are necessary. Furthermore, since a purely online algorithm may not be needed in reality, a recommender needs to flexibly support both of purely online and mini-batch update based on merging.

As the author showed in Sec. 1, the state-of-the-arts [1, 3, 6] are infeasible due to the lack of the above properties.

3. ONLINE ITEM RECOMMENDATION USING MATRIX SKETCHING

This section describes the proposed online item recommendation framework. Sec. 3.1 first states the key idea that anomaly detection and item recommendation can be discussed interchangeably, and Sec. 3.2 introduces a state-of-the-art online anomaly detection technique. Finally, the details of the proposal are clarified in Sec. 3.3.

3.1 Similarities between Anomaly Detection and Online Item Recommendation

This paper argues that **anomaly detectors can be seen as an online item recommender**, because both of them deal with a very similar problem. That is, anomaly detectors and item recommenders respectively find dissimilar and similar samples from captured patterns of the past events. Additionally, since both problems tackle dynamic data, their research fields share common challenges. In spite of the obvious similarity, this view has never been explicitly pointed out in the literature to the best of the author's knowledge.

It should be noted that anomaly detectors are generally categorized into *outlier* and *change-point* detectors. Both types of anomalies are strongly related to online item recommendation. In terms of outliers, finding suddenly-observed unforeseen patterns is a similar challenge to making reasonable recommendation for new users and items. At the same time, change-points can be interpreted as a trend in data streams; working around with the shifting (i.e., dynamic) patterns is a crucial challenge for online item recommenders.

Importantly, it is clear that all properties of online item recommenders described in Section 2 are also necessary for anomaly detectors as follows:

1. **Online-updating.** Since anomaly detection directly affects to system reliability, anomalies should be detected as fast as possible by using up-to-date models.
2. **Implicit feedback.** In a context of anomaly detection, a term "feedback" indicates single data point in a system, and the task is binary prediction to infer whether a data point is anomaly or not. This setting is exactly same as implicit-feedback-based recommendation which makes prediction for a unary target value.
3. **Feature-expressiveness.** Anomalies are usually detected by a combination of various factors monitored in a target system. For example, log files provide many different features such as timestamp and the number of requests.
4. **Usability.** Complex hyperparameters and confusing scores are not preferred because explanation of detectors' output is important in practice to make decision.
5. **Parallelizability.** Modern huge back-end systems are highly distributed, and data points may come from multiple data streams. Thus, the anomaly detectors should be parallelizable.

Therefore, the author connects the field of anomaly detection with online item recommendation.

3.2 Streaming Anomaly Detection using Matrix Sketching

Sketching is a technique to efficiently approximate particular properties of massive data, with strong theoretical guarantees. Recently, Liberty [4] proposed a matrix sketching technique, frequent directions (FD), and it had been proved that a huge matrix $A \in \mathbb{R}^{m \times n}$ $(m \ll n)$ can be approximated by a tiny sketched matrix $B \in \mathbb{R}^{m \times \ell}$ $(\ell < m)$ as $AA^{\mathrm{T}} \approx BB^{\mathrm{T}}$. In particular, matrix A and B satisfy the following property:

$$AA^{\mathrm{T}} - BB^{\mathrm{T}} \succeq 0 \text{ and } ||AA^{\mathrm{T}} - BB^{\mathrm{T}}|| \leq 2||A||_F^2/\ell,$$

where $\succeq 0$ indicates that a matrix is positive semidefinite. Thanks to the above property, orthonormal bases of A can be efficiently approximated by singular value decomposition (SVD) of the much smaller matrix B.

Huang and Kasiviswanathan [2] took advantage of FD's fast, iterative sketching algorithm and proposed a streaming anomaly detection framework. A key idea of their approach is to sketch a series of "normal" vectors to a tiny matrix B. By the orthogonal projection of a newly observed unit vector $\mathbf{x}$ onto the orthonormal bases U_ℓ obtained from $\mathrm{SVD}_\ell(B)$, an anomaly score can be defined as $a = ||(\mathbb{I} - U_\ell U_\ell^{\mathrm{T}})\mathbf{x}||$; larger scores indicate that the vector is far from a "normal" vector space.

Note that, they actually extended discussion about FD to randomized matrix sketching for computational efficiency, but we now focus on the original FD-based matrix sketching for simplicity. It can be easily extended to the randomized variant in the future.

3.3 Sketching User-Item Interactions

This paper proposes a novel online item recommender inspired by the matrix-sketching-based anomaly detector. In short, for a set of users U and items I, recommendation and update are done as Alg. 1 and Alg. 2, respectively. Here, m is the number of dimensions of a feature vector which represents an observed user-item interaction, and sketch size ℓ is a small integer. B is initialized by $O \in \mathbb{R}^{m \times \ell}$. Meanwhile, Fig. 2 illustrates the whole procedure.

First, Alg. 1 follows a concept of anomaly scores introduced in [2]. When we have the orthonormal bases U_ℓ derived from the past user-item interactions, the length of the orthogonal projection of a vector $\mathbf{x}'_{ui}$ onto U_ℓ (i.e. item score) represents how much the vector is similar to the past events; items which take smaller scores are more likely to be recommended.

Next, Alg. 2 updates a sketched matrix B as described in [4]. Since ℓ is a small integer, $\mathrm{SVD}_\ell(B)$ can be efficiently computed, and the procedure works well as an online algorithm. Tracking U_ℓ is also important to compute scores in the recommendation step.

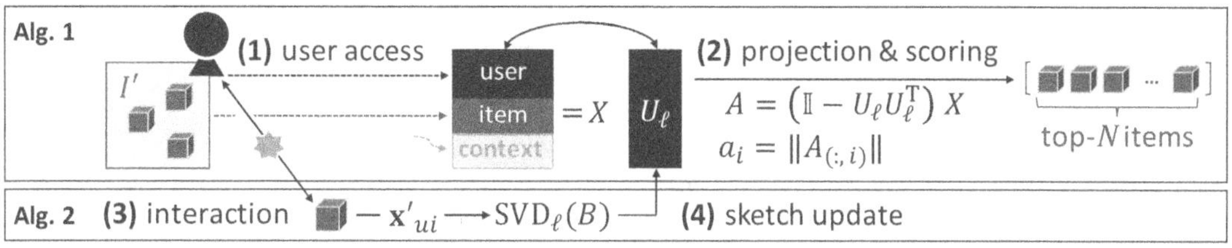

Figure 2: Overview of our new online item recommendation framework. In Alg. 1, (1) a recommender first creates a matrix X for the user-item pairs, and (2) top-N recommendation is launched based on the orthogonal projection. If (3) a user interacts with an item, Alg. 2 constructs a vector $\mathbf{x}'_{ui}$ and (4) updates the orthonormal bases U_ℓ by matrix sketching.

Algorithm 1 Recommend to a user $u \in U$ ((1) in Fig. 1)

Input: $U_\ell \in \mathbb{R}^{m \times \ell}$, Set of target items $I' \subseteq I$, Recommendation size N

Create feature vectors $\mathbf{x}_{ui} \in \mathbb{R}^m$ for every $i \in I'$
Normalize $\mathbf{x}'_{ui} \leftarrow \mathbf{x}_{ui}/\|\mathbf{x}_{ui}\|$
Create a matrix $X \leftarrow [\mathbf{x}'_{u1}, \cdots, \mathbf{x}'_{ui}, \cdots, \mathbf{x}'_{u|I'|}]$
$A \leftarrow (\mathbb{I} - U_\ell U_\ell^\mathrm{T})\, X \in \mathbb{R}^{m \times |I'|}$
Compute scores $a_i \leftarrow \|A_{(:,i)}\|$ for each column of A
Sort items $i \in I'$ by a_i in an **ascending** order
return Top-N items

Algorithm 2 Update for an interaction between $u \in U$ and $i \in I$ ((3) in Fig. 1)

Input: $B \in \mathbb{R}^{m \times \ell}$

Create $\mathbf{x}_{ui} \in \mathbb{R}^m$ for an observed (u, i) interaction
Normalize $\mathbf{x}'_{ui} \leftarrow \mathbf{x}_{ui}/\|\mathbf{x}_{ui}\|$
$j \leftarrow$ index of the leftmost all-zero column in B
$B_{(:,j)} \leftarrow \mathbf{x}'_{ui}$
$[U_\ell, \Sigma_\ell, V_\ell] \leftarrow \mathrm{SVD}_\ell(B)$
$\hat{\Sigma}_\ell \leftarrow \mathrm{diag}\left(\sqrt{\sigma_1^2 - \sigma_\ell^2}, \sqrt{\sigma_2^2 - \sigma_\ell^2}, \ldots, \sqrt{\sigma_{\ell-1}^2 - \sigma_\ell^2}, 0\right)$
$B \leftarrow U_\ell \hat{\Sigma}_\ell$
return B, U_ℓ

Matrix sketching holds attractive properties [2, 4], and hence our online item recommender satisfies **usability**. Clearly, item scores are always in a [0.0, 1.0] range as shown in Alg. 1. In addition, we only have one simple hyperparameter ℓ thanks to discussions about error bounds on FD; setting a very tiny integer to ℓ is sufficient. For instance, Huang and Kasiviswanathan [2] simply used $\ell = \sqrt{m}$ as a reasonable choice.

In terms of **parallelizability**, Liberty [4] showed that, for distributed sketch matrices B_1 and B_2, they are successfully mergeable by just sketching $B' = [B_1, B_2] \in \mathbb{R}^{m \times 2\ell}$ to $B \in \mathbb{R}^{m \times \ell}$. This fact also suggests that FD works well both on purely online and mini-batch fashion; more than one vectors can be sketched at once.

It should be noticed that a user-item interaction is represented by a feature vector $\mathbf{x}_{ui}$ in our framework. The simplest representation is concatenating quantitative variables and one-hot-encoded categorical variables just like FMs [5], and pairwise feature representation as demonstrated in [1] is also available. In either case, the vectors can represent not only user (item) features but also contextual variables which describe a set of circumstances.

4. EVALUATION

4.1 Experimental Setup

We consider three types of time-stamped datasets, Click, ML100k and ML1M. Click is a synthetic dataset which contains randomly generated users' impressions for five ad variants, following to a rule-based procedure introduced in [1]. ML100k is binalized MovieLens 100k data; only 5-starred rating events were extracted like [6]. ML1M is also binalized version of the MovieLens 1M data which behaves similarly to ML100k, but larger than that. Each time-stamped dataset was separated into three parts: 20% for batch training, 10% for batch validation and 70% for incremental evaluation. Details of this evaluation procedure are explained in [3, 6].

Similarly to [3], $\mathbf{x}_{ui}$ was flexibly designed by concatenating as much as possible user, item and contextual features instead of the user-item 2-dimensional data. As a result, $m = 55$ for Click, and $m = 73$ for ML100k and ML1M. We also examine the following baselines:

- **Popularity** is a non-personalized recommender which always recommends the most popular items as a reference.
- **iMF**[1] [6] is an incremental variant of MF. This method only uses the user-item 2-dimensional data.
- **iFMs**[2] [3] are an incremental version of FMs. One-hot-encoded user/item IDs are incorporated into $\mathbf{x}_{ui}$.

4.2 Results and Discussions

The author first examined whether our framework **Sketch** outperforms state-of-the-art personalized recommenders, iMF and iFMs. We set $\ell = 1$ for Click and $\ell = \sqrt{m} = 8$ for ML100k and ML1M, and compared the results on recall@N and mean percentile rank (MPR) as shown in Table 1. On the Click data, Sketch showed the best accuracy both on recall@1 and MPR. In case of the MovieLens datasets, while recall@10 was worse than iFMs on the smaller 100k data, Sketch became much better than iFMs on the larger 1M data. This results indicate that complex hyperparameters of iFMs were rapidly unfitted as a result of online update, and Sketch demonstrated more robust results as we expected. It should be noted that, even though the accuracy of iMF was consistently poor, its running time was much faster than the feature-based recommenders. Here is a trade-off between accuracy and efficiency.

Remarkably, the popularity-based recommender was the best on the MovieLens data. Thus, using item scores as a part of personalized/non-personalized hybrid recommenders

[1] $\lambda = 0.01$, $\eta = 0.002$, $k = 40$ for ML100k and ML1M, and $\lambda = 0.01$, $\eta = 0.0003$, $k = 2$ for Click.

[2] $\lambda_0 = 2.0$, $\lambda_\mathbf{w} = 8.0$, $\lambda_{V_k} = 16.0$, $\eta = 0.004$, $k = 40$ for ML100k and ML1M, and $\lambda_0 = \lambda_\mathbf{w} = \lambda_{V_k} = 0.01$, $\eta = 0.00006$, $k = 2$ for Click

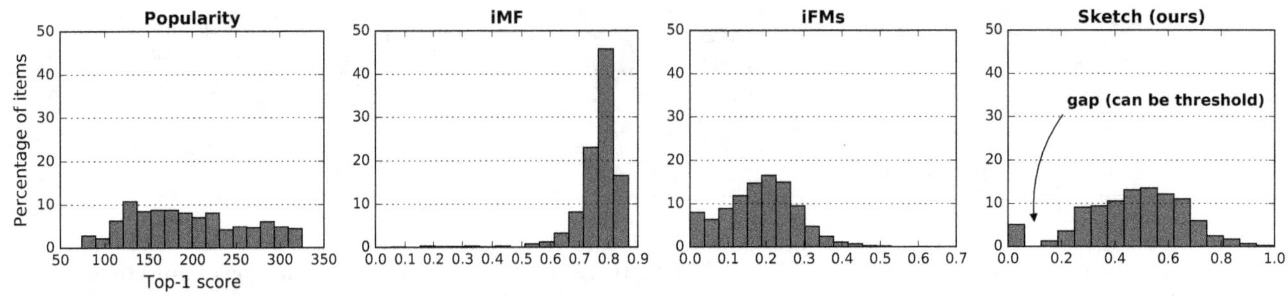

Figure 3: Distributions of top-1 item scores for each method on ML100k. Top-N largest-scored items are recommended in Popularity, and the other methods recommend top-N smallest-scored items.

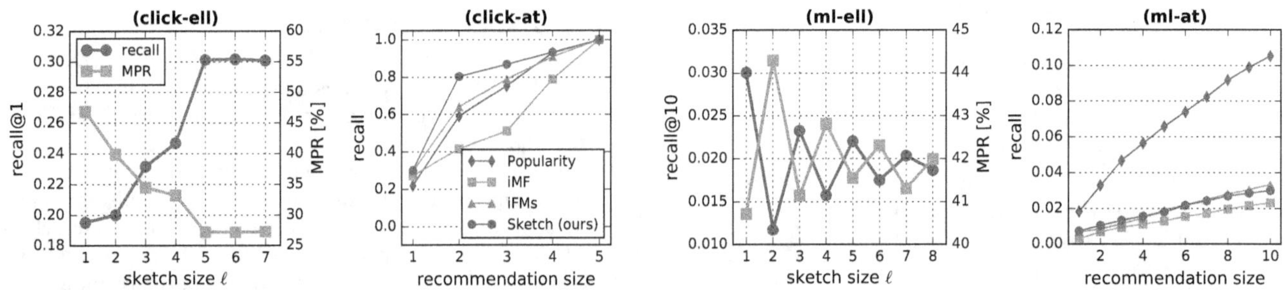

Figure 4: Relationship between accuracy and hyperparameters. Higher recall@N and lower MPR are better on the y-axis. **(click-ell)**: Different sketch size from 1 to $\sqrt{m} = 7$ on Click. **(click-at)**: Different recommendation size on Click. **(ml-ell)**: Different sketch size from 1 to $\sqrt{m} = 8$ on ML100k. **(ml-at)**: Different recommendation size on ML100k.

Table 1: Overall accuracy and running time. The best personalized recommender's accuracy is written in **bold**.

Method	recall@N	MPR [%]	Avg. time [sec.]	
			recommend	update
Click (@1)				
Popular	0.22089	37.62505	–	–
iMF	0.27251	50.27011	0.00002	0.00003
iFMs	0.29612	34.07363	0.00321	0.00026
Sketch	**0.30092**	**27.29092**	0.00190	0.00066
ML100k (@10)				
Popular	0.10538	17.10795	–	–
iMF	0.02318	40.91159	0.00017	0.00003
iFMs	**0.03349**	**27.51833**	0.02388	0.00142
Sketch	0.03005	40.72182	0.00650	0.00039
ML1M (@10)				
Popular	0.08454	12.14989	–	–
iMF	0.01249	42.18032	0.00061	0.00003
iFMs	0.01379	**27.84364**	0.30973	0.00605
Sketch	**0.02451**	37.67139	0.01626	0.00044

might be a requirement for getting more reasonable results. In that sense, we are now interested in distribution of item scores as illustrated in Fig. 3. Unlike the other methods, Sketch showed a gap between 0.0 and 0.2. We can infer that the items placed where score < 0.1 are particularly close to a space spanned by U_ℓ, and thresholding the scores leads a hybrid recommender. On the other hand, unnatural scores of iMF and iFMs are not suggestive.

Finally, by using Click and ML100k, Fig. 4 demonstrates accuracy of the various ℓ and cut-off @N to discuss limitations of the proposal. One thing we can observe is that larger ℓ does not always lead higher accuracy as shown in **(ml-ell)**. Even though attractive properties of the sketching technique help us to find promising ℓ, extra effort might be necessary to achieve the best accuracy.

5. CONCLUSION

This paper has proposed a matrix-sketching-based online item recommender. The matrix sketching technique has made the proposed framework highly usable and robust. In the future, **parallelizability** need to be evaluated in a realistic parallel environment, and scalability and efficiency should be improved from a practical point of view.

6. REFERENCES

[1] M. Aharon et al. OFF-Set: One-pass Factorization of Feature Sets for Online Recommendation in Persistent Cold Start Settings. In *Proc. of RecSys 2013*, pages 375–378, Oct. 2013.

[2] H. Huang and S. P. Kasiviswanathan. Streaming Anomaly Detection Using Randomized Matrix Sketching. *PVLDB*, 9(3):192–203, Nov. 2015.

[3] T. Kitazawa. Incremental Factorization Machines for Persistently Cold-Starting Online Item Recommendation. `arXiv:1607.02858 [cs.LG]`, July 2016.

[4] E. Liberty. Simple and Deterministic Matrix Sketching. In *Proc. of KDD 2013*, pages 581–588, Aug. 2013.

[5] S. Rendle. Factorization Machines with libFM. *ACM TIST*, 3(3), May 2012.

[6] J. Vinagre et al. Fast Incremental Matrix Factorization for Recommendation with Positive-only Feedback. In *Proc. of UMAP 2014*, pages 459–470, July 2014.

Designing Search Tasks for Archive Search

Jaspreet Singh, Avishek Anand
L3S Research Center, Leibniz Universität Hannover.
Appelstr. 9a
30167 Hanover, Germany
{singh,anand}@L3S.de

ABSTRACT

Longitudinal corpora like legal, corporate and newspaper archives are of immense value to a variety of users, and time as an important factor strongly influences their search behavior in these archives. While many systems have been developed to support users' temporal information needs, questions remain over how users utilize these advances to satisfy their needs. Analyzing their search behavior will provide us with novel insights into search strategy, guide better interface and system design and highlight new problems for further research. In this paper we propose a set of *search tasks*, with varying complexity, that IIR researchers can utilize to study user search behavior in archives. We discuss how we created and refined these tasks as the result of a pilot study using a temporal search engine. We not only propose task descriptions but also pre and post-task evaluation mechanisms that can be employed for a large-scale study (crowdsourcing). Our initial findings show the viability of such tasks for investigating search behavior in archives.

1. INTRODUCTION

Text archives can be loosely defined as a collection of timestamped documents with the level of curation depending on the context. Companies, governments, individuals, libraries and countless other organizations are continuously archiving documents for future reference and research. Such longitudinal corpora are not only important for historical research but also in retrospectively investigating scenarios in the legal and corporate world. While web search is geared towards popularity and recency, archive search is exclusively related to the past and time plays a vital role when searching.

For instance, consider a historian who wants to know why chloroform was not used during childbirth in the Victorian age. Using the British Newspaper Archive's search engine [1], she formulates her intent with the keywords `chloroform child birth 1800s`.

Ideally the system should help her uncover that chloroform was first used in 1841 during child birth by Dr.James Chester who found that chloroform did not pose any threat to mother and child. However widespread usage in hospitals was delayed due to the opposition of the church, till Queen Victoria used it in 1853 during the birth of Prince Leopold. The softening of the church's stance then came in for much critique and debate in the late 1800s.

CHIIR '17, March 07-11, 2017, Oslo, Norway

DOI: http://dx.doi.org/10.1145/3020165.3022153

Researchers in the field of Temporal Information Retrieval (TIR) have developed novel retrieval models [12, 5, 19], query suggestion algorithms [8], indexing frameworks [4] and exploratory search interfaces [18, 2, 15] to directly address such scenarios and information needs. However, little work has been done to understand how users interact with specialized search engines and interfaces for specific search tasks.

We intend to address these concerns by devising a large-scale experiment that will allow us to investigate the following questions: (i) How do people interact with a temporal search system when searching for information in a text archive? (ii) Are the new retrieval models and interface elements useful for completing a search task? We hope that our work will shed light on user search strategy and help guide the design and development of such specialized search engines. In this short paper, we tackle the first hurdle of conducting such a study: devising *search tasks* for archive search. Research in Interactive IR has led to the creation of a plethora of standardized tasks but the information needs are generic and mostly intended for web search. On the other hand our tasks are tailored to a news archive – The New York Times Newspaper Archive (1987 - 2007) [17]. We selected this particular archive over others for the following reasons: (i) easily available for a small fee (ii) clean XML storage format (iii) spans a large period of time (unlike web corpora).

We created 27 search topics related to various domains using a cognitive complexity framework. We build directly on work by Kelly et. al. [10] but differ in the nature of the tasks and corpus. Additionally the tasks are designed with scale in mind, meaning the pre and post-tests suggested are simpler to evaluate. We conducted a pilot study to confirm previous findings and refine our tasks before eventually using it for a future large-scale (crowd sourced) study. The participants were given access to a temporal search engine with two contrasting ranking methods: simple textual relevance (prevalent in commercial systems) and a diversification based approach designed specifically for archives [19]. Additionally, they had the option of visualizing the publication history of the query on a timeline, so often used in state-of-the-art temporal exploratory search systems. Figure 1 shows the user interface of the search engine.

2. BACKGROUND

One of the major challenges for TIR, as outlined in [3], is to understand how people search when their information intent is inherently temporal. Temporal information needs are either explicit (e.g. olympics 2016) or implicit (e.g. wtc bombing) [7]. Implicit temporal queries can be ambiguous – wtc bombing can refer to 9/11 or the 1993 bombings. Alternatively, [19] introduces the concept of a historical query intent where the user wants an overview of a broad

Figure 1: Search User Interface of our Temporal Search Engine. The top of the user interface consists of a retrieval model selector with two choices: (i) Textual Relevance (default option, a language model with dirichlet smoothing) (ii) HistDiv (temporal diversification based ranking [19]). The bottom of the user interface is occupied by a timeline visualizing the publication history of a query. The timeline can be opened and closed by clicking on the yellow button. It is visible by default.

topic across time, implying that temporal diversity is inherent to the intent. Several retrieval models have been suggested for these special intents [5, 12, 19] along with prototype systems that integrate them with timeline based visualizations in exploratory search interfaces [18, 2, 15]. However we do not know how user search experience and behavior is affected when using these systems.

To study this, a set of simulated search tasks is necessary. [16] describes a search task as a goal oriented activity carried out using search systems. Kelly et. al. [10] recently laid the groundwork for researchers to design their own search tasks based on Anderson and Krathwohl's taxonomy of educational objectives [11]. It consists of 6 types of cognitive processes of increasing complexity: remember, understand, apply, analyze, evaluate and create; as well as an associated target outcome. For instance, the outcome of a remember task is a fact whereas the outcome of an analyze task is a prioritized list of facts. Previous attempts to create search tasks and queries for newspaper archives [6, 14] have either relied on experts and/or logs but fail to consider varying levels of complexity.

To the best of our knowledge, no search tasks have been designed to specifically study user search behavior in archives. There exists work like [9] dedicated to applying conventional IR techniques to historical archives, however, interactive IR remains relatively unexplored. While previous work has shown that more complex search tasks lead to increased user interaction with the search engine [13], we wish to more specifically investigate how users interact with timeline visualizations and the ability to switch between retrieval models when completing these search tasks.

3. SEARCH TASK CREATION

3.1 Document Corpus

Unlike more general search behavior studies that focus on web search, we had to select an appropriate document corpus for our study. We selected the New York Times Annotated Corpus [17] which consists of 1.8 million news articles published between 1987 and 2007. The documents are stored in XML format and can be easily indexed. The documents are timestamped, explicitly categorized and also contain entity annotations.

3.2 Tasks

When creating tasks, we kept two factors in mind: (i) the tasks must be relevant for the NYT corpus (ii) the tasks must be amenable to crowd sourcing. By amenable here we mean search tasks which negate the effect of a crowd worker's prior knowledge and the outcome of which can be easily evaluated at scale. We selected 3 domains: politics, sports and science and technology. Within each domain we carefully selected topics that are relatively unpopular for a global audience. For example, in sports (basketball) we chose Allen Iverson over Michael Jordan. We also selected only 3 levels of Krathwohl and Anderson's model: remember, understand and analyze. It was more challenging to design plausible tasks for the other levels when using news archives. We created 3 topics for each domain and complexity level resulting in a total of 27 search tasks.

To motivate crowd workers and measure task performance, we intend to compensate workers for participation and based on their performance in a post-search quiz. This is different from lab based studies like [10] where participants are given fixed rewards and required to either copy-paste text from documents as evidence or write an explanation. Furthermore this requires manual judgment to grade performance whereas quizzes can be evaluated automatically. Table 1 shows an example of a search task and corresponding quiz for each complexity level. The type of quiz was selected based on target outcomes suggested in [10].

- **Remember**: A remember search task entails the search for a single fact. We created search tasks where the user has to search for the date of a particular event. The post-search quiz is a fill-in-the-blank statement.
- **Understand**: Understanding tasks are more complex since they require the user to compile a list of facts from more

Process	Target Outcome	Time	Post-Search Quiz
Remember	Fact	2 min.	Fill-in-the-blank
When was the Internet Explorer browser released by Microsoft?			Internet Explorer was released in the year ______
Understand	List (set)	10 min.	True or False
Newt Gingrich was Speaker of the House in the United States Congress in the late 90s. Although he constantly battled President Clinton at the time, he won several accolades and spurred significant reforms. However he resigned from his post after just 4 years because his party lost faith in him. Why did this happen?			Newt Gingrich officially departed the House of Representatives in 1997 Newt Gingrich is a Republican. Newt Gingrich called for the United States federal government shutdown of 1995 and 1996. Newt Gingrich was ousted after an ethics violation Newt Gingrich was charged with running a politically biased TV advertisement.
Analyze	List (prioritized), Description	15 min.	Chronological Ordering
Allen Iverson had a glittering career in the world of basketball. You are tasked with writing his biography and must chronicle his rise to stardom. Which teams did he play for both in college and the NBA? What were his major accolades in the NBA?			Iverson joins Georgetown Iverson wins MVP in the all star game and reaches the NBA playoff finals Iverson named NBA Rookie of the Year Iverson joins the Philadelphia 76ers Iverson joins the Denver Nuggets

Table 1: Examples of Search Tasks and Quizzes corresponding to Cognitive Processes and their Target Outcomes. All tasks and quizzes are available at http://bit.ly/ArchiveSearchTasks.

than one document. We created tasks that needed the user to explain a certain incident in the past. All search tasks in this category ask the user "Why did ...", followed by the incident. The post-search quiz is a set of statements that the user has to decide are true or false. In our pilot study, we include a "don't know" option as well.

- **Analyze**: Analyze tasks force the user to not only assimilate information but also order the facts learned. We created search tasks where the goal was to write a biography for a given entity, ensuing that the user has to identify, compile and summarize facts. The post-search quiz was an order the facts challenge where users have to chronologically order a set of statements.

We further set an arbitrary time limit for each task in order to make the study tractable. All tasks are made available to the public for further research. Notice that the search tasks are entity centric. We selected entities that had at least 1000 articles published about them in our corpus. We created the quizzes by consulting Wikipedia and searching the corpus. While we are aware that some of our search tasks can be solved by simply looking up Wikipedia, our intention is to simulate the kind of tasks people would carry out when working with much older or specialized archives which are difficult to obtain.

4. PILOT STUDY

We conducted a pilot study with 6 participants and a sample of 6 topics (2 from each category) to confirm if (a) the tasks are varied in complexity (b) the tasks are well defined and (c) the features and interface of the search engine are useful for these tasks.

4.1 Temporal Search Engine

Each participant had access to the same search engine and interface. The SERP is shown in Figure 1. Next to the query text field is a countdown timer informing participants of the time left. There is also a "Done" button to terminate the task early and start the post-search quiz and questionnaire. The timeline provides the user with visual cues for important time periods that she can refine her search with. The timeline is created by aggregating the top 1000 articles returned based on month of publication. We highlight important time periods using a simple burst detection algorithm. Users can interact with the timeline in 2 ways - click and drag across the timeline to filter by an arbitrary time interval or filter by directly clicking on a highlighted burst. Note that in this paper we do not wish to study the effects of the user interface but instead wish to check if the features are even used in any of the tasks. Hence we do not use variants of the search interface in the pilot study.

4.2 Study Setup

We recruited 6 graduate students from our department to complete 3 search tasks each. All participants were given the same instructions explaining the user interface and the retrieval models. Participants completed their tasks remotely and were asked to send us an email with any feedback they may have. We used the pre and post search questionnaires from [10] to measure task difficulty, engagement and interest. We also appended the following questions to the post-search questionnaire: Was the timeline useful for this task? Was the ability to switch between rankings useful for this task? Was the time provided sufficient?

To check for prior knowledge in the pre-search test, participants were asked to rate how well they know the history of the entity in question (before they are shown the search task) on a 5 point Likert scale. For future studies, participants claiming to know the entity well will be assigned a different task. Participants were asked to perform the study on desktops or laptops only. They were shown a random task from each category in random order.

4.3 Results and Discussion

All users completed a task from each category. All users also reported low prior knowledge of the entity in question and also moderate interest in the search task which are desirable traits. We also asked participants how often they searched for news on the web at the start of the study. Only 1 participant claimed to have never searched for news while the majority searched once a week. The pre-search questionnaires showed that participants found remember tasks to be the most defined, followed by understand tasks and then analyze. We found the oppposite trend for the question "How difficult do you think it will be to search for information for this task using this search engine?", with remember tasks being considered

Task	Queries	Timeline	Clicks
Remember	3	1	2
Understand	7	2	6
Analyze	13	7	11

Table 2: Search Log Statistics from the Pilot Study. Values are averaged and rounded up across all participants. Timeline refers to the average number of times users chose to filter results using the timeline. Note that we consider a search string with the selected retrieval model as a new "query"

the easiest. Interestingly all 3 types were reported to have a well defined outcome with no discernible difference in the responses.

Participants were shown the post-search questionnaire only after completing the quiz. This allowed participants to objectively measure if they had performed well and then report experienced task difficulty and complexity. We found that all participants answered the quiz for remember tasks correctly but had average performance in other task types. The first result we noticed was that even though all tasks seemed well defined, users felt that it is was hard to determine when they had gathered enough information for analyze and understand tasks. Additionally in both task types, only one participant felt the time allotted was sufficient. Participants also found it difficult to decide if a document is relevant or not. This can be directly attributed to the nature of the corpus – most news articles tend to be long and highly descriptive. They all usually report significant incidents and deciding which ones to read based on a snippet and title is harder than web search. Finally, from our logs we found that analyze tasks resulted in the highest number of interactions (clicks, queries, timeline usage), followed by understand and remember tasks (Table 2). An interesting insight here was that users tended to use both retrieval models for the same query string in quick succession.

All participants also reported being highly engaged by the task. They also agreed that the timeline was between moderate to highly useful for all task types. The ability to switch retrieval models was considered useful for understanding and analyzing tasks and unnecessary for remember tasks. The proportion of queries using HistDiv was slightly less than 50% in all cases. In their email correspondences, 3 participants felt that note taking would be a useful feature to add. Based on these results, we refined our search tasks and setup in the following way: (a) increased time limit for understanding and analyze tasks (b) indications regarding the type of post-search quiz to make it easier to decide when to stop (c) emphasizing the lead paragraph of a news article (which usually summarizes the article) when users decide to read a result.

5. CONCLUSION

To study search behavior and interfaces designed for archive search, we designed a set of search tasks based on directives from Kelly et al. [10]. The tasks are tailored to the New York Times archive which spans 20 years from 1987 to 2007. We also provide pre and post-search tests specific to each task and complexity level to make evaluation of user performance more scalable. Based on a pilot study, we found that the tasks have the desired effect of increasing difficulty and search activity. We identified weaknesses in our setup like the lack of time and hard-to-discern document relevance. The results show that the tasks and system, with minor modifications, are viable for a crowdsourcing based experiment to study user search behavior in archives.

6. ACKNOWLEDGMENTS

This work is funded by the ERC under the grant 339233 (ALEXANDRIA).

7. REFERENCES

[1] British newspaper archive http://www.britishnewspaperarchive.co.uk/.

[2] O. Alonso, K. Berberich, S. Bedathur, and G. Weikum. Neat: News exploration along time. In *Proceedings of ECIR*, 2010.

[3] O. Alonso, J. Strötgen, R. A. Baeza-Yates, and M. Gertz. Temporal information retrieval: Challenges and opportunities. *TWAW*, 2011.

[4] A. Anand, S. Bedathur, K. Berberich, and R. Schenkel. Temporal index sharding for space-time efficiency in archive search. In *Proceedings of ACM SIGIR*, 2011.

[5] K. Berberich, S. Bedathur, O. Alonso, and G. Weikum. A language modeling approach for temporal information needs. In *Proceedings of ECIR*, 2010.

[6] L. Braun, F. Wiesman, and I. Sprinkhuizen-Kuyper. Information retrieval from historical corpora. In *Proceedings of the DIR*, pages 106–112. Citeseer, 2002.

[7] R. Campos, G. Dias, A. M. Jorge, and A. Jatowt. Survey of temporal information retrieval and related applications. *ACM Comput. Surv.*, 47(2), 2014.

[8] D. Gupta and K. Berberich. Identifying time intervals of interest to queries. In *Proceedings of the 23rd ACM CIKM*, 2014.

[9] A. Järvelin, H. Keskustalo, E. Sormunen, M. Saastamoinen, and K. Kettunen. Information retrieval from historical newspaper collections in highly inflectional languages: A query expansion approach. *Journal of the Association for Information Science and Technology*, 2015.

[10] D. Kelly, J. Arguello, A. Edwards, and W. Wu. Development and evaluation of search tasks for iir experiments using a cognitive complexity framework. In *Proceedings of ACM ICTIR*, 2015.

[11] D. R. Krathwohl. A revision of bloom's taxonomy: An overview. *Theory into practice*, 41(4), 2002.

[12] X. Li and W. B. Croft. Time-based language models. In *Proceedings of ACM CIKM*, 2003.

[13] J. Liu, M. J. Cole, C. Liu, R. Bierig, J. Gwizdka, N. J. Belkin, J. Zhang, and X. Zhang. Search behaviors in different task types. In *Proceedings of the Conference on Digital libraries*. ACM, 2010.

[14] M. Maslov, A. Golovko, I. Segalovich, and P. Braslavski. Extracting news-related queries from web query log. In *Proceedings of the 15th International Conference on World Wide Web*, WWW '06, 2006.

[15] A. Mishra and K. Berberich. Exposé: Exploring past news for seminal events. In *Proceedings of WWW*. ACM, 2015.

[16] P. Peter Willett, B. Wildemuth, L. Freund, and E. G. Toms. Untangling search task complexity and difficulty in the context of interactive information retrieval studies. *Journal of Documentation*, 70(6):1118–1140, 2014.

[17] E. Sandhaus. The new york times annotated corpus. *Linguistic Data Consortium, Philadelphia*, 6(12):e26752, 2008.

[18] J. Singh, W. Nejdl, and A. Anand. Expedition: A time-aware exploratory search system designed for scholars. In *Proceedings of the ACM SIGIR*, 2016.

[19] J. Singh, W. Nejdl, and A. Anand. History by diversity: Helping historians search news archives. In *Proceedings of the ACM CHIIR*, 2016.

Identifying Useful and Important Information within Retrieved Documents

Piyush Arora Gareth J. F. Jones
ADAPT Centre, School of Computing,
Dublin City University, Dublin 9, Ireland
{parora,gfjones}@computing.dcu.ie

ABSTRACT

We describe an initial study into the identification of important and useful information units within documents retrieved by an information retrieval system in response to a user query created in response to an underlying information need. This study is part of a larger investigation of the exploitation of useful and important units from retrieved documents to generate rich document surrogates to improve user search experience. We report three user studies using a crowdsourcing platform, where participants were first asked to read an *information need* and *contents of a relevant document* and then to perform actions depending on the type of study: i) write important information units *(WIIU)*, ii) highlight important information units *(HIIU)* and iii) assess importance of already highlighted information units *(AIHIU)*. Further, we discuss a novel mechanism for measuring similarities between content annotations. We find majority agreement of about 0.489 and pairwise agreement of 0.340 among users annotation in the AIHIU study, and average cosine similarity of 0.50 and 0.57 between participant annotations and documents in the WIIU and HIIU studies respectively.

1. INTRODUCTION

Document surrogates are a primary way in which users interact with potentially interesting documents in information retrieval (IR) applications. Classically document surrogates are intended to enable users to assess the potential relevance of a document, rather than to provide important and useful information from the document itself to directly address the information need underlying the current search or more generally to improve the user's topical knowledge. The primary focus in IR has been on optimizing topical *relevance* by retrieving documents deemed *relevant* to the user's information need [5]. More recently it has been proposed that research and evaluation in IR should take a more sophisticated view of the objective of IR to include measuring features such as *utility* of retrieved information, the user's knowledge, or some combination of these parameters [1, 12]. In response to this IR researchers have begun to look beyond traditional topical relevance to evaluation metrics such as *usefulness*, *effort* and *readability* [3, 10, 16] to capture and satisfy user needs effectively but at the *document* or *IR system* level. However, in general only parts of a document will be of interest to the user. Recognising this there has been recent work to examine this topic. For example, Habernal et al. focused on finding sentence level relevant information within a document. In this work the authors specified detailed guidelines of relevance for each topic separately [4], which makes the task of sentence level annotation quite complex and laborious in general. Also of interest to this topic is previous work on XML and passage retrieval [6, 14] which looked at passages and the sentence level, but focused only on topical relevance. To the best of our knowledge no previous work has explored sentence level or other sub-document units to measure metrics such as usefulness and importance of text within a document.

We believe identifying useful and important information units at the sub-document level can be used in the generation of richer surrogate representations of documents to facilitate more meaningful user engagement with retrieved information in search [2, 15]. These useful and important information units offer alternative mechanisms to provide answers to user information needs, as in the case of question-answering systems and presenting information cards to the users [13]. As part of our investigation of this proposal, in this paper we study annotation of important and useful information within documents judged relevant to an information need. In particular we focus on consensus and agreement between users' annotations and judgments of annotated content.

CHIIR '17, March 07-11, 2017, Oslo, Norway

DOI: http://dx.doi.org/10.1145/3020165.3022154

2. EXPERIMENTAL INVESTIGATION

In this section, we introduce the design of the user studies and dataset used for our experiments.

2.1 Users study design

Participants were presented with a series of user information needs and a single relevant document for each one. Participants were recruited through the *Prolific* crowdsourcing platform[1], where each participant worked with just one of the interaction studies: WIIU, HIIU or AIHIU. Our study is composed of three types of user studies as follows:

Study-1 (WIIU): Re-writing important information units: Participants identify and re-write in their own words important and useful information units from within the document that satisfies the information need. We adopt the definition of information unit (iUnit) from the NTCIR Mobile click task [8], where information units are defined as relevant and atomic pieces of information, where *Relevant* means that a textual unit provides useful factual information to the user; *Atomic* means that a textual unit cannot be broken down into multiple units without loss of the original semantics.

[1] https://www.prolific.ac/

Study-2 (HIIU): Highlighting important information units: Following previous work on XML and Passage retrieval [6, 14], participants highlight important and useful information units from within the document that satisfies the information need.

Study-3 (AIHIU): Assessing already highlighted information units: Participants assess already highlighted information units on a scale of [1-4]. The first author of this paper manually identified and highlighted topically related textual units from the documents to be categorized by the users between 4 classes of relevance and importance: i) C1: Highly relevant and important, ii) C2: Fairly relevant and important, iii) C3: Slightly relevant and important and iv) C4: Neither relevant nor important.

Research Contribution: The main contribution of this paper is the study of three different methods of how people analyze information beyond the document level to find and assess important and useful units within a document. We find similarity values between user annotations when they highlight and write information units for a given relevant document and agreement values among users when assessing information units. We also discuss a novel technique for measuring similarities between human annotations and retrieved documents.

Our studies focus on the following specific research questions:

RQ-1: How can we compare and measure user annotations? (the WIIU and HIIU studies)

RQ-2: What is the agreement among users while assessing information units already marked in a document? (the AIHIU study)

2.2 Dataset

We used data from the TREC 2012 session track for our study [7]. We selected 3 information needs for this dataset and at random one relevant document from the *qrels* for each of the three information needs. Since this is a comprehensive and cognitively intensive task for our participants, we opted to concentrate on detailed descriptive analysis of a small number of documents for this initial study, with the main goal of analyzing important and useful richer units within a document.

Differences in the user's topic familiarity can influence their search behaviour [9], thus to ensure people are familiar with the topics, we carefully chose following three simple and generic topics from the TREC data set:

- T0: Wedding Traditions
- T1: Smoking Cessation
- T2: Junk Food

2.3 Study Procedures

Participant Training: To carry out the user studies, topics were organised and always presented in the same order as described below for user training and test data collection:

WIIU: One sample topic (T0) was used to familiarize participants with the task and the other two topics to collect test annotations [2] (T1 and T2).

HIIU: One sample topic (T0) was used to familiarize the participants with the task and the other two topics to perform annotations[2] (T1 and T2).

AIHIU: All three topics were used to perform annotations[2] (T0, T1 and T2).

Data Collection:

Annotations[2] were collected using Prolific crowdsourcing platform. Table 1 shows the demographics of the participants.

Study type	Users	Age Range	Demographics	Nationality
WIIU study	7	21-48	5 M & 2 F	4 US & 3 UK
HIHU study	7	21-35	3 M & 4 F	7 UK
AIHIU study	7	20-43	4 M & 3 F	5 UK & 2 US

Table 1: Participants Demographics Information

All participants were native English speakers. In accordance with standard crowdsourcing practice for this type of work, they were paid between 8-9 euros on a per hour basis.

After conducting a pilot run with 5 volunteers locally within our lab, we carried the user studies in two phases:

Phase-1 *WIIU and HIIU studies*: For each study we recruited seven multiple annotators as described in Table 1, to read documents and find useful and important information at textual level. Each study had 3 information needs, one information need was used for training to get familiar with the task and the other two were used to obtain the annotations as discussed in Section 2.2.

Phase-2 *AIHIU study*: In this method we asked the annotators to assess already highlighted textual units as discussed in Section 2.1.

3. EXPERIMENTS AND RESULTS

In this section we summarize the data collected and the results obtained in our three user studies.

3.1 Data Collection & Analysis

We collected following information from users:

i) Information units identified by the user (**WIIU and HIIU studies**)

ii) Assessment of highlighted information units on a scale of [1-4] with reasons (**AIHIU study**).

We carried out data analysis for the information units collected for the WIIU and HIIU studies. While writing information units in the WIIU study, participants rephrased the textual information, and in the HIIU study they freely highlighted the textual content. Thus calculating normal agreement across users is hard since the text boundaries are flexible and quite variable in nature. Hence we calculated word overlap and similarity between the information units and the document to analyze users response. This gives us a rough approximation of the consensus between participant annotations. We explore two different mechanisms to analyze information units for a given document:

a) *Quantitative approach:* We hypothesize that calculating the overlap of words, tokens and common nouns between participant annotations and documents can give a meaningful indication of agreement across participant responses. Thus for each participant we calculate overlap between the combined information units and the document in terms of number of words (W_O), tokens (U_W) and Nouns (N_N). We used NLTK toolkit [3] to perform part of speech tagging to extract Nouns from the document and information units.

b) *Qualitative approach:* We calculated the following two similarity scores between the information units and document to analyze user's annotations effectively.

1) *Cosine similarity (COS_S):* The cosine similarity between the document and the information units combined together.

2) *Word2Vec similarity (W2V_S):* We used *Word2Vec* vectors,

[2] "annotation" is used interchangeably, depending on the user study it means one of the three: find and write information units, highlight information units or assess already highlighted information units

[3] http://www.nltk.org/

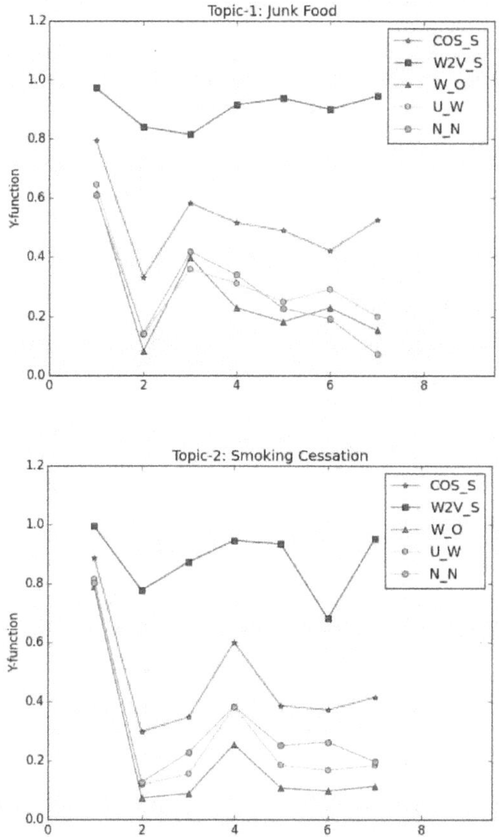

Figure 1: WIIU study

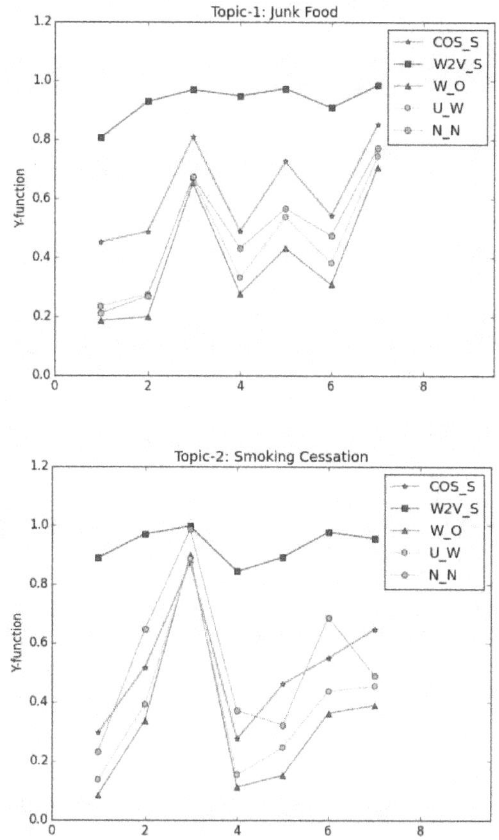

Figure 2: HIIU study

distributional representations of words, computed using neural networks [11] to calculate the cosine similarity between the centroid of all the word vectors in the document and the centroid of all the word vectors in the information units combined together. Word vectors were obtained using the Gensim toolkit [4].

3.2 Results

This section details the results of our three user studies. Figure 1 and 2 represent the participant annotation similarity and overlap scores for the WIIU and HIIU studies, across 7 users for T1 and T2 respectively. Table 2 details average users annotation similarity and overlap scores for WIIU and HIIU studies. Using different factors such as COS_S, W2V_S, W_O, U_W and N_N for measuring the similarities provide a holistic method to evaluate the annotations as looking at just one factor e.g. COS_S can be biased towards the length and number of information units.

Table 3 shows the agreement values for the AIHIU study. For each annotation we had 7 annotators and 4 classes. Because of the variance in terms of the distribution of classes and multiple annotators the scores of Fleiss Kappa, Pairiwse Cohen's Kappa and Krippendoff's kappa were quite low 0.012, 0.054 0.015 respectively. Thus we show only the majority agreement values in Table 3. These indicate the scores when majority of the users (>=4) agreed with the annotation class. We also tried reducing the 4 class relevance scale to 3 classes by combining class C2 and C3 i.e. "fairly relevant and important", and "slightly relevant and important". Agreement scores between three classes are also shown in Table 3.

[4]https://radimrehurek.com/gensim/models/word2vec.html

Study type	COS_S	W2V_S	W_O	U_W	N_N
WIIU_T1	0.523	0.903	0.270	0.313	0.285
WIIU_T2	0.472	0.879	0.217	0.286	0.321
HIIU_T1	0.623	0.931	0.395	0.454	0.486
HIIU_T2	0.517	0.932	0.334	0.387	0.534

Table 2: Comparison across different methods

4. ANALYSIS AND DISCUSSION

In this section we analyze the results of our user studies.

4.1 Study based Observations

WIIU study: More text written as information units results in better cosine similarity due to the increase in overlap of words. However, word2vec similarity results indicate that even with a lower number of units the similarity is higher than 80%. Some participants also rephrase the units, thus the cosine similarity and overlap scores decrease but the word2vec similarity is still high which is evident in Figure 1.

HIIU study: In the easier task of highlighting participants actually highlighted most of the text. The results here have quite a lot of noise due to the flexibility of free choice of the starting and ending points of the highlighted text with no constraints on the length of the textual piece to be highlighted. Thus it may be more apt to get annotators to mark documents at fixed sentence level and be more specific in the annotation guidelines in the future.

Results are more consistent between users when they write information units as compared to when they highlight information units, this is indicated by the frequent ups and down in the lines plot as shown in Figure 1 and 2. In the WIIU and HIIU studies partici-

Study type	No. of units	4 class relevance	3 class relevance
AIHIU_T0 (maj agr)	14	0.500	0.787
AIHIU_T1 (maj agr)	19	0.421	0.840
AIHIU_T2 (maj agr)	14	0.571	0.857
Average (maj agr)	47	0.489	0.829
Pair Agr	47	0.340	0.430

Table 3: Agreement for the AIHIU studies, Maj Agr: means majority agreement, Pair Agr: means pairwise agreement, calculating agreement of 2 annotators at a time and averaging over all the combinations.

pants reported that it is quite challenging to identify important and useful text when they read documents. Some people encounter new information and find everything useful and important, whereas others who know about the topic can be too hard and restrictive when judging the importance and usefulness of textual information without strict guidelines.

AIHIU study: The majority agreement averaged across three topics is 0.489 and the pairwise agreement is 0.340 as shown in Table 3. This is on similar lines to the agreement values reported for XML retrieval [6, 14]. Assessing information units as important and useful introduces a subjective aspect depending on the participant's prior knowledge, further assessment of these units at 4 levels of categories makes it challenging to get satisfactorily agreement between multiple annotators.

4.2 Issues with the study

We are aware of three shortcomings with the study:

1) The number of users was limited, we had 7 data points for each task. On average participants took about 15-20 minutes to complete each task. This limited us to have each participant working with just one of the interaction studies: WIIU, HIIU or AIHIU.

2) This is a preliminary study with 3 topics and 1 relevant document for each of the three topics. Further studies needs to be carried out with more topics and documents to draw effective conclusions.

3) Flexibility of choosing starting and ending points while highlighting text makes it challenging to calculate agreement between multiple annotators and needs further exploration.

5. CONCLUSION AND FUTURE WORK

In this work, we investigated the location and analysis of important and useful information within relevant documents using three different user study methods. We investigated two research questions:

RQ-1: How can we compare and measure user annotations (WIIU and HIIU studies)? – In this work, we calculated a combination of different measures such as textual overlap (including words, tokens and noun), cosine and word2vec similarity to compare and measure user's annotations, as just using the cosine similarity can be biased towards the length and number of information units. These measures collectively can give an approximation of the overlap between user annotations where it is difficult to measure direct agreement between annotations.

RQ-2: What is the agreement among users while assessing information units already marked in a document (AIHIU study)? – We calculated the majority agreement which is about 0.489 and the pairwise agreement which is about 0.340 among the users while categorizing information units into one of the four classes.

The objective of this study was to explore the potential to analyze information within documents beyond relevance to measures like importance and usefulness of information within documents. Though the number of data points is limited in this initial study, they indicate that it is realistic to annotate beyond document level to evaluate metrics such as useful, important and relevant information. The results and analysis indicate that we can look beyond the document level, but that it would be more practical to work with fixed boundary units such as sentence level rather than free annotation of textual units. In future work, we will explore the topics opened up in this study further with larger numbers of participants. Additionally, the results of this work will contribute to our broader objective of creation of richer document surrogate and summaries, and effective presentation of information to users to promote for effective search and engagement, and emerging areas such as improving learning through search.

Acknowledgment: This research is supported by Science Foundation Ireland (SFI) as a part of the ADAPT Centre at Dublin City University (Grant No: 12/CE/I2267).

6. REFERENCES

[1] A. Al-Maskari and M. Sanderson. A review of factors influencing user satisfaction in information retrieval. *JASIST, 2010*, 61(5):859–868.

[2] P. Arora and G. J. F. Jones. Position paper: Promoting user engagement and learning in search tasks by effective document representation. In *Proceedings of SAL workshop, SIGIR 2016*.

[3] M. Cole, J. Liu, N. Belkin, R. Bierig, J. Gwizdka, C. Liu, J. Zhang, and X. Zhang. Usefulness as the criterion for evaluation of interactive information retrieval. *Proc. HCIR*, pages 1–4, 2009.

[4] I. Habernal, M. Sukhareva, F. Raiber, A. Shtok, O. Kurland, H. Ronen, J. Bar-Ilan, and I. Gurevych. New collection announcement: Focused retrieval over the web. In *Proceedings of SIGIR 2016*, pages 701–704.

[5] K. Järvelin and J. Kekäläinen. Ir evaluation methods for retrieving highly relevant documents. In *Proceedings of SIGIR 2000*, pages 41–48.

[6] J. Kamps, J. Pehcevski, G. Kazai, M. Lalmas, and S. Robertson. Inex 2007 evaluation measures. In *International Workshop of the Initiative for the Evaluation of XML Retrieval*, pages 24–33. Springer, 2007.

[7] E. Kanoulas, B. Carterette, M. Hall, P. Clough, and M. Sanderson. Overview of the TREC 2012 Session Track. 2012.

[8] M. P. Kato, M. Ekstrand-Abueg, V. Pavlu, T. Sakai, T. Yamamoto, and M. Iwata. Overview of the ntcir-11 mobileclick task. In *NTCIR*, 2014.

[9] D. Kelly and C. Cool. The effects of topic familiarity on information search behavior. JCDL '02, pages 74–75. ACM, 2002.

[10] J. Mao, Y. Liu, K. Zhou, J.-Y. Nie, J. Song, M. Zhang, S. Ma, J. Sun, and H. Luo. When does relevance mean usefulness and user satisfaction in web search? In *Proceedings of SIGIR 2016*, pages 463–472.

[11] T. Mikolov, K. Chen, G. Corrado, and J. Dean. Efficient estimation of word representations in vector space. *arXiv preprint arXiv:1301.3781*, 2013.

[12] T. Saracevic. Relevance: A review of the literature and a framework for thinking on the notion in information science. part iii: Behavior and effects of relevance. *JASIST, 2007*, 58(13):2126–2144.

[13] M. Shokouhi and Q. Guo. From queries to cards: Re-ranking proactive card recommendations based on reactive search history. In *Proceedings of SIGIR 2015*, pages 695–704.

[14] A. Trotman and S. Geva. Passage retrieval and other xml-retrieval tasks. In *Proceedings of the SIGIR 2006 Workshop on XML Element Retrieval Methodology*, pages 43–50, 2006.

[15] R. W. White, J. M. Jose, and I. Ruthven. Using top-ranking sentences to facilitate effective information access. *JASIST, 2005*, 56(10):1113–1125.

[16] E. Yilmaz, M. Verma, N. Craswell, F. Radlinski, and P. Bailey. Relevance and effort: An analysis of document utility. In *Proceedings of CIKM 2014*, pages 91–100.

Telling How to Narrow it Down: Browsing Path Recommendation for Exploratory Search

Mostafa Dehghani[1] Glorianna Jagfeld[2] Hosein Azarbonyad[3]
Alex Olieman[1] Jaap Kamps[1] Maarten Marx[3]

[1]Institute for Logic, Language and Computation, University of Amsterdam, The Netherlands
[2]Institute for Natural Language Processing, University of Stuttgart, Germany
[3]Informatics Institute, University of Amsterdam, The Netherlands
{dehghani,h.azarbonyad,olieman,kamps,maartenmarx}@uva.nl, glorianna.jagfeld@ims.uni-stuttgart.de

ABSTRACT

Supporting exploratory search tasks with the help of structured data is an effective way to go beyond keyword search, as it provides an overview of the data, enables users to zoom in on their intent, and provides assistance during their navigation trails. However, finding a good starting point for a search episode in the given structure can still pose a considerable challenge, as users tend to be unfamiliar with exact, complex hierarchical structure. Thus, providing look-ahead clues can be of great help and allow users to make better decisions on their search trajectory.

In this paper, we investigate the behaviour of users when a recommendation engine is employed along with the browsing tool in an exploratory search system. We make use of an exploratory search system that facilitates browsing by mapping the data on a hierarchical structure. We designed and developed a path recommendation engine as a feature for this system, which given a text query, ranks different browsing paths in the hierarchy based on their likelihood of covering relevant documents. We conduct a user study comparing the baseline system with the featured system.

Our main findings are as follows: We observe that, using the baseline system the users tend to explore the data in a breadth-first-like approach by visiting different data points at the same level of abstraction to choose one of them to expand and go deeper. Conversely, with browsing path recommendation (BPR) as a feature, the users tend to drive their search in a more depth-first-like approach by quickly going deep into the data hierarchy. While the users still incline to explore different parts of the search space by using BPR, they are able to restrain or augment their search focus more quickly and access smaller but more promising regions of the data. Therefore, they can complete their tasks with less time and effort.

Keywords: Exploratory Search, Recommendation, BPR, ExPoSe.

1. INTRODUCTION

There are several information needs requiring sophisticated human-computer interactions that currently remain unsolved or poorly supported by major search applications. One of these cases is exploratory search, which refers to search tasks that are open-ended, multi-faceted, and iterative, like learning or topic investigation [5]. This type of search often occurs in a domain unknown or poorly known to the searchers which can make it hard for them to formulate proper queries for retrieving useful documents [3].

Exploratory search is composed of two main activities, *exploratory browsing* and *focused searching* [9]. Exploratory browsing refers to activities that aim at better defining the information need and raising the understanding of the information space. Focused searching corresponds to activities like query refining and results' comparisons after the information need has been shaped more clearly. Based on this composition, an exploratory search system needs to provide its users a connected space of information to browse and investigate, as well as facilities to adjust the focus of their search towards useful documents.

Using structured data to organize unstructured information is one of the promising approaches for supporting complex search tasks, including exploratory search [6]. Structure in the data provides overviews at different levels of abstraction and empowers the users to explore the data from different points of view. However, it may still be difficult to find useful paths of exploration and clues can help the users [1].

The main aim of this paper is *to investigate the user behavior in exploratory search when a recommendation engine for browsing paths is provided along with the browsing system.*. To do so, we have employed the *ExPoSe-Browser* (Exploratory Political Search Browser) as the baseline system and built a recommendation engine as a supplementary feature for the system. We have conducted a user study involving exploratory search tasks which revealed general differences of the browsing behaviour of the subjects using the two different systems.

We break down the main goal of the paper into two concrete research questions:

RQ1 *What is the effect of providing browsing path recommendations on user browsing behaviour in exploratory search?*

RQ2 *Does browsing path recommendation assist users in exploratory search?*

We demonstrate that in general, providing suggestions for paths for browsing and exploring the data helps the users to not only discover more promising regions of the search space and be more satisfied, but also to quickly narrow down their search, leading to shorter search sessions. In the rest of this paper, we first introduce the case study system in Section 2. Then we describe our experimental setups and presents the results in Section 3. In Section 4, we conclude.

CHIIR '17, March 07 - 11, 2017, Oslo, Norway

ISBN 978-1-4503-4677-1/17/03...$15.00

DOI: http://dx.doi.org/10.1145/3020165.3022155

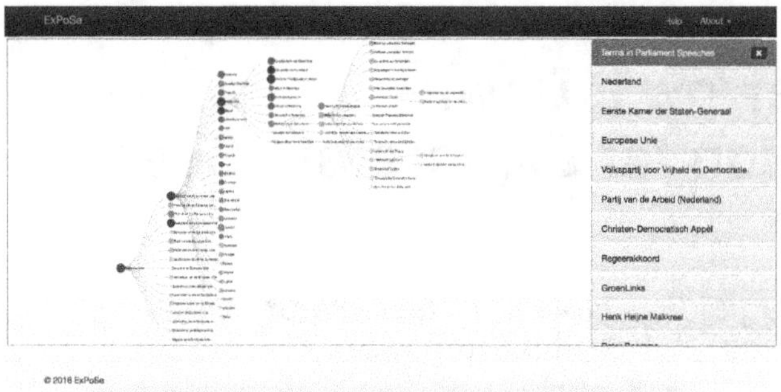

(a) A sample expanded hierarchy for exploring Dutch parliamentary proceedings in search of "European union". Left panel provides the hierarchies of topics based on Wikipedia categorical structure and right panel demonstrates the entities and speeches related to the selected topic.

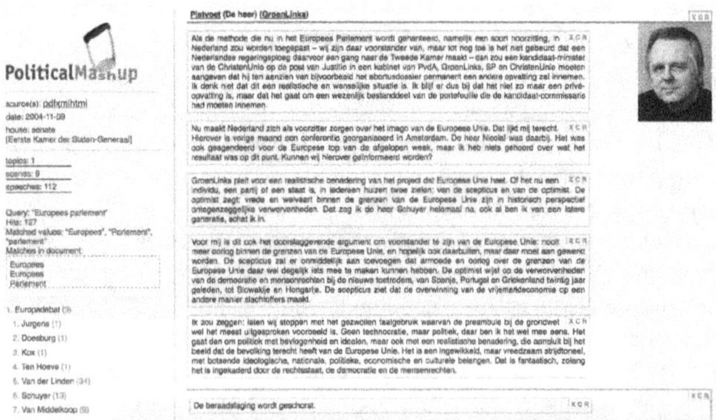

(b) A sample of visited speech by a user in search of "European union". The page contains information and the content of whole debate and the searched entity is highlighted.

Figure 1: Exploratory Political Search (ExPoSe) System.

2. BPR

Browsing the search space is an important element in exploratory search. While organizing data into a structured format improves the browsability, difficulties on deciding the direction of exploration might remain. In this section, we introduce the ExPoSe-Browser as the system we employed in our case study and explain the BPR engine we added as a supplementary feature to the system.

2.1 ExPoSe-Browser System

The ExPoSe-Browser [2, 4] is an exploratory search system that provides a hierarchical grouping of parliamentary speeches based on Wikipedia categories. More precisely, it enables its users to browse and investigate the parliamentary proceedings from an arbitrary point of view. First, the user has to chose the point of view from the set of Wikipedia categorie. Then, the ExPoSe-Browser makes a projection of the parliamentary speeches to the Wikipedia categorical structure with the point of view as the root of the hierarchy. This empowers the user to dive into the data from an abstract level to the detailed information by traversing the hierarchical structure.

The projection process is based on Wikipedia named entities mentioned in the parliamentary speeches. A customized entity linker for parliamentary conversation [7, 8] is employed to recognize and disambiguate the general named entities as well as domain specific entity types like politicians and political parties from all the speeches. Then ExPoSe-Browser lets the user select a sub-hierarchy from Wikipedia's category hierarchy[1] onto which mentioned entities from the text are projected. In the selected hierarchy, each node is a category which represents a topic. Its descendant nodes are its sub-topics. Parliamentary speeches are grouped into the nodes in the hierarchy based on the categorical memberships of entities mention in them.

Based on the debates and entities related to the categories in the hierarchy, the system calculates the importance and recency of each category. The importance of each node demonstrates how much the topic of that category is addressed in the parliamentary debates, based on the frequency of entities related to this category. The recency of each node shows how recently the topic of this category was discussed in the debates. Importance and recency are visualized by the size and color of the nodes in the user interface. Nodes can be expanded to display the next level of the hierarchy. Furthermore, the list of the speeches categorized under each node can be accessed as well as the full content of the speeches with the related entities highlighted in the text. In summary, the ExPoSe-Browser provides an overview of the data at different levels of abstraction and implicitly offers a faceted interface by clustering the data into different topical aspects. Moreover, the users can explore multiple alternative browsing paths by going-back-and-forth functionalities.

As an example of the type of complex search that can be addressed with ExPoSe-Browser, assume a user is interested in analyzing the relation between national laws of the Netherlands and European union legislation. A reasonable approach is to investigate when EU legislation was discussed in the Dutch parliament and in the context of which (proposed) Dutch laws. In other words, it is desirable to see how debates within the parliament of the Netherlands can be projected onto the topics related to the European Parliament in terms of both the subject matter and time . Using the ExPoSe-Browser, user is able to browse and investigate Dutch parliamentary proceedings regarding topics related to EU from a very abstract level (categories - Figure1a) to a very detailed level (entities/content of speeches - Figure1b).

2.2 Path Recommendation

We design and implement a recommendation engine for suggesting paths of browsing and exploration as a supplementary plugin for the ExPoSe-Browser system. In general, the BPR engine, given a text query, provides a ranking of paths based on their likelihood of leading to speeches relevant to the query (Figure 1).

More precisely, the recommendation engine, for a given text query, calculates the similarity of the query with the full content of all speeches. Then, it assigns a score to each entity based on its occurrence in different speeches and their corresponding scores. Afterwards, it integrates the normalized scores of all entities under each category as the likelihood score of the category given the searched query. Finally, the likelihood score is mapped to the weight of the path from the root of the hierarchy to the category and the thickness of each edge in the hierarchy is determined by the weights of all paths that pass through the edge.

Providing a ranking of paths to speeches instead of ranking the speeches themselves can be considered as a preview clue that brings a limited amount of certainty to the exploration process while its bias is not strong enough to completely deter the users from exploring the space.

3. EXPERIMENTS

In this section, we present a user study we conducted to investigate the effect of BPR on user behaviour in exploratory search. First, we describe our experimental setups, then we present the results of the experiments.

[1] Formally, Wikipedia's category system is modeled as a directed acyclic graph rather than a tree structure.

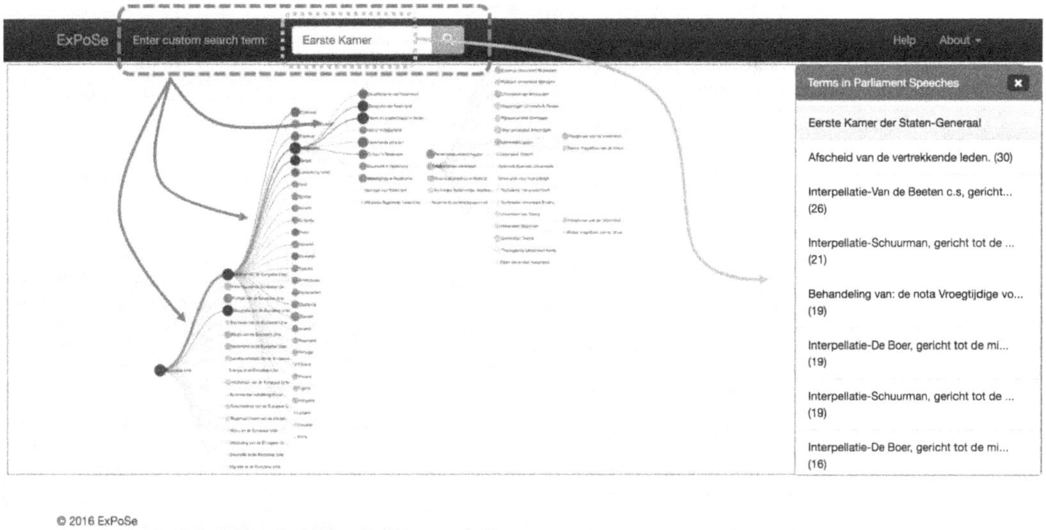

Figure 2: BPR for Exploratory Political Search Browser (ExPoSe-Browser) System.

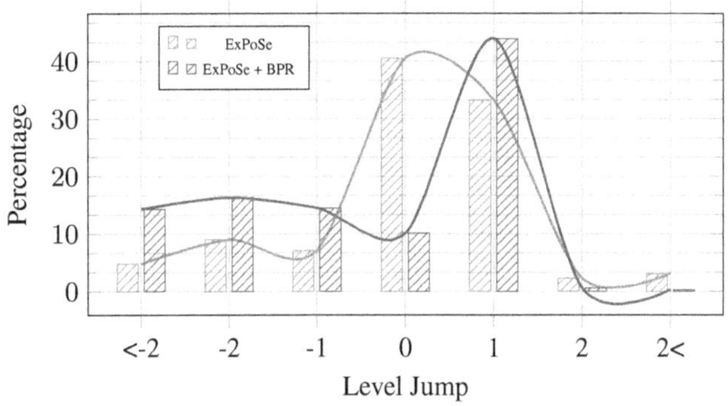

Figure 3: Distribution of different level jumps: positive and negative jumps mean toward lower and higher levels respectively.

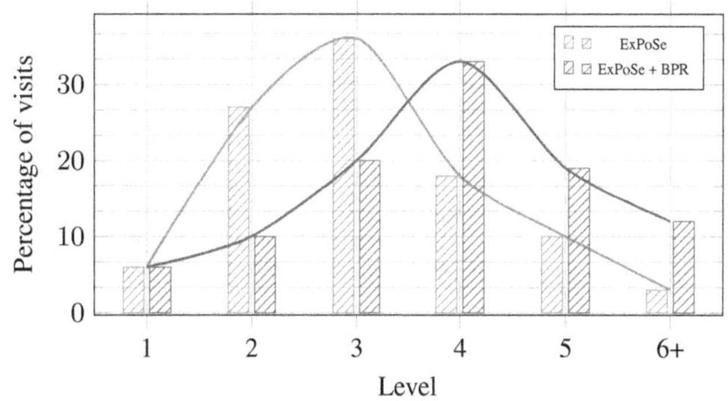

Figure 4: Distribution of level visits.

3.1 Experimental Setup

Twelve participants were enrolled in this study who had an average age of 27 (SD = 2.14). Four participants were male and eight female. Three participants were undergraduate students, nine were graduate students. All participants had more than 10 years of computer experience and a fairly high ability of online search. All participants were inexperienced in the political domain. We compiled eight general search tasks for which there is no concrete answer. Briefly, the tasks were to summarize the attitude/opinion of the Dutch parliament on specific topics: *Immigration*, *Islam*, *World War II*, *Tax*, *Holocaust*, *Dutch Golden Age*, *EU Membership of the UK*, and *EU membership of Greece*.

Each participant was given two different tasks to complete using the baseline system and then two other tasks to complete using the featured system. The tasks were distributed among the participants and systems in such a way that each task was completed three times with the baseline system and three times with the featured system, each time by different participants. The overall number of search sessions was 48, consisting of an equal number of search sessions with the baseline and featured system. Prior to working on the tasks, the users were trained to work with the systems and got to know their features. During the experiments, they were given a short and clear description of the tasks. They were asked to provide a summary of two to three paragraphs of the information obtained in each search session. All interactions of the users with the systems were logged during the experiments.

3.2 Effect of Path Recommendation

In this section, first, we address our first research question: "What is the effect of providing browsing path recommendations on user browsing behaviour in exploratory search?"

In each search session, the users could to move back-and-forth across the hierarchy and visit different nodes at different levels. In order to investigate and compare the node visits in two systems, for each system, we count the number of different level jumps across all sessions. The level jump can be zero, which means the currently visited node is at the same level as the last visited node. A positive level jump indicates that the currently visited node is at a lower level than the last visited node (forward move). A negative level jump means the currently visited node is at a higher level than the last visited node (backward move).

Figure 3 shows the percentage of different level jumps in both systems. According to the plots in the figure, in the baseline system, users tend to explore the nodes at one level (high percentage of zero-jumps) and then choose one of them to go to the next level, which is a breadth-first-like traversal model of the data. However, in the featured system with BPR, the users mostly choose to quickly descend in the hierarchy, which is a more depth-first-like traversal model of the data. Moreover, in the featured system, there is a fairly high percentage of negative jumps compared to the baseline system,

Table 1: Statistics from search sessions for both systems. The given numbers are per-session statistics, averaged over all search sessions.

System	avg. num. of root selection	avg. num. of node expansion	avg. num. of entity list loading	avg. num. of speech list loading	avg. num. of speech content loading	avg. session duration (min)
ExPoSe	1.2 (SD=0.33)	16.4 (SD=4.1)	29.5 (SD=8.4)	16.7 (SD=8.7)	36.3 (SD=8.7)	31.6 (SD=7.5)
ExPoSe + BPR	1.3 (SD=38)	9.7 (SD=2.2)	21.1 (SD=3.16)	12.4 (SD=2.5)	18.4 (SD=3.7)	23.1 (SD=6.1)

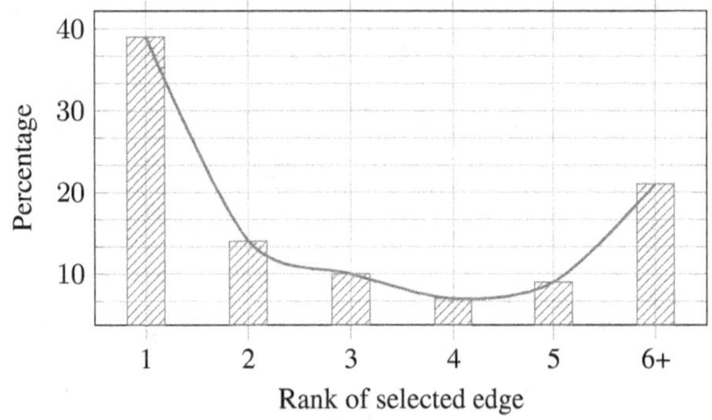

Figure 5: Distribution of ranks of selected edges.

which demonstrates that users backtrack to try other paths from higher levels, probably to cover different aspects of the topic.

Figure 4 presents the distribution of node visits over different levels during the search sessions for both systems. Based on the plots, in average, users visited deeper levels of the hierarchies when they used the featured system. Figures 3 and 4 demonstrate that BPR makes users more confident to quickly narrow down their search space and deepen their exploration path. Additionally, they feel less risk to conduct back-and-forth moves in the search space.

In another analysis, we investigate the chance of an edge being selected to be pursued by the user according to its rank given from the BPR. Figure 3 demonstrates the percentage of times that edges in different ranks are selected. As can be seen, although edges with the top rank were selected in almost %40 of cases, the users also tried paths with lower ranks. Thus, BPR did not decrease the chance of exploration.

Now, we address our second research question: "Does browsing path recommendation assist users in exploratory search?"

We extracted statistics from all search sessions to study the difference between two systems in terms of the search system quality and user satisfaction. Table 1 presents the statistics of different actions per session by users averaged over all search sessions in both systems. As can be seen, in the featured system, the average number of nodes expanded in the hierarchy in each session is much lower compared to the baseline system. Moreover, the average number of requests for displaying more detailed information like the list of entities, the list of speeches, or content of speeches under each node is lower than the baseline system. The average duration of search session is also lower in the featured system.

Furthermore, we asked two experts in the political domain to rate the quality of the summaries generated by the users as an indicator for their understanding of the topic on a 10-point scale. Summaries generated using the featured system get fairly higher ratings (M=7.73, SD=2.10), compared to the summaries generated using the baseline system (M=5.36, SD=3.31).

Considering the statistics from Table 1 along with the ratings given to the summaries generated by the users, we conclude that with BPR, users can complete their complex tasks better and by making less effort and spending less time.

4. CONCLUSIONS

The main aim of this paper was *to investigate the user behavior in exploratory search when a recommendation engine for browsing paths is provided along with the browsing system.*

We designed a BPR engine and employed it in the ExPoSe-Browser system, our baseline exploratory search system to investigate the change in the behaviour of the users. We observed that providing BPR leads to a depth-first-like traversal by users since it brings some certainty into the decision-making process of the users and makes them able to quickly deepen their search. However, without path recommendation, they need to explore different options at each level which corresponds to a breadth-first-like strategy for exploration. We also found that using BPR, users still tend to explore different parts of the search space. But they adjust their search focus to make less effort and spend less time for completing their tasks.

In future work, we can improve the BPR engine by making it adaptive to the user's browsing history. As the analytical future work, we are going to study the effect of the complexity of tasks in the same setting. We are also interested to study to which extend providing recommendations in the different parts of an exploratory search system like query suggestion, node expansion hints, etc. helps.

Acknowledgments

This research is funded in part by Netherlands Organization for Scientific Research through the *Exploratory Political Search* project (ExPoSe, NWO CI # 314.99.108), and by the Digging into Data Challenge through the *Digging Into Linked Parliamentary Data* project (DiLiPaD, NWO Digging into Data # 600.006.014).

References

[1] A. Azman and I. Ounis. Browsing recommendation based on the intertemporal choice model. In *International Conference on Flexible Query Answering Systems*, pages 215–226, 2009.

[2] M. Dehghani, A. Olieman, and H. Azarbonyad. Discovering links in political conversations. Technical report, University of Amsterdam, 2015.

[3] A. Diriye, M. L. Wilson, A. Blandford, and A. Tombros. Revisiting exploratory search from the hci perspective. In *HCIR 2010*, pages 99–102, 2010.

[4] ExPoSe. Exploratory political search project. http://humanities.uva.nl/~kamps/expose/, 2015. Netherlands Organization for Scientific Research.

[5] G. Marchionini. Exploratory search: From finding to understanding. *Commun. ACM*, 49(4):41–46, 2006.

[6] N. Marie. *Linked data based exploratory search.* PhD thesis, Université Nice Sophia Antipolis, 2014.

[7] A. Olieman, H. Azarbonyad, M. Dehghani, J. Kamps, and M. Marx. Entity linking by focusing dbpedia candidate entities. In *Proceedings of the First International Workshop on Entity Recognition & Disambiguation*, ERD'14, pages 13–24, 2014.

[8] A. Olieman, J. Kamps, M. Marx, and A. Nusselder. A Hybrid Approach to Domain-Specific Entity Linking. In *Joint Proceedings of the Posters and Demos Track of 11th International Conference on Semantic Systems (SEMANTiCS'15) and 1st Workshop on Data Science: Methods, Technology and Applications (DSci'15)*, pages 55–58, Vienna, 2015. URL http://arxiv.org/abs/1509.01865.

[9] R. W. White and R. A. Roth. Exploratory search: beyond the query-response paradigm (synthesis lectures on information concepts, retrieval & services). *Morgan and Claypool Publishers*, 3, 2009.

Incorporating Task Analysis in the Design of a Tool for a Complex and Exploratory Search Task

Tugba Kulahcioglu*
Dept. of Computer Science
Rutgers University
Piscataway, NJ 08855, USA
tugba.kulahcioglu@rutgers.edu

Dmitriy Fradkin
Corporate Technology
Siemens Corporation
Princeton, NJ 08540, USA
dmitriy.fradkin@siemens.com

Sridharan Palanivelu
Corporate Technology
Siemens Corporation
Princeton, NJ 08540, USA
sridharan.palanivelu@siemens.com

ABSTRACT

Due to its nature, a complex and exploratory search task is not directly actionable; it needs to be decomposed into actionable sub-tasks. Achieving this decomposition is usually not trivial for non-expert users. Also, the users need additional support to decrease their cognitive workload, regardless of their experience level.

A tool designed for a specific task should handle the above issues. In this paper, we present a design approach that can help achieve this, and exemplify this approach using the search task of patent infringement discovery. We apply hierarchical task analysis to analyze a successful goal decomposition scenario for the task. This kind of decomposition makes explicit the tasks that are most responsible for the cognitive workload of the user. We then apply cognitive analysis to reveal the knowledge that enables such decomposition. Finally, we use these findings to design the tool in a way that reduces the load on the user and enables achieving decomposition for non-expert users.

Keywords

Goal based decomposition; information retrieval; search tool design; complex and exploratory search; requirements analysis

1. INTRODUCTION

An exploratory search typically has the goal of learning or investigating a topic, and it requires iterations of search [17]. The goal is usually not sufficiently clear to enable the user to take search actions directly [7]. Thus, it needs to be decomposed into actionable sub-tasks. This decomposition can be relatively easy for expert users, but it can become a bottleneck for others. In such a case, users would first look for ways to decompose the task, which would make the task more difficult and time-consuming [3].

*This work was done while the author was an intern at Corporate Technology, Siemens Corporation.

CHIIR '17, March 07-11, 2017, Oslo, Norway

DOI: http://dx.doi.org/10.1145/3020165.3022156

In [5], Aula and Russel discuss explorativeness of the search together with complexity of the information problem. A complex search would typically involve multiple search tasks-sessions along with a need for different information resources. Complex searches increase the cognitive workload of the user, and lead to new requirements, such as note-taking [5].

Ideally, a tool designed specifically for a complex and exploratory search task should help users overcome these challenges [19]. It should guide the users to implement a successful goal decomposition, and support them in handling the cognitive workload of the task. Achieving this requires answering the following questions:

1) What is the knowledge that non-expert users lack to implement a successful decomposition for the task?

2) What are the sub-tasks that increase the cognitive workload of the users?

We suggest answering the above questions by using hierarchical decomposition of the search task and cognitive analysis of the search knowledge through this decomposition.

Hierarchical goal-decomposition is a task analysis method that connects the problem domain with the solution domain by recursively decomposing the goals until solution actions are reached [18][12]. In our case, the solution actions are the actionable search tasks. This kind of decomposition makes it easier to understand the sub-tasks that increase the cognitive workload, because these tasks do not decompose into a search task. Instead, they require cognitive processing.

Bhavnani and Bates have carried out cognitive analysis of the search knowledge aiming to reveal the declarative and procedural knowledge that enables goal decomposition for expert users [8]. We carry out a similar analysis using the sub-tasks obtained by the hierarchical decomposition to reveal the enabling knowledge behind a successful decomposition.

Application of these methods makes it possible to design the tool by making structural design decisions (such as using vertical search engines) and adapting related support mechanisms (such as keyword suggestion).

We exemplify the suggested method using the patent infringement discovery task. Patent infringement discovery mainly aims to find any unauthorized use of a patented invention [2]. Discovering patent infringements is a complex and exploratory search task, since, from the goal formulation alone, it is not clear which steps need to be taken to find relevant information. Even after defining these steps, the problem decomposes into multiple complex search processes, each a typical representative of a complex search problem.

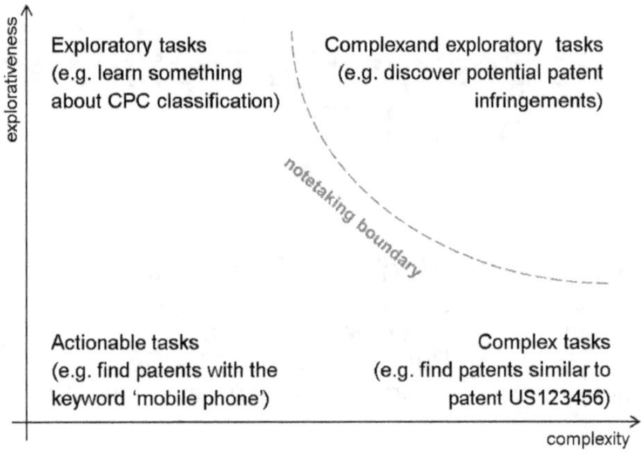

Figure 1: Task examples from patent infringement discovery. Figure adapted from [5].

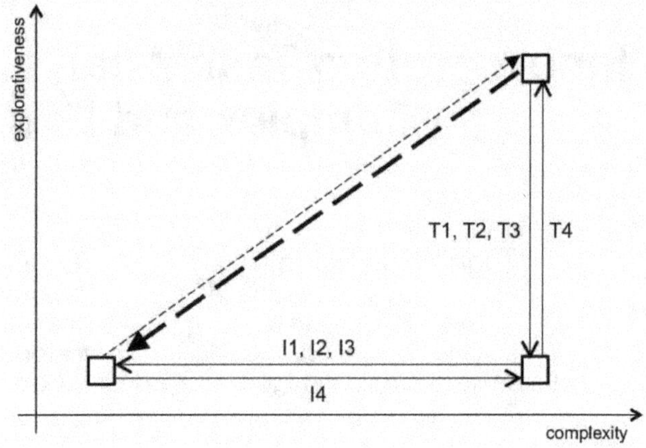

Figure 2: Illustration of task decomposition for patent infringement discovery. T1-T4 and I1-I4 refer to sub-tasks marked in Figure 3.

The rest of the paper is organized as follows. We first analyze patent infringement discovery as a complex and exploratory search problem in Section 2. In Section 3, we propose a decomposition strategy for that problem and analyze the enabling declarative and procedural knowledge. In Section 4, we present our design choices that are based on the previous analysis. We present related work in Section 5, and then discuss future work and conclude in Section 6.

2. PROBLEM ANALYSIS

We examine patent infringement discovery using the two-dimensional classification proposed by [5]. Figure 1 illustrates the two-dimensional problem classification together with related task samples from different levels.

On the top-right is the task of discovering potential patent infringements. This task is abstract because there is no straightforward way to achieve it using search. This goal is also complex, because it is composed of many sub-tasks requiring multiple sessions (typically days/weeks of work) and multiple resources.

On the top-left is the task of learning more about CPC (Cooperative Patent Classification) [1], an international classification system that is used to classify patent publications. Compared to the top-right corner, this problem is simple because it is possible to learn something about CPC with a single search. It is still abstract because it is not clear what we need to learn.

On the bottom-right is the task of finding patents similar to a specified patent. Compared to the above problems, this goal is concrete because what we need is clear. However, it is still a complex problem which may require multiple searches/sessions.

On the bottom-left is the task of finding patents with a specified keyword. This search task is one of the many that are needed to find the results for the tasks discussed above. It is a concrete and simple task. It is concrete because it is clear how to solve the problem. And since the solution requires only one search, it is also simple.

The main task of discovering potential patent infringements (top-right) needs to be reduced into actionable tasks (bottom-left) using task decomposition. The bold hypotenuse arrow line in Figure 2 represents this task reduction.

3. GOAL DECOMPOSITION AND ITS COGNITIVE ANALYSIS

Here we present a hierarchical goal decomposition[1] approach for the patent infringement discovery task and analyze this decomposition's enabling knowledge components. Figure 3 summarizes this decomposition and corresponding cognitive analysis using three different knowledge layers that are discussed in the following subsections.

3.1 Task Layer

In the task layer, the main task is decomposed into four sub-tasks. The first three sub-tasks find relevant products, publications and patents; whereas the last task combines results from previous sub-tasks and analyzes them together to make a decision.

The declarative knowledge needed in that step is that it is possible to find clues for a patent infringement in the forms of products, patents and publications. That follows a procedural strategy of 'find each-analyze all', which represents finding relevant results in different forms (such as product and publication) and analyzing them together. Without the former knowledge, it is not possible for users to implement the latter strategy. This is mainly the reason novice users have difficulty carrying out this search task.

3.2 Intermediate Layer

In the intermediate layer, we expand the task of finding relevant patents (T3) from the task layer as an example decomposition. It decomposes into four sub-tasks which is a result of a four-step strategy of extracting search parameters, searching with these parameters, expanding these parameters and searching, and collecting all relevant results during these tasks. This decomposition requires the declarative knowledge of the existence of patent-specific search resources and CPC classes [1]. In other words, this decomposition can only be possible when the user have this knowledge.

[1]Please note that, although carried out with the help from a domain expert, this analysis does not aim to achieve the best possible decomposition. Rather, we aim to have a sample decomposition that could be used to illustrate the suggested design approach.

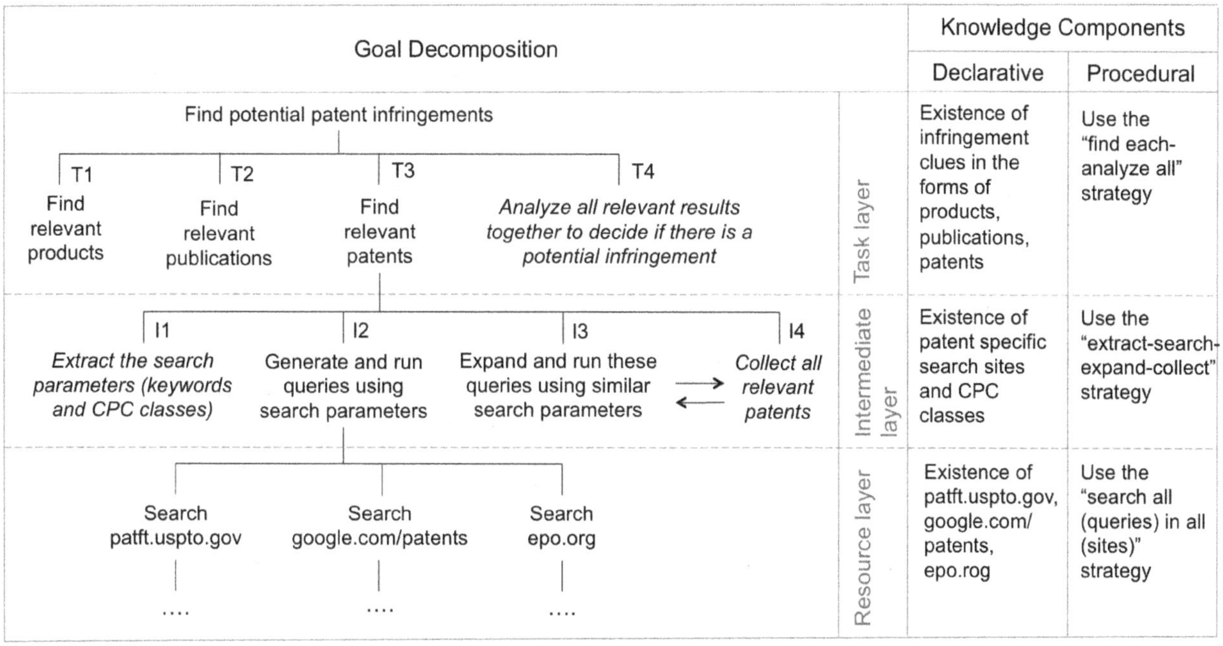

Figure 3: Goal decomposition and enabling knowledge components[2]. The codes next to some of the tasks are used to refer to these tasks throughout the paper. Figure 2 can be checked for an illustration of how these tasks contribute to the decomposition. Figure adapted from [8].

3.3 Resource Layer

In the resource layer, we expand the search task with the initial search parameters (I2) into three further sub-tasks, each focusing on searching a specific resource. If a user is not aware of these resources, then this decomposition would become a challenge for them. They will first need to find a list of such resources. The procedural knowledge used in that level is the need to perform searches in all data sources. This strategy is more generic compared to others.

4. DESIGN DECISIONS

The analysis in the previous section answers the questions mentioned in the introduction. The next step, as a part of the proposed approach, is to make design decisions for the search tool based on this analysis.

4.1 Enabling Goal Decomposition

The cognitive analysis in Figure 3 reveals that users should be aware of different forms of infringements; and for each of these forms, they need to know the specific web-sites.

To enable goal decomposition for all users, a useful design choice can be the use of vertical search engines. Vertical search leverages domain knowledge and focuses on domain specific search tasks to achieve a deeper relevance [13].

It can support 'find each' strategy by creating a vertical search engine for each of the infringement forms, namely products, publications and patents. By embedding these vertical search engines to the tool, the user can be guided to implement searches in each domain.

A vertical search engine can also support the 'search in all' strategy by searching in all of the specified resources for a domain. It also makes it possible to allow expert users to modify these resources, or to assign different preferences.

4.2 Reducing Cognitive Workload

Some tasks can be decomposed further until their actionable sub-tasks can be implemented through a search. However, there are some tasks in this decomposition that could not be decomposed into actionable sub-tasks, and they require cognitive efforts to implement. These tasks are T4, I1 and I4; and they are italicized in Figure 2.

One approach to support task I1 is to automatically suggest search parameters, such as keywords and CPC classes, that are relevant to input patent [21]. Parameter suggestion is especially difficult for patents since they are typically long documents written in a formal language with many domain-specific words and phrases [15].

To support task I4, there should be a mechanism in the tool allowing the users to save the results that they consider relevant. Otherwise, users would need to store these results using external tools, which can substantially increase the workload. Since these results would be coming from different searches, it could be useful if the tool could keep track of the search parameters they are associated with.

Supporting task T4 also requires saving the results from different verticals, but on top of that, it would be helpful to provide a clustering mechanism to associate results from these verticals with each other. That could help user to come up with stronger infringement clues.

The support mechanisms for tasks I4 and T4 are particularly important because patent search is a recall oriented information problem, and it typically requires handling an enormous number of results [16].

[2]In addition to the knowledge components analyzed, these tasks also require knowledge in the domain of the input patent in general. A future direction could be to integrate domain and search knowledge dimensions into this analysis.

5. RELATED WORK

Goal decomposition has been used in different fields, including requirements engineering [20] and database design [10]. Previous studies indicate that decomposing a problem leads to better understanding and thus constructing a better response [18][4][9]. Bhavnani and Bates applies cognitive analysis to the decomposition process to understand the search knowledge behind the decomposition [8] and we have applied that method in this study.

Patent information retrieval possesses its own challenges [15], which caused it to evolve as a separate branch in Information Retrieval [14]. These challenges include query extraction and expansion, and the need of high recall and its evaluation. Query expansion and other patent retrieval related topics are surveyed in [22]. Also, there has been studies investigating user requirements of patent search tools [11][6].

6. CONCLUSIONS

The proposed approach aims to facilitate the design decisions which would make a complex and exploratory task easier to implement for non-expert users, and decrease the cognitive workload caused by the complexity of its sub-tasks. It is achieved by:

1. Building an ideal task decomposition
2. Analyzing necessary declarative/procedural knowledge
3. Identifying sub-tasks with high cognitive-demand
4. Making design decisions based on the above steps

The approach summarized above is domain independent, and we exemplified it for the patent infringement discovery task. In addition to the previously mentioned advantages, this approach could help developers to carry out a structured task-based evaluation by assessing the contribution of each sub-task (hence each support method) to its ancestor. Such kind of decomposition and aggregation of evaluation criteria may lead to a better assessment of support methods [18].

7. REFERENCES

[1] Cooperative patent classification. http://www.cooperativepatentclassification.org. Accessed: 2016-04-05.

[2] USPTO about patent infringement? http://www.uspto.gov/patents-maintaining-patent/patent-litigation/about-patent-infringement. Accessed: 2016-04-05.

[3] A. Al-Maskari and M. Sanderson. The effect of user characteristics on search effectiveness in information retrieval. *Information Processing and Management*, 47(5):719 – 729, 2011. Managing and Mining Multilingual Documents.

[4] J. S. Armstrong, W. B. Denniston, and M. M. Gordon. The use of the decomposition principle in making judgments. *Organizational Behavior and Human Performance*, 14(2):257–263, 1975.

[5] A. Aula and D. M. Russell. Complex and Exploratory Web Search. In *Information Seeking Support Systems*, 2008.

[6] L. Azzopardi, W. Vanderbauwhede, and H. Joho. Search system requirements of patent analysts. In *Proceedings of the 33rd International ACM SIGIR Conference on Research and Development in Information Retrieval*, SIGIR '10, pages 775–776, New York, NY, USA, 2010. ACM.

[7] N. J. Belkin. The human element: helping people find what they don't know. *Commun. ACM*, 43(8):58–61, 2000.

[8] S. K. Bhavnani and M. J. Bates. Separating the knowledge layers: Cognitive analysis of search knowledge through hierarchical goal decompositions. *Proceedings of the American Society for Information Science and Technology*, 39(1):204–213, 2002.

[9] A. R. Dennis, J. S. Valacich, T. Connolly, and B. E. Wynne. Process structuring in electronic brainstorming. *Information Systems Research*, 7(2):268–277, 1996.

[10] L. Jiang, T. Topaloglou, A. Borgida, and J. Mylopoulos. Incorporating goal analysis in database design: A case study from biological data management. In *Proceedings of the 14th IEEE International Requirements Engineering Conference*, RE '06, pages 196–204, Washington, DC, USA, 2006.

[11] H. Joho, L. A. Azzopardi, and W. Vanderbauwhede. A survey of patent users: An analysis of tasks, behavior, search functionality and system requirements. In *Proceedings of the Third Symposium on Information Interaction in Context*, IIiX '10, pages 13–24, New York, NY, USA, 2010. ACM.

[12] B. Kirwan and L. K. Ainsworth, editors. *A Guide to Task Analysis: The Task Analysis Working Group.* Taylor & Francis, 1 edition, Sept. 1992.

[13] B. Long and Y. Chang. *Relevance Ranking for Vertical Search Engines.* Morgan Kaufmann Publishers Inc., San Francisco, CA, USA, 1st edition, 2014.

[14] M. Lupu and A. Hanbury. Patent retrieval. *Foundations and Trends in Information Retrieval*, 7(1):1–97, 2013.

[15] M. Lupu, K. Mayer, J. Tait, and A. J. Trippe, editors. *Current Challenges in Patent Information Retrieval*, volume 29 of *The Information Retrieval Series.* Springer, 2011.

[16] W. Magdy. Toward higher effectiveness for recall-oriented information retrieval: A patent retrieval case study, Jan 2012.

[17] G. Marchionini. Exploratory search: From finding to understanding. *Commun. ACM*, 49(4):41–46, Apr. 2006.

[18] S. Munro, S. Liaskos, and J. Aranda. The mysteries of goal decomposition. In *Proceedings of the 5th International i* Workshop 2011, Trento, Italy, August 28-29, 2011*, pages 49–54, 2011.

[19] E. Toms. Complex tools for complex tasks. *Gäde et al.[4]. URL http://ceur-ws. org*, 1338, 2015.

[20] A. van Lamsweerde. Goal-oriented requirements engineering: A guided tour. In *5th IEEE International Symposium on Requirements Engineering (RE 2001), 27-31 August 2001, Toronto, Canada*, page 249, 2001.

[21] X. Xue and W. B. Croft. Automatic query generation for patent search. In *Proceedings of the 18th ACM Conference on Information and Knowledge Management*, CIKM '09, pages 2037–2040, New York, NY, USA, 2009. ACM.

[22] L. Zhang, L. Li, and T. Li. Patent mining: A survey. *SIGKDD Explor. Newsl.*, 16(2):1–19, May 2015.

Analysis of Children's Queries and Click Behavior on Ranked Results and Their Thought Processes in Google Search

Jacek Gwizdka
School of Information, University of Texas at Austin
1616 Guadalupe St, Austin, TX 78701, USA
chiir2017@gwizdka.com

Dania Bilal
School of Information Sciences, University of Tennessee
1345 Circle Park, Suite 451, Knoxville, TN 37996
dania@utk.edu

ABSTRACT
We investigate query characteristics and click behavior on SERPs of children in grades 6 and 8 (ages 11 and 13, respectively). We employ Retrospective Think-Aloud (RTA) protocol to elicit children's thought processes while clicking on results and to identify the sources of information that shaped these processes. We analyze the effect of grade level and task type on query characteristics and click behavior. Early findings show statistical significance across the three tasks in relation to query characteristics and between younger and older children in relation to query entry duration, count of web pages visited and count of result pages clicked on in SERPs. Our study confirms findings reported in previous research, including large-scale search logs studies, and reveals new findings in some areas.

1. INTRODUCTION
Early studies of children's interaction with search engines revealed that children ages 11-13 years do not go beyond the first page of results [1–3]. A study of children ages 7, 9, and11 years in using Google [4, 5] confirmed this finding. Recent studies [6–9] have confirmed that young users click on the top-ranked results more often than they do on the middle- or lower-ranked results in a SERP. However, a study by [10] showed that children's clicks on lower ranked results are more frequent than on top-ranked results. These studies provide insights in children's query analysis (e.g., query formulations and reformulations), performance, and time on task, among others. Yet, we have little understanding of how children's thought processes influence their click behavior while interacting with a search engine. Similarly, scant studies have elicited the sources of information that shape these processes. That is, the "information authority" influencing their decision-making process. In the present study, we report on the characteristics of children's click behavior on results on Google SERPs and elicit the sources of information that have shaped this behavior. We also analyze their query characteristics in relation to task type and grade level, and we use these two factors to determine effect on children's click behavior. We discuss whether leveraging children's click behavior on SERPs can be used to improve results ranking and to inform query characteristics in relation to task type and grade level or age, as well as to design digital information literacy. We investigate the following research questions:

RQ-1: Do children's query entry and length while interacting with a Google SERP vary by: a. grade level, and by b. Task type

CHIIR '17, March 07-11, 2017, Oslo, Norway
 ISBN 978-1-4503-4677-1/17/03…$15.00
DOI: http://dx.doi.org/10.1145/3020165.3022157

RQ-2: Does the order of result ranks clicked by children on a Google SERP vary by: a. grade level, and b. task type?

RQ-3: What are children's thought processes while clicking on a Google SERP, and what are the sources of information have shaped these thoughts?

2. RELATED WORK
Studies of children's interaction with search engines [1–3] found that children in seventh grade (ages 11-13 years) did not go beyond the first page of results and seldom scrolled down pages to explore results. A later study in using Google revealed that children ages 7, 9, and 11 years clicked on the top-ranked results and did not go beyond the sixth-ranked result on a result page [4, 5]. A follow-up longitudinal study confirmed these findings [7]. A recent study of Chinese students in grades 7-12 showed that 74% browsed the first results page; and all of them tended to click on the top-ranked results but also clicked on the lower-ranked results if they did not find the information sought.

A large-scale study of query logs in DMOZ Directory, Kids and Teens section [10] showed that children's clicks on the tenth-ranked results from the first results page were more frequent than those on upper ranked positions. Also, younger users tended to click more on lower ranked results than teens or mature teens. The query logs study of three German search engines designed for children ages 6-13 years [8], found that most children visited only the first results page and looked at the first three results. A large-scale search logs study of Yahoo! revealed that users ages 6-12 years tended to click on higher-ranked results, especially those ranked "0" (i.e., any kind of special results such as link to news, shopping); and the click distribution of teenagers (ages 13-15 and 16-18 years) differed considerably from that of younger children (ages 6-7, 8-9, and 10-12 years). Children and teenagers as a group were less likely than adults to click on a result below the third-ranked position. However, as a group, younger children were less likely than teenagers to click on results below the third ranked-position on a page [10].

Eye tracking studies of children's query analysis and click behaviors are scant. Our recent study [11] revealed that children's eye fixations on a Google SERP varied by age (11 vs. 13 years) and that age had a more significant effect than task type in relation to time on task, query length, and result rank, among other factors. The reviewed literature shows patterns of similarity in children's web behavior, especially in terms of viewing the first SERP. However, it highlights differences in relation to clicking on ranked results in a SERP. Given that log analysis data do not involve actual participants, they fall short of explaining young users' thought processes while interacting with SERPs.

3. THEORETICAL FRAMEWORK
This study works from the cognitive psychology theoretical position that is concerned with "the study of how people perceive, learn, remember, and think about information." [13, p.3], and that prescribes judgment and decision-making as types of thought

processes that are "used to select from among choices or to evaluate opportunity." [12]. To that end, we examine children's thought processes while clicking on results on modified Google SERPs. Specifically, we determine reasons that trigger the clicking behavior and identify the sources of information that have shaped this behavior. We build upon the understanding that task type is one of the primary factors that is likely to impact users' interaction with information retrieval systems (IRs). Additionally, we draw upon the theory of cognitive development that describes children's abilities at different stages of development based on age or intellectual maturity level [12, 13]. Accordingly, we compare the click behavior of children ages 11 and 13 years while interacting with modified Google SERPs.

Table 1. Search tasks

Factual Tasks (Task 1)
Grade 6: *Alexander the Great was the son of King Philip II. After Philip II died, Alexander the Great became the King of Macedonia. Search Google and find when Alexander the Great became the King of Macedonia, and how old he was at that time. Write the answers below.*
Grade 8*: On October 28, 2014, a rocket carrying students' science experiments exploded shortly after takeoff. Search Google and find the name of the city or state where the rocket exploded. Also find one of the students' science projects or experiments the rocket carried and what the project or experiment was about. Write the answers below.*
Research/Informational Task (Task 2)
All Grades: *The Earth's climate is currently changing. Scientists call this climate change Global Warming. Search Google and find credible and useful information that discusses or explains some of the evidence or examples that scientists are finding. Also, find and name two credible and useful specific examples of scientific studies that you would research further if you were to write a report on this subject. Write the examples and name the two studies below.*

4. METHOD

We used Tobii eye-tracker X2-60 for collecting eye-gaze (not reported here), and Tobii Studio for collecting quantitative data (interaction logs) and qualitative data (e.g., thought processes). We employed the Retrospective Think-Aloud protocol for the latter [11]. We recruited children from private schools (non-governmental) and public schools (governmental). We started recruiting from one private school in the southern part of the US but due to the low number of children who participated (11) in the first phase of the data collection (private school), we employed the snowballing approach, which resulted in fifteen additional participants, totaling 26 participants. Of these, three children took part in the pilot study and we excluded them from the data analysis. We sought consents from the respective academic institutions, parents, and the private school's administration. The final sample consisted of 23 children from public and private schools and one child-participant from a home schooling program. Participants' demographics and background are diverse (e.g., male, female; White, African-Americans; low to high socioeconomic conditions). The present paper reports on analyzed data for 14 children (6 from sixth grade and 8 from eighth grade).

4.1 Search Tasks

We used three search tasks, two assigned (one fact-finding and one research-informational) and one fully self-generated [3]. For detail see [11].

4.2 Search System

Children performed searches using a web page with a search interface we have created that communicated with a proxy server, which retrieved data in the background from the Google search engine. Architecture of our system is described in [14]. We used our own interface to achieve control over the display of search results (Fig. 1). We limited the number of results per each Google SERP to seven to ensure that the interaction is accurately tracked on each line of result text. Screen coordinates of a search result HTML element were automatically saved by using a JavaScript we inserted into the search page; see details in [11, 14].

Figure 1. Modified Search Engine Results Page (SERP)

4.3 Procedure

Data collection took place in a User Experience Lab located at one of the author's academic institution. We introduced the purposes of the study and asked the child-participant to follow the instructions appearing on the computer screen to perform each task. We also provided the child with a written version of each task to use during the interaction. We remained in proximity with the child to provide assistance as needed. The child-participant performed the factual task session first, which we saved upon completion and followed by an RTA interview that one of the authors conducted. We employed the same procedures for searching Google on both the research-informational task and the fully self-generated task. The exception in the latter was that the child's parent had to be approved the selected topic. Interactions with Google SERPs and associated pages were stored in a database on a remote proxy server.

4.4 Variables Analyzed

The independent variables in our analysis were grade level (grade 6 or age 11and grade 8 or age 13), and task type (see Table 1). The first group of dependent variables is at the query level (Table 2).

Table 2. Dependent Variables at the query level

Variable	Description
query entry duration	time spent entering a query
query length in words	length of a query in words
count of SERPs	number of SERPs visited per query
total SERPs duration	total time spent on SERP pages per query

The second group of dependent variables (Table 3) describes the children's behavior from the perspective of examining search results displayed on a SERP and of clicking on selected results (associated web pages). We distinguished first visits to the result pages from subsequent visits. In addition to considering result pages visited directly from a SERP, we considered all web pages visited by following links from a SERP and associated pages

Table 3. Dependent Variables at the SERP level

Variable	Description
count of results clicked on SERP	number of visited result pages from a given SERP
time on result pages [s]	time spent on result pages visited from a SERP
web page count	number of all web pages visited by following links from a given SERP (also done for 1st visits)
web page duration	time spent on all web pages visited by following links from a given SERP (also for 1st visits)
mean click distance from SERP	how many pages (clicks) away from SERP were opened (also done for 1st visits to SERPs)
max click distance from SERP	maximum number of pages (clicks) away from SERP were opened (also for 1st visits to SERPs)
rank of 1st result clicked	rank of a first result clicked on a SERP
mean result rank clicked	mean rank of a result clicked on a SERP
max result rank clicked	highest rank of a result clicked on a SERP

5. RESULTS

We report the findings for fourteen child-participants, six in sixth grade (age 11) and eight in eighth grade (age 13).

5.1 Query level by task

At the query level, there was a significant difference across the three tasks in relation to query entry, query length, number of SERPs visited per query for each task, total SERPs visited by task, and total duration on a SERP per task (Table 4). Pairwise comparisons show that tasks 1 and 3 differ significantly on all measures (underlined in Table 4) except for the count of the SERPs visited. Tasks 1 and 2 differed significantly on query length ($p<.001$), while tasks 2 and 3 differed significantly on query entry duration ($p=.009$), count of visited SERPs ($p=.014$), and total duration of SERP visits ($p=.001$) (shaded cells in Table 4).

Table 4. Results at the query level across the three tasks

Variable	Task 1 mean (SD)	Task 2 mean (SD)	Task 3 mean (SD)	χ^2	p[1]
query entry duration [s]	35 (39)	28 (34)	9 (9.5)	225	<.001
query length [words]	8.8 (3.5)	4.9 (2.7)	5.3 (2.9)	339	<.001
count of SERPs visited per query	3 (1.7)	4 (2.4)	2.6 (1.9)	309	.033
total SERP duration [s]	119 (94)	118 (81)	49.8 (55)	294	.001

[1] Asymp. Sig. (2-tailed).

5.2 Query level by grade level

We found significant differences between younger and older children. Younger children took longer time to enter queries and visited more SERPs per query (M=4.3) than older children (M=2.9) (Table 5). The differences in query length or in total duration on SERPs between the two groups were approaching significance.

Table 5. Results at the query level by grade level

Variable	6th grade mean (SD)	8th grade mean (SD)	M-W U	p[1]
query entry duration [s]	26 (14)	18 (23)	225	.005
query length [words]	7.9 (3.8)	6 (3)	339	.066
count of SERPs	4.3 (2.6)	2.9 (1.7)	309	.039
total SERP duration [s]	132 (92)	84 (79)	294	.059

[1] Asymp. Sig. (2-tailed)

5.3 Clicks at the SERP level by grade level

We found significant difference in the number of results clicked on SERPs between younger and older children. Younger children clicked on more results than older children (Table 6). The maximum position of ranked results clicked was also significantly different between the two groups. Younger children clicked more often on results in lower-ranked positions than older children, from the first- to the fourth-ranked positions. However, the rank of the 1st result clicked was not significantly different between the two groups. Younger children tended to click more on 1st or 2nd top-ranked results, while older children clicked anywhere between the first- and sixth-ranked result. A few other variables approach significance. For example, time spent on result pages directly clicked from SERPs was 430 seconds for younger children vs. 233 second for older children. The overall number of 1st visits to all web pages (i.e., including links followed from other web pages and not only from SERPs) approached significant difference between the two groups. Additionally, younger children visited more pages than older children (Table 6).

5.4 Thought processes and sources of information

The Retrospective Think-Aloud interviews tapped into the children's mindset and explored their thoughts and judgment for clicking on results on a SERP. Here we report these thoughts for younger children only (grade 6, age 11). We are coding and analyzing the rest of the collected data (including data from grade 7 students). Those who clicked on the 1st result on a SERP had different thoughts. For example, one child said: "I usually pick the first result that pops up". In asking why so, the child said: "because it is the most trustworthy or the most viewed one. If the result is not good, I go to the next one, I just go down." It seems that this child's selection style is sequential in nature [1]. Another child indicated that reading the summary of the 1st result and the title helps to make a decision to click or not, a decision confirmed in a previous study [7]. "Convenience" was conveyed by another child. When prompted, the child explained "convenience" as the result "had the answer I needed." It seems that this child did not articulate well the meaning of "convenience." Other thoughts on choosing the 1st top-ranked result: "helpful I can understand it, ability to read it, "familiarity" with the site" (referring to National Geographic), "it's not complicated." This comment refers to the readability of the result. Other thoughts were: "I think it's the most recent one so it's most accurate," "It captured my eyes a little bit," "habit…I don't have to scroll down…," and "I was going in order."

Table 6. Results at the SERP level for grade levels

Variable	6th grade mean (SD)	8th grade mean (SD)	M-W U	p[1]
count of results clicked on SERP	3.6 (2.2)	2.2 (1.5)	172	.026
time on result pages [s]	430 (335)	233 (244)	183	.056
web page 1st visit count	4.2 (3.3)	2.5 (1.9)	193	.077
web page 1st visit duration [s]	467 (360)	297 (261)	199	.438
mean click distance from SERP	1.07 (.19)	1.11 (.27)	254	.480
max click distance from SERP	1.29 (.72)	1.3 (.61)	258	.549
rank of 1st result clicked	1.36 (.5)	2 (1.4)	225	.222
mean result rank clicked	3 (1)	2.7 (1.47)	228	.300
max result rank clicked	4.86 (2.2)	3.5 (1.96)	181	.048

[1] Asymp. Sig. (2-tailed).

Not all younger children indicated the source of information that influenced the click decision. Those who did mentioned they had learned it in school. In future work, we will report on the differences in thought processes between younger and older children, explore the type of digital information literacy programs offered in schools attended by the participants, and gather school librarians' perspectives on to the participants' thought processes.

6. DISCUSSION

The age of our group of young users, tasks they performed, context, and methodology are different from those used in previous studies of children's interaction on the Web including Google. Nevertheless, we found both similar and inconsistent patterns in the query analysis and click behavior reported in previous studies. As to the task type, there was no statistically significant effect of search task at the SERP level, but there were significant effects of task type at the query level. Children formulated shorter queries on the research task and longer queries on the factual task and seemed to put less effort into the fully self-generated task. As was mentioned earlier, the study by [15] found little difference in the number of query characters between navigational and non-navigational queries by children's age level (10 to 12 and 13-15). Additional analysis of the data could provide a better explanation of the differences found in the present study. It is plausible that the difference we found is due to the specific search topics used in our study.

Overall, younger children in grade six (age 11) were less discriminating in what they clicked on, more exhaustive in the exploration of results, and slower in formulating somewhat longer queries than older children (grade eight, age 13). They also seemed to make less deliberate choice in choosing which result to click. Their click behavior showed that they started clicking on the top two-ranked results in a SERP. This may be due to their thought processes while clicking on results as reported in the previous section. Convenience, habit, and sequence are examples of these thoughts. It seems that older children's clicking behavior was based more often on reading result snippets and not just on the ranked position of a result in a SERP. While they tended to click on the top-ranked results (Mean rank=2), the range of their clicks was on results ranked 1-6, confirming the results by [8] and [15]. However, this finding is inconsistent with [4, 5] in terms of the age group or with [10]. Analysis of the additional click data should provide a deeper understanding of this click behavior across all child-participants.

7. CONCLUSIONS

Younger and older children had some misconception about the meaning of ranked results in Google SERPs, indicating an inadequate level of education in this area. The strong effect of children's age or grade level, query characteristics, and click behavior provides a basis for future research. While this study employed a small sample compared to large-scale logs studies, it unveiled some patterns of similarities and differences in the findings, warranting further investigation. The early findings from this study provide basis for further investigations of children's query analysis, click behavior, and thought processes while interacting with Google. We will analyze the additional quantitative and qualitative data we have collected from the children in both grade levels (6 and 7) and compare their behavior and thought processes to those in 7th grade. This analysis should allow us to draw more definite conclusions and to overcome some of the limitations of this work.

ACKNOWLEDGMENTS

This research has been supported, in part, by Google Faculty Research Award to Dania Bilal and Jacek Gwizdka.

8. REFERENCES

[1] Bilal, D. 2000. Children's use of the Yahooligans! Web search engine: I. Cognitive, physical, and affective behaviors on fact-based search tasks. *Journal of the American Society for Information Science*. 51, 7 (Jan. 2000), 646–665.

[2] Bilal, D. 2001. Children's use of the Yahooligans! Web search engine: II. Cognitive and physical behaviors on research tasks. *Journal of the American Society for Information Science and Technology*. 52, 2 (Jan. 2001), 118–136.

[3] Bilal, D. 2002. Children's use of the Yahooligans! Web search engine. III. Cognitive and physical behaviors on fully self-generated search tasks. *Journal of the American Society for Information Science and Technology*. 53, 13 (Nov. 2002), 1170–1183.

[4] Druin, A. et al. 2009. How Children Search the Internet with Keyword Interfaces. *Proceedings of the 8th International Conference on Interaction Design and Children* (New York, NY, USA, 2009), 89–96.

[5] Druin, A. et al. 2010. Children's Roles Using Keyword Search Interfaces at Home. *Proceedings of the SIGCHI Conference on Human Factors in Computing Systems* (New York, NY, USA, 2010), 413–422.

[6] Duarte Torres, S. and Weber, I. 2011. What and How Children Search on the Web. *Proceedings of the 20th ACM International Conference on Information and Knowledge Management* (New York, NY, USA, 2011), 393–402.

[7] Foss, E. et al. 2012. Children's search roles at home: Implications for designers, researchers, educators, and parents. *Journal of the American Society for Information Science and Technology*. 63, 3 (Mar. 2012), 558–573.

[8] Gossen, T. 2015. *Search engines for children: search user interfaces and information-seeking behaviour*. Springer Verlag.

[9] Dan Wu and Weiping Cai 2016. An empirical study on Chinese adolescents' web search behavior. *Journal of Documentation*. 72, 3 (Apr. 2016), 435–453.

[10] Duarte Torres, S. et al. 2010. An analysis of queries intended to search information for children. *Proceedings of the third symposium on Information interaction in context* (New York, NY, USA, 2010), 235–244.

[11] Bilal, D. and Gwizdka, J. 2016. Children's Eye-fixations on Google Search Results. *Proceedings of the 79th ASIS&T Annual Meeting* (Silver Springs, MD, USA, 2016), 53:1–6.

[12] Piaget, J. and Inhelder, B. 2008. *The Psychology of The Child.* Basic Books.

[13] Sternberg, R.J. and Sternberg, K. 2016. *Cognitive Psychology*. Cengage Learning.

[14] Wei, X. et al. 2014. YASFIIRE: Yet Another System for IIR Evaluation. *Proceedings of the 5th Information Interaction in Context Symposium* (New York, NY, USA, 2014), 316–319.

[15] Duarte Torres, S. et al. 2014. Analysis of Search and Browsing Behavior of Young Users on the Web. *ACM Trans. Web.* 8, 2 (Mar. 2014), 7:1–7:54.

Do Highlights Affect Comprehension? Lessons from a User Study

Samuel Dodson
iSchool
University of British Columbia
Vancouver, BC Canada
dodsons@mail.ubc.ca

Luanne Freund
iSchool
University of British Columbia
Vancouver, BC Canada
luanne.freund@ubc.ca

Rick Kopak
iSchool
University of British Columbia
Vancouver, BC Canada
r.kopak@ubc.ca

ABSTRACT

A largely unquestioned assumption in social reading is that publicly shared annotations improve reading outcomes. In this study, we explore the specific assumption that relevant and irrelevant passive highlighting affects comprehension. Participants were divided by cognitive style based on their degree of Field Dependence-Independence [20]. We found that irrelevant highlights had significant negative effects on reading comprehension for Field Independents (FIs), but not Field Dependents (FDs). This is a surprising result because FDs typically rely on external cues to structure and help process information, whereas FIs use internal cues. This suggests that highlighting cues information but does not structure it.

CCS Concepts

• *Information systems~Collaborative and social computing systems and tools* • *Information systems~Users and interactive retrieval* • *Human-centered computing~HCI design and evaluation methods* • *Applied computing~Collaborative learning*

Keywords

annotation; comprehension; highlighting; reading; social reading

1. INTRODUCTION

Highlighting is a common form of text annotation widely used to facilitate reading, especially when reading to learn. Given the connection between reading, highlighting, and learning, it was not surprising that Marshall's [11] seminal study of annotations found that most second-hand textbooks examined were thoroughly highlighted. The practice of highlighting has carried over from print to digital reading environments, most of which offer tools for highlighting. Features such as Popular Highlights on the Amazon Kindle go even further by storing and aggregating highlights and displaying them to readers as a layer of social information complementary to the original text.

The underlying assumption of such systems is that both active (made by the reader during the act of reading) and passive (made by previous readers) highlights have a positive effect on reading outcomes, such as increased comprehension, retention, and engagement. However, very little research exists to support this assumption, particularly in the digital context. This paper reports on a study of passive, or social highlights, and investigates their effect on comprehension, an important outcome of human information interaction and a key component of learning.

CHIIR '17, March 07 - 11, 2017, Oslo, Norway

ACM 978-1-4503-4677-1/17/03...$15.00
DOI: http://dx.doi.org/10.1145/3020165.3022158

2. PREVIOUS WORK

Marshall [11] identified multiple uses of highlights: as signals for future use; as place marks for a specific passage to be referenced later; and, to focus attention on the text, especially when a passage is difficult to read. Of these, the first is most applicable to passive highlights, which signal to readers the most important or interesting sections of the text. There is some evidence that highlights that cue key passages increase recall regardless of whether they were actively created by the reader or passively encountered [5, 9, 10]. However, one of the concerns with passive highlights, is that they may be of poor quality. If we consider that the effectiveness of highlights relies upon the von Restorff effect [15], which predicts that an item that stands out from its background is more likely to be remembered than items that do not, we have to acknowledge that poor quality highlights may interfere with readers' ability to make sense of, and learn from, highlighted text [14]. Readers may simply jump from one highlighted passage to the next, without assessing the quality or relevance of the highlights, as was found in [3].

Silvers and Kreiner [18] studied the effects of relevant and irrelevant highlighting on text comprehension in a two-phase study with three conditions: no highlighting (control), relevant highlighting, and irrelevant highlighting. They found that the participants performed similarly in the relevant and control conditions, but the irrelevant highlighting had a significant negative effect on comprehension. The same negative impact of irrelevant highlights was observed even after warning participants that the highlights may be irrelevant. We were intrigued by these results and decided to test them in a digital context. We also wondered if individual differences between readers may have influenced the results.

The way readers interact with information is affected by their cognitive styles [1, 12]. One of the most studied cognitive styles is Field Dependence-Independence (FDI) [20] [17, 19]. Messick [12] describes the difference as follows: "The field independent person tends to articulate figures as discrete from their backgrounds and to easily differentiate objects from embedding context, while the field dependent person tends to experience events globally in an undifferentiated fashion" (p. 5). FDs use external cues to guide their information processing, while FIs use internal ones. As a result, FDs are more likely to use the existing structure of a field, whereas FIs create their own [21].

While FDI was originally a measure of perceptual ability (to structure or restructure visual fields), it has been found to affect other tasks, such as problem solving [19], cognitive restructuring ability [6], and attention to relevant cues [2]. In the context of reading, FDs are more likely to use the pre-existing structure of a text while FIs are better at focusing their attention on relevant information and ignoring distractions [7]. It is especially difficult for FDs to focus on the most important information when they are presented with distracting cues, such as irrelevant highlights [7]. When a field is well-structured, however, FDs can perform as well as FIs [21], suggesting that relevant highlighting could be used as an aid for FDs.

Given the prevalence of passive highlights in current social reading systems, we decided to test the assumptions that seem to underlie their design: that highlights of any kind improve the reading experience. Our research questions were as follows:

- Does the existence of relevant highlights improve text comprehension?
- Does the existence of irrelevant highlights reduce text comprehension?
- Are the effects of highlighting on comprehension influenced by cognitive style, specifically FDI?

3. METHODS

To answer these questions, we conducted a within-subjects experiment with 29 participants. Following the approach used by Silvers and Kreiner [18], participants were asked to read texts in three conditions: those with irrelevant highlights, those with relevant highlights, and a control with no highlights. We updated and improved the methods used in [18] by using lengthier texts presented in digital format with no more than 15% of the text highlighted, as suggested in [9]. We designed our own comprehension tests based on a recognized model of text comprehension [8]. Details of the methods are presented in the following sections.

Texts were three general interest articles from *Scientific American* of approximately 3,000 words each and presented in plain html format with charts and images removed. In the relevant highlighting condition passages that contained concepts or facts central to the overall meaning, or gist of the article were emphasized. Relevant highlights were created where at least two of the three researchers highlighted the same passage. Irrelevant highlights emphasized passages that at least two of the three researchers identified as informative, but peripheral to the main themes of the text. We then carefully trimmed the highlights down to include no more than 15% of the text in accordance with the findings of [9, 10].

The highlighting condition was the manipulated variable, with each participant reading one text in each condition. The Group Embedded Figures Test (GEFT) [24] was used to measure Field Dependence-Independence. Following Demick [4], participants who scored at, or below, the median GEFT score were classified as Field Dependent (FD) (M=10.33, SD=2.66, N=15) and those who scored above as Field Independent (FI) (M=10.33, SD=2.66, N=14). The primary dependent variable was comprehension, measured through tests administered after each text was read. Tests questions were designed in accordance with the Construction-Integration model [8] to assess microstructural and macrostructural comprehension, and were of three types: multiple choice matching questions; Sentence Verification Technique (SVT) questions [16]; and an open-ended summary question.

A convenience sample of 29 undergraduates (14 males, 15 females) was recruited via listservs and posted advertisements. Sessions lasting 1.5 hours were run with groups of 10 participants randomly seated in a large computer lab. Computers were pre-set to display the articles. Instructions, pre- and post-session questionnaires, and comprehension quizzes were provided in print format.

Participants completed a consent form, a demographics and reading habits questionnaire, and the GEFT (on paper). Then they were told their task was to read three articles and complete a comprehension quiz for each. The scenario was to imagine the articles had been assigned for an upcoming class discussion for which they had limited time to prepare. Participants were given five minutes to read each article. This was done to encourage efficient reading strategies, such as the use of highlights, and to simulate typical online reading behaviors [13].

The three articles were counterbalanced to reduce ordering effects but all participants experienced the conditions in the same order: relevant, control, irrelevant. This was to limit a negative carry-over effect that we observed in the pilot test when the irrelevant highlights were assigned first and subsequent highlights were ignored. After reading an article, participants were given seven minutes to complete the corresponding comprehension quiz. They were not allowed to look at the test until they had finished reading the article and were not able to refer to the article once they started the test. After completing the reading tasks, participants completed a post-session questionnaire asking about their experiences and their thoughts on the usefulness of the highlights. They received a $20 honorarium for participating.

The 3 researchers scored the open-ended summary responses independently using a rubric, compared scores, and reached a consensus score for each to ensure inter-scorer reliability. Data were analyzed using ANOVA and an alpha level of 0.05 was used for all statistical tests.

4. RESULTS

Comprehension scores for each condition were compared to measure the effects of highlighting on comprehension. Comprehension was measured using multiple choice, open-ended summary, and SVT questions. An overall measure, which averaged the scores from the three measures, was also used. The highest possible comprehension score for each measure is 100. Differences were found between measures of comprehension used in the study. Most previous studies have only used multiple choice as a measure of comprehension; these results found differences between the measures of comprehension, which may provide an argument for pairing other measures of comprehension with multiple choice.

Table 1 shows the mean overall comprehension scores for the three conditions, and are reported for all participants, FIs, and FDs. Across all three groups, the highest means were achieved in the control condition and lowest in the irrelevant.

The mean comprehension scores for all participants on the multiple choice and summary questions did not vary significantly across the three conditions; however, there was a significant effect of condition on the comprehension scores in the SVT question ($F(2,56) = 4.360, p = .017$). *Post hoc* tests, using the Bonferroni correction, indicated that SVT scores in the irrelevant condition

(M=53.09) were significantly lower than in the control (M=60.99) ($p = .006$), but the scores in the relevant condition (M=59.13) did not differ from the other conditions. When we combined the comprehension scores into an overall measure, there was a borderline significant effect of condition ($F(2,56) = 2.998, p = .058$) showing the same trend as for the SVT scores.

Table 1: Descriptive statistics of the overall measure.

		Condition					
		Relevant		Control		Irrelevant	
Group	n	*M*	*SD*	*M*	*SD*	*M*	*SD*
All	29	59.13	17.02	60.99	14.09	53.09	12.76
FD	15	62.70	15.43	64.06	11.94	54.30	13.58
FI	14	55.31	18.36	57.71	15.86	51.80	12.19

The mean comprehension scores of the FDs were relatively consistent across conditions. One-way within-groups ANOVAS showed no evidence of significant differences between comprehension scores across conditions for any of the measures.

For FIs, some differences did arise by condition. One-way within-groups ANOVAs show no evidence of significant differences by condition for the multiple choice and summary questions, but there was a significant difference for the SVT question ($F(2,26) = 3.405, p = .049$). A *post hoc* pairwise t-test, using the Bonferroni correction, indicates that scores in the irrelevant condition were significantly lower than the control ($p = .023$). Comprehension scores in the relevant condition were also lower than the control ($p = .053$).

In a post-session questionnaire participants were asked to describe what they thought of the highlights and whether some were more useful than others. Reactions to the highlights were mixed. Of the 29 participants, eight indicated that the highlights were very helpful, 13 claimed the quality of the highlights varied, while 8 found the highlights unhelpful.

There was an even distribution of FDs and FIs among these response groups, suggesting that there was no effect of cognitive style on attitudes towards the highlighting conditions. Positive responses tended to emphasize that highlights helped with focus and overall understanding. P28 reflected that "Reading the highlights helped to get the gist of what [the] article was talking about but didn't help with the little details". P15 added "I tended to focus on the highlights."

P21 stated, "I thought the highlights were distributed between helpful and useless". P14 added, "I found the highlights to be very helpful, especially in the first article [the relevant condition], the third article highlights [the irrelevant condition] made me skim the surrounding information". P5 stated, "While skimming, I felt like I had to read them [the highlights], which was obnoxious when they weren't helpful".

Among those who had a negative response to both highlighting conditions, there was a split between those that claimed to have ignored all the highlights and those that looked at them, but did not find them useful. Several participants used words such as "annoying" and "distracting" to describe the highlights. Two participants said that they do not value highlighting. P10 said "I didn't really notice the highlights, because I was focused on reading. I believe highlights are most helpful, when done by the reader." P23 added, "I didn't find the highlighting useful. If I wasn't the one to highlight, the highlight just gets in the way". Four participants said they ignored the highlights. P9 said "did not pay much attention to the highlights, felt they were distracting as they pulled my focus away from the article when I was reading." P4 "noticed them but didn't really analyze them."

5. DISCUSSION

How do relevant and irrelevant highlights affect comprehension? The results provide no evidence that relevant highlights improve comprehension for any of the groups, and some evidence that irrelevant highlights negatively affect comprehension. Mean comprehension scores were lowest in the irrelevant highlighting condition across all groups in most measures. Statistical testing provided some evidence to support this trend, indicating that comprehension scores were significantly lower in one measure for the irrelevant condition than in the control condition for all participants and FI groups. For FIs, there is even limited evidence that relevant highlights may be more detrimental to comprehension than no highlights at all.

These results validate the earlier work of Silvers and Kreiner [18], showing no benefit of relevant highlights and some negative effect of irrelevant highlights. Furthermore, this study shows that the effects of highlighting observed by Silvers and Kreiner extend to longer texts in digital reading environments. Together, these results suggest passive highlighting provides little benefit in terms of comprehension for these participants. For most individuals, reading texts without highlights results in higher comprehension than when presented with any kind of highlights.

A unique contribution of this work was its exploration of the effects of cognitive style. In examining the effects of relevant and irrelevant highlights within the FD and FI groups, our results showed that the comprehension of FDs was not significantly affected by the different conditions, while FIs seemed to be negatively affected by both irrelevant and relevant highlights. Both FDs and FIs performed best without highlighting. There was some variation in comprehension between groups and measures; however, mean comprehension was generally highest in the control and lowest in the irrelevant condition. Differences between relevant–control and irrelevant–control pairings were insignificant for FDs. While the relevant–control comparison was also insignificant for FIs, the irrelevant–control pairing was significant in the SVT measure. This finding suggests that readers' cognitive styles may be an important factor in the understanding of texts with passive highlighting. Contrary to what we would expect from the literature, FIs, rather than FDs, were affected by passive highlights. Given that FDs rely on external structuring to process information, we were surprised that the highlighting conditions had no effect on FDs' comprehension. We expected a positive effect of relevant structuring in the form of highlights, and negative effects of the control, which did not structure the text, and the irrelevant, in which the text was poorly structured. Similarly, we assumed that FIs would be unaffected by highlighting, because these individuals use internal rather than external processes to make sense of information. However, the comprehension scores for FDs were similar across conditions. The comprehension scores for FIs indicated that the irrelevant highlights were an impediment. There was even limited evidence that the relevant highlights interfered with comprehension.

One explanation for these two surprising results is that FDs and FIs engaged at different levels with the highlights. FDs' comprehension was not influenced by the highlights. FDs are known to accept the presentation of a text as given, so these individuals may have expended little or no effort assessing the relevance of the highlights. It was also found that highlights negatively affected FIs' understanding of the texts. These individuals may have spent great effort assessing the quality or relevance of the highlights, distracting them from their task in this study. Given that these results are contrary to our expectations, we must question how FDs and FIs interact with passive annotations. Future research could provide answers by measuring participants' visual attention through eye tracking.

In general, these results challenge the assumption that passive, or "social" highlights, benefit readers by helping them make sense of, and, learning from, texts. For some readers, passive highlights, whether relevant or irrelevant, may be a form of distraction and annoyance. This does not preclude benefits of highlights on different reading processes and outcomes, such as reading efficiency, navigation, re-finding information, and engagement, which may be the focus of our future research.

6. CONCLUSION

This study furthers our understanding of the effects of highlighting on reading comprehension through three contributions. No previous work on relevant and irrelevant highlights explored the effects of 1) readers with different cognitive styles, 2) the length of texts, or 3) presentation in digital reading environments. This study validates previous work [18], by showing that relevant highlights do not positively affect comprehension, while irrelevant highlights may have a negative effect on comprehension.

The results of the study are limited to passive highlights. Future work could use techniques such as eye tracking to collect more data on reading processes and consider measuring different reading outcomes, such as efficiency and engagement. It would also be useful to compare the effects of passive highlights with active highlighting. Work built upon the findings of this study will be significant in the development of digital reading environments that may better support readers' understanding and engagement with texts.

7. REFERENCES

[1] Ausburn, Lynna J, and Floyd B Ausburn. 1978. "Cognitive styles: Some information and implications for instructional design." *Educational Communication and Technology* 26 (4): 337–54.

[2] Berger, Elizabeth, and Leo Goldberger. 1979. "Field dependence and short-term memory." *Perceptual and Motor Skills* 49: 87–96.

[3] Chi, Ed H, Michelle Gumbrecht, and Lichan Hong. 2007. "Visual foraging of highlighted text: An eye-tracking study." In *Human-Computer Interaction: HCI Intelligent Multimodal Interaction Environments*, 589–98. Berlin, Germany: Springer.

[4] Demick, Jack. 2014. "Group Embedded Figures Test: Manual." Menlo Park, ca: Mind Garden, Inc.

[5] Fowler, Robert L, and Anne S Barker. 1974. "Effectiveness of highlighting for retention of text material." *Journal of Applied Psychology* 59 (3): 358–64.

[6] Goodenough, Donald R. 1976. "The role of individual differences in field dependence as a factor in learning and memory." *Psychological Bulletin* 83 (4): 675–94.

[7] Kent-Davis, J, and Kathryn F Cochran. 1989. "An information processing view of field dependence-independence." *Early Child Development and Care* 51 (1): 31–47.

[8] Kintsch, Walter. 1998. *Comprehension: A paradigm for cognition*. Cambridge, England: Cambridge University Press.

[9] Lorch, Robert F, Jr. 1989. "Text-signaling devices and their effects on reading and memory processes." *Educational Psychology Review* 1 (3): 209–34.

[10] Lorch, Robert F, Jr, Elizabeth Pugzles Lorch, and Madeline A Klusewitz. 1995. "Effects of typographical cues on reading and recall of text." *Contemporary Educational Psychology* 20 (1): 51–64.

[11] Marshall, Catherine C. 1997. "Annotation: From paper books to the digital library." In *Proceedings of the Second ACM International Conference on Digital Libraries*, 131–40. New York, NY: ACM.

[12] Messick, Samuel. 1976. *Individuality in learning*. San Francisco, CA: Jossey-Bass Publishers.

[13] Nielsen, J. (1997, October). How users read on the web. Retrieved from https://www.nngroup.com/articles/how-users-read-on-the-web/

[14] Nist, Sherrie L, and Mark C Hogrebe. 1987. "The role of underlining and annotating in remembering textual information." *Literacy Research and Instruction* 27 (1): 12–25.

[15] Restorff, Hedwig von. 1933. "Über die wirkung von bereichsbildungen im spurenfeld." *Psychologische Forschung* 18 (1): 299–342.

[16] Royer, James M, Barbara A Greene, and Gale M Sinatra. 1987. "The sentence verification technique: A practical procedure for testing comprehension." *Journal of Reading*, 414–22.

[17] Shipman, Stephanie, and Virginia C Shipman. 1985. "Cognitive styles: Some conceptual, methodological, and applied issues." *Review of Research in Education*, 229–91.

[18] Silvers, Vicki L, and David S Kreiner. 1997. "The effects of pre-existing inappropriate highlighting on reading comprehension." *Literacy Research and Instruction* 36 (3): 217–23.

[19] Witkin, Herman A, and Donald R Goodenough. 1981. "Cognitive styles: Essence and origins field dependence and field independence." *Psychological Issues*, no. 51: 1–141.

[20] Witkin, Herman A, R B Dyk, H F Fattuson, Donald R Goodenough, and S A Karp. 1962. *Psychological differentiation: Studies of development*. New York, NY: Wiley.

[21] Witkin, Herman A, Donald R Goodenough, and Philip K Oltman. 1979. "Psychological differentiation: Current status." *Journal of Personality and Social Psychology* 37 (7): 1127–45.

[22] Witkin, Herman A, Philip K Oltman, Evelyn Raskin, and Stephen A Karp. 1971. *A manual for the embedded figures tests*. Palo Alto, ca: Consulting Psychologists Press.

Slide Over Here: The Various Adjacencies of Co-borrowed Ebooks

Dana McKay
University of Melbourne
Parkville, Melbourne
Victoria 3010, Australia
danamckay@gmail.com

George Buchanan
University of Melbourne
Parkville, Melbourne
Victoria 3010, Australia
george.buchanan@unimelb.edu.au

ABSTRACT
One of the major failings of ebook collections is the lack of readily available browsing mechanisms particularly in academic libraries. This stands in sharp contrast to the library shelves, and is bemoaned by readers as a reason to avoid the use of ebooks. Nonetheless earlier work has identified limited ebook co-borrowing; in this paper we address the relationships between these ebooks with a view to understanding how readers accessed them in a single session.

Keywords
User studies; libraries; information behaviour; information seeking, browsing.

1. INTRODUCTION AND BACKGROUND
It is clear from repeated studies beginning in 1993 [9] that shelf arrangements affect how readers borrow library books. Not only do we witness shelf arrangement affecting borrowing patterns in both observational [19] and log based studies [9; 12; 14], but readers tell us that browsing the shelves is an important book discovery mechanism [17]. There is no such shelf option for ebooks, a fact decried by users of both public [18] and academic [10] libraries. There are a number of systems [7; 16; 22] in early development that may provide readers with an option to browse digitally, however most of these thus far include physical books only, and none has been thoroughly tested.

Some may argue that search results provide an ebook browsing experience, but library search typically only displays a very limited number of results, and few readers will look beyond the first two pages at most [20]. True browsing, as defined by Bates [1], requires a rich and varied scene from which information seekers can select and sequentially examine objects of interest. It has been noted that by this definition, the library shelves are a near-ideal browsing engine [7]

Another online system that is frequently discussed in the context of ebook browsing is Amazon's 'customers who bought...' feature, however this system (like ordinary search) requires seeding with search terms. Choosing search terms is difficult [3], and even Amazon shows only a small number of alternative books.

CHIIR '17, March 07 - 11, 2017, Oslo, Norway

978-1-4503-4677-1/17/03...$15.00
DOI: http://dx.doi.org/10.1145/3020165.3022159

Despite the difficulty readers are likely to have in finding related ebooks, our earlier work [14] demonstrated a limited number of co-borrowings—that is, books that were borrowed in a single reading session by a single user. One criticism of our earlier work is that it is challenging to determine whether co-borrowings of items from the physical shelves occur due to their related topic, or whether they are encouraged specifically by shelf co-location and therefore browsing. In this paper we address both issues by looking for explanations for ebook co-borrowing. There are many possible ways in which ebook co-borrowings may occur. The first of these is that the ebooks in question may bear a close topical relationship—this relationship may not be apparent in a standard library classification scheme, it is a known failing of such schemes that related books are often shelved apart—but if we examine more than one classification scheme topic relationships are likely to be apparent. Another way that co-borrowings can occur is more weakly-related books appearing in search results together and being discovered together in this way. The third likely reason for ebook co-borrowing is a reader meeting two separate information needs (for example for two separate assignments) within a single information seeking session.

We attempt to determine, for a set of ebook loans from an academic library spanning four months, which explanation is best for any given co-borrowing. We use borrowing logs, which include classification metadata from both Dewey Decimal (DDC) and Library of Congress (LoC) classification schemes, and a two-level subject hierarchy allowing a fine grained investigation into the impact of topic. A side effect of this approach is that we can determine, at least for our ebook set, which classification scheme is a better fit for demonstrating topic relationships in this ebook collection. We also compare topic relationships with search as an explanation for co-borrowing.

By investigating the many possibilities for co-borrowing ebooks, we are attempting to understand the impact lack of shelves, so bemoaned by library users, has on actual use and usage patterns. We also hope to discover preferences about classification approach that can (possibly) be used to support the design of more flexible, human-centred information systems.

In the main part of the paper we describe the logs and discuss our method, then give the results of our analysis. Finally we discuss our results in the context of the existing literature

2. METHOD
This paper follows a long tradition of log analysis to understand user behaviour in both physical [9] and digital libraries [15]. It is also the most recent in our own series of works examining borrowing patterns [11-14], and as such builds on the methods we have presented earlier. In this section we will briefly describe the collection we analysed, then address the methods used specifically within this paper.

The ebook collection we used is works purchased from a single ebook provider by Swinburne, a small, research active university in Australia. The provider logs several pieces of metadata for each use of a book, including book title, anonymous user key, start date and time and duration of use, pages accessed and broken down by view copy and print, and for each book one or more LoC codes, DDC codes and subject headings. The ebook collection in question allows 'browsing' of books prior to creating a 'loan'. Loans are created when a reader prints or copies any material, views more than 20 pages of a book or interacts with a book for more than five minutes. To create a loan the reader has to click 'yes' on a dialog box, a positive affirmation of interest in the content of the book at hand. We examined only data from loans, activity analogous to actually borrowing physical books. The sample data is a complete set of ebook data from March through to July of 2013, totalling 13,640 unique ebook loans.

At the time of the study the ebooks in this collection could not be downloaded, meaning useful sections of works had to be read on screen, printed or copied. As such there is no activity analogous to borrowing a number of books in a single transaction, as one would with print. As such we determined that books borrowed together were those where a second book was borrowed within 30 minutes of finishing using the first; this is the same metric we use in earlier work [14].

We divided use into sessions, where each session was a single reader accessing one or more books with no more than a 30 minute break. We identified 12579 sessions, generated by 4957 unique readers. 875 were multi-book; these included 1935 books. The remaining 11704 sessions were singleton loans.

The collection uses three separate classification schemes for books: DDC; LoC and a collection-specific subject hierarchy. Each book is assigned to one or more points in each classification scheme. To compare classification schemes we looked at the distances between co-borrowed books within each scheme.

For each classification scheme we generated a sorted library file (like a single long shelf) showing all books in the library, even those that had never been borrowed. For the Subject scheme we sorted books alphabetically by title within classes. To compare schemes we then calculated the distance between co-borrowed pairs in each scheme. Where a book had more than one classification within a scheme, we took the shortest distance. This follows the process used in the previous work [14]. Each pair of co-borrowed books thus had separate distances for Dewey, LoC and Subject schemes. Where the either book had no classification headings, then the two were not counted as co-borrowings for the classification system being used. However, fewer than 70 books lacked an assignment under any classification.

For search, a different mechanism was used to calculate distance. We used the title data for each book, and for each co-borrowed pair, created a list of the title keywords shared by both books. These words were used as query terms, and a search was done against and index of all titles, using the log-rule matching algorithm. This produced a ranked list of all matching documents. The difference of the relative rank of the two documents in the sorted result list was used as their distance in the search condition. Where there were no common title words, the two books were eliminated as search co-borrowings.

As a final note, as each search produces a unique ordering, and that as an ideal, a book will be a top match for itself, there is a difference in the treatment of search and browse neighbours. In the case of search neighbours are only available in one direction (usually seen as 'down' on screen). In contrast, in the vast majority of cases a book has neighbours both before and after it in the hierarchy, or on the shelf to both left and right. Thus, there are ten books within five places to its left and right, whereas for a (top) search result, the same ten neighbours all lie 'below' it. We corrected for this in data processing.

3. RESULTS

First we report our findings regarding the relationships between the different subject classifications and the co-borrowing loans seen in the collection. Then, we compare search against these hierarchies, to see which better accounts for the collection's co-borrowing, and report in detail the relationship between topics and the level of co-borrowing in different parts of the collection. Finally, we note finer details that compare browse and search.

3.1 Subject Shelving versus Search

We compiled data for classifications using all three methods used in the ebook library: 1) Dewey decimal; 2) Library of Congress and 3) Subject headings. The latter is specific to the system being used, and has 35 main headings, two of which ('Engineering' and 'Science') have eight further sub-headings apiece. This creates a simple two-level classification scheme.

We detected 44 erroneous records in our loans file (out of 13640) resulting in a change in mean from our earlier published work. Means are shown in Table 1 below.

Table 1: distances between co-borrowing by classification

	Mean	Median
DDC	3243.3	1191
LoC	2927.11	578
Subject Headings	2779	886

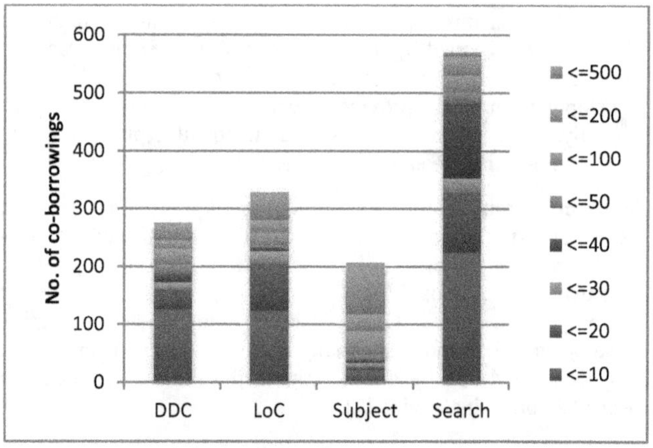

Figure 1: co-borrowing matches by classification, within different rank/shelf distances

We collated the data for the number of co-borrowings at distances of 10, 20, etc. up to 500 books away, summarised in Figure 1 and Table 2. Note, as per Section 2, there are slightly different treatments for browse and search to provide a like-for-like comparison. The different distance lists were tested against each other using a four-way Kruskal-Wallis test, producing $p<0.001$ ($H=487.15$, $df=3$). Closer study confirmed that, as the table suggests, search is markedly the most effective, and subject heading the least effective, but the differences between the Dewey and LoC organisation are not significant ($p=0.087, H=2.936, df=1$).

Table 2: co-borrowing matches by classification, within different rank/shelf distances

Distance	DDC	LoC	Subject	Search
10	127	124	21	225
20	161	205	27	328
30	173	227	34	353
40	187	232	39	483
50	203	237	47	502
100	231	259	89	531
200	245	281	118	564
500	276	328	207	570
> 500	1253	1201	1322	959

We also examined the pattern of co-borrowings across the Subject hierarchy, to establish how often books in the same subject heading were borrowed together. In total, there were 4313 co-borrowings; of these, 1004 loan pairs shared one or more categories in the subject hierarchy. We further investigated to see if there were topic effects—i.e. subjects that had disproportionate rates of co-borrowings within their topic. The ten largest classifications, by holding count, are seen in Table 3.

Table 3: Summary of co-borrowing by Subject classification

Subject	Books	Co-borrowed books	Co-borrowed in class
Business	4319	461	124
Social Science	3512	1067	310
Medicine	1626	278	68
Engineering	1364	445	127
Psychology	1124	323	15
Education	1099	680	211
Computer Science	1068	212	49
Science	892	112	13
Fine Arts	700	15	11
Political Science	591	86	7

There were marked patterns—e.g. "Business", which contains a total of 4319 books, and accounts for a high proportion of solo loans, was involved in 461 co-borrowings, of which 124 had both books in the subject. In contrast, Computer Science has 1068 books and 212 co-borrowings, of which 49 co-borrowings are within-subject. However, the highest rate of co-borrowings in a sizable subject was in Education, where 1099 books had 688 co-borrowings of which 211 within-subject. This indicates that even for ebooks, there are clear co-borrowing topic effects. Similarly co-borrowing within topic is not evenly distributed by topic, even considering book holdings, borrowing rates or co-borrowing rates. These differences were strongly significant, though very small subject holdings had to be eliminated to avoid null-values. A chi-squared test of the rate of co-borrowing versus expected values by holding rate, for example, produced $p<0.0001$, $\chi^2=9213$, df=28.

Turning back to a global comparison of the different classification hierarchies, we look at what we term the number of neighbour co-borrowings—co borrowings within 5 books of each other in any organization. DDC yielded 129 neighbour borrowings, LoC 147. The difference between these figures is not statistically significant due to the low level of neighbour co-borrowing generally. In contrast, the subject ordering produced a mere 31 neighbour co-borrowings, and this difference was statistically significant ($p<0.001$, $\chi2=83.29$, df=2).

These figures are a stark contrast to the relative position of books using even a simplistic keyword search. We used shared title words for co-borrowed ebooks to determine how many occurred in the top ten rankings for such a search. This accounted for 268 neighbour co-borrowings, rather a higher figure than any of the topic relationships discussed above. Given that search is the only mechanism by which readers can locate ebooks that are not known items, the dominance of search as a predictor of co-borrowing is unsurprising.

We then analysed how often these documents were also close on the shelf organisations above, and what the relative distances were in both potential methods of discovery. Any document pair that could only be explained by one method was counted separately. The distance between documents for both methods was not used to limit the data. For the co-borrow pairs that were comparable, the shelf distance was shorter for 85 cases, tied for 8 cases, and the search distance was shorter for 353 pairs. The data was further characterised by the median shelf distance being 1004 (rather lower than the general pool) for browsing, and a mere 31 for search. A Mann-Whitney test produced $z=13.23$, $r=0.384$, $p<0.001$. Several different tests led to the same conclusion, that search was a significantly better predictor of co-borrowing than shelving location.

4. DISCUSSION AND CONCLUSIONS

Browsing the shelves, and the proximity of material in the physical library is long reported as supporting information discovery [5; 10]. Teasing out the distinction between serendipitous moments at the shelves and the simple fact that books shelved together are semantically related [21] is difficult, though, and this has been one of the major criticisms of our earlier work [11-14]. By investigating co-borrowing in a collection for which no semantic presentation such as the shelves exists, we can speculate on the effect of presentation on these discovery experiences.

It is clear from our data that topic similarity is by any means not as important in ebook data as shared keywords, thus readers at the electronic shelves are not borrowing books they might see and find relevant if they were standing at the physical shelves. It is not merely the semantic relationships between neighbouring books that has driven the neighbour effect seen in our earlier work [12-14]; it is also the presentation of these books in close visual proximity, an arrangement that affords browsing [1].

None of this is to say the shelves are a perfect information seeking resource—they clearly aren't [2]—nor that ebooks represent a threat to intellectualism, as some have argued [4]. It does reinforce, however, the urgent need for online browsing systems.

The 'cluster hypothesis' in information retrieval [6] has long suggested that matches to a search are naturally clustered, and it is perhaps more likely that the shared classifications that we do see may well be emerging from that phenomenon, rather than users in fact browsing a hierarchy online.

Our choice of keywords was (necessarily) naïve, as we had no means of obtaining any search terms that users actually used to retrieve these documents. As we created synthetic search terms purely from document titles, it is very probable that we both under-report the amount of co-borrowing related to searching the collection. It is also likely in the case of search that we report a greater nominal distance down the ranked list than users actually experienced, especially given users' known parsimony when reading pages of results [20]. This clearly demonstrates that readers are unlikely to have typed in a number of searches to find books (another critique of our earlier work) and suggests instead exactly what we would expect in the simplest case: readers are using what they find in the first page of search results, whether it is the most relevant material to their needs or not.

Looking in more detail at our results, we see clear topic differences; this is something that has been noted in earlier studies of ebook use [8]. Targeting efforts to improve the ebook browsing experience on those fields where co-borrowing is already high is likely to be an effective starting point.

5. CONCLUSION

In this study we have investigated the ways in which ebooks borrowed within a single information session by the same user are related. Search accounts better for relationships than any measure of semantic similarity. On one hand this result is to be expected, there is no semantic presentation of ebooks. On the other, it reinforces a clear need for ebook browsing systems: readers have said they want them; their behaviour at physical shelves demonstrates the value of browsing, and this study shows that topic relationships are not enough for ebooks to be found together in search. How best to provide that experience, with all the potential advantages of an online system over physical shelves, remains a question for future work.

6. ACKNOWLEDGMENTS

Our thanks to the library of Swinburne University of Technology for permitting our access to the user log data.

7. REFERENCES

[1] Bates, M.J., 2007. What is browsing--really? A model drawing from behavioural science research. *Inform Res 12.*

[2] Blandford, A., Rimmer, J., and Warwick, C., 2006. Experiences of the Library in the Digital Age. In *Proc CCCDT 06* (Tavros, Greece), FOHW.

[3] Borgman, C.L., 1996. Why are online catalogs *still* hard to use? *JASIS 47*, 7, 493-503. DOI= http://doi.org/10.1002/(SICI)1097-4571(199607)47:7<493::AID-ASI3>3.0.CO;2-P.

[4] Cull, B.W., 2011. Reading revolutions: online digital text and implications for reading in academia. *First Monday 16*, 6.

[5] Hancock-Beaulieu, M., 1993. Evaluating the impact of an online library catalogue on subject searching at the catalogue and at the shelves. *J Doc 46*, 4, 318-338. DOI= http://doi.org/10.1108/eb026863.

[6] Hearst, M.A. and Pedersen, J.O., 1996. Reexamining the cluster hypothesis: scatter/gather on retrieval results. In *Proc SIGIR 96* (Zurich, Switzerland), ACM, 76-84. DOI= http://doi.org/10.1145/243199.243216.

[7] Kleiner, E., Rädle, R., and Reiterer, H., 2013. Blended shelf: reality-based presentation and exploration of library collections. In *Proc CHI 13* (Paris, France), ACM, 577-582. DOI= http://doi.org/10.1145/2468356.2468458.

[8] Littman, J. and Connaway, L.S., 2004. A Circulation Analysis of Print Books and E-Books in an Academic Research Library. *Libr Resour Tech Serv 48*, 256-262.

[9] Losee, R.M., 1993. The relative shelf location of circulated books: A study of classification, users, and browsing. *Libr Resour Tech Serv 37*, 2, 197-209.

[10] Makri, S., Blandford, A., Gow, J., Rimmer, J., Warwick, C., and Buchanan, G., 2007. A library or just another information resource? A case study of users' mental models of traditional and digital libraries. *JASIST 58*, 3, 433-445. DOI= http://doi.org/10.1002/asi.20510.

[11] Mckay, D. and Buchanan, G., 2016. You can check it out but it will never leave: Characterising ebook borrowing patterns. In *Proc CHIIR 2016* (Carrboro, NC), ACM, 203-212. DOI= http://doi.org/10.1145/2854946.2854970.

[12] Mckay, D., Buchanan, G., and Chang, S., 2015. Tyranny of Distance: Understanding Academic Library Browsing by Refining the Neighbour Effect. In *Proc TPDL 15* (Poznan, Poland), Springer, 280-294. DOI= http://doi.org/10.1007/978-3-319-24592-8_21.

[13] Mckay, D., Smith, W., and Chang, S., 2014. Lend me some sugar: Borrowing rates of neighbouring books as evidence for browsing. In *Proc DL 2014* (London, UK), 145-154. DOI= http://doi.org/10.1109/JCDL.2014.6970161.

[14] Mckay, D., Smith, W., and Chang, S., 2015. Down the Superhighway in a Single Tome: Examining the Impact of Book Format on Borrowing Interactions. In *Proc OZCHI 16* (Melbourne, Australia), ACM, 517-525. DOI= http://doi.org/10.1145/2838739.2838766.

[15] Nicholas, D., Huntington, P., Jamali, H.R., and Tenopir, C., 2006. Finding Information in (Very Large) Digital Libraries: A Deep Log Approach to Determining Differences in Use According to Method of Access. *J Acad Libr 32*, 2, 119-126. DOI= http://doi.org/10.1016/j.acalib.2005.12.005.

[16] Pearce, J. and Chang, S., 2014. Exploration without Keywords: The Bookfish Case. In *Proc OzCHI 2014* (Sydney, Australia), ACM, 76-79. DOI= http://doi.org/10.1145/2686612.2686639.

[17] Rowlands, I. and Nicholas, D., 2008. Understanding Information Behaviour: How Do Students and Faculty Find Books? *J Acad Libr 34*, 1 (1//), 3-15. DOI= http://doi.org/10.1016/j.acalib.2007.11.005.

[18] Saarinen, K. and Vakkari, P., 2013. A sign of a good book: readers' methods of accessing fiction in the public library. *J Doc. 69*, 5, 736-754. DOI= http://doi.org/10.1108/JD-04-2012-0041.

[19] Saarti, J., 1997. Feeding with the spoon, or the effects of shelf classification of fiction on the loaning of fiction. *Inform Serv Use 17*, 2/3, 159. DOI= http://doi.org/10.3233/ISU-1997-172-312.

[20] Spink, A., Wolfram, D., Jansen, M.B.J., and Saracevic, T., 2001. Searching the web: The public and their queries. *JASIST 52*, 3, 226-234. DOI= http://doi.org/10.1002/1097-4571(2000)9999:9999<::AID-ASI1591>3.0.CO;2-R.

[21] Svenonius, E., 2000. *The Intellectual Foundation of Information Organization*. MIT Press, Boston, MA.

[22] Thudt, A., Hinrichs, U., and Carpendale, S., 2012. The bohemian bookshelf: supporting serendipitous book discoveries through information visualization. In *Proc CHI 12* (Austin, TX), ACM, 1461-1470. DOI= http://doi.org/10.1145/2207676.2208607.

Skip or Stay: Users' Behavior in Dealing with Onsite Information Interaction Crowd-Bias

Seyyed Hadi Hashemi Jaap Kamps
University of Amsterdam, Amsterdam, The Netherlands
{hashemi|kamps}@uva.nl

ABSTRACT

Mobile devices and the internet of things blend our virtual online behavior with our actions in the real-world. The physical context creates numerous external factors that play a role in the user's online interactions, thus creating new external biases in the collected information interaction logs. Our general aim is to improve our understanding of onsite users' behavior, which allow us to create better online and onsite contextual suggestion systems. We focus on the cultural heritage domain and have collected onsite users' information interaction logs of visits in a museum. This prompts the question: How to understand users' behavior in order to be able to predict their onsite behaviors? Our main findings are the following: First, users behave differently in different onsite contextual situations. Second, there is a significant dependency between users' onsite behaviors and other users, who are interacting with next point of interests (POIs). Third, we have proposed a contextual Skip-Or-Stay behavior classifier based on four different pairwise contextual features that significantly improves a defined baseline based on all the considered evaluation metrics. Fourth, we have analyzed the importance of different contexts in the Skip-or-Stay behavior predictions.

Categories and Subject Descriptors: H.3.3 [**Information Storage and Retrieval**]: Information Search and Retrieval—*Query formulation, Search process, Selection process*

Keywords: Behavioral dynamics; Bias; Internet of things; Onsite logs

1. INTRODUCTION

The last years witnessed the emergence of interests in understanding users' onsite behavior in different domains like tourists [2, 6] and cultural heritage [3]. To this aim, they become interested in logging users' onsite information interactions. However, due to many external noises and biases in the onsite information interaction logs, understanding users' behavior is challenging and difficult. Existence of onsite biases in onsite logs prompts the questions: how users behave in existence of external factors in physical spaces? Is it possible to predict users' behaviors using contextual information in the existence of onsite biases?

In the search domain, biases in query logs have been studied for a long time [1, 4]. For example, eye tracking studies for understanding how users interact with search results show a position rank bias in users click behavior, in which users tend to click on the top of the ranked list rather than the bottom [1]. Trust bias is another online bias, which is studied for using clickthrough data as implicit feedback [4]. Biases have also been studied in user click models, helping to better understand users' behavior [5].

Although users' online behaviors in interacting with search engines are well studied, there are a few studies on users' onsite behavior. Some of the biases in users' onsite information interactions are studied in [3], which found a "walk-through" position bias in users' onsite behaviors. Walk-through position bias is users' tendency in visiting point of interests one after the other, based on proximity in the real world, from check-in to check-out stations, even though users are free to visit any POI at any order. However, this users' tendency to visit POIs in a particular order is affected by other external factors leading to further, new biases in onsite information interaction logs. Specifically, as there are other visitors the next POI might be busy by another user, which leads to creation of a crowd-bias in onsite logs.

Existence of a user crowd in the physical space leads to two different users' onsite behaviors, namely, skip or stay. As it is shown in Figure 1, assume $user_a$ is interacting with POI2 and $user_b$ is interacting with POI3. Then, what would happen if $user_a$ wants to see another POI, but the next POI (i.e., POI3) is busy? *Skip behavior* is the case that $user_a$ skips the POI3 and prefers to visit another POI. *Stay behavior* is the case that $user_a$ waits until $user_b$ is satisfied by interacting with the POI3 and leaves the POI.

In this paper, we study users' behavior in dealing with the crowd-bias, and how their behaviors affected in different contexts. In fact, our main aim is to study the question: *How do users behave in the presence of a crowd of users in the physical space?* Specifically, we answer the following research questions:

1. *How does the context of an onsite session affect on users' behavior?*
2. *Is the Skip-Or-Stay behavior of users dependent on characteristics of users interacting with the next POI? Is it possible to effectively predict Skip-Or-Stay behavior using contextual information?*

CHIIR '17, March 07-11, 2017, Oslo, Norway

DOI: http://dx.doi.org/10.1145/3020165.3022160

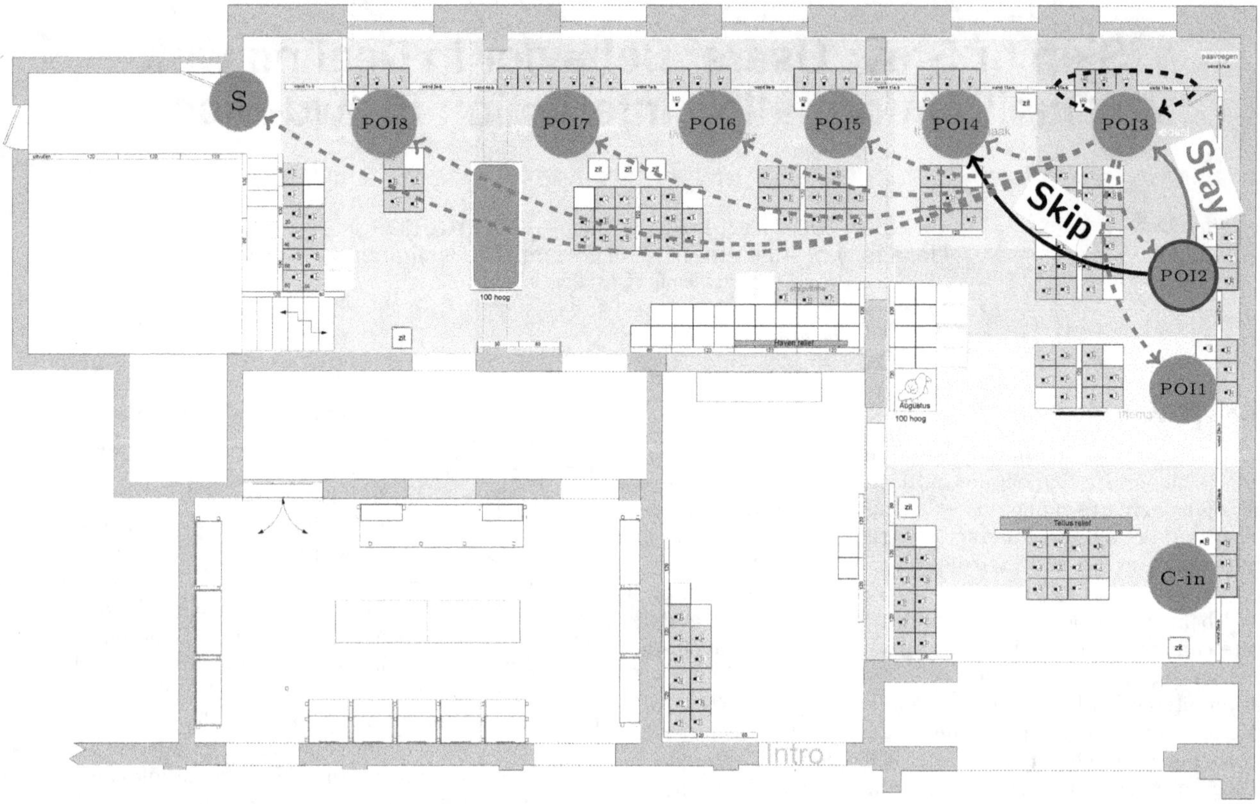

Figure 1: Skip-Or-Stay examples in onsite users' behavior. The figure indicates skip or stay behavior of a user at POI2. Stay behavior is shown by red edges and skip behavior is shown by black edges. Behaviors of the $user_a$ at the POI2 is shown by lines and behaviors of $user_b$ at the POI3 is shown by dashed lines. C-in is the check-in station and the S is the check-out station.

3. *What is the importance of each context in understanding users' Skip-Or-Stay behavior?*

The rest of the paper is organized as follows. Section 2 details the experimental data being used in this research. Section 3 studies the impact of different contexts on users' onsite behavior. Section 4 details our Skip-Or-Stay classification model. Section 5 is devoted to studying contribution of different contexts in understanding users' onsite behavior and Skip-Or-Stay prediction. Finally, Section 6 presents our conclusions and future work.

2. EXPERIMENTAL DATA

The dataset of this study is based on onsite information interaction logs collected at an archaeological museum. In the exhibition, RFID cards are provided as a key to access some additional information about objects being shown in the museum. Users can enter their preferences at the beginning of the museum exhibition in order to personalize the content being shown in all of the POIs. These preferences are the perspectives of the narratives, as well as language, gender and the user's age range.

After checking in, users are free to put their keys on RFID readers of POIs to unlock contents being shown about objects at the POIs. Each POI contains 3 different archeological objects. Users are free to interact with POIs in any order. They can watch short movies, interacting with 3D photos of POIs' objects, or read contents about objects being shown at POIs. At last, users might check out in a summary station, in which they might leave their name, birth date and email address. In this paper, five months onsite logs of the museum with more than 21,000 sessions are used.

In our collected onsite information interaction logs, about 16,000 out of 21,000 sessions either did not have any interactions with POIs or they did not check out at the summary station. We exclude all sessions have not checked in at any POI at the exhibition. We also exclude sessions that did not check out at the summary station as users who did not visit the whole exhibition and for whom we do not have all implicit judgements of their interests in POIs. As a result of this preprocessing step, 5,017 out of 21,000 high-quality onsite information interaction sessions remain for creating the test collection. Using the remained 5,017 sessions leads to creation of 2,001 cases that users came to a decision of Skip-Or-Stay behavior.

3. IMPACT OF CONTEXT ON USERS' BEHAVIOR

This section studies different users' behavior in dealing with the crowd-bias, aiming to answer our first research question: *How does the context of an onsite session affect on users' behavior?*

In this experiment, we consider language, age-range, gender and chosen perspective of narratives as explicit context

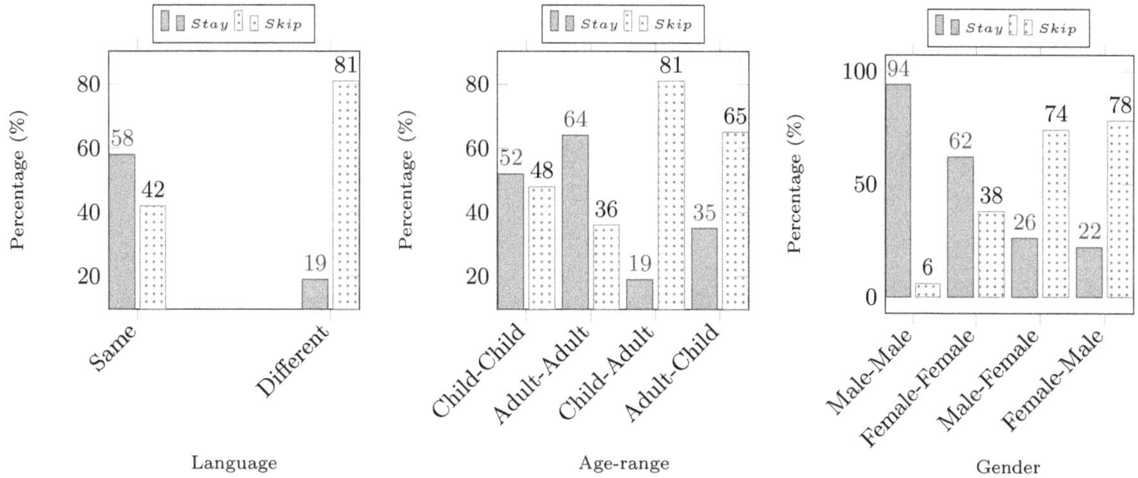

Figure 2: Impact of a sample of different contextual information on onsite users' behavior.

given explicitly at the physical environment. Then, we consider pairwise context of pairs of users as context in our study. For example, if gender of $user_a$ is "male", and gender of $user_b$ who is interacting with the next POI is "female", the pairwise gender context is $< Male, Female >$.

In this study, languages can be either "English" or "Dutch", age-range is either "Adult" or "Child", and perspectives are "Lowlands", "Egypt" or "Rome". As shown in Figure 2, each pair of users having different pairwise context, generally behave differently in staying or skipping the next busy POI.

Figure 2 shows pairwise contexts having a same language prefer to stay, however, users tend to skip the busy POI taken by a user speaking a different language. As another example, adults generally prefer to skip a POI taken by a child, however, they tend to stay if the next POI is taken by an adult. Interestingly, users prefer to gently skip a POI that is taken by a user having an opposite gender. On the other hand, users tend to stay at the POI in the case the next POI taken by another user having a same gender. To conclude, there are variety of onsite Skip-Or-Stay behaviors in different pairwise contexts, which seems very helpful in discriminating stay behavior from the skip behavior.

4. SKIP-OR-STAY BEHAVIOR PREDICTION

This section answers our second research question: *Is the Skip-Or-Stay behavior of users dependent on characteristics of users interacting with the next POI? Is it possible to effectively predict Skip-Or-Stay behavior using contextual information?*

We first detail how we classify users' Skip-Or-Stay behavior in the given pairwise context based on the pair of users. To this aim, we have used Logistic classifier, in which variable $c = 1$ indicates Stay behavior and $c = 0$ is the skip behavior. Specifically, $P_\theta(c = 1|u_a, u_b, p)$ is the probability of user u_a to stay at the next POI p and wait till the user u_b leave the POI, where θ is unknown parameters that are learned using maximum likelihood estimation (MLE) based on the train set.

Let U be a set of onsite users and P be a set of POIs available in the physical environment. Given the class label l for behaviors of user u_a while next POI is busy by user u_b in the train set, the likelihood L of the train set is as follows:

$$L = \prod_{i=1}^{|U|}\prod_{j=1}^{|U|}\prod_{k=1}^{|P|} P_\theta(c = 1|u_i, u_j, p_k)^l P_\theta(c = 0|u_i, u_j, p_k)^{1-l},$$

in which we assume class labels l are generated independently and $i \neq j$. We model $P_\theta(c = 1|u_i, c_j, p_k)$ by logistic function on a linear combination of features. Then, we optimize the unknown parameters θ by maximizing the following log likelihood function:

$$\theta^* = argmax_\theta \sum_{i=1}^{|U|}\sum_{j=1}^{|U|}\sum_{k=1}^{|P|}(l) log P_\theta(c = 1|u_i, u_j, p_k) + (1 - l) log P_\theta(c = 0|u_i, u_j, p_k).$$

To test the Skip-Or-Stay classification, in order to avoid overfitting, we have done 5-fold cross-validation, in which we leave one fold out as a test set and keep the rest as a train set. We repeat the process for all the 5 folds and report the average of the evaluation metrics. In this experiment, Precision of skip class (i.e., $P(Skip)$ in Table 1), Precision of stay class (i.e., $P(Stay)$), *Accuracy* and $F1$ are considered as evaluation metrics.

In order to test our proposed onsite user behavior classifier using pairwise context, we have defined a user behavior classifier using pointwise context as a baseline. Pointwise context is the explicit contexts given by users onsite. The only difference of the baseline with the proposed Skip-Or-Stay classifier is considering independency of users' behavior to the user interacting with the next POI.

As it is shown in Table 1, Skip-Or-Stay classifier using the pairwise contextual features significantly improves the baseline that gets independent pointwise contextual features as input based on all the defined evaluation metrics. In particular, the proposed Skip-Or-Stay classifier has 37% improvement in term of *Accuracy* and 59% improvement in term of $F1$ over the baseline. We perform significance testing in terms of all metrics using a paired t-test, treating p-values lower than 0.05 as statistically significant.

This experiment shows that users' Skip-Or-Stay behavior is not independent on other users in the physical environment. In fact, improvement of the Skip-Or-Stay classifier,

Table 1: Comparison of Skip-Or-Stay classification based on pairwise context and pointwise context. * indicates a statistically significant ($p < 0.05$) improvement.

Method	P(Skip)	P(Stay)	Acc.	F1
Pointwise	43.41	55.76	52.73	44.77
Pairwise	**76.18**	**70.42**	**72.42**	**71.06**
Improvement	**75.49***	**26.30***	**37.34***	**58.72***

which uses pairwise contextual features created based on users' behavior dependency on users interacting with the next POI, over the baseline is a proof for this conclusion.

5. CONTEXTS IMPORTANCE IN UNDERSTANDING USERS' ONSITE BEHAVIOR

This section answers our third research question: *What is the importance of each context in understanding users' Skip-Or-Stay behavior?*

To this aim, by assuming that contextual features obtaining greater weights in the training phase of the successful logistic regression classifier are more important than other contextual features, we consider the trained weights of the contextual features in the logistic classifier as an importance indicator.

To be able to compare the weights being optimized in each fold of the 5-fold cross validation, we have normalized learned weights of the logistic classifiers in each fold and mapped weights to values between -1 and 1. Then, we average the weights over the 5 folds. As it is shown in Figure 3, pairwise age-range and gender contextual features are relatively more important in Skip-Or-Stay behavior prediction in comparison to pairwise language and chosen perspective contextual features.

To conclude, this section shows different contexts has different importance and contribution in prediction of users' onsite behavior. Specifically, language is less important than the gender. The reason could be the ability of majority of Dutch people to fluently speak English. Therefore, it causes less limitations in users' onsite communications and behaviors. On the other hand, age-range and gender has a considerable impact in users' onsite behavior variance, which leads to greater weights and importance in comparison to language and chosen perspective as contextual information.

6. CONCLUSIONS

The main focus of this paper is to study users' behaviors in dealing with onsite external factors that create bias in onsite information interaction logs. Specifically, we observed a crowd-bias in the onsite logs, in which the user's tendency to visit POIs one after another is affected by other users occupying the next POI. An analysis based on more than 5,000 onsite sessions shows that different pairs of users with different pairwise contextual features behave differently in skipping the next busy POI or staying at the next busy POI till the POI becomes free. We defined four different pairwise contextual features, namely, language, age-range, gender and the chosen narrative perspective. In order to understand users' onsite behavior and predict their behavior, we have studied dependency of users' behaviors on other

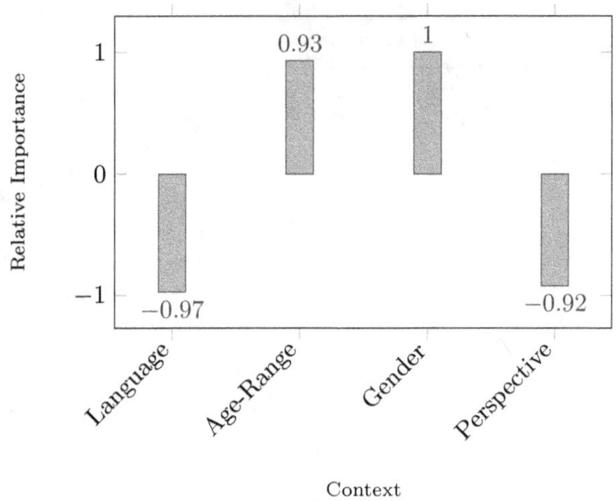

Figure 3: Relative importance of different contextual information on onsite users' behavior.

users interacting with the next POIs. The result of this study proves that user's behavior is more predictable by a users' behavior dependency assumption using pairwise contextual information in comparison to a Skip-Or-Stay classification based on pointwise contextual features with users' behavior independency assumption. Moreover, a study on contexts importance in understanding users' onsite behavior shows that different contexts contribute differently in prediction of the users' onsite behaviors. We realized that users pairwise age-range and gender contextual features have relatively more contribution in users' onsite behavior prediction in comparison to pairwise language and chosen perspective contextual features. As future work, we are going to investigate the effects of considering users' onsite behavior (e.g., Skip-Or-Stay behavior) in the unseen POI recommendation model based on onsite human information interactions.

Acknowledgments

This research is funded by the European Community's FP7 (project meSch, grant # 600851).

References

[1] L. A. Granka, T. Joachims, and G. Gay. Eye-tracking analysis of user behavior in www search. In *SIGIR*, pages 478–479, 2004.

[2] I. Guy. The role of user location in personalized search and recommendation. In *Proceedings of the 9th ACM Conference on Recommender Systems*, RecSys '15, pages 236–236. ACM, 2015.

[3] S. H. Hashemi, W. Hupperetz, J. Kamps, and M. van der Vaart. Effects of position and time bias on understanding onsite users' behavior. In *Proceedings of the 2016 ACM on Conference on Human Information Interaction and Retrieval*, CHIIR '16, pages 277–280. ACM, 2016.

[4] T. Joachims, L. Granka, B. Pan, H. Hembrooke, and G. Gay. Accurately interpreting clickthrough data as implicit feedback. In *SIGIR*, pages 154–161, 2005.

[5] Y. Zhang, W. Chen, D. Wang, and Q. Yang. User-click modeling for understanding and predicting search-behavior. In *KDD*, pages 1388–1396, 2011.

[6] O. Zoeter. Recommendations in travel. In *Proceedings of the 9th ACM Conference on Recommender Systems*, RecSys '15, pages 234–234. ACM, 2015.

Exploring the Role of Named Entities in Automatic Indexing

Anne-Stine Ruud Husevåg
2nd year PhD Student
Supervised by Prof. Ragnar Nordlie
Department of Archivistics, Library and Information Science
Oslo and Akershus University College of Applied Science, Oslo, Norway
Anne-Stine.Husevag@hioa.no

ABSTRACT

Due to a major digitization effort, the Norwegian Broadcasting Corporation, NRK, has made Norwegian cultural heritage from the last century of radio and TV available to the public. It is impossible to manually go through and index all the digitized material, and automatic methods are required. This PhD project explores the possible role and usefulness of named entities in an automatic indexing process. This is done by annotating named entities in textual documents from NRK (textual description in metadata records and subtitles), analyzing differences in various genres and document types, and surveying potential users. Different methods for extracting the most salient named entities will be investigated. This project encompasses both multimedia indexing, information behavior and different forms of evaluation.

Keywords

Named entities; Multimedia indexing; Metadata

1. MOTIVATION

Advances in information technology and web access of the past decade have triggered several digitization efforts by libraries, archives, and other cultural heritage institutions. The Norwegian Broadcasting Corporation, NRK, is one of them. Digitization is the first step in making cultural expressions available to a broader public, but indexing is vital to the information retrieval process. Because of the increasing amount of content that cultural heritage institutions have made available, the need to develop and refine indexing processes is rapidly growing. It may take a cataloguer up to three times the length of a TV-program to manually annotate keywords, depending on the genre [1]. Gustman et al. found that the process of creating a three-sentence summary of a clip and any necessary person objects, and then linking appropriate thesaurus descriptors and persons to the clip took about 15 hours for each hour of video [2]. Indexing content is an integral part of any collection of material and vital to the information retrieval process. Indexing multimedia material is a complex process, but automatic processing of text from subtitles is relatively simple, and therefore has a huge potential in terms of future implementation and actual use.

CHIIR '17, March 07-11, 2017, Oslo, Norway
ACM 978-1-4503-4677-1/17/03.
http://dx.doi.org/10.1145/3020165.3022166

The aim of this research is to improve search functions by better indexing, and to facilitate the generation of automatic recommendations, both inside the NRK archive and to other resources. Cultural expressions are often connected to places, persons, things or events in various ways. It is likely that different cultural institutions have information about the same entities, but these connections are not visible to users and researchers today. Semantic Web technology, in particular linked data, is often seen as a potential solution to this problem [3], [4]. An important first step in creating linked data is to identify which entities it will be useful to link to other entities, and I hope that my contribution to the research field can show how this language technology can be most useful for future users of broadcasting archives.

2. RESEARCH QUESTIONS

The overarching topic in this project is to explore the usefulness of Named Entity Recognition (NER) as a method for facilitating automatic indexing of broadcast material. My research questions are as follows:

1. Are named entities more salient content descriptors than other words?
    a. To what extent do users use named entities when searching for and describing content?
    b. To what extent do trained librarians use named entities when describing content?
    c. Are some entity types more salient than other types, and is this different in different genres and material?
    d. What characterizes salient entities?
2. What methods are best suited to extract the most salient named entities from subtitles?
    a. Will these approaches find the same entities that users use when searching?
3. How can recognition of named entities improve linking between documents?
    a. To what extent are users interested to learn more about named entities mentioned in a program?

b. Will similarity measures based on named entities alone give a different result than similarity measures based on descriptions in metadata records or the full text from subtitles?

3. METHODOLOGY

Data for this project is collected from different sources, mainly subtitles and metadata records from NRK, but also input from potential users. Information from users is collected through a questionnaire. In collaboration with other researchers from Oslo and Akershus University College of Applied Science, I have annotated named entities in a corpus of metadata records and subtitles from two different categories of programs: culture and news. We chose to develop our own annotation tool to allow annotations on specific levels adapted to our projects. It also enabled us to annotate the material with the same entity types as the other Norwegian researchers on NER have used in their projects, in order to be able to compare our results with earlier research. Our joint efforts and annotating tool is discussed in detail in [5].

The annotated entities can be analyzed in many different ways. The focus in my project is to compare named entities from different programs and data sources. The comparison of named entities used to describe programs from different genres, and subtitles and metadata records for the same TV programs is particularly interesting. When named entities are used in metadata records and in input from potential users, they may be perceived as more salient than other named entities. An increased understanding of the differences between salient and non-salient named entities would improve methods for automatic indexing. When comparing methods for extracting the most salient named entities, the metadata records are made by trained librarians and acts as a gold standard. I will rank the named entities according to types and frequency (both simple counts and tf-idf), and also by frequency and type of relations to other named entities.

4. PROGRESS MADE SO FAR

I have begun the work by analyzing entity types, name density and name frequencies in subtitles and metadata records from different TV programs. The analysis shows that the name density in metadata records is much higher than the name density in subtitles, implying that named entities are important in the descriptions of this kind of material. The findings indicate that named entities with high frequencies in the subtitles are more likely to be mentioned in the metadata records, and that differences in frequencies have a higher discriminatory value for some entity types. Personal names, geographical names and names of organizations where the most prominent entity types in both the news subtitles and news metadata, while persons, works and locations are the most frequent in culture programs. A paper describing these findings will be presented at the 15th European Networked Knowledge Organization Systems (NKOS) Workshop in Hannover September 9th 2016.

After having conducted a pilot study, a survey has been sent to new students at the beginning of the school year, asking them to watch clips from NRK. The students will then be asked to provide the search terms they would have used if they wanted to find this clip again, the terms they would have used to index this clip in order to help others find it, and finally what clips or information resources they would like to see after having watched this clip.

5. FUTURE PLANS

I plan to finish the survey data collection and analyse the survey results in the autumn of 2016. Combined with the analysis of entity types, name density and name frequencies in subtitles and metadata records, this will hopefully result in an article about the importance of named entities in content descriptions of broadcasting material. I will also categorise the answers to the question about what the potential users wanted to watch after they see the clips from NRK, and examine whether the subtitles contain enough information to make this links automatically. In 2017, I will test and evaluate different methods for choosing the most salient named entities from subtitles and further explore the possible role of named entities in a future recommendation system.

6. REFERENCES

[1] L. Gazendam, C. Wartena, V. Malaisé, G. Schreiber, A. de Jong, and H. Brugman, 'Automatic Annotation Suggestions for Audiovisual Archives: Evaluation Aspects', *Interdiscip. Sci. Rev.*, vol. 34, no. 2–3, pp. 172–188, Sep. 2009.

[2] S. Gustman, D. Soergel, D. Oard, W. Byrne, M. Picheny, B. Ramabhadran, and D. Greenberg, 'Supporting access to large digital oral history archives', in *Proceedings of the 2nd ACM/IEEE-CS joint conference on Digital libraries*, 2002, pp. 18–27.

[3] R. Engels, *Åpen og samordnet tilgang til kulturarven: anbefalinger for en vellykket tilstedeværelse i den digitale kulturelle verden*. Oslo: ABM-utvikling, 2010.

[4] G. Kobilarov, T. Scott, Y. Raimond, S. Oliver, C. Sizemore, M. Smethurst, C. Bizer, and R. Lee, 'Media Meets Semantic Web – How the BBC Uses DBpedia and Linked Data to Make Connections', in *The Semantic Web: Research and Applications*, L. Aroyo, P. Traverso, F. Ciravegna, P. Cimiano, T. Heath, E. Hyvönen, R. Mizoguchi, E. Oren, M. Sabou, and E. Simperl, Eds. Springer Berlin Heidelberg, 2009, pp. 723–737.

[5] K. Tallerås, D. Massey, A.-S. R. Husevåg, M. Preminger, and N. Pharo, 'Evaluating (linked) metadata transformations across cultural heritage domains', in *Metadata and semantics research*, Springer, 2014, pp. 250–261.

Investigating Mobile Social Media Users' Behaviors in Tourism Collaborative Information Seeking

Jannatul Fardous
(PhD Student)
School of Information Technology & Mathematical Sciences
University of South Australia
Contact: 61402498578
jannatul.fardous@mymail.unisa.edu.au

Dr. Jia Tina Du
(Principal Supervisor)
School of Information Technology & Mathematical Sciences
University of South Australia
Contact: 61883025269
Tina.Du@unisa.edu.au

Dr. Kim-Kwang Raymond Choo
Dr. Songshan (Sam) Huang
(Co-Supervisors)
The University of Texas, San Antonio
University of South Australia
raymond.choo@utsa.edu
Sam.Huang@unisa.edu.au

ABSTRACT

Leisure travelers most often travel in groups with family, relatives or friends. It is argued that tourist information search tends to be more collaborative than a completely individual decision-making exercise. Collaborative information seeking (CIS) deals with collaboration in searching for information. In recent years, social media has been steadily increasing as an important information source for tourists who access social media frequently through their mobile devices. Research has shown that travelers rely more on the suggestions and reviews provided by experienced tourists for their travel planning and decision-making. Tourists undertake social search during which they exploit their social networks/relationships to improve the search process. However, limited research has investigated social media users' behaviors in collaborative search for tourism information. What is the role of social media in supporting of collaborative tourism information search, including collaborative search patterns and strategies in social environments, has remained unknown. This research aims to investigate mobile social media users' behaviors in collaborative search for tourism information. Using the Grounded Theory approach, a conceptual framework of mobile social media users' tourism CIS behavior will be built. Questionnaire survey and semi-structured in-depth interviews will be employed to collect users' search experiences.

Keywords

Collaborative information seeking (CIS); social media; tourism

1. MOTIVATION

Collaborative information seeking (CIS) refers to the activities where members of a team or group engage in identifying an information need, formulating a query, retrieving information, evaluating it and applying it to resolve the need [6,13,15]. CIS also involves communication regarding the information need, sharing the retrieved information and coordinating the information retrieval activities between members of the group.

CHIIR '17, March 07-11, 2017, Oslo, Norway
ACM 978-1-4503-4677-1/17/03.
http://dx.doi.org/10.1145/3020165.3022167

In CIS environments, collaborators communicate with each other in order to seek information from multiple sources and share the retrieved information across.

However, the social interactions of collaborators and use of social media have not been considered yet for information seeking and sharing purposes during CIS. For instance, in tourism, a tourist relies and trusts more on the user generated contents (e.g. personal opinions, thoughts, experiences and stories) than official sources [11]. Thus, social media can be integrated in CIS domain during information seeking and travel planning process. Social media users post their travel-related experiences in social media platform with their reviews on destination places, environment at destination, activities at destination, foods, accommodation and cultures etc.

In recent years, social media plays an important role in various domains of our everyday life including travel planning. For instance, there are many tourists who look up to social media as the most trusted source of information due to information shared by people they know each other. Besides, Facebook has emerged as a popular and trustworthy source for tourism-related information [1, 3, 16, and 21]. In social media environment, people seek recommendations on products and services from friends, classmates and other acquaintances as credible and reliable source of information and thus, they depend more on social media for needed information before making any purchase decision [2]. In the United States, nearly half of the Facebook users were found to alter their trip planning (e.g. destination and hotel) due to the influence of social media [14]. Nowadays, many tourism organizations have opened their tourism pages in Facebook and Twitter to promote tourism and attract tourists to visit a particular country for holidays, such as Tourism Australia and South Australia Tourism Commission have Facebook page and Twitter account to attract tourists via social media [19, 20].

Some research has shown that social interactions via social media can be an important and influential aspect of such tasks in tourism domain. A recent study [18] revealed that tourist interacts with different groups of people, such as intragroup and intergroup, around him/her for information seeking activities during travelling. But their study [18] utilized such social interactions when a tourist seeks information individually not in CIS contexts. The role of social media has not been studied during CIS activities.

Considering the potential aspects of social interactions in CIS activities, this research aims to explore how to make use of such interactions for seeking and obtaining useful and effective information needed for travel planning and during the trip.

In our preliminary study [9], we found that tourists use social media in CIS context for obtaining and validating information at different stages of trip planning. Therefore, the findings of this research will present an in-depth understanding on employing social media for tourism collaborative information seeking.

2. RESEARCH QUESTIONS

This research project aims to investigate mobile social media users' behaviors in collaborative search for tourism information.

Specifically, the project will address the following five research questions:

1. **Why do mobile social media users employ social media platforms both in travel planning process and during traveling?**
   Social media have become an integral part of people's lives in various occasions, for instance, sharing experiences and thoughts, obtaining information and staying connected with friends and family. Recently, this article [5] revealed that social media plays a key role to influence people in travel planning and decision-making. In addition, it also helps travellers to seek information during traveling time. However, the role of social media such as why and when tourists use social media platforms while planning a trip or when they are traveling is an under-studied topic.
2. **What are the types of social interactions and social media platforms do they utilize during collaborative information seeking and how do they influence tourism information search?**
   Due to the widespread use of social media, people are more connected than before and thus, can obtain any needed information synchronously and asynchronously or by scanning reviews. During CIS activities for tourism information, tour members may communicate with their friends and family members through social media as well as review posts like photos/videos and experiences shared by experienced tourists with the purpose of obtaining authentic tourism information for an upcoming tour. This research question will explore types of social interactions including other forms of social media that tourists employ during information seeking. Further, it will examine the impacts of social interactions and other forms of social media on information seeking activities.
3. **How do they collaborate with other social media users as well as other forms of social media for tourism information seeking?**
   There is an increasing trend in seeking information using smart mobile devices as mobile devices have the capabilities to accessing websites via high-speed Internet [8]. Since literature has shown that mobile device users frequently access social media for various purposes including travel information seeking, this project aims to reveal how tourists collaborate with other social media users and different forms of social media as well as accompanying tourists for tourism information seeking and sharing. This research question is used to examine the behavioural characteristics (e.g. how tourists' search information, and what type of information they search for etc.).
4. **What are the impacts of social media during trip planning and traveling time in CIS context?**
   Social media plays an increasingly important role in online tourism domain. Travelers search and share information, organise trips and elucidate their travel stories and experiences through different forms of social media, for example blogs and microblogs (e.g. blog, twitter), online communities (e.g. Facebook, Instagram and TripAdvisor), media sharing sites (e.g. YouTube), social bookmarking sites (e.g. Delicious), social knowledge sharing sites (e.g. Wikitravel) and other tools in collaborative way [9]. But there is limited study which investigates the impacts of social media during trip planning and traveling time.
5. **Why and how do they share travel-related information on social media like Facebook?**
   The emergence of social media has enabled tourists to share their experiences, which turned to an important information source to potential travellers during trip planning [22]. This research question will explore why and how travellers share their travel-related knowledge on social media platform.

3. METHODOLOGY

The research methodology that will be used is the Grounded Theory approach. Grounded theory is often referred to as the methodology in qualitative studies where researchers build a theory regarding a phenomenon by systematically gathering and analyzing relevant data (Strauss & Corbin, 1990). The Grounded Theory methodology has been extensively used in the field of information seeking and retrieval [4] as well as in online tourism [7,12].

Table 1 illustrates the research questions and data collection techniques which are undertaken and will be employed throughout this study.

Table1: Research questions and data collection techniques

Research questions	Data collection techniques
Research question 1	Questionnaire survey
Research question 2	Questionnaire survey
Research question 3	Semi-structured interviews
Research question 4	Semi-structured interviews
Research question 5	Semi-structured interviews

4. PROGRESS MADE SO FAR

In order to achieve the research goals, we designed and conducted questionnaire survey using an online tool SurveyGizmo (https://www.surveygizmo.com/) between February and March 2016. 108 participants participated in this survey where 63 participants participated under trip planning category and 45 participants took part in during traveling category. We used both online (44.44%) and printed (55.56%) versions of the questionnaire to collect data. The questionnaire consists of both multiple choice and open-ended questions concerning social media usage by tourists in trip planning and during traveling, ways of collaboration with tour mates and social media, types of sources they rely and trust more during collaborative information seeking. We used SPSS and content analysis to analyze multiple choice and open-ended questions.

The survey results based on trip planning activities show that the majority (73.8%) of participants used social media at the beginning of the trip planning to obtain information, followed by nearly half of participants utilized it at the middle of trip planning to obtain information and 41% of participants used it to validate information at the end of the planning. Social media was identified as mostly (80.95%) used media for information seeking and followed by communication apps (30.16) and face-to-face (4.76%). From the survey we also discovered that tourists used two different types of information sources, such as human and non-human for information searching. We found human source like friends (59.02%) and family members (45.90%) were the two main source for tourists. Non-human source like social media pages of tourism websites (18.03%) and blogs, forums and others (13.12%) were also used by tourists during trip planning. Another human source such as colleague and acquaintances (8.20%) was the least employed media for information seeking.

5. FUTURE PLAN

Now we are analyzing further data gathered from survey. We are also about to conduct in-depth interviews. Based on the survey data and in-depth interviews, we intend to develop a conceptual framework as well as in-depth knowledge in CIS activities using social media. In addition, since social media is widely used platforms for information sharing, searching and communicating, we will investigate the motivations of tourists why they share information on such platforms. We also plan to develop a CIS tool integrating features of social media if time allows.

6. REFERENCES

[1] Brown, V. R., & Vaughn, E. D. 2011. The writing on the (Facebook) wall: The use of social networking sites in hiring decision. *Journal of Business and Psychology*, 219–225.

[2] Chu, S.-C., & Kim, Y. 2011. Determinants of consumer engagement in electronic word-of-mouth (eWOM) in social networking sites. *International Journal of Advertising*, 30(1), 47–75.

[3] Cox, C., Burgess, S., Sellitto, C., & Buultjens, J. 2009. The role of user-generated content in tourists' travel planning behavior. *Journal of Hospitality Marketing & Management*, 18(8), 743–764.

[4] Du, J. T., Liu, Y.-H., Zhu, Q. H., & Chen, Y. J. 2012. Behaviours of information seeking, information judgments, information use and sharing by marketing professionals. *In Proceedings of the 2012 Information Seeking in Context (ISIC): The Information Behaviour Conference*, September 4-7, Japan.

[5] European Travel Commission. 2014. Digital trends travellers and tocial media. Retrieved December 15, 2014, from http://etc-digital.org/digital-trends/social-networking-and-ugc/travellers-and-social-media/regional-overview/latin-america/

[6] Hansen, P., Shah, C., & Klas, C.-P. (Eds.). 2015. *Collaborative Information Seeking*. Cham: Springer International Publishing.

[7] Ho, C.-I., Lin, M.-H., & Chen, H.-M. 2012. Web users' behavioural patterns of tourism information search: from online to offline. *Tourism Management*, 33(6), 1468–1482.

[8] Imgraben, J., Engelbrecht, A., & Choo, K-KR. 2014. Always connected, but are smart mobile users getting more security savvy? A survey of smart mobile device users. *Behaviour & Information Technology*, 33(12), 1347–1360.

[9] J, Fardous, Du, J. T., Choo, K-KR, Huang, SS and Hansen, P. 2016. Exploring collaborative information search behavior of mobile social media users in trip planning. *In the proceedings of iConference,* March 22-25, Wuhan, China.

[10] Leung, D., Law, R., van Hoof, H., & Buhalis, D. 2013. Social media in tourism and hospitality: A literature review. *Journal of Travel & Tourism Marketing*, 30(1–2), 3–22.

[11] Milano, R., Baggio, R., & Piattelli, R. 2011. The effects of online social media on tourism websites. *In ENTER* (pp. 471–483). Innsbruck, Austria: Springer Vienna.

[12] Papathanassis, A., & Knolle, F. 2011. Exploring the adoption and processing of online holiday reviews: A grounded theory approach. *Tourism Management*, 32(2), 215-224.

[13] Poltrock, S., Grudin, J., Dumais, S., Fidel, R., Bruce, H., & Pejtersen, A. M. 2003. Information Seeking and Sharing in Design Teams. *In Proceedings of the 2003 International ACM SIGGROUP Conference on Supporting Group Work* (pp. 239–247). NY, USA.

[14] Ráthonyi, G. 2013. Influence of Social media on touriSm–eSpecially among Students of the University of Debrecen. Retrieved from http://ageconsearch.umn.edu/bitstream/152233/2/18_Rathonyi.pdf

[15] Shah, C. 2014. Collaborative information seeking. *Journal of the Association for Information Science and Technology*, 65(2), 215–236.

[16] Stankov, U., Lazic, L., & Dragicevic, V. 2010. The extent of use of basic Face book user-generated content by the national tourism organizations in Europe. *European Journal of Tourism Research*, 3(2), 105–113.

[17] Strauss, A., & Corbin, J. M. 1990. *Basics of qualitative research: Grounded theory procedures and techniques*. Thousand Oaks, CA, US: Sage Publication, Inc.

[18] Tan, E., & Goh, D. 2015. A study of social interaction during mobile information seeking. *Journal of the Association for Information Science and Technology*, 66(10), 2031–2044.

[19] @TourismAus. 2009. Tourism Australia. Retrieved October 12, 2014, from https://twitter.com/TourismAus

[20] @tourismsa. 2013). South Australian Tourism Commission (SATC). Retrieved October 12, 2014, from https://twitter.com/tourismsa

[21] Vance, K., Howe, W., & Dellavalle, R. P. 2009. Social internet sites as a source of public health information. *Dermatologic Clinics*, 27(2), 133–136.

[22] Zeng, B., & Gerritsen, R. 2014. What do we know about social media in tourism? A review. *Tourism Management Perspectives*, 10, 27–36.

Automatic Simulation of Users for Interactive Information Retrieval

Maram Barifah
2nd year PhD Candidate
Università della Svizzera italiana (USI), Faculty of Informatics, Lugano, Switzerland
maram.barifah@usi.ch
Prof. Fabio Crestani and Dr. Monica Landoni

ABSTRACT

Hiring and engaging real users for conducting user studies is costly and time consuming. Therefore, simulating users has been proposed as a resource saving solution. Simulation helps to predict users' performance with retrieval systems and could provide researchers with much needed insights. There is a growing body of research in simulating users but most of the research conducted in the field is based only on data about how real users interact with the Information Retrieval System (IRS) leaving out aspects describing information seeking behaviours and individual differences. Consequently, essential data about users is not accounted thus the models are less realistic. To overcome this issue, an alternative approach is proposed. It concerns looking at user behaviour and analysing all the influencing factors that contribute to the user profile in order to produce representative user models. Thus, the aim of this research is to build real user profiles in order to produce more realistic user simulation. We will achieve that by capturing information seeking behaviour through user studies and selecting those factors and attributes that make our user models more realistic and operational at the same time. Furthermore, the proposed approach will allow to reduce the number of real users needed to evaluate the system.

Keywords

Interactive information retrieval; evaluation; simulation; information seeking behaviour; user profile; persona

1. MOTIVATION

Due to the simulation's ability to save user time, reduce expenses, make experiments reproducible, and expand data sets by producing natural, varied and consistent interactions from little data [16], simulation has become a preferable tool for the evaluation. Researchers try to incorporate human behaviour's models into evaluation of IRSs. Based on the literature, the continuum of the users' simulation can be anchored to formal models from one side and conceptual and descriptive models from the other side. The conceptual and descriptive models are more user-centric, they simulate the users' interactions and the information seeking behaviours. The aim of such models is to gain a deep understanding of the users' information seeking behaviour or to investigate theories of such behaviour. Examples of such models are *Bates' Berry Picking Model* [4] and *Ingwersen and Järvelin model of information seeking research* [7]. Azzopardi criticises the previous models as they are merely descriptive. Therefore, he emphasises the importance of formal (mathematical) models [2, 3].

As we move along the continuum, the next type of simulation is predictive and explanatory models. This type of simulation considers the interactions of the users with the systems and develops formal models and theories. The aim of such models is explaining and predicting search behaviour. The search process and the users behaviour, including querying, scanning and selecting documents, stopping and marking documents are modelled to simulate user interactions. Such models and theories formalise the relationship between the interactions of the users with the costs and gains of the IRS. *Information Foraging Theory* [17], and *The interactive Probability Ranking Principle model* [10] are examples of such models.

At the other end of the spectrum are the formal (mathematical) models. This type of simulation intends to improve the traditional evaluation (Cranfield-styled) measures by combining them with user models. This type of simulation aims to introduce techniques based on user modeling that are informed by users' behaviours studies and tries to translate user models into evaluation measures. An example is modeling user variance in time-biased gain [20]. However, the formal models are criticised for being less realistic than the descriptive models. Cole states that effective simulation should be based on real user interactions and tasks [8]. Thus, user studies can not be ignored. Therefore, this research can be placed in the middle of the continuum as an attempt to answer if it is possible to build users models by starting from user profiles.

User profiling is not a new phenomena in IRS domain. It has been used widely to overcome the problems of the overload of the information and the retrieval of the non relevant documents [1, 21]. Examples of applying user profiles in the domain of IRS are [14, 1]. Generally, the purpose of adapting user profiles in IRS is to improve the performance of the systems [12]. The aim of this research is to use the user profiling paradigm, which is based on the influencing attributes that shape the user behaviour, to overcome some

CHIIR '17, March 07-11, 2017, Oslo, Norway
ACM 978-1-4503-4677-1/17/03.
http://dx.doi.org/10.1145/3020165.3022168

of the limitations of the existing user models, too descriptive and conceptual in nature versus those of formal models that lack of real details.

2. RESEARCH QUESTIONS

This research aims at addressing two questions:

1. To what extent can the proposed user models replace the real users?
2. What are the significant attributes of specific users profiles that can produce valuable models?

The final aim of the research would be to propose an evaluation methodology that can replace some real users with simulated users, still maintaining the power and the sufficiency of the original evaluation.

3. METHODOLOGY

Two users studies will be conducted as follows.

3.1 Identifying an IIR system

RERO Doc[1] has been chosen to conduct the study. RERO Doc is a digital library which is the network of the libraries of Western Switzerland. RERO Doc had between February - June (2016) 643,342 accesses from different parts of the world including Switzerland, France, US, Germany, Algeria and many others. The users search for different domains including Nursing, Economics, Teaching, Computer Science and others. RERO Doc provides various document types such as books, articles, theses, periodicals, research reports,etc. The users conduct several activities include searching, checking bibliographics records, and uploading files. The following phases summary the study.

3.2 Phase I: Experiment I

For the first study, an experiment of real users in naturalistic setting will be conducted where various real users of RERO Doc will do research-tasks based on their information needs. The following tools will serve to collect their data.

3.2.1 Pre-questionnaire

The questionnaire is divided into three sections, gathering demographic, task and system information. The purpose of this questionnaire is to identify the most significant attributes that will characterize RERO Doc users. The most influential attributes of the users of the digital library have been identified based on the literature of the information seeking behavior [13, 18]. This includes demographic information such as age, gender, and academic status. Task information includes a description of the task, initial queries, task difficulty, task urgency and motivation. System information involves search experience, degree of familiarity, and frequency of using the system.

3.2.2 Log analysis

To understand the interactive behavior of the users of RERO Doc, the transaction logs will be analyzed. Search log analysis provides insights to the users' search behavior including navigation methods, use of the advance search procedure, levels of user activities i.e. number of sessions conducted and number of viewed pages [13, 15, 11]. In particular, three main elements will be analyzed [11, 13]:

[1]https://doc.rero.ch

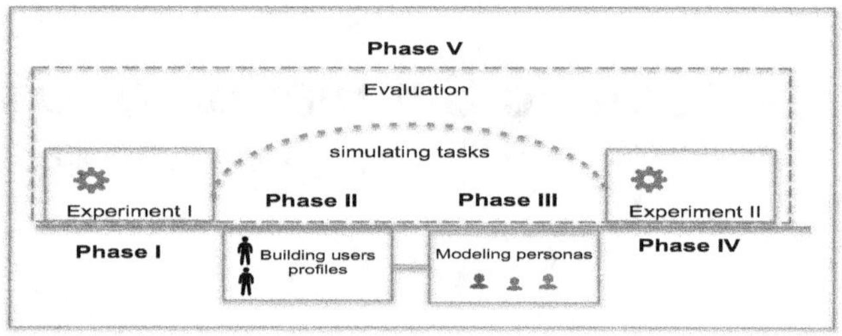

Figure 1: The phases of the study

1. *Sessions,* including changes in queries during a session, the duration of a session, number of pages viewed and number of documents downloaded
2. *Queries,* including queries issued, queries modifications, mean length of search queries, the use of logic and modifiers, and the types of queries i.e. unique, modified, identical, and repeat query
3. *Terms,* including the most highly used search terms and the number of search terms

3.2.3 Post-questionnaire

Because it is almost impossible to gauge the satisfaction of the search results in relation to the information needs of the users by analyzing the logs, the users will fill a post session questionnaire. The questionnaire will measure certain criteria including the users satisfaction, task completion, sufficiency of information gathering, efforts to locate useful information and relevance judgment.

3.3 Phase II: Building users profiles

Based on the previous phase, different users profiles will be built. As searching the digital library is a dynamic process, the hybrid user profiling method will be used which is a combination of implicit and explicit methods [19]. The static attributes about the users will be extracted explicitly from the pre and post session questionnaires. Other dynamic data such as search interactions, query modifications, and search history are obtained implicitly from the search logs analysis [11]. The aim of this phase is to build real user profiles comprising the most significant attributes that represent various users of RERO Doc to be used on phase III.

3.4 Phase III: Modeling personas

In this phase, we will compute multiple personas for each type of users. The potential RERO Doc users are researchers, teachers, professors, and students (undergraduate and postgraduate). A persona is "a fictional individual created to describe a specific user" [9]. Personas are built starting from user profiles to create a typical yet realistic user. Our personas will act as placeholders to the real users. The attributes of the personas are extracted from phase II.

3.5 Phase IV: Experiment II

In this phase we will apply Borlund's simulated work task situations method [6]. Based on experiment I, we will design simulated work task situations extracted from the real information needs of the real users. Such information needs are embodied in RERO Doc users' issued queries and their relevance assessments. After that, we will recruit a small sample of real users and generate a higher number of personas. Later, we will run a second user study where the combination of real users and personas will evaluate the same system of experiment I.

3.6 Phase V: Evaluation

We will evaluate the performance of our proposed IIR evaluation method by comparing between the result of experiment I and experiment II. In summary, the IIR system in experiment I will be evaluated only by real users while in experiment II the IIR system will be evaluated by the combination of real users and personas.

3.7 Result and data analytics

We are planning to use one of the Rasch model software because of the Rasch model ability to generate valid quality information and accurate probabilistic inferences. Measuring various variables of the information seeking behaviour attributes requires a robust approach and the Rasch model is one of the best established tools for such measuring. Also, Rasch measurement will facilitate the transformation of the ordinal raw observed data into linear measures [5].

4. PROGRESS MADE SO FAR

The required steps to conduct the study have been finalised including contacted RERO Doc administration to participate in this study and signed ethical approval. Currently, we are conducting a pilot study of the previous detailed methodology on USI digital library [2]. The users of this digital libraries are academic staff and students of USI. We also designed the pre and post session questionnaires. The aim of this study is to validate the proposed methodology and the data collection tools including the log analysis software that we plan to use, and identify the potential obstacles and limitations.

5. FUTURE PLAN

Possibly, phase I and phase II will end by December 2016. Phases III and IV are scheduled to be completed by July 2017. The evaluation and the result analysis are likely to be completed by March 2018.

6. REFERENCES

[1] R. Arezki, P. Poncelet, G. Dray, and D. W. Pearson. Information retrieval model based on user profile. In *Artificial Intelligence: Methodology, Systems, and Applications*, pages 490–499. Springer, 2004.

[2] L. Azzopardi. Modelling interaction with economic models of search. In *Proceedings of the 37th international ACM SIGIR conference on Research & development in information retrieval*, pages 3–12. ACM, 2014.

[3] L. Azzopardi and G. Zuccon. Building and using models of information seeking, search and retrieval. In *SIGIR 2015: 38th Annual ACM SIGIR Conference*, pages 1107–1110, 2015.

[4] M. J. Bates. The design of browsing and berrypicking techniques for the online search interface. *Online review*, 13(5):407–424, 1989.

[2]https://en.bul.sbu.usi.ch

[5] T. Bond and C. M. Fox. *Applying the Rasch model: Fundamental measurement in the human sciences.* Lawrence Erlbaum, 2007.

[6] P. Borlund. Experimental components for the evaluation of interactive information retrieval systems. *Journal of Documentation*, 59(1):71–90, 2000.

[7] T. Catarci and S. Kimani. Human-computer interaction view on information retrieval evaluation. In *Information Retrieval Meets Information Visualization*, pages 48–75. Springer, 2012.

[8] M. J. Cole. Simulation of the iir user: Beyond the automagic. *Simulation of Interaction*, page 1, 2010.

[9] C. Courage and K. Baxter. *Understanding Your Users: A practical guide to user requirements Methods.* Elsevier, 2005.

[10] N. Fuhr. A probability ranking principle for interactive information retrieval. *Information Retrieval*, 11(3):251–265, 2008.

[11] S. Jones, S. J. Cunningham, R. McNab, and S. Boddie. A transaction log analysis of a digital library. *International Journal on Digital Libraries*, 3(2):152–169, 2000.

[12] S. Lainé-Cruzel, T. Lafouge, J.-P. Lardy, and N. B. Abdallah. Improving information retrieval by combining user profile and document segmentation. *Information Processing & Management*, 32(3):305–315, 1996.

[13] Y. Li and D. Hu. Interactive retrieval using simulated versus real work task situations: Differences in sub-facets of tasks and interaction performance. *Proceedings of the American Society for Information Science and Technology*, 50(1):1–10, 2013.

[14] B. Mianowska and N. T. Nguyen. A method for collaborative recommendation in document retrieval systems. In *Intelligent Information and Database Systems*, pages 168–177. Springer, 2013.

[15] D. Nicholas, P. Huntington, H. R. Jamali, I. Rowlands, and M. Fieldhouse. Student digital information-seeking behaviour in context. *Journal of Documentation*, 65(1):106–132, 2009.

[16] O. Pietquin and H. Hastie. A survey on metrics for the evaluation of user simulatinons. *Knowledge Engineering Review*, 28(01):59–73, 2013.

[17] P. Pirolli and S. Card. Information foraging. *Psychological review*, 106(4):643, 1999.

[18] D. Sawadogo, R. Champagnat, and P. Estraillier. User profile modelling for digital resource management systems. In *The 22nd Conference on User Modeling, Adaptation and Personalization*, 2014.

[19] S. Schiaffino and A. Amandi. Intelligent user profiling. In *Artificial Intelligence An International Perspective*, pages 193–216. Springer, 2009.

[20] M. D. Smucker and C. L. Clarke. Modeling user variance in time-biased gain. In *Proceedings of the Symposium on Human-Computer Interaction and Information Retrieval*, page 3. ACM, 2012.

[21] V. Snášel, A. Abraham, S. Owais, J. Platoš, and P. Krömer. User profiles modeling in information retrieval systems. In *Emergent Web Intelligence: Advanced Information Retrieval*, pages 169–198. Springer, 2010.

WebSAIL: Computer-based Methods for Enhancing Web Search Literacy

Ioannis Karatassis
Institute for Information Systems
University of Duisburg-Essen
47048 Duisburg, Germany
karatassis@is.inf.uni-due.de

ABSTRACT

Recent studies reveal that most Web search engine users lack of appropriate search strategies for finding information efficiently and effectively, and overestimate their capabilities in the domain of Web search. As a consequence these users spend more time in searching for information and also do not always find the best results. They eventually miss out on important information and may not even be aware of this fact, especially in more complex Web search tasks. Users get frustrated after failing at finding information they are looking for and abandon the search session at worst. We launched the WebSAIL project to tackle these deficits by promoting Web search literacy. Different methods (i.e., a tutorial, scaffolding, and gamification) will be used for training. In the end we will compare the applied methods to determine whether Web search literacy can be enhanced at all, whether acquired knowledge is long-lasting and which method has the biggest impact on the enhancement of Web search literacy.

CCS Concepts

•**Applied computing** → **Interactive learning environments;** *Computer-assisted instruction;*

Keywords

web search, web search literacy, web search competence, gamification, scaffolding, tutorial

Author Information

Second year PhD student. Supervisor: Prof. Dr.-Ing. Norbert Fuhr, University of Duisburg-Essen, Germany.

1. INTRODUCTION

Today search engines are de facto the first address for users to satisfy their information needs. Despite of this many of those users have very little knowledge how to use Web search engines effectively [3]. We say these users are little Web search literate. As a consequence they do not always find the best results, eventually spend more time in searching [10, 2] or even miss out on important information. This is especially the case in complex Web search tasks [2]. Furthermore, a study by Stark et al. [15] found out that most users overestimate their Web search literacy. Aula et al. [2] observed the search behavior of users during search tasks. They found that even highly skilful searchers sometimes struggle with finding information they are looking for and end up with issuing a number of different queries or even giving up after becoming frustrated.

Web search engines try to tackle these problems by providing additional search features to their users usually on request. However, these options are normally ignored by users because of either their complexity in use or their existence is not known to the users. We launched a project named WebSAIL to guide users in performing better Web search and enhancing their overall Web search literacy (WSL). One of the aspects of WebSAIL is to give users awareness of their limited Web search literacy and provide a smooth adaptation to Web search by applying training methods such as a tutorial, scaffolding and gamification. In our research we aim to investigate whether these methods are helpful at all and if so, which is the best approach for improving the Web search literacy.

In summary our research questions are the followings:

- RQ1 Can we enhance Web search literacy by training users with either a tutorial, scaffolding or gamification?
- RQ2 Which one of these approaches leads to the best results?
- RQ3 If we improve Web search literacy by using the methods, will they last long or will they be just temporarily? I.e., will the users continue using the collected knowledge in their future search or will they just continue searching as before?

The paper is structured as follows: First we define Web search literacy (Section 2) and then we describe in Section 3 the WebSAIL project in detail. For the purpose of testing and training users, we implemented a task-based application (Section 4) which we plan to enhance with the methods tutorial, scaffolding and gamification (Section 5). Finally we describe our future plan in Section 6.

2. WEB SEARCH LITERACY

We define Web search literacy as the ability to identify, locate and effectively use information on the Web. In order to identify and locate effectively information a user is looking for, she has to be familiar with the following Web search concepts: searchability, linguistic functions, query language, ranking, search tactics, search stratagems and search strategies. From this we can conclude that Web search literate users are aware of the mentioned Web search concepts and are capable of applying them intuitively in order to perform a good Web search.

3. WEBSAIL

The name WebSAIL stands for Web search literacy, Awareness, Interface complexity and Long-term effects. The ultimate goal of the project is to enhance Web search literacy through training methods embedded into a task-based Web application. In order to motivate users

CHIIR '17 March 07-11, 2017, Oslo, Norway

ACM ISBN 978-1-4503-4677-1/17/03.

DOI: http://dx.doi.org/10.1145/3020165.3022171

enhancing their WSL we first have to detect and disclose Web search deficits to them. Most Web search engine users are not aware of their deficits leading to ignorance of any support provided by search engines or tutorials focusing on improving retrieval effectiveness.

As mentioned before Web search engines share some common advanced functionalities to improve results. However, these functionalities are hardly used by users. Even if they are used, they are not applied correctly. Web search engine users not only have to be aware that a certain additional search functionality exists but also be able to identify when this specific feature is needed and embed it correctly into a suitable search strategy. As Aula et al. have shown, even good searchers formulate diverse queries, try more advanced operators and spend more time on the search tasks when facing difficulties with finding relevant pieces of information [2].

Speaking about search strategies, we refer to Bates' information search tactics [4] which have been very influential since they were published in 1979. Smith [14] extracted a set of tactics useful in the practice and teaching of internet searching. However, not all of them are applicable in Web search. A subgoal of WebSAIL is, thus, to identify suitable tactics for Web search which can be transformed into appropriate tasks.

Besides increasing awareness with regard to search deficits and training users in using both simple and complex search interfaces effectively, we want to find out whether acquired skills are long-lasting. However, we assume that once users learn to perform better search that for instance decreases the time they spend on their entire search activity, they will continuously adopt the techniques brought by WebSAIL to their daily search actions.

4. WEB APPLICATION

The Web application features solutions for tackling the challenges described in Section 3. When it comes to evaluation, test persons will have to solve a number of tasks. Thus, we will be able to get an overview of their actual knowledge. The application comprises two types of tasks: quiz (Section 4.1) and fact-finding (Section 4.2). Moreover the baseline application provides neither feedback to users nor any kind of hints and serves only for testing knowledge. As mentioned before, a number of training methods exist. However, in order to train users we plan to embed a tutorial, scaffolding and gamification into the baseline Web application one at a time.

4.1 Quiz

In quiz tasks we will focus on the theoretical aspects of Web search literacy. The type is intended to comprise questions related to the structure, functioning and provided functionalities of search engines. Even more complex features like search operators (i.e., the query language) can be evaluated. In a quiz task a question is presented to the users. To solve the task she can either select items from a pre-defined set of answers or simply enter an answer into a provided text field. The tasks themselves can be used to evaluate knowledge and for training the user. In quiz the training effect can be achieved, e.g., by revealing correct answers and providing feedback upon task completion.

4.2 Search Hunt

A more challenging task type than quiz is fact-finding (what we named search hunt) where the user is presented with a question and has to find the correct solution using a Web search interface. The interface is connected to the Bing Search API[1] as well as the Google Books API[2] and uses all their provided features, e.g., we can search for common result types like web, images, news, video, or books, use type related filters, or display instant query suggestions.

Search hunt tasks can be designed in a way reflecting everyday information needs and hence train users in satisfying them. We may think of creating tasks intended to use specific Web search strategies or Web search operators in order to find the solution effectively. However, a user is not required to use any Web search strategy. When evaluating a user's solution to a specific task we may think of rating the user's competence high in case she used a suitable strategy rather than just trying to issue a number of diverse queries to find the solution she is looking for. Hence, through search hunt tasks not only query crafting skills can be improved, but also the ability to use search engine functionalities correctly and to locate desired information more efficiently and effectively.

5. TRAINING METHODS

The following sections describe the methods we plan to evaluate for enhancing Web search literacy. We will embed them into the baseline Web application described in Section 4 in order to train users.

5.1 Tutorial

Interactive learning environments typically use step-by-step demonstrations and individual feedback to support users [12]. Here we distinguish between intelligent tutoring systems that provide users with adaptive sequence of problems and personalized hints [8, 1] and software tutorials [5] that often use step-by-step demonstrations. We plan to demonstrate strategies step-by-step to solve tasks properly by integrating software tutorials into our Web application. Acquired basic strategies are intended to be used and adapted as needed in satisfying regular information needs.

5.2 Scaffolding

Another effective method of teaching procedures is by providing scaffolding. The strategy aims at analysing procedures and providing actions to continue based on predefined case bases [11]. Scaffolding does not aim at teaching complete strategies rather than giving the user a number of actions tailored to the current progress. Transferred to our application, the system will contain a case base fed with search sessions in advance (as described in Section 6). In each step of a search process, the system will analyse the current search state and provide the user with useful actions that she can perform in order to continue the search. By providing users with search actions, we intend them to develop complete search strategies in order to solve search tasks efficiently and effectively.

5.3 Gamification

Gamification refers to "the use of game design elements in non-game contexts" [7] with the aim to foster user engagement and is most often manifested in the form of points, badges and leaderboards (also called the PBLs) [7, 6]. Gamified applications make use of the fact that games are fun [13] and aim therefore to invoke the same psychological experiences as games do [9] in order to keep users motivated.

With this in mind, we will enrich the baseline Web application (see Section 4) by game design elements such as points, levels, leaderboards and badges. Users will be rewarded with points for solving tasks correctly and can level-up when they exceed a point threshold. Rewards in the form of badges can be obtained by either reaching a certain game state, executing a certain action or solving a task with a good strategy. Leaderboards and progress bars show progress and aim at encouraging users to not only complete a task efficiently, but also compete with other searchers.

6. FUTURE PLAN

To achieve WebSAIL's goals, we designed a Web application which is capable of entailing quiz (see Section 4.1) and fact-finding tasks

[1]https://www.microsoft.com/cognitive-services/en-us/bing-web-search-api

[2]https://developers.google.com/books

(see Section 4.2). In order to create good tasks we first have to gather empirical data about Web search behavior. As training effects caused by WebSAIL can differ among target groups, our focus lies on students. By analysing what they are searching for and how they search, we will be able to detect actual deficits in search processes. For this purpose, we implemented a browser plugin that is capable of tracking Google search sessions and distributed across numerous subjects. Data will be tracked for a period of 3 months. Afterwards we will use this information to detect signals that suggest a user is having trouble in a search session. Based on the definition of Web search literacy and detected signals in daily search sessions we will create suitable tasks to test and train the students at a later time during evaluation.

Since we will have our task pool at the time, we can then focus on answering RQ1 – RQ3. It should be noted that we aim to obtain conclusions about the extended systems. This can only be achieved when we disclose any bias that will occur when an application is used more than once (repeated evaluation using the same system). For avoiding such a bias we will perform the following:

First, we will assign students randomly into the groups X and Y. They will have to participate in three evaluation sessions in total. In session one, group X-subjects will use our baseline system and subjects from group Y will use one of the extended systems, without using the baseline system. Session two will be conducted one week after session one. This time, both groups X and Y will use the baseline application. In session two the tasks will differ from session one. However, we will make sure that they have the same complexity.

In both sessions we will record WSL. The X-group-users will give us the difference between the WSL scores obtained on the same system: scores recorded at session one and scores recorded at session two. These scores will give us conclusion about the impact of re-using the same system after a short period. Similarly, we will obtain score differences for the Y-group-users and compare them to the X-group user scores. With this comparison we will be able to obtain direct conclusion about our extended systems. This means if the Y-group-scores are higher than the X-group-user scores then we know that the improvement did not happen because of re-using the system but rather because the WebSAIL components helped users to improve their ability to perform better search. With these we will be able to answer our first two research questions (RQ1, RQ2).

The third evaluation session is intended to investigate whether training effects are still preserved (RQ3). That is the reason why it is conducted several months after the second session. Subjects participated in session one and two will be invited again to test their state of knowledge using our baseline application.

References

[1] J. R. Anderson, A. T. Corbett, K. R. Koedinger, and R. Pelletier. Cognitive tutors: Lessons learned. *The Journal of the Learning Sciences*, 4(2):167–207, 1995.

[2] Anne Aula, Rehan M. Khan, and Zhiwei Guan. How does search behavior change as search becomes more difficult? In *Proceedings of the SIGCHI Conference on Human Factors in Computing Systems*, CHI '10, pages 35–44, New York, NY, USA, 2010. ACM. ISBN 978-1-60558-929-9. .

[3] Scott Bateman, Jaime Teevan, and Ryen W. White. The search dashboard: How reflection and comparison impact search behavior. In *Proceedings of the SIGCHI Conference on Human Factors in Computing Systems*, CHI '12, pages 1785–1794, New York, NY, USA, 2012. ACM.

[4] Marcia J. Bates. Information search tactics. *Journal of the American Society for Information Science*, 30(4):205–214, 1979. ISSN 1097-4571. .

[5] Lawrence Bergman, Vittorio Castelli, Tessa Lau, and Daniel Oblinger. DocWizards: a system for authoring follow-me documentation wizards. In *In Proc. ACM symposium on User interface software and technology*, pages 191–200. ACM Press, 2005.

[6] Yukai Chou. Points, Badges, and Leaderboards: The Gamification Fallacy. http://yukaichou.com/gamification-study/points-badges-and-leaderboards-the-gamification-fallacy/., 2015. Accessed May 19, 2016.

[7] Sebastian Deterding, Dan Dixon, Rilla Khaled, and Lennart Nacke. From Game Design Elements to Gamefulness: Defining "Gamification". In *Proceedings of the 15th International Academic MindTrek Conference: Envisioning Future Media Environments*, MindTrek '11, pages 9–15, New York, NY, USA, 2011. ACM. ISBN 978-1-4503-0816-8. .

[8] K. D. Glazewski and P. A. Ertmer. Scaffolding Disciplined Inquiry in Problem-Based Learning Environments. *International Journal of Learning*, 12(6):397–306, 2005.

[9] Kai Huotari and Juho Hamari. Defining Gamification: A Service Marketing Perspective. In *Proceeding of the 16th International Academic MindTrek Conference*, MindTrek '12, pages 17–22, New York, NY, USA, 2012. ACM. ISBN 978-1-4503-1637-8. .

[10] Neesha Kodagoda and B L William Wong. Effects of low & high literacy on user performance in information search and retrieval. In *Proceedings of the 22Nd British HCI Group Annual Conference on People and Computers: Culture, Creativity, Interaction - Volume 1*, BCS-HCI '08, pages 173–181, Swinton, UK, UK, 2008. British Computer Society.

[11] Sascha Kriewel. *Support in Finding and Performance of Search Strategies in Digital Libraries (in German)*. PhD thesis, University of Duisburg-Essen, Germany, 2010. URL http://duepublico.uni-duisburg-essen.de/servlets/DocumentServlet?id=22266.

[12] Eleanor O'Rourke, Erik Andersen, Sumit Gulwani, and Zoran Popović. A Framework for Automatically Generating Interactive Instructional Scaffolding. In *Proceedings of the 33rd Annual ACM Conference on Human Factors in Computing Systems*, CHI '15, pages 1545–1554, New York, NY, USA, 2015. ACM. ISBN 978-1-4503-3145-6. .

[13] Karolien Poels, Yvonne de Kort, and Wijnand Ijsselsteijn. "It is Always a Lot of Fun!": Exploring Dimensions of Digital Game Experience Using Focus Group Methodology. In *Proceedings of the 2007 Conference on Future Play*, Future Play '07, pages 83–89, New York, NY, USA, 2007. ACM. ISBN 978-1-59593-943-2. .

[14] Alastair G. Smith. Internet search tactics. *Online Information Review*, 36(1):7–20, 2012.

[15] Birgit Stark, Dieter Dörr, and Stefan Aufenanger, editors. *Die Googleisierung der Informationssuche : Suchmaschinen zwischen Nutzung und Regulierung (in German)*. Number 10 in Media Convergence / Medienkonvergenz. De Gruyter, Berlin/Boston, 2014. ISBN 978-3-11-033821-8.

A Generative Framework to Query Recommendation and Evaluation

Matthew Mitsui
6th Year PhD Candidate
Supervisor: Chirag Shah
Department of Computer Science
Rutgers University
New Brunswick, NJ, USA, 08901
mmitsui@cs.rutgers.edu

ABSTRACT

In practice, query recommenders in Web search typically recommend queries directly from a query log or iteratively refine a user's current context to make recommendations. These approaches either limit themselves to queries in the log or do not take necessary exploratory leaps in their recommendations. Moreover, they do not directly incorporate the encompassing, driving information needs and tasks. The author first shows that user queries may not necessarily be the best to use for recommendations and moreover proposes a framework for generating novel queries for query recommendation, using an approximation of need.

CCS Concepts

•**Information systems** → **Query suggestion;** *Personalization;* Document topic models; Retrieval effectiveness;

Keywords

Search session analysis; Diversity; User simulations; Query recommendation

1. MOTIVATION AND RESEARCH QUESTIONS

In the classic machine learning problem of classification, algorithms can be divided into two categories: 1) discriminative methods and 2) generative methods [10]. In the former, a classification algorithm directly finds the best classification label y for a data point x by directly computing $p(y|x)$. Generative approaches assign class labels more indirectly by learning $p(x, y)$, from which $p(y|x)$ (and hence the most likely class label) can be computed. To illustrate the difference, consider a logistic regression classifier (discriminative classifier) and Naive Bayes (generative classifier). For e-mail spam classification, a logistic regression classifier accepts a list of values (e.g., word frequencies from the message) and outputs a label (e.g., whether the e-mail is spam). It can discover which terms are important in distinguishing spam but cannot determine the frequencies of terms in spam and non-spam documents. Yet Naive Bayes learns the probability of each word $x_1, x_2, ..., x_n$ in the vocabulary separately for each class label so could theoretically generate spam and non-spam documents by sampling from these distributions.

Query recommendation falls into a very similar framework as above. "Generative" approaches recommend queries by taking a user's context and modifying queries the user previously issued in the session, such as by substituting query terms or incrementally adding terms to a query [4]. As with Naive Bayes, they could generate any possible query with a compact representation, such as a language model over the possible terms. However, they make incremental refinements and do not take the necessary exploratory leaps often required of recommendations. As found by [11], recommendations are useful to people in the late stage of a long task, who issued several refinements and need a fresh start.

"Discriminative" query recommenders can offer more exploratory leaps more quickly. They select recommendations strictly from a query log - i.e., queries that have been issued in the past by users of a retrieval system. Some calculate explicit transition probabilities between queries in a log - as in a Markov model - to recommend likely subsequent queries from a user's context [3]. Others compute pairwise matrix similarities; [12] recommended queries that fell within a threshold similarity to balance relevance and diversity. These approaches rely on similarity measures or transition probabilities between queries to compute recommendations. Changing similarity thresholds can more heavily emphasize diverse or homogeneous recommendations. Moreover, the set of potential queries determined wholly by the input of users of an information retrieval system. However, such approaches can scale poorly, as they can require a matrix of up to size $|Q|$, where Q is the number of queries and is exponential in the number of possible words.

The expansive query recommendation literature suggests a genuine need for query recommendations. Yet most work fails to consider the motivating task, even though there has been extensive work to theoretically model searchers' task structures [5] and to automatically extract searchers' tasks from web logs [6]. One recent query recommendation approach extracted the task - as a set of related queries - and topic - as a word distribution - and combined these to create tailored query recommendations [7]. Even then, such

CHIIR '17, March 07-11, 2017, Oslo, Norway
ACM 978-1-4503-4677-1/17/03.
http://dx.doi.org/10.1145/3020165.3022172

an approach does not immediately address the coverage of information needs of users. Hence, the following research questions are proposed to address at the doctoral consortium:

- To what extent, in terms of effectiveness and efficiency, can current discriminative and generative approaches to query recommendation be outperformed by a generative approach that generates queries directly from an information need?
- How can such an approach be evaluated in the absence of relevance judgments for documents?

2. PROPOSED METHODOLOGY

Query recommenders generally follow the following flow of information: 1) A recommender generates a background model of words, documents, queries, or some combination. 2) It uses the background model to map a user's log data - queries and clicks - to a context model. 3) It determines (implicitly or explicitly) what information or documents a user should view next. 4) This determination is converted into a query recommendation. The same framework is followed here. As a proposed methodology, the author will attempt to show where discriminative methods such as query graphs fall short and where compact but smart generative methods are necessary. Attempts will be made to incorporate task and need information to create tailored recommendations and compare it to previous state-of-the-art recommenders.

3. PREVIOUS WORK

3.1 Case for a Generative Approach

Previous work from the author has suggested user queries can be less effective for recommendation than other approaches [9], calling for something beyond the discriminative recommender. In a Mechanical Turk task, participants guessed the query that generated a list of top 10 results, as on the first page of a Web search engine. The stimuli given in the Mechanical Turk task were real results from real queries issued to the Google Search API [1], given as titles, URLs, and result snippets, with the underlying query hidden.

User guesses were then issued to the same API and compared against the original results and those of simple algorithms for guessing the query, given the same 10 results. A portion of the analysis is given in Figure 1. It shows that if the query length is known, an algorithm can greatly outperform users in guessing the underlying query. The best algorithm used a simple bag-of-words approach and output the most frequent words. Since an algorithm could guess the underlying query, it stands to reason that given a method for effectively determining a related set of relevant information (here as the top 10 results), an effective generative query recommendation can be given. Further recall that "discriminative" query recommenders largely select users' previous queries as candidates for recommendation. The results also suggest that even if a user is given an ideal set of information to search for, the user will issue a query that is less effective than that of a simple algorithm. This means users may issue suboptimal queries, which are in turn candidates for discriminative recommenders and can affect recommendation quality.

[1]https://www.google.com/cse/

	Titles	*Snippets*	*Titles+Snippets*
Users	0.66	-	-
Freq	0.76	0.86	0.87
Freq (P)	0.53	0.60	0.59
Skipgram	0.66	0.73	0.78
Skipgram (P)	0.47	0.48	0.50

Figure 1: User and algorithmic performance in guessing queries, in Jaccard distance. (P) indicates a simple probabilistic model of query length, otherwise the query length is given. Results for the most frequent words (Freq) and most frequent skipgram.

Algorithm	Tech.	Health	Ent.	Art
Session	**11.63%**	14.74%	7.89%	7.35%
ORTH	9.97%	**26.34%**	**16.42%**	**40.68%**
LDA-SG	9.21%	20.03%	8.39%	31.02%

Figure 2: Recommendation performance of a discriminative approach (ORTH), our method [8] (LDA-SG), and user sessions (Session). Columns are for performance in Technology, Health, Entertainment, and Art search topics.

3.2 Attempting a Generative Approach

How, then, can a full generative pipeline be implemented: a background model, user context, a mapping to information needs, and ultimately a recommendation? The author approximated this notion of "information need" with a simpler topic-based approach in previous work [8]. For the background model, a Latent Dirichlet Allocation (LDA) topic model and a skip-gram model were pre-trained on a single web corpus, comprising 5 topics. LDA modeled a user's context - previous search queries and results - as a distribution over topics the user has seen so far. The "need" was approximated as a topic that was relevant but still diverged from the viewed topics. The skipgram model controlled phrases that were suggested as queries, so quality of queries would not degrade. This model completely generated queries by operating at the level of topic first and working down, using a simple (albeit naive) approach to modeling "need".

This approach was compared to an entirely discriminative approach from [12]. Users' sessions from a real lab study (searching on the same 5 Web corpus topics) were injected with recommendations. Some results are given in Figures 2 and 3. The proposed approach recommends queries that may give entirely unknown web pages that do not have a relevance score, which is also possible in a cold-start scenario with no relevance judgments. Therefore, traditional metrics such as Normalized Discounted Cumulative Gain (NDCG) will not work. Alternative approaches to precision and recall were hence used. A penalty score was used for precision: the percent of words or topics in recommended results that belonged to a different Web page topic than the one under recommendation. "Topicality" was measured at a URL-based level, using the Open Directory Project (ODP) mapping from URLs to topics.[2] ODP was also used previously to mine query intention [2] and to evaluate recommenders. Recall was measured with the coverage of ODP topics. The new recommender can improve diversity, with some cost in relevance. In some cases, it outperforms a discriminative approach, showing promise with future improvements.

[2]http://www.dmoz.org

Unit of Measure	Tech.	Health	Ent.	Art
Words	0.06%	1.11%	1.15%	0.83%
ODP topics	11.01%	15.73%	12.69%	4.32%

Figure 3: Penalty scores for the combined LDA and skipgram approach.

4. FUTURE PLAN

4.1 Future Methodology

While work such as [7] shows that task and topic information can be combined in a hybrid model, [9] suggests query logs may not be effective as a direct source for query recommendations. A very coarse LDA model of "need" fueled recommendations and showed that topical recall can be improved with loss in precision with a simple model. Yet this shows that a more accurate method of determining relevant information or needs is required. For future research the author must address 1) improvements to the recommender, 2) datasets to use, and 3) methods for evaluation.

One direction for improvement is a better topic model that better separates topics, such as correlated LDA, which can create incremental improvements. For the data set, other established query logs with long sessions will be used in addition to the current data, such as the TREC Session Track[3]. While this was used for the Mechanical Turk task to give a set of queries, it has not yet been used for the LDA-based query recommender. Lastly, evaluation should compare more baselines, including a generative one like [4] and a combined topical and query graph model like [7].

4.2 Research Issues and Considerations

There are several additional issues worth exploring to improve future research in this area. The first most pressing issue to address for this research is the evaluation metric. While ODP has been used in the past, traditional URL-based metrics such as NDCG are by far the most common. Yet for this type of generative recommender, the URLs in recommended queries may not have been manually annotated for relevance. Since lack of relevance judgments is also a problem for cold-start search tasks in general, it is a more universal problem. A possible direction of discussion is the development of a general, reasonable method of evaluation in addition to (or in place of) the previous metrics. How useful can such metrics be in the absence of relevance judgments, and how can they be empirically validated? On a related note, perhaps it would be better to use simulated users as in [1], evaluating which documents simulated users find useful instead of which relevant ones are discovered.

Another discussion point is potential components to add to a query recommender that 1) incorporate task and information need and 2) do not generate from a seed query, to test the viability of such a general framework. This requires refinements to models of task, need, and topic. One possibility is to model task and need as weighted combinations triples (as in the Resource Description Framework), to sample a subset of these for a recommendation, and to transform them into a query. Another complementary approach is to focus on modeling "needs" in a taxonomy, as [5] did with task facets, and optimize filling information gaps. Such an approach would also complement the precision-based performance of [7]. These are suggestions are fueled by the belief that generative query recommenders that operate at the level of "information" rather than "queries" are a frontier worth exploring.

[3]http://ir.cis.udel.edu/sessions/index.html

5. ACKNOWLEDGMENTS

This work has been supported by an ACM SIGIR Student Travel Grant. It was also funded by grants NSF IIS #1423239 and IMLS #LG-81-16-0025.

6. REFERENCES

[1] L. Azzopardi, D. Kelly, and K. Brennan. How query cost affects search behavior. In *Proceedings of the 36th International ACM SIGIR Conference on Research and Development in Information Retrieval*. ACM, 2013.

[2] R. Baeza-Yates, L. Calderón-Benavides, and C. González-Caro. The intention behind web queries. In *Proceedings of the 13th International Conference on String Processing and Information Retrieval*. Springer-Verlag, 2006.

[3] Q. He, D. Jiang, Z. Liao, S. C. H. Hoi, K. Chang, E.-P. Lim, and H. Li. Web query recommendation via sequential query prediction. In *Proceedings of the 2009 IEEE International Conference on Data Engineering*. IEEE Computer Society, 2009.

[4] R. Kraft and J. Zien. Mining anchor text for query refinement. In *Proceedings of the 13th International Conference on World Wide Web*. ACM, 2004.

[5] Y. Li and N. J. Belkin. An exploration of the relationships between work task and interactive information search behavior. *Journal of the American Society for Information Science and Technology*, 2010.

[6] C. Lucchese, S. Orlando, R. Perego, F. Silvestri, and G. Tolomei. Identifying task-based sessions in search engine query logs. In *Proceedings of the Fourth ACM International Conference on Web Search and Data Mining*. ACM, 2011.

[7] R. Mehrotra and E. Yilmaz. Terms, topics & tasks: Enhanced user modelling for better personalization. In *Proceedings of the 2015 International Conference on The Theory of Information Retrieval*. ACM, 2015.

[8] M. Mitsui and C. Shah. Multi-word generative query recommendation using topic modeling. In *Proceedings of the 10th ACM Conference on Recommender Systems*. ACM, 2016.

[9] M. Mitsui and C. Shah. Query generation as result aggregation for knowledge representation. In *Proceedings of the 50th Hawaii International Conference on System Sciences*, 2017.

[10] A. Y. Ng and M. I. Jordan. On discriminative vs. generative classifiers: A comparison of logistic regression and naive bayes. In *Advances in Neural Information Processing Systems 14*. MIT Press, 2002.

[11] X. Niu and D. Kelly. The use of query suggestions during information search. *Inf. Process. Manage.*, 2014.

[12] H. Vahabi, M. Ackerman, D. Loker, R. Baeza-Yates, and A. Lopez-Ortiz. Orthogonal query recommendation. In *Proceedings of the 7th ACM Conference on Recommender Systems*. ACM, 2013.

Using Information Foraging Theory to Understand Search Behavior in Different Environments

Kevin Ong
RMIT University
Melbourne, Australia
kevin.ong@rmit.edu.au

ABSTRACT

The aim of this research proposal is to understand the extent in which Information Scent, part of Information Foraging Theory, influence the perception of relevance of retrieved search engine result pages (SERPs) in different environments (desktop and mobile). Firstly, we planned to investigate how previously found correlations between information scent and search behavior on desktop SERPs may also applicable on mobile. Secondly, we investigate if the differences in search behavior are also caused by SERP visibility and/or physical input behavior in different environments. Lastly, we would like to observe the extent in which changing snippet length can affect web search behavior. The perception of relevance on SERPs might be similar in both environments because the arrangement of SERPs on both mobile and desktop are identical; or different because the visibility of search results is less on mobile compared to desktop, due to limited screen sizes. We wanted to study the extent of which the physical limitations might significantly impact search behavior in different environments due to expected "hidden scent". We conducted two user studies to observe these phenomenon and seek to understand search behavior by manipulating the SERPs presented to users. We observed both similarities and differences in web search behavior between the environments. On the desktop, increasing information scent led to lower positions of search results saved as relevant and lower positions of mouse hover. However, on mobile, increasing relevant search results beyond the initial screen size, reduced the number of documents examined.

Categories and Subject Descriptors

H.3.3 [**Information Storage and Retrieval**]: Information Search and Retrieval—*search process; selection process*

Keywords

Search Behavior; Search Strategies; Query Reformulation; Information Foraging Theory

CHIIR '17 March 07-11, 2017, Oslo, Norway

ACM ISBN 978-1-4503-4677-1/17/03.

DOI: http://dx.doi.org/10.1145/3020165.3022173

1. INTRODUCTION

Information Foraging Theory [4] is a theory that seeks to predict how rational information seekers behave when finding relevant information. They seek to maximize information gain by minimizing the cost of information seeking. Information Scent, part of Information Foraging Theory, has been observed to alter web search behavior when SERPs were intentionally manipulated. Past work [8] found that stronger information scent, increased document examinations and clicked deeper on the search results. We seek to understand if this behavior is also consistent on mobile.

1.1 Motivation

The rise of mobile search[1] meant that, unlike traditional desktop search, perception of relevance of search results will be constrained. Regardless of the direction that modern mobile engine is taking, understanding how "hidden scent[2]" can affect search behavior is worth investigating because if the expected "hidden scent" plays a role in searching, we may need to evaluate searching in different environments differently.

While mobile phones typically have the smallest screens compared to tablets or desktops, they have the highest mobility and timely access to up-to-date information. These differences suggest different devices types may satisfy different information needs [5]. However, there are reasons to expect similarities as well. They are similar because they all provide access to roughly the same Internet sources with similar amounts of information. We are motivated to use Information Foraging Theory to understand how the extent in which Information Scent affect search behavior in different environments.

2. RESEARCH QUESTIONS

The main research questions are as follows:

Research Question 1 (RQ1): *To what degree, can mobile and desktop web search behavior be explained by Information Scent Theory?*

Wu et al. [9] found that while interacting with SERPs more relevant search results, searchers examined more documents and clicked deeper in the search result list; also found searchers

[1] http://selnd.com/2aJcPv1

[2] relevant search results not immediately seen

to more likely abandon queries, if relevant results are only located lower on the SERPs. We want to study if the phenomenon would happen regardless of the environments. Therefore, we gave the searchers same topics for both environments and observe if they would behave differently. Addressing this question can enable us to extend our knowledge on the applicability of Information Foraging Theory in different environments.

Research Question 2 (RQ2): *To what degree, does mobile and desktop query reformulations affected by Information Scent and typing fluency [3]?*

We seek to address if users' propensity for query reformulation is influenced by Information Scent and/or typing fluency. There are two distinct forms of search strategies [7]. We want to investigate how different environments (between desktops and mobiles) may reflect changes in search strategies. Addressing this question will enable a better understanding of information seeking behavior that is influenced by user's physical characteristics. By extending this work to individually measure typing characteristics of each query issue by users, we can test the validity of using typing characteristics to categorize users into task familiarity and topic expertise. This can potentially be extended to voice search and visually handicapped information seekers.

Research Question 3 (RQ3): *To what degree, does snippet length affect search behavior in different environments?*

We will like to explore the impact that different snippet length have on user's web search behavior. Previously, Cutrell and Guan [1] have identified that lengthening snippets aided users in information-seeking tasks. However, Song et al.[5] have observed that navigational tasks on portable devices (tablets and smartphones) are diminishing due to availability of app store on smartphones. By focusing our attention on information-seeking tasks, how much will user information seeking behavior change, due to different snippet lengths. To this aim, we will also investigate how different snippet lengths can affect search behavior across different environments.

3. METHODOLOGY

In this section, we will demonstrate how the research questions can be addressed. The methodology is ongoing for RQ1 and RQ2 and planned for RQ3.

RQ1 & 2: Comparative user studies: In the first stage, we conducted two user studies to compare users on mobile phones and desktops using previous research framework [8]. We created both mobile and desktop search interfaces to capture the data from the user studies. By conducting user studies of our own and comparing against previous study, we can validate previous study's results and adopt appropriate measures to conduct further experiments. We split both user studies into 2 groups: Information Scent Level (**ISL**) and Information Scent Pattern (**ISP**). ISL refers to increasing level of topically relevant search results on the SERPs while ISP refers to different distribution of four topically relevant search results on the SERPs. There are two views on relevance, topicality or user-utility [6]. We estimated user utility by taking the top queries for the topics from previous experiment [8] to construct our SERPs before the experiments. The SERPs were constructed based on concepts that were relevant to the topic questions. Non-relevant search results were included to vary the level of information scent. We acknowledged users might still issue queries that was significantly different from our pool. Therefore, they were instructed to find topically relevant results after their searches. We also recorded typing characteristics for each query that every user issued. They can then potentially be used to build user profiles on search experiences and task familiarity.

RQ3: Crowd experiment: To identify the effects of search snippet length on information needs, we plan to do the following experiments:

Create a desktop experiment with various length of search snippets with prefixed tasks: Using TREC collections to build tasks and relevant results with varying length of search snippets and conduct the experiment on crowd-sourced workers.

Create a simulated mobile and tablet experiment with varying search snippet length with prefixed tasks: Using previous experiment resources, we will run our experiments on simulated displays on crowd-sourced workers. The displays will be simulated by predefining screen size on desktop-sized screens to smaller dimensions to fit typical tablets and smartphone sizes.

4. PROGRESS

We have concluded the user studies and are currently analyzing the results for **RQ1**.

4.1 Measurements

Below is a subset of the measurements taken from the user studies:

- **Time**: Time spent examining search results for the first query per task
- **NumPage**: Number of SERP paginations for each task.
- **NumExam**: Number of documents examined for each search result set.
- **DRS**: Deepest rank scrolled into view. Lowest search result position that becomes visible in the viewable area during a search. If the participant paginate to second page, search depth ranges from 11 – 20.
- **DRH**: Deepest rank hover (for desktop experiment). Lowest search result position that the mouse hovered over for at least 0.5 seconds. If users did not hover the mouse at all, the value will be 0.
- **ROA**: Rate Of Abandonment, the rate of not clicking or saving any document as relevant after the initial query submission for each task.
- **DRT**: Deepest position on the first SERP saved as relevant by the users.
- **TTotal**: Total number of search results on the first SERP saved as relevant per task per participant.
- **TRele**: Total number of relevant search results on the first SERP (according to ISL/ISP conditions) saved by the users.

On Tables 1 and 2, Information Scent Level - Low (**ILL**), Information Scent Level - Medium (**ILM**) and Information Scent Level - High (**ILH**) referred to the number of *topically relevant* [6] search results presented to the users, arranged in ascending level of information scent from 1 to 3 to 5 from the top position on the SERPs. Details of the distribution can be found in previous work [8]. It shows that both on desktop and mobile, users tended to mark more documents (as well as more relevant documents) as relevant as ISL increased. Users also looked at more results (DRS) when more relevant

Table 1: Increasing Information Scent Level (ISL) conditions

ISL	Desktop			Mobile		
Measures	**ILL**	**ILM**	**ILH**	ILL	ILM	ILH
Time	47.92 (28.19)	57.37 (38.11)	**62.94 (39.85)**	43.42 (21.00)	**61.61 (43.81)**	53.39 (26.20)
NumPage	.31 (.47)	.46 (.51)	**.49 (.51)**	.28 (.45)	**.31 (.47)**	**.31 (.47)**
NumExam	.39 (.49)	.40 (.81)	**.69 (1.16)∗**	.19 (.40)	**.56 (.91)**	.31 (.92)∗
DRS	12.44 (5.18)∗	14.17 (5.38)⁑	**14.34 (5.41)⁑**	10.83 (5.60)∗	11.17 (5.74)⁑	**11.69 (5.19)⁑**
DRH	6.11 (7.04)	7.89 (6.85)	**8.64 (6.92)**	–	–	–
ROA	39%	23%	**17%**	**28%**	11%	11%
DRT	.53 (.56)⁑∗	1.86 (1.44)	**3.17 (2.55)**	1.42 (2.13)⁑∗	2.42 (1.65)	**3.69 (2.45)**
TTotal	.53 (.56)∗	1.60 (1.33)	**2.37 (1.88)**	.92 (.91)∗	1.86 (1.25)	**2.78 (1.74)**
TRele	.50 (.51)	1.49 (1.09)	**2.26 (1.80)**	.61 (.49)	1.64 (1.07)	**2.61 (1.55)**

The significant differences between same condition (desktop ILL -> mobile ILL) in both environments is indicated on the table.
Chi-Square Test: ∗p < .05, ⁑p < .01, ⁑∗p < .001, ⁑⁑p < .0001

Table 2: Statistical difference between conditions

	ISL	
Measure	**Desktop**	**Mobile**
NumPage	1.41	0.63
NumExam	3.85	7.00∗
DRS	3.77	1.21
DRH	16.08⁑∗	–
ROA	2.60	4.00
DRT	65.11⁑⁑	37.40⁑⁑
TTotal	39.20⁑⁑	33.67⁑⁑
TRele	37.62⁑⁑	44.45⁑⁑

The significant differences across the conditions are indicated.
Chi-Square Test: ∗p < .05, ⁑p < .01, ⁑∗p < .001, ⁑⁑p < .0001

search results were present in both environments. When comparing between both environments, while more search results scrolled into view on desktop, the depth of search results saved as relevant by users was lower on desktop compared to on mobile when there was only 1 relevant result (ILL condition). This suggest that users were less likely to save relevant documents (less than 1) when the number of relevant search results were too few. Conversely, it also suggested that mobile users were more tolerant of non-relevant search results for ILL condition by saving some non-relevant (more than 1) search results as relevant. On mobile, we can only display 2–3 search results due to the smaller screen. We observed that displaying 5 relevant search results did not increase the number of documents clicked by users. In fact, click-through rate were lower when more snippets were present from 3 to 5 relevant search results. We speculated that by having enough number of relevant search results, users were able to determine any of the search results were relevant by just viewing the snippets. This is, however, different on desktop, the number of examined documents increased with increasing number of relevant search results. In terms of statistical significance, the varying information scent level influenced search behavior in terms of DRT, TTotal and TRele in general, DRH on desktop and NumExam on mobile.

4.2 Future plan

We have identified a correlation between ISL and search behavior. In future work, we intend to study if Information Scent also affect query reformulations in different environments. Given that we also collected typing behavior, we will like to analyze if query reformulations behavior is influenced by typing fluency (that is if the ease of typing on query reformulations). We will analyze if Information Scent influenced query reformulations in terms of session-level, task-level or query-level differences [2].
Additionally, we will also like to conduct a follow-up experiment to understand if varying snippet length on both mobile and desktop crowd-source experiments have an influence on search behavior. We plan to combine both typing behavior and snippet length to build new user models based on Information Foraging Theory to predict web search behavior in different environments. Keystroke biometrics are already used in other areas such as for user authentication.[3] It is plausible that user characteristics such as their search experience and even topic familiarity may be informed by their typing behaviors, such as typing speed, rhythm and pauses.

5. REFERENCES

[1] Cutrell, E., and Guan, Z. What Are You Looking For?: An Eye-tracking Study of Information Usage in Web Search. In *Proceedings of SIGCHI* (2007), pp. 407–416.

[2] Jiang, J., and Ni, C. What Affects Word Changes in Query Reformulation During a Task-based Search Session? In *Proceedings of CHIIR* (2016), pp. 111–120.

[3] Oppenheimer, D. M. The secret life of fluency. *Trends in Cognitive Sciences 12*, 6 (2008), 237–241.

[4] Pirolli, P., and Card, S. Information Foraging. *Psychological Review 106*, 4 (1999), 643–675.

[5] Song, Y., Ma, H., Wang, H., and Wang, K. Exploring and exploiting user search behavior on mobile and tablet devices to improve search relevance. In *Proceedings of WWW* (2013), pp. 1201–1212.

[6] Tombros, T., and Crestani, F. Users' perception of relevance of spoken documents. *JASIST 51*, 10 (2000), 929–939.

[7] White, R., and Drucker, S. M. Investigating Behavioral Variability in Web Search. In *Proceedings of WWW* (2007), pp. 21–30.

[8] Wu, W.-C., and Kelly, D. Online search stopping behaviors: An investigation of query abandonment and task stopping. *77th ASIS&T Annual Meeting* (2014).

[9] Wu, W.-C., Kelly, D., and Sud, A. Using Information Scent and Need for Cognition to Understand Online Search Behavior. In *Proceedings of SIGIR* (2014), pp. 557–566.

[3] http://www.keytrac.net/

Missing Information in the Classroom and Misinformed by the Crowd: Developing Analytical Skills for Understanding Online Controversies

Alamir Novin
University of British Columbia
1961 East Mall, Vancouver, BC, Canada
alamir.novin@ubc.ca

ABSTRACT

At the heart of this research is the role freedom of speech and freedom of access plays in the information era. Prior research found that while our access to information is rising, so is our level of spreading misinformation. This research will build on these prior studies to argue that our biases lead us to share less meaningful knowledge constructs. To tackle this problem this study integrates the fields of Human-Computer Interactions (to study our implicit biases), Social Network Analysis (to research the spread of biases), Information Visualization (to study the representation of bias) and Collaborative Information Behaviour (to observe the dialogical reconciliation of biases). The research will build on prior research to explore how students contextualize the various biases in the science controversies that they encounter online. Two objectives have been set to be accomplished by the end of this research: 1) develop a strategy for classrooms to equip students with skills for evaluating online science information and 2) develop recommendations for how online interfaces can present information that contextualizes conflicting information in a science controversy.

Keywords

search engine results page; SERP; bias; biases; heuristics; document genre; document order; collaboration; collaborative information behavior; collaborative information seeking;

1. Introduction

The National Science Board (2014) reported that the Internet has become the public's primary source for encountering science information. The report cautioned that even though the public has greater access to scientific information on the Internet, they are also at risk of believing more misinformation (2014). Addressing the effects of online misinformation on the public requires the development of students' information literacy and online search strategies. A recent study found that young people still have a difficult time thinking critically about online sources, such as differentiating between advertisements and search results [2]. Students often trust lists produced by search algorithms over their own analytical skills [3], even though search algorithms can influence our opinions and decisions [4]–[6].

CHIIR '17, March 07-11, 2017, Oslo, Norway
ACM 978-1-4503-4677-1/17/03.
http://dx.doi.org/10.1145/3020165.3022174

Locally in Vancouver, Canada, the Curriculum for Information Technology [7] has not developed "achievement indicators" for primary school students to "evaluate information retrieved electronically for authenticity, bias, and timeliness" (p.82).

Developing achievement indicators requires understanding not only how students evaluate bias results in a search engine, but how the information is used. Current researchers in information retrieval are expounding on the importance of studying more complete models of information use, from the interactions users have with systems [8], the usefulness of its information, its influences [9], and the outcome of the retrieval [10]. Researching these factors requires tailoring the work task to the information environment and participants [10]. Therefore, understanding students' searching and learning about science controversies will require making observations that look beyond their comprehension of science information [11] to understand how students contextualize the *conflicting information* in scientific controversies presented by search engines. An *explanatory sequential mixed methods* approach [12] is required when the quantifiable data, such as a student's academic achievements in science, can be contextualized by qualitative information, such as a student's socio-cultural influences [13], [14].

2. Motivation and Research Questions

In a study that will be published in the Conference on Human Information Interaction and Retrieval (CHIIR 2017), my supervisor, Dr. Eric Meyers, and I found that the way students summarize science controversies can be influenced by the way a search engine presents information. We suggested that students can mitigate the influences of the biased results if they collaborate while searching, thereby remaining open to multiple perspectives [15]. I will be building on this prior research to explore how students contextualize the various biases in the science controversies that they encounter online. The central research question being investigated is: *If students collaboratively contextualize various perspectives on science controversies that they find online, will they be able to produce a more comprehensive understanding in their assignments?* By investigating this question, I hope to achieve two tangible objectives that will work together to help contextualize online information for students: 1) develop a strategy for classrooms to equip students with skills for evaluating online science information and 2) develop recommendations for how online interfaces can present information that contextualizes conflicting information in a science controversy.

3. Methods

This study will use an *explanatory sequential mixed methods* approach to examine two groups of young students at a primary school in British Columbia. I am currently in contact with several classroom teachers and school educational psychologists in British Columbia who have expressed interest in allowing me to conduct my research within their classroom. The classrooms are related to media studies where students are collaborating to understand various online science controversies. One group of students will be required to collaborate by using the Internet to share their information searches via a web application. The web application was developed for my Masters' thesis and it maps the searches of different users in relation to each other. By recording the sharing of information within a group of students, this study can lay out a clear causal relationship between the gathering of information by one student and the use of that information if it appears in the output of another student's assignment. The second group of students will function as a control group. They will also collaborate on assignments, but sharing their search results will be presented as only an option and not a requirement. The experiences, sharing of search results, and writing outputs of the two groups will be compared. How the students comprehend the science controversies and mitigate their biases is the focus of the analysis.

4. Progress

For my Masters' thesis, I used my fellowship funding to develop online software that helped to contextualize science debates for an online community of journalists. During my thesis defense, I was encouraged by members of my committee, specifically Dr.Brian Gabrial and Dr.David Secko, to build on my research progress by looking at the field of education and information sciences. I joined UBC's doctoral program in Library, Archival and Information Studies and am honoured to have Dr. Eric Meyers support me as my supervisor. Dr. Meyers is widely recognized in the field for his award-winning research in children's education and student information practices. My dissertation is strongly supported by his expertise in the major areas of my research. Most importantly, our ongoing research into how student groups collaborate together provides a growing and dynamic knowledge base to draw from. Having passed the qualifying exams of my program this year, I am now at the beginning stages of my research proposal.

5. Future Plans

After working with my school contacts on a reasonable start time, the project involves three research phases: (i) Training the students in sharing information searches through the developed web application (1 week), (ii) surveying the experience of the students while sharing their data (4 months), and (iii) testing the comprehensiveness of the resulting assignments produced by the students (4 months). The study is then completed by performing a quantitative analysis with a panel of teachers to rank the accuracy and comprehensiveness of the assignments that used the software (2 months). An analysis of the findings and write up will take 6 months. After these stages, I will complete the revisions and defense of my dissertation in 6 months, for a total of two years.

6. References

[1] "National Science Board (2014) Science and Engineering Indicators." National Science Foundation, Arlington, VA., 2014.

[2] Ofcom, "Children and Parents: Media Use and Attitudes Report," Nov. 2015.

[3] E. M. Meyers, "Access denied: how students resolve information needs when an ideal document is restricted," in *Proceedings of the 2012 iConference*, 2012, pp. 629–631.

[4] N. J. Belkin, M. Cole, and J. Liu, "A model for evaluation of interactive information retrieval," presented at the Proceedings of the SIGIR 2009 Workshop on the Future of IR Evaluation, 2009, pp. 7–8.

[5] R. Epstein and R. E. Robertson, "The search engine manipulation effect (SEME) and its possible impact on the outcomes of elections," *Proc. Natl. Acad. Sci.*, p. 201419828, Aug. 2015.

[6] E. Hargittai, "Digital Na(t)ives? Variation in Internet Skills and Uses among Members of the 'Net Generation,'" *Sociol. Inq.*, vol. 80, no. 1, pp. 92–113, Feb. 2010.

[7] "BC Grade 8 Curriculum for Information Technology," 2015. [Online]. Available: https://www.bced.gov.bc.ca/irp/curric_grade_packages/gr8curric_req.pdf. [Accessed: 23-Nov-2015].

[8] D. Kelly, "Methods for evaluating interactive information retrieval systems with users," *Found. Trends Inf. Retr.*, vol. 3, no. 1—2, pp. 1–224, 2009.

[9] D. Case, "Sixty years of measuring the use of information and its sources: from consultation to application," *Libr. Digit. Age LIDA Proc.*, vol. 13, 2014.

[10] P. Borlund, "Interactive Information Retrieval: An Introduction," *J. Inf. Sci. Theory Pract.*, vol. 1, no. 3, pp. 12–32, Sep. 2013.

[11] D. M. Kahan, A. R. Landrum, K. Carpenter, L. Helft, and K. H. Jamieson, "Science Curiosity and Political Information Processing," *Adv. Polit. Psychol. Forthcom.*, 2016.

[12] J. Creswell, *Research Design - Qualitative, Quantitative, and Mixed Methods Approach*, vol. 3. Sage, 2014.

[13] C. Hewson and D. Laurent, "Research Design and Tools for Internet Research," in *The Sage Handbook of online Research Methods*, Fielding, Lee, and Blank, Eds. Sage, 2008.

[14] R. M. Lee, N. Fielding, and G. Blank, *The Internet as a Research Medium: An Editorial Introduction to The Sage Handbook of Online Research Methods*. Sage, 2008.

[15] A. Novin and E. Meyers, "Making Sense of Online Science: Exploring 'Bias' in the Search Engine Result Page," in *Conference on Human Information Interaction and Retrieval*, 2017.

The Long Term Effects of Search Query Examples on the Search Behaviours of Non-native Users of Government E-Services

David Brazier
2nd year PhD
Northumbria University
Dr Morgan Harvey

ABSTRACT

Interacting with information in an on-line capacity is common place for the majority of people nowadays. However, there still remains a considerable section of society whose skills, knowledge and experience in such activities are creating significant barriers to essential services. This research aims to investigate the information interaction behaviours of English as a second language users of on-line governmental services in the UK. Work has already begun on identifying what this user group understands by the term governmental service and the skills and information needs necessary to interact with such services on-line. Findings from the study of searching in a second language (English) in contextually relevant search situations show that despite performing to the best of their abilities, deeming that they were bookmarking documents of relevance to the task and that the tasks were easy, the participants were only choosing documents that were partially or tangentially relevant. This shows that despite their confidence in their overall performance these users were not able to correctly determine their actual performance and would suggest there is scope for search systems to support the information interaction of said users.

Keywords

Information interaction; search; e-government; information literacy; information behaviour

1. MOTIVATION

Government initiatives, such as the UK's 'digital by default', have been instigated in a response to the proliferation of digital services and Internet-based technologies. This has seen the UK government running both standard services (face-to-face, telephone and postal) and digital services simultaneously but it is not inconceivable that standard services will (eventually) be phased out.

CHIIR '17 March 07-11, 2017, Oslo, Norway

ACM ISBN 978-1-4503-4677-1/17/03.
DOI: http://dx.doi.org/10.1145/3020165.3022175

For those who find Internet technologies an everyday tool this is no great concern, however, there are members of society who currently rely on face-to-face encounters with staff or the skills, knowledge and experience of their friends, family or community members when their own is lacking. Information and digital divides place importance on the IT literacy and abilities of the user [4] so in instances where these social groups are unavailable or their knowledge and experience are inadequate this can have adverse effects for the more vulnerable members, who may already face significant barriers.

Research into the information interaction of users whose first language is not English is growing [1, 2, 4] but there still remains much that can be done in understanding their search behaviours [12] and in turn help facilitate those most at risk of falling prey to the 'digital divide' and segretation from essential governmental services. This project serves to add to the research (and this knowledge area) by exploring the ideas of information seeking as an activity [8] and expanding on the work of Harvey, Hauff and Elsweiler [6] by adapting methods of improving the users own abilities and knowledge through the utilisation of search query examples. In this process the user submits an initial query, are then offered high quality examples as alternatives to the original query which lead to users recognising positive aspects and are then able learn to produce higher-quality queries themselves.

2. RESEARCH QUESTIONS

The overall research question of this project is to look at "What are the long term effects of search query examples on the search behaviours of non-native users of government e-services". The following sub-questions were then formulated to facilitate this research:

- How do English as a second language (ESL) users search for information?
- How does this differ from native English language users?
- Can potential differences be supported by the search system?
- What are the long term effects of such support?

3. METHODOLOGY

Before tackling the research questions it is, perhaps, prudent to determine not just what the users needs are but what they know, firstly, of what constitutes governmental services but also what systems are pre-existing and whether there is a need for such functionality as search query examples [6].

Participatory action research is a methodology widely used in a number of fields [11] by facilitating the identification of user needs and developing relevant and validated systems in association with the users [7, 9, 10] and has potential to be utilised in an Information Retrieval setting [5, pp. 92].

As a result, a pilot study to set context, upon which the three sub-questions could then be based, has been devised in line with similar studies [13]. The objective of the first sub-question is identifying the needs of the user and how they search for information. The first stage of this is to be addressed as part of the pilot study, The second stage will employ a mixed methods approach, utilising recorded observation of participants undertaking search tasks and manual log analysis of their interactions, and post study semi structured discussion to determine their experiences and perceptions [4]. This second stage will also look to conclude the action research aspect of the study by not only identifying how these users search for information but also to help understand why they interact with search systems as they do and allow the users the opportunity to identify if existing services are fit for purpose and offer solutions should this not be the case.

Comparison of behaviours against those of English language natives (those whose first language is English) will follow with the use of identical methods to ensure similarities and/or differences in interactions can be adjudged with some level of certainty, and in the process accomplish sub-question two. The third and fourth sub-questions will then look to adapt the approach of searching by example [6] on a longitudinal scale (somewhere between 10 weeks and 6 months) with time-scales determined by the implementation date in conjunction with the time remaining of the PhD project.

4. PROGRESS SO FAR

To date the pilot study has been concluded. Identification of the types of services users would use was made by involving 7 international PhD students (who ESL users) at a UK university, 6 of whom also took part in the second stage of the study. The students were recruited and tasked with identifying: what a government service entailed; which would be deemed most useful (to the group); and the information needs, information sources and skills that would be required to successfully utilise the e-service.

From this information, four search tasks were designed to reflect realistic information seeking situations as part of the second stage. This study incorporated a search retrieval experiment, with participants using the Google search engine to bookmark documents of most relevance to completion of the tasks. This was followed by a post study discussion whereby they could voice their experiences and put forward possible solutions and recommendations to any issues they encountered.

10 international PhD students from a UK university took part in this study with each a ESL user. Findings from the study of searching in a second language (English) in contextually relevant search situations show that despite performing to the best of their abilities, deeming that they were bookmarking documents of relevance to the task and that the tasks were easy, the participants were choosing documents that were non-relevant or tangentially relevant. This shows that despite their confidence in their overall performance these users were not able to correctly determine their actual performance and would suggest there is scope for search systems to support their information interaction [3]. Due to the nature of governmental services the implications of these findings could have detrimental effect to the user in a real world scenario. Gaining a further understanding why these issues arise may inform development of future systems and techniques to mitigate these problems.

Although the findings show promise, the low participant numbers limit the ability to offer generalisable indications of ESL user behaviours. It is for this reason that the second stage study has been extended - with a view to gaining additional users. Work has already begun on this in conjunction with ongoing progress into the study of native English language speakers, that is users who use English as a first language.

5. FUTURE PLAN

The plan for the immediate future is to complete the remainder of the two studies in order to be able to complete sub-questions one and two and offer comparative evidence of the user groups.

Over the remaining time of the PhD the aim is to build on the idea of creating a bespoke search system to test the repeated effect of users exposure to search query examples [6] which will help achieve the project objective of whether these users can be supported by the search system and the effects of such support over an extended period. It is hoped that this will result in recommendations for search user interface design, and training activities and material to meet the needs of users.

6. REFERENCES

[1] B. Berendt and A. Kralisch. A user-centric approach to identifying best deployment strategies for language tools: the impact of content and access language on web user behaviour and attitudes. *Information Retrieval*, 12(3):380–399, 2009.

[2] T. Bogers, M. Gäde, M. Hall, and M. Skov. Analyzing the influence of language proficiency on interactive book search behavior. *iSchools*, 2016.

[3] D. Brazier and M. Harvey. Strangers in a strange land: A study of second language speakers searching for e-services. In *CHIIR 2017 -Conference on Human Information Interaction and Retrieval, 7th - 11th March 2017, Oslo, Norway*, 2017. (in press).

[4] P. Chu, E. Jozsa, A. Komlodi, and K. Hercegfi. An exploratory study on search behavior in different languages. In *Proceedings of the 4th Information Interaction in Context Symposium*, pages 318–321. ACM, 2012.

[5] N. Ford. New cognitive directions. In *New directions in cognitive information retrieval*, pages 81–96. Springer, 2005.

[6] M. Harvey, C. Hauff, and D. Elsweiler. Learning by example: training users with high-quality query suggestions. In *Proceedings of the 38th International ACM SIGIR Conference on Research and Development in Information Retrieval*, pages 133–142. ACM, 2015.

[7] S. M. C. Lau and S. Stille. Participatory research with teachers: toward a pragmatic and dynamic view of equity and parity in research relationships. *European Journal of Teacher Education*, 37(2):156–170, 2014.

[8] A. Lloyd, M. A. Kennan, K. M. Thompson, and A. Qayyum. Connecting with new information landscapes: information literacy practices of refugees. *Journal of Documentation.*, 69(1):121–144, 2013.

[9] J. McDonagh and D. Coghlan. The art of clinical inquiry in information technology-related change. *Handbook of action research*, pages 372–378, 2001.

[10] F. Millerand and K. S. Baker. Who are the users? who are the developers? webs of users and developers in the development process of a technical standard. *Information Systems Journal*, 20(2):137–161, 2010.

[11] P. Reason and H. Bradbury. *Handbook of action research: Participative inquiry and practice.* London : Sage Publications, 2nd edition, 2008.

[12] G. Rózsa, A. Komlodi, and P. Chu. Online searching in english as a foreign language. In *Proceedings of the 24th International Conference on World Wide Web Companion*, pages 875–880. International World Wide Web Conferences Steering Committee, 2015.

[13] R. B. Tavares, M. Hepworth, and S. M. D. S. Costa. Investigating citizens' information needs through participative research: a pilot study in candangolândia, brazil. *Information Development*, 27(2):125–138, 2011.

Interactive Search in Video & Lifelogging Repositories

Frank Hopfgartner
University of Glasgow
Glasgow, UK
frank.hopfgartner@glasgow.ac.uk

Klaus Schoeffmann
Klagenfurt University
Klagenfurt, Austria
ks@itec.aau.at

ABSTRACT

Due to increasing possibilities to create digital video, we are facing the emergence of large video archives that are made accessible either online or offline. Though a lot of research has been spent on video retrieval tools and methods, which allow for automatic search in videos, still the performance of automatic video retrieval is far from optimal.

At the same time, the organization of personal data is receiving increasing research attention due to the challenges that are faced in gathering, enriching, searching and visualizing this data. Given the increasing quantities of personal data being gathered by individuals, the concept of a heterogeneous personal digital libraries of rich multimedia and sensory content for every individual is becoming a reality.

Despite the differences between video archives and personal lifelogging libraries, we are facing very similar challenges when accessing these multimedia repositories. For example, users will struggle to find the information they are looking for in either collection if they are not able to formulate their search needs through a query. In this tutorial we discussed (i) proposed solutions for improved video & lifelog content navigation, (ii) typical interaction of content-based querying features, and (iii) advanced content visualization methods. Moreover, we discussed and demonstrate interactive video & lifelog search systems and ways to evaluate their performance.

1. MOTIVATION

This tutorial addressed two separate, yet similar challenges, namely interactive search in video and lifelogging repositories. In Section 1.1, we first introduce current challenges in the video retrieval domain. Section 1.2 then introduces open research challenges when dealing with lifelogging material.

1.1 Interactive Video Search

Over the last two decades, there has been a lot of research on content-based video retrieval to solve the problem of finding the proper scene of interest in a large video archive (e.g., [1, 4, 5, 6, 11, 16, 17, 20, 22, 25, 15]). Video retrieval tools use content-based indexing methods to perform automatic annotation with content descriptors for color, texture, shape, and semantic concepts. The extracted information is used to provide retrieval functions through different querying modes [13]: *query-by-text*, *query-by-example image* (or example clip), *query-by-sketch*, and by *query-by-filtering* (e.g. through semantic concepts). The user first formulates a query, initiates the retrieval engine that looks for matching video segments, and then browses the results, which are typically lists of keyframes extracted from the result segments.

Retrieval approaches commonly use interactive *relevance feedback* methods to keep the human in the loop after the query and to learn which results are relevant in order to adapt the search in another iteration to the user's needs ([3, 12, 24]). However, the actual search process with video retrieval tools is mostly automatic and a *black box* for the user. Interaction is limited to the *query-formulation* and *results-browsing* phases. Research on video retrieval mainly focuses on improving the performance of the retrieval engine (i.e., the querying itself), with less focus on the user and her interaction with the system [26].

There are well-known issues with video retrieval applications. First, there is the *usability gap*. A user is often not able to express her needs and thoughts through text, a problem that is already apparent for an image ("*An image is worth a thousand words.*") but much worse for a video segment consisting of many images. In fact, most video retrieval tools operate on images (i.e., keyframes of shots) and provide image query features. Additionally, the issue of *polysemy* is a challenging problem in text-based search, which can only be partially solved through relevance feedback. Similarly, an automatic retrieval tool cannot easily determine the user-dependent relative importance (i.e., weight) of a query term and hence often returns too many irrelevant results. When considering the query-by-example approach, it turns out that users rarely have a good example image or example clip at hand, which is similar to the target scene they are looking for. The query-by-sketch approach is also not very convenient for users, because most users typically cannot draw a sufficiently good sketch for a scene they want to find, although they would immediately recognize it when they see it. Query-by-filtering (e.g., for a semantic concept like '*car*', for example) in a large video collection is often also not very helpful for a user, since the returned result list is typically way too long and the confidence of concept detection is still not good enough.

CHIIR '17 March 07-11, 2017, Oslo, Norway

ACM ISBN 978-1-4503-4677-1/17/03.
DOI: http://dx.doi.org/10.1145/3020165.3022161

Finally, there is another challenging problem that affects the content-based indexing phase, namely the *semantic gap*, which is the discrepancy between the semantics a user can derive from an image and the information a computer can extract from pixel values [23]. The semantic gap seriously limits the achievable performance of visual information retrieval tools.

1.2 Lifelogging

Recent technological advances have introduced new types of sensors (informational sensors, physical sensors) and devices (for example Google Glass or Apple's Watch) which allow the individual to compile vast archives of personal data.

The activity of recording personal bio signals and metrics using software and tools is referred to as self-tracking. Different reasons can be found that motivate people to start recording and analyzing personal data. A large share of self-trackers include people with chronic medical conditions who rely on technology to track their personal well-being. Other self-trackers are motivated to observe and to increase their personal fitness and wellness levels [18]. These individuals can be considered as part of the *Quantified Self* (QS) movement that uses instruments to record numerical data on all aspects of our lives: input (food consumed, surrounding air-quality), states (mood, arousal, blood oxygen levels), and performance (mental, physical). Such self-monitoring and self-sensing, which combines wearable sensors and wearable computing, is also sometimes referred to as *Lifelogging*, although lifelogging describes the process of recording and storing any type of personal data rather than just user-centric sensor data. Captured over a long period of time, such personal data can provide a detailed picture of the activities of an individual and will require search, summarization and knowledge extraction tools to make them valuable. Therefore it comes as no surprise that Lifelong Digital Libraries are receiving increasing attention within the research community [7].

One of the early adopters of lifelogging techniques is Gordon Bell of Microsoft. Within the "MyLifeBits" project [2], they captured all of their personal data in digital form and created software that allowed them to access this data. The goal of this technology was to create a personal archive, or a "portable, infallible, artificial memory" that can be exploited to increase job productivity, serve as a basis for medical treatment, improving performances in school and many other scenarios. Another lifelogging pioneer is Steve Mann, who uses wearable computing to create a record of his life. He performed significant studies on visual memory prosthetics that transformed his eye into a camera and his body into a Web server. He refers to this technique as 'cyborg logging' or 'glogging'. Wearable cameras play an important role in research on lifelogging since analyzing camera data streams can reveal a lot of information. One wearable lifelogging device, the SenseCam [14], automatically captures images every 30 seconds, resulting in thousands of recorded images per day. It is a camera with a fish-eye lens, about the size of a cigarette packet. The camera is usually worn around the neck and can be set to take photographs when triggered by such things as changes in the light, ambient heat or body temperature. The SenseCam has since been improved with new models and competing devices available for purchase. The SenseCam has received a lot of attention from scientific researchers who focused in 100+ papers on various aspects of lifelogging. For a detailed description of state-of-the-art lifelogging techniques, see Gurrin et al. [10].

2. OBJECTIVES

As mentioned above, various issues and challenges arise when interacting with multimedia content. In this tutorial, we gave an overview of existing video & lifelog search interfaces that illustrate different methods to approach named challenges and issues. The participants learned best practice on how to interact with multimedia content and how to apply this knowledge in their own project. Following an introduction of the subject matter, we highlighted the need for interactive video search and outlined well-known issues and current research areas. Moreover, we introduce the research area of lifelogging and highlight similarities between both fields.

Focusing on video search, we presented different graphical user interfaces that are designed to address these challenges. We started by presenting commercial and academic video search systems that represent the state-of-the-art in video search. In order to illustrate the limitations of video search, we began by providing an introduction into video content analysis. In particular, we focused on the segmentation of videos into different units of retrieval (i.e., video shots and semantically coherent scenes), argued for the selection of appropriate keyframes and explained how to index these video materials. Then, we overviewed methods for video content presentation, namely abstraction and summarization of video content and methods for video content visualization. After that, we introduced different methods to interact with video content. We showcased the advantages of browsing and exploration of video content, methods to navigate through the content, querying and sketching interfaces.

Focusing on the lifelogging domain, we first provided an introduction to this upcoming technology. After presenting approaches on how to capture heterogeneous datastreams of lifelogs, we outlined state-of-the-art techniques to analyze this data. Then, we presented different methodologies to visualize and access lifelog data.

Following this session, the participants learned how to evaluate the performance of video & lifelog search engines. We introduced the de-facto standard evaluation protocol that is applied for scientific performance evaluation. Furthermore, we introduced popular Academic evaluation campaigns, namely the Known-Item search task promoted by TRECVid [21], the Video Browser Showdown [19] which has been organized as part of the Multimedia Modeling Conference, and the Personal Lifelog Access & Retrieval Task NTCIR-Lifelog [9] that is organized as part of the Japanese conference series on the Evaluation of Information Access Systems (NTCIR). The aim of this task is to begin the comparative evaluation of information access and retrieval systems operating over personal lifelog data. As part of this, a dataset consisting of anonymized lifeless gathered by a number of individuals over an extended period is released [8]. In 2017, NTCIR-Lifelog includes four subtasks, two of which focus on unser-centred interaction and retrieval: In the Lifelog Semantic Access Task (1), participants have to retrieve a number of specific moments in a lifelogger's life. The Lifelog Insight Task (2) aims to gain insights into a lifelogger's life as promoted by the Quantified Self community.

3. REFERENCES

[1] Y.A. Aslandogan and C.T. Yu. Techniques and systems for image and video retrieval. *Knowledge and Data Engineering, IEEE Transactions on*, 11(1):56–63, Jan 1999.

[2] Gordon Bell and J. Gemmell. *Your Life, Uploaded: The Digital Way to Better Memory, Health, and Productivity.* Plume, 2010.

[3] C. Breiteneder and H. Eidenberger. Content-based image retrieval in digital libraries. In *Digital Libraries: Research and Practice, 2000 Kyoto, International Conference on.*, pages 288–295, 2000.

[4] Shih-Fu Chang, John R. Smith, Mandis Beigi, and Ana Benitez. Visual information retrieval from large distributed online repositories. *Communications of the ACM*, 40(12):63–71, December 1997.

[5] Tat-Seng Chua and Li-Qun Ruan. A video retrieval and sequencing system. *ACM Transactions on Information Systems*, 13(4):373–407, October 1995.

[6] P Geetha and Vasumathi Narayanan. A survey of content-based video retrieval. *Journal of Computer Science*, 4(6):474, 2008.

[7] Cathal Gurrin and Frank Hopfgartner. Lifelong digital libraries. In *Proceedings of the 15th ACM/IEEE-CS Joint Conference on Digital Libraries*, JCDL '15, pages 287–287. ACM, 2015.

[8] Cathal Gurrin, Hideo Joho, Frank Hopfgartner, Liting Zhou, and Rami Albatal. NTCIR lifelog: The first test collection for lifelog research. In *Proceedings of the 39th International ACM SIGIR conference on Research and Development in Information Retrieval, SIGIR 2016, Pisa, Italy, July 17-21, 2016*, pages 705–708, 2016.

[9] Cathal Gurrin, Hideo Joho, Frank Hopfgartner, Liting Zhou, and Rami Albatal. Overview of ntcir-12 lifelog task, 2016.

[10] Cathal Gurrin, Alan F. Smeaton, and Aiden R. Doherty. Lifelogging: Personal big data. *Foundations and Trends in Information Retrieval*, 8(1):1–125, 2014.

[11] Alexander G. Hauptmann and Michael G. Christel. Successful approaches in the TREC video retrieval evaluations. In *Proceedings of ACM Multimedia*, pages 668–675, New York, NY, USA, 2004. ACM.

[12] Alexander G. Hauptmann, Wei-Hao Lin, Rong Yan, Jun Yang, and Ming-Yu Chen. Extreme video retrieval: Joint maximization of human and computer performance. In *Proceedings of ACM Multimedia*, pages 385–394. ACM, 2006.

[13] Daniel Heesch, Peter Howarth, Joao Magalhaes, Alexander May, Marcus Pickering, Alexei Yavlinsky, and Stefan Rüger. Video retrieval using search and browsing. In *TREC Video Retrieval Evaluation Online Proceedings*, 2004.

[14] Steve Hodges, Lyndsay Williams, Emma Berry, Shahram Izadi, James Srinivasan, Alex Butler, Gavin Smyth, Narinder Kapur, and Ken Wood. Sensecam: A retrospective memory aid. In *Proceedings of the 8th International Conference on Ubiquitous Computing*, UbiComp'06, pages 177–193, Berlin, Heidelberg, 2006. Springer-Verlag.

[15] Frank Hopfgartner, Jana Urban, Robert Villa, and Joemon M. Jose. Simulated testing of an adaptive multimedia information retrieval system. In *International Workshop on Content-Based Multimedia Indexing, CBMI '07, Bordeaux, France, June 25-27, 2007*, pages 328–335, 2007.

[16] Yu-Gang Jiang, Chong-Wah Ngo, and Jun Yang. Towards optimal bag-of-features for object categorization and semantic video retrieval. In *Proceedings of the 6th ACM International Conference on Image and Video Retrieval*, CIVR '07, pages 494–501, New York, NY, USA, 2007. ACM.

[17] Michael S. Lew, Nicu Sebe, Chabane Djeraba, and Ramesh Jain. Content-based multimedia information retrieval: State of the art and challenges. *ACM Transactions on Multimedia Computing, Communications, and Applications*, 2(1):1–19, February 2006.

[18] Na Li and Frank Hopfgartner. To log or not to log? swot analysis of self-tracking. In Stefan Selke, editor, *Lifelogging: Theoretical Approaches and Case Studies About Self-Tracking.* Springer Verlag, Zurish, June 2016.

[19] Klaus Schoeffmann, David Ahlström, Werner Bailer, Claudiu Cobârzan, Frank Hopfgartner, Kevin McGuinness, Cathal Gurrin, Christian Frisson, Duy-Dinh Le, Manfred del Fabro, Hongliang Bai, and Wolfgang Weiss. The video browser showdown: a live evaluation of interactive video search tools. *IJMIR*, 3(2):113–127, 2014.

[20] Nicu Sebe, MichaelS. Lew, Xiang Zhou, ThomasS. Huang, and ErwinM. Bakker. The state of the art in image and video retrieval. In ErwinM. Bakker, MichaelS. Lew, ThomasS. Huang, Nicu Sebe, and XiangSean Zhou, editors, *Image and Video Retrieval*, volume 2728 of *Lecture Notes in Computer Science*, pages 1–8. Springer Berlin Heidelberg, 2003.

[21] Alan F. Smeaton, Paul Over, and Wessel Kraaij. Evaluation campaigns and trecvid. In *MIR '06: Proceedings of the 8th ACM International Workshop on Multimedia Information Retrieval*, pages 321–330, New York, NY, USA, 2006. ACM Press.

[22] Alan F. Smeaton, Peter Wilkins, Marcel Worring, Ork de Rooij, Tat-Seng Chua, and Huanbo Luan. Content-based video retrieval: Three example systems from trecvid. *International Journal of Imaging Systems and Technology*, 18(2-3):195–201, 2008.

[23] A. W M Smeulders, M. Worring, S. Santini, A. Gupta, and R. Jain. Content-based image retrieval at the end of the early years. *Pattern Analysis and Machine Intelligence, IEEE Transactions on*, 22(12):1349–1380, Dec 2000.

[24] Cees Snoek, Kvd Sande, OD Rooij, Bouke Huurnink, J Uijlings, van M Liempt, M Bugalhoy, I Trancosoy, F Yan, M Tahir, et al. The mediamill trecvid 2009 semantic video search engine. In *TRECVID*, 2009.

[25] Cees G. M. Snoek and Marcel Worring. Concept-based video retrieval. *Foundations and Trends in Information Retrieval*, 2(4):215–322, April 2009.

[26] Marcel Worring, Paul Sajda, Simone Santini, David A. Shamma, Alan F. Smeaton, and Qiang Yang. Where is the user in multimedia retrieval? *MultiMedia, IEEE*, 19(4):6–10, Oct 2012.

Building Cost-Benefit Models of Information Interactions

Leif Azzopardi
University of Strathclyde
Glasgow, United Kingdom
leifos@acm.org

ABSTRACT

Modeling how people interact with search interfaces has been of particular interest and importance to the field of Interactive Information Retrieval. Recently, there has been a move to developing formal models of the interaction between the user and the system, whether it be to: (i) run a simulation, (ii) conduct an economic analysis, (iii) measure system performance, or (iv) simply to better understand user interactions and hypothesise about user behaviours [7]. In such models, they consider the costs and the benefits that arise through the interaction with the interface/system and the information surfaced during the course of interaction. In this half day tutorial, we will focus on describing a series of cost-benefit models that have been proposed in the literature and how they have been applied in various scenarios. The tutorial will be structured into two parts. First, we will provide an overview of Decision Theory and Cost-Benefit Analysis techniques, and how they can and have be applied to a variety of Interactive Information Retrieval scenarios. For example, *when do facets helps?*, *under what conditions are query suggestions useful?* and *is it better to bookmark or re-find?* The second part of the tutorial will be dedicated to building cost-benefit models where we will discuss different techniques to build and develop such models. In the practical session, we will also discuss how costs and benefits can be estimated, and how the models can help inform and guide experimentation. During the tutorial participants will be challenged to build cost models for a number of problems (or even bring their own problems to solve).

Keywords

Search Behaviour, User Models, Retrieval Strategies, Evaluation

CHIIR '17 March 07-11, 2017, Oslo, Norway

ACM ISBN 978-1-4503-4677-1/17/03.

DOI: http://dx.doi.org/10.1145/3020165.3022162

1. OVERVIEW AND BACKGROUND

An emerging area of research within Interactive Information Retrieval (IIR) is the development of cost-benefit models that characterize the cost and benefits of interaction with a particular interface or particular features within the interface. Such models have been used for various purposes, such as:

1. controlling the number of interactions a simulated user can perform in a given period of time [16, 17],
2. approximating the time spent examining the results in a ranked list, e.g., within time biased measures [35, 37],
3. analyzing and empirically evaluating the costs and benefits of different interfaces [8, 28, 32] and
4. estimating the cost of different courses of interaction to determine the most efficient course of action [4, 27, 31].

Essentially, these lines of research explicitly consider the *cost* that the user incurs, as opposed to traditional performance measures, which typically only consider the *gain* or *benefit* that the user receives from such actions. Thus such models/measures of cost-benefit complement and extend the existing research on measuring the utility of searching; and do so from a user perspective [10]. IIR systems often provide various features and functions, such as query suggestions and relevance feedback, that a user may or may not decide to use. The decision to take such a particular option has associated costs and may lead to some benefit. Thus, a savvy user would take decisions that maximises their net benefit. Given this premise, it is possible to design interfaces that reduce costs and increase benefits. Further, such models also help to understand why users select one action over another and let us hypothesise about how a user would interact under different conditions. Through the tutorial we will describe an array of models and draw a number of insights into different decisions, provide explanations for observed behaviours and show how it is possible to generate numerous testable hypotheses from the models. The tutorial will be composed of two parts: (1) Theory and (2) Practice. In the theory sessions we will cover how: cost-benefit analysis and decision theory, and how it can be applied, followed by descriptions and explanations of a series of cost (and benefit) models that have been developed in the context of interactive information retrieval and searching. In the practical sessions we will focus on explaining how to building such models, how to use the models in practice, along with a discussion on how to estimate and measure costs/benefits in IIR. Then participants, in groups, will undertake a series of activities, where they are challenged to build and develop a cost model for IIR. *Participants are free to bring along their own problem, or work on the problems provided in class.* The tutorial will conclude with a discussion of solutions along with a summary of the challenges and future directions for modeling costs in IIR.

2. TUTORIAL OVERVIEW

As previously mentioned the first half of the tutorial will be focused on theory and existing work, and the second half will be focused on how to build such models and a practical session.

2.1 Costs, Benefits and the Economics of Search

In the first session we will briefly provide the context and motivation for developing formal models of Information Seeking and Retrieval (ISR). To begin, we will discuss and describe various conceptual and descriptive models of ISR, including Bates' Berry Picking Model [18] and the ISR framework proposed by Ingwersen and Kalvero [25], along with other such models (e.g. [40, 29, 21]). This will provide the background for the tutorial where we point out the limitations of such models and motivate the need to develop models that are not only descriptive in nature, but which help us to hypothesise and explain observed behaviours. We will then provide an overview of Cost-Benefit Analysis techniques and Decision Theory, before describing a series of different models which attempt to answer various questions like:

- who should search more the student or the professor? [20]
- how should facets be organised to reduce the cost of interaction? [27]
- how long a user's query should be? [13]
- should the user pose a specific or vague query?
- should the user take a suggestion or re-formulate?
- when should a user employ relevance feedback? [26]
- when would the "find similar" functionality be worthwhile to the user?
- when should a user stop searching? [19, 24, 36]
- should a user examine many documents and issue few queries, or vice versa? [2, 4]

In describing the different models, we will explore and explain how different parameters affect the decisions at play. This will provide a number of insights into how these models can be used to inform experimentation, and guide further research.

2.2 How To Build Cost-Benefit Models

In the next session (after lunch), we will focus on how to build cost models and how to use them to generate hypotheses using various methods (analytical, graphical and computational) [39, 30]. The essence of such models is to develop a cost function and a benefit function given the different interactions that users can perform. Given these functions, it is then possible to establish under what conditions cost is minimized and/or benefit is maximized. Alternatively, given the cost/benefit function for various interaction/choices it is possible to compare when one choice is preferable to another. This section will explore the following topics:

- Decision Making and Cost Models [23, 30].
- Optimality and Rationality [34, 33, 38].
- What choices are available? What are the limitations?
- What are the interactions, costs and benefits?
- What will vary? Parameters?
- Define the problem and the goal
- Construct a cost and benefit function
- What method to choose: analytical, graphically, computational
- Solve, plot, compute
- Draw inferences and generating hypotheses
- How to estimate costs / benefits
- How to design/construct experiments based upon the models

To help illustrate how to undertake the model building process, we will use an example based on the simple scenario of finding the first highly relevant document in a result list [14]. We will describe how we can characterize the problem, enumerate the different variables, and show how the different variables impact the overall cost and the design of the interface. Given this scenario, we will show how we can devise a number of experiments to empirically test and explore the model - and discuss how it is possible to estimate various costs and benefits.

The final session of the tutorial will be dedicated to building models. For example, participants will be given a context such as a user trying to find an app on a mobile phone or tablet. The goal here is to find the app that the user wants to use. So the focus will be on building a cost function to model the different ways in which the user can find the app, e.g. search or browse. To add realism to the scenario, we will consider different types of users, ones that can remember where the app is, and those who cant (i.e., best and average/worse cases) as well as consider how screen size and app icon size can be modelled to arrive at an optimal size and layout for such interaction. During the practical session, participants will be encouraged to abstract away the details to form a representation of the problem, and identify the main variables that are likely to influence the interaction (i.e., the number of apps on the phone, the number of apps per screen page, the cost of moving between screens, etc.). These will be used to formulate the costs, then we will be able to reason about when it is better to search for an app and when it is better to browse. We will also consider alternative designs, such as presenting the most used apps first, or a hierarchical browsing structure, and whether they are likely to be more efficient or not, or under what circumstances.

3. INTENDED LEARNING OUTCOMES

By the end of the tutorial, participants should be able to:

- Understand the context and rationale for formal models;
- Describe and explain different types of cost/benefit models;
- Define and create a cost/benefit model;
- Explain and infer the predicted user behaviour given the cost models;
- Generate hypotheses regarding user behavior given the cost and benefit models.

4. BIOGRAPHY

Dr. Leif Azzopardi has been recently awarded a Chancellor's Fellowship at the University of Strathclyde within the Department of Computer and Information Sciences. Prior to this appointment, he was a Senior Lecturer in the School of Computing Science at the University of Glasgow. His research focuses on building formal models for Information Retrieval - usually drawing upon different disciplines for inspiration, such as Quantum Mechanics, Operations Research, Microeconomics, Transportation Planning and Gamification. Central to his research is the theoretical development of statistical language models for Information Retrieval, where his research interests include:

- Models for the retrieval of documents, sentences, experts and other information objects [15, 22];
- Probabilistic models of user interaction and the simulation of users for evaluation [1, 5, 6];
- Microeconomic models of information interaction, specifically how cost and effort affect interaction and performance with search systems [2];
- Methods which assess the impact of search technology on society in application areas such as, search engine bias and the accessibility of e-Government information [?, 9], and;
- Search for fun (i.e. the SINS of users) [3].

He received his Ph.D. in Computing Science from the University of Paisley in 2006, and he received a First Class Honours Degree in Information Science from the University of Newcastle, Australia, 2001. After undertaking Post Doctoral Research Positions at the University of Amsterdam and University of Strathclyde, he was awarded an RCUK Fellowship at the University of Glasgow in 2006. He has given numerous invited talks on Formal Models of Information Seeking and Retrieval throughout the world and lectured at the Information Foraging Summer School (2011, 2012 and 2013), the Autumn School of Information Foraging and Retrieval (2016), the Symposium of Future Directions in Information Access (2007-2013), and various universities throughout the world.

Acknowledgements This tutorial is builds upon the work developed in collaboration with Dr. Guido Zuccon [11, 12]. *Thanks Guido!*

5. REFERENCES

[1] L. Azzopardi. Query side evaluation: an empirical analysis of effectiveness and effort. In *Proceedings of the 32nd international ACM SIGIR conference on Research and development in information retrieval*, pages 556–563. ACM, 2009.

[2] L. Azzopardi. The economics in interactive information retrieval. In *Proc,of the 34th international ACM SIGIR conference*, pages 15–24. ACM, 2011.

[3] L. Azzopardi. Searching for unlawful carnal knowledge. In *Proceedings of the SIGIR Workshop: Search for Fun*, volume 11, pages 17–18, 2011.

[4] L. Azzopardi. Modelling interaction with economic models of search. In *Proc. of the 37th ACM SIGIR Conference*, pages 3–12, 2014.

[5] L. Azzopardi and M. de Rijke. Automatic construction of known-item finding test beds. In *Proceedings of SIGIR '06*, pages 603–604, 2006.

[6] L. Azzopardi, M. de Rijke, and K. Balog. Building simulated queries for known-item topics: an analysis using six european languages. In *Proc. of the 30th annual international ACM SIGIR conference*, pages 455–462. ACM, 2007.

[7] L. Azzopardi, K. Järvelin, J. Kamps, and M. D. Smucker. Sigir 2010 report workshop on the simulation of interaction. *SIGIR Forum*, 44:35–47, 2011.

[8] L. Azzopardi, D. Kelly, and K. Brennan. How query cost affects search behavior. In *Proceedings of the 36th International ACM SIGIR Conference on Research and Development in IR*, pages 23–32, 2013.

[9] L. Azzopardi and V. Vinay. Retrievability: An evaluation measure for higher order information access tasks. In *Proc. of the 17th ACM CIKM*, pages 561–570, 2008.

[10] L. Azzopardi and G. Zuccon. An analysis of theories of search and search behavior. In *Proceedings of the 2015 International Conference on The Theory of Information Retrieval*, ICTIR '15, pages 81–90, 2015.

[11] L. Azzopardi and G. Zuccon. Building and using models of information seeking, search and retrieval: Full day tutorial. In *Proceedings of the 38th International ACM SIGIR Conference on Research and Development in Information Retrieval*, SIGIR '15, pages 1107–1110, 2015.

[12] L. Azzopardi and G. Zuccon. Advances in formal models of search and search behaviour. In *Proceedings of the 2016 ACM International Conference on the Theory of Information Retrieval*, ICTIR '16, pages 1–4, 2016.

[13] L. Azzopardi and G. Zuccon. An analysis of the cost and benefit of search interactions. In *Proceedings of the 2016 ACM on International Conference on the Theory of Information Retrieval*, ICTIR '16, pages 59–68, New York, NY, USA, 2016. ACM.

[14] L. Azzopardi and G. Zuccon. *Two Scrolls or One Click: A Cost Model for Browsing Search Results*, pages 696–702. 2016.

[15] K. Balog, L. Azzopardi, and M. de Rijke. Formal models for expert finding in enterprise corpora. In *Proceedings of the 29th Annual International ACM SIGIR Conference on Research and Development in Information Retrieval*, SIGIR '06, pages 43–50, 2006.

[16] F. Baskaya, H. Keskustalo, and K. Järvelin. Time drives interaction: simulating sessions in diverse searching environments. In *Proceedings of the 35th ACM conference on research and development in information retrieval (SIGIR)*, pages 105–114, 2012.

[17] F. Baskaya, H. Keskustalo, and K. Järvelin. Modeling behavioral factors ininteractive information retrieval. In *Proceedings of the 22nd ACM international conference on Conference on information and knowledge management*, pages 2297–2302, 2013.

[18] M. J. Bates. The design of browsing and berrypicking techniques for the online search interface. *Online Information Review*, 13(5):407–424, 1989.

[19] U. Birchler and M. Butler. *Information economics.* Routledge, 2007.

[20] M. D. Cooper. A cost model for evaluating information retrieval systems. *Journal of the American Society for Information Science*, pages 306–312, 1972.

[21] S. Erdelez. Information encountering: a conceptual framework for accidental information discovery. In *Proceedings of an international conference on Information seeking in context*, pages 412–421. Taylor Graham Publishing, 1997.

[22] R. T. Fernández, D. E. Losada, and L. A. Azzopardi. Extending the language modeling framework for sentence retrieval to include local context. *Information Retrieval*, 14(4):355–389, 2011.

[23] F. S. Hillier and G. J. Lieberman. Introduction to operations research. *NY, US*, 2001.

[24] J. Huang and A. Kazeykina. Optimal strategies for reviewing search results. In *Proceedings of the Twenty-Fourth AAAI Conference on Artificial Intelligence*, AAAI'10, pages 1321–1326. AAAI Press, 2010.

[25] P. Ingwersen and K. Järvelin. *The Turn: Integration of Information Seeking and Retrieval in Context.* Springer-Verlag New York, Inc., 2005.

[26] K. Järvelin. Interactive relevance feedback with graded relevance and sentence extraction: simulated user experiments. In *Proceedings of the ACM conference on Information and knowledge management (CIKM)*, pages 2053–2056, 2009.

[27] A. Kashyap, V. Hristidis, and M. Petropoulos. Facetor: cost-driven exploration of faceted query results. In *Proceedings of the 19th ACM conference on Information and knowledge management (CIKM)*, pages 719–728. ACM, 2010.

[28] D. Kelly and L. Azzopardi. How many results per page?: A study of serp size, search behavior and user experience. In *Proceedings of the 38th International ACM SIGIR Conference on Research and Development in Information Retrieval*, SIGIR '15, pages 183–192, 2015.

[29] C. C. Kuhlthau. Developing a model of the library search process: Cognitive and affective aspects. *RQ*, pages 232–242, 1988.

[30] K. G. Murty. Optimization models for decision making: Volume. *University of Michigan, Ann Arbor*, 2003.

[31] P. Pirolli and S. Card. Information foraging. *Psychological Review*, 106:643–675, 1999.

[32] D. M. Russell, M. J. Stefik, P. Pirolli, and S. K. Card. The cost structure of sensemaking. In *Proceedings of the INTERACT/SIGCHI*, pages 269–276, 1993.

[33] H. A. Simon. A behavioral model of rational choice. *The quarterly journal of economics*, 69(1):99–118, 1955.

[34] H. A. Simon. Theories of bounded rationality. *Decision and organization*, 1:161–176, 1972.

[35] M. D. Smucker and C. L. Clarke. Time-based calibration of effectiveness measures. In *Proceedings of the 35th International ACM SIGIR Conference on Research and Development in IR*, pages 95–104, 2012.

[36] M. D. Smucker and C. L. Clarke. Modeling optimal switching behavior. In *Proceedings of the 2016 ACM on Conference on Human Information Interaction and Retrieval*, CHIIR '16, pages 317–320, 2016.

[37] M. D. Smucker and C. P. Jethani. Human performance and retrieval precision revisited. In *Proceedings of the 33rd ACM conference on research and development in information retrieval (SIGIR)*, pages 595–602, 2010.

[38] G. J. Stigler. The economics of information. *The journal of political economy*, 69(3):213–225, 1961.

[39] H. R. Varian. How to build an economic model in your spare time. *American Economist*, 41:3–10, 1997.

[40] T. D. Wilson. Human information behavior. *Informing science*, 3(2):49–56, 2000.

Second International Workshop On the Evaluation of Collaborative Information Seeking and Retrieval (Ecol'17)

Leif Azzopardi
University of Strathclyde
Glasgow, UK
Leif.Azzopardi@strath.ac.uk

Jeremy Pickens
Catalyst Repository Systems
Palo Alto, CA, USA
jpickens@catalystsecure.com

Chirag Shah
Rutgers University
New Brunswick, NJ, USA
chirags@rutgers.edu

Laure Soulier
Sorbonne Universités, UPMC
Univ Paris 06, LIP6 UMR 7606
75005 Paris, France
laure.soulier@lip6.fr

Lynda Tamine
Université de Toulouse UPS IRIT
Toulouse, France
tamine@irit.fr

ABSTRACT

The workshop on the evaluation of collaborative information retrieval and seeking (ECol) is held in conjunction with the ACM SIGIR Conference on Human Information Interaction & Retrieval (CHIIR) in Oslo, Norway. To make the workshop active and the participant pro-active, we released datasets and tools so as to help researchers contributing to the formalization of evaluation frameworks for challenging collaborative tasks. The workshop is split into two parts. First, a presentation session. Then, the afternoon is devoted to group discussion addressing challenges of evaluating and designing models for social and collaborative search.

Keywords

Collaborative information retrieval, social information retrieval, task, evaluation

1. INTRODUCTION

The paradigm of Collaborative Information Seeking (CIS) and Retrieval (CIR) refers to methodologies and technologies that support collective-knowledge sharing within a work team in order to solve a shared complex problem [5]. Accordingly, the main underlying challenge is to satisfy the mutual beneficial goals of both individual users and the collaborative group while maintaining a reasonable level of cognitive effort underlying users' interactions [11]. Indeed, collaborative search is also known as a social process [4] in which users leverage from other users' interactions and social signals (e.g., bookmarks and annotations). In the recent years, several studies [7, 16, 8] have been carried out to understand the behavioral process of users in terms of question asking on search engines vs. social networks. In this context, social platforms (e.g., social networks [9, 2] and community question-answering [6, 3]) have been acknowledged as a place where users collaborate to solve an information need. This provides numerous opportunities for new and novel research within the field of CIR/CIS where the gap between social and collaborative search can be brought together.

However, the evaluation for CIS/CIR and social & collaborative IR models are still challenging, as there are a variety of confounding factors such as the multi-user and multi-level contexts, the exploratory aspect of the search through multi-session search activities, the multiplicity of relevance factors, the individual vs. collective value of relevance, the search interfaces supporting the collaborative interactions as well as the social interactions themselves. While, substantial research advances in the evaluation of non-collaborative information retrieval and seeking tasks have been achieved through international evaluation campaigns such as TREC, CLEF and NTIR, to date and to our knowledge, no standardization effort has been achieved for the evaluation of CIS/CIR and social-CIR. During the first ECol Workshop there was strong consensus that there is an important need to investigate the evaluation challenge in CIS/CIR/social-CIR with the aim of creating common evaluation frameworks that would foster the research area.

A first edition of this workshop has been organized at CIKM 2015 in which we discussed about the issue of evaluation in CIS/CIR [14]. The second edition of the ECol Workshop[1] [14] focuses the discussion and provides concrete contributions in developing such an evaluation framework for the unique challenges in CIS/CIR and social-collaborative IR. To make the workshop active and the participant pro-active, we release datasets and tools so as to help researchers contributing to the formalization of evaluation frameworks for challenging collaborative tasks (that we will identify).

Finally, we hope that this workshop will be beneficial for the community in both short- and long-term. First, this would allow to understand relevance factors or design standard evaluation frameworks. Second, provided resources (datasets, tool, and tasks) would remain available for the whole community, facilitating in the future comparable and reproducible experiments.

2. SCOPE AND NOVELTY OF THE WORKSHOP

These last years and particularly since 2005, CIS and CIR have became emerging topics that have been addressed in

[1]https://www.irit.fr/ECol2015/

CHIIR '17, March 7–11, 2017, Oslo, Norway.

ACM ISBN 978-1-4503-4677-1/17/03.

DOI: http://dx.doi.org/10.1145/3020165.3022164

several IR and IS conferences including CIKM and SIGIR conferences [1, 14]. While the potential of collaboration has been highlighted with respect to individual settings, other challenges remain and need to be thoroughly explored. Despite most of experimental evaluations have been done with the objective of highlighting the synergic effect of the proposed contributions, there is an important need for the future to discuss about what should be evaluated in terms of collaboration aspects (e.g. cognitive effort, mutual beneficial goal satisfaction, collective relevance...). Moreover, it does not exist standard framework as proposed in ad-hoc information retrieval through the evaluation campaign, as those proposed by TREC, INEX, CLEF, etc.

While a follow on from our previous workshop, this workshop has two distinguishing and novel elements: (i) it has a specific focus on social IR and collaborative IR evaluation, bridging the gap within this space, and (ii) it provides datasets, tools and new tasks for participants and others to undertake evaluations and explore this space. We believe that formalizing evaluation frameworks for a such domain would lead researchers to investigate this research area and propose new social-collaborative models.

Participants will have different ways to participate to the workshop:

- Use the **provided** datasets/tools to propose an evaluation framework for the **identified** tasks.
- Use their **own** datasets/tools to propose an evaluation framework for the **identified** tasks.
- Use the **provided** datasets/tools to propose an evaluation framework for a task **they have identified**.
- Propose an evaluation framework **without** support of datasets/tools for a task **we/they have identified**.
- Designing **possible tasks** (with/without proposing models and evaluation frameworks) on provided or their own datasets.

This opens future research directions and would lead to the design of evaluation frameworks. This would also enable comparable contributions in terms of evaluation framework and constructive discussions throughout the workshop.

3. RELEASED DATASETS AND TOOLS

To make the workshop interactive and also in a long-term objective in the field, we share resources and tools:

- Datasets:
  - Social-based datasets: tweet collections about two crises, respectively the Ebola virus epidemic and the hurricane Sandy[2] [13, 15].
  - Collaborative search logs[3] [12].
- Tools:
  - Coagmento collaborative interface [10].
  - Open-source version of Coagmento for doing user-studies on github[4].

[2]https://figshare.com/collections/expac/3283118
[3]http://infoseeking.org/data.php#cis2010
[4]https://github.com/InfoSeeking/CoagmentoCollaboratory

4. EXAMPLES OF TOPICS

Taking into consideration the release of datasets and tools, we will propose different topics that would guide participants in their contributions. For each topic, participants would be invited either to design the task or formalize the evaluation framework (including metrics, datasets, ground truth, baselines, etc.). Below we list examples of topics:

- Recommending social collaborators (experts, answerers, sympathizers).
- Collaborative ranking on social platforms (criteria: federated, novelty, diversity, interactive, time consideration).
- Identifying impacting factors on search effectiveness (failure, success, struggling).
- Preserving data privacy through multi-level CIR.
- Exploratory search (knowledge acquisition, multi-faceted search).
- Collaborative intent understanding.

5. INTENDED PROGRAM COMMITTEE

- Thilo Boehm, University Hagen - Germany
- Luanne Freund, University of British Columbia - USA
- Martin Halvey, University of Strathclyde - UK
- Preben Hansen, Stockholm University - Sweden
- Ryan Kelly, University of Bath - UK
- Simon Knight, University of Technology Sydney - Australia
- Stephann Makri, University of London - UK
- Jian-Yun Nie, University de Montreal - Canada
- Takehiro Yamamoto, Department of Social Informatics, Graduate School of Informatics, Kyoto University - Japan

6. REFERENCES

[1] *CIR '11: Proceedings of the 3rd International Workshop on Collaborative Information Retrieval*, New York, NY, USA, 2011. ACM. 605110.

[2] D. Castilho, P. Melo, D. Quercia, and F. Benevenuto. Working with friends: Unveiling working affinity features from facebook data. In *ICWSM*, 2014.

[3] S. Chang and A. Pal. Routing questions for collaborative answering in community question answering. In *ASONAM*, pages 494–501. ACM, 2013.

[4] B. M. Evans and E. H. Chi. An elaborated model of social search. *IP&M*, 46(6):656–678, 2010.

[5] J. Foster. Collaborative information seeking and retrieval. *Annual Review of Information Science and Technology*, 40(1), 2006.

[6] B. Li and I. King. Routing questions to appropriate answerers in community question answering services. In *CIKM*. ACM, 2010.

[7] M. R. Morris, J. Teevan, and K. Panovich. What do people ask their social networks, and why?: A survey study of status messages. In *CHI*, pages 1739–1748, 2010.

[8] A. Oeldorf-Hirsh, M. R. Morris, J. Teevan, and G. Darren. To search or to ask: The routing of information needs between traditional search engines and social networks. In *ICWSM*, 2014.

[9] S. A. Paul, L. Hong, and H. Chi. Is twitter a good place for asking questions? a characterization study. In *ICWSM*, 2011.

[10] C. Shah. Coagmento- a collaborative information seeking, synthesis and sense-making framework. In *Integrated demo at CSCW 2010*, 2010.

[11] C. Shah and R. González-Ibáñez. Evaluating the synergic effect of collaboration in information seeking. In *SIGIR*, pages 913–922, 2011.

[12] C. Shah and R. Gonzalez-Ibanez. Collaborative information seeking lab experiments dataset. http://infoseeking.org/data.php#cis2010, 2017.

[13] L. Soulier, L. Tamine, and G. Nguyen. Answering twitter questions: a model for recommending answerers through social collaboration. In *CIKM*, pages 267–276, 2016.

[14] L. Soulier, L. Tamine, T. Sakai, L. Azzopardi, and J. Pickens. Report on the first international workshop on the evaluation on collaborative information seeking and retrieval (ecol'2015). *SIGIR Forum*, 50(1):42–48, 2016.

[15] L. Tamine, L. Soulier, L. Ben Jabeur, F. Amblard, C. Hanachi, G. Hubert, and C. Roth. Social media-based collaborative information access: Analysis of online crisis-related twitter conversations. In *HT*, pages 159–168. ACM, 2016.

[16] J. Teevan, D. Ramage, and M.-R. Morris. Twitter search: A comparison of microblog search and web search. In *WSDM*, pages 35–44, 2011.

Second Workshop on Supporting Complex Search Tasks

Nick Belkin, Rutgers University
Toine Bogers, Aalborg Univ. Copenhagen
Jaap Kamps, University of Amsterdam
Diane Kelly, Univ. Tennessee Knoxville
Marijn Koolen*, Huygens ING Amsterdam
Emine Yilmaz, University College London

ABSTRACT

There is broad consensus in the field of IR that search is complex in many use cases and applications, both on the Web and in domain specific collections, and both professionally and in our daily life. Yet our understanding of complex search tasks, in comparison to simple look up tasks, is fragmented at best. The workshop addresses many open research questions: What are the obvious use cases and applications of complex search? What are essential features of work tasks and search tasks to take into account? And how do these evolve over time? With a multitude of information, varying from introductory to specialized, and from authoritative to speculative or opinionated, when to show what sources of information? How does the information seeking process evolve and what are relevant differences between different stages? With complex task and search process management, blending searching, browsing, and recommendations, and supporting exploratory search to sensemaking and analytics, UI and UX design pose an overconstrained challenge. How do we evaluate and compare approaches? Which measures should be taken into account? Supporting complex search tasks requires new collaborations across the fields of CHI and IR, and the proposed workshop will bring together a diverse group of researchers to work together on one of the greatest challenges of our field.

1. INTRODUCTION

One of the current challenges in information access is supporting complex search tasks. A user's understanding of the information need and the overall task develop as they interact with the system. Supporting the various stages of the task involves many aspects of the system, e.g. interface features, presentation of information, retrieving and ranking. Many search systems treat the search process as a series of identical steps of submitting a query and consulting documents. Yet information seeking research has shown that users go through different phases in their search sessions, from exploring and identifying vague information needs, to focusing and refining their needs and search strategies, to finalizing their search. To be able to support exploring and discovering strategies we need to understand the characteristics of different tasks including open-ended, leisure-focused sessions. This is a highly complex problem that touches upon and bridges areas of information seeking, interactive information retrieval, system-centered (ranking, evaluation) and user interface design.

The background for this workshop is derived from the Interactive Track (2014–2016) of the Social Book Search Lab at CLEF [8], which investigates scenarios with complex book search tasks and develops systems and interfaces that support the user through the different stages of their search process. But the aims of the workshop are broader and addresses all aspects of supporting complex search tasks.

2. GOALS AND OBJECTIVES

The overall goal of the workshop is to create and foster an interdisciplinary forum where researchers can exchange and contribute to the development of alternative experiments and prototypes. The main aim is to better understand how to support complex search tasks, addressing many open research questions to be explored, including:

Context What are the obvious use cases and applications of complex search? In what sense are these "complex"? What generic characteristic do they share? How can search become an integral part of its context, and the context integral part of search?

Tasks What are essential features of work tasks and search tasks to take into account? And how do these evolve over time? How can complex tasks be decomposed into manageable sub-tasks, and partial results composed into comprehensive answers? How can we monitor and support task progress?

Heterogeneous sources With a multitude of information, varying from introductory to specialized, and from authoritative to speculative or opinionated, when to show what sources of information? When to show more or other types of information than directly requested by the searcher? Do we know when the user has gotten enough?

Search process How does the information seeking process evolve and what are relevant differences between different stages? What search tactics and search strategies

*Corresponding organizer.

CHIIR '17 March 07-11, 2017, Oslo, Norway

ACM ISBN 978-1-4503-4677-1/17/03.
DOI: http://dx.doi.org/10.1145/3020165.3022163

are effective? How can we promote the use of effective search strategies? How does the information need evolve and what are relevant success criteria for the end result and intermediate steps? How can we cast these as effective complex queries, and how to (interactively) construct such queries?

UI and UX Does the need of complex task and search process management, blending searching, browsing, and recommendations, and supporting exploratory search to sense-making and analytics, make UI and UX design an over-constrained challenge? What affordances are required and in what stage of the search process? How can we make the search process transparent to the user? How and when does the initiative shift between system and user? How can interfaces support various user groups and their special needs?

Evaluation How do we evaluate and compare approaches? How can we design realistic evaluation campaigns for interactive search? Can we carve out one or a range of generic aspects testable on a suitable benchmarks? Is there enough empirical evidence to ground simulated interactive search? What kind of novel retrieval models are needed to combine topical, contextual and preferential aspects?

3. WORKSHOP FORMAT

SCST 2017 will be a half day workshop on supporting complex search tasks—a *work*shop proper where discussion is central, and all attendees are active participants.

We will start the workshop with a full round of introductions of all participants, making everyone feel welcome and part of the workshop. Then, the workshop continues with two short keynotes to set the stage and ensure all attendees are on the same page. One from an academic perspective, by *Mark Hall (Edge Hill University, UK)*, and one from an industry perspective, by *Jussi Karlgren (Gavagai, Sweden)*.

Next, we will have presentations of contributed papers, with each paper getting a 1-minute boaster and a poster presentation in an interactive poster session. There will be a light-weight submission format where authors can submit short $2 + 1$ page research and position papers, allowing for max. 2 pages of narrative text and an additional page for tables/figures/notes/references. We will allow accepted papers to be extended to four pages in the camera-ready version, so that comments of the reviewers can be implemented in full.

The second half of the workshop consists of 3-4 breakout groups, seeded from the open research questions (see §2) and the contributed papers, each group thoroughly prepared by a chair who guides the discussion, with examples from relevant IR evaluation campaigns such as the TREC Session and Tasks Tracks and the SBS Interactive and Suggestion Tracks, and from concrete examples of complex support systems with their UX and UI challenges. One of the topics will be an Interactive IR task that is planned for the TREC Tasks Track.[1] Finally, the breakout groups report to the audience and a panel of experts, with continued discussion on what we have learned.

The discussion will continue during a social event in a more informal way over food and drinks, deep into the Oslo night. The organizers have gained a proud reputation for their open and inclusive workshops, leading to new research collaborations, other workshops, and new evaluation tracks.

The workshop will bring together a varied group of researchers—bridging CHI and IR in a natural way—with experience covering both user and system centered approaches, to work together on the problem and potential solutions, and identify the *barriers* to success and work on ways of addressing them.

The format allows us deal with a relatively large number of participants while still preserving the interactive workshop character – the last edition at ECIR'15 had 41 paid registrations (and the head count was even higher on the day of the workshop).

All accepted papers will be published in the workshop proceedings (CEUR-WS). A report of the workshop including a summary of the break-out discussions will be published as a SIGIR Forum report.

4. RELATED WORKSHOPS

This workshop is a follow-up to the first SCST workshop at ECIR 2015 ([5, 6]) and is closely related to the Interactive Track of the CLEF Social Book Search Lab of 2015 and 2016 [7, 8]. The Interactive track is focused on the domain of book search, whereas the proposed workshop addresses issues around the search process and system interaction from a broader perspective.

Some of the organizers were involved in the *SIGIR 2011 Workshop on "Entertain me" Supporting Complex Search Tasks* [2] and in the spin-off TREC Contextual Suggestion Track [3, 4]; in related discussion within the *SWIRL '12: Strategic Workshop on Information Retrieval in Lorne* [1]; and the *NSF Task-Based Information Search Systems Workshop* [9]. There is a broad research agenda emerging that attracts interest from research in all areas of HCI and IR.

The workshop builds on the results of the earlier discussion, and through the CLEF Social Book Search Lab [10] has already been pushing this line of research with a range of user studies, novel user interfaces, and analysis of large scale social data. The workshop will be held to have a more focused discussion based on the results so far.

The workshop will provide a comprehensive overview of current work on supporting complex tasks in a variety of settings, and fosters new collaboration within across the fields of CHI and IR, on one of the most important topics in the coming years.

5. ACKNOWLEDGMENTS

We thank the CHIIR workshop chair Preben Hansen and the local organizers for their support. We also thank the programme committee members for their timely and constructive reviews.

REFERENCES

[1] J. Allan, B. Croft, A. Moffat, and M. Sanderson. Frontiers, Challenges, and Opportunities for Information Retrieval: Report from SWIRL 2012 the Second Strategic Workshop on Information Retrieval in Lorne. *SIGIR Forum*, 46(1):2–32, May 2012.

[2] N. J. Belkin, C. L. Clarke, N. Gao, J. Kamps, and J. Karlgren. Report on the SIGIR Workshop on "En-

[1]Information about the 2017 Tasks Track is available at http://www.cs.ucl.ac.uk/tasks-track-2017/

tertain Me": Supporting Complex Search Tasks. *SIGIR Forum*, 45(2):51–59, Jan. 2012.

[3] A. Dean-Hall, C. L. A. Clarke, J. Kamps, P. Thomas, and E. M. Voorhees. Overview of the TREC 2012 Contextual Suggestion Track. In E. M. Voorhees and L. P. Buckland, editors, *The Twenty-First Text REtrieval Conference Proceedings (TREC 2012)*. National Institute for Standards and Technology: NIST Special Publication 500-298, 2013.

[4] A. Dean-Hall, C. L. A. Clarke, J. Kamps, P. Thomas, N. Simon, and E. M. Voorhees. Overview of the TREC 2013 Contextual Suggestion Track. In E. M. Voorhees, editor, *The Twenty-Second Text REtrieval Conference (TREC 2013) Notebook*. National Institute for Standards and Technology. NIST Special Publication 500-302, 2014.

[5] M. Gäde, M. Hall, H. Huurdeman, J. Kamps, M. Koolen, M. Skov, E. Toms, and D. Walsh, editors. *Proceedings of the first international workshop on Supporting Complex Search Tasks*, volume 1338 of *CEUR Workshop Proceedings*, 2015. CEUR-WS.org. URL http://ceur-ws.org/Vol-1338.

[6] M. Gäde, M. M. Hall, H. C. Huurdeman, J. Kamps, M. Koolen, M. Skov, E. Toms, and D. Walsh. Report on the First Workshop on Supporting Complex Search Tasks. *SIGIR Forum*, 49(1):50–56, 2015.

[7] M. Gäde, M. M. Hall, H. C. Huurdeman, J. Kamps, M. Koolen, M. Skov, E. Toms, and D. Walsh. Overview of the SBS 2015 Interactive Track. In L. Cappellato, N. Ferro, G. J. F. Jones, and E. SanJuan, editors, *Working Notes of CLEF 2015 - Conference and Labs of the Evaluation forum, Toulouse, France, September 8-11, 2015.*, volume 1391 of *CEUR Workshop Proceedings*. CEUR-WS.org, 2015. URL http://ceur-ws.org/Vol-1391/78-CR.pdf.

[8] M. Gäde, M. M. Hall, H. C. Huurdeman, J. Kamps, M. Koolen, M. Skov, T. Bogers, and D. Walsh. Overview of the SBS 2016 interactive track. In *Working Notes of CLEF 2016 - Conference and Labs of the Evaluation forum, Évora, Portugal, 5-8 September, 2016.*, volume 1609 of *CEUR Workshop Proceedings*, pages 1024–1038. CEUR-WS.org, 2016. URL http://ceur-ws.org/Vol-1609/16091024.pdf.

[9] D. Kelly, J. Arguello, and R. Capra. NSF Workshop on Task-based Information Search Systems. *SIGIR Forum*, 47(2):116–127, Jan. 2013.

[10] M. Koolen, T. Bogers, M. Gäde, M. M. Hall, I. Hendrickx, H. C. Huurdeman, J. Kamps, M. Skov, S. Verberne, and D. Walsh. Overview of the CLEF 2016 Social Book Search Lab. In *Experimental IR Meets Multilinguality, Multimodality, and Interaction - 7th International Conference of the CLEF Association, CLEF 2016, Évora, Portugal, September 5-8, 2016, Proceedings*, volume 9822 of *Lecture Notes in Computer Science*, pages 351–370. Springer, 2016.

NeuroIIR: Challenges in Bringing Neuroscience to Research in Human-Information Interaction

Jacek Gwizdka
School of Information
University of Texas at Austin
Austin, TX, USA
chiir2017@gwizdka.com

Javed Mostafa
Info. Science & BRIC
UNC at Chapel Hill
Chapel Hill, NC, USA
jm@unc.edu

ABSTRACT
The workshop will be the second in a series, building upon a successful workshop held at the SIGIR 2015 conference. The main aim is to focus on a narrow but highly important set of topics that have been identified in the last workshop and are of importance to IR and IIR researchers. The core theme of the workshop will be challenges is using and applying neurophysiological experimental methodologies and their applicability and adaptation in the context of IR and IIR research studies. The goal will be to clarify some of the major neurophysiological methodological concepts and constructs relevant to IR and IIR, expand awareness of critical parameters associated with neurophysiological devices and equipment, and provide a foundation to researchers to enable them to apply appropriate neurophysiological modalities for specific types of IR and IIR research investigations. Discussions on establishing reference tasks and standard data sets and launching a special journal issue on key topics will round out the event.

Keywords
Neuroscience; Experimentation; Human-Information Interaction; Information Retrieval; Measurement; Neuro-physiological methods and tools.

1. RATIONALE, SCOPE AND NOVELTY
There is a growing interest in the use of neurophysiological (NP) methods in IR and IIR research. Researchers view NP approaches as potentially offering deeper insights into human interactions with information and wish to utilize NP-methods to generate complementary experimental data. The fact that several IR and IIR research projects on NP have secured the best-paper awards recently in major conferences and scholarly venues [1–4], that the last workshop concentrating on the intersection of NP with IR (which we describe below) held in the SIGIR 2015 Conference attracted a large attendance and, that the only *Perspective paper* accepted (out of 10 submitted) in the first CHIIR event held in 2016 explored NP approaches in IIR [5], are strong indicators of the increasing prominence of this interdisciplinary area.

A second workshop, to be held at CHIIR 2017, will allow us to reach a broader community – colleagues who work at the intersection of IR/IIR and HCI. In particular, the CHIIR 2017 conference venue will make it easier to reach European colleagues, many of whom are engaged in related work.

CHIIR '17, March 07-11, 2017, Oslo, Norway
ACM 978-1-4503-4677-1/17/03.
http://dx.doi.org/10.1145/3020165.3022165

2. TOPICS AND PURPOSE
The proposed workshop is a follow up to our first international workshop on NP approaches in Information Retrieval Research (NeuroIR'2015 @ SIGIR) [6]. The previous workshop, being the first of its kind, had deliberately selected a board scope. We plan to significantly narrow the scope in the second meeting and concentrate on certain critical areas that have been identified in the first workshop. A major barrier identified in the last workshop is the lack of understanding and development of *experimental methods* that are unique to the neuro-physiological area. Specifically, conducting information seeking activities, while wearing specialized devices or being inside scanning equipment (required for certain neuro-physiological experiments) introduces particular challenges in conducting information seeking experimental studies. Developing a deeper and clearer understanding of the wide variety of parameters (e.g., specific types filters used in EEG monitoring generate unique and characteristic wave patterns that represent different types of brain activities) is essential in accurately operating the neuro-physiological equipment and tuning them for particular types of information interaction events. Furthermore, a solid foundation in NP methodologies, as they have been adopted for IR and IIR experimental studies will be beneficial in understanding how to interpret the experimental evidence generated by the common (and widely used) NP tools and matching the appropriate NP tools with the correct IR/IIR interaction phenomena that are under consideration in a study. Beyond NP methodologies and associated tools, two other topics that will receive significant attention in the planned event are: 1) IR and IIR reference tasks and standard data sets that researchers can use to cross-validate and compare their research efforts with other researchers and 2) community building and dissemination of NP research findings through a special issue of JASIST, whose outline and sub-topics will be developed in the workshop.

3. FORMAT AND PLANNED ACTIVITIES
This will be a half-day workshop with a mixture of presentations (including paper and poster presentations) and interactive activities (including panel discussions and group activities). We aim to devote at least half the workshop time to interactive discussions and break-out group sessions that will be focused on working out solutions to identified challenges. We also plan a poster display as a way of allowing selected participants to share their early stage research and experiences with NP tools.

Before the workshop:

A workshop website is at http://neuroir.org, through which workshop participation and paper submissions will be solicited.

Papers will be reviewed and selected based on peer-review; selected authors will be invited to present their work.

Workshop schedule:

1. Lunch
2. During lunch, posters will be set up in the workshop room.
3. Introduction to the workshop by the organizers (15 min).
4. Paper presentations and Q&A. Three papers will be selected for presentation (5 min per paper + 5min Q&A) (30 min).
5. Break-out group working discussions. Depending on the number of workshop participants, we plan to form two-three groups. Each group will focus on one topic: 1) experimental methods; 2) matching NP tools with IR/IIR phenomena under study; 3) reference tasks and standard data sets (45 min).
6. Coffee break and poster presentations (30 min).
7. Summary of breakout groups and general discussion (30 min).
8. Expert panel (45 min).
9. Closing (15 min).
10. Optional workshop participant dinner (later in the evening).

Activities after the workshop:

The workshop website will be maintained post-workshop; a report will be written up for submission to SIGIR Forum; all participants will be invited to submit their manuscripts to the JASIST special issue.

4. PROGRAM COMMITTEE

- Ioannis Arapakis, Yahoo Labs, Spain
- Ofer Bergman, Bar-Ilan University, Israel
- Vincent N. Carrasco, Info. Science, UNC at Chapel Hill, USA
- Kelly Giovanello, Neuroscience, UNC at Chapel Hill, USA
- Sampath Jayarathna, Computer Science, California Polytechnic University
- Yasher Moshfeghi, CS, U Glasgow, UK
- Henning Muller, Medical Imaging & Informatics, Switzerland
- Frank Pollick, Psychology, University of Glasgow, UK
- Tuukka Ruotsalo, HIIT, Finland
- Erin Treacy Solovey, iSchool, Drexel, USA
- Max Wilson, University of Nottingham, UK

5. HIGHLIGHTS

Panel. The workshop will end with an expert discussion panel. We will invite five panelists.

Journal special issue. A special issue to be published in the Journal of the Association for Information Science and Technology (JASIST) is being planned. Note that one of the workshop organizers, Javed Mostafa, currently serves as JASIST's editor-in-chief.

6. PARTICIPANTS AND SUBMISSIONS

We will solicit *research experience* and *research highlights* papers. Papers in the first category will be reviewed for their depth of experience and potential impact on the workshop audience. Only three of them will be selected for oral presentation. Other research experience and research highlights papers will be considered for a lunch-time poster presentation. The main goal for a poster session is to exchange experiences based on cutting-edge and emerging work and learn about other colleagues' research engagements, and to contribute to community building. Selection of papers and posters will be conducted at two levels. Members of the program committee will be assigned responsibilities to conduct the first level review. At least two reviewers will be assigned per research experience paper and at least one member will review each research highlights paper. Our planned event will welcome participants beyond those who submitted papers or presentations to the workshop.

Accepted papers will be published as open-access CEUR-WS proceedings.

7. REFERENCES

[1] Moshfeghi, Y. et al. 2013. Understanding Relevance: An fMRI Study. *Advances in Information Retrieval*. P. Serdyukov et al., eds. Springer Berlin Heidelberg. 14–25.

[2] Moshfeghi, Y. et al. 2016. Understanding Information Need: An fMRI Study. *Proceedings of the 39th International ACM SIGIR Conference on Research and Development in Information Retrieval* (New York, NY, USA, 2016), 335–344.

[3] Gwizdka, J. 2013. Looking for Information Relevance In the Brain. *Gmunden Retreat on NeuroIS 2013* (Gmunden, Austria, Jun. 2013), 14.

[4] Arapakis, I. et al. 2009. Enriching User Profiling with Affective Features for the Improvement of a Multimodal Recommender System. *Proceedings of the ACM International Conference on Image and Video Retrieval* (New York, NY, USA, 2009), 29:1–29:8.

[5] Mostafa, J. and Gwizdka, J. 2016. Deepening the Role of the User: Neuro-Physiological Evidence As a Basis for Studying and Improving Search. *Proceedings of the 2016 ACM on Conference on Human Information Interaction and Retrieval* (New York, NY, USA, 2016), 63–70.

[6] Gwizdka, J. and Mostafa, J. 2016. NeuroIR 2015: SIGIR 2015 Workshop on Neuro-Physiological Methods in IR Research. *SIGIR Forum*. 49, 2 (Jan. 2016), 83–88.

[7] Cole, M.J. et al. 2013. Inferring user knowledge level from eye movement patterns. *Information Processing & Management*. 49, 5 (Sep. 2013), 1075–1091.

[8] Wang, S. et al. 2016. Using Wireless EEG Signals to Assess Memory Workload in the n-Back Task. *IEEE Transactions on Human-Machine Systems*. 46, 3 (Jun. 2016), 424–435.

[9] Gwizdka, J. 2016. Differences in Reading between Word Search and Information Relevance Decisions – Evidence from Eye-tracking. *Gmunden Retreat on NeuroIS 2016* (Gmunden, Austria, Jun. 2016), 6.

Author Index

www.ingramcontent.com/pod-product-compliance
Lightning Source LLC
LaVergne TN
LVHW080008210926
848481LV00011B/2970
* 9 7 8 1 4 5 0 3 5 4 4 6 2 *